Corporate Entrepreneurship and Growth

The International Library of Entrepreneurship

Series Editor: David B. Audretsch
Ameritech Chair of Economic Development and Director,
Institute for Development Strategies
Indiana University, USA

1. Corporate Entrepreneurship and Growth
   Shaker A. Zahra

Future titles will include:

Women and Entrepreneurship: Contemporary Classics
Candida G. Brush, Nancy M. Carter, Elizabeth J. Gatewood, Patricia G. Greene and Myra M. Hart

The Economics of Entrepreneurship
Simon C. Parker

Entrepreneurship and Technology Policy
Albert N. Link

Entrepreneurship and Economic Growth
A. Roy Thurik and Martin Carree

Technological Entrepreneurship
Donald S. Siegel

Corporate Entrepreneurship and Growth

Edited by

Shaker A. Zahra

Robert E. Buuck Chair in Entrepreneurship
University of Minnesota, USA

THE INTERNATIONAL LIBRARY OF ENTREPRENEURSHIP

An Elgar Reference Collection
Cheltenham, UK • Northampton, MA, USA

Published by
Edward Elgar Publishing Limited
Glensanda House
Montpellier Parade
Cheltenham
Glos GL50 1UA
UK

Edward Elgar Publishing, Inc.
136 West Street
Suite 202
Northampton
Massachusetts 01060
USA

A catalogue record for this book is available from the British Library.

ISBN   1 84542 478 6

Printed and bound in Great Britain by MPG Books Ltd, Bodmin, Cornwall

Contents

Acknowledgements

The editor and publishers wish to thank the authors and the following publishers who have kindly given permission for the use of copyright material.

Administrative Science Quarterly for article: Robert A. Burgelman (1983), 'A Process Model of Internal Corporate Venturing in the Diversified Major Firm', *Administrative Science Quarterly*, **28**, 223–44.

Blackwell Publishing Ltd for articles: Pramodita Sharma and James J. Chrisman (1999), 'Toward a Reconciliation of the Definitional Issues in the Field of Corporate Entrepreneurship', *Entrepreneurship: Theory and Practice*, **23** (3), Spring, 11–27; Jeffrey G. Covin and Morgan P. Miles (1999), 'Corporate Entrepreneurship and the Pursuit of Competitive Advantage', *Entrepreneurship: Theory and Practice*, **23** (3), Spring, 47–63; Shaker A. Zahra, Anders P. Nielsen and William C. Bogner (1999), 'Corporate Entrepreneurship, Knowledge, and Competence Development', *Entrepreneurship: Theory and Practice*, **23** (3), Spring, 169–89; Shaker A. Zahra, Daniel F. Jennings and Donald F. Kuratko (1999), 'The Antecedents and Consequences of Firm-Level Entrepreneurship: The State of the Field', *Entrepreneurship: Theory and Practice*, **24** (2), Winter, 45–65; Julian Birkinshaw, Rob van Basten Batenburg and Gordon Murray (2002), 'Venturing to Succeed', *Business Strategy Review*, **13** (4), Winter, 10–17; Morgan P. Miles and Jeffrey G. Covin (2002), 'Exploring the Practice of Corporate Venturing: Some Common Forms and Their Organizational Implications', *Entrepreneurship: Theory and Practice*, **26** (3), Spring, 21–40.

Copyright Clearance Center for articles: Robert A. Burgelman (1983), 'A Model of the Interaction of Strategic Behavior, Corporate Context, and the Concept of Strategy', *Academy of Management Review*, **8** (1), 61–70; Shaker A. Zahra (1996), 'Governance, Ownership, and Corporate Entrepreneurship: The Moderating Impact of Industry Technological Opportunities', *Academy of Management Journal*, **39** (6), December, 1713–35; Donald F. Kuratko, R. Duane Ireland and Jeffrey S. Hornsby (2001), 'Improving Firm Performance Through Entrepreneurial Actions: Acordia's Corporate Entrepreneurship Strategy', *Academy of Management Executive*, **15** (4), 60–71.

Elsevier for articles: Ian C. MacMillan, Zenas Block and P.N. Subba Narasimha (1986), 'Corporate Venturing: Alternatives, Obstacles Encountered, and Experience Effects', *Journal of Business Venturing*, **1**, 177–91; Robin Siegel, Eric Siegel and Ian C. MacMillan (1988), 'Corporate Venture Capitalists: Autonomy, Obstacles, and Performance', *Journal of Business Venturing*, **3**, 233–47; Hollister B. Sykes (1990), 'Corporate Venture Capital: Strategies for Success', *Journal of Business Venturing*, **5**, 37–47; Shaker A. Zahra (1991), 'Predictors and Financial Outcomes of Corporate Entrepreneurship: An Exploratory Study', *Journal of Business*

Venturing, **6**, 259–85; Shaker A. Zahra and Jeffrey G. Covin (1995), 'Contextual Influences on the Corporate Entrepreneurship–Performance Relationship: A Longitudinal Analysis', *Journal of Business Venturing*, **10**, 43–58; Scott Shane, S. Venkataraman and Ian MacMillan (1995), 'Cultural Differences in Innovation Championing Strategies', *Journal of Management*, **21** (5), 931–52; Igor Filatotchev, Mike Wright, Trevor Buck and Vladimir Zhukov (1999), 'Corporate Entrepreneurs and Privatized Firms in Russia, Ukraine and Belarus', *Journal of Business Venturing*, **14**, 475–92; Shaker A. Zahra and Dennis M. Garvis (2000), 'International Corporate Entrepreneurship and Firm Performance: The Moderating Effect of International Environmental Hostility', *Journal of Business Venturing*, **15**, 469–92; Stewart Thornhill and Raphael Amit (2000), 'A Dynamic Perspective of Internal Fit in Corporate Venturing', *Journal of Business Venturing*, **16**, 25–50; Jeffrey S. Hornsby, Donald F. Kuratko and Shaker A. Zahra (2002), 'Middle Managers' Perception of the Internal Environment for Corporate Entrepreneurship: Assessing a Measurement Scale', *Journal of Business Venturing*, **17** (3), 253–73; Gregory G. Dess, R. Duane Ireland, Shaker A. Zahra, Steven W. Floyd, Jay J. Janney and Peter J. Lane (2003), 'Emerging Issues in Corporate Entrepreneurship', *Journal of Management*, **29** (3), Special Issue on Entrepreneurship, 351–78; Kenneth Husted and Christian Vintergaard (2004), 'Stimulating Innovation Through Corporate Venture Bases', *Journal of World Business*, **39**, 296–306.

Federal Reserve Bank of Atlanta for article: Paul A. Gompers (2002), 'Corporations and the Financing of Innovation: The Corporate Venturing Experience', *Federal Reserve Bank of Atlanta Economic Review*, **87** (4), Fourth Quarter, 1–17.

Harvard Business School Publishing Corporation for article: Donald A. Schon (1963), 'Champions for Radical New Inventions', *Harvard Business Review*, **41** (2), March–April, 77–86.

Institute for Operations Research and the Management Sciences for articles: Danny Miller (1983), 'The Correlates of Entrepreneurship in Three Types of Firms', *Management Science*, **29** (7), July, 770–91; Deborah Dougherty (1992), 'Interpretive Barriers to Successful Product Innovation in Large Firms', *Organization Science*, **3** (2), May, 179–202; Diana L. Day (1994), 'Raising Radicals: Different Processes for Championing Innovative Corporate Ventures', *Organization Science*, **5** (2), May, 148–72.

Palgrave Macmillan for article: Michael H. Morris, Duane L. Davis and Jeffrey W. Allen (1994), 'Fostering Corporate Entrepreneurship: Cross-cultural Comparisons of the Importance of Individualism Versus Collectivism', *Journal of International Business Studies*, **25** (1), First Quarter, 65–89.

The Regents of the University of California for articles: Henry Chesbrough (2000), 'Designing Corporate Ventures in the Shadow of Private Venture Capital', *California Management Review*, **42** (3), Spring, 31–49; Gina Colarelli O'Connor and Mark P. Rice (2001), 'Opportunity Recognition and Breakthrough Innovation in Large Established Firms', *California Management Review*, **43** (2), Winter, 95–116.

John Wiley & Sons Limited for articles: William D. Guth and Ari Ginsberg (1990), 'Guest Editors' Introduction: Corporate Entrepreneurship', *Strategic Management Journal*, **11**, 5–15; Donald F. Kuratko, Ray V. Montagno and Jeffrey S. Hornsby (1990), 'Developing an Intrapreneurial Assessment Instrument for an Effective Corporate Entrepreneurial Environment', *Strategic Management Journal*, **11**, 49–58; Julian Birkinshaw (1997), 'Entrepreneurship in Multinational Corporations: The Characteristics of Subsidiary Initiatives', *Strategic Management Journal*, **18** (3), 207–29; Gregory G. Dess, G.T. Lumpkin and J.G. Covin (1997), 'Entrepreneurial Strategy Making and Firm Performance: Tests of Contingency and Configurational Models', *Strategic Management Journal*, **18** (9), 677–95; Bruce R. Barringer and Allen C. Bluedorn (1999), 'The Relationship Between Corporate Entrepreneurship and Strategic Management', *Strategic Management Journal*, **20** (5), 421–44.

Every effort has been made to trace all the copyright holders but if any have been inadvertently overlooked the publishers will be pleased to make the necessary arrangement at the first opportunity.

In addition the publishers wish to thank the Marshall Library of Economics, Cambridge University, the Library of the University of Warwick, and the Library of Indiana University at Bloomington, USA for their assistance in obtaining these articles.

Introduction

Shaker A. Zahra

The study of corporate entrepreneurship (CE) has grown rapidly over the past two decades. Despite persistent debates about its domain and contributions (Sathe, 2003), CE is now integrated into almost every major research conference on entrepreneurship around the globe. Researchers have also made strides in discussing, analyzing and documenting the effects of CE on organizational performance, both financial and non-financial (Ahuja and Lampert, 2001; Baden-Fuller, 1995; Kuratko, Ireland and Hornsby, 2001; Zahra, Jennings and Kuratko, Chapter 18, this volume). CE has become an important component of the business curriculum in undergraduate and graduate programs in the USA and elsewhere. Some universities have also developed research centers and executive development programs on the topic.

These major achievements in the study and teaching of CE cover some persistent and thorny issues that have limited research progress. For instance, what do we mean by CE? What are the theoretical foundations of CE research? How and when does CE contribute to value creation? With a growing emphasis on organizational growth as a way of creating value, prior research does not seem to offer much guidance on how best to use CE initiatives to nurture, achieve and cultivate this growth. Though these issues have been the subject of discussion and debate, scholars remain divided in their conclusions.

There is agreement that companies could use CE to sail against the winds of change, prosper and achieve growth. Therefore, in this Introduction I will cover issues associated with the entrepreneurial mindset that underlies CE; analyze the various dimensions of CE; discuss how CE could lead to organizational growth; discuss how companies can design effective corporate venturing programs that allow them to create value and learn new skills and capabilities; analyze the various antecedents of CE, highlighting the importance of fit; explore the implications of the dynamic interplay between a firm's CE and competitive strategy; and discuss the effect of national culture on CE. In discussing these themes, I will highlight key research findings research to date and issues of importance for future research.

Transplanting and Cultivating the Entrepreneurial Mindset

Most CE research is predicated on the proposition that managers and individual employees could be inspired to act entrepreneurially, introduce innovations of different types, and harvest these innovations through profitability and growth (Block and MacMillan, 1993; Bowman, 1999; Brazeal, 1993; Kanter, 1983; Morris, 1998; Sathe, 2003). There is a belief that managers and their companies can create an environment that stimulates individual creativity by encouraging collaborative work and fostering a desire to assume the financial, political and reputational risks necessary to create and manage new businesses within existing organizational boundaries. Proponents of this view believe that an entrepreneurial mindset is essential in making these changes desirable and possible (Morris, 1998; Munk, 1998; Pinchot, 1985). This mindset emphasizes alertness in identifying, evaluating, and choosing particular opportunities for development. It centers also on agility in assembling and deploying resources to achieve desired outcomes. Achieving this agility demands creative thinking that overcomes key cognitive barriers that stifle effective opportunity recognition and definition. As such, an entrepreneurial mindset involves thinking creatively and perhaps differently about the industry, its structure, and competitive dynamics. It probes different scenarios of possible trajectories of an industry's evolution. This mindset induces changes not only in how the industry is organized but also in how it is defined and perceived, and how companies within the industry relate to each other and to other companies in other industries.

An ethos supportive of such CE activities usually revolves around making people secure enough to initiate new ventures and tolerate the risks associated with their emergence, development, and growth. This ethos lies in people's minds, as they ponder whether an opportunity actually exists, what this opportunity is all about, how big it is, and how its evolutionary trajectory might look. The rules that guide the decisions that managers and employees contemplate are frequently vague and imprecise. Managers can only create the context that makes people feel safe enough to express their views, come forward and share their ideas, and explore various opportunities (Kanter, 1982; Morris, Davis and Allen, Chapter 30, this volume; Sathe, 2003). Managers shape this context by being supportive of subordinates' initiatives, and shielding them against bureaucracy and potential retaliation from existing power centers that work hard to protect the status quo.

A key and promising development in the study of organizational entrepreneurial mindsets is the recent introduction of cognitive concepts and methods of inquiry into the study of intrepreneurs' decision-making behaviors. Probing entrepreneurs' belief systems can only sharpen our understanding of the informal processes associated with the discovery and definition of opportunities within established firms, and how these processes might unfold over time. This research also gives us a more realistic perspective of how individuals in a company see where different opportunities lie and how they can create the political support and organizational momentum necessary to pursue these opportunities.

Ethnographic methods are powerful in deciphering the sequence of events shaping the evolution of different CE initiatives, the changes that occur in them as they are considered and analyzed by different groups in the organization, and the factors that lead companies to adopt particular CE initiatives but reject others. I think this is an important turning point. For a long time, researchers have been preoccupied with documenting the effects of CE on organizational performance. As a result, they have failed to examine the ecology of CE projects and how it comes to bear on their adoption and rejection (Burgelman, 1991). This gap in the literature is surprising because of the acknowledged importance of informal CE activities and the fact that many of them never receive the formal recognition and support of management. Given the criticality of these autonomous activities for successful CE, it would be crucial to identify the factors that make some of them acceptable to management. Therefore, attention should be given to the nature and consequences of CE ideas and ventures. The context in which these projects are proposed and analyzed should also be considered. For example, researchers should consider the champions who support and lobby CE ideas (Zahra, 2005) and the political clout champions have in their organization.

From a Mindset to Behavior: Dimensions of CE

One of the most persistent and frustrating issues in the literature is the absence of a unified and widely accepted definition of the CE concept. Most researchers accept Danny Miller's (Chapter 16, this volume) definition that CE has three dimensions: innovativeness, proactiveness, and risk taking. Innovativeness refers to a firm's investment in and commitment to product, process and organizational innovation. Not only does innovation transform a company (Quinn, 1985), but it also creates new market spaces in which new competencies provide avenues for growth (Kim and Mauborgne, 1999; Markides, 1997, 1998). Proactiveness denotes a firm's disposition and actual commitment to beating the competition by being first to the market with new products, systems or processes. Risk taking signals a firm's willingness to assume the various risks associated with new venture creation even when the payoff is uncertain.

Some researchers have also shown that the dimensions of innovativeness, proactiveness and risk taking form a single, multidimensional measure of CE (Knight, 1997). Zahra et al. (Chapter 18, this volume), however, note that while prior researchers are justified in using Miller's definition, they do so to capture the richness of informal CE activities that occur within the organization. Informal activities are an important part of what employees, middle managers and senior executives do as they promote innovation and create momentum for change in their companies. Zahra (Chapter 17, this volume) argues that CE definitions should embody both formal and informal dimensions and offer a measure of informal CE activities, calling for further research on these informal activities ('intrapreneurship'). Despite these calls for research, we do not know much about the content of intrapreneurial activities.

Birkinshaw's (Chapter 1, this volume) research highlights the importance of intrapreneurial activities in redefining what the firm does and how it goes about accomplishing its goals. Focusing on subsidiaries of multinational corporations (MNCs), Birkinshaw offers a number of important explanations of these activities, including internal competition and the quest for strategic variety. Some of these activities are deliberate, seeking to overcome stagnation within the firm. Others are spontaneous and improvisational in nature, reflecting middle managers' recognition of emerging opportunities that could transform their companies' businesses and create new growth options. This distinction between 'deliberate' and 'improvisational' CE efforts echoes the early work of Burgleman (1983; Chapters 2 and 28, this volume) who separated 'induced' from 'autonomous' strategic behaviors that he observed while studying corporate venturing activities.

Guth and Ginsberg (Chapter 3) have attempted to integrate definitions of CE, proposing that various CE definitions fall under two categories: innovation and venturing. Unlike Miller (Chapter 16, this volume), however, Guth and Ginsberg adopt a broader view of innovation, not limiting it to only radical new product development. Guth and Ginsberg also distinguish internal from external venturing activities, noting that the organizational motivations for undertaking each are different. Zahra (1993) used Guth and Ginsberg's definition to show that CE activities (innovation and venturing) based on a firm's environment and the payoff from innovation versus venturing activities also varies from one competitive environmental setting to another. More recently, Husted and Vintergaard (Chapter 5, this volume) have argued compellingly that corporate venturing activities could stimulate innovation and spur growth, providing additional and thoughtful evidence that companies could gain considerably from nurturing and sustaining CE activities.

Sharma and Chrisman (Chapter 6, this volume) have enriched the field by reviewing, categorizing and defining the various dimensions of CE. Their classification offers an important and rich foundation for careful theoretical and empirical work that establishes the dimensionality of the CE construct and, if multiple dimensions do exist, the relationship between these dimensions and their potential links to key organizational performance outcomes such as profitability and growth.

Other researchers have also examined the dimensions of corporate entrepreneurship. For example, Covin (1991) and Covin and Slevin (1989) have refined Miller's (Chapter 16, this volume) measure, setting the stage for fruitful empirical analysis. Zahra (Chapter 17, this volume) has extended Miller's (Chapter 16, this volume) work by considering informal CE activities. Hornsby, Kuratko, and Montagno (1999) also have developed an instrument to measure corporate entrepreneurial environments, capturing the willingness or disposition of a firm's managers to support and foster CE activities in its operations.

The above discussion highlights the continuing interest in conceptualizing and measuring CE activities. Though attention has centered on these issues, researchers have not probed the mindset that underlies these behaviors. What are the characteristics of this mindset? How different is this mindset from individual entrepreneurs' mindsets? Is there a significant difference between these different mindsets in terms of how people spot and evaluate opportunities and proceed to assemble the resources necessary to pursue them? Are there significant differences also in the motivations to exploit these opportunities? These are simple but important questions that deserve recognition and exploration in future research, especially as many advise companies to emulate the behaviors and strategies of independent entrepreneurs to stimulate CE in their operations. Gaining an appreciation of the similarities and differences in the mindsets that underlie independent entrepreneur versus CE could also be beneficial in devising effective strategies to implement entrepreneurial activities.

CE and Organizational Growth

Several studies have made clear that CE could foster organizational growth. For instance, Zahra (Chapter 17, this volume; 1993) reported a positive association between his measures of CE and sales and revenue growth. Wiklund (1999) also found a positive association between CE and revenue growth. Zahra and Covin (Chapter 26, this volume) also reported a positive association between changes in CE and organizational growth. These results of the studies just cited, however, suffer from several limitations that include survivor bias, the use of cross-sectional designs that preclude making firm causal inferences, and short time windows that make it difficult to assess the long-term contributions of CE to organizational growth. CE researchers have not been consistent with their conceptualization and measurement of growth.

Most prior research on the link between CE and organizational growth has been *atheoretical*. Researchers have advanced several explanations for the positive relationship between CE and organizational growth. The most common is that CE leads to new venture creation by combining resources and uncovering opportunities for growth. Resource combinations are important for creating growth options, within existing operations and in new market arenas. Some resource combinations are likely to be radically new and therefore enable the organization to pursue new avenues for growth. Missing from this literature, however, is a systematic effort that documents the various types of resource recombinations that might occur within the various CE processes. Also, we do not know if these combinations are different from those already noted by Schumpeter (1934). If these combinations are qualitatively different, then one could easily see how CE might introduce variety into incumbent firms' strategic repertoire.

A second explanation is that CE leads to the creation of new knowledge that is useful in finding new opportunities and creatively exploiting them to achieve growth. Zahra, Nielsen, and Bogner (Chapter 33, this volume) have advanced this view, arguing that CE activities could generate new knowledge that serves as a foundation for conceptualizing and locating new opportunities, revising where and how a company competes, and refining the competitive advantage the firm can develop in new market arenas. Zahra et al. (Chapter 33, this volume) also suggested that CE activities can help infuse the organization with new ideas based on the knowledge created internally, offering a basis for exploring new growth options. This knowledge could also infuse new mental models that alter the way managers view their markets and competition and define their firms' competitive priorities. These mental models could underlie the processes by which companies proceed to revise their industries and the rules that govern competition in them. Keil (2004) has also shown that external modes of CE could also create and exploit new knowledge in existing or new market arenas, intensifying the momentum for growth.

A serious weakness of the literature is the lack of attention to linking a firm's intellectual capital base to its CE activities. Indeed, there has been little effort devoted to theorizing about and empirically exploring the links that might exist between different components of a firm's intellectual capital and various CE activities. Therefore, we do not know that a firm's effective human resource and intellectual capital management practices can stimulate and sustain different CE activities. Moreover, we do not know how changes in a firm's knowledge base, epitomized in its intellectual capital, influence the intensity and direction of future CE activities. This gap in the literature is surprising, given the huge investments that companies make in assembling and upgrading their human resource bases. With the growing interest in the knowledge-based theory of the firm, one would have expected greater recognition of the effect of the stocks (amounts) and flows (changes) of intellectual capital on CE activities, both domestic and international. Knowledge *stocks* could be harvested to attain profitability. Knowledge *flows* can significantly influence the pace and direction of a firm's growth (Dierickx and Cool, 1989).

Designing Effective Corporate Venturing Programs

There is agreement in the literature that venturing is one of the key dimensions of CE, and that venturing could be internal or external in focus (Keil, 2004). Internal venturing focuses on pursuing opportunities within a company's various ongoing operations (Zahra and Yu, 2005). External venturing stresses exploiting opportunities outside the boundaries of a firm's existing (traditional) operations. Companies use internal *and* external venturing to redefine their business concepts, explore new business models, and revitalize their operations. Despite nearly two decades of research, the conditions under which the internal and external modes of corporate venturing complement vs. substitute each other are not well understood, highlighting a topic of immense interest for future research.

Companies often use a portfolio of CE initiatives. In developing this portfolio, companies are apt to consider their current and future core competencies; desired growth vectors and levels; implications for business and other types of risks; and operational and strategic synergies and their effects on shareholders' value. Companies need to retain some degree of strategic coherence while venturing into the unknown. This is a difficult task to manage, but it is one of senior executives' most important responsibilities. This task is further complicated by the fact that managers cannot predict the evolutionary paths of various CE activities. As March (1991) proposes, experimentation induces unpredictability and variance. Senior executives cannot know a priori how CE activities will develop.

Researchers have studied the process of internal corporate venturing. Prior research documents the importance of internal venturing; the organizational and environmental conditions that stimulate venturing activities; the various approaches that companies can follow in their venturing; and the financial and non-financial (e.g., organizational learning) consequences of internal venturing. Prior studies have also highlighted the critical importance of having champions at different levels of the organization to promote and sustain internal venturing. Similarly, researchers have also investigated the structural, cognitive and political obstacles of internal venturing and how managers could overcome them.

Future researchers need to examine further the roles champions play in formal and autonomous CE ventures. To be sure, Schon (Chapter 23, this volume) discusses the different types of champions, motives, and skills. Shane (1994) has explored the differences between champions and non-champions. Shane, Venkataraman, and MacMillan (Chapter 24, this volume) have explored the influence of national cultures on championing behavior. Still, we know little about these differences, even though it is well understood that they could determine the fate of CE activities. It is important also to investigate the fate of these champions, especially those that sponsor and promote radical CE ideas and initiatives. Researchers readily acknowledge that champions risk losing their jobs and undermining their own reputations as they push for particular CE initiatives. Aside from a few case studies, we do not know how organizations treat these champions and what happens to their careers.

In recent years, researchers have examined how internal venturing supports organizational learning and the emergence and development of new capabilities (Zahra et al., Chapter 33, this volume) – including dynamic capabilities. This research is in its infancy but indicates that internal venturing could be an important forum for creating new knowledge that allows the firm to develop new routines that become the foundation of new skills and capabilities. This emerging literature also reveals that senior managers' recognition of this knowledge and organizational learning as potentially valuable strategic resources is crucial to revising a firm's strategic repertoire. Moreover, the effective integration of this knowledge promotes the firm's ability to develop those capabilities that allow it to compete differently in current or new markets. An important future research avenue is how internal venturing can enhance organizational growth, especially in revenue and profitability, through the creation of new capabilities.

The role of internal and external venturing activities in creating new knowledge deserves further recognition because it underscores the importance of organizational learning and knowledge creation in revitalizing the firm's competitive repertoire. Knowledge is a key foundation of competitive strategy and the source of competitive advantage, especially in hypercompetitive business environments. If CE results in new types of knowledge, then researchers should document how and which new knowledge is created; how this knowledge is shared, evaluated, and integrated into the firm's various activities; what are the various roles that managers at different organizational levels play in these processes; and how new knowledge is diffused in the organization. Currently, little is known about when new knowledge displaces the present knowledge and what happens to existing organizational routines and systems as a consequence. New knowledge does not always 'add' to existing knowledge; it can suppress or even displace it, possibly confounding the firm's ability to conceptualize the market, its competition and its performance.

Infusion of new knowledge through CE can have serious organizational consequences. It could revise how the organization views its business and core competencies; how it structures its operations; and how it determines who holds power in the firm. Changes in the stocks and flows of knowledge can also profoundly alter these power centers, inducing tensions and conflicts about organizational priorities, resource allocations, and strategic choices. These issues are at the core of the processes of organizational evolution and influence a firm's competitive performance. Greater attention to these issues would help to bring about greater clarity about how entrepreneurship shapes organizational renewal and, as a result, evolution.

Keil (2004) discusses the key forms of external venturing. In turn, the diversity of these modes highlights the potential synergies and trade-offs that might exist between the various approaches open to companies as they venture externally to seek and to capture their potentially differential effects on a firm's financial performance, particularly profitability and growth. Some have also analyzed the efficacy of different modes of external venturing on organizational learning (Keil, Maula and Zahra, 2004), suggesting that companies can acquire new knowledge from the outside and use it in their operations. This knowledge can stretch the firm's cognitive map, fostering its ability to conceive of different and new competitive arenas and develop new ways to compete. Yet, the literature also indicates that three activities are essential to benefit from external venturing activities in promoting organizational learning. First, the firm has to have the requisite absorptive capacity to spot, value, acquire, assimilate and use external knowledge. As Zahra and George (2002) suggest, each of these activities requires a different set of organizational skills. Spotting and valuing relevant information requires effective environmental scanning. Assimilating and absorbing this knowledge requires effective and multifunctional integration. Exploiting this knowledge demands an ability to envision industry evolution and a capacity to innovate. Second, there is a need for the effective integration of external knowledge into the firm's operations by the firm's senior managers (Zahra and Nielsen, 2002). This integration could be formal or informal. Third, there is the need to manage the co-evolution of the firm and its capabilities in ways that inform and shape the development of its corporate and competitive strategies. Consequently, senior executives should have a vision for their organization's evolution and how this evolution fits with industry conditions.

Corporate venture capital (CVC) is one type of external venturing. CVC has been the subject of much discussion in recent years (Chesbrough, 2002; Chesbrough and Socolof, 2000; Keil, Maula and Zahra, 2004). CVC investments connect established companies to new ventures' networks in and outside their industries and make it possible to cast a wide net as they seek to capture knowledge about potential technological and industry changes. Some CVC investments are financial in nature, with established companies reaping primarily financial gains from these investments (Chesbrough, 2002; Chesbrough and Socolof, 2000). Other CVC investments are made with specific strategic objectives in mind, bringing new knowledge into a company's operations. This new knowledge enables incumbents to spot technological discontinuities, learn about emerging market trends, identify potential competitors, define changing success factors in the industry, and determine potential alliance partners or acquisition targets (Keil et al., 2004). Research has only begun to explore the various conditions under which such strategic investments add value to incumbents and allow them to learn and develop new competencies. This research should also investigate the strategic and financial implications of CVC for those new ventures that receive such funding. Further, we do not know much about the changing relationship between incumbents and the new ventures in which they invest and the factors that create trust between these two groups of firms, enabling them to learn from each other and form beneficial alliances that lead to greater innovation and higher financial performance.

Recently, some have studied the portfolio of internal and external (e.g., CVC) venturing activities that firms pursue. Key questions explored in recent research are: What is the optimal venturing portfolio that maximizes organizational performance? What are the key factors that determine this 'optimal portfolio'? When does external venturing complement vs. substitute internal venturing? Is there a virtual venture cycle, where an increase in external venturing also promotes internal venturing? Alternatively, is there a vicious cycle where external venturing consumes management resources and attention, depressing internal venturing activities? When does such a vicious (or virtuous) cycle exist? When and how does the cycle shift from virtuous to vicious venturing activities? What are the key factors that determine changes in the composition of a firm's portfolio of internal and corporate external venturing activities? How do companies manage the tensions that arise in the course of reorienting their internal and external venturing efforts as a consequence of CVC? By answering these questions, we can begin to appreciate the learning effects of CVC and other types of CE activities.

CVC can also help incumbents develop a constellation of beneficial relationships that add value. Therefore, it would be worthwhile to investigate the organizational structures and systems that companies create to manage these relationships. Reviewing the literature, it quickly becomes evident that there is little systematic documentation in the way that companies structure these relationships, how and when they interact with the new ventures in which they invest, and how they collate the knowledge they glean from these relationships and exploit it into their own operations. CVC managers also have to balance the need for building trust with the new ventures in which they invest and their own needs to learn about emerging technologies and business models. Case studies and large-scale research could clarify these issues, improving our understanding of the political and organizational factors that limit incumbents' ability to learn from their growing networks, especially those formed with new ventures through CVC investments.

Antecedents of CE: The Nexus of Structure, Organization and Environment

A cursory review of the CE literature would suggest that considerable effort has been devoted to studying the antecedents of CE. Without a doubt, this is the most widely researched area in CE. Researchers have investigated the independent and interactive effects of the firm's external environment (Miller, Chapter 16, this volume; Zahra, Chapter 17, this volume; 1993), organizational structures (Covin and Slevin, 1989; Miller, Chapter 16); managerial incentives and ownership (Zahra, Chapter 22, this volume; Zahra, Neubaum and Huse, 2000), organizational culture (Day, Chapter 20, this volume), ideology (Chung and Gibbons, 1997), among others. Other researchers have studied the effect of managerial decision making, styles and roles in promoting CE (Kuratko et al., 2001).

Given the number of studies reporting on these issues to date, it is fair to ask: What are the general conclusions one can derive from prior research? I believe that there are only a few conclusions that one can generalize with some confidence. One conclusion is a need for an organic structure to promote CE. The value of this structure in inducing and enhancing CE is greater when a firm's external environment is dynamic, as Covin and Slevin (1989) found out. Structural organicity makes it possible to implement CE initiatives and, in addition, gather the information necessary to explore avenues for innovation and change. When organic structures prevail, the flow of information within the firm's systems and operations makes it easier to spot opportunities and explore their strategic relevance. Organic structures also create a sense of empowerment, one that makes managers and employees feel able and willing to assume the risks of strategic change.

Another key conclusion from prior research is the need to achieve fit between the firm's portfolios of CE activities with its external environment. Given that the environment is subject to much dynamism, fit is temporary at best. This places considerable pressure on senior managers to scan their environments and reconsider their portfolio of CE activities and achieve fit. Organizational structures and systems are often too difficult to change, and organizational cultural norms are even more difficult to alter in the short term.

A third general finding from research is the critical importance of senior management in promoting CE efforts, even those that emanate informally. Senior executives articulate the need for CE, provide the context with which these activities might flourish, and define the strategic relevance of its contributions. Equally important, senior managers select, evaluate and compensate middle managers who, for the most part, are often the champions of CE initiatives.

Looking at the voluminous body of research on the antecedents of CE, it is tempting to suggest a need to move on and explore other topics. This would be a premature conclusion, given that several issues remain unexplored. Researchers have yet to explore the relationships between these antecedent conditions and different CE dimensions over time and how changes in these relationships could influence organizational performance. Such longitudinal research would help address another issue: Do certain structural variables enhance particular CE initiatives while handicapping others? If so, how do managers address the potential tradeoffs that might exist in this regard? Is there a process of 'sequential attention' at play, where managers focus on aligning a particular structure with a given CE activity and, once success is achieved, then focus on other initiatives? If this is the case, how can we reconcile this decision-making process with findings using survey methods that highlight the importance of overall fit between structure and CE? Are these results valid?

Probing the links between antecedent conditions and CE draws attention to the possible substitution that might exist among a firm's structure, leadership, strategy, and culture. For instance, does the use of particular organizational structures reduce the need for formal leadership of CE activities? If this is true, what does this tell us about prior research findings emphasizing the central role of leadership and management support in promoting CE? Further, we need to know if certain types of leadership do well in ensuring the success of certain CE initiatives. Knowing this can provide clarity about the organizational strategies intended to prepare such leaders and effectively match them with the various CE activities that the firm is undertaking.

A related issue that has not received sufficient recognition is the role of informal champions vs. official leaders within CE. It would be beneficial, therefore, to investigate when these roles supplement, augment or substitute each other.

The Interplay Between Entrepreneurship and Strategy

Early research has highlighted the role of formal and informal CE activities in defining a company's business, strategic arena, and growth options. This research has shown that informal (autonomous) CE activities broaden the firm's search, allowing it to supplement formal (induced) strategic moves. Barringer and Bluedorn (Chapter 27, this volume) have analyzed the important link between CE and strategy. Hoskisson and Busenitz (2000) have discussed the implications of CE for diversification, a key corporate strategy. These authors make it clear that the CE–diversification link has serious implications for organizational learning and the development of new capabilities.

It is reassuring to know that researchers recognize the valuable contributions that CE can make to the firm's business definition and strategic re-orientation. Missing from the literature is a systematic effort to delineate the implications of CE for organizational evolution and how this evolution might take place under different resource and environmental conditions. One reason for the absence of such an integrative framework is the complexity of the process of organizational evolution itself. Cognitive, technical, political and organizational variables frequently combine to define the nature of this evolution, its process, and consequences. Path dependencies and external variables also influence the direction, speed and magnitude of this evolution.

Future research could also improve our thinking about the influence of CE on competitive strategy. As used in the literature, CE is an organization-wide phenomenon whose objective is to improve firm performance. As noted throughout this Introduction, the new knowledge CE activities generate could provide a foundation for new skills and capabilities that could be used to revise the firm's competitive strategies. We see some evidence of this important role of CE in recent research on entrepreneurial activities within subsidiaries; these activities create new competencies to compete differently in different countries and world regions (Birkinshaw and Hood, 1998). The same logic applies to the various divisions of the large, established corporation.

For years, researchers have viewed corporate entrepreneurs as mariners sailing against the wind. With much at stake, these entrepreneurs have to work behind the scene or underground (Pinchot, 1985). Much has changed over the past 20 years, with companies' growing recognition of the potential value added of CE for growth. Thus, corporate entrepreneurs can influence organizational thinking about potential market arenas and how best to compete in them. CE, therefore, could become the forerunner of corporate-wide radical strategic change.

National Culture and CE

One of the most exciting trends in the CE literature is the growing attention to international issues (Dess et al., Chapter 34, this volume; Kemelgor, 2002). Researchers across the world's six major continents have explored different facets of CE and how they might influence organizational profitability and growth. Researchers have also examined how national cultural variables might influence the propensity to support and pursue CE (Zahra, Neck and Kelley, 2004). Though the studies seeking to clarify the links between national cultural variables and CE remain few in number, they are informative. They report that national cultural variables influence organizational cultures and personality variables. In turn, organizational cultures and personality variables often determine the intensity and types of CE activities.

Research linking national cultures and CE is important for several reasons. National cultures define the meaning and measurement of risk as the penalties and rewards associated with taking such risks. In some countries (e.g., the USA), being an entrepreneur is respected and highly rewarded. In other countries (e.g., Denmark), taking the risks associated with entrepreneurship is not widely accepted. In addition to defining the nature and desirability of risks, national cultures influence planning and investment horizons, the acceptable period in which a person or firm could invest without expecting returns. Traditionally, Japanese and Korean companies have shown a strong proclivity to invest patiently in new product and market development. In contrast, US companies appear to have shorter planning and investment horizons, possibly reflecting the powerful influence of the stock market and national values. Differences in investment horizons, no doubt, determine companies' investments in CE and the returns they might expect from these activities.

National cultures also offer an interesting explanation of why countries might differ in their entrepreneurial activities and why certain activities might flourish in one society but not in another. Understanding the sources of this variability can help explain observed differences in the rates of innovation as well as the level of technological and economic development across countries. It also provides rich insights as to why countries might differ significantly in their global competitiveness. By identifying national cultural variables that foster CE, government officials and public policy makers have a foundation from which to bring about changes that can spur their national companies' innovation.

Moreover, with increased flows of knowledge from other countries and companies, building institutional absorptive capacity assumes greater strategic relevance in the contest for global technological supremacy. Korea's rise to the ranks of a global technological leader is a case in point, where a country has worked hard to build institutional absorptive capacity to assimilate knowledge gained from other countries and then infuse it into its established companies. Singapore has done the same thing in its bid to become a global powerhouse in information technology. Similarly, India's global leadership in the software industry has benefited from having this capacity. Likewise, Costa Rica's growing semiconductor industry has benefited from building and then harvesting its institutional absorptive capacity. These examples serve as a reminder of the need for researchers to explore the importance of public policy choices for CE activities that flourish in some countries but not others. Conversely, it is relatively easy to see how the success of certain CE activities in some leading national organizations could inspire governments and public policy makers to target certain economic sectors for future development as national innovation hubs.

As noted earlier, one area where CE research has increased is the study of MNCs and their subsidiaries. This interest is understandable given MNCs' importance in the global economy, their role in transferring knowledge and technology, and their proven ability to harvest innovations on a worldwide scale. Moreover, increasingly subsidiaries enjoy greater autonomy from their parent MNCs and many have proceeded to capitalize on the unique resources (especially knowledge) that exist in their local markets through innovation. Some subsidiaries have also shown great creativity in cultivating local knowledge in developing original innovations or revising their existing products and goods. Successful subsidiary innovations might be diffused throughout their parent MNCs' networks.

The growing prominence of MNCs and their subsides as centers for innovation and entrepreneurship suggests several questions for future research: Why are some subsidiaries more entrepreneurial than others? What are the relative contributions of these firms' location, resources, mission, management, and culture? Where do CE ideas emanate in these subsidiaries? How are they evaluated, by whom, and against which criteria? How do subsidiaries transfer their best practices to the MNC's network? What are the strategies that subsidiaries use in this regard? How does the parent MNC cultivate or integrate the diverse innovations their subsidiaries develop? What is the effect of subsidiaries on their parent MNCs' entrepreneurialism? How do CE initiatives shape MNCs' growth paths and speed of growth?

Conclusion

Research on CE has grown rapidly over the past two decades. This research has been uneven in its coverage of critical issues associated with the initiation and effective implementation of different CE activities. This Introduction has highlighted progress made to date and the key issues that deserve greater scrutiny and attention in future research. Clearly, opportunities for future research on CE abound, offering considerable room for the use of multiple qualitative and quantitative research methods. The implications of CE for the creation of capabilities that define the competitive arena and determine the future paths of growth especially in international markets are of special research interest. Future research on CE promises to continue to accelerate, speaking to a worldwide audience.

References

Ahuja, G. and Lampert, C.M. (2001), 'Entrepreneurship in the large corporation: A longitudinal study of how established firms create breakthrough inventions', *Strategic Management Journal*, **22**, 521–43.

Baden-Fuller, C. (1995), 'Strategic innovation, corporate entrepreneurship and matching outside-in to inside-out approaches to strategy research', *British Journal of Management*, **6**, S3–S16.

Birkinshaw, J. and Hood, N. (1998), 'Multinational subsidiary evolution: Capability and charter change in foreign-owned subsidiary companies', *Academy of Management Review*, **23**, 773–95.

Block, Z. and MacMillan, I.C. (1993), *Corporate Venturing: Creating New Businesses Within the Firm*, Boston, MA: Harvard Business School Press.

Bowman, C. (1999), 'Why we need entrepreneurs, not managers', *General Management Review*, **1** (1), 15–23.

Brazeal, D.V. (1993), 'Organizing for internally developed corporate ventures', *Journal of Business Venturing*, 8 (1), 75–90.

Burgelman, R.A. (1983), 'Corporate entrepreneurship and strategic management: Insights from a process study', *Management Science*, **29** (12), 1349–64.

Burgelman, R.A. (1991), 'Intraorganizational ecology of strategy making and organizational adaptation: Theory and field research', *Organizational Science*, **2**, 239–62.

Chesbrough, H.W. (2002), 'Making sense of corporate venture capital', *Harvard Business Review*, **80** (3), 9–100.

Chesbrough, H.W. and Socolof, S.J. (2000), 'Creating new ventures from Bell Labs technologies', *Research Technology Management*, **43** (2), 13–18.

Chung, L.H. and Gibbons, P.T. (1997), 'Corporate entrepreneurship: The roles of ideology and social capital', *Group and Organization Management*, **22**, 10–30.

Covin, J.G. (1991), 'Entrepreneurial versus conservative firms: A comparison of strategies and performance', *Journal of Management Studies*, **28** (5), 439–62.

Covin, J. and Slevin, D. (1989), 'Strategic management of small firms in hostile and benign environments', *Strategic Management Journal*, **10** (1), 75–87.

Dierickx, I. and Cool, K. (1989), 'Asset stock accumulation and the sustainability of competitive advantage', *Management Science*, **35**, 1504–11.

Hornsby, J.S., Kuratko, D.F. and Montagno, Ray V. (1999), 'Perception of internal factors for corporate entrepreneurship: A comparison of Canadian and U.S. managers', *Entrepreneurship: Theory and Practice*, **24** (2), 9–25.

Hoskisson, R.E. and Busenitz, L.W. (2000), 'Market uncertainty and learning distance in corporate entrepreneurship entry mode choice', in Hitt, M., Ireland, D., Camp, M. and Sexton, D. (eds), *Strategic Entrepreneurship: Creating a New Mindset*, New York: Blackwell, 151–72.

Kanter, R.M. (1982), 'The middle manger as innovator', *Harvard Business Review*, **60** (4), 95–105.

Kanter, R.M. (1983), *The Change Masters*, New York: Simon and Schuster.

Keil, T. (2004), 'Building external corporate venturing capability', *Journal of Management Studies*, **41**, 799–825.

Keil, T., Maula, M. and Zahra, S. (2004), 'Explorative and exploitative learning from corporate venture capital: Model of program level factors', *Best Paper Proceedings Academy of Management Meetings 2004*, New Orleans, LA, USA, 6–11 August, 2004.

Kemelgor, B.H. (2002), 'A comparative analysis of corporate entrepreneurial orientation between selected firms in the Netherlands and the USA', *Entrepreneurship and Regional Development*, **14** (1), 67–88.

Kim, W.C. and Mauborgne, R. (1999), 'Creating new market space', *Harvard Business Review*, **77** (January–February), 83–93.

Knight, G.A. (1997), 'Cross-cultural reliability and validity of a scale to measure firm entrepreneurial orientation', *Journal of Business Venturing*, **12** (3), 213–26.

Kuratko, D.F., Ireland, R.D. and Hornsby, J.S. (2001), 'Improving firm performance through entrepreneurial actions: Acordia's corporate entrepreneurship strategy', *Academy of Management Executive*, **15** (4), 60–71.

March, J.G. (1991), 'Exploration and exploitation in organizational learning', *Organization Science*, **2** (1), 71–87.

Markides, C. (1997), 'Strategic innovation', *Sloan Management Review*, **38** (3), 9–23.

Markides, C. (1998), 'Strategic innovation in established companies', *Sloan Management Review*, **39** (3), 31–42.

Morris, M.H. (1998), *Entrepreneurial Intensity*, Westport, CT: Quorum Books.

Munk, N. (1998), 'The new organization man', *Fortune*, 16 March, 68–72.

Pinchot, G., III (1985), *Intrapreneuring*, New York: Harper and Row.

Quinn, J.B. (1985), 'Managing innovation: Controlled chaos', *Harvard Business Review*, **63** (3), 73–84.

Sathe, V. (2003), *Corporate Entrepreneurship: Top Managers and New Business Creation*, Cambridge, UK: Cambridge University Press.

Schumpeter, J. (1934), *The Theory of Economic Development*, Cambridge, MA: Harvard University Press.

Shane, S.A. (1994), 'Are champions different from non-champions?' *Journal of Business Venturing*, **9**, 397–421.

Wiklund, J. (1999), 'The sustainability of the entrepreneurial orientation–performance relationship', *Entrepreneurship Theory and Practice*, **24** (1), 37–49.

Zahra, S.A. (1993), 'A conceptual model of entrepreneurship as firm behavior: A critique and extension', *Entrepreneurship Theory and Practice*, **17** (4), 5–21.

Zahra, S. (2005), 'Championing corporate ventures', in Hitt, M. and Ireland, D. (eds), *The Blackwell Encyclopedia of Management (Volume 3): Entrepreneurship*, New York: Blackwell, 28–30.

Zahra, S. and George, G. (2002), 'Absorptive capacity: A review, reconceptualization and extension', *Academy of Management Review*, **27** (2), 185–203.

Zahra, S. and Nielsen, A.P. (2002), 'Sources of capabilities, integration and technology commercialization', *Strategic Management Journal*, **23**, 377–98.

Zahra, S. and Yu, J. (2005), 'Internal venturing', in Hitt, M. and Ireland, D. (eds), *Blackwell Encyclopedia of Management (Volume 3): Entrepreneurship*, New York: Blackwell, 157–59.

Zahra, S., Neubaum, D.O. and Huse, M. (2000), 'Entrepreneurship in medium-size companies: Exploring the effects of ownership and governance systems', *Journal of Management*, **26** (5), 947–76.

Zahra, S., Neck, H. and Kelley, D. (2004), 'International corporate entrepreneurship and the evolution of organizational competence', in Shepherd, D. and Katz, J. (eds), *Advances in Entrepreneurship Research*, New York: JAI Press, 145–71.

Part I
Corporate Entrepreneurship:
Importance and Key Dimensions

Strategic Management Journal, Vol. 18:3, 207–229 (1997)

ENTREPRENEURSHIP IN MULTINATIONAL CORPORATIONS: THE CHARACTERISTICS OF SUBSIDIARY INITIATIVES

JULIAN BIRKINSHAW
Institute of International Business, Stockholm School of Economics, Stockholm, Sweden

This paper defines initiative as a key manifestation of corporate entrepreneurship, and examines the types of initiative exhibited in a sample of six subsidiaries of multinational corporations. From a detailed analysis of 39 separate initiatives, four distinct types are identified, which we refer to as 'global,' 'local,' 'internal' and 'global–internal hybrid,' to correspond to the locus of the market opportunity whence each arose. Two important conclusions are indicated. First, entrepreneurship at the subsidiary level has the potential to enhance local responsiveness, worldwide learning and global integration, a much broader role than previously envisioned. Second, the use of contextual mechanisms to create differentiated subsidiary roles has its limitations because each initiative type is facilitated in different ways. © 1997 by John Wiley & Sons, Ltd.

INTRODUCTION

The ability of the large multinational corporation (MNC) to leverage the innovative and entrepreneurial potential of its dispersed assets is a fundamental strategic imperative (Bartlett and Goshal, 1989). While some studies have explicitly confronted the challenge of entrepreneurship in MNCs (e.g., Ghoshal, 1986), research has tended to focus on either the organizaation of the existing activities of the MNC or on corporate entrepreneurship as a generic managerial issue (Ghoshal, 1986: 6). As stated by Hedlund and Ridderstråle (1992: 5) the dominant theme in prior MNC research—particularly from a theoretical perspective—has been 'on the exploitation of givens (i.e., existing product–market combinations) rather than on the creation of novelty.' The need for research that explicitly links MNC management with studies of corporate entrepreneurship is therefore substantial.

The current paper examines initiatives in MNC

subsidiaries. An *initiative* is defined here as a discrete, proactive undertaking that advances a new way for the corporation to use or expand its resources (Kanter, 1982; Miller, 1983). An initiative is essentially an entrepreneurial process, beginning with the identification of an opportunity and culminating in the commitment of resources to that opportunity. In this sense, the term is narrower than related constructs such as 'internal corporate venture' (Burgelman, 1983a) which involve both the initiative and the ongoing management of the resultant business activity. Several prior studies have used the initiative construct (e.g., Burgelman, 1991; Cohen and Machalek, 1988; Sathe, 1985).

Subsidiary is defined here to be any operational unit controlled by the MNC and situated outside the home country. This definition ensures that the artificial notion of a single parent–subsidiary relationship is avoided. The reality in most MNCs today is that subsidiaries have a multitude of linkages with other corporate entities in the home county and worldwide (Ghoshal and Bartlett, 1991), but academic research has—for the most part—continued to work on the basis of a single parent–subsidiary relationship. By working at the

---

Key words: multinational corporation; subsidiary; initiative; corporate entrepreneurship

CCC 0143–2095/97/030207–23
© 1997 by John Wiley & Sons, Ltd.

Received 5 May 1995
Final revision received 23 April 1996

initiative level this study breaks new ground in that it documents activities at a sub-subsidiary unit of analysis.

Why study initiative in MNC subsidiaries rather than in the parent company? The simple answer is that despite the compelling logic for tapping into local markets through the subsidiary network (Bartlett and Ghoshal, 1986), many corporations appear to neglect the creative potential of their subsidiaries. Thus, subsidiary initiative may be a relatively rare and underresearched phenonemon but its potential value to the MNC is high. While the most common form of subsidiary initiative is probably the identification and pursuit of a new product opportunity in the local market, this paper takes the concept further by showing that three other forms of subsidiary initiative can also be identified. The paper puts forward a conceptual framework, based on the network theory of the MNC (Ghoshal and Bartlett, 1991) through which subsidiary initiative can be better understood, and then describes the results of a detailed inductive study of 39 initiatives. The major contribution of the paper is the finding that subsidiary initiative has the potential to enhance local responsiveness, worldwide learning *and* global integration, a much broader role than previously envisioned.

This paper is organized as follows. First, the literature on corporate entrepreneurship is reviewed, in broad terms and then specifically in terms of MNC subsidiary management. Second, the network theory of the MNC is used to build a conceptual framework in which three types of subsidiary initiative are identified. Each type of initiative is also identified in the extant literature. Third, the research methodology is described. Fourth, the findings from the study are discussed—this section includes the identification and description of a fourth type of initiative, and a systematic description of the salient characteristics of all four types. Finally, the implications of the study for MNC management theory and for corporate entrepreneurship are discussed.

CORPORATE ENTREPRENEURSHIP AND INITIATIVES

Corporate entrepreneurship is receiving increasing levels of research attention, and was the focus of a recent special issue of the *Strategic Manage-*

ment Journal (Guth and Ginsberg, 1990). In broad terms, three forms of corporate entrepreneurship can be identified (Stopford and Baden-Fuller, 1994): (1) the creation of new business activities within the existing organization; (2) the transformation or renewal of existing organizations; and (3) the enterprise changing the rules of competition in its industry. The focus of this study is on the first of these forms: the creation of new business activities within the existing enterprise.

There is a broad recognition, however, that the generation of new business activities or 'new combinations' (Schumpeter, 1934) alone does not constitute entrepreneurship. A research and development group, for example, has a clear mandate to innovate, but the behavior expected of its employees falls within established norms and guidelines. Entrepreneurship suggests more: a predisposition towards proactive and risk-taking behavior (Covin and Slevin, 1991; Miller, 1983); use of resources beyond the individual's direct control (Kirzner, 1973; Stevenson and Jarillo, 1990); or a 'clear departure from existing practices' (Damanpour, 1991: 561). Kanter (1982) proposed the following distinction between 'basic' and entrepreneurial activities:

> Basic accomplishments ... are part of the assigned job and require routine and readily available means to carry them out. In contrast innovative accomplishments are strikingly entrepreneurial. They are sometimes highly problematic and generally involve acquiring and using power and influence. (1982: 97)

On the basis that within-firm corporate entrepreneurship involves a departure from existing practices or 'a *new way* for the corporation to use or expand its resources' (Kanter, 1982), the literature suggests two distinct models, which will be termed focused and dispersed corporate entrepreneurship respectively. Initiative, the focal construct in this research, is a manifestation of the dispersed approach.

Focused corporate entrepreneurship (also called corporate venturing) works on the premise that entrepreneurship and management are fundamentally different processes that require different modes of organization to occur effectively (Burns and Stalker, 1961; Galbraith, 1982; Kanter, 1985). This is typified by the New Venture Division, whose mandate is to identify and nurture new business opportunities for the corporation (Burgelman, 1983a; Kuratko, Montagno and Hornsby, 1990; Sykes, 1986). The new venture division is typically a semi-autonomous entity with little formal structure, integration across traditional functional areas, availability of 'patient money,' and management support for risk taking and creativity (Galbraith, 1982; Kanter, 1985; Kuratko et al., 1990; Quinn, 1985; Sathe, 1985). There are many examples of corporations that have pursued this approach to corporate entrepreneurship, including 3M, Kodak, and Exxon (Ginsberg and Hay, 1995; Sykes, 1986). Note that the mandate of a new venture division is fundamentally broader and more ambiguous than that of a research and development group, where the set of tasks and responsibilities can be fairly narrowly defined. In Schollhammer's terms (1982), the new venture division is a case of 'incubative' entrepreneurship while the R&D group is 'administrative' entrepreneurship.

Dispersed corporate entrepreneurship (also called intrapreneurship) rests on the premise that every individual in the company has the capacity for both managerial and entrepreneurial behavior *more or less simultaneously*. Rather than hiving off separate groups or divisions to be entrepreneurial, while the rest are left to pursue the ongoing managerial tasks (Galbraith, 1982), the dispersed approach sees the development of an entrepreneurial culture or posture as the key antecedent to initiative (Covin and Slevin, 1991; Goshal and Bartlett, 1994; Kanter, 1985; Stopford and Baden-Fuller, 1994). The design of an 'organic' (Burns and Stalker, 1961) or 'integrative' (Kanter, 1985) organization creates the facilitating conditions, but entrepreneurship is actually driven by the actions of employees who—for whatever reason—choose to pursue risky or uncertain ventures 'for the good of the organization' (Barnard, 1938: 200). The challenge for corporate management is to instill the personal involvement and commitment in its employees that drives entrepreneurship (Ghoshal and Bartlett, 1994).

Dispersed corporate entrepreneurship therefore assumes a latent dual role for every employee, consisting of (a) the management of ongoing activities and (b) the identification and pursuit of new opportunities (Kirzner, 1973; Penrose, 1959; Stevenson and Jarillo, 1990). The advantage of this approach over the focused approach is that a greater diversity of opportunities will be sensed, because the entrepreneurial capability is dispersed throughout the organization, rather than restricted to a new venture division. The major disadvantage of this approach is that managerial responsibilities typically 'drive out' entrepreneurial responsibilities (Hedlund and Ridderstråle, 1992; Kanter, 1986) because they are more clearly defined and have more immediate rewards. Unless it is well managed the dispersed approach can actually inhibit entrepreneurship (Drucker, 1985).

Initiative, as used in this paper, is the primary manifestation of dispersed corporate entrepreneurship. The initiative process is bounded by the identification of an opportunity at the front end and the commitment of resources to the undertaking at the back end. Note that the long-term success of the resultant business activity is a secondary issue. The entrepreneurial challenge is to move from an idea to a commitment of resources; the managerial challenge is to make the resultant business activity profitable. It is important, moreover, to recognize that the focused and dispersed approaches are complementary rather than alternative. For example, an opportunity identified in a subsidiary may be nurtured and developed in the new venture division; equally, an innovation by the new venture division may inspire further innovation by an operating division. Clinical evidence suggests that successful entrepreneurial companies such as 3M and HP do indeed exhibit both approaches (Kanter, 1985; Peters and Waterman, 1982; Pinchott, 1985).

INITIATIVE IN MNC SUBSIDIARIES

Parent–subsidiary relationships in MNCs have been studied for many years (Martinez and Jarillo, 1989). Most early research focused narrowly on facets of the parent–subsidiary relationship such as centralization, formalization, coordination and control (Brandt and Hulbert, 1977; Cray, 1984; Hedlund, 1981; Negandhi and Baliga, 1981; Picard, 1980). More recently, new conceptualizations of the MNC such as the heterarchy (Hedlund, 1986) or the transnational corporation (Bartlett and Ghoshal, 1989) enabled a more holistic understanding of the subsidiary as a semi-autonomous entity within a differentiated system. Within this broad school of thought, two distinct views of the subsidiary can be discerned, with direct parallels to the two types of corporate entrepreneurship described in the previous section.

The first perspective viewed the subsidiary as having a 'role' in the MNC. Bartlett and Ghoshal (1986) made the observation that national subsidiaries can take one of four generic roles, based on the strategic importance of the local environment and the competence of the subsidiary. They further suggested that the MNC's structure should reflect this heterogeneity, so that certain subsidiaries receive, for example, much greater strategic autonomy than others. This study and others in the same genre (e.g., Ghoshal and Nohria, 1989; Gupta and Govindarajan, 1991; Jarillo and Martinez, 1990) shared a number of underlying characteristics: first, an implicit parent company perspective, in that subsidiaries were modeled in terms of 'relative capabilities' (vs. sister subsidiaries); second, the belief that the subsidiary's role was determined by the parent company and essentially assigned to the subsidiary in question; and third, the notion that the subsidiary's role was enacted through the definition of an appropriate set of coordination and control mechanisms (its structural context in Bower's, 1970, terms).

This model is entirely consistent with the description of focused corporate entrepreneurship above. Certain subsidiaries are given the responsibility for innovating or pursuing initiatives, while others are given implementational roles. These roles are enacted through the structural context of the MNC. As shown by Ghoshal and Bartlett (1988), autonomy, local resources, normative integration and interunit communication are associated with creation (of innovations) in subsidiaries, but negatively associated with adoption and diffusion.

The second perspective focused directly on the subsidiary level of analysis. This perspective envisioned a much greater element of strategic choice on the part of subsidiary management than the subsidiary role perspective. Thus, the subsidiary's strategy was constrained (rather than defined) by the structural context, and subsidiary managers had considerable latitude within the imposed constraints to shape a strategy as they saw fit. This body of research was predominantly Canadian, stretching back to Safarian's (1966) work on the foreign ownership of Canadian

industry and with key contributions from Crookell (1986), D'Cruz (1986), Poynter and Rugman (1982) and White and Poynter (1984, 1990). In part because of the high levels of foreign ownership in Canadian industry, academic thinking has pushed towards subsidiary managers utilizing their strategic discretion rather than simply responding to parental decree. White and Poynter (1984: 69), for example, noted that subsidiary mangers 'Will have to adjust their strategies to successfully deal with changed circumstances . . . Through the careful development of local capabilities the subsidiary manager can contribute to the evolution of the Canadian subsidiary's strategy.' This is consistent with the dispersed approach to corporate entrepreneurship. As suggested by White and Poynter (1984) and others, creativity and innovation should be endemic to the national subsidiary as the driver of its strategy. The subsidiary has ongoing managerial responsibilities but at the same time it has the responsibility to respond to entrepreneurial opportunities as they arise.

In summary, entrepreneurship in MNC subsidiaries is a subject that has received limited research attention but that can be informed by the broader literature on corporate entrepreneurship. As with the literature on corporate entrepreneurship, the implication here is not that one model of subsidiary management is superior to the other in terms of entrepreneurial capability but that the two are complementary. In particular, proponents of the subsidiary role perspective have made the observation that complete control of the national subsidiary through contextual mechanisms is neither possible nor desirable (e.g., Prahalad and Doz, 1981). There is clearly an interesting trade-off between control and autonomy in the parent–subsidiary relationship, and the fact that subsidiary 'role' research favors control and subsidiary 'strategy' research favors autonomy is essentially a function of the opposing perspectives of parent and subsidiary managers.

CONCEPTUAL DEVELOPMENT

As defined above, an initiative is viewed as a discrete, proactive undertaking that advances a new way for the corporation to use or expand its resources. For the purposes of this research, this definition was subject to two additional constraints. First, the entrepreneurial thrust had to come from subsidiary managers, rather than those at head office. Second, the initiative had to lead to international responsibilities for the subsidiary, such as exporting intermediate products to affiliates or managing a product line on a global basis. This condition was set to exclude trivial initiatives. MNCs are becoming increasingly global in the configuration and coordination of their value-adding activities (Porter, 1986), and subsidiaries are likewise recognizing the interdependence of their activities with those of the global network. Particularly in a country such as Canada where the national market is small and the cross-border flows with the United States large, the likelihood of any new activity attracting corporate support is substantially enhanced when it has international scope.

Conceptual framework

Notwithstanding the question of personal motivation, the origin of an initiative lies in the identification of an opportunity to use or expand the corporation's resources. In Kirzner's (1973) words, it is an 'alertness to hitherto unnoticed market opportunities' that stimulates the entrepreneur to act. In similar fashion, Stevenson and Jarillo (1990: 23) saw entrepreneurship as '... a process by which individuals—either on their own or inside organizations—pursue opportunities without regard to the resources they currently control.'

From the perspective of the MNC subsidiary, the notion of *a market opportunity* is usually understood in terms of its national market. The traditional role of the subsidiary was first to adapt the MNC's technology to local tastes, and then to act as a 'global scanner,' sending signals about changing demands back to head office (Vernon, 1966, 1979). More recently, it has been recognized that subsidiaries often have unique capabilities of their own, as well as critical links with local customers and suppliers. In such situations, the subsidiary's ability to pursue local opportunities itself, and subsequently to exploit them on a global scale, is an important capability (Bartlett and Ghoshal, 1986; Harrigan, 1983; Hedlund, 1986).

To view market opportunity solely in terms of the subsidiary's *local* relationships is, however, somewhat restricting. There is a growing body of

research that models the MNC as an interorganizational network (Forsgren and Johanson, 1992; Ghoshal and Bartlett, 1991), in which the subsidiary has multiple linkages to other entities both inside and outside the formal boundaries of the MNC. Viewed in this way, the national subsidiary sits at the interface of three 'markets:' (1) the local market, consisting of competitors, suppliers, customers, and regulatory bodies in the host country; (2) the internal market, which is comprised of head office operations and all corporate-controlled affiliates worldwide; and (3) the global market, consisting of competitors, customers and suppliers that fall outside the local and internal markets. This conceptualization is depicted in Figure 1. Global market relationships, of course, do not exist in all cases, but increasingly subsidiaries are taking on specialized roles and responsibilities within the MNC that give them access to international customers and suppliers (Roth and Morrison, 1992). Again using Kirzner's definition, three types of initiative are immediately suggested, namely *local market initiative, internal market initiative,* and *global market initiative.* These are defined by the locus of the market opportunity in each case.

How much evidence is there for these types of initiative? No systematic research appears to have been done on either internal market or global market intiatives, while Ghoshal (1986) is the only detailed prior study on local market initiatives. The remainder of this section, then, will pull together the limited body of research that exists to provide a grounding for the current study. In addition to the locus of opportunity (by which the types are defined), three additional sets of characteristics will be considered: the facilitating conditions (i.e., those elements of the subsidiary's structural context that foster an environment in which initiative can occur), the intiative process; and the intended outcome. Figure 2 illustrates these elements. This framework is very similar to those used in several other process research studies, including Mintzberg, Raisinghani, and Theoret (1976) and Nutt (1993). Note that the relationships between these elements is not one of linear causality. Facilitating conditions and process, for example, probably interact with and reinforce one another, rather than one defining the other. Thus, the elements could best be described as configurations (Meyer, Tsui, and Hinings, 1993), which are 'tight con-

212   *J. Birkinshaw*

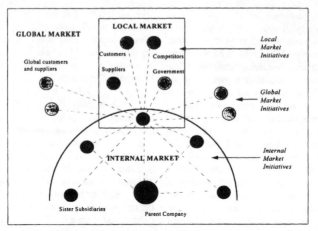

Figure 1.   Conceptual model of the national subsidiary and three types of initiative

stellations of mutually supportive elements'
(Miller, 1986: 236).

Local market initiatives

There are several well-documented cases of local
market initiatives in the literature: examples
include Philips UK's development of Teletext
technology (Bartlett and Ghoshal, 1986) and Alfa
Laval U.S.'s invention of the milking machine in
1917 (Hedlund and Ridderstråle, 1992). These
two cases were both inspired by local product
and/or market needs and subsequently exploited
on a global scale.[1]

In terms of facilitating conditions, Ghoshal's
(1986) detailed study of innovation in MNCs
identified local resources, local autonomy, normative integration, subsidiary–HQ communication,
and intrasubsidiary communication as factors that
were positively associated with the 'creation'
process. No other work has systematically
addressed this issue, though several Canadian
studies have hinted at the conditions in which
local market initiatives occur (e.g., Etemad and
Dulude, 1986). Some insight into the initiative

Figure 2.   Organizing framework for process study

process can also be inferred from these studies.
It appears to be quite protracted, involving considerable effort from subsidiary management to
develop the concept in the first place, and even
more effort to get it accepted in other countries.
However, this is not significantly different from
the generic innovation process (e.g., Howell and
Higgins, 1990), or from the process that can be
inferred from prior studies of global or internal
market initiatives (see below). There is thus considerable scope for new insight in this area.
Finally, the intended outcome, according to Bartlett and Ghoshal (1986), is to enhance worldwide learning.

---

[1] Note that in theory local market initiatives could remain
within the local market, e.g., if a product is designed specifically for a segment of the local market. In practice, the
sample used in this study exhibited no incidences of local
initiatives that stayed local: all went on to become international products.

Global market initiatives

These are driven by unmet product or market needs among *nonlocal* suppliers and customers. In theory, the subsidiary could potentially interact with any customer or supplier in the world, but evidence in the literature suggests that such initiatives probably occur as extensions to existing relationships.[2] Consider the case of Litton Systems Ltd. (Science Council of Canada, 1980). Litton developed an international business in the 1960s (through a local market initiative) around an inertial navigation system. On the basis of its worldwide customer base it then identified additional opportunities in related areas, and went on to develop products such as air traffic control systems and radar systems. These latter product introductions were global initiatives, because the locus of opportunity was outside the subsidiary's local market.

With the exception of the Science Council of Canada study, no evidence of global market initiatives was found in the literature. This is perhaps surprising, in that there are several examples of subsidiary companies taking on international product responsibilities (e.g., Hedlund, 1986; Roth and Morrison, 1992), which would naturally provide the circumstances in which global initiatives could transpire. In terms of the characteristics of global market initiatives, the Science Council of Canada suggested (a) that local autonomy, local resources and existing international responsibilities were facilitating conditions, and (b) that the intended outcome was to leverage the subsidiary's existing capabilities into related areas. However, these should be viewed as very tentative propositions because they arose from only three case studies. There was, unfortunately, no substantive insight into the initiative process, except insofar as it appeared to mirror the generic process described above.

Internal market initiatives

The concept of an internal market initiative is somewhat unusual, in that it arises through 'market opportunities' identified in the corporate sys-

tem. The best way of explaining the concept is through an example: the quote below is with regard to Dow Chemical's internal market (White and Poynter, 1990: 56):

> The internal product sourcing relationship between a manufacturing plant and a commercial department can be 'challenged' at any time ... If the U.S. market for polyethylene could be sourced at lower out-of-pocket cost from a Dow Canada plant than elsewhere, that adjustment would be made.

The initiative in this case would be the Canadian plant challenging the incumbent in-house manufacturer for the rights to polyethylene production, on the basis that the incumbent was either not operating efficiently or was operating in a country where factor costs put it at a comparative disadvantage *vis-à-vis* the challenging plant. This type of initiative is thus subtly different from the other two types, because it is directed towards cost reduction rather than revenue enhancement.

The concept of an internal market, in which divisions or subsidiaries of a single company pursue competitive exchange relationships with one another, is well established in academic writing (e.g., Galunic and Eisenhardt, 1994; Halal, 1993) and is widely used in many large corporations. As before, however, the internal market *initiative* is implicit in prior research. Galunic and Eisenhardt (1994), for example, discussed competition from other subsidiaries as a stimulus for charter loss; and White and Poynter's description of the horizontal organization (above) included a clear example of subsidiary initiative that was not labeled as such. The characteristics of internal market initiatives can thus be inferred from the existing literature as follows: (a) local resources, some decentralization of decision making, good relationships with the parent company and shared decision premises as facilitators of initiative; (b) an entrepreneurial selling process, again very similar to that seen in other types of initiative; and (c) efficiency in global operations and desire for local value-added as the intended outcomes. Table 1 represents a summary of prior research.

In conclusion, this section set forth a conceptualization of subsidiary initiative that is consistent with the emerging body of literature on interorganizational networks, but which at the same

---

[2] This point is substantiated by the body of literature on internationalization which sees international relationships growing incrementally through experience and existing contacts (e.g., Johanson and Vahlne, 1977).

214   *J. Birkinshaw*

Table 1.   Previous research on three forms of subsidiary initiative

Locus of market opportunity (definition)	Local market initiative	Internal market initiative	Global market initiative
Facilitating factors	● Local resources, local autonomy, normative integration, sub.–HQ communication, intra-sub. communication (Ghoshal, 1986)	● Local resources, some decentralization (Galunic and Eisenhardt, 1994) ● Local resources, good relations with parent (Science Council of Canada, 1980) ● Horizontal network and shared decision premises (White and Poynter, 1990)	● Local resources, local autonomy, existing international responsibilities (Science Council of Canada, 1980)
Process	● No discernible difference between process models in all three types. Generic model indicates a protracted selling process by subsidiary management to parent management (Etemad and Dulude, 1986; Science Council of Canada, 1980)		
Intended outcome	● Enhance worldwide learning (Bartlett and Ghoshal, 1986) ● Maximize global innovation (Harrigan, 1983)	● Efficiency of global operations and local value-added (Science Council of Canada, 1980; White and Poynter, 1990)	● Leverage existing subsidiary capabilities into related areas (Science Council of Canada, 1980)

time suggests a much broader opportunity set for the subsidiary than previously thought. The three initiative types have been identified to varying degrees in the literature, so our *a priori* expectations are not sufficiently clear that research propositions can be explicated. The objective of the remainder of this paper is thus twofold: (1) to assess the validity of this conceptualization; and (2) to describe the facilitating conditions, the process, and the outcomes of the types of subsidiary initiative that are identified.

RESEARCH METHODOLOGY

Sampling methodology

Defining the research sample posed two methodological problems. The first problem was that many MNC subsidiaries have never undertaken initiatives, so it was necessary to identify a sample of subsidiaries that *had* undertaken intiatives.[3] The

---

[3] Note that this does not impart a bias to the results: the research objective was to understand the characteristics of subsidiary initiatives, not to understand why some subsidiaries undertake them while others do not.

second problem was identifying a sample of initiatives from the sample subsidiaries. The decision was made to research the entire set of initiatives in a small number of companies, on the grounds that the quality of data was a critical element of this study. The alternative of a one company–one initiative study would also have been possible, but would have entailed very few respondents per initiative, and therefore less richness in the data. If a single initiative had been studied for each subsidiary there would have been a danger of selection bias towards the respondents' more memorable—but not necessarily representative—initiatives. A third problem was anticipated but did not materialize, namely the identification of initiatives that met the definitions posed at the outset. Kanter (1982: 99) noted that the delineation between an entrepreneurial activity (i.e., an initiative) and a managerial activity is much easier in practice than it is in words, and this study bore out her observation. Likewise, the stated need for all initiatives to lead to international responsibilities never created any methodological problems, in that every initiative identified, even the local market type, quickly (i.e., within 24 months) led to international sales.

The following sampling methodology was adopted. Using the *Financial Post 500* index, a list of subsidiaries was drawn up with the following restrictions: (1) Canadian subsidiaries of U.S.-owned MNCs; (2) with 1992 sales revenues of greater than $200 million; and (3) participating in a global industry (Morrison, 1990). These criteria were selected on the basis that a case research design should intentionally limit the variance in the sample to make cross-case analysis meaningful (Parkhe, 1993; Yin, 1984). There were also strong *a priori* reasons for the size and global industry restrictions, in that the strategic imperatives for smaller subsidiaries (which may be sales-only) and subsidiaries in nonglobal industries (with limited cross-border trade flows) are not germane to the management of the mature MNC. One additional criterion was also developed, namely clear evidence of initiative. By picking out those subsidiaries with an established record of success in taking the initiative or gaining international responsibilities we were able to avoid approaching companies that did not exhibit the necessary levels of entrepreneurship. Approximately 40 subsidiaries met all these criteria.

Subsidiaries from this sample were then approached on a convenience basis. Two of four initial selections agreed to participate fully. As research in these two subsidiaries progressed, additional subsidiaries were approached, and over the course of 9 months four more were added (with a further two declining to participate). The decision to stop at six sites was based on the principle of redundancy (Yin, 1984), in that no substantive additional insights appeared to be forthcoming towards the end of the study. The data collection period lasted from November 1993 to August 1994. Some basic facts about the subsidiary sample are displayed in Table 2.[4]

In each sample company, initiatives were identified through discussions with senior managers. The major initiatives, particularly those that had resulted in new international responsibilities, were identified immediately, but some careful investigation was required to pick out smaller or less-successful initiatives. It was only towards the end of the research that some of the more interesting failures were uncovered, presumably because respondents' comfort level with the researcher increased with time. Between 3 and 10 initiatives were identified in each company to give a total sample size of 39 initiatives (Table 3).

Data collection methods

The two primary sources of data were (1) semi-structured interviews with subsidiary and parent company managers, and (2) a questionnaire filled out by the key individual for each initiative. These data were complemented by business plans and other company documents, and secondary data compiled through a CD ROM library search. Interviews followed a carefully prepared protocol, with a mixture of specific questions ('What was the proposed dollar investment in this project?') and open-ended questions ('How did this initiative arise in the first place?). For each initiative the intention was to speak to every manager who was actively involved. Thus, between 2 and 10 managers were interviewed for each initiative. In 65 percent of cases one or more parent managers involved in the initiative were interviewed. Interviews were taped and transcribed, and notes were also taken. A total of approximately 1500 pages of data were assembled through this process.

The questionnaire was put together towards the end of the research, as a means of validating the qualitative interview findings. Questions were drawn up to measure the emerging constructs, such as the nature of the market opportunity or the level of selling by subsidiary management. Following a careful preparation process, in which four academicians and three subsidiary managers (not in the sample) provided feedback on wording and design, the questionnaire was mailed to the key respondent for each of the 39 initiatives. Thirty-five questionnaires were returned, and in the four remaining cases the questionnaire was filled in by an independent research assistant following a careful reading of the interview transcripts.[5]

---

[4] The six subsidiaries in the final sample appeared to be typical of the larger sample of 40 subsidiaries. Their average sales revenues in 1993 were $550 million compared to $440 million in the larger sample. Furthermore, informal interviews were subsequently conducted in a further 12 of the 40 companies, with qualitatively very similar findings to those reported here.

[5] More specifically, the research assistant completed a questionnaire for *every* initiative (i.e., all 39) based on his reading of the transcripts. Interrater reliability for the 35 questionnaires where both the key respondent and the research assistant had completed them was 0.64 (using Cohen's kappa; Perreault and Leigh, 1989). Consistent with Nunnally (1978) this is

216   *J. Birkinshaw*

Table 2. Subsidiary sample

Company	Principal industry	Approximate size (1993 revenues)	Number of interviews
A	Industrial and consumer products	$600 million[a]	22
B	Chemicals	$450 million	19
C	Computer hardware/software	$500 million	15
D	Computer hardware/software	$800 million	19
E	Industrial products	$420 million	14
F	Engineering systems	$420 million	11

[a]Figures are in Canadian dollars.

Data analysis

Five constructs were measured using question-naire data.[6] The nonparametric Kruskal–Wallis test was conducted on these measures to determine whether there were any significant differences between the means of the different initiative types. Qualitative data were analyzed using the procedures recommended by Miles and Huberman (1984), which emphasize the use of tables and diagrams for reducing and visualizing data. The analysis was undertaken by both the researchers, and discrepancies reconciled through discussion. The qualitative findings were summarized in the form of a case history, and sent to the lead respondent to verify that the case was a fair portrayal of what actually happened. Specific constructs were then abstracted from the case studies and compared to the quantitative findings. The results section (below) provides both sets of data so that the convergence between the qualitative and quantitative techniques can be judged.

---

acceptable for the early stages of a research program. It was therefore decided that the research assistant's responses were a reasonable proxy in the four cases where no response was forthcoming.

[6] Questions, all on 5-point Likert scales except the last one, were as follows. AUTONOMY: (a) What level of strategic autonomy did the Canadian subsidiary have?; PROVEN RESOURCES: (a) To what extent did the subsidiary have previous international responsibilities? (b) To what extent did the subsidiary have a track record of success getting projects approved? PARENT–SUBSIDIARY COMMUNICATION: (a) What was the extent of the relationship between the parent and subsidiary management? INTERNAL SELLING: (a) What was the extent of the selling process followed by subsidiary management? (b) How active was the Canadian president's involvement in pursuing the initiative? APPROVAL: (a) What was the immediate outcome (explicit approval, implicit approval, rejection)?

RESEARCH FINDINGS

Types of subsidiary initiative

The conceptual framework suggested that three types of initiative should be identifiable, on the basis of the locus of the market opportunity (i.e., local, internal and global). This proposition was confirmed to the extent that all three putative types were in evidence, but in addition there emerged in the course of the research a fourth type that was essentially a hybrid between the internal market and global market forms. This hybrid type took the form of subsidiary management identifying and bidding for an embryonic corporate investment. For example, in one case subsidiary management read in the corporate long-range plan that a new plant was scheduled 4 years hence. They recognized a fit with the Canadian subsidiary's capabilities so they built a case for making the investment in Canada and solicited support for their proposal at head office. In this case the initial market opportunity was identified by head office managers but subsidiary management proactively pursued it. Thus, there was a heavy element of internal selling, to persuade head office management that the subsidiary was the appropriate site for investment, but the initial market opportunity was clearly global.

The hybrid case can best be understood in terms of the locus of opportunity vs. the locus of pursuit,[7] in that its locus of opportunity was global but its locus of pursuit was internal. In all the other three forms the locus of opportunity coincided with the locus of pursuit. This state of

---

[7] We are indebted to an anonymous reviewer for suggesting this distinction.

Table 3. Initiative sample

Sub.	Initiative	Outcome	Interviews
A	Initial proposal to manufacture in Ontario	Success	2
A	Proposal for plant extension in Manitoba	Success	2
A	Proposal to bring conversion to Ontario (a)	Failure	2
A	Proposal to bring conversion to Ontario (b)	Success	3
A	Proposal to bring finishing to Canada	Success	2
A	Proposal to consolidate production in Canada	Success	3
A	Bid for major new tape plant	Success	3
A	Restructure of sales and marketing organization	Success	8
A	Bid for plant extension	Success	5
A	New library security product	Mixed	2
B	Bid for new chemical facility in Canada	Failure	1
B	Incremental investment in Canadian plant	Success	4
B	Business management shifted to Canada	Success	5
B	Toll manufacture brought in-house	Success	7
B	Bid for new formulation of major product	Success	5
B	New dispensing product for major product	Success	2
B	Proposed technological innovation in Canada	Failure	2
C	New digital screen technology	Success	7
C	System controller product	Success	6
C	Cutting equipment innovation	Success	3
C	Electronics for defense missile	Success	3
C	Airport terminal product innovation	Success	4
C	New generation terminal product	Success	2
C	Second generation missile electronics	Failure	2
C	Communication network product	Failure	2
D	Local hardware company acquisition	Mixed	5
D	Industrial terminal product innovation	Mixed	6
D	New high-technology terminal	Success	6
D	Regional product development center	Success	10
D	Software development center	Mixed	3
D	New information protocol center	Success	3
E	Export of valve to Europe	Success	4
E	Export of switch manufacture to U.S.	Success	5
E	Rationalization of North American production	Success	10
E	Designation of two SBUs in Canada	Success	6
E	Software system for building controls	Mixed	1
F	Software/hardware system for oil flow	Success	6
F	New PC network management product	Success	5
F	Local high-tech company acquisition	Success	6

affairs serves to underline the complexity of the subsidiary's role within the 'interorganizational network' of the MNC. Rather than just focusing on one type of market opportunity at a time, there is also the need to reconcile emerging global opportunities with internal capabilities. We might argue that this is the job of the corporate center, but the evidence shows that the proactive subsidiary can also take on parts of that role itself.

Table 4 lists the number of cases found of each initiative type, with a description to facilitate understanding. In terms of methodology, the fourth type (the hybrid) emerged during the data collection process. Then, during the data analysis

218   *J. Birkinshaw*

Table 4.   Four types of initiative

Initiative type	Number of cases	Number of failures	Description
Local market initiative	13	2	Seek to develop a new product, market, or process through opportunities that are first identified in the subsidiary's home market
Internal market initiative	12	1	Promote the redistribution of existing corporate assets or resources such that they are more efficiently deployed. In the Canadian context the objective is typically to reconfigure a branch plant in the light of the North American Free Trade Agreement
Global market initiative	9	1	Seek to build on an existing mandate or proven capability to meet a perceived international product or market opportunity
Hybrid initiative	5	1	Seeks to attract a global investment which has already (in principle) received corporate support

stage each initiative was assigned by the lead researcher to one of the four types. The research assistant replicated the process, on the basis of the interview transcripts, and made the same assignment as the lead researcher in 37 of 39 cases. The remaining two were discussed and agreement was eventually reached regarding the appropriate type. Next, a discriminant analysis was undertaken on the questionnaire data, to check whether the four types could be distinguished on the basis of the 'drivers' of initiative.[8] This analysis yielded Wilks lambdas of 0.06, 0.23 and 0.54 respectively for the three canonical discriminant functions, representing a very high level of separation between the four groups. In sum, 33 of the 39 cases were correctly classified by this procedure, or 85 percent of the total. This is an excellent result, and provides further confirmation of the validity of the typology.[9]

Facilitators of initiative

Local market initiatives

The 13 cases of local market initiatives suggested an interesting duality to the roles of subsidiary autonomy and parent–subsidiary communication as facilitators of initiative that had not been identified before. At the formative stage autonomy had to be high and communication correspondingly low so that subsidiary resources could be applied to the opportunity without head office interference; at the more advanced stage of viability a higher level of communication and a lower level of autonomy were more appropriate, in that subsidiary management had typically to achieve sponsorship for the business in question from a U.S.-based operating division. In one case a subsidiary manager built a $20 million business from nothing in 4 years, but took a further 4 years to find a 'home' with one of the major corporate business groups. His observation was that autonomy had helped him to move quickly early on, but was a liability as he attempted to enlarge the business and integrate it into the corporate network.

In terms of resources, it became apparent in the course of the study that *proven* resources (i.e., those which were recognized by parent management) were a more important facilitator of intiative than resources *per se*.[10] However, in

---

[8] The seven initiative drivers were: (1) desire to consolidate operations with those of the parent; (2) creation of a North American free-trade environment; (3) routine product or business upgrade on existing product; (4) business opportunity defined by a parent request for proposal; (5) a product–market opportunity arising through interaction with local customers; (6) a product–market opportunity arising through interaction with international customers; and (7) desire by subsidiary management to enhance local value-added.

[9] As discriminant analysis assumes multivariate normality and equivalent variance–covariance matrices, neither of which was wholly present given the small sample size, this result should be interpreted with caution.

[10] This finding is consistent with process models of strategy such as Bower (1970) in which resource allocation decisions are typically made on the basis of the individual's track record rather than on purely economic or technological arguments.

the specific case of local market initiatives, the sample companies only exhibited moderate levels of proven resources. Respondents commented that the subsidiary had to have sufficient experience and/or expertise to pursue opportunities as they arose, but without the high levels of proven resources that were necessary to succeed with some of the other types.

Respondents observed that *internal market initiatives* were facilitated most effectively by the credibility of the subsidiary in the eyes of the parent company, which was a function, in turn, of the subsidiary's high level of proven resources. In cases where the subsidiary had already built up a number of world product mandates through prior initiatives, subsequent initiatives progressed much more smoothly. Credibility was also a function of a high level of parent–subsidiary communication and, by the same token, a fairly low level of autonomy in that subsidiary managers had to be working very closely with their U.S. counterparts. As described by one respondent:

It is awfully important that we have a close association [with the U.S. management]. We are talking frequently about what are the issues in their business, what are their problems, what are the opportunities that we can offer to help them solve their problems. That is important to do.

One facilitator of internal market initiatives that had not been identified in prior research was the global orientation (Perlmutter, 1969) of the senior management in the United States. Some were essentially ethnocentric in their approach, which created enormous obstacles for subsidiary management; others took a geocentric attitude which streamlined the entire process, as the following quote suggests.

[The general manager] had a kind of 'let's do the right thing then tell everyone' attitude. Let's not be political about this, let's collaborate and do the right thing. What's right to do here is not what's right for our own camp, it's what's right for the corporation. So we got backing on this and got him interested. He then adopted it and became the overall mentor for it, and kept up the momentum.

Global market initiatives appeared to be facilitated by high autonomy, a high level of proven resources, and a correspondingly low level of parent–subsidiary communication. The importance of autonomy was underlined by one case

in which the subsidiary had achieved great success in building a viable international business, but where the parent company had then curtailed its autonomy because of corporate financial difficulties. Pursuing intiatives suddenly became a time-consuming and frustrating process, as this quote suggests:

The basic dilemma facing [the general manager of the subsidiary] is lack of investment. If he wants $100,000 to develop a product the customer is paying for he has to make a couple of visits to head office, which might take three months. By the time approval is granted, the opportunity has passed.

Proven resources here referred to a history of successful initiatives and an accumulation over time of specialized and valued capabilities. All the subsidiaries undertaking global market initiatives in this study were essentially building on existing international responsibilities or world mandates (Etemad and Dulude, 1986). With regard to parent–subsidiary communication, most respondents felt that initiative was facilitated by low levels of communication. This is not to suggest that communication is damaging, but that it is a low priority and is liable to be limited in a high-autonomy subsidiary. This quote is indicative of the level of parent–subsidiary communication that was observed:

... [The head office boss] was looking at the numbers, and 'other income' was quite large. He said 'What's that?' and [his colleague] said 'that's the electronics group up in Canada.' So my head office boss called me and said, 'We don't know what you're doing up there, but keep it up.' Isn't that representative of the relationship!

Hybrid initiatives were facilitated by very similar factors to internal market initiatives. That is, the credibility of the subsidiary with head office decision-makers was felt to be critical, and this was typically a function of moderate to high levels of proven resources, strong parent–subsidiary communication and relatively low autonomy. One subsidiary president commented on the nature of the bid process in his company:

You end up with a couple of sites that come pretty close and one that will have a minor advantage economically, but sitting in an operating committee in the States, what really swings you is the credibility of the organization that's asking for the order.

220   *J. Birkinshaw*

The fact that the market opportunity in the hybrid initiative was global had little bearing on the facilitating conditions, because the entire process was internal to the MNC. The evidence, in fact, suggested that hybrid initiatives required the highest level of 'selling' of all four types, which in turn necessitated a high level of ongoing parent–subsidiary communication.

Triangulation of qualitative and quantitative data

The questionnaire data that tapped into the three main constructs under discussion is displayed in Table 5. The nonparametric Kruskal–Wallis test was conducted to determine whether there were any significant differences between the means of the four initiative types. Despite the small sample size (between 5 and 13 observations for each type), two significant results were recorded, both consistent with the qualitative data. First, the high level of autonomy in global market initiatives was confirmed, in relation to all other types. Second, parent–subsidiary communication was different (at a marginal level of significance) across the types, with local and global initiatives exhibiting low levels of communication and internal and hybrid initiatives exhibiting high levels. The two measures selected as proxies for proven resources (existing international responsi-

bilities and a record of success with initiatives) were not able to distinguish between initiative types, though there was a suggestion that proven resources were slightly lower in local market initiatives. While consistent with the qualitative data, this finding is at odds with Ghoshal's (1986) observation that local innovations are associated with high levels of local resources.

Taken together, the quantitative and qualitative data provided several important new insights into the facilitators of subsidiary initiative. Internal market and hybrid initiatives exhibited a higher level of integration (in terms of parent–subsidiary communication and low autonomy) than previous studies suggested, and appeared to rely on geocentrically minded parent company managers to be successful; local market initiatives appeared to be facilitated by a careful balance between autonomy and integration; and global market initiatives were exhibited only where the subsidiary was *very* autonomous. The fact that autonomy was apparently so critical to the global market type is interesting, because *a priori* one might not expect local and global market initiatives to be significantly different. This evidence suggests that subsidiaries can not easily build world mandate businesses while at the same time remaining integrated with the rest of the corporation, but it is at odds with several studies that have suggested this is a desirable combination (e.g., Bartlett and Ghoshal, 1989; Roth and Morrison, 1992).

Table 5. Questionnaire data on initiative facilitators

	Local market initiative	Internal market initiative	Global market initiative	Global–internal hybrid initiative	Kruskal–Wallis ANOVA (*F*/sig.)	Pairs significantly different
Subsidiary autonomy	3.0	2.6	4.4	2.8	11.2/0.01	Global with all others
Specialized resources:						
(a) Existing international responsibilities	3.2	3.7	4.1	3.6	3.1/0.38	None
(b) Record of success with initiatives	2.9	3.8	3.4	4.0	4.3/0.23	None
Parent–sub. communication	3.1	3.9	3.0	4.2	7.4/0.06	Local and hybrid

All measures on 5-point likert scales where 5 = high; 1 = low.

Initiative processes

The qualitative findings shed considerable light on the initiative process, though in broad terms they were consistent with expectations. Two distinct processes were identified: one internally focused and the other externally focused. The *internally focused* process was exhibited by internal market initiatives and hybrid initiatives, in that formal corporate approval was necessary for resources to be made available. There was therefore a high level of selling, first of all by middle-level managers to their superiors in the subsidiary, and subsequently by the top subsidiary managers to their superiors in head office. This process is encapsulated by the following quote by a middle-level manager regarding an internal market initiative:

> I said really we should make a play for [this business], and started to build the argument. I sounded out the [U.S. business manager]: 'What are the possibilities here? What about running the business from Toronto? What do you think about it?' He basically thought it had merit, and he coached me. But my sales effort was not to try to convince U.S. people beyond my sphere of influence, it was really to get the people here convinced, to provide them a position that they could then embellish. So I worked with them and ultimately [the Canadian President] was the guy to say 'We would like to do this' at a very senior level in head office.

While much of the internal selling took the form of an upward progression through the hierarchy (Bower's 1970 'impetus'), there was also some evidence of horizontal selling as well. Many middle managers in the subsidiary were on global business teams, and were thus in a position to influence their head office and international peers, and subsidiary top management were typically connected into an extensive lateral network through which support for initiatives could be built. The following quote illustrates the extensive selling process undertaken by one subsidiary CEO:

> First he had to get approval (for the initiative) from the operations committee, who report directly to the chairman. Then he went to the sector meetings, where you had the division VPs. There were three of them. ... He then went to a couple of other corporate bodies, typical places where you would showcase this kind of thing— the marketing council, the technical council as

well, which is a huge group of the laboratory managers. So having cascaded it down he tried to pick large bodies where he would get to the level below division VP.

The concept of a horizontal organization superimposed on the traditional M-form has been documented by several academics (Bartlett and Ghoshal, 1993; Hedlund, 1986; White and Poynter, 1990). In terms of subsidiary initiatives, it was a valuable source of support, though typically only as a complement to the vertical chain of command through which resource allocation occurred.

Were there any differences between the observed process in internal market initiatives and hybrid initiatives? The distinguishing characteristic was the level of involvement of parent company management, in that hybrid initiatives always had parent management support in principle from the start, whereas internal market initiatives had to build their own support. This created a rather subtle difference in process: internal market initiatives were iterative, involving several rounds of credibility building with parent management and refining of proposals; hybrid initiatives were 'take-it-or-leave-it' proposals in which parent management typically had to choose between several directly competing courses of action.

The local market and global market initiatives were *externally focused*. Head office approval was typically implicit, so the majority of the effort on the part of subsidiary management was dedicated to building a viable product for local and global customers respectively. In the case of local market initiatives the subsidiary usually took responsibility for developing the concept using local development funds or bootlegged resources, without the support—and sometimes even without the knowledge—of the parent company. As stated in the previous section, approval from the parent was only sought on average several years later when the business had become viable. In the case of global market initiatives the subsidiary almost always had authority to invest in new projects within the subsidiary's existing charter (Galunic and Eisenhardt, 1994). The appropriate parent company division was kept informed of all such investments, but they did not intervene in the process. Championing was thus relegated to an internal subsidiary activity, as middle managers sought to convince the subsidiary general manager that their initiative should be pursued.

In general terms, then, the initiative process took one of two forms, neither of which corresponded precisely to the classic formulation of Bower (1970). Where resource allocation was a centralized phenomenon (i.e., with internal market and hybrid initiatives), horizontal systems complemented the vertical chain of authority as a means of building legitimacy and momentum for the initiative. Where resource allocation was decentralized, selling occurred primarily within the subsidiary and head office approval was implicit. It is not clear to which extent this finding is specific to the sample, which was deliberately skewed to favor initiative-taking subsidiaries. Bartlett and Ghoshal (1993) observed that their 'new' organizational model, which included a very similar extension to the Bower model of resource allocation, was induced from a sample of leading-edge companies, some of which were the same as used in the current study. Thus there is some suggestion that these processes may not be representative of the population of MNCs. Future research will be necessary to examine this question.

Triangulation of qualitative and quantitative data

The questionnaire data that tapped into the two constructs under discussion are displayed in Table 6. The nonparametric Kruskal–Wallis test was conducted on the two internal selling measures; the approval process data were nominal so

they are presented in raw form. The results provide strong support for the qualitative findings discussed above. Both local and global initiative types exhibited a lower level of internal selling than their internal and hybrid counterparts, and this difference was significant for the subsidiary president's selling activity. Equally, the approval process was predominantly implicit for the local and global types (13 out of 19 cases), and explicit for the internal and hybrid types (14 out of 15 cases). In sum, there appears to be a very clear split between the two broad processes.

Initiative outcomes

Setting aside the five that were not successful, the 34 remaining initiatives all led to increased sales, investment from head office, and new jobs. As Table 7 shows, however, the differences in these measures between types were mostly small. The only substantive difference, in fact, was that the internal market and hybrid initiative types both involved higher levels of capital investment than the other two. This is presumably a function of the resource allocation system in the MNC. Where subsidiary managers had the authority to approve the initiative (as with local and global market types) they proceeded in an incremental fashion, investing relatively small sums each time. Where approval was centralized at the head office, investments were typically larger. As with the data on facilitating conditions and the initiative process, this process emphasized the simi-

Table 6. Questionnaire data on initiative process

	Local market initiative	Internal market initiative	Global market initiative	Global–internal hybrid initiative	Kruskal–Wallis ANOVA (*F*/sig.)	Pairs significantly different
Internal selling: (a) by subsidiary management	3.6	4.1	3.3	3.8	3.9/0.27	None
(b) by subsidiary president	2.8	3.8	2.4	3.8	7.3/0.06	Local and internal; Global and internal
Nature of approval process	4 explicit 8 implicit 1 rejected	10 explicit 1 implicit 1 rejected	2 explicit 5 implicit 2 rejected	4 explicit 0 implicit 1 rejected	–	Local and global different to internal and hybrid

All measures on 5-point likert scales (except approval process) where 5 = high; 1 = low.

Table 7. Initiative outcomes

	Local market initiatives	Internal market initiatives	Global market initiatives	Hybrid initiatives
Average new investment in subsidiary as a result of approval	$2.2 million	$4.8 million	$1.7 million	$8.6 million
Average new sales for subsidiary within two years	$5.2 million	$10.5 million	$7.8 million	$9.2 million
Long term outcomes stated by respondents (subjective)	Local value-added Customer responsiveness New business for MNC	Local value-added Competitive subsidiary operations Integrated production	Specialized capability Local value-added Development of center of excellence	Local value-added Optimally located new facility

larity between the hybrid and internal market initiative types.

Qualitatively, the outcomes of the four types of initiative were markedly different. Local market initiatives led, in the first instance, to an enhanced service to local customers, but as they developed they led to new business opportunities for the MNC as a whole. Two of the 13 cases in this study became 'blockbuster' products (with revenues in 1994 of $50 million and $110 million respectively), while the rest led to niche businesses, or businesses that lasted a few years and were then phased out. Local market initiatives can therefore be viewed as enhancing worldwide learning as well, in that opportunities identified in the Canadian market were addressed and then applied in other countries. More broadly, local market initiatives are also instrumental to the imperative of corporate adaptation and renewal, in that they provide the variety that the MNC's systems can then select against (Burgelman, 1991). Without the diversity of opportunities and ideas that local market initiatives represent, the MNC's ability to adapt to changing environmental demands would be severely constrained.

Internal market initiatives, as predicted, led to a rationalization of activities between Canada and the United States, and hence a more efficient corporate system. Typically a branch plant went from producing a broad range of products for the

Canadian market to one or two products on a North American or global basis. Overall volumes stayed the same (initially at least), but both U.S. and Canadian plants increased their export sales. There were also cases of rationalization in administrative functions: in one case, for example, product management was relocated to Canada to be more closely integrated with the associated manufacturing. Both outcomes are symptomatic of the shift in MNCs towards a geographical concentration of value activities (Porter, 1986).

The outcome of the global market initiatives in the study was the maintenance and development of a specialized corporate capability. That is, each initiative sought to build a new product or market around an existing business line using the distinctive capabilities resident in that subsidiary. The term 'center of excellence' was used by respondents in this regard, with the implication that the parent company and other subsidiaries also stood to benefit from those capabilities. In terms of the corporate objectives identified at the outset, then, this is another facet of worldwide learning. Tangentially, it does suggest that the concept of worldwide learning is multifaceted, with at least two separate characteristics: (1) the transfer of information about customer needs within the corporate network, as achieved through local market initiatives; and (2) the transfer of proprietary technology and other capabilities within the corporate network, as achieved through global market initiatives. Both appear to be important strategic imperatives for the MNC.

Finally, hybrid initiatives had a similar outcome to the internal market type, in that they led to a geographically concentrated value activity serving the North American or global market. The four successful cases identified in this study made use of both the comparative advantages of Canada (relative to the United States) such as cheap power and a low-cost, low-turnover workforce, and also the specialized capabilities of the subsidiary. This is a facet of the global integration imperative, but it is actually superior to the rationalization process that internal market initiatives promote because it results (in theory at least) in the positioning of the value-adding activity at the optimum global location, rather than an existing location. Table 8 provides a summary of the findings: it is similar in format to Table 1, so the findings can be easily compared to the *a priori* expectations.

DISCUSSION

MNC subsidiary management

A major contribution of this study is its documentation of an internal subsidiary phenomenon, in contrast to most previous research that has concerned itself more with aspects of the parent–subsidiary relationship. Many recent studies (Bartlett and Ghoshal, 1993; Birkinshaw, 1995; Humes, 1993; Quelch, 1992) have suggested that the parent–subsidiary relationship is multifaceted, in that it varies across business units and operates at multiple levels of management. By focusing here on the initiative as the unit of analysis the problem of defining a parent–subsidiary relationship was circumvented. Certain initiatives were found to be specific to a single plant so involved a single relationship with a U.S. manufacturing director; others involved the whole spectrum of business units and all their relationships with their U.S. counterparts. In all cases, however, it was possible to examine a generic process based around the nature of the initiative, rather than a

Table 8. Summary of findings from current study

	Local market initiative	Internal market initiative	Global market initiative	Hybrid initiative
Facilitating conditions	• Low parent–sub. communication (quantitative) • High autonomy at first • Moderate proven resources (qualitative)	• High parent–sub. communcation • Low autonomy • Strong proven resources, hence credibility • Geocentric perspective in parent company (all qualitative)	• High autonomy • Low parent–sub. communication (quantitative) • Strong proven resources (qualitative)	• High parent–sub. communication • Low autonomy • Strong proven resources, hence credibility • Geocentric perspective in parent company (all qualitative)
Process	• Low to moderate internal selling • Implicit approval process[a] (qualitative and quantitative)	• High internal selling • Explicit approval process[b] (qualitative and quantitative)	• Low internal selling • Implicit approval process[a] (qualitative and quantitative)	• High internal selling • Explicit approval process[b] (qualitative and quantitative)
Intended outcome	• New business for the MNC; local opportunity leveraged worldwide (qualitative)	• Rationalization of existing activities; increased efficiency (qualitative)	• Enhancement and international leverage of an existing product line or business (qualitative)	• Optimum global siting of new value-adding activity (qualitative)

[a]The global market initiative process involved somewhat less internal selling and greater levels of implicit approval than the local market initiative process.
[b]The internal market and hybrid initiative processes differed only in subtle ways. Hybrid initiatives involved significantly earlier parent involvement than local market initiatives, but the magnitude of the investment in question coupled with the competitive nature of the bid meant that a stronger selling effort was typically observed. The internal market initiative process, by contrast, tended to be slightly more incremental in nature, often taking several years to come to fruition.

somewhat artificial conceptualization of the parent–subsidiary relationship.

This research also embraced a broader conceptualization of subsidiary initiative than had previously been identified. Taking Ghoshal (1986) as the definitive piece of work in this area, subsidiary initiatives can be focused either on local market opportunities ('local for local innovations') or on global market opportunities ('local for global' or 'global for global' innovations). This research has shown, in addition, that initiatives can be internally focused, towards a rationalization of existing activities or the promotion of new ones. Viewed in this way, the subsidiary suddenly has the potential to enhance the local responsiveness, global integration *and* worldwide learning capabilities of the MNC. This is a significantly broader role than previous research has suggested. The implication is that the MNC that is able to harness the full entrepreneurial capabilities of its subsidiaries stands to gain competitive advantage.

How can the subsidiary's entrepreneurial capabilities be most effectively harnessed? The first challenge is to create an appropriate structural context, that is, one that facilitates entrepreneurship. Ghoshal's (1986) research showed that *ceteris paribus* high autonomy, specialized resources, high normative integration and high interunit communication were associated with subsidiary initiative. This study suggested a more complex set of relationships. Autonomy, for example, was shown to be positively associated with local and global market initiatives and negatively associated with internal market and hybrid initiatives.[11] Likewise, the other facets of structural context actually varied between initiative types as well. The implication is that a single structural context cannot facilitate all four types of initiative. If a subsidiary is highly integrated with its parent, for example, it can easily pursue internal market and hybrid initiatives, but less easily undertake local or global market initiatives.

The implicit trade-offs that the parent company faces in shaping the subsidiary's structural context are reduced when one recognizes that the subsidiary is itself differentiated. One division of the subsidiary can be closely integrated with its par-

ent; another may be largely autonomous. GE Canada, for example, has 11 divisions each one of which has a unique relationship to its respective parent division in the United States. Furthermore, the subsidiary's structural context and its assigned role are not cast in stone. Over time a successful initiative-taking subsidiary would expect to impact its own strategic context (Burgelman, 1983b) and hence its perceived role within the MNC. One of the subsidiaries in this study, for example, built a new business from scratch in Canada. As the division in question grew it developed an international customer base and a unique set of capabilities so that eventually it operated as a stand-alone global business. Over this period its emphasis shifted from local market initiatives to global market initiatives, and correspondingly its structural context also changed to accommodate its new role.

In sum, the idea that subsidiary roles can be differentiated through contextual mechanisms (Bartlett and Ghoshal, 1986) is a powerful one, but not without its limitations. This study has shown that context needs to be differentiated at the sub-subsidiary level (typically the division, business unit or plant) if the full scope of initiative types is to be facilitated. It has also suggested that a more dynamic approach to role and context management is appropriate, given that the subsidiary's opportunity set and internal capabilities are continually evolving.

The second challenge facing the MNC that is attempting to enhance the entrepreneurial capabilities of its subsidiaries is to develop an entrepreneurial culture, i.e., one that motivates its employees to take the initiative. The review of the corporate entrepreneurship literature identified this as a key imperative, but the current study was not able to shed light on it. By focusing on six companies that had all successfully pursued initiatives, it would be reasonable to deduce that all had relatively entrepreneurial cultures. Future research, in which a sample of initiative-taking subsidiaries is compared with a sample of noninitiative-taking subsidiaries, will be necessary to understand exactly what an entrepreneurial culture means for a MNC.

Corporate entrepreneurship

Entrepreneurship in this paper was defined as alertness to market opportunity. While this con-

---

[11] Qualitatively, the evidence suggested a *causal* relationship between autonomy and initiative in the directions indicated, though this cannot be verified with the quantitative data.

ceptualization is well accepted in the literature (Kirzner, 1973; Stevenson and Jarillo, 1990), traditional usage was extended by modeling 'market' to include entities both internal and external to the MNC. This insight, in turn, led to a recognition that there were two distinct entrepreneurial processes at work in the sample companies: (1) 'internal entrepreneurship' (internal and hybrid initiatives) in which initiatives were subject to corporate selection mechanisms such as legitimacy and approval; and (2) 'external entrepreneurship' (local and global initiatives) in which initiatives were subject to environmental selection mechanisms such as customer acceptance and survival. The concept that the corporation can create its own variation–selection–retention mechanism is, of course, not new (e.g., Burgelman, 1991), but the data in this case provided strong empirical support for what is a relatively underresearched phenomenon.

To what extent did a sample of MNC subsidiaries make this research on corporate entrepreneurship a special case? The Canadian setting is interesting (and rich in data) because the recent transition to North American Free Trade, and the perceived threat to Canadian operations, has induced many Canadian subsidiaries to actively look for ways to add value. Furthermore, the problems of building relationships and gaining credibility with decision-makers are all exacerbated by the geographical and (relatively minor) cultural distances between subsidiary and head office. In addition, the concepts of 'local' and 'global' initiative are clearly designed to apply to foreign subsidiaries and not domestic entities. Notwithstanding these facts, our position is that the subsidiary context implies a difference of degree rather than of kind. It is a small stretch (conceptually and physically) to move a subsidiary plant in London, Ontario to Buffalo, New York, so we suggest that the issues illuminated here are no less portable. While the primary focus of the research was obviously on MNC subsidiary management, the implications for corporate entrepreneurship are substantial.

CONCLUSION

The objective of this paper was to document an empirical investigation of subsidiary initiatives, and to understand them in terms of the existing theory of the MNC. The key finding was that four types of subsidiary initiative can be identified. Previous research by Ghoshal (1986) had indicated that subsidiary initiatives can be focused either on local market or global market opportunities. This research demonstrated, in addition, that initiatives can be internally focused, towards a rationalization of existing activities or towards the promotion of new ones. This finding has two implications: first, it suggests that the subsidiary has the potential to drive the local responsiveness, global integration *and* worldwide learning capabilities of the MNC, a much broader role than previously recognized; second, it indicates that the differentiation of subsidiary roles through contextual mechanisms (Bartlett and Ghoshal, 1986) has its limitations. Both of these implications are explored in the discussion.

This study had a number of limitations. First, the sample was drawn from a single country, which was appropriate given the state of knowledge about subsidiary initiatives (Parkhe, 1993; Yin, 1984) but also limiting with regard to external validity. Subsequent research in other countries and with parents of other nationalities is the important next step in building knowledge about subsidiary initiatives. Second, the sample was selected to include only those subsidiaries with some record of success with initiatives. This, again, was appropriate given the need to understand the characteristics of initiatives, but it begs the question 'What factors are responsible for promoting initiative in some subsidiaries and stifling it in others?' Now that the types of initiatives are better understood a follow-up study addressing this question can be conducted.

In terms of the methodology, three limitations were evident. The first was the challenge of collecting data on failed initiatives. For a variety of reasons managers were reluctant to dwell on their less auspicious moments, so a small number of failed initiatives may have been missed in the sample companies. This problem could potentially be mitigated by spending longer in the company, but there are clear trade-offs in terms of diminishing returns and potentially alienating time-constrained managers. A real-time study would also solve this problem, but would be very time intensive. Equally problematical were those initiatives that died out before they took off. Rather than being failures *per se*, such initiatives simply did not register as important in the minds of the respondents. Again, a real time study would be the only way to circumvent this concern. Finally, the questionnaire was deliberately short to ensure a high response rate, but this meant that one- and two-item construct measures were used. For future research greater attention needs to be given to the development of a valid and reliable measurement instrument.

Future research, then, is recommended in two directions. The first thrust should be towards a comprehensive understanding of the initiative phenomenon in other MNC settings, and in a larger sample of subsidiaries. Of interest here is not only the generalizability of the *initiative* characteristics identified in the current study, but also the characteristics of *subsidiaries* that exhibit initiatives. The second research thrust should be directed towards the personal motivation of employees to pursue initiatives. While the current study identified the intended outcomes behind initiatives, it was unable to inform the discussion of why certain individuals choose to pursue entrepreneurial opportunities while others do not. If we are to build a complete model of subsidiary initiative, the critical element may be the personal motivation and the spark of creativity that sets the whole process in motion.

ACKNOWLEDGEMENTS

The thoughtful comments of Nick Fry, Paul Beamish, Sumantra Ghoshal, Allen Morrison and Rod White are gratefully acknowledged. Financial assistance was provided by the Plan for Excellence, Richard Ivey School of Business. Research assistance from Laura MacLellan and Nigel Owens is also acknowledged.

REFERENCES

Barnard, C.I. (1938). *The Functions of the Executive.* Harvard University Press, Cambridge, MA.

Bartlett, C. A. and S. Ghoshal (1986). 'Tap your subsidiaries for global reach', *Harvard Business Review*, **64**(6), pp. 87–94.

Bartlett, C. A. and S. Ghoshal (1989). *Managing across Borders: The Transnational Solution.* Harvard Business School Press, Cambridge, MA.

Bartlett, C. A. and S. Ghoshal (1993). 'Beyond the M-Form: Toward a managerial theory of the firm', *Strategic Management Journal*, Winter Special Issue, **14**, pp. 23–46.

Birkinshaw, J. M. (May–June 1995). 'Is the country manager an endangered species?', *International Executive*, pp. 279–302.

Bower, J. L. (1970). *Managing the Resource Allocation Process.* Irwin, Homewood, IL.

Brandt, W. K. and J. M. Hulbert (Winter 1977). 'Headquarters guidance in marketing strategy in the multinational subsidiary', *Columbia Journal of World Business*, 12, pp. 7–14.

Burgelman, R. A. (1983a). 'A process model of internal corporate venturing in the diversified major firm', *Administrative Science Quarterly*, **28**, pp. 223–244.

Burgelman, R. A. (1983b). 'A model of the interaction of strategic behavior, corporate context and the concept of strategy', *Academy of Management Review*, **8**(1), pp. 61–70.

Burgelman, R. A. (1991). 'Intraorganizational ecology of strategy making and organizational adaptation: Theory and field research', *Organization Science*, **2**(3), pp. 239–262.

Burns, T. J. and G. Stalker (1961). *The Mangement of Innovation.* Tavistock Publications, London.

Cohen, L. E. and R. Machalek (1988). 'A general theory of expropriative crime: An evolutionary ecological model', *American Journal of Sociology*, **94**, pp. 465–501.

Covin, J. G. and D. P. Slevin (Fall 1991). 'A conceptual model of entrepreneurship as firm behavior', *Entrepreneurship Theory and Practice*, pp. 7–25.

Cray, D. (1984). 'Control and coordination in multinational corporations', *Journal of International Business Studies*, **15**(3), pp. 85–98.

Crookell, H. H. (1986). 'Specialization and international competitiveness'. In H. Etemad and L. S. Dulude (eds.), *Managing the Multinational Subsidiary.* Croom Helm, London, pp. 102–111.

Damanpour, F. (1991). 'Organizational innovation: A meta-analysis of effects of determinants and moderators', *Academy of Management Journal*, **34**, pp. 555–590.

D'Cruz, J. R. (1986). 'Strategic management of subsidiaries'. In H. Etemad and L. S. Dulude (eds.), *Managing the Multinational Subsidiary.* Croom Helm, London, pp. 75–89.

Drucker, P. (1985). *Innovation and Entrepreneurship.* Harper & Row, New York.

Etemad, H. and L. S. Dulude (1986). *Managing the Multinational Subsidiary.* Croom Helm, London.

Forsgren, M. and J. Johanson (1992). *Managing Networks in International Business.* Gordon & Breach, Philadelphia, PA.

Galbraith, J. (Winter 1982). 'Designing the innovating organization', *Organizational Dynamics*, pp. 5–25.

Galunic, D. C. and K. M. Eisenhardt (1994). 'The evolution of intracorporate domains: Division charter losses in high-technology, multidivisional corporations', working paper, INSEAD.

Ghoshal, S. (1986). 'The Innovative Multinational: A Differentiated Network of Organizational Roles and Management Processes', unpublished doctoral dissertation, Harvard Business School.

Ghoshal, S. and C. A. Bartlett (1988). 'Creation, adoption and diffusion of innovations by subsidiaries of multinational corporations', *Journal of International Business Studies*, **19**(3), pp. 365–388.

Ghoshal, S. and C. A. Bartlett (1991). 'The multinational corporation as an interorganizational network', *Academy of Management Review*, **15**(4), pp. 603–625.

Ghoshal, S. and C. A. Bartlett (1994). 'Linking organizational context and managerial action: The dimensions of quality of management', *Strategic Management Journal*, Summer Special Issue, **15**, pp. 91–112.

Ghoshal, S. and N. Nohria (1989). 'Internal differentiation within multinational corporations', *Strategic Management Journal*, **10**(4), pp. 323–337.

Ginsberg, A. and M. Hay (1995). 'Confronting the challenges of corporate entrepreneurship: Guidelines for venture managers', *European Management Journal*, **12**(4), pp. 382–389.

Gupta, A. K. and V. Govindarajan (1991). 'Knowledge flows and the structure of control within multinational corporations', *Academy of Mangement Review*, **16**(4), pp. 768–792.

Guth, W. D. and A. Ginsberg (1990). 'Guest editors introduction: Corporate entrepreneurship', *Strategic Management Journal*, Summer Special Issue, **11**, pp. 5–15.

Halal, W. E. (1993). *Internal Markets*. Wiley, New York.

Harrigan, K. R. (1983). 'Innovation within overseas subsidiaries', *Journal of Business Strategy*, pp. 47–55.

Hedlund, G. (1981). 'Autonomy of subsidiaries and formalization of headquarters–subsidiary relationships in Swedish MNCs'. In L. Otterbeck (ed.), *The Management of Headquarters–Subsidiary Relations in Multinational Corporations*. Gower Publishing, Aldershot, Hampshire, U.K., pp. 27–76.

Hedlund, G. (1986). 'The hypermodern MNC: A heterarchy? *Human Resource Management*, **25**, pp. 9–36.

Hedlund, G. and J. Ridderstråle (1992). 'Towards the N-Form corporation: Exploitation and creation in the MNC', working paper, Stockholm School of Business, RP 92/15.

Howell, J. M. and C. A. Higgins (1990). 'Champions of technological innovation', *Administrative Science Quarterly*, **35**, pp. 317–341.

Humes, S. (1993). *Managing the Multinational Corporation: Confronting the Global–Local Dilemma*. Prentice-Hall International, Hertfordshire.

Jarillo, J. -C. and J. I. Martinez (1990). 'Different roles for subsidiaries: The case of multinational corporations in Spain', *Strategic Management Journal*, **11**(7), pp. 506–512.

Johanson, J. and J. -E. Vahlne (1977). 'The internationalization process of the firm: A model of knowledge development and increasing foreign market commitments', *Journal of International Business Studies*. **1**, pp. 23–32.

Kanter, R. M. (July–August 1982). 'The middle manager as innovator', *Harvard Business Review*, pp. 95–105.

Kanter, R. M. (1985). *The Change Masters*. Simon & Schuster, New York.

Kanter, R. M. (1986). 'Supporting innovation and venture development in established companies', *Journal of Business Venturing*, **1**(1), pp. 47–60.

Kirzner, I. M. (1973). *Competition and Entrepreneurship*. University of Chicago Press, Chicago, IL.

Kuratko, D. F., R. V. Montagno and J. S. Hornsby (1990). 'Developing an intrapreneurial assessment instrument for an effective corporate entrepreneurial environment', *Strategic Management Journal*, Summer Special Issue, **11**, pp. 49–58.

Martinez, J. I. and J.-C. Jarillo (Fall 1989). 'The evolution of research on coordination mechanisms in multinational corporations', *Journal of International Business Studies*, pp. 489–514.

Meyer, A. D., A. S. Tsui and C. R. Hinings (1993). 'Configuration approaches to organizational analysis', *Academy of Management Journal*, **36**(6), pp. 1175–1195.

Miles, M. B. and M. Huberman (1984). *Qualitative Data Analysis: A Sourcebook of New Methods*. Sage, Newbury Park, CA.

Miller, D. (1983). 'The correlates of entrepreneurship in three types of firms', *Management Science*, **29**, pp. 770–791.

Miller, D. (1986). 'Configurations of strategy and structure', *Strategic Management Journal*, **7**(3), pp. 233–249.

Mintzberg, H., D. Raisinghani and A. Theoret (1976). 'The structure of unstructured decision processes', *Administrative Science Quarterly*, **21**, pp. 246–274.

Morrison, A. J. (1990). *Strategies in Global Industries: How U.S. Businesses Compete*. Quorum Books, Westport, CT.

Negandhi, A. R. and B. R. Baliga (1981). 'Internal functioning of American, German and Japanese multinational corporations'. In L. Otterbeck (ed.), *The Management of Headquarters–Subsidiary Relations in Multinational Corporations*. Gower Publishing, Aldershot, Hampshire, U.K., pp. 106–120.

Nunnally, J. C. (1978). *Psychometric Theory* (2nd ed.) McGraw-Hill, New York.

Nutt, P. (1993). 'The formulation processes and tactics used in organizational decision-making', *Organization Science*, **4**(2), p. 226–251.

Parkhe, A. (1993). '"Messy" research, methodological predispositions, and theory development in international joint ventures', *Academy of Management Review*, **18**(2), pp. 227–268.

Penrose, E. T. (1959). *The Theory of the Growth of the Firm*. Basil Blackwell, Oxford.

Perlmutter, H. V. (January–February 1969). 'The tortuous evolution of the multinational corporation', *Columbia Journal of World Business*, pp. 9–18.

Perreault, W. D. and L. E. Leigh (1989). 'Reliability of nominal data based on qualitative judgements', *Journal of Marketing Research*, **XXVI**, pp. 135–148.

Peters, T. J. and R. H. Waterman (1982). *In Search of Excellence*. Harper & Row, New York.

Picard, J. (1980). 'Organizational structures and integrative devices in European multinational corporations', *Columbia Journal of World Business*, **15**, pp. 30–35.

Pinchott, G. III (1985). *Intrapreneuring*. Harper & Row, New York.

Porter, M. E. (1986). *Competition in Global Industries*. Harvard Business School Press, Boston, MA.

Poynter, T. A. and A. M. Rugman (Autumn 1982). 'World product mandates: How will multinationals respond?' *Business Quarterly*, pp. 54–61.

Prahalad, C. K. and Y. L. Doz (Summer 1981). 'An approach to Strategic Control in MNCs', *Sloan Management Review*, pp. 5–13.

Quelch, J. A. (1992). 'The new country managers', *McKinsey Quarterly*, pp. 156–165.

Quinn, J. B. (1985). 'Managing innovation: Controlled chaos', *Harvard Business Review*, **63**(3), pp. 73–84.

Roth, K. and A. J. Morrison (1992). 'Implementing global strategy: Characteristics of global subsidiary mandates', *Journal of International Business Studies*, **23**(4), pp. 715–736.

Safarian, A. E. (1966). *Foreign Ownership of Canadian Industry*. McGraw-Hill, Toronto.

Sathe, V. (1985). 'Managing an entrepreneurial dilemma: Nurturing entrepreneurship and control in large corporations'. In J. A. Hornaday, E. B. Shils, J. A. Timmons and K. H. Vesper (eds.), *Frontiers of Entrepreneurship Research*. Babson College, Wellesley, MA, pp. 636–657.

Schollhammer, H. (1982). 'Internal corporate entrepreneurship'. In D. Sexton and K. H. Vesper (eds.), *Encyclopedia of Entrepreneurship*. Prentice-Hall, Englewood Clilffs, NJ, pp. 209–223.

Schumpeter, J. A. (1934). *The Theory of Economic Development*. Harvard University Press, Cambridge, MA.

Science Council of Canada (1980). *Multinationals and Industrial Strategy: The Role of World Product Mandates*. Science Council of Canada, Supply and Services Canada, Ottawa.

Stevenson, H. H. and J.-C. Jarillo (1990). 'A paradigm of entrepreneurship: Entrepreneurial management', *Strategic Management Journal*, Summer Special Issue, **11**, pp. 17–27.

Stopford, J. M. and C. W. F. Baden-Fuller (1994). 'Creating corporate entrepreneurship', *Strategic Management Journal*, **15**(7), pp. 521–536.

Sykes, H. B. (1986). 'The anatomy of a corporate venturing program: Factors influencing success', *Journal of Business Venturing*, **1**, pp. 275–293.

Vernon, R. (May 1966). 'International investment and international trade in the product cycle', *Quarterly Journal of Economics*, pp. 191–207.

Vernon, R. (1979). 'The product cycle hypothesis in a new international environment, *Oxford Bulletin of Economics and Statistics*', **41**, pp. 255–267.

White, R. E. and T. A. Poynter (Summer 1984). 'Strategies for foreign-owned subsidiaries in Canada', *Business Quarterly*, pp. 59–69.

White, R. E. and T. A. Poynter (Autumn 1990). 'Achieving worldwide advantage with the horizontal organization', *Business Quarterly*, pp. 55–60.

Yin, R. K. (1984). *Case Study Research*. Sage, Beverly Hills, CA.

[2]

A Process Model of
Internal Corporate Ven-
turing in the Diversified
Major Firm

Robert A. Burgelman

This paper reports findings of a field study of the internal
corporate venturing (ICV) process in a diversified major
firm. It presents a grounded process model of the interlocking key activities of managers at different levels in the
organization, which constitutes the strategic process by
which new ventures take shape. Successful ICV efforts are
shown to depend on the availability of autonomous entrepreneurial activity on the part of operational level participants, on the ability of middle-level managers to conceptualize the strategic implications of these initiatives in more
general system terms, and on the capacity of top management to allow viable entrepreneurial initiatives to change
the corporate strategy.•

This paper examines the management of new ventures in a firm
of the "diversified major" or "related business" type. Such
firms are large agglomerates of widely diverse yet related
businesses grouped into divisions whose general managers
report to corporate management. In recent years, a substantial
literature has emerged on the relationships between strategy,
structure, degree of diversification, and economic performance
in the divisionalized firm (Chandler, 1962; Williamson, 1970;
Wrigley, 1970; Rumelt, 1974; Galbraith and Nathanson, 1979;
Caves, 1980). The actual processes of corporate entrepreneurship and strategic change, however, remain less well
understood. This is probably because these processes in such
firms are complex and are difficult and costly to research. While
large, diversified firms are clearly not representative of business organizations in general (Aldrich, 1979), they represent
such a large proportion of the total industrial activity in the
developed economies that efforts to construct a theory of
corporate entrepreneurship would seem valuable (Arrow,
1982).

The research reported here investigates the process through
which a diversified major firm transforms R&D activities at the
frontier of corporate technology into new businesses through
internal corporate venturing (ICV). These new businesses enable the firm to diversify into new areas that involve competencies not readily available in the operating system of the
mainstream businesses of the corporation (Salter and
Weinhold, 1979). Previous systematic research of ICV has not
clearly distinguished between new product and new business
development and has investigated the ICV development process only up to the "first commercialization" phase (von Hippel,
1977). The present study specifically examines the relationship
between project development and business development,
showing how new organizational units developed around new
businesses become integrated into the operating system of the
corporation either as new freestanding divisions or as new
departments in existing divisions. The rationale for studying
projects utilizing new technologies is that the strategic management problems involved in corporate entrepreneurship are
likely to be most accentuated and most identifiable in projects in
which innovative efforts are radical (Zaltman, Duncan, and
Holbek, 1973).

Ansoff and Brandenburg (1971) discussed the strategic management problems of diversification through internal development in the divisionalized firm, and proposed that corporations

© 1983 by Cornell University.
0001-8392/83/2802-0223/$00.75
•
This paper is based on the author's doctoral
dissertation, which received a Certificate of
Distinction for Outstanding Research in the
field of Strategic Management, Academy
of Management and General Electric Company, 1980. L. Jay Bourgeois, Arthur P.
Brief, David B. Jemison, Leonard R. Sayles,
Stephen A. Stumpf, and Steven C. Wheelwright have made useful comments on
earlier drafts of this paper. The constructive
comments of three anonymous ASQ reviewers have contributed significantly to
this final version. Support from the
Strategic Management Program of Stanford University's Graduate School of Business is gratefully acknowledged. My
thanks also to Barbara Sherwood for excellent administrative assistance.

create separate units within the corporate structure to facilitate new venture development. During the seventies, many large corporations adopted the new venture division (NVD) design (Hanan, 1976; Hutchinson, 1976). Fast (1979), however, showed that new venture divisions often occupy a precarious position within the corporate structure because of erratic changes in corporate strategy or in the political position of the NVD in the corporate context. Argyris and Schön (1978) provided anecdotal evidence of the various problems that impede the effectiveness of the NVD in divisionalized firms. The present study further elucidates the management problems inherent in internal corporate venturing.

Frohman (1978), Quinn (1979), and Maidique (1980) suggested categories of specialized roles to conceptualize the innovation process in organizations. The present study uses a different approach, documenting the key activities of persons on different hierarchical levels within the organization. The flow of these interlocking activities is represented in a process model of internal corporate venturing. Such a model is useful to elucidate the "generative mechanisms" (Pondy, 1976) of corporate entrepreneurship. It indicates how the entrepreneurial activities of individuals combine to produce entrepreneurship at the level of the corporation, as well as how forces at the level of the corporation influence the entrepreneurial activities of these individuals.

METHODOLOGY AND RESEARCH DESIGN

A qualitative method was chosen as the best way to arrive at an encompassing view of ICV. Concerns of external validity were traded off against opportunities to gain insight into as yet incompletely documented phenomena. The caveats pertaining to field methods described by Kimberly (1979) are in order.

ICV project development has a ten- to twelve-year time horizon (Biggadike, 1979), and a truly longitudinal study was thus beyond the available resources. Instead, a longitudinal-processual approach (Pettigrew, 1979) was adopted. The ICV process was studied exhaustively in one setting. Data were collected on six ongoing ICV projects that were in various stages of development. The historical development of each case was traced and the progress of each case during a fifteen-month research period was observed and recorded. These materials formed the basis for a comparative analysis of the six projects. This approach should not be confused with the so-called "comparative method" of early sociology, which used, often selectively, cross-sectional data to support a priori theories — most aptly called metaphors — of stages of development (Nisbet, 1969). No such theory guided the present research, nor is one proposed as a result of it.

In fact, because of the exploratory nature of the study and the objective of generating a descriptive model of as yet incompletely documented phenomena, Glaser and Strauss's (1967) strategy for the discovery of "grounded theory" was adopted. This strategy requires the researcher " . . . at first, literally to ignore the literature of theory and fact on the area under study, in order to assure that the emergence of categories will not be contaminated by concepts more suited to different areas" (Glaser and Strauss, 1967: 37). It also requires joint collection,

Internal Corporate Venturing

coding, and analysis of the data. Data must be collected until patterns have clearly emerged and additional data no longer add to the refinement of the concepts.

The lack of previous research at the ICV project level of analysis made it fairly easy to follow these guidelines. By the same token, great uncertainty existed as to what conceptual framework would emerge from the data. Throughout the research period, idea booklets were used to write down new insights and interpretations of data already collected. These ongoing, iterative conceptualization efforts resulted in the creation of a new set of terms for the key activities in ICV and provided the bits and pieces out of which the conceptual framework finally emerged.

Research Setting

The research was carried out in one large, U.S.-based, high-technology firm of the diversified major type which I shall refer to as GAMMA. GAMMA had traditionally produced and sold various commodities in large volume, but it had also tried to diversify through the internal development of new products, processes, and systems so as to get closer to the final user or consumer and to catch a greater portion of the total value added in the chain from raw materials to end products. During the sixties, diversification efforts were carried out within existing corporate divisions, but in the early seventies, the company established a separate new venture division (NVD). Figure 1 illustrates the structure of GAMMA at the time of the study.

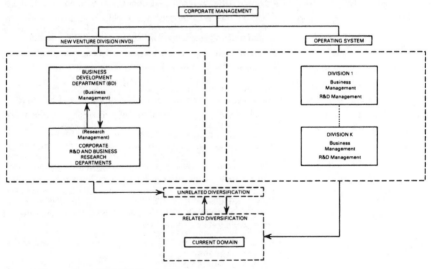

Figure 1. The structure of GAMMA Corporation.

Data were obtained on the functioning of the NVD. The charters of its various departments, the job descriptions of the major positions in the division, the reporting relationships and mechanisms of coordination, and the reward system were studied. Data were also obtained on the relationships of the NVD with the rest of the corporation. In particular, the collaboration between the corporate R&D department and divisional R&D groups was studied. Finally, data were also obtained on the role of the NVD in the implementation of the corporate strategy of unrelated diversification to help explain why it had been created, how its activities fit in the corporation's Strategic Business Unit system, and how it articulated with corporate management. These data describe the historical evolution of the structural context of ICV development at GAMMA before and during the research period. The bulk of the data was collected in studying the six major ICV projects in progress at GAMMA at the time of the research.

Fermentation Products was in the earliest stage of development. The new business opportunity was still being defined and no project had been formally started. Five people from this project were interviewed, some several times, between November 1976 and August 1977.

Fibre Components was a project for which a team of R&D and business people were investigating business opportunities and their technical implications. Five people in this group were interviewed between January 1977 and May 1977.

Improved Plastics had reached a point where a decision was imminent as to whether the project would receive venture status and be transferred from the corporate R&D department to the venture development department of the NVD. Seven people from this project were interviewed, some several times, between February 1977 and April 1977.

Farming Systems had achieved venture status, but development had been limited to the one product around which it had been initially developed. Efforts were being made to articulate a broader strategy for further development of the venture. This was achieved during the research period and an additional project was started. Seven people were interviewed, some several times, between November 1976 and August 1977.

Environmental Systems had also achieved venture status, but was struggling to deal with the technical flaws of the product around which its initial development had taken place. It also was trying to develop a broader strategy for further development. It failed to do so, however, and the venture was halted during the research period. Six people from the project were interviewed between March 1977 and June 1977.

Medical Equipment was rapidly becoming a mature new business. It had grown quickly around one major new product, but had then developed a broader strategy that allowed it to agglomerate medically related projects from other parts of the corporation and to make a number of external acquisitions. After the research period, this venture became a new free-standing division of the corporation. Eleven people were interviewed, some several times, between June 1976 and September 1977.

Data Collection

In addition to the participants in the six ICV projects, I interviewed NVD administrators, people from several operating divisions, and one person from corporate management. All in all, sixty-one people were interviewed. Table 1 indicates the distribution of persons interviewed over job categories.

Internal Corporate Venturing

Table 1

Distribution of Persons Interviewed, by Job Title

	Number:
Top management of the New Venture Division (NVD)	
Director of NVD	2
Director of corporate R&D Department	1
Director of Business Research Department	1
Director of Business Development Department	2
Participants from corporate R&D Department	
R&D managers	4
Group leaders	10
Bench scientists	6
Participants from Business Research Department	
Business managers	2
Business researchers	4
Participants from Business Development Department	
Venture managers	5
Business managers	1
Technology managers	3
Group leaders in venture R&D group	3
Marketing managers	4
Marketing researchers	2
Operations managers	4
Project managers	1
Administration of NVD	
Personnel managers	1
Operations managers	1
Participants from other operating divisions	
R&D managers	1
Group leaders	2
Corporate management	
Executive staff	1
Total	61

The interviews were unstructured and took from one and a half to four and a half hours. Tape recordings were not made, but the interviewer took notes in shorthand. The interviewer usually began with an open-ended invitation to tell about work-related activities, then directed discussion toward three major aspects of the ICV development process: (1) the evolution over time of a project, (2) the involvement of different functional groups in the development process, and (3) the involvement of different hierarchical levels in the development process. Respondents were asked to link particular statements they made to statements of other respondents on the same issues or problems and to give examples, where appropriate.

A major benefit from this approach was that it was possible to interview more people than originally planned. Respondents mentioned names of relevant actors and were willing to help set up interviews with them. It was thus possible to interview the relevant actors in each of the ICV cases studied and to record the convergence and divergence in their views on various key problems and critical situations throughout the development process. In some cases, it was necessary to go back to a previous respondent to clarify issues or problems, and this was always possible. After completing an interview, the interviewer made a typewritten copy of the conversation. All in all, about 435 legal-size pages of typewritten field notes resulted from these interviews.

The research also involved the study of documents. As could be expected, the ICV project participants relied little on written procedures in their day-to-day working relationships with other participants. One key set of documents, however, was the set of written corporate long-range plans concerning the NVD and each of the ICV projects. After repeated requests, I received permission to read the plans on site and to make notes. These official descriptions of the evolution of each project between 1973 and 1977 were compared with the interview data.

Finally, occasional behavioral observations were made, for example when other people would call or stop by during an interview or in informal discussions during lunch at the research site. These observations, though not systematic, led to the formulation of new questions for further interviews.

A PROCESS MODEL OF ICV

A Stage Model

As the research progressed, four stages of ICV development were identified — a conceptual, a pre-venture, an entrepreneurial, and an organizational stage. Table 2 indicates the stages reached in each project, the number of projects observed for each stage, and the number of real time observations of each stage.

Table 2

Stages of Development Reached by Six ICV Projects

Project	Conceptual	Stages Pre-venture	Entrepreneurial	Organizational
Medical Equipment	*	*	*	*
Environmental Systems	*	*	*	
Farming Systems	*	*	*	
Improved Plastics	*	*		
Fibre Components	*	*		
Fermentation Products	*			
Projects observed	6	5	3	1
Real time observations	1	2	2	1

Note: An asterisk indicates that the project reached this stage prior to the conclusion of the study.

This research design thus resulted in seven case histories. At the project level, the comparative analysis of the six ICV cases allowed the construction of a grounded stage model that described the sequence of stages and their key activities. At the level of the corporation, the research constituted a case study of how one diversified major firm went about ICV and how the corporate context influenced the activities in each stage of development of an ICV project.

A stage model describes the chronological development of a project. It provides a description of the development activities and problems in a series of stages, which is convenient for narrative purposes. Such a model, however, is somewhat deceptive because it does not capture the fact that strategic activities take place at different levels in the organization simultaneously as well as sequentially and, sometimes, in a different order than would be expected.

Internal Corporate Venturing

ICV Process

The process-model approach proposed by Bower (1970) for strategic capital investment projects permits one to connect the project and corporate level of analysis and to depict simultaneous as well as sequential strategic activities. Subsequent research has established the usefulness and generalizability of the process-model approach for conceptualizing strategic decision making in and around projects other than capital investment in large, complex firms (Hofer, 1976; Bower and Doz, 1979).

The inductively derived process model for ICV at GAMMA presented below shows how managers from different generic levels in the organization got involved in the development of ICV projects. The first step was to map the stages of ICV development onto the *definition* and *impetus* processes of the model. The definition process encompassed the activities involved in articulating the technical-economic aspects of an ICV project. Through the impetus process, it gained and maintained support in the organization. Definition and impetus were identified as the *core* processes of ICV.

The second step was to map the corporate-level findings onto the *strategic context* and *structural context* determination processes, which make up the corporate context in which ICV development takes shape. Structural context refers to the various organizational and administrative mechanisms put in place by corporate management to implement the current corporate strategy. It operated as a selection mechanism on the strategic behavior of operational and middle-level managers. Strategic context determination refers to the process through which the current corporate strategy was extended to accommodate the new business activities resulting from ICV that fell outside the scope of the current corporate strategy. Strategic and structural context determination were identified as the *overlaying* processes of ICV.

The third step was the documentation of the managerial activities that constitute these different processes.

Figure 2 maps the activities involved in ICV onto the process model. It shows how the strategic process in and around ICV is constituted by a set of key activities (the shaded area) and by a set of more peripheral activities (the nonshaded area). These activities are situated at the corporate, NVD, and operational levels of management.

Figure 3, which can be superimposed on Figure 2, shows how these different activities interlock with each other, forming a pattern of connections. The relative importance of activities is indicated by the different types of line segments. The data also suggested a sequential flow of activities in this pattern, as indicated by the numbers in Figure 3.

Figure 3 shows that ICV is primarily a bottom-up process and depicts the key role performed by middle management. Looking at Figure 3, entrepreneurial activities at the operational and middle levels (1, 2, 3) can be seen to interact with the selective mechanisms of the structural context (5). These selective mechanisms can be circumvented by activating, through organizational championing (6), the strategic context, which allows successful ICV projects to become retroactively ratio-

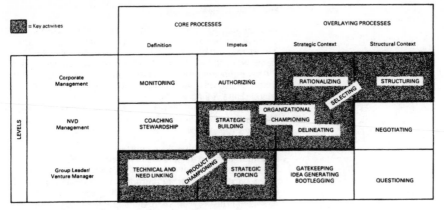

Figure 2. Key and peripheral activities in a process model of ICV.

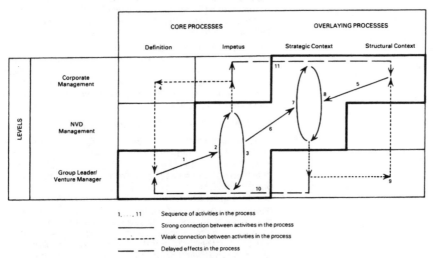

Figure 3. Flow of activities in a process model of ICV.

nalized by corporate management in fields of new business delineated by the middle level (7, 8). These parts of the pattern, represented by the full line segments in Figure 3, constitute the major forces generated and encountered by ICV projects.

The finely dotted lines in Figure 3 (4, 9) represent the connection between the more peripheral activities in the ICV process and their linkages with the key activities. Corporate management was found to monitor the resource allocation to ICV projects. Middle-level managers managed these resources and facilitated collaboration between R&D and business people in the definition of new business opportunities; however, these activities seemed to support, rather than drive the definition process. In the same fashion, authorizing further development was clearly the prerogative of corporate management, but this

Internal Corporate Venturing

was a result, not a determinant of the impetus process. In the strategic context determination process, gatekeeping, idea generating, and bootlegging activities by operational level participants were all found to be important in developing a basis for further definition processes but seemed to be more a result of the process than a determinant of it. In the process of structural context determination, questioning of the structural context by operational level participants and efforts by middle managers to negotiate changes in it seemed to be reactive rather than primary.

The broken line segments in Figure 3 (10, 11) indicate two important delayed effects in the ICV process. First, the successful activation of the process of strategic context determination encouraged further entrepreneurial activities at the operational level, thus creating a feedforward loop to the definition process (10). Second, corporate management attempted to influence the ICV process primarily through its manipulations of the structural context. These manipulations appeared to be in reaction to the results of the previously authorized ICV projects. This created a feedback loop (11) between the core and overlaying processes.

Figures 2 and 3 and the preceding overview of the process model can now serve as a road map for detailed examination of the interlocking key activities that constitute the major driving forces in the four processes — definition, impetus, strategic context determination, and structural context determination — that together constitute ICV.

DEFINING NEW BUSINESS OPPORTUNITIES

The case data of the present study suggest that the definition process of an ICV project encompasses the conceptualization and pre-venture stages of the development process. As the definition process takes shape, an idea for a new business opportunity evolves into a concrete new product, process, or system around which a pre-venture team of R&D and business people is formed. As a result of the successful technical and market development efforts of this pre-venture team, a project grows into an embryonic business organization. These stages take place in the context of the corporate R&D department. Critical for the definition of new business opportunities are *linking processes* and *product-championing* activities.

Linking Processes

In all of the cases studied, the initiation of the definition process involved a double linking process. Technical linking activities led to the assembling of external and/or internal pieces of technological knowledge to create solutions for new, or known but unsolved, technical problems. Need linking activities involved the matching of new technical solutions to new, or poorly served, market needs.

In five out of six cases, the definition of the new business opportunity had its origin in technical linking activities in the context of ongoing research activities in the corporate R&D department. In the Fibre Components case, the idea came from a business-oriented manager, but once the idea was to be made concrete, technical linking activities began to dominate the definition process there, too. This suggests "technology first" (Schön, 1967) as the dominant mode of conceiving of a new

1
This is how the originator of the medical
equipment venture recounted a story that
illustrated the importance of integrating
technical and marketing considerations in
the definition process:

In 1968, we had a think tank session in
Connecticut. A scientist from our
government-sponsored lab, I found out,
was working on a new way to handle and
transfer blood samples, an entirely new
concept, . . . but the scientist had very
fixed ideas about how the product
should look as a commercial product. . . .

An outside group also had discovered
the existence of the scientist's idea and
followed closely his recommendations.
It was a small company, with a sales
volume of some eight million dollars. I
decided not to make "Chinese copies" of
their approach. I insisted on doing market research, and actually spent two
months full-time doing this. We ended
up with a radical departure from the
scientist's approach; we used only the
nucleus of his physical concepts. We had
found out some advisable product
characteristics from our market research, which led, for instance, to a
broader-sized "reader." We also combined the analyzer with a computer.

A further discussion of how this integration
is achieved and of the issues related to the
collaboration between R&D and business
people in the definition process is provided
in Burgelman (1980).

2
In the words of the group leader:

As with most new ideas, people would
give little time to it. People "knew" that
SURF was "unpractical," so the divisions
did not really get involved, except in an
informal way.

3
Argyris and Schön (1978: 214) noted a
similar phenomenon in their Mercury case,
in which key participants were those who
could recognize "a Mercury problem." In
the present study, however, initiators were
more concerned with avoiding the work on
projects that would be perceived by top
management as *not* a GAMMA problem.
Projects were avoided in those areas in
which there had been failures in the past, in
those where there might be risk to the
corporation's image, or in areas having special legal liabilities.

4
Said the group leader:

But these pumps are costly, and people
at the management level are afraid to
commit themselves to such outlays. At
that time, however, an engineer came on
the project. He knew of the corporate
surplus lists and got some old pumps.
We rebuilt them and showed that we
could pump 35 percent to 49 percent
solutions. Having showed that, we could
now get the pumps we needed.

venture. However, the case data also suggest that the continued viability of a project depended to a very great extent on
the integration of technical and marketing considerations in the
definition process.[1]

An important characteristic of ICV project definition was its
autonomy from current corporate strategy. ICV project initiators
perceived their initiatives to fall outside the current strategy but
felt that there was a good chance for them to be included in
future strategic development if they proved to be successful.
For instance, in the Improved Plastics project, SURF was a
process through which cheap plastics — a major business of
GAMMA — could be given certain properties of expensive
plastics. However, since knowledgeable and influential people
at GAMMA were convinced that SURF could not work because
it was too violent a process, it was very difficult to obtain formal
support for work in this area.[2] The leader of the efforts in SURF
persisted, however, and was capable of developing an application of the process with plastic aerosol bottles. Later on, it
turned out that they had focused their efforts on the wrong size
bottles for commercial application, but in the meantime a basis
for corporate support had been demonstrated.

The key position in the definition process turned out to be that
of group leader, a first-line supervisory position, in the corporate
R&D department. This person had sufficient direct involvement
in the research activities to perform technical linking activities,
sufficient contact with the business side to be aware of market
needs and start the need linking activities, and sufficient
experience of the corporate tradition to know what might be
included in corporate strategy.[3] Fermentation Products, Improved Plastics, Farming Systems, and Medical Equipment all
clearly illustrated the importance of the group leader in the
definition process. Fibre Components and Environmental Systems involved higher levels of management in a very superficial
way in the initiating phase, but it was the group leader who was
able to perform the concrete linking activities, and the higher
level involvement soon became very remote even in these two
cases.

Product Championing: Linking Definition and Impetus

Because group leaders were most deeply involved in the
definition process, they tended to take on the product-
championing activities (Schön, 1967) that formed the connection between the definition and impetus processes. Product
championing was required to turn a new idea into a concrete
new project in which technical and marketing development
could begin to take shape. These activities required the ability to
mobilize the resources necessary to demonstrate that what
conventional corporate wisdom had classified as impossible
was, in fact, possible. To overcome difficulties in resource
procurement resulting from this conventional wisdom, product
champions acted as scavengers, reaching for hidden or forgot-
ten resources to demonstrate feasibility. SURF, for instance,
demonstrated the validity of its need for pumps by using
modified pumps from the corporate reserve list.[4]

Product championing also set the stage for the impetus process by creating market interest in the new product, process, or
system while, from the corporate point of view, it was still in the
definition process. To do so, the product champion sometimes

Internal Corporate Venturing

cut corners in corporate procedures, as in a case where unauthorized selling efforts were started from the R&D site before the project had become an official venture.[5] ICV projects of the nature investigated in this study thus had to be fought for by their originators. Hiding their efforts until they could show positive results clearly had survival value for product champions. Once such positive results were available, however, pressure began to build to give a project venture status and to transfer it to the business development department, where the impetus process took further shape.

The importance of product championing was especially clear in the cases where it was lacking. In the Fibre Components case, a product champion had not yet emerged, and this hampered the momentum of the project. The more careful balance between the technical and business considerations fostered in this case seemed to make the emergence of a champion more difficult. In Improved Plastics, the original product champion returned to more basic research, and the subsequent reorganization of the pre-venture team with greater balance between R&D and business people made the emergence of a new product champion more difficult. In the Farming Systems, Environmental Systems, and Medical Equipment cases, however, a product champion was able to develop a single product or system around which an embryonic business organization could be formed.

IMPETUS

The impetus process of an ICV project encompasses the entrepreneurial and organizational stages of development. Major impetus was received when a project was transferred with venture status to the business development department. At this time it acquired its own organization, general manager, and operating budget, thus becoming an embryonic new business organization in the department. In the course of the impetus process, the embryonic business grew into a viable one-product business and then, possibly, into a more complex new business with several products. The impetus process reached its conclusion in the decision to integrate this new unit into the operating system of the corporation as a freestanding new division or as a major new department of an existing division. The data indicate that there were no clear general criteria that guided the decisions to transfer projects to the business development department. Although formal screening models existed and the participants in all cases were very able in quantitiative analysis, there was little reliance on formal analytical techniques in the ICV process. This is understandable, since each project was unique and could not easily be judged by prior experience. Not surprisingly, the transfer decision thus tended to be greatly influenced by the success of the product-championing activities. The latter allowed a project to reach a threshold level of commercial activity which, in turn, created pressure for it to be given venture status. Farming Systems, Environmental Systems, and Medical Equipment all manifested this pattern. The data on these cases also indicate that after a project was transferred, its further development was highly dependent on the combination of *strategic forcing* and *strategic building* activities and their corollary forms of *strategic neglect*. These activities together give shape to the impetus process.

5

As the product champion in this case explained:

When we proposed to sell the ANA product by our own selling force, there was a lot of resistance, out of ignorance. Management did numerous studies, had outside consultants on which they spent tens of thousands of dollars; they looked at XYZ Company for a possible partnership. Management was just very unsure about its marketing capability. I proposed to have a test marketing phase with 20 to 25 installations in the field. We built our own service group; we pulled ourselves up by the "bootstrap." I guess we had more guts than sense.

Strategic Forcing

In the first phase of the impetus process, product-championing activities were transformed into strategic forcing by the entrepreneurial venture manager. This transformation happened naturally, because, in the cases studied, the product champion had become the venture manager. Even though normative theory might question this practice, there were very strong pressures to let the technically oriented product champion become the venture manager. These pressures were in part motivational, because product champions were attracted by the opportunity to become general managers, but they also resulted because there was nobody else around who could take over and maintain momentum. Strategic forcing required that the venture manager concentrate his efforts on the commercialization of the new product, process, or system. In particular, it required a narrow and short-term focus on market penetration.

The Medical Equipment case illustrates successful strategic forcing. Under the impulse of a product champion/venture manager, this ICV project doubled its sales volume each year for five consecutive years. This created the beachhead for further development into a new, mature business.[6] Such successful strategic forcing created a success-breeds-success pattern that allowed the new venture to maintain support from top management and facilitated collaboration from people in other parts of the corporation who liked to be part of the action of a winner. In addition, the success of strategic forcing allowed the emerging venture organization to acquire substantial assets that could not easily be disposed of, thus committing the corporation.[7]

The Environmental Systems case, on the other hand, illustrates unsuccessful strategic forcing. In this case, premature commercialization caused strategic forcing to degenerate into mere selling, and technical people were forced to spend their time correcting the technical flaws of systems already sold. The resulting failure-breeds-failure pattern led first to a reduction of the control of the product champion/venture manager, then to management-by-committee, then to the termination of the venture.

The corollary of successful strategic forcing, however, was strategic neglect of the development of the administrative framework of the new venture. Strategic neglect refers to the more or less deliberate tendency of venture managers to attend only to performance criteria on which the venture's survival is critically dependent; that is, those related to fast growth. To carry out the strategic forcing efforts, the entrepreneurial venture manager attracted or was assigned generalist helpers who usually took care of more than one of the emerging fuctional areas of the venture organization. This was inexpensive and worked sufficiently well until the volume of activity grew so large that operating efficiency became an important issue. Also, as the new product, process, or system reached a stage of maturity in its life cycle, the need for additional new product development was increasingly felt. To deal with the operating problems and to maintain product development, some of the generalists were replaced with functional specialists who put pressure on the entrepreneurial venture man-

6

In the words of the venture manager:

We were convinced that we could develop simultaneously domestically and internationally. We were fearless, and, management being ignorant, we just started to do it. What we did was, in fact, a parallel international new development. That made our sales 55 percent larger and allowed a larger profit fraction. If we had not done this, we might have lost the business.

7

In the words of one of the key participants in a venture:

The mechanism is to double each year your size. The next step is then to acquire assets that are not easily disposed of. Then management cannot get rid of you that easily, and you can relax if you have a bad year.

Internal Corporate Venturing

ager to pay more attention to administrative development. In the cases studied, this led to severe friction between the venture manager who continued to be pressured by forces in the corporate context to maintain a high growth rate, and the functional specialists.[8]

In the successful Medical Equipment venture, the venture manager neglected the administrative development of the venture and experienced increasingly strong conflicts with the professional functional managers brought in to replace the generalists. This became a problem especially in manufacturing. The venture manager also neglected to maintain close relationships with the corporate R&D group and focused everything on development efforts related to the original product. The venture R&D group, seeking its own identity, sealed itself off from corporate R&D.[9] One of the problematic results of this was that the flow of new product development never got under control. Eventually, the organizational problems and the difficulties in new product development required the replacement of the venture manager.

This study of ICV thus reveals an important dilemma in the process of radical corporate innovation. Successful strategic forcing is required if a project is to gain and maintain impetus in the corporate context. Yet, the very success of strategic forcing seems to imply strategic neglect of the administrative development of the venture. This, in turn, leads to the ironic result that the new product development may become a major problem, and to the tragic result that the entrepreneur may become a casualty in the process of gaining a beachhead for the venture.

Strategic Building

Successful strategic forcing was a necessary, but not sufficient, condition for the continuation of the impetus process. Strategic forcing had to be supplemented by strategic building activities if the project was to overcome the limitations of a one-product venture and maintain the growth rate required for continued support from corporate management. Strategic building took place at the level of the business development (BD) department manager (the venture manager's manager). Thus, consistent with Kusiatin's (1976) and von Hippel's (1977) findings, the present study identifies the venture manager's manager as a key position in the ICV process.

Strategic building involved the articulation of a master strategy for the broader field of new business development opened up by the product champion/venture manager and the implementation of this strategy through the agglomeration of additional new businesses with the original venture. This involved negotiating the transfer of related projects from other parts of the corporation and/or acquisition of small companies with complementary technologies from the outside.

The Medical Equipment case illustrates successful strategic building. From year to year, the written long-range plans showed an increase in depth of understanding of what the real opportunity was. Strategic plans grew more specific, and there was a progression in identifying problems and solving them. Based on this articulation of the principles underlying success, the BD manager negotiated the transfer of one major medically

8

Arrow (1974) uses "salutory neglect" to denote the situation in which problems for which there are no satisfactory solutions are not placed on the agenda of the organization. Strategic neglect, independently observed in the present study, has a similar meaning. Arrow points out that neglect is never productive. In the long run, and from the perspective of the larger system, this may be true, and of course the larger system will, in time, correct for neglect. From the perspective of the entrepreneurial actor, however, strategic neglect of administrative issues was the necessary cost of forcing growth.

9

In the words of one person who was transferred from corporate R&D to the venture:

We were, at the time, basically separated from the group in the venture. The group there wanted to identify itself. They did it to such an extent that they put a wall between themselves and us. . . . In a way, it was ironic. We were funded by the venture, and the technology that we developed was not accepted by them!

related project from one of the divisions and was able to identify suitable acquisition candidates and convince top management to provide the resources to get them.

Strategic building was iterative in nature. The evolving master strategy reflected the learning-by-doing that resulted from the assessment of the success of the strategic forcing efforts of the venture manager. The BD manager learned to understand the reasons for the success of these efforts and used this insight to further articulate the strategy. This, in turn, increased his credibility and provided a basis on which to claim further support of the venture.[10]

The Environmental Systems case illustrates how failure to understand the nature of the opportunity prevented further progress. Over a five-year period, the long-range plans remained vague about what the opportunity was. There was no progress in terms of identifying and then solving problems. An acquisition was actually made, but it turned out to be as much technically flawed as the original system around which the venture was formed.

The Farming Systems case illustrates how the impetus received from fairly successful strategic forcing can slow down, and even halt, when strategic building is lacking. Only after a new BD manager took over and an analysis was made of the underlying principles of the business opportunity did the impetus process pick up again. The new BD manager discarded the original product, which had been the vehicle for strategic forcing, and articulated a new master strategy that led first to the redirection of the R&D efforts and then to the acquisition of two small companies with complementary technology.

Strategic building, like strategic forcing, was accompanied by strategic neglect in the Medical Equipment case. Because forces in the corporate context emphasized fast growth, the BD manager got absorbed in the search and evaluation of companies that could be acquired, in negotiations with divisions to transfer related projects, and in courting top management. The coaching of the venture manager was, again more or less deliberately, neglected, which seemed to suit the venture manager. As a result, the emerging administrative problems in the venture organization deteriorated from petty and trivial to severe and disruptive, and some high-quality people left the venture.

The personal orientations of the venture managers further reinforced this tendency in the cases in my study. The venture manager of Medical Equipment complained about a lack of guidance from the BD manager, but he also pointed out that the situation gave him leeway for his mistakes. Furthermore, he pointed out that because the venture was growing very fast, there was little time for coaching. He also admitted that his style was probably considered a bit "adversarial" by the BD manager, and that this did not facilitate the coaching process.

The venture manager of Environmental Systems also complained about a lack of guidance.[11] This manager, however, admitted that he had been eager to get the venture manager's job in spite of his lack of experience. Others in the venture organization pointed to this manager's stubbornness and lack of responsiveness to others' inputs.

10

Explaining his approach, one BD manager said:

First, I look for demonstrated performance on an arbitrarily chosen — sometimes not even the right one — tactic. For instance, developing a new analyzer may not be the right move, but it can be done and one can gain credibility by doing it. So, what I am really looking for is the ability to predict and plan adequately. I want to verify your claim that you know how to predict and plan, so you need a "demonstration project" even if it is only an experiment. The second thing that I look for is the strategy of the business. That is the most important milestone. The strategy should be attractive and workable. It should answer the questions where you want to be in the future and how you are going to get there. . . . And that, in turn, allows you to go to the corporation and stick your neck out.

11

Right after his replacement, this manager observed:

I should have gotten help from my management — counseling and education. Most venture managers tend to come from the technology side because these ventures require a lot of high technology input. But in the technology area there is relatively little need for broad general management skill development. I was lacking that kind of judgment.

Internal Corporate Venturing

The present study thus suggests a second important dilemma in the strategic management process. The BD manager can spend more time trying to guide the impetuous venture manager, but this may both interfere with the strategic forcing efforts of the venture manager and limit the time available to the BD manager for strategic building activities. Or, he can leave the venture manager alone and let him run his course until the problems in the growing venture organization require his replacement, but by that time the venture itself should have reached a viable position in terms of commercial activity. The data suggest that the forces exerted by the corporate context — the emphasis on fast growth — seem to favor the second of these possibilities.

Successful strategic forcing and strategic building created a new business organization with several products and a sales volume of about 35 million dollars in the case of Medical Equipment, but important managerial problems remained to be solved. First, the effects of the strategic neglect of the administrative framework of the venture became particularly pronounced. This administrative instability was exacerbated by the fact that there was not yet a strong common orientation, and there was still a lot of opportunistic behavior on the part of some key participants in the venture organization, who seemed to work more to improve their resumes to get a better position elsewhere than for the overall success of the venture. Also, the delayed effects of the strategic neglect of new product development in the original area of business manifested themselves. Furthermore, strategic building efforts had led to the creation of a complex new business organization, where growth could no longer be maintained solely by the hard work of the venture manager. New strategies for the different business thrusts had to be generated by the organization, but this required that people work in a strategic planning framework in which the concerns of the different new business thrusts could be traded off and reconciled, and the participants were still learning to do this.

In addition to these internal managerial problems, this new venture also had to cope with the problem of securing its position in the corporation. The venture's size made it visible in the external and internal environments, and corporate management became increasingly aware of the differences in modus operandi between the new business and the rest of the corporation and of the effects of these differences on the corporate image. NVD management thus was faced with the problem of convincing corporate management that the new venture was compatible with the rest of the corporation and was moving toward institutionalization.

STRATEGIC CONTEXT

For institutionalization to take place, an area of new venturing must become integrated into the corporation's concept of strategy. Adaptation of corporate strategy at GAMMA involved complex interactions between managers of the NVD and corporate management in the process of *strategic context* determination.

Strategic context determination refers to the political process through which middle-level managers attempt to convince top management that the current concept of strategy needs to be changed so as to accommodate successful new ventures. Strategic context determination constitutes an internal selection mechanism that operates on the stream of autonomous strategic behavior in the firm. The key to understanding the activation of this process is that corporate management knows when the current strategy is no longer entirely adequate but does not know how it should be changed until, through the selection of autonomous strategic initiatives from below, it is apparent which new businesses can become part of the business portfolio.[12]

Critical activities in this process involve *delineating* new fields of business development and *retroactive rationalizing* of successful new venture activities. The link between the process of strategic context determination and the impetus process of a particular new venture is constituted by *organizational championing* activities.

Organizational Championing: Linking Impetus and Strategic Context Determination

The case data indicate that during the impetus process, organizational championing activities became the crucial link between the emerging new business organization and the corporate context. Organizational championing involved the establishment of contact with top management to keep them informed and enthusiastic about a particular area of development. This, in turn, involved the ability to articulate a convincing master strategy for the new field, so as to be able to communicate where the development was leading and to explain why support was needed for major moves. These activities were also performed at the level of the business development manager.

Organizational championing was, to a large extent, a political activity. The BD manager committed his judgment and put his reputation on the line. Astute organizational champions learned what the dispositions of top management were and made sure that the projects they championed were consistent with the current corporate strategy. More brilliant organizational champions were able to influence the dispositions of top management and make corporate management see the strategic importance of a particular new business field for corporate development.

Organizational championing required more than mere political savvy, however. It required the rare capacity to evaluate the merit of the proposals and activities of different product champions in strategic rather than in technical terms. Thus, in the Medical Equipment venture, a sound master strategy for the new venture and corresponding strategic building moves allowed the organizational champion to convince top management that the medical field was an attractive and viable one for the corporation. In the Environmental Systems venture, on the other hand, the failure to come up with a master strategy prevented the organizational champion from obtaining the resources needed to straighten out the technological problems of the new venture and prevented him from engaging in strategic building. His organizational championing was limited to gaining more time, but eventually top management concluded that the opportunity just wasn't there. Finally, in the

12
The identification of the process of strategic context determination leads to a major extension of the process model. It suggests that the corporate context is more complex than was revealed by Bower's (1970) study of strategic capital investment projects. These projects were situated in the operating system of the corporation. Even though they were clearly strategic because of the large amounts of resources involved, they did not require a change in the business portfolio of the corporation. These projects fell within the scope of and were induced by the current concept of strategy of the corporation.

Internal Corporate Venturing

Farming Systems venture, new impetus was developed as a result of the involvement of the same person who was the organizational champion in Medical Equipment.

Delineating

Through organizational championing based on strategic building, middle-level managers were capable of delineating in concrete terms the content of new fields of business development for the corporation. It is a critical finding of this study that these new fields became defined out of the agglomeration of specific commercial activities related to single new products, processes, or systems, developed at the level of venture projects rather than the other way around. Delineating activities were thus iterative and aggregative in nature. This was clearly reflected in the written long-range plans of the NVD in 1975, which stated: "Instead of dealing with an ever-growing number of separate arenas, the NVD should henceforth focus its attention on a critical few major fields, within each of which arenas may be expanded, grouped together, or added."

Retroactive Rationalizing

To be sure, corporate management, too, got involved in the process of strategic context determination. Top management gave indications of interest in venture activity in certain general fields and expressed concern about the fit of ongoing ICV activities with corporate resources and strategy. In the final analysis, however, corporate management's role was limited to rejecting or rationalizing, retroactively, the ICV initiatives of lower-level participants in fields delineated by middle-level management.

These findings corroborate and extend the findings of previous research. They confirm the critical role of middle-level managers in shaping the strategy of internal development in the diversified major firm (Kusiatin, 1976). More generally, these findings also extend Kimberly's (1979) observation of the paradox that the success of a new, nonconformist unit creates pressures in the larger organizational context toward conformity, thereby affecting the very basis of success. Entrepreneurial and institutional existence seem to be inherently discrete states, and middle-level management needs to bridge the discontinuity.

STRUCTURAL CONTEXT

Given the limited substantive involvement of corporate management in the process of strategic context determination, how do they try to exert control over the ICV process? The present study suggests that they did so by *structuring* an internal selection environment.

Structuring

As in the situation studied by Bower (1970), corporate management relied on the determination of the structural context in its attempts to influence the strategic process concerning ICV. The structural context includes the diverse organizational and administrative elements whose manipulation is likely to affect the perception of the strategic actors concerning what needs to be done to gain corporate support for particular initiatives. The creation of the NVD as a separate organizational unit, the definition of positions and responsibilities in the departments of the NVD, the establishment of criteria for measuring and evaluating venture and venture-manager performance, and the assignment of either entrepreneurially or administratively inclined managers to key positions in the NVD all seemed intended to affect the course of ICV activity.

The corporate level seemed dominant in the determination of structural context. Corporate management's manipulations of the structural context seemed to be guided primarily by strategic concerns at their level, reflecting emphasis on either expansion of mainstream businesses or diversification, depending on perceptions at different times of the prospects of current mainstream businesses.

These changes in structural context did not reflect a well-conceived strategy for diversification, however, and seemed to be aimed at consolidating ICV efforts at different levels of activity rather than at guiding and directing these efforts. The NVD was created in the early seventies because people in the divisions had been engaging in what some managers called a "wild spree" of diversification efforts. Corporate management wanted to consolidate these efforts, although at a relatively high level of activity. Key managers involved in those earlier decisions pointed out that the direction of these consolidated efforts was based on preceding lower level initiatives that had created resource commitments, rather than on a clear corporate strategy of diversification.

The lack of a clear strategy for directing diversification was also evident in 1977, when significant changes in the functioning of the NVD took place. The newly appointed NVD manager pointed out that corporate management had not expressed clear guiding principles for further diversification beyond the emphasis on consolidation and the need to reduce the number of fields in which ICV activity was taking place.

Selecting

Structural context determination thus remained a rather crude tool for influencing ICV efforts. It resulted in an internal selection environment in which the autonomous strategic initiatives emerging from below competed for survival. In all the ICV cases, strong signals of fast growth and large size as criteria for survival were read into the structural context by the participants. This affected the process, if not so much the specific content, of their behavior. The importance of product championing, strategic forcing, strategic building, and the corresponding forms of strategic neglect would seem to indicate this. The inherent crudeness of the structural context as a tool for influencing the ICV process provided, of course, the rationale as well as the opportunity for the activation of the strategic context determination process discussed earlier.

CONCLUSIONS AND IMPLICATIONS

The preceding discussion of a process model of ICV does not, to be sure, treat the entire range of phenomena associated with new ventures (Roberts, 1980) and corporate entrepreneurship (Peterson, 1981). Reasons of focus as well as space constraints prevent discussion of issues such as management of the interfaces between business and R&D people and structural and managerial innovation associated with the separate new venture division.

Internal Corporate Venturing

The purpose here has been to construct a grounded model and to use this model as a framework for insights into the generative mechanisms of one form of corporate entrepreneurship in one type of large business organization. Verification is necessary to identify the generalizable relationships embedded in the process model generated in this paper and to identify the contingency factors that might explain variance across organizations in these relationships. The major insights gained from this exploratory study of the ICV process are recapitulated below and some major implications are briefly discussed.

First, the findings suggest strongly that the motor of corporate entrepreneurship resides in the autonomous strategic initiatives of individuals at the operational levels in the organization. High-technology ventures are initiated because entrepreneurially inclined technologists, usually at the group-leader level, engage in strategic initiatives that fall outside the current concept of corporate strategy. They risk their reputations and, in some cases, their careers, because they are attracted by the perceived opportunity to become the general manager of an important new business in the corporation. This stream of autonomous strategic initiatives may be one of the most important resources for maintaining the corporate capability for renewal through internal development. It constitutes one major source of variation out of which the corporation can select new products and markets for incorporation into a new strategy. Second, because of their very nature, autonomous initiatives are likely to encounter serious difficulties in the diversified major firm. Their proponents often have to cope with problems of resource procurement, because they attempt to achieve objectives that have been categorized by the corporation as impossible. Because such initiatives require unusual, even unorthodox, approaches, they create managerial dilemmas that are temporarily resolved through the more or less deliberate neglect of administrative issues during the entrepreneurial stage. The success of the entrepreneurial stage thus depends on behaviors that, paradoxically, have a high probability of eliminating the key actors from participation in the organizational stage. There seems to be an inherent discontinuity in the transition from entrepreneurial to institutionalized existence, as well as a possible asymmetry in the distribution of costs and benefits for the actors that may underlie the myth of the entrepreneur as tragic hero in the large corporation.

Third, the study of ICV elucidates the key role of middle-level managers in the strategy-making process in the diversified major firm. The venture manager's manager performs the crucial role of linking successful autonomous strategic behavior at the operational level with the corporate concept of strategy. Both the continuation of the impetus process of a particular ICV project and the change of the corporate strategy through the activation of the process of strategic context determination depend on the conceptual and political capabilities of managers at this level. The importance of this role seems to confirm the above-mentioned discontinuity between entrepreneurial activity and the mainstream of corporate activity.

Fourth, corporate management's role in the ICV process seems to be limited to the retroactive rationalization of autonomous strategic initiatives that have been selected by both the external environment at the market level and the internal corporate environment. Top management's direct influence in the ICV process is through the manipulation of structural context. These manipulations, however, seem to be predicated less on a clearly formulated corporate strategy for unrelated diversification than on concerns of consolidation. Ironically, from this perspective, the establishment of a separate, new venture division may be more a manifestation of corporate management's uneasiness with autonomous strategic behavior in the operating system than the adaptation of the structure to implement a clearly formulated strategy. The present study thus suggests that the observed oscillations in ICV activity at GAMMA may have been due to the lack of articulation between these manipulations of the structural context and a corporate strategy for unrelated diversification. It also provides further corroboration for the similar findings of Fast (1979) on the unstable position of NVDs in many corporations and for Peterson and Berger's (1971) suggestion that top management may view corporate entrepreneurship more as insurance for coping with perceived environmental turbulence than as an end in itself.

Implications for Organization Theory and Strategic Management

The research findings presented in this paper can be related to the current discussions in organization theory of the validity of rational versus natural selection models to explain organizational growth and development (Pfeffer and Salancik, 1978; Aldrich, 1979; Weick, 1979). Relatively successful, large diversified major firms like GAMMA would seem to be representative of the class of organizations that have sufficient control over their required resources to escape, to a great extent, the tight control of external selection and to engage in strategic choice (Child, 1972; Aldrich, 1979). The detailed, multilayered picture of the strategic management process presented in this paper suggests, however, that these strategic choice processes, when exercised in radical innovation, take on the form of experimentation and selection, rather than strategic planning. This is fundamentally different from the view that administrative systems "program" their own radical change (Jelinek, 1979).

Further research is needed to establish the conditions under which different systems for innovation in organizations can be adequate. The limited evidence of the present study, however, suggests that the tight coupling implied in the institutionalized approach may be inadequate for organizations with multiple, mostly mature technologies in their operating system. In an organization like GAMMA, there seems to be relatively little opportunity for generating radical innovation from within the operating system through the imposition of a strategic planning approach.

Large, complex business organizations have separate variation and selection mechanisms. Previously unplanned, radically new projects at the product/market level are generated from the relatively unique combination of productive resources of such firms. Not all of these projects are adopted, not so much because the market may turn out to be unreceptive but because they must overcome the selection mechanisms in the internal administrative environment of the firm, which reflect, normally,

Internal Corporate Venturing

the current strategy of the corporation, i.e., the retained wisdom of previously selected strategic behavior. Thus, the experimentation and selection model draws attention to the possibility that firms may adopt externally unviable projects or may fail to adopt externally viable ones and provides a clue to why firms occasionally produce strange innovations.[13] This analysis posits a conceptual continuity between internal and external selection processes, analogous to Williamson's (1975) analysis of external and internal capital markets, to explain the existence of the conglomerate form of the divisionalized firm. Because corporate entrepreneurship, as exemplified by the ICV activities in this paper, seems to differ from traditional individual entrepreneurship, as well as from traditional organizational economic activity, it may be necessary to devise different arrangements between the corporate resource providers and their entrepreneurial agents. Further research, both theoretical and empirical, would seem useful here.

The insights generated by the present study also have some implications for further research on the management of the strategy-making process in general. Comparative research studies of a longitudinal-processual nature, carried out at multiple levels of analysis, are necessary to document and conceptualize the multilayered, more or less loosely coupled network of interlocking, simultaneous, and sequential key activities that constitute the strategy-making process. Following Bower (1970), the present study has found it useful to focus the research on a particular strategic project rather than on the strategy-making process in general. This is consistent with Quinn's (1980: 52) observation that top managers "deal with the logic of each subsystem of strategy formulation largely on its own merits and usually with a different subset of people." A concrete focus, it would seem, is more likely to produce data on the vicious circles, dilemmas, paradoxes, and creative tensions that are embedded in the strategy-making process.

Comparative analysis of process models of various strategic projects could produce grounded concepts and categories that would initially be somewhat rudimentary and evocative. Hopefully, these would stimulate the imagination of other scholars and provide the base for more formal and precise concepts of managerial activity in the strategy-making process. Eventually, this could lead to a general theory of the management of strategic behavior in complex organizations and to the conceptual integration of content and process, formulation and implementation.

The present study may then be viewed as an attempt to augment the substratum of rudimentary and evocative concepts and categories. One result of this attempt is the identification of the new concepts of autonomous strategic behavior and strategic context determination and categories of key strategic activities. Further research along these lines may be able to provide a clearer understanding of the interactions between strategy, structure, and managerial activities and skills.

[13]
In the course of the present study, anecdotal evidence for the emergence of very unusual projects was amply available. In one case, a scientist pulled out a file with a whole series of such abortive projects, e.g., the mining of gold from sea water.

REFERENCES

Aldrich, Howard E.
1979 Organizations and Environments. Englewood Cliffs, NJ: Prentice-Hall.

Ansoff, H. I., and R. G. Brandenburg
1971 "A language for organization design, Part II." Management Science, 17: B717–B731.

Argyris, Chris, and Donald A. Schön
1978 Organizational Learning. Reading, MA: Addison-Wesley.

Arrow, Kenneth J.
1974 The Limits of Organization. New York: Norton.
1982 Innovation in Large and Small Firms. New York: Price Institute for Entrepreneurial Studies.

Biggadike, Ralph
1979 "The risky business of diversification." Harvard Business Review, 56: 103–111.

Bower, Joseph L.
1970 Managing the Resource Allocation Process. Boston: Graduate School of Business Administration, Harvard University.

Bower, Joseph L., and Yves Doz
1979 "Strategy formulation: A social and political view." In Dan E. Schendel and Charles W. Hofer (eds.), Strategic Management: 152–166. Boston: Little, Brown.

Burgelman, Robert A.
1980 "Managing innovating systems: A study of the process of internal corporate venturing." Unpublished doctoral dissertation, Columbia University.

Caves, Richard E.
1980 "Industrial organization, corporate strategy, and structure." Journal of Economic Literature, 18: 64–92.

Chandler, Alfred D., Jr.
1962 Strategy and Structure. Cambridge, MA: MIT Press.

Child, John
1972 "Organization structure, environment, and performance: The role of strategic choice." Sociology, 6: 1–22.

Fast, Norman D.
1979 "The future of industrial new venture departments." Industrial Marketing Management, 8: 264–279.

Frohman, Alan L.
1978 "The performance of innovation: Managerial roles." California Management Review, 20: 5–12.

Galbraith, Jay R., and Daniel A. Nathanson
1979 "The role of organizational structure and process in strategy implementation." In Dan E. Schendel and Charles W. Hofer (eds.), Strategic Management: 261–286. Boston: Little, Brown.

Glaser, Barney J., and Anselm L. Strauss
1967 The Discovery of Grounded Theory. Chicago: Aldine.

Hanan, Mack
1976 New Venture Management. New York: McGraw-Hill.

Hofer, Charles W.
1976 "Research on strategic planning: A survey of past studies and suggestions for future efforts." Journal of Business and Economics, 28: 261–286.

Hutchinson, John
1976 "Evolving organizational forms." Columbia Journal of World Business, 11: 48–58.

Jelinek, Mariann
1979 Institutionalizing Innovation. New York: Praeger.

Kimberly, John R.
1979 "Issues in the creation of organizations: Initiation, innovation, and institutionalization." Academy of Management Journal, 22: 435–457.

Kusiatin, Ilan
1976 "The process and capacity for diversification through internal development." Unpublished doctoral dissertation, Harvard University.

Maidique, Modesto A.
1980 "Entrepreneurs, champions, and technological innovations." Sloan Management Review, 21: 59–76.

Nisbet, Robert A.
1969 Social Change and History. New York: Oxford University Press.

Peterson, Richard A.
1981 "Entrepreneurship and organization." In Paul Nystrom and William Starbuck (eds.), Handbook of Organizational Design: 65–83. New York: Oxford University Press.

Peterson, Richard A., and David G. Berger
1971 "Entrepreneurship in organizations: Evidence from the popular music industry." Administrative Science Quarterly, 16: 97–106.

Pettigrew, Andrew M.
1979 "On studying organizational cultures." Administrative Science Quarterly, 24: 570–581.

Pfeffer, Jeffrey, and Gerald R. Salancik
1978 The External Control of Organizations. New York: Harper & Row.

Pondy, Louis R.
1976 "Beyond open system models of organizations." Paper presented at the Annual Meeting of the Academy of Management, Kansas City, August 12.

Quinn, James B.
1979 "Technological innovation, entrepreneurship, and strategy." Sloan Management Review, 20: 19–30.
1980 Strategies for Change. Homewood, IL: Irwin.

Roberts, Edward B.
1980 "New ventures for corporate growth." Harvard Business Review, 57: 134–142.

Rumelt, Richard P.
1974 Strategy, Structure, and Economic Performance. Boston: Graduate School of Business, Harvard University.

Salter, Malcolm S., and Wolf A. Weinhold
1979 Diversification through Acquisition. New York: Free Press.

Schön, Donald A.
1967 Technology and Change. New York: Delacorte.

von Hippel, Eric
1977 "Successful and failing internal corporate ventures: An empirical analysis." Industrial Marketing Management, 6: 163–174.

Weick, Karl E.
1979 The Social Psychology of Organizing. Reading, MA: Addison-Wesley.

Williamson, Oliver E.
1970 Corporate Control and Business Behavior. Englewood Cliffs, NJ: Prentice-Hall.
1975 Markets and Hierarchies. New York: Free Press.

Wrigley, Leonard
1970 "Divisional autonomy and diversification." Unpublished doctoral dissertation, Harvard University.

Zaltman, Gerald, Robert L. Duncan, and Jonny Holbek
1973 Innovations and Organizations. New York: Wiley.

[3]

Strategic Management Journal, Vol. 11, 5–15 (1990)

GUEST EDITORS' INTRODUCTION: CORPORATE ENTREPRENEURSHIP

WILLIAM D. GUTH and ARI GINSBERG
Stern School of Business, New York University, New York, New York, USA

When Schendel and Hofer (1979: 515) formally proposed a new way of viewing the business policy and planning field a little over a decade ago, they identified a number of areas in which research needs and opportunities existed 'to modify, broaden, and test the strategic management paradigm.' Among those they suggested was the topic of 'entrepreneurship and new ventures.' In discussing the importance of this topic within the rubric of strategic management, Schendel and Hofer pointed out that the 'birth process is necessary; and survival, regardless of size requires a renewal of key ideas on which the organization is built' (p. 526).

Entrepreneurship involves the identification of market opportunity and the creation of combinations of resources to pursue it (Kirzner, 1973; Schumpeter, 1934). The *de novo* development of new businesses within established firms reflects the process of corporate entrepreneurship. Renewal of key ideas on which organizations are built also reflects the process of corporate entrepreneurship; renewal of key ideas requires the ability to manage transformation and discontinuous change. As argued by Stevenson and Jarillo-Mossi (1986: 14), 'if a company wishes to continue to be entrepreneurial, it must convince everyone that change is the company's overriding goal.'

The topic of corporate entrepreneurship encompasses two types of phenomena and the processes surrounding them: (1) the birth of new businesses within existing organizations, i.e. internal innovation or venturing; and (2) the transformation of organizations through renewal of the key ideas on which they are built, i.e.

strategic renewal. Studies of corporate entrepreneurship have tended to focus on internal innovation or venturing. However, we believe that studies of strategic renewal will command increasing attention in corporate entrepreneurship research.

This special issue focuses on the state of theory, methods, and findings in corporate entrepreneurship research. We proposed a special issue of the *Strategic Management Journal* on corporate entrepreneurship to Dan Schendel for several reasons: (1) policy analysts and business leaders have increasingly recognized the need for widespread revitalization of corporations and have called for greater emphasis on entrepreneurial activity within large companies; (2) scholars and practitioners have become increasingly attentive to questions that concern the management of organizational transformation and strategic renewal; and (3) we were convinced that a special *SMJ* issue could facilitate progress in the development and testing of theories on corporate entrepreneurship by clarifying and presenting a more coherent view of current research.

THE DOMAIN OF CORPORATE ENTREPRENEURSHIP

In his introduction to last year's special issue on strategic leadership, Donald Hambrick (1989) observed that compared to the topic of the previous special issue—strategy content—the domain of strategic leadership was relatively diffuse and unmapped. In focusing this special issue on the topic of corporate entrepreneurship,

0143-2095/90/050005-11$05.50

we too have set sail on a relatively uncharted sea; for despite the growing interest in corporate entrepreneurship, there appears to be nothing near a consensus on what it is. Some scholars, emphasizing its analog to new business creation by individual entrepreneurs, view corporate entrepreneurship as a concept that is limited to new venture creation within existing organizations (Vesper, 1985). Others argue that the concept of corporate entrepreneurship should encompass the struggle of large firms to renew themselves by carrying out new combinations of resources that alter the relationship between them and their environments (Baumol, 1986; Burgelman, 1983a; Kanter, 1989).

In our call for papers for this special issue we decided to cast our net based on a broad, rather than a narrow, view of corporate entrepreneurship. In constructing a list of phenomena that fall under this broad conception, we were heavily influenced by Schumpeter's (1934) view of the entrepreneur as one who 'carries out new combinations.' As applied to entrepreneurial activities in large, complex organizations, this definition implies that the essential ingredient in corporate entrepreneurship is that decisions are made and actions are taken that result in new combinations of resources being carried out (Ellsworth, 1985). This carrying out of new combinations translates into changes in strategy that alter the *pattern* of resource deployment in an existing firm versus changes in strategy that modify the *magnitude* of resource deployment (Ginsberg, 1988).

Changes in the pattern of resource deployment—new combinations of resources in Schumpeter's terms—transform the firm into something significantly different from what it was before—something 'new.' This transformation of the firm from the old to the new reflects entrepreneurial behavior. Corporate venturing, or new business development within an existing firm, is only one of the possible ways to achieve strategic renewal. Corporate venturing may or may not be directed at, or result in, strategic renewal.

Strategic renewal is different from financial restructuring, though in current practice they are sometimes linked (Lewis, 1990). Strategic renewal involves the creation of new wealth through new combinations of resources. This includes actions such as refocusing a business

competitively, making major changes in marketing or distribution, redirecting product development, and reshaping operations. In addition, strategic renewal includes making acquisitions resulting in new combinations of resources for businesses within the acquiring firm. In contrast, financial restructuring is directed at financing an exisiting combination of resources in a way that yields a higher return to shareholders. This includes actions such as increasing leverage and stock repurchase programs.

Thus far, we have argued that all changes in firms' pattern of resource deployment stemming from the carrying out of new combinations should be considered in the domain of corporate entrepreneurship. From this perspective, research on venturing within established firms only looks at one aspect of corporate entrepreneurship.

We turn now to an overview of research on corporate entrepreneurship based on this broader perspective.

A FRAMEWORK FOR MAPPING CORPORATE ENTREPRENEURSHIP RESEARCH

The guest editor of the previous special issue, Donald Hambrick, attempted to put strategic leaders 'back into the strategy picture.' Although his discussion centered on top managers, middle managers also have a role in strategic leadership. The 'autonomous strategic behavior' of middle managers 'provides the raw material—the requisite diversity—for strategic renewal' (Burgelman, 1983a). Top management actions and responses in relation to the autonomous strategic behavior of middle managers may significantly influence the frequency and success of entrepreneurial effort in the firm.

Building on earlier models of strategic management (Guth, 1971; Schendel and Hofer, 1979; Hambrick, 1989), Figure 1 portrays the theoretical connections that can be drawn from corporate entrepreneurship to the other conceptual elements of the field of strategic management. Researchers in strategic management generally agree that organization form/conduct includes strategy, structure, and management process (Hambrick, 1989). Increasingly, organization theorists argue for including core organization values or beliefs among the conduct variables,

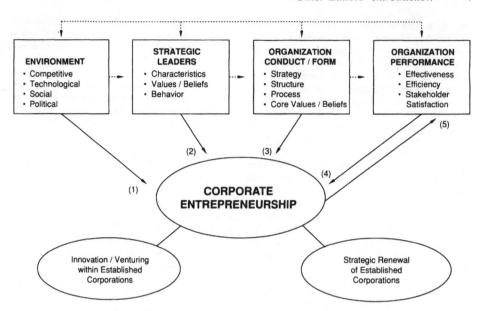

Figure 1:   Fitting Corporate Etrepreneurship Into Strategic Management

pointing to the fundamental role these play in effective and efficient implementation of strategy structure, and process (Tushman and Romanelli, 1985). Empirical research on the relationships between core organizational values/beliefs and other conduct variables is in an early stage of development in the field. There seems to be some agreement, however, that conduct variables must be configured in relation to each other, such that significant change in one variable—such as strategy—must be accompanied by change in the others, or the organization (viewed as a system) will lose effectiveness and/or efficiency (Miller and Friesen, 1980). Without getting into many possible multi-way interactions and feedback loops, we have identified five classes of inquiry into corporate entrepreneurship (see the numbered lines in Figure 1).

1. Environment influences corporate entrepreneurship

Examples of previous research findings in this category include:

   (a) The impact of major environmental shifts, such as deregulation, can influence changes

in strategy in a non-random way, with organizations (in the aggregate) moving away from one generic strategy towards other generic strategies (Zajac and Shortell, 1989).

   (b) The more dynamic and hostile the environment, the more firms will be entrepreneurial (Miller, 1983).

   (c) Industry structure affects opportunities for successful new product development (Cooper, 1979).

Clearly, changes in industry competitive structures and the technologies underlying them affect corporate entrepreneurship. Opportunities for new products and services stem from development of new technology and/or commercialization of technologies developed by others. Both opportunities and problems stem from the potential of the firm and its competitors in an industry to find new combinations of resources that lead to competitive advantage.

2. Strategic leaders influence corporate entrepreneurship

Examples of previous research findings in this category include:

8   *W.D. Guth and A. Ginsberg*

(a) The management style of top managers affects the level and performance of new corporate ventures (Kanter, 1983).

(b) Middle manager effectiveness at building coalitions among peers and higher-level managers in support of their entrepreneurial ideas affects the degree of success in their implementation (Burgelman, 1983b).

(c) Banks that are more innovative are managed by more highly educated teams, who are diverse with respect to their functional areas of expertise (Bantel and Jackson, 1989).

Many would argue that entrepreneurial behavior in organizations is critically dependent on the characteristics, values/beliefs, and visions of their stategic leaders. The role of both individual managers and management teams in corporate entrepreneurship warrants considerable further research.

3. Organization form/conduct influences corporate entrepreneurship

Examples of previous research findings in this category include:

(a) Firms pursuing strategies of acquisitive growth have lower levels of R&D intensity than firms pursuing strategies of internal growth through innovation (Hitt *et al.*, 1989).

(b) Creating new business venture units in larger organizations does not affect the level of sales from new products (Hisrich and Peters, 1984).

Bureaucratic structures and management processes are widely regarded as anathema to innovation and change within organizations. Yet there have been reports in the literature of high levels of new product introduction in organizations observed to have highly bureaucratic structures and processes (Sathe, 1985). More rigorous empirical research is needed on the combined effects of organization structure, strategy, and core organizational values/beliefs on corporate entrepreneurship.

4. Organizational performance influences corporate entrepreneurship

Examples of previous research findings in this category include:

(a) Successful firms make more radical and more frequent product and process innovations than unsuccessful firms (Mansfield, 1963).

(b) Organizations which experience performance downturns tend to innovate new practices and change strategic directions only after prolonged decline leads to changes in top management (Tushman, Virany, and Romanelli, 1985).

Innovation and radical change may be precipitated when firms have excess resources that allow them to seize upon opportunities that arise; they also may be induced by crises or severe external threats. More research is needed to shed light on questions concerning the conditions that moderate the influence of organizational performance on innovation and strategic renewal. For example, in what kinds of competitive environments do successful firms make more radical and more frequent product innovations? Under what conditions does renewal take place without change in top management?

5. Corporate entrepreneurship influences performance

Examples of previous research findings in this category include:

(a) Scale of entry in new product introductions affects performance (Biggadike, 1979).

(b) Independent, venture-backed start-ups, on average, reach profitability twice as fast and end up twice as profitable as corporate start-ups (Weiss, 1981).

(c) Early entry in new-product markets does not affect performance (Cooper, 1979).

The short-run performance orientation of many managements has often been cited as a deterrent to innovation and change. It is clear that new ventures often take several years to turn into contributors to overall corporate profit performance. Organizational re-creations may often have short-run negative performance consequences. Defining success and failure of corporate entrepreneurship is a major issue not well addressed in the literature.

From the above perspective on findings and issues in corporate entrepreneurship research, we turn now to a discussion of the papers in this special issue.

THE PAPERS

The review process yielded nine papers for the special issue out of 62 submitted. The reviewers used two criteria in the first cut: (1) Is the paper currently or potentially publishable on criteria used by *SMJ*? (2) Does the paper meet the additional criterion of contribution to the theme of the special issue? The reviewers, in consultation with the guest editors, subjected those that remained to one additional criterion: (3) Did the paper reach its potential in time to meet the publication schedule for the special issue? Table 1 classifies the accepted papers on six dimensions:

1. The primary Figure 1 focus: the strategic management relationships, as numbered in Figure 1.
2. The research question addressed: these vary widely from why it is difficult for corporate venture managers to use social transaction strategies to what factors affect major change in stagnating companies.
3. The primary aspect of corporate entrepreneurship studied: five of the papers focus on innovation/venturing within existing organizations and four focus on strategic renewal of existing organizations.
4. The unit of analysis: seven of the papers focus on the organization and two focus on individual new products or ventures within the organization.
5. Key concepts and theories: a wide variety of concepts and theoretical perspectives are used in the papers to study corporate entrepreneurship.
6. The theoretical intent and method: eight of the nine papers intend to build theory; one intends to test theory. The theory-building papers employ a variety of methods.

The first five papers examine corporate entrepreneurship as entrepreneurial processes, or venture activities, within existing firms. Howard Stevenson and Jose-Carlos Jarillo, in their paper, 'A Paradigm of Entrepreneurship: Entrepreneurial Management,' develop a view of corporate entrepreneurship, which they argue facilitates the application of previous findings in individual entrepreneurship research. Building on earlier work to conceptualize entrepreneurship based on extensive case observation of individual entrepreneurs (Stevenson and Gumpert, 1985),

the authors develop propositions about characteristics of organizations that affect the degree of entrepreneurial behavior they will exhibit.

Michael Hitt, Robert Hoskisson, and Duane Ireland, in their paper, 'Mergers and Acquisitions and Managerial Commitment in M-Form Firms,' analyze the impact of corporate acquisitive growth strategies on managerial commitment to innovation in acquiring firms. This theory construction study focuses on an important issue in the trend among large companies to pursue growth through acquisition. Their analysis persuasively leads to the major proposition that such strategies result in reduction of entrepreneurial effort to develop new technologies and products. While new wealth may be created by some synergistic acquisitions, the preponderance of evidence is that mostly neutral and sometimes negative results are achieved by acquiring firms. The authors' hypothesis that acquisitive growth strategies reduce entrepreneurial efforts raises serious questions not only about the long-run implications of these strategies for firms that pursue them, but also for the American economy as a whole, given the high frequency of acquisition efforts among large American firms. Empirical research suggested by this study promises to yield findings of major importance to corporate strategists and public policy analysts.

The next paper, by Donald Kuratko, Ray Montagno, and Jeffrey Hornsby, 'Developing an Intrapreneurial Assessment Instrument for An Effective Corporate Entrepreneurial Environment,' examines the organizational context within which new products/ventures develop. Using a quasi-experimental design within one organization and factor-analytic techniques, this study empirically documents a parsimonious set of organizational context factors that may encourage or inhibit venturing behavior among middle-level managers. Prior to this study, much of the research on the influence of organizational context variables on intrapreneurship was based on case studies or anecdotal evidence. More rigorous empirical methods, like those used in this study, are needed to develop theory in this important area of corporate entrepreneurship. As yet, there is no systematic evidence regarding the impact on venturing behavior of effectively managing the factors documented in this study.

The next paper, by Deborah Dougherty, 'Understanding New Markets for New Products',

10   *W.D. Guth and A. Ginsberg*

Table 1. Classification of papers

Author(s)	Primary Figure 1 focus	Specific research question	Primary aspect of corporate entrepreneurship studied	Unit of analysis	Key theories	Contribution and method
Stevenson and Jarillo	2,3	What view of entrepreneurship facilitates the application of previous findings to the field of corporate entrepreneurship?	Innovation/venturing	Organization	Organizational inducements; individual learning	Theory-building; conceptual
Hitt, Hoskisson and Ireland	3	How does an acquisitive growth strategy affect managerial commitment to innovation?	Innovation/venturing	Organization	Risk preferences; organization form and control	Theory-building; conceptual
Kuratko, Montagno, and Hornsby	2,3	What factors foster new venture creation within an organization?	Innovation/venturing	Organization	Organizational inducements	Theory-building; quasi-experimental; factor analysis
Dougherty	3,5	Why is understanding new markets difficult for innovators in large firms?	Innovation/venturing	Individual products	Enactment, selection, retention	Theory-building; case studies; descriptive statistics
Starr and MacMillan	3,5	Why are new venture managers in corporations less able/willing to use social transaction strategies for resource acquisition than individual entrepreneurs?	Innovation/venturing	New ventures	Social exchange	Theory-building; case studies

continued overleaf

Author		Question			Concepts	Method
Meyer, Brooks, and Goes	1	How does discontinuous change at the industry level of analysis impact entrepreneurial responses of organizations?	Strategic renewal	Organization	Punctuated equilibrium; quantum speciation	Theory-building; industry case study
Singh	3,5	Does the transformation in governance structure of management buyouts result in major improvements in performance?	Strategic renewal	Organization	Incentive for entrepreneurship	Theory-testing; logistic regression
Grinyer and McKiernan	4,5	What factors affect major change in stagnating companies?	Strategic renewal	Organization	Aspirations; organizational learning; inertial forces	Theory-building; case studies; descriptive statistics
Lant and Mezias	1,5	How do different entrepreneurial search strategies impact the performance of a population of firms over time when faced with discontinuous environmental change?	Strategic renewal	Organization	Organizational learning	Theory-building; simulation

12   *W.D. Guth and A. Ginsberg*

examines why the process of understanding new markets is difficult for innovators of new products in large firms. In her grounded theory study of 18 new product innovation cases embedded in five firms, the author found three distinct market knowledge creation cycles operating at the departmental, interdepartmental, and project-to-firm levels.

Developing knowledge about new markets for new products in established firms is a more complex process than in start-up firms. The structure and processes in place to manage established products may inhibit or enhance development of knowledge about new opportunities. Dougherty's study suggests that how departmental, interdepartmental, and project-to-firm knowledge cycles are managed in established firms may be critical to new product success or failure.

Jennifer Starr and Ian MacMillan's paper, 'Resource Cooptation via Social Transactions: Resource Acquisition Strategies for new Ventures,' analyzes resource acquisition strategies of individual entrepreneurs, and explores why social transaction strategies used frequently and extensively by individual entrepreneurs may be more difficult for corporate venture managers to pursue. They argue that social transactions strategies reduce the investment required in new ventures and, among other virtues, increase the amount of 'network' commitment and support available to new ventures. Both these outcomes serve to increase returns on investment and the speed with which these returns are achieved, compared to ventures developed without extensive use of social transaction strategies. Starr and MacMillan's paper provides an interesting theoretical explanation for Weiss's (1981) empirical findings that independent start-ups dramatically outperformed corporate ventures in terms of the time it took them on average to become profitable, and in terms of return on investment. Their paper is indicative of the potential for advancement of knowledge about corporate entrepreneurship through cross-fertilization with theory and findings from independent entrepreneurship.

The next four papers examine corporate entrepreneurship as strategic renewal. In analyzing the impact of industry-level change on organizational responses, Alan Meyer, Geoffrey Brooks, and James Goes conceptualize four types of industry-level change—adaptation, metamor-

phosis, evolution, and revolution—and argue that less is known about the strategic management implications of revolutionary industry change than the other three. They studied the hospital industry in the San Francisco area over the period from the 1960s through the 1980s, noting that the type and level of change in the industry varied at different points in that period. Their analysis identified corresponding patterns of change among firms within the industry, highlighting the entrepreneurial responses of these firms to the revolutionary industry level changes of the 1980s. Their paper develops researchable propositions that are linked to their study. The occurrence of revolutionary change during the past decade in a number of industries, e.g. financial services, electric power, and airline transportation, provides a plethora of opportunities for researchers to contribute to our understanding of the impact of such change on corporate entrepreneurship.

Harbir Singh, in his paper, 'Management Buyouts: Distinguishing Characteristics and Operating Changes Prior to Public Offering,' also focuses on corporate entrepreneurship as a process of strategic renewal or rebirth. His study centers on the controversial issue of whether or not radical transformations in the ownership and governance structure of management buyouts result in radical (and positive) changes in the firm's post-buyout operations, or whether they simply induce a market correction in the value of the assets involved. Put simply, do management buyouts result in new wealth creation?

Singh's findings support those who see management buyouts as resulting in increased entrepreneurial drive in the management of their assets. Managers of the firms in his large sample demonstrated a willingness to make drastic changes in the operations of their respective firms, and to maintain large holdings of their stock when their firms went public. Although concern remains about the high levels of debt normally associated with management buyouts, Singh hypothesizes that management buyouts may be a sign of a new era of governance of firms and divisions. From the point of view of corporate entrepreneurship, management buyouts of divisions of larger firms may be a manifestation of failure of those larger firms to solve the problem of providing incentives to division managers to seek opportunity through new combinations of resources.

In the next paper, 'Generating Major Change in Stagnating Companies,' Peter Grinyer and Peter McKiernan examine how the 25 firms they studied changed to 'sharp-bend' their performance from stagnation or decline relative to their competitors to sustained superior performance. Drawing on earlier work, including Cyert and March (1963), the authors develop a model that predicts why and how organizations change radically. They confront this model with the data from their more general longitudinal study of the sharp-bending companies (Grinyer, Mayes, and McKiernan, 1988).

Their findings about the frequency, type, and conditions surrounding the organizational transformations observed are interesting in relation to corporate entrepreneurship as strategic renewal. These findings suggest that, for the sharp-bending firms, external and internal 'triggers' for organizational change provided opportunity for strategic renewal, which was seized by old or new top managers in many of the firms. There was no support in the data for the authors' proposition that managers make strategic changes only after finding functional changes inadequate.

The last of the papers examining corporate entrepreneurship as strategic renewal is by Theresa Lant and Stephen Mezias, 'Managing Discontinuous Change: A Simulation Study of Organizational Learning and Entrepreneurship.' Using a simulation methodology, this study develops theory about longitudinal patterns of entrepreneurship across a population of organizations, and the implications of different patterns for organizational performance. Among the many intriguing findings of their study is that firms with adaptive strategies do less well over the long run than firms with imitative strategies, under conditions of high environmental ambiguity.

Longitudinal research on strategic renewal, involving field study methods, tends to be rather costly and difficult to implement. Lant and Mezias's paper applies an innovative methodology that makes it possible to address theoretical issues in corporate entrepreneurship that might be prohibitively expensive to investigate solely through traditional methods.

CONCLUSION

In a recent article on the state of American management, Walter Wriston, one of America's most respected managers, observes that 'today, the spirit of the entrepreneur has entered the mainstream of U.S. management. Entrepreneurship is transforming the corporate bureaucracy' (1990: 79). We believe that corporate entrepreneurship will become an increasingly important topic over the next decade, as competitive, technological, social, and political change in the environment of U.S. firms continues to accelerate. Strategic management research that contributes to increasing the frequency and success of corporate entrepreneurship will, in our view, be highly valued in the academic and practitioner communities.

Of course, such research needs to be theory-based and confronted with good data. Theory development has not progressed in the area of corporate entrepreneurship as far as it has in some other streams of research in strategic management. That the overwhelming majority of papers submitted for review were theory-building in intent, rather than theory-testing, did not surprise us. One of our principal objectives in proposing the special issue was to facilitate progress in theory development on corporate entrepreneurship.

Identifying corporate entrepreneurship topics in need of further systematic research is easy in the sense that there is much room for across-the-board theoretical and methodological progress. However, deciding on specific topics most in need of study is rather challenging. The topics of the previous two special issues—strategy content and strategic leadership—and the topic of the next special issue—global strategy—provide some useful leads. Among the most interesting strategy content questions identified by Montgomery (1988) are those that relate to the scope of the firm—the combination of markets in which firms participate. Of particular interest are the questions of why firms participate in multiple and particular combinations of markets, and what accounts for the performance differences repeatedly observed across firms. Among these questions, we would include: What impact does participation in particular combinations of markets have on strategic renewal? What accounts for performance differences between entry into new markets through internal venturing versus acquisition? The flourishing economics literature on transaction cost analysis and principal–agent relations holds much promise for explaining the transformation of organizational governance

14   *W.D. Guth and A. Ginsberg*

structures, and the governance needs of internal venturing in established firms.

Among the strategic leadership topics identified by Hambrick (1989: 13) as most in need of study were: 'the processes by which some executives inspire and energize large organizations.' To this we would add 'inspire and energize large organizations to innovate and renew themselves.' Another is the question of how managers learn and develop and how they broaden and upgrade their repertoires. The answer to this question is part of the solution to the puzzle of what it takes to make corporate entrepreneurship work.

Changes in the international environment have presented researchers in the field of strategic management with challenges and opportunities that entail the application of methods and concepts previously employed in domestic settings. Such opportunities and challenges extend to the study of corporate entrepreneurship in a global context. Of particular interest are such questions as: What specific difficulties confront multi-national corporations engaging in strategic renewal? How can cross-border strategic alliances be used to facilitate corporate venturing within established firms? How does increasing global market opportunity and competition affect new venture strategies within existing firms?

Although diverse, the research questions covered by papers in this special issue address only a very small portion of the topics in need of further study in corporate entrepreneurship. An important objective for the special issue was to encourage and challenge researchers in the field of strategic management to contribute to this important area of inquiry.

In concluding, we want to thank the organizations and many individuals who contributed to this project. The Center for Entrepreneurial Studies, Stern School of Business, New York University provided administrative support for the project. Loretta Poole managed the logistics of the reviewing process with skill, patience, and resolve. Mary Lou Schendel handled the final editing process with forbearance and great charm. Dan Schendel, from beginning to end, gave freely of his entrepreneurial spirit, his experience, and his wisdom.

Finally, we thank the authors who submitted their papers and the referees who reviewed them. The authors of the submitted papers provided the intellectual raw materials for the special issue.

The reviewers listed at the end, shaped the final outcome with their constructive criticisms and judicious evaluations of the papers.

REFERENCES

Bantel, K. A. and S. E. Jackson. 'Top management and innovations in banking: Does the composition of the top team make a difference?', *Strategic Management Journal*, **10**, 1989, pp. 107–125.

Baumol, W. J. 'Entrepreneurship and a century of growth'. *Journal of Business Venturing*, **1**(2), 1986, pp. 141–145.

Biggadike, R. 'The risky business of diversification', *Harvard Business Review*, May–June 1979, pp. 103–111.

Burgelman, R. A. 'Corporate entrepreneurship and strategic management', *Management Science*, **29**(12), 1983a, pp. 1349–1364.

Burgelman, R. A. 'A process model of internal corporate venturing in the diversified major firm', *Administrative Science Quarterly*, **28**, 1983b, pp. 223–244.

Cooper, R. G. 'The dimensions of industrial new product success and failure', *Journal of Marketing*, **43**, 1979, pp. 93–103.

Cyert, R. and J. March. *A Behavioral Theory of the Firm*, Prentice Hall, Englewood Cliffs, NJ, 1963.

Ellsworth, R. R. 'Entrepreneurship in big business: the impossible dream?' In John J. Kao and Howard H. Stevenson (eds), *Entrepreneurship: What It Is and How to Teach It*. Harvard Business School, Boston, MA, 1985, pp. 282–308.

Ginsberg, A. 'Measuring and modelling changes in strategy: Theoretical foundations and empirical directions', *Strategic Management Journal* **9**, 1988, pp. 559–575.

Grinyer, P. H., D. Mayes and P. McKiernan. *Sharpbenders: The Secrets of Unleashing Corporate Potential*, Basil Blackwell, Oxford, UK, 1988.

Guth, W. 'Formulating organizational objectives and strategy: A systematic approach', *Journal of Business Policy* **2**(1), 1971, pp. 24–31.

Hambrick, D. 'Guest editor's introduction: Putting top managers back in the strategy picture', *Strategic Management Journal*, **10**, 1989, pp. 5–15.

Hisrich, R. D. and M. P. Peters. 'Internal venturing in large corporations: The new business unit', *Frontiers of Entrepreneurship Research*, Babson College, Wellesley, MA, 1984, pp. 321–342.

Hitt, M. A., R. E. Hoskisson, R. D. Ireland and J. D. Harrison. 'Acquisitive growth strategy and relative R&D intensity: The effects of leverage, diversification and size', *Academy of Management Best Paper Proceedings*, 1989, pp. 22–26.

Kanter, R. M. *The Change Masters: Innovation and Entrepreneurship in the American Corporation*, Simon & Schuster, New York, 1983.

Kanter, R. M. *When Giants Learn to Dance*, Simon & Schuster, New York, 1989.

Kirzner, I. M. *Competition and Entrepreneurship*, University of Chicago Press, Chicago, IL, 1973.

Lewis, W. W. 'Strategic restructuring: A critical requirement in the search for corporate potential'. In Rock, M. and H. Rock (eds), *Corporate Restructuring*, McGraw-Hill, New York, 1990, pp. 43–55.

Mansfield, E. 'Size of firm, market structure, and innovation', *Journal of Political Economy*, 71(6), 1963, pp. 556–576.

Miller, D. 'Entrepreneurship correlates in three types of firms', *Management Science*, 29, 1983, pp. 770–791.

Miller, D. and P. Friesen, 'Archetypes of organizational transition', *Administrative Science Quarterly*, 25, 1980, pp. 268–298.

Montgomery, C. 'Guest editor's introduction to the special issue on research in the content of strategy', *Strategic Management Journal*, 9, 1988, pp. 3–8.

Sathe, V. 'Managing an entrepreneurial dilemma: Nurturing entrepreneurship and control in large corporations', *Frontiers of Entrepreneurship Research*, Babson College, Wellesley, MA, 1985, pp. 636–656.

Schendel, D. E. and C. W. Hofer, 'Research needs and issues in strategic management'. In Schendel, D. and C. Hofer (eds), *Strategic Management*, Little, Brown, Boston, MA, 1979, pp. 515–530.

Schumpeter, J. A. *The Theory of Economic Development*. Harvard University Press, Cambridge, MA, 1934.

Stevenson, H. H. and D. E. Gumpert. 'The heart of entrepreneurship', *Harvard Business Review*, March–April 1985, pp. 85–94.

Stevenson, H. H. and J. C. Jarillo-Mossi. 'Preserving entrepreneurship as companies grow', *Journal of Business Strategy*, 6(1), 1986, pp. 10–23.

Tushman, M. L. and E. Romanelli. 'Organizational evolution: Metamorphosis model of convergence and reorientation'. In Staw, B. and L. Cummings (eds) *Research in Organizational Behavior*. JAI Press, Greenwich, CT, Vol. 7, 1985, pp. 171–222.

Tushman, M. L., B. Virany and E. Romanelli. 'Executive succession, strategic reorientations and organizational evolution', *Technology in Society*, 7, 1985, pp. 297–313.

Vesper, K. H. 'A new direction, or just a new label?' In J. J. Kao and H. H. Stevenson (eds), *Entrepreneurship: What It Is and How to Teach It*, Harvard Business School, Boston, MA, 1985, pp. 62–76.

Weiss, L. E. 'Start-up businesses: A comparison of performances, *Sloan Management Review*, Fall 1981, pp. 37–53.

Wriston, W. B. 'The state of American management', *Harvard Business Review*, January–February 1990, pp. 78–83.

Zajac, E. and S. M. Shortell. 'Changing generic strategies: Likelihood, direction and performance implications', *Strategic Management Journal*, 10, 1989, pp. 413–430.

[4]

Strategic Management Journal, Vol. 11, 49–58 (1990)

DEVELOPING AN INTRAPRENEURIAL ASSESSMENT INSTRUMENT FOR AN EFFECTIVE CORPORATE ENTREPRENEURIAL ENVIRONMENT

DONALD F. KURATKO, RAY V. MONTAGNO and JEFFREY S. HORNSBY
College of Business, Ball State University, Muncie, Indiana, U.S.A.

The implementation of corporate entrepreneuring or intrapreneurship is becoming an important activity for growth-oriented businesses. However, very little empirical research exists that attempts to measure the effectiveness of an environment or culture for the implementation of intrapreneurial ideas. This study attempted to assess the factor structure of intrapreneurship culture through the development of the intrapreneurship assessment instrument (IAI). This instrument was used to assess the effectiveness of an ongoing intrapreneurship training program in a Fortune 500 company.

INTRODUCTION

Recently there has been a growing interest in the use of 'intrapreneurship' as a means for corporations to enhance the innovative abilities of their employees and, at the same time, increase corporate success through the creation of new corporate ventures. However, the creation of corporate entrepreneurship activity is difficult since it involves radically changing internal organizational behavior patterns.

The need to pursue corporate entrepreneurship has arisen from a variety of pressing problems including: (1) required changes, innovations, and improvements in the marketplace to avoid stagnation and decline (Miller and Friesen, 1985); (2) perceived weaknesses in the traditional methods of corporate management (Hayes and Abernathy, 1980); and (3) the turnover of innovative-minded employees who are disenchanted with bureaucratic organizations (Kanter, 1985; Pinchott, 1985; Goddard, 1987). This loss is intensified by the new appeal of entrepreneurship as a legitimate career (Ronstadt, 1987) and the increased development of the venture capital industry capable of financing more new

ventures (Timmons and Bygrave, 1986; Henderson, 1988).

However, the pursuit of corporate entrepreneuring as a strategy to counter these problems creates a newer and potentially more complex set of challenges on both a practical and theoretical level. On a practical level, organizations need some guidelines to direct or redirect resources towards establishing effective intrapreneuring strategies. On a theoretical level, researchers need continually to reassess the components or dimensions which predict, explain, and shape the environment in which corporate entrepreneuring flourishes. While there have been a number of studies focusing on various factors contributing to or enhancing the establishment of corporate venturing, this study attempted to identify empirically a set of dimensions that both researchers and practitioners can utilize.

The identification of the various dimensions or factors of intrapreneurship, of course, is a broad arena to consider and the initial objective of this research is to verify the existence of a generalized set of perceived ambient internal conditions that can facilitate intrapreneurial activities. This approach has been taken as opposed to trying to

0143–2095/90/050049–10$05.00

50   *D. F. Kuratko, R. V. Montagno and J. S. Hornsby*

identify specific issues that may affect unique intrapreneurial projects.

Intrapreneurship defined

Pinchott (1985) defined intrapreneurship as entrepreneurship inside of the corporation. He proposed that as intrapreneurs, individuals will 'champion' new ideas from development to complete profitable reality. Other authors have expanded this definition by including the need to recognize that entrepreneurial activities revolve around organizational sanctions and resource commitments for the purpose of innovative results (Burgelman, 1984; Kanter, 1985; Alterowitz, 1988). While on the surface this concept may appear straightforward, a number of authors have concluded that intrapreneurship may take several forms. Schollhammer (1982) proposed five broad types of internal entrepreneurship which he labeled administrative, opportunistic, imitative, acquisitive, and incubative. While each of these represents a strategic form of corporate entrepreneurial activity and each poses specific problems and challenges to the organization, the incubative form approximates the activity that served as the foundation for the current study. Incubative entrepreneurship refers to the creation of semi-autonomous units within the existing organization for the purpose of: sensing external and internal innovative developments; screening and assessing new venture opportunities; and initiating and nurturing new venture developments.

Vesper (1984) developed three major definitions of corporate venturing which he identified as (1) new strategic direction; (2) initiative from below; and (3) autonomous business creation. Vesper's study illustrates that corporate venturing could be any one of these individual types, as well as any or all possible combinations. Similar to Schollhammer's incubative form, the 'initiative from below' approach, where an employee undertakes something new (i.e. an innovation), best represents the type of corporate entrepreneuring activity for which the current study was designed. It is felt that these forms are most sensitive to the perceived climate within the organization. While all these forms of intrapreneuring are considered important, the current approach was to focus on the factors which are essential in developing a perceived entrepreneur-

ial environment for employees. If managers feel the atmosphere within their organization does not support their efforts, intrapreneuring will probably not occur.

Studies in corporate entrepreneuring

The process of creating a comprehensive and valid understanding of intrapreneuring requires a technique for assessing and describing the organization. Therefore, the purpose of this paper is to analyze the existence of certain factors in a corporate setting and to develop an instrument which will be useful in diagnosing the degree of intrapreneurship culture in an organization.

The existing body of literature on corporate entrepreneuring has evolved from a number of sources. Ellis and Taylor (1988) found that most research reflected obervations of case studies from field work, large sample studies (usually from information based upon the Strategic Planning Institute Profit Impact of Marketing Strategies data base), or contributions from practitioners that have developed intrapeneurial projects. However, Ellis and Taylor (1988) point out that the studies to date have produced little clarity on the most effective factors for corporate entrepreneuring. The importance of each contribution at this point, however, cannot be minimized in a field that is just emerging and potentially may have great impact on corporations' future directions. This study attempts to build upon the previous research and add some clarity to the growing list of organizational factors.

A number of researchers have attempted to examine particular factors which are associated with success in corporate entrepreneurial ventures. For example, issues such as financial factors (Von Hippel, 1977), incentive and control systems (Sathe, 1985; Block and Ornati, 1987), market and entry approaches (Roberts and Berry, 1985; Hobson and Morrison, 1983), and market-driven vs. technology-driven demand (Ellis and Taylor, 1988), have been examined as possible causal factors in the success or failure of corporate entrepreneurial activity.

In addition, specific obstacles to corporate entrepreneuring have been identified. MacMillan, Block and Narasimha (1986) cited operational difficulties, inadequate planning, unrealistic corporate expectations, inadequate corporate support, and misreading the market, as major obstacles to successful new business development.

More recently Sykes and Block (1989: 159) suggested 10 corporate management practices that serve as the major obstacles in corporate venturing. The practices that were examined ranged from enforcement procedures to avoid mistakes to uniform compensation procedures. Their recommendations for corporate venturing success included assessing and choosing affordable risks and, most importantly, making venturing a 'mainstream' function of the business. This last recommendation suggests the need for an 'environment' within the corporation that supports corporate entrepreneurial activity. This would suggest a number of factors such as management support, incentives, organizational structure, resources, and risk-taking, are needed to develop an intrapreneurial environment. Quinn (1985) also addressed the issue of environment when he identified a number of factors for large corporations seeking innovative activity which included developing the atmosphere and vision for such activity and structuring the organization for innovation. These changes were recommended to counter the bureaucratic barriers to innovation of inappropriate incentives, top management isolation; short time horizons, and excessive bureaucracy.

Sathe (1985) suggested that the dilemma of a large institution trying to nurture an atmosphere for entrepreneurial activity while maintaining corporate controls, could be managed if disciplined reporting systems were balanced with a strong entrepreneurial culture of mutual trust and open communication. While the reward versus risk ratio was a factor in the study, employees' willingness to take a risk was related more to the overall organizational culture. Thus, the risk of individual entrepreneuring will relate strongly to support, structure, resources, etc.

In order to further identify the different factors involved in the 'entrepreneurial atmosphere or culture', Burgleman (1983) suggested that innovation in organizations is the result of two distinct processes, both of which are related to corporate strategic concepts. The first of these is what he calls induced strategic behavior. Burgleman suggests that induced strategic behavior is an outcome of strategy while the

second process, autonomous strategic behavior, actually influences corporate strategy. While induced strategic behavior is seen as the official path for innovation, Burgleman proposes that as long as operational-level participants see opportunities that exceed the 'opportunity set' proffered by top management, autonomous strategic behavior (intrapreneurship) will occur.

Given this potential, it must be assumed that differing conditions within corporations are more or less likely to see innovative behavior beyond that of the induced strategic type. Miller (1983) looked at the entrepreneurial activities of the firm as a whole and correlated a number of macro-level variables such as company type, environment, structure, and decision-making with entrepreneurship. His general findings were that firm type (i.e. simple, planning, and organic) did moderate the relationship between the firms's entrepreneurial behavior and several of the other variables identified. The main conclusion that can be drawn for the purposes of the current study is that varying conditions within a firm do, in fact, affect entrepreneurial behavior.

While Miller's factors were not intended to measure micro-level differences, the effects on variables like centralization, which were found to be moderated by company type, do suggest specific configurations of micro-policies and procedures which can lead to more successful intrapreneurship. In fact, a number of researchers have examined more micro-level factors and their influence on the success of innovative ventures. Souder (1981) found that the presence of six specific management practices was associated with the positive outcomes in 100 new ventures in 17 organizations. These factors were early identification of intrapreneurs, formal license (or authority to proceed), sponsorship, appropriate location, discretionary powers, and informal influence. While this study made no attempt systematically to measure these factors, it does offer support for their influence.

Fry (1987) and Kanter (1985) also identified a similar set of factors that seem to be associated with successful intrapreneuring. Some of the additional factors that they identify are resource availability (including both time and material), appropriate rewards and treatment of unsuccessful venture champions (a venture champion is defined as one who develops and coordinates a new product or service within the organization). In examining the climate for entrepreneurial start-ups, Katz and Gartner (1988) proposed four properties (intentionality, resources, boundary, and exchange) as key elements that should be studied in understanding new organizations. Bird (1988) also advanced the importance of intentionality for implementing entrepreneurial ideas. Intentionality can best be described as conscious behavior that is directed as intrapreneurial activity. Concomitant with the intentionality of the intrapreneur is the intention of the organization to foster innovative behavior. This can be likened to the expectation in 3M that an individual can 'steal' 15 percent of his or her time to work on an innovative idea (Fry, 1987), or to the notion of tolerated autonomous strategic behavior (Burgleman, 1983).

Other studies demonstrate similar types of conditions that companies need to address. Hisrich and Peters (1986) studied a number of *Fortune* 1000 firms and established nine characteristics needed for a good environment within which new business units can be created. Among these characteristics are top management support, resources, experimentation, and multi-disciplined teamwork. Schuler (1986) outlined the essential structural practices that corporations need to implement in order for entrepreneurship to be facilitated in organizations. Structural freedom and support, along with flexible policies and procedures, were highlighted by Schuler as distinguishing elements to be addressed.

In attempting to specifically classify the intrapreneurial environment, Sykes (1986) proposed a framework for factors that affect corporate venture success. Based upon his experience with Exxon Enterprises between 1970 and 1980 where 37 new high-technology ventures were created, the author established a framework for classifying factors involved in corporate venturing. The framework broadly classified the factors into extrinsic or environmental factors and intrinsic factors which related to the venture itself. Extrinsic factors were divided into two categories. The structural factors of technology, market, organization, and people were summed up as the overall degree of structural congruence. The procedural factors of control, selection of venture managers, incentive compensation, and financing were dealt with as differences between the corporate environment and an independent ven-

ture environment. Intrinsic factors were also subdivided into two categories: product-related (market and technical risk levels) and managerial (relative experience). Sykes, however, admitted the limitation of his framework to a case study approach and called for additional studies to confirm the implications of his factors.

While the literature illustrates a wide variety of entrepreneurial factors, there are a few elements that are consistent throughout the writings in this field. One is the appropriate use of rewards (Fry, 1987; Sathe, 1985; Block and Ornati, 1987; Scanlan, 1981; Souder, 1981; Kanter, 1985). These theorists stress that any reward system in order to be effective, must consider goals, feedback, emphasis on individual responsibility, and rewards based on results. A second element is management support which relates to willingness of managers to facilitate entrepreneurial projects (Hisrich and Peters, 1986; Sykes, 1986; Souder, 1981; Sykes and Block, 1989; ·MacMillan *et al.*, 1986; Quinn, 1985). Resources (which includes time) and their availability are a third element recognized in many of the writings. Employees must perceive the availability of resources for innovative activities (Sathe, 1985; Von Hippel, 1977; Souder, 1981; Sykes, 1986; Hisrich and Peters, 1986; Katz and Gartner, 1988; Kanter, 1985; Sykes and Block, 1989). A fourth consistent element is organizational structure which is identified in various ways yet always appears as an essential factor (Souder, 1981; Sathe, 1985; Hisrich and Peters, 1986; Sykes, 1986; Burgelman, 1983; Schuler, 1986; Bird, 1988; Sykes and Block, 1989). Finally, risk-taking appears as a consistent element in that employees and management must have a willingness to take a risk and have a tolerance for failure should it occur (MacMillan *et al.*, 1986; Sathe, 1985; Sykes, 1986; Burgelman, 1983; Quinn, 1985; Kanter, 1985; Bird, 1988; Sykes and Block, 1989).

As indicated by the literature presented, much of the work that has been conducted concerning the existence of a specific set of conditions which contributes to an intrapreneurial environment is the result of case studies, surveys, and anecdotal evidence. While this provides a good basis for determining the domain of these concepts, it has produced a number of diverse factors. More rigor is needed in actually establishing the validity of the ideas present in the literature. A beginning point in any research of this type woud be to construct an instrument that would assess the various dimensions that make up this area.

Based on an analysis of the most consistent elements in the literature, a multidimensional scale consisting of five factors was hypothesized to summarize the major subdimensions of the concept of intrapreneuring in organizations. These dimensions were: management support for intrapreneurship, reward and resource availability, organizational structure and boundaries, risk-taking, and time availability. Subsumed under each of these factors were various procedures and policies that may exist in an organizational setting which reflect many of the points cited earlier in this paper.

METHOD

Overview

This study was a quasi-experimental design set in a *Fortune* 500 firm in the midwest. The study attempted to achieve two goals. The first was to examine the factor structure and reliability of an instrument (the intrapreneurial assessment instrument, IAI) designed to assess the intrapreneurial culture of an organization. A secondary goal was to investigate the utility of the IAI by using it to assess the degree of change in corporate culture as a result of a training program intended to introduce intrapreneurial concepts. The IAI's factor structure, reliability, and utility were assessed using the subordinates of managers who participated in the training program.

Sample

Data for both the factor analysis and the assessment of training effectiveness (demonstrating the utility of the IAI) were collected from 111 low- to mid-level managers of the Associated Group (formerly the Blue Cross/Blue Shield of Indiana). The Associated Group represents a class of firms that recently moved into an environment that is less regulated. One of the most important outcomes of decreased regulation has been the growth of competition from alternative health-care providers. As a result the organization has found itself in the position of attempting to develop innovative products and services.

The subjects in the sample were the subordinates of 25 senior-level managers who participated in an intrapreneurial training program (ITP) conducted by two of the authors. The sample was obtained by asking each of the 25 managers to identify five subordinates from whom data could be collected. This process of identifying the sample is explained further in the 'Procedure' section. The responding subordinates had an average tenure in the organization of 10.0 years.

A separate sample of 23 managers similar to those used in the experimental sample was utilized to assess the test–retest reliability of the instrument. This sample was obtained from a portion of the organization whose managers did not participate in the ITP.

Procedure

The IAI was first administered to subordinates of managers who participated in a training program that was conducted over six consecutive weeks. During the fourth session trainees were asked to have their subordinates participate by completing the IAI. Each trainee identified at least five subordinates whom they closely supervised. It was pointed out that these were not to be necessarily their best subordinates, but rather a cross-section of the people who worked for them. The IAI was delivered via company mail with the assistance of a human resource manager in the organization. Pre-addressed, business reply envelopes were provided so completed questionnaires could be sent directly to the researchers. Respondents were assured confidentiality and asked to provide their names. After 2 weeks a follow-up survey was sent to anyone who had not responded. Out of approximately 150 surveys sent, 111 were returned, representing a response rate of 74 percent.

Four months after the first survey was sent, the post-measure was taken. The procedure used was basically the same as for the pre-measure. That is, the initial survey was distributed by the company through interoffice mail, and follow-ups were handled by the researchers. Of the 111 surveys sent out, 87 were returned. This resulted in complete data for 87 individuals, or a 78 percent response rate for the second round of data collection. Given the voluntary nature

54   *D. F. Kuratko, R. V. Montagno and J. S. Hornsby*

of participation, this response rate compares favorably with other research of this type.

In addition, the same follow-up procedures were utilized with the reliability sample. Of 23 initial participants, retest responses were received from 16 individuals. This represents a response rate of 70 percent and is similar to the experimental sample.

Instrument

The intrapreneurial assessment instrument (IAI) was developed to identify the dimensional structure of organizations with respect to their ability to foster intrapreneurial activity. Initially, 28 items were constructed around an hypothesized five factors. The existence of five factors was determined on the basis of two processes. First, a review of the existing literature on intrapreneuring, corporate entrepreneuring, and innovation in corporations was conducted (Von Hippel, 1977; Scanlan, 1981; Souder, 1981; Burgelman, 1983; Miller, 1983; Vesper, 1984; Kanter, 1985; Sathe, 1985; Quinn, 1985; Roberts and Berry, 1985; Sykes, 1986; MacMillan *et al.*, 1986; Schuler 1986; Hisrich and Peters, 1986; Block and Ornati, 1987; Ellis and Taylor, 1988; Katz and Gartner, 1988; Bird, 1988; Sykes and Block, 1989). In addition, the authors used their experience in intrapreneuring organizations to confirm the logic of the factors. It appeared that although there were a number of different names given to factors by various writers in the field, the most consistent factors seemed to fall into five distinct categories. Therefore, the initial five factors were: (1) management support for intrapreneurship; (2) organizational structure; (3) risk-taking; (4) time availability; and (5) reward and resource availability.

The original items in the IAI were developed using the same strategy as for the factors. However, in addition to those methods, the managers who were participants in the training program were asked to critique suggested items and recommend any additional ones. The resulting questionnaire contained 28 items.

Reliability assessment

The items were formatted on a five-point scale asking subjects to indicate the degree to which the item described the atmosphere in their immediate workplace, with '1' being very descriptive and '5' being not at all descriptive. Eleven of the items were worded in a negative manner and were reverse-scored for analysis purposes. Internal consistency and test–retest reliability measures were assessed using SPSSx.

Training program

While not strictly a part of this research, the ITP served as a manipulation to induce the change in respondents' perceptions of their work atmosphere. It is not the intent to elaborate completely on the content of the training program here, but a detailed description of the program is presented in Kuratko and Montagno (1989). However, a brief summary of the program is presented to provide a general understanding of the training program designed to introduce an intrapreneurial environment in the company.

The training program was intended to create an awareness of intrapreneurial opportunities in the organization. The program consisted of six 4-hour modules, each designed to move participants to the point of being able to support intrapreneurship in their own work areas. The modules and a brief summary of their contents were as follows:

1. *Introduction*—This consisted of a review of management and organizational behavior concepts, definitions of intrapreneurship and related concepts, and a review of several intrapreneurship cases.
2. *Personal creativity*—This module attempted to define and stimulate personal creativity. It involved a number of creativity exercises and had participants develop a personal creative enrichment program.
3. *Intrapreneuring*—A review of the current literature on the topic of intrapreneuring was presented here, as well as in-depth analyses of several intrapreneuring organizations.
4. *Assessment of current culture*—A climate survey (not the research instrument) was administered to the training group for the purposes of generating discussion about the current facilitators and barriers to change in the organization.
5. *Business planning*—The intrapreneurial business planning process was outlined and explained. The specific elements of a business

plan were identified and illustrated. An example of an entire business plan was presented.

6. *Action planning*—In this module participants worked in teams and created action plans designed to bring about change to foster intrapreneurship in their own workplaces.

This program was designed based on a review of the literature in intrapreneuring, and thus represents an attempt to operationalize the factors discussed in the literature review.

The 'Results' section contains factor analysis results, item statistics, and subscale reliabilities, as well as an analysis of changes which took place in the work environment.

RESULTS

Factor analysis

The results of the principal components factor analysis, based on a varimax rotation, suggested a three-factor solution instead of the hypothesized five factors. The resulting factors were management support for intrapreneurship (nine items), organizational structure (six items), and resource availability (six items). Essentially, the hypothesized time availability factor was integrated into rewards and resource availability and the hypothesized risk-taking factor was integrated into the top management support factor. The factor structure was similar for both the pre- and post-training analyses and the number of items was reduced from 28 to 21. These factors, item descriptors, and factor loadings can be found in Table 1.

Item analysis and test–retest reliability

The item analysis of the three scales suggested in the factor analysis revealed that the scales were highly reliable given the number of items in each scale. The resulting coefficient alpha reliabilities were 0.76, 0.75, 0.68 for management support for intrapreneurship, organizational structure, and resource availability, respectively. A further description of the item statistics for each scale can be found in Table 2.

As previously mentioned, test–retest reliability was assessed using a sample of managers from part of the organization not influenced by the training program. The test–retest reliability coefficient was 0.67 ($p < 0.005$).

Repeated measures ANOVA

In order to assess whether the IAI is effective for measuring the impact of an intrapreneurship training program, a repeated measures ANOVA was computed on the changes that employees perceived took place in their work environment. The results of this analysis can be found in Table 3. As shown there, the IAI was able to measure a significant change in the company's environment after the ITP was completed. Specifically, statistically significant changes were found for management support for intrapreneurship and resource availability ($p < 0.05$).

CONCLUSIONS

This study attempted to begin to organize the large body of theory and research on corporate entrepreneuring. Specifically, the results demonstrate support for the existence of an underlying set of environmental factors that need to be recognized for organizations introducing intrapreneurial concepts. The three factors that were identified (management support for intrapreneurship, organizational structure, and resource availability) are an initial effort to provide a parsimonious description of the conditions needed to foster entrepreneurial activity within corporations.

From a theoretical perspective this research provides a beginning step in the understanding of an important topic. As pointed out previously, the literature on this subject is primarily subjective in that most writers have developed conceptual models that are never empirically tested or make conclusions based upon case studies. An examination of the factors and the items of which these models are composed cleary suggests the lack of clarity that currently exists in the realm of corporate entrepreneuring. In light of this, the current study focused upon internal ambient factors impacting intrapreneurial behavior.

This focus distinguishes this research from other climate or culture research that tends to concern itself with more generalized assessments of organizations. This is an important issue. The purpose here is to suggest that if intrapreneuring

56   *D. F. Kuratko, R. V. Montagno and J. S. Hornsby*

Table 1.   Rotated factor structure for intrapreneurship assessment instrument*

	Factor loading
Scale 1: Management support for intrapreneurship	
1. Management encouragement for activities	0.56
2. Decision-making power	0.37
3. Senior managers encourage bending rules	0.32
4. Top management experience with innovation	0.64
5. Top management sponsorship	0.67
6. Individual risk-takers are often recognized whether eventually successful or not	0.64
7. Encouragement for calculated risks	0.67
8. 'Risk-taker' is considered a positive attribute	0.68
9. Small and experimental projects are supported	0.55
Scale 2: Organizational structure	
1. Second chances after mistakes	0.50
2. Mistakes as learning experiences	0.60
3. Important to look busy	0.46
4. Difficult to form teams	0.69
5. Concern for job descriptions	0.76
6. Defining turf is important	0.73
Scale 3: Reward and research availability	
1. Availability of funds	0.54
2. Lack of funding	0.59
3. Problems with company budget process	0.66
4. Additional rewards/compensation	0.63
5. Options for financial support	0.56
6. Problem solving time with co-workers	0.55

*Item descriptors are abbreviated.

is to take place in an organization then certain, but not all, aspects of an organization's climate must be addressed. Obviously, this study does not confirm that assertion, but it does support the notion that there are a set of dimensions, identified initially from applied writings, that are relatively reliable and stable. From an applications perspective this can give direction to an organization which might be considering trying to develop a more intrapreneurial climate.

The second part of the study has additional implications. To begin, the IAI instrument can be used as an assessment tool for the evaluation of training in intrapreneurship. The results of the analysis using the instrument indicate that perceptions of the environment on the factors measured were affected by the training program.

Another implication is that the instrument can be used as a diagnostic tool for determining the areas where changes may be needed if an

organization is considering introducing intrapreneurship.

Obviously there are certain limitations to this study that must be acknowledged. Primary among these is the lack of experimental controls in the evaluation of the training program. Due to the limitations imposed by the organization, however, this could not be helped.

In sum, this research has served several purposes. First it has provided some empirical evidence as to the existence of a structure associated with intrapreneuring within an organization. Next, it suggests that intrapreneurship training may be effective in altering individual perceptions of the work environment.

More research is needed to refine both the concept of intrapreneuring and the environment which fosters it; however, this research seems to provide a basis for beginning the process.

Developing an Intrapreneurial Assessment Instrument   57

Table 2. Item statistics for intrapreneurship assessment instrument scales

Item	Corrected item-total correlation	Alpha if item deleted
Scale: Management support for intrapreneurship (scale alpha = 0.76)		
1	0.47	0.73
2	0.33	0.75
3	0.23	0.76
4	0.42	0.74
5	0.54	0.72
6	0.52	0.72
7	0.44	0.73
8	0.46	0.73
9	0.53	0.72
Scale: Organizational structure (scale alpha = 0.75)		
1	0.37	0.75
2	0.53	0.71
3	0.41	0.74
4	0.50	0.72
5	0.60	0.69
6	0.57	0.70
Scale: Resource availability (scale alpha = 0.68)		
1	0.48	0.61
2	0.39	0.64
3	0.45	0.62
4	0.38	0.65
5	0.49	0.61
6	0.27	0.68

Table 3. Repeated measures ANOVA results for intrapreneurship assessment instrument scales

Source	SS	DF	MS	F
Scale: Management support for intrapreneurship				
Within cells	11.49	81	0.14	
Time	0.74	1	0.74	5.20*
Scale: Organizational structure				
Within cells	19.94	79	0.25	
Time	1.06	1	1.06	4.18*
Scale: Resource availability				
Within cells	12.63	84	0.15	
Time	0.26	1	0.26	1.74

$p < 0.05$.

REFERENCES

Alterowitz, R. *New Corporate Ventures*, John Wiley & Sons, New York, 1988.

Bird, B. 'Implementing entrepreneurial ideas: The case for intention', *Academy of Management Review*, **13**, 1988, pp. 442–453.

Block, Z. 'Some major issues in internal corporate venturing', *Frontiers of Entrepreneurship Research*, Babson College, Wellesley, MA, 1983, pp. 382–389.

Block, Z. and O. A. Ornati. 'Compensating corporate venture managers', *Journal of Business Venturing*, **2**, 1987, pp. 41–51.

Brandt, S. C. *Entrepreneuring in Established Companies*. Dow Jones/Irwin Co., Homewood, IL, 1986.

Burgleman, R. A. 'Corporate entrepreneurship and strategic management: Insights from a process study', *Management Science*, December 1983, pp. 1349–1363.

Burgelman, R. A. 'Designs for corporate entrepreneurship', *California Management Review*, **26**, 1984, pp. 154–166.

Drucker, P. F. *Innovation and Entrepreneurship*, Harper & Row, New York, 1985.

Ellis, R. J. and N. T. Taylor. 'Success and failure in internal venture strategy: An exploratory study', *Frontiers of Entrepreneurship Research*, Babson College, Wellesley, MA, 1988, pp. 518–533.

Fry, A. 'The Post-It-Note: An intrapreneurial success', *SAM Advanced Management Journal*, Summer 1987, pp. 4–9.

Garvin, D. A. 'Spinoffs and the new firm formation process', *California Management Review*, **25**, 1983, pp. 3–20.

Goddard, R. W. 'Recharge the power shortage in corporate America', *Personnel Journal*, March 1987, pp. 38–42.

Hayes, R. H. and W. J. Abernathy. 'Managing our way to economic decline', *Harvard Business Review*, July–August 1980, pp. 67–77.

Henderson, J. W. *Obtaining Venture Financing*, Lexington Books, Lexington, MA, 1988.

Hisrich, R. D. 'The inventor: A potential source for new products', *Mid-Atlantic Journal of Business*, Winter 1985/86, pp. 67–79.

Hisrich, R. D. and M. P. Peters. 'Establishing a new business venture unit within a firm', *Journal of Business Venturing*, **1**, 1986, pp. 307–322.

Hobson, E. L. and R. M. Morrison. 'How do corporate start-up ventures fare?' *Frontiers of Entrepreneurship Research*, Babson College, Wellesley, MA, 1983, pp. 390–410.

Kanter, R. M. 'Supporting innovation and venture development in established companies', *Journal of Business Venturing*, **1**, 1985, pp. 47–60.

Kanter, R. M. 'How to be an entrepreneur without leaving your company', *Working Woman*, November 1988, pp. 44–47.

Katz, J. and W. B. Gartner. 'Properties of emerging organizations', *Academy of Management Review*, **13**, 1988, pp. 429–441.

Kuratko, D. F. and R. V. Montagno. 'Intrapre-

58   *D. F. Kuratko, R. V. Montagno and J. S. Hornsby*

neurship: Developing innovation in the corporate culture', *Training and Development Journal*, **43**(10), 1989, pp. 83–86.

MacMillan, I. C., Z. Block and P. N. Subba Narasimha. 'Corporate venturing: Alternatives, obstacles encountered, and experience effects', *Journal of Business Venturing*, **1**, 1986, 177–191.

Miller, D. 'The correlates of entrepreneurship in three types of firms', *Management Science*, **29**, 1983, pp. 770–791.

Miller, D. and P. Friesen. 'Innovation in conservative and entrepreneurial firms: Two models of strategic management', *Strategic Management Journal*, **3**, 1985, pp. 1–25.

Pinchott, G. *Intrapreneuring*, Harper & Row, New York, 1985.

Quinn, J. B. 'Managing innovation: Controlled chaos', *Harvard Business Review*, May–June 1985, pp. 73–84.

Roberts, E. B. and C. A. Berry. 'Entering new business: Selecting strategies for success', *Sloan Management Review*, Spring 1985, pp. 3–17.

Ronstadt, R. 'The educated entrepreneurs: A new era of entrepreneurial education is beginning', *American Journal of Small Business*, Spring 1987, pp. 37–53.

Sathe, V. 'Managing an entrepreneurial dilemma: Nurturing entrepreneurship and control in large corporations', *Frontiers of Entrepreneurship Research*, Babson College, Wellesley, MA, 1985, pp. 636–656.

Scanlan, B. K. 'Creating a climate for achievement', *Business Horizons*, March–April 1981, pp. 5–9.

Schollhammer, H. 'Internal corporate entrepreneurship'. In C. Kent, D. Sexton and K. Vesper (eds), *Encyclopedia of Entrepreneurship*, Prentice Hall, Englewood Cliffs, NJ, 1982.

Schuler, R. S. 'Fostering and facilitating entrepreneurship in organizations: Implications for organization structure and human resource management practices, *Human Resource Management*, **25**, 1986, pp. 607–629.

Souder, W. 'Encouraging entrepreneurship in large corporations', *Research Management*, May 1981, pp. 18–22.

Sykes, H. B. 'The anatomy of a corporate venturing program', *Journal of Business Venturing*, **1**, 1986, pp. 275–293.

Sykes, H. B. and Z. Block. 'Corporate venturing obstacles: Sources and solutions', *Journal of Business Venturing*, **4**, 1989, pp. 159–167.

Timmons, J. A. and W. D. Bygrave. 'Venture capitals' role in financing innovation for economic growth', *Journal of Business Venturing*, **1**, 1986, pp. 161–176.

Vesper, K. H. Three faces of corporate entrepreneurship: A pilot study.' *Frontiers of Entrepreneurship Research*, Babson College, Wellesley, MA, 1984, pp. 294–320.

Von Hippel, E. 'Successful and failing internal corporate ventures: An empirical analysis', *Industrial Marketing Management*, **6**, 1977, pp. 163–174.

[5]

ELSEVIER

Available online at www.sciencedirect.com

SCIENCE @ DIRECT·

Journal of World Business 39 (2004) 296–306

www.socscinet.com/bam/jwb

Stimulating innovation through corporate venture bases

Kenneth Husted[1], Christian Vintergaard[*]

*Department of Management, Politics, and Philosophy, Copenhagen Business School,
Blaagaardsgade 23 B, DK-2200 Copenhagen N, Denmark*

Abstract

A common shortcoming, both in the literature on corporate venturing and in practice, is insufficient or no attention to the ability and responsibility of firms to stimulate and influence the creation of innovative ideas that can lead to new ventures. This paper focuses on the initial process of corporate venturing and explores how corporate venture management can stimulate the generation of genuinely original and dynamic ideas by establishing and maintaining a venture base. The following concrete actions are proposed in order to promote and improve the functionality of the venture base: take responsibility, secure access, acquire network capabilities, gain competencies in how to influence the vision and agendas in knowledge-creating networks, contextualize, and invite to discussion at an early stage. The paper is mainly conceptual in nature but draws on 22 semistructured interviews conducted between 2000 and 2002 with managers of corporate venturing departments at six multinational Danish firms in knowledge-intensive industries. The interviews are used to illustrate the main arguments of the paper.
© 2004 Elsevier Inc. All rights reserved.

Keywords: Corporate venturing; Venture base; Innovation; Knowledge networks

1. Introduction

Since the early 1990s, corporate venturing has become a significant method for business development (Block & MacMillan, 1993; Burgelman, 1983, 1985; Gompers & Lerner, 1999). The popularity is mainly due to the presumed ability of corporate venturing to facilitate continuous growth by embracing high-level innovation and accessing cutting-edge technological development. To some companies, corporate venturing has become a core concept in their strategic planning (Burgelman, 1983).

* Corresponding author. Tel.: +45-38153630; fax: +45-38153635.
E-mail addresses: kh.lpf@cbs.dk (K. Husted), cv.lpf@cbs.dk (C. Vintergaard).
[1] Tel.: +45-38153630; fax: +45-38153635.

1090-9516/$ – see front matter © 2004 Elsevier Inc. All rights reserved.
doi:10.1016/j.jwb.2004.04.008

Corporate venturing has also received considerable attention in academic literature (McNally, 1997). Much of this attention has been focused on the later stages of the venturing process (Block, 1982; Block & MacMillan, 1993), such as the organizational setup of the corporate venture activity (Block & MacMillan, 1993), the criteria for developing a portfolio of ventures into a winning entity (MacMillan & Day, 1987), the development and growth of a venture (Simon, Houghton, & Gurney, 1999), and possible exit strategies (Gompers & Lerner, 2001). In practice, too, we find a strong focus on the later stages of the venture process. Corporate venture firms often rely heavily on their ability to develop firms around "winning" ideas and too little on how they can promote the development of a continuous flow of high quality ideas.

This paper suggests that one of the most crucial aspects of a corporate venturing strategy is the ability to secure a steady flow of genuinely innovative ideas.

K. Husted, C. Vintergaard / Journal of World Business 39 (2004) 296–306   297

It further argues that corporate venture firms need to stimulate the flow of ideas by participating actively in the process of developing and shaping new ideas. In other words, corporate venture firms must work systematically with their venture base from where new ideas for ventures emerge. The venture base is defined as the web of internal and external sources of opportunity-creating activities that can foster new ideas for ventures based on the knowledge production of the sources themselves or a combination of knowledge resources.

The development of genuine high technology innovations (from the venture base) demands a combination of scientific skills and intellectual capacity that exceeds the capabilities of an individual corporation (Powell, Koput, & Smith-Doerr, 1996; Seufert, Von Krogh, & Bach, 1999). In particular, when learning and knowledge for innovation is dispersed, learning about new opportunities depends on participation in a network of knowledge-generating relations (Powell, 1998). Since the venture base transcends organizational boundaries, we will apply a network perspective on the very complex process of shaping the venture base. The paper also draws on the insight of the new production of scientific knowledge as taking place in close interaction between knowledge-creating institutions with various norms, values, and justification criteria. As a consequence of this Mode 2 production of knowledge, ideas will not only be conceived and shaped in an individual institution, but also in the interplay between a number of network-organized players. Finally, the paper will provide arguments for how corporate venture companies can influence the venture base in order to increase the quality and flow of original ideas.

2. The study

Our study is based on 22 semistructured interviews conducted at six multinational Danish firms between 2000 and 2002. The six companies all had corporate venturing departments, though with some variation in their level of experience. At one end of the scale, one of the firms had more than 20 years' experience in corporate venturing and a number of extremely successful exits, and at the other were two firms with less than two years' experience and no exits at all. The

other three companies included in the study all had between four and eight years' experience in corporate venturing activities.

All interviewees had held positions in corporate venturing at top and middle management level for at least two years. This was an important criterion for their selection as study participants. Each interview lasted between 2 and 3 hr. All interviews were tape-recorded and transcribed verbatim.

The interviews served an important role in drawing our attention to barriers faced by corporate venturing units in the early stages of the venturing process, especially in terms of ensuring a sufficient inflow of genuinely innovative ideas from which selection could take place. In the paper, the findings of the study will primarily be presented as quotations and serve to underpin and illustrate the theoretical arguments.

3. Corporate expectations of venturing

Corporate venturing is a strategy for business development. It involves investment in high-risk activities that generate new businesses within or closely related to the activities of the parent corporation, i.e., it is a business development strategy that seeks to generate new businesses for the corporation in which it resides (Von Hippel, 1977). Corporate venturing can be used strategically to encourage corporate renewal in the parent organization (Elfring & Foss, 1997), as a growth driver by investing in ventures with high growth potential, or to diversify the core business of the parent by investing in ventures in diverse industries (Block & MacMillan, 1993). The ideas for new businesses can originate either inside the organization or externally. Activities hosted by the corporate venturing unit will often be new to the organization and require the parent company to extend their resources by acquiring new equipment, people or knowledge (Biggadyke, 1979). Moreover, corporate venturing activities are characterized by a significantly higher risk or failure rate and greater uncertainty (Block & MacMillan, 1993). The characteristics below appear to distinguish corporate venturing from other business development strategies such as takeovers, corporate R&D, traditional venture capital financing, and joint ventures (Albrinck, Hornery, Kletter, & Neilson, 2001).

Firstly, a corporate venture involves a significantly higher risk of failure or substantial losses than the core business of the organization and is therefore often characterized by greater uncertainty. Furthermore, the ventures undertaken are typically subject to less strict management of internal costs than usual research and development activities (Block & MacMillan, 1993). A corporate venture should involve an activity new to the organization, defined broadly as new products, processes, and technologies that can contribute to the organization.

Secondly, in a corporate venturing setup the returns on investments are partly financial and partly strategic (McNally, 1997). The aim is that ventures will be managed separately at some time in the future. A venture is a semiautonomous entity optimally controlled by one manager. While returns on pure venture capital investments are based solely on financial measures, corporate venturing investments are also strategic in the sense that they aim to develop the base business of the corporation (Burgelman & Doz, 2001). The reason for undertaking a venture is to increase and/or improve the resource base of a company and/or its competitive situation in the market while at the same time offering a potential financial gain.

Thirdly, corporate venturing often operates over a longer time frame than traditional business development: compared to the traditional business development process, the aim is to manage developments that extend beyond the development time for current activities. Many of the technologies and services are projected so far into the future that the organization has only a vague idea of the actual outcome. The consequence of long time frames is also reflected in the measures of new venture success (Albrinck et al., 2001), which should emphasize value creation and long-term returns, such as capitalized ROI at the time of exit. In the early stages, measures tend to focus on reaching specific milestones. Funding is provided based on these well-defined achievements, sometimes by outside investors in order to provide the new venture target with external validation (Gompers & Lerner, 1999).

Fourthly, corporate ventures are expected to yield above average returns. The return is tightly linked to the risk associated with the investment, as investors believe they can gain an above average return by seeking and discovering market inefficiencies.

A corporate venture relationship is commonly based on resource exchanges between a parent company and a portfolio of small ventures. Our interviews in the case organizations also illuminate the range of corporate incentives for engaging in corporate venturing. One manager points to the ability of corporate venturing to increase corporate agility. He states:

> The aim of the investments was 'speed to market' ... [we] wanted to get onto the market quickly when the decision [concerning the venture division] had been made. (Venture manager, telecommunications industry)

Other managers emphasize the strategic value:

> The ventures are to be used strategically. The projects are not to be sold at their peak, but used more strategically. Utility has to be seen in terms of new products and technological features complementing our existing portfolio of activities. (Venture manager, high technology industry)

> The decision [to go into corporate venturing] was strategic as we wanted to be better able to meet the technological development while simultaneously creating synergies between future ideas and present services. (Venture manager, telecommunications industry)

In order to achieve these benefits the parent company is expected to contribute both financial resources and knowledge resources in management, marketing, production, etc.—all resources to which small ventures seldom have access. Well-established technology and knowledge-based companies in particular find corporate venturing useful to increase their speed and levels of innovation, while maintaining many of the advantages of large resource pools. The relevance of choosing corporate venturing as a business development strategy also relates to the characteristics of the business environment, with the following characteristics particularly conducive to establishing corporate venturing activities (Gompers & Lerner, 1999; McNally, 1997):

- The industry is subject to changes on many fronts emanating from small firms.
- The firm is under threat from new entrants to the market with new technologies that undermine its current capabilities.

K. Husted, C. Vintergaard/Journal of World Business 39 (2004) 296–306   299

- Future business will depend on new capabilities that are not currently central to the organization.
- Retention of key staff in technical departments has become a challenge.
- The corporation is being approached with numerous investment proposals by both internal and external sources.

Companies with a strong technology base are often more inclined to participate in corporate venturing. Such companies frequently see an additional advantage in the contribution of corporate venturing to technological intelligence. Through evaluating and cooperating with small ventures with a different understanding and perspective on technology, the parent company creates a "window on technology." This window is expected to accelerate product development, the ability to recognize new market developments, and the development of new technologies—all crucial competences in volatile and uncertain environments (Block & MacMillan, 1993). In our empirical data, we also find strong indications that access to innovation is a major reason for undertaking corporate venturing:

> [Working with corporate venturing] improves the internal ethos in the direction of innovation ... it teaches the employees to think in innovative paths. (Venture manager, telecommunications industry)

Corporate venturing is seen predominantly as a way for large, established companies to transform their organizations through a process of strategic renewal based on the acquisition of new capabilities (Zahra, 1996; Zahra & Covin, 1995). The strategy is a transformation of large corporations often operating in mature or stagnant business areas (Ginsberg & Hay, 1994). At the same time, it is a strategy to seek new ways to be innovative and flexible and to gain knowledge that may be parlayed into future revenue streams (Greene, Brush, & Hart, 1999).

Many of the characteristics discussed above could not be developed and exploited by other types of business development strategies, but require the structure and strategy that this concept brings. The arguments above emphasize this specific type of business development strategy, but also stress what is often the most essential input in a corporate venture, namely original ideas.

4. Ideas—the raw material

One of the features of corporate venturing activities is the expectation of above average returns on successful investments. Therefore, the business idea, around which a potential new venture is formed, should also reflect the possibility of achieving an above average return. Taking a Schumpeterian view (Schumpeter, 1934, 1950), one could argue that successful entrepreneurial development of new combinations of resources is a kind of rent for a significant period of time. In this view, even if a resource does not yield rents in the long run, as long as the process of adjustment to the zero-rent state is slow, substantial quasi-rents may still be earned in the middle run. This type of competition is not the traditional one based on price but rather the continuous and universal search for substitutes to replace the less desirable.

Corporate venture firms need access to a significant flow of high quality ideas from which selection can take place (Burgelman, 1983). If the corporate venture does not have access to an appropriate number of unique ideas, the venture unit will not be able to create a sufficient number of profitable ventures and will eventually cease (Block & MacMillan, 1993). As observed by a corporate venture manager in a pharmaceutical company:

> I see the greatest obstacles to development in the venture market to be associated with competencies—of the entrepreneurs and the venture capital providers—these are greater than the structural and legislative constraints.

A top venture manager makes a similar observation in the high technology industry:

> The lack of unique ideas is the most serious obstacle to further growth in the number of ventures.

Corporate venturing needs a critical population of ideas and certain requirements in the quality and innovativeness of these ideas. A further important point is that aiming for one viable business idea often leads to positive spillovers to other potential projects (Haddad & Harrison, 1993).

Current corporate venturing literature has recognized these elements, but has paid only limited attention to the initial stage of providing a steady flow of high quality and innovative ideas for venturing

300 *K. Husted, C. Vintergaard / Journal of World Business 39 (2004) 296–306*

opportunities. In most of the literature on corporate venturing, the flow of ideas is often viewed as rich and generous or is not treated explicitly at all. For example, Burgelman (1983) almost ignores the idea stage when discussing the conceptualization and pre-venture stages of the development process: "As the definition process takes shape, an idea for a new business opportunity evolves into a concrete new product, process or system around which a pre-venture team of people is formed. As a result of the successful technical and market development efforts of this pre-venture team, it grows into an embryonic business organization. These stages take place in the context of the corporate R&D department" (Burgelman, 1983: 231).

However, it may not be so straightforward. The characteristics of corporate venturing as a business development strategy as outlined above emphasize that corporate venturing requires innovative ideas away from the core business in order to fulfill expectations. Only a very small proportion of incoming proposals receive capital from investors (Gompers & Lerner, 1999). This may indicate a lack of highly innovative and viable proposals that meet the criteria for corporate venturing activities.

For many companies, the most significant impediment to create renewal and growth is too few and too traditional mainstream ideas (Block & MacMillan, 1993; Tidd, Bessant, & Pavitt, 2001). Block and Macmillan's (1993) analysis of how to influence the idea population focuses on explaining under what conditions the internal and external environments are good sources of new ideas. Their starting point is that corporate venture firms should be receptive to ideas generated both inside and outside the organization. However, they do not consider whether firms should take more active steps to encourage the development of innovative and viable ideas, nor do they discuss in any detail how corporate ventures should ensure access to ideas.

A common feature of all the discussed characteristics of corporate venturing as business development is the need for genuine and viable business ideas. Gompers and Lerner (2001) argue that some organizations, particularly research-based organizations, establish corporate venturing activities because they have a surplus of ideas that they cannot utilize or capture value from within their mainstream activities.

However, we also see that the creativity and ability in these organizations to generate new and innovative ideas wanes as the most innovative people become involved in established ventures.

The data also indicate strongly that venture managers experience a shortage of truly innovative ideas and view this as a major impediment to the development of the corporate venturing activity:

> The greatest challenge for our corporation at present is to gain access to the ideas that are in the market. Filling the idea pipeline is the foundation for the success of our corporate venture department. (Venture manager, high technology industry)

> ... there are no restrictions in the venture department—the only restriction is within the individual employee, though they are restricted by not being entrepreneurial enough. (Top venture manager, high technology industry)

> The lack of unique ideas is the most serious obstacle to further growth in the number of ventures. (Venture manager, high technology industry)

The respondents share the view that not only is it crucial to have sufficient critical mass in the population of ideas, but also that they face a serious shortage of genuinely innovative ideas. They also point to the failure of the research systems to provide them with a steady supply of genuine input and innovations.

> A key problem in our area is to attract a sufficient number of investment proposals that are based on research at an international [high] level. (Venture capitalist, middle manager)

> The government should provide students with a high-level basic education and develop fundamental research at the universities. There are too many unambitious researchers at the universities who are not given the proper incentives [to provide ideas]. (Venture capitalist, middle manager)

This further illustrates the importance of focusing on the main input to the corporate venture process, namely ideas that can subsequently be turned into ventures. When analyzing the elements that are central to the concept, it seems obvious that a central activity to corporate venturing should be those processes that facilitate the generation and shaping of new venture ideas.

K. Husted, C. Vintergaard/Journal of World Business 39 (2004) 296–306   301

We have argued that the main challenge in corporate venturing is to ensure a steady supply of original ideas. In the next section, we will discuss the features of the venture base of a firm. It will also be argued that an additional benefit in allocating managerial attention to designing an appropriate venture base is that the underlying knowledge will become socially robust. Particularly for systemic innovations, this can lead to faster acceptance in the market and coordinated action in the value chain. This challenge can be addressed by studying the firms' venture base.

5. Insights into the venture base

Corporate venture units have different strategies for addressing a slow and insufficient inflow of new ideas for ventures activities. One option is to focus on more mature technologies and firms, and develop the venture portfolio by acquiring small, technology-based companies. Another option is to expand the scope for new potential ventures by exploring activities less related to the core business activities of the parent company. A third option to boost the portfolio is through invitations to co-invest with other investment funds. In this section, as an alternative to the strategies mentioned, we suggest that one of the most crucial aspects of a corporate venturing strategy is the ability to secure a steady flow of genuinely innovative ideas. Following this line of argument, corporate venture firms need to stimulate this flow by participating actively in the process of developing and shaping new ideas. Corporate venture literature has already observed that ideas for venturing activities spring from the venturing bases of firms (Block & MacMillan, 1993; Hanan, 1976). The venture base refers to the opportunity-creating activities that can foster new ideas for ventures. These activities are embedded in knowledge-creating actions that will lead to innovation. However, surprisingly little attention has been paid to developing an understanding of how these venture bases function and under what conditions they can systematically generate ideas leading to breakthroughs. A venture base is made up of the opportunity-creating activities of a firm and its environment, which can serve as major resources for starting new ventures (Block, 1982). It is argued in this paper that the ability of the venture base to attract and shape

innovative ideas is grounded in the capacity of the venture base to span organizational boundaries and its ability to contextualize the knowledge production underlying the innovations.

Block and MacMillan (1993) is one of the few works to touch on the importance of ensuring the full commitment of the overall organization to the venture bases. The arguments concerning the venture base provided by Block and MacMillan (1993) are, however, primarily from an internal perspective and mainly address the topic of constructing a venture base in order to gain maximum benefit from existing in-house competencies. The argument also rests on the belief that a single person or a small group of individuals is sufficient to create new and innovative ideas capable of changing current paradigms. However, as also illustrated by the following quotes, the internal source of ideas is seldom sufficiently rich to provide the corporate venture organization with a critical mass of ideas:

> Even though we have come quite far in the establishment of a corporate venture department here at our company, we are constantly faced with the problem of finding internal ideas with great potential . . . (Venture manager, high technology industry)

> We search for unique ideas at universities and conferences, virtually everywhere researchers meet and exchange ideas or search for partners . . . (Top venture manager, biotechnology industry)

> We are dependent on inventions generated by the external market enabling us to create new ventures . . . (Top venture manager, high technology industry)

Moreover, radical new knowledge creation is not likely to occur within the boundaries of a formal organization with its restricting rigidities and bureaucracies. Today, it seems more likely that cooperation between a number of participants increases the chances of new and innovative developments. Arora and Gambardella (1990) and Powell et al. (1996) argue that the locus of innovation should be thought of as a network of interorganizational relations. It has proved to be valuable to analyze knowledge creation as a social activity embedded in a dense web of social, economic, contractual, and administrative relationships. Since sources of innovation are more commonly

302 *K. Husted, C. Vintergaard/Journal of World Business 39 (2004) 296–306*

found in the interstices between organizations with various perspectives, learning occurs within the context of participation and invitation to a community and may require various kinds of organizations and organizational practices to access that community (Powell et al., 1996). It has even been stressed that competition should no longer be regarded as a game with a zero-sum outcome (Thurow, 1980), but rather as a positive-sum relationship in which new competencies and resources develop, in tandem with advances in knowledge.

Interorganizational learning in networks is viewed as conducive to innovation because the dynamics of knowledge creation are endogenous to a particular network of actors (Lane & Lubatkin, 1998). The building and the harvesting of a venture base demand capabilities that greatly exceed those of an individual person or single firm. Knowledge creation occurs in the context of a network community, one that is fluid and evolving rather than tightly bound or static (Powell et al., 1996). Thus knowledge creation is an ongoing social construction process, which is linked to the conditions and context under which learning takes place. In this way, the venture base becomes transorganizational, relying on activities in networks between firms, universities, consultants, customers, suppliers, national laboratories, and media.

A number of statements from the corporate venturing managers interviewed also underline the importance of focusing on the early stages of the venturing process in the form of the venture base. For example, on their sources of innovations and their effort in accessing and interacting with these sources, they state:

> We are aware of our increasing dependence on universities such as the University of Southern Denmark—we are initiating many activities to ensure that we can establish our brand as a venture company. It's a new situation for us. (Venture manager, high technology industry)

> We have located our business on [a science park] to benefit from the creative research environment— we know that we must build relationships with scientists and universities to gain access to ideas. (Venture manager, pharmaceutical industry)

The last statement in particular illustrates a corporate awareness of learning and innovations as a phenomenon that occurs in relationships in which new competencies and resources develop, in tandem with advances in knowledge. Within these networks, corporate venture firms need to learn how to transfer knowledge across partnerships to enable them to keep pace with the most promising scientific or technological developments and through these actions develop a more genuine and unique venture base. Similarly, venture managers state that a central requirement for corporate venture firms is to generate venture ideas in collaboration with their environment:

> Idea generation is a process where one has to draw inspiration from outside while remembering what competencies one possesses oneself. (Venture manager, high technology industry)

> We are dependent on the research results developed at technical universities. So far, we have been very dependent on the ideas that were created at the Technical University of Denmark [DTU]. To be as close as possible to the innovative environment, part of our own activities are located at DTU. (Venture manager, high technology industry)

The corporate venture firms with access to a more diverse set of competencies and activities and those with more experience in collaborating stand a better chance of developing opportunity-creating activities in information-rich positions.

Participating in this kind of broad network also ensures the creation of a high level of socially robust knowledge, which can prove useful in new venture generation in the next stage. Gibbons et al. (1994) suggest a model for knowledge production, referred to as Mode 2 (as opposed to Mode 1). In Mode 2, knowledge is carried out in a context of application: it is characterized by transdisciplinarity and heterogeneity and is more plentiful and transient. "Mode 2 is more socially accountable and reflexive. It includes a wider, more temporary and heterogeneous set of practitioners, collaborating on a problem defined in a specific and localized context" (Gibbons et al., 1994: 3). In contrast, Mode 1 is organized hierarchically and tends to preserve its form. Mode 1 is most often identical to what is meant by "science." In short, we are experiencing a shift from Mode 1 science, which is expert, discipline-bound and self-referential, to Mode 2 knowledge production.

K. Husted, C. Vintergaard/Journal of World Business 39 (2004) 296–306 303

In terms of production and development, the venture base context is of crucial importance. However, not simply context in the sense that greater attention must be paid to the end users of science—not even in the sense that context helps to define scientific problems and to select appropriate methodologies—but in the more fundamental sense as a result of its contextualization into reliable knowledge. This kind of knowledge is being progressively redefined—or superseded by—knowledge that is socially robust (Nowotny, Gibbons, & Scott, 2001). In this connection, the venture base is developed and shaped during the process of contextualization in order to generate opportunity-creating activities that are socially robust.

Late modern innovative developments are increasingly characterized by interdisciplinary collaboration in contexts of application resulting in the hybridization of knowledge production. Participatory procedures involving scientists, stakeholders, active citizens, and users of knowledge are needed to transform knowledge claims into trustworthy, socially robust, usable knowledge about the realities that matter in social and environmental changes and in the transition to sustainability. As illustrated in the quotations below, some of the interviewees have started to work on the boundaries of the corporate venture and other organizations such as research institutions:

> Much of our work to get new products and ideas is done in collaboration with researchers and students at the technical universities. (Venture manager, high technology industry)

> You should help researchers by providing them with what they need to develop their idea ... Recently, I lent equipment to a researcher in order for him to carry out his research ... If the researchers ever need to collaborate with a company, I think we will be top of his list ... (Venture manager, biotechnology industry)

Following this line of argument, the aim is to further ground and test the developments to socially robust knowledge as this would: (1) become valid not only to the corporate venture company but also outside the organization, (2) gain validity through the involvement of an extended group of experts, and (3) include "society" as the genesis. In order for this to happen, a space needs to be created where the transdisciplinary

can meet and where problems are formulated and negotiated, i.e., an agora. During this process, a better understanding of the content of the venture base will emerge, and interested parties will have the opportunity to reply in a public space or network formation.

The conditions for systematic knowledge creation and utilization in the corporate venture base do not emerge or develop spontaneously, but require a much more deliberate and reflexive design of the venture base, supporting value creation by embodying truly innovative ideas in new ventures controlled by the firm. This kind of value creation is dependent on a certain degree of coordination of both knowledge creation and use in the venture base among the individuals in organizations and across organizations. These design and coordination efforts converge around shared social processes. Until now, such efforts have mostly emerged sporadically and as a result of self-organization, but for firms that have chosen corporate venturing as their growth strategy, there is an increased urgency for intentionally designing and developing their venture bases. The following section outlines these main challenges for corporate venture mangers.

6. Nursing the base: management recommendations

This paper argues that, because of its significance, the venture base demands special attention. In the section below, a number of concrete actions will be proposed to promote and improve the ability of the venture base to generate original ideas. There are at least six areas that managers need to consider in relation to their venture base.

6.1. Take responsibility

It is often taken for granted (both in the academic and the business community) that the bases and thereby venture ideas appear from nowhere or serendipitously in the external environment and that no initiatives are necessary to facilitate them. However, companies cannot be passive, rather they need to take active part in creating the bases from which ideas can spring. These actions should be focused both on encouragement of employees and on engagement in sources of innovation outside the organization. Therefore, parent companies need to take responsibility for knowledge production in networks and in the process of conceptualizing knowledge (Munk & Vintergaard, in press).

6.2. Secure access

In order for a corporate venture company to engage in network formation, it must also have something to offer in terms of its own level of knowledge production, reputation, etc. Companies will not become part of a value-creating network unless they can contribute something that is not already present in the network. Powell et al. (1996) argue that a partnering decision depends on each partner's size and position in the "value-chain" and the level of technological sophistication. They further argue that to remain current in a rapidly moving field an organization must be involved in the research process. Passive recipients of new knowledge are less likely to appreciate technological advances or be able to respond rapidly. In industries where knowledge is crucial, companies must be experts in both in-house research and in cooperative research with external partners, such as university scientists, research hospitals, and skilled competitors.

In addition to focusing on their ability to secure access to external knowledge and their ability to assess the value of and assimilate the external knowledge, companies must also consider the organizational economics involved in any relationship. An effective win–win situation for the actors in a network, for example, the research-based institutions and corporate ventures, is to share the value potential created in the network by offering equity in the venture.

6.3. Network capabilities

Companies need to learn to interact and create networks in order to be able to manage the venture base. Seufert et al. (1999) argue that individuals in an organization should be able to recognize personally relevant knowledge within the organization which can be exploited in the organization. The ability to create and participate in a network and to contextualize one's knowledge should be viewed as something that can be learned, but also something that often depends on personal traits.

6.4. Competencies in how to influence the vision and agendas in knowledge-creating networks

An important part of managing the venture base is to take an active part in influencing agendas in the network. Doing this will enhance the content of the venture base as resource allocation and focus are shifted in a desirable direction. In order to achieve such a position, the corporate venture must nevertheless learn where and how to access or structure a network formation and a community for contextualization. Huxham and Vangen (2000) argue that: "Structures thus play an important leadership role because they determine such key factors as who has an influence on shaping a partnership agenda, who has power to act, and what resources are tapped."

They further argue that when the structure of collaboration is part of a system of multiple overlapping partnerships, the influence on the agenda may be even more significant. By taking active part in influencing the agendas in a network, corporations will also have a greater chance of gaining a central position within it.

6.5. Contextualization

In order to shape the venture base during the process of contextualization, there are strong demands on the company to disseminate and negotiate new knowledge to a wide range of stakeholders. These types of stakeholder must hold central positions and originate from a transdisciplinary background. The dissemination and negotiation can occur both through formal and informal processes and events, such as committees, workshops, and seminars and telephone, fax, and e-mail, through which the communications of collaboration take place. Informal processes may take many forms and may be important for a number of reasons. The way in which and the frequency with which members communicate, for example, are obvious components of processes. Similarly, some processes obviously encourage members to share information and develop a common understanding of issues, whereas others hinder active communication (Huxham & Vangen, 2000).

6.6. Invite to discussion at an early stage

A common error in the phases of building a venture base is that the process of contextualization occurs too

K. Husted, C. Vintergaard / Journal of World Business 39 (2004) 296–306   305

late in the development. As a consequence, the final business proposal will receive a lower evaluation due to both a lack of quality and a lack of appropriateness. Therefore, corporations must overcome the traditional paradigm of "knowledge hoarding" and create new methods and incentives for knowledge sharing. Even though knowledge sharing is a necessity for the venture base to develop, knowledge-sharing hostility both at individual and organizational levels hampers such development (Husted & Michailova, 2002).

Based on analysis of the characteristics and corporate expectations of corporate venturing as a business development strategy, we conclude that the underlying generation and shaping of ideas should be of central concern to corporate venture managers. This paper has elaborated on this initial process of corporate venturing and explored how to design and benefit from setting up a venture base. In order to foster innovation from the venture base, it is important to realize that innovation is not created in an individual firm or between firms of homogenous character, but in the interfaces and overlaps between various industries and disciplines. Many corporate venture firms work with a number of preferred partners at a local level and maintain working relationships with a number of international players in the venture capital market. However, the conditions for value creation through the incorporation of truly innovative ideas in new ventures controlled by the firm do not emerge or develop spontaneously. To enable corporate venturing to contribute continuously to value creation in an organization, managers need a much more deliberate and reflexive design of the venture base, supporting value creation by embodying truly innovative ideas in new ventures controlled by the firm.

References

Albrinck, J., Hornery, J., Kletter, D., & Neilson, G. (2001). Adventures in corporate venturing. *Strategy and Business, 22:* 119–129.

Arora, A., & Gambardella, A. (1990). Complementarity and external linkages. *The Journal of Industrial Economics, 38*(4): 361–379.

Biggadyke, R. (1979). The risky business of diversification. *Harvard Business Review, 57:* 103–111.

Block, Z. (1982). Can corporate venturing succeed? *The Journal of Business Strategy, 3*(2): 21–34.

Block, Z., & MacMillan, I. C. (1993). *Corporate venturing— Creating new businesses within the firm.* Cambridge, MA: Harvard Business School Press.

Burgelman, A. R., & Doz, L. Y. (2001). The power of strategic integration. *MIT Sloan Management Review, 42*(3): 28–38.

Burgelman, R. A. (1983). A process model of internal corporate venturing in the diversified major firm. *Administrative Science Quarterly, 28:* 223–244.

Burgelman, R. A. (1985). Managing the new venture division: Research findings and implications for strategic management. *Strategic Management Journal, 6*(1): 39–54.

Elfring, T., & Nicolai, F. J. (1997). *Corporate renewal through internal venturing and spin-offs—Perspectives from organisational economics.* Revised Draft. Copenhagen Business School.

Gibbons, M., Scott, P., Nowotny, H., Limoges, C., Schwartzmann, S., & Trow, M. (1994). *The new production of knowledge—The dynamics of and research in contemporary science societies.* London: Sage Publications.

Ginsberg, A., & Hay, M. (1994). Confronting the challenges of corporate entrepreneurship: Guidelines for venture managers. *European Management Journal, 12:* 382–389.

Greene, P., Brush, C., & Hart, M. (1999). The corporate venture champion: A resource based approach to role and process. *Entrepreneurship Theory and Practice, 23*(3): 103–122.

Gompers, P. A., & Lerner, J. (1999). *The venture capital cycle.* Cambridge, MA: MIT Press.

Gompers, P., & Lerner, J. (2001). The venture capital revolution. *Journal of Economic Perspectives, 15*(2): 145–169.

Haddad, M., & Harrison, A. (1993). Are there positive spillovers from direct foreign investment? Evidence from panel data for Morocco. *Journal of Development Economics, 42*(1): 51–75.

Hanan, M. (1976). *Venture management.* New York: McGraw-Hill.

Husted, K., & Michailova, S. (2002). Diagnosing and fighting knowledge sharing hostility. *Organizational Dynamics, 31*(1): 60–73.

Huxham, C., & Vangen, S. (2000). Leadership in the shaping and implementation of collaboration agendas: How things happen in a (not quite) joined-up world. *Academy of Management Journal, 43:* 1159–1176.

Lane, P. J., & Lubatkin, M. H. (1998). Relative absorptive capacity and interorganizational learning. *Strategic Management Journal, 19*(5): 461–477.

McNally, K. (1997). *Corporate venture capital: Bridging the equity gap in the small business sector.* London: Routledge.

Munk, B. K., & Vintergaard, C. (in press). Accentuating the role of venture capitalists in systems of innovation. *(VEST) Journal for Science and Technology Studies, 17*(1).

Nowotny, H., Gibbons, M., & Scott, P. (2001). *Re-thinking science. Knowledge and the public in an age of uncertainty.* Oxford: Polity Press.

Powell, W. W. (1998). Learning from collaboration: Knowledge and networks in the biotechnology and pharmaceutical industries. *California Management Review, 40*(3): 228–240.

Powell, W. W., Koput, K. W., & Smith-Doerr, L. (1996). Interorganizational collaboration and the locus of innovation: Networks of learning in biotechnology. *Administrative Science Quarterly, 41*(1): 116–146.

Schumpeter, J. A. (1934). *The theory of economic development.* Cambridge: Harvard University Press.

Schumpeter, J. A. (1950). *Capitalism, socialism, and democracy.* New York: Harper and Brothers.

Seufert, A., Von Krogh, G., & Bach, A. (1999). Towards knowledge networking. *Journal of Knowledge Management, 3:* 180–1090.

Simon, M., Houghton, S. M., & Gurney, J. (1999). Succeeding at internal corporate venturing: Roles needed to balance autonomy and control. *Journal of Applied Management Studies, 8*(2): 145–159.

Thurow, L. C. (1980). *The zero-sum society: Redistribution and the possibilities for economic change.* New York: Basic Books, Perseus Book Group.

Tidd, J., Bessant, J., & Pavitt, K. (2001). *Managing innovation: Integrating technological, market and organizational change.* Chichester: Wiley.

Von Hippel, E. (1977). Successful and failing internal corporate ventures: An empirical analysis. *Industrial Marketing Management, 6:* 163–174.

Zahra, S. A. (1996). Governance, ownership, and corporate entrepreneurship: The moderating impact of industry's technological opportunities. *Academy of Management Journal, 39*(6): 1713–1735.

Zahra, S. A., & Covin, J. G. (1995). Contextual influences on the corporate entrepreneurship-performance relationship: A longitudinal analysis. *Journal of Business Venturing, 10*(1): 43–59.

[6]

1042-2587-99-233$1 50
Copyright 1999 by
Baylor University

Toward a Reconciliation of the Definitional Issues in the Field of Corporate Entrepreneurship

Pramodita Sharma
James J. Chrisman

Although authors generally agree on the nature of entrepreneurial activities within existing firms, differences in the terminology used to describe those activities have created confusion. This article discusses existing definitions in the field of corporate entrepreneurship, reconciles these definitions, and provides criteria for classifying and understanding the activities associated with corporate venturing.

Scholars have begun to pay increasing attention to entrepreneurial activities within existing organizations (e.g., Birkinshaw, 1997; Burgelman, 1983; Caruana, Morris, & Vella, 1998; Drucker, 1985; Guth & Ginsberg, 1990; Kanter, 1983; Miller, 1983; Pinchot, 1985; Zahra, 1986, 1995, 1996). Unfortunately, and similar to the study of entrepreneurship in general, there has been a striking lack of consistency in the manner in which these activities have been defined. A number of scholars have expressed concern about this lack of universally acceptable definitions (e.g., Jennings & Lumpkin, 1989; Stopford & Baden-Fuller, 1994; Wortman, 1987; Zahra, 1991). Although the choice of definitions in behavioral sciences generally remains subject to debate (Hoy, 1995), a clearly stated set of definitions is necessary for scientific understanding, explanation, and prediction (McKelvey, 1982). Moreover, clearly stated and agreed-upon definitions makes it easier for researchers to build on each other's work, and for practitioners to decide whether research findings are applicable to their situation. Because the field of corporate entrepreneurship is still in its infancy, the time is ripe to work on the clarification of existing terminology.

This article represents one effort to systematize the use of terminology in the field of corporate entrepreneurship. To do this we first review some of the existing definitions and illustrate how they are contradictory. This review is conducted to provide a grounding from which a framework of definitions can be developed that covers the field of corporate entrepreneurship. In developing this framework we go from a general to a specific point of view in order to clarify the existing boundaries of the field, reconcile the various terms used to describe the phenomena of interest, and illustrate the territory they cover.

Each of the definitions we will propose are broad, by intention. We are of the opinion that broad definitions of concepts are preferable to narrow definitions at this stage in the field's development for several reasons. First, broad definitions are less likely to exclude as-yet-unspecified problems, issues, or organizations that are potentially important or interesting. Therefore, starting broad makes it less likely that the definitions will become outmoded and in need of revision as new issues are discovered. Furthermore, broad definitions are more amenable, and more resilient, to the discovery and classification of unique populations and subpopulations of firms and events since they avoid premature or arbitrary decisions about the variables that delineate one group from another. Broad definitions make it possible for the natures of different organizations and events to emerge through empirical research and theories of differences. Finally, broad definitions are more likely to be acceptable to most scholars since most will find a place for the topic or sites of research that are of interest to them. In sum, broad definitions better reflect the early stage of development of the field, avoid the need for excessive retrenchment as new knowledge becomes available, and provide considerable latitude for a theoretical and empirical process to emerge that will eventually permit the unique parts of the whole to be classified, defined, and understood in relation to that whole.

After we have presented our framework of definitions pertaining to corporate entrepreneurship, we then proceed to discuss some of the critical constructs by which internal corporate venturing efforts might be classified to illustrate the possibilities of the approach taken. We focus on internal corporate venturing because it is the sub-area that has been perhaps the most thoroughly studied thus far and is, therefore, the most amenable to further classificatory efforts.

EXISTING DEFINITIONS

Entrepreneurship

Before discussing existing definitions in the field of corporate entrepreneurship, we briefly turn our attention to the term "entrepreneurship." Entrepreneurship has meant different things to different people (Gartner, 1990; McMullan & Long, 1990). The historical development of the term has been documented by various authors (e.g., Gartner, 1988; Hisrich, 1986; Livesay, 1982; McMullan & Long, 1983). The earliest reference of the term has been traced to Richard Cantillon's work (1734). To him, entrepreneurship was self-employment with an uncertain return (McMullan & Long, 1990).

In a recent study, Gartner (1990) identified two distinct clusters of thought on the meaning of entrepreneurship. The first group of scholars focused on the characteristics of entrepreneurship (e.g., innovation, growth, uniqueness, etc.) while the second group focused on the outcomes of entrepreneurship (e.g., creation of value). Scholars who subscribe to the notion that entrepreneurship should be defined by its characteristic attributes appear to be the largest group, accounting for 79% of Gartner's sample. Among members of this group, most seem to rely on variations of one of two definitions of entrepreneurship: Schumpeter's (1934) or Gartner's (1988).

To Schumpeter (1934), an entrepreneur is a person who carries out new combinations, which may take the form of new products, processes, markets, organizational forms, or sources of supply. Entrepreneurship is, then, the process of carrying out new combinations. In contrast, Gartner states that "Entrepreneurship is the creation of organizations" (1988, p. 26). Gartner was careful to specify that this was not offered as a definition but rather as "an attempt to change a long held and tenacious viewpoint in the entrepreneurship field" toward "what the entrepreneur does, not who the entrepreneur is" (p. 26). Nevertheless, it is clear from the literature that a large number of researchers in entrepreneurship have employed this definition, including Gartner himself (e.g., Bygrave, 1993; Gartner, Bird, & Starr, 1991; Learned, 1992).

Whereas both these definitions have merit, it should be clear that despite their overlaps, each covers a somewhat different territory. Thus, while the carrying out of new combinations (i.e., an innovation of product, process, etc.) may result in the creation of a new organization, it does not necessarily have to do so. Likewise, the creation of a new organization may involve a new combination; however, there are many new organizations that can make no claim to innovative activity. The debate about what entrepreneurship is will surely rage on for the foreseeable future in spite of the best arguments of scholars on any side of the debate. Yet there are clear advantages to attempts to reconcile the language used in the field, as ambiguity in terminology holds back the development of cohesive, explantory, or predictive theories (Low & MacMillan, 1988). As explained below, in this article, we seek definitions that do not exclude what has been termed entrepreneurship or corporate entrepreneurship in the past, are most likely to cover those aspects of entrepreneurship and corporate entrepreneurship that will draw the attention of scholars in the future, and will facilitate the reconciliation of the theory and research on entrepreneurship and corporate entrepreneurship.

Corporate Entrepreneurship Terminology

In recent years, the entrepreneurial abilities of corporate organizations has become a major subject of discussion both among practitioners and academicians. With this broadening of perspective, entrepreneurship has become more a hypothetical and abstract term attached to any individual or group creating new combinations (e.g., Lumpkin & Dess, 1996; Pass, Lowes, Davies, & Kronish, 1991), either on their own or attached to existing organizations. This is reflected in some academic writings. For example, Covin and Slevin (1991) have suggested that the three entrepreneurial postures of risk taking, innovativeness, and proactiveness, brought forth by Miller (1983), can be applied to corporate processes as well as to new independent ventures. Collins and Moore (1970) have differentiated between "independent" and "administrative" entrepreneurs, with the former creating new organizations from scratch, and the latter creating new organizations within or adjunct to existing business structures. More recently, Lumpkin and Dess (1996) have stated that launching a new venture can be done either by a start-up firm or an existing firm.

Although there is an increasing recognition of the entrepreneurial activities within existing firms, ambiguities continue to plague attempts to define such activities. In fact, the language problem is, if anything, more acute when entrepreneurship is applied to a corporate setting. While the terms "entrepreneurship" or "independent entrepreneurship" are used to describe entrepreneurial efforts of individuals operating outside the context of an existing organization, a variety of terms are used for the entrepreneurial efforts within an existing organization such as corporate entrepreneurship (Burgelman, 1983; Zahra, 1993), corporate venturing (Biggadike, 1979), intrepreneuring (Pinchot, 1985), internal corporate entrepreneurship (Jones & Butler, 1992), internal entrepreneurship (Schollhammer, 1982; Vesper, 1984), strategic renewal (Guth & Ginsberg, 1990), and venturing (Hornsby, Naffziger, Kuratko, & Montagno, 1993). A list of definitions used in the literature for these related terms is presented in Table 1.

Definitional Ambiguities

A careful examination of Table 1 reveals that the same term is sometimes used differently by different authors, and some authors use different terms to describe the same phenomenon. Examples of these definitional ambiguities are provided below and highlighted in Table 2.

Table 1

Existing Definitions

Author/s & Yr.	Definition suggested
	CORPORATE ENTREPRENEURSHIP
Burgelman (1983)	Corporate entrepreneurship refers to the process whereby the firms engage in diversification through internal development Such diversification requires new resource combinations to extend the firm's activities in areas unrelated, or marginally related, to its current domain of competence and corresponding opportunity set (p 1349).
Chung & Gibbons (1997)	Corporate entrepreneurship is an organizational process for transforming individual ideas into collective actions through the management of uncertainties (p 14)
Covin & Slevin (1991)	Corporate entrepreneurship involves extending the firm's domain of competence and corresponding opportunity set through internally generated new resource combinations (p 7, quoting Burgelman, 1984, p 154)
Guth & Ginsberg (1990)	Corporate entrepreneurship encompasses two types of phenomena and the processes surrounding them (1) the birth of new businesses within existing organizations, i e , internal innovation or venturing, and (2) the transformation of organizations through renewal of the key ideas on which they are built, i e strategic renewal (p 5).
Jennings & Lumpkin (1989)	Corporate entrepreneurship is defined as the extent to which new products and/or new markets are developed An organization is entrepreneurial if it develops a higher than average number of new products and/or new markets (p 489).
Schendel (1990)	Corporate entrepreneurship involves the notion of birth of new businesses within on-going businesses, and the transformation of stagnant, on-going businesses in need of revival or transformation (p 2)
Spann, Adams, & Wortman (1988)	Corporate entrepreneurship is the establishment of a separate corporate organization (often in the form of a profit center, strategic business unit, division, or subsidiary) to introduce a new product, serve or create a new market, or utilize a new technology (p 149)
Vesper (1984)	Corporate entrepreneurship involves employee initiative from below in the organization to undertake something new An innovation which is created by subordinates without being asked, expected, or perhaps even given permission by higher management to do so (p 295)
Zahra (1993)	Corporate entrepreneurship is a process of organizational renewal that has two distinct but related dimensions innovation and venturing, and strategic renewal (p 321).
Zahra (1995, 1996)	Corporate entrepreneurship — the sum of a company's innovation, renewal, and venturing efforts Innovation involves creating and introducing products, production processes, and organizational systems Renewal means revitalizing the company's operations by changing the scope of its business, its competitive approaches or both It also means building or acquiring new capabilities and then creatively leveraging them to add value for shareholders Venturing means that the firm will enter new businesses by expanding operations in existing or new markets (1995, p 227, 1996, p 1715)
	INTERNAL CORPORATE ENTREPRENEURSHIP
Jones & Butler (1992)	Internal Corporate Entrepreneurship refers to entrepreneurial behavior within one firm (p. 734)
Schollhammer (1982)	Internal (or intra-corporate) entrepreneurship refers to all formalized entrepreneurial activities within existing business organizations Formalized internal entrepreneurial activities are those which receive explicit organizational sanction and resource commitment for the purpose of innovative corporate endeavors — new product developments, product improvements, new methods or procedures (p. 211)
	CORPORATE VENTURING
Biggadike (1979)	A Corporate venture is defined as a business marketing a product or service that the parent company has not previously marketed and that requires the parent company to obtain new equipment or new people or new knowledge (p 104)
Block & MacMillan (1993)	A project is a Corporate venture when it (a) involves an activity new to the organization, (b) is initiated or conducted internally, (c) involves significantly higher risk of failure or large losses than the organization's base business, (d) is characterized by greater uncertainty than the base business, (e) will be managed separately at some time during its life, (f) is undertaken for the purpose of increasing sales, profit, productivity, or quality (p 14)
Ellis & Taylor (1987)	Corporate venturing was postulated to pursue a strategy of unrelatedness to present activities, to adopt the structure of an independent unit and to involve a process of assembling and configuring novel resources (p. 528)
von Hippel (1977)	Corporate venturing is an activity which seeks to generate new businesses for the corporation in which it resides through the establishment of external or internal corporate ventures (p 163)

continued overleaf

Table 1

Continued

Author/s & Yr.	Definition suggested
	VENTURE, INTERNAL VENTURES, INTERNAL CORPORATE VENTURING, NEW BUSINESS VENTURING
Hornsby, Naffziger, Kuratko, Montagno (1993)	Venture may be applied to the development of new business endeavors within the corporate framework (p 30)
Roberts & Berry (1985)	Internal ventures are a firm's attempts to enter different markets or develop substantially different products from those of its existing base business by setting up a separate entity within the existing corporate body (p 6)
Stopford & Baden-Fuller (1994)	New Business Venturing occurs when 'individuals and small teams form entrepreneurial groups inside an organization capable of persuading others to alter their behavior, thus influencing the creation of new corporate resources' (p 522)
Zahra (1996)	Venturing means that the firm will enter new businesses by expanding operations in existing or new markets (p 1715)
Zajac, Golden, Shortell (1991)	Internal corporate Venturing involves 'the creation of an internally-staffed venture unit that is semi-autonomous, with the sponsoring organization maintaining ultimate authority' (p 171)
	INTRAPRENEURSHIP
Nielson, Peters, & Hisrich (1985)	Intrapreneurship is the development within a large organization of internal markets and relatively small and independent units designed to create, internally test-market, and expand improved and/or innovative staff services, technologies or methods within the organization This is different from the large organization entrepreneurship/venture units whose purpose is to develop profitable positions in external markets (p 181)
Pinchot III (1985)	Intrapreneurs are any of the "dreamers who do " Those who take hands-on responsibility for creating innovation of any kind within an organization They may be the creators or inventors but are always the dreamers who figure out how to turn an idea into a profitable reality (p ix)
	STRATEGIC or ORGANIZATIONAL RENEWAL
Guth & Ginsburg (1990)	Strategic renewal involves the creation of new wealth through new combinations of resources (p 6)
Stopford & Baden-Fuller (1994)	Organizational renewal alters the resource pattern of business to achieve better and sustainable overall economic performance To be sustainable, more pervasive effort is needed, involving more than a few individuals and the finance function (p 522)
Zahra (1993, 1995, 1996)	Renewal means revitalizing a company's business through innovation and changing its competitive profile It means revitalizing the company's operations by changing the scope of its business, its competitive approaches or both It also means building or acquiring new capabilities and then creatively leveraging them to add value for shareholders (1995, p 227, 1996, p 1715)
	Renewal has many facets, including the redefinition of the business concept, reorganization and the introduction of system-wide changes for innovation Renewal is achieved through the redefinition of a firm's mission through the creative redeployment of resources, leading to new combinations of products and technologies (1993, p 321)

Burgelman (1983) defines corporate entrepreneurship as "the process whereby the firms engage in diversification through internal development. Such diversification requires new resource combinations to extend the firm's activities in areas unrelated, or marginally related, to its current domain of competence" (p. 1349). Biggadike (1979), on the other hand, describes corporate venturing as "marketing a product or service that the parent company has not previously marketed and that requires the parent company to obtain new equipment or new people or new knowledge" (p. 104). Taking a still different approach, Ellis and Taylor (1987) define corporate venturing as "a strategy of unrelatedness to present activities, to adopt the structure of an independent unit and to involve a process of assembling and configuring novel resources" (p. 528).

Table 2

Examples of Some Definitional Ambiguities

	Authors and terms used		
Characteristics	**Ellis & Taylor (1987)** **CV**	**Burgelman (1983)** **CE**	**Biggadike (1979)** **CV**
Extent of innovation	assembling & configuring novel resources	requires new resource combinations	requires obtaining new equipment, or people, or knowledge to introduce a new product or service
Relatedness to existing businesses	unrelated to present activities	activities in areas unrelated or marginally related to current domain of competence	
Structural autonomy	independent unit		

CE – Corporate Entrepreneurship

CV – Corporate Venturing

It is observed that all three definitions describe the creation of a new business in an area that requires innovative resource combinations. A closer observation of these definitions, however, also reveals differences in the degree of restrictiveness. Burgelman restricts corporate entrepreneurship to diversification into activities unrelated or marginally related to a firm's area of competence. Biggadike's definition, on the other hand, does not necessarily limit the venturing effort in this way. Thus, an existing competence could still come into play as long as the venture extended that competence in some manner, that is, through the need for new equipment, people, or knowledge. The difference in restrictiveness suggests that Burgelman's corporate entrepreneurship is a subset of Biggadike's corporate venturing.

Ellis and Taylor agree with the requirement of unique resources and with Burgelman's conception of an unrelated activity but add another level of restrictiveness into the definition by specifying the structural arrangement of the venture in relation to the corporation. Their definition would include only those venturing efforts that involved the creation of a new venture division as a setting for such efforts. Thus, firms that engaged in venturing within a pre-existing corporate structure would fall outside Ellis and Taylor's definition. As a consequence, the firms that fit Ellis and Taylor's (1987) definition of corporate venturing constitute a subset of the firms that would fit Burgelman's definition of corporate entrepreneurship. In turn, Burgelman's corporate entrepreneurship appears to be a subset of Biggadike's (1979) concept of corporate venturing.

Perhaps the most widely accepted definition of corporate entrepreneurship was proposed by Guth and Ginsberg (1990). They say that corporate entrepreneurship encompasses the birth of new businesses within existing businesses and the transformation (or rebirth) of organizations through a renewal of their key ideas. Their definition of corporate entrepreneurship not only contains Biggadike's definition of corporate venturing (which contains Burgelman's, etc.), it also introduces, in a different context, the interplay of the idea of new organizations and new combinations that characterizes the debate found in the literature on entrepreneurship. While we follow Guth and Ginsberg (1990) in this article, it is important to illustrate the inconsistencies in these definitions because using the same terminology to describe markedly broader and narrower concepts is not conducive to the advancement of the field.[1]

In summary the need for a framework that will help clarify the definitional ambiguities that exist in the field of corporate entrepreneurship becomes obvious from these examples, a task we turn to below.

A DEFINITIONAL FRAMEWORK

Although organization creation and innovation[2] are generally regarded as key factors in entrepreneurship (Stopford & Baden-Fuller, 1994), the challenges that entrepreneurs face vary according to whether they are operating independently or as a part of an existing organization. This necessitates two things: first, a need to clarify the definition of entrepreneurship; and second, a need to differentiate between the settings in which entrepreneurship takes place.

Entrepreneurship

For the sake of clarification in terminology and in recognition of the entrepreneurial efforts of individuals working in a corporate setup, the following definitions of entrepreneurship and entrepreneurs are proposed (Gartner, 1988; Schumpeter, 1934; Stopford & Baden-Fuller, 1994; Zahra, 1993, 1995, 1996).

> *Entrepreneurship* encompasses acts of organizational creation, renewal, or innovation that occur within or outside an existing organization.

> *Entrepreneurs* are individuals or groups of individuals, acting independently or as part of a corporate system, who create new organizations, or instigate renewal or innovation within an existing organization.

The conditions that define entrepreneurship are related to newness in the sense of strategy or structure.[3] Thus, the creation of an organization as defined by Gartner (1988) is entrepreneurial since it entails fundamental strategic and structural decisions (Cooper, 1979). Likewise, the renewal or rebirth of an existing organization is entrepreneurial in the sense that it represents a radical departure from predominant and historic strategic or structural patterns. Innovation is also an entrepreneurial activity since it involves new combinations that may dramatically alter the bases of competition in an industry, or lead

---

1 There is an interesting difference in the attempts to define individual or independent entrepreneurship on the one hand and corporate entrepreneurship on the other. Many of those who study entrepreneurs seem bent on limiting the field to individuals who create new organizations *and* new combinations (cf. Gartner, 1990) On the other hand, the definition proposed by Guth and Ginsberg (1990) makes it clear that corporate entrepreneurship can involve *either* the creation of new organizations *or* new combinations. Thus, corporate entrepreneurship is defined more broadly than some would like to define entrepreneurship This means that activities considered entrepreneurial in a corporate setting might not be considered as such if undertaken outside an existing company.

2. An innovation is distinguished from an invention An innovation brings something into new use, whereas an invention brings something new into being (Rogers, 1962) The criteria for success of an invention are technical, whereas for an innovation the criteria are commercial (Burgelman & Sayles, 1986).

3 By strategy we mean the manner in which an organization aligns its key resources with its environment Thus, strategy includes an organization's core competencies, resource deployments, competitive methods, and scope of operations at either the business unit or corporate level (cf Hofer & Schendel, 1978, Porter, 1980, Prahalad & Hamel, 1990). By structure we mean simply the manner in which an organization goes about implementing its strategy (cf. Galbraith & Nathanson, 1978)

to the creation of a new industry (Schumpeter, 1934; Stopford & Baden-Fuller, 1994), even though it may not be immediately manifested in organizational creation or renewal. However, while the above definition recognizes the centrality of innovation to entrepreneurship, it does not require that the birth or rebirth of an organization be accompanied by a Schumpeterian innovation (Stopford & Baden-Fuller, 1994), only that it consist of actions that materially affect the nature of the organization (Schollhammer, 1982). Put differently, both creation and renewal would subject the organization in question to the "liability of newness" as put forth by Stinchcombe (1965). The extent of this liability for an organization will vary according to the extent of its departure from its existing strategy or structural patterns, as well as the extent of newness of the product, service, technology, processes, etc., in a particular marketplace.

Thus, the presence of an innovation is viewed as a *sufficient* condition for entrepreneurship but not a *necessary* one, because organizational creation or renewal can occur in the absence of innovation. Newness or uniqueness of an innovation is a matter of degree both in terms of the tangible characteristics and in terms of the relevant market. Furthermore, new to the marketplace does not necessarily mean that the innovation is sold or consumed, as in the case of a new organizational form or a new process development. Since innovation may vary in its amount and impact, it is very difficult and, indeed, counterproductive to attempt to specify the precise level of innovation necessary for entrepreneurship. Therefore, we take the position that for the purpose of defining entrepreneurship, it is preferable to treat innovation as an entrepreneurial act rather than as the only act that makes the occurrence of entrepreneurship possible.

It should be apparent that despite the breadth of this definition it is highly consistent with the prevalent views of entrepreneurship (Gartner, 1990; Schumpeter, 1934) and corporate entrepreneurship (e.g., Zahra, 1995). Furthermore, the definition of entrepreneurship proposed allows for further distinctions between independent and corporate entrepreneurship to be made in a manner that is internally consistent.

Independent and Corporate Entrepreneurship

Following the lead of Collins and Moore (1970), entrepreneurial activities undertaken independently and those undertaken within the context of an organization are differentiated as "independent entrepreneurship" and "corporate entrepreneurship." Thus:

Independent entrepreneurship is the process whereby an individual or group of individuals, acting independently of any association with an existing organization, create a new organization.[4]

Corporate entrepreneurship is the process whereby an individual or a group of individuals, in association with an existing organization, create a new organization or instigate renewal or innovation within that organization.

Strategic Renewal and Corporate Venturing

As mentioned earlier, a number of authors (e.g., Guth & Ginsberg, 1990; Schendel, 1990; Zahra, 1995, 1996) have suggested that within the realm of existing organizations, entrepreneurship encompasses three types of phenomenon that may or may not be

---

4. Since organizational renewal obviously involved major strategic or structural changes to an existing organization, it cannot be considered independent entrepreneurship, by definition. Furthermore, organizational creation can occur in the presence or absence of innovation, as discussed above. Therefore, to include innovation in this definition would be redundant

interrelated: (i) the birth of new businesses within an existing corporation; (ii) the transformation of existing organizations through the renewal or reshaping of the key ideas on which they are built; and (iii) innovation. While the first has been referred to as internal corporate venturing (Zajac, Golden & Shortell, 1991), intrapreneurship (Pinchot, 1985), corporate new venture division (Sandberg, 1992), internal innovation, internal venturing (Guth & Ginsberg, 1990), and so on, the second has been called strategic renewal (Guth & Ginsberg, 1990), strategic change, revival, transformation (Schendel, 1990), strategic departure, new product development (Vesper, 1984), reorganization, redefinition (Zahra, 1993), organizational renewal (Stopford & Baden-Fuller, 1994), etc. In this discussion the terms strategic renewal and corporate venturing are used.

Strategic renewal refers to the corporate entrepreneurial efforts that result in significant changes to an organization's business or corporate level strategy or structure. These changes alter pre-existing relationships within the organization or between the organization and its external environment and in most cases will involve some sort of innovation. Renewal activities reside within an existing organization and are not treated as new businesses by the organization.

Corporate venturing refers to corporate entrepreneurial efforts that lead to the creation of new business organizations within the corporate organization. They may follow from or lead to innovations that exploit new markets, or new product offerings, or both. These venturing efforts may or may not lead to the formation of new organizational units that are distinct from existing organizational units in a structural sense (e.g., a new division).

Thus, both strategic renewal and corporate venturing suggest changes in either the strategy or structure of an existing corporation, which may involve innovation. The principle difference between the two is that corporate venturing involves the creation of new businesses whereas strategic renewal leads to the reconfiguration of existing businesses within a corporate setting.[5]

External and Internal Corporate Venturing

As noted above, corporate venturing may or may not lead to the formation of organizational entities that are distinct from the existing entities within an organization. In fact, corporate ventures may or may not reside within the domain of the existing organization (von Hippel, 1977). Based on these options, corporate venturing can be classified either as external or internal.

External corporate venturing refers to corporate venturing activities that result in the creation of semi-autonomous or autonomous organizational entities that reside outside the existing organizational domain.

Some examples of external corporate ventures are those formed as a result of joint ventures, spin-offs, and venture capital initiatives. Although these may vary in their

---

5. However, as our previous discussion has suggested, there may be instances where innovation occurs in an existing organization in the absence of either corporate venturing or strategic renewal efforts. Although these instances may be rare it is important to clarify the nature of these innovations for the purpose of completeness. To be entrepreneurial in the absence of organizational creation or renewal the innovation must be of the Schumpeterian (1934) variety or, in other words, involve the introduction of an original invention or idea into a commercially usable form that is new to the marketplace and has the potential to transform the competitive environment as well as the organization (Stopford Baden-Fuller, 1994).

degree of separateness from the parent company, their common feature is that they reside outside the domain or boundaries of the existing organization.

> *Internal corporate venturing* refers to the corporate venturing activities that result in the creation of organizational entities that reside within an existing organizational domain.

The relationship between the terms discussed above is diagrammatically presented in Figure 1. It is observed that at every step down the hierarchy a new limiting criterion is added, resulting in a set of internally consistent definitions that conform with previous usages (Table 3).

TOWARD A CLASSIFICATION OF INTERNAL CORPORATE VENTURES

Up to this point we have been concerned with a reconciliation of the definitions of the key terms used in the field of corporate entrepreneurship. As noted at the outset of this article, we have chosen to define these terms broadly. However, it should be clear that phenomena such as internal corporate venturing may take many forms. Indeed, a comparison of the definitions of Biggadike (1979), Burgelman (1983), and Ellis and Taylor (1987) emphasizes this point. As we move from abstract concepts to concrete

Figure 1

Hierarchy of Terminology in Corporate Entrepreneurship

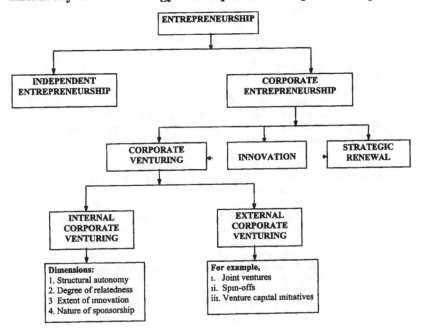

Table 3

Unique Features of Corporate Entrepreneurship Terminology

Terms	Unique Criteria
Entrepreneurship	organizational creation, renewal, or innovation, within or outside existing organizations
Independent entrepreneurship	organizational creation, + by individual(s) not associated with an existing corporate entity
Corporate entrepreneurship	organizational creation, renewal, or innovation, + instigated by an existing organizational entity
Strategic renewal	organizational renewal involving major strategic and/or structural changes + instigated by an existing organizational entity, + resides within existing organizational domain
Corporate venturing	organizational creation, + instigated by an existing organizational entity + treated as new businesses
Innovation	introduction of something new to marketplace + potential to transform competitive environment and organization + usually occurring in concert with corporate venturing or strategic renewal
External corporate venturing	organizational creation, + instigated by an existing organizational entity, + treated as new businesses, + resides outside existing organizational domain
Internal corporate venturing	organizational creation, + instigated by an existing organizational entity, + treated as new businesses, + reside within existing organizational domain.
Dimensions of internal corporate venturing	1 Structural autonomy 2 Relatedness to existing business(es) 3 Extent of innovation 4 Nature of sponsorship

solutions, it is desirable to classify groups or populations of organizations or events that share a large number of common characteristics and differ sharply from other groups or populations on those same characteristic dimensions. The problem of classification is best addressed by a combination of theoretical and empirical methods. Thus, while we can have a purely theoretical debate about what actions or situations to which the entrepreneurial or corporate venturing labels should be attached, it is more difficult to effectively classify discrete types of such phenomena without empirical research. However, we can develop theories about the nature of the differences that distinguish one population from another to guide empirical investigation. In this vein we will discuss the dimensions that appear to differentiate discrete types of internal corporate ventures. We chose internal corporate ventures because of personal interest, their importance to the field, and because they have received considerable attention in the literature, and are, therefore, perhaps the best understood aspect of corporate entrepreneurship.

Although internal corporate venturing activities are located within existing organizations, they are created in different ways, have different relationships with the corporate parent, involve different levels of innovation, and differ in strategic importance. These distinctions suggest that internal corporate ventures may vary in terms of at least four dimensions that may materially influence their subsequent development and performance: structural autonomy, relatedness to existing businesses, extent of innovation, and nature of sponsorship. In turn, these variations suggest that a classification of internal corporate ventures is possible. Although it is beyond the scope of this article to develop such a classification in full, each of the relevant dimensions is discussed briefly below as a starting point for empirical investigations.

Structural Autonomy

This refers to the extent to which the internal corporate venturing activities of a corporation are embedded within its existing organizational units. Put differently, this dimension addresses the crucial decision of where to locate the venture within an organization. The options vary from totally embedding the venture within the ongoing operations of an existing division to creating a separate new-venture division isolated from the rest of the organization and reporting directly to top management (Block & MacMillan, 1993; Kanter, Richardson, North, & Morgan, 1991). Block and MacMillan (1993) suggest that the ideal place to locate a venture will depend on its needs for managerial attention, resources, learning opportunities, and protection from corporate antagonism.

Different authors have focused on internal corporate ventures with different levels of structural autonomy, and these differences have influenced their definitions of terms as well as their descriptions of the phenomenon. For example, Burgelman and Sayles (1986) studied new venture divisions. This choice of setting may have influenced their restrictive definition of corporate entrepreneurship and may also explain the nature of the model by which they seek to describe the venturing process. However, Pinchot's (1985) work indicates that relationships among the critical components of the process may vary somewhat for ventures initiated within the structure of an existing division. Overall, this suggests that differences in the structural autonomy of internal corporate ventures may have a material effect on the venturing process.

Degree of Relatedness to Existing Business

The second dimension on which the internal corporate venture may vary is the degree of relatedness of the new business to existing businesses in terms of product offerings, markets, or core competencies and resources required. This construct may vary from being closely related to completely unrelated to the organization's present activities, leading to a variation in the challenge provided and the learning required for effectively managing the internal corporate venture (Block & MacMillan, 1993; Sorrentino & Williams, 1995).

Extent of Innovation

While the degree of relatedness to existing businesses refers to the degree of newness of the venture to the organization, the extent of innovation refers to the degree of newness of a venture in the marketplace. This dimension may vary from ventures that are simply imitative entries to those innovative entries that are potentially "frame-breaking" (Stopford & Baden-Fuller, 1994). Although imitative ventures will require considerable learning on the part of an organization, some lessons may be learned from experiences of pioneering competitors. For the ventures that are completely new to the marketplace, and perhaps even create new markets, the firm in question is the pioneer and faces considerably greater challenges as a consequence.

Nature of Sponsorship

This dimension is related to the degree of formal authorization for the venture. Zahra (1993) has suggested that ventures may vary from being formal or induced (sponsored by an organization) to informal or autonomous (entrepreneurial efforts based on employees' initiative without formal organizational sponsorship). This view has been extended by Day (1994), whose research supported the existence of "top-down," "bottom-up," and "dual-role champions" in entrepreneurial processes within internal corporate ventures.

Sponsorship has received considerable attention in the corporate entrepreneurship literature. While Covin and Slevin (1991) and Burgelman (1983) have focused on formal entrepreneurial efforts, other authors (e.g., Kanter, 1983; Pinchot, 1985) have focused on informal entrepreneurial efforts. The challenges and opportunities for entrepreneurship vary according to the nature of sponsorship. For example, in case of autonomous entrepreneurial efforts, the role of an organizational champion and sponsor is extremely important, whereas it may not be as critical in the case of formally induced efforts.

Reconciliation of Definitions

Based on the discussion presented in this article it is now possible to clarify the relationships between the definitions of Biggadike (1979), Burgelman (1983), Ellis and Taylor (1987), and Guth and Ginsberg (1990). First, it should be clear that we follow Guth and Ginsberg (1990) in defining coporate entrepreneurship as an activity comprising corporate venturing, strategic renewal, and innovation. Second, it should also be clear that Biggadike's (1979), Burgelman's (1983), and Ellis and Taylor's (1987) definitions all involve internal corporate venturing efforts but that each defines somewhat different types of internal corporate venturing. Thus, Biggadike's (1979) definition comprises all those internal corporate ventures that involve some amount of innovation regardless of the venture's degree of relatedness to the parent, structural autonomy, or sponsorship. Burgelman (1983), on the other hand, does not specify the degree of structural autonomy or sponsorship but makes it plain that the venture must be innovative and unrelated to the parent's existing businesses. Finally, Ellis and Taylor (1987) specifically exclude any venture that is not structurally autonomous, innovative, and unrelated to the parent, although either a formally or informally sponsored venture that possesses those characteristics would qualify.

As shown in Table 4, if we assume that each of the four dimensions by which internal corporate ventures might be classified can take one of two states, Biggadike's (1979) definition encompasses eight of the 16 possible types of internal corporate ventures. Burgelman's (1983) contains four of those types, and Ellis and Taylor's (1987) consists of two.[6] This reconcilation not only illustrates the consistency of the definitional framework proposed in this article, but also illustrates how it might be utilized by researchers to reconcile the findings of those and other studies.

For example, all else held equal, Biggadike's (1979) findings are generalizable to the most situations. However, because his study does not distinguish between different types of innovative internal corporate ventures, generalizations must be made with the greatest caution; the averages across types may not apply strongly to any single type. Conversely, Ellis and Taylor's (1987) work is the least generalizable across internal corporate ventures because of the restrictiveness of their definition. On the other hand, this restrictiveness also means that one can have a higher degree of confidence in the generalizations that can be made. Of course, Burgelman's (1983) definition and study falls somewhere in-between in terms of the extent and reliability of the generalizations that can be made from his research.

Admittedly, not all of the definitions previously used will fit as neatly into the framework proposed in this article as the ones discussed above. Nevertheless, the frame-

---

6. The classification scheme shown in Table 4 is meant for illustrative purposes Thus, while it might be a good starting point for clarifying internal corporate ventures, it is not our intention to suggest that this is how internal corporate ventures should be classified.

Table 4

A Tentative Classification of Internal Corporate Ventures and a Reconciliation of Previous Definitions

Extent of innovation	Relatedness to parent	Structural autonomy	Nature of sponsorship	Definitions used		
Innovative	Unrelated	Autonomous	Formal	Biggadike	Burgelman	Ellis & Taylor
			Informal	(1979)	(1983)	(1987)
		Embedded	Formal			
			Informal		↓	↓
	Related	Autonomous	Formal			
			Informal			
		Embedded	Formal			
			Informal	↓		
Imitative	Unrelated	Autonomous	Formal			
			Informal			
		Embedded	Formal			
			Informal			
	Related	Autonomous	Formal			
			Informal			
		Embedded	Formal			
			Informal			

work does provide a standard term of reference by which definitions and research findings can be compared and harmonized.

CONCLUSION

A review of the literature of corporate entrepreneurship reveals an ambiguity in terminology used. Although various authors agree on the features that are unique in corporate entrepreneurship, they often use different terms to express themselves. While this is not uncommon in behavioral sciences in general, and in new emerging disciplines in particular, an acceptance of a common set of terminology is necessary for scientific progress. This article represents one effort to systematize the terminology in corporate entrepreneurship.

A framework for the clarification and reconciliation of definitions was developed with the aim of providing a set of criteria for each descriptor. Moreover, a hierarchy of criteria was developed for the different terms. Finally, the basis for developing a system of classification for internal corporate ventures was proposed. While more work needs to be done, it is hoped that our efforts to put forward a set of internally consistent definitions and specify the criteria that differentiates one descriptor from another will provide a step toward a common terminology in the field of corporate entrepreneurship. Regardless, we believe that the clarification of the various elements that constitute corporate entrepreneurship should be of immediate value to the field.

REFERENCES

Biggadike, R (1979). The risky business of diversification. *Harvard Business Review, 57*(3), 103-111.

Birkinshaw, J (1997) Entrepreneurship in multinational corporations: The characteristics of subsidiary initiatives. *Strategic Management Journal, 18*(3), 207-229

Block, Z., & MacMillan, I C. (1993). *Corporate venturing· Creating new businesses within the firm.* Boston: Harvard Business School Press.

Burgelman, R. A. (1983) Corporate entrepreneurship and strategic management Insights from a process study *Management Science, 29,* 1349-1364

Burgelman, R A. (1984) Designs for corporate entrepreneurship. *California Management Review, 26*(2) 154-166

Burgelman, R A., & Sayles, L R (1986) *Inside corporate innovation: Strategy, structure, and managerial skills* New York: Free Press.

Bygrave, W D. (1993) Theory building in the entrepreneurship paradigm *Journal of Business Venturing, 8,* 255-280.

Cantillon, R. (1734). *Essai sur la nature du commerce en general.* [Essay on the nature of general commerce] (Translated by Henry Higgs) London· MacMillan

Caruana, A , Morris, M H , & Vella, A (1998) The effect of centralisation and formalization on entrepreneurship in export firms *Journal of Small Business Management, 36*(1), 16-29

Chung, L H , & Gibbons, P. T (1997) Corporate entrepreneurship· The roles of ideology and social capital *Group and Organization Management, 22*(1), 10-30

Collins, O , & Moore, D G (1970). *The organization makers* New York· Appleton

Cooper, A. C (1979) Strategic management· New ventures and small business. In D E. Schenedel & C W Hofer (Eds), *Strategic management A new view of business policy and planning,* pp 316-327 Boston Little, Brown.

Covin, J G , & Slevin, D. P. (1991) A conceptual model of entrepreneurship as firm behavior. *Entrepreneurship Theory and Practice, 16*(1), 7-25

Day, D. L. (1994). Raising radicals· Different processes for championing innovative corporate ventures *Organization Science, 5,* 148-172

Drucker, P (1985) *Innovations and entrepreneurship.* New York Harper & Row

Ellis, R J., & Taylor, N. T (1987) Specifying entrepreneurship In N. C. Churchill, J. A. Hornaday, B A. Kirchhoff, O. J Krasner, & K H Vesper (Eds), *Frontiers of entrepreneurship research,* pp. 527-541 Wellesley, MA: Babson College.

Galbraith, J R., & Nathanson, D. A (1978). *Strategy implementation. The role of structure and process* St. Paul, MN West

Gartner, W B. (1988) "Who is an entrepreneur?" is the wrong question *American Journal of Small Business, 12*(4), 11-32

Gartner, W. B (1990). What are we talking about when we talk about entrepreneurship? *Journal of Business Venturing, 5,* 15-28

Gartner, W B , Bird, B. J , & Starr, J. A. (1991). Acting as if Differentiating entrepreneurship from organizational behavior *Entrepreneurship Theory and Practice, 16*(3), 13-31

Guth, W D , & Ginsberg, A (1990) Guest editors' introduction Corporate entrepreneurship *Strategic Management Journal, 11*(Summer), 5-15

Hisrich, R. D. (1986) *Entrepreneurship, entrepreneur, and venture capital* Lexington, MA· Lexington Books

Hofer, C. W , & Schendel, D E (1978). *Strategy formulation· Analytical concepts* St Paul, MN. West

Hornsby, J. S , Naffziger, D. W., Kuratko, D. F , & Montagno, R. V. (1993) An integrative model of the corporate entrepreneurship process *Entrepreneurship Theory and Practice, 17*(2), 29-37

Hoy, F. (1995). Researching the entrepreneurial venture. In *Advances in entrepreneurship, firm emergence, and growth,* Vol. 2, 145-174. Greenwich, CT. JAI Press.

Jennings, D. F., & Lumpkin, J R. (1989). Functioning modeling corporate entrepreneurship: An empirical integrative analysis *Journal of Management, 15*(3), 485-502.

Jones, G R., & Butler, J. E. (1992) Managing internal corporate entrepreneurship: An agency theory perspective. *Journal of Management, 18,* 733-749.

Kanter, R. M. (1983). *The change masters* New York· Simon & Schuster

Kanter, R. M., Richardson, L., North, J., & Morgan, E. (1991). Engines of progress· Designing and running vehicles in established companies; The new venture process at Eastman Kodak, 1983-1989 *Journal of Business Venturing, 6,* 63-82.

Learned, K. E. (1992). What happened before the organization? A model of organizational formation *Entrepreneurship Theory and Practice, 17*(1), 39-48.

Livesay, H. C. (1982). Entrepreneurial history In C. A. Kent, D L. Sexton, & K. H Vesper (Eds.), *Encyclopedia of entrepreneurship.* Englewood Cliffs, NJ. Prentice Hall.

Low, M B., & MacMillan, I. C. (1988) Entrepreneurship· Past research and future challenges. *Journal of Management, 14*(2), 139-161

Lumpkin, G. T., & Dess, G. G. (1996) Clarifying the entrepreneurial orientation construct and linking it to performance. *Academy of Management Review, 21*(1), 135-172

McKelvey, B. (1982). *Organizational systematics: Taxonomy, evolution, classification.* Berkeley: University of California Press.

McMullan, W. E., & Long, W. A. (1983). The meaning of entrepreneurship. *American Journal of Small Business, 8*(2), 47-59

McMullan, W. E., & Long, W. A. (1990) *Developing new ventures· The entrepreneurial option.* Orlando, FL· Harcourt Brace Jovanovich.

Miller, D. (1983) The correlates of entrepreneurship in three types of firms *Management Science, 29*(7), 770-791

Nielson, R. P., Peters, M. P., & Hisrich, R D. (1985). Entrepreneurship strategy for internal markets— Corporate, nonprofit, and government institution cases *Strategic Management Journal, 6*(2), 181-189

Pass, C., Lowes, B., Davies, L , & Kronish, S. J. (1991). *The Harper Collins dictionary of economics.* New York: HarperCollins.

Pinchot, G III (1985). *Intrapreneuring.* New York. Harper & Row.

Porter, M E (1980). *Competitive strategy.* New York: Free Press.

Prahalad, C. K , and Hamel, G. (1990). The core competence of the corporation *Harvard Business Review, 68*(3), 79-91.

Roberts, E. B , & Berry, C A (1985). Entering new businesses· Selecting strategies for success. *Sloan Management Review, 26*(3), 3-18.

Rogers, E. M. (1962). *Diffusion of innovation* New York· Free Press.

Sandberg, W. R. (1992) Strategic management's potential contributions to a theory of entrepreneurship. *Entrepreneurship Theory & Practice, 16*(3), 73-90.

Schendel, D (1990) Introduction to the special issue on corporate entrepreneurship. *Strategic Management Journal, 11*(Summer), 1-3

Schollhammer, H (1982) Internal corporate entrepreneurship. In C. A. Kent, D. L. Sexton, & K. H. Vesper (Eds.), *Encyclopedia of entrepreneurship,* pp. 209-229. Englewood Cliffs, NJ. Prentice Hall.

Schumpeter, J. A. (1934). *The theory of economic development.* New Brunswick, NJ· Transaction Publishers

Sorrentino, M., & Williams, M. L. (1995). Relatedness and corporate venturing· Does it really matter? *Journal of Business Venturing, 10*(1), 59-73

Spann, M S., Adams, M., & Wortman, M. S (1988). Entrepreneurship: Definitions, dimensions, and dilemmas. *Proceedings of the U.S Association for Small Business and Entrepreneurship,* 147-153

Stinchcombe, A L. (1965). Social structure and organizations In J G March (Ed.), *Handbook of organizations,* pp. 142-193. Chicago: Rand McNally

Stopford, J M , & Baden-Fuller, C. W. F. (1994). Creating corporate entrepreneurship. *Strategic Management Journal, 15*(7), 521-536.

Vesper, K. H. (1984) Three faces of corporate entrepreneurship· A pilot study. In J. A. Hornaday, F. Tarpley, Jr., J. A Timmons, & K H Vesper (Eds.), *Frontiers of entrepreneurship research,* pp. 294-326 Wellesley, MA. Babson College.

von Hippel, E (1977) *The sources of innovation.* New York. Oxford University Press.

Wortman, M. S , Jr. (1987) Entrepreneurship An integrating typology and evaluation of the empirical research in the field. *Journal of Management, 13*(2), 259-279.

Zahra, S A. (1986). A canonical analysis of corporate entrepreneurship antecedents and impact on performance *Proceedings of the Academy of Management,* 71-75

Zahra, S. A. (1991). Predictors and financial outcomes of corporate entrepreneurship: An exploratory study *Journal of Business Venturing, 6*(4), 259-285.

Zahra, S. A. (1993) A conceptual model of entrepreneurship as firm behavior A critique and extension. *Entrepreneurship Theory and Practice, 17*(4), 5-21.

Zahra, S. A. (1995) Corporate entrepreneurship and financial performance· The case of management leveraged buyouts *Journal of Business Venturing, 10*(3), 225-247.

Zahra, S A. (1996). Governance, ownership, and corporate entrepreneurship· The moderating impact of industry technological opportunities. *Academy of Management Journal, 39*(6), 1713-1735.

Zajac, E. J , Golden, B R , & Shortell, S M. (1991) New organizational forms for enhancing innovation· The case of internal corporate joint ventures. *Management Science, 37*(2), 170-185.

Pramodita Sharma is Assistant Professor of Management at Dalhousie University

James J. Chrisman is Associate Dean, Director of Ph.D and MBA Thesis program and Professor of Venture Development in the Faculty of Management at the University of Calgary.

The authors are indebted to William D Guth, W Ed McMullan, the editors, and two anonymous reviewers for their comments on earlier drafts of this manuscript.

An earlier version of this paper was presented at the 10th annual meeting of the U S Association for Small Business and Entrepreneurship

Please direct correspondence concerning this article to Pramodita Sharma

Part II
Designing Effective Corporate Venturing Programs

Business Strategy Review, 2002, Volume 13 Issue 4, pp 10-17

Venturing to succeed

Julian Birkinshaw, Rob van Basten Batenburg and Gordon Murray

Corporate venturing reached a peak of popularity at the height of the dot-com boom. But that was only the latest in a series of popularity peaks for an idea that has been around for 40 years. In spite of slipping out of corporate fashion, corporate venturing will return once again. The question is whether organisations will have learned the lessons in making the idea work.

Corporate venturing is the process of actively investing in small start-up businesses by large firms. Typically, corporate venturing is managed through a separate entity – a venture unit – which is given the responsibility of identifying suitable start-ups to invest in, adding value to those businesses, and deciding whether and when to exit them. There are many different types of venture units and often they end up performing several different functions. The common element, however, is that they all make active investments in start-up businesses.

Over the last two years we have spoken to executives in 50 venture units in eight different countries and gathered questionnaire data from a further 50. While many companies got out of corporate venturing altogether in the last couple of years, many others have persevered and a few have thrived. This article highlights the key factors that appear to separate the winners from the losers.

Before describing the results of our research, it is useful to provide some context on the phenomenon of corporate venturing.

Since the 1960s, corporate venturing has gone through three cycles. The first ended in 1973 with the oil price shock and the ensuing recession. The second began in the early 1980s and was fuelled by the growth of the computer and electronics sectors. It came to an end in the late 1980s (again because of recession). The third wave began during the great 1990s technology boom, and it peaked in 2000 before falling steeply. This latest wave was driven by a combination of new technologies (the Internet, microprocessors, telecommunications, biotechnology and so on) and also a bubble economy that made it seemingly possible to make very quick returns by investing in exciting new technologies.

In 2001 the total number of firms investing in corporate venture capital fell by about a quarter (with a further fall in 2002) but even during this downturn a number of new investing firms have also emerged. The total invested amounts have been estimated to be $7.6bn, based on 2001 investment figures gathered by Venture One. (See Figure 1)

The current slowdown has been due to a number of well-known factors – the collapse of high-technology stocks, a loss of faith in most Internet-based business plans and a number of high-profile corporate failures. Companies that have got out of corporate venturing over the last three years include British Airways, Reuters, Vodafone, British Gas, Marks and Spencer

11 Julian Birkinshaw, Rob van Basten Batenburg and Gordon Murray

Figure 1
Annual CVC investments and active CVC investors 1980-Q2/2002

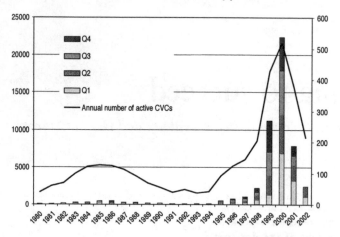

and Compaq. Corporate venture capital investments in the US fell by two thirds in 2001, though by comparison Europe has remained at a relatively higher level of investment (approximately €544m , which is 46 per cent down) according to *Real Deals* magazine. Corporate venturing in the US, in other words, seems to have suffered more than in Europe, in large part because the business environment in Europe had some catching up to do.

Increasing research and understanding
Academic thinking on corporate venturing provides some perspectives on how these cycles emerged as they did. The first academic studies looked at the various different structural forms of corporate venture units. They also documented many of the internal tensions that make corporate venturing difficult and showed that in most cases venture units failed to deliver value to their parent companies. While the oil price shock of 1973 killed off the first wave, the lack of success that most corporations experienced meant that corporate venturing did not return into vogue for another 10 years.

The second wave suffered from many of the same afflictions as the first, perhaps in part because it was focused in the computer and electronics industries, which had no prior experience with venturing. Again, problems emerged and most corporations struggled to gain a return on their investment. In his book

Venture Capital and Private Equity, Joshua Lerne describes three structural failures that can be identified in the approach to corporate venturing adopted during this period: most venture units had multiple goals rather than one clear mission; there was not sufficient management commitment to venturing, with the result that the necessary skills were not developed; and compensation schemes were not aligned to the growth of the ventures, with most venture managers paid on salary rather than in accordance with the new wealth created by the businesses in their portfolio.

During the 1990s considerable progress was made in understanding these problems through the enormous growth of the venture capital (VC) industry. VCs were true specialists in creating new businesses and they achieved their success through very disciplined investing, developing highly specialised skills, aligning incentives and creating strong external business networks. As corporate venturing took off again during the 1990s many venture units drew explicitly from the VC model. Well-known venture units including Intel Capital, Xerox Technology Ventures and Lucent's New Venture Group all adopted the VC model in an overt way and with considerable success.

However, the current proliferation of literature on corporate venturing offers mixed views on whether the VC model is entirely appropriate. Most studies acknowledge the wide variety of different forms of corporate venturing that have emerged and suggest that the appropriate model is highly contingent on the strategy adopted by the parent firm. There is also a sense that while the VC model has been effective at delivering financial gains, it has not delivered the strategic benefits that corporations typically seek.

Our sense is that the learning from the VC industry has been extremely valuable and it still has some way to go before it permeates the entire corporate venturing industry. However, there is a danger in adopting the VC model wholesale because ultimately most corporate venturing units are attempting to deliver strategic value back to their parent companies and this cannot be done with complete independence.

Key success factors

Our research revealed a number of different corporate venturing models from the pure "portfolio" investments made by some corporate venture capital firms through to internally focused "incubators". While there are obviously some important differences between these different models, in terms of such things as their objectives and the types of start-up operations they invest in, there are some broad key success factors that apply to all cases. None of these success factors will come as a great surprise. What is surprising is the number of venture units that have failed to follow them.

Develop clear goals – and a structure to deliver on them

Corporate venture units are established for a wide variety of reasons – making a company more entrepreneurial, providing a window on new technologies, making a strong financial return. But the more objectives venture unit managers have to balance, the more difficult it is to make smart investment decisions. Those units with single-minded objectives can build a focused organisation with the specific skills they need. Those units with multiple and conflicting objectives end up being stuck in the middle – they cater for many different types of investment opportunity, their skill sets become diluted and they are rarely the partner of choice for an external VC.

Clear goals can take many forms. The most common model, as exemplified by Innovacom and Lucent Venture Partners, is to focus on financial returns within a particular technology space. Ericsson Business Innovation focuses on creating the next core business

Nokia: two main criteria

for Ericsson. BT Brightstar is concerned fundamentally with spinning out under-utilised technology in BT's labs. The most interesting model is the Nokia Venture Organisation, which has three dedicated venture units as well as a number of related activities. While on the face of it these venture units have the potential to get in each other's way, each one was formed for a particular purpose. The result is a set of highly focused and clearly defined units.

Many other venture units have struggled to define clear goals. One London-based unit that was created at the height of the dot-com boom was given a broad mandate to pursue both internally focused and externally focused opportunities with the intention of providing both a strong financial return and delivering on a number of strategic goals. The result of this lack of focus was a stuck-in-the-middle venture unit that opportunistically followed whatever business opportunities came its way without a clear position on such things as the use of VC partners, investment levels or linkages to the parent company. After two years the unit was folded back into the parent company.

> Corporate venturing requires distinct capabilities that can only be built up through experience

Build specialised capabilities

Venture capitalists often view corporate venture units as poor relations – they see them as short-term funds with blurred objectives typically managed by corporate executives who do not have the networks, experience

13 Julian Birkinshaw, Rob van Basten Batenburg and Gordon Murray

---

Nokia Ventures Organisation

In the late 1990s Nokia realised that it needed a more structured ventures organisation as a way to create and develop new businesses outside the natural development path or current focus of core businesses. It was realised that different corporate venturing situations required different solutions.

As explained by Johan Schmidt, who leads one of the venture groups, "it enables us to look at opportunities outside the current business and on a longer time horizon". Ultimately Nokia's model developed into one New Ventures Organisation (NVO), responsible for co-ordinating the different venturing activities and reporting directly to the president of the company. It thus ensures close alignment with the corporate strategy.

Nokia separated its venture activities according to two main criteria: the primary business driver and the future link with Nokia's core business. In fact, as layers of an onion, it has built several corporate venture groups around Nokia Mobile Phones and the Nokia Networks, the existing core of the company, in order to deal with new venture opportunities.

The first layer is a strategic planning group called Insight and Foresight, an organic business function within the Nokia Ventures Organization, identifying new opportunities based on market and technology disruptions and contributing to the advanced business development of the existing core. Business ideas from this process may grow into the next layer as concrete business plans.

The second layer, New Growth Business, looks at internal business opportunities that have a high

likelihood of a future link with the core business, and the main driver is to create strategic new businesses. The structure is a small team, within NVO, and organically a part of the Nokia organisation.

The third layer is the Nokia Early Stage Technology Fund. It is a closed Fund, with all money coming from Nokia, investing in ideas with high growth potential. Its focus is on ideas coming from inside the company that have a possible future link with Nokia's core business. The driver for this fund is creating strategic options as well as a return.

The final layer is a very outward-looking closed fund, Nokia Venture Partners. It operates at arms length to the parent organisation and is structured as a venture capital fund, with Nokia as the largest general partner. The driver is therefore return on investment, and it invests in new ventures that are non-core to Nokia. However, it has a very clear investment focus on new ventures that operate in the telecommunications and networking business. Here, Nokia can add value through technical expertise in the due diligence phase and gets an insight into new technologies, markets and business models being developed in the outside world.

In summary, the different structures of Nokia Ventures Organization overlap somewhat, but they reflect very well the distinction in different roles that a ventures organisation can play for a corporation. The success is due in some part to the direct support from the top-management, through which it gets high visibility and support throughout the organisation. The high level of support also seems to have a direct and positive effect on the entrepreneurial culture within the corporation.

---

or discipline needed to successfully build new businesses. While this point has less validity than it used to, the underlying argument is unassailable – that corporate venturing requires distinct capabilities that can only be built up through experience.

These capabilities include a system for sensing and evaluating new ideas, networks and contacts to build the management team for a new venture and a disciplined approach to funding that kills off unpromising ventures quickly.

While this is an obvious point, it is surprising how many corporate venture units have been established without any attempt to buy in these capabilities or develop them in a systematic fashion. At the height of the dot-com boom, for example, many large corporations sank tens of millions into venture funds with complete disregard for the capabilities and discipline needed to realise a return on those funds. Today, venture units are far more savvy though many still work on the incorrect assumption that they can get up to speed on the finer points of venture investing in a few months flat. They cannot – it takes years.

Building specialised capabilities can be done in a variety of ways. One obvious approach is through partnership. Unilever, for example, partnered with a London-based VC when it established its Unispark venture unit in 1998. Lucent, Intel and Nokia all worked with VCs in their early days and still have external partners in some of their funds. Roche has an internally focused venture unit but an integral part of its venture programme is commercial skills training for the hundreds of people every year who come forward with promising ideas.

Separate, separate, separate

It's the oldest story of them all. Venture units work on new ideas that do not fit with the mainstream business so they need to be separated otherwise the ideas will be killed. At the same time, however, it is also recognised that too much separation is bad because the potential strategic benefits from venturing will never be realised.

Our initial bias in this study was towards greater integration with the parent company but the evidence pushed us the other way. Our analysis reveals a strong correlation between separation and venture unit performance. At least in the early stages, it is imperative that venture units create distance between themselves and their parent companies. This distance can include such things as having a separate fund (rather than corporate funds subject to internal review), a high level of decision-making autonomy, strong links to the VC community, and incentives based on carried interest and bonuses. These are all ways of preventing the venture unit managers from being second-guessed by their corporate parents.

One particular issue is worth highlighting here. If the venture unit is investing in potentially disruptive technology, should they seek approval or sign-off from the relevant business unit? Some people we spoke to felt business unit sign-off was essential – to ensure their support in developing the idea and to facilitate their eventual adoption of that technology. Others disagreed and argued that business unit sign off would kill any potentially disruptive technology. Our research finds some evidence for the latter point of view. In other words, the more successful units typically were the ones that did not require business unit sign off on new ideas.

Build links back to parent when you are established

It is rarely enough for the venture unit to be successful purely as a stand-alone entity. Even financially driven venture units are looking to make investments in companies that will offer some strategic benefits to their parent companies. And for such benefits to occur there have to be operational linkages back from the venture unit to the corporation. These linkages can take many forms – business unit employees helping with due diligence, business unit executives taking board seats on portfolio companies, explicit partner agreements between portfolio companies and the parent company and so on.

Johnson & Johnson Development Corporation, one of the most successful venture organisations, actively cultivates linkages between its portfolio companies and the relevant business units. Intel Capital will often work with Intel Architecture Labs on due diligence studies.

The challenge here is to reconcile the need for linkages with the need for separation. Our belief is that complete separation is necessary in the early stages of development. But once the venture unit has established itself – with some proven winners and a positive return on investment – it can begin to cultivate links back to the parent company.

High-level sponsorship and critical mass

Venture units are by definition misfits. And misfits are always the first things to be killed off whenever high-level strategic changes are made or whenever problems arise. To survive these periodic culls, the venture unit needs committed sponsorship from the highest level, preferably the CEO or president of the company. All of the real success stories in corporate venturing – including Nokia, Intel, J&J and Lucent – have CEO-level support. Many of the others have much more mixed levels of sponsorship.

High-level sponsorship does not equate to the line of reporting or to the presence of senior executives on the board of advisors. Rather it means there is a senior executive prepared to stick his/her neck out for the venture unit when it loses money for its first five years of operation. The term "air cover" is often used to describe this phenomenon – someone in a senior position who pushes back all criticism of the venturing activities while the venture managers get on with doing their job.

15 Julian Birkinshaw, Rob van Basten Batenburg and Gordon Murray

Related to high-level sponsorship is the issue of critical mass. Corporate venturing is all about managing a portfolio – on the basis that the few big winners will make up for the many under performers and outright losers. Research from the financial markets tells us that you need a portfolio of 30 or so companies to balance out the risks from individual companies and to a large extent the same logic applies to corporate venture units. So if a venture unit only makes 10 investments in the first three years, it is almost certainly below critical mass.

Evidence from our research suggests that most internally focused venture units are below critical mass. And indeed, in some cases we are seeing consolidation underway. Siemens, for example, has now pulled together its various venturing funds under a single management structure.

Linking corporate venturing to the broader corporate strategy agenda

The second set of insights from our study is concerned with the link between corporate venturing and the broader strategic agenda of the parent company. It is self-evident that such linkages should exist. However, there are many different models in terms of how the relationship between the venture unit and the parent company is structured and there are significant variations in terms of how the venture unit evolves over time. A number of specific points can be made.

First, corporate venturing should be viewed as one approach to corporate development alongside others such as acquisition, strategic investment and alliance rather than as a stand-alone activity.

Alcatel: *clear on the logic*

Figure 2
The venture life-cycle

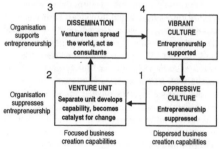

Many companies, including Philips, Sun and Alcatel, are very clear on this logic. For example, if a potentially interesting start-up company is identified they will examine its prospects, capabilities and strategic fit and only then will they decide whether to build a relationship with it through the venture unit or through an alliance or acquisition. The aim is to match the investment or development "vehicle" with the opportunity in such a way that the long-term value creation potential is optimised. This is easily said but it requires a high level of co-ordination to work – which is hard to deliver on while also giving autonomy to the venture unit.

Second, corporate venturing should never be viewed as a permanent solution.

Our opinion is that "business creation" should be viewed as a corporate capability that ideally exists throughout the organisation. The venture unit can therefore be seen either as a "second-best" solution in corporations that feel they will never be able to win over the mainstream business units or as an "agent of change" whose role is to build specialised capabilities in venturing.

Indeed, our research suggests that one way of looking at corporate venturing is through a life-cycle model (see Figure 2). Most companies sit at stage 1 of the model – new business development is suppressed and the few entrepreneurs that the company has are dispersed throughout the organisation. Companies like this occasionally see new businesses emerge but only through the dedicated effort of the lone entrepreneur who succeeds despite the system.

The creation of a venture unit takes the company into stage 2 of the model. While the organisation as a whole does not support entrepreneurship, the creation of a focused and dedicated unit provides it with a "centre of excellence" in which the necessary skills and capabilities around new venture development can be built. Assuming the venture unit has critical mass and high-level support it can begin to generate support for the concept of new venture development, and it can act as a catalyst for change.

In the next stage (stage 3), the venture unit managers start providing their services to other parts of the organisation, helping new business ideas to get established without the protection afforded by a distinct venture unit. And in the final stage (stage 4), the venture unit managers essentially work themselves out of a job. They push the process out into the mainstream business units, giving individuals in those units responsibility to make their own investment and development decisions and closing down the central unit.

This model has support among companies that we have studied. Hewlett Packard, for example, argues that is has no corporate venturing activity but it frequently makes strategic investments as an integral part of its ongoing business development process. Royal Sun Alliance had a separate venture unit for several years but folded it back into its corporate strategy activity when it became apparent that closer integration with the mainstream business units was necessary. Marks and Spencer essentially did the same and ensured that all the individuals from its venture unit were given senior jobs back in the mainstream business to ensure that their learning was not lost.

Third, there are a number of corporate-level capabilities that venturing can help to develop.

Many companies are trying to develop a broad capability in business creation. But underneath that are a number of very specific capabilities important to a company's long-term success that corporate venture units are well positioned to help develop. These include:

- *An entrepreneurial mindset among employees.* For example, BT's Brightstar venture unit was created to uncover the "hidden value" in BT's R&D laboratories but a secondary – and no less important – goal was to change the culture in the organisation to make individuals more commercially minded and entrepreneurial.

- *Commercial capabilities throughout the company.* For example, Roche's venturing process has involved training large numbers of people in business plan development so that they can effectively pursue their new ideas. Lonie Shoff, who runs the unit, observed that in his view the single biggest change they have brought about is a broader understanding of business concepts and models.

- *Networking inside and outside the company.* Venture units are perfectly positioned to create linkages between their parent company and the VC community and such links are an invaluable source of new business ideas and fresh thinking. Venturing also demands high levels of networking by managers across the various different parts of the corporation.

- *Market sensing.* In a rapidly changing world, companies need to be very responsive to new opportunities as they arise. And again corporate venturing units potentially offer a strong market-sensing capability that can benefit the entire corporation. For example, when Unilever created Unispark its intention was primarily to grow and amplify the set of new ideas that were coming into the company. Likewise, Diageo's venture unit invests a lot of time in brainstorming and new idea creation processes.

- *The discipline of funding and killing projects.* Large companies have traditionally been relatively bad at phasing the funding of new projects and even worse when it comes to killing off projects that have not met their objectives. Venture units have learnt from their VC cousins how to do this properly and again this is a capability that top management can and should infuse into the corporation as a whole.

Prospects for venturing

What are the prospects for corporate venturing in the coming years? There are several reasons to be pessimistic.

The economy in North America and Europe is struggling, new business scandals are seemingly emerging every week and there is still a backlash underway against anything associated with the excesses of the dot-com era (including corporate venturing). So most

17 Julian Birkinshaw, Rob van Basten Batenburg and Gordon Murray

companies do not want to use their diminishing capital available in seemingly risky ventures.

On the other hand, corporate venturing still has many supporters. One of the enduring lessons of the dot-com era is that companies need to take disruptive technological change seriously and have to invest in the development of new businesses to protect themselves from that threat.

Corporate venturing is never easy but it is beginning to be recognised as something that far-sighted companies cannot do without. Our prognosis is that there will be a gradual reduction in corporate venturing activity over the next couple of years but for many large corporations it will remain firmly on the agenda, as an engine of corporate innovation and growth.

The key findings from this research project are available in a report, Corporate Venturing – State of the Art and Prospects for the Future. *The research involved interviews with executives in more than 40 companies in eight countries and the collection of systematic data on 95 corporate venture units worldwide.*

Julian Birkinshaw (jbirkinshaw@london.edu) is associate professor of strategic and international management at the London Business School. He was the research leader in this corporate venturing study. He is the author of four books, including Leadership the Sven-Goran Eriksson Way *(2002) and* Entrepreneurship in the Global Firm *(2001. He is currently writing a book on corporate venturing, due out next year (*Inventuring, *McGraw Hill, 2003).*

Rob van Basten Batenburg (rbastenbatenburg@london.edu) is a Sloan Fellow of London Business School and has worked as an independent strategy consultant, entrepreneur and research associate. He executed this corporate venturing study.

Gordon Murray (gmurray@london.edu) is an associate professor of entrepreneurial management at the Department of Entrepreneurship, London Business School, and worked for international corporations and in UK government service before becoming a full-time business school academic.

Resources

Alterowitz R and Zonderman J. *New Corporate Ventures: How to Make Them Work*, John Wiley & Sons, 1988, New York USA.

Block Z and Macmillan I C. *Corporate Venturing, Creating new Businesses within the Firm*, Harvard Business School Press, 1993, Boston (MA), USA.

Basten Batenburg, R A J van "In search for the key drivers for success" in *Corporate Venture Capital*, London Business School Masters Thesis, August 2001, LBS.

Burgelman R A & Syles L R. *Inside Corporate Innovation, Strategy, Structure and Managerial Skill*, The Free Press, New York 1988.

Burgelman R A. "Managing the Internal corporate venturing process", *Sloan Management Review*, Winter 1984, pp 33-48.

Chesbrough H. "Making sense of corporate venture capital", *Harvard Business Review*, 2002.

Day J D, Mang P Y, Richter A and Roberts J. "The innovative organisation: why new ventures need more than a room of their own", *McKinsey Quarterly*, 2001 - 2, pp. 21-31.

Hamel G. "Bringing the Valley inside", *Harvard Business Review*, Sept-Oct 1999.

Laurie D L. *Venture Catalyst*, Nicholas Brealey Publishing, London, 2001

Lerner J. *Venture Capital and Private Equity: a Casebook*, John Wiley & Sons Inc, New York 2000.

Murray G and Maula M *Corporate Venture Capital and the Creation of US Public Companies: The impact of sources of Venture Capital on the performance of Portfolio Companies*, forthcoming in Hitt MA, Amit R, Lucier C and Shelton B (Eds.).

Pinchot C and Pellman R. *Intrapreneuring in Action: A Handbook for Business Innovation*, Berrett-Koehler Publishers Inc, 1999, San Fransisco USA.

Reid, G C. *Venture Capital Investment: An Agency Analysis of Practice*, Routledge, New York, 1998

The Corporate Venture Capital Directory and Yearbook, 2000; Ibid, 2001 , Asset Alternatives Inc, Wellesley (MA), USA.

Zider B. "How venture capital works", *Harvard Business Review*, Nov-Dec 1999.

[8]

CORPORATE VENTURING:

ALTERNATIVES, OBSTACLES

ENCOUNTERED, AND

EXPERIENCE EFFECTS*

IAN C. MACMILLAN, ZENAS BLOCK, and
P. N. SUBBA NARASIMHA
New York University

EXECUTIVE SUMMARY

In this study of a relatively small number of corporate executives with line experience in corporate venturing, some clues are uncovered that could help those corporations contemplating the initiation of acquisition, joint venturing, or corporate start-up activities to avoid or overcome the obstacles that our sample of managers encountered.

The preliminary indications are:

1. *Joint ventures appear to be a highly useful way of starting off in venturing activity while at the same time reducing the initial risk.*
2. *The excutives in this sample indicated that experience at venturing resulted in improvement in venturing performance, **but only after several venture attempts**. From this observation, two suggestions appear reasonable: 1) Start venturing with few relatively small ventures and keep ventures relatively small until experience is gained. Start perhaps with joint ventures to learn your way in and "graduate" to grass-roots start ups once significant learning has taken place; and 2) The experience gained will reside in people who may have been part of an unsuccessful venture, perhaps several unsuccessful ventures. If this experience is to be useful, the people who have gained it need to be retained and recycled to other new ventures.*
3. *Although some of the obstacles perceived by the executives diminish with experience, others do not. Regardless of experience, inability to plan for new ventures is a recurrently cited obstacle, as is the inability of the corporation to provide adequate support to the venture.*

The last point may be the most significant observation in this study. Prevailing corporate values call for the ability to plan and to meet the plan as one of the primary measures of managerial competence. New ventures, however, rarely conform to plan, especially the quantitative projections.

Address correspondence to Prof. Ian C. MacMillan, Center for Entrepreneurial Studies, New York University, 100 Trinity Place, New York, New York 10006.

*The authors wish to acknowledge support from the Center for Entrepreneurial Studies at New York University.

178   MacMILLAN ET AL.

As a result, corporate support either dwindles when plans are not achieved or desperate spending efforts are made to achieve unachievable planned results, which often result in large losses. Very different planning methods are needed for ventures, methods that, in the highly uncertain surroundings of venturing activity, address what realistic corporate expectations should be, how progress should be measured and venture managers evaluated, and in what ways and at what times support will be provided by the parent corporation. These are discussed in the main body of the article.

INTRODUCTION

This article is concerned first with assessing the types of obstacles a firm faces when venturing and second in whether, after several attempts by an existing corporation at starting up new businesses, that firm "learns" to overcome the start-up obstacles encountered in its first ventures.

Our interest in this subject was piqued by a number of studies of the corporate start-up phenomenon that indicated the difficulties that firms experience with such start ups. For instance, Biggadike (1979), in his study of start-up businesses, found that his sample of (largely Fortune 500) companies experienced considerable delays before success was achieved in the form of profits and net positive cash flow.

Schon (1963) was one of the first researchers to explicitly argue that any start-up activity is up against a significant and a very natural resistance in existing organizations. An organization *must* build a high commitment to existing products and technologies or it will be "perpetually and fruitlessly shifting gears." He points out that radical change creates radical disruption, which is anathema to bureaucracy. The bureaucracy therefore acts to protect and reestablish the status quo, stifling the start-up effort (Hlavacek and Thompson 1975).

Kanter (1983) points out another reason for which modern organizations tend to stifle start ups—the large modern organization has erected huge barriers to the exercise of entrepreneurial initiative by excessive specialization and compartementalization of jobs, administered by an onerous hierarchy that confines lower-level members to very narrowly specified activities.

The fact that firms appear to have great difficulty at start ups leads one to ask whether or not there are better alternatives than attempting a full-scale, grass-roots start up. Roberts (1980) and Roberts and Berry (1985) identified a spectrum of alternative approaches, whereby a firm can avoid some of the obstacles to success by using a venture partner with compensating skills.

Roberts and Berry's range of possible alternatives are: internal development, internal start ups, licensing, various forms of joint ventures, acquisitions, and "educational" participation in venture capital markets. They suggest that a firm is ill advised to attempt venturing in areas in which the prerequisites for competing and the firm's skills and experience are mismatched. Fast (1981) goes further and suggests that inexperienced firms should begin by participating in venture-capital funds to observe and learn venturing before starting to venture themselves.

Weiss (1981) and Fast (1981) found major differences in performance between independent, venture-capital-backed start ups and Biggadike's (1979) data for corporate start ups. On average, the independents reach profitability twice as fast and end up twice as profitable as the Biggadike corporations. Thus, a compelling argument can be made for letting the venture capitalists weather the problems of start up and then acquire the resulting ongoing firm. Because the samples for all the independent start-up studies were drawn from the venture-capital supported firms in the *Venture Economics* database, we concluded that venture capitalists probably have an experience base that allows them to anticipate, avoid, or overcome the obstacles that large firms encounter.

However, nowhere in the literature was any reference made to changes in corporate venturing performance as it relates to experience nor were direct comparisons in venture performance made between alternative venturing modes (start up, joint venture, or acquisition).

This gap in the literature caused us to decide that some benefit could be derived from a study that allowed us to add modestly to the database on corporate venturing and venturing experience: to learn which obstacles senior executives with experience in venturing perceived as important; whether these obstacles existed to an equal extent in the three different venture modes; and whether a relationship exists between experience and the perception of obstacles encountered by line managers involved in actual ventures.

Accordingly, senior managers from 85 firms from a variety of industries who were participants in an advanced executive program at a major university were approached. Of these, 31 who identified themselves as having been involved as line managers in some form of business venture (start up, joint venture, and/or acquisition) agreed to participate in this study.

Because our interest was on the obstacles perceived by these respondents, our first step was to ask them to list any major obstacles they had encountered to successful implementation of their ventures. These responses were collated into a single list, and, at a meeting of the group, each item was clarified by the manager who had identified that obstacle.

In order to obtain a list with a manageable number of obstacles, the respondents were then requested to identify the five most serious obstacles they had encountered. In order to qualify for the final list, an item required identification by at least three respondents. It was this process that resulted in the 27 obstacles used in the study.

The items were then classified into the broader categories of venturing problems as shown in the subheadings of Table 1.

In the final step of the study, managers were asked to fill out a questionnaire that had been developed from Table 1. Three separate questionnaires were administered—one each for acquisitions, joint ventures, and corporate start ups.

Each manager was asked to indicate:

1. The number of times his or her business unit had attempted that mode of venturing in the past decade, ranging from never through five or more;
2. On a seven-point scale, the effectiveness with which the most recent venture was carried out—ranging from not at all effective through extremely effective; and
3. On a seven-point scale, the degree to which each of the items in Table 1 was an obstacle in his or her most recent venture; ranging from little or no extent to a great extent.

Thirty responses to this stage were obtained. Respondents' businesses ranged in sales from $7.5 million to $16 billion and were from a moderately diverse set of industries: food, medical, petroleum, pharmaceutical, manufacturing, chemicals, plastics, electronics, construction, and financial services.

We identified a number of problems with this research design, stemming mainly from the fact that it is a self-report study. It was not possible under the circumstances to get multiple responses from *other* managers in the companies involved, so reliability of the

180   MacMILLAN ET AL.

TABLE 1   Obstacles to Successful New Business Development

	Acquisitions[a]	Joint Ventures[a]	Start Ups[a]
I. Misreading the Market			
Imperfect market analysis	3.5	2.5	4.0[b]
Underestimation of competition	3.9	2.5	3.7[b]
Underestimation of initial selling effort needed	3.3	2.4	3.4[b]
Underestimation of customer's risk in supporting venture and reluctance to take this risk	2.1	1.7	2.2
Underestimation of barriers to entry in market	2.4	2.4	2.8
Unexpected customer education and training requirements	2.2	1.9	2.8[b]
II. Inadequate Corporate Support (Commitment and Resources)			
Lack of real commitment to venture	2.4	2.9	3.2
Lack of clear mission for new unit	2.6	2.2	3.0
Lack of entrepreneurial talent in company	3.6	3.4	3.6
Competition for resources within company	2.5	2.4	3.6[b,c]
Lack of fit with corporate stategy	2.7	2.2	2.6
III. Unrealistic Corporate Expectations			
Impatience within company to get results	3.6	3.7	4.0
Unrealistic payback criteria	3.1	2.9	3.1
Overcontrol by corporation	2.9	2.0	2.3
Excessive corporate cost allocations	2.5	2.5	3.1
Underestimation of riskiness of venture	3.6	3.6	3.8
Refusal to acknowledge weaknesses	3.2	3.2	4.1
IV. Inadequate Planning			
Poor cost estimation	3.2	2.2	3.2[b]
Underestimation of funds needed	3.5	3.1	3.6
Unanticipated regulatory problems	1.9	2.6	2.5
Lack of contingency plans	3.5	3.1	3.1
No clear definition of failure	2.5	2.5	2.6
V. Operational Difficulties			
Debugging time underestimated	3.5	2.5	3.4
Quality-control maintenance	2.5	2.6	2.9
Disruption of ongoing operations	2.6	2.2	2.8
Incorporation of new unit into ongoing operations	3.0	2.8	3.3
Venture-incurred excess fixed costs	2.5	2.4	2.8

[a]Sample sizes: acquisitions, 22; joint ventures, 17; start ups, 24.
[b]Significant difference ($p < 0.05$) between joint venture and start up.
[c]Significant difference ($p < 0.05$) between acquisition and start up.

responses is challengeable, particularly because the measures of effectiveness and of the difficulty of the obstacles required subjective judgment on the part of the respondents.

Furthermore, because the respondents had all been involved in managing the venture itself, they would tend to overrate its success and to project obstacles to the corporate level, as Hill and Hlavacek (1972) found in their study.

The results, however, do appear to provide some new insights into the effects of experience in venturing, as well as corroboration of many propositions offered by other authors, as will be seen below. Because a variety of different results emerged from this study, we shall combine results and discussion in each of several sections.

RESULTS AND DISCUSSION

Obstacles Encountered: Start Ups Versus Other Venturing Modes

Table 1 lists the mean value of the responses to the individual items in the list. It is clear from the results that joint venturing consistently, and systematically, encounters fewer obstacles than do start ups (sign test: $p < 0.001$) and that acquisitions also encounter significantly less obstacles than do start ups (sign test: $p < 0.05$). Note that this applies only to those obstacles identified in the study; obviously our sample could not exhaust all possible venturing obstacles. From those cases in which there are significant differences in Table 1, it is also clear that joint ventures create significantly fewer problems when it comes to reading the initial market.

We were initially surprised by the low values obtained for the mean scores on the obstacles. On reflection, we feel that the explanation lies in the research design—the fact that the respondents would rate the one or two major obstacles they faced in their most recent venture as high and that other obstacles would then be rated low relative to these major obstacles. If different major obstacles were encountered by different respondents, most of the obstacles would tend to be rated low, leading to low means in general.

We scanned the distributions of the original responses for each of the obstacles, seeking those with the most frequent scores of 5 or more—obstacles that had been cited as significant obstacles by several respondents. Some interesting patterns were found, as reported in Table 2.

The following obstacles were cited as serious by more than 25% of respondents for *every* mode:

- Refusal by corporate level to recognize weaknesses;
- Impatience within corporation for results;

TABLE 2 Obstacles Frequently Cited as Serious by Respondents[a]

	Start Ups[b]	Acquisitions[b]	Joint Ventures[b]
Refusal by corporation to recognize weaknesses	42	32	35
Underestimation of funds required	37	27	23
Impatience in corporation for results	33	32	35
Lack of entrepreneurial talent	29	36	35
Lack of contingency planning	25	36	29
Debugging problems	33	36	c
Underestimation of competition	29	41	c
Unrealistic payback period expected	29	23	c
Underestimation of risk	29	32	c
Unique to Start Ups			
Excessive corporate cost allocations	25	c	c
Lack of commitment	25	c	c
Difficulties of incorporation in ongoing operations	25	c	c
Lack of clarity of mission	25	c	c
Imperfect market analysis	42	c	c
Underestimation of initial selling effort	29	c	c

[a]All figures are percentages of managers who rated difficulty of obstacles as 5 or higher.
[b]Sample sizes: start ups, 24; acquisitions, 22; joint ventures, 17.
[c]Fewer than 20% of the respondents rated these items as 5 or higher.

182 MacMILLAN ET AL.

- Underestimation of funds required;
- Lack of entrepreneurial talent; and
- Lack of contingency plans.

In addition, the following obstacles were cited by at least 25% of the managers as being serious problems for at least two modes of venturing: underestimation of risk involved; underestimation of the competition; unrealistic payback requirements; and unexpected debugging problems.

Nearly all these problems are related to planning and estimates of the future and were sufficiently serious to a large enough percentage of ventures reported to warrant suggestion that specific and different planning methodologies are necessary for venturing. The problem of lack of entrepreneurial talent is directly related to the problems of planning and misestimation mentioned above, because entrepreneurial talent is what is needed to cope with the continuous flow of surprises that result from the inevitable misestimations by firms that enter into new and unknown markets and products.

The critical difference between conventional planning and planning for new ventures is the lack of corporate knowledge upon which to anchor new venture plans—and hence this lies at the heart of the monitoring and control of new ventures. A conventional business has a sufficient idea of market conditions, operating procedures, and competitive actions on which to base its plan, yet firms still have difficulty in meeting plans.

In the face of the almost complete ignorance of market and production conditions that the venturing firm faces, the venture manager cannot be expected to match accomplishments with a set of prearranged deadlines (Block and MacMillan 1985).

A balance must be struck between imposing some fiscal and management discipline and the ludicrousness of forcing managers to blindly produce according to a set of projections made in ignorance.

The solution to this problem may lie in the ways in which the *independent* entrepreneur is handled by the banks and venture capitalists. For instance, Shapero (1984) has suggested that monitoring and control of the venture be handled in much the same way as the banker handles the small-business entrepreneur. The bank does not attempt to get involved in the day-to-day operation of the business but controls by imposing key performance goals and then setting a limited number of financial controls that set rather broad boundaries on the actions the business can take. The idea is that as long as the entrepreneurs operate within these constraints, they are free to act as they please, but once these limits are violated a meeting with the banker is required.

Fast (1981) takes a somewhat different but complementary approach:

> One of the major difficulties of venturing within a large corporation is the setting of realistic budgets and benchmarks against which performance is measured. For the independent start-up, this task is less difficult. The major reason is that there are very clear go/no-go decision points that center around rounds of financing. An entrepreneur who starts a venture and receives venture capital funding has made it over the first hurdle, but he is aware that within a year or two, he will probably need additional financing. Thus, he must perform credibly so as to make his company attractive for the next round of financing. Performing exactly as planned is not critical in his case. [The key issue is whether] he can adapt to both unforeseen difficulties and opportunities and end up showing progress and promise. This is quite different from the corporate environment, where the venture's performance is typically evaluated by how closely it adheres to plan. There is a much greater emphasis on doing what was promised rather than opportunistically adapting and responding to the unforeseen.

Another element to the plan-execution process is very significant for ventures: the learning opportunity. In a longitudinal follow-up of their original study, Maidique and Zirger (1984) have identified a critical benefit of the venturing process that has only been recognized implicitly in other research: the learning benefit. They suggest that the venturing process is characterized by three highly beneficial learning processes that take place as the venture progresses: 1) customers and distributors "learn by using" (i.e., only by using the product do they begin to understand its benefits and limitations, and thus venturing firms learn what the real needs are); 2) the firm "learns by doing" (i.e., only by making the product and delivering it to the market does the firm learn the technical and marketing challenges it faces); 3) the firm "learns by failing" (i.e., even in failure the seeds of future successes can be sown. Maidique and Zirger (1984) uncovered many cases in which spectacular successes were achieved from the ashes of failure.

Of particular import in planning is the need for rapid development of an understanding of the ill-defined market and vaguely determined market needs. In study after study this has been cited as a critical challenge (von Hippel 1977; Cooper 1979; Maidique and Zirger 1984). One would therefore expect that a significant proportion of early milestones should revolve around gathering market information.

In addition to insuring that venture managers are not bound to ill-advised attempts to meet unrealistic projections, milestone planning has another advantage. At each milestone a decision point is reached—the next step of the venture may be approved, accelerated, slowed down, aborted, or redirected, based on a realistic assessment of the new information obtained since the last milestone. This helps eliminate many of the problems identified by Myers and Sweezy (1978), who in their study found many cases in which projects had been killed prematurely and many *other* cases in which firms had persisted far beyond what was justified.

OBSTACLES UNIQUE TO CORPORATE START UPS

Table 2 listed several obstacles for which more than 25% of the respondents cited serious problems that were unique to corporate start ups. Three of these are the consequences of corporate actions rather than problems of venture management (inappropriate corporate cost-allocation procedures; problems incorporating the unit into ongoing operations; and lack of corporate commitment). These results provide support for Block's (1982) argument regarding the disruptive effects of corporate behavior on venture success: Block suggested that venturing is seriously compromised by inflexible corporate design and inadequate corporate support and attention.

These results also reinforce the literature arguing that success at corporate start ups is highly dependent on the creation of a supportive entrepreneurial culture in the corporation. For instance, Hill and Hlavacek (1977) in their survey of 100 firms found that an entrepreneurial environment was one of the distinguishing characteristics of firms with successful corporate ventures. In the literature, three major components to this appear to be top management commitment, top management support, and top management style (MacMillan 1986).

Top Management Commitment

Fast (1981) ascribes lack of top management commitment as a major contributor to the failure of dozens of attempts at corporate venturing in the 1970s. Maidique (1980) argues that regardless of the size or stage of evolution of a firm, venturing will fail if top management

184   MacMILLAN ET AL.

is not commited to change. Quinn and Mueller (1963) suggest that mere statement of commitment is not enough, that success requires tough-minded and constant attention to fostering change in the organization to prevent it from becoming comfortable with the status quo.

Top Management Support

To reinforce management commitment, serious top management support is needed (Quinn 1985). In his comprehensive study, Fast (1979) identified a variety of important ways in which support for venturing activity can be given: by budget allocations (for funds and staff); by indirect budget allocations (by making other departments commit resources); by supporting venture management's proposals; and by siding with venture management when arbitrating conflicts. Fast goes on to suggest that such support is a delicate issue: too much support for venture managers alienates them from the rest of the organization and exposes them politically. Roberts (1980) and Maidique and Hayes (1984) argue that another, critical way of providing support is by assuring that potential ventures can have access to a variety of funding channels rather than to a single, formal route for necessary funds.

Top Management Style

According to researchers, the most critical issue in fostering an entrepreneurial culture lies in management style. Kanter's (1983) research results indicate that internal entrepreneurship cannot thrive in the absence of a flexible and collaborative style. Maidique and Hayes's (1984) multicase study suggests that this open, collaborative climate be accompanied by a management style that encourages rapid attacking of problems, is more tolerant of failure, has high levels of communication across *and* between levels, allows individual workers time to pursue their own ideas, and encourages hands-on management. To these Roberts (1980) would add: management must create an environment in which the burden of proof lies on the people who want to stop a new idea.

In Table 2 another major obstacle unique to corporate start ups was identified: lack of clarity regarding the mission of the venturing activity.

The problem of mission—what should be the scope and reach of new venturing activity?—is a knotty one (MacMillan 1986). Hill and Hlavacek (1972) found that a broad mission was an important correlate for venturing success by new venture teams. By 1977, however, Dunn found that the failed venture divisions in his study had all been given very broad missions.

The resolution of this apparent inconsistency probably lies in the research results of Fast (1979) and Roberts and Berry (1985), which suggest that *relatedness* to the firm's current activities is the important issue when it comes to defining mission: the further away from "base" a firm is, the most likely it will run into problems. Fast suggests that the primary reasons for this are that related activities benefit from three major advantages: maximum skills transfer is possible; the new activity can be implemented with small incremental cost; and high levels of commitment from management are secured with minimal effort.

The final two major obstacles unique to corporate start ups are shown in Table 2: imperfect market analysis and the resulting underestimation of an initial selling effort needed to break into this market. Apparently, firms that launch corporate start ups are prone to enter markets that seem attractive but that are really inappropriate.

Considerable research indicates what to seek by way of appropriate markets. Cooper (1979) and von Hippel (1977) undertook two important studies that systematically compared successful ventures with unsuccessful ones, drawing on the earlier SAPPHO results of Rothwell (1972) and Rothwell et al. (1974). As a result of these studies, market characteristics can be classified into two categories (MacMillan 1986).

1. Inhibiting market conditions: very competitive, dynamic markets (Cooper 1979); markets with rapid rates of new-product introduction (Cooper 1979); markets in which there exists a high proportion of satisfied customers (Cooper 1979; Hobson and Morrison 1983); highly fragmented markets (MacMillan and Day 1985); and markets in which recent major technological innovation has occurred (Hambrick and MacMillan 1985).
2. Facilitating market conditions: high market growth rates (Cooper 1979); customers who know, and interact intensively with, the parent firm (Maidique and Zirger 1984; Quinn 1985); markets rich in technological opportunities (Hambrick and MacMillan 1985); markets in which there are dominant competitors (MacMillan and Day 1985); and markets in which customers initiated the new-product idea (von Hippel 1978).

One of the most important market characteristics, which appears to permeate all these studies, is the degree to which the venture satisfies a clear user need in the target market (Rothwell 1972; Cooper 1979; von Hippel 1977; Maidique and Zirger 1984; Quinn 1985; Rich and Gumpert 1985). E. von Hippel (1977) found that two successes out of three attempts satisfied a market need, whereas six failures out of six attempted to "sell" a technical capability. Maidique and Zirger (1984) point out that a particularly beneficial combination for venturing is a market in which the customer base is well known, interaction between the firm and customer is intense, and market need is real—so that the emerging venture can create a product or service for which benefit to cost is clearly identifiable to both venturers and customers. E. von Hippel (1977) found that the best of all worlds occurs when the user need has high "proximity" to the firm's technological strengths. Roberts (1968) also found support for such technical proximity.

This concludes the discussion of the obstacles encountered by the sample of managers involved in corporate venturing activity. The next issue of interest in the study was whether or not experience benefits exist for those firms that attempt several start ups.

EXPERIENCE EFFECTS AND START-UP PERFORMANCE

As a first step in exploring the experience issue, the responses for corporate start ups were partitioned into two groups: those cases for which three or fewer attempts had been made and those cases for which four or more attempts had been made. Each subsample was then further subdivided into cases wherein the respondents rated the effectiveness of their *most recent venture* as 3 or less or as 4 or more.

The results of this partitioning are reported in Table 3. Experience benefits appear to exist: executives with firms that had made three or fewer attempts at corporate start ups rated their firms much lower in effectiveness than did those whose firms had made four or more attempts. One potential problem here is that the subjective judgment of effectiveness by respondents can easily lead to a significantly higher proportion of "effective" ventures than we are led to believe from the previous research. This optimistic bias, however, should apply equally to inexperienced and experienced venturers, so we concluded that the results in Table 3 are a clear indication that the company that has attempted several ventures does achieve improvement in effectiveness, at least as perceived by the managers involved in corporate start ups. This experience effect only seems to occur after more than three venturing attempts.

186   MacMILLAN ET AL.

TABLE 3   Start-up Experience Versus Effectiveness

	Three Start-Up Attempts or Fewer		Four Start-Up Attempts or More	
	Effectiveness Ratings of 3 or Lower	Effectiveness Ratings of 4 or Higher	Effectiveness Ratings of 3 or Lower	Effectiveness Ratings of 4 or Higher
Number of Corporate Start Ups	5	4	1	15

Companies that made few attempts at start ups (three or fewer)—in other words, companies without experience—were as likely to be rated ineffective as effective.

Companies that made many attempts at start ups (four or more) were rated effective, rather than ineffective ($t = 3.50; p < 0.01$; one-tail test of differences in proportions). In other words, companies with experience were much more likely to be rated effective than ineffective.

Companies that made many attempts at start ups reported significantly more effective start ups than did those that made few ($t = 2.81; p < 0.01$; one-tail test of differences in proportions). In other words, companies with experience in start ups were significantly more effective than were those without experience.

Experience Effects for Specific Obstacles to Start Ups

Our next concern was with the degree to which experience with corporate start ups reduces *specific* obstacles to venture success. To test this, we ran correlations between the number of attempts at startup and respondents' ratings of the degree of difficulty of each of the obstacles. Results are reported in Table 4 (note that Table 4 lists only those cases for which significant correlations between number of attempts and the obstacle were found).

Distinct areas can be identified in which firms are able to "learn" how to overcome

TABLE 4   Correlation Between Experience and Obstacles to Corporate Start Ups[a]

I. Misreading of Market	
Imperfect market analysis	-0.32[b]
Underestimation of competition	-0.49[d]
Underestimation of selling effort	-0.29[b]
Underestimation of reluctance of customer	-0.28[b]
II. Inadequate Corporate Support	
(No significant correlations)	
III. Unrealistic Corporate Expectations	
Overcontrol by corportation	-0.36[c]
Excessive corporate cost allocations	-0.57[c]
Underestimation of risk of venture	-0.26[b]
IV. Inadequate Planning	
Lack of contingency plans	-0.52[d]
No clear definition of failure	-0.29[b]
V. Operational Difficulties	
Debugging time required	-0.53[d]
Incorporation of unit into ongoing operations	-0.32[b]
Venture incurs excessive fixed costs	-0.52[d]

[a]Only significant Pearson coefficients are reported.
[b]$p < 0.1$.
[c]$p < 0.05$.
[d]$p < 0.01$.

obstacles and in which they are not. For instance, firms appear to be able to learn to do a better job of reading the initial market, solving operational problems, and becoming more realistic in their expectations regarding the venture. Firms apparently do not learn from their past inadequacies in planning and particularly cannot learn to provide adequate support for the venture (which reintroduces the previously identified need for creation of supportive entrepreneurial climates in firms).

Factor Analysis of Obstacles

In order to see whether or not the obstacles identified in Table 1 fall into natural groupings, we factor analyzed the responses. Because Table 1 contains a large number of items (27) and small samples sizes for each mode, we pooled all responses (this is to some extent justified by the fact that for only a few items were significant differences in means obtained in Table 1.) The initial factor analysis, with all 27 items, yielded four factors. This analysis was scanned, and items that did not load heavily (< 0.50) on any factor were dropped. Twelve items were retained, and the factor analysis was rerun with these 12 items for the pooled sample of 63 responses.

The four factors that emerged are shown in Table 5: unrealistic corporate expectations, misreading of initial market, inadequate corporate support, and operational distress. These appear to be the four broad classes of problem that our sample of corporate venturers experienced.

As a rough check, the factor analysis was then repeated for the subsample of 24 startups, despite the fact that there were twelve items. Essentially the same four factors were identified, indicating no major differences in the corporate start-up subsample and the pooled sample.

After identifying these four more generic classes of venturing obstacles, we decided to see how they correlated with effectiveness and which of these generic problems benefit from experience effects. The weighted-factor scores, therefore, were calculated for each corporate start-up response and the correlation between this factor score and the respondents' assessment of effectiveness was calculated. In addition, the correlation between number of attempts at start up and effectiveness at the most recent start up was determined.

From Table 6 we see once again that effectiveness of corporate start ups is highly correlated with number of attempts at start up. This is further evidence of an experience effect. There is also a significant negative correlation between effectiveness and the misread factor for start ups. This emphasizes the need for paying serious attention to systematic market analysis before embarking on a venture.

There are also modestly significant negative correlations between unrealistic corporate expectations and effectiveness and operational difficulties and effectiveness, indicating that there also could be significant benefits for firms that devote serious time to thinking through and developing realistic expectations for their ventures and to paying careful attention to operations management.

Table 7 lists the correlations between number of attempts and the weighted-factor scores for each of the factors.

Here we see significant negative correlations between number of attempts and the factors misread and operations: once again indicating an experience benefit gained from reading the market or overcoming operational problems. Most firms, however, do not seem to be able to "learn" to be more realistic in their expectations regarding start ups or to "learn" to provide adequate support to the start ups.

188   MacMILLAN ET AL.

TABLE 5   Results of Final Factor Analysis

	I Corporate Expectations (Expect)	II Misread Market (Misread)	III Corporate Support (Support)	IV Operational Distress (Opers)
Impatience	57	.19	.35	.07
Payback	.62	.11	.08	.03
Definition of failure	.72	.07	.08	.15
Poor market analysis	.46	.60	.12	.19
Underestimated competition	.25	.84	.18	.14
Underestimated effort	−.02	.72	.40	.16
Lack of commitment	.34	.11	.51	−.03
Lack of entrepreneurs	.38	.28	.53	.17
Customer education	−.07	.18	.63	.15
Internal competition	.23	.12	.57	.24
Debugging time	.30	.36	.06	.68
Quality control	.00	.07	.20	.65

TABLE 6   Correlation of Effectiveness with Attempts and Generic Problems[a]

	Attempts	Corporate expectations	Misread market	Corporate support	Operational distress
Correlation with effectiveness	0.76	−0.28	−0.47	−0.10	−0.33
t Values	5.48[d]	−1.37[b]	−2.50[d]	−0.47	−1.64[b]

[a]*N* = 24.
[b]*p* < 0.10 (one-tail test).
[c]*p* < 0.05 (one-tail test).
[d]*p* < 0.01 (one-tail test).

TABLE 7   Correlation of Attempts with Generic Startup Problems[a]

	Corporate expectations	Misread market	Corporate support	Operational distress
Correlation with start-up attempts	−0.20	−0.45	0.13	−0.30
t-Values	−0.96	−2.36[d]	0.61	1.48[b]

[a]*N* = 24.
[b]*p* < 0.10 (one-tail test).
[c]*p* < 0.05 (one-tail test).
[d]*p* < 0.01 (one-tail test).

SUMMARY

Overall, the study has provided us with some interesting insights: we were able to identify a number of obstacles to corporate venturing and identify the degree of seriousness of these obstacles for three different modes of venturing. Managers who pursued a joint venturing mode generally reported less difficulty with these obstacles than did managers pursuing independent start ups. In addition, in most cases managers pursuing the acquisition mode also reported fewer problems with these obstacles than did managers attempting corporate start ups.

For corporate start ups, we found evidence of experience benefits. Managers from experienced firms reported considerably greater effectiveness at start ups, but only those managers in firms that had made three or more attempts at start up.

For corporate start ups we also found evidence of experience benefits for several specific obstacles, especially those in the areas of assessing the market, improving operations, and holding more realistic expectations of the venture. This evidence was further supported when we analyzed the factors for experience effects. On the other hand, little evidence was found to show that companies were able to learn how to plan start ups better or to learn to provide adequate corporate support for such start ups.

IMPLICATIONS FOR MANAGEMENT

The results above have important implications for management, particularly for firms embarking on a venturing mode for the first time. These implications are discussed below.

Joint Venturing is a Seriously Entertainable Alternative

Roberts' advice to explore joint venturing options appears to be well heeded: the results from Table 1 indicate that although obstacles to joint venturing exist, they are consistently fewer than the obstacles to grass-roots start ups, particularly as far as reading initial markets are concerned. Thus, the beginner venturing firm should give serious consideration to "learning its way in" to venturing by initially undertaking joint ventures.

A Deliberate Experience-Building Strategy Can Deliver Benefits

We saw that those managers who reported several start-up experiences also reported a substantial improvement in reported effectiveness. The implications of this for venturing are significant: first, because ventures tend to require substantial resources, a real danger exists that a firm may attempt one or two ventures and then abandon all venturing efforts in despair just as its venture managers are starting to gain experience. Second, the company that is starting to venture may need to be aware that the initial ventures are not likely to be highly successful per se but that the experience benefits can be substantial. This suggests selecting modest initial ventures, with relatively low resource requirements, as a vehicle for "learning" to be effective at venturing.

The fact that the obstacles are generally less severe for joint ventures than for start ups suggests that we can take the idea of deliberately learning to venture one step further: firms can start by joint venturing to assure that maximum initial learning at minimum cost is achieved, particularly because this appears to result in far fewer serious problems of misreading the initial market. Once the necessary experience base is built, the joint-venturing strategy can be abandoned in favor of grass-roots corporate start ups.

Capitalize on Experience Benefits

Table 4 indicated several areas in which experience benefits seemed to accrue to the survey respondents. In particular, firms appear to learn not to misread their market, not to expect too much too soon, and to manage their launch operations more effectively. It may be

190   MacMILLAN ET AL.

possible to capitalize on these benefits by consciously managing this learning. Much more effective and rapid learning can take place if the management consciously and systematically treats every success and failure in the venture as data points from which to extract as much learning as possible. Creating an atmosphere in which constant attention is given to learning why things went, or did not go, as planned is therefore important.

Recognize and Manage the Blind Spots in the System

Table 4 also indicated that the large firm appears unable to learn to plan ventures well or to provide enough support. If it can't learn by experience then it must learn by conscious management of those problems. Corporate officers and venture managers alike should pay inordinate and special attention to these two issues before a venture is launched. Block (1982) asserts adamantly that planning based on normal business operations is inadequate due to the inherent uncertainties involved in venturing. Planning according to a purely temporal budget is inappropriate: like venture capitalists, firms should plan according to key milestones, with designated commitments of resources to each stage. This is probably the only realistic approach for start ups.

A different and possibly more appropriate approach to new venture "planning" might be to utilize the milestone-triggered process described by Block (1982): after establishing objectives for the venture, the significant milestones that are required to reach each of these objectives are defined. Planning should then be focused on getting from milestone to milestone, with subsequent resource allocations dependent on what is *learned* with each successive milestone achievement or failure. Evaluation of the venture managers should then be based on their resourcefulness and their ability to learn and adapt to the emerging realities, rather than to ability to plan and to meet that plan.

CONCLUSION

In concluding, if we can assume that the experience factor indicated in this study does produce learning and improved venture performance, management options are clear for the firm with little experience in venturing:

- Start with joint ventures if at all possible;
- Start with small ventures;
- Expect some early failures and consciously use them to learn;
- Look for evidence of improvement after three or four ventures; and
- Make sure that the experience is not lost by removing the people who are learning from it.

REFERENCES

Biggadike, R. May-June 1979. The risky business of diversification. *Harvard Business Review* 103–111.

Block, Z. Fall 1982. Can corporate venturing succeed? *Journal of Business Strategy* 3(2):21–33.

Block, Z., and MacMillan, I. Sept./Oct. 1985. Growing concern: Milestones for successful venture planning. *Harvard Business Review*.

Burgelman, R.A. 1983. A process model of internal corporate venturing in the diversified major firm. *Administrative Science Quarterly* 28:223–244.

Cooper, R.G. Summer 1979. The dimensions of industrial new product success and failure. *Journal of Marketing* 43:93–103.

Dunn, D.T. Oct. 1977. The rise and fall of ten new venture groups. *Business Horizons* 32–41.

Fast, N.D. March 1981. Pitfalls of corporate venturing. *Research Management* 21–24.

Fast, N.D. 1979. The future of industrial new venture departments. *Industrial Marketing Management* 8:264–273.

Hambrick, D.C., and MacMillan, I.C. 1985. Efficiency of product research and development in business units: The role of strategic context. *Academy of Management Journal* 28(3):527–547.

Hill, R.M., and Hlavacek, J.D. 1977. Learning from failure: Ten guidelines for venture management. *California Management Review* 19(4):5–23.

Hill, R.M., and Hlavacek, J.D. July 1972. The venture team: A new concept in marketing organization. *Journal of Marketing* 36:44–50.

Hlavacek, J.D., and Thompson, V.A. April 1975. Bureaucracy and venture failure. *Academy of Management Review*.

Hobson, E.L., and Morrison, R.M. 1983. How do corporate start-up ventures fare? *Frontiers of Entrepreneurship Research*. Wellesley, Mass.: Babson College, pp. 390–410.

Kanter, R.M. 1983. *The Change Masters*. New York: Simon and Schuster.

Kitching, J. Nov.-Dec. 1967. Why mergers miscarry. *Harvard Business Review* 84–97.

MacMillan, I.C., and Day, D.L. Jan. 1985. Corporate venturing into industrial product businesses: Agressive entry can pay. Working Paper: New York University Center for Entrepreneurial Studies. New York.

MacMillan, I.C. 1986. Progress in research on corporate venturing. In Sexton D.L. and Smilor, R.W: The Art and Science of Entrepreneurship. Cambridge, MA: Ballinger.

Maidique, M.A. Winter 1980. Entrepreneurs, champions and technological innovation. *Sloan Management Review*.

Maidique, M.A., and Hayes, R.H. Winter 1984. The art of high-technology management. *Sloan Management Review* 17–31.

Maidique, M.A., and Zirger, B.J. Nov. 1984. The Stanford Innovation Project, Phase 1: A study of success and failure in high technology innovation. *IEEE Transactions on Engineering Management* EM-31(4):192–203.

Myers, S., and Sweezy, E.E. March-April 1978. Why innovations fail. *Technology Review* 40–46.

Quinn, J.B. May-June 1985. Managing innovation: Controlled chaos. *Harvard Business Review* 73–84.

Quinn, J.B., and Mueller, J.A. Jan.-Feb. 1963. Transferring research results to operations. *Harvard Business Review* 49–66.

Rich, S.R., and Gumpert, D.E. May-June 1985. How to write a winning business plan. *Harvard Business Review* 156–163.

Roberts, E.B. July-Aug. 1980. New ventures for corporate growth. *Harvard Business Review* 134–142.

Roberts, E.B. 1968. A basic study of innovators: how to keep and capitalize on their talents. *Research Management* 11(4):249–266.

Roberts, E.B., and Berry, C.A. Spring 1985. Entering new businesses: Selecting strategies for success. *Sloan Management Review* 3–17.

Rothwell, R. 1972. Factors for success in industrial innovations. In *Project SAPPHO—A Comparative Study of Successes and Failures in Industrial Innovation*. Brighton, England: SPRU.

Rothwell, R., Freeman, C., Horsley, A., Jervis, V.T.P., Robertson, A.B., and Townsend, J. 1974. SAPPHO updated—Project SAPPHO phase II. *Research Policy* 3:258–291.

Schon, D.A. March-April 1963. Champions for radical new inventions. *Harvard Business Review* 77–86.

Shapero, A. 1984. Intracorporate entrepreneurship: A clash of cultures. Working Paper: Ohio State University.

von Hippel, E. Jan. 1978. Successful industrial products from customer ideas. *Journal of Marketing* 39–49.

von Hippel, E. 1977. Successful and failing internal corporate ventures: An empirical analysis. *Industrial Marketing Management* 6:163–174.

Weiss, L.E. Fall 1981. Start-up businesses: A comparison of performances. *Sloan Management Review* 23(1):37–53.

[9]

1042-2587-02-263$1.50

Exploring the Practice of Corporate Venturing: Some Common Forms and Their Organizational Implications

Morgan P. Miles
Jeffrey G. Covin

This study explores the domain of corporate venturing using a theoretically grounded classification typology as an organizing scheme. The typology is applied in a field study of
corporations that are active in venturing and based in the United Kingdom or the United
States. Corporate venturing is classified into four generic forms by the focus of entrepreneurship and the presence of investment intermediation: (1) direct-internal venturing; (2)
direct-external venturing; (3) indirect-internal venturing; and (4) indirect-external venturing.
A managerial decision framework is offered to assist corporate executives in selecting
potentially appropriate forms of corporate venturing, given specific venturing objectives
and corporate circumstances.

Corporate entrepreneurship's (CE) potential to rejuvenate and revitalize corporations is often and increasingly acknowledged. Top executives are commonly viewing CE
as an important tool for business development, revenue growth, and as a promising path
to enhance financial returns (see, for example, Rind, 1981; Sykes, 1986; Block &
MacMillan, 1993; Chesbrough, 2000). Hamel (2000) proposes that constantly increasing
shareholder expectations are causing many corporations to view CE as an essential
mechanism for creating new markets through revolutionary business concept innovation.
Academic interest in CE has also increased, and empirical evidence now regularly
suggests that various forms and manifestations of CE are often linked to enhanced
financial performance (for example, see Naman & Slevin, 1993; Zahra & Covin, 1995;
Morris & Sexton, 1996; Knight, 1997, 2000; Wiklund, 1999).

Associated with the increased practitioner and academic attention to CE is an ac-
companying recognition that the effective practice of CE involves some risks and non-
obvious choices. For example, CE often operates as a "strategic lever," potentially
amplifying the reputational and financial implications of both fortunate and less fortunate decisions. Two high-profile companies illustrate this point: Lucent and Procter &
Gamble. Writings by Chesbrough and Socolof (2000), Leifer, McDermott, O'Connor,
Peters, Rice, and Veryzer (2000), and others suggest that Lucent is something of an
exemplar in the arena of corporate venturing, having received much recognition in the
business press for its New Ventures Group. Whitney's (1997) case study and substantial
anecdotal evidence reported by Pearson (1992) and others suggest that Procter & Gamble
is an equally active participant in the corporate venturing arena. However, shareholders

and employees in both companies have recently suffered tremendous financial losses, resulting in both Lucent's and Procter & Gamble's CEOs being replaced. The failure of these executives has been attributed to their inability to fully comprehend and manage the potential risks and negative consequences of adopting venturing as a regular part of their firms' business activity (see, for example, Ip & Bryan-Low, 2000; Jarvis, 2000; Young & Lubin, 2000).

Moreover, from an academic standpoint, solid theoretical frameworks and empirically grounded, managerially useful prescriptions involving CE have not progressed as quickly as enthusiasm for the practice (see, for example, Amit, Glosten, & Muller, 1993; Bygrave, 1993; Guth, 1995; Brazeal & Herbert, 1999). In short, while the value-creating potential of CE is increasingly recognized, current knowledge regarding the role, risks, and effective conduct of entrepreneurial activities in corporations remains quite limited.

The present study was designed to extend the CE knowledge base through the development of a typology that describes the domain of one manifestation of CE: corporate venturing. Based on a review of the previous corporate venturing research, interview data derived from a field study of corporate venturing practitioners, and anecdotes from the popular press, this article was prepared with two specific purposes in mind: (1) to identify the benefits, risks, and prescriptions associated with the conduct of four generic forms of corporate venturing; and (2) to propose a tentative decision framework for choosing among these four forms based on the cumulative results of current observations.

MAPPING THE DOMAIN OF CORPORATE VENTURING

Many writers on the topic of corporate venturing have recognized that such activity can be either internally or externally focused. For example, Sharma and Chrisman (1999, pp. 19-20) propose that external venturing "refers to corporate venturing activities that result in the creation of semi-autonomous or autonomous organizational entities that reside outside the existing organizational domain," while internal ventures are "activities that result in the creation of organizational entities that reside within an existing organizational domain." Likewise, Ginsberg and Hay (1994), for example, categorized venturing as one approach to CE based on the focus of entrepreneurship (internal or external to the organization) and the level of integration with the firm (fully integrated or as an autonomous unit).

Among those who recognize the internal-external distinctions in the focus of venturing, there are differences in the requirement that the venture activity must have originated within the firm. Sharma and Chrisman (1999, p. 19) defined corporate venturing as "entrepreneurial efforts that lead to the creation of new business organizations within the corporate organization." By contrast, Withers (1995, 1997) conceptualizes venturing as a vehicle for infusing into corporations dynamic, entrepreneurial activities that originated in independent entrepreneurial firms. Rind (1981) developed a "spectrum of corporate venturing strategies" ranging from internal ventures that are directly controlled by the corporation to equity investing in new external ventures. Sykes's (1986) study of Exxon's corporate venturing activities confirmed the importance of externally originating entrepreneurial activity as part of a firm's venturing strategy. The corporate venturing typology adopted in the current research is consistent with this recognition that corporate venturing can involve businesses that originated inside or outside the organization.

The presence of investment intermediation is another variable of relevance in the context of corporate venturing, and a variable around which a venturing typology might be developed. For example, Withers (1995) categorizes the principal modes of corporate venturing by the presence of investment intermediation. Specifically, corporate venturing may occur in the form of direct investment of capital by the larger firm in the smaller firm (typically combined with management assistance and technology sharing) or indirect corporate venturing, where the larger firm invests in a venture capital fund that serves as a financial intermediary between the corporation and the entrepreneurial ventures in which the investments are made.

Thus, investment intermediation, in the context of corporate venturing, can be described as present when an independent financial investment mechanism (i.e., a financial investment mechanism operating outside the corporation's operating or strategic budgets, typically a venture capital fund) links the corporation and the venture itself. The presence of investment intermediation in corporate venturing is largely a function of the corporation's (1) level of commitment to entrepreneurial initiatives; (2) preferred degree of control over the initiatives; (3) ability to accept and manage entrepreneurial risks; and (4) desired level of market diversification (e.g., Jolly & Kayama, 1990). Investment intermediaries add value to the venturing activity of the corporation by, for example, (1) pooling funds from various sources, resulting in diversification and the amelioration of risks faced by corporate investors; (2) minimizing the costs to the corporation of due diligence assessments; and (3) subjecting the venture to objective, market-based assessments. In the past, firms such as Exxon, General Electric, DuPont, and AT&T made sizable investments in corporate venture capital funds (see, for example, Rind, 1981; Hardymon, DeNino, & Salter, 1983; Sykes, 1986). Currently, firms such as Lucent, 3M, Nortel Networks, and Procter & Gamble, among many others, are major venture capital investors (see Chesbrough, 2000; Chesbrough & Socolof, 2000; Leifer et al., 2000; Rice, O'Connor, Leifer, McDermott, & Standish-Kuon, 2000).

The present study builds on prior corporate venturing theory and research in creating a classification typology that frames the diverse scope of potential venturing activities. The authors propose that the domain of corporate venturing can be captured by a typology consisting of four generic forms of corporate venturing, partitioned by (1) the focus of entrepreneurship (internal to the firm vs. external to the firm [adapted from Rind, 1981; Sykes, 1986; Jolly & Kayama, 1990; Ginsberg & Hay, 1994; McNally, 1997; Sharma & Chrisman, 1999]) and (2) the presence of investment intermediation between the corporate parent and the venture (from the corporation directly investing in the venture to an indirect investment made through an independent venture fund [adapted from Rind, 1981; Hardymon, DeNino, & Salter, 1983; Sykes, 1986; Withers, 1995, 1997]). Selected classification frameworks from previous studies are summarized in Table 1. Table 2 summarizes the proposed classification framework, which includes (1) direct-internal venturing; (2) direct-external venturing; (3) indirect-internal venturing; and (4) indirect-external venturing. Table 3 offers summary definitions of the four forms of corporate venturing.

THE STUDY

This article is part of a long-term project aimed at delineating the generic benefits and risks of various forms of corporate venturing. The first phase of this project entailed an extensive review of the literature pertaining to corporate venturing and resulted in the development of the previously discussed typology of corporate venturing forms. In the second phase of this project, the corporate venturing typology was applied in a field study to better understand how corporate venturing is currently being practiced. The field study consisted of a series of 24 extensive personal interviews and 21 site visits with executives from 11 firms that had been identified by both the researchers and the

Table 1

A Comparison of Selected Typologies of Corporate Venturing

Author	Types of Corporate Venture Activities	Key Classification Dimension[s]
Roberts (1980)	Venture capital Venture nurturing Venture spin-off New-style joint ventures Venture merging & melding Internal venturing	Required corporate involvement
Rind (1981)	New venture division Wholly-owned ventures New-style joint ventures Direct venture capital	Required corporate management attention
Sykes (1986)	Internal ventures Venture capital investments	Internal or external to the corporation
Jolly & Kayama (1990)	Company-wide task forces Informal, voluntary teams Corporate support staff New venture department New venture company	Level of corporate control Internal or external to the corporation
Ginsberg & Hay (1994)	Internal corporate venturing Entrepreneurial partnering	Where the focus of entrepreneurial activity resides
Sharma & Chrisman (1999)	External corporate venturing Internal corporate venturing	Where the new venture resides

sponsors of the study as having a long-term and active interest in corporate venturing. The firms targeted in the study include AT&T's Cambridge Research Lab, British Gas Technology, British Telecom, Cable & Wireless, Chevron, The Generics Group, GM/ Saturn, Minnesota Mining and Manufacturing (3M), Procter & Gamble, The Technology Partnership, and Unilever. Top executives from eight ventures associated with the corporations studied were also interviewed to gain insight from the perspective of venture

Table 2

A Typology of Corporate Venturing

		Presence of Investment Intermediation	
		Direct Investment in the Venture through the Corporation's Operating or Strategic Budgets	Indirect Investment in the Venture Using Financial Intermediaries
Focus of Entrepreneurship	Internal to the Corporation	Direct-Internal Venturing	Indirect-Internal Venturing
	External to the Corporation	Direct-External Venturing	Indirect-External Venturing

Table 3

Summary Definitions of the Four Forms of Corporate Venturing

Form of Venturing	Defining Characteristics
Direct-Internal	New ventures are funded without financial intermediation (directly through the operating or strategic budgets) and developed within the domain of the corporation by corporate employees.
Direct-External	The corporation, without using a dedicated new venture fund, acquires or takes an equity position in an external venture.
Indirect-Internal	The corporation invests in a venture capital fund designed to encourage corporate employees to develop internal ventures. The venture capital fund typically originates and operates within the corporation and is managed by corporate employees.
Indirect-External	The corporation invests in a venture capital fund that targets external ventures in specific industries or technology sectors. The venture capital fund may originate outside the corporation and be managed by persons who are not corporate employees, or the fund may originate within the corporation and be managed by corporate employees.

managers. In addition, opportunistic discussions were held with government policy-makers, venture capitalists, and industry experts to understand more fully the art and practice of corporate venturing.

An "enquiring" qualitative analysis technique, based on Savage and Black's (1995) discussion of firm-level epistemological strategies, was utilized when conducting the interviews. This technique involves the use of open-ended interviews that allow for probing follow-on questions. Each interview was begun using a structured protocol of general questions pertaining to corporate venturing activities. The interviews evolved based on the executives' responses to the open-ended questions. Extensive notes were taken to fully capture the data, and each executive was provided the opportunity to read and correct a written transcript of the interview. To ensure the accuracy of the collected data, executives were contacted when there were apparent discrepancies between publicly published material and their responses.

It is important to note that the corporations studied were not pre-selected to conform to any *a priori* distribution within the typology's cells, but were included based on their interest in and experience with corporate venturing. Moreover, typed summaries of the interviews and a draft of this article were made available to the interviewees to ensure accuracy in how the firm's venturing activities were described and classified. Classification of a firm into one or more of the forms of corporate venturing required consensus among authors (who independently and identically sorted the firms based on the interview transcripts) and the interviewees.

The interviews took place in the United States and the United Kingdom during the latter half of 1999. Key events and theoretically significant data (e.g., new product introductions, acquisition announcements) were corroborated when possible with additional materials provided from publicly available sources such as the corporation's homepage and annual reports, published articles, interviews, and cases, and regulatory filings, such as securities and tax documents. A list of the questions used as the protocol for the corporate manager and venture manager interviews will be furnished by the authors on request.

THE FOUR FORMS TYPOLOGY OF CORPORATE VENTURING

Corporations often concurrently engage in multiple forms of venturing. Nonetheless, the four forms of corporate venturing are discussed separately below in order to elucidate their fundamental differences. Table 4 identifies the forms of corporate venturing associated with the corporations that participated in the field study.

Direct-Internal Venturing

The simplest form of corporate venturing, where employees with a business idea are permitted or encouraged to develop and then commercially exploit that idea within the corporate structure, is termed direct-internal venturing. Direct-internal venturing implies that the idea was generated within the corporation and funded, developed, and commercialized utilizing internal resources.

A good example from the current study of the effective use of the direct-internal form of venturing is provided by The Generics Group, a small, highly innovative technology design and development firm. The Generics Group has a policy of accepting

Table 4

Study Firms by Modes of Corporate Venturing

Mode of Corporate Venturing	Corporation
Direct-Internal	AT&T Lab, Cambridge
	British Gas Technology (B-G)
	British Telecom (BT)
	Cable & Wireless (C&W)
	GM/Saturn
	Procter & Gamble (P&G)
	The Generics Group
	The Technology Partnership (TTP)
	3M
	Unilever
Indirect-Internal	British Telecom (BT)
	Procter & Gamble (P&G)
	The Generics Group
	The Technology Partnership (TTP)
	3M
Direct-External	AT&T Lab, Cambridge
	British Gas Technology (B-G)
	Cable & Wireless (C&W)
	Chevron
	The Generics Group
	The Technology Partnership (TTP)
	3M
Indirect-External	British Gas Technology (B-G)
	British Telecom (BT)
	Cable & Wireless (C&W)
	Chevron
	GM/Saturn
	Procter & Gamble (P&G)
	The Generics Group
	The Technology Partnership (TTP)
	3M
	Unilever

consulting projects based, in part, on the synergistic venturing opportunities the projects may create. The intellectual capital and capabilities gained through The Generics Group's technology consulting are often leveraged to develop new ventures, ultimately creating additional value for The Generics Group's shareholders. The Generics Group's venturing experience fits well with Dougherty's (1995) observations on the symbiotic interactions between a corporation's core competencies and the creation of new internal ventures.

3M is well known for its long-standing support of direct-internal venturing (see, for example, Rind, 1981; Rice et al., 2000). 3M has a management control system that allocates business resources to support the creation and development of innovation ideas and "formal business project" funds that support subsequent commercialization. 3M also encourages "autonomous" innovation by designating 15% of its technical personnel's time as slack time that may be used to pursue pet innovation projects.

Other organizations, such as AT&T's Cambridge Research Lab (AT&T's European-based R&D organization that is focused on the development of communications technology), rely primarily on emergent (vs. planned) entrepreneurial behavior and have a much more informal, but highly successful, venturing philosophy. Managers at the Cambridge Research Lab (CRL) mentioned during their interview that internally originating entrepreneurial projects with high commercial potential tend to "float to the top," are internally supported and funded, and may even be given priority over more conventional or explicitly induced work. Alan Jones, one of AT&T's CRL executives, suggested that to CRL a new venture is simply an innovative "technology seeking a market."

Based on the authors' collective observations, direct-internal venturing appears to offer two primary advantages over other forms of venturing: (1) it can create real options by developing the organization's capabilities, tangible resources, and intangible resources, such as tacit knowledge (see, for example, Kogut & Kulatilaka, 1994; McGrath 1995, 1997, 1999; Luehrman, 1998); and (2) the innovative activities associated with venturing can help make autonomous entrepreneurial behavior acceptable and bring about desirable cultural change and human resource development within the organization. Combined, these advantages can help a firm to better recognize and exploit entrepreneurial opportunities. Procter & Gamble's and Saturn's experiences demonstrate these points.

Procter & Gamble induces direct-internal venturing through a formal support program designed to encourage intrapreneurs to constantly refresh the corporation's product mix and re-energize the innovation-inducing aspects of the corporate culture. Mike Clasper, President of P&G's Global Home Care and New Business Development Division, stated that P&G wants "venturing to help (1) enhance sales; (2) create new behavior-changing/frame-breaking brands; and (3) change the corporate culture at P&G, making it faster and more innovative." Moreover, direct-internal venturing provides brand managers an attractive alternative to traditional product development and family branding for corporations attempting to enter new markets or capitalize on new technologies. Specifically, risks to brand equity can be managed by using direct-internal venturing to create venture-specific "stand-alone" brands when entering new product, market, technology, or regulatory arenas. Hence, direct-internal venturing allows the corporation to preserve its hard-won brand equity and corporate reputation by creating an alternative brand to compete with or supplement its core brand in specific markets.

Saturn was designed as the organizational vehicle created to revolutionize GM's new small car strategy. Saturn was developed as an autonomous company and was an alternative to the previous GM small car product development projects in terms of branding strategy, organizational structure, culture, research and development, technology, production, human resource management, and marketing (Stavro, 1985; Lewandowski & MacKinnon, 1992; Taylor, 1993). Aaker (1994, p. 130) observed that "the Saturn miracle simply would not have happened at Chevrolet," it required a separate and autonomous organizational structure. Saturn was conceived as a business experiment with a unique business orientation, directed at different markets, and with technologies and management systems that are vastly different from those of the corporate parent, GM. Roger Smith, former chair of GM, "conceived the Saturn project as a laboratory in which to re-invent" GM and its culture (Hartley, 1995, p. 259).

Despite the aforementioned benefits of direct-internal venturing, this venturing form is the most costly in terms of managerial involvement. Resource commitments also tend to be high, since widespread "slack" must often be created to allow for independent, employee-driven creative activities. Moreover, venture intrapreneurs who do not feel highly valued and supported by the corporation may choose to leave the corporation, often starting rival businesses (Pinchot, 1985).

Direct-internal venturing can also contribute to intra- and inter-departamental conflicts and "turf wars," often fueled by disagreements over how corporate funds should be allocated. Bill Betts, manager of corporate communications for Saturn, mentioned during his interview that at GM there were many turf battles over the resources that were going to support Saturn, and there is still resentment by some mainstream GM people who want Saturn brought back into the larger corporation.

The fear of failure and corresponding unwillingness to accept the risks of venturing are two common and related problems associated with both direct and indirect forms of internal venturing. These problems surfaced in numerous interviews, including those with executives from British Gas Technology, Chevron, P&G, Cable & Wireless, and Unilever. Successful direct-internal venturing demands an explicit and honest discussion and a shared understanding of the likelihood and consequences of venture failure. Regarding the likelihood of failure, British Gas's manager for corporate venturing, Richard Rudman, stated that "B-G feels that out of 100 (potential) deals, 3 would be profitable." Biggadike's (1979) study of the performance of Fortune 500 firms' internal corporate venturing suggests that "it takes an average of 10 to 12 years before the ROI of the ventures equals that of mature businesses," and ventures typically do not exhibit positive returns until years 7 or 8. However, as McGrath (1999) notes and Chesbrough (2000) supports, there is growing evidence that entrepreneurial failure often results in the firms "falling forward" by generating and retaining valuable new tacit knowledge, insights, and a better understanding of what Dougherty (1995) terms "core incompetencies." A large display at the 3M Innovation Center in Bracknell, England, has put the consequences of failure into proper perspective. In the words of William McKnight, a former CEO of 3M,

> Mistakes will be made. But if a person is essentially right, the mistakes he or she makes are not as serious in the long run as the mistakes management will make if it undertakes to tell those in authority exactly how they must do their job. Management that is destructively critical when mistakes are made kills initiative, and it is essential that we have many people with initiative if we are to grow.

To conclude, direct-internal venturing is the most researched form of venturing (see, for example, von Hippel, 1977; Fast, 1979, 1981; Roberts, 1980; Rind, 1981; Burgelman, 1983a, b, c, 1984a, b; Roberts & Berry, 1985; Sykes, 1986; Block & MacMillan, 1993; David, 1994; Simon, Houghton, & Gurney, 1999; Chesbrough, 2000; Chesbrough & Socolof, 2000; Leifer et al., 2000; Rice et al., 2000; Thornhill & Amit, 2001). Nonetheless, many of this form's advantages, including the ability to create desirable cultural change, generate new tacit knowledge, and develop real options, while prominent themes in the authors' interviews, have not been given equivalent attention in the literature. As such, these foci would appear to be potentially fruitful themes for future research.

Direct-External Venturing

Direct-external venturing takes place when, without using a dedicated new venture fund, a corporation acquires or purchases equity in an external entrepreneurial firm, often with the objective of facilitating the transfer of technology, resources, capabilities between the business entities. The specific relationship a corporation has with an external venture can be quite varied. Roberts (1980), for example, suggests that corporations may simply provide funding in exchange for equity in the external venture or provide much more (including, for example, management and technical assistance) and, thereby, enter into a "nurturing" relationship with the venture. Direct-external venturing may also include corporate "partnering" where larger companies develop strategic partnerships with smaller, more entrepreneurial firms, as in Landau's (1987) description of the 1966 partnership between Atlantic Richfield (ARCO) and Halcon. This venturing effort provided the smaller firm, Halcon, with enhanced access to capital and markets, and ARCO with innovative technologies and entrepreneurial management.

Anecdotal evidence suggests that partnering, whereby the corporate parent has a "hands-on" relationship with the external venture, may be an increasingly common manifestation of the direct-external form of venturing. Sahakian (1998) suggests that partnering with smaller firms can provide larger corporations with enhanced flexibility, increased market share, and potential access to new competencies. Moreover, the financial promise of corporate investments in external ventures seems to be a key driver of the growing corporate interest in external venturing. Chan, Kensinger, Keown, and Martin (1997) documented the pecuniary benefits of partnering for corporate parents. The hope of realizing consistently superior rates of return has recently attracted many corporations to the direct-external form of venturing. By "spiking their portfolios" with strategically related external business investments, corporations are sometimes able to realize tremendous financial success (Ip, McWilliams, & McGee, 2000). However, among the firms we interviewed, the anticipated financial benefits of direct-external venturing were often downplayed relative to the more strategic benefits. Our interview with Graham Wylie, CEO of XAAR PLC, exemplifies this point.

XAAR is a small, entrepreneurial firm that, at the time of the study, was the only source of marketable technology for ink jet printing (HP and Canon will not license their technology). One of XAAR's major Japanese customers, Dainippon Screen (DNS), took an equity position in XAAR prior to the float of XAAR's IPO in 1997. DNS's direct-external venture investment in XAAR greatly enhanced XAAR's financial reputation, providing much-needed credibility prior to XAAR's IPO. The financial and reputational value of this well-timed equity investment in XAAR by DNS was tremendous and contributed to XAAR's very successful IPO float. Significantly, Graham Wylie felt that while DNS fully understood the reputational value to XAAR of its equity investment, DNS viewed the investment as primarily a relationship-building tool and not simply a financial investment. According to Wylie, DNS had no intention of simply "putting the stock (XAAR's) in a drawer, and forgetting about it." Rather, DNS's equity investment was viewed by both parties as a way to nurture the strategic relationship between DNS and XAAR.

Direct-external corporate venturing has numerous general advantages for the large corporation, including (i) access to new markets, innovative technologies, and other forms of learning through the relationship with the smaller firm; (2) enhanced reputation, particularly for "old economy" companies that partner with innovative "new economy" firms (creating a "bricks and clicks" partnership); (3) potential tax benefits in certain regulatory environments; (4) enhanced potential for financial gain, and (5) enhanced access to acquisition candidates (see, for example, Roberts, 1980; Siegel, Siegel, & MacMillan, 1988; Inland Revenue, 1999). Not surprisingly, some organizations, such as the Confederation of British Industry (CBI, 1999), regard external venturing as the most promising form of corporate venturing.

The downside risks associated with direct-external venturing are few. However, the risks are potentially significant. One major risk area involves the potential to damage the corporation's reputation and the possibility of legal liability if there are differences in the social, environmental, or ethical conduct of the large corporation and its smaller partner. Corporate reputation is a valuable but fragile intangible asset that can influence a corporation's ability to create wealth for its shareholders (see Caves & Porter, 1977; Chauvin & Hirschey, 1994; Lusch & Harvey, 1994; Fombrun, 1996; Miles & Covin, 2000). While a study by Robideaux, Miles, and White (1993) found no empirical evidence that smaller, entrepreneurial U.S. firms behave in a less socially responsible manner than large U.S. corporations, the risk to the large corporation's reputation and relationships with its stakeholders, nonetheless, must be considered in the venturing decision. The effect on the large corporation's reputation is increasingly salient with multinational venture relationships becoming more accepted in the race to reach global markets. Major corporations must realize that venture partners from diverse cultures may face quite different cultural, ethical, and regulatory constraints and often have very different expectations of the other partner's behavior.

A second type of downside risk pertaining to direct-external venturing is when internal stakeholders perceive they are not obtaining their "fair share" of resources due to the external venture investments made by the corporation. In times of capital rationing or periods of cost cutting, direct-external venturing may cause conflicts over capital and other resource allocations within the corporation. For example, one of the study's firms, Cable & Wireless (a large British telecommunications firm) closed its Silicon Valley-based venturing operation, C&W Innovation, due to C&W Innovation's inability to justify its resource allocation policies. Other business units competing for scarce resources within Cable & Wireless perceived that C&W Innovation was not being held accountable to the same corporate financial performance standards as the rest of the corporation. Since C&W Innovation's funding was part of the larger corporation's regular operating budget, the rest of the corporation granted no special allowances for the unit's poor financial performance.

A third issue with direct-external venturing relates to corporate governance and the level of diversification corporate stockholders prefer. Zahra (1996), in a recent empirical study of the relationship between the components of corporate entrepreneurship, corporate governance mechanisms, and ownership in large U.S. industrial corporations, found that venturing was positively and strongly related to high levels of executive ownership and institutional ownership. Zahra's (1996) research suggests that corporate executives, due to a lack of career mobility, may promote corporate entrepreneurship as a path to diversify the firm's holdings and manage their personal portfolio risks. This suggests that when managers promote direct-external venturing, it may be simply to benefit themselves and not in the best interests of the stockholders. In addition, stockholders may prefer to directly invest their funds into small, entrepreneurial firms without the costs added by the corporation's due diligence requirements.

Overall, our field study and related anecdotal evidence suggest that direct-external venturing is most effective when used to create mutually beneficial long-term strategic relationships between organizations with complementary capabilities and resources. The synergism created may enhance the larger corporation's ability to recognize and exploit entrepreneurial opportunities while providing the smaller firm with needed resources, relationships, and capabilities. However, prior to engaging in direct-external venturing, both parties should carefully consider their shareholders' preferences as well as the relationship's potential impact on corporate reputation and internal budgeting and control processes.

Indirect-Internal Venturing

Indirect-internal venturing occurs when the corporation invests in a venture capital fund designed to encourage corporate employees to develop internal ventures. The venture capital fund typically originates and operates within the corporation and is managed by corporate employees. The primary difference between direct-internal and indirect-internal venturing is the source of venture support and funding. If the entrepreneurial activities are directly supported by the corporation through its operating or strategic budgets, then the activity is direct-internal venturing. However, if there is a separate, independent investment intermediary that functions as an internal corporate venturing fund, then the venturing is termed indirect-internal. This investment intermediary could be a "captive fund," owned by the corporation, funded with corporate resources, and managed by a corporate-wide venture board (see, for example, Leifer et al., 2000); or it could be organized as a partnership between the corporation and external venture capital investors (see, for example, Kambil, Eselius, & Monteiro, 2000).

3M has adopted the indirect-internal form of venturing. Specifically, 3M utilizes competitive innovation grants called Alpha/Genesis grants where there is a dedicated source of funding that operates internally and autonomously (i.e., separate from the operating budget) at the corporate level. Procter & Gamble's approach to indirect-internal venturing is similar to 3M's in that a separate corporate-level fund is potentially accessible by ventures that are not able to garner sufficient support through traditional funding sources. Notably, P&G's venturing support system is based on the recognition that most internal ventures tend to be merely adaptations and extensions of the status quo. P&G uses indirect-internal venturing mechanisms to support dynamic "frame-breaking, industry creating" ventures. Mike Clasper, President of P&G's Global Home Care and New Business Development Business Division, stated that

> In (P&G's) Global Home Care unit there are groups right under the president in charge of 'designing the future' and a group assigned with maintaining on-going and current operations. They are not the same teams. P&G feels that if there is not a separate 'Corporate New Venture' group, innovations will be mostly incremental and not behavior and/or frame breaking innovations.

With its autonomous, corporate-level new venture group, P&G is trying to change its culture. Whitney (1997) reports on the creation and development of P&G's centralized Corporate New Ventures department (CNV) and how it was designed to revitalize P&G's culture and product mix. The CNV department serves as an autonomous venturing organization, where projects that cannot get adequate support in the more mainstream global business units can be considered for venture funding at the corporate level.

Indirect-internal venturing has the advantage of encouraging "bottom-up" or emergent entrepreneurial behavior. In some companies (e.g., 3M) the venture champion's direct supervisor need not be "in the loop" unless the venture proposal is funded. This can reduce the fear of failure and encourage more employees to consider venturing, potentially creating a more entrepreneurial cultural. Moreover, as in the case of two of the firms studied (The Technology Partnership and The Generics Group), funds provided by the investment intermediary can sometimes be used to buy the venture teams' time back from their former business units, thus allowing the teams to devote all their efforts to the entrepreneurial project.

Reliance on a specific form of indirect-internal venturing may also increase the speed with which corporations introduce new ventures. Kambil et al. (2000) discuss how the financial and operating involvement of certain external partners in a corporation's new business creation activity can often hasten the start-up process. In particular, Kambil et al. (2000) note that the involvement of external equity partners with experience relevant to the corporation's new ventures can often reduce business ramp-up time when the venture differs significantly in its technological or market focus from its corporate parent.

On the negative side, the risks and costs associated with direct-internal venturing, discussed previously, also apply to indirect-internal venturing. To reiterate, some of the more significant concerns include the possibility of significant financial losses as well as the potential for debilitating conflict between the new venture and established units. Additionally, the possible involvement of an external equity partner in the corporation's internal business creation activity will typically necessitate the sharing of financial rewards with that partner, which can create resentment among company insiders who would have preferred to engage in independent venturing.

On the whole, what makes indirect-internal venturing particularly attractive is the forced objectivity of an "independent" third party assessment—i.e., the venture capital unit's assessment—of the feasibility of the venture and its value in the market. The aforementioned problems notwithstanding, indirect-internal venturing ideally results in new business activity not being benchmarked against current business activity, with a corresponding absence of explicit resource competition. Thus, indirect-internal venturing may allow for a more rational allocation of a corporation's overall venturing resources.

Indirect-External Venturing

In indirect-external corporate venturing the corporation invests in a venture capital fund that targets external ventures in specific industries or technology sectors. There are at least two common variants of this form of venturing. The venture capital fund may originate outside the corporation and be managed by persons who are not corporate employees. In this case, the corporation typically operates as one of several investors in a venture capital fund, and the corporation's interest in the external ventures targeted by the fund may be strategic or merely financial. The venture capital fund may also originate within the corporation and be managed by corporate employees. Other variants of the indirect-external form of venturing have also been observed. Brody and Ehrlich (1998) note that corporations not wanting to "go it alone" as venture capitalists can (1) co-venture, becoming part of a syndicate with independent venture capital firms; (2) hire a VC firm to run a "dedicated fund" where the corporation is the only investor; or (3) invest in a targeted "pooled fund" with other investors. The commonality among each of these indirect-external venturing variants is the corporation's investment in a venture capital fund that targets external ventures. Typical of such a venturing approach would be, for example, Royal Dutch/Shell Group's recent creation of a dedicated venture capital fund designed to help the company make informed equity investments in strategically related "new economy" firms (McGee, 2000).

Indirect-external venturing is sometimes used to create and expand markets for the corporation's products and technologies. Sechler (2000) reports that Compaq's new $100 million genomics and life-sciences fund requires that the start-ups funded "commit up front to buying Compaq computer systems and services." The potential of the indirect-external form of venturing to expand demand for a corporation's products is evident in Brody and Ehrlich's (1998, p. 51) observations regarding Adobe Systems' experience:

> Adobe Systems . . . launched a $40 million venture fund in 1994 to invest in companies strategic to its core business, such as Cascade Systems Inc., and Lantana Research Corporation. So successful has this effort been in boosting demand for its core products that Adobe recently launched a second $40 million fund.

Moreover, corporations are increasingly recognizing indirect-external venturing as an efficient alternative to traditional R&D activities. For example, Matsushita Electric Industrial Company in 1998 created a venture fund in the Silicon Valley to directly invest $50 million in innovative start-ups, with the objective of using the investment in new ventures to capture, exploit, and commercialize new internet-based technologies (Wysocki, 2000). Matsushita intends to use indirect-external venturing to "invest, incubate, and introduce the start-ups into Matsushita's network," leveraging Matsushita's internal innovative capabilities (Wysocki, 2000).

Other benefits may accrue to corporations practicing indirect-external venturing. For example, in cases where the corporation participates in an external venture fund with multiple investors, the corporation's due diligence costs per screened venture may be reduced, with due diligence assessments typically being shared among fund investors. Additionally, through its involvement with the venture fund the corporation may be privy to venture-specific information allowing the corporation to acquire tacit knowledge about new markets, horizon technologies, or the attractiveness of potential acquisition candidates.

The downside risks of indirect-external venturing tend to be limited to the corporation's financial investment. Intangible resources such as reputation, brand equity, and intellectual capital are not typically at risk. However, the upside benefits are also limited. While indirect-external venturing can provide access to new markets and technologies for the corporation and possibly help the corporation to identify acquisition candidates, it does not typically involve direct transfers of technology, capabilities, or intellectual property rights between the corporation and the ventures. As with direct-external venturing, the principal benefits sought through indirect-external venturing are often financial in nature.

The hoped-for financial benefit of the indirect-external form of venturing was observed in one of the study's firms. Specifically, indirect-external venturing was one of three approaches to corporate venturing that British Gas Technology (BG) adopted in 1988 in an attempt to rejuvenate its organization which had been privatized only two years before. Top management at BG hoped to achieve three objectives with corporate venturing: (1) generate strategic benefits; (2) change BG's culture from a public sector monopoly-minded culture to an entrepreneurial, market-driven culture; and (3) generate superior financial returns. While the indirect-external form of venturing had no impact on the achievement of the first two objectives at BG, it was credited by a BG executive we interviewed with helping the firm to achieve its financial objectives. Chevron's experience with indirect-external venturing also yielded partially positive results. As in the case of British Gas Technology, indirect-external venturing appeared to have had no effect on Chevron's culture. However, according to our interview with Herb Long, Chevron's Manager of Strategic Planning, indirect-external venturing has allowed Chevron to explore alternative technologies and market opportunities without a major commitment of resources or risk to corporate reputation.

Still, the prospect of significant financial gain appears to be at the core of why many companies engage in the indirect-external form of venturing. As demonstrated most vividly by Microsoft's and Intel's experiences in the late 1990s, indirect-external venturing can sometimes be effectively used to "spike" corporate financial returns when core operations are not as profitable as external venture investments (Ip et al., 2000; Takahashi 2000). Takahashi (2000) reported that Intel's portfolio of high-tech "investment" businesses increased in value from $500 million in 1997 to $8.2 billion in 1999. Due to recent stock market declines, the taking of equity positions in external ventures for purely financial purposes is decreasing in popularity (Williams, 2001). Nonetheless, the possibility of great wealth appreciation will likely remain a major point of appeal for the indirect-external form of venturing.

TOWARD A MANAGERIAL DECISION FRAMEWORK FOR DETERMINING THE SUITABILITY OF VARIOUS CORPORATE VENTURING FORMS

While there are many attractive aspects to each of the corporate venturing forms, the identification of appropriate forms for the achievement of specific corporate objectives is often challenging. In response to this challenge, a corporate venturing decision framework is offered based on the venturing considerations suggested by Jolly and Kayama (1990), including the corporate management's need for control over the venture, ability and willingness to commit resources toward venturing, and entrepreneurial risk-accepting propensity. This framework also incorporates the three venturing objectives most commonly identified by interviewees in the current study, including (1) organizational development and cultural change, (2) strategic benefits and the creation of real options, and (3) quick financial returns.

Table 5 indicates the forms of venturing that may be most suitable for the achievement of various objectives given specific corporate circumstances. Since corporations often have multiple venturing objectives, multiple forms of venturing can be appropriate for any given corporation. The specific entries in Table 5 are offered as hypotheses. The rationale underlying the pattern reflected in these entries follows.

Regarding the matter of when a direct versus indirect investment approach to venturing is appropriate, it seems plausible that corporate managements with greater venture-control needs will favor a direct approach due to the "hands-on" benefit such an approach offers. An indirect investment approach distances, in some respects, the locus

Table 5

Potentially Appropriate Forms of Corporate Venturing in Various Corporate Contexts

Corporate Management's Needs & Biases	Corporate Venturing Objectives		
	Organizational Development & Cultural Change	Strategic Benefits/ Real Option Development	Quick Financial Returns
Need for Control of Venture			
High	D-I	D-I, D-E	D-E
Low	I-I	I-I, I-E	I-E
Ability & Willingness to Commit Resources to Venturing			
High	D-I, I-I	D-I, D-E, I-I, I-E	D-E, I-E
Low	I-I	I-I, I-E	I-E
Entrepreneurial Risk Accepting Propensity			
High	D-I, I-I	D-I, D-E, I-I, I-E	D-E, I-E
Low	None	I-I, I-E	I-E

D-I: Direct-Internal venturing

D-E: Direct-External venturing

I-I: Indirect-Internal venturing

I-E: Indirect-External venturing

of venture activity from corporate management's oversight and, thus, may be more acceptable to corporate managements with low control needs. Corporate managements that are strongly committed to venturing and accepting of the associated risks may find the direct and indirect approaches equally palatable. Those managements low on these dimensions, by contrast, may prefer the indirect mode because it limits exposure to venturing's downside risks.

Many corporations initiate corporate venturing as a means to build an innovative or entrepreneurial capability. These corporations are responding to a perceived entrepreneurial imperative; they recognize that they must embrace innovation or their long-term viability will be jeopardized. Venturing represents the mechanism by which the corporations hope to become more change accepting and change competent. Corporations with these characteristics are herein defined as those with an "organizational development and cultural change" objective. In our field study, corporations exhibiting this objective include, for example, GM/Saturn, Procter & Gamble, and British Telecom. An internal venturing focus is posited as most appropriate for corporations with the organizational development and cultural change objective. This proposal is based on our belief that, in general, entrepreneurial cultures and the capabilities they enable cannot be acquired from external sources; they must emerge from within, and this requires an internal venturing focus.

A second common driver of corporate venturing activity is the desire to more fully appropriate value from current organizational competencies, or to strategically reinvent or stretch the corporation. While these desires may seem dissimilar on a superficial level, they both relate to using venturing as a means to explore business opportunities in which the corporation ought to be involved, or at least better understand. Corporations with this aspiration are herein defined as those with a "strategic benefits/real options development" objective. In our field study, corporations exhibiting this objective include, for example, 3M, The Generics Group, and AT&T's Cambridge Research Lab.

As shown in Table 5, an internal focus and an external focus are both posited as being appropriate for corporations with this objective. We believe, more specifically, that those corporations most effective at employing venturing for the purpose of strategic benefits/real options development will often *combine* the internal and external modes. This proposal is based on the assumption that most firms' long-term, strategic interests will be best served if they do not rely solely on the internal development of new businesses or the acquisition of external ventures that fit with where the corporation wants to go. Rather, internal and external venturing can function as effective complements. For example, internal venturing may enable corporations that also practice external venturing to develop "absorptive capacity" (see Cohen & Levinthal, 1990) such that the capabilities of acquired ventures can be appropriated and assimilated into the corporation for future use. And external venturing enables corporations that also practice internal venturing to pursue business opportunities in arenas deemed strategically important to the corporation, but which are beyond the corporation's capacity to successfully or quickly exploit.

As evidenced by numerous examples in the popular business press (see Williams, 2001), the promise of quick financial returns represents yet a third reason why many firms initiate corporate venturing programs. Quite commonly, venturing in new business arenas is used as a means to circumvent the profitability caps inherent to one's core product-market segments or industries. The new business activity usually takes place in a related but more lucrative arena than that in which the corporation operates. However, some corporations employ venturing purely for the cash expected to be thrown off by the ventures in which the corporation has invested, with little or no expectation that those ventures must somehow fit the corporate strategy. In our field study, corporations motivated by the possibility of quick financial returns from venturing include, for example, Chevron, Cable & Wireless, and British Gas Technology.

We believe that an external venturing focus may best fulfill a desire for quick financial returns from venturing. Investments in internal corporate venturing initiatives typically have multi-year payback periods, and the returns from such investments are often highly uncertain (Block & MacMillan, 1993). "Patient money" is required. These realities become moot if the corporation invests in external ventures that have demonstrated capacities to generate superior returns. Of course, corporate venturing investments under such a scenario are subject to their own set of risks, such as post-acquisition performance deterioration. Moreover, it is arguable that picking portfolios of high-potential and high-flying ventures is best left to the financial investment community where such capabilities are their forte. Thus, even though our interviews and substantial anecdotal evidence suggest that the desire for quick financial returns *is* a driver of corporate venturing activity, perhaps this, ideally, would not be the case. Our point here is that *if* quick financial returns are sought through venturing, they will most likely be realized by adopting an external focus.

SUMMARY AND CONCLUSION

This paper has proposed a typology of corporate venturing based on the two dimensions of focus of the entrepreneurship (internal or external to the corporation) and presence of investment intermediation. Using this typology as an organizing scheme for the interpretation of interview data, the authors were able to uncover and compare the major advantages and disadvantages of the various manifestations of corporate venturing.

This effort is timely in that more and more corporations are experiencing frustration in their efforts to "be entrepreneurial." Because of the difficulties large bureaucracies have in trying to innovate, increasing numbers of such firms (or so the anecdotal evidence suggests) are turning to external means to implement venturing. Investment in, or the acquisition of independent, highly entrepreneurial firms, appears to be increasingly employed as a substitute for the internal development of the corporation's own entrepreneurial potential. Likewise, many companies are exploring joint venturing options in order to spread business risks, hasten the start-up process, or overcome internal venturing capability inadequacies (Kambil et al., 2000).

Such a shift in corporate philosophy regarding the way one ought to become more entrepreneurial has long-term implications for the practice of corporate venturing. In particular, corporate executives, if they are to effectively manage their firm's venturing activities, need to be more familiar with the benefits and risks associated with the corporate venturing options. Toward this end, this paper has summarized some of the primary potential benefits and costs or concerns associated with four common forms of corporate venturing. This paper has also offered a preliminary decision framework for choosing among these corporate venturing options. Future research into corporate venturing activity might focus on further clarifying the conditions under which various options should be chosen. Additional promising research objectives include the identification of contextual factors that encourage or discourage the use of particular venturing options, process attributes associated with successful corporate venturing, and change models for effectively balancing "mainstream" and "newstream" (e.g., venturing) activities in the evolving organization.

REFERENCES

Aaker, D. A. (1994). Building a brand: The Saturn story. *California Management Review, 36*(2), 114-133.

Amit, R., Glosten, L., & Muller, E. (1993). Challenges to theory development in entrepreneurship research. *Journal of Management Studies, 30*(5), 815-834.

Biggadike, R. (1979). The risky business of diversification. *Harvard Business Review, 57*(3), 103-111.

Block, Z., & MacMillan, I. C. (1993). *Corporate venturing: Creating new businesses within the firm.* Boston: Harvard Business School Press, 1-17.

Brazeal, D. V., & Herbert, T. T. (1999). The genesis of entrepreneurship. *Entrepreneurship Theory and Practice, 23*(3), 29-45.

Brody, P., & Ehrlich, D. (1998). Can big companies become successful venture capitalists? *The McKinsey Quarterly, 2,* 51-63.

Burgelman, R. A. (1983a). A process model of internal corporate venturing in the diversified major firm. *Administrative Sciences Quarterly, 28*(2), 223-244.

Burgelman, R. A. (1983b). Corporate entrepreneurship and strategic management: Insights from a process study. *Management Science, 29*(12), 1349-1364.

Burgelman, R. A. (1983c). A model of the interaction of strategic behavior, corporate context, and the context of strategy. *Academy of Management Review, 8*(1), 61-70.

Burgelman, R. A. (1984a). Managing the internal corporate venturing process. *Sloan Management Review, 25*(2), 33-48.

Burgelman, R. A. (1984b). Designs for corporate entrepreneurship in established firms. *California Management Review, 26*(3), 154-166.

Bygrave, W. D. (1993). Theory building in the entrepreneurship paradigm. *Journal of Business Venturing, 8*(3), 255-280.

Caves, R., & Porter, M. (1977). From entry barriers to mobility barriers. *Quarterly Journal of Economics, 91,* 421-434.

Chan, S. H., Kensinger, J. W., Keown, A. J., & Martin, J. D. (1997). Do strategic alliances create value? *Journal of Financial Economics, 46*(2), 199-221.

Chauvin, K. W., & Hirschey, M. (1994). Goodwill, profitability, and the market value of the firm. *Journal of Accounting and Public Policy, 13,* 159-180.

Chesbrough, H. (2000). Designing corporate ventures in the shadow of private venture capital. *California Management Review, 42*(3), 31-49.

Chesbrough, H., & Socolof, S. (2000). Creating new ventures from Bell Lab technologies. *Research Technology Management, 43*(2), 13-17.

Cohen, W. M., & Levinthal, D. A. (1990). Absorptive capacity: A new perspective on learning and innovation. *Administrative Science Quarterly, 35,* 128-152.

Confederation of British Industry (CBI). (1999). *Connecting companies: Using corporate venturing for growth.* London: Confederation of British Industry.

David, B. L. (1994). How internal venture groups innovate. *Research Technology Management, 37*(2), 38-43.

Dougherty, D. (1995). Managing your core incompetencies for corporate venturing. *Entrepreneurship Theory and Practice, 19*(3), 113-135.

Fast, N. D. (1979). The future of the industrial new venture department. *Industrial Marketing Management, 8*(4), 264-273.

Fast, N. D. (1981). Pitfalls of corporate venturing. *The International Journal of Research Management, 14*(2), 21-24.

Fombrun, C. (1996). *Reputation: Realizing value from the corporate image.* Boston: Harvard Business School Press.

Ginsberg, A., & Hay, M. (1994). Confronting the challenges of corporate entrepreneurship: Guidelines for venture managers. *European Management Journal, 12*(4), 382-389.

Guth, W. D. (1995). Theory from field research on firm-level entrepreneurship: A normal science overview. *Entrepreneurship Theory and Practice, 19*(3), 169-173.

Hamel, G. (2000). *Leading the revolution.* Boston: Harvard Business School Press.

Hardymon, G. F., DeNino, M. J., & Salter, M. S. (1983). When corporate venture capital doesn't work. *Harvard Business Review, 83*(3), 114-121.

Hartley, R. F. (1995). *Marketing mistakes.* New York: John Wiley and Sons.

Inland Revenue. (1999). *Corporate venturing relief: A technical note by the Inland Revenue.* London.

Ip, G., & Bryan-Low, C. (2000). Plunge in tech shares hurts Intel's earning from portfolio sales. *The Wall Street Journal,* October 12, C1, C2.

Ip, G., McWilliams, G., & McGee, S. (2000). Portfolio profits boost firms' bottom line, but stir controversy. *The Wall Street Journal,* January 20, A1, A6.

Jarvis, S. (2000). P&G's challenge. *Marketing News, 34*(18), 1, 13.

Jolly, V. K., & Kayama, H. (1990). Venture management in Japanese companies. *Journal of Business Venturing, 5*(4), 249-269.

Kambil, A., Eselius, E. D., & Monteiro, K. A. (2000). Fast venturing: The quick way to start web businesses. *Sloan Management Review, 41*(4), 55-67.

Kogut, B., & Kulatilaka, N. (1994). Options thinking and platform investments: Investing in opportunity. *California Management Review, 36*(2), 52-72.

Knight, G. (1997). Strategy and entrepreneurship in a developing free trade area: The case of the textiles/ apparel industry in Canada. *International Journal of Management, 14*(2), 237-249.

Knight, G. (2000). Entrepreneurship and marketing strategy: The SME under globalization. *Journal of International Marketing, 8*(2), 12-32.

Landau, R. (1987). Corporate partnering can spur innovation. *Research Management, 30*(3), 21-26.

Leifer, R., McDermott, C. M., O'Connor, G. C., Peters, L. S., Rice, M. P., & Veryzer, R. W. (2000). *Radical innovation: How mature companies can outsmart upstarts.* Boston: Harvard Business School Press, 1-17.

Lewandowski, J. L., & MacKinnon, W. P. (1992). What we learned at Saturn. *Personnel Journal, 71*(12), 30-32.

Luehrman, T. A. (1998). Strategy as a portfolio of real options. *Harvard Business Review, 76*(5), 89-99.

Lusch, R. F., & Harvey, M. G. (1994). The case for an off-balance-sheet controller. *Sloan Management Review, 35*(Winter), 101-105.

McGee, S. (2000). Shell starts 'new economy fund.' *The Wall Street Journal,* November 9, C22.

McGrath, R. G. (1995). Advantage from adversity: Learning from disappointment in internal corporate ventures. *Journal of Business Venturing, 10,* 121-142.

McGrath, R. G. (1997). A real options logic for initiating technology positioning investments. *Academy of Management Review, 22*(4), 974-996.

McGrath, R. G. (1999). Falling forward: Real options reasoning and entrepreneurial failure. *Academy of Management Review, 24*(1), 13-30.

McNally, K. (1997). *Corporate venture capital: Bridging the equity gap in the small business sector.* London: Routledge.

Miles, M. P., & Covin, J. G. (2000). Environmental marketing: A source of reputational, competitive, and financial advantage. *Journal of Business Ethics, 23*, 299-311.

Morris, M. H., & Sexton, D. L. (1996). The concept of entrepreneurial intensity: Implications for company performance. *Journal of Business Research, 36*(1), 5-14.

Naman, J. L., & Slevin, D. P. (1993). Entrepreneurship and the concept of fit: A model and empirical tests. *Strategic Management Journal, 14*(2), 137-153.

Pearson, A. E. (1992). Corporate redemption and the seven deadly sins. *Harvard Business Review, 70*(3), 65-84.

Pinchot, G. (1985). *Intrapreneuring: Why you don't have to leave the corporation to become an entrepreneur.* New York: Harper and Row.

Rice, M. P., O'Connor, G. C., Leifer, R., McDermott, C. M., & Standish-Kuon, T. (2000). Corporate venture capital models for promoting radical innovation. *Journal of Marketing Theory & Practice, 8*(3), 1-10.

Rind, K. W. (1981). The role of venture capital in corporate development. *Strategic Management Journal, 2*(2), 169-180.

Roberts, E. B. (1980). New ventures for corporate growth. *Harvard Business Review, 58*(4), 134-142.

Roberts, E. B., & Berry, C. A. (1985). Entering new businesses: Strategies for success. *Sloan Management Review, 26*(3), 3-17.

Robideaux, D. R., Miles, M. P., & White, J. B. (1993). Codes of ethics and firm size: A stakeholder approach to strategic planning. *International Journal of Value-Based Management, 6*(1), 49-60.

Sahakian, C. (1998). The dangerous dozen common partnering mistakes. *Strategy & Leadership, 26*(4), 40.

Savage, G. T., & Black, J. A. (1995). Firm-level entrepreneurship and field research: The studies in their methodological context. *Entrepreneurship Theory and Practice, 19*(3), 25-34.

Sechler, B. (2000). Venture investing has become a marketing tool. *The Wall Street Journal,* November 13, B17.

Sharma, P., & Chrisman, J. J. (1999). Toward a reconciliation of the definitional issues in the field of corporate entrepreneurship. *Entrepreneurship Theory and Practice, 23*(3), 11-28.

Siegel, R., Siegel, E., & MacMillan, I. C. (1988). Corporate venture capitalists: Autonomy, obstacles, and performance. *Journal of Business Venturing, 3*(3), 233-247.

Simon, M., Houghton, S. M., & Gurney, J. (1999). Succeeding at internal corporate venturing: Roles needed to balance autonomy and control. *Journal of Applied Management Studies, 8*(2), 145-159.

Stavro, B. (1985). Dealing with the doubters. *Forbes, 135*(6), 39-41.

Sykes, H. B. (1986). The anatomy of a corporate venturing program: Factors influencing success. *Journal of Business Venturing, 1*(3), 275-293.

Takahashi, D. (2000). Intel rolls dice on tech upstarts—and hits jackpot. *The Wall Street Journal,* February 8, C1, C3.

Taylor, A. (1993). Blah car, bad book. *Fortune, 128*(14), 187.

Thornhill, S., & Amit, R. (2001). A dynamic perspective of internal fit in corporate venturing. *Journal of Business Venturing, 16*(1), 25-50.

von Hippel, E. (1977). Successful and failing internal corporate ventures: An empirical analysis. *Industrial Marketing Management, 6*(3), 163-174.

Whitney, D. (1997). *Corporate new ventures at Procter and Gamble.* Case 9-897-088, Harvard Business School, Boston, MA.

Wiklund, J. (1999). The sustainability of the entrepreneurial orientation-performance relationship. *Entrepreneurship Theory and Practice, 24*(1), 37-47.

Williams, M. (2001). Little gain, less venturing: Company investments slow. *The Wall Street Journal,* July 5, C1, C15.

Withers Solicitors. (1995). *Gateway to growth: A study of corporate venturing.* London.

Withers Solicitors. (1997). *Window on technology: Corporate venturing in practice.* London.

Wysocki, B. (2000). U.S. incubators help Japan hatch ideas. *The Wall Street Journal,* June 12, A1.

Young, S., & Lubin, J. S. (2000). Lucent outs McGinn as CEO and chairman. *The Wall Street Journal,* October 24, B1, B4.

Zahra, S. A. (1996). Governance, ownership, and corporate entrepreneurship: The moderating impact of industry technological opportunities. *Academy of Management Journal, 39*(6), 1713-1735.

Zahra, S. A., & Covin, J. G. (1995). Contextual influences on the corporate entrepreneurship-firm performance relationship: A longitudinal analysis. *Journal of Business Venturing, 10*(1), 43-58.

Morgan P. Miles is Professor of Marketing at Georgia Southern University.

Jeffrey G. Covin is the Samuel and Pauline Glaubinger Professor of Entreprenueurship at the Kelly School of Business at Indiana University.

The field research for this study was conducted when the first author was a Senior Research Associate for the Judge Institute of Management, Cambridge University.

This project was sponsored by the University of Cambridge's Judge Institute of Management, 3i corporation (Europe's largest venture capital corporation), Georgia Southern University, and Indiana University's Kelley School of Business. The authors thank John Butler for his editorial guidance, the three anonymous reviewers for helpful insights and suggestions, and Larry Glaubinger for his financial support of this project.

[10]

Opportunity Recognition and Breakthrough Innovation in Large Established Firms

Gina Colarelli O'Connor
Mark P. Rice

"Every day, I try to go out and grab lightning."
—Terry Fadem, Director, New Business Development, DuPont Corporation

"**G**rabbing lightning" is how Terry Fadem characterized opportunity recognition associated with breakthrough innovations. In recent annual surveys of the members of the Industrial Research Institute (a professional association of the technology leaders of R&D-intensive firms), "making innovation happen" and "managing R&D for business growth" were cited as the number one challenges facing IRI members (in 1998 and 1999 respectively). Opportunity recognition is the bridge that connects a breakthrough idea to the initial innovation evaluation process—which in turn leads to the formation of a formally established commercialization effort.

During the 1980s, U.S. and European firms were competitively challenged by Asian firms in many industries, e.g., memory chips, office and factory automation, consumer electronics, and auto making.[1] In response, these firms dramatically increased their competencies in managing continuous improvement and incremental innovation in existing products or processes, with an emphasis on cost competitiveness, quality improvements, and efficiency.[2] In the past decade, there has been growing awareness that managerial practices had simply shifted from one incomplete approach to an alternative but equally incomplete approach. According to Gary Hamel: "Most companies long ago reached the point of diminishing returns in their incremental improvement programs. Radical, non-linear innovation is the only way to escape the ruthless hyper-competition that has been hammering down margins in industry after

Opportunity Recognition and Breakthrough Innovation in Large Established Firms

industry."[3] Although achieving excellence in ongoing operations and incremental innovation has been critical for regaining competitiveness, the demand for corporate growth and improved financial performance from senior management and from shareholders has catalyzed an intense and renewed interest in the discovery, development, and commercialization of breakthrough innovations.

Since 1995, we have followed the evolution of twelve radical innovation projects in ten large, established firms. In this article, we examine how these firms undertook the recognition of opportunities associated with breakthrough innovations, which from their perspective had the potential to "change the game." In this context, opportunity recognition is defined as the match between an unfulfilled market need and a solution that satisfies the need.[4] In our twelve projects, breakthrough innovations arose out of invention, or insights based on new combinations of technologies and processes. The technical discovery or insight typically originated with a scientist or engineer, who frequently was not prepared—either through training or life experience—to make the cognitive leap from a technical idea to an envisioned and articulated business opportunity. Markets might not yet exist and would have to be imagined,[5] or current markets might be transformed to such an extent by the innovation that it was difficult for the scientist or engineer to discern the business model that might emerge. The opportunity recognizer, typically a research manager or senior scientist, was able to link the breakthrough technical idea with a need in the marketplace— one that already existed, but was unfulfilled, or one that could be created. What is striking is that this act must happen not just once, but many times for a single breakthrough innovation project to come to fruition in the market (as Figure 1 shows). Thus the problem of enhancing the capacity for opportunities to be recognized in a sustained manner is critically important to any firm interested in breaking new ground.

Creative ability lies within individuals, and the degree of creativity varies across individuals.[6] Opportunity recognition is a creative act. In and of itself, it is not an organizational process.[7] Yet to simply rely on individuals is an inefficient use of an organization. As Amabile and others have noted,[8] while individual creativity is a critical factor, there are a number of management actions and attitudes that can be put in place to enhance the likelihood that the creative side of individuals will be developed, motivated, and directed in useful ways.

Writers in the fields of innovation management and organizational learning have identified a number of problems that established organizations face in enabling the recognition of breakthrough opportunities. Christensen provides numerous examples of leading firms that have been unable to recognize the import of novel technologies, developed either within or external to their organizations, to the future of their own industries and markets.[9] Indeed, the classic business strategy literature emphasizes the importance of organizational experience with familiar technologies and markets in maintaining continuous streams of successful new products.[10] Other writers show that the ability to create and depend on efficient routines, considered a critical aspect of organizational

Opportunity Recognition and Breakthrough Innovation in Large Established Firms

FIGURE 1. Opportunity Recognition—Initial and Recurring—within the Radical Innovation Lifecycle

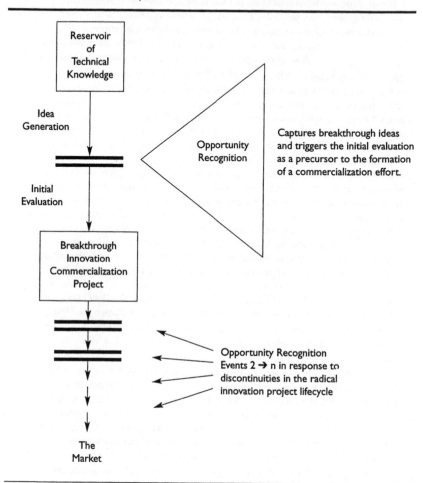

learning and successful performance may, in fact, prevent firms from sensing opportunities that would drag them beyond those programmatic practices, i.e., the domain of breakthrough innovation.[11] Van de Ven identifies the human problem of managing attention.[12] In accordance with the observations of Christensen, he notes that the more successful an organization is, the more difficult it is to trigger people's thresholds to attend to new ideas, needs, and opportunities. Finally, Tushman and O'Reilly elucidate the need for, and challenges associated with, building ambidexterity into organizations; that is, to manage current operations and simultaneously develop dramatically new and different ones to cope with turbulent environments.[13] These writings focus on the dual importance of the individual and the organizational context, i.e., the role of the creative individual in seeing an opportunity and championing it,[14] and the role of organizational context and organizational learning mechanisms that can facilitate and support the creativity required of opportunity recognizers.

Much of the literature on the topic of opportunity recognition focuses on the nature and importance of the phenomenon rather than on how to enhance the firm's capacity to support it. A number of writers offer prescriptions regarding the capabilities and sensitivities firms must possess to be effective at opportunity recognition. For example, since the development of a breakthrough innovation may take a decade or more, the ability to anticipate the direction and timing of technological development and to identify technological alternatives will be critical.[15] Shifts in technology, market, and competition need to be recognized and interpreted within the context of the firm's environment.[16] Companies must be able to imagine markets that do not presently exist, and invest in their development ahead of the competition.[17] It is important for a firm to extend its view beyond current operating practice to imagine how a discontinuity may develop and look at the potential discontinuity in the context of all possible scenarios.[18] It is interesting that these writers refer to the capacity of the company for opportunity recognition without offering guidelines for enabling them. In contrast, in our study opportunity recognition was itself a discontinuous act based on individual initiative rather than a process or practice of the firm.

The literature does recognize the importance of individuals through its consideration of the roles of technical and market gatekeepers, but it does not tie them specifically to the act of opportunity recognition. The firm that initiates discontinuous innovation must be dependent on, and responsive to, information from outside the organization.[19] Gatekeepers provide a link between internal and external sources of information, acquiring, translating, and disseminating new information.[20] Technical, or information, gatekeepers link technical information they gain through external sources with product development and process improvement, generating new technical possibilities.[21] Market gatekeepers possess competence in the application of technology to potential new markets.[22] They insure the innovation is meeting a market need—information that will likely change as the project evolves. While these writers provide rich description of the roles involved in opportunity recognition, they do not explore how firms can enhance the likelihood that it will happen as a result of the presence of gatekeepers. To whom should technical and market gatekeepers provide such information? How might the organization structure itself to be most receptive to the information? How can the organization enable opportunity recognition, an individual act, and leverage it efficiently?

This article aims to contribute to the understanding of the initiation of breakthrough innovation projects and of the role of recurring opportunity recognition events in sustaining these projects in the face of multiple discontinuities in the radical innovation lifecycle (see Figure 1). We add to the growing body of descriptive literature on innovation processes so richly developed by Van de Ven and his colleagues, whose research program has worked across organizational domains, organizational sizes, and both product and process innovations.[23] While they have plowed new ground in describing the complexity of the innovation process, there is room for a more focused look at key aspects of that process, and for constraining the domain of innovation more tightly to look at specific contexts. In this study, the context is the large established organization that is concerned with creating value through the application of breakthrough technology to changing markets.

Though the firms in our study exhibited a variety of organizational mechanisms for supporting opportunity recognition, in general they were implemented in ad hoc fashion with varying degrees of success. None have implemented a sustained, comprehensive, and disciplined approach. In this article, we examine several alternative approaches through which organizations may be able to systematically stimulate and support opportunity recognition.

Research Design and Cases

Defining Radical Innovation

We define a radical or breakthrough innovation as the creation of a new line of business—new for both the firm and the marketplace. By "new" we mean a product or process either with unprecedented performance features or with already familiar features that offer potential for a 5-10x (or greater) improvement in performance, or a 30-50% (or greater) reduction in cost. By this definition, CT and MRI were discontinuous innovations in the field of diagnostic imaging, but none of the subsequent incremental and generational improvements in the technologies were. The first PCs were discontinuous innovations, but the many subsequent improvements were not.

Multiple Case Study Methodology

Case study research involves the examination of a phenomenon in its natural setting. It is especially appropriate for research in new topic areas, where the focus is on understanding "how" or "why" questions concerning a contemporary set of events, and the objective is on gaining insights to build a theory rather than on testing hypotheses.[24] Multiple cases are generally regarded as more robust than single case studies, in that comparisons across cases allow for a greater robustness in the development of insights and a consideration of their context dependency.[25]

To guard against post hoc rationalization of the reasons and motives for particular actions, a prospective approach to data collection was taken. That is, firms were enlisted for their participation while the cases were ongoing. In order to qualify for participation, projects had to have been formally identified, with an associated team and a budget. We collected data about the project's history on our first round of interviews, but from there we collected data in real time as the team was being confronted with successes and challenges in the course of the project's development. To date, 5 of the projects have been introduced into the marketplace to varying degrees of success, 5 are still under development, and 2 have been abandoned.

Information gathering techniques have included in-depth interviews, surveys, reviews of project documentation, and teleconferences. Where possible, copies of materials prepared for early evaluation boards were also collected and analyzed. All interviews were taped and transcribed. We gathered information from a variety of company representatives associated with each project from a variety of functional perspectives.

During the first year of the study, the participant firms hosted a minimum of two site visits and provided access to the appropriate individuals—senior managers, project managers and project team members-—who could provide both historic and current information and insights with respect to the research questions of interest. As some projects are beginning to move into operating units, new transitional team members are being added to our interviews.

Following Miles and Huberman,[26] the transcripts and documents were reviewed and coded in a systematic manner. Any comment that bore on the issue of opportunity recognition and early evaluation was highlighted and collected on a summary sheet for each project. Where individuals within a project team gave conflicting data, it was so noted. The summary sheets were then compared to aggregate the data and draw comparisons and contrasts.

The Sample of Cases

This study is sponsored by the Industrial Research Institute (IRI), an association of R&D managers and Senior Technology Officers of *Fortune 1000* firms in the United States. The IRI is our sampling frame, and it therefore must be noted that our results cannot be generalized to all types of innovations, but only to those whose earliest development was housed in a central R&D function. While the initial opportunity recognition that led to several of the projects actually occurred outside R&D, the work was, in all cases, quickly centralized in R&D due to the high levels of technical uncertainty associated with them.

The unit of analysis is the project, not the firm or a division of the firm. Members of the IRI volunteered projects within their firms for observation. R&D managers were asked to consider projects that were currently formally identified as projects, with an associated assignment of personnel and a budget, and that had the potential to have the market impact described above in our definition of radical innovation. The firms were Air Products and Chemicals, Analog Devices, DuPont, General Electric, General Motors, IBM, Nortel (now Nortel Networks), Polaroid, Texas Instruments, and United Technology Corporation's Otis Elevator division.[27] A brief description of the projects follows.

- Air Products and Chemicals Corporation developed an ionic transport membrane (ITM) for separating oxygen from air and is working on systems to meet the needs of three different application domains. The firm believes that the oxygen produced through the new system will offer a 30% cost improvement over current systems in use, and has the potential to completely change the current delivery system in medical and metal cutting applications areas, resulting in new to the world features.

- Analog Devices has developed a micro-electro-mechanical (MEMS) accelerometer, a small microchip that can measure changes in speed. While the application possibilities are nearly endless (e.g., virtual reality games, medical applications to detect changes in the rate of heart pulse), ADI initially used this technology to help move itself into the automotive market space. Even there, potential applications are numerous, but the initial market disruption was to replace electro-mechanical airbag sensors with accelerometers. The cost to the automotive market for the airbag system fell from approximately $500 to $100 per unit.

- Dupont's Biomax, is a polyester material that can be recycled or decomposed. It holds up under normal commercial conditions for a time period established through product specifications. The material decomposes at the right time and under the right conditions. It is environmentally safe at every stage of its decomposition. Chemically, Biomax® represents a new family of highly versatile polymers based on traditional polyethylene terephthalate (PET) technology. Its biodegradable qualities are made possible by the water-soluble (hydrolyzable) linkages in its molecular chain. These linkages dissolve as they make contact with water, causing the entire molecular chain to break apart. The remnants are consumed by microbes, which convert them into carbon dioxide and water. The material itself can be made into fibers, films, or resins. This makes it suitable for countless agricultural, industrial, and consumer product applications: mulch containers, mulching film, seed mats, plant pots, disposable eating utensils, blister packs, yard waste bags, parts of disposable diapers, blown bottles. In the United States alone, where the average household creates over three tons of disposable waste each year, the number of potential applications for Biomax® is immense; its development represents a potentially huge business for DuPont and an important solution to the mounting problem of solid waste in developed countries.

- Dupont's Electron Emitter is a fiber that emits light at a rate significantly faster than any known source. The most promising application areas are in electronic display technologies. Prior to this discovery, Dupont was not involved in the displays business at any level.

- GE is well known for its advances in medical diagnostic technology, particularly with respect to imaging systems. One of the most controversial recent innovations in that industry is the advance of Digital X-ray technology. Digital X-ray not only allows for dramatic improvement in the specificity of the image, but also can be sent as a stream of data to a diagnostic bank. That alone allows for remote diagnosing, and has wide ranging implications for staffing of highly paid radiologists at local hospitals and clinics. GE has found a way to combine Digital X-ray technology with Fluoroscopy, a technology that allows the filming and digitization of movement within the body. The combined benefit provides a leap in benefits in the medical imaging field that GE believes will be the next "game-changer."

- GM's focus on alternative power systems for automobiles is widely known. One of the innovation paths down which they, and their counterparts, have been travelling for some time is that of the hybrid electric vehicle. The concept is that power comes from both electrical and conventional engines, each of which is drawn upon at the speeds at which it performs most efficiently. Those technologies, combined with several others such as regenerative braking, could serve to offer a vehicle capable of exceptional gas mileage (50-80 miles/gallon) and exceedingly low emissions of pollutants.

- IBM has commercialized a new microchip based on an alloy of Silicon and Germanium (SiGe), which promises to become the basis for high-performance new transistors with switching speeds up to four times faster than those of traditional semiconductors. SiGe chips also offer several other important additional benefits. First, they can operate using only a fraction of the normal power requirements for competing technologies, such as Gallium Arsenide (GaAs) based chips. Secondly, SiGe can be manufactured with the same costly fabrication equipment used to make conventional silicon chips, potentially avoiding billions in new capital investments. The most promising application arenas are in telecommunications, which is based on analog technology, an arena in which IBM had not previously participated.

- IBM's second project is the confluence of display, power, and memory technologies to enable the creation of an "electronic book" that could be used to store vast amounts of data such as technical manuals, doctor's files, or newspaper articles, could be portable, and could receive written information as well as be highly readable.

- NetActive is a spin-off venture of Nortel Networks, though it began as an internal organizational innovation. The innovation is a software capability that allows NetActive to encode game publishers' software in such a way that a user could obtain the application for a fraction of the normal purchase price. The customer must then initialize its use over the internet, and choose from a variety of usage options that allow single use, usage for a specified period of time, or purchase, all with differing fee structures. The customer's credit card is then charged for the given usage selection. Game software and utility software such as tax filing programs are the current most promising applications.

- Polaroid applied highly innovative manufacturing technology from its traditional product arenas to the creation of low-cost, high-capacity memory storage devices.

- Texas Instrument's Digital Light Processor is based on the MEMS device described above. The TI projector creates a screen image by bouncing light off of 1.3 million microscopic mirrors squeezed onto a 1 square-inch chip, each mirror has the ability to angle itself independently in order to best reflect light.

Potential applications exist in the hard copy markets, home movie projection systems, and large screen movie theaters, to name but a few. The first that TI is commercializing are large screen movie projection systems. Movie theater owners can now receive movies from Hollywood producers on Digital Video Disks or even by satellite rather than on heavy reels. Theaters will no longer be limited by a finite number of film prints, so they have increased flexibility in show times and the number of screens showing a particular movie.

- United Technologies' Otis Elevator division has devoted considerable energy to solving the problem of the "mile high building." In the commercial construction industry, limits on building height are not based on any technical constraints other than the problem of the elevator systems. Current systems are limited by the weight of the cable that pulls the elevator. Once the cable gets too long (more than 130 stories), it becomes too heavy to lift. Designing parallel elevator shafts and moving people from one shaft to the other is the current solution to very tall buildings, but at some point, that solution becomes uneconomic because the amount of the building's real estate needed to house the shafts is too high in proportion to the amount available for rent. Otis has developed a system of people movement that solves the problem. It allows for elevator cars to become separated from the shaft, and to move onto other shafts. A combination of horizontal and vertical movement allows for a conservation of shaft space, and opens up the opportunity for thinking about conveyance systems in a completely different light.

Observations

Opportunity recognition for radical innovation is highly dependent on individual initiative and capacity, rather than routine practices and procedures of the firm. Opportunity recognizers are in positions in the organization that allow them to make their cognitive leap. Opportunity recognition can be characterized as reactive or proactive. On the one hand, individuals may be alert and ready to react to ideas and information that have the potential to become an opportunity. On the other hand, through their own initiative or via a challenge from a superior, they may take on the responsibility of searching through the organization for ideas that can be developed into opportunities for significant new products or businesses.

The report of the initial opportunity recognition that led to the establishment of DuPont's Electron Emitter project is illustrative. The research manager for the scientist who discovered the light-emitting properties of a material under consideration for use in composites recognized that it might be of interest to the electronic materials business unit. The research manager contacted Terry Fadem, the director of New Business Development, and encouraged him to attend the technical review at which the scientist would present his discovery. The initial act of opportunity recognition by the research manager triggered a second act of opportunity recognition, which in turn led to a technology evaluation effort.

Corporate executives seldom play the role of opportunity recognizer. In 10 of our 12 cases, a low- to mid-level research manager completed the initial act of opportunity recognition. However, opportunity recognizers are not necessarily the champions who provide the energy and persistence required to ensure that the project receives appropriate management attention.[28] In the majority of cases in the study, the scientists who have envisioned, worked toward, and discovered the discontinuous innovations have some idea of the applications for their innovations, but they have a limited understanding of the market. The scientists' research managers, who have recognized the opportunities associated with their discontinuous innovations, have sufficient understanding of the market which, when combined with their technical expertise, allows them to recognize business opportunities. The leap in thinking required is illustrated by one of the research managers:

> "Although I didn't do much with the business unit that would ultimately market this technology, I knew something about the field. It did seem important to me. If you look at the history of innovation in this field, there really hasn't been much. This . . . really had the potential to change the game."

Early conceptualizations of the commercial opportunity are made and excitement is generated not based on projections of financial cash flows, market share gains or wins, or the typical rules of the game that large corporations establish. Every one of our participant teams could articulate a number that the market promise had to be in order for this to be considered "an opportunity" by the conventional corporate standards. For example, "if it isn't a $250 million market, we aren't interested" was typical of the comments they had heard. Those sorts of estimates, however, bordered on the ridiculous for many of these projects. Market uncertainty is simply too high and costs of production, at the outset, are impossible to predict. Rather, the recognition of the opportunity lay in a conceptualization of what the delivered benefits of the technology might be, and how rich and robust those were. The idea was that, if those benefits could be delivered, the market would definitely be "big enough." There was no consideration of the timing over which the market would develop to become big enough to recoup the enormous investment required.

As a breakthrough innovation project proceeds, there is an increased commitment of financial and human resources. In this domain, investment is typically staged, rather than committed for the entire development path. Hence, higher-level technical and business managers along with external partners frequently engage in opportunity recognition, as a triggering mechanism for the opportunity evaluation process leading to decision making about commitment of resources. The research manager, as the first to identify the opportunity, acts as the initial catalyst to set off this chain reaction in which technical and business managers at various levels of the organization engage in the opportunity recognition process.

Opportunity Recognition and Breakthrough Innovation in Large Established Firms

One example of the multiple levels of opportunity recognition is the General Motors hybrid-electric vehicle project. Initial technical development began in 1969. Because of the inability to overcome technical hurdles at that time, the project was shelved. In the late 1980s, two research managers and a research engineer had adopted a practice of getting together every week or two for informal technology reviews, primarily to consider ideas volunteered from random individuals and customers outside the firm.[29] The review of one of those ideas triggered the occurrence of opportunity recognition—the "big bang" that became the catalyst for the formation of the project (the first opportunity recognition). In the process of explaining why a particular idea violated the laws of thermodynamics, an insight by the research engineer caused the group to come up with a new way to look at the technology, which could meet a well-understood market need if a set of technical hurdles could be overcome.

The research manager, using funds under his control, set up a technology evaluation team in early 1989. The results of the evaluation were sufficiently positive to cause the research manager to approach the head of the research division, who in turn recognized the opportunity (the second opportunity recognition) and committed substantial funding. Two years later, one of the project leaders moved to a development organization, beginning a period in which parallel and complementary efforts were being conducted in the research group and in the development group. Within twelve months, both projects were in danger of losing funding, due to the downturn in the firm's sales revenue and market share. The two project managers decided to stage a technology demonstration for all the corporate executives "to try to save our butt."

Although the demonstration appeared to be successful, the director of the development group informed his project director: "You did a good show, but we got orders to close you down. Our budgets can't handle you." That same evening one of the senior executives, who had seen the demonstration earlier that day, called the director of the development group and said, "That's good stuff. You've got to keep that going somehow" (the third opportunity recognition). The project was resurrected and would continue, albeit under tight budgetary restrictions. One month later, the director of the development group presented the concept to a senior official in a federal agency. The senior official recognized the opportunity (the fourth opportunity recognition) and agreed to champion the project for federal funding, which was authorized about a year later.

In the case of GE Digital X-Ray, there were seven key occurrences of opportunity recognition, involving: the research scientist (1984); someone from the outside firm (1987); the research manager (1987); the first head of the business unit (1988); the head of central research (1992); the CEO (1993); and the second head of the business unit (1997). This pattern of multiple instances of opportunity recognition, and the necessity for an ability to articulate the opportunity to many constituents, arose in every one of our cases. For radical innovations, this occurrence is a matter of life and death of the project.

Given the high degree of technical and market uncertainty associated with breakthrough innovation, the understanding of the opportunity often changes over the course of the project, requiring a repeat of the opportunity recognition process that may result in a new or substantially redefined opportunity. To appreciate this, it is important to understand the difference between ongoing project evaluation and additional occurrences of opportunity recognition subsequent to the initial occurrence that may be required due to discontinuities in the project development path. When an opportunity related to a radical innovation is recognized, invariably assumptions are made related to the uncertainties associated with the discontinuous innovation. Ongoing project evaluation occurs through project reviews, which typically focus on achievement of milestones along the project development path envisioned on the basis of these assumptions. They are, in a sense, incremental steps along the path, are evaluative in nature, and do not involve the cognitive leap required for opportunity recognition.

When a major milestone is missed or a key assumption turns out to be wrong, a discontinuity along the project development path occurs. For those managers who do not have the capacity or willingness to make the cognitive leap required for opportunity recognition, this discontinuity will be a project killer, or at least a major setback for the project. For those who do have the capacity or willingness, it will be the trigger for a new occurrence of opportunity recognition.

For example, initial technical research for the project that ultimately became Texas Instruments' Digital Light Processor was conducted in the mid-1970s. Opportunity recognition first occurred with respect to this technology in 1978, when an application domain was identified. Prototypes were developed by 1980, and the technical breakthrough was incorporated into a consumer product in 1983. Within a year, the product was abandoned. At this point the project could have died, but two new potential applications were recognized, and middle and senior research managers and senior corporate management continued to provide financial support to sustain the project. In 1987, a critical technical breakthrough occurred which transformed the nature of the technology. Even so the project was in danger of being killed off. A major new potential application of interest to federal agencies emerged in 1989. Senior research managers succeeded in attracting federal funding and additional funding from an outside corporate partner that kept the project alive. In cases where a technical or market development reaches a dead end, it requires idea generation and opportunity recognition that result in a dramatic redirection of the project.

In another example, discontinuities in the development path of Dupont's Biodegradable Material project required reoccurrence of opportunity recognition. First, when the initial application was killed by the business unit, the manager of the research team identified a new market opportunity through industry contacts. He precipitated the development of a new product that embodied a characteristic of the original product that was not deemed important in the original application but which was the technical breakthrough for the new product. Next, when anticipated government regulations requiring biodegradable diapers did not materialize, a key customer pushing for the development of the technology suddenly became disinterested. A non-application specific (strategic) opportunity was recognized as important for the firm by the director of the business development group in central research, however, and the project was maintained on life support, with one person and almost no budget. Finally, a senior technical researcher in another business unit recognized an opportunity associated with a new application for this technology in a market of interest to his business unit, and reinvigorated the effort.

Again, this pattern is repeated in nearly every one of the twelve cases in the sample. When the technical and/or market assumptions related to an opportunity turn out to be incorrect, a project associated with a discontinuous innovation faces a high probability of being killed (as it should be if no attractive alternative opportunity emerges). At these critical junctures, a new occurrence of opportunity recognition is required to sustain the project. In some instances it is the same individuals who engage in the new instance of opportunity recognition, and in other instances, different individuals, even in other business units, recognize new opportunities. In most of the instances, a senior researcher or research manager engaged in the subsequent occurrences of opportunity recognition.

Although opportunity recognition is usually an act of individual initiative, informal networks play an important role in propagating waves of opportunity recognition within and external to the firm. The twelve projects in this study have undergone long gestation periods. Eleven of the twelve originated more than 10 years ago, and several can be traced back more than twenty years. The youngest project in the set, one based on the lightning-paced information technology industry, is entering its seventh year of development. While personnel turnover is inevitable under these conditions, for ten of the twelve projects, one or more of the early champions have been involved for the entire life of the project, although sometimes in different positions.

The capacity of the firm for opportunity recognition is related to the continuity of the informal network of individuals engaged in the conversion of breakthrough innovations into new ventures. *Upward networks* (access to senior managers) provide protection and access to pockets of money, while the broad-based *lateral and downward networks* appear to provide information, confirmation of the recognizer's perception of the opportunity, and other resources.

In the case of IBM's Silicon Germanium project, the opportunity was based on a scientific breakthrough that was in conflict with commonly accepted research results that turned out to be incorrect. In addition, the market for the technology represented a market discontinuity for the firm. As a result, there was substantial resistance on both market and technical dimensions to recognizing the opportunity. The well-established network of the research manager was critical to success in getting the opportunity recognized at multiple levels in the organization and in getting the opportunity re-recognized when market-related discontinuities occurred along the project development path.

First, in order to prove the initial research assumptions incorrect, he needed access to a fabrication line. No such resources were available to him, since this research was not funded at the time. He called a manufacturing specialist that he knew in another business unit and "called in [his] chits with him." In other words, were it not for the informal relationship he had with someone in a business unit, he would not have had access to the resources he needed. Later in the project, the research manager used his network of connections to potential customers to provide testimonials for his senior management about the potential of the technology in a new application market. A manager previously connected to an earlier incarnation of the project by that time held a manufacturing manager position. Because of his history with the technology and the research manager, he recognized the new opportunity and played a key role in enabling the pursuit of this new market. Four years later, this same individual became a vice president in the business unit in which the innovation is being commercialized and is a strong advocate for the innovation, even against a strong organizational resistance.

The evidence here is of senior management behaving as a protector within a resistant organization, and lateral networks providing resources (the fabrication line) and confirmation of the value of the opportunity (other scientists he met at professional conferences who were employed by potential customer firms). In seven of our twelve cases, senior managers behaved as protectors of potentially game changing opportunities. Thus, in more than half our sample, the project would have died had it not been for the project champion gaining access to a senior manager sponsor (Vice-President or above) and convincing him that the project was important. Senior managers provided protection from conventional forms of evaluation or from organizational resistance that arose in reaction to some of these projects. Rather than basing their decisions on promise of specific economic payback hurdles, sponsors commonly cited both their gut feelings that the project could have significant impact on the long-term success of the firm and their trust in the project champion. Thus they recognize the potential opportunity, rather than relying on the safety of a traditional evaluation process that uses criteria inappropriate for a breakthrough innovation. Many of the projects would "fall between the cracks" of the existing businesses of their corporations. The sponsor of each of these projects worked to keep them alive (even unofficially), and encouraged business units to adopt them. Thus, upward networks provide paths around conventional organizational processes that become pathological when applied to radical innovation.

The implication of these stories is that networks are efficient and cost effective. They are based on personal friendships, histories, and favors. Organizations today that are not promoting or leveraging long-term employment, job rotation, and building of networks may be missing opportunities to help their people think and act creatively.

Summarizing the Observations

Taken together, these data suggest that the process for moving from a firm's reservoir of technical knowledge to the initiation of a project with potentially game-changing opportunity appears to be almost capricious and, to a large extent, dependent on chance events, supra-normally motivated individuals, and rich informal systems, many of which have been destroyed with early retirements and downsizing activities. Further, the individuals in positions to see opportunities aren't always as motivated as the champion literature would lead one to believe.[30] Criteria applied by opportunity recognizers in the initial evaluation of breakthrough innovations are different from the conventional criteria applied to decision making regarding incremental innovation. The initial assessment is highly dependent on an individual's capacity to clarify the ways a technology can be used to substantiate a large enough market. This requires distinctive skills and access to many varying types of people to test early assumptions. It also requires multiple waves of opportunity recognition as the project confronts discontinuities, critical sponsors come and go, corporate strategies change, and the project's development path takes it into unexpected domains. All of this points to the need for sustained effort and mechanisms to help make the transitions easier.

Improving the Organizational Capacity for Opportunity Recognition

Based on the observations, following are methods that can help build an opportunity recognition capability in established organizations along with mechanisms to improve the gaps and potential difficulties.

Articulating a Call to Action

There are actions managers can take that establish a context to encourage idea generation and opportunity recognition. When senior managers communicate a need for breakthrough ideas, they get a response. These communications can either happen explicitly, as singular events, or be part of the fabric of the firm's culture. For example, Jerry Junkins, former CEO of Texas Instruments, announced the need to "find businesses in the white spaces between our existing business units." The Digital Light Processor project was one of several results of that call. At Nortel, a new ventures group was set up and began issuing Requests for Proposals for new business ideas. Their first taker was the group that is now the NetActive project. This was originally a group of individuals who had been assigned in one of the business units to "play in the idea sandbox" to try to develop applications for broadband technologies that were diffusing into homes. A number of ideas were generated, but this one did not exactly fit the bill of broadband communication. Had the Requests for Proposals not been issued, it may never have gone beyond the limits of the sandbox. In both of these instances, the message was simply a call for new directions for growth, which was currently being limited by the operating units' focus on current customers, current business models, and current combinations of technologies. It was a clear message about a need for new growth in any domain, and about organizational receptivity to new ideas.

A large percentage of our projects ensued from management's articulation of strategic intent to grow in a particular technology or market domain. A well-known example is the case of Jack Welch's commonly known order to "be Number 1 or Number 2 in all of our lines of business." This, in itself, provided an impetus for a mid-level researcher working in avionics at GE's Corporate R&D center to recognize the potential for the fluoroscopy technology he was developing as having possible applications in medical systems. He then made his counterpart in the medical systems group of the R&D lab aware of it. Similarly, it was Analog Devices' president Jerry Fishman's explicit statement of strategic intent during the early 1980s to "get into automotive" that motivated the effort that ultimately led to the accelerometer device as an airbag actuator, and subsequently into numerous other applications.

Investing in Organizational Enablers for Opportunity Recognition

Beyond the direct attention that senior management can give to stimulating breakthroughs, there are a number of activities organizations can engage in that help connect opportunity recognizers to internal and external sources of information. These activities reinforce the opportunity recognizers and steep them in diverse types of data that they use as fodder in making connections. Rather than simply relying on individuals to pursue access to a wide variety of sources of data on their own, R&D organizations can build enabling activities into people's jobs to increase the probability that opportunity recognition will occur.

Although we saw no evidence of firms providing special professional development programs to enhance the skills of opportunity recognizers, some of the firms did have mechanisms to stimulate divergent thinking among personnel in a position to engage in idea generation and opportunity recognition. For example, research scientists at GE described periodic conferences that brought together people from GE Medical Systems and Corporate Research and Development in which "people would talk about things that were a little bit more radical, wilder ideas and so forth. [These meetings promoted] cross-fertilization of ideas and exposure to what other people were doing." Interactions with other scientists in the opportunity recognizer's technical discipline and associated professions played an important role in our cases. Attendance at professional conferences and interactions with research labs and universities stimulated the recognition of a number of opportunities. Other enabling activities included think tanks, brown bag lunches with world-renowned scholars and researchers in particular fields of expertise that may become arenas of strategic focus for the firm, technology forecasting exercises, and idea generation sandboxes. These activities are frequently put in place for some short period of time when a new manager comes in and are the first to be cut when budgets need tightening. Yet these activities were a part of the genesis of each project we observed. Project team participants bemoaned the fact that, while management was benefiting from those activities through a current project, they would have no similarly enabling activities in the future.

Sustaining Attention: The Need for a Project Oversight Board

Strategic priorities in organizations shift over time. Firms that purport to value investments in potential breakthroughs are not consistent supporters. A senior technical manager in one of our participant companies described a recurring 17-year cycle during which strategic attention to the development of discontinuous innovations, opportunity recognition, and pursuit of new business opportunities waxed and waned.[31]

Changing expectations create inefficiencies in organizations, especially in the realm of highly uncertain, long development span, high investment opportunities. The stops and starts documented in these projects result, in part, from changing strategic contexts. The long investment horizon required, turnover in senior management, resistance posed by operating units that perceive it as a threat to their existing product lines and revenue models, and resistance from corporate funding boards as the project continues to require investment over long periods of time, all require some need for continuity, reminder of purpose, and continued articulation of the strategy.

We have documented the positive impact on opportunity recognition of senior management's articulation of strategic intent for growth. We have also documented the requirement for renewed opportunity recognition over time and across organizational sub-units as the players change. There is a need for an oversight board for each innovation project that protects the project from turnover in senior management champions and changes in key breakthrough innovation players, sub-units, and strategic contexts. The purpose of such a board would be to continue to articulate the opportunity in a manner meaningful to the firm, rather than to subject it to re-recognition by players who may not understand it or feel threatened by it. Hence, the board should include individuals with a long-term strategic view of the importance of breakthrough innovation who can make the long-term commitment to board participation needed to provide continuity and perseverance. Appropriate company outsiders (such as key members of project alliance partners or technical experts) should be considered for inclusion on the board. The firms in our study that structured such boards without including external members subjected the project to the normal bureaucratic haggling that comes with typical corporate resistance. Those that built the board based on needed expertise and alliances were more likely to succeed.

Promoting and Nurturing Informal Networks

Opportunities are frequently recognized by developing boundary-spanning capabilities in individuals. A broad-based awareness and sensitivity to business issues has been mentioned as a key component of opportunity recognition. For research managers who are most often the initial opportunity recognizers, sensitization to the key lines of business, current and potential customers, and future market directions enhances their effectiveness in this role. While we are not suggesting that they become market research specialists, our results point to the importance of the multi-dimensionality required of these individuals. The active promotion of informal networks is an activity management could undertake to allow researchers to gain this sensitivity. As one of the Senior Managers described the process:

> "The true genesis of the idea is technical. The vast number of ideas comes from the technical side. But they come from [technical people] with an understanding of market needs...They [get this through] interacting with their counterparts on the operating side. It's important that the scientists have enough [market] knowledge, and that knowledge either comes from their own experiences or working with the development folks."

Developing Organizational Structure Mechanisms that Support Breakthrough Innovation

Since opportunity recognizers are not always driven to champion the idea, it is imperative that organizations develop mechanisms to make it easy for opportunity recognizers to come forward. These mechanisms enhance the organization's capacity for radical innovations by focusing on and supporting three types of opportunity recognizers: *gatherers, hunters,* and *radical innovation hubs.*

Gatherers are passive opportunity recognizers. A good R&D manager can understand the potential business implications of a breakthrough idea brought to him by a bench scientist. These individuals have the experience, skill, judgment, and motivation to be alert and receptive to the ideas that bubble up out of the normal R&D environment. Not everyone is equipped to be an effective gatherer. They must have enough scientific or engineering knowledge to understand a technical concept, and they must also be sufficiently "market wise" to envision the technology's potential impact on the market. First-line or mid-level research managers or senior scientists usually play the role of gatherer.

Hunters are active seekers of opportunities in organizations. Their mandate is to search for opportunities among the activities in research labs and other arenas of the organization known to be sources of innovative ideas. Their skills and experiences are similar to the gatherers', but they are more oriented towards marketing and business development, with a broad rather than a specialist technical background. They use their extensive networks in the organization to quickly and inexpensively make connections between technologies they uncover and potential market applications. They often extend themselves outside of the organization as well. A key skill that a hunter must develop is the ability to articulate the opportunity in a compelling way for management. One hunter described his job as follows:

> "I was brought in to manage long-term product and market strategy. I started looking through R&D to find out where there was intellectual property that I could leverage into the marketplace. I was actively scanning and I knew [he] had been running around evangelizing the technology for two or three years. They hadn't made any progress. They just weren't able to build a case that got it recognized and funded. What we had here was a [Corporate Research] Fellow, one of the smartest guys in the world, but he couldn't get the attention to tilt this thing up."

A *Radical Innovation Hub* is a known home for ideas. Creating an organizational repository for ideas is an important approach to establishing idea receiving and opportunity recognition capacities in organizations. The hub's staff should have the skills and talents necessary to be opportunity recognizers themselves. They can convene informal and formal evaluation teams (experts from outside the organization if necessary), record evaluation outcomes, and provide feedback to idea generators. If the decision is made to form a team, the hub staff can play the role of catalyst. If the initial evaluation turns out to be negative, the hub staff can provide shelf space to store the idea for possible future use. Although we have seen several partial manifestations of a radical innovation hub in a few of our case studies, most firms don't have one. Just as there needs to be an organizational mechanism for capturing the results of opportunity recognition, there also needs to be a capacity for taking the results of a positive evaluation and establishing and supporting a breakthrough innovation project team. Clearly managing the handoffs between individuals and organizational structures is critically important for the survival and progress of breakthrough innovation projects. Hence, the individuals responsible for these sets of activities must be skillful at managing organizational interfaces.

We have observed several models of hunters, gatherers, and hubs that have not functioned well. The first is the single Business Development Manager located in Central R&D, whose job is to behave as a hunter and evaluator. This person floats from project to project within R&D to evaluate and guide the commercial development aspect of each project. In this case, the floater became so involved with one project that he ultimately joined the development team. The advantage of building the hub capability was lost. A new person had to be found to begin the process again. It was known as a rotational job position.

The second model we have seen is an informal group of scientists within R&D that convened monthly, under the direction of the R&D manager, to review ideas that came from anywhere. This was the fertile ground from which the technical insight sprang for one of our projects. However, there were two challenges associated with this board's structure. First, it served as a technical review only. There were no business development personnel on the board, and so early questions about markets and costs were not considered. Secondly, the

board was not a permanent fixture. The monthly r
R&D manager retired, and the firm no longer enga

The successful hub, then, will require a sta'
experiences, known within the organization as tʰ
ideas, and skilled at evaluating and helping artici
nologies. Persistence and organizational staying

Conclusions

Though developing a robust and persistᵁ...
recognition has proven to be a difficult challenge for these nɪɪɪʋ, ...
within the sample have aided the opportunity recognition practice. The in-depᵁ.
descriptions and insights of these firms can contribute to grounded theory development and offers the potential to improve practice for the technology-inten-
sive, established firm. Systematic methods to enable opportunity recognizers
to leverage their skills are imperative for those organizations that compete based
on technological innovation.

Notes

1. J.G. Morone, *Winning in High Tech Markets* (Boston: MA: Harvard Business School Press, 1993).
2. Frederick Betz, *Strategic Technology Management* (New York, NY: McGraw-Hill, 1993); D. Gerwin, "Integrating Manufacturing into the Strategic Phases of New Product Development," *California Management Review*, 35/4 (Summer 1993): 121-134; G. Hamel and C.K. Prahalad *Competing for the Future* (Boston, MA: Harvard Business School Press, 1994).
3. G. Hamel, *Leading the Revolution* (Boston, MA: Harvard Business School Press, 2000).
4. M.P. Bhave, "A Process Model of Entrepreneurial Venture Creation," *Journal of Business Venturing*, 9 (1994): 223-241. See also I.M. Kirzner, *Competition and Entrepreneurship* (Chicago: The University of Chicago Press, 1983), wherein on p. 81 the author states: "The important feature of entrepreneurship is...the ability to perceive opportunities which others have not yet noticed...to see where new products have become unsuspectedly valuable to consumers and where new methods of production have, unknown to others, become feasible." Our thanks to an anonymous reviewer for reminding us of this reference.
5. Hamel and Prahalad, op. cit.
6. Most researchers in the field of creativity acknowledge that the level of creativity varies across people, and they note the power of organizational support mecha-nisms to help encourage creative actions. See for example A. van Gundy, "Organizational Creativity and Innovation," in Scott G. Isaksen, ed., *Frontiers of Creativity Research: Beyond the Basics* (Buffalo, NY: Bearly Limited, 1987), pp. 358-381.
7. T.M. Amabile, "A Model of Creativity and Innovation in Organizations," in B.M. Staw and L.L. Cummings, eds., *Research in Organizational Behavior*, Vol. 10 (Green-wich, CT: JAI Press, 1988). See also H.L. Angle, "Psychology and Organizational Innovation," in A.H. Van de Ven, H.L. Angle, and M.S. Poole, eds., *Research on the*

Management of Innovation: The Minnesota Studies (New York, NY: Ballinger, 1989), pp. 135-170.

8. T.M. Amabile, "The Delicate Balance in Managing for Creativity," *R&D Innovator* (August 1994); T.M. Amabile, "How to Kill Creativity," *Harvard Business Review*, 76/5 (September/October 1998): 76-87; T.M. Amabile, R. Conti, H. Coon, J. Lazenby, and M. Herron, "Assessing the Work Environment for Creativity," *Academy of Management Journal*, 39/5 (October 1996): 1154-1184.

9. C.M. Christensen, *The Innovator's Dilemma: When New Technologies Cause Great Firms to Fail* (Boston, MA: Harvard Business School Press, 1997).

10. H.I. Ansoff, *The New Corporate Strategy* (New York, NY: John Wiley & Sons, 1988); C.K. Prahalad and G. Hamel, "The Core Competence of the Corporation," *Harvard Business Review*, 68/3 (May/June 1990): 79-91; R.P. Rumelt, *Strategy, Structure and Economic Performance* (Cambridge, MA: Harvard University Press, 1974).

11. A.S. Miner, "Structural Evolution Through Idiosyncratic Jobs: The Potential for Unplanned Learning," *Organization Science*, 1 (May 1990): 195-210; M.L. Tushman and P. Anderson, "Technological Discontinuities and Organization Environments," *Administrative Science Quarterly*, 31 (September 1986): 439-465; R.A. Burgelman, "A Process Model of Internal Corporate Venturing in the Diversified Major Firm," *Administrative Science Quarterly*, 28 (June 1983): 223-244; D. Dougherty and C. Hardy, "Sustained Product Innovation in Large, Mature Organizations: Overcoming Innovation-to-Organization Problems," *Academy of Management Journal*, 39/5 (1996): 1120-1153.

12. A.H. Van de Ven, "Central Problems in the Management of Innovation," *Management Science*, 32/5 (May 1986): 590-607.

13. M.L. Tushman and C.A. O'Reilly III, "Ambidextrous Organizations: Managing Evolutionary and Revolutionary Change," *California Management Review*, 38/4 (Summer 1996): 8-30.

14. J.M. Howell and C.A. Higgins, "Champions of Technological Innovation," *Administrative Science Quarterly*, 35 (1990): 317-341; D. Day, "Raising Radicals: Different Processes for Championing Innovative Corporate Ventures," *Organization Science*, 5 (1994): 148-172; S.K. Markham, "A Longitudinal Examination of How Champions Influence Others to Support Their Projects," *Journal of Product Innovation Management*, 15 (1998): 490-504; S.K. Markham and A. Griffin, "The Breakfast of Champions: Associations between Champions and Product Development Environments, Practices and Performance," *Journal of Product Innovation Management*, 15 (1998): 490-504.

15. See, for example, Richard N. Foster, "Timing Technological Transitions," in M.L. Tushman and W.L. Moore, eds., *Readings in the Management of Innovation* (Cambridge, MA: Ballinger, 1988). See also Betz, op. cit.

16. Mark B. Myers and Richard S. Rosenbloom, "Research Management and Corporate Renewal," Conference on the Future of Industrial Research, Harvard Business School, February 1993.

17. Gary Hamel and C.K. Prahalad, "Corporate Imagination and Expeditionary Marketing," *Harvard Business Review*, 69/4 (July/August 1991): 81-92.

18. Paul Strebel, *Breakpoints: How Managers Exploit Radical Business Change* (Boston, MA: Harvard Business School Press, 1992).

19. J. Gluck, "Radical Innovation through Creative Leadership," in R.L. Kuhn, ed., *Handbook for Creative and Innovative Managers* (New York, NY: McGraw-Hill, 1988). See also Betz, op. cit.

20. Michael L. Tushman and David Nadler, "Organizing for Innovation," *California Management Review*, 28/3 (Spring 1986): 74-92.

21. Edward B. Roberts and Alan R. Fusfeld, "Staffing the Innovative Technology-Based Organization," *Sloan Management Review*, 22/3 (Spring 1981): 19-33. See

also Michael J. Martin, *Managing Technological Innovation and Entrepreneurship* (Reston, VA: Reston Publishing Company, Inc., 1984)

22. Robert A. Burgelman, "A Process Model of Internal Corporate Venturing in the Diversified Major Firm," *Administrative Science Quarterly*, 28/2 (1983): 223-244. See also Martin, op. cit.

23. A.H. Van de Ven, H.L. Angle and M.S. Poole, eds., *Research on the Management of Innovation: The Minnesota Studies* (New York, NY: Harper & Row, 1989). See also A.H. Van de Ven, "Central Problems in the Management of Innovation," *Management Science*, 32/5 (1986): 590-607; A.H. Van de Ven and D. Pollay, "Learning While Innovating," *Organization Science*, 3/1 (February 1992): 92-116; Y.T. Cheng and A.H. Van de Ven, "Learning the Innovation Journey: Order Out of Chaos?" *Organization Science*, 7/6 (November/December 1996): 593-614.

24. K.M. Eisenhardt, "Building Theories from Case Study Research," *Academy of Management Review*, 14/4 (1989): 532-550.

25. R.K. Yin, *Case Study Research* (Thousand Oaks, CA: Sage Publications, 1994).

26. M.B. Miles and A.M. Huberman, *Qualitative Data Analysis*, 2nd edition (Thousand Oaks, CA: Sage Publications, 1994).

27. For a more detailed description of the characteristics of these projects, see G.C. O'Connor, "Market Learning and Radical Innovation: A Cross Case Comparison," *Journal of Product Innovation Management*, 15/2 (March 1998): 151-166.

28. This observation implies that relying on the literature about championing behavior may not be leading us in the right direction in our thinking about opportunity recognition. We find they are two independent sets of skills.

29. The informal technology review practice has been discontinued since the research managers' retirement, which reinforces our point that these practices are ad hoc and dependent on individual initiative.

30. In this regard, the champion literature suffers from a fundamental methodological flaw. Typically the researcher identifies champions after a project's been initiated, and then studies his behaviors, attitudes, and skills. What this implies is that the literature has not identified those who recognized opportunities but elected *not* to champion them, which is something we identify in this work.

31. Parry Norling and Robert J. Statz, "How Discontinuous Innovation Really Happens," *Research-Technology Management*, 41/3 (May 1998): 41-44.

[11]

A DYNAMIC PERSPECTIVE

OF INTERNAL FIT IN

CORPORATE VENTURING

STEWART THORNHILL
York University, Toronto, Ontario, Canada

RAPHAEL AMIT
The University of British Columbia, Vancouver, BC, Canada

EXECUTIVE SUMMARY

Managers of corporate parents and their ventures have long been faced with the question of how closely to tie the parent and venture. A close connection may enable a venture to capitalize on the competencies and resources of the parent. However, venture autonomy could prevent corporate inertia and bureaucracy from constraining venture growth.

The lack of consensus on this issue leads us to the first of two complementary research questions that we address in this paper: "What is the effect of internal strategic fit between a corporate parent and its venture on venture performance?" We suggest that a tight fit is positively associated with venture performance because of the venture's access to its parent's resources.

Managers and researchers alike have often observed that growing enterprises are dynamic entities. In the case of corporate ventures, this implies that the relationship between parent and venture evolves over time. Our second research question directly addresses this issue by asking: "Does the relationship between a corporate parent and its venture(s) evolve over time, and if so, how?"

We identify two dimensions of the fit between corporate parents and their ventures: relational and economic. A relational fit reflects organizational culture and structure, while an economic fit is a function of the needs of the venture and the resources of the parent. We develop a series of hypotheses and test them with survey data from 97 Canadian corporate ventures. For the purposes of this study, we define success as the ability of a firm to meet internal milestones on schedule.

We find that the degree of fit between a corporate parent and its venture does affect the success of a venture, and that success is associated with high levels of awareness, commitment, and connection. Further, the relational dimension of the parent-venture interface appears to have a greater association with venture success than does the economic dimension.

Our data support the idea that the parent-venture relationship is dynamic in nature as ventures in our sample generally lessened their economic connections with their parents as they matured (or vice-versa). We did find, however, that the relational bonds remained more or less intact. The exceptions to

Address correspondence to Dr. Stewart Thornhill, York University, Schulich School of Business, 4700 Keele Street, Toronto, ON, M6P 2R7, Canada; Phone: (416) 736-2100 (x77908); Fax: (416) 736-5687; E-mail: sthornhill@ssb.yorku.ca

The authors are most grateful for the generous financial support of the Social Sciences and Humanities Research Council of Canada (Grant # 412930005). The authors are also grateful to the editor and the two anonymous JBV reviewers for their valuable comments and suggestions.

Journal of Business Venturing **16**, 25–50

0883-9026/01/$–see front matter
PII S0883-9026(99)00040-3

26 S. THORNHILL AND R. AMIT

these general trends were an increasing emphasis on financial targets along with decreasing CEO involvement as ventures matured. Both of these findings make intuitive sense. Greater financial independence is accompanied by greater financial accountability. And, as a venture gains in both independence and accountability, there is less need for the CEO to provide "air cover." These two issues aside, the basic model of enduring relational ties and diminishing economic ties was supported. As well, the increasing accountability is consistent with our expectation that a close connection is preferable to high venture autonomy. © 2000 Elsevier Science Inc.

Firms with growth aspirations have several ways of reaching their goals. Mergers, acquisitions, and joint ventures are a few of the better-known approaches to firm growth. Another route, which is of interest to both managers and researchers, is corporate venturing—growing a business from the inside out. The motives for launching a corporate venture include improving corporate profitability, (Zahra 1991), generating strategic renewal (Guth and Ginsberg 1990), fostering innovation (Baden-Fuller 1995) and gaining knowledge that may be parlayed into future revenue streams (McGrath, Venkataraman, and MacMillan 1994).

Researchers have acknowledged the importance of the corporate venture (CV) as a vehicle for firm growth (Arrow 1982; Burgelman 1983) and have addressed several issues unique to this growth mechanism. The literature addresses the performance implications of corporate ventures (Biggadike 1979), the relationship between CV performance and environmental context (Covin and Slevin 1994; Tsai, MacMillan, and Low 1991; Zahra 1993), the role of compensation practices within corporate ventures (Block and Ornati 1987), and the influence of CV champions (Day 1994). The relationship between a corporate parent (CP) and its corporate venture has also been studied (Miller, Spann, and Lerner 1991; Sorrentino and Williams 1995). Little has been done, however, to empirically test whether the connection, or fit, between parent and venture influences CV performance. Although some authors have argued that high levels of relatedness between CP and CV are desirable (Dougherty 1995; MacMillan, Block, and Narasimha 1986), others have contended that tight coupling is antithetical to venture success (Burgelman 1983; Ginsberg and Hay 1994; Sykes and Block 1989). In his report on 37 ventures at Exxon Enterprises, Sykes (1986) identified reasons both for and against the practice of allowing venture autonomy.

The lack of consensus on this issue leads us to the first of two complementary research questions that we address in this paper: "*What is the effect of internal strategic fit between a corporate parent and its venture on venture performance?*" Following the resource-based view of the firm (Penrose 1959; Wernerfelt 1984), which argues that competitive advantage derives from idiosyncratic capabilities that firms develop internally, we suggest that a tight fit is positively associated with venture performance because of the venture's access to its parent's resources. This position, along with several specific hypotheses, is developed in the sections that follow.

A number of studies have argued that corporate venturing is a dynamic process, that is, one in which the relationship between parent and venture evolves as the venture matures (Burgelman 1983; Garud and Van de Ven 1992; Schrader and Simon 1997; Sykes 1986). Our second research question addresses this issue by asking: "*Does the relationship between a corporate parent and its venture(s) evolve over time, and if so, how?*"

In the following sections, we develop a model of the CP-CV relationship that incorporates the economic and relational dimensions of firm growth within a dynamic, evolutionary framework. This perspective is anchored in both the extant literature and a series of interviews with corporate venture managers. We formulate specific hypotheses from the model and test them with survey data from a sample of 97 Canadian corporate ventures. Finally, we present and discuss the results of the empirical tests.

CONCEPTUAL DEVELOPMENT

Corporate Venturing

Our review of the literature on the processes and outcomes of corporate venturing (summarized in Table 1) reveals a few points of general agreement. First, it is generally agreed that corporate venturing has a positive effect on firm performance (Biggadike 1979; Zahra 1991, 1993; Zahra and Covin 1995), although such benefits are not guaranteed and ventures may take several years to become profitable. Second, ventures go through a series of stages as they mature (Garud and Van de Ven 1992; McGrath et al. 1994; Schrader and Simon 1997). Though a number of classification schemes have been suggested in the literature, there is general agreement that the nature of CVs is dynamic, not static. Third, and in keeping with the evolutionary nature of the ventures themselves, there is almost unanimous agreement that milestones are the best method for evaluating CV performance (Block and MacMillan 1993; Block and Ornati 1987).

Although it is reassuring that there are some areas of convergence in the literature, there are also several areas on which there is little or no agreement. Researchers disagree, for example, about the desired tightness of coupling or fit between parent and venture. The degree of fit may be thought of as a continuum, anchored at one end by what Sykes (1986) refers to as "total congruence." In this case, "the 'venture' is no more than a new product extension by an existing operating division, and, even if innovative, would probably not qualify as 'internal venturing'" (Sykes 1986, p. 281). At the other end of the continuum is an independent entrepreneurial enterprise (Miller et al. 1991; Schrader and Simon 1997). The debate revolves around which point on this spectrum is optimal for corporate venture performance.

The advantages of a close fit between parent and venture include resource sharing (e.g., access by the venture to the parent's suppliers and distributors) and the availability of internal corporate capital. On the other hand, ventures with greater autonomy may be free from the entrenched bureaucratic processes of the corporate parent and more flexible in their response to changing internal and external demands. Effective corporate venturing has been described as a balancing act with needs for creativity and change on one side and demands for cohesiveness and complementarity on the other (Lengnick-Hall 1992; Tushman and Nadler 1986).

The few studies that have directly addressed internal fit have yielded mixed results. Ginsberg and Hay (1994), for example, argued that the flexibility associated with autonomy facilitates CV success. Similar conclusions were presented by Dougherty (1995) and Block (1989), based on the premise that the pressures and rigidities emanating from a corporate parent adversely affect venture performance. A similar argument contends that management practices that work for large corporations are inappropriate for ventures (Block 1983; Kanter 1985; Sykes and Block 1989).

A study of 88 industrial product corporate ventures from the PIMS STR4 database found that relatedness between corporate parents and ventures does not affect venture performance (Sorrentino and Williams 1995). This finding echoes the results of a similar study, also using PIMS data, in which the reporting level for CVs was found to have

TABLE 1 Summary of Corporate Venturing Research

Author(s)	Research Question(s)	Finding(s)
Baden-Fuller (1995)	Proposition: competitive advantage flows from the capacity to manage internal change, a capacity which is closely connected to corporate entrepreneurship	Strategic innovations are not necessarily profitable. Corporate entrepreneurship is not the only way to stimulate innovation is established firms.
Biggadike (1979)	What are the performance implications of corporate venturing?	Of the ventures studied, 18% achieved profitability in 2 years, 38% in 4 years. Median performance was 7% ROI in years 7 and 8. Companies should start fewer ventures with more resources rather than many with less. The time it takes to reach profitability can be reduced by spending more earlier to obtain market share.
Birkinshaw (1997)	An exploratory study on initiatives in MNC subsidiaries	Two distinct entrepreneurial processes: (1) internal—initiatives subject to corporate selection mechanisms, and (2) external—initiatives subject to local environmental selection mechanisms (e.g., customer acceptance)
Block (1983)	How can corporate ventures succeed?	There are five pivotal decisions which can impact venture success: format, management and compensation, venture plan approval, positioning, and financing triggers.
Block (1989)	How can firms reduce the costs of corporate venture failure?	Two principal causes of large losses: (1) incorrect assumption and (2) pressures within the parent which inhibit altering or aborting venture strategies.
Block and Ornati (1987)	What compensation practices are in use among corporate ventures and do they impact performance?	"... the incentives and compensation used are not correlated with the rate of success ... (but) the compensation systems used weren't much of an incentive" (p. 44).
Burgelman (1983)	What are the processes by which a large diversified firm transforms new technology into new businesses through internal corporate venturing?	"Because corporate entrepreneurship ... seems to differ from traditional individual entrepreneurship, as well as from traditional organizational economic activity, it may be necessary to devise different arrangements between the corporate resource providers and their entrepreneurial agents" (p. 243).
Caruana, Morris, and Vella (1998)	How do centralization and formalization impact entrepreneurial behavior in export firms?	"The results suggest that entrepreneurial behavior is negatively affected by increases in centralization and size but positively influenced by increased formalization" (p. 24).
Chung and Gibbons (1997)	What is the role of culture in corporate entrepreneurship?	1. As superstructure, culture provides an ideology for organizational members 2. As a sociostructure, culture provides social capital which in turn enables the emergence of competitive advantage.

(continued)

TABLE 1 *continued*

Author(s)	Research Question(s)	Finding(s)
Covin and Slevin (1994)	What is the impact of industry technological sophistication and the strategy-related characteristics of entrepreneurial firms?	Industry technological sophistication moderates the strength of the relationships between many strategic and firm performance. The modes of competition differ for entrepreneurial firms in high and low technology industries.
Day (1994)	How does the championing process explain innovativeness in corporate venturing?	Ventures requiring modest resources may survive with low level champions and have the potential to be radically innovative. Top level champions are required for high-profile, expensive, innovative ventures.
Dougherty (1995)	How can managers assure an effective connection between ventures and the firm's core competencies?	Connecting core competencies with new products is problematic because of the existence and persistence of rigid core incompetencies with which the competencies have little interplay. Incompetencies must be managed so that competencies can be assessed.
Garud, and Van de Ven (1992)	What guides the development of a venture under conditions of uncertainty and ambiguity?	Three different periods: agenda setting, expansion, and contraction. Negative outcomes lead to greater involvement by corporate sponsors.
Hornsby, Naffziger, Kuratko and Montagno (1993)	Introduction of a model that describes the intrapreneurship process from initial decision to implementation	"Intrapreneurship is multidimensional and relies on the successful interaction of several activities rather than events occurring in isolation." (p. 35)
Jennings and Lumpkin (1989)	What differences exist between conservative and entrepreneurial firms?	In entrepreneurial organizations: decision making is more participative, performance objectives are jointly determined, and managers are not penalized for the failure of risky projects.
Knight (1989)	Examination and comparison of innovative practices in large and small firms	CV obstacles includes: lack of entrepreneurial talent, lack of CV fit with corporate strategy, and lack of commitment to the venture. IVs encountered problems with market assessment and operational and financial issues.
Lengnick-Hall (1992)	Can configurations for strategy and design of CVs be defined and tested and does the level of cohesion between strategy and CV design affect market performance with profitability?	Firms that are highly cohesive experience fewer obstacles and problems. Cohesiveness may be more advantageous for lean, value driven firms than for rigid firms requiring more resource diversity and organizational slack.

(continued)

30 S. THORNHILL AND R. AMIT

TABLE 1 *continued*

Author(s)	Research Question(s)	Finding(s)
MacMillan, Block, and Narasimha (1986)	What obstacles face firms wishing to launch CVs?	Firms should attempt to acquire experience by starting with joint ventures or small ventures.
McGrath (1995)	What are the management opportunities inherent in CV disappointments?	Redirection is an important alternative to shutting down unsuccessful CVs. Linkages between a CV and other SBUs can facilitate the benefit of knowledge transfer if a CV fails.
McGrath, Venkataraman, and MacMillan (1994)	Development of a framework which combines extant CV theory with the RBV to depict CV potential for yielding future rents.	Ventures evolve through a series of developmental stages. CV progress should be assessed in terms of the development of new competencies and their subsequent exploitation.
Miller and Camp (1985)	What differences exist between the strategies of successful and unsuccessful corporate ventures?	Successful strategies differ between young ventures and matures SBUs (e.g., low cost strategy is better for mature SBUs while differentiation is more suitable for adolescent CVs)
Miller, Gartner, and Wilson (1989)	What is the effect of entry order on market share and competitive advantage among corporate ventures?	"Overall, pioneers typically gain significantly greater market share and some types of competitive advantage compared to followers (specifically, product and technological advantages)" (p. 203)
Miller, Spann, and Lerner (1991)	What is the impact of resource sharing, reporting level, and the relationship between sharing and reporting level?	Resource sharing benefits quality advantages but hurts cost advantages. No main effects for reporting level. Reporting level moderated quality and cost advantages of resource sharing (highest performance with lowest reporting levels).
Miller, Wilson and Adams (1988)	What is an appropriate measure for evaluating corporate venture success?	Velocity (V = product of regression coefficient of ROI over time (beta) and coefficient of determination (r-sq.) fit the observed data in 78% of the cases.
Pearce, Kramer and Robbins (1997)	What managerial behaviors indicate an entrepreneurial orientation and how are such behaviors evaluated by subordinates?	"Overall, this study developed and validated a scale of entrepreneurial behaviors and found that corporate entrepreneurship was well received by subordinates even when such behaviors were counter to the preexisting culture" (p. 158)
Schrader and Simon (1997)	1) Do IVs and CVs emphasize different resources? 2) Do IVs and CVs pursue different strategies? 3) Do IVs and CVs differ in performance? 4) Do IVs and CVs differ in the relationship between resources, strategies, and performance?	1) IVs placed importance on external capital and brand development; CVs developed proprietary knowledge and marketing. 2) IV's concentrated on customer service & specialty products & had greater strategic breadth. 3) No performance differences 4) Broad strategies improved IV performance and degraded CV performance.

(continued)

TABLE 1 *continued*

Author(s)	Research Question(s)	Finding(s)
Sorrentino and Williams (1995)	Does relatedness determine CV success?	"The degree to which a venture is related to its parent firm does not explain performance results or the entry strategy decisions at the venture level" (p. 70) [Performance is evaluated by market share]
Sykes (1986)	What factors determine corporate venture success?	"The data provide strong evidence that venture managers' prior experience in the venture's target market area and their general managerial experience are the factors most important to venture financial success" (p. 290).
Thornhill, Amit, and Belcourt (1998)	What are the influences of venture strategies, venture capabilities, and environmental hostility on corporate venture performance?	Corporate venture profitability is positively associated with venture age and negatively associated with environmental hostility. Differentiation appears to be an appropriate strategy in benign environments, while aggressive marketing and innovation are called for in hostile competitive conditions.
Tsai, MacMillan, and Low (1991)	What is the relative importance of environment and strategy for CV performance?	Both environment and strategy are important to CV success. Munificent markets are good; hostile markets are not. Quality strategy improves market share at the expense of ROI. Low prices and high promotion improve both market share and ROI.
Zahra (1991)	(1) What are the antecedents of corporate entrepreneurship? (2) What is the association between CV and company performance?	(1) CV activities increased as environments were perceived as increasingly dynamic, hostile, and heterogeneous. (2) There was a positive relationship between CV and company performance.
Zahra (1993)	What is the relationship between external environment, corporate entrepreneurship and financial performance?	CV activities differ in different environments. CV is associated with company financial performance.
Zahra (1995)	What is the impact of LBOs on corporate entrepreneurship?	Changes in corporate entrepreneurship activities after LBOs were positively associated with changes in company performance.
Zahra (1996a)	What is the relationship between corporate ownership, industry, and corporate entrepreneurship?	Executive stock ownership and long-term institutional ownership are positively associated with CV. Conversely, short-term institutional ownership is negatively associated with it, as is a high ratio of outside directors on a company's board. Finally, an industry's technological opportunities moderate the associations observed between corporate governance and ownership variables and corporate entrepreneurship.

(continued)

32 S. THORNHILL AND R. AMIT

TABLE 1 *continued*

Author(s)	Research Question(s)	Finding(s)
Zahra (1996b)	(1) Do CVs and IVs vary in their technology strategies? (2) Do the dimensions of technology strategy influence the performance of CVs and IVs differently?	Both research questions can be answered in the affirmative: "The results suggest that the two venture types follow different paths to achieve success. The high performing IV focuses its R&D spending on pioneering a few new products. Conversely, the CV benefits from investing more in R&D to develop many products and by protecting these products with patents . . . the CV uses both internal and external R&D sources" (p. 310).
Zahra and Covin (1995)	What is the CV–performance relationship in different industry contexts?	CV is positively associated with firm performance and the strength of the relationship increases over time. Hostile environments reward CV activities more than do benign environments.

no main effects on venture performance (Miller et al. 1991). However, Lengnick-Hall (1992) presented evidence in favor of a close fit in her study of 86 firms sampled from the *Business Week 1000*. Based on the results of discriminant analysis, she concluded that "the price of neglecting organizational consistency is increased organizational problems" (Lengnick-Hall 1992, p. 147).

Internal Strategic Fit

Our model of the relationship between a firm and its corporate venture(s) borrows from the grounded theory methodology of Glaser and Straus (1967). We conducted 17 semi-structured interviews, 1 to 2 hours in length, with senior executives and venture managers of nine large Canadian corporations that had engaged in a wide range of corporate ventures. Our analysis of the interview transcripts guided our construction of a model in which the parent and venture interact on the basis of economic drivers (based on the resources of the parents and needs of the venture) and relational drivers (flowing from the structures and cultures of the parent and venture).

The economic aspect of the CP-CV relationship was expressed by one venture manager in his observation that "Certainly the deep pockets of (the parent company) helped because I had lost a lot of money." The nature of the economic ties is complex and often difficult to manage, a sentiment expressed by another senior executive who stated that "We're probably under-funding. . . . We're hobbling our young entrepreneurs too much." Yet, the same executive was quick to qualify his remark: ". . . but, then again, I'm not so sure that that doesn't create innovation."

Our interviews also revealed a relational dimension to the CP-CV structure. In the words of one CEO, "I think that building a new business is very much about managing relationships." Two of our interviewees also drew analogies between child-rearing and corporate venturing. This metaphor not only captures the relational issue; it also encompasses the evolving, dynamic nature of the relationship.

The economic dimension pertains to issues such as investment and compensation, while the relational dimension involves issues such as the levels of support and trust that exist between a venture and its corporate parent. These categories are similar to the intrinsic and extrinsic dimensions proposed by Sykes (1986). Under his typology, the extrinsic dimension captures the relationship between a venture and its corporate sponsor and includes structural and procedural sub-dimensions. The intrinsic dimension pertains to the characteristics of the venture itself and is divided into product-related and managerial facets. Although Sykes's dimensions are respectively parent-focused and venture-focused, our dimensions portray the parent-venture relationship in distinct economic and relational terms.

Economic Dimension

Our interviews revealed four aspects of the economic dimension of the parent-venture relationship. The first stems from the parent's reasons for launching a venture. Ventures launched with the objective of earning a target return on investment may be run very differently from ventures launched for defensive (responding to competitors' initiatives) or developmental purposes. McGrath (1995) argued that ventures must be able to demonstrate "market worth," (i.e., economic viability) without which they will be unlikely to survive. The prospect of turning a profit should also enhance support within corporate top management, further enhancing the likelihood of venture success. We anticipated that ventures that are anchored in well-developed business plans with articulated, profit-based objectives would experience greater success than those that are not.

This raises the issues of performance evaluation and accountability. There are many ways to evaluate the success of a venture. For the purposes of this study, we define success according to a venture's ability to meet milestones on schedule (see *Method* section below). While there are as many different types of milestones as there are new ventures (e.g., target shipping dates, market share, ROI), profitability eventually enters the discussion. Block and MacMillan (1993) observed that lax financial controls are among the more common causes of corporate venture failure. We anticipated that firms that evaluate their ventures on the basis of financial targets would be successful more often than those that eschew financial benchmarks.

Another dimension of corporate venturing is the capital stake that the parent commits to a venture. How much the parent invests, whether the funds are sunk and/or restrict redeployment, and whether funds are delivered as promised all send signals to the venture team and external stakeholders such as clients, competitors, and suppliers about the level of commitment of the parent (Ghemawat 1991). We expected that economic commitments in the form of large, specialized, non-recoverable investments would be associated with venture success.

The fourth facet of the economic relationship concerns the degree of congruence between the practices of a parent and its venture. This dimension speaks directly to the issue of tight fit versus autonomy. Are venture managers compensated differently than the managers of the parent company? Are training budgets larger? Is the budgeting process more flexible? Our preliminary interviews and subsequent theory development led us to predict that firms that maintain consistency in the administration of compensation and budgeting practices between parent and venture would be more successful than firms allowing autonomy among their ventures' financial practices. In other words, *we expected to see greater success among firms that treat their ventures more like divisions of the parent than like stand-alone entities*. This reflects our belief that corporate ventures that do not maintain close connection with the parent forego the resource-based competitive advantages of the parent, and thus hinder their own prospects for success. We thus have the following hypotheses:

H1: Ventures selected on the basis of economic decision making (e.g., rate of return) are more successful than those that are not.

H2: Venture success is associated with the use of financial targets.

H3: Venture success is associated with large, specialized investments of capital by the parent company.

H4: Venture success is associated with uniform financial practices between parent and venture.

Relational Dimension

Ventures often have to compete with other CVs or with other corporate divisions for a limited pool of resources. However, ventures can diminish the effects of competition by operating under the mentorship of a chief executive. Champions are often critical to the survival and success of internal ventures (Day 1994; Frost and Egri 1990). We predict that ventures that obtain top management sponsorship, in the form of active support from the parent CEO and the CEO running interference for the venture, experience greater success than those that lack such support.

Another element of the relational dimension involves the visibility or preeminence of the venture within the parent company. Hornsby, Naffziger, Kuratko, and Montagno (1993) identified both management support and time availability as factors that contribute to the success of a corporate venture. Venkataraman, MacMillan, and McGrath (1992) emphasized the need to manage both the hierarchical processes and the institutional context within which corporate venturing activities take place. Preeminence may flow from efforts on the part of the venture manager to secure buy-in at the senior management levels of the parent company. Preeminence will also be indicated by the position of the venture on the parent's business agenda.

A third element of the relational dimension is confidence, or trust. Barney and Hansen (1994) have identified trustworthiness as a potential source of competitive advantage. Ventures that have faith that the parent will not abandon them when the going gets tough, and whose parents have solid track records of meeting commitments, should be more likely to succeed than ventures without such qualities.

A final aspect of the parent-venture relationship mirrors the issue of economic connection and consistency. We predict that autonomy, as indicated by empowerment of venture employees and managers and a strong culture within the venture, is negatively related to venture success. We thus have the following hypotheses:

> *H5:* Venture success is associated with active protection and support by the parent CEO.
>
> *H6:* Venture success is associated with preeminence in the eyes of the parent.
>
> *H7:* Venture success is associated with high levels of commitment and trust between parent and venture.
>
> *H8:* Venture success is associated with low levels of venture autonomy.

Parent-Venture Dynamics

Because of the dynamic nature of the parent-venture relationship, longitudinal studies of venture performance are highly valued and in high demand. Yet they tend to be the exception rather than the norm in entrepreneurship and strategy research. Those studies that have taken a longitudinal approach tend to be characterized by small sample sizes that limit their scope and generalizability. Although our survey is fundamentally cross-sectional, we capture some of the dynamic nature of the CP-CV relationship by asking respondents about parent and venture practices in progressive stages of venture growth and maturity. Our approach is exploratory and the following propositions are tentative, yet we believe that our research is a step in the direction of capturing the dynamic processes underlying the growth of corporate ventures.

We propose that the relationship between a CP and CV evolves as a venture matures but that the economic and relational dimensions of the CP-CV fit evolve in different ways. When a corporate parent launches a venture, the venture is critically dependent on the economic resources of the parent. As the venture begins to grow, this dimension may become less important. The relational ties between parent and venture, on the other hand, do not necessarily diminish in importance as a function of venture maturity. Returning to our original position that *the connection between CP and CV enables a venture to capitalize on the idiosyncratic, distinctive competencies of the parent,* we contend that maintaining close relational fit serves a venture well, regardless of its stage of development. This view of the evolution of the economic and relational ties between parent and venture is captured in the following propositions:

P1: Economic ties tend to diminish between parent and venture as a venture matures.

P2: Relational ties tend to remain consistently strong between parent and venture as a venture matures.

METHODS

Sample

Our initial sample frame comprised 2,614 of Canada's largest companies. We sent a screening letter to these firms asking if they had developed any new business units as part of their growth strategy. A business was considered "new" if it had developed any three of the following: new markets, new methods of distribution, new products/services, and/or new technology. A total of 448 firms responded, 261 in the affirmative.

The interview phase of our research project, supported by an extensive review of the corporate venturing and strategic management literature, served as the foundation for a detailed survey of practices and processes. The survey, which we pilot tested with senior managers of parent corporations and their ventures, was sent to the CEOs of the 261 firms that had responded positively to our initial mailing. One follow up letter and a phone call to initial non-respondents yielded a total of 102 completed surveys.

Our rationale for using a mail survey as our method of data collection is consistent with Schrader and Simon (1997), who noted that "A survey was the most appropriate means of collecting data, because secondary sources did not contain detailed information regarding companies' resources, strategies, and performance. . . . Privately owned IVs (independent ventures) do not publish annual reports, and data on CVs are often subsumed into the sponsors' reports." (1997, p. 54).

Of the 102 responses that we received, one firm was excluded because we felt that its reported venture age (38 years) made it inappropriate to include that firm with a group of relatively young corporate ventures. Four other firms were excluded due to non-response to an item on milestone attainment which we use as the dependent variable of our study (see *Measures* below). The 97 remaining ventures have a mean age of 3.4 years (with a standard deviation of 3.4 years). The majority of the ventures (82%) are 5 years old or younger. Of the 448 firms that responded to our initial screening letter, we were able to obtain information about industry membership, revenue, and assets for 312 firms. Within the smaller sample of 97 firms that responded to our survey and were retained for analysis, this data is available for 56 firms. Table 2 contains summary information about the population frame, the initial response subset, and the final sample. There appears to be some over-representation in our sample in construction, manufacturing, and trade, and under-representation in agriculture and natural resources. However, it is not clear whether this is an artifact of our sample or representative of less corporate venturing in agriculture and natural resources. The mean values for assets and revenues of firms in the population frame, the initial response set, and the final sample do not differ significantly when compared by *t*-test. Thus, while not perfectly representative in terms of industry affiliation, our sample appears to be representative for size and revenue characteristics.

Corporate Entrepreneurship and Growth

TABLE 2 Sample and Population Frame Characteristics

Sector	Final Sample	Initial Respondents	Population Frame
# of firms in total	97	448	2,614
# of firms with asset & revenue data	56	312	2,367
Assets ($M)	1,268 (2,930)	1,127 (6,418)	1,198 (9,136)
Revenues ($M)	546 (1,419)	430 (1,090)	391 (1,407)
Agriculture and natural resources	19 %	34 %	36 %
Construction, manufacturing, and trade	27 %	20 %	18 %
T.C.U. and F.I.R.E	28 %	31 %	29 %
Accommodation and consumer goods	7 %	9 %	12 %
Other	19 %	6 %	4 %

Most of the firms (80%) had prior venturing experience. Of those, 77% described their previous ventures as positive experiences. The reasons most often cited for launching corporate ventures were to complement existing products/services and develop new competencies. Other, less common reasons cited for venturing include the utilization of idle resources, and offensive or defensive moves relative to competitors' actions. The firms in our sample all chose to launch ventures in the same industry as the parent's primary business. We were thus unable to evaluate the potential influence of line-of-business similarity with this data.

Measures

Performance Criteria

Measuring the performance of corporate ventures shares many of the difficulties associated with evaluating the performance of small, entrepreneurial firms. The complexity of the issue has been addressed in the literature (Covin and Slevin 1989; Naman and Slevin 1993; Sandberg and Hofer 1987; Sapienza, Smith, and Gannon 1988) although it remains far from being resolved. Covin and Slevin (1989) identified three reasons for using subjective performance measures of small-firm performance over more objective, hard numerical data: (1) the inability and/or unwillingness of firms to provide financial data (Fiorito and LaForge 1986), (2) the difficulty of interpretation and comparison of data due to differing firm objectives (Cooper 1979), and (3) the influence of industry effects (Miller and Toulouse 1986). Their solution to the problem of performance evaluation was to create a weighted average performance index for firms based upon the product of 'importance' scores and 'satisfaction' scores on a series of questions about various financial criteria (e.g., sales, cash flow, profit margin).

A similar approach was used by Venkatraman (1990) who operationalized performance with three indicators, two of which reflect managerial satisfaction and a third that evaluates the performance of the competition. He argued that such measures are reasonable proxies for often unobtainable secondary-source data.

Respondents to our survey were asked to indicate on a scale of one to seven the degree to which they agreed or disagreed (1 = strongly disagree, 7 = strongly agree) with the statement that their venture had been able to meet milestones on schedule. We then categorized firms as either High or Low performers on the basis of their responses to this question. Fifty-two ventures, which gave responses of 5 or higher, were classified as High performers while 45 ventures (with responses of 4 or less) were Low performers. Milestones included such measures as profit, revenue, market share, customer satisfaction, and technical objectives. Roughly half of the ventures (52%) relied primarily on measures of profitability such as ROI and ROA.[1] The milestones were typically established with input from both the parent company and the venture.

Economic Measures

Eleven items on the survey addressed the economic interaction between parent and venture. The first of these asked what proportion of the parent's capital budget had been invested in the venture to date. This item was designed to capture the level of financial commitment of the parent. Another item asked if the venture offered the best potential rate of return among alternative growth opportunities. The remaining nine items were designed to capture the dynamic processes of a growing business unit. Respondents were asked to answer questions categorized by the stage of development of the venture: *Early*, *Middle*, and *Established*. The *Early* stage was defined in the survey as commencing with financial investment in the venture and continuing until the venture began to generate revenue. The *Middle* stage begins with the beginning of a revenue stream and continues until the venture realizes a profit. At this point, the venture has become *Established*. Nineteen of the ventures in our sample described themselves as early stage entities and, consequently, responded only to the early stage portion of multi-stage survey items. Forty-nine firms were in the middle stage and 29 classified themselves as established. Samples of the multi-stage question format are included in the Appendix.

Our decision to adopt this unique format in our questionnaire stemmed from the preliminary interviews in which managers consistently noted that many aspects of the parent-venture relationship evolve as the venture itself matures. Pilot testing of our survey indicated that managers easily grasped the intent of the multi-stage questions and were receptive to describing the dynamic process of venture management.

The multi-stage, economic survey items asked whether funds promised to the venture are ever diverted, whether they are sunk, whether the investment restricts alternative venturing activities, and whether the investments in the venture are highly specialized. They also inquired into the relative budgets and compensation systems of parent and venture, the use by the venture of the parent's systems, and whether the venture is accountable to financial targets.

Relational Measures

The relational measures included one single-stage question that asked if the parent would withdraw support if the venture were to experience adverse conditions. The remaining eight items in this category were of the multi-stage format described above. Items included the level of support provided by the CEO, whether the venture manager works to obtain buy-in, the importance of venture culture, the venture's position on

---

[1] Many of the respondents indicated that they used multiple milestones, including both financial and non-financial measures of performance. As such, we were not able to control for the specific type of milestone(s) used.

TABLE 3   Mean Scores of Survey Items by Venture Stage and Performance Category

	Early Stage			Middle Stage			Established Stage		
	High	Low	Diff.[a]	High	Low	Diff.	High	Low	Diff.
Economic Dimension									
Venture offered best rate of return (H1)[b]	5.56	4.89	0.67**	5.24	5.65	−0.41	6.14	6.28	−0.13
Venture must meet financial targets (H2)	4.77	4.86	−0.09						
Level of investment in venture (H3)	2.77	2.48	0.29						
Venture restricts alternate venturing (H3)	3.86	3.43	0.43	3.50	2.91	0.59†	2.80	2.42	0.38
Investments in the V are specialized (H3)	5.52	5.40	0.12	5.39	5.03	0.36	5.50	4.09	1.41**
Funds in the Venture are sunk (H3)	5.54	6.24	−0.70	4.92	5.62	−0.69	4.10	4.93	−0.83
Funds are not diverted from venture (H3)	6.04	6.26	−0.22	6.15	6.06	0.09	6.06	6.36	−0.30
Importance to V of Parent's resources (H3)	6.33	5.76	0.57*	5.75	6.00	−0.25	5.07	6.00	−0.93
Venture budgeting is more flexible (H4)	4.33	4.43	−0.10	3.83	3.94	−0.11	3.15	3.40	−0.25
Venture compensation is different (H4)	3.35	3.49	−0.14	3.14	3.35	−0.21	3.45	3.71	−0.26
Venture has larger training budget (H4)	2.82	3.56	−0.74*	2.79	3.46	−0.67†	2.68	3.06	−0.39
Venture must use parent's systems (H4)	4.60	3.74	0.86*	4.57	4.00	0.57†	4.56	3.53	1.03*
Relational Dimension									
CEO actively supports venture (H5)	6.38	6.39	−0.01	6.26	5.95	0.32	6.27	5.53	0.74*
CEO runs interference for venture (H5)	4.39	5.07	−0.68	4.07	4.69	−0.61	3.41	3.81	−0.40
V manager works to obtain buy-in (H6)	5.75	4.85	0.90**	5.74	4.94	0.80*	5.82	4.80	1.02*
V near top of P's business agenda (H6)	4.83	4.38	0.45	4.90	4.18	0.73*	4.73	3.71	1.01*
P would withdraw if V in trouble (H7)	3.39	4.31	−0.92**						
P has record of meeting commitments (H7)	5.67	5.50	0.17	5.67	5.46	0.21	5.76	5.27	0.49†
Decision-making power of V EEs (H8)	4.21	4.89	−0.67*	4.10	4.97	−0.88*	4.28	5.00	−0.72†
Decision-making power of V manager (H8)	4.38	4.73	−0.35	4.05	4.94	−0.89*	4.24	4.87	−0.63
Importance of venture culture (H8)	6.18	5.93	0.25	6.07	5.71	0.37	6.03	5.87	0.16
Venture is protected from politics (H8)	4.16	4.29	−0.13	4.05	4.34	−0.29	3.85	5.06	−1.21*
Identification with V as distinct entity (H8)	4.90	6.17	−1.27**	4.66	5.57	−0.92*	4.96	5.80	−0.84
V EE sense of autonomy from Parent (H8)	4.49	5.07	−0.58†	4.50	5.24	−0.74*	4.41	5.60	−1.19*

[a] Superscripts indicate p-values for 1-tailed *t*-test: † < 0.10; * < 0.05; ** < 0.01.

[b] All responses are on a 7-point scale anchored by strongly disagree (1) and strongly agree (7) except the investment question which is scaled as follows: (1) < 1%; (2) 1%–5%; (3) 6%–10%; (4) > 10% of parent's capital budget. Items not reported for the middle and established stages were not framed in a multi-stage format.

40 S. THORNHILL AND R. AMIT

TABLE 4 Composite Mean Score Comparisons between High and Low Performing Ventures

	Early			Middle			Established		
	# Var[a]	F[b]	Prob[c]	# Var	F	Prob	# Var	F	Prob
Economic									
H3: Large, specialized investments	5	1.69	0.15	5	1.22	0.32	5	1.08	0.40
H4: Uniform financial practices	4	1.92	0.12	4	1.02	0.40	4	0.91	0.47
Relational									
H5: CEO protection and support	2	1.70	0.19	2	1.96	0.15	2	1.99	0.15
H6: Venture preeminence	2	3.57	0.03	2	3.39	0.04	2	3.30	0.05
H8: Low venture autonomy	6	3.99	0.00	6	1.75	0.13	6	1.20	0.34

[a] # Var indicates the number of dynamic survey items used to evaluate the hypothesis (e.g., H3 evaluates restriction of alternate venturing, specialization of investments, sunk funds, diversion of funds, and importance of parent resources; a total of 5 dynamic variables. The level of investment by the parent is not multi-stage and is not included in the calculation of Hotelling's T^2).
[b] The F-test statistic is derived from Hotelling's T^2 by the formula F = (N-p-1)/(N-2)*p))*T^2. In this equation, N = n$_1$ + n$_2$ = the total number of observations; p indicates the total number o variables being evaluated (e.g., p = 5 for H3) (Stevens 1996).
[c] P-values are based on a null hypothesis that the mean vectors of the hgh and low performers are equal. (H$_0$: Hi = Lo).

the parent's business agenda, whether the venture is protected from politics, and the parent's track record of meeting commitments to the venture.

Analysis

The mean scores to the survey items, for the high and low performers, respectively, in each of the three stages of venture development are presented in Table 3. Simple means tests allowed us to evaluate hypotheses 1, 2, and 7, but the remaining hypotheses were operationalized by several multi-stage variables that should be tested concurrently. For this, we employed two tests, one on the mean scores themselves and the other on composite factor scores. In the first test, we used Hotelling's T-squared in each of the three stages of venture maturity. Results of this procedure for Hypotheses 3, 4, 5, 6, and 8 are presented in Table 4. For these multi-item hypotheses, we also used principal components analysis to derive factor scores for the combined variables associated with each hypothesis (the item regarding venture autonomy was reverse coded for consistency with the other variables in H4). Eigenvalues and alpha values for the factors are included in the Appendix (Table A.1). Once factor scores were derived, we ran logistic regression analyses for each of the three stages of venture development. The results of the logistic analyses are presented in Table 5.

We also used Hotelling's T-squared in our evaluation of the dynamic propositions of our model (P1, P2). Table 6 contains results of our within-firm comparisons of responses to the multi-stage survey items. First, the difference scores for each venture were calculated between the early and middle stages and between the middle and established stages. Only middle and established firms could be evaluated on their evolution from early-to-middle stage and only for established firms could these results be compared with the middle-to-established stage transition phase. The means of the difference scores, for all ventures in each transition phase, are presented in the columns labeled "Diff." in Table 6. Two separate tests were then performed for each variable. First, the mean difference was evaluated against a null hypothesis that the mean is equal to zero. If we could reject the null hypotheses, then we could conclude that the item varies with increasing venture maturity. Second, we compared the relative change between stages

TABLE 5   Logistic Regression of Factor Scores

	Early[a]	Middle	Established
H3: Large, specialized investments	−0.16	0.26	−0.35
H4: Uniform financial practices	−0.47	−0.34	−0.96
H5: CEO protection and support	−0.49[†]	−0.68[†]	−1.40
H6: Venture preeminence	0.92**	1.14*	1.02
H8: Low venture autonomy	−0.13	−0.30	0.78
Constant	0.33	0.44	1.88*
Observations	61	48	27
Chi-squared	13.81*	11.63*	5.74
Pseudo R²	17	0.18	0.22
Log Likelihood	−34.71	−26.40	−10.07

ª Superscripts indicate p-values: $^†< 0.10$; $*< 0.05$; $**< 0.01$.

across the groups of high and low performing ventures. In this case, the null hypothesis was that the change among the high-performers is the same as the change among the low-performers. F-statistics and p-values are provided for each test.

In addition to testing the changes of individual variables as the ventures matured, we were also interested in the aggregate changes of the variables that jointly formed our multivariate hypotheses. Tests were performed for the joint changes of the variables which represent Hypotheses 3, 4, 5, 6, and 8 (i.e., the vectors of mean difference scores are compared). Finally, we combined all economic variables and all relational variables, respectively, to evaluate the net change of the economic and relational dimensions in the parent-venture relationship.

RESULTS

Parent/Venture Strategic Fit

Although firms have numerous reasons for engaging in corporate venturing, our results indicate that a venture's anticipated rate of return significantly distinguishes the high performers in our sample from the low performers, as predicted by H1 (Table 3).

Our hypothesis regarding the use of financial targets (H2), however, is not supported by the data. The differences in mean scores indicate a greater use of financial targets by low performers in all three stages, although the results are not statistically significant. We observe, however, that the use of financial targets increases among all firms as the ventures mature.

Our expectation that venture success would be associated with significant, financial resource commitments by the corporate parent (H3) is not supported by the data. In fact, an inspection of the mean responses among high and low performers (Table 2) indicates that, contrary to our predictions, the low-performers reported sunk funds and non-diversion of funds to a greater extent than did the high-performers. The logistic regression also fails to support H3—none of the coefficients for the three stages of venture maturity is significant for the factor variable on investment (Table 5). One other noteworthy finding is that high-performers relied less on parent resources as they matured, while the opposite is evident for the low-performers, although this finding is not statistically significant when tested for within-venture mean differences.

Our prediction that successful ventures would be distinguished by uniform financial

TABLE 6 Dynamic Evolution of Parent-Venture Relationship

	Diff[a]	Early to Middle Stage				Diff	Middle to Established Stage			
		H₀: Diff=0		H₀: Hi=Lo			H₀: Diff=0		H₀: Hi=Lo	
		F[b]	Prob	F	Prob		F	Prob	F	Prob
Economic										
H2 Venture must meet financial targets	0.92	60.60	0.00	0.00	0.95	1.00	36.03	0.00	0.73	0.40
H3 Venture restricts alternate venturing	-0.39	9.77	0.00	0.03	0.85	-0.56	7.58	0.01	2.54	0.12
H3 Investments in the V are specialized	-0.11	0.76	0.39	0.01	0.92	-0.12	0.45	0.51	7.62	0.01
H3 Funds in the venture are sunk	-0.58	17.14	0.00	0.00	0.96	-0.82	17.95	0.00	0.88	0.35
H3 Funds are not diverted from venture	-0.16	3.74	0.06	1.35	0.25	0.00	0.00	1.00	0.76	0.39
H3 Importance to V of P's resources	-0.47	10.71	0.00	1.98	0.17	-0.56	12.35	0.00	0.76	0.39
Test of combined H3 Diff. scores		7.90	0.00	0.74	0.60		7.63	0.00	0.54	0.75
H4 Venture budgeting is more flexible	-0.43	13.00	0.00	0.15	0.70	-0.42	11.63	0.00	1.13	0.24
H4 Venture compensation is different	0.11	2.33	0.13	0.05	0.83	0.11	0.42	0.52	1.64	0.21
H4 Venture has larger training budget	-0.13	1.95	0.17	0.50	0.48	-0.13	1.52	0.22	0.01	0.91
H4 Venture must use parent's systems	0.11	0.65	0.42	0.80	0.37	0.17	1.00	0.32	0.53	0.47
Test of combined H4 Diff. scores		4.50	0.00	0.50	0.74		3.63	0.01	1.23	0.31
Test of combined Economic hypotheses		5.70	0.00	0.86	0.56		5.20	0.00	1.40	0.92
Relational										
H5 CEO actively supports venture	-0.19	6.52	0.01	4.68	0.03	-0.09	0.66	0.42	1.58	0.22
H5 CEO runs interference for venture	-0.30	5.55	0.02	0.31	0.58	-0.38	8.52	0.01	2.37	0.13
Test of combined H5 Diff. scores		5.16	0.01	2.10	0.13		3.77	0.03	3.10	0.06
H6 V manager works to obtain buy-in	0.12	1.33	0.25	0.26	0.61	0.02	0.03	0.87	0.71	0.41
H6 near top of P's business agenda	0.00	0.00	1.00	0.40	0.53	0.04	0.08	0.78	1.19	0.28
Test of combined H6 Diff. scores		0.66	0.52	0.36	0.70		0.04	0.96	1.47	0.24
H7 CP record of meeting commitments	-0.10	0.74	0.39	0.26	0.61	-0.10	0.30	0.59	0.13	0.72
H8 Decision making power of V EEs	-0.08	0.64	0.43	1.00	0.32	0.02	0.02	0.88	0.05	0.82
H8 Decision making power of V mgr	-0.05	0.31	0.58	0.24	0.63	0.06	0.19	0.67	0.00	0.96
H8 Importance of venture culture	-0.01	0.04	0.84	0.05	0.82	-0.10	1.09	0.30	0.06	0.81
H8 Venture is protected from politics	0.00	0.00	1.00	0.04	0.85	0.02	0.01	0.93	0.02	0.89
H8 Identify with CV as distinct entity	-0.35	4.19	0.05	3.76	0.06	0.26	2.56	0.12	5.15	0.03
H8 CV sense of autonomy from CP	0.02	0.02	0.88	1.06	0.31	0.00	0.00	1.00	1.19	0.28
Test of combined H8 Diff. scores		1.23	0.31	1.30	0.28		0.58	0.74	1.16	0.36
Test of combined Relational hypotheses		1.48	0.18	1.16	0.34		1.47	0.22	1.13	0.39

[a] The difference score is obtained by subtracting the earlier period from the later period for a given venture. The number reported in the Diff. column of this table is the average of the within venture difference scores for all ventures. Mean difference scores for the high and low performers, respectively, are not reported.

[b] The F-test statistic is derived from Hotelling's T^2 by the formula $F=((N-p-1)/(N-2)p))T^2$. In this equation, $N = n_1 + n_2 =$ the total number of observations; p indicates the total number of variables being evaluated (e.g., $p = 5$ for H3) (Stevens 1996).

practices between parent and venture (H4) is partially supported by the data. Use of the parent's systems is positively and significantly associated with high performance in all three stages. Differences between parent and venture in their budgeting, compensation, and training practices are associated with low performance, as predicted, yet the differences are statistically significant only in the case of training budgets in the early and middle stages. Tests of the combined mean vectors of the H4 variables indicated a low level of statistical significance in the early stage and virtually no significant differences between high and low performers in the middle and established stages, although the sign of the differences does correspond to our hypothesis. The logistic regression coefficients are not statistically significant for the H4 factor variables.

The items regarding protection and support of the venture at the CEO level (H5) yield mixed results. Active CEO support is significant in the established stage of successful ventures. However, having the CEO run interference for the venture is more pronounced for the less successful ventures. The combined test of the two variables yields results of weak statistical significance, yet because the two variables are quite different in nature (CEO support predominates among high performers while having the CEO run interference is more characteristic of the low performers), the meaning of this result is not clear. The factor variables in the logistic analysis produce negative coefficients of weak statistical significance, consistent with the influence of the CEO interference item among the sub-sample of low performers.

Venture preeminence in the eyes of the parent (H6) does, however, distinguish firms that met milestones on schedule from those that did not. Ventures that were near the top of the parent's business agenda and whose managers worked to obtain buy-in of the parent are among the success stories of our sample. The univariate results are confirmed by Hotelling's T-squared, yielding significance at the 0.05 level in all three stages. As well, the logistic analysis indicates significant, positive coefficients in the early and middle stages and a non-significant positive coefficient in the established stage.

Our expectation that successful firms would believe that the parent would not withdraw support if the venture experienced adverse conditions (H7) is supported by a single-stage survey item. As well, the direction of the difference between high and low performers on a multi-stage assessment of the parent's track record of meeting commitments is consistent with our prediction, although the difference is statistically significant only in the established stage.

Finally, our hypothesis regarding the level of autonomy of the venture (H8) is partially supported by the data. Indications of high venture autonomy are characteristic of the low performers, although the degree of statistical significance varies across the individual items. The strongest differences are evident in the items pertaining to relative decision making authority of venture managers and employees, the level of identification of employees relative to parent or venture, and the perceived sense of autonomy of the venture from the parent. In these instances, the data strongly and significantly support the notion that close ties are associated with venture success. The combined tests of mean differences indicate a strong difference between high and low performers in the early stage, and moderate to weak differences in the middle and established stages, respectively. The combined factor variables run in the logistic analysis are not significant predictors of venture performance.

Our proposition that the economic ties between parent and venture would diminish with venture maturity (P1) is strongly supported (Table 6). In the early-to-middle stage transition phase, the combined test of H3 and H4 variables (Hotelling's T^2) indicate decreasing mean responses with significance at the 0.01 level. The combined test of all multi-stage economic variables is also negative (as predicted) and significant at the 0.01 level. These results are also found across the middle-to-late transition phase. The sole exception to the pattern of decreasing economic connection between parent and venture is found in the H2 variable—use of financial targets—which is strongly and significantly negative (significant at the 0.001 level). It appears that although economic dependence decreases with increasing venture maturity, accountability increases. The level of economic change across the phases of venture maturity is not significantly different between the high and low performers.

The predicted stability of relational ties (P2) is also generally supported although, as is the case for P1, there is one important exception. The individual and combined significance tests for the relational, multi-stage variables for H6, H7, and H8 do not allow us to reject the null hypothesis of no change from the early-to-middle stage. The same is true of the middle-to-late stage transition. We infer from this that the relational ties do not differ across stages. The one relational aspect that does evolve across the stages of venture maturity is H5—CEO interference and support. In this case, the mean scores of both variables decrease with increasing venture maturity. The relational difference scores across the transition phases do not differ significantly when we compare the high and low performing ventures.

DISCUSSION

The hypotheses developed in this paper address the effects of the economic and relational dimensions of parent-venture strategic fit on venture performance. The eight hypotheses fall into 3 general categories: H1, H2, H5, and H6 pertain to *characteristics* of a specific venture; H3 and H7 address the level of parent-venture *commitment*; and H4 and H8 speak directly to the level of *connection* or autonomy that exists between parent and venture. The hypotheses and the results of our empirical investigation are summarized in Table 7.

Of the four hypotheses related to venture-specific characteristics, two are supported by the data, one gives mixed results, and one—use of economic performance criteria—is not supported. The hypotheses on *commitment* and *connection* are fully or partially supported in the relational dimension, yet they receive only partial support or no support when evaluated in economic terms. In fact, sunk funds are significantly associated with low performance, contrary to our expectations.

From these findings, we conclude that the degree of fit between a corporate parent and venture does affect the success of a venture, and that success is associated with high levels of awareness, commitment, and connection. Further, the relational dimension of the parent-venture interface appears to have a greater association with venture success than does the economic dimension.

Our second research question, regarding the dynamic nature of the parent-venture relationship (P1 and P2) is also addressed in Table 5. Support is found for our model in that ventures generally lessened their economic connections with their parents as they mature (or vice-versa) while the relational bonds remain more or less intact. The exceptions to these general trends are an increasing emphasis on financial targets and decreasing CEO involvement as ventures mature. Both of these findings make intuitive sense. Greater financial independence (the defining characteristic of the stages in our model) is accompanied by greater financial accountability. And, as a venture gains in

TABLE 7 Summary of Hypotheses and Results

	Economic Dimension		Relational Dimension	
	Hypotheses	Results	Hypotheses	Results
Characteristics of the Venture	H1: Success assoc. with ROR selection criteria	Supported	H5: Success assoc. with CEO protection and support	Mixed results
	H2: Success assoc. with economic performance criteria	Not supported	H6: Success assoc. with preeminence in eyes of parent	Supported
Commitment	H3: Success assoc. with large, sunk investments	Not supported	H7: Success assoc. with commitment and trust	Supported
Connection	H4: Success assoc. with uniform financial practices	Partial support	H8: Success assoc. with low autonomy	Partial support
Dynamic	P1: Diminishing economic ties as venture matures	Supported	P2: Consistently, strong relational ties as V matures	Supported

both independence and accountability, there is less need for the CEO to provide "air cover." These two issues aside, the basic model of enduring relational ties and diminishing economic ties is supported most notably in the areas of *commitment* and *connection*. As well, the increasing accountability is consistent with our expectation that close connection is preferable to high venture autonomy.

Our finding that the degree of change in the parent-venture relationship does not differ between high and low performers may be due to a number of factors. The simplest of these is that there is no difference. However, it may be that our relatively crude measurement instrument, coupled with a fairly small sample size, is not sensitive enough to allow us to detect differences that may be quite subtle. Larger-scale studies of a truly longitudinal design may address this issue with greater power and precision. Another area that may prove to be of value in future research is the possible interaction of the relational and economic aspects of the CP-CV interface. Although beyond the scope of this paper, it is an issue that may yield interesting insights into the dynamic processes of corporate venture development.

Two aspects of this research that differ from other studies are our use of a multi-stage questionnaire format and our criteria for venture success. With respect to the first issue, the dynamic trends within the parent-venture managerial processes support our use of the multi-stage format. Although our survey is strictly a cross-sectional method of data collection, containing all of the weaknesses of retrospective, self-reported data, the format was well received and allowed respondents to indicate which practices changed over time and whether they had improved or degraded. Future development of this data collection method may yield additional insights into the evolutionary nature of management and decision processes.

The issue of how to define "success" is still unresolved (see Miller, Wilson, and Adams 1988). Any method or measure of venture performance has both strengths and weaknesses and an "ideal" criterion is yet to be defined. The prevalent use of milestones by corporations, and the near unanimous support for this method of performance evaluation in the academic and practitioner press, convinced us that this was a useful way to categorize corporate ventures.

CONCLUSION

We have taken a dynamic, multi-dimensional approach in our investigation of corporate venturing. We have identified distinct relational and economic dimensions of the parent-venture relationship. Contrary to conventional wisdom, our data indicate that a close fit between a corporate parent and its venture is positively associated with venture performance. Further, our multi-stage survey instrument allows us to confirm that the relationship between parent and venture evolves as the venture matures, and that the nature of the changes are consistent with consistently strong relational ties, low venture autonomy, and decreasing economic connection.

Although there is still a pressing need for longitudinal studies of corporate ventures, this paper hints at the type of findings that may result as we move from static, cross-sectional research designs to those that can capture the dynamic processes underlying the growth of corporate ventures. Like any organization, corporate ventures have the potential to grow and flourish or contract and wither away. As we improve our ability to identify and measure dynamic elements within organizations, we will improve our ability to understand the dimensions that underlie the processes of venture growth.

Given the prevalence of corporate venturing as a growth mechanism, it is important to continue to explore these dimensions, their components, and the way they interact during venture growth and development.

REFERENCES

Arrow, K.J. 1982. *Innovation in Large and Small Firms.* New York: Price Institute for Entrepreneurial Studies.

Baden-Fuller, C. 1995. Strategic innovation, corporate entrepreneurship and matching outside-in to inside-out approaches to strategy research. *British Journal of Management* 6(Special Issue):S3–S16.

Barney, J.B., and Hansen, M.H. 1994. Trustworthiness as a source of competitive advantage. *Strategic Management Journal* 15(Special Issue):175–190.

Biggadike, R. 1979. The risky business of corporate diversification. *Harvard Business Review* May–June:103–111.

Birkinshaw, J. 1997. Entrepreneurship in multinational corporations: The characteristics of subsidiary initiatives. *Strategic Management Journal* 18(3):207–229.

Block, Z. 1983. Can corporate venturing succeed? *The Journal of Business Strategy* 3(2):21–33.

Block, Z. 1989. Damage control for new corporate ventures. *Journal of Business Strategy* 10(2):22–28.

Block, Z., and MacMillan, I.C. 1993. *Corporate Venturing: Creating New Businesses within the Firm.* Boston: Harvard Business School Press.

Block, Z., and Ornati, O.A. 1987. Compensating corporate venture managers. *Journal of Business Venturing* 2(1):41–51.

Burgelman, R.A. 1983. A process model of internal corporate venturing in a diversified major firm. *Administrative Science Quarterly* 28(1):223–244.

Caruana, A., Morris, M.H., and Vella, A.J. 1998. The effect of centralization and formalization on entrepreneurship in export firms. *Journal of Small Business Management* 36(1):16–29.

Chung, L.H., and Gibbons, P.T. 1997. Corporate entrepreneurship: The roles of ideology and social capital. *Group and Organization Management* 22(1):10–30.

Cooper, A.C. 1979. Strategic management: New ventures and small business. In D.E. Schendel and C.W. Hofer, eds., *Strategic Management: A New View of Business Policy and Planning.* Boston: Little, Brown, and Company.

Covin, J.G., and Slevin, D.P. 1989. Strategic management of small firms in hostile and benign environments. *Strategic Management Journal* 10(1):75–87.

Covin, J.G., and Slevin, D.P. 1994. Corporate entrepreneurship in high and low technology industries: A comparison of strategic variables, strategy patterns and performance in global markets. *Journal of Euromarketing* 3(3):99–127.

Day, D.L. 1994. Raising radicals: Different processes for championing innovative corporate ventures. *Organization Science* 5(2):148–172.

Dougherty, D. 1995. Managing your core incompetencies for corporate venturing. *Entrepreneurship: Theory and Practice* 19(3):113–135.

Fiorito, S.S., and LaForge, R.W. 1986. A marketing strategy analysis for small retailers. *American Journal of Small Business* 10(4):7–17.

Frost, P.J., and Egri, C.P. 1990. Influence of political action on innovation: Part I. *Leadership and Organization Development Journal* 11(1):17–25.

Garud, R., and Van de Ven, A.H. 1992. An empirical evaluation of the internal corporate venturing process. *Strategic Management Journal* 13(Special Issue):93–109.

Ghemawat, P. 1991. *Commitment: The Dynamics of Strategy.* New York: Free Press.

Ginsberg, A., and Hay, M. 1994. Confronting the challenges of corporate entrepreneurship: Guidelines for venture managers. *European Management Journal* 12(2):382–389.

48 S. THORNHILL AND R. AMIT

Glaser, G.B., and Strauss, A.L. 1967. *The Discovery of Grounded Theory: Strategies for Qualitative Research.* Chicago: Aldine.

Guth, W.D., and Ginsberg, A. 1990. Guest editors' introduction: Corporate entrepreneurship. *Strategic Management Journal* 11(Special Issue):5–15.

Hornsby, J.S, Naffziger, D.W., Kuratko, D.F., and Montagno, R.V. 1993. An interactive model of the corporate entrepreneurship process. *Entrepreneurship: Theory and Practice* 17(2): 29–37.

Jennings, D.F., and Lumpkin, J.R. 1989. Functioning modeling corporate entrepreneurship: An empirical integrative analysis. *Journal of Management* 15(3):485–502.

Kanter, R.M. 1985. Supporting innovation and venture development in established companies. *Journal of Business Venturing* 1(1):47–60.

Knight, R.M. 1989. Technological innovation in Canada: A comparison of independent entrepreneurs and corporate innovators. *Journal of Business Venturing* 4(4):281–288.

Lengnick-Hall, C.A. 1992. Strategic configurations and designs for corporate entrepreneurship: Exploring the relationship between cohesiveness and performance. *Journal of Engineering and Technology Management* 9(2):127–154.

MacMillan, I.C., Block, Z., and Narasimha, P.N.S. 1986. Corporate venturing: Alternatives, obstacles encountered, and experience effects. *Journal of Business Venturing* 1(2):177–191.

McGrath, R.G. 1995. Advantage from adversity: Learning from disappointment in internal corporate ventures. *Journal of Business Venturing* 10(2):121–142.

McGrath, R.G., Venkataraman, S., and MacMillan, I.C. 1994. The advantage chain: Antecedents to rents from internal corporate ventures. *Journal of Business Venturing* 9(5):351–369.

Miller, A., and Camp, B. 1985. Exploring determinants of success in corporate ventures. *Journal of Business Venturing* 1(1):87–105.

Miller, A., Gartner, W. B., and Wilson, R. 1989. Entry order, market share, and competitive advantage: A study of their relationships in new corporate ventures. *Journal of Business Venturing* 4(3):197–209.

Miller, A., Spann, M.S., and Lerner, L. 1991. Competitive advantages in new corporate ventures: The impact of resource sharing and reporting level. *Journal of Business Venturing* 6(5):335–350.

Miller, A., Wilson, R., and Adams, M. 1988. Financial performance patterns of new corporate ventures: An alternative to traditional measures. *Journal of Business Venturing* 3(4): 287–300.

Miller, D., and Toulouse, J.M. 1986. Strategy, structure, CEO personality and performance in small firms. *American Journal of Small Business* 10(3):47–62.

Naman, J.L., and Slevin, D.P. 1993. Entrepreneurship and the concept of fit: A model and empirical tests. *Strategic Management Journal* 14(2):137–153.

Pearce, J.A., Kramer, T.R., and Robbins, D.K. 1997. Effects of managers' entrepreneurial behavior on subordinates. *Journal of Business Venturing* 12(2):147–160.

Penrose, E. 1959. *The Theory of the Growth of the Firm.* London: Basil Blackwell.

Sandberg, W.R., and Hofer, C.W. 1987. Improving new venture performance: The role of strategy, industry structure, and the entrepreneur. *Journal of Business Venturing* 2(1):5–28.

Sapienza, H.J., Smith, K.G., and Gannon, M. J. 1988. Using subjective evaluations of organizational performance in small business research. *American Journal of Small Business* 12(3): 45–53.

Schrader, R.C., and Simon, M. 1997. Corporate versus independent new ventures: Resource, strategy, and performance differences. *Journal of Business Venturing* 12(1):47–66.

Sorrentino, M., and Williams, M.L. 1995. Relatedness and corporate venturing: Does it really matter? *Journal of Business Venturing* 10(1):59–73.

Stevens, J. 1996. *Applied Multivariate Statistics for the Social Sciences.* Mahwah, NJ: Lawrence Earlbaum Associates.

Sykes, H.B. 1986. Lessons from a new ventures program. *Harvard Business Review* 64(3):69–74.

Sykes, H.B., and Block, Z. 1989. Corporate venturing obstacles: Sources and solutions. *Journal of Business Venturing* 4(3):159–167.

Thornhill, S., Amit, R., and Belcourt, M. 1998. Determinants of corporate venture performance: An empirical study of firm and industry effects. *Proceedings of the Administrative Sciences Association of Canada Annual Conference* 19(21):80–90.

Tsai, W.M., MacMillan, I.C., and Low, M.B. 1991. Effects of strategy and environment on corporate venture success in industrial markets. *Journal of Business Venturing* 6(1):9–28.

Tushman, M., and Nadler, D. 1986. Organizing for innovation. *California Management Review* 3(1):73–84.

Venkataraman, S., MacMillan, I.C., and McGrath, R.G. 1992. Progress in research on corporate venturing. In D. Sexton and J. Kasarda, eds., *State of the Art in Entrepreneurship Research.* Boston: PWS-Kent Publishing Co.

Venkatraman, N. 1990. Performance implications of strategic coalignment: A methodological perspective. *Journal of Management Studies* 27(1):19–41.

Wernerfelt, B. 1984. A resource-based view of the firm. *Strategic Management Journal* 5(2):171–180.

Zahra, S.A. 1991. Predictors and financial outcomes of corporate entrepreneurship: An exploratory study. *Journal of Business Venturing* 6(4):259–285.

Zahra, S.A. 1993. Environment, corporate entrepreneurship, and financial performance: A taxonomic approach. *Journal of Business Venturing* 8(4):319–340.

Zahra, S.A. 1995. Corporate entrepreneurship and financial performance: The case of management leveraged buyouts. *Journal of Business Venturing* 10(3):225–247.

Zahra, S.A. 1996a. Governance, ownership, and corporate entrepreneurship: The moderating impact of industry technological opportunities. *Academy of Management Journal* 39: 1713–1735.

Zahra, S.A. 1996b. Technology strategy and new venture performance: A study of corporate-sponsored and independent biotechnology ventures. *Journal of Business Venturing* 11(4): 289–321.

Zahra, S.A. and Covin, J.G. 1995. Contextual influences on the corporate entrepreneurship-performance relationship: A longitudinal analysis. *Journal of Business Venturing* 10(1):43–58.

APPENDIX

Sample items from corporate venturing survey

Many of the following questions ask for a response in three time periods. Please indicate, for your venture, approximately when each stage as defined below occurred. If your venture has not reached the Established Stage, for example, respond only for the stages appropriate to your venture.

Early Stage—First financial investment in the venture: 19__
Middle Stage: The Venture has begun to generate revenue: 19__
Established Stage: The Venture has become profitable: 19__

50 S. THORNHILL AND R. AMIT

28. Venture employees are empowered with greater decisions making authority than are their counterparts in the parent company:			54. The budget for training venture personnel is proportionally greater than the training budget of the parent company:		
Strongly	7 ○	7 ○	7 ○	Strongly	7 ○	7 ○	7 ○

Strongly   7 ○   7 ○   7 ○   Strongly   7 ○   7 ○   7 ○
Agree   6 ○   6 ○   6 ○   Agree   6 ○   6 ○   6 ○
               5 ○   5 ○   5 ○   5 ○   5 ○   5 ○
               4 ○   4 ○   4 ○   4 ○   4 ○   4 ○
               3 ○   3 ○   3 ○   3 ○   3 ○   3 ○
Strongly   2 ○   2 ○   2 ○   Strongly   2 ○   2 ○   2 ○
Disagree   1 ○   1 ○   1 ○   Disagree   1 ○   1 ○   1 ○

               Early   Middle   Established   Early   Middle   Established
               Stage   Stage   Stage   Stage   Stage   Stage

TABLE A.1 Alpha Scores and Eigenvalues for Composite Variables

	Alpha Coefficient	Eigenvalue (Early)	Eigenvalue (Middle)	Eigenvalue (Established)
Economic				
H3: Large, specialized investments	0.74	1.41	1.44	1.16
H4: Uniform financial practices	0.85	1.60	1.59	1.86
Relational				
H5: CEO protection and support	0.80	1.27	1.09	1.09
H6: Venture preeminence	0.85	1.27	1.30	1.43
H8: Low venture autonomy	0.91	2.69	2.88	2.94

Part III
Corporate Venture Capital
and Corporate Entrepreneurship

[12]

Designing Corporate Ventures in the Shadow of Private Venture Capital

Henry Chesbrough

"The search for innovation needs to be organizationally separate and outside of the ongoing managerial business. Innovative organizations realize that one cannot simultaneously create the new and take care of what one already has. They realize that maintenance of the present business is far too big a task for the people in it to have much time for creating the new, the different business for tomorrow. They also realize that taking care of tomorrow is far too big and difficult a task to be diluted with concern for today. Both tasks have to be done. But they are different. Innovative organizations, therefore, put the new into separate organizational components concerned with the creation of the new."—Peter Drucker[1]

Since Drucker's advice of a generation ago, many companies have tried to separate their new business endeavors from their current business structures in an attempt to stimulate greater innovation and generate additional business growth. These attempts have generally met with only temporary success. The general pattern is a cycle that starts with enthusiasm, continues into implementation, then encounters significant difficulties, and ends with eventual termination of the initiative. Yet, within a few years, another generation of businesses undertakes the effort anew, and the cycle occurs again.

For example, in the 1960s and early 1970s, 25% of the *Fortune 500* had a corporate venturing program.[2] These were largely disbanded, though, during the late 1970s. Then in the early 1980s, as the independent venture capital market grew again, corporations renewed their interest in corporate venturing. These initiatives were again discontinued after the market downturn in 1987.

Useful comments on this paper have been received by Stephen Socolof, Stefan Thomke, and Steven Wheelwright. Support for this research was provided by the Division of Research of the Harvard Business School.

Then, as the extended bull market of the 1990s has gained momentum, corporations have again re-introduced corporate venturing activities.[3]

While the cycle appears to continue, the method of structuring these corporate ventures appears to have changed. The most recent cycle of corporate venturing has utilized venture capital structures to motivate employees to become more entrepreneurial and take more risk. Adobe, Intel, Lucent, Sun Microsystems, Texas Instruments, and Xerox, among others, have all introduced corporate venture capital programs to promote greater innovation. Is this a step forward or is the corporate venturing cycle simply going to run its course one more time until the market turns down again?

Exxon's Natural Experiment in Corporate Venturing

A remarkable natural experiment at Exxon usefully contrasts corporate venturing and private venture capital.[4] It suggests that there is something different about venture capital. As part of its strategic mission to diversify its businesses away from an exclusive reliance on the petroleum industry in the 1970s, Exxon embarked on a two-fold corporate venturing program. One portion of the program was a series of external financial investments alongside private venture capital funds, to be followed by a second program of internal ventures that were to be started and managed in a special unit inside Exxon. The Exxon strategy was to probe and assess new venture opportunities via external investment, then invest in the most promising of these venture opportunities via internal venture organizations.

There were 18 such external investments made under the first program, starting around the year 1975. Exxon invested approximately $12 million in these external startup companies. These performed well financially: of the 18 ventures in which Exxon invested alongside other private investors, three of them were sold to other companies at a profit, and five went public via an initial public offering (IPO). By 1982, Exxon's investments in these firms were worth $218 million, for an internal rate of return of approximately 51% per annum (assuming all investments were made in 1975, and making no adjustment for inflation). This was an impressive success in financial terms, whether compared to Exxon's overall rate of return or to the median return of similar vintage private venture capital funds.

Following through on its strategy, Exxon then initiated 19 internal venture activities to commercialize the most promising areas identified through its external investment programs. One might have expected the internal programs to fare even better, due to their narrower focus on areas where significant opportunity had already been demonstrated through the external investment probes.

To the contrary, Exxon's financial results were dramatically *lower* from these internal ventures than those from its external investments. None of the 19 entities achieved an external liquidity event (such as the sale of the company to an outside firm or an IPO). None of the 19 ever managed to reach a break-even point, where their revenues were covering their costs. Exxon terminated and wrote off all of the internal ventures.[5]

Exxon's experience in the 1970s is worth recalling today. Many corporate venture capital programs are being justified on grounds similar to those of Exxon: utilize private equity investing to identify promising growth areas in markets near those of the corporation and then utilize those investments to leverage the parent company's business. As the Exxon example shows, though, it is a long road from identifying a potential opportunity to realizing that potential in a new venture within the parent company.

In many respects, it has gotten more challenging to design corporate venture programs since Exxon's aborted experiment. Independent venture capital was a quiescent cottage industry in the mid-1970s, confined to a handful of enterprising partnerships on the East Coast and West Coast of the United States. There were 50 active venture investors in 1978 who had raised $300 million over the previous 18 months.[6] Giant enterprises such as Exxon had little to worry about from such a small source of money.

These days, any corporate venture program that has any chance of success must be designed in the shadow of independent venture capital. This is due in no small part to the sheer growth and velocity of the independent venture capital sector. In 1998, it raised over $13 billion and has raised over $21 billion in the first nine months of 1999.[7] This enormous and growing pool of money lures many talented managers and technical staff out of successful established companies into startup companies.[8] This group of experienced personnel, who are willing to take greater risks in return for greater rewards, is exactly the same pool of talent that most corporate venturing programs hope to leverage. External venturing with outside venture capitalists is an increasingly viable and attractive option for these personnel, one that casts a long shadow over corporate venturing initiatives.

Clearly, the impressive rise of independent venture capital has changed the world of corporate venturing. However, there are important lessons to be learned from the past, as Exxon's experience demonstrates. In order to design successful corporate ventures in this new environment, it is helpful to re-examine the past history of corporate venturing and to interpret that history against some salient characteristics of independent venture capital. Armed with these insights, we will then consider how to design corporate ventures in the shadow of independent venture capital. One promising example of such a design is that of Lucent Technologies' New Ventures Group. While its approach is no panacea, it has clearly thought through the problem of how to stimulate greater innovation within Lucent in the presence of a vibrant venture capital industry. Indeed, one appealing aspect of Lucent's approach is that it leverages outside venture capital when that helps advance Lucent's objectives.

Designing Corporate Ventures in the Shadow of Private Venture Capital

Previous Research on Corporate Venturing

The first academic evaluations of corporate new venture organizations were rather cautious in their assessments. Von Hippel reported that when the parent firm had significant prior experience in that market (vs. having experience with the technology, which was *not* associated with better outcomes), the new venture was much more likely to succeed.[9] He also noted the problems that venture sponsors faced in building and sustaining internal support for new ventures from the top management of the company. The problem for a sponsor was one of adverse selection: over time, the best performing ventures gradually migrated to other divisions, or went off on their own. The remaining ventures became the "problem children" for the sponsor of the new venture division, and this was not a way to boost the sponsor's career within the firm.

Norman Fast conducted another study that attempted to explain the factors that were associated with the success of "new venture divisions" (NVDs).[10] In addition to the issues Von Hippel identified above, Fast found a surprising third problem encountered by NVDs inside an organization: the problem of new venture *success*. Fast found that successful NVDs were often viewed as threatening to established businesses in the parent firm. This threat arose from the ability of the new venture to compete for corporate resources.[11] As the venture realized greater success, it required more resources, and these resources were perceived to diminish the amount of corporate resources available to other businesses in the firm.

Kenneth Rind further explored the potential inherent conflicts of interest that can arise between the sponsoring firm and the new venture it is trying to cultivate.[12] He noted that if the venture was serving a market already served by the parent firm, that might constrain the venture's marketing options so that they didn't conflict with those of the parent firm. A further issue that Rind identified was the problem of the governance: the costs required to manage a new venture successfully would be incurred early in the venture's life under one NVD manager, while the benefits to those investments, if they indeed occurred, would arise later on under another manager. This could create perverse incentives for new venture managers to avoid costly, risky decisions, because they will incur the costs of those decisions, yet may not be around to receive credit for their subsequent benefits.

One could think of compensation mechanisms that might resolve this intertemporal governance issue. However, such mechanisms do not appear in empirical surveys of corporate venture programs. A study by Block and Ornati examined the compensation practices of firms when they establish new venture divisions.[13] They reported that most of the companies using corporate venture programs in their survey do *not* compensate venture managers any differently from their other managers.

Why would so many companies eschew the opportunity to provide a higher risk/reward compensation package to new venture managers to motivate and reward risk-taking behavior? The primary reason mentioned by Block and Ornati's survey respondents was maintaining internal equity. Managers at similar levels in other parts of the company would see it as unfair that a peer manager received a disproportionately higher compensation level because of the performance of the new venture unit.[14] One venture capitalist made a telling remark to Block and Ornati: "The only reason for our existence is the inability of corporations to provide the financial incentives which can be achieved in an independent startup."[15]

A study by Siegel, Siegel, and MacMillan studied the potential conflict between two frequently cited rationales for new venture businesses.[16] One rationale is strategic: to exploit the potential for additional growth latent in the company. A second rationale is financial: to create additional revenue and profit in the new venture itself. Siegel et al. point out that to maximize the financial return from the new venture, firms are best advised to provide complete autonomy to the new venture's managers. However, if the primary motivation for the venture is strategic, then providing this greater autonomy increases the potential likelihood of conflict with the established businesses of the company. Here, the firm may need to intervene in order to manage the potential conflicts between the new venture and the established business. Such intervention will likely have the effect of lowering the autonomy and hence reducing the financial performance of new ventures.[17]

Overall, previous studies of corporate venturing activities have reported significant difficulties for the sponsoring companies. There are problems with developing the relevant market experience. There are problems of adverse selection. There are conflicts between the strategic objectives of new ventures and their financial objectives. There are issues of compensation and internal equity. There are even problems of resource allocation if a new venture actually succeeds. Despite Drucker's admonition, it is not easy to manage the separation of the current business from the new business.

Venture Capital as a Benchmark Reference for Corporate Venture Designers

One very useful reference point for considering the issues in utilizing corporate venturing structures to pursue innovation opportunities is the independent venture capital model of launching and growing new companies. One reason to make this comparison is that private venture capital is an increasingly important part of the commercialization of new technology in the U.S. economy. A second reason is that many of the organizational issues that arise in corporate venturing are addressed in a very different manner in ventures financed through private venture capital. A third reason is that there are many cases where a promising innovation diffused out of a corporation and was only able to be commercialized outside the firm, funded through venture capital.[18]

The general topic of venture capital is an extensive one.[19] The focus here is to abstract from research on how venture capital structures new ventures and to create a set of stylized facts that provide a contrasting benchmark with which to assess the efficacy of internal corporate venturing.

An initial stylized fact is that the venture capital model aligns incentives between the venture capitalist (VC) and the investing limited partners that provide the capital for investment, and the model similarly aligns incentives between the VC and the entrepreneur in whom the VC invests.[20] If the venture proves to be successful, the entrepreneur's success directly generates economic value for the VC, and the VC's gain-sharing arrangement with its limited partners assures that 70% to 80% of that gain is readily distributed to the limited partners by the end of the fund.

A second stylized fact is that the financing of new ventures is carefully staged, with small financial commitments offered initially, along with the option (but not the obligation) to invest more later, pending the achievement of certain milestone events[21] by the venture. This use of contingent, staged financing imposes tremendous constraints and discipline upon the venture. These constraints force the venture to focus on only the most essential elements of its business plan necessary to achieve positive cash flows. At each stage of financing, there is a credible threat to discontinue further financing. Note that under these arrangements, the problem of zero-sum bargaining for internal corporate resources does not arise.

A third stylized fact is the intensive oversight provided by venture capitalists to firms in their portfolio. One survey by Gorman and Sahlman found that VCs visited their portfolio companies an average of 19 times each year, with over 100 hours of direct contact between the VC and managers of the venture.[22] One important manifestation of this intensive oversight was demonstrated by Lerner, who found that VCs generally increased their participation during times of CEO crisis.[23] This increased monitoring allows VCs to gather information that may not be gathered by corporate venture sponsors. In addition, it provides a faster decision cycle. VCs' intensive monitoring gives them the information necessary to commit to a course of action in a short amount of time. Their arrangements with their limited partners mean that their decisions will stand without further review by other levels of management.

A fourth stylized fact is that VCs are structured so as to be indifferent to what business model portfolio companies use to achieve their success. By construction, the VCs have no established assets and no business model that might be put at risk by the activities of a new venture. By contrast, Hellman noted that corporate venture investing would likely be strongly affected by whether the activities of the venture were complementary to—versus a substitute for—the activities of the corporate investor.[24] Corporations would have a vested interest in supporting startups that build upon their current businesses and technologies, but they would rationally pay less for startups that threaten those assets. Similarly, corporations would support startups that leverage the

Designing Corporate Ventures in the Shadow of Private Venture Capital

TABLE 1. Comparison of Corporate Venture (CV) and Venture Capital (VC) Structures, Relative to Specific Organizational Attributes

Attribute	CV	VC
Incentive Intensity	weaker	strong
Financial Discipline on Downside	weaker	strong
Monitoring	Internal	External, including outside Board
Discovering Alternative Business Models	constrained	unconstrained

corporation's existing business model, but would underfund those that required a very different model to achieve their objectives.[25]

These four stylized attributes of the independent VC model are compared with the attributes of corporate venturing in Table 1. This comparison helps us understand what happened at Exxon and what might happen to poorly designed corporate venture programs today as well. Consider first the incentive alignment in the structure of venture capital. This proved to be very difficult to replicate in Exxon's corporate venture program. Obviously, providing stock grants for Exxon's corporate stock to venture managers would blend the performance of a tiny startup with that of a huge oil company. Other, more specific surrogate equity measures, such as phantom stock, ran into conflicts with the internal norms of equity with the compensation of other, "similar" Exxon managers.

The incentive differences also worked the other way. If a private VC venture fails to meet its milestones, its top managers might be replaced[26] or the venture might even be shut down. By contrast, Sykes reported that Exxon tolerated poor venture performance from its venture managers.[27] When milestones were missed, the managers essentially renegotiated, setting new targets for the following period. This supports Sahlman's speculation: "Should the [internal] project not be successful, team members probably will find other tasks within the corporation, provided they have not been guilty of gross incompetence or malfeasance. Though the pecuniary rewards for success are modest, so too can be the consequences of failure."[28]

Consider next the method of financing new ventures. The VC projects were carefully staged, with infusions of capital meted out when and if milestones were met and new information justifying additional investment was obtained. By contrast, Sykes reported that Exxon's internal venture decisions had to run a gauntlet composed of many organizational levels.[29] To minimize the frequency of these delays, venture managers asked for, and received, significant sums of money for their projects up front. These infusions of capital only were reviewed annually in the corporate budget cycle.

It was harder for Exxon to make timely decisions as well. Sykes wrote that, "During the early stages of the venture when expenditures are low, most decisions [were] delegated to the venture management or to those directly

Designing Corporate Ventures in the Shadow of Private Venture Capital

TABLE 2. Potential Advantages of Corporate Venture (CV)
vs. Venture Capital (VC) Structures

Attribute	CV	VC
Time Horizon	indefinite	tied to fund length
Scale of Capital Invested	potentially large	smaller
Coordination of Complementarities	extensive	limited
Retention of Group Learning	strong	weak

supervising the venture management. As the venture grows and needs larger financial or functional resources from the parent, the reviews extended wider and higher."[30] This delayed the time it took to make decisions for the venture. Worse, these decisions over the fate of the venture increasingly involved people who had spent little or no time monitoring the venture previously. Whenever the venture deployed a business model different from that of Exxon, these senior level reviews likely resulted in less support and funding because the new venture did not leverage Exxon's current resources.

Designing Corporate Ventures in the Shadow of Venture Capital

It is clear that any corporate venturing activity in the foreseeable future in the United States will take place in an environment in which independent venture capital is a significant and growing reality. It is not enough, however, for corporate venturing to be managed to be more like private venture capital (though corporate ventures may benefit from adopting certain practices employed by private venture capitalists). If corporate venturing is to endure beyond the next downturn in the equity markets, it must offer some structural advantages over private venture capital in its ability to manage the development and commercialization of new technologies. If these structural advantages cannot be identified and then leveraged, company shareholders reasonably will ask why corporations don't simply return excess cash for the shareholders to invest themselves.[31]

While the evidence to date is fragmented, there may in fact be some advantages for corporations in commercializing new technological opportunities through external venture structures. It is premature to claim that these structural differences can sustain corporate venturing activity in the shadow of private venture capital, but at least they provide a potential rationale for doing so. These potential advantages are listed in Table 2.

One difference may seem trivial, the difference of time. Approximately two-thirds of venture funds in the U.S. are organized as limited partnerships.[32] These venture funds are created with a limited lifetime, generally between seven

Designing Corporate Ventures in the Shadow of Private Venture Capital

and ten years.[33] This limited horizon acts to enforce the incentive alignment between limited partners and the general VC partner by ensuring that gains earned through successful investments are returned to the limited partners and not simply "rolled over" into new risky investments. The limited horizon also provides a safeguard of last resort for the limited partners. If the general partner has performed poorly despite the other incentive alignment features in the fund, the limited partners can take their proceeds at the termination of the fund and simply go elsewhere.

Corporations, by contrast, have an indefinite life span. There is no "end of the fund" pressure to gain liquidity for venture positions that have yet to either be sold or go public. This difference suggests one implied structural advantage or corporations over private venture capital firms: the ability to fund and sustain longer-term projects. Any new VC fund takes some period of time to invest its proceeds after the fund closes its financing. At the other end, winding up the portfolio and achieving liquidity for the fund's investments also takes time. Corporate ventures may enjoy an advantage here for projects that require an expected duration of as little as six years to deliver value, and that advantage grows as the time needed to deliver value increases.

A second potential advantage is one of scale. While venture firms aggressively syndicate larger investments and can deploy increasingly large sums of money collectively as a result, the aggregate amount of investment they make in individual ventures remains substantially below that of the largest corporations. This advantage has proved to be important in the past. Alfred Chandler analyzed the limits of "personal capitalism" in Britain in comparison with the ability of U.S. and German corporations to amass the capital needed to finance the large investments required to drive the development of the chemicals, railroad, and steel industries.[34] To take a more recent (and admittedly extreme) example, the development of the IBM System 360 was said to have required over $4 billion in 1963 dollars.[35] In today's dollars, that amount exceeds the combined total annual spending of all venture capital firms in the United States. As a practical matter, this second advantage is likely to matter in only a small number of cases, as firms seldom invest sufficient sums of money in their corporate venture activities to benefit from this advantage.[36]

A third potential structural advantage stems from the corporation's ownership of important physical, knowledge-based, and other intangible complementary assets. To the extent that these assets cannot be freely traded, but can only be controlled through owning the corporation itself, then the corporation enjoys a structural advantage over private VCs in coordinating complementary technology developments. When venture activities complement these corporate assets, corporations potentially could benefit more from their realization than would private venture investors.[37]

In addition, certain technologies require the development of complementary technologies in order to deliver value, and corporations would likely have advantages over private venture capitalists in coordinating these complementarities.[38] One recent large sample study by Gompers and Lerner comparing corporate venture investments and private venture investments found that when corporations invested in activities that were related to their own line of business, their returns actually were competitive with those of private VC funds.[39] Corporate investments in unrelated activities were found to earn an inferior return, both in comparison with related investments and with private venture capital. This suggests that corporate investments in related venture activities are able to compete with private venture capital.

The evidence to date of this advantage is taken from complementarities in technology. However, the principle of corporations leveraging complementarities with non-tradable corporate assets in their venture activities can be extended to all such assets. Knowledge-based assets, for example, can support a structural advantage over private venture capital provided that this knowledge accrued to the corporation and did not simply reside in a few people's heads. Another non-tradable asset that can offer leverage is an intangible asset such as a brand or the company's reputation. This rationale of complementarities is the primary rationale used to justify the many corporate venture investments of the Intel Corporation.[40]

A final potential structural advantage stems from the very weakness of incentive systems in providing strong risk/reward packages to its employees. The same inability to pay high bonuses or large amounts of stock to individual employees also works on the downside: corporations do not punish failure as fully as private venture firms do. Because of this, and because most new ventures fail for both VCs and for corporations, *the potential exists for companies to retain more learning from these failures.* Instead of disbanding the firm, breaking up the team, and scattering people to their individual job searches (as would be done in the failure of a private VC-financed venture), corporations could conduct post-mortem learning activities with the team in place.[41] Some portion of the team then could be deployed on a new opportunity, while others could evangelize the positive elements of the experience back in the rest of the corporation. In this process, other venture attempts that built upon the experience of the prior attempt might meet with greater success.

The advantage of this is embodied in the concept of "intelligent failure."[42] There is a human tendency to block out the experience from a failed endeavor. In the context of commercializing technology, much valuable information from a failed venture may be lost as a result. It is not by accident that many of the most successful technology entrepreneurs have had at least one failure in their own past experience. Much can be learned from failures, if one has the will and ability to do so.

Some anecdotal evidence exists that some corporations do "fail forward" to some degree.[43] 3M has a reputation as a company that will acknowledge and even celebrate certain "noble failures." Some HP managers have commented that David Packard used to say, "If you're not failing once in a while, you're not taking enough risk." In a recent presentation by senior IBM managers, one of them said that, "If you haven't been yelled at by a senior manager lately, you're not doing your job." Xerox PARC's famous Computer Science Laboratory, which was the birthplace of many of PARC's most storied discoveries, is now run by a manager who was the initial leader of one recent failed spinout venture.

These structural disadvantages of corporate venturing shown in Table 1, combined with the potential advantages in Table 2, comprise a set of design principles that can inform the design of new corporate ventures in the shadow of independent venture capital.

One Innovative Corporate Venture Design: Lucent's New Ventures Group

One organization has recently embarked on a corporate venture design that was developed with the shadow of private venture capital very much in mind. Lucent created its New Ventures Group (NVG) in 1997 in order to commercialize technologies out of its Bell Laboratories that did not fit with any of Lucent's established businesses.[44] In addition to capturing value from these technologies, Lucent also wished to speed up the time it took for its technologies to go into its mainstream businesses as well.

Lucent was careful to conduct extensive external benchmarking activities to determine whether and how to utilize corporate money to finance new technology ventures. Some of this benchmarking activity involved discussion with other companies who had experience with this activity, including Intel, 3M, Raychem, Thermo-Electron, and Xerox. The planning staff also held numerous discussions with the private venture capital community to understand how their approach to financing and commercializing new technologies worked.

Lucent learned early on that it needed to craft an operating model to blend the incentives, risk taking, and speedy decision making of private venture capital with the deep technological resources and the culture of Bell Laboratories. The key challenge for the NVG was to graft a more entrepreneurial spirit onto the culture of the organization. This required faster decisions, more individual risk taking, and greater individual identification with the business opportunities latent in the deep technical resources of the company.

To manage the cultural change process, the NVG consciously created what became known internally as "the phantom world." The phantom world did not exist outside of Lucent; it was a hybrid constructed out of a pure venture capital organization and a large technology-based company. It could be thought of as a "half-way house," which would enable people and ideas that weren't ready or able to go out directly to obtain pure venture capital to develop their ideas further within Lucent. By being sensitive about the cultural gaps that had to be bridged, and by being sensible about the right mix of risk and reward to offer, the phantom world created a launching pad for ideas to move out of Bell Labs into markets outside of Lucent's traditional business channels.

Designing Corporate Ventures in the Shadow of Private Venture Capital

TABLE 3. Lucent's NVG Portfolio, as of Q4, 1999

GROUP 1: Internal NVG Venture Companies

EC&S
Full View
Lucent Public Safety Systems
NetCalibrate
Savaje

GROUP 2: Syndicated NVG Venture Companies

Face2Face
Lucent Digital Radio
Persystant
Siros
Talarian
Veridicom
VideoNet
Visual Insights
Watchmark

GROUP 3: Ventures That Have Experienced Liquidation Events

Elemedia*
Lucent Digital Video*
Maps on Us
Noteable*
Speech

* re-acquired by Lucent

Through the end of 1999, the NVG had invested in 19 ventures. Most ventures have been in the Internet, networking, software, and wireless and digital broadcast spaces, which are of strategic interest to Lucent. While most investments have yet to achieve liquidity, the five ventures that have reached liquidity have brought in an 80% return on invested capital for NVG's fund.[45]

The 19 ventures can be grouped into four categories, as is depicted in Table 3. The first group is the internal ventures that the NVG is managing on its own. There are five venture companies in this group. The second group is comprised of those ventures that the NVG started, but have now syndicated with other VC firms, so that the risks, rewards, and governance are shared with them. There are nine companies in this group. The third group consists of venture companies that have had external liquidity events, either an IPO, or an acquisition. There are five companies in this last group. Three of these last five ventures were actually re-acquired by Lucent.

Table 4 shows how Lucent's design of NVG took the structural advantages and disadvantages of corporate venturing (in comparison with private venture capital) into account. NVG has not tried to fully emulate the incentives offered by private venture capital. Instead, they have developed a hybrid compensation system that provides greater rewards than commonly available through Bell Labs, and they do impose some modest amount of risk on employees who wish to join a venture sponsored by NVG. However, the risks and rewards are far less extreme than what are found in private VC-financed structures.

This has important implications for the people whom the NVG chose to launch new ventures. The NVG managers needed the founder of each venture to personally commit himself or herself to the success of the venture, even as the NVG was making a financial commitment to the venture. This commitment included the willingness of each founder to forego his or her annual bonus, in return for shares in more risky "phantom stock" that would pay off only if the venture succeeded. Fringe benefits within the ventures were also usually less than that in Lucent overall, so founders needed to accept that as well. Some Lucent researchers, when they realized the commitment involved, chose to remain researchers. Others, though, were excited about the opportunity to

Designing Corporate Ventures in the Shadow of Private Venture Capital

TABLE 4. Design of Lucent's NVG Operating Model in Comparison with Internal Business Development (BD) and Private Venture Capital (VC) Models

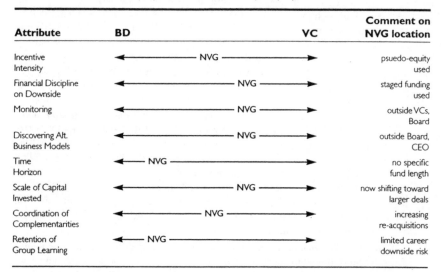

Attribute	BD	VC	Comment on NVG location
Incentive Intensity	◄———— NVG ————►		psuedo-equity used
Financial Discipline on Downside	◄———— NVG ———►		staged funding used
Monitoring	◄———— NVG ———►		outside VCs, Board
Discovering Alt. Business Models	◄———— NVG ———►		outside Board, CEO
Time Horizon	◄— NVG ————————►		no specific fund length
Scale of Capital Invested	◄———— NVG ———►		now shifting toward larger deals
Coordination of Complementarities	◄——— NVG ——►		increasing re-acquisitions
Retention of Group Learning	◄— NVG ————————►		limited career downside risk

become entrepreneurs and to carry their research out of the lab and into the market.

The NVG operating model in Table 4 also influences the type of people who can be brought in from outside to help launch new ventures from within Lucent. A pure entrepreneur with no experience of operating within a larger company would likely be unable to function effectively in the NVG operating model. He or she might never have seen corporate overhead charges, annual operating plans, and company-wide occupational safety, environmental, or other corporate policy and personnel initiatives. There is an opposing pull from the pure VC model as well. Managers hired from outside of Lucent, and some internal Lucent researchers, seek a truly independent venture capital style arrangement. This involves substantial equity options, a commitment to achieve liquidity for that stock, and a pursuit of financial success no matter what the cost or impact is upon the parent companies' business. The NVG model strikes a balance between the pure corporate development model on the one hand and the pure VC model on the other in terms of the incentives it provides to hire an outside CEO.

The NVG operating model in Table 4 emulates some of the governance features of private venture capital. The money is given to individual ventures through staged financing increments, very much like rounds of investment by venture capital firms. In nine of the ventures, NVG even syndicated later rounds of investment with outside venture firms, and invited the outside venture partners onto the Board of the venture. This helps provide diligent monitoring and oversight and allows NVG ventures to access some of the external VC network of contacts in order to help identify appropriate CEO candidates and promising business model approaches. To date, most NVG ventures have hired an outsider to serve as CEO for the venture and have pursued a wide variety of business models. Importantly, they have shifted business models when it became clear that an initial model was not working. Thus, the NVG model makes intelligent use of independent VC firms (and in turn, selectively sharing the profits from these ventures) in the pursuit of its objectives.

However, the NVG has also taken care to leverage the potential structural advantages of corporate venturing noted above. While the managers of NVG are measured on their return on invested capital, there is no fixed life of the fund and no associated "end of fund" drive for liquidity. To date, the funds invested have been kept deliberately modest, but NVG managers are beginning to build credibility within Lucent from their initial investment results. As their credibility increases, NVG managers are beginning to evaluate larger-scale initiatives that most venture capital firms would not consider. This will allow the NVG to enjoy potential scale advantages in the future.

NVG managers are particularly interested in projects that can exploit one of more complementarities with Lucent's assets. Much of NVG's due diligence process involves extended discussions with internal Lucent business managers to identify important industry trends and missing elements in Lucent's internal offerings and to assess the ability of Lucent's channels to support new product and service offerings. These discussions help to validate the business potential of a new venture. They also help to align the ventures with the overall strategic direction of Lucent's businesses.

Lucent has also taken steps to retain group learning from the experience of its NVG ventures. Lucent employees have the ability to rejoin the company if the venture does not succeed, preserving some institutional memory of a failed venture (though the outside CEO typically is expected to leave the company). Another benefit is that other Lab staff that do not spin off into new ventures are nonetheless being influenced by the NVG process. The presence of the NVG provides a potential alternative path to market for Bell Labs technologies, and this is viewed positively by many Bell Labs researchers. Lucent is even finding that there are recruiting advantages to its NVG program. The biggest competition it has for new Ph.D. hires is not from other research laboratories; rather, it is from startup firms. The NVG is helping Lucent recruit new Ph.D. scientists and engineers who appreciate joining a world-class research organization that also might provide a spinout opportunity for their ideas down the road.

The NVG process also appears to be achieving its goal of serving as an impetus for Bell Labs technologies to move off of the shelf. Once the NVG group has identified a promising technology within Bell Labs, the Lucent business units have only a limited amount of time to consider whether or not to take over the technology themselves and fund its further development. In the past, the business units could wait and see whether a technology would become important, and this often delayed the introduction of new technologies to the market. When the NVG serves notice that it is interested in commercializing an internal technology, that effectively becomes a forcing function that has increased the speed with which technology is moving out of Bell Labs into the market.

Once the technology is taken into the market by the NVG, the NVG process also provides more rapid feedback on the value of the technology to Lucent. The three instances to date where Lucent reacquired an NVG venture arose when it became clear that the technologies were too important to Lucent to have them managed independently of the company. This strategic value would not likely have been visible had the technologies continued to sit on the shelf. The ability to take them to market through new ventures allowed the market to provide a "second opinion" to the earlier judgment of Lucent's business managers, who judged earlier that the technologies were not yet ready for the market.

The NVG has evolved its approach in the two years since it began operation. It has learned to invest more time and effort up front in performing due diligence on prospective investments. To that end, it now specializes its managers in specific investment areas, such as wireless communications or e-commerce, so that due diligence can be performed more rapidly. It also has moved from seeking to supply all of the financing of its ventures to seeking to syndicate funding with outside venture firms in most instances. The composition of its boards has changed as a result, from knowledgeable technologists and consultants to partners of venture capital firms with a sizeable financial stake in the venture. These outside board members add an important independent perspective and often bring a network of useful contacts as well.

In addition to accessing these external contacts, the NVG is building closer contacts with both lab researchers and managers within Bell Laboratories, and increasingly with business unit managers within Lucent's ten business groups. These latter links also have proven to be increasingly valuable to the NVG, both as a source of opportunities for new ventures and also for learning about market trends and needs. These enhanced connections with the external marketplace have sped up the NVG's due diligence process and have improved its effectiveness in spotting important opportunities. They also increase the awareness of and appreciation for technical opportunities within Lucent's business groups. Ironically, NVG's early interest in technologies has caused some Bell Labs technologies to move directly into the business groups that might otherwise have been overlooked by those businesses. This is one contribution that NVG makes to Lucent that is not formally measured.

Conclusion

Corporate venturing has had a checkered past, rising and falling with the public equity markets. The recent surge in private venture capital makes the design of corporate ventures even more problematic, as these ventures must compete with independent venture capital for entrepreneurial talent latent in the firm. To sustain themselves through the down phase of the next cycle, corporate venturing structures must be designed to operate in the shadow of independent venture capital.

While they may do well to mimic certain VC practices, corporate venture structures ultimately will only work if they can deliver strategic benefits to their sponsoring companies. To realize these benefits, these structures must do more than mimic independent venture capital. They must leverage the potential advantages of corporate ventures. To be sure, in these days of munificent public equity markets and abundant IPOs, the potential advantages of corporate venturing versus independent venture capital have yet to assert themselves. However, corporate structures do differ in their time span, their scale, their management of strategic complements, and their ability to learn from venture failures. In less exuberant equity markets, these advantages could become more salient.

Lucent's NVG is one structure that illustrates how corporate venture structures can be designed in this new environment. Its structure balances many aspects of private venture capital with other aspects of its corporate mission. It is consciously a hybrid, lying between a pure venture capital model and a pure corporate development model. It works closely with Lucent's businesses, yet it retains an independent ability to select technologies and take them to market. It seeks to exploit Lucent's resources to the fullest, but is free to pursue whatever business model it wishes to use for a new venture. Its managers are compensated on their return on their investment and even reacquired ventures are purchased at market prices. Its returns so far have been impressive, yet it has managed not to antagonize the senior managers of the parent firm.

However effective Lucent's NVG ultimately turns out to be, it is likely to be more effective than a corporate venturing strategy that either ignores venture capital on the one hand or simply seeks to emulate all of the practices of private venture firms on the other. The way forward is to acknowledge that the corporate context differs in important ways from that of private venture capital and then to design corporate venture structures that flow from the logic of those contextual differences. Lucent's NVG provides one example of such a structure.

Notes

1. Peter Drucker, *Management: Tasks, Responsibilities, Practices* (New York, NY: Harper & Row, 1974), p. 799.
2. Norman Fast, "The Rise and Fall of Corporate New Venture Divisions," (Ann Arbor, MI: UMI Research Press, 1978).

3. Matthew Yost, "The State of Corporate Venturing: The Number of Active Programs Levels Off as Corporations Complete Shifts Back to Core Businesses," *Corporate Venturing* (June1994). Block and MacMillan think the cycle historically has run about every 10 years. Zenas Block and Ian Macmillan, *Corporate Venturing: Creating New Businesses Within the Firm* (Cambridge, MA: Harvard Business School Press, 1993), p. 13.

4. This section closely follows Sykes' first hand account of this experience. Hollister Sykes, "The Anatomy of a Corporate Venturing Program: Factors Influencing Success," *Journal of Business Venturing*, 1 (1986): 275-293.

5. The amount written off is not reported by Sykes [ibid.].

6. Bradley Graham, "World of Venture Capitalists Becomes More Complicated," *Washington Post*, October 1, 1978, p. M1.

7. Venture One, "3Q'99 Venture Capital Financings Top 8 Billion Dollars," November 2, 1999, http://www.v1.com/news/press/Q399PRFinancings.htm

8. Henry W. Chesbrough, "The Differing Organizational Impact of Technological Change: A Comparative Theory of National Institutional Factors," *Industrial and Corporate Change*, 8/3 (1999): 447-485.

9. Eric Von Hippel, "An Exploratory Study of Corporate Venturing—A New Product Innovation Strategy Used by Some Major Corporations," unpublished dissertation, Carnegie Mellon University, 1973; Eric Von Hippel, "Successful and Failing Internal Corporate Ventures: An Empirical Analysis," Industrial Marketing Management, 6 (1977): 163-174.

10. Fast, op. cit.

11. Joseph Bower, "Managing the Resource Allocation Process," Division of Research, Harvard Business School, 1970.

12. Kenneth Rind, "The Role of Venture Capital in Corporate Development," *Strategic Management Journal*, 2 (1981): 169-180.

13. Zenas Block and Oscar Ornati, "Compensating Corporate Venture Managers," *Journal of Business Venturing*, 2 (1987): 41-51.

14. This is consistent with problems of measurement that frustrate most pay-for-performance incentive systems in large corporations. Zenger finds that engineers have highly inflated beliefs about their relative performance versus that of their peers, and therefore regard large variations in compensation as arbitrary and unfair. The result is a "leveling" effect that dampens salary incentive increases. Todd Zenger, "Compensating for Innovation: Do Small Firms Offer High-Powered Incentives that Lure Talent and Motivate Effort?" working paper, John M. Olin School of Business, Washington University, St. Louis, MO, May 24, 1996; Todd Zenger, "Explaining Organizational Diseconomies of Scale in R&D: The Allocation of Engineering Talent, Ideas, and Effort by Firm Size," *Management Science*, 40 (1994): 708-729.

15. Block and Ornati, op. cit., p. 44.

16. R. Siegel, E. Siegel, and I. MacMillan, "Corporate Venture Capitalists: Autonomy, Obstacles and Performance," *Journal of Business Venturing*, 3/3 (1988): 233-247.

17. This is a specific instance of a more general problem. See Williamson for a seminal discussion of "the problem of selective intervention," or why a large company cannot do everything a small company can do, and more. Oliver E. Williamson, *The Economic Institutions of Capitalism* (New York, NY: Free Press, 1985), Chapter Six.

18. Douglas Smith and Robert Alexander, *Fumbling the Future: How Xerox Invented, Then Ignored, The First Personal Computer* (New York, NY: William Morrow & Co., 1988); Michael Hiltzik, *Dealers of Lightning: Xerox PARC and the Dawn of the Computer Age* (New York, NY: HarperCollins, 1999).

Designing Corporate Ventures in the Shadow of Private Venture Capital

19. For reviews, see William Sahlman, "The Structure and Governance of Venture-Capital Organizations," *Journal of Financial Economics*, 27/2 (October 1990): 473-521; William Sahlman, "Insights from the American Venture Capital Organization," Harvard Business School working paper #92-047, 1992; William Bygrave and Jeffrey Timmons, *Venture Capital at the Crossroads* (Boston, MA: Harvard Business School Press, 1992); Josh Lerner, "Venture Capitalists and the Oversight of Private Firms," *Journal of Finance*, 50/1 (1995): 301-318; Thomas Hellman, "The Allocation of Control Rights in Venture Capital Contracts," *Rand Journal of Economics*, 29/1 (1998): 57-76.

20. Sahlman (1990), op. cit.

21. These milestones might include the creation of a working prototype unit, or the receipt of an initial customer order, or reaching a breakeven point on a cash basis.

22. Michael Gorman and William Sahlman, "What Do Venture Capitalists Do?" *Journal of Business Venturing*, 4 (1989): 231-248.

23. Lerner, op. cit. The objection might arise, why do entrepreneurs voluntarily bear such risk, and enter into arrangements that entail such significant oversight and financial discipline? Hellman [op. cit.] provides one answer. He studies a model of a wealth-constrained entrepreneur who faces a tradeoff between retaining more control vs. receiving better financial terms. Because the entrepreneur's effort is non-contractible, VCs will rationally offer better financial terms to entrepreneurs who agree to accept these constraints on their control rights.

24. Thomas Hellman, "A Theory of Corporate Venture Investing," working paper, Graduate School of Business, Stanford University, 1996.

25. Henry Chesbrough and Richard Rosenbloom, "The Dual-Edged Role of the Business Model in Leveraging Corporate Technology Investments," paper delivered at the NIST conference on Managing Technical Risk, the John F. Kennedy School of Government, Harvard University, September 1999.

26. James Baron, M. Diane Burton, and Michael Hannan, "The Road Taken: Origins and Evolution of Employment Systems in Emerging Companies," *Industrial and Corporate Change*, 5/2 (1996): 239-276.

27. Sykes, op. cit.

28. Sahlman (1992), op. cit., p. 25.

29. Sykes, op. cit.

30. Ibid.

31. Michael Jensen, "Agency Costs of Free Cash Flow, Corporate Finance, and Takeovers," *American Economic Review*, 76/2 (1986): 323-330; Michael Jensen, "Eclipse of the Public Corporation," *Harvard Business Review*, 67/5 (September/October 1989): 61-75.

32. Sahlman (1992), op. cit., p. 6,

33. Sahlman (1990; 1992), op. cit.

34. Alfred D. Chandler, *Scale and Scope: The Dynamics of Industrial Capitalism* (Cambridge, MA: Harvard University Press, 1990).

35. Emerson Pugh, Lyle Johnson, and Jack Palmer, *IBM's 360 and Early 370 Systems* (Cambridge, MA: MIT Press, 1991).

36. It does suggest an alternative strategy for corporate venturing, though, that lies outside the scope of this article. This strategy would rely on venture capital to fund, organize, and govern early stage endeavors, and it would focus corporate internal venture activity on selectively acquiring later stage ventures and grow them from there, rather than start them from scratch.

37. Hellman (1996), op. cit.

38. Henry Chesbrough and David Teece, "When is Virtual Virtuous: Organizing for Innovation," *Harvard Business Review*, 74/1 (January/February 1996): 65-74.

Designing Corporate Ventures in the Shadow of Private Venture Capital

39. Paul Gompers and Josh Lerner, "The Determinants of Corporate Venture Capital Success: Organization Structure, Incentives, and Complementarities," Harvard Business School working paper #99-009, 1998.
40. Brian Taptich, "The New Startup," *Red Herring* (October 1998), pp. 52-56.
41. Cusamano and Selby describe Microsoft's extensive use of post mortem analyses, which are written at the end of every major development project. Importantly, these analyses are widely shared within the top management of the company, and with future project leaders of related projects. Michael Cusamano and Richard Selby, *Microsoft Secrets: How the World's Most Powerful Software Company Creates Technology, Shapes Markets, and Manages People* (New York, NY: Free Press, 1995). See Sinofsky and Thomke for a practical note regarding the effective management of post mortem analysis. Steven Sinofsky and Stefan Thomke, "Learning from Projects: Note on Conducting a Postmortem Analysis," Harvard Business School Case #N9-600-021, September 3, 1999.
42. Dorothy Leonard, *Wellsprings of Knowledge* (Cambridge, MA: Harvard Business School Press, 1995), p. 118.
43. To be sure, many corporations do *not* do much to proactively learn from their failures. The argument here is that there is the *potential* for corporations to do more than private VC firms; not that most corporations in fact are doing so.
44. See Chesbrough and Socolof for a more complete description of Lucent's New Ventures Group. This section draws heavily from that paper. Henry Chesbrough and Stephen Socolof, "Commercializing New Ventures from Bell Labs Technology: The Design and Experience of Lucent's New Ventures Group," *Research-Technology Management* (March 2000), pp. 1-11.
45. This is a cash-on-cash return and excludes markups taken on private companies in subsequent rounds.

[13]

Corporations and the Financing of Innovation: The Corporate Venturing Experience

PAUL A. GOMPERS

The author is a professor of business administration at Harvard Business School and a research associate at the National Bureau of Economic Research. He thanks VentureOne for making this project possible through generous access to its database of venture financings. He thanks Harvard Business School's Division of Research for financial support.

orporate internal investments in innovative activities, including research and development, have often been maligned for their ineffectiveness (Jensen 1993). Over the past forty years, corporations have attempted to capture the value from waves of technology and innovation. But during much of this time, corporations saw young, nimble start-ups capitalize on opportunities that the corporations saw first.

Why have corporations had difficulty bringing innovations to market? Many of the best ideas have languished, unused, whether because of internal resistance (for example, from managers who did not want to see a product launched that competed with one of their offerings) or an inability to execute on the initial insight. In other cases, defecting employees started new firms that turned those ideas into blockbuster commercial successes. The achievements of fast-growing technology firms such as Microsoft and Cisco Systems—many of which relied on acquisitions rather than on internal research and development (R&D) for the bulk of their new ideas—also made conventional approaches to innovation look lackluster by comparison. In response to these factors, many corporations entered the venture capital market in hopes of spurring their own innovative capacity.

Corporations have good reason to explore new ways of stimulating innovation. All too often, their investments in traditional R&D laboratories have generated paltry returns as researchers have focused on incremental product advances or on academic ideas with little relevance to the corporation (Henderson 1993; Henderson and Cockburn 1996). Worse, even when these corporate laboratories managed to come up with truly innovative ideas, other organizations—especially venture-backed start-ups—have sometimes seized the opportunity to commercialize them.

But how can companies best stimulate innovation in a corporate setting? The venture capital industry's success may be difficult to replicate. Though total disbursements from the venture industry during 1975–2000 proved considerably less than the R&D spending of either IBM or General Motors alone, venture-backed firms have scored remarkable successes (Reinganum 1989; Lerner 1997).

This paper explores the history, structure, and performance of corporate venture programs in the United States. It chronicles the cyclical nature of the industry over the past forty years, a time during which corporate venture capital programs were often halted before the full fruits from the investment activity could be realized. This study shows that the corporate venture capital market in the United States has gone through three waves of activity that track the overall independent venture capital market.

The paper next explores the experience of corporate venture investment using a detailed microlevel data set. The analysis finds that such investments are increasingly made in related industries—that is, over time, the strategic fit between corporate venture capital investments and the parent corporation's business has increased. In addition, contrary to previous assumptions, corporate venture capital investments have, on average, been more successful than independent venture capital investments. This success is exclusively associated with strategic corporate venture investments—that is, nonrelated investments have much lower success rates. This study concludes that corporations appear to be learning many of the best practices from the independent venture capital sector. The success of corporate venture investing has increased over time.

Types of Corporate Venturing

Large corporations have long been attracted to venture capital investing. Many of these efforts have been motivated by a desire to gain access to cutting-edge technologies for strategic reasons. Sometimes these strategic goals far outweighed any consideration of financial return for corporate investors, allowing financial investors to treat these corporations as later-stage, valuation-insensitive investors. This behavior led many independent venture capitalists to introduce early-stage technology companies to corporate investors only during later rounds of financing, when portfolio companies required large amounts of cash raised at extremely high valuations to preserve the venture capitalists' percentage ownership. This practice created situations in which corporations invested in companies that were often significantly overvalued and made it difficult for corporate investors to achieve acceptable financial returns. As a result, many corporate investors reached the conclusion that it was not possible to achieve both financial and strategic goals in doing early-stage technology investing.

Corporations used several models to achieve their strategic and financial objectives for venture capital investments. Each of these models, however, created problems that ultimately caused corporations to fail to reach their goals.

Internal corporate venture group. Some corporations created internal corporate venture groups to analyze venture capital opportunities and make investments. Problems typically arose with this strategy because it limited deal flow to those companies that wanted to be associated with that particular corporation. Entrepreneurs were limited by this structure because, while they could receive excellent depth of assistance in the corporation's area of expertise, they were forced to sacrifice breadth of available resources. In addition, early-stage entrepre-

neurs were often concerned about protecting their intellectual property and wanted to avoid alliances that could threaten their position. For example, a small high-technology company in a precarious financial situation might be reluctant to approach IBM or Sony directly for funding. Therefore, the very companies in which these corporations wanted to invest were usually the ones that never made it to their doorsteps.

Dedicated external fund. Other corporations placed investment capital in a dedicated fund that existed as a separate entity outside the corporation. This structure did not solve many entrepreneurs' concerns because they still needed to feel comfortable with forming an alliance with the particular corporation sponsoring the fund. Since corporations were able to use only dedicated external funds to attract entrepreneurs that wanted to be aligned with them, the corporations were not able to allocate assets across industry areas besides their own even though diversification through pooled investments might have produced better risk management and higher financial returns. In addition, a dedicated external fund often frustrated a corporation's desire to gain strategic leverage with start-up companies. The corporation's relationship was too distant for the corporation's employees to work closely with the entrepreneurs.

Passive limited partner in a venture fund. Existing venture funds gave corporations the opportunity to become passive limited partners and make diversified investments in entrepreneurial companies.[1] The venture capitalists managing these funds typically had little incentive to involve corporations in early investments. Instead, the venture capitalists would send corporate limited partners deals at later stages for passive investment at fairly high valuations.[2] In addition, this structure did not allow corporations to achieve strategic objectives since the corporations, as passive investors, did not have direct relationships with the entrepreneurs. The "information flow" to corporations depended on the venture capitalists' goodwill.

The History of Corporate Venturing Investments

The first corporate venture funds emerged in the mid-1960s—about two decades after the initial institutional venture capital funds formed.[3] Since that time, corporate venturing has undergone three boom-and-bust cycles that closely track the independent venture capital sector. Corporations have typically entered the corporate venture capital market after the independent sector showed signs of success (Gompers and Lerner 1998a). All too often, however, corporations overbuilt capacity without carefully thinking out the implications (Block and Ornati 1987). This strategy invariably led to retrenchment.

The first wave. As traditional venture capital funds fueled the success of corporations such as Digital Equipment Corporation, Memorex, Raychem, and Scientific Data Systems, large companies took notice, reviewing these successes as new potential opportunities. Large companies began establishing divisions that emulated venture capitalists. During the late 1960s and early 1970s, more than 25 percent of the Fortune 500 firms set up such programs (Rind 1981).

At one end of the spectrum, large corporations financed new firms that were already receiving venture capital from independent venture capital organizations. Most of these efforts, such as General Electric's Business Development Services, Inc., invested directly in start-ups. This strategy let managers tailor their firms' portfolios to their particular technological or business needs. In other cases, the corporations simply provided funds to a separate venture capital firm. This separate firm would in turn invest the money in entrepreneurial organizations.

At the other end of the spectrum, projects such as DuPont Corporation's Development Department and Ralston Purina's New Venture Division sought to promote new ventures internally. These programs encouraged the companies' own product engineers and scientists to forge ahead with their innovations—and provided financial, legal, and marketing support. In some cases, these units were separate legal entities, which at times also had outside equity investors. More typically, however, the corporate parent retained ownership of the program.

In 1973, the market for new public offerings—the primary avenue through which venture capitalists exit successful investments—dried up as small technology stocks experienced very poor returns. Returns of independent venture funds shrank, and commitments to the independent venture capital sector fell. Corporations, in light of the declining market, began scaling back their own venturing initiatives. The typical corporate venture program begun in the late 1960s was dissolved after just four years.

The second wave. The independent venture industry's prospects brightened again in the late 1970s and early 1980s. Two regulatory changes had

a dramatic impact on venture capital commitments (Gompers and Lerner 1998c). First, the top capital gains tax rate was reduced in 1978. Second, the Department of Labor eased pension investment restrictions in 1979, allowing pension managers to invest substantial amounts into venture capital funds. In addition, several new technological innovations, including personal computer hardware and software, provided an opportunity for new companies to exploit new markets. The flow of funding into the venture capital industry grew, and the number of active venture organizations proliferated.

Corporate venturing increased shortly thereafter. By 1986 corporate funds managed $2 billion, or

> The venture capital industry expanded once again in the late 1990s, fueled in large part by the highly visible successes of telecommunications and Internet-related companies.

nearly 12 percent of the total pool of venture capital. Whereas the earlier wave of corporate venturing had taken aim at a broad range of investment opportunities, now high-tech and pharmaceutical companies—such as Control Data, EG&G, Eli Lilly, and Monsanto—led the charge.

The boom of the early 1980s, however, was soon followed by another retrenchment. In 1987, the stock market crashed and the market for new public offerings again deflated. As in the past, returns and fund-raising by independent partnerships shrank as well. Chart 1 provides a profile of this relationship. This time, corporations scaled back their commitment to venture investing even more dramatically. By 1992 the number of corporate venture programs had fallen by one-third, and their capital under management represented only 5 percent of a much smaller venture pool.

The third wave. The venture capital industry expanded once again in the late 1990s, fueled in large part by the highly visible successes of telecommunications and Internet-related companies. As rates

---

1. For a discussion of typical independent venture capital fund structures, see Gompers and Lerner (1996, 1999).
2. For a discussion of staging and its implications for investors, see Gompers (1995).
3. This history of corporate venture capital is based on Fast (1978); Hardymon, DeNino, and Salter (1983); Venture Economics (1986); and assorted press accounts. It is largely based on the history of corporate venture capital presented in Gompers and Lerner (1998b).

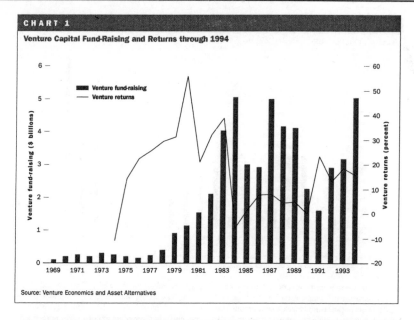

CHART 1

Venture Capital Fund-Raising and Returns through 1994

Source: Venture Economics and Asset Alternatives

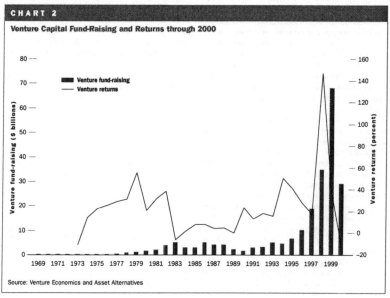

CHART 2

Venture Capital Fund-Raising and Returns through 2000

Source: Venture Economics and Asset Alternatives

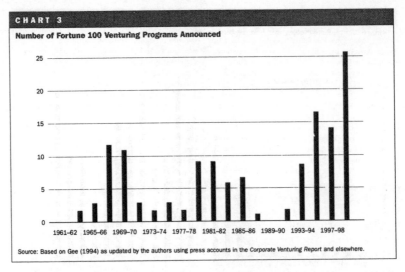

CHART 3

Number of Fortune 100 Venturing Programs Announced

Source: Based on Gee (1994) as updated by the authors using press accounts in the *Corporate Venturing Report* and elsewhere.

of return on venture capital investments rose, corporations once again became attracted to the opportunity of corporate venturing. Chart 2 graphs the pace of venture capital fund-raising through 2001 and median rates of return on venture capital investments through 2000. The graph shows the dramatic expansion in returns along with the unprecedented rise in fund-raising. During this period, many corporations had decided to reevaluate the innovation process itself. For much of the century, large corporations had typically relied on central R&D laboratories to crank out new product ideas. Now, these organizations began exploring other ways to access new ideas—including joint ventures, acquisitions, and university-based collaborations. Corporate venture programs gave corporations the opportunity to capitalize on these relationships.

The rapid diffusion of the Internet and its power to either enhance or cannibalize "bricks-and-mortar" businesses intensified this interest. Corporations everywhere realized that e-commerce presented both an opportunity and a threat. However, many organizations lacked the internal resources to explore these new opportunities. Corporate venturing provided one solution. For example, the Tribune Company, the Sony Corporation, and United Parcel Service all instituted efforts to invest in on-line businesses.

Finally, numerous venture capital groups, looking for strategic-partnering opportunities, expressed interest in collaborating with corporations. In earlier years, traditional venture investors had approached

corporate investors with a mix of caution and skepticism. The waxing and waning of corporate interest—which historically had fluctuated more wildly than cycles in the venture industry had—made many venture capitalists nervous.

But as the venture capital sector grew increasingly crowded in the late 1990s, the venture community adopted a different attitude. Venture capitalists increasingly saw corporate investments as a potential strategic advantage. And a new focus on revolutionary business strategies—such as customer-relationship management—woke up venture groups to their own limitations. A corporate partner, some venture firms surmised, might provide the knowledge and experience that venture organizations needed to improve their own skills and professionalism. Such groups forged partnerships with corporations, not only accepting money from them as investors but also structuring unique collaborations that sought to draw upon the expertise of the large organization.

Corporate Venture Activity

Corporate venture capital activity is difficult to measure, but Chart 3 provides some measure of the level of activity. Chart 3 graphs the number of corporate venture capital programs announced publicly by Fortune 100 companies. The three historical "waves" show up prominently in the graph. The number of programs established during the 1962–98 period totals well above 100. Though not all corporations established venturing programs during these decades, many that did often set up more than one. In addition, a single company might abandon and revive a series of such programs.

Another indicator of the size of the corporate venturing effort can be seen in Table 1, which shows the fifteen largest corporate venture capital programs in 2000 and their capital under management. The table shows that the types of firms engaged in corporate venturing come from a diverse set of industries. Many are high-technology leaders in their fields, such as Intel and Siemens. Others are relatively low-technology or financial companies, including Comdisco, Time Warner, and Visa International.

> In addition to strategic fit, market knowledge, and resources, the way a corporation approaches its venture program influences its chances of success.

The overall scope of corporate venture activity over recent years is shown in Table 2, which compiles the number and (in latter years) the size of venture investments made directly by corporations. These numbers do not include cases in which companies committed capital to independent venture groups, which then invested the funds. Nor do they reflect instances in which a financial services organization or a subsidiary of an operating corporation (for instance, Goldman Sachs or GE Capital) made an investment. The table demonstrates the tremendous growth of corporate venturing during the third wave. The number of corporate venture investments increased nearly twenty-fold over sixteen years, and the amount of corporate venture investments that could be tracked amounted to nearly $8 billion in 1999.[4]

Empirical Analysis

Data description. VentureOne, established in 1987, collects data on firms that have obtained venture capital financing. The VentureOne database used in this analysis includes firms that have received early-stage equity financing from venture capital organizations, corporate venture capital programs, and other organizations.

The companies are initially identified from a wide variety of sources, including trade publications,

company Web pages, and telephone contacts with venture investors. VentureOne then collects information about the businesses through interviews with venture capitalists and entrepreneurs. Among the data collected are the names of the investors, the amount and valuation of the venture financings, and the industry, history, and current status of the firm. Data on the firms are updated and validated through monthly contacts with investors and firms.[5] VentureOne then markets the database to venture funds and corporate business development groups (see Gompers and Lerner 2000 for a detailed discussion of the database).

For this analysis, the VentureOne data were supplemented when necessary. Some firms in the VentureOne sample were missing information, such as an assignment to one of the 103 VentureOne industry classes or information on the firm's start date. To determine this information, a variety of reference sources were consulted, including Corporate Technology Information Service's *Corporate Technology Directory* (1996), Dun's Marketing Services' *Million Dollar Directory* (1996), Gale Research's *Ward's Business Directory of U.S. Private and Public Companies* (1996), National Register Publishing Company's *Directory of Leading Private Companies* (1996), and a considerable number of state and industry business directories in the collections of Harvard Business School's Baker Library and the Boston Public Library. Several electronic databases were also employed: the Company Intelligence and Database America compilations available through LEXIS's COMPANY/USPRIV library and the American Business Disk CD-ROM directory.

The investors in the VentureOne database were diverse. They included individuals, institutional investors such as pension funds, traditional independent venture funds (such as Kleiner, Perkins, Caufield & Byers), and funds sponsored by corporations, financial institutions, and government bodies. In order to understand the impact of organizational structure, many of the analyses below concentrate on two types of funds: independent venture partnerships and corporate funds. As discussed above, other hybrid venture funds, such as those affiliated with commercial and investment banks, were eliminated because many of these closely resembled traditional venture organizations.

To identify independent and corporate venture capital organizations, the analysis used an unpublished database of venture organizations assembled by Venture Economics' Investors Services Group. Venture Economics is a unit of Securities Data Company and tracks the venture capital industry. The

TABLE 1	
Corporate Venture Capital Fund	
Corporate sponsor	Capital under management
Electronic Data Systems	1,500
General Electric	1,500
Andersen Consulting	1,000
Comdisco	500
Time Warner	500
Times Mirror	500
Visa International	500
Intel Corporation	450
AT&T	348
Hikari Tsushin	332
News Corporation	300
ValueVision International	300
Comcast	250
PECO Energy	225
Siemens	210

Note: The estimated capital under management is shown in millions of current dollars in 2000. If the corporation organizes multiple programs, these are consolidated. Some corporations do not make formal commitments in advance to their venture programs or do not disclose the size of these commitments. These firms are not included on the list. Among the largest corporate venture capital programs falling into these categories are those of Cisco, Dell, Johnson & Johnson, and Microsoft.

Source: Asset Alternatives (2000)

TABLE 2		
Number of Corporate Venture Capital Investments		
	Number of rounds	Dollar volume of rounds
1983	53	
1984	91	
1985	139	
1986	129	
1987	152	
1988	179	
1989	202	
1990	233	
1991	249	
1992	214	
1993	198	
1994	193	
1995	65	193
1996	101	369
1997	229	708
1998	391	1,449
1999	936	7,968

Note: The series reporting number of investments before 1995 and in and after 1995 may not be strictly comparable. For 1995 and after, the dollar volume of these investments (in millions of 2000 dollars) is also reported.

Source: Asset Alternatives (2000)

organization was known as Capital Publishing when it was established in 1961 to prepare a newsletter on federally chartered small business investment companies (SBICs). Since 1977 the company has maintained a database on venture partnerships, which includes over 2,000 venture capital funds, SBICs, and related organizations. The Investors Services Group database is used in preparation of directories, such as the Venture Economics annual volume *Venture Capital Performance*. The database is compiled from information provided by venture capitalists and institutional investors. This analysis excluded from either classification a variety of other organizations that make private equity investments, including individual investors, SBICs, funds sponsored by banks and other financial institutions, and funds associated with financial subsidiaries of nonfinancial corporations (such as General Electric Capital). To determine whether a

company was a nonfinancial corporation, the firm directories noted above were consulted to determine the main lines of business in the year of the investment and thus draw as sharp a contrast as possible between corporate and independent funds.

In some cases, it was difficult to ascertain if an investor was a corporate venture organization. Some U.S. and several European companies invest in companies through traditional venture capital partnerships. For example, Eastman Kodak not only makes direct equity investments but also invests through a partnership called Aperture Partners, in which it is the sole limited partner. While many of these cases were identified for this analysis, some affiliations may have been missed. In other cases, independent venture organizations also cater to corporate investors. A prominent example is Advent, a Boston-based company that organizes comingled funds for financial investors and other funds for

4. Because many corporations do not report their private investments in entrepreneurial firms, these figures should be regarded as conservative estimates of the level of corporate venture capital activity. The true level would be higher.

5. Information about the financing of private firms is typically not revealed in public documents, and investors and entrepreneurs may consider this to be sensitive information. VentureOne seeks to overcome this reluctance by emphasizing that its database also helps firms obtain financing. In particular, firms can alert investors whether they intend to seek further private financing or intend to go public in upcoming months.

TABLE 3

Distribution of the Sample

| | | Number of investments | | Number of | Dollar |
	Total	Corporate VC	Independent VC	rounds	amount
1983	1,841	53	1,013	436	2,219
1984	2,249	91	1,206	550	2,905
1985	2,593	139	1,382	625	2,910
1986	2,557	129	1,381	592	2,394
1987	2,675	152	1,397	642	3,065
1988	2,599	179	1,385	611	2,687
1989	2,866	202	1,490	720	3,069
1990	2,826	233	1,455	784	3,640
1991	2,890	249	1,472	757	3,207
1992	3,166	214	1,699	911	3,891
1993	3,118	198	1,586	931	4,532
1994	2,984	193	1,601	947	4,973
Total	32,364	2,032	17,067	8,506	39,492

Note: The table depicts the number of venture capital investments in the VentureOne sample by year between 1983 and 1994 as well as the number of financing rounds (a round may consist of several investments by different investors) and the aggregate amount of funding disbursed (in millions of 1994 dollars). Similar tabulations of the number of investments are presented for corporate and independent venture funds.

Source: VentureOne

single corporate limited partners. From the Venture-One database, it is usually difficult to determine whether the private equity group is investing from its traditional partnerships or from one of its corporate funds.

Finally, the corporate venture capital investments were characterized by the degree of fit between the corporation and the portfolio firm. From information in the corporate annual reports for the 1983, 1989, and 1994 fiscal years, investments were classified as to whether there was a direct fit between one of the corporation's lines of business during the period and the portfolio firm, whether there was an indirect relationship, or whether there was no apparent relationship. In the analyses below, investments are denoted as having a strategic fit only if there was a direct relationship between a line of business of the corporate parent and the portfolio firm. The results are robust to expanding the definition to include indirectly related transactions as well: for example, when a corporate fund invests in a firm that is a potential supplier to or customer of the corporate parent. Not all investments were classified. In some cases, the relationship could not be determined. In others, only the proximate annual reports could be obtained; in particular, it was difficult to obtain the 1983 and 1989 annual reports for many of the foreign firms.

The analysis was limited to investments in privately held firms between 1983 and 1994. While VentureOne has sought to "back-fill" its database with information on earlier venture investments, its coverage of the 1970s and early 1980s is poor. Furthermore, there was concern that VentureOne's methodology may have introduced selection biases. While the database does not include all venture investments between 1983 and 1994, it provides a reasonable view of the activity in the industry during this period.[6] Investments made after 1994 were not included because I wish to assess the outcomes of the investments: it may take several years until the fate of venture-backed firms is clear. I also eliminated a variety of investments outside the scope of this analysis, such as purchases of shares of publicly traded firms and other financings.

Summary statistics. After presenting an overview of the sample, I undertake empirical analyses of the ultimate success of corporate and other venture investments.

Table 3 provides an overview of the sample by year. After the deletions noted above, the sample consists of 32,364 investments. Investments by independent venture funds represent over one-half of the total transactions in the sample. Corporate venture investments represent a much smaller share, about 6 percent. Chart 4 presents the fraction of investments that are corporate venture capital investments by year. Because on average about four investors participate in each financing round, the number of rounds, 8,506, is significantly smaller. In

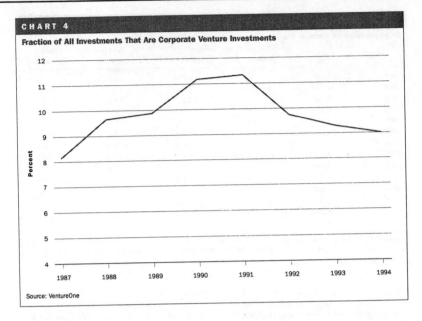

CHART 4

Fraction of All Investments That Are Corporate Venture Investments

Source: VentureOne

the analyses below, patterns are analyzed on both the investment and round level.[7]

Table 4 provides a comparison of four categories of investments: the total sample, investments by corporate and independent venture capital organizations, and corporate investments in which there was a strategic fit between the parent and the portfolio firm. In general, the corporate investments closely resemble those of the other funds:

- *Status at the time of investment.* Corporate funds tend to invest slightly less frequently in start-up and mature private firms. Instead, they are disproportionately represented among companies in the middle stages, such as "development" or "beta."[8]
- *Location of the firm.* The sample disproportionately includes investments in firms based in California. This idiosyncrasy reflects VentureOne's

greater coverage of this region, particularly in the early years (see Gompers and Lerner 2000 for a discussion). While corporate venture investments as a whole are slightly more common in California than other venture investments, corporate invest-ments with a strong strategic fit are more frequent elsewhere.

- *Industry of the firm.* Venture capital investments tend to focus on a few high-technology industries. This pattern is even stronger for corporate venture investments with a strategic focus.
- *Maturity of the firm and investment characteristics.* Corporate venture funds tend to invest in later and larger financing rounds and in slightly older firms than other venture funds do.

Trends and determinants of investment relatedness. This section explores the trends and

---

6. See Gompers and Lerner (2000) for an analysis of the comprehensiveness of the VentureOne database over time. Concerns about selection biases are addressed by repeating the analyses below using observations from only 1988 to 1994, when VentureOne's coverage of the industry was much more comprehensive. The results are little changed.

7. The reader may note that the dollar amounts reported here are greater in some years than the cumulative disbursements from venture capital funds reported elsewhere (for example, Kortum and Lerner 1998). This disparity reflects the fact that the VentureOne data represent total financings from all sources for privately held venture-backed firms rather than just funds from venture capital organizations.

8. See the appendix for definitions of stages, regions, and industries.

TABLE 4

Characteristics of Firms at the Time of Investment

	Entire sample	Corporate VC only	Corporate VC and strategic fit	Independent VC only
Status at time of investment				
Start-up	9.8	7.1	6.4	10.4
Development	30.5	33.6	35.9	31.2
Beta	4.1	5.5	6.4	4.1
Shipping	45.5	44.4	42.9	44.8
Profitable	7.6	6.9	5.6	7.3
Restart	2.4	2.5	2.8	2.3
Location of firm				
All western United States	59.7	63.7	59.6	60.8
California	51.6	53.7	51.3	52.7
All eastern United States	24.1	25.2	29.1	23.4
Massachusetts	12.8	14.0	16.5	12.6
Industry of firm				
Medical	25.5	25.9	24.2	24.2
Computer hardware	16.7	17.0	16.2	16.8
Communications	14.5	14.2	22.1	15.5
Computer software/on-line services	15.1	15.1	14.0	16.2
Other	28.1	27.9	23.5	27.3
Round of investment				
Mean	2.4	2.8	2.9	2.4
Median	2	3	3	2
Age of firm at time of investment				
Mean	3.9	4.0	4.2	3.8
Median	3.0	3.3	3.4	2.8
Amount invested in venture round				
Mean	6.1	6.2	6.0	5.7
Median	4.3	4.5	4.7	4.2

Note: The sample consists of 32,364 investments in privately held venture-backed firms between 1983 and 1994. The table presents the stage of the firm's development at the time of the investment, the geographic location of the firm, the industry of the firm, the ordinal rank of the venture round, the age of the firm at the time of the investment (in years), and the amount of the investment in the financing round (in millions of 1994 dollars). Separate tabulations are presented for investments by corporate venture firms, corporate funds where there was a strategic fit between the parent and portfolio firms, and independent venture funds.

Source: VentureOne

determinants of whether corporate venture capital investments are made in related industries or not. As the previous discussion made clear, many corporate venture capital efforts have failed when they made investments in companies in totally unrelated markets. It is often believed that large existing players in an existing market can add value to new entrants. Understanding when and how corporate venture groups choose to invest in related compa-

nies is critical to determining whether corporate investments can add value.

Chart 5 shows the fraction of the corporate venture capital investments that are made in related industries. One surprising observation is that a large fraction of investment is in related industries. In each year of investment, at least 68 percent of investments made by corporate venture capital groups are in companies in a related industry. It also

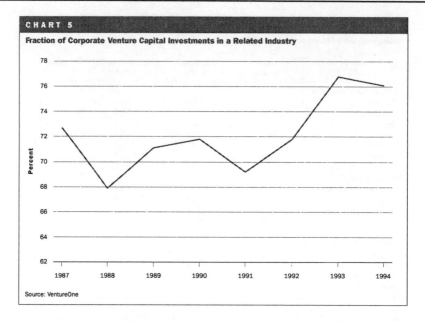

CHART 5

Fraction of Corporate Venture Capital Investments in a Related Industry

Source: VentureOne

appears that the fraction of the investments made in related industries has increased over the sample period. By the end of the sample, between 76 percent and 77 percent of the investments were being made in related industries.

Table 5 undertakes a regression analysis to understand the determinants of investment relatedness. The dependent variable is a dummy that equals one if the corporate investment is in a related industry. The independent variables include the age of the firm, a time trend to understand whether the rate of related investments have increased over time, the stage of development of the company, and a dummy variable that equals one if the company is headquartered in Massachusetts or California.

Not surprisingly, the probability of a corporate investment being made in a related industry increases over time. In fact, each year the probability of a related investment increases by 3.5 percent. It therefore appears that corporations were learning about the value of related investments during the decade.

It also appears that investments in early-stage companies are more likely to be in a related industry than investments in later-stage companies. Firms

in the development stage or the beta stage are significantly more likely to be in related industries. This tendency is also encouraging. Existing players in an industry can provide significant value to young, entrepreneurial firms. Large corporations are also likely to get the most value from investing in the younger start-ups.

Finally, there are interesting geographical differences in the rate of related investments. Corporate venture investments in Massachusetts are far more likely to be in related industries than are investments in California or in the rest of the country. The rate of related investments in California is no different than in the rest of the country. Perhaps the types of venture capital firms in Massachusetts create an environment that is more accepting of corporate investments by industry leaders.

Success of venture investments. Even though these complex motives—and benefits—make it hard to compare the success of corporate versus independent venturing, a pattern does emerge if one examines the data. In fact, in making a comparison, let's look only at corporate venture investments made between 1983 and 1994 to ensure that those efforts had time to ripen.[9]

---

9. For a discussion of return in the venture capital industry, see Venture Economics (1988, 1997).

TABLE 5				
Logit Regression Analyses of Strategic Fit of Corporate Investments				
	Was the corporate investment in a related industry?			
Age of firm at time of financing	0.0105	[1.16]	0.0116	[1.28]
Time trend	0.0351	[2.38]	0.0358	[2.42]
Firm is in development stage?	0.524	[2.96]	0.506	[2.86]
Firm is in beta stage?	0.697	[3.02]	0.6860	[2.97]
Firm is in shipping stage?	0.184	[1.02]	0.179	[0.99]
Firm is in profitable stage?	−0.180	[−0.72]	−0.176	[−0.70]
Firm is in restart stage?	0.456	[1.54]	0.463	[1.56]
Firm based in California?			0.098	[1.05]
Firm based in Massachusetts?			0.362	[2.92]
Log likelihood		−2,878.1		−2,880.8
χ²-statistic		67.71		70.01
p-value		0.000		0.000
Number of observations		2,032		2,032

Note: The sample in the regressions consists of 2,032 corporate investments in privately held, venture-backed firms between 1983 and 1994. The dependent variable is a dummy that takes the value of one if the firm is in an industry that is related to the parent of the corporation sponsoring the venture investment. Independent variables include the age of the firm at the time of the investment, a time trend, firms based in California and Massachusetts, the status of the firm at the time of the investment, the industry of firm (not reported), and a constant (not reported). All dummy variables take on the value of one if the answer to the posed question is in the affirmative. Absolute *t*-statistics are reported in brackets.

Source: VentureOne

The status of the firms in the spring of 1998 is determined from the VentureOne database. Table 6 presents the outcomes for four classes of investors as well as tests of the statistical significance of the differences between them. Firms backed by corporate venture groups are significantly more likely to have gone public than those financed by other organizations and are less likely to have been liquidated. These differences are particularly strong for those investments in which there was a strategic tie between the corporate parent and the portfolio firm. These comparisons may be influenced, however, by differences between the firms backed by corporate and other venture investors.

The evidence is striking: In more than 30,000 investments into entrepreneurial firms by venture capital organizations of all types, corporate efforts appear to be at least as successful as those backed by independent venture organizations (using such criteria as the probability of a portfolio firm's going public). As Table 6 shows, 35 percent of the investments by corporate funds went to companies that had gone public by the end of the sample period as opposed to 31 percent for independent funds. The differences persist even when different criteria for success are used: for instance, firms that went public or were acquired at a valuation that was at least three times that of the original investment.

It might be thought that these results are just consequences of the fact that corporate groups often invest in later financing rounds. By this point in many investee firms' development, uncertainties have cleared up and prospects have brightened. As it turns out, the same results ensued even when controls for a portfolio firm's age and profitability at the time of the original investment are added.

The success is not uniform, as the final column of the table reveals. The success of a venturing effort varies with the "tightness" of fit between the corporation and the portfolio firm—that is, whether the corporate parent and the investee are in the same line of business. To assess this fit, one can examine corporate annual reports and classified investments. The success of a corporate program depends on the presence of a direct, strategic overlap between corporate parent and investee. As just one illustration, the probability of going public by the end of the sample period is 39 percent for companies that had this kind of alignment compared with much lower percentages for nonaligned firms.

To address this concern, I examine these patterns in a regression framework in Table 7. I estimate logit regressions, alternatively using each investment and each financing round as observations. I seek to explain the probability that the investment had gone public by the spring of 1998 or the probability that the

TABLE 6

Status of Corporate and Independent Venture Investments

Status at end of analysis	Entire sample	Corporate VC only	Independent VC only	Corporate VC and strategic fit
Initial public offering completed	31.1	35.1	30.6	39.3
Registration statement filed	0.7	0.2	0.7	0.3
Acquired	29.0	29.0	30.3	27.5
Still privately held	20.6	21.1	19.7	18.3
Liquidated	18.7	14.6	18.7	14.7

Note: The sample consists of 32,364 investments in privately held venture-backed firms between 1983 and 1994. The table presents the eventual outcome of the firms as a percentage of the sample. Separate tabulations are presented for investments by corporate venture firms, corporate funds where there was a strategic fit between the parent and portfolio firms, and independent venture funds.

Source: VentureOne

TABLE 7

Logit Regression Analyses of Firms in Spring 1998

	Observations are investments			
	Did firm go public?		Did firm go public, register, or have favorable acquisition?	
Age of firm at time of financing	-0.02 [5.52]	-0.02 [0.50]	-0.02 [6.17]	-0.02 [6.13]
Round number	0.13 [11.39]	0.13 [11.18]	0.13 [11.48]	0.13 [11.29]
Corporate venture investment?	0.15 [2.54]	-0.19 [1.31]	0.12 [2.15]	-0.23 [1.64]
Independent venture investment?	-0.003 [0.09]	-0.002 [0.07]	0.07 [2.54]	0.07 [2.56]
Corporate investment and strategic fit?		0.52 [3.15]		0.57 [3.55]
Firm based in California?	0.30 [9.29]	0.29 [8.96]	0.23 [7.44]	0.22 [6.98]
Firm based in Massachusetts?	0.36 [7.83]	0.36 [7.75]	0.24 [5.26]	0.23 [5.04]
Firm is in development stage?	0.44 [7.73]	0.42 [7.27]	0.38 [6.99]	0.35 [6.41]
Firm is in beta stage?	0.25 [2.83]	0.22 [2.50]	0.14 [1.60]	0.11 [1.24]
Firm is in shipping stage?	0.38 [6.28]	0.36 [5.95]	0.30 [5.20]	0.28 [4.82]
Firm is in profitable stage?	1.32 [17.08]	1.30 [16.61]	1.10 [14.77]	1.08 [14.27]
Firm is in restart stage?	-0.56 [4.20]	-0.56 [4.19]	-0.43 [3.64]	-0.45 [3.71]
Log likelihood	-14,743.6	-14,252.0	-15,477.4	-14,973.7
χ^2-statistic	2,409.9	2,362.4	2,065.5	2,025.7
p-value	0.000	0.000	0.000	0.000
Number of observations	24,515	23,740	24,515	23,740

Note: The sample in the first four regressions consists of 32,364 investments in privately held, venture-backed firms between 1983 and 1994; in the fifth and sixth regressions, the sample consists of 8,506 financing rounds of privately held, venture-backed firms between 1983 and 1994. The dependent variable in the first, second, fifth, and sixth regressions is a dummy variable that takes on the value of one if the firm had gone public by the spring of 1998. In the third and fourth regressions, the dummy takes the value of one if the firm had gone public, filed a registration statement, or been acquired at twice the postmoney valuation (in inflation-adjusted dollars) at the time of the investment by the spring of 1998. Independent variables include the age of the firm at the time of the investment, the ordinal rank of the investment round, and dummy variables denoting investments by corporate and independent venture capital funds, corporate venture investments where there was a strategic fit with the portfolio firm, firms based in California and Massachusetts, the status of the firm at the time of the investment, the year of the investment (not reported), the industry of firm (not reported), and a constant (not reported). All dummy variables take on the value of one if the answer to the posed question is in the affirmative. Absolute t-statistics are reported in brackets.

Source: VentureOne

firm had gone public, filed a registration with the U.S. Securities and Exchange Commission (a preliminary step before going public), or been acquired for a valuation of at least twice the postmoney valuation of the financing.[10] As independent variables, I use the age of the firm at the time of the investment and the ordinal rank of the investment round. I also employ dummy variables denoting investments by corporate and independent venture capital funds, corporate venture investments in which there was a strategic fit with the portfolio firm, firms based in California and Massachusetts, the status of the firm at the time of the investment, the year of the investment, the industry of the firm, and a constant.

> While corporate venture investing suffers from many of the same problems that have affected fads in venture capital investing as a whole, corporate venture investments have a successful track record.

The results are consistent with the univariate comparisons above. Corporate venture investments are significantly more successful than other investments. (In most of the regressions, independent venture investments are also more successful though the effect is smaller in magnitude and statistical significance.) When the dummy variable denoting corporate venture investments with a strategic fit is added to the regressions, the corporate venture dummy variable becomes insignificant (and frequently negative). Corporate venture investments in general do not perform better—only those with a strategic fit. These results seem consistent with the complementarities hypothesis above.

A Clinical Look at the Corporate Venture Evidence

In addition to strategic fit, market knowledge, and resources, the way a corporation approaches its venture program influences its chances of success (Siegel, Siegel, and MacMillan 1988; Sykes 1990). In companies whose venture programs do not succeed, managers have made two fatal mistakes:

- They never created consensus inside the organization about the program's objectives and its potential benefits to the company.

- They failed to build relationships and establish credibility outside the corporation. (In many instances, they assumed that the corporation's name alone would ensure success.)

Solidifying internal cohesion. Many corporations plunge into corporate venturing without realizing that how they design the program matters. As a result, conflict can arise over the program's objectives—and can even force the dissolution of the effort. For instance, as discussed earlier, departments that feel threatened by or otherwise uncomfortable with the program might push to have it terminated. Or the venture unit's interests and the corporation's goals may be unaligned—for example, venture personnel are rewarded solely on financial return whereas the corporation makes strategic goals a priority.

Exxon Enterprises, whose venture capital effort ranks among the most spectacular failures in the field, suffered the consequences of internal dissension.[11] The oil giant (called Esso at the time), seeking to diversify its product line, launched its venture program in 1964. The program began with a mandate to exploit technology in Exxon's corporate laboratories: for example, making building materials out of petroleum derivatives.

In the late 1960s, however, the fund managers decided to make minority investments in a wide variety of industries, from advanced materials to air-pollution-control equipment to medical devices. In the late 1970s, the strategy changed yet again—the program now focused solely on systems for office use. Finally, in 1985, Exxon abandoned the venture effort entirely. Each shift in corporate strategy had brought on waves of costly write-downs. The information-systems effort alone generated an estimated $2 billion in losses for the corporation.

What explains this disaster? In part, the corporate venture team came to the project with scant investment experience and made numerous poor decisions. But equally important, senior managers at Exxon could not agree on the program's overarching purpose. Moreover, various divisions at Exxon insisted on detailed reviews of the program. These reviews consumed so much time that they distracted the fund managers' attention away from the selection and oversight of investments. Meanwhile, various organizations within the corporation had a hand in structuring the program. For instance, Exxon's human resources staff complained that the venture firms' compensation schemes did not mirror those of the overall corporation. In the late 1970s, human resources succeeded in replacing the venture staff's separate stock-option schemes with a standard salary-plus-bonus plan. An exodus of fund managers soon followed.

Internal consensus is particularly important in venture programs with strong strategic objectives. The $100 million Java Fund, launched in 1996 by Kleiner, Perkins, Caufield & Byers, is one example of a fund that gave a number of corporations a chance to invest primarily for strategic reasons.[12] The fund specifically invested in companies that used Java, a programming language developed by Sun Microsystems that runs on a wide variety of operating systems and challenged Microsoft Windows. In addition to raising capital from traditional limited partners (such as the Harvard, Stanford, and Yale University endowments), the fund also tapped firms such as Cisco, IBM, Netscape, Oracle, and, of course, Sun. Even though these firms competed intensely with each other, they all wanted to see this programming language take root because it would level the playing field with their formidable competitor Microsoft.

Cultivating external relationships. Good relationships with independent venture firms are also essential to the success of corporate programs. Why? Particularly today, the venture capital business is highly competitive. Identifying and gaining access to attractive opportunities can be difficult for new players. Meanwhile, investors have to make decisions quickly, often with scant information about an opportunity. Close ties between corporate venture efforts and traditional venture firms can

- bring promising opportunities to the corporate fund's attention,
- bring early-stage transactions—which often have lower valuations and more strategic potential— to the corporate fund's attention,
- ensure that venture capitalists deal with corporate capitalists professionally and respectfully, and
- let corporate groups tap into independent groups' knowledge.

Despite all these potential benefits, relations between corporate and independent venture groups continue to be somewhat strained. The venture capital community is close-knit; many leading firms have syndicated transactions with each other for decades. Though these firms' skepticism about corporate venture funds has abated somewhat, a residual amount remains. Furthermore, unscrupulous venture groups have been known to exploit naive corporate investors, offering them overpriced investments or withholding bad news about potential investees.

To make relationship building even more difficult, it takes time for corporations to build credibility in the eyes of independent venture capitalists. Many corporations launch venture programs assuming that their names alone will earn them instant respect. They then discover that their venture program is not going anywhere without "road shows" with venture groups, conference presentations, and press releases to publicize the company's activities.

There are several important lessons to be learned from these accounts:

- Form an appropriately sized fund. Too small a fund suggests a limited commitment by the corporation to the program; too substantial an effort leads to speculation that the corporation does not understand the dangers associated with growing too quickly.
- Recruit one or more of the fund's investment professionals from the venture capital community.
- Articulate a clear investment strategy.
- Simultaneously invest in venture capital partnerships specializing in similar technologies.
- Consider joint ventures (1) with a specific venture capitalist firm (for instance, Softbank and K-Mart formed a collaboration called BlueLight[13]), (2) with several other corporations and a venture capitalist firm (such as Kleiner Perkins' Java Fund), and (3) with a number of venture capitalist firms. (For instance, Sutter Hill Ventures, Technology Crossover Ventures, and buyout fund Bain Capital joined in mid-2000 with the consulting firm eLoyalty to establish the eLoyalty Ventures Fund.[14])

10. The postmoney valuation is defined as the product of the price paid per share in the financing round and the shares outstanding after the financing round. In calculating the valuations, VentureOne converts all preferred shares into common stock at the conversion ratios specified in the agreements. Warrants and options outstanding are included in the total as long as their exercise price is below the price per share being paid in the financing round.
    The results are also robust to the use of a third dependent variable, the probability that the firm has not been liquidated by the spring of 1998.
11. The discussion of Exxon Enterprises is based on the Venture Economics study cited above.
12. The account of the Java Fund relies on Fisher (1996) and on <www.kpcb.com/keiretsu/initiative_old_list.php?initiative=10>.
13. The BlueLight Fund is discussed in Chesbrough and Rotelli (2000).
14. The eLoyalty Fund is documented in Leibowitz (2000).

Conclusions

This paper has explored the experience of corporations' investments in young, entrepreneurial firms. Historically, the media and academics have maligned corporate investments in venture capital and highlighted visible failures. This study, however, finds quite a different result. Corporate venture investments have waxed and waned in tandem with the independent venture capital industry. Many of today's leading technology corporations are extremely active in the sector. In addition, corporate venture capital groups have been increasingly willing to invest in start-ups in related industries. The probability of making investments in related companies increases with early-stage companies. Finally, the paper shows that corporate investments are at least as successful as independent venture capital investments. In addition, the probability of success is substantially higher for corporate venture investments in related industries.

While corporate venture investing suffers from many of the same problems that have affected fads in venture capital investing as a whole, corporate venture investments have a successful track record. The experience of recent corporate programs, many of which have been initiated by companies that can trace their own history to venture capital investments, bodes well for the future of corporate venturing.

APPENDIX

Definitions of Firm Categorizations

Investment Stages

Start-up: Company with a skeletal business plan, product, or service development in preliminary stages.

Development: Stage at which product or service development is under way but the company is not generating revenues from sales.

Beta: For companies specializing in information technology, the phase at which the product is being tested by a limited number of customers but not available for broad sale. For life sciences companies, beta is synonymous with a drug in human clinical trials or a device being tested.

Shipping: The stage at which the product or service is being sold to customers and the company is deriving revenues from those sales but expenses still exceed revenues.

Profitable: The stage at which the company is selling products or services and the sales revenue yields a positive net income.

Restart: The stage at which the firm is recapitalized at a reduced valuation, accompanied by a substantial shift in the product or marketing focus.

Industry Groups

Computer hardware: Firms whose primary lines of business are personal computing, minicomputers or workstations, mainframe computers, CAD/CAM/CAE systems, data storage, computer peripherals, memory systems, office automation, source data collection, multimedia devices, and computer networking devices.

Computer software: Firms whose primary lines of business are compilers, assemblers, and systems, applications, CAD/CAM/CAE/CASE systems, recreational and home, artificial intelligence, educational, multimedia software, and on-line services.

Communications: Firms whose primary lines of business include modems, computer networking, fiber optics, microwave and satellite communications, telephone equipment, pocket paging, cellular phones, radar and defense systems, television equipment, teleconferencing, and television and radio broadcasting.

Medical: Firms whose primary lines of business include biotechnology, pharmaceuticals, diagnostic imaging, patient monitoring, medical devices, medical lab instruments, hospital equipment, medical supplies, retail medicine, hospital management, medical data processing, and medical lab services.

Regions

Eastern United States: Firms whose headquarters are located in Connecticut, Delaware, the District of Columbia, Maine, Maryland, Massachusetts, New Hampshire, New Jersey, New York, Pennsylvania, Rhode Island, Vermont, and West Virginia.

Western United States: Firms whose headquarters are located in Alaska, Arizona, California, Colorado, Hawaii, Idaho, Montana, Nevada, New Mexico, Oregon, Utah, Washington, and Wyoming.

Source: Adapted from VentureOne (1998)

REFERENCES

Asset Alternatives. 2000. *The corporate venturing direc-tory and yearbook*. Wellesley, Mass.: Asset Alternatives.

Block, Zenas, and Oscar A. Ornati. 1987. Compensating corporate venture managers. *Journal of Business Venturing* 2 (1987): 41–52.

Chesbrough, Henry W., and Mary Teichert Rotelli. 2000. Hotbank: Softbank's new business model for early stage venture incubation. Harvard Business School Case No. 9-600-100.

Corporate Technology Information Services. 1996 (and earlier years). *Corporate technology directory*. Woburn, Mass.: Corporate Technology Information Services.

Dun's Marketing Services. 1996 (and earlier years). *Million dollar directory*. Parsippany, N.J.: Dun's Marketing Services.

Fast, Norman D. 1978. *The rise and fall of corporate new venture divisions*. Ann Arbor, Mich.: UMI Research Press.

Fisher, Lawrence M. 1996. $100 million fund will finance Java-based ventures. *New York Times*, August 22, D4.

Gale Research. 1996 (and earlier years). *Ward's busi-ness directory of U.S. private and public companies*. Detroit: Gale Research.

Gee, Robert E. 1994. Finding and commercializing new businesses. *Research/Technology Management* 37 (January/February): 49–56.

Gompers, Paul A. 1995. Optimal investment, monitoring, and the staging of venture capital. *Journal of Finance* 50:1461–89.

Gompers, Paul A., and Josh Lerner. 1996. The use of covenants: An analysis of venture partnership agreements. *Journal of Law and Economics* 39:463–98.

———. 1998a. Venture capital distributions: Short- and long-run reactions. *Journal of Finance* 53:2161–184.

———. 1998b. The determinants of corporate venture capital success: Organizational structure, incentives, and complementarities. In National Bureau of Economic Research Conference Volume on Concentrated Owner-ship. Cambridge, Mass.: NBER.

———. 1998c. What drives venture capital fundraising? *Brookings papers on economic activity: Microeco-nomics 1998*: 149–92.

———. 1999. An analysis of compensation in the U.S. venture capital partnership. *Journal of Financial Economics* 51:3–44.

———. 2000. Money chasing deals? The impact of fund inflows on private equity valuations. *Journal of Financial Economics* 55:281–325.

Hardymon, G. Felda, Mark J. DeNino, and Malcolm S. Salter. 1983 When corporate venture capital doesn't work. *Harvard Business Review* 61 (May/June): 114–20.

Henderson, Rebecca 1993. Underinvestment and incom-petence as responses to radical innovation: Evidence from the photolithographic alignment equipment indus-try. *Rand Journal of Economics* 24:248–70.

Henderson, Rebecca, and Iain Cockburn. 1996. Scale, scope, and spillovers: The determinants of research pro-ductivity in drug discovery. *Rand Journal of Eco-nomics* 27:32–59.

Jensen, Michael C. 1993. Presidential address: The mod-ern Industrial Revolution, exit, and the failure of internal control systems. *Journal of Finance* 48 (July): 831–80.

Kortum, Samuel, and Josh Lerner. 1998. Does venture capital spur innovation? Boston University and Harvard University. Unpublished working paper.

Leibowitz, Alissa. 2000. Bain, Sutter, and TCV to invest in eLoyalty Fund. *Venture Capital Journal* 40 (September): 16–18.

Lerner, Josh. 1997. An empirical examination of a tech-nology race. *Rand Journal of Economics* 28:228–47.

National Register Publishing Company. 1996 (and earlier years). *Directory of leading private companies, including corporate affiliations*. New Providence, Wilmette, N.J.: National Register Publishing Company.

Reinganum, Jennifer R. 1989. The timing of innovation: Research, development, and diffusion. In *The Handbook of Industrial Organization*, edited by R. Schmalensee and R.D. Willig. New York: North-Holland.

Rind, Kenneth W. 1981. The role of venture capital in corporate development. *Strategic Management Jour-nal* 2:169–80.

Siegel, Robin, Eric Siegel, and Ian C. MacMillan. 1988. Corporate venture capitalists: Autonomy, obstacles, and performance. *Journal of Business Venturing* 3:233–47.

Sykes, Hollister B. 1990. Corporate venture capital: Strategies for success. *Journal of Business Venturing* 5:37–47.

Venture Economics. 1986. Corporate venture capital study. Unpublished manuscript.

———. 1988. *Exiting venture capital investments*. Needham, Mass.: Venture Economics.

———. 1997. *Investment benchmark reports—venture capital*. New York: Venture Economics.

VentureOne. 1998. *VentureOne 1997 Annual Report*. San Francisco: VentureOne.

[14]

CORPORATE VENTURE
CAPITALISTS: AUTONOMY,
OBSTACLES, AND
PERFORMANCE

ROBIN SIEGEL, ERIC SIEGEL,
and IAN C. MACMILLAN
The Wharton School

EXECUTIVE SUMMARY

This report presents the results of a formal study of the corporate venture capital community in the United States, and is based upon responses to a questionnaire completed by 52 corporate venture capitalists (CVCs).

The central question addressed in this study involves which approach to corporate venture capital is most likely to produce successful results.

This question was addressed via cluster analysis which segregated the CVC community into two broad classes—"pilots," which are marked by substantial organizational independence and "copilots," which are highly dependent on corporate management with respect to venture funding and decision authority.

Pilots achieve equal or higher levels of performance, and are plagued by far fewer obstacles, than their highly dependent counterparts. The results suggest the following:

1. The corporate venture fund should be established as an independent entity and should have access to a committed, separate pool of funds. This will enable CVCs to respond aggressively to, and manage, investment opportunities with minimal corporate interference. Such an independent entity will defuse justifiable concerns on the part of entrepreneurs related to such interference.

2. The fund should be managed by skilled venture professionals who may be drawn from the independent venture community or the small but growing pool of experienced CVCs. Corporate executives may comprise a part of the management team.

3. If the corporate venture fund hopes to attract top quality managers, it must be prepared to offer compensation and authority commensurate with their skill level. In short, corporate venture capitalists should be treated like independent venture capitalists. By organizing the

Address correspondence to: Eric Siegel, Snider Entrepreneurial Center, 3200 Steinberg-Dietrich Hall, The Wharton School, University of Pennsylvania, Philadelphia, PA 19104.

The authors are indebted to the Snider Entrepreneurial Center at the Wharton School and Coopers & Lybrand. Joel Gazes and Cheryl Suchors of Coopers & Lybrand shared their considerable expertise through each stage of the study. Jennifer Starr at Wharton was invaluable in assisting us with data analysis.

Journal of Business Venturing 3, 233–247

0883–9026/88/$3.50

© 1988 Elsevier Science Publishing Co., Inc., 52 Vanderbilt Ave., New York, NY 10017

      fund as an independent entity, the political problem associated with establishing compen-
      sation levels above those of the corporation can be minimized.

    4. *All CVCs should establish a primary focus on the realization of financial objectives (i.e.,*
      return on investment). Strategic benefit objectives are not necessarily ill advised so long as
      they do not interfere with sound financial decision making. When they do, the corporate
      venture capital process is likely to become less effective. For instance, a corporate venture
      fund should only confine itself to investing in a few industries if there are sufficient high-
      grade investment opportunities within those industries to ensure adequate deal flow. The
      venture fund should not be pressured. Investments that appear exciting from a corporate
      perspective, for technological or marketing reasons, but are not financially attractive may
      well drain resources rather than produce opportunities.

    5. *Venture proposals failing on financial criteria might be referred to other parts of the cor-*
      poration with the purpose of exploring an alternate relationship (e.g., a development contract
      or joint venture). If this is appealing to the corporation, a mechanism such as a corporate
      liaison or reporting system might be established to facilitate the flow of information.

    6. *A corporation should be willing to make a complete commitment of talent and capital if it*
      establishes its own corporate venture fund. The corporation should then be willing to accept
      a limited role. If the corporation is unable to accept a limited role with respect to its own
      fund, it may be best for it to participate as an investor in a traditional fund, where such
      limitations will be enforced. However, this latter approach may significantly dilute or elim-
      inate potential for strategic benefits.

INTRODUCTION

This report presents the results of a formal study of the corporate venture capital community
in the United States. We were drawn to this area of study for three primary reasons.

    First, an activity that combines the enormous resources of corporate America with the
volatile nature of new ventures holds the promise of dramatic gain or loss. Some corporate
venture funds have started and thrived while others have started, sputtered, and finally
discontinued operations.

    Secondly, the very term "corporate venture capital" implies a contradiction. Large
corporations are generally considered to be nonentrepreneurial relative to the way they make
decisions and operate. Yet venture capitalists necessarily must function in an entrepreneurial
environment. This raises questions as to how the two cultures may be reconciled.

    Finally, there has been little study of this activity to date. What has been done is more
case oriented rather than focusing broadly on the corporate venture capital community. For
instance, Hardymon, DeNino, and Salter (1983) studied the effectiveness of corporate venture
capital in three major corporations. More recently, Sykes (1986) presented a detailed examination of Exxon's corporate venture capital activity.

    It was hoped that as a result of this study we would better understand:

- The objectives of corporate venture capitalists (CVCs);
- The manner in which CVCs pursue these objectives including their decision-making
  process and how they organize their efforts;
- The results of corporate venture capital activity as reflected in obstacles that they encounter
  and their performance; and
- Perhaps most important, what approach to corporate venture capital is most likely to
  produce successful results.

    The application of the above understanding should have the following practical benefits:

1. Existing CVCs will become more familiar with the activity of their peers and this knowledge should help them to fine-tune their efforts.
2. Corporations contemplating entering the field will be better able to formulate expectations and ultimately achieve their goals.
3. Entrepreneurs seeking corporate venture capital will better understand this important financial resource, hereby improving the efficiency of the venture capital market.

METHODOLOGY

The first stage of the study involved interviews with seven prominent CVCs. The purpose was to determine which questions they would most like to see answered. The interviews also gave us a better feel for the diversity of interests, organizations and modes of operation which characterize the corporate venture capital community.

Next, a questionnaire was designed which focused on:

The objectives of the CVC,

Decision-making criteria used to select ventures,

Obstacles encountered in the corporate venture capital process,

Assessments of CVC performance,

The approval process,

Compensation arrangements,

Investment funding arrangements,

Sources of investment opportunities, and

The favored form of structuring deals.

All responses, with the exception of those related to organization, were scaled on a four-point scale.

The questionnaire was mailed to a list of 142 corporate venture capitalists. We received 52 responses giving us a response rate of over 35%, thus indicating a high level of interest in the study. Twenty-nine of these respondents were Fortune 100 companies.

In interpreting the results, the usual selection and social acceptance biases associated with self-report questionnaire responses need to be taken into account.

RESULTS

Objectives

As shown in Table 1, the objective considered most important by CVCs is return on investment. However, the high standard deviation for this objective indicates that there is not high consensus as to the importance of this objective. In fact, nearly 42% of the respondents listed return on investment as less than essential.

Of the objectives related to strategic benefits, the most important was exposure to new technologies and markets.

Investment Criteria

Means and standard deviation for the responses related to investment criteria appear in Table 2. In general, CVCs appear to screen ventures in a manner similar to that of the independent

TABLE 1   Objectives of Corporate Venture Capital Firms

Objective	Mean	SD
Exposure to new technologies and markets	3.12	1.01
Potential to manufacture or market new products	2.39	1.15
Potential to improve manufacturing processes	1.88	0.92
Potential to acquire companies	2.13	0.14
Return on investment	3.38	0.80

Scale: 1, irrelevant; 2, desirable; 3, important; 4, major objective.

venture capitalists. Criteria related to the entrepreneur appears to take priority over product, market, or financial considerations. This is consistent with past studies examining the investment criteria of independent venture capitalists, such as the study conducted by MacMillan, Siegel, and SubbaNarasimha (1985).

However, our findings show that CVCs do deviate in some respects from the independent venture capitalists in the study by MacMillan et al. (1985). Some CVCs heavily weigh corporate strategic considerations whereas others appear to focus less intently on some of the qualities of the entrepreneur. These departures are most evident when examining the 10 criteria most frequently rated as essential by CVCs, reported in Table 3, and comparing these results with those found in the study by MacMillan et al. (1985).

Three new evaluation criteria are included among those most frequently rated as essential. These include the entrepreneur's familiarity with the product, the attractiveness of the venture's market or industry to the corporation, and whether the products fit with the corporation's long-term strategy. The first of these criteria was not included in the earlier study, but it seems likely that independent venture capitalists would also deem it to be important. The latter two criteria relate to strategic benefits to the corporation, and clearly would be irrelevant to independent venture capitalists. Significantly, both of these strategic benefit criteria correlate negatively with the criterion that the entrepreneur have demonstrated leadership ability in the past. In other words, those CVCs that focus on strategic benefit appear to be more willing to tolerate the absence of an entrepreneur with demonstrated leadership ability to head up a new venture.

Generally, CVCs also consider financial return and liquidity to be less important than do independent venture capitalists. This is not surprising given that CVCs are more concerned with strategic benefit than with financial return.

Three evaluation criteria that are considered to be much less important by CVCs than independent venture capitalists are indicated in Table 4. All three of these criteria relate to the entrepreneur.

In summary, the fundamental differences between CVC criteria and those of independent venture capitalists is that CVCs will sacrifice financial and entrepreneur quality criteria to achieve strategic fit for the corporation. As we shall see below, this is a sacrifice of dubious value.

Obstacles Confronting CVCs

In order to understand the challenges that CVCs face, we asked them to rate the effect of two sets of obstacles: those which relate to dealings with corporate management (i.e., those

TABLE 2 Investment Criteria

Criterion	Mean	SD
1. *The Entrepreneur's Personality*		
Capable of sustained effort	3.65	0.52
Able to evaluate and react well to risk	3.47	0.58
Articulate in discussing venture	2.96	0.63
Attends to detail	2.80	0.76
Able to accept criticism	2.58	0.86
Has personality compatible with mine	2.10	0.74
2. *The Entrepreneur's Experience*		
Thoroughly familiar with product	3.42	0.61
Thoroughly familiar with market	3.60	0.63
Demonstrated leadership ability in past	3.12	0.70
Has a track record relevant to venture	2.85	0.67
Has assembled a functionally balanced management team	2.77	0.83
3. *Characteristics of the Product*		
Product is proprietory or can otherwise be protected	3.10	0.73
Product has been developed to point of a functioning prototype	2.67	0.79
Product enjoys demonstrated market acceptance	2.29	0.72
Products fits with the corporation's long-term strategy	2.77	1.20
4. *Characteristics of the Market*		
The target market enjoys a significant growth rate	3.19	0.72
The venture will stimulate an existing market	2.50	0.70
The venture will create a new market	2.44	0.67
Competition in the market will be minimal during the first three years	2.37	0.77
The venture is in a market or industry which is attractive to my company	2.81	1.19
5. *Financial Considerations*		
The venture generates a return equal to at least 10 times the investment within 5–10 years	2.94	0.79
The investment can easily be made liquid	2.15	0.92
My company will be the controlling investor in the venture	2.12	1.13
My company will have a minority position in the venture	1.88	1.03
Venture's long-term sales potential will have a material impact on corporate performance	1.96	0.97
Size of specific investment should be no greater than 10%–20% of total funds available to venture activity	2.12	1.00

Scale: 1, irrelevant; 2, desirable; 3, important; 4, essential.

238   R. SIEGEL ET AL.

TABLE 3   The Criteria Most Frequently Rated as Essential by Corporate Venture Capitalists vs. Independent Venture Capitalists

	Venture capitalist (%)	
Criterion	Corporate	Independent
Capable of sustained effort	67	64
Familiar with market	67	62
Able to evaluate and react well to risk	48	NA
Market/industry attractive to corporation	39	NA
Product fits with corporation's long-term strategy	˙37	NA
Target market enjoys significant growth rate	35	43
Product can be protected	31	29
Entrepreneur has demonstrated leadership ability	31	50
Return 10 time investment in 5–10 years	28	50

to whom the CVCs must report), and those which relate to the corporate venture capital activities per se. Means and standard deviations for these obstacles appear in Table 5, while obstacles rated by more than 25% of the respondents as either having a significant or destructive impact appear in Table 6.

Obstacles Related to Corporate Management

The most damaging obstacle CVCs report in their dealings with corporate management is the lack of a clear mission regarding venture activity. Other obstacles receiving high ratings relative to corporate management include inadequate financial commitment, underestimation of the risk involved in venture investing, and lack of patience related to the time required for new ventures to achieve success. It is clear that lack of understanding and plain interference on the part of the parent corporation are major sources of frustration in the eyes of CVCs.

Obstacles Related to Executing the Venture Activity Itself

The most important obstacle related to the venture activity itself is an incompatibility between corporate and entrepreneurial cultures. This is closely followed by the lack of authority to make independent decision, the inability of corporations to attract qualified venture managers, and a pervasive concern by entrepreneurs that their ventures will be subverted to satisfy the

TABLE 4   Criteria Included in Top Ten for Independent but not for Corporate Venture Capitalists

Criterion	CVC (%)	IVC (%)
Articulate in discussing venture	18	31
Track record relevant to venture	15	37
Investment can easily be made liquid	10	44

TABLE 5 Obstacles

	Means	SD
1. *Obstacles Related to Corporate Management*		
Lacks clear mission regarding venture activity	2.25	0.97
Lacks patience related to time required for new venture to achieve success	2.06	1.04
Has made inadequate financial commitment	2.08	1.02
Underestimates the riskiness of venture investing	2.06	0.95
Is inflexible in dealing with venture activity	1.77	0.90
Does not encourage support from other areas within the corporation	1.75	0.90
2. *Obstacles Related to Venture Activity Itself*		
Lack of authority to make independent decisions	2.14	0.87
Inability to attract qualified venture managers	2.10	0.90
High turnover rate for venture managers	1.69	0.86
Inadequate deal flow	1.71	0.76
Difficulty liquidating an investment	1.64	0.75
Lack of opportunity to participate in syndications	1.51	0.62
Entrepreneurs fear that their ideas will be stolen	1.51	0.70
Entrepreneurs fear that venture will be controlled to satisfy corporate objectives rather than those of the venture	1.94	0.86
Incompatibility between corporate and entrepreneurial cultures	2.19	0.95

Scale: 1, no impact; 2, minimal impact; 3, significant impact; 4, destructive impact.

corporation's objectives. Once again, the responses reflect frustration with the inability to make decisions without corporate interference, and an inability for the corporation to understand even as it is interfering.

The Relationship Between Criteria and Obstacles

We computed a correlation matrix which included all criteria and obstacles examined in the study. As indicated in Table 7, we found that the following three strategic benefit criteria correlated with a number of obstacles:

1. The product fits with the corporation's long-term strategy.

TABLE 6 Obstacles Frequently Ranked as Having a Significant or Destructive Impact

Obstacle	%
Lacks clear mission	42.0
Incompatibility between cultures	40.0
Inadequate financial commitment	39.0
Corporate management lacks patience	37.0
Lack of authority	33.0
Inability to attract qualified venture managers	33.0
Corporate management underestimates riskiness	31.0
Entrepreneur fears control by corporation	25.0

TABLE 7   Selected Correlations Between Criteria and Obstacles

Correlation	Product fit	Attractive Mkt/Ind	Control
1. *Obstacles–Corporate Relations*			
Lacks clear mission	0.05	0.16	0.38^c
Lacks patience	0.11	0.27^c	0.27^b
Has made inadequate financial commitment	0.05	0.05	0.39^c
Underestimates riskiness	0.12	0.27^a	0.33^b
Inflexible	0.17	0.16	0.28^b
Does not encourage support from other areas	−0.30	0.15	0.36^c
2. *Obstacles–Venture Activity*			
Lack of authority	0.32^b	0.38^c	0.45^c
Inability to attract qualified venture managers	0.11	0.06	0.24^a
High turnover rate	−0.14	−0.11	−0.14
Inadequate deal flow	0.27^a	0.28^b	0.54^c
Difficulty liquidating investments	0.05	0.09	0.09
Lack of opportunity to participate in syndications	0.21	0.16	0.03
Entrepreneurs fear idea will be stolen	0.21	0.33^b	0.11
Entrepreneurs fear corporate control over venture	0.39^c	0.52^c	0.35^c
Incompatiblity between cultures	0.50^c	0.45^c	0.43^c

$^a p < 0.1$.
$^b p < 0.05$.
$^c p < 0.01$.

2. The venture is in a market or industry which is attractive to my company.
3. My company is, or will have, the option to be the controlling investor in the venture.

Four obstacles correlate positively with each of these three criteria—lack of authority to make independent decisions, inadequate deal flow, fear by entrepreneurs that the venture will be controlled to satisfy the corporation's objectives, and incompatibility between corporate and entrepreneurial cultures. This we take as strong evidence that an insistence on corporate strategy criteria causes serious problems in the execution of the CVC's activity, at least in the eyes of the CVC managers.

Furthermore, CVCs who indicate that the option to be a controlling investor is a condition for funding ventures also indicate that corporate management:

● lacks a clear mission regarding venture activity,
● makes inadequate financial commitment to venture activity,
● is impatient regarding the time it takes for new ventures to succeed,
● is inflexible, and
● does not encourage support of the activity from other areas within the corporation.

To us this strongly suggests that when corporate management encroaches on the decision-making process for venture investing, the corporation becomes less appealing as a source of funds to the entrepreneur. Further, in extreme situations, when the corporation requires complete control of the venture, the potential for conflict not only arises between the CVC and the entrepreneur, but also between the CVC and corporate management.

Organization

We next asked a series of questions which focus on how corporations organize their venture capital effort. Frequency of distributions for these responses are reported in Table 8.

Approval Process and Funding

The majority of the CVCs surveyed are given little authority to select which ventures should be funded without approval from corporate management. Of the total, 51% of the venture professionals indicated that formal approval from corporate management was required for *all* deals. Another 15% of the CVCs require approval for deals over a designated size. Thus, nearly two-thirds of all CVCs require formal approval on projects of significant size.

Nearly half of the CVCs surveyed get their deals funded on an ad hoc basis (46%).

Compensation

The majority of CVCs surveyed are compensated in a manner which has little or nothing to do with the performance of their company's investment portfolio. It typically takes several years or longer for ventures to mature into successful companies, yet 61% of the CVCs surveyed reported that they were compensated either by a base salary only or by a base salary plus a short-term bonus. Only 24% of the CVC (15% of the respondents did not answer the question) indicated that their compensation was linked to the performance of their company's venture activity over the long term (either through a bonus or direct equity participation in the fund).

Source and Structure of Deals

The most important source of deals for CVCs is via direct contact from entrepreneurs. This is closely followed by other venture funds in terms of importance. Because many CVCs have a different orientation than independent venture capitalists, we suspected that CVCs might experience problems in networking with other venture capitalists. As a result, they might have access to few deals and few opportunities to participate in syndications. This suspicion appears to be unfounded. The relatively high ranking of venture funds as a valuable source of deals and the relatively low rating of the two obstacles "inadequate deal flow" and "lack of opportunity to participate in syndications" suggest that CVCs' interaction with the venture capital community is quite adequate.

There was a high consensus that direct equity was the best approach to structuring a deal. Objectives of the CVC did not appear to influence structure.

Performance

One important area that we hoped to better understand was the level of performance being achieved by the CVCs. Since performance is not easily quantified, particularly when associated with strategic benefits, we asked respondents to report their general levels of satisfaction relative to their various objectives. The means and standard deviations for responses to this question appear in Table 9.

As a caveat, responses related to performance must be reviewed with care given the self-report nature of this study, the general way in which the question was asked, and the subjectivity involved in rating one's own performance.

TABLE 8   Organizational Issues—Frequency of Responses

Issue	%
1. *Approval Process*	
Approval from corporate management is not required	11.0
Approval from corporate management is required but the process is typically a formality	21.0
Approval from corporate management is required above a designated deal size and is based upon their thorough evaluation	15.0
Approval from corporate management is required on all deals and is based upon their thorough evaluation	51.0
Did not respond	2.0
2. *Compensation*	
Base salary only	31.4
Base salary plus bonus based on venture activity's performance over short-term	29.4
Base salary plus bonus based on venture activity's performance over long-term (over 5 years)	13.7
Base salary plus direct participation in venture fund	9.8
Did not respond	15.7
3. *Funding*	
A separate pool of funds is specifically earmarked for venture capital investment on a one-time basis	48.1
A separate pool of funds is specifically earmarked for venture capital investment on a periodic basis	26.9
Deals are funded on an ad hoc basis	19.2
Did not respond	5.8
4. *Most Valuable Source of Deals*	
Venture funds	34.6
Departments within my company	25.0
Financial intermediaries	7.0
Lawyers	0.0
Accountants	0.0
Direct contact by entrepreneurs	28.8
Did not respond	4.6
5. *Favorite Form of Structuring Deals*	
Direct equity participation	66.0
Joint venture	6.0
Licensing agreement	4.0
Development contract	2.0
Other	22.0

TABLE 9   Performance

Parameter	Mean	SD
Exposure to new technologies and markets	2.80	0.70
Return on investment	2.47	0.95
Opportunities to manufacture and market new products	2.41	0.97
Acquisition candidates	2.30	0.87
Opportunities to improve manufacturing processes	1.75	1.04

Scale: 1, unsatisfactory; 2, satisfactory; 3, highly satisfactory; 4, outstanding.

TABLE 10 Experience Effects

	More experienced: More than 10 deals n = 21		Less experienced: Less than 10 deals n = 24	
	Mean	SD	Mean	SD
Obstacles[c]				
Corporate management lacks clear mission	2.05[a]	1.07	2.54	0.88
Corporate management lacks patience	1.80[a]	1.08	2.42	0.97
Corporate management underestimates riskiness	1.86[a]	0.96	2.48	0.85
Lack of authority	1.90[a]	0.86	1.90	0.97
Inadequate deal flow	1.43[a]	0.60	1.96	0.82
Entrepreneurs fear corporate control	1.67[b]	0.80	2.26	0.81
Incompatibility between cultures	1.81[b]	0.87	2.58	0.93
Performance				
Return on investment	2.76[a]	1.04	2.19	1.03
Funding[d]	2.10[b]	0.87	2.71	0.75
Approval Process[e]	2.62[b]	1.24	3.46	0.88

[a] $p < 0.05$, one-tail t-test for differences between means.
[b] $p < 0.01$, one-tail t-test for differences between means.
[c] Only variables where mean scores of the two groups showed statistically significant differences were included in this chart. For complete list of variables included in the questionnaire see Table 5 for obstacles, Table 8 for organization, and Table 9 for performance.
[d] The lower the mean the more likely a separate fund is set aside rather than funding on an ad hoc basis.
[e] The lower the mean, the greater the authority given to CVCs to make independent investment decisions.

We find that CVCs judge their own performance to be at minimum satisfactory with respect to all measures except the opportunity to improve manufacturing processes.

Experience Effects

A study by MacMillan, Block, and SubbaNarasimha (1986) suggested that there are significant experience effects in venturing activities and piqued our interest to explore whether there were similar effects for corporate venture capital activity.

Therefore, we compared responses of those CVCs who had made more than 10 deals with those who had made less than 10 (CVCs having made exactly 10 deals were not included in this part of the analysis, so that the differences between the experienced and less experienced CVCs would be more pronounced). We thought that experience would be best measured by number of deals transacted rather than years in business, since a CVC who had been in existence for several years but had made few deals would still be relatively inexperienced. The results are presented in Table 10.

It is clear that the more experienced CVCs learn to ameliorate the impact of a number of obstacles that plague less experienced CVCs. In particular, they learn over time to overcome some of the key problems identified above, developing some proficiency at handling the relation with the corporation and more expertise at attracting deals from nervous entrepreneurs. They also learn to deliver return on investment. So, as they gain experience, they begin to behave more like independent venture capitalists—they receive more authority and a more certain financial commitment from the corporation. They are also able to reduce the impact of a number of obstacles (which are unique to corporate venture capital) and their performance in return of investment improves.

244   R. SIEGEL ET AL.

TABLE 11   Profiles of Clusters[e]

	Copilots n = 32		Pilots n = 20	
	Mean	SD	Mean	SD
Objectives				
Exposure to new technologies and markets	3.47[c]	0.80	2.53	0.67
Manufacture or market new products	2.65[a]	1.02	2.00	1.26
Improve manufacturing processes	2.09[a]	0.94	1.53	0.77
Acquisition of companies	2.53[c]	1.14	1.50	0.83
Return on investment	3.15[b]	0.85	3.75	0.55
Criteria				
Able to accept criticism	2.40[a]	0.81	2.85	0.88
Has personality compatible with mine	1.93[a]	0.74	2.35	0.67
Demonstrated leadership ability	2.91[b]	0.64	3.45	0.69
Track record relevant to venture	2.62[c]	0.61	3.20	0.62
Product fits with corporation's longterm strategy	3.19[c]	0.97	2.10	1.25
Market industry attractive to corporation	3.34[c]	0.90	1.95	1.09
Return 10 × investment in 5–10 years	2.73[a]	0.78	3.25	0.72
Option to be controlling investor	2.51[b]	1.09	1.50	0.89
Investment easily made liquid	1.90[b]	0.83	2.55	0.94
Material impact on corporation's performance	2.31[c]	0.90	1.40	0.82
Size of investment = 10–20% total funds	1.90[a]	0.84	2.45	1.14

[a] $p < 0.05$, one-tail t-test for differences between means.
[b] $p < 0.01$, one-tail t-test for differences between means.
[c] $p < 0.001$, one-tail t-test for differences between means.
[d] $p < 0.06$, one-tail t-test for differences between means.
[e] Only variables where mean scores of the two groups showed statistically significant differences were included in this table. For a complete list of variables related to criteria see Table 2.

Cluster Analysis

The observation that the more experienced venture capital firm secured more antonomy and also reduced the obstacles while simultaneously achieving better financial performance led to another question which has been the focus of considerable discussion in the corporate venturing area: how much autonomy should be allowed? We hypothesized that the autonomy of the CVC in relation to its corporate parent would be a significant determinant of effectiveness of venture activity. We therefore subjected the responses to a cluster analysis using the SAS cluster procedure with the responses to the items on funding procedure and approval procedure as independent variables. Each of these sets of items were treated as a 1 to 4 scale, with low score indicating the highest dependency on corporate and a high score indicating high autonomy. The two cluster solution revealed a large group of highly controlled CVCs (62% of respondents) and a smaller group of highly autonomous CVCs (38% of respondents).

The small cluster we dubbed "pilots" because these members have far greater authority to make investment decisions and the parent corporation makes a far more permanent and reliable financial commitment to corporate venture activity. The large cluster we dubbed "copilots" because this group enjoys significantly less independence: respondents must share

TABLE 12 Comparisons of Cluster Obstacles and Performance[e]

	Copilots $n = 32$		Pilots $n = 20$	
	Mean	SD	Mean	SD
Obstacles				
Corporation lacks clear mission	2.44[a]	0.98	1.95	0.88
Corporate management lacks patience	2.25[a]	1.02	1.75	1.02
Corporate management is inflexible	1.93[a]	0.91	1.50	0.83
Lack of authority	2.45[c]	0.72	1.95	0.88
Inadequate deal flow	1.71[a]	0.85	1.64	0.51
Entrepreneurs fear idea will be stolen	1.69[b]	0.78	1.21	0.42
Entrepreneurs fear corp. control	2.16[a]	0.78	1.60	0.88
Incompatibility between cultures	2.44[b]	0.80	1.80	1.06
Performance				
Acquisition candidates	2.48[a]	0.92	1.91	0.94
Return on investment	2.28[d]	1.07	2.75	0.97
Source of deals[f]				
Venture funds	2.68[a]	1.44	1.83	1.38
Departments within company	2.35[a]	1.52	3.42	1.73
Accountants	5.30[a]	0.92	4.38	1.50

[a]$p < 0.05$. one-tail *t*-test for differences between means.
[b]$p < 0.01$. one-tail *t*-test for differences between means.
[c]$p < 0.001$, one-tail *t*-test for differences between means.
[d]$p < 0.06$, one-tail *t*-test for differences between means.
[e]Only variables where mean scores of the two groups showed statistically significant differences were included in this table. For a complete list of variables included in the questionnaire see Table 5 for obstacles, Table 8 for organizational characteristics and Table 9 for performance.
[f]The lower the mean, the more favored the source of funding.

decision-making authority with corporate management and the corporation's financial commitment is considerably more uncertain, since capital is contributed on a periodic or deal by deal basis.

Unfettered by constraints imposed by the corporation, one might expect the pilots to behave in a way that is similar to independent venture capitalists. Conversely, one would expect the copilots to be significantly influenced by corporate dictate.

Our expectations were borne out by the responses of the two groups with respect to objectives and investment criteria, as indicated in Table 11.

Almost all of the pilots regarded return on investment as a major objective of venture investing. In their screening of ventures, this group places relatively heavier emphasis on entrepreneurial talent and leadership and financial considerations than do the copilots. Criteria related to strategic benefits weigh less heavily in their investment decisions.

Copilots attach greater importance to strategic benefits. Almost all consider at least one strategic objective to be essential. Of the 32 respondents in this cluster 19 consider return on investment a less than essential objective. The investment criteria of this group reflect the corporate priorities in their criteria. Strategic benefits are much more important then criteria relating to the entrepreneur and to financial performance.

In order to determine which was the more effective of the pilot and copilot approaches, responses relative to obstacles and performance were compared. These results are reported in Table 12.

There were eight instances in which the impact of obstacles were assessed differently by the two clusters. *In every instance*, the copilots assessed the obstacles as being more damaging than did the pilots. Four of the obstacles—corporate managements' lack of a clear mission, lack of flexibility, lack of patience regarding venture activity, and inability to relinquish control to the CVC—appear to be a direct result of the intimate organization relationship between the corporation and its copilot CVC. This close relationship also seems to magnify obstacles related to the appeal of the corporation as a source of funds: the entrepreneurs' fear of corporate control and their fear that their ideas will be pirated, a general incompatibility between corporate and entrepreneurial cultures, and inadequate deal flow are all viewed as more serious by the copilots than by the pilots.

This is very strong evidence that when it comes to corporate venture capital, close control appears to become a serious impediment to such activity.

This argument is further supported by the results on performance. We expected pilots to report better performance with respect to return on investment, and copilots to report better performance with respect to achieving strategic benefits. However, while pilots do report higher satisfaction in achieving return on investment generally, *they do no worse* than copilots in achieving strategic benefits (the only exception to this is exposure to acquisition opportunities).

To check that we were not merely seeing a "replay" of the experience effect discussed above, we tested to see whether pilots had done significantly more deals than copilots. This was not the case, indicating that while CVCs tend to gain pilot status with experience, it is pilot status that is important for performance, whether the CVC is experienced or not.

We take the above results as strong and convincing evidence that the pilots' approach to corporate venture capital organization is generally more effective than a copilot approach. A desire to identify acquisition opportunities seems to be the only excuse for employing the latter approach. And even then, there are difficulties associated with the acquisition portfolio companies funded by corporate venture capital (Hardymon, Denino, and Salter 1983).

At this point, one might conclude that if corporate venture capital is to be successful, CVCs should simply be made clones of independent capitalists.

Our interpretation of the data is that this view is too extreme. In particular, a few copilots were able to achieve *outstanding* performance relative to strategic benefit objectives, as were some pilot CVCs. Clearly further study is needed in order to determine how CVCs successfully integrate financial and strategic considerations, and which benefits are most likely to be achieved.

In summary, we review our two major findings. First, autonomy and a firm commitment of capital (the pilot approach) are necessary conditions to provide an environment conducive to effective corporate venture capital operations. This approach has far less obstacles to effective CVC operations. Secondly, the pilot approach is successful in producing both return on investment (no surprise) and strategic benefit (something of a surprise). It appears that a primary emphasis on strategic benefits increases problems with obstacles. These findings are especially noteworthy given that 62% of our respondents are organized using the copilot approach to corporate venture capital.

REFERENCES

Hardymon, G., De Nino, J., and Salter, M.S. 1983. *Harvard Business Review*

MacMillan, I.C., Block, Z., and SubbaNarasimha, P.N., 1986. Corporate venturing: Alternatives, obstacles and experience effects. *Journal of Business Venturing* 1(2):177–192.

MacMillan, I.C., Siegel, R., and SubbaNarasimha, P.N. 1985. Criteria used by venture capitalists to evaluate new venture proposals. *Journal of Business Venturing* 1(1):119–128.

MacMillan, I.C., Zemann, L., and SubbaNarasimha, P.N. 1986. Criteria distinguishing successful from unsuccessful ventures in the venture screening process. *Journal of Business Venturing* 2(2):123–138.

Sykes, H.B. 1986. Anatomy of a corporate venturing program: factors influencing success. *Journal of Business Venturing* 1(3):275–294.

Tyebjee, T.T., and Bruno, A.V. 1984. A model of venture capital investment activity. *Management Science* 30(9):1051–1066.

[15]

CORPORATE VENTURE
CAPITAL: STRATEGIES
FOR SUCCESS

HOLLISTER B. SYKES
New York University

EXECUTIVE SUMMARY

Currently, about 80 major companies have venture capital programs that were started for strategic reasons—to help foster new business development. Yet the results have been mixed. Some companies consider their programs successful. Others have doubts. Others have quit.

To explore causes for this disparity of results, survey data were gathered from 31 major corporations through questionnaires and follow-up interviews. Only strategic investment programs, where the motivating purpose is to assist corporate new business development, were covered. Programs conducted solely for financial return were excluded. Data on two modes of venture capital investment were obtained: venture capital investment (VCI) directly in new ventures and investment in venture capital limited partnerships (VCLPs) managed by private venture capital firms.

Corporations were asked to rate, on a five-level scale, the overall contribution (added value) of their programs in meeting their strategic objectives. In the survey, eight factors were probed to determine their possible effect on the strategic value rating. Four of these factors appear to have a significant influence on strategic value: choice of primary strategic objective, type and frequency of communications with the ventures or VCLPs, return on portfolio investment, and mode of investment (VCI vs. VCLP).

Objectives that produce a mutually supportive environment, such as formation of corporate/venture business relationships, are more likely to lead to success. Objectives that induce a potential conflict of interest between the corporations and the venture, such as venture acquisition, may lead to a nonproductive environment and failure of the relationship.

Modes of communication that involve direct and frequent contact between the corporation and the venture regarding areas of special or mutual interest produce the highest strategic value. Of questionable value are routine reports and attendance at venture board meetings.

Reported return on investment for those programs that had been in operation for five or more

Address correspondence to Professor Hollister B. Sykes, Graduate School of Business Administration, New York University, 100 Trinity Place, New York, NY 10006.

Journal of Business Venturing 5, 37–47
©1990 Elsevier Science Publishing Co., Inc., 655 Avenue of the Americas, New York, NY 10010

0883-9026/90/$3.50

38 H. B. SYKES

years averaged 14 to 15%. Portfolio ROI% was positively related to strategic value in the case of investment in VCLPs, but no significant relationship was found in the case of VCI investments.

Comparison of the strategic value of direct vs. VCLP investment showed opinion predominantly in favor of direct investment if only one strategy were chosen. However, as the interviews brought out, the two programs can serve somewhat different purposes and be complementary to one another. The most effective combination is one in which the VCLP investments provide contacts with the venture capital community and "deal flow" and the direct investments enhance specific business relationships such as marketing or research agreements.

The implication of these results for corporate investors is that program strategic success can be significantly enhanced by a proactive approach involving frequent interaction with the ventures or venture capital firms regarding specific issues of mutual interest. One of the most effective channels for interaction is through the formation of business relationships ("strategic partnerships" in current parlance). Financial returns will probably be acceptable and additive to any strategic returns.

INTRODUCTION

The sole investment objective of the private venture capitalist is return on capital. On the other hand, the primary objective of most corporate venture capital programs is strategic. The impact of possible capital gains on total corporate results is viewed as minor compared with the potential for development of new business.

In the 1960s a number of major U.S. corporations began to experiment with venture capital as a supplement to internal new business development activities. Direct venture capital investment (VCI) programs were started at Dow, DuPont, Exxon, Ford, General Electric, Grace, Hercules, Singer, and Union Carbide, among others. The strategic objectives of these programs were to provide a "window" on potential new business growth areas and to provide a source of potential acquisitions for entry into these new areas.

The "window" concept appeals because history demonstrates that major new business growth areas have evolved from new products originally developed by innovative small companies. Melberg and Fast (1980) and Klein (1987) recommend venture capital investment as a way to provide early insight into the potential for a new business market or technology. However, venture capital investment as a means to acquire independent new ventures often hasn't worked out. Hardymon et al. (1983) note that the venture capital opportunities available to a corporation are restricted by a number of factors that diminish the chance of strategic success.

One difficulty with the "window" concept noted by Hardymon et al. (1983) and Rind (1981) is that corporate exposure to a venture's proprietary technical or marketing information can be a legal problem. As a solution Rind recommended investment in venture capital limited partnerships (VCLPs) in order to insulate the corporation from direct exposure.

In a formal research study of corporate venture capital, Siegel et al. (1988) concluded that the best *financial performance* is obtained when the corporate venture capital group has nearly independent autonomy and a committed source of funds. However, these attributes did not appear to differentiate *strategic performance*, except possibly in a negative direction when the primary strategic objective was acquisition.

Over 100 major U.S. corporations have, at one time or another, tried venture capital investment as an aid to new business development. Since 1980, the number of corporate programs has increased threefold. However, as many as one quarter of the companies who have tried such investing have since stopped, and a number of others have questioned the value of the activity. Those continuing investment are trying new approaches to improve results. A few consider their programs to be very successful.

This range of experience could result from random distribution, but it seems probable that certain management approaches work better than others. From prior experience and talks with personnel at a number of companies with active venture capital programs, we assembled a list of eight factors, one or more of which were believed to affect program success:

1. Choice of primary strategic objective
2. Type and frequency of contact between the corporation and the ventures or venture capital limited partnerships (VCLPs)
3. Mode of investment (direct VCI vs. investment in one or more VCLPs)
4. Portfolio financial return
5. Corporate venture capital manager experience and compensation
6. Organizational position of the primary corporate contact
7. Source of direct (VCI) investment opportunities
8. Number of corporate investors in the same VCLP

By use of a questionnaire, these eight factors were probed to determine their possible effect on the perceived strategic value of the venture capital programs. To measure strategic value, the corporate personnel were asked to rate, on a five-level scale, the overall contribution (added value) of their programs toward meeting the corporate new business development (strategic) objective.

Based solely on statistical measures, the first four factors had the most significant effect on strategic value. The results related to these factors will be reviewed in some depth, followed by a brief commentary on findings related to the other factors. Results are reported on two levels: statistical analysis of data obtained from questionnaires sent to each corporation and interpretive comments based on interviews with the corporations.

STUDY SCOPE

Venture capital investment as used herein is defined as the purchase of non-publicly traded equity in an *independently* managed start-up or growth company. Therefore, this study does not include internally developed and managed corporate ventures. Also, this study is concerned with only "strategic" venture capital investments—those undertaken for the primary purpose of assisting corporate new business development. Investment programs managed strictly for financial return, such as corporate pension fund investments or the investments of GE's former GEVENCO affiliate, are not part of this study.

Two generic modes of strategic corporate venture capital investment are followed: investments managed through an independent venture capital limited partnership (VCLP) and direct venture capital investment (VCI) in individual ventures. Data on both modes were obtained and analyzed in this study and will be referred to by the abbreviations VCI and VCLP.

DATA BASE

Eighty-six corporations known to have venture capital investment programs were asked to respond to a questionnaire covering their objectives and investment management practices. Thirty-three provided data for the questionnaire. Two of these responses fell outside the scope of this study, leaving 31 usable for analysis. The data were supplemented through personal or telephone follow-up interviews.

TABLE 1   Investment Profile for Companies in the Study

Median per company	VCI group	VCLP group
Time since first investment, years	4	4
Number of investments, total	4	6.5
Investment rate, $M/year	2.3	4.9

Of the 31 companies, 25 had made investments in venture capital limited partnerships and 26 had made direct investments in individual ventures. Twenty companies had made both kinds of investments. This provided an opportunity to compare the two modes of investment for relative strategic value.

The fractional (38%) response rate raises the question of nonrespondent bias. To check this we called all of the nonrespondent companies and determined that 21 (24%) did not have adequate records to respond because of limited programs or because their programs had been abandoned and 11 (13%) had a corporate policy against replying to such inquiries. Only 21 (24%) would not respond at all. We attribute this to work priorities rather than any reluctance to reveal their program results. Consequently, we estimate that about 60% of those companies that could have provided useful data were sampled and that the data are reasonably representative.

Annual revenues for all but two companies in our sample were in excess of $1 billion. All were industrial or communications companies. The median investment profile for those corporations making VCI and VCLP investments is summarized in Table 1.

PROGRAM STRATEGIC VALUE RATING

The major dependent variable in this study is a five-level rating (-1, 0, $+1$, $+2$, $+3$) by the corporate respondents which measured their perception of the overall strategic value of the program to their corporation. Only 36 to 40% of the companies rated program value at the highest level of $+2$ or $+3$. Twenty to 24% said the program was of nil (0) to negative (-1) overall strategic value. The distribution of the value ratings is depicted in Figure 1.

Because the perceived strategic value rating (referred to as "VALU") is a qualitative and personal judgment, personal bias of the respondents could affect the answers. To test for bias, the VALU data were sorted into two groups. The "a" group included those respondents employed by or directly responsible for the VC program. All other respondents were included in the "b" group. A chi-squared test indicated that correlation of VALU with the group type was not significant ($p > .5$ for the VCI data and $p > .2$ for the VCLP data). However, the "a" group comprised 70 to 80% of the respondents. If there was bias among this group, we believe it reasonable to assume that it affected the absolute rather than relative valuations.

PRIMARY STRATEGIC OBJECTIVE VS. VALUE

Venture capital investment is a strategy that has been recommended (Melberg and Fast 1980; Klein 1987; Rind 1981) to meet various corporate new business development objectives. A list of possible strategic objectives, drawn from our prior discussions with corporate venture

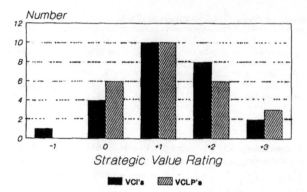

FIGURE 1 Distribution of value ratings.

capital groups, was provided in the questionnaire. Respondents were asked to rank them in order of their program priority. Table 2 lists the strategic objectives and the mean of the priority rankings for each investment mode (VCI vs. VCLP).

Identification of new business opportunities (the "window" objective) and development of business relationships ranked at the top of the list. Typical business relationships include agreements under which the corporation markets products developed by the venture or the venture conducts research in its area of specialization for the corporation.

Our primary interest was to determine whether choice of primary objective resulted in significant differences in rated strategic value of the overall program. For instance, Hardymon et al. (1983) had questioned the efficacy of venture capital–related acquisitions. To test this, the objective ranked #1 by each respondent was compared with their program strategic value ranking (VALU). Table 3 lists the mean of the VALU rankings for each group of companies that cited the same first-priority objective.

In the VCI group, the acquisition objective yielded the lowest mean VALU rating. Of the five companies who listed acquisition as their primary objective, the two with the most experience (investing for five or more years) gave their programs the lowest VALU ratings. Their overall program valuations were −1 and 0, both lower than the five-company mean. In the VCLP group, the acquisition objective also scored a low mean value. To test the

TABLE 2 Strategic Objective Rankings

	Mean priority ranking	
Strategic objective	VCIs	VCLPs
Identify new opportunities	2.0	2.9
Develop business relationships	2.4	2.7
Find potential acquisitions	3.3	3.8
Learn how to do venture capital	—	4.0
Change corporate culture	4.2	—
Assist spin-outs from the corporation	4.7	4.7

TABLE 3   Relation of Primary Strategic Objective to VALU

Primary strategic objective	Count	Mean VALU	SD	TSp*
VCI group				
Identify new opportunities	10	1.60	0.84	.021
Develop business relationships	9	1.33	1.00	.054
Change corporate culture	1	1.00	—	—
Find potential acquisitions	5	0.40	0.89	base
VCLP group				
Identify new opportunities	6	1.67	0.82	.054
Develop business relationships	12	1.50	1.00	.056
Find potential acquisitions	2	1.00	0	base
Learn how to do venture capital	4	0.25	0.50	.041

*Significance of mean VALU differences tested by two-sample *t* tests of each mean relative to the "base" mean VALU.

significance of differences in VALU rankings for the objectives, two-sample *t* tests were performed and are listed in the column headed "TSp".[1]

The numerical results were directionally supported by our interviews with the company representatives. Several commented that initiating venture capital investments with the intention of using them as an option for future acquisition induces a negative environment. The better entrepreneurs and venture capitalists don't want to lose the option of taking the venture public at some point.

COMMUNICATIONS VS. STRATEGIC VALUE

Achievement of any of the *strategic* objectives would, of course, depend on effective communication between the corporate managers and the venture or VCLP managers. The questionnaire provided a list of types of contact, drawn from previous interviews, and asked the frequency of each. To compare type and frequency of communication with VALU, the companies were grouped into three samples according to VALU rating. The first sample, the "failures," includes programs with VALU ratings of −1 and 0. The second, or middle sample includes all data from programs with a VALU rating of 1. The third sample, the "successes," includes programs with VALUs of 2 and 3. The mean frequencies of each type of communication for the "failure" and "success" samples were compared for significance by a two-sample *t* test.

Table 4 summarizes the types of communication examined and the two-sample significance for the "failure"/"success" pair, referred to by the abbreviation "TSp."

Data on frequency and type of VCI contact showed significant two-sample VALU differences in only two instances: corporate requests for expert advice from the ventures and meetings with the ventures regarding business relationships. However, this significance was not confirmed by Pearson correlation of the complete spectrum of frequency data because of wide scatter of data in the middle group (VALUs of 1). Routine contacts and commu-

---

[1]The relationship between pairs of continuous variables was tested for significance by two-sample *t* tests of means. Because of the small sample size, significance tests were calculated assuming samples with separate variances. All significance figures are reported as one-tailed probabilities that the null hypothesis is true. Two-sample probabilities are indicated by the abbreviation "TSp."

TABLE 4 Relation of Frequency of Communication to VALU

Type of communication	"Failures"			"Successes"			
	n	Mean	SD	n	Mean	SD	TSp
VCI group							
Corporate requests for expert advice from a venture	3	0	0	6	5.00	4.10	.020
Corporate meetings with ventures regarding business relationships	4	0.25	0.50	6	8.33	6.71	.020
Periodic reports by ventures on their activities	4	7.00	3.83	6	9.50	3.89	.175
Investment opportunities submitted by the ventures to the corporation	2	2.50	3.54	5	103	272	.186
Board meetings attended by corporate representatives	5	4.40	4.51	8	6.13	3.80	.249
Venture requests for expert advice from the corporation	4	3.25	4.57	6	5.17	3.43	.253
VCLP group							
Corporate requests for meetings with the VCLP managers	4	0.25	0.50	7	2.43	1.40	.004
Investment referrals from VCLPs	3	2.33	0.58	8	27.1	31.4	.032
Corporate/venture contacts initiated by the corporation	4	0.75	0.96	7	6.14	6.79	.043
VCLP requests for advice from the corporation	3	2.67	2.31	8	13.6	15.3	.044
Corporate/venture contacts initiated by the VCLP	3	1.00	1.00	7	21.0	35.1	.093
VCLP routine reports on venture activities	3	4.33	1.53	7	3.20	1.10	.169
VCLP routine reports on deals seen	3	5.00	6.24	6	6.40	4.59	.377
Corporate requests for investment advice from VCLPs	4	2.25	2.06	8	3.13	3.27	.293

nication, such as periodic reports by the ventures on their activities and attendance at board meetings, were of intermediate or questionable value by both statistical methods.

The VCLP data provided a more definitive confirmation of the VCI results. Direct communications between the corporation and the ventures or VCLP regarding items of special interest (such as investment referrals) were of significant value. Periodic routine reports were of questionable value. Moreover, the significance of the VCLP two-sample differences shown in Table 4 was confirmed by Pearson correlations using the complete spectrum of data.

Formation of Business Relationships

Communication between the corporation and individual ventures concerning some activity of mutual interest would be expected to be more meaningful than routine meetings or standardized information exchange. As demonstrated by the communication data, such interaction is likely to result from the formation of business relationships such as research contracts or marketing arrangements. Data on the number of business relationships formed in the course of each program were obtained and compared with the strategic value rating.

In Table 5, the corporate programs are grouped in ranges according to the number of business relationships entered. Mean program VALU ratings are listed for each group.

44 H. B. SYKES

TABLE 5 VALU vs. Number of Business Relationships

Number of business relationships entered	Mean VALU	Count	SD	Mean VALU significance	
				TSp*	TSp*
VCI group					
0	0	6	0.6	base	.003
1–2	1.2	5	0.4	.003	base
3–4	1.4	7	0.5	.001	—
4+	2.0	5	0.7	.001	.035
VCLP group					
0	0.7	10	0.5	base	.065
1–2	1.3	6	0.8	.065	base
3–4	1.5	2	0.7	.195	—
4+	2.5	4	0.6	.005	.016

*Significance of mean VALU differences tested by two-sample t tests of each mean relative to the "base" mean VALU.

For both types of programs, two-sample t tests indicate a significant relationship between the perceived strategic program value and the number of business relationships entered. Pearson correlations of VALU vs. number of business relationships entered confirmed these results ($R = .60, p = .001$ for the VCI group; $R = .75, p = .001$ for the VCLP group). To test whether time was a factor, Pearson correlations were also run on VALU vs. the number of relationships entered *per year*. For the VCI group, $R = .4$ and $p = .03$; for the VCLP group, $R = .8, p = .006$.

Our interviews supported the statistical findings. Respondents stressed that communication between the venture and those corporate units having a specific strategic interest is necessary for an effective relationship. Also, there were some strong opinions that the most valuable communication was at direct working relationship meetings with individuals in the ventures, rather than at board meetings.

A number of company representatives said they would not make an equity investment in a new venture unless there was some kind of business relationship involved. One said, we will "continue to invest only in companies where we have a contractual business relationship," and "an operating division must sponsor and take responsibility."

A representative of one of the companies expressed doubts that "pure" equity investments (meaning without concurrent business relationships) would yield insights that couldn't as well be obtained through a business relationship.

Contacts with the Investment Community

A good "deal flow" is considered necessary to provide a wide choice for investment. The VCLP data indicated that there was significant value in the investment referrals to the corporation by the VCLP managers. In the VCI survey we collected data on the sources of investment referrals. Venture capitalists were the most frequent sources (an average of 27% vs. the next highest referral source, corporate personnel, at 20%).

Contacts with the investment community, primarily venture capitalists, are developed through VCLP investments and coinvestments with the VCLPs in individual ventures. Effective working relationships are built over time, usually by coinvesting. For example, we found a significant (Pearson $p = .038$) relationship between the percentage of referrals from venture capitalists and the number of years the VCI program had been in operation. The average percentage of referrals from this source was 42% for those programs with terms of five years or more, versus an average of 22% for those programs in operation for less than five years.

STRATEGIC VALUE OF VCI VS. VCLP INVESTMENT

An obvious issue is whether one mode of investment is more effective than the other. And, is it useful to have both types of programs? During interviews each respondent was asked to compare the relative *strategic* value of direct investment in ventures vs. investment in limited partnerships. From the 20 companies that had both types of programs, we obtained 17 responses. Of these, 10 favored direct VC investments (VCIs), six were neutral, and one favored VCLP investments.

Although qualitative opinion was predominantly in favor of direct investment, given only one choice, the respondents noted that the two programs can serve somewhat different purposes and be complementary to one another. This distinction was most evident from the comments of those individuals in companies that had been active for many years in both types of programs. In their opinion, the most effective strategy is a combination of both modes of investment. The VCLP investments *provide contacts with the venture capital community and "deal flow,"* and the direct investments *enhance specific business relationships.* Investment first in VCLPs provides a useful learning experience, although it should not be the primary objective.

RETURN ON INVESTMENT VS. STRATEGIC VALUE

Unlike independent venture capital funds, most corporations do not make venture capital investments primarily for investment return. Those few who have done so generally set up the venture capital program as a more autonomous operation, which in several cases (GE, Grace, and Inco) has eventually resulted in spin-out of the activity as an independent fund, often including other institutional investors as limited partners. (Data from these companies were eliminated from our data base.)

Strategic value ratings were compared with reported ROI% to determine whether there was a significant relationship. A positive relationship to rated VALU was found in the case of the VCLP programs (Pearson $R = .53$, $p = .02$), but was less significant for the VCI programs ($R = .36$, $p = .12$). These results could mean that higher financial returns increase strategic value *or* that the strategic value ratings were biased by the level of ROI% achieved.

Although return on investment is not a primary corporate objective, it seems logical that if a venture cannot survive commercially, it is a poor prospect as a "window" on opportunity. More critically, it would be a poor candidate for a business relationship. The spokesman for one corporation stated that they have a policy of investing only in those ventures in which venture capitalists have already invested. He considered this an important test of economic viability.

Our ROI data showed no correlation with the number of years the VCI or VCLP programs had been in operation, which would indicate no experience effect. However, factors other than experience are involved, for example the methods of evaluating portfolios before there are earnings or public trading of the shares and the time it takes for failures to show up.

In assessing average financial results of the venture capital programs, we excluded data from those programs that had been in operation for four years or less. The averaged annual ROI for the nine VCI programs that had been in operation for five years or more was 15%. Four reported returns of 10% or less, and four reported returns of more than 20%. The average ROI for 11 VCLP programs was similar, at 14%. Five reported returns of 10% or less, and four reported returns of more than 20%.

On balance it can be concluded that strategic investment programs for the past few years have had a positive financial effect. So the strategic benefits, if any, did not come at an average net cost to the companies.

OTHER FACTORS

The primary *source of investment opportunities* for direct investment was referrals from venture capitalists. As noted previously, the percentage of referrals from venture capitalists increased significantly with the term of the venture program. However, we found no significant correlation between program strategic value and the dominant source of referrals.

Neither the *term of the program* nor the years of *venture capital experience* of the corporate program managers showed a significant correlation with strategic value. However, there was a very significant correlation (Pearson $p = .006$) between the term (years) of the program and the number of corporate venture capital program personnel who left each year to join private venture capital firms.

The *primary contact person* between the corporation and a venture, after the investment has been made, can be from several organizational locations, e.g., the venture capital program group, R&D department, or line operating divisions. We found no significant strategic value associated with these three locations or the *position level* of the contact person. However, a spokesman for one of the highest-rated programs expressed the opinion that, to satisfy the "window" objective, the primary contact should be a high-level person with broad contacts throughout the corporation and credibility with both top and operating management.

In the last few years *"focused" VCLPs*, dedicated to serving the specific business area interests of a sole corporate investor, have made an appearance. This is almost like having a direct investment portfolio, except independently managed. Our data were too sparse to compare this mode of investment with investment in the more common VCLPs which have multiple investors (limited partners). Only two companies in our survey were sole investors in at least one VCLP in addition to being one of three or more investors in other VCLPs. Both companies reported that the sole investor relationship was more strategically effective.

MANAGEMENT IMPLICATIONS

Several implications for management can be derived from the results of the statistical analysis supplemented by the interview comments. One failure mode of corporate venture capital may be pursuit of the wrong objective. Objectives that produce a potential conflict of interest between the corporation and the venture can lead to a nonproductive environment and failure of the relationship. Objectives that produce a mutually supportive environment can lead to success.

Corporate conflict of interest objectives include:

- A unilateral corporate desire for acquisition
- Expectation of strategic information input in exchange for equity investment only

Mutually supportive objectives include:

- Investment for the primary purpose of building a viable, independent company (the venture capitalist's objective)
- Establishment of mutually beneficial business relationships, such as marketing agreements
- Corporate assistance to the venture in areas of the corporation's expertise in return for a window on emerging technologies and markets

The working relationship between the corporation, the venture, and the venture capital community will be improved by emphasis on organizational and management strategies that:

- communicate awareness of each other's specific needs and interests between the individuals concerned,
- balance the needs of one party with the motivation to fill those needs by the other party, and
- build long-term relationships.

Corporations should continue to employ venture capital investment as one mode of remaining alert to new opportunities for business development in areas that relate to or could be extensions of their existing business. Use of venture capital to explore entirely new, unrelated business areas also may be of value, but development of effective communication channels and implementation of follow-on strategies will be more difficult because it will be more difficult to find areas for mutually beneficial business relationships.

REFERENCES

Hardymon, G. F., DeNino, M. J., and Salter, M. S. May–June 1983. When corporate venture capital doesn't work. *Harvard Business Review* 114:120.

Klein L. E., Winter 1987. How a venture capital initiative can help the corporate 'intrapreneur': A case study. *Business Development Review* 1(4):22–27.

Melberg, R. S., and Fast, N. D. 1980. Identifying new business opportunities. *SRI International, Business Intelligence Program*. Guidelines No. 1053, November.

Rind, K. W. 1981. The role of venture capital in corporate development. *Strategic Management Journal* 2:169–180.

Siegel, R., Siegel, E., and MacMillan, I. C. Summer 1988. Corporate venture capitalists: Autonomy, obstacles, and performance. *Journal of Business Venturing* 3(3):233–247.

Part IV
Antecedents and Consequences of Corporate Entrepreneurship

[16]

MANAGEMENT SCIENCE
Vol. 29, No. 7, July 1983
Printed in U.S.A.

THE CORRELATES OF ENTREPRENEURSHIP IN THREE TYPES OF FIRMS*

DANNY MILLER†

The objective of the research was to discover the chief determinants of entrepreneurship, the process by which organizations renew themselves and their markets by pioneering, innovation, and risk taking. Some authors have argued that personality factors of the leader are what determine entrepreneurship, others have highlighted the role played by the structure of the organization, while a final group have pointed to the importance of strategy making. We believed that the manner and extent to which entrepreneurship would be influenced by all of these factors would in large measure depend upon the nature of the organization. Based upon the work of a number of authors we derived a crude typology of firms: *Simple* firms are small and their power is centralized at the top. *Planning* firms are bigger, their goal being smooth and efficient operation through the use of formal controls and plans. *Organic* firms strive to be adaptive to their environments, emphasizing expertise-based power and open communications. The predictiveness of the typology was established upon a sample of 52 firms using hypothesis-testing and analysis of variance techniques. We conjectured that in *Simple* firms entrepreneurship would be determined by the characteristics of the leader; in *Planning* firms it would be facilitated by explicit and well integrated product-market strategies, and in *Organic* firms it would be a function of environment and structure. These hypotheses were largely borne out by correlational and multiple regression analyses. Any programs which aim to stimulate entrepreneurship would benefit greatly from tailoring recommendations to the nature of the target firms.
(ENTREPRENEURSHIP; CONTINGENCY THEORY; PLANNING; ORGANIZATIONAL STUDIES)

1. Introduction

Entrepreneurship can be defined and studied in a broader, less restrictive manner than tradition seems to dictate. There has been a strong tendency to identify entrepreneurship with a dominant organizational personality, generally an independent-minded owner-manager who makes the strategic decisions for his firm (Cole [7], Redlich [39], Hartman [17], Collins and Moore [8], Shapero [46]). The emphasis has been upon the innovative abilities of this individual, and generally it is the entrepreneur as actor who has been the focus of the research. This paper shifts the emphasis somewhat, looking at the entrepreneurial activity of the *firm*. With the growth and complexification of organizations, there is continually a need for organizational renewal, innovation, constructive risk-taking, and the conceptualization and pursuit of new opportunities, a pursuit that often goes beyond the efforts of one key manager. The entrepreneurial role stressed by Schumpeter [45] is socially vital but it can be performed by entire organizations which are decentralized. It can easily exceed or even circumvent the contributions of one central actor. In some firms, organizational renewal is performed by a traditional entrepreneur. In other firms, it is the province of a head office "planning" or "ventures" department. And in still other organizations it may be performed at lower levels of the hierarchy in R & D, engineering, marketing or even production departments. But what is most important is not who is the critical actor, but the *process* of entrepreneurship itself and the organizational factors which foster and impede it. These are the foci of the paper.

*Accepted by Arie Y. Lewin; received June 15, 1981. This paper has been with the author $2\frac{1}{2}$ months for 1 revision.
†McGill University and Ecole des Hautes Etudes Commerciales, Montreal.

Previous literature causes us to treat entrepreneurship as a multidimensional concept encompassing the firm's actions relating to product-market and technological innovation (Schumpeter [45], Cole [7], Cooper [10]), risk taking (Collins and Moore [8], Miller and Friesen [31], Kets de Vries [21]), and proactiveness (Miller and Friesen [30], Mintzberg [33]). An entrepreneurial firm is one that engages in product-market innovation, undertakes somewhat risky ventures, and is *first* to come up with "proactive" innovations, beating competitors to the punch. A nonentrepreneurial firm is one that innovates very little, is highly risk averse, and imitates the moves of competitors instead of leading the way. We can tentatively view entrepreneurship as a composite weighting of these three variables. A formal statistical justification for this will be presented later.

Much has been written on the determinants of entrepreneurship. Different works stress different determinants. For example, Shapero [46], Collins and Moore [8], Collins, Moore and Unwalla [9], Kets de Vries [21] and Toulouse [50] have stressed the importance of personality factors, psychodynamic characteristics, and the socio-cultural background of the chief executive in fostering entrepreneurial behavior. In contrast, March and Simon [27], Burns and Stalker [4], V. Thompson [48], J. Thompson [49], and Hage and Aiken [15] have called attention to the environmental and structural aspects of the firm that seem to promote innovation and entrepreneurial activity. Finally, Ackoff [1], Miller and Friesen [30], [31] and Mintzberg [33] have stressed the decision making and strategy factors promoting entrepreneurship.

Not only do the various authors place different emphases upon the different determinants of entrepreneurship, debates also abound about the impact of a given variable. Take the case of centralization. Authors such as Thompson [49], Normann [35] and Hage and Dewar [16, p. 285] have argued that centralization will promote innovation, the latter being vital to entrepreneurship. According to Thompson [49, pp. 153–154]:

> diffusion of power to the point where no inner circle emerges with sufficient stability to give direction to the organization . . . [may result in] administrative behavior [which is] problem oriented, not aggressive, and . . . safety oriented, not innovative.

But a very different message emanates from another body of literature. Burns and Stalker [4], Thompson [48], and Litwak [26] have pointed out the advantages that expertise-based power and extensive delegation of decision making authority have in *promoting* innovation. We shall try to show that this conflict and many others in the literature are due to the failure to distinguish among company types in examining the correlates of entrepreneurship (Miller [29]). The central theme of this paper as well as its main finding is that the correlates of entrepreneurship vary in a systematic and logical way from one type of firm to another.

The paper is structured as follows. First we describe three common but very different types of firms and briefly outline some hypothesized determinants of entrepreneurship for each. Then we proceed to describe our samples and variables and to validate our typology of firms using hypothesis testing and analysis of variance techniques. Finally, we present our findings on the correlates of entrepreneurship for each type of firm.

2. Company Types and Their Entrepreneurial Correlates

Our first task was to arrive at a predictive typology of firms that would focus upon *common* but very *different* types. While there are many such typologies in the literature, most of these deal independently with either environment, structure, or strategy making (see the review by Carper and Snizek [5]). We wished to adopt a typology that dealt with all three classes of variables since each has been shown to influence the nature of entrepreneurship (Kets de Vries [21]; Toulouse [50]). The work by Mintzberg [33], [34] afforded this opportunity. His three modes of strategy making (Mintzberg [33]), and five structural configurations [34], three of which relate quite naturally to his strategy making modes, served as a promising basis for our typology. Aside from breadth of scope, a key strength of Mintzberg's work is that it represents the outcome of an exceedingly thorough and widely acclaimed synthesis of the literature in policy and organizational theory.

But there were also some problems in using Mintzberg's types. A major shortcoming is that they have not been empirically validated. Thus, it was necessary for us to establish the generality and predictiveness of his typology in our research. Second, Mintzberg did not directly make the link between his strategy-making modes and his structures. This task fell to us. Fortunately little judgement was needed since Mintzberg [33] discusses the environmental and structural contexts of each of his strategy-making modes. A third problem was that it would have been impossible to accurately and parsimoniously measure all of Mintzberg's [34] structural attributes in a questionnaire study such as ours. Thus we have focussed mostly upon his [33] environmental and strategy-making variables and have employed rough surrogates for only a subset of his structural [34] variables. Fourth, since entrepreneurship was our dependent variable, each of the three types had to be defined to allow considerable variation in the degree of entrepreneurship. Finally, because leader personality has been shown to be critical to entrepreneurship (Shapero [46]; Miller, Kets de Vries and Toulouse [32]), we decided to go beyond Mintzberg's work to take this into account.

As a result of these problems, our three types are only loosely based upon those discussed by Mintzberg [33], [34]. It is suggestive of the generality of the typology however that each type recalls many of the ones described by other organizational theorists. Essentially, our *Simple* firms are those which pursue Mintzberg's [33] 'Entrepreneurial' mode of strategy making, and possess his [34] 'Simple' structure. Our *Planning* firms are those which have adopted his 'Planning' mode of strategy-making and his 'Machine Bureaucracy' structure. Finally, our *Organic* firms conform to Mintzberg's [33] 'Adaptive' mode of strategy making and suggest his 'Adhocracy' [34] structure. While these types do not exhaust the population of business firms, they do tend to be rather *common* and quite *different* from one another and this is *all* we intended to accomplish with the typology. We hypothesized that the determinants of entrepreneurship would be different for each of the three types.

Type One. Simple Firms: The Leadership Imperative

These are small firms operating in homogeneous environments and generally run by owner-managers. Ease of entry makes markets hostile and the small size of firms leaves them susceptible to threats from competitors. Power is highly centralized in the hands of one or two top administrators. Such centralization is often practical since the firm tends to be so simple and undiversified. One man can usually master its intricacies and effectively control it. Simple firms are partly represented by Mintzberg's [33] entrepreneurial firms, and by his [34] simple structures, by Pugh et al.'s [37] implicitly structured organizations, and by Filley and House's [13] 'stage two' firms. According to Mintzberg [34, p. 306]:

> The *simple structure* is characterized, above all, by what is not—elaborated. Typically, it has little or no technostructure (e.g. planning and control personnel), few support staffers, and minimal differentiation among its units. Coordination is effected largely by direct supervision.

Strategy making in these firms tends to be intuitive rather than analytical. It is performed by men who have a 'feel' for their business, not by staff planners and technocrats. There is generally little planning, time horizons are short, and the focus is upon operating matters rather than visionary master plans (Filley and House [13]). Finally, strategies are not explicitly or formally elaborated but reside as the implicit and often vague vision of the leaders.

In Simple firms we expect there to be a "leadership imperative" driving entrepreneurship. This is largely because the orientation of the firm is tied so closely to one central actor. Three prime factors, all of them leadership-related, are expected to determine the level of entrepreneurship. These include the personality, the power, and the store of knowledge of the leader (the italicized terms in our hypotheses are the names of the variables we measured in our data base).

(H1-1) Because the leader is the driving force behind the Simple firms, his personality will be a key determinant of entrepreneurship. His '*locus of control*' (Rotter [42]) may be especially crucial. The work by Miller et al. [32] and Shapero [46] shows that 'internal' leaders, those confident of their ability to control their environment, are the most likely to be entrepreneurial.

(H1-2) *Centralization* of decision making power is also expected to be positively correlated with entrepreneurship. Where the leader has arrogated most of the power to himself, he is freer to embark upon innovations and entrepreneurial ventures (Wilson [53]; Sapolsky [44]; Normann [35]).

(H1-3) In small Simple firms, the chief executive often acts as the brain. We propose that the more knowledge he has about emerging markets, products, and technologies, the greater the number of innovative ideas he will have and the higher the level of entrepreneurship. Two key sources of such ideas will be environmental *scanning* (Aguilar [3]; Carter and Williams [6]) and discussions with *technocrats* (Hage and Aiken [15]).

To summarize, in small centralized firms, entrepreneurship is predominantly influenced by the leader: his personality, his power, and his information. He is in a position sufficiently powerful to override structural and environmental obstacles to entrepreneurship. He can also resist entrepreneurial activity in the face of environmental incentives and structural pressures.

Type Two. Planning Firms: The Strategic Imperative

The emphasis or objective of Planning firms is smooth, efficient, and regular functioning. Firms try to buffer themselves from their rather stable and predictable environments and to function with a machine-like harmony. This aim tends to be reflected by the structure of the organization, principally by the use of elaborate control and planning systems, the extensive use of structural integration devices such as committees and task forces, a low to moderate level of interdepartmental differentiation, and a powerful central group of managers and technocrats who dominate decision making. Typically, the firm has an abundant store of slack resources. The Planners of Mintzberg [32], the Analyzers of Miles and Snow [28], and in part the machine bureaucracies discussed by Mintzberg [34], Burns and Stalker [4] and Crozier [11] represent our Planning firms.

According to Mintzberg [33] there are three central *strategy making* features characterizing the planning mode: the analyst plays a major advisory role in strategy making; there is a systematic analysis of the costs and benefits of competing proposals; and there is a careful integration of decisions. The stable environment allows a somewhat mechanistic orientation, making it easier and safer for the firm to buffer itself from external uncertainties. It is too difficult to plan or to use sophisticated control systems when the ground rules keep changing.

What factors are likely to determine entrepreneurship here? Some might be tempted to say that these firms will be anything but entrepreneurial. But Planning firms often pursue a systematic, orderly process of innovation and product-market renewal. We anticipate that entrepreneurial activity will be mainly a function of the strategy pursued by Planning firms—hence our title "the strategic imperative." Specifically we hypothesize the following (variable names are italicized):

(H2-1) The *explicitness* and *integration* of product-market strategies are likely to be the critical factors influencing entrepreneurship. Vague and disjointed strategies increase the natural danger that Planners will begin to focus exclusively on internal matters such as operating efficiency.[1] If there is a clear and well articulated product-market strategy, it draws attention to the big picture: the distinctive competence of the firm, its ultimate mission, its business scope, and present and future target markets (Ansoff [2]; Steiner [47]).[2]

(H2-2) Because power is centralized, the *locus of control* of the chief executive is again expected to be important, as was the case in the Simple firms.

(H2-3) Planners' efforts to buffer themselves from their environment make them far less responsive to it (Burns and Stalker [4]; Mintzberg [34]). Thus we predict that environmental *dynamism* and *hostility* will *not* correlate significantly with entrepreneurship for samples composed of Planners.

(H2-4) Only planned, regular, and predictable entrepreneurship is palatable to Planners. This can be as easily undertaken by firms with 'mechanistic' structures as those with 'organic' ones (the former are *centralized*, have restricted hierarchial *communication*, high *integration*, low *differentiation* and tight formal *controls*). Either type of structure will do. Thus for Planners, we predict that our structural variables will *not* relate significantly to the level of entrepreneurship. This goes against the predictions of Zaltman et al. [54], Lawrence and Lorsch [24], and indeed most of the literature on organizations.

To recap, the level of entrepreneurship in the Planning firms is expected to be largely a function of the explicitness and integration of the product-market strategy. Clear, explicit, well-integrated strategies may make executives focus regularly on the need for product-market renewal. Vague, implicit product-market strategies increase the likelihood that Planners will develop too much of a preoccupation with operating problems and efficiency at the expense of giving sufficient attention to the prospects of products and markets.

Type Three. Organic Firms: The Environmental and Structural Imperatives

These are perhaps the most interesting firms highlighted by recent literature. Their structures correspond roughly to those of Mintzberg's [34] adhocracies, as well as

---

[1] In the Simple firms, an explicit strategy is not needed to induce innovation. The dominant leader's private visions of the future are enough to guide the firm. But in the larger and more complex Planning firms many managers must be involved in decision making. Unless product-market strategies are articulated explicitly enough to guide these managers, the firm can lose its sense of direction and thus begin to ignore product-market posture. The Planner's natural compulsion to pursue efficient and mechanical operation will then thwart entrepreneurship and the status quo will prevail. The focus becomes operations instead of mission, maintenance instead of progression.

[2] It can be argued that product-market strategies might be explicit and integrated but still oriented towards the status quo. There can, in other words, be an explicit strategy of conservatism. But we think this is unlikely in the case of most Planners. Any focus on product-market mission by the many staff technocrats and experts will induce them to be more concerned with seizing innovative opportunities and avoiding obsolescence. Decisions tend to be made analytically in these firms, and product-market analysis will tend to lead to product-market entrepreneurship (Ansoff [2]). Where product-market strategies are too vague and fragmented to command the attention of managers, the focus will more likely be upon the production and operating problems which are an abiding obsession in Planning firms.

Burns and Stalker's [4] organic firms, and Lawrence and Lorsch's [24] plastics firms, while strategy making behavior recalls Mintzberg's [33] adaptive mode. The firms tend to operate in dynamic environments where customer tastes, product-service technologies, and competitive weapons often change unpredictably. Because product-market innovations are common in such firms, managers often find themselves dealing with a rather diverse array of customers, that is, with a heterogeneous market.

To cope with the very complex environment firms adopt a rather organic structure. Organizations try to be responsive to their challenging environments. Adaptation is facilitated by five structural devices. First, much authority is delegated to lower level personnel. The adaptive task is too difficult to be done exclusively at the top of the firms. Second, much use is made of technocrats such as scientists and engineers in creating product and technological innovations (Hage and Aiken [15]). Third, firms engage in much scanning of the environment to discover important challenges and opportunities (Carter and Williams [6]). Fourth, firms are highly differentiated as diverse contingencies posed by the environment require individuals and departments with very different abilities (Wilson [53]; Lawrence and Lorsch [24]). Finally, there is a need for extensive and open internal communication among organizational members so that they can work jointly on complex innovative projects (Thompson [48]; Litwak [26]; Burns and Stalker [4]).

Strategy making epitomizes Mintzberg's [33] adaptive mode. It emphasizes careful but quick analysis of issues and is performed by many levels of managers. There is often no time for lengthy studies. Also, planning horizons cannot be very long in the face of the turbulent environment. Finally, strategies cannot be explicitly conceptualized *or* articulated since they must change rapidly. In fact, complex, detailed and tightly integrated strategies may be too confining for Organic firms (Mintzberg [33]).

Because Organic firms strive to be adaptive, their entrepreneurial efforts will reflect the demands of their environments and the capacities of their structures (hence the "environmental-structural imperative"). More specifically:

(H3-1) The more *dynamic* and *hostile* the environment, the more firms will be entrepreneurial. Dynamism and hostility require innovation. Since firms try to tailor their actions to the environment, they will gear entrepreneurial efforts to the demands of their markets (Burns and Stalker [4]; Thompson [49]).

(H3-2) Structure will importantly influence entrepreneurship. For example, delegation (*decentralization*) of authority to lower level experts allows the most knowledgeable people to help the firm adapt and innovate (Hage and Aiken [15]). The use of *technocrats* increases the store of innovative ideas. Organizational *differentiation* provides the mix of skills necessary to develop these ideas (Lawrence and Lorsch [24]). And finally, effective and open internal *communications* bring together those with different skills so that they can collaborate effectively on innovative projects (Litwak [26]; Rogers and Shoemaker [41]).

(H3-3) The *locus of control* of the CEO will have *little* influence upon entrepreneurship in Organic firms. Power is decentralized and the entrepreneurial effort is carried out by many lower level managers such as technocrats and department heads.

(H3-4) While in Planning firms *an explicit* and *integrated strategy* should boost entrepreneurship, this is less true of Organic firms. Consciousness of strategy may unite the efforts of technocrats and help them to work together more effectively toward a central goal. But extremely detailed, tightly integrated, longstanding product-market strategies will serve to constrain adaptive behavior and curtail entrepreneurship. They will reduce the flexibility so necessary to Organic firms.

To summarize, the two key classes of entrepreneurial determinants in Organic firms will be environment and structure. The more challenging the firms' environments, the

DANNY MILLER

TABLE I

Expected Type Attributes and Hypothesized Determinants of Entrepreneurship

	Simple: Att.[1]	Hyp.[2]	Planning: Att.	Hyp.	Organic: Att.	Hyp.
Size	c[3] Small		c Large		Medium	
Locus of Control		(−)		(−)		(0)
Environment						
Dynamism	Medium		Low	(0)	High	(+)
Heterogeneity	Low		Medium		High	(+)
Hostility	High		Low	(0)	Medium	(+)
Organization/Structure						
Scanning	Low	(+)	Medium		High	(+)
Controls	Low		c High	(0)	Medium	
Communication				(0)	c High	(+)
Resources	Low		High		Medium	
Centralization	c High	(+)	c Medium	(0)	c Low	(−)
Technocratization	Low	(+)	Medium		c High	(+)
Differentiation	Low		Medium	(0)	High	(+)
Integration	Low		High	(0)	Medium	
Strategy/ Decision Making						
Analysis	Low		High		Medium	
Futurity	Low		c High		Medium	
Explicitness of Product-Market Strategy	Low		High	(+)	Medium	(+)
Strategic Integration	Medium		High	(+)	Low	(−)
Entrepreneurial Imperative	Leadership (personality, power & knowledge)		Strategy		Environment & Structure	

[1] *Att.* stands for attributes of the types. High, Medium and Low are ranks relative to the other two groups. Where the space is left blank, the authors discussing the types tend to be noncommital.

[2] *Hyp.* signifies hypothesized relationship with entrepreneurship. Signs indicate an expected positive (+) or negative (−) correlation with entrepreneurship on the basis of our hypotheses. (0) indicates that we expect an insignificant relationship. A blank space indicates 'no opinion.'

[3] Variables preceded by a 'c' are those that were used as classifactory criteria.

greater their need to be entrepreneurial; the more organic their structures, the better they are able to recognize and fulfill this need.

Table I summarizes the features of the three types of firms and highlights the expected determinants of entrepreneurship in each. It is notable that for each type a different category of variables is expected to be related to the level of entrepreneurship: in the Simple firm it is the leader's personality, power and knowledge, in the Planning firm it is strategy and leader personality, and in the Organic firm it is environment and structure.

3. Methodology

The Variables and Questionnaires

In order to test the hypotheses derived in the last section we employed a lengthy questionnaire to gather information on variables of environment, organization structure, decision making style, strategy, and entrepreneurship. The questionnaire is available from the author. We measured a number of distinct indicants and aspects for each variable to ensure that it would be broadly and thoroughly represented. Scale

TABLE II

Selection Criteria and Variable Means and Standard Deviations for the Types

		Type One: Simple Arms		Type Two: Planning Firms		Type Three: Organic Firms		All Types	
	Selection Criteria:	N. of Employees < 500 Centralization > 5		N. of Emp. > 500 Controls & Futurity > 4 Centralization & Analysis > 4		Centrali- zation < 4 Technocra- tization > 4 Communication > 4			
	Sample Size	18		18		13		52	
		M.	S.D.	M.	S.D.	M.	S.D.	M.	S.D.
Cronbach Alpha	Variables								
	Sales ($MM)	18	33	405	923	493	518	230	639
	N. of Employees (00's)	2	3	44	100	31	36	22	66
	Locus of Con- trol of Leader	6.0	2.2	4.4	1.9	4.4	1.6	5.4	3.2
	Environment								
0.74	Dynamism	4.0	1.8	3.7	1.1	4.2	1.2	3.9	1.5
0.84	Heterogeneity	3.4	1.4	4.5	1.3	5.2	1.5	4.1	1.6
0.55	Hostility	4.4	1.3	4.0	1.0	4.2	1.0	4.2	1.1
	Organization/Structure								
0.74	Scanning	4.3	1.7	5.1	1.3	5.4	1.3	4.7	1.4
0.69	Controls	3.5	1.7	5.6	0.7	4.9	1.8	4.4	1.7
0.87	Communication	5.0	0.9	4.9	1.2	4.5	1.5	4.9	1.1
0.68	Resources	4.1	1.6	4.9	1.0	4.5	1.2	4.3	1.3
0.79	Centralization	6.2	0.4	5.0	0.8	3.5	0.7	5.1	1.2
0.69	Technocratization	3.2	1.9	4.6	1.4	5.4	1.1	4.0	1.7
0.88	Differentiation	2.7	1.0	4.0	1.7	4.8	1.4	3.5	1.8
0.71	Integration	4.9	1.3	5.2	1.0	4.3	1.2	4.8	1.2
	Decision Making/Strategy								
0.62	Analysis	3.6	1.3	4.8	0.9	4.7	1.4	4.0	1.3
0.83	Futurity	3.4	1.5	5.5	0.5	4.2	1.7	4.1	1.5
N/A	Explicitness of Strategy	3.4	1.9	4.8	1.3	4.2	1.4	3.9	1.6
0.46	Strategic Inte- gration	4.5	1.2	4.7	1.0	4.2	1.1	4.3	1.1
	Entrepreneurship								
0.77	Innovation	3.2	1.8	3.8	1.3	4.1	1.6	3.5	1.6
0.81	Proactiveness	3.9	2.0	4.9	1.0	4.7	1.1	4.3	1.5
0.91	Risk Taking	3.2	1.3	3.9	1.1	3.8	1.1	3.6	1.2
0.88	Average (Entrep.)	3.4	1.3	4.2	0.8	4.2	1.1	3.8	1.2
0.74	Av. Cronbach Alpha for all variables								

items were averaged to obtain the variable scores. Table II presents the construct reliability indices of each of our variables. In every instance, the Cronbach alpha measure, which averaged 0.74 for all variables, well exceeded the guidelines set up by Van de Ven and Ferry [52, pp. 78–82] for measuring organizational attributes. The standard of comparison for scales were all other firms unless other polarities were specified.

There are many ways to describe personality, but we were concerned mainly with factors that relate to entrepreneurship. The literature points very strongly to "locus of control" (Rotter [42]) as a critical characteristic influencing entrepreneurial behavior. Shapero [46], Kets de Vries [21], and Miller, Kets de Vries, and Toulouse [32] have established that entrepreneurial behavior such as risk taking, innovation, and proactiveness are strongly associated with locus of control. Specifically, the more "internal" the executive, that is, the more he feels he has control over his environment and his destiny, the more entrepreneurial his behavior. In contrast, if he believes that outcomes influencing his life are principally due to chance or to elements beyond his control, he is much less likely to take risks or to be innovative and proactive. We measured locus of control using Rotter's [42] well-known internal-external scale.

Data Sample

Our data sample consists of 52 business firms that range in size from sales of less than $2,000,000 to those of over $1 billion. Mean sales are $237 million and the standard deviation is $649 million. The average number of employees is 2270. Firms are in industries as varied as retailing, furniture manufacturing, broadcasting, pulp and paper, food, plastics, electronics, chemicals, meatpacking, publishing, construction and transportation. No industry represents more than 8% of the sample. Still, we cannot pretend here to have a random sample since its geographic area is restricted to the Montreal region. The firms were chosen by teams of second-year MBA students according to convenience of access and the cooperativeness of the top level executives. However, because of the broad representation of types and sizes of businesses, and because no one type of firm dominates the sample, these exploratory findings should have a high degree of generality.

All responses to the questionnaire were obtained by interviews. This ensured that executives could have any vague items explained to them and it removed any problem of missing data. While it is difficult to estimate a response rate, most interviewing teams were able to obtain cooperation from the first company they contacted. About 30% of the teams approached two or three firms before they were able to gain admission to the firm to carry out their field study.

All respondents used in the analysis had the rank of Divisional Vice President or higher. In 67% of the cases, more than one respondent per firm completed the questionnaire. In such cases, the ratings of the highest ranking respondent were used. Where responses differed by more than two points on the scales among the respondents, responses were averaged. This happened for 8% of the scores. In 73% of the cases, the data was supplied by the chief executive. Inter-rater reliability was adequate across all of the variables. The scores of the raters were significantly correlated at beyond the 0.001 level of significance for all the variables. In cases of diversified and divisionalized companies, each division was treated as a separate entity to ensure that questions could be answered unambiguously. Thus, five of the "firms" in the sample were really the "divisions" of three different organizations. In every case the divisions represented profit centers and were controlled on the basis of their financial performance.

4. Validating the Typology

Because Mintzberg's [33], [34] work was conceptual rather than empirical, it was necessary to establish the predictiveness of the typology. Two methods were used to do this. The first classifies firms using only a few structural and strategy making characteristics, and then attempts to determine whether the remaining characteristics are in line with those attributed to each type. The second method entails performing analyses of variance to establish whether the groups of firms are significantly different from one another in the manner predicted.

Let us consider the first method of assessing the typology. Firms were classified into one of the three types (or as outliers) using a selection of attributes that Mintzberg

([33], [34] and personal communication) deemed central to each type. (It is likely however that other classification criteria could have been used without significantly altering our results.) Simple firms were classified according to their small size ($<$ 500 employees) and high centralization of power (score of >5 on the 7-point scale). Planning firms had to be large ($\geqslant$ 500 employees) and centralized (score of $\geqslant$ 4) and to make use of sophisticated controls (>4), long-range planning (futurity >4) and much analysis of decisions (>4). Finally, Organic firms were classified as those having a low centralization score ($\leqslant$ 4), open internal communications ($\geqslant$ 4) and high technocratization (>4).

Having classified the firms using these criteria, the problem was to assess the predictiveness of the typology. In other words, given the classification is it possible to accurately predict the characteristics of the types summarized in Table I? This was easy to establish. We trichotomized our variables into low, high and medium ranks. These terms signified that relative to other groups the average variable score for the type was the lowest of the three, the highest, or "in between" respectively. For three variables (controls, technocratization and futurity) the *high* rank was used as a classification criterion. It was thus necessary only to predict the low and medium ranks for these variables.

As we can see from comparing Table I and Table II, 35 out of the 37 ranks were classified correctly. We erred only on the integration variable. The probability of arriving at so accurate a classification under the null hypothesis of ignorance was less than 0.00001, a most significant *p*-value. Thus our typology seems to be quite predictive.

We can get some intuitive grasp of the face validity of the typology by taking the example of the Simple firm. The classification criteria for admission to this category were small size and extremely centralized power. It is encouraging that the group of companies defined by these criteria had all of the following attributes that were listed on Table I and in our descriptions. That is, as we can see from Table II, compared to Planning and Organic firms, Simple firms were in a less heterogeneous and more hostile market, had the smallest technocratic component, and were the least differentiated. Their use of control systems was minimal, while their decision making was intuitive (i.e. the least analytical). Strategies were the least explicitly articulated. The same predictiveness was also manifested for the Planning and Organic groups.

The second method of validating the typology consisted of a series of one-way analyses of variance. Since the means of variables used to define groups were forced to differ significantly across types, these were of course excluded from our analysis. However, where a variable was used to define only one group, a *t*-test was used to compare the means on that variable for the remaining groups to see if they differed as predicted. The results were presented on Table III. As we can see the analysis of variance shows the variable means of groups to be significantly different in the predicted direction according to the *F*-statistic for heterogeneity, resources, differentiation, integration, analysis, explicitness of strategy, proactiveness, risk-taking and average entrepreneurship. The *t*-tests show significant differences along the controls, technocratization, and futurity variables. Thus, our groups of firms are significantly different along most attributes. Their characterization as Simple, Planning, and Organic types seems to be quite accurate.

5. Findings

We shall for purposes of relevance and brevity focus upon the relationships between the independent variables and our aggregate entrepreneurship variable. The latter is simply an arithmetic average of the scores on the innovation, proactiveness, and

DANNY MILLER

TABLE III

Analysis of Variance and t-Tests for the Three Types
for Nonclassificatory Variables[1]

	F-ratio[2]	t-statistic[3]	
Dynamism	1.0		
Heterogeneity	5.7**		
Hostility	1.2		
Scanning	1.8		
Controls		2.3*	(29)
Resources	2.9˙		
Technocratization		2.5**	(34)
Differentiation	6.1**		
Integration	2.9˙		
Analysis	6.2**		
Futurity		1.4˙	(29)
Explicitness of Strategy	5.9**		
Strategic Integration	0.8		
Innovation	0.7		
Proactiveness	3.8*		
Risk Taking	2.5˙		
Enterpreneurship	3.6*		

[1] Variables of size, communication, and centralization were omitted since these were used to classify firms or were not predicted to differ among types. Variables used to generate groups cannot be used to establish the predictiveness of any typology.

[2] The F-ratio presented has 2, 46 degrees of freedom. The symbols ˙, *, and ** indicate statistical significance at the 0.10, 0.05 and 0.01 levels respectively.

[3] Where a variable was used for purposes of classification for one group only, the differences in means for the other groups were tested using a t-test. The degrees of freedom are presented in brackets.

risk-taking variables. As we noted at the outset, the literature shows entrepreneurship to be a multidimensional concept comprising three dimensions: innovation, proactiveness, and risk taking (Toulouse [50]; Kets de Vries [21]). In general, theorists would not call a firm entrepreneurial if it changed its technology or product-line ("innovated" according to our terminology) simply by directly imitating competitors while refusing to take any risks. Some proactiveness would be essential as well. By the same token, risk-taking firms that are highly levered financially are not necessarily considered entrepreneurial. They must also engage in product-market or technological innovation. Thus our focus upon the composite dimension is intuitively reasonable.

The Cronbach Alpha coefficient for the seven-item entrepreneurial variable is 0.88. Also, the correlations between entrepreneurship and its component variables of innovation, proactiveness, and risk-taking are 0.82, 0.76, and 0.80 respectively (all correlations are significant at beyond the 0.001 level). Finally, in 79% (114/144) of the cases, correlations that are significant (not significant) between aggregate entrepreneurship and the independent variables are significant in the same direction (not significant) for innovation, proactiveness, and risk-taking variables.

In cases where the correlational findings for the aggregate entrepreneurial variable are not representative of most of its component variables, we shall mention this in the text. Readers who are interested in the relationships between the innovation, proactiveness, and risk-taking variables and the independent variables can find these in Appendix I.

The correlational and regression results are given on Tables IV and V. Stepwise regressions were run merely to isolate the joint effects of the key variables. The small

ENTREPRENEURSHIP CORRELATES IN THREE TYPES OF FIRMS   781

TABLE IV

Product-Moment Correlations of Variables with Entrepreneurship for Three Types

	Simple Firms	Planning Firms	Organic Firms	All Types
Locus of Control of Leader	− 0.66**[1]	− 0.43*	− 0.16	− 0.64**
Environment				
Dynamism	0.09	− 0.06	0.52*	0.35**
Heterogeneity	0.18	0.22	0.44˙	0.41**
Hostility	0.24	0.12	0.50*	0.26*
Organization/Structure				
Scanning	0.41*	0.21	− 0.01	0.26*
Controls	0.12	0.13	− 0.11	0.11
Communication	− 0.09	0.27	0.38˙	0.08
Resources	− 0.10	− 0.11	− 0.18	− 0.07
Centralization	0.40*	− 0.06	− 0.60*	− 0.01
Technocratization	0.51*	0.36˙	0.53*	0.46**
Differentiation	0.19	0.34˙	0.10	0.46**
Integration	0.31˙	−0.11	0.00	0.10
Decision Making/Strategy				
Analysis	− 0.10	0.20	0.42˙	0.19˙
Futurity	0.15	0.10	0.37˙	0.25*
Explicitness of				
Strategy	0.24	0.69**	0.43˙	0.39**
Strategic Integration	0.02	0.33˙	−0.31	− 0.09
Entrepreneurship				
Innovation				0.82**
Proactiveness				0.76**
Risk-Taking				0.80**

[1]The symbols ˙, *, and ** indicate that the correlations are significant at the 0.10, 0.05, and 0.01 levels respectively.

TABLE V

Multiple Regressions for Entrepreneurship in the Three Types of Firms

Simple Firms:
    Entrepreneurship = 0.31 − 0.35 Locus of Control + 0.84 Centralization*
        Beta: − 0.61   − 0.29
        Partial F: 11.1   2.5
           Overall $F = 8.03$, d.f. 2, 15, $p = 0.005$, $R = 0.72$, $R^2 = 0.52$, Adj.$R^2 = 0.45$

Planning Firms:
    Entrepreneurship = 1.40 + 0.41 Explicit. Strat. +0.19 Technoc'n.
        Beta: 0.68   0.33
        Partial F: 17.1   4.1
           Overall $F = 10.9$, d.f. 2, 15, $p = 0.005$, $R = 0.77$, $R^2 = 0.59$, Adj.$R^2 = 0.54$

Organic Firms:
    Entrepreneurship = 3.2 − 0.96 Centraliz'n. +0.53 Explicit. Strat. +0.40 Technoc'n.
        Beta: − 0.57   0.65   0.41
        Partial F: 13.3   19.6   6.7
           Overall $F = 13.8$, d.f. 3, 10, $p = 0.001$, $R = 0.91$, $R^2 = 0.82$, Adj.$R^2 = 0.76$

*In adding variables to the regression, a cutoff point of 2.0 was used for the partial F ratio. Variables not meeting this criterion would not explain a significant amount of variance even at the 0.10 level.

sample sizes make the regression results quite tentative. A cutoff of 2.0 for the partial F ratio was used to ensure that only the most relevant variables would be included. Before proceeding with a discussion of each hypothesis it might be useful to summarize the findings. In general, most of the hypotheses are confirmed and there is a high degree of explanation of the dependent variable for each type.

Simple firms show the expected high correlations of entrepreneurship with locus of control and centralization, as well as with scanning and technocratization. No other correlations are significant. Thus, all variables contributing to entrepreneurship in Simple firms appear to be leader-related, namely, personality, power, and knowledge from scanning and technical advice. Together, locus of control and centralization explain 52% of the variance in entrepreneurship.

As predicted, the major correlates of entrepreneurship for the *Planners* are the explicitness of strategy, and leader locus of control. Environmental and most structural variables seem to matter hardly at all, with the possible exceptions of technocratization and differentiation. The latter may provide the variety and expertise necessary for innovation. Explicitness of strategy and technocratization together explain 59% of the variance of entrepreneurship.

Finally, for Organic firms many structural, decision making, and environmental variables seem to correlate with entrepreneurship, while locus of control does not. Again this generally conforms with our predictions. Table V shows that collectively centralization, explicitness of strategy, and technocratization explain 82% of the variance in the dependent variable.

6. Discussion

Simple Firms and the Leadership Imperative

The findings presented in Tables IV and V leave little doubt that leadership related factors are the most correlated with entrepreneurial activity in the Simple firms. These are of at least three varieties: the leader's personality as portrayed by his locus of control score, his power, and his knowledge of markets and products. We can discuss each factor in turn.

H1-1. Our hypothesis 1-1 is strongly borne out. Locus of control is very significantly correlated with entrepreneurial activity in the Simple firm. The more "internal" the leader, that is, the more he believes events to be subject to his own control and influence, the more likely it is for his firm to undertake entrepreneurial projects. This is consistent with the findings of Shapero [46] and Miller, Kets de Vries and Toulouse [32]. In contrast, "external" leaders will feel that events are beyond their influence; they will be more passive in dealing with their environments. Since leaders dominate the Simple firms so thoroughly, their personalities are a critical factor, indeed, according to our findings, the *most* critical factor in determining entrepreneurship. As we can see from Table IV, personality far overrides the impact of environmental, structural, and decision making factors upon entrepreneurship in the Simple firms. Here, entrepreneurship requires an entrepreneur.

H1-2. Hypothesis 1-2 correctly predicted that centralization would correlate with entrepreneurship in the Simple firm. The more powerful the leader, the more entrepreneurial the company. This supports the arguments of Hage and Dewar [16], Normann [35] and Thompson [49], cited earlier, but not those of Burns and Stalker [4], Thompson [48] and Litwak [26]. Having leadership divided among several partners of a small firm can paralyze action when there are dissenting views. The partners may veto one anothers' proposals so that no entrepreneurial programs can be implemented. In contrast, where a leader has unchallenged authority, he can confidently make entrepreneurial decisions without having to be concerned about their ultimate acceptability to other managers. As we shall see, however, things are very different in Organic firms.

H1-3. As expected, we found a positive correlation between scanning and entrepreneurship (also suggested by Tushman [51] , Carter and Williams [6], and Rogers and

Shoemaker [41]). Because in Simple firms the entrepreneurial task usually falls upon one person, his knowledge of the environment, that is, of customer wants, sources of supply, and competitor strategies, will provide the information necessary for an aggressive competitive strategy. Notice from Appendix I that scanning does not correlate with innovation, merely with proactiveness and risk taking. In our sample of Simple Firms scanning sometimes resulted in reducing the level of innovation to avoid the depletion of resources.

There is also a positive correlation between technocratization and entrepreneurship. Where leaders are frequently in touch with scientists, engineers or even marketing experts, they are more likely to become informed of new product opportunities and to engage in entrepreneurial activity. Also, technocrats enjoy working at the forefront of their fields and want to develop professionally. They may thus try to sell the entrepreneur on new ideas so that they can have more variety and challenge at their jobs (Hage and Aiken [15]; Zaltman et al. [54]).

Moving beyond our original hypotheses, it is noteworthy that in Simple firms, entrepreneurship is so very tied up with the leader's personality, power, and information that *almost nothing else seems to count*. Neither environment, structure, nor decision making styles seem to correlate with entrepreneurship.

Simple firms could be entrepreneurial in stable environments and conservative in dynamic ones. Environment just did not seem to matter. During the course of interviews, the chief executives of several small firms claimed not to belong to any industry. They said their firms were unique and followed a niche strategy. These men tended not to view industry factors as constraints. Entrepreneurship seemed to be much more a function of the leader's goals and character than of external events.

The structural variables so often identified in the literature as being facilitators of entrepreneurship also seemed extraneous in the context of the Simple firm. For example, internal communication, differentiation, and integration were uncorrelated with entrepreneurship, contradicting the arguments of Burns and Stalker [4], Lawrence and Lorsch [24] and others. One possible explanation for this is that in Simple firms acts of entrepreneurship and innovation also tend to be simple. They do not involve complex projects that require the collaboration of diverse groups of specialists. The low level administrative complexity does not call for elaborate structures. Entrepreneurship can be the domain of one man. For the same reason, the analytical, future-oriented, integrated strategies advocated by Ansoff [2], Ackoff [1], and Steiner [47] seem to play no role in boosting entrepreneurship in Simple firms. These techniques are required mainly when the innovative project is complex to design and administer, not when it can be handled by one or two top executives.

To conclude, our hypotheses about the Simple firm are borne out. Our use of the phrase "leadership imperative" to describe the genesis of entrepreneurship seems appropriate.

Planning Firms and the Strategic Imperative

Earlier, we postulated that for Planners two types of obstacles must be surmounted before entrepreneurial activity can take place. The first is the tendency to focus exclusively inwards in the pursuit of efficiency and operating stability. The second is the tendency to become monolithic, to concentrate only upon the production function of the firm. The first tendency can produce an automaticity of operation that causes entrepreneurial activities to be neglected. The second may accord too much power to those who dislike the disruptive nature of organizational or product-market renewal.

Our results in Tables IV and V show that there are four safeguards against both tendencies: the two most significant ones, explicitness of strategy and top executive

784   DANNY MILLER

locus of control were hypothesized. The others, differentiation and technocratization, were not.

H2-1.   This hypothesis is strongly confirmed by our data. There are indeed high correlations of entrepreneurship with the explicitness of strategy and strategic integration variables. Sporadic, disruptive bursts of unpredictable innovation may be unpalatable to Planners. But regular, predetermined entrepreneurial activity which follows an explicit master plan can be more readily systematized and prepared for. It can be fit more easily into the operations of the "machine" since its scope and dimensions are carefully defined to begin with. Instead of having to adapt to uncertain and unforeseen challenges, the firm can broaden its product-market field in a planned and consistent direction. This approach is used by firms such as ITT (Sampson [43]) and IBM (Rogers [40]). However, it can only occur where strategies are explicitly articulated, well established and integrated.

When product-market strategies have been explicitly formulated, and when these established strategies strongly and regularly guide decision-making, executives will continually be reminded of the broader objectives of the firm. They will think more of product-market renewal and of the need to incorporate entrepreneurial activity in an orderly way (Ansoff [2]). The tendency towards conservatism will have been combatted as the firm begins to stress growth and opportunity over the efficiency and stability of internal operations.

H2-2.   As predicted, another correlate of entrepreneurship in the Planning sample is the leader's locus of control. Because strategy making power is quite centralized, the personality of the top executive plays a key role in determining entrepreneurship, for much the same reasons that were given in the analysis of the Simple firm. The CEO can overcome the obstacles of automaticity and a monolithic staff with his innovative directives. It is notable, however, that the correlation between locus of control and entrepreneurship is less significant in Planning firms than in Simple firms, probably because Planning firms are more elaborate and many individuals besides the CEO get involved in strategy making. The leader's role and influence are reduced so his personality is no longer quite so critical in determining entrepreneurship.

Locus of control is not however correlated with the innovation component of entrepreneurship in Planning firms (cf. Appendix I). Innovation is a complex process in large firms and so is likely to be influenced by the excellence of technocrats and R & D departments. While the leader can himself set the tone for risk taking and competitive aggressiveness, his personality must be complemented by the skills of others in order to boost innovation.

H2-3.   Hypothesis 2-3 is strongly supported: the environment does not serve as a stimulus to entrepreneurship. Planning firms try to operate mechanically. Thus they buffer their operating cores from the environment (Mintzberg [34]). Extensive controls, plans, and close sub-unit integration induce smooth and regular functioning, while a stable, munificent environment and ample slack resources make such functioning possible. Litwak [26] discusses the inability of such rule-bound, mechanical structures to respond to nonroutine events. The organization starts to ignore the environment by design, erecting elaborate and rigid "castles" (Hedberg, Nystrom and Starbuck [19]). This in turn causes it to ignore the environment by *necessity* since there is no longer sufficient flexibility to adjust to unpredictable external pressures.

Possible exceptions to this trend can be found in the significant relationships shown in Appendix I between innovation and environmental hostility and heterogeneity. We believe these may be due to the effect of the large organization *upon* its environment rather than vice-versa. That is, by innovating, many firms enter into different segments of the market, boosting heterogeneity. They also create greater challenges for competitors who usually decide to fight back. So competition escalates.

H2-4. Hypothesis 2-4 was only partially confirmed. As we predicted, most structural variables do not correlate significantly with entrepreneurship in Planning firms. The regulated and planned entrepreneurial projects of Planners may be just as compatible with mechanistic as with organic structures. For example, open communications or extensive decentralization are not necessary to very orderly and structured entrepreneurship. To our surprise, however, two structural variables did seem to be important to entrepreneurship: differentiation and technocratization (cf. Table IV).

Differentiation allows a greater diversity of talent and experience to co-exist within the organization. When managers collectively are familiar with different product lines, technologies, and areas of expertise, their diversified bank of experience may help them to generate and implement more entrepreneurial ideas (Hoffman and Maier [20]; Wilson [53]). Familiarity with diverse markets can combine with knowledge of assorted production techniques and design procedures to suggest interesting innovation opportunities. Conservatism can also be combatted by hiring technocrats such as scientists and design engineers. These individuals may collectively constitute an effective pressure group that lobbies *for* change in the face of the production and workflow design people who lobby against it (Zaltman, Duncan, and Holbek [54]).

But the above results are highly tentative. It is true that correlations of entrepreneurship with differentiation and technocratization were significant at the 0.10 level. However, we can see from Appendix I that the correlations were not significant for the proactiveness and risk-taking components of entrepreneurship. In other words, technocratization and differentiation are correlated *only* with innovation. Perhaps this is because in Planning firms, technocrats rather than chief executives are responsible for most of the innovation. Innovation may be greatly facilitated by technocratization and the diversity of managerial personnel. But risk taking and proactiveness are more strongly influenced by the explicitness of product-market strategy and the personality of the leader.

It is now possible to summarize the findings for the Planning firms. We stressed earlier that Planners make an effort to buffer themselves from their environments. Thus they do not gear their levels of entrepreneurship to the external circumstances which they face. Neither environmental dynamism, heterogeneity nor hostility relate significantly to entrepreneurship. Instead, entrepreneurial activity depends upon *internal* initiative. We argued that this initiative comes largely from the product-market strategy and the personality of the leader. The "strategic imperative" seems to be borne out for the Planning sample.

Organic Firms and the Environmental/Structural Imperatives

H3-1. We hypothesized that Organic firms would be adaptive; that they would tailor their levels of entrepreneurial activity to the demands of the environment. This is strongly reflected by the results in Table IV. Dynamism and hostility are significantly correlated with entrepreneurship. This finding is not surprising. It is much in line with the predictions of Burns and Stalker [4], and their followers (Miller [29], Harvey and Mills [18], Cooper [10], Downs [12, p. 172]). Indeed researchers have come to expect that organizations will adjust to challenges by innovating and updating their strategies. What *is* surprising is that Organic firms are the *only* ones in our sample that seem to gear their innovative and entrepreneurial responses to their environments. Simple firms and Planning firms do not.

It is interesting also that environmental heterogeneity is related to entrepreneurship. But here, the direction of causality is especially ambiguous. It may be that market heterogeneity gives managers broader experience so that they perceive more entrepreneurial opportunities. Firms may begin to apply lessons learned in one market to their other markets. Conversely, entrepreneurial activity may cause a growth in product-lines or entry into more diverse markets, thereby boosting heterogeneity. Since the last possibility seems to apply equally well to Simple and Planning groups which do *not* show a significant correlation between entrepreneurship and heterogeneity, we may very tentatively favour the first causal direction.

H3-2.   The hypothesis that many structural variables would correlate highly with entrepreneurship in Organic firms was generally confirmed. Organic firms face the most dynamic and hostile environments and, unlike Planners, make deliberate efforts to be open and responsive to the external challenges they face. This involves making quick responses which cannot be well planned or programmed, and requires *ad hoc* collaboration among diverse groups of specialists and technocrats as new products or technologies are developed. An Organic structure thus becomes critical in mediating between environment and entrepreneurship (Burns and Stalker [4]). Table IV shows that many structural variables seem to be correlated with entrepreneurship. Technocratization (Hage and Aiken [15]), delegation of authority (Thompson [48]), and open internal communications (Burns and Stalker [4]) all seem to induce firms to engage in entrepreneurial endeavours. They make decsion makers aware of the need for change and provide the expertise, resources, and collaborative framework necessary to do so.

It is instructive that *de*centralization rather than centralization is related to entrepreneurship in the Organic firms. This is the opposite of what we found for Simple firms and vindicates the predictions of Burns and Stalker [4], Read [38], Thompson [48] and Hage and Aiken [15, pp. 510–511]. It seems the controversy over the influence of centralization shows hope of being resolved if we control for the type of firm. Where the firm and the innovative task are simple, having one powerful man in control speeds things up and avoids political obstacles to change. But where the adaptive task and the environment are as complex as they are in Organic firms, it is impossible for the leader to effectively shoulder a major portion of the burden of entrepreneurship. It is necessary for authority to be shared with those who are in the best position to devise, understand and implement innovations. Power is useless to entrepreneurship when capability is lacking.

We were quite surprised that scanning and differentiation did not correlate more highly with entrepreneurship and are at a loss to explain this convincingly. Most of the firms in the Organic sample scored high on these variables. Perhaps then the threshold levels of the variables were attained and they could no longer induce or facilitate entrepreneurship. For example, it may be that once differentiation is high enough to combat any monolithic tendency that lies in the way of innovation, it ceases to have any effect. Certainly further research is needed on these questions.

H3-3.   Hypothesis 3-3 was also confirmed. Because decision making power is so diffuse in Organic firms, the personality of the leader does not have a significant impact upon entrepreneurship which is performed by many individuals at many levels of the organization. The chief executive does not dominate Organic firms as he does Simple or Planning firms. Thus entrepreneurial activity seems more a function of the nature of the environment and the adequacy of the organization structure for innovation. It is not determined by personality.

H3-4.   We can turn now to our final hypothesis. We expected that an explicit and well articulated product-market strategy would help to give managers of Organic firms some integrated vision of where to go, thereby facilitating the harmonious collaboration among those working on entrepreneurial endeavours. Such a strategy helps to avoid fragmentation and divided goals, and thus ensures a more concerted entrepreneurial effort. .This indeed seems to be the case according to the figures of Table IV.

The strategic integration variable may have the opposite effect however. It reflects the extent to which an *established* strategy tends to guide decision making and is resistant to change. In Organic firms, the turbulent environment dictates that strategies must constantly be revised and updated. Strategies cannot be rigid without becoming anachronistic and interfering with the process of innovation (hence the weak negative correlation). Recall that strategic rigidity and stability were not harmful in the calm settings of the Planners. Perhaps they made entrepreneurial product-market objectives that much clearer and more compelling. But rigidity seems out of place on Organic firms and may hinder their adaptive efforts.

The decision-making variables of analysis and futurity also appear to be significantly associated with entrepreneurship. It may be that the Organic firms only become entrepreneurial in order to meet and exploit external challenges. This requires a careful analysis of the environment, the methodical selection of the best plan from among different possible courses of action, and the prediction of market-related factors. Decision-making variables have much the same impact as communication, centralization, and technocratization in helping the firm to better understand external contingencies and to adequately provide for them.

To conclude our discussion of the Organic firms, we should point out that the focus upon an environmental-structural imperative for entrepreneurship is incomplete. All environmental and most of the predicted structural variables did in fact correlate with entrepreneurship. But the decision making variables of analysis and futurity seemed also to be important, as did the two strategy variables. *All* classes of variables seemed to be related to entrepreneurship in Organic firms.

Perhaps this is because the Organic firms have so many interdependencies among all classes of variables. Given that their goal is to adapt to the environment, the nature of environment will influence structure and strategy. Strategy and structure can in turn influence decision making and entrepreneurship. In other words, in Organic firms there may be tightly interdependent constellations of variables. For example, highly dynamic and uncertain environments will breed technocratic, decentralized, organic structures, flexible but well-articulated strategies, a great analytical effort to master uncertainty, and a high level of entrepreneurship. In stable and more predictable environments, most of these variables will shift. There will be fewer technocrats, more centralization, less internal communication, less analytical decision making, more rigid strategies, and less entrepreneurship (Khandwalla [22]).

7. Conclusion

In our discussion we have often referred to entrepreneurial "determinants" and "imperatives". These causal terms were used simply to make our conjectures more coherent. Unfortunately, the correlational data give us no adequate grounds for inferring causality. There remains much doubt about the direction of influence between entrepreneurship and the "independent" variables. There can however be little doubt about the truth of the central thesis of the paper: namely, that entrepreneurship is integrally related to variables of environment, structure, strategy, and leader personality, and that these relationships vary systematically and logically from one type of firm to another. Miller and Friesen [31] pursue this theme further.

It is instructive to now turn back to Table IV and examine its final column of correlations. As we can see, any exclusive focus upon a sample-wide analysis would have concealed the dramatic differences that occurred among our three subsamples. The aggregated sample reveals, for example, that there is a strong relationship between locus of control and entrepreneurship. This is just as Shapero [46] and Miller, Kets de

Vries, and Toulouse [32] would have predicted. But while the relationship holds true for Simple and Planning firms, it is not true for Organic firms. Similarly, environment is shown to have many significant relationships with entrepreneurship, again bearing out the literature; but most of the significance is due to the adaptive Organic firms. Planners' entrepreneurial activity is not influenced by the environment.

Another misleading aggregate result is the completely insignificant correlation shown between entrepreneurship and centralization. This seems to have been due to two dramatically opposed results: a significant positive correlation for the Simple firms, and a significant negative correlation for the Organic firms.

The only uniformly significant result is that between technocratization and entrepreneurship. It seems that no matter what kind of firm we are dealing with, the presence of technocrats will boost entrepreneurship. Their scientific interests, expertise and desire for learning and career development may cause them to perceive and to wish to implement ideas for innovation and organizational renewal. But for this, as well as for many of our other findings, the reverse causal direction is also plausible, namely, that entrepreneurship generates complex innovative projects that require firms to hire technocrats.

The theme of the paper as well as its central finding seem to have practical importance. Different firms probably do require very different kinds of forces to

APPENDIX I

Product-Moment Correlations of Variables with Entrepreneurship for Three Types

	Simple Firms				Planning Firms			
	ENT.	I.	P.	R.	ENT.	I.	P.	R.
Locus of Control of leader	−0.66**	−0.44*	−0.44*	−0.61**	−0.43*	−0.08	−0.42*	−0.45*
Environment								
1. Dynamism	0.09	0.09	0.05	0.05	−0.06	0.24	−0.06	−0.33˙
2. Heterogeneity	0.18	0.26	0.18	−0.13	0.22	0.46*	0.24	−0.27
3. Hostility	0.24	0.46*	−0.03	0.10	0.12	0.44*	0.00	−0.25
Organization/Structure								
4. Scanning	0.41*	0.03	0.44*	0.45*	0.21	0.18	0.32*	−0.04
5. Controls	0.12	0.04	0.16	0.04	0.13	0.18	0.14	−0.06
6. Communication	−0.09	−0.29	−0.16	0.40*	0.27	0.02	−0.01	0.54**
7. Resources	−0.10	−0.19	−0.11	0.13	−0.11	0.03	−0.01	−0.27
8. Centralization	0.40*	0.31˙	0.24	0.35˙	−0.06	−0.28	0.14	0.06
9. Technocratization	0.51*	0.45*	0.33˙	0.34˙	0.36˙	0.47*	0.19	0.04
10. Differentiation	0.19	0.29	−0.02	0.17	0.34˙	0.55**	0.07	0.03
11. Integration	0.31˙	0.06	0.09	0.69**	−0.11	−0.42*	−0.28	0.48
Decision Making/ Strategy								
12. Analysis	−0.10	−0.28	0.03	0.07	0.20	0.24	0.13	0.04
13. Futurity	0.15	0.18	−0.10	0.33˙	0.10	0.13	−0.06	0.10
14. Explicitness of Product-Market Strategy	0.24	0.15	0.22	0.18	0.69**	0.51*	0.54**	0.46*
15. Strategic Integration	0.02	−0.03	0.08	−0.02	0.33˙	0.10	0.34˙	0.29
16. Enterpreneurship								
16a. Innovation	0.74**				0.70**			
16b. Proactiveness	0.74**				0.68**			
16c. Risk-Taking	0.72**				0.72**			

The symbols ˙, *, and ** indicate that the correlations are significant at the 0.10, 0.05, and 0.01 levels respectively.

stimulate entrepreneurship. There seem to be very few panaceas for promoting entrepreneurial activity. In Simple firms the focus may have to be upon the leader. If he has the wrong personality or inadequate power, entrepreneurship will be rare. In Planning firms, entrepreneurship may best be stimulated by explicit entrepreneurial product-market strategies, strategies which ritualize and systematize innovation and entrepreneurship. This will ensure that entrepreneurship is focussed upon in addition to the routine internal operating matters. It will also minimize the disruptiveness of entrepreneurship, a trait that is particularly unpalatable to firms that try to function mechanically. Finally, Organic firms may tend to be entrepreneurial according to the demands of their environments and the capacities of their structures. Any change agent wishing to stimulate entrepreneurship would probably be wise to focus upon these distinctions. The need to seek out common organizational types before making predictions about behaviour and performance is a topic pursued in much greater detail by Miller and Friesen [31].[3]

[3] The author would like to thank Professors Peter H. Friesen, Jean-Marie Toulouse, Manfred F. R. Kets de Vries, and Henry Mintzberg for their comments on an earlier draft of this paper. This research was supported in part by grants EQ 1162 of the Government of Quebec, and by John Labatt Ltd.

APPENDIX I (*continued*)

Product-Moment Correlations of Variables with Entrepreneurship for Three Types

| | Organic Firms | | | | All Types | | |
ENT.	I.	P.	R.	ENT.	I.	P.	R.
− 0.16	− 0.01	− 0.29	− 0.20	− 0.64**	− 0.45	− 0.70	− 0.62
0.52*	0.48*	0.38˙	0.47*	0.35**	0.36**	0.20˙	0.16
0.44˙	0.38*	0.60*	0.17	0.41**	0.49**	0.35**	0.15
0.50*	0.60*	0.29	0.33	0.26*	0.43**	0.02	0.04
− 0.01	0.03	0.21	− 0.27	0.26*	0.08	0.36**	0.18
− 0.11	− 0.08	0.06	− 0.26	0.11	0.07	0.19	0.05
0.38˙	0.29	0.01	0.65**	0.08	0.01	− 0.03	0.39**
− 0.18	− 0.11	0.01	− 0.38˙	− 0.07	− 0.05	− 0.07 −	− 0.01
− 0.60*	− 0.44˙	− 0.44˙	− 0.69**	− 0.01	− 0.03	− 0.16 −	− 0.13
0.53*	0.54*	0.24	0.46˙	0.46**	0.44**	0.34**	0.27*
0.10	0.08	0.14	0.03	0.46**	0.48**	0.24*	0.29*
0.00	− 0.06	− 0.15	0.23	0.10	− 0.03	− 0.04	0.36
0.42˙	0.50*	0.42˙	0.11	0.19˙	0.10	0.20˙	0.18˙
0.37˙	0.40˙	0.48*	0.06	0.25*	0.21˙	0.15	0.26*
0.43˙	0.60*	0.44˙	− 0.01	0.39**	0.35**	0.30˙	0.27*
− 0.31	− 0.14	− 0.22	− 0.47	− 0.9	− 0.11	− 0.01 −	− 0.10
0.91**				0.82**			
0.86**				0.76**			
0.79**				0.80**			

References

1. ACKOFF, R. L., *A Concept of Corporate Planning*, Wiley Interscience, New York, 1970.
2. ANSOFF, H. I., *Corporate Strategy*, McGraw-Hill, New York, 1965.
3. AGUILAR, F., *Scanning the Business Environment*, Macmillan, New York, 1967.
4. BURNS, T. AND STALKER, G., *The Management of Innovation*, Tavistock, London, 1961.
5. CARPER, W. AND SNIZEK, W., "The Nature and Types of Organizational Taxonomies: An Overview," *Acad. Management Rev.*, Vol. 6 (1980), pp. 65–75.
6. CARTER, C. AND WILLIAMS, B., *Industry and Technical Progress: Factors Governing the Speed of Application of Science*, Oxford University Press, London, 1957.
7. COLE, A. H., "An Approach to the Study of Entrepreneurship," *J. Econom. History*, Suppl. VI. (1946), pp. 1–15.
8. COLLINS, O. AND MOORE, D. G., *The Organization Makers*, Appleton-Century-Crofts, New York, 1970.
9. COLLINS, O., MOORE, D. G. AND UNWALLA, D., *The Enterprising Man*, Bureau of Business and Economic Research, Graduate School of Business, Michigan State University, East Lansing, 1967.
10. COOPER, A. C., "Technical Entrepreneurship: What do We Know?," *Research and Development Management*, Vol. 3 (1973), pp. 59–64.
11. CROZIER, M., *The Bureaucratic Phenomenon*, Univ. of Chicago Press, Chicago, 1964.
12. DOWNS, A., *Inside Bureaucracy*, Little, Brown & Co., Boston, 1966.
13. FILLEY, A. AND HOUSE, R., *Managerial Process and Organizational Behavior*, Scott, Foresman, Glenview, Ill., 1969.
14. GALBRAITH, J. *Designing Complex Organizations*, Addison-Wesley, Reading, Mass., 1973.
15. HAGE, J. AND AIKEN, M., *Social Change in Complex Organizations*, Random House, New York, 1970.
16. —— AND DEWAR, R., "Elite Values versus Organizational Structure in Predicting Innovation," *Admin. Sci. Quart.*, Vol. 18 (1973), pp. 279–290.
17. HARTMAN, H., "Managers and Entrepreneurs: A Useful Distinction," *Admin. Sci. Quart.*, Vol. 3 (1959), pp. 429–451.
18. HARVEY, E. AND MILLS, R., "Patterns of Organizational Adaptation: A Political Perspective," in M. Zald (Ed.), *Power in Organizations*, Vanderbilt University Press, Nashville, Tenn., 1970.
19. HEDBERG, B., NYSTROM P, AND STARBUCK, W., "Camping in Seesaws: Prescriptions for a Self-Designing Organization," *Admin. Sci. Quart.*, Vol. 21 (1976), pp. 41–65.
20. HOFFMAN, L. R. AND MAIER, N. R. F., "Quality and Acceptance of Problem Solutions by Members of Homogeneous and Heterogeneous Groups," *J. Abnormal and Soc. Psychol.*, Vol. 62 (1961), pp. 401–407.
21. KETS DE VRIES, M. F. R., "The Entrepreneurial Personality: A Person at the Crossroads," *J. Management Stud.*, Vol. 14 (1977), pp. 34–57.
22. KHANDWALLA, P., *The Design of Organizations*, Harcourt, Brace, Jovanovich, New York, 1977.
23. KLATT, L., *Small Business Management: Essentials of Entrepreneurship*, Wadsworth, Belmont, Cal., 1973.
24. LAWRENCE, P. R. AND LORSCH, J., *Organization and Environment*, Harvard University Press, Boston, 1967.
25. LILES, P. R., *New Business Ventures and the Entrepreneur*, Irwin, Homewood, Ill., 1974.
26. LITWAK, E., "Models of Bureaucracy Which Permit Conflict," *Amer. J. Sociol.*, Vol. 67 (1961), pp. 177–184.
27. MARCH, J. G. AND SIMON, H. A., *Organizations*, Wiley, New York, 1958.
28. MILES, R. E. AND SNOW, C. C., *Organizational Strategy, Structure and Process*, McGraw-Hill, New York, 1978.
29. MILLER, D., "Strategy, Structure and Environment: Context Influences Upon Some Bivariate Associations," *J. Management Stud.*, Vol. 16 (1979), pp. 294–316.
30. —— AND FRIESEN, P. H., "Archetypes of Strategy Formulation," *Management Sci.*, Vol. 24 (1978), pp. 921–933.
31. —— AND FRIESEN, P. H., *Organizations: A Quantum View*, Prentice-Hall, Englewood Cliffs, N.J., in press.
32. ——, KETS DE VRIES, M. F. R. AND TOULOUSE, J.-M., "Top Executive Locus of Control and Its Relationship to Strategy, Environment and Structure," *Acad. Management J.*, Vol. 25 (1982), pp. 237–253.
33. MINTZBERG, H., "Strategy-Making in Three Modes," *California Management Rev.* (Winter 1973), pp. 44–53.
34. ——, *The Structuring of Organizations*, Prentice-Hall, Englewood Cliffs, N.J., 1979.
35. NORMANN, R., "Organizational Innovativeness: Product Variation and Reorientation," *Admin. Sci. Quart.*, Vol. 16 (1961). pp. 203–215.
36. PERROW, C., *Complex Organizations: A Critical Essay*, Scott, Foresman, Glenview, Ill., 1972.

37. PUGH, D. S. HICKSON, D. J. AND HININGS, C. R., "An Empirical Taxonomy of Structures of Work Organizations," *Admin. Sci. Quart.*, Vol. 14 (1969), pp. 115–126.
38. READ, W., "Upward Communication in Industrial Hierarchies," *Human Relations*, Vol. 15 (1962), pp. 3–15.
39. REDLICH, F., "The Origin of the Concepts of Entrepreneur and Creative Entrepreneur," *Explorations in Entrepreneurial History*, Vol. 1 (1949), pp. 145–166.
40. RODGERS, W., *Think: A Biography of the Watsons and IBM*, Stein & Day, New York, 1969.
41. ROGERS, E. M. AND SHOEMAKER, F., *Communication of Innovations: A Cross-Cultural Approach*, Free Press, New York, 1971.
42. ROTTER, J. B., "Generalized Expectancies for Internal Versus External Control of Reinforcement," *Psychol. Monographs*, Vol. 80 (1966), (1, Whole No. 609).
43. SAMPSON, A., *The Sovereign State of ITT*, Stein & Day, New York, 1973.
44. SAPOLSKY, H., "Organizational Structure and Innovation," *J. Business*, Vol. 40 (1967), pp. 497–510.
45. SCHUMPETER, J., *The Theory of Economic Development*, Cambridge University Press, Cambridge, 1934.
46. SHAPERO, A., "The Displaced, Uncomfortable Entrepreneur," *Psychology Today*, Vol. 11, No. 7 (November 1975), pp. 83–89.
47. STEINER, G., *Top Management Planning*, Macmillan, New York, 1969.
48. THOMPSON, V. A., *Modern Organization*, Knopf, New York, 1961.
49. THOMPSON, J. D., *Organizations in Action*, McGraw-Hill, New York, 1967.
50. TOULOUSE, J. M., *L'Entrepreneurship au Quebec*, Les Presses H. E. C., Montreal, 1980.
51. TUSHMAN, M. L., "Special Boundary Roles in the Innovation Process," *Admin. Sci. Quart.*, Vol. 22 (1977), pp. 587–605.
52. VAN DE VEN, A., AND FERRY, D., *Measuring and Assessing Organizations*, Wiley, New York, 1980.
53. WILSON, J. Q., "Innovation in Organization: Notes Toward a Theory," in J. D. Thompson (Ed.), *Approaches to Organizational Design*, Univ. of Pittsburgh Press, Pittsburgh, 1966, pp. 193–218.
54. ZALTMAN, G., DUNCAN, R. AND HOLBEK, J., *Innovations and Organizations*, Wiley, New York, 1973.

[17]

PREDICTORS AND
FINANCIAL OUTCOMES
OF CORPORATE
ENTREPRENEURSHIP:
AN EXPLORATORY STUDY

SHAKER A. ZAHRA
George Mason University

EXECUTIVE SUMMARY

Today, there is considerable scholarly and managerial interest in corporate entrepreneurship; that is, those activities that enhance a company's ability to innovate, take risk, and seize opportunities in its markets. Corporate entrepreneurship centers on creating new business by penetrating new markets, pursuing new business, or both.

Despite the growing recognition and use of corporate entrepreneurship, little empirical research has been done on its antecedents and potential association with company financial performance. To fill this gap in the literature, this study proposes a model that identifies potential environmental, strategic, and organizational factors that may spur or stifle corporate entrepreneurship. The model also highlights the potential associations between corporate entrepreneurship and corporate financial performance.

Building on the existing literature, the study advances five hypotheses that operationalize the model. The hypotheses are tested using data from 119 of the Fortune 500 industrial firms, covering the period 1986 to 1989. This exploratory study's results indicate that: (1) environmental dynamism, hostility, and heterogeneity (multiplicity and complexity of environmental components) intensify corporate entrepreneurship; (2) growth-oriented strategies are associated with increased corporate entrepreneurship, whereas a strategy of stability is not conducive to corporate entrepreneurship; (3) the scanning, formal communication, and integration components of formal organizational structure are positively related to corporate entrepreneurship—increased differentiation and extensive controls stifle corporate entrepreneurship; (4) clearly defined organizational values, whether relating to competitors or employees, are positively associated with corporate entrepreneurship; and (5)

Address correspondence to Prof. Shaker A. Zahra, Department of Management, School of Business Administration, George Mason University, Fairfax, VA 22030.

I acknowledge with appreciation the helpful comments by Jeff Covin, Ari Ginsberg, Dan Jennings, William Schulte, Jr., and two anonymous reviewers on earlier drafts of this paper. Katherine Swenson, Jaideep Puri, and Patricia H. Zahra's editorial suggestions have also improved this manuscript significantly. I gratefully acknowledge the financial support from George Mason University and its School of Business Administration.

Journal of Business Venturing **6**, 259–285

© 1991 Elsevier Science Publishing Co., Inc., 655 Avenue of the Americas, New York, NY 10010

0883-9026/91/$3.50

260   S.A. ZAHRA

corporate entrepreneurship activities are associated with company financial performance and re-duced systematic risk.

INTRODUCTION

The 1980s witnessed the emergence of corporate entrepreneurship as a centerpiece in or-ganizational efforts aimed at enhancing product innovativeness, risk-taking, and proactive responses to environmental changes (Covin and Slevin 1988; Miller 1983; Pinchot 1985; Slevin and Covin 1989; Wortman 1987). Corporate entrepreneurship offered a means of revitalizing large corporations' ability to innovate and compete effectively, improve employee morale and productivity, enhance financial performance, and reduce business risk (Serpa 1987). However, despite the proliferation of writings on the topic, only a few studies have systematically examined the effect of corporate entrepreneurship on company performance (e.g., Biggadike 1979; Block 1989; Miller and Camp 1985; Zahra 1986). As a result, evidence on the utility of corporate entrepreneurship has been tentative and largely testimonial in nature. This has raised concern that corporate entrepreneurship was fast becoming a managerial fad (Duncan et al. 1988). Also, this absence of credible evidence on the utility of corporate entrepreneurship has been compounded by a lack of attention to identifying its antecedents. Thus, conditions under which corporate entrepreneurship becomes viable are unclear. For this reason, executives looking to the literature for guidance on corporate entrepreneurship will find it replete with case studies and illustrative examples that lack a unifying framework. Such a framework is essential to set the stage for research on corporate entrepreneurship, and for guiding executive actions to stimulate corporate entrepreneurship.

OBJECTIVE AND FOCUS

This exploratory study addresses two questions: (1) what are the antecedents of corporate entrepreneurship? and (2) what is the association between corporate entrepreneurship and company performance? To answer these questions, this study presents and empirically tests a model of the precursors and effects of corporate entrepreneurship in large, well-established organizations. The model posits that a combination of environmental, strategic, and com-pany-related variables jointly influences corporate entrepreneurship efforts. Therefore, whereas each variable may independently influence corporate entrepreneurship, only by examining their simultaneous effects can corporate entrepreneurship's major precursors be reliably understood. A second proposition underlying the model is that pursuit of corporate entre-preneurship is positively associated with superior corporate financial performance. To set the stage for this research, and appreciate the value of the proposed model and this study's empirical findings, corporate entrepreneurship must first be defined.

CORPORATE ENTREPRENEURSHIP

Today, there is no universally acceptable definition of corporate entrepreneurship (Jennings and Lumpkin 1989; Wortman 1987). Authors use many terms to refer to different aspects of corporate entrepreneurship; intrapreneurship (Pinchot 1985), internal corporate entrepre-neurship (Schollhammer 1982), corporate venture (Ellis and Taylor 1987), and internal corporate venture (Burgelman and Sayles 1986). Regardless of the label, corporate entre-preneurship refers to the process of creating new business within established firms to improve organizational profitability and enhance a company's competitive position (for a review, see Ronen 1988) or the strategic renewal of existing business.

Corporate entrepreneurship entails creating new business by redefining the firm's products (or services) or by developing markets. Redefinition of a firm's products involves revising the concept of the existing business by developing or introducing new products, services, or technologies (Rule and Irwin 1988). Revising the business occurs through adding new business to a firm's portfolio through acquisitions and joint ventures, or internal developments, product introductions, and market development, or both. For instance, Boeing has recently established a joint venture (with two other companies) to market the financial packages Boeing offers its customers.

Within the context of corporate entrepreneurship, market development can occur by locating new markets for existing products (MacMillan and Day 1987). An example is Heinz's recent emphasis on the institutional market, such as prisons, to increase ketchup sales (Kotler 1989). Market development can also occur through creating markets for products newly developed by the firm, as in Rubbermaid's recently formed joint venture with a Dutch chemical group, DSM, to produce and market housewares and plastic furniture in Europe, the Middle East, and North Africa. The same principle underlies McDonnel Douglas' venture, which will sell IBM products to its customers, thereby providing additional services to Douglas' existing markets (Kanter 1990).

Creation of a new business through market and product developments requires risk-taking and careful articulation of the firm's competitive posture or altering the rules of the competitive game (Murray 1985). Therefore, corporate entrepreneurship also embodies administrative processes aiming to seize opportunities in the firm's competitive environment (Ellis and Taylor 1987; Zahra 1989). These innovative managerial practices can take place at almost every functional area within the corporation, with the intent of creating momentum to increase innovations in products or markets (Morris et al. 1988). Thus, corporate entrepreneurship takes place at the corporate, division (business) or project levels in a company (Morris and Gordon 1987). A noteworthy example of such functional corporate entrepreneurship is Zenith Electronic's marketing venture with Hewlett-Packard, whereby Zenith has expanded its laptop market presence.

Corporate entrepreneurship activities can be internally or externally oriented (MacMillan et al. 1986). Internal activities are typified as "the development within a large organization of internal markets and relatively small and independent units designed to create internal test-markets or expand improved or innovative staff services, technologies, or production methods within the organization" (Nielson et al. 1985, p. 181). These activities may cover product, process, and administrative innovations at various levels of the company (Burgelman and Sayles 1986; Kanter 1989; Zahra 1989). External efforts entail mergers, joint ventures, or acquisitions. For example, in 1984, Rubbermaid entered the toy industry by acquiring Little Tikes, a successful toymaker. Even though internal and external corporate entrepreneurship complement each other, the factors that lead to their pursuit are not well understood.

Whether internal or external in focus, corporate entrepreneurship activities can be formal or informal (Burgelman and Sayles 1986). Although some firms designate a unit to spearhead corporate entrepreneurship activities, not all initiatives originate from these units. Informal efforts occur autonomously, with or without the blessing of the official organization (Ronen 1988). Such informal activities can result from individual creativity or pursuit of self-interest, and some of these efforts eventually receive the firm's formal recognition and thus become an integral part of the business concept (Burgelman and Sayles

1986). Because informal projects are so pervasive, a comprehensive definition of corporate entrepreneurship must incorporate both formal and informal aspects of corporate venturing, as follows:

> Corporate entrepreneurship refers to formal and informal activities aimed at creating new business in established companies through product and process innovations and market developments. These activities may take place at the corporate, division (business), functional, or project levels, with the unifying objective of improving a company's competitive position and financial performance. Corporate entrepreneurship also entails the strategic renewal of an existing business.

CORPORATE ENTREPRENEURSHIP CORRELATES

Building on the literature, Figure 1 suggests that a firm's external environment, corporate strategy, and internal organizational factors may influence the intensity of corporate entrepreneurship activities. Each of these sets has multiple components that vary in their potential association with corporate entrepreneurship. An understanding of these potential antecedents would require attention to their joint effect.

Environment

Companies innovate and venture in anticipation of, or response to, their external environment (Zahra 1986). An environment poses challenges and offers new opportunities to which firms

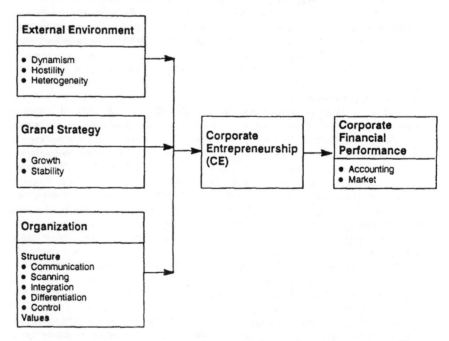

FIGURE 1.   A model of predictors and financial outcomes of corporate entrepreneurship.

must respond creatively through corporate entrepreneurship. An environment also serves as a rich source of ideas for new product developments. Suppliers, buyers, and competitors provide incentives for companies' innovation and venturing.

Dynamism refers to the perceived instability of a firm's market because of continuing changes (Keats and Hitt 1988). Opportunities emerge from the dynamism of an industry where social, political, technological, and economic changes bring about new developments that can enrich a company's niche.

Increased dynamism is hypothesized to be conducive to the pursuit of corporate entrepreneurship, because dynamism creates opportunities in a firm's markets, as in the packaged-goods industry which introduced over 10,000 new products in 1988 alone (Fannin 1989). Changes in the external environment open many new windows of opportunity, thus spurring a company's quest for new innovative ventures to benefit from these developments. Dynamism also intensifies rivalry by encouraging entry into the market. This entry is usually supported by newer technologies and innovative marketing practices than those already in the industry (Oster 1990). When entry occurs and competition intensifies, the environment becomes volatile, thereby increasing the risk of failure for companies (Keats and Hitt 1988). To cope with this volatility, companies may diversify into new fields, thereby altering their concept of business. Still, others may emphasize internal developments (new products) for existing markets, or engage in new marketing, production, or administrative processes to control cost and expedite response to the environment (Haskins and Petit 1988). Corporate entrepreneurship helps to respond to these new competitive forces, either through innovations or imitating competitors' practices. As a result, companies that view their environments as dynamic will emphasize corporate entrepreneurship, as depicted in Figure 1.

A hostile environment creates threats to a firm's mission, through increasing rivalry in the industry or depressing demand for a firm's products (or services), thereby threatening the very survival of the firm. Hostility denotes the perceived adverseness of an environment for a firm's mission (Miller and Friesen 1984).

Environmental hostility is also expected to stimulate the pursuit of corporate entrepreneurship. Faced with unfavorable environmental conditions, a company may opt to differentiate its products through intensive marketing and advertising activities in order to sustain customer loyalty or increase penetration of existing segments. And, if hostility continues to intensify in the firm's principal markets, these companies consider novel business ideas to replace or supplement their additional business core through internal developments, external joint venturing, or diversification (Keats and Hitt 1988). Heinz offers a case in point. Known for its ketchup business, Heinz also had a baby food division. With rising concern over health and slowing birth rates, Heinz's two primary divisions were experiencing declining sales and profits. To reverse this trend, Heinz has embarked on a dual program of internal developments and acquisitions. Schmid (1989), Heinz's CEO, summarizes the thrust of internal development as being "Our low-cost operator programs, marketing of big brands, and development of new products . . ." (p. 17). Acquisitions involved Weight Watchers, Friteco, Inc. (later expanded into Ore-Ida Vended Products, Inc.), and a number of acquisitions in the pet food market (e.g., 9-Lives). The company has used these acquisitions to strengthen its position in the USA and abroad. Overall, as depicted in Figure 1, increased environmental hostility in a firm's primary industry is predicted to be associated with increased pursuit of corporate entrepreneurship.

Opportunities also emerge from the heterogeneity of the environment, where developments in one market create new pockets of demand for a firm's products in related areas. Heterogeneity indicates the existence of multiple segments, with varied characteristics and needs, that are being served by the firm. Hence, a heterogeneous environment is perceived to be complex because of the multiplicity of the needs with which the company must contend (Dess and Beard 1984). In particular, "This dimension refers to the number of different organizationally relevant attributes or components of the environment" (Miles 1980, p. 223). For instance, two companies may compete in the same industry and serve the same customer groups but will perceive the environment quite differently. One firm may perceive the environment as manageable (simple); the other views it as complex and uncontrollable. These perceptual differences arise from the experience of companies with the external environment.

Increased environmental heterogeneity is predicted to be associated with greater use of corporate entrepreneurship. Heterogeneity means diversity of customer needs and expectations among the different segments served by the firm (Miller and Friesen 1984, p. 157). This diversity offers a company many opportunities for additional innovation and market development, aids a firm in adopting successful entrepreneurial ventures from one line of business to another, and enables it to learn from competitors (Keats and Hitt 1988). In addition, because perceived heterogeneity is interpreted to mean increased complexity of a firm's environment, companies may undertake ventures to reduce this uncertainty. Some companies may use joint ventures, and others may use administrative innovations to develop creative ways to manage environmental complexity. Thus, according to Peterson and Berger (1971) and Wilson (1966), greater environmental heterogeneity is associated with increased organizational innovations, hence corporate entrepreneurship. This discussion leads to the study's first hypothesis:

H1:   Environmental dynamism, hostility, and heterogeneity are associated positively with corporate entrepreneurship.

Grand Corporate Strategy

Figure 1 suggests that, in addition to the characteristics of the firm's environment, grand corporate strategy is an important predictor of corporate entrepreneurship activities. A number of authors have highlighted the importance of fit between corporate entrepreneurship activities and corporate strategy as a prerequisite for their success and improved company performance (Burgelman and Sayles 1986; MacMillan et al. 1986). When a venture is congruent with the strategy, the probability of its adoption increases (MacMillan et al. 1986) because it will be viewed as a means of actualizing a company's mission. Conversely, when a venture does not match the thrust of strategy, it will be viewed as risky because it falls beyond the firm's areas of expertise and grand strategy.

Grand corporate strategy is the persistent theme that dominates organizational mission and goals and guides the deployment of a company's resources. Operationally, there are four such strategies: internal growth, external growth, stability, and retrenchment (Hitt et al. 1982). Because of their different orientations, Figure 1 suggest that these strategies are expected to vary in their associations with corporate entrepreneurship.

Specifically, growth strategies are predicted to stimulate corporate entrepreneurship. An internal growth strategy calls for extensive "in-house" innovation and venturing, in almost every functional area within a corporation. These innovations aim to strengthen a company's position in existing markets by offering novel, product-improving service, or reducing cost.

It also means initiating ventures to expand the scope of the market through product introduction.

Firms that follow an external-growth strategy are also expected to support corporate entrepreneurship. An external-growth strategy calls for aggressive expansion by broadening the scope of business and markets. Corporate entrepreneurship offers a means of revising the firm's business concept through imitating competitors' ventures or by purchasing new technologies whether they were developed inside or outside the industry, or by acquiring entrepreneurial firms (Betz 1987).

In contrast to growth-oriented firms, corporations that follow a stability strategy will be less disposed to pursue corporate entrepreneurship. A strategy of stability usually requires making only incremental increases in the scope of business and focuses on maintaining past rates of financial performance without making significant changes in the firm's competitive posture or patterns of resource allocations (Hitt et al. 1982). Consequently, firms that follow the stability option are expected to implement only a few corporate entrepreneurship projects.

Retrenchment strategies call for drastic measures—such as reduction in corporate assets, scope of operations, or the labor force—for companies to regain their competitive strengths. Because firms undergo this strategy in response to severe performance problems and because of the temporary nature of this strategy, no hypothesis on the relation of corporate entrepreneurship and retrenchment is offered in this article. This discussion leads to the second hypothesis:

H2: Growth-oriented grand corporate strategies will be positively associated with pursuit of corporate entrepreneurship. In contrast, a stability strategy will be negatively associated with corporate entrepreneurship.

Organizational Factors

The literature highlights the importance of organizational factors for the pursuit of corporate entrepreneurial activities (Burgelman and Sayles 1986; Jennings and Lumpkin 1989; Kanter 1986; Slevin and Covin 1989). These variables form the context within which employees and executives perceive opportunities for new ventures. Organizational variables also constitute the context within which corporate entrepreneurship ventures are evaluated, accepted, or rejected (Zahra 1986).

Organizational correlates of corporate entrepreneurship fall into two broad categories: tangible and intangible. Tangible variables pertain to the properties of the formal organizational structure and its receptivity to the emergence and adoption of corporate entrepreneurship. Intangible variables include dominant organizational values, primarily a company's persistent belief system. These values determine how a firm views itself and the world at large, and define appropriate ways of relating to competitors (Hall and Zahra 1990; Schein 1985; Zahra et al. 1987). Both tangible and intangible organizational variables can enhance or impede corporate entrepreneurship, as presented in Figure 1 and discussed below.

Tangible organizational variables center on the properties of a company's formal organizational structure, especially: communication, scanning, integration, differentiation, and control. As presented in Figure 1, these properties may influence corporate entrepreneurship in different ways.

Communication. The quality and amount of communication are of crucial importance to the successful initiation and implementation of corporate entrepreneurship (Peters and

266   S.A. ZAHRA

Waterman 1982). Communication helps in introducing new ideas to the firm and in familiarizing company employees with recent industry trends. Communication exposes employees and executives to new ideas and focuses their attention on the opportunities and threats in the external environment, thereby creating a basis for exploring novel ventures. Communication also promotes interdisciplinary cooperation, which is essential for the success of these initiatives (Kanter 1986). These projects often require attention to complex financial, technical, and administrative issues that cross departmental boundaries: communication brings together different units in pursuit of viable corporate entrepreneurship activities. Consequently, some companies have implemented new organizational designs that promote formal communications among departments associated with a new venture (Kanter 1989). Finally, formal communication is necessary to promote awareness of a company's progress in ve... turing activities. As formal communication increases, the pursuit of corporate entrepreneurship is expected to intensify, as depicted in Figure 1.

Organizational communication can be formal and informal, and both are invaluable to successful corporate entrepreneurship (Pinchot 1985). However, in this preliminary effort, emphasis is on formal communication, which is more observable and easier to measure than informal communication. Future research should explore the important association between informal communication and corporate entrepreneurship.

Scanning refers to formal efforts to collect, analyze, and interpret data about the firm's external environment and the competition (Daft et al. 1988). Scanning facilitates the timely acquisition of relevant data on industry trends and changes, thereby permitting the accumulation of information on new ventures initiated in the industry that may be of interest to the firm. Scanning also alerts senior executives to threats and opportunities in their firms' environment. As a result, it is predicted that increased scanning will be positively associated with increased corporate entrepreneurship activities.

Integration is a third structural component that influences corporate venturing and innovation. It refers to formal organizational activities that aim to tie different units or levels within the hierarchy, through exchange of information among different units (Kanter 1986). This integration helps to disseminate corporate entrepreneurship ideas, and generate support among different units and levels in the firm for certain ventures. Yet, as in the case of differentiation, excessive integration requires extensive use of rigid controls which, in turn, may impede corporate entrepreneurship activities. In fact, two studies (Covin and Slevin 1988; Jennings and Lumpkin 1989) suggest that extensive reliance on integration may hinder venturing activities. As a result, a negative association is hypothesized to exist between excessive integration and corporate entrepreneurship.

Differentiation reflects the division of labor within the organization. Differentiation is associated with corporate entrepreneurship because it helps to promote a strong identification with the mission of organizational units and commitment to their formal goals (Daft 1988; Kanter 1989). This differentiation builds commitment to areas of expertise and profession. Through specialization and commitment, employees develop a thorough familiarity with the goals and objectives of their units and companies. In turn, this usually manifests itself in the employees' desire to ensure the success of their units. These committed employees may contribute ideas for new ventures for the corporation. In addition, as differentiation increases, organizational efforts to facilitate communication among units will intensify. These efforts foster exchange of creative venturing or innovation ideas. Finally, as Keats and Hitt (1988) observe, this differentiation also results in increased specialization among personnel in certain products (or markets). These expert employees are, thus, in a position to examine new trends in their industry, evaluate their relevance to the firm's mission, and develop novel solutions or projects that take advantage of these trends. Overall, increased differentiation is predicted to be positively associated with corporate entrepreneurship.

A caveat about the predicted positive association between differentiation and corporate entrepreneurship is in order. Increased differentiation can stifle formal communication. And, if carried to an extreme, it must be counterbalanced with extensive, formal controls to ensure coordination among units that may stifle venturing and innovation initiatives.

Controls. Some formal controls are essential to the selection of corporate entrepreneurship projects (Kanter 1989). These controls enable a company to separate promising corporate entrepreneurship ventures from less valuable projects. However, the excessive use of formal controls may stifle the pursuit of corporate entrepreneurship (MacMillan et al. 1986). Champions of corporate entrepreneurship projects may become frustrated because of the red tape or the need to "go through channels" to receive formal support for their ideas. Increased reliance on formal controls is, therefore, predicted to be negatively associated with corporate entrepreneurship.

The above discussion on structure leads to a third hypothesis:

H3: Formal communication, scanning, and differentiation will be positively associated with corporate entrepreneurship. Formal controls and integration will be negatively associated with corporate entrepreneurship.

Values

Specific organizational values are also predicted to be positively associated with corporate entrepreneurship (Kanter 1989; Peters and Waterman 1982). Organizational values embody managerial philosophies and ideals and the formal norms that guide employee behavior. Two aspects of company values are recognizable: individual-centered and competition-focused (Deal and Kennedy 1982; Schein 1985). Individual-centered values focus on the way a company views and treats its employees (Bettinger 1989; Kanter 1986, 1989). Positive individual-centered values held by a firm often promote individual creativity and encourage risk taking (Zahra et al. 1987). These values center on creating an internal climate that enhances integration of employee and company goals, and intensifies the level of employees' commitment to the company. These factors encourage employees to explore viable means to ensure successful organizational performance because employees will be disposed to contribute new ideas or take on new ventures to ensure company success. Merck, Hewlett-Packard, Kodak, and 3M are well known for their strong commitment to their employees, and for encouraging them to experiment and take risks.

Competitive values reflect a firm's assumptions about the appropriate approaches that executives and employees should follow in pursuing company goals (Hall and Zahra 1990; Schein 1985). In firms that encourage agile and aggressive responses to environmental moves as the *modus operandi,* corporate entrepreneurship efforts will flourish. In these companies, employees and executives will be disposed to monitor industry trends, to experiment with new ideas, and to initiate new corporate ventures to capitalize on emerging opportunities in the marketplace, and as a result, venturing activities will intensify. Thus:

H4: Clearly articulated organizational values that are employee (person)-supportive and competition-oriented are positively associated with corporate entrepreneurship.

Corporate Entrepreneurship and Financial Performance

Companies embark on corporate entrepreneurship for a variety of reasons: to seize opportunities that complement or extend their existing business, to better utilize resources, to excite employees and improve morale, or to retain managerial talent (Burgelman and Sayles 1986; Kanter 1989; Pinchot 1985). Collectively, these factors may enhance a company's productivity and enhance its competitive position. Hence, as depicted in Figure 1, corporate entrepreneurship is expected to be positively associated with corporate financial performance.

Organizational performance has two components: accounting and market-based. The accounting component refers to a firm's ability to generate above the "going market" profits. This is usually evidenced in a firm's earnings per share (EPS), net income-to-sales, growth in revenue, and similar measures.

The market-based performance component relates to the level of risk associated with a firm's stock portfolio. Because systematic risk is assumed to be common to all market participants, attention usually centers on unsystematic risk, i.e., the portion that is distinct to a firm's portfolio (Franks et al. 1985). Unsystematic risk reflects the stock market appraisal of corporate actions, including those that pertain to corporate entrepreneurship. When corporate entrepreneurial projects are emphasized, capital markets are likely to respond. Once approved, new venture activities are usually publicized in corporate ceremonies and documents, press releases, and trade publications. If judged positively by external markets, the unsystematic portion of risk declines, showing confidence in these initiatives—an indication of a successful market performance. These ventures help to stabilize or improve corporate earnings, thereby reducing a company's non-diversifiable risk. Thus:

H5: Corporate entrepreneurship is positively associated with corporate financial performance; that is, positively with accounting measures and negatively with market-based criteria.

This study's hypothesized association between corporate entrepreneurship and subsequent financial performance does not preclude the possibility that a reverse relationship exists between these variables. Indeed, some financially successful companies (e.g., 3M and Hewlett-Packard) have been actively engaged in corporate entrepreneurship. Future examinations may explore the interactive link between past performance and pursuit of corporate entrepreneurship.

Summary

Corporate entrepreneurship represents an important development in the quest for improved corporate performance. A proposed model suggests that three sets of variables influence the pursuit of corporate entrepreneurship: environment, strategy, and internal organization. As the above discussion indicates, this exploratory study focuses primarily on the direct effect of these three sets of variables on corporate entrepreneurship. Finally, future studies may explore the associations of interactions (or joint) of these variables with corporate entrepreneurship. The model also suggests that corporate entrepreneurship will be associated with company performance. These two propositions provide a basis for an exploratory study that is reported below.

METHOD
Data Collection
Sample

Data were collected using mailed questionnaires and secondary financial sources. The questionnaires were sent to 450 companies that appeared on the *Fortune 500* list of U.S. industrial corporations. (The remaining 50 companies were excluded because they participated in a pretest study by the author that resulted in the current survey instrument.) The questionnaire was directed to the companies' CEOs (or highest-ranking executives). Although only one mailing was used due to cost constraints, 119 valid responses were received, for a 26.4% response rate. Response rates for academic research from the *Fortune 500* typically fall within the 20 to 30% range (Tootelian and Gadeake 1987).

This study emphasized the *Fortune 500* manufacturing population because of its acknowledged importance to the U.S. national economy, and the fact that these companies are usually on the cutting edge in developing corporate entrepreneurship because of rising international competition and the maturity of many of their primary industries.

Non-Response Bias

Firms that participated in this study were compared with others in their industries (by the two-digit *Fortune* classification) on four dimensions: company size (measured by both total number of full-time employees and total assets); growth in EPS over the past 10 years; *Fortune's* estimated growth in return to investors (ROI) over the past 10 years; and dividends per share for the three years that preceded data collection. Using the *t* test, no significant differences were found between responding and non-responding firms on these four variables. This suggested the absence of systematic differences in corporate size and financial status between respondents and non-respondents on the four chosen dimensions. Still, generalizations of the results to other *Fortune 500* should be made with caution because they may differ from respondents on other variables that have not been examined here. Also, because *Fortune 500* are among the largest U.S. companies, the results may not apply to other sectors of the economy.

Respondents

As mentioned, the survey targeted the CEOs (or the highest-ranking corporate officers) because of their positions, which give them a unique and comprehensive view of corporate entrepreneurship activities. These individuals typically have an appreciation of a company's "total picture," and are intimately familiar with the firm's environment, strategy, structure, and performance (Hambrick 1981). These executives are also frequently called upon to evaluate major new ventures, to approve financial support for these projects, and are involved in evaluating ongoing activities. Still, because some researchers contend that other senior executives and managers at different levels of the hierarchy are usually involved in corporate entrepreneurship initiation and implementation (e.g., Burgelman and Sayles 1986; Kanter 1989; Pinchot 1985), future research may benefit from collecting additional data from these individuals to minimize potential source bias.

270   S.A. ZAHRA

Variables and Measures

Both secondary and primary data sources were used to gauge the variables in Figure 1. The "Appendix" presents the variables, measures, and relevant Cronbach alpha-coefficient, which is an index of scale internal consistency (reliability).

Environment

Dynamism, hostility, and heterogeneity were measured using multi-item indices, which appear in the "Appendix." Two observations on these measures are essential. First, some of the scale items ("Appendix") refer to the firm's "industry." This is done in keeping with the literature. Whereas the majority of *Fortune 500* corporations are diversified, prior research suggests that the "environment of a firm's core business becomes the dominant focus or frame of reference for most corporate-level decisions" (Keats and Hitt 1988). This view has been supported in a number of sound empirical studies (e.g., Dess and Beard 1984; Hill and Hoskisson 1987; Hitt and Ireland 1985; Prahalad and Bettis 1986) and conceptual models (Dess et al. 1990; Porter 1980). Accordingly, emphasis on the firm's primary industry in examining its environment provides a basis for understanding corporate entrepreneurship; changes in the firm's primary industry are important to understanding corporate entrepreneurship.

Second, an extensive body of research suggests that executives' perceptions of their firms's core (major) business play a most crucial role in mapping corporate responses to opportunities and threats (Dess et al. 1990; Hitt et al. 1982; Weick 1979). Therefore, data were collected from senior executives about their perceptions of their environment. These measures of the environment were correlated with objective data in order to ensure their validity. Data on R&D were collected from *Business Week* and *Forbes*. Data on hostility and heterogeneity were collected from *Fortune 500*; all for the 1986–1989 period.

Dynamism was correlated with average change in corporate R&D expenditure for a three-year period. R&D was emphasized because it was an important source of environmental dynamism (Daft 1988). For each of the three years, change in R&D was calculated by subtracting the percent of corporate sales allocated to R&D in a given year from the preceding year's allocation and then dividing the result by the past year's spending. The product of this process was then divided by three to determine average change in R&D allocation. This average was then correlated with the dynamism score, using Pearson's simple correlation. The two measures were significantly associated at $p < 0.001$ ($r = 0.40$, $n = 103$). This suggested that while the dynamism and R&D measures were distinct, they converged in gauging "dynamism."

In order to validate the hostility scale, it was correlated with data on the rate of growth in industry-wide sales (using two-digit standard industrial classifications; SIC) for a period of three years. The inverse ratio (1/growth) was used to indicate hostility; it showed lower growth in industry sales. Correlation between objective and subjective scale data was positive ($n = 110$, $r = 0.32$, $p < 0.001$). This moderate association showed that hostility was associated with lower growth rates in industry sales. Other factors may have caused an industry's environment to be hostile, including radical technological changes, influx of new competitors, and new regulatory actions by the government. Thus, the moderate association between subjective and objective indicators of hostility reflected the influence of only one factor. Overall, then, this moderate association indicated that the subjective (survey-based) hostility scales captured environmental unfavorability (Daft 1988).

The heterogeneity scale was validated using the approach suggested by Grossack (1965) and Keats and Hitt (1988). Grossack (1965) emphasized the notion of dynamic concentration where industries moved toward or away from dominance of sales by large firms. To derive this index, market shares (defined as company sales/industry sales) in the data collection year (t_0) were divided by shares 3 years earlier. A high score on the index implied increasing heterogeneity. The objective and subjective (see "Appendix") indices were correlated positively ($n = 112$, $r = 0.37$, p < 0.001).

The overall results supported the construct validity of the environmental measures. In addition, coefficient alpha (see "Appendix") reaffirmed the measures' reliability.

Strategy and Organization

The "Appendix" presents the measures of strategy, structure, and values.

Financial Performance

Performance data were collected for three periods: same year, one-year lag, and a two-year lag. This allowed comparison of contemporaneous and lagged correlations between corporate entrepreneurship and performance.

Four accounting performance criteria were used: EPS, *Fortune's* estimate of the 10-year ROI, net income-to-sales, and the standard deviations of return on assets (RA). The ROI and net income-to-sales measures gauged corporate entrepreneurship's contribution to superior company performance. Profits from corporate entrepreneurship contribute to overall corporate revenues. The standard deviation of RA indicated the volatility of corporate earnings. This volatility arose from many sources, including erosion of a firm's competitive position in traditional markets. New corporate entrepreneurship ventures were believed to reverse such an erosion by generating new income, thereby stabilizing earnings. EPS reflected corporate entrepreneurship's contribution to shareholders' wealth.

Risk was measured by the average *Value Line* beta values. The beta value reflected an external assessment of company stock and performance by an independent venerable financial institution, *Value Line*.

Entrepreneurship

Measuring corporate entrepreneurship proved to be a most challenging task because of the complexity of the concept and the limited empirical research in this area. As noted by other researchers, a psychometrically valid measure of corporate entrepreneurship did not exist (Covin and Slevin 1988; Jennings and Lumpkin 1989; Morris et al 1988; Morris and Gordon 1987). To ensure accuracy and comprehensiveness, this study employed four indicators of corporate entrepreneurship, as follows:

(1) An index of corporate entrepreneurship was developed based on CEOs' responses to nine items ($\alpha = 0.86$), as reported in the "Appendix." The index covered formal and informal aspects of corporate entrepreneurship. It was based on the theoretical and empirical studies by Burgelman (reviewed in Burgelman and Sayles 1986), Miller (1983), and Morris and Gordon (1987). The corporate entrepreneurship index was validated by correlating it with the measure developed by Miller (1983). Miller's index (9 items, $\alpha = 0.81$) covered three areas: product innovation, risk-taking, and proactiveness. The simple correlation between Miller's index and the new corporate entrepreneurship scale was significant ($r = 0.49$, p < 0.001). This coefficient supported the validity of the new scale and, at the same

time, its distinctiveness from the Miller index. This latter measure only gauged a firm's *disposition* toward, rather than actual engagement in, corporate entrepreneurship activities— and covered the formal aspects of corporate entrepreneurship, thereby ignoring less formalized corporate entrepreneurship efforts. In contrast, the new scale incorporated items that covered these informal aspects.

(2) Percentage of sales derived from new lines of business was used as a second measure of corporate entrepreneurship. It was defined as the percentage of sales derived from new business divisions that did not exist five years earlier. This measure defined corporate entrepreneurship as creating new business within established companies (Murray 1985).

(3) Percentage of sales derived from new products or brands was the third indicator of corporate entrepreneurship. Data emphasized products or brands that did not exist five years earlier.

(4) Externally oriented corporate entrepreneurship was measured in two ways: by the number of joint ventures in which the firm participated over the past three years, and by the number of SIC added to the firm's business over the past three years. Executives provided data about joint ventures, whereas secondary sources (e.g., annual and 10K reports, *Fortune, Forbes,* and the *Wall Street Journal,* 1985–1989) were used to collect data on new SIC business.

Data on sales from new business (measure #2 above), sales from new products (measure #3), and joint ventures (measure #4 above) were cross-validated using data from 20 vice presidents, each representing one firm. Correlations between survey and vice presidents' responses averaged 0.78. This was interpreted as indicating the reliability of senior executives' data on sales from new businesses, new products, and the number of joint ventures.

ANALYSIS AND RESULTS

Preliminary Analyses

Table 1 presents Pearson's correlations among the four corporate entrepreneurship indicators and the variables relating to the environment, strategy, and organization. To calculate these correlations, dummy coding of the categorical strategy measure was necessary. This meant that the retrenchment strategy was dropped in order to retain growth and stability strategies, emphasized in H1. Table 1 shows the means, standard deviations, and intercorrelations among the variables.

Data in Table 1 suggested that measures of the environment, strategy, and organization might be interdependent. To determine the absence of extreme multicolinearity, the sample was split into two, then three, groups to determine if the pattern of correlations would change. In addition, a series of analyses suggested by Berry and Feldman (1985) were conducted. Collectively, these analyses indicated that a serious multicolinearity problem did not exist.

Precursors of Corporate Entrepreneurship

The correlations in Table 1 suggested that measures of corporate entrepreneurship were interrelated, as would be expected. Therefore, canonical analysis was considered the appropriate analytical tool because it produced combinations of criteria and predictors such

TABLE 1 Means, Standard Deviations, and Intercorrelations Among the Study's Variables (N = 119)

Variables	Means	SD	1	2	3	4	5	6	7	8	9	10	11	12	13	14	15	16	17
1. Dynamism	13.4	6.4	—																
2. Hostility	38.6	11.6	31	—															
3. Heterogeneity	18.4	9.6	07	23	—														
4. Internal growth	0.3	0.6	10	08	−17	—													
5. External growth	0.5	0.4	21	03	34	06	—												
6. Stability	0.4	0.3	−23	−08	05	−08	−12	—											
7. Communication	45.3	12.4	17	24	33	29	16	18	—										
8. Person value	17.7	5.4	−18	22	27	16	12	25	28	—									
9. Competition value	41.6	4.8	23	19	28	12	26	21	24	29	—								
10. Scanning	18.7	5.4	26	32	26	17	36	13	39	12	26	—							
11. Differentiation	16.2	4.4	09	28	19	28	28	18	24	14	18	31	—						
12. Integration	39.6	15.0	12	19	17	26	12	14	16	17	−10	29	13	—					
13. Control	16.1	6.1	−17	23	24	31	−17	28	23	19	26	38	06	36	—				
14. CE (overall)	47.3	11.6	27	34	40	23	34	09	43	42	19	40	27	18	−21	—			
15. New business	11.2	10.3	19	23	26	19	30	07	17	21	28	09	18	42	23	49	—		
16. New products	23.7	14.3	23	19	18	26	27	04	28	19	21	24	20	27	28	43	46	—	
17. Joint venture	3.1	3.7	30	26	29	−14	23	12	11	08	02	19	−13	−04	08	29	31	27	—

*Intercorrelations are two decimal points; correlation should be at least 0.16 to be significant at $p < 0.05$.

that the linear composites were maximally associated. Hair et al. (1987) provided an extensive discussion of canonical analysis procedures and limitations. The results from canonical analysis appear in Table 2.

Overall Patterns

The results of canonical analysis in Table 2 suggested the following three points:

(1) Although canonical analysis produced canonical (linear) composites equal to the number of variables in the smaller function (in this case, five), only two functions were significant ($p < 0.05$) and were shown in Table 2. The other three were ignored because they were not meaningful.

(2) Redundancy analysis was conducted in order to determine the shared variance between predictors (environment, strategy, and organization) and criterion variables (the four corporate entrepreneurship indicators) in each function. This index was the multivariate analog of R^2 in multiple regression analysis. It indicated the amount of variance in corporate entrepreneurship that was explained by the predictor set. A redundancy index was calculated by multiplying the root (eigenvalue) by the average square of loadings. For instance, in the first function, the root was the square of the canonical correlation, $(0.89)^2 = 0.79$. For the criterion set (still, function #1), average square loadings was calculated as follows: $[(0.89)^2 + (0.52)^2 + (0.76)^2 + (0.44)^2] = 0.434$. The redundancy index was calculated by multiplying 0.79 by 0.434, producing 0.34. The same procedure was followed for the second function (redundancy = 0.16). This meant that predictors explained 34 and 16% of the variations in the four corporate entrepreneurship indicators in the first and second function, respectively.

(3) The structure coefficients (loadings) indicated that the first function was dominated

274 S.A. ZAHRA

TABLE 2 Canonical Results of Associations of Environment Characteristics, Strategy, and Structure with Corporate Entrepreneurship

	Functions			
	#1		#2	
Variables	Standardized coefficient	Structure coefficient	Standardized coefficient	Structure coefficient
Criterion set				
Index (overall)	0.46	0.89	0.31	0.54
New business sales	0.30	0.52	0.44	0.86
New product sales	0.43	0.76	0.30	0.62
No. of joint ventures	0.31	0.44	0.46	0.89
Predictor set				
Dynamism	0.28	0.49	0.18	0.42
Hostility	0.51	0.42	0.33	0.31
Heterogeneity	0.44	0.50	0.19	0.59
Growth strategy	0.21	0.40	0.09	0.33
Stability	−0.39	−0.20	−0.40	−0.18
Communication	0.41	0.53	0.14	0.68
Scanning	0.39	0.44	0.60	0.56
Differentiation	−0.28	−0.42	0.26	0.50
Integration	−0.28	0.37	−0.13	−0.30
Control	0.13	−0.26	−0.28	−0.41
Person values	0.31	0.56	0.23	0.32
Competition values	0.46	0.30	0.47	0.49
$p <$	0.001		0.01	
Canonical correlations (CR)	0.89		0.54	
Root (CR^2)	0.79		0.29	

by internal, formal corporate entrepreneurship activities directed at increasing new product sales. This was evidenced by the significant large loadings of 0.89 and 0.76 for the corporate entrepreneurship index and new product sales, respectively (function 1, column 2).

The second function manifested corporate entrepreneurship activities pertaining to new business creation and pursuit of joint ventures. This was evidenced by the high coefficients for new business sales (loading = 0.86) and joint ventures (loading = 0.89). These results suggested that function 2 was dominated by externally oriented corporate entrepreneurship.

Testing Hypotheses 1 to 4

The results on hypotheses 1 to 4 are summarized below:

Hypothesis 1 suggested that environmental characteristics of dynamism and heterogeneity and hostility were associated positively with corporate entrepreneurship. Canonical analysis supported this prediction. As reported in Table 2, the loadings associated with dynamism, hostility, and heterogeneity were positive, exceeding the suggested cutoff point of 0.30 (Hair et al. 1987). Overall, the results indicated that companies emphasized corporate entrepreneurship as they perceived their environment as becoming increasingly dynamic, hostile, and heterogeneous.

Hypothesis 2 suggested that growth-oriented strategies were positively associated with corporate entrepreneurship, whereas stability strategies were negatively related to corporate enterpreneurship. The hypothesis was generally supported; growth strategies had positive and significant loadings on the two functions. Stability strategy had negative loadings on both functions. However, the loadings were below 0.30, thereby indicating that a stability strategy lacked association with corporate entrepreneurship.

Hypothesis 3 covered five dimensions of the formal organizational structure as they related to corporate entrepreneurship. The results regarding this multifaceted hypothesis were mixed, as follows: (1) As predicted, communication was significantly and positively associated with corporate entrepreneurship (with loadings of 0.53 and 0.68) on the two functions; (2) the postulated positive association between scanning and corporate entrepreneurship was supported (with loadings of 0.44 and 0.56) on the two functions; (3) the results on differentiation and integration were mixed—the two variables varied in their association with corporate entrepreneurship; these two variables were associated in opposite directions with external and internal corporate entrepreneurship; and finally (4) control was negatively associated with corporate entrepreneurship on the two functions. The loadings (of -0.26 and -0.41, respectively) implied that increased formal controls were associated with lower corporate entrepreneurship, especially the externally oriented type. Care must be exercised in interpreting the results of the control variable because its loading on the first function was below 0.30, and the control measure itself was not comprehensive in its coverage. Still, increased formal controls were associated negatively with corporate entrepreneurship activities.

Hypothesis 4 suggested that person-related and competition-oriented values were positively associated with corporate entrepreneurship. The four loadings relating to these variables were significant and positive, thereby supporting hypothesis 4. The loadings suggested that person-related values were especially germane in the case of internal corporate entrepreneurship. Conversely, competition-oriented values were especially relevant in the case of externally oriented corporate entrepreneurship ventures.

The results on H1 to H4 raised an important question: What was the effect of the joint association of environment, strategy, and organizational variables on corporate entrepreneurship? (Unfortunately, the large number of interactions (3 environmental × 3 strategies × 7 organizational scales) relative to the sample size ($n = 119$) made it impossible to examine these joint effects. Had such an analysis been performed, it would have rendered the results of canonical analysis unstable, if not meaningless. Future research should consider these joint effects.

Testing Hypothesis 5

A positive association was posited between corporate entrepreneurship activities and company financial performance. Simple contemporaneous and lagged correlations were used to test this hypothesis. Contemporaneous correlations showed the associations between corporate entrepreneurship and performance criteria at the same time period (t_0). Lagged correlations reflected one- and two-year gaps between the time corporate entrepreneurship measures and performance criteria were collected. Using lagged correlations was desirable because corporate entrepreneurship took time to pay off (Biggadike 1979; Block 1989). Given the dearth of empirical studies, there was no a priori length for this time lag. This problem was compounded by the fact that data on actual company performance were available only for two years after the survey data were collected. As a result, analyses were conducted for

276   S.A. ZAHRA

TABLE 3   Associations between Corporate Entrepreneurship and Corporate Financial Performance

	Overall Index	New Business Sales	New Product Sales	Joint Ventures
Contemporaneous				
EPS	0.16*	0.29***	0.17*	0.16*
ROI	0.26*	0.14	0.21*	0.12
New income to sales	0.22*	0.17*	0.14	0.17*
RA	−0.19*	0.25*	0.20*	0.19*
Beta	−0.26*	−0.22*	−0.27*	0.10
One-year lag				
EPS	0.20*	0.30**	0.17*	0.14
ROI	0.26**	0.16*	0.22*	0.14
Net income to sales	0.26**	0.17*	0.11	0.13
RA	−0.20*	0.24**	0.22*	0.18*
Beta	−0.31***	−0.22*	−0.19*	0.17*
Two-year lag				
EPS	0.33***	0.28**	0.19*	0.19*
ROI	0.29***	0.14	0.25*	0.14
Net income to sales	0.27**	0.17*	0.17*	0.11
RA	−0.28**	0.25**	0.22*	0.18*
Beta	−0.33***	−0.29*	−0.23*	−0.20*

*$p < 0.05$.
**$p < 0.01$.
***$p < 0.001$.

one- and two-year lags, as reported in Table 3. Future studies may examine longer time frames.

Table 3 shows that 50 of the 60 possible correlations between corporate entrepreneurship and performance measures (83.3%) were significant at $p < 0.05$. Corporate entrepreneurship measures were also positively associated with accounting performance criteria, with the exception of the negative associations between the overall corporate entrepreneurship index and standard deviations of return on assets (RA). This meant that corporate entrepreneurship was positively associated with accounting performance measures. The magnitude of correlations was stable within the contemporaneous and lagged analyses, thereby indicating that short-term improvements in financial performance through corporate entrepreneurship were incremental.

Table 3 also showed that the associations between the four corporate entrepreneurship measures and beta values were negative in 11 of the 12 cases, with the exception of the insignificant association with joint ventures.

Overall, the results from accounting and risk-related measures supported Hypothesis 5, which suggested positive association between corporate entrepreneurship and company performance.

DISCUSSION

This exploratory study has advanced a model of the potential antecedents of corporate entrepreneurship (environment, strategy, and organization), and the association between corporate entrepreneurship and company financial performance. Four observations emerge from this study's data and results.

(1) The study highlights two components of corporate entrepreneurship: internal and external. Internal entrepreneurship centers on reviving the existing business through innovation and venturing. External entrepreneurship centers on broadening and, sometimes, revising the concept of the business. This suggests a need to simultaneously explore internal and external corporate entrepreneurship that enhances product and business development as a means of improving company performance. That is, future studies need to incorporate measures of both internal and external corporate entrepreneurship.

(2) The results supported the model presented in Figure 1. In particular, the results were consistent with theory on the association of environment and strategy with corporate entrepreneurship. High environmental dynamism, hostility, and heterogeneity were conductive to the pursuit of entrepreneurship. Likewise, even though growth-oriented strategies were associated positively with entrepreneurship, the relationship between a stability strategy and corporate entrepreneurship was negative. The results were also consistent with theory on organizational values; well-articulated values (centering on the employees as individuals and competition) were conducive to corporate entrepreneurship.

The results on organizational structure were not universally consistent with predictions. Although communication and scanning were associated positively with corporate entrepreneurship, the results on differentiation, integration, and control were mixed. Associations varied according to the two corporate entrepreneurship dimensions: differentiation was negatively associated with internal, but positively with external, corporate entrepreneurship. The negative association might have resulted from the fragmentation of effort associated with corporate entrepreneurship when differentiation was carried to an extreme. Conversely, the positive association between differentiation and external corporate entrepreneurship might have resulted from the increased access to innovation and venturing ideas from outside sources because of the increased specialization and professional contacts of a firm's staff.

The opposite situation was observed in the case of integration: it was positively associated with internal corporate entrepreneurship, perhaps because of unity of effort resulting from increased coordination. However, integration was associated negatively with external corporate entrepreneurship, perhaps because of a lack of focus and poor coordination. These differences in associations with the internal and external components of corporate entrepreneurship were consistent with the findings of Jennings and Lumpkin (1989).

The results about control need to be interpreted with caution. Although a reliable index was used in this study, it might not have fully captured the effect of control on corporate entrepreneurship ventures. Nevertheless, as predicted, control was negatively associated with both internal and external corporate entrepreneurship activities, perhaps because increased controls added rigidity to the structure, thereby stifling initiative and, ultimately, corporate entrepreneurship.

(3) Although the internal and external dimensions of corporate entrepreneurship were interrelated, they varied in their associations with different antecedents, as summarized in Table 4. Table 4 emphasized the canonical results (in Table 2), particularly the size of loadings. Although there were no formal tests of differences in loadings in constructing Table 4, a difference of 0.10 between two loadings was considered significant. This intuitive cutoff point was conservative.

Table 4 shows that many of the same environmental, strategic, organizational variables were associated with the internal and external dimensions of corporate entrepreneurship.

TABLE 4 Summary of Predictors of Internal and External Corporate Entrepreneurship

	Types	
Predictors	Internal	External
Environment		
Dynamism	+	+
Hostility	+ +	+
Heterogeneity	+	+
Strategy		
Growth	+	+
Stability	×	×
Organization		
Structure		
Communication	+	+ +
Scanning	+	+ +
Differentiation	−	−
Integration	+	−
Control	×	+ +
Values		
Person	+ +	+
Competition	+	+ +

+ , Positive association between a variable and a component of corporate entrepreneurship.
+ + , Stronger positive association between a variable and this corporate entrepreneurship type than the other type.
− , Negative association between a variable and a component of corporate entrepreneurship.
− − , Negative association between a variable and this corporate entrepreneurship type than the other type.
× , Not significant.

Still, these two dimensions varied in the magnitude of their associations with antecedent variables. For instance, hostility and person-centered values were more germane to internal than external entrepreneurship. On the other hand, scanning, communication, competition-based values and controls were more relevant to the external than internal ventures. By delineating variables associated with internal and external dimensions of corporate entrepreneurship, this study offered a basis for further theory building. Again, scholars need to recognize these differences as they construct future models or theories of corporate entrepreneurship.

(4) Corporate entrepreneurship was associated positively with measures of financial performance. Although causal inferences could not be made about the direction of this relationship because of the cross-sectional design of the study, the current results offered preliminary evidence that corporate entrepreneurship activities were positively associated with company performance (Biggadike 1979; Miller and Camp 1985). And, even though some previous research has shown that it took corporate ventures seven or eight years to pay off, the current results indicated that the associations between the intensity of corporate entrepreneurship and financial performance criteria were almost instantaneous and grew, albeit incrementally, over time. Hence, there might be short- and long-term financial benefits from pursuing corporate entrepreneurship activities. This finding should be viewed as tentative. The current study focused on the corporate level of analysis whereas previous research by Biggadike (1979) and Miller and Camp (1985) stressed the business level of the analysis. In addition, these previous studies employed longitudinal designs, thereby making it feasible

to discern patterns of association between corporate entrepreneurship and financial performance.

The above encouraging results on the association between corporate entrepreneurship and company performance should be interpreted with caution because the correlations were moderate in size. These moderate coefficients reflected a number of corporate realities. Some corporate entrepreneurship ventures were in their infancy; it would take several years before they would pay off. In addition, a number of researchers (Block 1989; Kanter 1989; Sykes 1986) have reported a number of corporate entrepreneurship failures. These cases of failure might have depressed the magnitude of the correlations between corporate entrepreneurship and company performance. A third explanation was that corporate entrepreneurship activities might influence profitability only on a limited scale. For instance, short-term profitability may suffer as a result of corporate entrepreneurship, whether internal or external. However, companies were willing to accept this reality because entrepreneurial ventures stimulated long-term growth which would compensate for the reduction in short-term profitability returns from these projects. Unfortunately, a shortcoming of this study was the absence of a measure of growth. Thus, the potential tradeoff between short-term profitability and long-term growth could not be tested in this study. This theoretically appealing tradeoff should be examined in future studies, by using indicators of both profitability and growth as a consequence of corporate entrepreneurship.

The implications of corporate entrepreneurship for short-term profitability can be understood within the context of organizational financial slack. When this slack is high, companies are willing to innovate and venture, thereby rejuvenating their business and improving their revenue. When this slack is low, companies will be constrained in investing in corporate entrepreneurship activities, and their profitability may not improve as is the case when slack is high. This argument suggests that the association between corporate entrepreneurship and financial performance may be bi-directional: past high performance (and high slack) are conducive to pursuit of corporate entrepreneurship and subsequent high performance. This interactive, bi-directional association between corporate entrepreneurship and financial performance needs to be examined in a longitudinal framework. This means that the current results on this study's hypothesis (H5) only look into one part of the interactive interplay between corporate entrepreneurship and financial performance.

IMPLICATIONS

The study has five implications for scholars and future researchers, as follows:

(1) Conceptual and field work is necessary in order to articulate the domain of corporate entrepreneurship. As recent comprehensive reviews suggest, definitional problems continue to plague this young area of research (Low and MacMillan 1988; Wortman 1987). Of particular interest is whether corporate entrepreneurship is a multidimensional or unitary concept. Whereas researchers recognize the multiplicity of corporate entrepreneurship components (Covin and Slevin 1988; Miller 1983; Miller and Camp 1985; Slevin and Covin 1989; Zahra 1986), little effort has been made to identify each of these dimensions and show how they relate to one another. Defining different corporate entrepreneurship dimensions would expedite progress in the field by enabling researchers to study the correlates and effects of each on company performance. In turn, this would encourage the development of theories that prescribe effective executive actions that spur particular types of corporate entrepreneurship.

(2) There is a need to develop a comprehensive framework for studying the predictors

and outcomes of corporate entrepreneurship. For instance, do we need to add additional variables to the proposed model of corporate entrepreneurship (Figure 1)? This exploratory study has examined the association of environment, strategy, and organization with corporate entrepreneurship. A related issue involves the nature of links among these variables; some researchers have suggested that a causal chain exists among them (Keats and Hitt 1988). Does such a causal order among the antecedent variables accentuate their collective impact on corporate entrepreneurship? If such a causal chain is identified, their effect on corporate entrepreneurship can be understood by using path analysis. Future studies may also explore the effect of interaction among the environment, strategy, and organizational predictors on the pursuit of corporate entrepreneurship (Kanter 1989).

Scholars may examine the association between each of the antecedent sets (environment, strategy, and organization) and corporate entrepreneurship. Each of these sets has been the subject of interest and extensive studies in the literature. Integrative studies that tie together multiple dimensions of these sets and their association with corporate entrepreneurship are necessary. For instance, successful internal and external corporate entrepreneurship activities in different environmental settings need to be isolated. Likewise, the potential bi-directional interplay between strategy and corporate entrepreneurship (e.g., a growth strategy encourages entrepreneurship, which further accelerates growth) deserves investigation. The present study examines only one aspect of these interactive, dynamic relationships. Future integrative efforts would enrich the field by developing fine-grained models and theories of how "antecedent" variables affect corporate entrepreneurship.

(3) The results invite replications, using data from *Fortune 500* or other populations, employing the same or different measures. For example, as the present study has focused specifically on the intensity of corporate entrepreneurship activities, future researchers may examine the effect of certain corporate entrepreneurship types (e.g., marketing, administrative, and technological) on financial performance. Alternatively, replications may contrast the predictors and effect of corporate entrepreneurship activities at the overall corporate, versus business, levels of the analysis. These refinements are necessary to better evaluate the contribution of corporate entrepreneurship at different organizational levels.

(4) The study has stressed the association between corporate entrepreneurship and company financial performance. Although consistent with the spirit of past findings, the results should be corroborated using alternative measures of risk or by exploring the effect of corporate entrepreneurship on non-financial performance criteria. As mentioned, companies often pursue corporate entrepreneurship for reasons other than stimulating performance improvements. These effects should be studied longitudinally to determine the time frame within which corporate entrepreneurship pays off optimally; to determine if a causal chain exists among predictors; and to examine the alternative plausible hypothesis that past, high company-performance (hence slack) may spur future corporate entrepreneurship activities. Past profitability may generate high financial slack, which encourages corporate venturing. Future empirical studies would help in refining this potential interactive link between corporate entrepreneurship and financial performance.

Future studies on the performance consequences of corporate entrepreneurship need to incorporate growth measures. Such studies will help in examining the potential tradeoffs between the short-term profitability and long-term growth objectives of corporate venturing.

(5) There is a growing body of empirical research on the processes associated with corporate entrepreneurship activities, but it consists primarily of case studies (Ellis and Taylor 1987). Scholars may employ different research approaches to document the processes and problems associated with the implementation of corporate entrepreneurship.

In conclusion, over the past decade corporate entrepreneurship has become a centerpiece in corporate efforts to improve financial performance, and to compete domestically and globally. The present study has presented a model of corporate entrepreneurship antecedents and the potential financial association of these ventures with financial performance. The study's encouraging results show that corporate entrepreneurship contributes to superior corporate financial performance.

REFERENCES

Berry, W. and Feldman, S. 1985. *Multiple Regression in Practice*. Beverly Hills, CA: Sage.

Bettinger, C. 1989. Use corporate culture to trigger high performance. *Journal of Business Strategy* 10(2): 38–42.

Betz, F. 1987. *Managing Technology*. Englewood Cliffs, NJ: Prentice-Hall.

Biggadike, R. 1979. The risky business of diversification. *Harvard Business Review* 79(5): 103–111.

Block, Z. 1989. Damage control for new corporate ventures. *Journal of Business Strategy* 10(2): 22–28.

Burgelman, R.A., and Sayles, L.R. 1986. *Inside Corporate Innovation Strategy, Structure and Managerial Skills*. New York: The Free Press.

Covin, J.G., and Slevin, D.P. 1988. The influence of organization structure on the utility of an entrepreneurial top management style. *Journal of Management Studies* 25:217–234.

Daft, R. 1988. *Organization Theory and Design*, 2nd ed. St. Paul, MN: West.

Daft, R., Sormunan, J., and Parks, D. 1988. Chief executive scanning, environmental characteristics, and company performance: an empirical study. *Strategic Management Journal* 8(2): 123–139.

Deal, T. and Kennedy, A. 1982. *Corporate Cultures: The Rites and Rituals of Corporate Life*. Reading, MA: Addison-Wesley.

Dess, G.G., and Beard, W.W. 1984. Dimensions of organizational task environments. *Administrative Science Quarterly* 29:52–73.

Dess, G.G., Ireland, R.D., and Hitt, M.A. 1990. Industry effects and strategic management research. *Journal of Management* 16:7–28.

Duncan, W.J., Ginger, P.M., Racks, A.C., and Jacob, T.D. 1988. Entrepreneurship and the reinvention of the corporation. *Business Horizons* 31(3): 16–19.

Ellis, J.R., and Taylor, N.T. 1987. Specifying entrepreneurship. *Frontiers of Entrepreneurship Research*. Wellesley, MA: Babson College p. 527–542.

Fannin, R. 1989. Where are the new brands? *Marketing & Media Decisions* 24(7): 20–27.

Franks, J.R., Broyles, J.E., and Carleton, W.T. 1985. *Corporate Finance: Concepts and Applications*. Boston, MA: Kent Publishing Company.

Grossack, I. 1965. Towards an integration of static and dynamic measures of industry concentration. *Review of Economics and Statistics* 7:301–308.

Hair, J., Jr., Anderson, R., and Tatham, R. 1987. *Multivariate Data Analysis*, 2nd ed. New York, NY: Macmillan Co.

Hall, E., and Zahra, S. 1990. Organizational culture: a methodological typology. *Southern Management Association Proceedings*, 285–287.

Hambrick, D.C. 1981. Strategic awareness within top management teams. *Strategic Management Journal* 2, 263–279.

Haskins, R., and Petit, T. 1988. Strategies for entrepreneurial manufacturing. *Journal of Business Strategy* 9(6): 24–28.

Hill, C.W., and Hoskisson, R.E. 1987. Strategy and structure in the multiproduct firm. *Academy of Management Review* 12:331–341.

Hitt, M.A., and Ireland, R.D. 1985. Corporate distinctive competence, strategy, industry and performance. *Strategic Management Journal* 6:273–293.

Hitt, M.A., Ireland, R.D., and Stadter, G. 1982. Functional Importance and Company Performance: Moderating Effects of Grand Strategy and Industry Type. *Strategic Management Journal* 3:315–330.

Jennings, D., and Lumpkin, J. 1989. Functionally modeling corporate entrepreneurship: an empirical integrative analysis. *Journal of Management* 15:485–502.

Learning Resources
Centre

282   S.A. ZAHRA

Kanter, R.M. 1986. Supporting innovation and venture development in established companies. *Journal of Business Venturing* 1(1): 47–60.

Kanter, R.M. 1989. *When Giants Learn to Dance*. New York, NY: Simon & Schuster, Inc.

Kanter, R.M. 1990. When giants learn cooperative strategies. *Planning Review* 18(1): 15–20, 22.

Keats, B.W., and Hitt, M. 1988. A causal model of linkages among environmental dimensions, macro organizational characteristics and performance. *Academy of Management Journal* 31:570–598.

Kotler, P. 1989. From mass marketing to mass customization. *Planning Review* 17(5): 10–47.

Low, M.B., and MacMillan, I.C. 1988. Entrepreneurship: past research and future challenges. *Journal of Management* 14:139–161.

MacMillan, I.C., Block, Z., and Narashima, P.N.S. 1986. Corporate venturing: alternatives, obstacles encountered, and experience effects. *Journal of Business Venturing* 1(2): 177–192.

MacMillan, I.C., and Day, D.L. 1987. Corporate ventures into industrial markets: dynamics of aggressive entry. *Journal of Business Venturing* 2(1): 29–39.

Miles, R.H. 1980. *Macro Organizational Behavior*. Santa Monica, CA: Goodyear Publishing.

Miller, A., and Camp, B. 1985. Exploring determinants of success in corporate ventures. *Journal of Business Venturing* 1(1): 87–105.

Miller, D. 1983. The correlates of entrepreneurship in three types of firms. *Management Science* 29:770–791.

Miller, D., and Friesen, P. 1984. *Organizations: A Quantum View*. Englewood Cliffs, NJ: Prentice-Hall.

Morris, M.H., Davis, D.L., and Ewing, J. 1988. The role of entrepreneurship in industrial marketing activities. *Industrial Marketing Management* 17:337–346.

Morris, M., and Gordon, P. 1987. The relationship between entrepreneurship and marketing in established firms. *Journal of Business Venturing* 2:247–259.

Murray, J. 1985. Marketing is home for entrepreneurial process. *Industrial Marketing Management* 10:93–99.

Nielsen, R.P., Peters, M.P., and Hisrich, R.D. 1985. Entrepreneurship strategy for internal markets— corporate, non profit, and government institution cases. *Strategic Management Journal* 6:181–190.

Oster, S. 1990. *Modern Strategic Analysis*. New York, NY: Oxford University Press.

Peters, T.J., and Water, R.H., Jr. 1982. *In Search of Excellence: Lessons from America's Best-Run Companies*. New York, NY: Harper & Row.

Peterson, R., and Berger, D. 1971. Entrepreneurship in organizations. *Administrative Science Quarterly* 16:97–106.

Pinchot, C. III. 1985. *Intrapreneuring*. New York: Harper & Row.

Porter, M. 1980. *Competitive Strategy*. New York: The Free Press.

Prahalad, C.K., and Bettis, R.A. 1986. The dominant logic: a new linkage between diversity and performance. *Strategic Management Journal* 7:485–501.

Ronen, J. 1988. Individual entrepreneurship and corporate entrepreneurship: a tentative synthesis. In G. Libecap, ed. *Advances in the Study of Entrepreneurship of Innovation, and Economic Growth*, Vol. 2. pp. 243–268. Greenwich, CT: JAI Press.

Rule, E.G., and Irwin, D.W. 1988. Fostering intrapreneurship: the new competitive edge. *Journal of Business Strategy* 9(3): 44–47.

Schein, E. 1985. *Organizational Culture and Leadership*. Homewood, IL: Irwin.

Schmid, W.G. 1989. Heinz covers the globe. *Journal of Business Strategy* 10:2, 17–20.

Schollhammer, H. 1982. Internal corporate entrepreneurship. In D.L. Sexton and K.H. Vesper, eds. *Encyclopedia of Entrepreneurship*. Englewood Cliffs, NJ: Prentice-Hall, Inc., pp. 209–223.

Serpa, R. 1987. Entrepreneurship in large corporations: a case history. In *Frontiers of Entrepreneurship Research*. Wellesley, MA: Babson College pp. 542–552.

Slevin, D., and Covin, J. 1989. Juggling entrepreneurial style and organization structure—how to get your act together. *Sloan Management Review* 31(2): 43–53.

Sykes, H.B. 1986. The anatomy of a corporate venturing program: factors influencing success. *Journal of Business Venturing* 1(3): 275–293.

Tootelian, D.H., and Gadeake, R.M. 1987. Fortune 500 list revisited 12 years later: still an endangered species for academic research. *Journal of Business Research* 5:359–363.

Weick, K. 1979. *The Social Psychology of Organizing*. Reading, MA: Addison-Wesley.

Wilson, J.Q. 1966. Innovation in organization: notes toward a theory. In J.D. Thompson, ed., *Approaches to Organizational Design*. Pittsburgh, PA: University of Pittsburgh Press, pp. 193–218.

Wortman, M.S., Jr. 1987. Entrepreneurship: an integrating typology and evaluation of the empirical research in the field. *Journal of Management* 13:259–279.

Zahra, S. 1986. A canonical analysis of corporate entrepreneurship antecedents and impact on performance. *Academy of Management Best Papers Proceedings*, 46th Annual Meeting, pp. 71–75.

Zahra, S., Floyd, S., and Pearce, J.A. II. November 1987. Strategy, culture and organizational performance: relationships in one industry. *Southern Management Association Proceedings* pp. 226–228.

Zahra, S. 1989. Organizational strategy, innovation and performance. *Academy of Management Best Papers Proceedings*, 49th Annual Meeting, pp. 349–353.

APPENDIX: STUDY MEASURES

Measures are based on data collected through a mail survey and from secondary financial sources, as reported below.

Environment

Perceived environmental dynamism, hostility, and heterogeneity were measured as follows:

(1) *Dynamism* (3 items; $\alpha = 0.79$). The items were: The rate of product obsolescence in our industry is high; In our industry, methods of production change often and in major ways; and Our firm must change its marketing practices frequently.

(2) *Hostility* (6 items, $\alpha = 0.82$). Items were: In our industry, actions of competitors are unpredictable; In our industry, demand and customer tastes are unpredictable; Declining markets for products are a major challenge in our industry; Tough price competition is a major challenge in our industry; Government interference is a major challenge in our industry; and Our business environment causes a great deal of threat to the survival of our company.

(3) *Heterogeneity* (3 items; $\alpha = 0.85$). Items were: We are a highly diversified conglomerate and operate in unrelated industries; Customers' buying habits vary a great deal from one line of our business to the other; and Market dynamism and uncertainty vary a great deal from one line of our business to the other.

All items relating to the environment were taken from Miller and Friesen (1984), and followed a seven-point Likert-type response format (1 = "strongly disagree" vs. 7 = "strongly agree").

Grand Strategy Types

The nominal scale developed by Hitt et al. (1982) was used. These authors have provided convincing evidence of the reliability of the scale.

284   S.A. ZAHRA

Organization

The following dimensions were measured.

(1) *Communication* (10 items; α = 0.86). The items followed a seven-point scale (7 = high vs. 1 = low.

Items	Quality	Frequency
Upward Communication		
a. Between middle management & senior management	——	——
b. Between employees & senior management	——	——
c. Between employees & middle management	——	——
Downward Communication		
a. Between middle management & senior management	——	——
b. Between employees & middle management employees	——	——
c. Between employees & senior management employees	——	——

Past research does not specify whether a summative (quality plus frequency) or multiplicative (quality × frequency) index of communication is a better predictor of corporate entrepreneurship. Therefore, two canonical analyses were run, one with the multiplicative and the second with the additive index. No differences were found between the two runs. Therefore, the results for the additive index are reported in this paper.

(2) *Scanning* (4 items; α = 0.81). An example item was, "We routinely track the policies and tactics of competitors."

(3) *Differentiation* (3 items; α = 0.64). An example item was, "The markets we participate in are very similar in terms of the required marketing, types of customers, pricing, etc."

(4) *Integration* (8 items, α = 0.68). An example item was, "We use task forces to facilitate interdepartmental collaboration on specific new projects."

The scanning, differentiation, and integration variables were measured using the items developed and validated by Miller and Friesen (1984), and followed a seven-point scale (1 = strongly disagree vs. 7 = strongly agree).

(5) *Control* (6 items; α = 0.70). Executives were asked to rate the extent to which several control devices were used to monitor progress in venturing activities and collect information on the performance of the projects. The items followed a seven-point Likert-type scale (1 = strongly disagree vs. 7 = strongly agree). Items were: All new ventures are subject to extensive review to determine their financial feasibility; Managers associated with a venture project must formally report its financial progress several times a year; Senior executives monitor different ventures closely to evaluate their performance; We conduct extensive reviews of the progress of different ventures; Our ventures are tightly controlled by top management; and There are many policies and procedures with which our employees must comply in initiating or maintaining a new venture.

(6) *Organizational Values*. Items followed seven-point semantic differentials, as follows:

(a) Person-centered (4 items, $\alpha = 0.73$): reward versus punishment; positive versus negative; person versus task; and participatory versus autocratic.

(b) Competition-related (8 items, $\alpha = 0.86$): open versus closed; aggressive versus passive; proactive versus reactive; leader versus follower; dominant versus submissive; quick versus slow; top versus bottom; and cooperative versus non-cooperative.

Organizational Performance

Four accounting measures were used: (1) average ROI; net income-to-sales ratio, EPS; and the standard deviations of RA. And risk was measured by the average beta estimates from *Value Line*. The rationale for these measures is discussed in the text.

Entrepreneurship

A scale consisting of nine items ($\alpha = 0.86$) was used to gauge corporate entrepreneurship. Responses followed a seven-point scale (1 = little emphasis to 7 = major emphasis). The items were: Implementing new programs to enhance innovation throughout the company over the past three years; Encouraging employee creativity and innovation; Soliciting employee ideas for new products and processes; Rewarding employees for creativity and innovation; Establishing a unit or department responsible for innovation and corporate development; Pursuing business opportunities developed outside your company; Training supervisors and managers in creativity and innovation techniques; Designating managers as champions of new ideas or innovations; and Emphasis on innovation in your company compared to your competitors.

[18]

1042-2587-99-242$1.50
Copyright 1999 by
Baylor University

The Antecedents and Consequences of Firm-Level Entrepreneurship: The State of the Field

Shaker A. Zahra
Daniel F. Jennings
Donald F. Kuratko

Empirical research into firm-level entrepreneurship spans over a quarter of a century. This article reviews the current state of this research by identifying key trends in 45 published empirical studies; examining the key issues addressed and methods used to examine them; and outlining six key areas that need greater attention in future research.

Research into the nature, antecedents and effects of firm-level entrepreneurial activities has grown rapidly over the past 25 years. Starting with Peterson and Berger's (1972) seminal study, this research has sought to identify organizational and environmental factors that affect a company's entrepreneurial activities. Earlier researchers gave special attention to the process by which established firms venture into new business fields and discussed the factors that influence the success of corporate ventures (Burgelman, 1983a, 1983b; Scholhammer, 1982). Likewise, Burgelman's (1983c) research into corporate venturing processes added considerable richness to the literature by documenting the interplay between autonomous and formal strategic behaviors that exist in a firm's entrepreneurial activities. Miller's (1983) paper, however, was a key turning point in the research on firm-level entrepreneurship. Authors from the U.S. and other countries have used Miller's theory and research instruments to examine the key linkages between environmental, strategic, and organizational variables, and a company's entrepreneurial activities. Research into these complex linkages continues to grow rapidly in scope and depth.

This article reviews the published research on the antecedents and consequences of firm-level entrepreneurship. It identifies issues covered, methods used, types of analyses conducted, and conclusions to be drawn from this research. The review also seeks to identify the shortcomings and contributions of past research efforts, hoping to set the stage for future research studies. Toward this end, the article outlines research questions worthy of greater attention in future study.

Two comments about the scope of this review are in order. First, given that several researchers (Jennings & Lumpkin, 1989; Covin & Slevin, 1991; Kuratko, Hornsby, Naffziger, & Montagno, 1993; Hornsby, Naffziger, Kuratko, & Montagno, 1993; Zahra, 1991, 1993a) have offered models of firm-level entrepreneurial activities, we have opted not to offer a new model. We believe that existing models are appropriate, but greater creativity is needed in testing the relationships depicted in, or proposed by, these models. Second, while we have reviewed diverse conceptual and empirical contributions as well as case studies, this paper emphasizes past empirical studies that have shaped the evolution of research in this area. Consequently, we have attempted to be as thorough and comprehensive as possible in assembling and reviewing these articles from refereed journals. This has led us to exclude some proceedings papers and book chapters. Still, we have made extensive use of many of these papers in developing our arguments and explaining key trends in the literature. Below, we present a listing of the articles we reviewed together with the variables we studied. In discussing each of these key variables, we have also stated the contributions and limitations of prior studies. Finally, the implications of our analysis of the state of the field for future research and scholarship are outlined.

ARTICLES REVIEWED

Table 1 presents the articles that we reviewed. These articles were selected from the journals identified by MacMillan (1993) as an appropriate publication forum for entrepreneurial research, with two exceptions. The first was Scholhammer's (1982) classification of internal corporate ventures and the second was Vesper's (1994) empirical classification of corporate ventures. Both classifications have been widely cited in the literature and, consequently, were included in the analysis.

As stated earlier, we examined only empirical studies so that we could follow the evolution of research in the area of firm-level entrepreneurship. The classification of variables used to construct Table 1 was developed simply by listing the variables mentioned in previous research. Thus, no a priori conceptual typology guided the development of the categories of the classification. Using this post hoc categorization of past writings has allowed us to capture the richness of the literature without imposing our biases or personal preferences on prior contributions.

PUBLICATION TIMELINE

A comprehensive search of the literature yielded 45 empirical papers on firm-level entrepreneurship. Table 1 shows that three papers appeared on the topic in the 1970s, 10 were published in the 1980s, and the remaining 32 papers were published in the 1990s. Three factors account for this dramatic increase in the number of papers published in the past decade. First, the growth of the field of entrepreneurship itself has added legitimacy to research into firm-level entrepreneurship. This growth also resulted in the creation of entrepreneurship-related journals that were especially interested in research into firm-level phenomena. Indeed, most of the papers on the topic have appeared in specialized entrepreneurship journals such as *Journal of Business Venturing (JBV)* and *Entrepreneurship Theory and Practice (ET&P)*. Second, the growth of publications in this area mirrored a societal interest in the U.S. and elsewhere in revitalizing established companies and improving their ability to innovate and take calculated risks. Third, the availability of reliable instruments that capture entrepreneurial activities has made it easier for researchers to examine this complex phenomenon. The instruments developed and validated by Miller (1983) have become the standard in this area. Covin and Slevin's (1988) extensions and refinements of this instrument were also influential in promoting empirical research on firm-level entrepreneurship.

TRENDS IN SAMPLES, LOCATION, AND DATA COLLECTION

Countries. Most past research into firm-level entrepreneurship has been conducted in

Table 1

Articles Reviewed

Conceptual Contribution	1	2	3	4	5	6	7	8	9	10	11	12	13	14	15	16	17	18	19
Schultz (1975)	X	X	X																X
Webster (1977)			X								X								
Roberts (1980							X					X	X						
Scholhammer (1982)							X	X	X	X	X								
Burgelman (1983)			X				X						X						
Gartner (1985)											X	X	X						
MacMillan & George (1985)			X				X						X						
Nielsen, Peters, & Hisrich (1985)				X															
Roberts & Berry (1985)						X	X		X			X							
Kanter (1985)		X	X				X					X			X		X		
Quinn (1985)	X	X	X								X					X			
Reich (1987)			X		X											X			
Wortman (1987)				X															
Gartner (1988)													X						
Rule & Irwin (1988)				X															
Sathe (1989)		X													X	X			
Guth & Ginsbert (1990)							X						X	X			X		
Howell & Higgins (1990)			X								X					X			
Kanter, North, Bernstein, & Williamson (1990)	X																	X	X
Starr & MacMillan (1990)							X												
Stevenson & Jarrillo (1990)				X	X										X				
Chittipeddi & Wallet (1991)	X	X		X					X										
Covin & Slevin (1991)	X	X	X															X	
Cunningham & Lischeron (1991)				X															
Fulop (1991)		X																	
Herron (1992)			X	X			X	X		X									
Lengnick-Hall (1992)				X		X	X		X										
Jones & Butler (1992)										X	X				X				X
Kelly (1993)																X			X
Zahra (1993a)	X	X	X													X	X		X
Kuratko (1993)															X	X			
Kuratko, Hornsby, Naffziger, & Montagno (1993)		X													X				
Ginsberg & Hay (1994)				X				X	X										
Stopford & Baden-Fuller (1994)	X	X		X										X				X	X
Dougherty (1995)														X					
Ghosal, Bauman, & Bartlett (1995)											X	X				X			X
Guth (1995)			X								X								X
Hill & Levenhapen (1995)		X	X																X
Krachhardt (1995)											X		X						

Table 1

Continued

Conceptual Contribution	1	2	3	4	5	6	7	8	9	10	11	12	13	14	15	16	17	18	19
Muzyka, Koning, & Churchill (1995)										X		X						X	X
Yeoh & Jeong (1995)						X													X
Rope & Hunt (1995)										X							X		
Brazeal & Herbert (1996)	X	X														X			
Dess, Lumpkin, & McGee (1996)																		X	X
Johnson (1996)													X					X	
Lumpkin & Dess (1996)	X	X	X			X	X	X	X	X				X				X	X
Teese (1996)			X				X	X						X				X	
Chung & Gibbons (1997)												X						X	X
Johannison & Monsted (1997)								X											X
Tercine, Harvey, & Buckley (1997)														X		X	X		
Tiessen (1997)			X		X	X													
Peterson & Berger (1971)						X							X	X					
Von Hipple (1977)							X										X		
Biggadike (1979)							X						X						
Fast (1981)							X						X						
Miller & Friesen (1982)	X	X	X													X		X	X
Miller (1983)	X	X	X																
Vesper (1984)						X	X	X											
Miller & Camp (1985)							X												
Covin & Slevin (1986)													X						
MacMillan, Block, & Subbanarsimha (1986)						X	X												
Hisrich & Peters (1986)							X									X	X	X	
Sykes (1986)		X					X					X				X	X	X	
Covin & Slevin (1988)																		X	
Jennings & Lumpkin (1989)		X											X					X	
Jennings & Young (1990)			X																
Kuratko, Montagno, & Hornsby (1990)					X						X								
Zahra (1991)																		X	
Larson (1992)			X		X														X
Russell & Russell (1992)																		X	X
Deshpande, Farley, & Webster (1993)			X																
Katz (1993)		X																	
Kolvereid, Shave, & Westhead (1993)							X												X
Morris, Avila & Aallen (1993)			X														X		

Table 1

Continued

Conceptual Contribution	1	2	3	4	5	6	7	8	9	10	11	12	13	14	15	16	17	18	19
Zahra (1993b)																		X	X
Zahra (1993c)			X											X					
Dougherty & Heller (1994)			X																
Morris, Davis, & Allen (1994)	X															X		X	X
Sebora, Hartman, & Tower (1994)			X											X		X			
Dougherty & Bowman (1995)			X								X					X			
Fiol (1995)			X																
Fisenhauer (1995)												X							
Morris & Lewis (1995)	X																		X
Sayles & Steward (1995)	X	X	X						X						X				
Scott (1995)			X																X
Zahra (1995)			X					X	X	X									
Brazeal (1996)			X											X		X			
Morris & Sexton (1996)																	X	X	
Zahra (1996)											X								
Dennis (1997)	X															X			
Kuratko, Hornsby, & Naffziger (1997)														X					
Park & Kim (1997)											X		X						
Pearce, Kramer, & Robbins (1997)	X										X					X			
Vesper & Gartner (1997)	X	X																	
Wright, Robbie, & Ennew (1997)										X		X							
Westhead & Wright (1998)												X						X	X

1 = Proactiveness, 2 = Risk Taking, 3 = Innovation, 4 = Intrapreneurship, 5 = Internal Alliances, 6 = External Alliances, 7 = Incubative Ventures, 8 = Initiative Venturing, 9 = Acquisitive Venturing, 10 = Opportunistic Venturing, 11 = Administrative, 12 = Venture Capital, 13 = Business Definition, 14 = Competitive Approach, 15 = Appropriate Use of Rewards, 16 = Management Support, 17 = Resource availability, 18 = Organizational Structure, 19 = Environment.

the U.S. or by researchers working in U.S.-based universities. Only a few studies have been published using data from non-U.S. companies including: Canadian (Miller, 1983), Norwegian (Knight, 1997), Japanese (Deshpande, Farley, & Webster, 1993); Swedish (Wiklund, 1998); and South African and Portuguese (Morris, Davis, & Allen, 1994) companies. However, more and more papers are being contributed by researchers from non-U.S. universities or by researchers using data from different countries. Researchers have also begun to explore factors that differentiate entrepreneurial research conducted in other countries from the U.S. model of scholarship. A noteworthy example is Huse and Landstrom's (1997) special issue devoted to European-based research on entrepreneurship. Without doubt, this research will increase our understanding of the profound effect of national cultures and unique resource endowments in promoting firm-level trend entrepreneurship.

Economic sectors studied. Another trend in published research into firm-level entrepreneurship is the predominance of data collected from manufacturing companies (85%). Service companies, which represent one of the fastest growing sectors in the global economy, have received only modest attention. One possible reason for the disproportionate attention given to manufacturing companies is the public concern over the global competitive status of manufacturing companies. Another reason is that some researchers do not understand service companies' operations.

Samples. Researchers have also relied for the most part on data collected from established companies (average age across samples = 42 years, sd = 3.5). This focus on established companies is understandable because of the interest in renewing and revitalizing companies' ongoing operations (Drucker, 1985; Peters & Waterman, 1982; Pinchot, 1985). However, with the exception of the Covin and Slevin (1990) study, we do not know the effect of the stages of the industry life cycle (ILC) on companies' entrepreneurial activities or whether the payoff from these activities varies across these stages. Economists (e.g., Porter, 1980) have long recognized the importance of inter-industry variations in explaining entrepreneurship and determining its effect on company performance.

Eighty-five percent of prior studies that have used manufacturing samples have also collected data from multiple industries. However, there is no uniformity in controlling for inter-industry variations, a factor that increases concern about the validity of past results. Only 37% of the studies controlled for industry effects. Even when statistical controls are used, we fear that researchers miss the opportunity to capitalize on inter-industry differences in structures and competitive dynamics in theorizing about the nature of entrepreneurship and its implications for company performance.

Researchers have also made extensive use of mail surveys in collecting data on entrepreneurial activities. Our analysis shows that 19% of the studies reviewed have used only mail surveys to collect data; 7% used interviews; 6% employed both interviews and mail surveys; and 68% used a combination of mail surveys and secondary data. The predominance of survey data is understandable because gaining access to information about companies' entrepreneurial activities is exceedingly difficult.

Reliance on surveys has well-known side effects such as an overemphasis on the content of entrepreneurial activities (rather than their process) and difficulties in making strong causal attributions. Use of survey data might have contributed to an overemphasis on the formal aspects of entrepreneurial activities, overlooking informal entrepreneurial activities and their contributions to a company's performance. As noted by several observers (Drucker, 1985; Kanter, 1985, 1989; Kuratko, 1993; Kuratko & Hornsby, 1996; Peters & Waterman, 1982; Pinchot, 1985; Wortman, 1987; Zahra, 1991), informal aspects of entrepreneurship can and do play an important role in enriching a company's performance. Field studies, experiments, and interviews can be more revealing about the role of autonomous entrepreneurial activities (Burgelman, 1983c, 1991).

We certainly do not suggest that mail surveys are not a viable approach to data collection; we have in fact made extensive use of them in our own research. Rather, we would like to see more energy devoted to using multiple sources of data in research on firm-level entrepreneurship in validating measures, testing hypotheses, and developing theories.

The problems associated with the use of survey data are further magnified by researchers' reliance on a single respondent. When mail surveys are used (87% of the articles reviewed), nearly all studies relied on a single respondent. Almost all past studies targeted CEOs or the firm's most senior managers who are assumed to know a great deal about companies' entrepreneurial activities (Zahra, 1991). A few studies (19%) have attempted to establish inter-rater reliability by contacting a second respondent (typically a senior executive). Of course, evidence of significant inter-rater reliability increases confidence in the quality of data used in prior studies. However, senior executives may not be fully aware of the many autonomous initiatives undertaken by their firms' divisions; middle managers are usually more positioned at the center of these activities (Burgelman, 1991; Floyd & Wooldrige, 1992; Peters & Waterman, 1982; Pinchot, 1985). Middle managers are also better informed about how formal and informal entrepreneurial activities unfold (Kanter, 1985) and therefore can better evaluate the success or failure of these efforts. Given that most prior studies have attempted to link entrepreneurial activities to the firm's overall financial performance, important insights can be gained from surveying or interviewing middle managers (Kuratko, Montagno, & Hornsby, 1990).

THE MANY FACES OF FIRM-LEVEL ENTREPRENEURSHIP

A close examination of published papers reveals that authors have not been consistent in the label they attach to the phenomenon they purport to study (Wiklund, 1998). Authors have used labels that include: entrepreneurship (Miller, 1983), corporate entrepreneurship (Peterson & Berger, 1971; Morris & Paul, 1987; Zahra, 1991, 1993a, 1993b, 1996; Zahra & Covin, 1995), intrapreneurship (Kuratko, 1993; Kuratko, Montagno, & Hornsby, 1990), entrepreneurial posture (Covin & Slevin, 1991), strategic posture (Covin & Slevin, 1988; Covin, Slevin, & Covin, 1990; Merz, Parker, & Kallis, 1990), and entrepreneurial orientation (Dess, Lumpkin, & Covin, 1997; Miles, Arnold, & Thompson, 1993). Yet, despite the ubiquity of labels used, most researchers have used Miller and Friesen's (1982) measure of firm-level entrepreneurship (Merz et al., 1990) or a modified version of this instrument (Covin & Slevin, 1988, 1991; Covin et al., 1990; Miles et al., 1993; Zahra, 1991).

Miller's (1983) conceptualization focuses on three related dimensions of firm-level entrepreneurship: proactiveness, innovation, and risk taking. Some earlier studies attempted to extend and modify Miller's (1983) conceptualization. Covin and Slevin (1988) extended Miller's measure to gauge a firm's entrepreneurial activities. Zahra (1991) argued that Miller's instrument captured disposition toward rather than actual entrepreneurship (Wiklund, 1998). Miller's measure did not capture, however, external entrepreneurial activities by the firm, focusing instead on internal entrepreneurial activities. Zahra (1991) further asserted that Miller's measure did not capture those informal entrepreneurial activities that take place in a firm (e.g., Pinchot, 1985; Wortman, 1987).

When Guth and Ginsberg (1990) reviewed the status of the field a decade ago, they concluded that firm-level entrepreneurship embodied two key components: innovation (of all types) and new business creation through venturing. However, we were able to locate only one study that captured both dimensions (Zahra, 1993b). Apparently, Miller's conceptualization has evolved into the instrument of choice in examining firm-level entrepreneurship. One unanticipated consequence of this practice is that research into corporate venturing, therefore, has not been fully integrated into discussions of firm-level entrepreneurship or entrepreneurial orientation.

Perhaps the time has come to conceptually integrate Miller's (1983) and Guth and Ginsberg's (1990) classifications of firm-level entrepreneurship. A unified typology (Zahra, 1991) would highlight three dimensions. The first is the content of the entrepreneurial act, which corresponds to Miller's (1983) conceptualization and Guth and Ginsberg's (1990) innovation and venturing. The second dimension focuses on the locus of this act; it separates internal from external entrepreneurial activities. Internal activities are conducted within a firm's boundaries, as happens when two divisions of the same company join forces to develop a new product. External entrepreneurial activities transcend the firm's boundaries, as occurs when a firm joins another to pursue new product development. The third and final dimension indicates the source of the entrepreneurial act: whether formal or informal. This last dimension corresponds directly to Burgelman's (1983c, 1991) distinction between autonomous and formal strategic actions. Combining these three dimensions produces an eight-cell matrix that represents different entrepreneurial activities that can occur within established companies. Each of these eight cells offers interesting research possibilities into the antecedents, process, and consequences of entrepreneurial activities.

While no single typology is all encompassing, the above classification (Figure 1) suggests that some dimensions of firm-level entrepreneurial activities have not been closely examined. Informal, whether internally or externally focused, entrepreneurial activities have not been studied, and more research is needed to understand the conditions that foster these activities. The cells overlooked in this typology are among the areas that are receiving attention beyond the traditional boundaries of the field of entrepreneurship. Formal alliances that support corporate venturing are one example. Another example is research on external networks, the ties that bond their members, and their effects on a company's innovation and risk taking. These issues are receiving attention from strategic management and international business scholars. Future entrepreneurship research would benefit greatly from examining these issues, thus filling voids in our knowledge of the nature, dimensions, and effects of these variables on firm-level entrepreneurship.

Figure 1

A Typology of Firm-Level Entrepreneurship

Locus on Entrepreneurial Activity

Internal	External	Internal	External
Informal	Informal	Informal	Informal
Formal	Formal	Formal	Formal
Venturing	Innovation	Venturing	Innovation

Method and Analysis

Understanding the contributions of past research requires that we consider several issues: the statistical treatment of the entrepreneurship construct; the statistical controls employed in past designs; and the types of analytical tools used.

Statistical treatment of the entrepreneurship construct. Most past studies (45%) used a measure of entrepreneurship as their dependent variable (76%). Most prior research examined the determinants of firm-level entrepreneurship by exploring the effects of a company's external environment, strategy, structure, and organizational culture. Researchers were keenly interested in uncovering those variables that enhanced companies' willingness to be entrepreneurial. This research, we believe, responded to a societal need to identify the sources of variations in entrepreneurial activities. Through the 1980s and 1990s, belief persisted that once these variables were identified and understood, strategic change and organizational renewal were achievable.

A smaller number of studies, however, treated entrepreneurship as an independent variable (Brazeal, 1993). Most of these studies have explored the effect of a company's entrepreneurial activities on financial or non-financial outcomes. In many ways, these studies enhanced the legitimacy of research into firm-level entrepreneurship by documenting the effects of entrepreneurship on company performance. Collectively, these studies suggested that entrepreneurship was a significant correlate of a company's performance.

Still a third group of researchers treated entrepreneurship as both a dependent and independent variable (Zahra, 1991). They sought to clarify the antecedents and effects of certain variables on firm-level entrepreneurship and examine the effect of entrepreneurship on an outcome variable such as the company's financial performance. Most of these studies were guided by the configuration approach that dominated the literature in the late 1980s and early 1990s. This approach focused on finding constellations of organizational variables that influenced entrepreneurship while determining their potential association with measures of performance.

Upon examining published studies, one cannot help but notice the general lack of attention to the lagged effect that might exist among the sets of antecedents, entrepreneurship, and performance variables examined. The overwhelming majority of prior studies give the reader the impression that antecedent variables affect entrepreneurship almost instantly, and that entrepreneurship improves company performance as quickly. We were able to find two studies that recognized the possibility that the effect of entrepreneurship is long-term in nature (Zahra, 1991; Zahra & Covin, 1995), and both of these studies have several limitations. One of these studies (Zahra, 1991) examined the effect of entrepreneurship on performance measures for only one or two years after the data for the entrepreneurship variable were collected. Obviously, the long-term effects of entrepreneurship on a company's performance are unclear. The other study (Zahra & Covin, 1995) used a three-year time lag, but the attrition among companies in the sample was so high that survivor bias might have been magnified in the results. Companies that survived might have pursued different entrepreneurial ventures from firms that failed, or pursued the same ventures but did so differently from failing companies. Whether this is true or not cannot be gleaned from the results. Further, many organizational changes have occurred in the firms studied by Zahra and Covin (1995), raising a question about the sources of performance differences observed in the sample.

In summary, most prior studies have treated "entrepreneurship" as either an independent or dependent variable. However, because these studies have not examined the lag effect that might exist between antecedent variables and entrepreneurship, and between entrepreneurship and outcomes (e.g., performance), the causal sequence among these variables is unclear.

Measures. There has been an unusually high degree of consistency in the way researchers measured firm-level entrepreneurship. Most researchers used the measures developed by Miller and Friesen (1982) and published by Miller (1983). This consistency is remarkable, especially because researchers have not used the same labels (or even the same constructs) in their research, as we noted earlier. Consequently, we fear that the quest for consistency has caused a serious *misfit* between construct and measures, raising a question about the meaning of what has been found and its theoretical and practical importance. One exception was the study by Jennings and Lumpkin (1989) in which they utilized the work of Schumpeter (1947), Ansoff (1965), and Hambrick (1983) to define firm-level entrepreneurship as the extent to which new products are developed. Jennings and Lumpkin (1989) also used archival data to measure new product additions.

Another source of concern is that few researchers have attempted to validate the popular measures developed by Miller and Friesen (1982), who were careful to show evidence of the reliability and validity of their measure. Zahra (1991, 1993b) correlated secondary and survey data to demonstrate the validity of Miller's (1983) index, supporting the reliability and validity of the measure. In another effort, Covin and Slevin (1988) used factor analysis to establish the dimensionality of a revised (expanded) measure of Miller's index. However, Jennings and Young (1990) found no significant difference between Jennings and Lumpkin's (1989) measurement of firm-level entrepreneurship and that of Miller and Friesen (1982). Thus, the dimensionality of Miller's measure has escaped close examination until recently, when Knight (1997) used LISREL to compare the stability (hence, comparability) of the structure of this measure using data from Norway and the U.S.

We appreciate the need for the use of consistent measures of entrepreneurship. Indeed, the Miller (1983) measure and the Covin and Slevin (1988) extensions have both served the field well, and no one can question their merit. We remain concerned that researchers might have prematurely agreed on a common measure without establishing its dimensionality or other psychometric properties. Triangulation also is clearly absent in this area of research, which opens the door for many interesting possibilities to be explored in future studies to validate, revise, and refine measures of firm-level entrepreneurship. In particular, these improvements should also emphasize a closer connection between constructs and empirical measures.

Statistical controls. Over the past decade researchers have become more attentive to the issues of reliability, evidenced by the fact that nearly all studies (84%) report a measure of internal scale consistency (usually Cronbach's alpha). They have also increased their attention to demonstrating internal reliability (73% of the studies). Further, researchers have controlled for variables that might affect the relationship between entrepreneurial activities and firm performance, including: company age (6%), size (14%), industry types (5%), and past performance (9%). While researchers have used different ways to perform these controls, it is clear that researches are aware that these variables can confound their results.

One variable that has not been recognized in prior research is a company's past entrepreneurial activities. The laws of inertia may work both ways: conservative companies are likely to behave in this way over time, while innovative and entrepreneurial companies are likely to engage in more and more entrepreneurial activities. Given that most past research has focused on companies' entrepreneurial "disposition" or "orientation," future researchers need to control for a company's past entrepreneurial orientation.

Analytical tools used. Most past studies have used regression analysis as the primary technique in analyzing their data (59%); one study used both cluster analysis and multivariate analysis of variance (Covin et al., 1990); one study used structural equation modeling (LISREL) techniques (Knight, 1997); one study used canonical analysis

(Zahra, 1991); and one study used time series analysis (Zahra & Covin, 1995). It is noteworthy, however, that the use of techniques other than regression analysis increased in the 1990s, reflecting on the growing maturity of research in this area, the entry of researchers with a strong grasp of these techniques, and the availability of databases that permit the use of advanced analyses. We anticipate and suggest even greater diversity in the use of the analytical techniques employed in future studies.

FUTURE DIRECTIONS

Throughout this analysis of the literature, we have attempted to outline areas of potential importance for future research. In this section, we will only highlight the most important conceptual, methodological, and analytical issues that deserve greatest attention in future studies.

(1) There is a need to explore different conceptualizations of firm-level entrepreneurship. Future researchers are encouraged to distinguish between entrepreneurial disposition (Miller, 1983; Covin & Slevin, 1988), orientation (Lumpkin & Dess, 1996) and actions (Zahra, 1991, 1993b). Orientation does not always gauge actions. Lumpkin and Dess (1996) have made an important contribution to the field by identifying the various dimensions of firm-level entrepreneurship, and their classification system can guide future research. Entrepreneurial actions can be captured by companies' actual strategic choices and moves; they embody the firm's innovations (process, product, and organization) and venturing activities, as noted by Guth and Ginsberg (1990). Researchers can also help validate the results reported in prior research and summarized in this review by using alternative classifications of firm-level entrepreneurship.

(2) The literature would benefit also from revisiting the various units of analysis used in research into firm-level entrepreneurship. To date, and perhaps predictably, the literature has focused on overall firm-level activities. Greater attention should be given to entrepreneurship at the divisional (strategic business unit) level of the analysis. A great many entrepreneurial activities occur at the level of organizational divisions (Kuratko, Montagno, & Hornsby, 1990; Peters & Waterman, 1982; Pinchot, 1985; Zahra, 1993a, 1993b).

Researchers need also to give attention to the antecedents and effects of particular entrepreneurial events. These events provide important glimpses into a company's unfolding entrepreneurial activities and, therefore, can help improve our understanding of the contributions of entrepreneurship to company performance (Pinchot, 1985). Prior researchers, who have shown a consistent interest in entrepreneurial disposition or orientation, have not given sufficient attention to the factors that encourage firms to undertake particular actions. For example, rather than using the creation of a new venture as an indicator of firm-level entrepreneurship (which it is), future researchers should consider isolating the factors that may have led a company to undertake such an effort (Kuratko, Hornsby, & Naffziger, 1997).

(3) Greater diversity in the geographic and industry scope is also needed in future research into firm-level entrepreneurship. One area that requires greater attention is the nature of entrepreneurial activities across national cultures. Most past research has used data collected from U.S. companies; future researchers need to explore the stability of these results by collecting data from other countries. A related area of potential interest is the effect of national cultures on entrepreneurship. Shane's (1993) research clearly shows that national cultures play a profound role in explaining the differences in rates of entrepreneurship among societies. Research by Morris et al. (1994) also shows that national cultural variables can also influence firm-level entrepreneurship activities. However, more studies are needed to show how national cultures affect the rates and types of firm-level entrepreneurship and the resultant outcomes of entrepreneurial activities.

One area that needs more research is the interaction of national and organizational cultures on firm-level entrepreneurship. These two variables have been analyzed separately, though theory clearly indicates that national cultures influence organizational cultures (Morris et al., 1994), which, in turn, determine firm-level entrepreneurship. Does this mean that organizational culture mediates the national culture-entrepreneurship relationship? An answer to this question must await future research.

(4) Different conceptualizations of the link between entrepreneurial activities and company performance are needed. Both the popular press and the practitioner-oriented literature claim that entrepreneurial activities are inherently linked to higher company performance. However, this relationship is an important empirical question. There is the implicit assumption that first-mover firms that incur the greatest business and financial risk and spend the most on innovative activities would always be rewarded in the marketplace. However, many firms, such as Lincoln Electric and Emerson Electric, which are stellar performers, aggressively pursue cost leadership strategies and deemphasize innovation and risk taking (Dess, Lumpkin, & McGee, 1996). Also, as noted by Nelson and Winter (1982), research has indicated that firms may enjoy a greater long-term benefit from imitation strategies than from high levels of innovativeness. Further, the notion of equifinality suggests that organizations can utilize different orientations to reach the same objective and achieve the same outcome(s). Consequently, there may be no performance differences between entrepreneurial and conservative firms (Jennings & Seaman, 1994). The relationship between performance and entrepreneurial activity remains a fruitful area for future research. Austrian economics would suggest a further need to examine different entrepreneurial actions (tactical vs. strategic) and relate them to a company's performance (see, Grimm & Smith, 1997).

(5) An area that needs more attention is the firm's international operations. Entrepreneurial activities abound in the firm's internationalization efforts (Zahra & Garvis, 2000). As companies expand globally, researchers have a golden opportunity to examine entrepreneurial orientations, activities, and processes. Researchers may study companies' international expansion activities or the joint activities of companies from different countries. Studying the entrepreneurial activities of the subsidiaries of multinationals is another fertile area for empirical research (Birkinshaw, 1997).

(6) Qualitative and quantitative studies should be combined in ways that enrich our understanding of firm-level entrepreneurship. These studies can help clarify the relative importance of antecedent variables on entrepreneurial activities or orientations. These studies can also help to define the effect of organizational context on entrepreneurial variables of interest. One notable area that would benefit from integrating qualitative and quantitative studies is the role of organizational cultures in explaining entrepreneurial activities or the effect of these activities on company performance. Another area that deserves attention is national cultures, as noted previously. A third area is the effect of top managers (or owners) on firm-level entrepreneurship. Ownership variables vary considerably across countries and, therefore, can influence a company's entrepreneurial activities quite differently. Future studies can improve our appreciation of how and why the characteristics of senior executives can affect a company's entrepreneurship. Obviously, research opportunities on the nature and process of entrepreneurship and its implications for organizational performance are abundant.

CONCLUSION

Research on firm-level entrepreneurship has grown in scope and depth over the past 25 years. This research has enriched and extended the literature in significantly and important ways. The results of the theoretical research during this time period suggest that companies that engage in entrepreneurial activities achieve superior performance. Our review of the state of the art in this area, however, indicates that many research questions still need attention. We hope our review encourages future researchers to continue to explore some of the important issues we have highlighted in this paper.

REFERENCES

Ansoff, I. (1965). *Corporate strategy.* New York: McGraw-Hill.

Biggadike, R. (1979). The risky business of diversification. *Harvard Business Review, 57*(3), 103-111.

Birkinshaw, J. (1997). Entrepreneurship in multinational corporations: The role of subsidiary initiative. *Strategic Management Journal, 18*(3), 207-229.

Brazeal, V. D. (1993). Organizing for internally developed corporate ventures. *Journal of Business Venturing, 8*(1), 75-90.

Brazeal, V. D. (1996). Managing an entrepreneurial organizational environment. A discriminant analysis of organizational and individual differences between autonomous unit managers and department managers. *Journal of Business Research, 35*(1), 55-67.

Brazeal, V. D., & Herbert, T. T. (1996). Towards conceptual consistency in the foundations of entrepreneurship: Change, innovations and creativity. Working Paper, California State Polytechnic University.

Burgelman, R. A. (1983a). A model of the interaction of strategic behavior, corporate context, and the concept of strategy. *Academy of Management Review, 8*(1), 61-70.

Burgelman, R. A. (1983b). Corporate entrepreneurship and strategic management: Insights from a process study. *Management Science, 29*(12), 1349-1363.

Burgelman, R. A. (1983c). A process model of internal corporate venturing in the diversified major firm. *Administrative Science Quarterly, 28*(2), 223-244.

Burgelman, R. A. (1991). Intraorganizational ecology of strategy making and organizational adaptation: Theory and field research. *Organizational Science, 2*(3), 239-262.

Chittipeddi, K., & Wallet, T. (1991). Entrepreneurship and competitive strategy for the 1990s. *Journal of Small Business Management, 29*(1), 94-98.

Chung, H. L., & Gibbons, T. P. (1997). Corporate entrepreneurship: The roles of ideology and social capital. *Group & Organization Management, 22*(1), 10-30.

Covin, J. G., & Slevin, D. P. (1986). The development and testing of an organizational level entrepreneurship scale. In R. Ronstadt, J. A. Hornaday, R. Peterson, & K. H. Vesper (Eds.), *Frontiers of entrepreneurship research—1986,* pp. 628-639, Wellesley, MA: Babson College.

Covin, J. G., & Slevin, D. (1988). The influence of organization structure on the utility of an entrepreneurial top management style. *Journal of Management Studies, 25*(3), 217-234.

Covin, J. G., & Slevin, D. P. (1990). New venture strategic posture, structure and performance: An industry life cycle analysis. *Journal of Business Venturing, 5*(2), 123-135.

Covin, J. G., & Slevin, D. (1991). A conceptual model of entrepreneurship as firm behavior. *Entrepreneurship Theory & Practice, 15*(4), 35-50.

Covin, J. G., Slevin, D., & Covin, T. J. (1990). Content and performance of growth-seeking strategies: A comparison of small Firms in high- and low-technology Industries. *Journal of Business Venturing, 5*(6), 391-412.

Cunningham, J., & Lischeron, J. (1991). Defining entrepreneurship. *Journal of Small Business Management, 29*(1), 45-61.

Dennis, W. J., Jr. (1997). More than you think: An inclusive estimate of business entries. *Journal of Business Venturing, 12*(3), 175-196.

Deshpande, R., Farley, J. U., & Webster, F. E. (1993). Corporate culture, customer orientation, and innovativeness in Japanese firms: A quadrad analysis. *Journal of Marketing, 57*(1), 23-37.

Dess, G. G., Lumpkin, G. T., & Covin, J. G. (1997). Entrepreneurial strategy making and firm performance: Tests of contingency and configurational models. *Strategic Management Journal, 18*(9), 677-695.

Dess, G. G., Lumpkin, G. T., & McGee, J. E. (1996). Linking corporate entrepreneurship to strategy, structure, and process: Suggested research directions. Working Paper, University of Kentucky.

Dougherty, D. (1995). Managing your core incompetencies for corporate venturing. *Entrepreneurship Theory and Practice, 19*(3), 113-136.

Dougherty, D., & Bowman, E. H. (1995). The effects of organizational downsizing on product innovation. *California Management Review, 37*(4), 28-45.

Dougherty, D., & Heller, T. (1994). The illegitimacy of successful product innovation in established firms. *Organization Science, 5*(2), 200-218.

Drucker, P. (1985). *Innovations and entrepreneurship.* New York: Harper & Row.

Fast, N. D. (1981). Pitfalls of corporate venturing. *Research Management,* March, 21-24.

Fiol, C. M. (1995). Thought worlds colliding: The role of contradiction in corporate innovation processes. *Entrepreneurship Theory and Practice, 19*(3), 71-91.

Fisenhauer, J. G. (1995). The entrepreneurial decision: Economic theory and empirical evidence. *Entrepreneurship Theory and Practice, 19*(4), 67-80.

Floyd, S. W., & Woodridge, B. (1992). Middle management involvement in strategy and its association with strategic type: A research note. *Strategic Management Journal, 13*(special issue), 153-167.

Fulop, L. (1991). Middle managers: Victims or vanguards of the entrepreneurial movement? *Journal of Management Studies, 28*(1), 25-44.

Gartner, W. B. (1985). A conceptual framework for describing the phenomenon of new venture creation. *Academy of Management Review, 10*(4), 696-706.

Gartner, W. B. (1988). "Who is an entrepreneur?" is the wrong question. *American Journal of Small Business, 12*(4), 11-32.

Ghoshal, S., Bauman, P. R., & Bartlett, C. (1995). Building the entrepreneurial corporation: New organizational processes, new managerial tasks. *European Management Journal, 13*(2), 139-158.

Ginsberg, A., & Hay, M. (1994). Confronting the challenges of corporate entrepreneurship: Guidelines for venture managers. *European Management Journal, 12*(4), 382-389.

Grimm, C. M., & Smith, K. G. (1997). *Strategy as action: Industry rivalry and coordination.* Cincinnati, OH: South-Western College Publishing.

Guth, W. D. (1995). Theory from field research on firm level entrepreneurship: A normal science overview. *Entrepreneurship Theory and Practice, 19*(3), 169-173.

Guth, W. D., & Ginsberg, A. (1990). Guest editor's introduction: Corporate entrepreneurship. *Strategic Management Journal,* 11, 5-16.

Hambrick, D. C. (1983). Some tests of the effectiveness and functional attributes of Miles and Snow's strategic types. *Academy of Management Journal, 26*(1), 5-26.

Herron, L. (1992). Cultivating corporate entrepreneurs. *Human Resource Planning, 15*(4), 3-15.

Hill, R. C., & Levenhapen, M. (1995). Metaphors and mental models: Sensemaking and sensegiving in innovative and entrepreneurial activities. *Journal of Management, 21*(6), 1057-1075.

Hisrich, R. D., & Peters, M. P. (1986). Establishing a new business venture unit within a firm. *Journal of Business Venturing, 1*(3), 307-322.

Hornsby, J. S., Naffziger, D. W., Kuratko, D. F., & Montagno, R. V. (1993). An interactive model of the corporate entrepreneurship process. *Entrepreneurship Theory & Practice, 17*(2), 29-37.

Howell, J. M., & Higgins, C. A. (1990). Champions of technological innovation. *Administrative Science Quarterly, 35*(2), 317-341.

Huse, M., & Landstrom, H. (1997). European entrepreneurship and small business research: methodological openness and contextual differences. *International Studies of Management & Organization, 27*(3), 3-27.

Jennings, D. F., & Lumpkin, R. J. (1989). Functioning modeling corporate entrepreneurship: An empirical integrative analysis. *Journal of Management, 15*(3), 485-502.

Jennings, D. F., & Seaman, S. L. (1994). High and low levels of organizational adaptation: An empirical analysis of strategy, structure, and performance. *Strategic Management Journal, 15*(6), 459-475.

Jennings, D. F., & Young, D. M. (1990). An empirical comparison between objective and subjective measures of the product innovation domain of corporate entrepreneurship. *Entrepreneurship Theory and Practice, 15*(1), 53-66.

Johannison, B., & Monsted, M. (1997). Contextualizing entrepreneurial networking: The case of Scandinavia. *International Studies of Management and Organization, 27*(3), 109-128.

Johnson, R. A. (1996). Antecedents and outcomes of corporate refocusing. *Journal of Management, 22*(3), 439-484..

Jones, G. R., & Butler, J. E. (1992). Managing internal corporate entrepreneurship: An agency theory perspective. *Journal of Management, 18*(4), 733-749.

Kanter, R. M. (1985). Supporting innovation and venture development in established companies. *Journal of Business Venturing, 1*(1), 47-60.

Kanter, R. M. (1989). *When giants learn to dance.* New York: Simon and Schuster.

Kanter, R. M., North, J., Bernstein, A., & Williamson, A. (1990). Designing and running entrepreneurial vehicles in established companies. *Journal of Business Venturing, 5*(6), 415-427.

Katz, J. A. (1993). How satisfied are the self employed: A secondary analysis approach. *Entrepreneurship Theory and Practice, 17*(3), 35-52.

Kelly, J. (1993). Executive behavior: Classical and existential. *Business Horizons, 36*(1), 16-27.

Knight, G. A. (1997). Cross-cultural reliability and validity of a scale to measure firm entrepreneurial orientation. *Journal of Business Venturing, 12*(3), 213-225.

Kolvereid, L., Shave, S., & Westhead, P. 1993). Is it equally difficult for female entrepreneurs to start businesses in all countries? *Journal of Small Business Management, 31*(4), 42-52.

Krackhardt, D. (1995). Entrepreneurial opportunities in an entrepreneurial firm: A structural approach. *Entrepreneurship Theory and Practice, 19*(3), 53-70.

Kuratko, D. F. (1993). Intrapreneurship: Developing innovation in the corporation. *Advances in Global High Technology Management-High Technology Venturing, 3,* 3-14.

Kuratko, D. F., & Hornsby, J. S. (1996). Developing entrepreneurial leadership in contemporary organizations. *Journal of Management Systems, 8*(1), 17-27.

Kuratko, D. F., Hornsby, J. S., & Naffziger, D. W. (1997). An examination of owner's goals in sustaining entrepreneurship. *Journal of Small Business Management, 35*(1), 24-34.

Kuratko, D. F., Hornsby, J. S., Naffziger, D. W., & Montagno, R. V. (1993). Implementing entrepreneurial thinking in established organizations. *SAM Advanced Management Journal, 58*(1), 28-35.

Kuratko, D. F., Montagno, R. V., & Hornsby, J. S. (1990). Developing an entrepreneurial assessment instrument for an effective corporate entrepreneurial environment. *Strategic Management Journal,* 11, 49-58.

Larson, A. (1992). Network dyads in entrepreneurial settings: A study of the governance of exchange relationships. *Administrative Science Quarterly, 37*(1), 76-104.

Lengnick-Hall, C. A. (1992). Innovation and competitive advantage: What we know and what we need to learn. *Journal of Management, 18*(2), 399-429.

Lumpkin, G. T., & Dess, G. G. (1996). Clarifying the entrepreneurial orientation construction and linking it to performance. *Academy of Management Review, 21*(1), 135-173.

MacMillan, I. C. (1993). The emerging forum for entrepreneurship scholars. *Journal of Business Venturing, 8*(5), 377-381.

MacMillan, I. C., Block, Z., & Subbanarasimha, P. (1986). Corporate venturing: Alternatives, obstacles encountered, and experience effects. *Journal of Business Venturing, 1*(2), 177-191.

MacMillan, I. C., & George, R. (1985). Corporate venturing: challenges for senior managers. *Journal of Business Strategy, 5*(3), 34-44.

Merz, G. R., Parker, B. J., & Kallis, M. J. (1990). Resource-related dependencies: Marketing strategies of technological-based firms. *European Journal of Marketing, 23*(4), 44-65.

Miles, M. P., Arnold, D. R., & Thompson, D. L. (1993). The interrelationship between environmental hostility and entrepreneurial orientation. *Journal of Applied Business Research, 9*(4), 12-23.

Miller, A., & Camp, B. (1985). Exploring determinants of success in corporate ventures. *Journal of Business Venturing, 1*(1), 247-259.

Miller, D. (1983). The correlates of entrepreneurship in three types of firms. *Management Science, 29*(7), 770-791.

Miller, D., & Friesen, P. H. (1982). Innovation in conservative and entrepreneurial firms: Two models of strategic momentum. *Strategic Management Journal, 3*(1), 1-25.

Morris, M. H., Avila, R. A., & Allen, J. (1993). Individualism and the modern corporation: Implications for innovation and entrepreneurship. *Journal of Management, 19*(3), 595-613.

Morris, M. H., Davis, D. L., & Allen, J. W. (1994). Fostering corporate entrepreneurship: Cross-cultural comparisons of the importance of individualism versus collectivism. *Journal of International Business Studies, 25*(1), 65-90.

Morris, M. H., & Lewis, P. S. (1995). The determinants of entrepreneurial activity: Implications for marketing. *European Journal of Marketing, 29*(7), 31-49.

Morris, M. H., & Paul, G. W. (1987). The relationships between entrepreneurship and marketing in established firms. *Journal of Business Venturing, 2*(3), 247-259.

Morris, M. H., & Sexton, D. L. (1996). The concept of entrepreneurial intensity: Implications for company performance. *Journal of Business Research, 36*(1), 5-13.

Muzyka, D., Koning, A. D., & Churchill, N. (1995). On transformation and adaptation: Building the entrepreneurial corporation. *European Management Journal, 13*(4), 346-362.

Nelson, R. R., and Winter, S. G. (1982). *An evolutionary theory of economic change.* Cambridge, MA: Belknap Press.

Nielsen, R. P., Peters, M. R., & Hisrich, R. D. (1985). Intrapreneurship strategy for internal markets— Corporate, nonprofit, and government institution cases. *Strategic Management Journal, 6*(2), 181-189.

Park, S. H., & Kim, D. (1997). Market valuation of joint ventures: Joint venture characteristics and wealth gains. *Journal of Business Venturing, 12*(2), 83-108.

Pearce, J. A. II, Kramer, T. R., & Robbins, D. K. (1997). Effect of managers' entrepreneurial behavior on subordinates. *Journal of Business Venturing, 12*(2), 147-160.

Peters, T. J., & Waterman, P. H. (1982). *In search of excellence: Lessons from America's best run companies.* New York: Harper & Row.

Peterson, R., & Berger, D. (1972). Entrepreneurship in organizations. *Administrative Science Quarterly, 16,* 97-106.

Pinchot, G. III. (1985). *Intrapreneuring.* New York: Harper & Row.

Porter, M. E. (1980). *Competitive strategy.* New York: Free Press.

Quinn, J. B. (1985). Managing innovation: Controlled chaos. *Harvard Business Review, 63*(3), 43-59.

Reich, R. B. (1987). Entrepreneurship reconsidered: The team as hero. *Harvard Business Review, 65*(3), 7-83.

Roberts, E. (1980). New ventures for corporate growth. *Harvard Business Review, 58*(4), 130-144.

Roberts, E. G., & Berry, C. A. (1985). Entering new businesses: Selecting strategies for success. *Sloan Management Review,* Spring, 3-17.

Ropo, A., & Hunt, J. G. (1995). Entrepreneurial process as virtual and vicious spirals in a changing opportunity structure: A paradoxical perspective. *Entrepreneurship Theory and Practice, 19*(3), 91-111.

Rule, E. G., & Irwin, D. W. (1988). Fostering intrapreneurship: The new competitive edge. *Journal of Business Strategy, 9*(3), 44-47.

Russell, R. D., & Russell, C. J. (1992). An examination of the effects of organizational norms, organization structure and environmental uncertainty on entrepreneurial strategy. *Journal of Management, 18*(4), 639-657.

Sathe, V. (1989). Fostering entrepreneurship in large diversified firms. *Organizational Dynamics, 18*(10), 20-32.

Sayles, L. R., & Steward, A. (1995). Belated recognition for work flow entrepreneurs: A case of selective perception and amnesia in management thought. *Entrepreneurship Theory and Practice, 19*(3), 7-23.

Scott, S. (1995). Uncertainty avoidance and the preference for innovation championing roles. *Journal of International Business Studies, 26*(1), 47-69.

Scholhammer, H. (1982). Internal corporate entrepreneurship. In C. A. Kent, D. L. Sexton, & K. H. Vesper (Eds.), *Encyclopedia of entrepreneurs, pp. 209-223. Englewood Cliffs, NJ: Prentice Hall.*

Schultz, T. W. (1975). The value of the ability to deal with disequilibria. *Journal of Economic Literature, 13*(3), 827-846.

Schumpeter, J. (1947). *Capitalism, socialism and democracy* (2nd ed.). New York: Harper & Row.

Sebora, C. T., Hartman, A. E., & Tower, B. C. (1994). Innovative activity in small businesses: Competitive context and organization level. *Journal of Engineering and Technology Management, 11*(3,4), 253-272.

Shane, S. (1993). Cultural influences on national rates of innovation. *Journal of Business Venturing, 8*(1), 59-73.

Starr, J. A., & MacMillan, I. C. (1990). Resource co-optation via social contracting: Resource acquisition strategies for new ventures. *Strategic Management Journal, 11,* 79-92.

Stevenson, H. H., & Jarillo, J. C. (1990). A paradigm of entrepreneurship: Entrepreneurial management. *Strategic Management Journal, 11*, 17-27.

Stopford, J. M., & Baden-Fuller, C. W. F. (1994). Creating corporate entrepreneurship. *Strategic Management Journal, 15*(7), 521-536.

Sykes, H. B. (1986). The anatomy of a corporate venturing program: Factors influencing success. *Journal of Business Venturing, 1*(3), 215-230.

Teece, D. J. (1996). Firm organization, industrial structure, and technological innovation. *Journal of Economic Behavior and Organization, 31*(2), 193-224.

Tercine, R., Harvey, M., & Buckley, M. (1997). Shifting organizational paradigms: Transitional management. *European Management Journal, 15*(1), 45-57.

Tiessen, J. H. (1997). Individualism, collectivism, and entrepreneurship: A framework for international comparative research. *Journal of Business Venturing, 12*(5), 367-384.

Vesper, K. H. (1984). Three faces of corporate entrepreneurship: A pilot study. In J. A. Hornaday, F. A. Tarpley, J. Timmons, & K. H. Vesper (Eds.), *Frontiers of entrepreneurship research*, pp. 294-320. Wellesley, MA: Babson College.

Vesper, K. H., & Gartner, W. B. (1997). Executive forum measuring progress in entrepreneurial education. *Journal of Business Venturing, 12*(5), 403-421.

Von Hipple, E. (1977). Successful and failing internal corporate ventures: An empirical analysis. *Industrial Marketing Management, 6*(3), 163-174.

Webster, F. A. (1977). Entrepreneurs and ventures: An attempt of classification and clarification. *Academy of Management Review, 2*(1), 54-61.

Westhead, P., & Wright, M. (1998). Novice, portfolio, and serial founders: Are they different? *Journal of Business Venturing, 13*(3), 173-204.

Wiklund, J. (1998). *Small firm growth and performance.* Unpublished doctoral dissertation, Jonkoping University.

Wortman, M. S., Jr. (1987). Entrepreneurship: An integrating typology and evaluation of the empirical research in the field. *Journal of Management, 13*(2), 207-222.

Wright, M., Robbie, K., & Ennew, C. (1997). Venture capitalists and serial entrepreneurs. *Journal of Business Venturing, 12*(3), 227-249.

Yeoh, P. L., & Jeong, I. (1995). Contingency relationships between entrepreneurship, export channel structure and environment: A proposed conceptual model of export performance. *European Journal of Marketing, 29*(8), 95-116.

Zahra, S. A. (1991). Predictors and financial outcomes of corporate entrepreneurship: An exploratory study. *Journal of Business Venturing, 6*(4), 259-285.

Zahra, S. A. (1993a). A conceptual model of entrepreneurship as firm behavior; A critique and extension. *Entrepreneurship Theory and Practice, 17*(4), 5-22.

Zahra, S. A. (1993b). Environment, corporate entrepreneurship and financial performance: A taxonomic approach. *Journal of Business Venturing, 8*, 319-340.

Zahra, S. A. (1993c). New product innovation in established companies: Associations with industry and strategy variables. *Entrepreneurship Theory and Practice, 18*(2), 47-70.

Zahra, S. A. (1995). Corporate entrepreneurship and financial performance: The case of management leveraged buyouts. *Journal of Business Venturing, 10*(3), 225-247.

Zahra, S. A. (1996). Governance, ownership and corporate entrepreneurship: The moderating impact of industry technology opportunities. *Academy of Management Journal, 39*(6), 1713-1735.

Zahra, S. A., & Covin, J. G. (1995). Contextual influences on the corporate entrepreneurship-performance relationship: A longitudinal analysis. *Journal of Business Venturing, 10*(1), 43-58.

Zahra, S. A., & Garvis, D. (2000). International corporate entrepreneurship and firm performance: The moderating effect of international environmental hostility. *Journal of Business Venturing,* in press.

Shaker A. Zahra is at Georgia State University.

Daniel F. Jennings is at Texas A&M University.

Donald F. Kuratko is at Ball State University.

We acknowledge with gratitude the comments of Julie Carleton and Patricia H. Zahra. The support of the Beebe Institute for the first author is also acknowledged with appreciation.

List of contributions (in chronological order) reviewed in this article

Conceptual Contributions

Schultz (1975)
Webster (1977)
Roberts (1980)
Scholhammer (1982)
Burgelman (1983[a])
Gartner (1985)
MacMillan & George (1985)
Nielsen, Peters, & Hisrich (1985)
Roberts & Berry (1985)
Kanter (1985)
Quinn (1985)
Reich (1987)
Wortman (1987)
Gartner (1988)
Rule & Irwin (1988)
Sathe (1989)
Guth & Ginsberg (1990)
Howell & Higgins (1990)
Kanter, North, Bernstein, & Williamson (1990)
Starr & MacMillan (1990)
Stevenson & Jarrillo (1990)
Chittipeddi & Wallet (1991)
Covin & Slevin (1991)
Cunningham & Lischeron (1991)
Fulop (1991)
Herron (1992)
Lengnick-Hall (1992)
Jones & Butler (1992)
Hornsby, Naffziger, Kuratko, & Montagno (1993)
Kelly (1993)

Zahra (1993a)
Kuratko (1993)
Kuratko, Hornsby, Naffziger, & Montagno (1993)
Ginsberg & Hay (1994)
Stopford & Baden-Fuller (1994)
Dougherty (1995)
Ghosal, Bauman, & Bartlett (1995)
Guth (1995)
Hill & Levenhapen (1995)
Krachhardt (1995)
Muzyka, Koning, & Churchill (1995)
Yeoh & Jeong (1995)
Ropo & Hunt (1995)
Brazeal & Herbert (1996)
Dess, Lumpkin, & McGee (1996)
Johnson (1996)
Kuratko & Hornsby (1996)
Lumpkin & Dess (1996)
Teece (1996)
Chung & Gibbons (1997)
Johannison & Monsted (1997)
Tercine, Harvey, & Buckley (1997)
Tiessen (1997)

Empirical Contributions

Peterson & Berger (1971)
Von Hipple (1977)
Biggadike (1979)
Fast (1981)
Miller & Friesen (1982)
Miller (1983)
Vesper (1984)
Miller & Camp (1985)
Covin & Slevin (1986)
MacMillan, Block, & Subbanarsimha (1986)
Hisrich & Peters (1986)
Sykes (1986)
Covin & Slevin (1988)
Jennings & Lumpkin (1989)
Jennings & Young (1990)
Kuratko, Montagno, & Hornsby (1990)
Zahra (1991)
Larson (1992)
Russell & Russell (1992)
Deshpande, Farley, & Webster (1993)
Katz (1993)
Kolvereid, Shave, & Westhead (1993)
Morris, Avila, & Allen (1993)
Zahra (1993b)
Zahra (1993c)

Dougherty & Heller (1994)
Morris, Davis, & Allen (1994)
Sebora, Hartman, & Tower (1994)
Dougherty & Bowman (1995)
Fiol (1995)
Fisenhauer (1995)
Morris & Lewis (1995)
Sayles & Steward (1995)
Scott (1995)
Zahra (1995)
Brazeal (1996)
Morris & Sexton (1996)
Zahra (1996)
Dennis (1997)
Kuratko, Hornsby, & Naffziger (1997)
Park & Kim (1997)
Pearce, Kramer, & Robbins (1997)
Vesper & Gartner (1997)
Wright, Robbie, & Ennew (1997)
Westhead & Wright (1998)

Part V
Organizational Structure
and Corporate Entrepreneurship

[19]

ORGANIZATION SCIENCE
Vol. 3, No. 2, May 1992
Printed in U.S.A.

INTERPRETIVE BARRIERS TO SUCCESSFUL PRODUCT INNOVATION IN LARGE FIRMS*

DEBORAH DOUGHERTY

*Management Department, The Wharton School, University of Pennsylvania,
2000 Steinberg-Dietrich, Philadelphia, Pennsylvania 19104-6370*

The development of commercially viable new products requires that technological and market possibilities are linked effectively in the product's design. Innovators in large firms have persistent problems with such linking, however. This research examines these problems by focusing on the shared interpretive schemes people use to make sense of product innovation. Two interpretive schemes are found to inhibit development of technology-market knowledge: departmental thought worlds and organizational product routines. The paper describes in some depth differences among the thought worlds which keep innovators from synthesizing their expertise. The paper also details how organizational routines exacerbate problems with learning, and how successful innovators overcome both interpretive barriers. The main implication of the study is that to improve innovation in large firms it is necessary to deal explicitly with the interpretive barriers described here. Suggestions for practice and research are offered.
(INNOVATION; NEW PRODUCTS; INTERDEPARTMENTAL COLLABORATION; INTERPRETATION)

Successful product innovation is vital to many firms. This paper builds on three findings in the literature to explore the product innovation process in large firms. The first finding is that the commercial success of a new product depends on how well the product's design meets customers' needs (Rothwell et al. 1974; Lilien and Yoon 1988). An effective design requires that technological possibilities for a product are linked with market possibilities, e.g., who are the users? what will they use the product for? The second finding is that collaboration among the technical, marketing, manufacturing, and sales departments contributes to a new product's success (Bonnet 1986; Dean and Susman 1989). The third finding is that product innovators often do not link technological and market issues, and often do not collaborate across departments (Cooper and Kleinschmidt 1986; Souder 1987).

This research seeks to explain why innovators fail to develop a comprehensive appreciation of their product in its market. Three implications are developed from the findings. First, collaboration is necessary to technology-market linking, which means that collaboration enhances the product's design along with improving the execution of the development process. Second, the styles in which people organize their thinking and action about innovation—their "interpretive schemes"—are major barriers to linking and collaboration. Like "culture," such schemes provide shared assumptions about reality, identify relevant issues, and help people make sense of those issues (Daft and Weick 1984; Bartunek 1984). In the case of product innovation, two interpretive schemes become interpretive barriers: (1) departments are like different "thought worlds," each focusing on different aspects of technology-market knowledge, and making different sense of the total; and (2) organizational routines separate rather than coordinate the thought worlds, further constraining joint learning. The third implication is that correcting the innovation problems caused by these interpretive barriers requires cultural solutions, not only structural ones.

*Accepted by Richard L. Daft; received August 1989. This paper has been with the author for two revisions.

179

OPCO—An Example

Before defining terms and then explaining how these implications arise, excerpts from a case in the research are presented to illustrate thought worlds and routines, and to introduce the research. The data management division of OPCO, a communications company, decided to develop and sell a software accounting system that would process credit card transactions over their data network. They purchased a start-up firm with a system under development to enter the business quickly, and, after several months additional work at OPCO, the service was introduced to the market. The system did not operate properly, however, and was cancelled. As suggested by the quotes below, the innovation encountered many problems. The quotes also suggest that the participants interpret issues with unique departmental perspectives. The business manager sees no need to talk with customers since he considers the market opportunity to be obvious. He feels, however, that they failed to position the product properly against competitors:

> [Interviewer: Did you talk to customers?] No, because we knew that this was needed. We could see some competitors getting into the business. ... We could see that this was logical for us to do, so we decided to go. ... Had we done some market research and defined needs more carefully, and figured out the dozens of pieces we would need for a full system, we'd be positioned with a much better strategy.

The technical director sees no "market" problems at all with the effort. He describes design problems, however, that perhaps could have been resolved had a thorough analysis of users and how they operate been carried out:

> There were no market problems with this product. ... Our mistake was we didn't understand the application in total. ... We had a difficult time trying to figure out the relationships between us here at the operating level and the retail establishments, and the relationships between them and their banks and credit card clearing houses. ... There were a lot of players involved, which is different from (our regular product), where we interface with one customer at a time. It looks very nice theoretically, but the more relationships there are, the more complex the recovery.

The sales support person downplays general positioning and technological design to blame instead their failure to specify which users in the market could best use the product:

> I have never seen a definition for this service. There are no criteria on what makes a good or bad customer for this product. ... One person here had a pretty good understanding of what kind of customer would benefit from a system like this. More people here should have known. We needed a brain transplant.

The innovators also followed established routines at OPCO Data to develop and launch this new service. These routines included project teams and matrices, structures that are recommended for innovation (e.g., Tushman and Nadler 1986), but all participants note how they did not work. The routines did not synthesize components of the innovation itself nor relevant knowledge, and they squashed interaction:

> We were not successful in fully integrating the new business within the organization. A new product is unique—it has different distribution, different billing, a myriad of things have to work out well. It is difficult for a small organization [referring to the business unit] to handle all these issues, so things fall apart. We didn't see the pitfalls (business manager).
>
> At OPCO we tend to categorize people into roles, and give people only what they need to know. ... There are little shadings of meaning that get lost in the requirements statement from marketing (technical director).

> They [from the small company] were a very tight group, and they all talked to one another all the time. But when we brought them here they were dispersed into our matrix...(sales support).

In hindsight at least, these innovators knew that they should link technological and market issues, but they did not. This case along with 17 others is analyzed to explain why.

Conceptual Background

Components of Technology-Market Linking

To understand problems with technology-market linking, it is first necessary to understand what that linking comprises. Research suggests that technology-market linking has a process and a content component. On the process side, linking involves the construction of new knowledge about the product and the market. Henderson and Clark (1990) suggest that nonroutine innovations require new "architectures," in which innovators break out of existing procedures and know-how and reconfigure components of design and procedure into a new framework. Freeman (1982) describes product innovation as a "complex coupling" between market needs and technologies over time. Linking technological and market possibilities is challenging, because choices must be made among multiple design options, each with different outcomes. At the same time the market may be new so it is difficult to determine who the most likely customers are and what they actually need (Clark 1985). Developing innovative products is thus a process of double loop learning (Argyris and Schon 1978), in which new insights are incorporated and the premises themselves are reconsidered.

On the content side, linking means that a complex array of specific insights must be gathered and brought together. Dougherty (1990) finds that successful new product developers had more insight into users' applications, technological trends, distribution systems, and market segments. Urban and von Hippel (1988) suggest that developers determine key trends in both the technology and market areas, and then search for "lead users" who can identify viable design specifications. According to Bonnet (1986), integration of R & D and marketing facilitates both the assessment of commercial viability and the optimization of design characteristics. Requisite knowledge for new products is thus multi-faceted, multi-leveled, and detailed.

Organizational Barriers to Technology-Market Linking

To understand why people do not link technology and market issues effectively, it helps to understand what prevents them from frame-breaking learning, and from gathering and connecting diverse insights. Organization research contains numerous references to interpretive schemes at the department and organization levels which may intervene in these necessary innovation processes. Departments can develop different perspectives through which they might separate rather than combine information, including cognitive orientations such as goals, time frames, and formality (Lawrence and Lorsch 1967), languages (Tushman 1978), perceptions (Dearborn and Simon 1958), occupational cultures (Van Maanen and Barley 1984), or power (Riley 1983).

At the organizational level, firms create "programs" (March and Simon 1958) or "routines" (Nelson and Winter 1982) which can inhibit new product development. According to Nelson and Winter, routines are regular and predictable behavior patterns, which, first, comprise the organizational memory. When the firm is in a state of routine operation, each person knows his or her job, and there is no need to know others' jobs. Second, routines represent a truce for intra-organizational conflict,

Corporate Entrepreneurship and Growth

which, as Perrow (1986) notes, binds the firm in a network of practices that are difficult to alter. Third, routines are standards which managers try to keep from changing.

Few organization studies have connected departmental differences and organizational routines directly to new product development and technology-market linking, however. Lawrence and Lorsch (1967)'s often cited insights concern ongoing businesses, not discrete new products. Several studies suggest that their cognitive differences do not differentiate departments for new product development (Harrison 1980; Gupta, Raj and Wilemon 1986). And, while organization theorists may refer to knowledge development (Galbraith 1982; Kanter 1983), most concentrate on structures and cultures for innovativeness in general, not for product innovation in particular.

Toward a More Complete Model

Fleck (1979) was the first to apply differences in interpretive schemes to innovation (or at least to scientific discovery—Douglas 1987). His views suggest how to integrate the insights outlined above into a more complete understanding of the organizational and interpretive processes underlying product innovation and technology-market linking. Fleck emphasizes the social basis of cognition, and adds that innovations often are epistemologically unsolvable by any one person. They require insights from a variety of specialties, called "thought collectives" or "thought worlds" as Douglas (1987) proposes to retranslate the term. A thought world is a community of persons engaged in a certain domain of activity who have a shared understanding about that activity. Microbiologists, plumbers, opera buffs, and organizational departments all can be viewed as thought worlds.

Departmental Thought Worlds. Two aspects of thought worlds are relevant to product innovation: their "fund of knowledge"—what they know, and their "systems of meaning"—or how they know. According to Fleck what is already known influences the method and content of cognition. Thought worlds with different funds of knowledge cannot easily share ideas, and may view one another's central issues as esoteric, if not meaningless. A thought world also evolves an internally shared system of meaning which provides a "readiness for directed perception" based on common procedures, judgements, and methods. These systems of meaning produce an "intrinsic harmony" for the thought world, so ideas that do not fit may be reconfigured or rejected outright.

For new product development, one could infer that departmental thought worlds would selectively filter information and insights. Because of specialization, a certain thought world is likely to best understand certain issues, but also to ignore information that may be equally essential to the total task. Their intrinsic harmony would also reduce the possibility for creative joint learning, since members of a department may think that they already know everything.

Organizational Routines. Fleck does not deal with organizations per se, but argues that the collective action necessary to innovation is motivated by pressure from the social context. "Collective work proper" (1979, p. 99) is different from additive work, as when people come together to lift a large rock. Rather, it refers to "the coming into existence of a special form, like a soccer match, conversation, or orchestra." This new social form alters the thought worlds' existing readiness for directed perception to allow new possibilities for discovery and new facts. Fleck studied the development of the Wassermann test for syphilis, and argues that the disease was undefined for 400 years in part because there were no means for collective action. Different groups such as astrologers, priests, pharmacists, and physicians operated with their own theories. If it were not for the "insistent clamor of public opinion for a blood test" (1979, p. 77), Wassermann would never have gathered the collective experience necessary to develop a test. Wassermann began with the incorrect immunology perspective that syphilis is caused by a virus. But because of external pressure, his persistence coupled with developments from chemistry, medicine, and laboratory thought worlds to uncover the actual cause of the disease (a spirochete). A new social form among these diverse groups emerged, and they *collectively* produced a test for the disease.

Fleck's dynamics can be combined with Nelson and Winter's (1982) routines to suggest that the organizational context affects the thought world's capacity to collaborate, inhibits the development of new knowledge, and keeps innovators from creating a new social form.

Research Questions. This study will explore these dynamics by addressing the following questions: (1) What are the different funds of knowledge and systems of meaning for new products in the departmental thought worlds, and how do they affect product innovation? (2) What are the routines that inhibit product innovation, and how do they affect collective action among the thought worlds?

Methods

Data regarding 18 new product efforts in five firms were collected by interviewing 80 people from different departments who worked on these products. Schall's (1983) multi-method analysis suggests that such interviews are a valid means to assess departmental interpretive differences. An embedded, multiple case design was used (Yin 1989) in order to consider the effects of organization and product success and failure on the findings (Bailyn 1977).

Organizations and Products

Two of the firms are in the computer/communications industries (OPCO and SALECO) and three are in the chemical materials industries (TECHCO, COMPCO, and PRODCO). All generate over $1 billion annually, employ over 20,000 people, and are over 35 years old. The criteria used to select products for the study are: (1) they incorporated new or unfamiliar technology for the firm and/or were marketed to new or unfamiliar users; (2) the products were almost or already introduced to the market, to eliminate variance due to development stage; and (3) some products were commercially successful, and some were failures. "Success" was defined as generating at least as much profit as planned and "failure" as cancellation after introduction.

Data were collected in two stages. First, eleven cases were studied at TECHCO and OPCO. At TECHCO, a manager in each of the six product groups in its industrial division was asked to suggest a product from his group that met the criteria. One said he was too busy, so five products were selected. At OPCO, managers directed me to their voice venture (one product), and their data division, where five more cases were studied. Only one of these eleven cases was successful as defined above, however, and even though six were in the market their profitability was still uncertain. A second stage of data collection was undertaken to add more successful cases. SALECO, COMPCO, and PRODCO were asked to identify one success already introduced, and one failure that had been introduced but cancelled. At COMPCO, people also described an uncertain product, and this was included.

Seventeen products were in the market, so all but one were in the post-introductory stage when people were interviewed. The products are described in Appendix A. In addition to success and failure, a new category labeled "uncertain" was made for

TABLE 1
Comparing Product Innovation Cases by Success Status

	Successful (4 cases)	Uncertain (7 cases)	Failed** (6 cases)
Comparisons			
Average Time in Development Before Introduction in Months (1)	31	26	23
Average Time After Introduction in Months	42	19	18
Unfamiliarity to Firm (% of cases): (2)			
% new technology	50%	63%	50%
% new manufacture	75	88	83
% new market segments	50	75	50
% new applications	100	88	67
% new distribution	100	100	67

**Successful = already introduced and meeting/exceeding expectations;
Uncertain = not meeting expectations but not cancelled (7 cases already introduced, 1 still in development);
Failed = already introduced and subsequently cancelled.
(1) The starting time is when the particular product began to be developed, not when underlying technologies were invented.
(2) If 2 of the participants said that the product was unfamiliar to the firm in this area, it was coded as unfamiliar.

the seven cases that were in the market but not generating profits as expected. Table 1 compares the successful, uncertain, and failed cases. The successful cases were in development longer on the average, but this difference is because of one case which took over five years. The uncertain cases, however, have been out on the market for less time than the successes. Post-introductory time may enhance success, since some of the uncertain cases will eventually become successful, while some will be cancelled. The success or failure might depend on the case's unfamiliarity to the firm. To compare cases on unfamiliarity, if two people said that the product was unfamiliar in any of the five areas noted, it was coded as such. As can be seen in Table 1, there is no difference in unfamiliarity by success status.

The People and the Interviews

At least two people who worked on each product were interviewed, and most were still working on the product. All were operational and middle level managers, and only six had less than four years experience with the firm. All interviews followed the same protocol: describe the product; outline your role; tell the story of the product; and describe customers, technology, and working relationships with others. The interviews were structured around these general questions, but unstructured regarding what the person chose to emphasize. The interviews lasted from about one hour to over two hours. Notes were taken and filled in as soon as possible afterwards. Table 2 summarizes the people interviewed by product, department, and firm.

Retrospective interviews have two important sources of potential distortion: memory failure and attribution bias. To guard against memory failure, people were asked regularly for dates and names to keep them grounded in particulars, and one person was reinterviewed briefly to clarify any conflicts in reported events. In addition, archival data were reviewed for three of the products, and no conflicts with people's stories were found. To check for attribution bias, the uncertain cases were compared

INTERPRETIVE BARRIERS TO SUCCESSFUL PRODUCT INNOVATION   185

TABLE 2
Number of People Interviewed by Department, Company, and Product Case

Company and Case:	Technical	Field	Manufacturing	Planners	Total
TECHCO (chemicals)					
*F Battery	1			1	2
U CRT Device	3	1	1		5
U Video Device	2	1			3
U Medical System	2	1		1	4
S Film Cover		1	2		3
Others		1		2	3
OPCO (communications)					
F Accounting System	2	1		1	4
F Document System	2			2	4
U Software System	1			2	3
U Text System	4	1	1	2	8
U Voice System	1	5	1	1	8
U Transmit System	1			2	3
Others				3	3
SALECO (computers)					
F System II	2		3	2	7
S System I	1	1		2	4
Others				2	2
COMPCO (chemicals)					
F Hardpoly	2	2		1	5
U Stretchpoly	1			1	2
S Hotpoly	1	1		2	4
Others		2		1	3
PRODCO (chemicals)					
F Pit Liner	1			1	2
S Roof Liner	1	1			2
Others				1	1
TOTAL	28	19	8	30	85**

*F = failure, U = Uncertain, S = Successful.
**Several people were interviewed twice, so figures add to more than 80.

to the successes and failures. Many of these people presented their product as a success, yet the measures of their knowledge matched the failed people's more closely, suggesting that attribution bias does not seriously affect the measures (see Dougherty 1987, 1990, for details). Failed developers may have underreported the knowledge they had due to attribution bias. I conclude that memory failure and attribution bias do not dominate the data, but they may distort the findings somewhat.

Since labels vary by firm, people were categorized into departments (used in the same sense as "function") based on their responsibilities when they worked on the product. Four labels are used: (1) technical: those who worked in research or engineering; (2) field: those who worked in sales or customer relations; (3) manufacturing: plant and purchasing people, or manufacturing engineers and (4) planners: those who handled market research or business analyses but were not in regular contact with customers.

Data Analysis and Findings

The findings and methods of analysis are interdependent, and are described together for each issue being studied.

186   DEBORAH DOUGHERTY

TABLE 3
Technology-Market Content Analysis of Interviews and
Cognitive Orientations by Department

Issues and Orientations	Technology	Field	Manufacturing	Planners	Statistic
% of Interview:					
Business Issues	23%	24	17	42	$F = 16.1$ $p = 0.000$
Customer Issues	17	28	10	18	$F = 12.9$ $p = 0.000$
Selling Issues	4	22	3	10	**Chi 2: $p = 0.000$
Technical Issues	49	21	27	23	$F = 27$ $p = 0.000$
Manufacturing Issues	8	6	39	6	$F = 71$ $p = 0.000$
Orientations mean ranks:**					
Long-Short time	34	33	25	44	**Chi 2: $p = 0.11$
Task-People	39	20	43	42	**Chi 2: $p = 0.006$

**The four departments do not have homogeneous variances on these measures, per a Bartlett test. The original measures were ranked by case from 1 to 71 (71 of the original 85 interviews are used in this analysis because "others" and people who did not work on the product prior to its launch were deleted). A Kruskall-Wallis test that compares mean ranks was run. The mean percentage is reported for the Selling Issues to be consistent with the other content measures, but the statistic is a Chi Square used for the K-W test on the ranked scores. Two orientation measures are the mean ranks, with the higher rank reflecting more long-term or task orientation.

Thought Worlds

Technology-Market Funds of Knowledge. The first research question asks what are the different funds of knowledge about technology-market issues in the different departmental thought worlds? It is assumed that the content of the thought worlds would be evident in the emphases in people's stories. To assess these emphases, a coding scheme to measure "technology" and "market" was developed with five categories: (1) product technology and design issues, (2) manufacturing (plant, suppliers, materials), (3) business issues including segments, competition, and size forecasts, (4) customer issues such as needs and problems, and (5) distribution or selling issues. The author coded each statement of each interview into one of these five areas. A research assistant coded a subset of interviews, and we had 80% agreement. Issues we disagreed over were redefined and all interviews were recoded by the author.

Measures were also developed for two of Lawrence and Lorsch's (1967) "cognitive orientations." Time orientation was measured by counting the number of statements that referred to events more than one year prior to the start of the product, or one year into the future beyond the date of the interview (divided by the number of pages to control for interview length). This assumes that people with a longer time orientation would discuss more long-term events. A task versus people orientation was measured by a ratio of statements that referred to working with people versus those that referred to a task in the development.

To make comparisons as similar as possible, only those people who worked directly on the product *prior* to introduction were included in the analysis. Table 3 summarizes the technology-market contents and cognitive orientations of each thought world using this subset of 71 interviews. One-way analyses of variance suggest differences on six measures, with long-short term orientation statistically significant at only $p = 0.11$. Planners dwell on business analyses in their stories and are the most long term, while technical people emphasize design issues. The field people discuss customer and distribution issues more often, and are the most people oriented.

If the departments are like thought worlds, however, one would also expect to see these differences regardless of company and success versus failure. Two-way analyses of variance between the thought world fund of knowledge measures and orientations were run by department and by company and success status to check on this expectation. See Appendix B for the results. The department has a main effect in five of the seven comparisons. There are also a few differences by company and success status, as discussed in the Appendix. Since the department main effect is found across the firms and success outcomes, however, these findings lend support to the idea that departmental thought worlds differ systematically on technology-market issues regardless of the firm or product status.

Systems of Meaning. The Fleck model suggests that departments not only know different things, but also know things differently. That is, each would have a different system of meaning through which its members interpret technology-market issues. To understand these systems of meaning, dimensions to describe them were developed following Strauss's (1987) methods for qualitative analysis. First, people's descriptions of other departments and frustrations with them, how they thought about customers, and what they considered important to product development were written onto separate coding sheets. These were then compared across department, case, and firm to search for underlying patterns or themes which summarized the essence of the departmental differences. Preliminary themes were discussed with colleagues and with several of the people interviewed.

Three final themes seem to most distinguish how the four thought worlds interpret technology-market linking and new products: (1) what people see when they look into the future, including issues that are most uncertain; (2) what people consider to be the critical aspects of the product development process; and (3) how people understand the development task itself. By looking at technology-market issues through the unique combination of these themes, people in each thought world understood the product in qualitatively different ways. Each thought world had an "intrinsically harmonious" perspective on the product which did not overlap extensively with perspectives held by other departments. Table 4 summarizes the unique understandings about product innovation which arise from these different systems of meaning.

These themes are first outlined, and then the different views they engender are illustrated with case material. The first theme captures the future orientation inherent in new product development. It also highlights the fact that people understand the future by in effect sighting along different emerging trends—technological change versus customer shifts versus market evolution (see Table 4). They make different sense of the nebulous future by looking at disparate aspects of it. What they see seems uncertain, while what they do not see does not seem particularly uncertain or even noteworthy. These contrasts can be seen in the OPCO excerpts. The business planner worried about positioning against competition while the field person worried about identifying the right potential customers. They partitioned the product into separate sources of uncertainty, which may have kept them from developing a more comprehensive understanding of the market.

The second theme comprises people's understanding of the development process itself. Each department concentrates on different subsets of the overall process. People do not ignore the activities they do not deal with directly, and do not merely

TABLE 4

Differences in the Thought World Systems of Meaning about Product Innovation

THEMES THAT DIFFERENTIATE THOUGHT WORLDS	THE TECHNICAL PEOPLE	THE FIELD PEOPLE	THE MANUFACTURING PEOPLE	THE PLANNING PEOPLE
What is seen when looking into future/uncertainties	Future comprises emergence of the technologies underlying the new product: design problems and their solution, new technical possibilities to include, new trends which might change development. Uncertainties comprise finding out what the design parameters are.	Future comprises shifts or trends in the users' uses of and need for this and related products. Uncertainties comprise how to get to buyers, discern if they like product, and how to adjust product for user.	Future limited to capabilities in plant, need careful shifts in operations. Uncertainties concern if manufacture is possible, what are the volumes.	Future comprises emerging business opportunities, competitive changes, new niches. Uncertainties concern developing market forecasts and income projections.
Aspects of development considered most critical	Focus on devising the product, specifying what it should do. Want to know what users want in product specifications. Market is seen as what the product does, and as such is rather obvious.	Focus on matching products to users, adjusting the product quickly to meet their shifting needs, creating the sale. Want to know who makes buying decision, what problems customers want to solve. Market is seen as what the buyer wants, and as such is difficult to develop.	Focus on the product's durability, quality, how many types of product. Want to know how good is good enough in product quality. The market is seen in abstract terms as product's performance.	Focus on developing the business case and general marketing plans. Want to know the best segment to be in, how to position the product in this segment. Market is seen as a general business opportunity.
How development task is understood	Task is to build the product—a hands-on, tactile activity. Product is real, has a physical presence, and is "neat."	Task is to develop relationships with buyers, which occurs when products change to meet their needs. Sense of task is one of urgency. Also hands-on but product is not real—it is a possibility.	Task is to build the capacity to build the product. Also hands-on, tactile, product is well built.	Task is to analyze alternate possibilities, determine income potential—a conceptual, abstract activity. Product is a business.

argue over relative priorities. Rather, they gloss over the concerns of others, and tend not to appreciate their complexities (Van Maanen 1979). Recall that OPCO's technical person saw no "market" problems for the product effort described. Had they identified a set of retailers who needed the service but who had simple transaction needs, however, perhaps they could have designed a workable system. As Table 4 suggests, each department seeks inputs from the others that differ from the others' primary focus. Technical people, for example, concentrate on solving design problems, and expect field people to tell them exactly what customers want in the design. Field people, however, cannot identify these "specs" because in their view users are uncertain. Rather, field people consider that product innovation is to meet *shifts* in customer needs, and expect technical people to produce alternate designs quickly.

The third category concerns how people understand the task itself. As Table 4 shows, all but the planners understand product development in concrete, hands-on terms, so all these departments have difficulty making sense of planners' reports. There are also significant differences within these three hands-on groups, however. The technical people think that the product has a specific reality, while field people think it is a possibility. These contrasting perspectives can seriously impede a dialogue over what the product is and how it should be developed. Excerpts from the interviews illustrate these thought worlds for product development.

The Technical People. The product's design dominates the technical people's understanding of product development. When they look into the future, they see ever emerging design possibilities and numerous technological trade-offs. For example, an engineer with SALECO's System II discussed the decision over the disk drive at some length:

> The diskette started as a single side, but we had technical problems with that. ... Also when we started there was no question that we'd do half size. That was a new technology so it had to be single sided. But a guy in the group said in a few months we could fix the problems, so let's take a risk and forget single sided and do double sided. That helped push the technology... (SALECO)

Consistent with this view of the future, technical people emphasize establishing the product's performance specifications rather than what the customer does with the product. This is a complex and often frustrating process, as this engineer's comments about a communication system illustrate:

> There were a lot of specs, but these were only detailed conceptually. They wanted "something like this." What ended up as a result is that the specs get interpreted more widely. You end up delivering something they didn't ask for. ... I was working with one or two people (at the customer organization). Then they show it to fourteen others who say: "Oh My God!! We didn't want that!!" (OPCO)

Technical people define the market in terms of what the product does, and may overlook business aspects such as how many people will pay how much for the product. For example, the market for the battery was defined as "battery users," not particular sets of industrial customers who might need a more permanent energy source. Most technical people view the development task as a tactile activity that results in something objectively real. By concentrating on technological possibilities, however, they may assume the market is obvious and that customer needs are straightforward.

The Field People. As field people look into the future, they see constantly emerging customer applications rather than changing technological possibilities. Such changes are more immediate, often shifting with the user's model changes or competitor's

190   DEBORAH DOUGHERTY

product or price changes, giving them a short-term, action orientation. Field people also seem to take a customer-by-customer view of the market. Consider:

> You need to listen to what the customers want; what is he ready to buy? what is he looking for?... You have to be specific, applications oriented. I want the least amount possible in the shortest time, but [engineering] may take three years. ... The more (engineering and operations) are buffered from customers, the more they tend not to understand the urgency. (OPCO)

Field people emphasize creating or crafting the sale, not the product, and describe this activity as vividly as the engineers discuss disc drives or communication networks. Explains a voice service field person:

> It's a blast to let it go. I never go on a one on one meeting. I always try to have a minimum of three people (from the prospective customer's organization) and I throw out functions until I find a use. ... It's the most amazing thing in the world. Usually there's at least one guy who's determined not to like the product. He sits pulled away from you like he won't let you penetrate his shield. But then after ten minutes he pops up in his chair and starts coming up with ideas...(OPCO)

To field people, the task is real but not tactile. Developing a new product means establishing new relationships and buying-selling arrangements. The relational nature of their work is evident in this quote:

> We know what they need. The market is obvious. But the selling process is complex. Who are they and what do they want is clear. But there are six or eight decision makers. No one says yes but anyone can say no. ... The production guy wants to know if his yield will be better... The quality control guy says 'will I have to change my tests?' The sales manager says 'will my customers like the finished product as well?' The purchasing guy says 'what will you do for me?'... You need to work with all these guys and their bosses. (COMPCO)

Note also that the speaker downplays the complexities of doing a market analysis by focusing on his own tasks. Field people concentrate on what the user wants to do with the product, but also assume that customer needs are unique or constantly changing.

The Manufacturing People. Manufacturing people worry about the plant or operations, and are concerned that the others do not appreciate their special inflexibilities. A person at COMPCO explained that manufacturing is very concerned that marketing will take orders for products they cannot produce. " ... I don't like (them) taking risks (they) don't know (they) are taking." It seemed that these inflexibilities push manufacturing people to live in the ever present now. The director of operations for the voice service explained his problems with the others as follows:

> Sales and marketing live in the future and my needs are today. They are forever saying "why don't we do this?," or "isn't that easy to do?" But based on limited capacity now I can't do that. It's the same with networking. Sales and engineering wanted to bring up all the nodes at once! We said no, let's test it and do it one at a time... They know, they hear, but they aren't involved (as closely). And they don't get the 5,000 calls from customers (when the system fails)... There needs to be more interface between those who design the future and those who live in the real world. (OPCO)

Note that, like the others quoted above, the person is aware of the others' concerns and issues, but emphasizes his problems over theirs.

Manufacturing people concentrate on reliability and quality, evaluating and defining the product in these terms. For example, a manufacturing engineer picked up a keyboard for the failed System II and threw it into a corner of the room to show how well built it was. "Look at that!" he said. "That's a damn fine keyboard!" (SALECO). It turns out that the system was a commercial failure (in part) because the keyboard was difficult to use. How often it could be thrown around was not a factor.

The Planning People. The future that planners see consists of emerging business possibilities such as the size of the market and total revenue potential. For planners, both the technological trends and specific customer applications pale into abstraction. As a planner at TECHCO put it: "We locate markets and make recommendations if it's worthwhile to enter them. And that depends on the margins, or the amount of money you will make." Analyzing "the business" also can be very frustrating and uncertain, as one explained:

> The environmental scan is the most difficult part. There isn't enough information available. We looked at traditional sources (of information) including market research firms. But the problem is they are guessing too, they develop scenarios. An awful lot of projecting from just a few numbers goes on in this business. (OPCO)

The information the planners need for their reports is difficult to gather, so they resort to modeling. For example, several people at OPCO spent three months developing a model to predict the size of an electronic data transfer market, and then they developed their business proposal around the estimate. To do such extensive analyses with such ambiguous data, planners cannot treat design and applications as constantly emerging. Instead they abstract these issues into more general scenarios. The nature of the planners' work is conceptual, not concrete, which means that their concrete-thinking colleagues will have trouble with their plans. For example, a technical person said: "It's hard to know what to do with reports we get from marketing." A field person said: "I'll take luck to market research any day."

Thought Worlds and Product Innovation. Interpretive differences between departmental thought worlds play a strong role in problems with collaboration over technology-market linking. From the outside looking in, one can see the conventional stereotypes for each department in the sketches above: technical people never settle on a design, field people are short term, manufacturing people always say no, and planning people are conceptual. But from the inside looking out, each thought world is truly concerned with the successful development of the product. And as can be seen, each has an important insight into the product or market that is essential to a new product's development. Each emphasizes different aspects of development, however, and conceives of the whole in a different way.

When seen from the perspective of thought worlds, the collaboration problem runs deeper than conflicts over personality types or goals. Indeed, to attempt to resolve the problem through negotiation over goals may only begin to touch on the divergent understandings which lay at the heart of the problem. Nor is the problem like the proverbial set of blind men touching a different part of an elephant. It is more like the tales of eye witnesses at an accident, or of individuals in a troubled relationship—each tells a "complete" story, but tells a different one. Despite their potential benefits, departmental thought worlds separate the market-technology issues, limiting the possibility of a comprehensive understanding. The thought worlds also focus inward, reducing the possibility of learning. These data suggest that, to overcome the thought worlds' "inherent tenacity" (Fleck 1979) to focus on their own perspectives, managers may need to proactively foster collective action.

Organizational Routines

It became clear from the research that the thought worlds did not operate independently from the organizational context, however. Next, the analysis seeks to identify the organizational routines that affect product innovation, and how they affect collective action among the thought worlds. Most people described how products are usually developed in their firm, so the data provide some insight into routines. Descriptions of usual practice for product development (including evaluating the product, making decisions, and determining market needs) were transcribed onto coding sheets. The same kinds of practices used for the new product were also extracted, and compared with the usual practices by success status.

The analysis suggested three important patterns. First, three routines encourage thought world separation and inhibit learning. These routines were systematically violated in the successful cases, followed in the failed cases, and followed partly in uncertain cases. Second, the successful innovators did create a new social order for innovation. Third, the routines in these firms were very strong. Breaking out of them to establish an innovative social order seemed to be an unusual and often temporary event.

Organizational Routines, New Products, and Thought Worlds. The three routines found to affect product innovation concerned interdepartmental relations, market definition, and product standards. The first routine governed thought world relations by prescribing narrow roles and limited relationships. People would routinely do their own work and expect the same of others. Even when interactive structures such as task forces were used routinely, relationships were constrained, so the possibility of creating a new collective order which produced cross-fertilization and mutual learning was limited. The second routine imposed a predetermined definition of technology-market issues on product efforts. This reduced people's search for new information as well as the likelihood of frame-breaking learning. The third routine imposed standards which did not fit these new products. The standards varied by firm, and included set pay-back periods, profit margins, quality, and use of inhouse facilities. Following them forced developers to redefine the new product as an established business, further reducing new learning.

Successful developers violated all three routines, and created a new social order for their collaborative efforts. They developed mutually adaptive interactions in which knowledge of the work was developed as the work unfolded, as Mintzberg (1979) describes. They also created an alternate definition of the product in its market that was grounded in actual use, and developed appropriate standards to evaluate their efforts. The outcome was collective action as Fleck (1979) describes it: each thought world rechanneled its readiness for directed perception from an inward to an outward focus so that their knowledge could join to produce new insights and new facts.

An Example of Routines at SALECO: System I vs. System II. To illustrate the routines and how successful developers stepped out of them to create a new social order, SALECO's successful System I is contrasted with its failed System II. Both products used similar technology and some of the same people, and the failure followed the success, so the comparison holds constant some of the effects of individuals, technology, and experience. Appendix A summarizes how the other cases related to their organization's routines.

SALECO is a computer and communications manufacturer which has dominated several niches in these markets. The director of market research explained that, until five or ten years previously, SALECO's products were self-contained "turnkey" operations. SALECO maintained close relations with their dependent, installed base of business users through an extensive sales force. These customers' changing needs were easily monitored with in-depth customer profiles; product development became a sequential and highly organized process which abstracted customers' needs into financial indicators. A planner explained that they would look at a price-performance curve, and come up with a new product that sits further down the curve. "We would know what the market requirement is, and would invent nuances on the technology to do it." Predetermined goals and specifications were used to coordinate complex interdepartmental relationships, managed in a matrix structure. "The market" was given, so little energy would routinely go into feretting out user needs. And, befitting a company with market dominance, product norms included high profit margins, high quality production, and complete control of the product by handling all aspects inhouse.

The successful System I violated these carefully orchestrated, big business-oriented, financials-focused product routines, while the failed System II followed them. One person explained the overall routine violation as follows:

> The unique thing was they cut off (the System I group) from the culture. Basically a few top executives decided to play Daddy Warbucks. They disconnected (the team leader) from the normal process of building business cases.

The System I team's interdepartmental relationships encouraged ideas to be heard and built on and enhanced appreciation of one another's contributions. They interacted extensively, and, according to a field person, all participated in all the aspects of the product. Thus, rather than separating various concerns into pre-established role behavior, all problems and ambiguities were addressed from all angles, producing a more comprehensive design. Rather than coordinate by the usual formal but abstract plans, one member said "...we had no formal business plan, but everybody knew what it was." They did not create a single group mind, however. One explained that each department considered itself to be the one most important to the project, but that the leader fostered a sense of appreciation:

> ...(the team leader) always listened to everyone when it came to making a decision, so even if his decision differed from your recommendation, you knew your information was as important as the others'.

Along with redefining relationships, they redefined the task, and perhaps stepped out of the usual political truce that Nelson and Winter (1982) describe. The group created a vivid view of the product in its market which was more simple yet more realistic than SALECO's usual abstractions of price-performance ratios, market penetration estimates, and volume projections. The team used these general data, but combined them with first-order, direct experience with customers. An engineer describes their technology-market linking in what is almost a field person's perspective, as follows:

> The first thing was to define what the product was, who would buy it, and what they would use it for... You have to get into the hearts and minds of users... If you can't explain the product in 30 seconds, you're dead.

People's descriptions of their development process were full of instances in which they broke out of usual perspectives. For example, they broke out of SALECO's notion of customers as business people, and came to appreciate the new users for themselves. According to a planner:

> I remember our first focus group. It was a riot. There was this guy out there in a green T-shirt, long side burns and a flat top, jeans, a belt with a big silver buckle, and cowboy boots. He happened to be the president of the local micro-computer club. It's frightening when you realize that on the other side of the oneway mirror there was a room full of men in [conservative business attire]. We had to understand that that guy was our new customer. It took a leap of faith.

Third, they broke most of SALECO's product norms and created new standards appropriate to the System I market. Instead of the usual inhouse manufacture which "made equipment you can drop off ten story buildings," according to one, the machine was assembled from off-the-shelf parts purchased externally. This more effectively met the needs of low price in a market where "industrial strength" durability was not critical. Instead of total control by SALECO, they designed an open architecture to allow others to write software for sale. The group even published a book explaining how outsiders could build on the machine with their own products. Instead of careful quality control, some of the external software had bugs in it—the number of applications was more important to this market than perfect operation.

Less than a year later, this business unit began work on a follow-on product aimed at both professionals and home use. A number of new people were involved, but so were many of the System I group, including the leader and the senior people who played "Daddy Warbucks." More like SALECO's usual product development, however, the plan was simply to continue the momentum begun by System I. Interdepartmental relationships seemed to have also reverted to routine, and the inwardness of thought worlds dominated the people's work. When asked to describe the System II organization, an engineer went to his board and drew a circle to show the System I team. Then he drew an arrow over to a matrix to represent the System II organization, with columns for departments, and rows for various products under development—SALECO's routine matrix form. A planner explained that some people from the first effort were not fully focused on this product, that several key people left, and that the group had lost what he called its "group think."

For the technology-market definition, System II developers relied on assumed applications and users, as usual. A market had been "analyzed" with the routine calculus of price-performance trade-offs and buyer potential, and not questioned again. The design had unique features but these were not tested with users. As it turns out, few users liked the product. An engineer explained:

> We didn't get the system into real scenarios to test out our premises. We were overconfident... We all thought we were very smart... We made a lot of decisions daily to change the product based on what we thought we understood about the market place.

A market researcher noted that perhaps some focus groups would have picked up the problem they found after introduction with certain features. But he said that the design and manufacturing process had generated such a momentum, that:

> We would have been disappointed with the negative feedback, but we would have gone on with (the design) anyway.

Third, the System II team followed some of SALECO's usual product standards that were appropriate to its large systems, but not, perhaps, for System II. In-house manufacturing rather than assembly was used, and reliability and durability were emphasized. According to a manufacturing person:

> The product was fantastic. But it was high priced. You can't cut price or quality. There is no way SALECO would sell a lower quality product. But then people would say why should I pay so much for this computer, instead of paying attention to all the enhancements we put on it... It has half-size disk drives... Our fundamental error was in the design of [a certain part]. It didn't have user flexibility. That got us a lot of negative press. But the function was great. It should have sold like hotcakes.

By following the usual product development routines, the System II team produced a high quality, rather expensive but durable machine—just what SALECO's routines are designed to produce. Unfortunately the team did not begin with an established market, which the routines also presume, so the system did not fit any real needs. Sales were not high enough to cover the manufacturing costs, so the company shut down the plant, laid off the factory workers, and cancelled the product.

Discussion

An extensive literature tells managers how they ought to develop new products, and how they ought to design their organizations for innovation. This study has examined product innovation in practice in order to understand why these prescriptions are not often achieved. The research is limited by its exploratory nature, and the fact that commitment, leadership, politics, and other possible factors have not been included. However, it describes how two interpretive schemes can become barriers to effective technology-market linking. Departmental thought worlds partition the information and insights. Each also has a distinct system of meaning which colors its interpretation of the same information, selectively filters technology-market issues, and produces a qualitatively different understanding of product innovation. Organizational product routines reinforce thought world separation by providing for only limited interaction, and further inhibit the kind of collective action that is necessary to innovation.

Implications for Theory and Practice

This research suggests two important implications for the study and practice of innovation. The first is that theorists and practitioners need to pay attention to the effects of thought worlds and organizational routines. Innovation is an interpretive process, so the management of innovation must involve the management of the interpretive schemes that shape and frame how people make sense of their work. Innovation requires *collective action*, or efforts to create shared understandings from disparate perspectives. The advocation of rational tools and processes, the infusion of market research information, and the redesign of structures, while important, are not enough.

The second implication is that the potential barriers these interpretive schemes may become need to be dealt with specifically and in depth. This study suggests three intermediary processes which together can help overcome the barriers. Innovators must: (1) use and build on the unique insights of each thought world, (2) develop collaborative mechanisms that deal directly with the interpretive as well as structural barriers to collective action, and (3) develop an organizational context for collective action that enables both. The work suggests that, unless all three processes occur together, the thought world boundaries and routines may dominate. If so, pitfalls will be overlooked, meanings lost, and communication curtailed, as was the experience of OPCO's accounting system developers.

Building on the Thought Worlds. Each thought world knows about aspects of technology-market knowledge that others may gloss over. All must actively contribute to the product design, and actively challenge each other, or the final design will be awry. This means that reservations or skunkworks comprised solely of R & D people, as some theorists suggest (e.g., Galbraith 1982), would not be effective. The management of innovation is not merely the management of the R & D group or the coordination of activities, it comprises the *collective* creation of the product in its market.

This analysis has gone beyond the general differences in orientations usually cited to identify specific interpretive differences that must be confronted and overcome for new products. As argued here, innovators from different departments may *not* conflict over general goals or even over such intermediate goals as being "market oriented." They do, however, have unique interpretations of these goals, along the themes described in Table 4. Technical and field people focus on customers and have a concrete view of development. This means that reports from the conceptual market researchers may not make any sense to them, and may be ignored. Field people's close view of customers could contribute important insights to design, but it may also keep them from summarizing specifications that technical people need. Technical people's search for a general design makes them seem unresponsive to field people's requests for specific changes. Manufacturing people worry that others do not understand the limits of the plant, and so may dig in their heels unless their concerns are handled openly. These differences can preclude the development of an optimal design by producing severe frustrations and perhaps withdrawals into separate thought worlds. They must be deliberately and directly addressed as they come up.

Developing Collaboration Mechanisms. Collaboration mechanisms need to take into account the interpretive dynamics that separate the thought worlds. Their "intrinsic harmony" prompts people to focus inward on their own tasks, and to fill in unknowns from their thought world. Thought worlds most likely always exist where tasks are specialized, so efforts to surmount them always have to be made. Participants on interdisciplinary teams may feel "drawn inward" into their thought world over time, especially if they have other assignments, as is often the case. The analysis suggests one important way to overcome the inward dynamic. As in the SALECO System I case, thought worlds can come to a similar understanding of the product in the user's hands, and innovators can perhaps build a comprehensive appreciation from this common view. Interdisciplinary responsibility for focus groups, market research plans, technology audits, and visits with users should enhance collaboration. Structures alone such as liaison and boundary spanner roles or project groups do not assure that these dynamics of separation will be overcome. A realistic customer focus may.

Developing the Context for Collective Action. This research also suggests that thought world barriers cannot be overcome unless aspects of the organizational context which foster separation are also overcome. The capacity for collective action depends in part on organization level interpretive dynamics. It is inferred that an innovative social order must be designed specifically for new products so that: (1) interactions between thought worlds are based on appreciation and joint development, (2) product definitions are based on collective, first-order customer knowledge, and (3) product norms are based on the specific market. It is inferred further that general organizational attributes such as a risk-taking climate, visionary leadership, and/or an integrative culture may not address these day-to-day practices, although perhaps they increase innovative activity. Moreover, routines, like thought worlds, are probably inertial, and thus always have to be overcome. No matter what the general organizational design, managers must foster ongoing processes of knowledge development, joint learning, and customer interactions.

Future Research

Research is necessary to clarify and test all these implications. This study has not considered the structural aspects of thought worlds that might affect their collective action. Fleck (1979), for example, theorizes that stability of membership, the strength of the established beliefs, the clarity of boundaries, and power relationships within the thought world can all have an effect. For departments, one could speculate that

INTERPRETIVE BARRIERS TO SUCCESSFUL PRODUCT INNOVATION 197

people's training, experience, and professionalization would affect thought world separation or integration. Studies might explore whether and how job rotation, team experience, and bringing the tacit thought world differences to conscious awareness improve the propensity for collective action. Research on the R & D-manufacturing relationship is perhaps the most advanced (Adler 1990, Dean and Susman 1989), and these insights can be elaborated to include all four departments. Other approaches for mapping frames of reference (Dunn and Ginsberg 1986) should expand our understanding of departmental differences.

The implications for organizational routines are the most potentially confounded by attribution bias and the limited number and types of firms in the study. Additional research is essential to define the routines that inhibit innovation and articulate more clearly how they work. Research should also identify the routines, if any, which can foster innovation. The literature contains numerous discussions of *general* organizational attributes and phenomena that presumably engender innovation (e.g., Kanter 1983; Galbraith 1982). An important next step is to understand the relationships between such general contexts and the specific tasks of innovation, including technology-market knowledge development and thought world collective action. Focused research which examines these dynamics directly, and longitudinal research which sorts out the causal relationships between interpretive barriers and other factors are necessary.

In conclusion, this work indicates that improvements in the new product success rate are possible if innovators combine the prescriptive models with attention to these interpretive barriers, and the *ongoing processes* necessary to overcome them. Rather than test theory, this study has applied theory to the problem of new product development. The insights are more practical than theoretical, but the findings support the growing literature that understanding the interpretive dynamics of innovation and change is crucial (Bartunek 1984; Schein 1985; Barley 1986). The results show that such dynamics apply to product innovation, and can be studied systematically. Continued research into these interpretive dynamics, along with continued efforts to join organization theory with insights from marketing and technology, should advance our understanding of the complex problem of product innovation in large firms.

Acknowledgements

The data on which this paper are based come from a study sponsored by the Marketing Science Institute and a pre-doctoral fellowship from the American Association of University Women. A grant from the Reginald Jones Center and a Doris and Michael Goldberg Fellowship from the Snider Center for Entrepreneurial Studies, both of the Wharton School, supported this analysis. I would like to thank Ed Schein, John Van Maanen, David Thomas, Larry Hirschhorn, Stew Friedman, and Marsha Wilkof for insightful critiques. This paper has also benefitted significantly from critiques by editor Richard Daft and three anonymous reviewers for *Organization Science*.

Appendix A. Summary of Cases and Their Relationships with Routines

This appendix provides a thumbnail sketch of products in this study. See Dougherty (1987) for a complete description of each case, and Dougherty (1990) for an analysis of development processes. Since the relationships with organizational routines are important, so the cases are reported by company rather than success status. All firms and products are disguised.

TECHCO: Producer of chemical based products. Routines for product development stress technological innovativeness, and market analyses routinely not done. High quality was also a standard. Product development usually begins in R & D; procedure was to include others in sequence as the product was ready for a business analysis and marketing plan. People interviewed in Fall 1985.

1. *Failed Battery*. A technologically unique no-leak battery; originally invented for a product line, but because of excess production capacity, TECHCO decided to sell battery to others. Toy manufacturers were

selected as market since toys were a big user of batteries; no analyses of needs, problems, etc. Introduced in late 1981. Product required redesign of toys, and was not widely available so toy companies were not interested. Cancelled after 3 years. *Routines*. A technology dominant task force used for development, sponsored by senior VP; market definition based on what the battery could do, not what users needed; standards of uniqueness and high quality met.

2. *Uncertain CRT Device*. Electronically transfers computer images to produce a hardcopy. Began in R&D. Introduced in Fall 1983. Sales very slow; an interdisciplinary team was set up after introduction, and they were redesigning the product and changing the distribution system. *Routines*. Technology driven, limited interdepartmental interaction; marketing research advised against the product but were ignored. Market defined as white collar office workers; development delayed until quality standards could be met.

3. *Uncertain Video Device*. Similar to CRT device, but captures television signals. Also began in R&D, developed for home use. Commercial division took it, so product redesigned for commercial use. Were design, manufacturing, and quality problems. Concerns over quality and technical design persist. *Routines*. Partially broke routines by doing a market test jointly with R&D and marketing people; interaction seemed good; hung up on established product standards based on chemicals (this was electronic).

4. *Uncertain Medical Hardcopy System*. A chemical and mechanical technology that produces hardcopy from medical diagnostics machines. Requires redesign by diagnostics manufacturers. Delayed for over a year because of manufacturing problems; in the interim a competitor came out with similar product at much less cost. Now looking for alternate markets and uses. *Routines*. Set up an interdisciplinary task force; good interaction except with manufacturing; market plans good but limited to existing markets, contrary to original plan. Hung up on usual markets and standards.

5. *Successful Film Cover*. Adapts a light-proof paper wrap TECHCO makes for other products to contain professional grade photography film purchased from others. Very "low-tech" but intended for new markets and applications. Test market sales exceeded projections, so introduction advanced by 6 months. *Routines*. Began in business unit; product champion incorporated manufacturing and purchasing people on informal or "bootleg" team; all visited users together; considerable market data gathered; design adjusted to meet particular problems. Violated product approval and quality procedures.

OPCO: An operating phone company whose routines stressed low risk ventures, short-term planning, and quarterly operations reviews of all businesses and senior managers. Corporate requires extensive analyses of all new business plans. OPCO's Data Division evolved a "fast-out" product routine to avoid the "corporate gauntlet." They sneaked their first product, the Text System, into the market. Interviews from February to April 1986.

1. *Uncertain Voice System*. (Not associated with OPCO Data) Electronically transfers voice to digitalized packets transmitted over network. One of the first uses of this technology, introduced in 1983; still losing money. *Routines*. Began by a planner; general plans with no applications analyses (files reviewed by author). No interdisciplinary work. During test discovered product redesigned for discovered market of interoffice uses; multiple market definitions still operate. A venture group formed 2 years after test market.

2. *Uncertain Text System*. Similar technology to voice but transfers text. Introduced in the early 1980's; sales growth high but competition is strong and earnings uncertain. *Routines*. Developed by a technical skunkworks, and introduced as a technology. Market plan based on the number of salespeople, not users or needs. Violated OPCO corporate's analysis, but followed technology driven, fast out routines in division. No interdisciplinary group or comprehensive market definition; these now being developed.

3. *Failed Document System*. Allows text system users to produce a hardcopy delivered overnight to people not on the network. System failed since some mail took 2 weeks; removed from the market. *Routines*. Business planning and technical development done separately. Technical and operational plan poor but chosen because it could be done by the end of the quarter. Original market defined in vague terms.

4. *Failed Accounting System*. Transacts credit card purchases for retailers over a network. System double-debited and double-credited, and then crashed. Removed from market. *Routines*. Followed usual planning process with little connection between technology and marketing; business plan was complete, but particular applications not examined for design. Followed fast-out standard.

5. *Uncertain Transmit System*. Product still in development. It will transmit data between manufacturers and suppliers. Plan created by an interdisciplinary team. The plan violates OPCO's standard for a 2-year payback, so developers were unsure if it would be approved.

6. *Uncertain Software System*. Product transfers software over the network, from terminal to terminal or downloading from a central file. Just introduced, and is being given 90 days to "make" it. Market very uncertain. *Routines*. Developed by a planner, with some interaction from technical people. Targeted market has changed because software firms initially agreed to cooperate but then refused. Market definition very general—now the "Fortune 1000." Followed standards of general business analyses.

SALECO: see text. Interviews Summer 1986.

COMPCO: Chemical materials producer. Has a dominant market position with a certain grade of plastic. Product development usually begins with requests from customers processed through field, and

INTERPRETIVE BARRIERS TO SUCCESSFUL PRODUCT INNOVATION 199

these requests are responded to quickly. Market need is always known, so little analysis is routinely done. COMPCO has 102 variations of basic plastic. Interviews Fall 1986.

1. *Failed Hardpoly.* Combines a harder polymer with its basic one, giving the plastic more strength yet a lower cost than the stronger polymer alone. Previous efforts to combine these polymers could not overcome certain problems. The material was introduced into an application but failed the heat test and was withdrawn. *Routines.* The material began in technical, not field, but was then treated as a typical user request. An interdisciplinary task force was appointed, as is the routine, but there was little interaction between departments, and field assumed that it would perform as they expected.

2. *Uncertain Stretchpoly.* Combines a flexible polymer with COMPCO's basic material, for added flexibility and water resistance. The material was introduced 2 years ago into automotive, but does not meet those needs, and new niches are being explored. *Routines.* Like hardpoly, the material began in research, contrary to routines, so it had no clear market demand. Some market research was not used, and they assumed it would fit into their major market, the automotive business. An interdisciplinary project team has since been set up, and they are actively monitoring the product.

3. *Successful Hotpoly.* This is a new kind of polymer for COMPCO, with much greater heat resistance, and it opens up new market areas for the firm. The material was introduced in later 1982; only 1 other firm made it. Initial sales slow; field was not selling the product, and they overestimated users' willingness to

TABLE B-1
Thought World Measures by Company

Thought World Measures	Weighted Mean Score				ANOVA results Dept effect Company effect Interaction effect (prodco, manuf not included)
	SALECO	OPCO	COMPCO	TECHCO	
% of Interview:					
Business Issues	32	27	29	33	D F = 12.7*
					C 0.9
					I 1.96**
Customer Issues	16	23	23	19	D F = 6.6*
					C 2.5**
					I 1.2
Selling Issues	12	12	17	9	D F = 12.5*
					C 1.6
					I 1.6
Technical Issues	32	32	25	29	D F = 31.3*
					C 1.5
					I 0.4
Manufacturing	7	5	6	8	D F = 0.5
					C 1.8
					I 0.3
Orientations mean ranks: Long-Short time	37	32	37	38	D F = 0.3
					C 0.7
					I 1.8
Task-People	38	29	32	38 33	D F = 2.6**
					C 1.0
					I 1.4

*$p < 0.05$.
**$p < 0.1$; Department df = 2, 48; Company df = 3, 48: interaction df = 6, 48.

adopt a new product. With changes in sales-rewards and market analyses hotpoly has become successful, and COMPCO is building a multi-million dollar plant. *Routines*. A new task force was set up from the beginning with everyone but field involved; senior management gave strong support; new business and market plans were made.

PRODCO: A chemical materials producer. The five interviews were not adequate to develop a general appreciation of PRODCO routines. Interviews Fall 1986.

1. *Failed Pit Liner.* The product is a membrane-like material that lines industrial waste pits, creating large containment areas. Previous materials had to be buried a foot underground to avoid exposure to the sun. A supplier created a new material that resisted the sun, or so they thought. PRODCO entered the pit business with the new material in the early 1970's. After 3 years, material decayed. All pits had to be replaced. It seems that usual routines were followed, but in this case failure was an "act of God."

2. *Successful Roof Liner.* The product is a membrane-like material (but does not decay in the sun) used for industrial roofs. It was introduced in 1981 and has become a multi-million dollar business. *Routines*. A separate business unit was created with people from all departments in it. They worked together extensively, and the product was designed based on first-order data from users. They violated PRODCO's usual distribution process, planning process, and reporting structure. The team continues to run the business.

Appendix B. Thought Worlds Controlling for Company and Success or Failure of Product

The market-technology knowledge and cognitive orientations were analyzed with a two-way ANOVA by department and company to see if the thought world differences held across company. Manufacturing people and the 4 PRODCO people were deleted from the analysis since there are so few of them, so the

TABLE B-2
Thought World Measures by Success Status

Thought World Measures	Weighted Mean Score			ANOVA results: Dept effect Success effect Interaction effect
	Successful	Uncertain	Failed	
% of Interview:				
Business Issues	32	25	24	D $F = 13.2^*$ S 2.0 I 1.38
Customer Issues	20	21	15	D $F = 4.12^*$ S 8.1* I 0.99
Selling Issues	13	10	8	D $F = 9.7^*$ S 1.3 I 1.3
Technical Issues	23	29	30	D $F = 20.7^*$ S 4.8* I 1.3
Manufacturing	14	14	17	D $F = 71.3^*$ S 2.5** I 2.3
Orientations mean ranks:				
Long-Short time	46	32	30	D $F = 3.08^*$ S 2.5** I 0.72
Task-People	25	40	44	D $F = 3.6^*$ S 3.4* I 0.60

*$p < 0.05$.
**$p < 0.1$; Department df = 3, 59; Success df = 2, 59; Interaction df = 6, 59.

results are for 4 firms and 3 departments. The figures in Table B-1 are the means by company, weighted by thought world—the mean for planners, technical and field was added and divided by 3 to adjust for the different proportions of thought worlds in each firm. There is one interaction effect, and subsequent analysis shows that OPCO's field people are below average on business issues. There is also one company effect; analysis indicates that SALECO is below average on customer issues. The results, overall, however, suggest that the differences by department reported in Table 3 hold regardless of company. These analyses are exploratory only since there are problems with the variances.

Table B-2 summarizes the means by success status (again, weighted so each thought world has an equal effect) on the 7 thought world measures. Analyses were also run without the manufacturing people to check for problems with the small cell sizes, and the results are similar. The department effect is found for all 7 measures. Successful developers also emphasize customer issues more and technology and manufacturing issues less. In addition, the successful developers are long term and people oriented, consistent with the qualitative result that they have a more comprehensive technology-market knowledge and more collaborative relationships. Since the successful cases have been out longer, the results may be biased by time. To check for this, uncertain and failed cases which have been out for less than 2 years were deleted and the analysis rerun. The results were similar, which suggests no time bias.

References

Adler, P. (1990), "Shared Learning," *Management Science*, 36, 938–957.

Argyris, C. and D. Schon (1978), *Organizational Learning: A Theory of Action Approach*, Reading, MA: Addison Wesley.

Bailyn, L. (1977), "Research as a Cognitive Process: Implications for Data Analysis," *Quality and Quantity*, 11, 97–117.

Barley, S. R. (1986), "Technology as an Occasion for Structuring: Evidence from Observations of CT Scanners and the Social Order of Radiology Departments," *Administrative Science Quarterly*, 31, 78–108.

Bartunek, J. M. (1984), "Changing Interpretive Schemes and Organizational Restructuring: The Example of a Religious Order," *Administrative Science Quarterly*, 29, 355–372.

Bonnet, D. (1986), "Nature of the R&D/Marketing Co-operation in the Design of Technologically Advanced New Industrial Products," *R&D Management*, 16, 117–126.

Clark, K. (1985), "The Interaction of Design Hierarchies and Market Concepts in Technological Evolution," *Research Policy*, 14, 235–251.

Cooper, R. (1983), "A Process Model for Industrial New Product Development," *IEEE Transactions on Engineering Management*, 30, 2–11.

————— and E. Kleinschmidt (1986), "An Investigation into the New Product Process: Steps, Deficiencies, and Impact," *Journal of Product Innovation Management*, 3, 71–85.

Daft, R. and K. Weick (1984), "Toward a Model of Organizations as Interpretive Systems," *Academy of Management Review*, 9, 43–66.

Dean, J. and G. Susman (1989), "Organizing for Manufacturable Design," *Harvard Business Review*, (January–February), 28–37.

Dearborn, D. and H. Simon (1958), "Selective Perception: A Note on the Departmental Identification of Executives," *Sociometry*, 140–144.

Dougherty, D. (1987), "New Products in Old Organizations: The Myth of the Better Mousetrap in Search of the Beaten Path," unpublished Doctoral Dissertation, MIT, Sloan School of Management.

————— (1990), "Understanding New Markets for New Products," *Strategic Management Journal*, 11, 59–78.

Douglas, M. (1987), *How Institutions Think*, London: Routledge and Kegan Paul.

Dunn, W. and A. Ginsberg (1986), "A Sociocognitive Network Approach to Organization Analysis," *Human Relations*, 40, 955–976.

Fleck, L. (1979), *Genesis and Development of a Scientific Fact*, T. Trenn and R. K. Merton (Eds.), translated by F. Bradley and T. Trenn; originally published 1935; Chicago: University of Chicago Press.

Freeman, C. (1982), *The Economics of Industrial Innovation*, Cambridge, MA: MIT Press.

Galbraith, J. (1982), "Designing the Innovative Organization," *Organization Dynamics*, (Winter), 5–25.

Glaser, B. and A. Strauss (1967), *The Discovery of Grounded Theory*, Chicago: Aldine.

Gupta, A., S. Raj and D. Wilemon (1986), "R&D and Marketing Managers in High-Tech Companies: Are They Different?", *IEEE Transactions on Engineering Management*, 33, 25–32.

Harrison, F. (1980), "Goal Orientations of Managers and Scientists: An Illusory Dichotomy," *IEEE Transactions on Engineering Management*, 27, 74–78.

Henderson, R. and K. Clark, (1990), "Architectures for Innovation: The Reconfiguration of Existing Product Technology and the Failure of Existing Firms," *Administrative Science Quarterly*, (March), (forthcoming).

Kanter, R. M. (1983), *The Change Masters*, New York: Simon and Schuster, Inc.

Lawrence, P. and J. Lorsch (1967), *Organization and Environment*, Boston: Harvard School of Business Administration Press.

Lilien, G. and E. Yoon (1988), "Determinants of New Industrial Product Performance: A Strategic Re-examination of Empirical Literature," *IEEE Transactions on Engineering Management*, 36, 3–10.

March, J. and H. Simon (1958), *Organizations*, New York: Wiley and Sons.

Mintzberg, H. (1979), *The Structuring of Organizations*, Englewood Cliffs, NJ: Prentice Hall.

Nelson, R. R. and S. G. Winter (1982), *An Evolutionary Theory of Economic Change*, Boston: Belknap Press.

Perrow, C. (1986), *Complex Organizations: A Critical Essay*, (3rd ed.), New York: Random House.

Quinn, J. B. (1985), "Managing Innovation: Controlled Chaos," *Harvard Business Review*, (May-June), 73–84.

Riley, P. (1983), "A Structurationist Account of Political Culture," *Administrative Science Quarterly*, 28, 414–437.

Rothwell, R., C. Freeman, A. Horsley, V. Jervis, A. Robertson and J. Crawford (1974), "SAPPHO Updated. Project SAPPHO Phase II," *Research Policy*, 32, 58–291.

Schall, M. (1983), "A Communication Rules Approach to Organizational Culture," *Administrative Science Quarterly*, 28, 557–581.

Schein, E. (1985), *Organizational Culture and Leadership*, San Francisco: Jossey-Bass.

Souder, W. (1987), *Managing New Product Innovations*, Lexington, MA: Lexington Books.

Strauss, A. (1987), *Qualitative Analysis For Social Scientists*, Cambridge: Cambridge University Press.

Tushman, M. (1978), "Technical Communication in R&D Laboratories: The Impact of Project Work Characteristics," *Academy of Management Journal*, 21, 624–645.

_____ and D. Nadler (1986), "Organizing for Innovation," *California Management Review*, 28, 74–92.

Urban, G. and E. von Hippel (1988), "Lead User Analyses for the Development of New Industrial Products," *Management Science*, 34, 569–582.

Van Maanen, J. (1979), "On the Understanding of Interpersonal Relations," In W. Bennis, J. Van Maanen, E. Schein, and F. I. Steele (Eds.), *Essays in Interpersonal Communication*, Homewood, IL: Dorsey Press, 13–42.

_____ and S. R. Barley (1984), "Occupational Communities: Culture and Control in Organizations," *Research in Organizational Behavior*, 6, Greenwich, CT: JAI Press, 287–365.

Yin, R. (1989), *Case Study Research: Design and Methods*, Newbury Park, CA: Sage.

A
Managerial Roles Within the Corporate Entrepreneurship Process

[20]

Raising Radicals: Different Processes for Championing Innovative Corporate Ventures

Diana L. Day

*Department of Management, The Wharton School, University of Pennsylvania,
Philadelphia, Pennsylvania 19104*

This paper is unusual in terms of its radical departure from prevalent theory, its empirical analysis of 136 internal corporate ventures, and its conclusions regarding bottom-up versus top-down championing of innovation and intra-entrepreneurship processes in organizations.

Arie Y. Lewin

Abstract

This study investigates the types of championing processes that explain the innovativeness of 136 internal corporate ventures. Current theory suggests that bottom-up champions create the most innovative ventures. In contrast, this paper argues that both bottom-up and top-down champions are suitable for developing innovative ventures. Using a broadly based sample of Fortune 1000 firms, the study supports both bottom-up and top-down processes including a special dual-role principal champion, who acts both as product champion and organizational sponsor. The functions or roles of these top management and dual-role champions are quite different from bottom-up champions and represent relatively unexplored top-down championing processes. Preliminary results show support for an emerging theory that top management champions arise when ventures are expensive and visible and when they represent new strategic directions or resource reconfigurations for the firm. In contrast, dual-role champions emerge from the firm's upper ranks when an innovative idea is highly uncertain but not technology-driven. The paper proposes an integrative view of championing in which any one of three types of championing processes may be the most relevant for a particular venture, depending on what it needs to achieve innovative outcomes.

(*Championing*; *Corporate Entrepreneurship*; *Internal Corporate Venturing*; *Innovation*; *Top Management*)

Introduction

Innovativeness stimulates economic development by fueling the engines of corporate growth (Schumpeter 1934, Penrose 1959). Without it, firms eventually wither and die. Because of this, scholars have focused on ways to improve innovativeness within established firms through internal venturing or corporate entrepreneurship (see Guth and Ginsberg 1990; Venkataraman, McGrath, and MacMillan 1992). Champions or "intrapreneurs" are one of the most crucial elements in determining the outcomes of such internal entrepreneurial efforts (Frost and Egri 1990). Ideas without champions rarely have the impetus to become formal corporate ventures, and the few that do are typically not successful (e.g., Rothwell et al. 1974, Green et al. 1990). As a result, almost all internal corporate ventures have at least one champion, and most have two or more (e.g., Rothwell et al. 1974, Witte 1977, Green et al. 1990).

Repeated anecdotal evidence and interviews with those involved, however, suggest that even when there are multiple champions, one champion typically stands out as the venture's principal champion. The venture's principal champion is the one whose involvement is viewed as the most crucial in the transformation of concept or prototype into new commercial business (Maidique 1980, Kidder 1981, Jelinek and Schoonhoven 1990, Frost and Egri 1990). Unfortunately, little systematic research on the principal champion exists from which we can assess his or her role in fostering innovative ventures. Further, prevailing views narrowly confine corporate entrepreneurship to a process by which champions and their innovations emerge from the depths of the organization when, in fact, champions may emerge from any level and location within the

1047-7039/94/0502/0148/$01.25

firm. Principal champions may also play multiple roles for innovations, and variations in their origins are likely to combine in ways previously not addressed in the literature. Hence, while it is clear that champions are essential, the origins and roles of the principal champion are not, nor is the relationship between those origins and roles and the venture's resulting innovativeness. The purpose of this paper is to explore whether and how the origins of the principal champion affect the innovativeness achieved by internal corporate ventures, where innovativeness is broadly defined as the degree to which the venture is the first to create a new market, relative to other firms, through the commercialization of a product based on new technology.[1]

Background: Internal Corporate Entrepreneurship Theory and Research
A rich body of literature suggests that perhaps the most effective process for creating innovative ventures is through originating, developing, and promoting them from the bottom up (Burgelman 1983a, b, Kimberly 1979, Mintzberg 1979, Quinn 1985). This research finds that highly innovative ventures typically emerge from the purposeful behavior of individuals or small groups in the lower levels of the organization, implying that principal champions originate from these levels (Burgelman 1983a, b, Kimberly 1979, Mintzberg 1979, Quinn 1985). While such a process seems logical, given that lower-level champions typically have the most current knowledge and expertise and are closer to the sources of information critical to innovative outcomes, the bottom-up view is limited.

Part of the controversy concerning the bottom-up view stems from the myth that one person with an idea makes heroic efforts to take the idea from conception to final commercialization. In fact, such a process is relatively rare. "The innovator as creative zealot, for example, championing his idea in the face of dragon-like bureaucracy, fighting his way to glory in the marketplace. 'It happens that way maybe one time in 30,' says McKinsey's Foster" (Kiechel 1988). In addition, as Schumpeter (1934) points out, it is not who originates the idea (e.g., the inventor) but the entrepreneur who transforms the idea or invention into a new commercial business who plays the key role in economic growth. Indeed, U.S. companies are fraught with good ideas and inventions from which they never realize the potential profits, e.g., transitors and AT&T; flat panel displays and RCA, user-friendly icon-based software and Xerox. Prototypes come out of the lab and if no one takes ownership of them, they are shelved, sold off

through licenses, or snatched by other companies which then market them and profit from the originator's inventive efforts. Clearly, ideas or inventions alone are not enough.

Many functions must be performed to transform an idea or prototype into a viable commercial business. Someone must originate the idea or concept, create a prototype, give the venture its impetus, define and create the entire product bundle, generate the necessary resources, mentor and monitor the venture's progress, and provide it with legitimacy internally and externally. To assume originating or even defining the idea is the most important is to ignore the realities that in different situations, other functions may be much more critical. In fact, many (e.g., Venkataraman et al. 1992) define a champion as the agent who helps the venture navigate the socio-political environment inside the corporation. Such a definition suggests a process where hierarchical power plays a much more important role.

Indeed, earlier literature had focused on the critical role that top managers must play, implying a process in which the critical functions of the principal champions are those related to resources and legitimacy (e.g., Quinn and Mueller 1963, Susbauer 1973, Maidique 1980, Roberts 1980). Some researchers have found that fostering innovation demands top management commitment (e.g., Block, MacMillan, and Subba Narashimha 1986), including direct and early championing (e.g., Maidique 1980; Imai, Nonaka, and Takeuchi 1985; Jelinek and Schoonhoven 1990) and venture support (e.g., Susbauer 1973, Maidique and Hayes 1984). In addition, champions who have greater power, responsibility, and experience have been associated with more successful innovations (Rothwell 1977), and corporate top management champions were specifically associated with more successful innovations (Green et al. 1990). Watson, former CEO of IBM, was well known for his critical role in the development of the IBM 360 (Maidique 1980); Morita, Sony's former chairman, was the key figure in Sony's development of the Walkman (Morita et al. 1986); and Tonaka, a managing director for Canon, played the central role in Canon's move into plain-paper copiers (Nonaka and Yamanouchi 1989). While it is not totally clear who really originated these ideas, all three innovations were given their *impetus* and *championed* from the top.

Unfortunately, much of the top-down championing literature is largely anecdotal or retrospective. Sound reasons do exist, however, for some ventures to have principal champions from the top. For example, the bottom-up view is based on keeping ventures largely invisible until they are proven viable (Quinn 1979, Burgelman 1983a), but some ventures, by their very nature, will be highly visible initially or from the early stages of development. As Tushman and Romanelli (1985) point out, executive leadership is critical to ventures that strategically reorient a firm. In addition, extremely costly ventures often require significant involvement by those with control over substantial resources. When ventures need legitimacy or significant resources a priori to achieve innovative outcomes, top managers are essential as their principal champions.

Given these divergent views, developing an integrated perspective on the origins and roles of principal champions in creating innovative ventures may foster a better understanding of the challenges different ventures face and the ways that championing can help overcome them. Despite the importance of principal champions in developing innovative ventures, prior empirical research on championing has not addressed either the functions that these champions provide in spawning innovative ventures or the conditions that lead to their emergence from different origins. This paper argues that, depending on the challenges a venture faces, some functions and thus power bases of the principal champion may be more crucial than others in creating radically innovative ventures.

Championing

Champions use their power and influence to help ventures navigate the complex socio-political maze inside their corporations. Power here is meant in the broadest sense: it may be based on hierarchical position, access to resources, technical expertise, and/or centrality in a sociometric network of information (Chakrabarti and Hauschildt 1989). Different championing functions require different power bases, and just as all functions are not equally important for all ventures, neither are all the bases of power on which these functions are built. In order for ventures to be innovative, they need principal champions with the appropriate bases of power for the types of challenges they face. In some situations, creating innovative ventures requires a principal champion who has the appropriate knowledge and expertise and is close enough to the necessary sources of information to help the venture achieve innovative results: a champion from the lower levels of the firm. For these types of ventures, staying largely invisible in the organization can allow them to avoid top management attention and thus conflicts with powerful opponents until they can demonstrate their suc-

cess. Unfortunately, some ventures cannot remain invisible and require a corporate top manager as their principal champion to give them the resources and legitimacy they need to face the challenges they will encounter. Finally, a third type of venture entails such great initial uncertainty that it requires a dual-role champion—someone who possesses both the relevant expertise and information and the appropriate hierarchical power and control over resources so that he or she can make and implement better decisions in the face of significant uncertainties. This implies three types of processes: bottom-up, top-down, and dual-role championing, each driven by a principal champion with the appropriate power base for the challenges of a particular type of venture.

Bottom-Up Championing

The critical tasks in creating highly innovative ventures are often those of linking and learning (Dosi 1984). To achieve radically innovative outcomes, some ventures require principal champions who can help provide the creative insight and essential linking functions—linking promising technical problems with internal and external scientific knowledge and technical developments in the lab with market demand (Burgelman and Sayles 1986). For effective learning to take place, those with the most current and relevant knowledge and expertise must interact with critical sources of information to evaluate and incorporate new information effectively. Those who come from the lower levels of the organization are likely both to be closer to the technological and market interfaces and to have the most current knowledge and expertise (Maidique 1980). Lower-level champions' abilities to provide these linking activities are also derived from the fact that they usually hold central positions in sociometric networks of communication (Becker 1970). Because they are at the center of such networks, they have access to more information that might prove useful to the venture. The expertise and centrality of these lower-level champions also imbue them with informal organizational power and influence (Pettigrew 1972, Brass 1984), allowing them to garner resources and build coalitional support, even when their hierarchical position may not grant them much direct power or control over such resources.

In this bottom-up, emergent view of championing, incremental innovation can be "induced" from the top down, but highly innovative ventures will be seen as "errors" and be "selected out" unless they remain largely invisible until they can demonstrate success

(Burgelman 1983a). Too much visibility early in the process can inhibit innovativeness for many ventures, generating more resources than can be employed effectively, creating pressures for quick results, and inviting potential critics to have their say before crucial problems can be identified, much less resolved (Quinn 1979, Burgelman and Sayles 1986). Principal champions from lower levels can help ventures remain invisible during this critical time. The development of Tom West's 32-bit minicomputer for Data General (Kidder 1981), Chuck House's electronic lens monitors for Hewlett-Packard, and Art Fry's Post-Its for 3M (Pinchot 1985) provide excellent examples of lower-level principal champions and bottom-up championing processes. If bottom-up, emergent processes are important to the resulting innovativeness of some internal corporate ventures, then principal champions from the lower levels should provide a good proxy of such processes, implying a positive relationship between principal champions from the lower levels of the organization and the venture's resulting innovativeness. Thus, the hypothesized main effect of the principal champion's hierarchical level is:

HYPOTHESIS 1.   *The lower the principal champion's hierarchical level, the more innovative the venture will be.*

The principal champion's organizational location is also important. Since, on average, many people from corporate headquarters have staff or support positions in corporate planning, accounting and control, legal, or public relations, principal champions from corporate headquarters are likely to make ineffective principal champions. In general, because of their background, training, and experience, they are unlikely to have the specific expertise or knowledge that might be important for the venture. If they had such knowledge and expertise, their organizational location makes it unlikely they would have close contact with the market or technology or that they would be perceived as experts by others they would need to influence. Their organizational and perhaps even geographic distance from key daily decision-making activities would also detrimentally affect their ability to form appropriate coalitions or influence the direction of critical decisions (Eisenhardt and Bourgeois 1988). In addition, because many corporate positions are staff positions, most people in them do not have significant hierarchical power or direct-line authority over substantial resources. These arguments lead to the following hypothesis of the main

effect of the principal champion's corporate organizational location:

HYPOTHESIS 2.   *In general, principal champions from corporate headquarters, particularly from staff positions, will be negatively associated with innovativeness.*

Top-Down Championing
Some might argue that a bottom-up, emergent process of championing is, or perhaps should be, the only model that firms follow for radically innovative ventures. Rather than viewing top managers as playing direct roles as principal champions, some researchers have outlined three distinct but limited roles for top managers: as orchestrators (Galbraith 1982), retroactive legitimizers (Burgelman 1983b), or judges and arbiters (Angle and Van de Ven 1989). As orchestrators, top managers influence the outcomes of specific ventures only indirectly, creating the right structures and climate for general innovation through the use of substantive (Galbraith 1982) and symbolic (Pfeffer 1981) actions and then allowing the "invisible hand" to operate (Kanter 1988, Venkataraman et al. 1992). Both in terms of substantive and symbolic action, 3M provides the consummate example of top managers as orchestrators, e.g., creating pools of resources for innovation, establishing formal policies and controls to encourage innovative activity, identifying "intrapreneurs" as heroes, and devising ceremonies and awards to call attention to entrepreneurial activities. As retroactive legitimizers, top managers endorse only those ventures that are proven successes, and then only after they have established themselves as such. Dave Packard's earlier rejection and ultimate endorsement of Chuck House's electronic lens monitor provides a dramatic example of a bottom-up process in which top management acted as a retroactive legitimizer (Pinchot 1985). Finally, senior top managers can act as judges or arbiters between those who champion the venture and those who criticize it (Angle and Van de Ven 1989). This noncommittal role is premised on the belief that institutional leaders should not be the principal champions for ventures; rather, they should keep some psychological distance, to avoid potential escalating commitment to risky projects whose failure might bankrupt the company. These limited roles for top managers are based on several legitimate concerns, including the potential for poor decision making that may result from information asymmetries (Schon 1967), selection biases toward the familiar (Hannan and Freeman 1977, DiMaggio and Powell

1983, Van de Ven 1986), and bankruptcy risks due to escalating commitment to costly and risky ventures (Angle and Van de Ven 1989).

Despite the above arguments, there are specific ventures in which the top management of the firm, either the corporation's CEO or his or her direct subordinate, needs to play a direct role as principal champion. In general, these ventures can be described as costly, high-profile ventures or ventures that represent decisive strategic reorientations of the firm. They embody substantial risks for the organization and significant threats to the status quo (Tushman and Romanelli 1985). Such ventures cannot remain invisible until they can demonstrate success. As a result, they typically engender strong selection pressures within the firm. These ventures will require the considerable resources and early legitimacy that only the organization's most powerful members, corporate top managers, can bestow.

Some ventures which are organizational misfits (MacMillan and McCaffery 1983) or incorporate architectural innovations (Henderson and Clark 1990), require new resource combinations that breach intraorganizational boundaries to integrate operating assets or disparate technologies across the firm. For example, IBM's strategic goal in the development of the system 360 series was to reduce costly switching resulting from programming incompatibilities by creating a single, integrated line of computers. To accomplish this goal, IBM developed a whole new computer architecture incorporating revolutionary new microcircuitry which was simultaneously compatible with its previous software. Creating the series required $5 billion in capital (more than its total assets or sales at the time), significantly different relationships with suppliers and buyers, and ultimately, several restructurings of the firm (Schon 1967, Maidique 1980). There are five reasons that Watson, then IBM's CEO, had to take a substantial, direct, and early role in championing the 360: (1) the venture required significant, high-level cooperation and coordination across all of the firm's existing core businesses; (2) the established political structure of the entire firm had to be changed to accommodate it; (3) the venture would have a significant strategic impact on important interorganizational relationships; (4) it required the commitment of substantial financial resources; and (5) it involved exceptional risks for the firm, all of which require the power and authority of the CEO. Based on these arguments, the 360 would never have been initiated, much less successfully launched, without Watson's initial and continuous involvement.

When ventures represent costly, radical, and potentially important strategic or cultural departures for the firm, initial legitimacy may prove essential, not just to the venture's ultimate innovativeness but to its pursuit from the onset and throughout the process. In fact, if innovations will clearly be costly to develop, bottom-up champions often do not emerge because they recognize that such projects are beyond the scope of what they can hope to accomplish without significant and continuous support from the top. Control Data's development of PLATO, the first computerized interactive learning system, might never have happened if William Norris, Control Data's Chairman, had not initially and continuously advocated the project. So opposed were the operating people to the idea that Norris had to use his own "chairman's budget" to get the project started. This venture required a new way of thinking: according to Robert Price, "[Plato] changes the whole philosophy of how we interface with users. It changes our approach to normal data processing applications to make them more usable and more tutorial. It changes our philosophy on how to support our customers and enables us to provide remote support" (Worthy 1987, p. 105). While PLATO was very costly and time-consuming to develop—taking 17 years and $900 million to build—its technology spinoffs affected virtually every CDC business and permeated nearly every revenue stream in the company. Unfortunately, this made calculating PLATO's true profits practically impossible, and therefore it was widely viewed as a failure. When Norris was asked upon his retirement what his greatest accomplishment was, however, he answered, without hesitation, PLATO (Worthy 1987).

Given that these ventures are costly and may either reconfigure the firm or create whole new strategic directions, they represent extremely risky propositions. If they fail, they could have significant reputational and financial repercussions for the firm, including the firm's demise. While such ventures should be relatively rare because of their substantial risks, not pursuing them may be equally risky to the firm's long-run survival and profits, as IBM has recently learned. Given that these ventures need top management's power to achieve their innovative results, it is critical that top management not avoid championing responsibilities for such important ventures.

These arguments, along with the anecdotal evidence, suggest a top-down process in which the CEO or his or her direct subordinate provides the impetus for a specific venture from an early stage in the process. These points lead to the following hypothesis of a top-down process, indicated by principal champions from corpo-

152

rate top management:

HYPOTHESIS 3. *Within corporate headquarters, the higher the level of the principal champion (i.e., CEOs and their direct subordinates), the greater the innovativeness of the venture.*

Dual-Role Championing

While top management champions may take on some functions of product champions, such as providing the impetus and advocating the venture, as well as some functions of organizational sponsors, such as granting resources and legitimacy, they are not involved in all the key functions of either role and rely on others to do those tasks. For example, top management champions do not usually become involved in the actual definition of the product, typically a function of product champions, nor do they always carry out the frequent mentoring and monitoring of the venture, customarily functions of the organization sponsor. In contrast, there is an essentially top-down process in which the principal champion plays dual roles, taking on most or all of the key functions as both the product champion and the organizational sponsor. As product champions, they are directly involved in product definition. As organizational sponsors, they coach and mentor the venture concerning key decisions (Souder 1984, Galbraith 1982, Burgelman 1983) or actually make those key decisions themselves (Galbraith 1982). A dual-role principal champion, who is both product champion and organizational sponsor, may provide the right mix of knowledge and information, as well as hierarchical power, to foster certain kinds of highly innovative ventures. The concept of dual-role champions, however, conflicts not only with what many believe but also with previous theory and empirical evidence.

Many are convinced that innovative ventures require multiple champions to overcome the challenges they must face (e.g., Venkataraman et al. 1992). As Quinn (1986, p. 74) said, "For a high probability of success, an innovation needs a mother (champion) who loves it emotionally and will stay with it when others would give up, a father (authority figure with resources) who can support it, and pediatricians (experts) who can see it through technical difficulties." Further, empirical studies have found that one-man shows are, in general, seldom successful (Souder 1984), and a tandem structure of one champion with know-how and another champion with power usually works best (Witte 1973). In addition to the empirical evidence, previous theory on the division and specialization of labor in management (Taylor 1916, Lawrence and Lorsch 1967) and, more specifically, in championing innovations

(Chakrabarti and Hauschildt, 1989) suggests that multiple champions provide the superior configuration for championing all types of innovations, including radical ones.

Unfortunately, this division of championing roles is typically associated with information and power asymmetries (Schon 1967). Because they are typically located at different levels, multiple champions may vary in the quality and quantity of their information about the technology, the market, and the true needs and potential of the venture, as well as information concerning the basis on which corporate sponsorship and resource allocation decisions will be made. They may also differ in the kinds and amounts of power each has, with those at lower levels of the organization having indirect power and influence based on their knowledge and expertise and those from higher levels having hierarchical authority and more direct power. Information and power asymmetries are problems in various authorization situations because " ... choices are made by people who often do not fully comprehend the proposals presented to them. Thus, in authorization, the comparative ignorance of the manager is coupled with the inherent bias of the sponsor" (Mintzberg, Raisinghani, and Theoret 1976, p. 260). Therefore, while a division of roles may allow each champion to contribute in the way that each is best suited, it implies that those who must make decisions about allocating resources to the venture and helping it obtain legitimacy are not necessarily the ones who have the most knowledge and information about the venture's true needs and potential.

While Schon (1967) and Mintzberg et al. (1976) seem to presuppose that these asymmetries are similarly problematic for all ventures or authorization problems, there are cogent arguments why this is not necessarily true. Some ventures begin as highly innovative ideas. Highly innovative ideas inherently entail significantly more uncertainty and risk. Because of the high degree of uncertainty in such situations, the probabilities of making poor decisions because of weak or erroneous information are increased. When there is a division of roles in such situations, the organizational sponsor is often tempted to be conservative in allocating resources and seeking or granting legitimacy for the venture, preferring to keep the venture as quiet as possible until more information is known. Thus, the sponsor will not have to face a highly visible and costly error if the venture turns out to lack merit. As a result, ventures pursuing highly innovative ideas may often be underfunded and lack the necessary legitimacy to get things done, which can slow the process and result in fewer innovative outcomes than might have been achieved. For example, because of underfunding, the venture team may decide to use a part that already exists rather than design one from scratch, even though the specifically designed part may serve the new technology better, or it may decide to use existing distribution channels, though the target market for the product may call for the development of new ones. If the principal champion performs functions of both the organizational sponsor and the product champion, then he or she should have better insight and understanding when making decisions, as well as sufficient hierarchical power to grant legitimacy and provide the appropriate funding to readily implement those decisions. As a result, information and power asymmetries are no longer a problem.

The Walkman provides an excellent example of the importance of dual-role champions for overcoming information and power asymmetries. The Walkman violated a strongly held belief among marketing and technical people that all radios had to provide a record function. As a result, significant uncertainties existed as to whether there was a market at all for the product. These uncertainties created substantial problems for the venture in two ways. First, simply to create the prototype required pulling together people from the tape-recorder division with others from the head-phone division—each contributing key elements to the new product form. No one in power in either division, however, believed a market existed for the product and, therefore, no one was willing to support it. Second, most believed that if a product were created, then the wisest entry strategy would include an entry price point of at least $249 (the break-even point), and preferably higher, with very limited initial production and promotion until significant market demand could be demonstrated. Because Morita believed so strongly in the product and its market potential, he used his hierarchical power to force the cooperation of the relevant divisions. He also spent a great deal of time "researching" and thinking about the market. Based on his own personal vision of the market potential, Morita believed that pricing was crucial to market success and insisted on a penetration pricing strategy at $165 to attract the youth market. He also recognized the need to educate potential customers about the use of this new product concept so he not only insisted on an extensive promotion budget but also used a wide variety of other promotional tools from hiring young people to wear them to wearing one himself at every possible opportunity. Morita provided the impetus for the venture, made most of the key decisions that led to

the venture's success, granted it resources so that the venture could price in advance of demand, and gave it legitimacy both internally and externally (Morita et al. 1986, pp. 79–83).

Tonaka, a managing director at Canon, provides another good example of a dual-role champion. Canon's senior management decided that diversifying into plain-paper copiers provided an important opportunity to use some of their new technology, but they also recognized the need for a whole new concept of the market and thus a different product concept that would not infringe on Xerox's patents. To grant the venture sufficient access to resources and hierarchical power, Tonaka was put in charge and quickly emerged as a strong champion for the venture (Tonaka and Yamanouchi 1989). Tonaka got very involved in learning about the product and its market so that he could successfully defend the venture against increasingly stronger attacks by its critics.

Dual-role champions appear most appropriate only for specific kinds of ventures. There is one type of venture in which a single, dual-role champion is unlikely to emerge, and if one does, he or she will be disadvantaged compared with multiple champions. For most ventures in which (radically new) technology plays a central role, as in many science-based, technology-driven ventures, dual-role champions are unlikely to be helpful in defining the product because their hierarchical position puts them at too great a distance from the state of the art in scientific knowledge; therefore, they cannot effectively provide the technological linking tasks critical for such ventures. These complex, science-based, technology ventures thrive best with a division of championing roles. In contrast, dual-role champions are more likely to emerge and be effective with marketing-driven ventures, in which dual-role champions, even from the organization's upper levels, are likely to maintain or initiate contact with the relevant market or follow forecasted trends that might lead to innovative outcomes.

Theory on the problems of information and power asymmetries indicates that having the knowledge and understanding of the product champion and the funding and mentoring experience of the organizational sponsor represented in the same person may provide some ventures with significant advantages over those that have a division of championing roles. These arguments lead to the following hypothesis:

HYPOTHESIS 4. *Dual-role champions who play both the role of principal champion and of organizational sponsor will be positively associated with innovativeness.*

154

The Effects of Corporate Characteristics and Other Venture Attributes

The effects of corporate characteristics and other venture attributes need to be considered in any study of venture championing. This study includes controls for corporate size, age, and diversity as well as pre-entry R & D investments, cannibalization, organizational location and complementary, supporting assets.

Corporate Size. Economic models of technological innovation stem from Schumpeterian theory (Schumpeter 1942), which identified innovation as a scale-intensive activity positively related to organizational size. Explanations for the large size-innovation relationship reflect: (1) the resource-hungry nature of contemporary innovation in building distribution and developing markets, which favors large firms over small (Hay and Morris 1979); (2) capital market imperfections that give the large firm an advantage because of the correlation between size and the availability and stability of internally generated funds to cover technological and market development; (3) complementaries between R & D and other nonmanufacturing activities that may be better developed within large firms (see Cohen and Levin 1989, for the last two explanations); and (4) market power in introducing innovations, which, again, favors large firms (see Fisher and Temin 1973).

Size could also have the opposite effect. The bureaucratic effects of size could undermine a venture's innovativeness (Cooper 1964). Behind this counterargument are organizational theories suggesting that smaller firms have shorter lines of communication and control (e.g., Maidique and Hayes 1984), lower levels of work-decreasing alienation (e.g., Bonjean 1966, Nelson 1968), and lower levels of organizational inertia (e.g., Hannan and Freeman 1977, Tushman and Romanelli 1985). Also, the venture capital industry has provided smaller firms with access to substantial capital with fewer market imperfections because the industry is more specialized and has greater access to information and control than the general stock market. These counterarguments, along with the lack of empirical research, specifically on size and innovativeness, as defined here, suggest the possibility of either a positive or negative relationship.

Others have argued that medium-sized firms may have most of the benefits of large firms without many of the negative effects of bureaucracy (e.g., Scherer 1965, Mansfield 1968, Hambrick and MacMillan 1985). These arguments suggest a positive curvilinear, not linear, relationship between size and innovativeness; in

other words, corporate size[2] should be positively related to innovativeness.

Corporate Age. Internal conditions may lead firms to ossify as they age, due to: (1) the retention of control in the hands of the original founders or members of their families; (2) pressures toward internal consistency; (3) the hardening of vested interests; and (4) the homogeneity of members' perceptions (Aldrich and Auster 1986). These conditions suggest a negative relationship between age and innovativeness.

Corporate Diversity. Since highly diversified firms are less dependent on any single business or technology, they have less incentive to make the substantial investments necessary for innovation. Highly diversified firms often grow through merger or acquisition rather than internal development and corporate entrepreneurship (e.g., ITT). Therefore, diversity is likely to reduce the level of innovativeness attained by a corporation. If corporate diversity, rather than product championing, significantly influences innovativeness, then controlling for this variable may be important.

Pre-entry R & D Investment. Internal corporate ventures that produce innovative products are expensive. Mansfield and colleagues (1981) found that technologically innovative products were significantly more costly than products that imitate. Imitations averaged 65% or less of innovators' costs. Therefore, investments made in R & D before market entry should be positively related to innovativeness. If innovativeness is largely determined by R & D expenditures, outspending others on R & D initially would allow ventures to be more innovative, suggesting a positive relationship.

Cannibalization, Organizational Location, and Complementary Supporting Assets. If a venture threatens to take sales away from a firm's existing business, political pressures may be generated within the firm that undermine the venture's innovativeness during its development. The location of the venture within the corporate structure—whether it is in an operating division or an autonomous subunit—may also influence the level of innovativeness attained. If the venture can draw on the firm's existing operating assets, then the possession of these assets may also play a role in its innovativeness. These factors are also controlled for in this study.

The hypotheses developed above were tested using data from a large sample of internal corporate ventures. Data were collected through questionnaires administered to venture teams at an early point in each venture's life, before the time when it could be known whether the venture would be successful or not. Consequently, this data on principal champions do not suffer from retrospective rationalizing or bandwagon effects.

Methodology

Sample

This study's 136 internal corporate ventures and their related innovations, all in manufacturing industries, were drawn from an ongoing start-up database initiated by Biggadike (1976). An internal corporate venture was defined as any start-up that: (1) originated internally; (2) was new to the company on at least two of the three dimensions of products, markets, or technologies; and (3) required significant investments of company resources to accomplish a result beyond the year in which the expenditure was made. In addition, ventures entering established markets had to be perceived as new entrants by competitors and customers alike. Included under this definition were ventures that launched new products, drawn from new technologies that would displace a company's existing product. Not included were product/service extensions of existing product lines, capacity additions, or brand introductions by existing businesses (Biggadike 1976).

The vast majority of the ventures in this database were launched between the mid-seventies and the early eighties. Given that the economic, behavioral, and political processes underlying championing are generally timeless, the data's age should not be a problem. The ventures included in the sample were typical of the venturing activities within their firms (Biggadike 1976). They ranged from those having poor initial financial results (i.e., losses of more than 11,680%) to those that were highly successful (i.e., profits in excess of 86%) with initial market shares varying from less than 5% to 100% of their target markets. Preliminary results from a follow-up study in progress show that more than half the ventures in this database were ultimately terminated sometime within the first five years. Therefore, there is little evidence that this sample is biased in favor of the most promising and ultimately successful ventures, a problem from which other studies of innovativeness or pioneering have sometimes suffered (e.g., Robinson and Fornell 1985). While many of these ventures were eventually terminated, none was terminated during the initial two years, part of the "honeymoon" period (Levinthal 1991). A few of the industries represented include chemical, pharmaceutical, electronic, computer, and consumer packaged goods, ranging from high-tech to marketing-driven firms. These firms or subsidiaries ranged in size from $84 million to $16.3 billion in sales, with the vast majority representing the Fortune 1000. Examples of these ventures include a new materials venture developed by a metals company for use in sporting goods equipment, a new polyester product developed by a rayon producer, and a new piece of equipment for hospital pharmacies introduced by a manufacturer of hospital ward equipment (Biggadike 1976).

While there is no way to determine the sample's true representativeness on the variables of interest for all Fortune 1000 companies, some comparisons might prove informative. For example, the innovations in this study took anywhere from less than one year to eleven years to develop, with an average of 2.5 years. In comparison, in a study of consumer products, "significant R&D" products took 3.5 years, "some R&D" products took 2.5, and "me-too" products took 1.5 (Urban and Hauser 1980).

Data Collection. Data on the first 40 ventures were collected by Biggadike from each venture's team and its management. Subsequent data were collected from the venture team and its management by a set of professional researchers that assisted them in interpreting the questionnaires. In addition, an instructional manual accompanied each questionnaire, giving examples with appropriate responses to illustrate each question, and one-day seminars were held to train all participating venture teams in responding to the questions. Each venture paid a significant fee to participate in this database, and in return, participants were provided with custom-tailored feedback on their venture relative to the other ventures in the study. Given that the usefulness of this feedback was essentially a function of how accurately each team reported its data, it was in every team's best interest to provide thorough and accurate data. The questions on which data were collected included general information about the type of business, the venture's relationship to other parts of the company, the venture's principal champion, its location in the company, and the nature of the venture and its competitive environment. In addition, data were collected over time on the venture's competitive strategy, its costs, and its performance. To measure corporate-level phenomena (e.g., firm age), I added data from secondary sources.

Variables

Because the hypotheses being tested concern venture-specific rather than general firm-level phenomena, all measures, except for four measures of corporate context, were operationalized specifically for a given venture, unlike most empirical work on innovation (Cohen and Levin 1989).

Dependent Measure. Sahal (1981) defined innovation as the *first* commercial or practical application of a new device or invention. Some studies tend to categorize the first entrant as the innovator and those who follow as imitators (Schmookler 1966, Sahal 1981), but other early entrants, who may introduce equally novel products or processes in terms of technology and design or make significant changes to the technology and design of the first, may also play an important role. The same is true of a venture's role in market development. Such entrants often face costs, risks, and potential rewards virtually equal to the first. Some theorists thus separate entrants into various roles, such as first-mover, pioneer, early follower, or late entrant, where the first-mover is literally the first to introduce a new technology or enter a new market. Pioneers are very early entrants who are involved in initially developing the technology or market. Early followers trail pioneers, after the technology has been introduced or the market created but before the competition is well established, and late entrants enter last, after the technology or market are well established. Others, however, have separated entrants based on their order (second, third, etc.) or elapsed time since first entry (Lieberman and Montgomery 1988). Each of these approaches has strengths and weaknesses. Entry role, rather than order or elapsed time, was selected here, however, both because the timing role was already in the database and because I believe this measurement best captures the relevant definition of intervals for a cross-industry study.

There is then a problem with defining the concept of "first-mover" or innovator. Some scholars recognize that there are at least two distinct dimensions on which innovations can be first—technological and market (Abernathy and Clark 1985, Lieberman and Montgomery 1988). For example, a venture can be a first-mover in terms of introducing a new technology but introduce it to a market that was already established for that product category; it could take an existing technology and introduce it to a new geographic market or new market segment making it a first-mover in the new market; or it could take a new technology and create a new market for it, making it a first-mover for both the technology and the market. Therefore, for the purposes of this study, a venture's innovativeness was broadly specified as the degree to which a venture is first to create a new market relative to other firms through the commercialization of a product based on new technology.

Innovativeness was then measured using an index built around measures of the three defining characteristics of innovativeness: (1) the timing of entry of the venture (i.e., first, pioneer, early follower, later entrant); (2) the life-cycle stage of the market at the time of entry (i.e., introductory, growth, mature, decline); and (3) the technological newness of the offering (i.e., the extent to which the product was new to the world, new technologically but not a new product, or simply an imitation of existing products). Index design followed methods outlined in Lansing and Morgan (1977). Conventional scaling methods based on factor analyses or coefficient alphas were deemed inappropriate, as they make little use of the variance among indicators of innovativeness, which an index can incorporate.

Each level of these three measures was assigned a value from 3 to 0, except for technological newness, which was scored from 3 to 1 because only three responses were possible. A score of 3 on any measure indicated the highest degree of innovativeness for that measure. The scores on the measures were summed to form an index of innovativeness with a range of 9 (the most) to 1 (the least innovative). Because there was no theoretical justification for differences in weighting, all measures were weighted equally in building the index. *Timing of entry* captures the degree to which the venture was first in terms of its role of entry. First entrants were scored as the most innovative (rated 3), followed by pioneers (rated 2), early followers (rated 1), and later entrants (rated 0). *Life cycle stage* is a proxy for the extent to which the venture created a new market. Whenever a new product/market is created, a new life cycle is initiated (Moore and Tushman 1982). Ventures that enter during the introductory stage typically are more involved in creating a new market than those entering during the growth, mature, or declining stages, because these ventures must develop the market to accept the new product category and discover the product design and features that will lead to the widest possible market acceptance (i.e., the dominant design). Ventures entering in the introductory stage of the life cycle were scored as the most innovative (rated 3), followed by ventures entering in the growth stage (rated 2), the mature stage (rated 1), and the decline stage (rated 0). *Degree of technological newness* measures the extent to which the venture commercialized new technology. If an innovation was a significantly new conceptualization in terms of the product and its technology (i.e., new to the world), it was scored as more innovative than a venture that introduced an established product based on new technology, which was scored as more innovative than imitative (i.e., same product, same technology). For example, EMI's introduction of the first CAT scanner would be classified as a new-to-the-world product. The introduction of digital watches would be classified here as an established product/new technology and would receive a score of 2. Finally, ventures introducing imitative products received the lowest score of 1—for example, the introduction of IBM-compatible PCs or clones by non-IBM manufacturers. Given that only three of the 136 ventures scored at the extremes—two scored 9 and one scored 1—this measure seems to capture important variations in a venture's innovativeness that would have been missed by selecting a narrower measure based on using any one of these indicators as a proxy. For example, a pioneer that entered by imitating the first entrant's product is distinguished from a pioneer that introduced a product based on a different technology, even if both entered in the introductory phase. A late-mover that entered in the mature stage did not receive the same score as one that entered in the decline phase, even though both products may be imitative. Therefore, the multiple indicators in this index recognize and capture important variance among each of these three indicators, providing a more accurate indication of a venture's degree of innovativeness.

Another advantage of this composite index is that it should be less biased and more objective than respondents' evaluations of how innovative the venture was. If the question for this variable had simply asked how innovative the venture was, it is likely that the resulting distribution would have been seriously biased upward. The distribution of responses on each of the three more fact-based questions suggests support for this contention. In this database only 8% indicated that they were first and only 30% that they were pioneers either in creating new markets or in introducing new technologies or both. In contrast, the value of the pioneering variable in the PIMS database has been questioned because more than 50% of its businesses indicated that they were pioneers (Buzzell and Gale 1987). From life cycle theory we know that most entrants enter in the introductory or growth stages of the

life cycle. In this database, the distribution of entrants was also skewed toward entering in the introductory and growth stages of the life cycle. While 42% described their technology as largely imitative, only 3% classified their innovations as new to the world (compared with 10% from Booz-Allen, et al. 1982). Given that this study included as new to the world only those that represented both a new product concept and a new technology, the lower percentage of new-to-the-world innovations here is not surprising. The distribution of this measure was skewed toward imitation, reflecting the predominance of imitative products in the real world.

Independent measures. Three variables were used to measure the origins and roles of the venture's principal champion. The identification of the principal champion was based on a consensus of the venture team's responses which may be problematic; however, previous research on championing has found a very high rate of agreement concerning champions' identities. For example, Howell and Higgins (1990) found in their study that 89% of their sample were in total agreement on the identity of the champion and even the 11% who had some variation as to who the champion was were largely in agreement. Two variables evaluated the main effects of the principal champion's hierarchical level (an interval measure) and organizational location within the firm (a dummy variable for corporate headquarters). The principal champion's hierarchical level was measured for five levels, from CEO, scored a 5, to four levels down (scored a 1). The variable was normally distributed encompassing the entire range from 5 to 1. It had a mean of 3.04 and a standard deviation of 1.29, with CEOs not only from corporate headquarters but also from subsidiaries or divisions of the corporation. The dummy variable for the principal champion's organizational location was scored 1 if the champion was from corporate headquarters and 0 otherwise. Of the 136 ventures, 40 were championed by someone from corporate headquarters.

A third interaction variable was created by multiplying the principal champion's hierarchical level within the organization times his or her organizational location. This third measure is based on Schein's (1980) argument for a conical model of organization design, in which a person's proximity to the core of the organization is not determined merely by his or her organizational location or level in the hierarchy, but by the combination of the two. When the interaction of level and location were both considered, there were 17 corporate CEOs, 11 direct subordinates, 6 that were two levels down, 1 that was three, and 5 that were four levels down in a corporate staff function who emerged as principal champions for a venture. It is important to point out here that the respondents in this study were primarily individuals from the venture team where venture teams were often quite distant from corporate top management. Since respondents are more likely to identify as principal champions those closer to the venture team whose actions they could directly observe, top management champions must have been highly active and visible to be selected.

Beyond the principal champion's origin is the question of whether the principal champion performed most of the key functions generally attributed to two separate individuals, such as the key functions of both product champion and organizational sponsor, making him or her a dual-role champion. A division of championing roles typically emerges when the principal champion can no longer perform all the key functions of product definition, monitoring resource allocation and legitimization because of the limits of his or her hierarchical level (Maidique 1980, Chakrabarti and Hauschild 1989). Therefore, it is highly unlikely that the principal champion's and the organizational sponsor's level will be the same unless the principal champion performs both roles. Instead, there are two patterns that typically emerge with a division of championing roles. In the more widely-recognized bottom-up pattern, the principal champion's emerges from a lower hierarchical level and the organizational sponsor emerges from a higher level with the venture team reporting to its organization sponsor (e.g., Bower 1970, von Hippel 1981, Burgelman 1983b). In the top-down process, the principal champion emerges from a higher hierarchical level but the champion who coaches and monitors the venture on a frequent basis is someone from a lower level. This lower level champion may be involved in product definition or that function may be performed by a third champion even lower in the organization—the pattern observed in the IBM 360's development. Therefore, ventures whose principal champion's and organizational sponsor's level were equal were assumed to have the one champion playing both roles—a dual-role champion. The venture's reporting level was used as a proxy for the level of the organizational sponsor on the argument that the organizational sponsor's primary functions of mentoring and monitoring are typically directly tied to the venture's reporting activities. The fact that 36% of the sample were identified as dual-role champions, which is very close to the percentages found in other studies that directly measure the number of champions and their roles (Witte

1977, Rothwell et al. 1974, Green et al. 1990), lends tentative support to this argument.

While clearly there was a division of championing roles among the 136 ventures (e.g., 29 ventures or 21% had at least three champions), 49 (36%) of the ventures had principal champions who also played the role of organizational sponsor, making them dual-role champions. Nine of those 49 were also the CEOs of their companies. Twenty-eight of the ventures had all of their champions from the top management team. More specifically, 38% (52 ventures) had principal champions from the top management team, and 58% (79 ventures) had organizational sponsors from the top management team. The model level for principal champions was one level down from organizational sponsors. Eighteen of the ventures, however, had organizational sponsors who were below the level of principal champion. These 18 had principal champions who were either corporate CEOs, their direct subordinates, or divisional CEOs or VPs. Thus, the principal champion sometimes delegated his or her responsibilities for frequent mentoring and monitoring.

Several control variables were also included to avoid potential problems with specification error. Control variables included corporate size, corporate size^2, corporate age, corporate diversity, pre-entry R&D expenditures/ served market size, cannibalism, organizational location, and supporting assets. The variables concerning cannibalism, organizational location, and supporting assets were controlled for in the reported analysis but are not presented here because the focus of this paper is on championing. For corporate level variables, the overall firm was used, unless the focal firm was a subsidiary that was independently managed, in which case the subsidiary's data were used. The variable used to measure corporate size was an interval measure based on the dollar volume of sales of the corporation or subsidiary, one of the most common measures of firm size. This measure is not the precise sales volume, but the midpoint of an interval to which all the firms of a given size were assigned to approximate their total sales dollars in millions while disguising the identity of individual companies. A total of 14 intervals were designated, from $84 million to $16.342 billion. Number of employees was also collected as a proxy for size, but because the data on employees were incomplete and the two measures were highly correlated; total sales was used as the measure for size. Natural logs were taken because the variable was skewed. To test for the effect of medium-sized firms, corporate size was squared to create the curvilinear relationship. If medium-sized firms are related to more

Table 1   Means or Percentages, Standard Deviations, and Correlations

Variable	Mean/ Percentage	Standard Deviation
1 Innovativeness	4.85	1.88
2 Princ Champ's Level	3.04	1.29
3 Corporate Princ Champ	29%	
4 Corp Princ Champ*Level	1.13	1.90
5 Dual-role Champions	36%	
6 Corp Size (Log)	6.50	1.53
7 Corp Size2	44.64	20.45
8 Age	49.57	27.95
9 Diversity	2.84	1.13
10 Pre-entry R&D/Mkt(Log)	-2.88	4.66
11 No Expertise	2%	
12 # Years of Dev	2.07	2.27
13 P&E Newness	74.40	18.43
14 Operating Relat > 30%	93%	
15 Cannibalism (Log)	0.51	1.13
16 Market Size$/Yr/1m	395.71	1299.34
17 Technically Driven	21%	
18 Market Driven	24%	
19 Oper Rel to Market > 50%	59%	

Table 1 (Continued)

	1	2	3	4	5	6	7	8	9	10	11	12	13	14	15	16	17	18	19
									Correlation Matrix										
1	1.0000																		
2	-0.1208	1.0000																	
3	-0.0873	0.4065	1.0000																
4	-0.0654	0.5892	0.9245	1.0000															
5	0.1480	0.3226	0.0870	0.1252	1.0000														
6	0.0745	-0.4400	-0.0785	-0.1863	-0.0219	1.0000													
7	0.0719	-0.4283	-0.0584	-0.1682	-0.0134	0.9936	1.0000												
8	-0.0969	-0.2070	-0.0190	-0.0496	0.0109	0.4032	0.3929	1.0000											
9	-0.0991	-0.0161	-0.0362	-0.0691	-0.0010	0.0076	-0.0024	-0.0340	1.0000										
10	0.2441	-0.1332	-0.0174	-0.0401	0.0339	0.2625	0.2532	0.0271	0.0251	1.0000									
11	0.1986	0.1120	0.1228	0.1478	0.2001	0.0353	0.0286	-0.0371	-0.0673	0.0597	1.0000								
12	0.0830	-0.1610	0.0948	0.0969	0.0590	0.3470	0.3458	0.1598	-0.0016	0.3254	0.0177	1.0000							
13	-0.0920	0.0351	0.1931	0.1946	-0.0432	0.1373	0.1346	0.0912	0.2142	0.1064	0.01462	0.0720	1.0000						
14	-0.1011	-0.1273	-0.1273	-0.1734	-0.0820	-0.0289	-0.0057	-0.0235	0.0346	-0.0647	-0.1495	-0.0042	-10.73	1.0000					
15	-0.0459	0.0377	-0.0057	-0.0246	0.0095	0.0583	0.0637	-0.0405	0.0059	0.1129	-0.0684	-0.0883	0.0302	0.1283	1.0000				
16	-0.0121	0.0413	0.0293	0.0520	0.0196	0.0288	0.0268	0.0314	0.1574	-0.0331	0.0465	0.0593	0.1110	0.0816	-0.0700	1.0000			
17	0.1032	-0.1131	-0.1291	-0.1218	-0.2306	0.0236	0.0218	0.0377	-0.0560	0.0969	-0.0765	-0.1349	-0.0628	0.1434	-0.0016	-0.0334	1.0000		
18	-0.1061	-0.0292	-0.0157	-0.0204	-0.0191	0.1258	0.1158	0.0854	0.0027	0.0284	0.0347	0.1440	-0.0337	0.1563	-0.0338	0.0789	-0.2824	1.0000	
19	-0.0353	-0.2191	-0.0501	-0.1070	-0.2123	0.1112	0.1174	0.0615	-0.1202	-0.0763	0.0239	0.0375	-0.0323	0.3367	0.0292	0.0997	0.0935	0.2175	1.0000

innovative ventures, then this squared term will be significant. Logs were also taken here because of skewedness. Age of the firm was measured by subtracting the founding year of the firm or subsidiary from the founding year of the venture. Corporate diversity was measured on a quasi-interval scale from 1 to 5 for the degree of relatedness. One was a single-business firm; 2 was vertically integrated; 3 was related-linked; 4 was related-constrained; and 5 was a conglomerate. Table 1 presents descriptive statistics and a correlation matrix of all the variables in this study.

Cannibalism was measured as the percentage of the venture's sales in the first two years of commercialization that would cannibalize sales from the firm's existing units. To make this variable more tractable, natural logs were taken to help normalize the distribution. Two measures were used to create dummy variables for organizational location: new venture incubators, temporary autonomy, or permanent autonomy. The first measure directly asked whether the venture was initially a separate entity or part of any established department, division, or subsidiary of the parent. This measure was then combined with a second measure that asked for the basis on which the venture was made part of an established division department or subsidiary with one of the choices being units that had the most experience in starting new businesses. This response was used to identify ventures located in new venture incubators. To be identified as temporarily autonomous, a venture's team had to have shown that it was initially separate and then to have given a basis for its being subsequently located in an established department, division, or subsidiary, which suggested that it was only temporarily autonomous. Those that showed that they were initially autonomous who did not respond to the question on the basis for locating within an established unit were assumed to be permanently autonomous. Ventures in operating-unit locations throughout, the alternative response to the first question, were treated as the omitted category in the analysis. To operationalize the concept of supporting assets, a composite index was created from the three major sources of supporting assets derived from shared operations—shared plant and equipment, shared marketing programs (e.g., sales force), and shared distribution channels. These main effects variables were variously combined to create three two-way interaction variables and one three-way interaction variable to capture theoretically relevant combinations of these main effects. For parsimony's sake, these variables are not discussed further here because they are not the focus of this paper. For a thorough discussion of the theory and measurement of these variables see Day 1994.

Analytic Methods

After presenting the analysis to test the central hypotheses on championing and innovativeness additional analyses will be introduced to test the broader theory on the underlying conditions that lead to the emergence of a particular champion.

The analyses of a venture's innovativeness at launch and the conditions that led to the emergence of a particular champion are not modeled here as part of a simultaneous system in explaining innovativeness, because, while principal champions clearly affect the decisions that are made during a venture's development, principal champions emerge early in a venture's evolution; as a result, the principal champion's hierarchical level and organizational location are predetermined rather than simultaneous events concerning the innovativeness of the venture when it is ultimately launched. Therefore, the effect of the origin of the principal champion on the innovativeness of the venture was modeled as a single equation.

Ordinary least squares multiple regression was used to analyze and test the hypothesized relationships between the study's variables and the innovativeness of the venture at launch. OLS was deemed appropriate because the dependent variable approximates a normally distributed, quasi-interval measure. The main tests of the hypotheses were performed using one-tailed *t*-tests, as appropriate to the hypotheses stated, except for corporate size, where a two-tailed test was used, because size could have either a positive or negative effect.

Analyses using unstandardized variables were performed, because differing means across the categories of the dummy variables in interaction models influence the interaction terms differently in the process of standardization (Althauser 1971, Allison 1977, Schoonhoven 1981) and, therefore, bias the coefficients that result from the standardization process. The differential impact from this standardization process also detrimentally affects significance tests.

Results

Regression diagnostics were used on the preliminary analysis to uncover problems that might bias the results (Belsley, Kuh, and Welsch 1980). While there were several observations with high leverage, further analysis suggested that none was particularly problematic. Outlier analysis, however, highlighted one observation

Table 2   Results of Hypotheses Tests on Championing

Innovativeness ($n = 135$)

Variable	Hyp#	Hyp Sign	Beta Coefficient (Standard Error)	Significance Level
Constant			7.28	***
			(2.74)	
Principal Champion's Hierarchical Level	1	−	−0.46	***
			(0.19)	
Corp Principal Champion	2	−	−1.72	**
			(0.90)	
Corp Princ Champ* Hierchical Level	3	+	0.52	**
			(0.25)	
Dual-role Champions	4	+	0.61	**
			(.035)	
Control Variables				
Corp Size		+,−	−0.01	
			(0.81)	
Corp Size^2		+	0.00	
			(0.06)	
Age		−	−0.01	*
			(0.01)	
Diversity		−	−0.20	*
			(0.14)	
Pre-entry R&D/mkt lg		+	0.08	***
			(0.03)	
R^2			0.25	***

Results on cannibalism, operating locations, operating relatedness and interactions among these were included in the analysis as controls but are not presented here because they are not the focus of this paper.

p-values:
* $0.05 < p < 0.10$
** $0.01 < p < 0.05$
*** $0.001 < p < 0.01$

as extremely troublesome. This observation was removed from the final analysis reported here. In addition, White's (1978) test was employed to check for heteroskedasticity because of questionable residual patterns. This test indicated a problem that was also corrected in the final reported analysis by using White's consistent covariance matrix. The OLS results, along with the hypothesis tests, are presented in Table 2.

Bottom-Up Championing
Evidence of the power base for a bottom-up process should be identifiable from testing hypotheses about the main effects of the principal champion's hierarchical level and organizational location (corporate versus

noncorporate). The coefficient for the principal champion's hierarchical level indicated a highly significant negative relationship with innovativeness. Thus, in general, the higher the principal champion's hierarchical level, the lower the venture's innovativeness, or, conversely, the lower the principal champion's hierarchical level, the higher the venture's innovativeness, thus supporting Hypothesis 1. A significant negative relationship between corporate principal champion, in general, and innovativeness supports Hypothesis 2, which postulates that those in corporate headquarters have difficulty in establishing power and influence based on expertise and knowledge, proximity to information, or hierarchical power because many occupy support positions and thus tend to be poorly suited as principal champions for developing radical innovations.

Top-Down Championing
To capture the top-down process of principal championing, an interaction variable was created from the principal champion's hierarchical level and organizational location (corporate versus other locations, e.g., operating units). In contrast to the negative coefficients for the main effects of these variables, the interaction variable had a significant positive relationship with innovativeness, thus supporting Hypothesis 3. Within corporate headquarters, the higher the principal champion's hierarchical level, the greater the innovativeness of the venture. The top two levels of this variable represent the top management of the corporation, i.e., the corporate CEO and his or her direct subordinates. Given that corporate top managers have the ultimate power not only to grant the venture legitimacy but also to endow it with nearly all the firm's resources, the significant positive relationship of this coefficient with innovativeness provides empirical support for the argument that some ventures require a top-down principal champion.

Dual-Role Champions
The results on the coefficient for dual-role champions, i.e., principal champions who are also the organizational sponsors, were significantly and positively related to innovativeness, supporting Hypothesis 4. This hypothesis was based on improving decision making by reconciling information and power asymmetries when ventures are highly uncertain. For one champion to have both the information to champion the venture and the power to sponsor and support it is best when decisions are highly uncertain and speed is important, as with some radical innovations.

Results for Control Variables

Neither corporate size nor corporate size^2 were correlated either positively or negatively with innovativeness. The results on age, however, indicate weak support for the argument that firms ossify as they age, and the bureaucratic effects of this ossification are detrimental to innovativeness within established firms. Corporate size and age were significantly positively correlated at the 0.40 level, indicating that they are related but not redundant, lending some support to Aldrich and Auster's (1986) contention that age and size represent separate, independent effects on established firms' abilities to innovate. Of the two, it appears that age is the more problematic for an established firm's innovativeness.

The coefficient on corporate diversity evidenced a weakly significant, negative relationship with innovativeness. These results indicate support for the argument that diversified firms have less incentive to make the substantial investments necessary to develop new technologies or launch new industries.

The results also show that pre-entry R&D/served market and innovativeness are positively related, as expected. This finding suggests that, all else being equal, more R&D investment does result in more innovative ventures. The fact that all of this study's hypothesized relationships were well supported, even after controlling for the effects of this variable, suggests that simply spending more money will only accomplish so much in creating innovative new ventures; appropriate champions also appear to be important.

As noted earlier, cannibalism, supporting assets, organizational location, and interactions among these variables were also controlled for in this study but are not reported here because the focus of this paper is on the championing of the venture.

Overall Results

While the focus of this study is on the individual coefficients in the model, it is also useful to understand how well the model in general and the specific study variables as a group explain the innovativeness of internal corporate ventures. An examination of the overall R^2 shows the extent to which the model's independent variables are useful in explaining innovativeness. The full model, containing both the focal and control variables, had an R^2 of 0.25, which is highly significant at the 0.001 level. While this R^2 suggests that much is left unexplained, these results are very promising, given the complexity of innovativeness. In a regression analysis of the championing variables alone, these variables explain 8% of the variance in innovativeness. Even after controlling for the effects of the corporate context and the pre-entry investments in R&D/served market, the championing variables added 6.8% in R^2, which is also significant based on an F test for the increase in R^2. These overall results suggest that the origins and roles of the principal champion are important in explaining the resulting innovativeness of internal corporate ventures.

Subsequent Analysis

The arguments in the theory section for the importance of two less-recognized processes, i.e., top-down or dual-role, for the innovativeness of certain ventures were premised on the nature of the challenges that those ventures faced. If corporate top-management champions or dual-role champions are not associated with the types of challenges outlined in the theory, then although the original hypotheses were supported, the underlying theory for why these differing processes occur would not be supported. Therefore, additional analyses are necessary to test the validity of these theoretical arguments in light of the results supporting top-down and dual-role processes.

In this subsequent analysis, I take the independent variables for corporate top management champions (i.e., principal champion from corporate headquarters x hierarchical level of principal champion) and the dual role champions as dependent variables. As independent variables, I introduce the conditions that were argued in the theory section to lead to the emergence of top management and dual-role champions. The goal is to examine whether these conditions are associated with each type of principal champion. These conditions are not modeled as part of a simultaneous system in explaining innovativeness, however, because, while principal champions clearly affect the decisions that are made during a venture's development, they emerge early in a venture's evolution; as a result, their hierarchical level and organizational location are predetermined rather than simultaneous events with regard to the innovativeness of the venture when it is ultimately launched. Therefore, since the champion's origin is predetermined, the conditions that lead to the emergence of these two less-understood, top management and dual-role champions are modeled as separate independent equations.

Top Management Champions. The theoretical arguments for the importance of top management champions were premised on the exceptional challenges that certain ventures face. More specifically, ventures requiring top-down processes tend to be highly visible and costly. They also pose substantial threats to the status quo because they represent new strategic directions for the firm or reconfigurations of existing businesses. Two measures were selected as proxies for the potential visibility and costliness of the venture. The first measure, the number of years the project was under development, was chosen on the assumption that the longer a project is under development, the more costly it will become and the more difficult it will be to keep it invisible. P & E newness was selected to capture the building of new plant and equipment, on the grounds that the more new plant and equipment construction that is involved, the more costly the project is likely to be and the more visible it is likely to become. Ventures that represent new strategic directions for the firm will often involve the creation of all new operating assets—new sales force, distribution channels, and manufacturing facilities. If a venture did not draw on at least some operating assets of other established businesses on any of these dimensions, it is likely to represent a relatively new strategic direction for the firm. Therefore, a dummy variable was created that was 1 if the venture drew even somewhat on any existing operating assets of the firm (30% or more), and 0 otherwise. If this proxy has a negative coefficient, then this result would support the position that corporate top management champions are associated with new strategic directions. Finally, to identify organizational misfits, i.e., ventures that required a reconfiguration of established businesses, a dummy was developed, again based on the extent of operational assets shared between the venture and other parts of the company. If the venture shared substantial operating assets, i.e., 50% or greater, on all the operating dimensions outlined above, then it is likely to be based on a reconfiguration of these assets; otherwise, it would have failed to meet the definition of a start-up venture and would not have been included in the dataset. Only nine ventures fit this proxy for organizational misfits.

A number of other variables are important as controls here. For example, some might argue that it is the innovativeness of the idea that attracts corporate top managers to become involved in championing a given venture, while others might argue that their conservatism would lead them to select fewer innovative ideas. No measure exists in the database to address this issue directly, but one does exist that measures the degree of familiarity that the venture team initially had with the product technology and its manufacture, distribution, marketing practices, and selling methods. If no one on the venture team was initially even somewhat familiar with any one of these aspects, perhaps the venture was so innovative that no knowledge about these aspects existed. Logically, if someone in the company had expertise on any of these dimensions, the venture team would have tried to recruit him or her for the team. Therefore, no expertise was selected as a proxy for the innovativeness of the idea. If this proxy is appropriate, it should be at least weakly positively correlated with the venture's innovativeness at launch, because the initial goals of the venture should be reflected to some extent in what it eventually achieves. It should not necessarily be strongly correlated, however, because this would imply that all a venture team must do is have innovative ideas to achieve innovativeness, suggesting that the activities that take place in the interim have little to do with what is achieved. In support of this proxy, no expertise was weakly positively correlated with innovativeness, as shown in Table 1. While number of years of development and P & E newness might also seem to be possible proxies for the initial innovativeness of the idea, neither was significantly correlated with the lack of expertise, the proxy for the innovativeness of the idea, nor with the measure of the venture's resulting innovativeness. Therefore, they seem to tap other dimensions of the venture.

The strategic importance of the venture may also be relevant. Burgelman (1984) argued that top management should be directly involved in ventures that are strategically important to the firm. As a proxy for strategic importance, the extent to which the venture may potentially cannibalize an existing business was selected as evidence of its strategic importance. In addition, the size of the potential market for the venture may also attract top management attention. An estimate of the potential market for the venture was created by multiplying the number of potential customers by their average purchase amount.

Corporate size and diversity may also be factors. It seems obvious that in small and medium-size companies, the distance between the top and bottom of the organization should be sufficiently short that corporate top managers could emerge as champions, not only because of their hierarchical power and control over resources but also because of their proximity to information. In more diversified firms, it should be more difficult for corporate top managers to manage the complexity of their existing businesses, much less emerge as principal champions for new directions.

DIANA L. DAY   *Championing Innovative Corporate Ventures*

Table 3   **Tobit Results for Subsequent Analysis of Corporate Champion* Level**

Variable Name	Corporate Principal Champion* Level ($n = 136$)	
	Coefficient	Significance Level
Constant	19.47 (9.37)	**
Years of Dev.	0.44 (0.22)	**
P&E Newness	0.09 (0.03)	****
Oper Rel > 30%	−3.72 (1.69)	**
Org. Misfits	3.20 1.76	*
No Expertise	4.14 (2.65)	
Cannibalism	0.08 (0.41)	
Mkt Size	0.00 (0.00)	
Corporate Size	−7.36 (2.80)	***
Corporate Size^2	0.50 (0.21)	**
Diversity	−0.35 (0.43)	
Psuedo R^2	0.22	***

p-values:
* $0.05 < p < 0.10$
** $0.01 < p < 0.05$
*** $0.005 < p < 0.01$
**** $0.0005 < p < 0.005$

Therefore, corporate diversity should be negatively related to the interaction variable "corporate champion times level," representing this top-down process.

To test for the possible significance of these variables, a tobit regression analysis was chosen over OLS, because the dependent variable, corporate top management champions, had a censored distribution. The results are reported in Table 3. The number of years of development and plant and equipment newness were significantly positively related to corporate top management champions, providing support for the contention that the venture's costliness and visibility are key conditions associated with the emergence of corporate top managers as principal champions. In addition, operating relatedness of greater than 30%, a dummy variable, was significantly negatively related to corporate top management champions, supporting the argument that such champions are likely to be involved with ventures that represent new strategic directions for the firm. Organizational misfits were also significantly positively associated with corporate top management champions, providing support for strategic reconfigurations as another type of venture in which top management champions are likely to emerge.

Among the control variables, the proxy for the innovativeness of the idea, no expertise, was neither significantly positively nor negatively correlated with corporate top management champions, as the results of a two-tailed test show. This suggests that it is not the innovativeness of the idea per se, or the lack thereof, that is associated with the emergence of corporate top managers as principal champions. Neither cannibalism, a proxy for the venture's strategic importance, nor the venture's potential market size was significantly related to corporate top management champions, suggesting that it is not the venture's strategic importance that drives involvement by top management either. Among the corporate variables, corporate size and corporate size^2 were both significantly related, corporate size negatively and corporate size^2 positively, indicating support for the contention that top management champions are more likely to arise in small to medium-sized firms. Diversity, however, was not significantly related. It is important to note here that even while controlling for the predictable results on corporate size, the variables representing the visibility, costliness, new strategic directions and strategic reconfigurations were all significant explanatory variables. The significance of the corporate size variables may be overstated, however, because they are likely to be positively correlated with top managers' previous training and experience with championing. It is more likely that corporate top managers who had technical or operating backgrounds would emerge as principal champions. In small and medium-sized firms, it is very likely that those who are CEOs or their direct subordinates will have technical or operating backgrounds. In addition, they may have either been the entrepreneur who started the company or a member of the company's original start-up team. Unfortunately, no measures of the training and past experiences of the principal champions were available in the database. The model's pseudo R^2 (Maddala 1983) was 0.21, which can be considered a good fit,

166

given the few variables included in the analysis and the lack of variables on the training and past experiences of the principal champion.

Dual-Role Champions. In contrast to top management champions, dual-role champions would be expected to emerge for the ventures with more innovative ideas because of the inherent uncertainty of such ideas. Dual-role champions are likely to be the only ones who can rise to the occasion in tackling the problems of information and power asymmetries. Again, as a proxy for the innovativeness of the idea, "no expertise" was used.

As stated in the theory section, dual-role champions are likely to arise from middle to upper levels because they must be sufficiently high in the organization to have control over the resources needed to carry out their decisions, suggesting a positive relationship between dual-role champions and the principal champion's hierarchical level. In addition, because technology-driven innovations are often very complex, most require multiple champions, with at least one serving as a technical champion on the project (see Chakrabarti and Hauschildt 1989). Thus, technologically complex or technology-driven ventures should be positively related to multiple champions, or, conversely, negatively related to dual-role champions. In contrast, dual-role champions are more likely to emerge when ventures are market-driven or address new markets for the firm because champions at higher levels of the organization are more likely to have information or insight on potential new markets from environmental scanning or other sources. Unfortunately, data on the specific origin of the idea or the importance of the technological versus market aspects of the idea are not available in the database. Ventures did indicate, however, whether the technological or market aspects of the venture provided the basis for its original location in an established operating unit, which may serve as a reasonable proxy for technologically-driven versus market-driven ventures. Therefore, dummy variables were created which equalled one if the venture had a technological or market basis for location and 0 otherwise. In addition, ventures that address new markets for the firm are not likely to have substantial market overlaps with other businesses in the firm, given that these are supposedly new markets. Therefore, ventures that have significant market overlap with the firm's existing markets are unlikely to have dual-role champions. To measure this, a dummy variable was created that equaled 1 if the venture had a 50% overlap with an established

Table 4   Logit Results for Subsequent Analysis of Dual-role Champions

Variable Name	Dual-Role Champions ($n = 136$) Coefficient	Significance Level
Constant	−1.01 (3.88)	
Princ Champ's Lvl	0.67 (0.19)	***
Tech Driven	−1.47 (0.62)	***
Market Driven	−0.29 (0.50)	
Oper Rel > 50% to Market	−0.66 (0.42)	*
Corporate Size	−0.54 (1.18)	
Corporate Size^2	0.06 (0.09)	
Diversity	−0.05 (0.18)	
Latent R^2	0.29	***

p-values:
* $0.05 < x < 0.10$
** $0.01 < x < 0.05$
*** $0.001 < x < 0.01$

division on any of the market dimensions of end users, distribution channels, or marketing programs, and 0 otherwise.

In addition, large firms should be positively correlated with a division of championing roles, because of the significant additional complexity involved in managing large firms (Chakrabarti and Hauschildt 1989)—or, conversely, small and medium-sized companies should be negatively associated with a division of labor, or positively related to a dual-role champion. In more diversified firms, it should be more difficult for dual-role champions to manage the complexity of relationships and threats singlehandedly; therefore, corporate diversity should be negatively related to dual-role champions.

To test for the significance of these variables, a binomial logit analysis was chosen over OLS, because the dependent variable, dual-role champions, was a qualitative 0-1 variable. The results are reported in Table 4. The initial analysis, using "no expertise" as a proxy for the innovativeness of the idea, indicated that the few ventures that had "no expertise" all had dual-role champions; thus lending support to the arguments proposed here. However, an analysis could not be run using this variable because it formed a perfect linear transformation of the dual-role champions.

The principal champion's hierarchical level was very significantly related to dual-role champions, as expected. Technology-driven ventures were significantly negatively related to dual-role champions, also as expected, while market-driven ventures were unrelated to dual-role champions. However, those that had any substantial overlap with the firm's existing markets (50% or more) were weakly negatively related to dual-role champions, as expected. Surprisingly, none of the corporate variables was significantly associated with dual-role champions, suggesting that it is the characteristics of the venture and not the firm that lead to the emergence of dual-role champions. This model's latent R^2 (Aldrich and Nelson 1984, Maddala 1983) was 0.31, which is relatively strong, given the few variables included in the analysis. This strong R^2 is largely a result of the strong positive correlation with the hierarchical level of these dual-role champions and the negative correlation with technology-driven ventures.

Discussion and Conclusions

The results suggest that the origins and roles of the principal champions for highly innovative ventures are much more diverse than previously thought. Principal champions arose from lower levels as well as middle and upper levels of the firm. They held positions in technical, operating or corporate locations. While the most common view of corporate entrepreneurship as a bottom-up, emergent process was supported both in its occurrence (i.e., slightly less than one-third of the ventures had principal champions from lower levels of the organization) and in the regression results, a second, though less frequent, corporate top-management process (occurring about 20% of the time) was also supported in the regression results. In addition, evidence of another essentially top-down process—dual-role championing (i.e., with champions, largely from middle to upper management)—was also found to be positively related to radically innovative ventures, providing another top-down exception to the general view of bottom-up championing.

The results of testing Hypothesis 3 provided the first evidence of an exception to the bottom-up, emergent view of corporate entrepreneurship and innovativeness. These results are contrary to the previous findings of rich process studies, perhaps because such top-down processes are somewhat rare in larger firms. Therefore, only in studies with large sample sizes are such processes likely to be observed. Such top-down championed ventures are very important to their firms, however, because, as the theory and the findings here suggest, they often represent major and costly strategic changes for the firm. Given that these ventures are costly and, more important, that they strike at the strategic core of the firm, these ventures represent significant survival risks for the firm (Singh, House, and Tucker 1986). If top management follows a bottom-up only model of corporate entrepreneurship and innovation and allows internal selection mechanisms to operate unchecked, despite the importance of a particular venture, then the survival risks for the firm could be even worse (Tushman and Romanelli 1985). Thus, understanding the importance of a direct role for corporate top management in some ventures is crucial. A few classics in corporate entrepreneurship and innovation have embodied this insight (Kanter 1988, Mintzberg 1979). This research, however, calls attention to the importance of this process and provides the explicit linkages between this process and the conditions that give rise to it.

The results on dual-role champions are contrary to previous findings on the importance of "tandem structures." Those previous studies, however, typically focused on technology-driven industries, in which dual-role champions are argued to be less appropriate. The research results from the subsequent analysis on dual-role champions provide empirical support for this argument. Thus, the conflict between this and previous research arises largely out of the more narrow focus of these previous studies. Future research could help develop a better understanding of the conditions under which a division of labor in championing roles is more effective, versus the conditions under which the negative effects of asymmetries may be more critical. While the theory and preliminary analysis here provide some initial insights, little qualitative research is available on these champions that could provide an understanding of the functions they perform or the way this process works. Given that dual-role champions have been largely ignored in previous research yet they make up 36% of the champions in this and other studies, more research needs to be done on these champions.

This study is based on a more comprehensive definition of innovativeness than previous work. The most innovative ventures in this study were not only the first to introduce a new product based on a new technology, but they also created a new market or industry in the process. Thus, the innovativeness measure here captures more broadly the process of "creative destruction" of industries through which economic progress is made (Schumpeter 1942). Further, the measurement of innovativeness employed here captures critical variations in the innovativeness of various entrants that previous research has ignored. As a result, the findings and the insights derived should be critical to further theory development in this area.

This study creates a more comprehensive picture than previous work of where venture ideas find their champions, but it has thus far contributed less to the debate about where the different types of champions find their venture ideas. The fact that lower-level champions, for example, typically have essential technical information and expertise does not imply that they always originate the ideas that they champion. Although a venture's principal champion is often the source of the original idea, regardless of hierarchical level, it is also possible that the ideas that are promoted by lower-level managers originated with others, such as the customers with whom they interact (von Hippel 1981). Extensive anecdotal evidence also suggests that CEOs, presidents, top management teams, chairmen of the board, and founders have originated many new ideas for innovations. For example, Morita originated the idea for the Walkman (Morita et al. 1986), Kloss, CEO of Advent Corporation, initiated and developed the first large-screen television, and the founder of Honda himself often worked directly on ventures with the company's young engineers (Kanter 1988, p. 191). Therefore, both upper- and lower-level managers may originate an idea, participate in its product definition or adopt someone else's idea and champion it. Whatever the source of the idea, the principal champion typically provides the creative insight about the potential value of the idea and nurtures its transformation into a viable new commercial business.

Ventures that can be developed on a modest set of resources, and thus can remain largely invisible to the entrenched power structure until they can demonstrate success, can achieve radically innovative results with a principal champion from the lower levels of the organization. These lower level champions should have the knowledge and access to information to make the critical decisions, along with sufficient power and influence to obtain the limited resources necessary. For ventures that require substantial resources during development, remaining invisible until they can demonstrate success is largely impossible. Principal champions from top management will be important for these ventures if they are to achieve radically innovative results. In addition, for ventures that require substan-

tial cooperation across businesses and for those that conflict with the established strategic direction, top management champions may be critical. Dual-role champions provide a viable solution to the problems of information and power asymmetries that are likely to be exacerbated by the high degree of uncertainty inherent in some ventures. While innovative ventures usually require one or more champions, having one champion—the right champion—as the principal champion is essential if it is to present an innovative solution to the world. Because firms use such innovations to change and grow, having the right champion to guide a venture from its infancy to its emergence into the market may make all the difference.

Endnotes

[1] This is not to suggest that being more innovative necessarily implies commercial success. While it may, theory suggests this is not necessarily so (Teece 1987, Lieberman and Montgomery 1988). To examine the link between the innovativeness of a venture and its commercial success involves examining a whole set of other characteristics (e.g., the appropriability of the innovation), which is beyond the scope of this study.

[2] The Sol C. Snider Entrepreneurial Center and Huntsman Center for Global Competition and Leadership at the Wharton School, University of Pennsylvania and the Strategic Planning Institute are gratefully acknowledged for their support of this research. In addition, the author would like to thank Ned Bowman, Kathleen Conner, Kathleen Eisenhardt, William Hamilton, Jerry Katz, John Kimberly, Dan Levinthal, Ian MacMillan, Marshall Meyer, Terry Oliva, Elaine Romanelli, Claudia Schoonhoven, Harbir Singh, Jitendra Singh, Sid Winter and especially Connie Helfat, as well as the participants from Northwestern's Strategy/Organization colloquium, for helpful comments on earlier drafts of this manuscript. Finally, the author owes a great debt of thanks to both the editor, Arie Lewin, and three anonymous reviewers for their insightful and thought-provoking comments.

References

Abernathy, W. J. and K. B. Clark (1985), "Innovation: Mapping the Winds of Creative Destruction," *Research Policy*, 14, 3–22.

Aldrich, H. and E. R. Auster (1986), "Even Dwarfs Started Small: Liabilities of Age and Size and Their Strategic Implications," *Research in Organizational Behavior*, 8, 165–198.

Aldrich, J. H. and F. D. Nelson (1984), *Linear Probability, Logit, and Probit Models*, Sage University Papers: Quantitative Applications in the Social Sciences, Beverly Hills, CA: Sage.

Allison, P. D. (1977), "Testing for Interaction in Multiple Regression," *American Journal of Sociology*, 83, 144–153.

Althauser, R. P. (1971), "Multicollinearity and Non-Additive Regression Models," in H. M. Blalock (Ed.), *Causal Models in the Social Sciences*, Chicago, IL: Aldine-Atherton, 453–472.

Angle, H. L. and A. H. Van de Ven (1989), "Suggestions for Managing the Innovation Journey," in *Research on the Management of Innovation*, New York: Harper&Row.

Becker, M. G. (1970), "Sociometric Location and Innovativeness: Reformulation and Extension of the Diffusion Model," *American Sociological Review*, 35, 2, 267–282.

Belsley, D. A., E. Kuh, and R. E. Welsch (1980), *Regression Diagnostics: Identifying Influential Data and Sources of Collinearity*, New York: John Wiley and Sons.

Biggadike, R. (1976), "Entry Strategy and Performance," Unpublished doctoral dissertation, Harvard University, Cambridge, MA.

Block, Z., MacMillan, I. C. and P. N. Subba Narasimha (1986), "Corporate venturing: Alternatives, Obstacles Encountered, and Experience Effects," *Journal of Business Venturing*, 1, 177–192.

Bonjean, C. M. (1966), "Mass, Class, and the Industrial Community: A Comparative Analysis of Managers, Businessmen, and Workers," *American Journal of Sociology*, 72, 2, 149–162.

Booz-Allen&Hamilton (1982). *New Products Management for the 1980s*, New York, Booz-Allen&Hamilton, Inc.

Bower, J. (1970), *Managing the Resource Allocation Process*, Boston, MA: Harvard Business School Press.

Brass, D. J. (1984), "Being in the Right Place: A Structural Analysis of Individual Influence in an Organization," *Administrative Science Quarterly*, 29, 519–539.

Burgelman, R. A. (1983a), "Corporate Entrepreneurship and Strategic Management: Insights from a Process Study," *Management Science*, 29, 12, 1349–1364.

____ (1983b), "A Process Model of Internal Corporate Venturing in the Diversified Major Firm," *Administrative Science Quarterly*, 28, 223–244.

____ (1984), "Design for Corporate Entrepreneurship in Established Firms," *California Management Review*, 26, 154–166.

____ and L. Sayles (1986), *Inside Corporate Innovation: Strategy, Structure, and Managerial Skills*, New York: Free Press.

Buzzell, R. D. and B. T. Gale (1987), *The PIMS Principles: Linking Strategy to Performance*, New York: Free Press.

Chakrabarti, A. K. and J. Hauschildt (1989), "The Division of Labour in Innovation Management," *R&D Management*, 19, 2, 161–171.

Cohen, W. M. and R. C. Levin (1989), "Empirical Studies of Innovation and Market Structure," in R. Schmalensee and R. D. Willig (Eds.), *Handbook of Industrial Organization, Volume II*, New York: Elsevier Science Publishers B. V.

Cooper, A. C. (1964), "R&D is More Efficient in Small Companies," *Harvard Business Review*, May/June, 75–83.

Day, Diana (1994). "The Curse of Incumbency: Cannibalism, Organizational Locations, and Innovativeness in Internal Corporate Venturing," *Organization Science*, forthcoming.

DiMaggio, P. J. and W. W. Powell (1983), "The Iron Cage Revisited: Institutional Isomorphism and Collective Rationality in Organizational Fields," *American Sociological Review*, 48, (April), 147–160.

Dosi, G. (1984), *Technical Change and Industrial Transformation*, New York: St. Martin's Press.

Dunne, T., M. J. Roberts and L. Samuelson (1988), "Patterns of Firm Entry and Exit in U. S. Manufacturing Industries," *Rand Journal of Economics*, 4, 495–515.

Eisenhardt, K. M. and M. J. Bourgeois (1988), "Politics of Strategic Decision Making in High-Velocity Environments: Toward a Midrange Theory," *Academy of Management Journal*, 31, 4, 737–770.

Fichman, M. A. and D. A. Levinthal (1988), "Honeymoons and the Liability of Adolescence: A New Perspective on Duration Dependence in Social and Organizational Relationships," *Academy of Management Review*, 16, 2, 442–468.

Fisher, F. M. and P. Temin (1973), "Returns to Scale in R and D: What Does the Schumptereian Hypothesis Imply?" *Journal of Political Economy*, 81, 56–70.

Frost, P. J. and C. P. Egri (1990), "Influence of Political Action on Innovation, Part II," *Leadership and Organization Development Journal*, 11, 2, 4–12.

____ and ____ (1991), "The Political Process of Innovation," *Research in Organizational Behavior*, 13, 229–295.

Galbraith, J. (1982), "Designing the Innovating Organization," *Organizational Dynamics*, 10, 5–25.

Green, S. G., S. K. Markham and R. Basu (1990), "Champion and Antagonist Roles in Innovation," Working Paper, Krannert School of Management, Purdue University.

Guth, W. and A. Ginsberg (1990), "Guest Editor's Introduction: Corporate Entrepreneurship," *Strategic Management Journal*, 11, 2, 5–16.

Hambrick, D. C. and I. C. MacMillan (1985), "Efficiency of Product R&D in Business Units: The Role of Strategic Context," *Academy of Management Journal*, 28, 3, 527–547.

Hanan, M. T. and J. Freeman (1977), "The Population Ecology of Organizations," *American Journal of Sociology*, 83, 929–984.

Hanan, M. T. and J. Freeman (1984), "Structural Inertia and Organizational Change," *American Sociological Review*, 49, April, 149–164.

Harrigan, K. R. (1980), *Strategies for Declining Businesses*, Lexington, MA: D.C. Heath and Company.

Hay, D. A. and D. J. Morris (1979), *Industrial Economics: Theory and Evidence*, Oxford; England: Oxford University Press.

Henderson, R. M. and K. B. Clark (1990), "Architectural Innovation: The Reconfiguration of Existing Product Technologies and the Failure of Established Firms," *Administrative Science Quarterly*, 35, 9–30.

Hill, R. M. and J. D. Hlavacek (1972), "The Venture Team: A New Concept in Marketing Organization," *Journal of Marketing*, 36, 44–50.

Hisrich, R. D. and M. P. Peters (1984), "Internal Venturing in Large Corporation: The New Business Venture Unit," in John A. Hornajay et al., (Eds.), *Frontiers of Entrepreneurship Research*.

Howell, Jane and Christopher Higgins, (1990), "Champions of Technological Innovation," *Administrative Science Quarterly*, 35 (2), 317–341.

Imai, K., I. Nonaka and H. Takeuchi (1985), "Managing the New Product Development Process: How Japanese Companies Learn and Unlearn," in K. Clarke, R. Hayes and C. Lorenz (Eds.) *The Uneasy Alliance: Managing the Productivity-Technology Dilemma*, Boston, MA: Harvard Business School Press, 337–381.

Jelinek, M. and C. B. S. Schoovhoven (1990), *Innovation Marathon*, New York: Basil Blackwell.

Kanter, R. M. (1988), "When a Thousand Flowers Bloom: Structural, Collective, and Social Conditions for Innovation in Organization," *Research in Organizational Behavior*, 10, 169–211.

Kidder, T. (1981), *The Soul of a New Machine*, Boston, MA: Atlantic-Little Brown.

Kiechel, W. III (1988), "The Politics of Innovation," *Fortune*, 131–132.

Kimberly, J. R. (1979), "Issues in the Creation of Organizations: Initiation, Innovation, and Institutionalization," *Academy of Management Journal*, 22, 437–457.

Kirzner, I. M. (1976), "Equilibrium versus Market Process," in E. G. Dolan (Ed.), *The Foundations of Modern Austrian Economics*, Kansas City: Sheed and Ward, 115–125.

Lansing, J. B. and J. N. Morgan (1977), *Economic Survey Methods*, Ann Arbor, MI: Survey Research Center.

Lawrence, P. R. and J. Lorsch (1967), *Organization and Environment*, Boston, MA: Harvard Business School.

Leibenstein, H. (1978), *General X-efficiency Theory and Economic Development*, New York: Oxford University Press.

Levinthal, D. A. (1991), "Random Walks and Organizational Mortality," *Administrative Science Quarterly*, 36, 3, 397–420.

Lieberman, M. B. and D. B. Montgomery (1988), "First-Mover Advantages," *Strategic Management Journal*, 9, 41–58.

MacMillan, I. C. (1983), "Preemptive Strategies," *Journal of Business Strategy*, 4, 16–26.

____ and D. L. Day (1987), "Corporate Ventures into Industrial Markets: Dynamics of Aggressive Entry," *Journal of Business Venturing*, 2, 29–39.

____, M. L. McCaffery, and G. van Wijk (1986), "Competitors' Responses to Easily Imitated New Products—Exploring Commercial Banking Product Introductions," *Strategic Management Journal*, 6, 75–86.

____ and M. L. McCaffery (1983), "Strategy for Financial Services: Cashing in on Competitive Inertia," *Journal of Business Strategy*, 58–65.

Maddala, G. S. (1983), *Limited-Dependent and Qualitative Variables in Econometrics*, Cambridge, MA: Cambridge University Press.

Maidique, M. A. (1980), "Enterepreneurs, Champions, and Technological Innovation," *Sloan Management Review*, 59–76.

____ and R. H. Hayes (1984), "The Art of High Technology Management," *Sloan Management Review*, 24, 18–31.

Mansfield, E. (1968), *Economics of Technological Change*, New York: Norton.

____, M. Schwartz and S. Wagner (1981), "Imitation Costs and Patents: An Empirical Study," *Economic Journal*, 91, (December) 907–918.

March, J. G. and H. A. Simon, *Organizations*, Wiley, New York, 1958.

Merton, R. K. (1957), *Social Theory and Social Structure* (2nd Edition), Free Press, Glencoe, IL.

Mintzberg, H. (1979), *The Structuring of Organizations*, Englewood Cliffs, NJ: Prentice-Hall.

____, D. Raisanghani and A. Theoret (1976), "The Structure of Unstructured Decision Processes," *Administrative Science Quarterly*, 21, 2, 246–275.

Mitchell, W. (1989), "Whether and When? Probability and Timing of Incumbents' Entry into Emerging Industrial Subfields," *Administrative Science Quarterly*, 34, 208–230.

Moore, W. L. and M. L. Tushman (1982), "Managing Innovation Over the Product Life Cycle," *Readings in the Management of Innovation*, in Michael L. Tushman and William L. Moore (Eds.), Cambridge, MA: Ballinger Publishing Company, 131–150.

Morita, A., E. M. Reingold, M. Shimomura (1986), *Made in Japan*, New York: E. P. Dutton Publishers.

Nelson, R. R. (1968), "A Diffusion Model of International Productivity Differences in Manufacturing Industry," *American Economic Review*, 38, 1219–1248.

____ and S. S. Winter (1982), *An Evolutionary Theory of Economic Change*, Cambridge, MA: Harvard University Press.

Nonaka, I. and T. Yamanouchi (1989), "Managing Innovation as a Self-Renewing Process," *Journal of Business Venturing*, 4, 299–315.

Penrose, E. T. (1959), *The Theory of the Growth of the Firm*, Oxford, England: Basil Blackwell.

Pettigrew, A. M. (1972), "Information Control as a Power Source," *Sociology*, 6, 187–204.

Pfeffer, J. (1981), "Management as Symbolic Action: The Creation and Maintenance of Organizational Paradigms," *Research in Organizational Behavior*, 3, 1–52.

____ (1978), *Organizational Design*, Arlington Heights, IL: AHM Publishing Corp.

Pinchot, G., III (1985), *Intrapreneuring*, New York: Harper and Row.

Porter, M. E. (1985), *Competitive Advantage: Creating and Sustaining Superior Performance*, New York: Free Press.

Quinn, J. B. (1979), "Technological Innovation, Entrepreneurship, and Strategy," *Sloan Management Review*, 20, 3, 19–30.

____ (1985), "Managing Innovation: Controlled Chaos," *Harvard Business Review*, May–June, 73–84.

____ and J. A. Mueller (1963), "Transferring Research Results to Operations," *Harvard Business Review*, January–February, 49–66.

Reinganum, J. F. (1983), "Uncertain Innovation and the Persistence of Monopoly," *American Economic Review*, 73, 741–748.

Roberts, E. B. (1980), "New Ventures for Corporate Growth," *Harvard Business Review*, July/August, 134–142.

Robinson, W. T. and C. Fornell (1985), "Sources of Market Pioneer Advantages: The Case of Industrial Goods Industries," *Journal of Market Research*, 22, 297–304.

Rosenberg, N. (1982), *Inside the Black Box*, Cambridge: Cambridge University Press.

Rothwell, R., (1977), "The Characteristics of Successful Innovators and Technically Progressive Firms (with Some Comments on Innovation Research)," *R&D Management*, 7, 3.

____, C. Freeman, A. Horlsey, V. T. P. Jervis, A. B. Robertson and J. Townsend (1974), "SAPPHO Updated: Project SAPPHO Phase II," *Research Policy*, 3, 258–291.

Rumelt, R. P. (1987), "Theory, Strategy and Entrepreneurship," in D. J. Teece (Ed.), *The Competitive Challenge*, 137–158, Cambridge, MA: Ballinger Publishing Company.

Sahal, D. (1981), *Patterns of Technological Innovation*, Reading MA: Addison-Wesley.

DIANA L. DAY *Championing Innovative Corporate Ventures*

Scannell, E. (1991), "The Secret History of the IBM PC 'Gamble'," *InfoWorld*, 13, 32, p. 47, 50.

Schein, E. H. (1980), *Organizational Psychology*, Englewood Cliffs, NJ: Prentice-Hall.

Scherer, F. M. (1965), "Firm Size, Market Structure, Opportunity, and the Output of Patented Inventions," *American Economic Review*, 55 (December), 1097–1125.

——— (1980), *Industrial Market Structure and Economic Performance* (2nd ed.), Chicago, IL: Rand McNally.

Schmalensee, R. (1983), "Advertising and Entry Deterrence: An Exploratory Model," *Journal of Political Economy*, August, 90, 636–653.

Schmookler, J. (1966), *Invention and Economic Growth*, Cambridge, MA: Harvard University Press.

Schon, A. (1967), *Technology and Change*, New York: Dell Publishing.

Schoonhoven, C. B. (1981), "Problems with Contingency Theory: Testing Assumptions Hidden within the Language of Contingency 'Theory.'" *Administrative Science Quarterly*, 26, 349–377.

Schumpeter, J. A. (1934), *The Theory of Economic Development*, Cambridge, MA: Harvard University Press.

——— (1942), *Capitalism, Socialism, and Democracy*, New York: Harper&Row.

Singh, J. V., R. J. House, and D. J. House (1986), "Organizational Change and Organizational Mortality," *Administrative Science Quarterly*, 31, 4, 587–611.

Souder, W. E. (1984), "Encouraging Entrepreneurship in the Large Corporation," *Research Management*, (May), 18–22.

Susbauer, J. C. (1973), "U. S. Industrial Intracorporate Entrepreneurship Practices," *R&D Management*, 3.

Takeuchi, H. and I. Nonaka (1986), "The New Product Development Game," *Harvard Business Review*, Jan.–Feb. 137–146.

Tang, M. (1988), "An Economic Perspective on Escalating Commitment," *Strategic Management Journal*, 9 (Special Issue), 79–92.

Taylor, F. W. (1916), "The Principles of Scientific Management," *Bulletin of the Taylor Society*.

Teece, D. J. (1980), "Economies of Scope and the Scope of the Enterprise," *Journal of Economic Behavior and Organization*, 1, 1980, 223–247.

Teece, D. J. (1987), "Profiting from Technological Innovation: Implications for Integration, Collaboration, Licensing and Public Pol-

icy," in D. J. Teece (Ed.), *The Competitive Challenge, Strategies for Industrial Innovation and Renewal*, Cambridge, MA: Ballinger, 1987.

Thaler, R. H. (1980), "Toward a Positive Theory of Consumer Choice," *Journal of Economic Behavior and Organization*, 1, 39–60.

Thompson, J. D. (1967), *Organizations in Action*, New York: McGraw-Hill.

Tushman, M. L. and P. Anderson (1986), "Technological Discontinuities and Organizational Environments," *Administrative Science Quarterly*, 31, 439–465.

——— and E. Romanelli (1985), "Organizational Evolution: A Metamorphosis Model of Convergence and Reorientation," in B. Staw and L. Cummings (Eds.), *Research in Organizational Behavior*, 7, 171–222.

Urban G. L. and J. R. Hauser (1980), *Design and Marketing of New Products*, Englewood Cliffs, NJ: Prentice-Hall.

Van de Ven, A. H. (1986), "Central Problems in the Management of Innovation," *Management Science*, 32, 590–607.

———, H. L. Angle and M. S. Poole (1989), *Research on the Management of Innovation: The Minnesota Studies*, Grand Rapids, MI: Harper & Row.

Venkataraman, S., R. G. McGrath and I. C. MacMillan (1992), "Progress in Research on Corporate Venturing," in Donald L. Sexton and John D. Kasarda (Eds.), *The State of the Art of Entrepreneurship*, Boston MA: PWS Kent.

Von Hippel, E. (1981), "Users as Innovators," in R. R. Rothberg, (Ed.), *Corporate Strategy and Product Innovation*, New York: Free Press, 239–252.

——— (1977), "Successful and Failing Internal Corporate Ventures: An Empirical Analysis," *Industrial Marketing Management*, 6, 163–174.

Wise, T. A. (1966), "IBM's 5,000,000,000 Gamble," *Fortune*, 14–19.

——— (1981), "Users as Innovators," in R. R. Rothberg (Ed.), *Corporate Strategy and Product Innovation*, New York: Free Press, 239–252.

White, H. (1978), "Heteroskedasticity Consistent Covariance Matrix and a Direct Test of Heteroskedasticity," *Econometrica*, 817–838.

Witte, E. (1977), "Power and Innovation: A Two Center Theory," *International Studies of Management Organization*, (Spring), 47–70.

Worthy, J. C. (1987), *William C. Norris: Portrait of a Maverick*, Cambridge MA: Ballinger Publishing Company.

Accepted by Arie Y. Lewin; received October 1992. This paper has been with the author for one revision.

[21]

ELSEVIER   Journal of Business Venturing 17 (2002) 253–273

JOURNAL
of BUSINESS
VENTURING

Middle managers' perception of the internal environment for corporate entrepreneurship: assessing a measurement scale

Jeffrey S. Hornsby[a,1], Donald F. Kuratko[a,*], Shaker A. Zahra[b,2]

[a]Department of Management, College of Business, Ball State University, Muncie, IN 47306, USA
[b]College of Business Administration, Georgia State University, Atlanta, GA 30302-4014, USA

Received 1 June 1999; accepted 1 June 2000

Abstract

This study assesses the measurement properties of a scale that measures the key internal organizational factors that influence middle managers to initiate corporate entrepreneurship activities. In this study, corporate entrepreneurship is used in a broad sense to include the development and implementation of new ideas into the organization. Using this definition, this study describes an instrument used to empirically identify the internal conditions that influence middle manager's participation in corporate entrepreneurship activities. During the last decade, the role of the middle manager in corporate entrepreneurial activity has been recognized in the literature. The empirical research on the internal organizational factors that may foster middle manager activity has been limited, both in volume and scope. However, the literature does converge on at least five possible factors. *The appropriate use of rewards:* The literature stresses that an effective reward system that spurs entrepreneurial activity must consider goals, feedback, emphasis on individual responsibility, and results-based incentives. This factor, therefore, highlights middle managers' role in this regard. *Gaining top management support:* The willingness of senior management to facilitate and promote entrepreneurial activity in the organization, including championing innovative ideas as well as providing necessary resources, expertise or protection. This factor captures middle managers' role in this area. *Resource availability:* Middle managers must perceive the availability of resources for innovative activities to encourage experimentation and risk taking. *Supportive organizational structure:* The structure must foster the administrative mechanisms by which ideas are evaluated, chosen, and implemented. Structural boundaries tend to be a major stumbling block for middle management in corporate entrepreneurial activity. *Risk taking and tolerance for failure:* Middle managers must perceive an environment that encourages calculated risk taking while maintaining

* Corresponding author. Tel.: +1-765-285-5327.
[1] Tel.: +1-765-285-5312.
[2] Tel.: +1-404-355-5839.

reasonable tolerance for failure. The literature on the internal factors was utilized to develop an assessment instrument called the Corporate Entrepreneurship Assessment Instrument (CEAI). The instrument contained 84 Likert-style questions that were believed to assess a firm's internal entrepreneurial environment. Understanding middle manager perceptions about the internal corporate environment is crucial to initiating and nurturing any entrepreneurial process. A scale such as the CEAI, therefore, could be very useful for companies that wish to embark on a strategic transformation through corporate entrepreneurship. The measurement properties of the CEAI, including a factor analysis and reliability assessment, were determined. Results confirmed that five distinct internal organizational factors, similar to those suggested in the literature, do exist. Based on how the items loaded on each factor, the factors were entitled management support, work discretion, organizational boundaries, rewards/reinforcement, and time availability. The reliability of each of these factors also met acceptable measurement standards. From a managerial perspective, the results indicate that CEAI can be a useful tool in diagnosing a firm's environment for corporate entrepreneurship, identifying areas where middle managers can make a significant difference, and develop strategies that can positively spur and sustain corporate entrepreneurship efforts. The results of such diagnosis can be useful in designing effective training programs for middle managers. © 2001 Elsevier Science Inc. All rights reserved.

Keywords: Corporate entrepreneurship; Middle managers; Entrepreneurial environment

1. Introduction

Guth and Ginsberg (1990) stated "strategic management research that contributes to increasing the frequency and success of corporate entrepreneurship will, in our view, be highly valued in the academic and practitioner communities." Yet, while many authors have continued to tout the importance of corporate entrepreneurship as a growth strategy and an effective means for achieving competitive advantage (Dess et al., 1999; Pinchott, 1985; Kuratko, 1993; Merrifield, 1993) the literature has been, until recently, anecdotal and testimonial in nature. Indeed, Zahra (1991, p. 260) observed a lack of compelling empirical evidence on the contributions of corporate entrepreneurship to organizational performance, a factor that raised concerns that corporate entrepreneurship may become just another managerial fad. Even though some research has attempted to fill this gap in the literature (Covin and Slevin, 1991; Zahra and Covin, 1995), there is still much more to be learned about the substance and process of corporate entrepreneurship.

Corporate entrepreneurship, also referred to as corporate venturing, or intrapreneurship, has been initiated in established organizations for purposes of profitability (Zahra, 1991), strategic renewal (Guth and Ginsberg, 1990) fostering innovativeness (Baden-Fuller, 1995), gaining knowledge for future revenue streams (McGrath et al., 1994), and international success (Birkinshaw, 1997). However, the concept of corporate entrepreneurship has been evolving over the last 25 years (Peterson and Berger, 1972; Hill and Hlavacek, 1972; Hanan, 1976; Quinn, 1979). Sathe (1989) defined corporate entrepreneurship as a process of organizational renewal. Other researchers have conceptualized corporate entrepreneurship as embodying entrepreneurial efforts that require organizational sanctions and resource

J.S. Hornsby et al. / Journal of Business Venturing 17 (2002) 253–273   255

commitments for the purpose of carrying out innovative activities in the form of product, process, and organizational innovations (Miller and Friesen, 1982; Covin and Miles, 1999; Burgelman, 1984; Kanter, 1985; Alterowitz, 1988; Naman and Slevin, 1993; Zahra and Covin, 1995).

While the concept of corporate entrepreneurship may appear straightforward, several authors have concluded that it may take several forms (Sharma and Chrisman, 1999). For instance, Schollhammer (1982) identified administrative, opportunistic, imitative, acquisitive, and incubative, as different forms of corporate entrepreneurial activities. Vesper (1984) developed three major definitions of corporate entrepreneurship, which he identified as (1) new strategic direction; (2) initiative from below; and (3) autonomous business creation. Vesper's study shows that corporate entrepreneurship could be any of these individual types, as well as any or all-possible combinations.

According to Damanpour (1991, p. 556) innovation would include "... the generation, development, and implementation of new ideas or behaviors. An innovation can be a new product or service, an administrative system, or a new plan or program pertaining to organizational members." In this context, corporate entrepreneurship centers on re-energizing and enhancing the ability of a firm to acquire innovative skills and capabilities. The present study follows this definition of corporate entrepreneurship that acknowledges the formal and informal aspects of these efforts (Pinchott, 1985), and recognizes the challenges of promoting entrepreneurship within an existing firm. These challenges demand a thorough understanding of the internal conditions that prevail within a firm. These conditions usually shape middle managers' views of (and interest in) corporate entrepreneurship efforts (Kuratko et al., 1990). They also determine middle managers' support of these activities. This support can determine the fate of corporate venturing activities (Kanter, 1985).

The decade of the nineties brought about a greater effort by researchers to conduct empirical studies that examine the antecedents of corporate entrepreneurial activities (Zahra and Covin, 1995). Accumulated research findings consistently suggest that internal organizational factors, in particular, play a major role in encouraging corporate entrepreneurship (Covin and Slevin, 1991). Zahra and O'Neil (1998) point out that the factors in the external environment and the organization interact, challenging managers to respond creatively and act in innovative ways. While there is no agreement on which key internal organizational factors stimulate corporate entrepreneurship, research emphasizes the vital role of middle managers in creating an environment that encourages innovation and entrepreneurship (Kanter, 1985; Floyd and Woolridge, 1990, 1992, 1994; Ginsberg and Hay, 1994; Pearce et al., 1997). Not only can middle managers stimulate interest in corporate entrepreneurship but they can also influence their subordinates' commitment to these activities once they are initiated; this commitment is necessary for a company to benefit from corporate entrepreneurship activities (Kuratko, 1993; Stopford and Baden-Fuller, 1994).

Despite the growing recognition of the role of middle managers in stimulating and sustaining corporate entrepreneurship, little is actually known about the specific factors that can influence middle managers to achieve this objective. One reason for this is the paucity of empirical studies on the topic. Most prior research has focused, instead, on the various activities of top managers in support of corporate entrepreneurship activities (Kanter, 1985) Moreover, little is known about how much weight middle managers place

256 J.S. Hornsby et al. / Journal of Business Venturing 17 (2002) 253–273

on different aspects of the firm's internal organization as a means of promoting or facilitating corporate entrepreneurship.

This study examines the key internal organizational factors that influence middle managers to stimulate corporate entrepreneurship by developing an instrument that measures these factors. To accomplish this purpose, the study uses data collected from 761 middle managers in 17 organizations. The focus on middle managers is consistent with the growing recognition of the key role these managers play in promoting or stifling corporate entrepreneurship efforts (Burgelman, 1983b; Floyd and Woolridge 1992, 1994; Pinchott 1985; Nonaka and Takeuchi, 1995). Results from the study can thus help to define middle managers' zone of influence and set the stage for their greater involvement in enhancing entrepreneurial activities.

Having defined the scope and goal of the paper, the following section focuses on the recognition of middle managers' involvement with corporate entrepreneurship. This is followed by examining the existing literature for the role of internal factors in stimulating (stifling) corporate entrepreneurship. This discussion is followed by an empirical study conducted to identify these key internal organization factors. The results of the study and their implications for research and managerial practice are discussed in the final section.

1.1. Middle managers and corporate entrepreneurship

To date, little systematic attention has been given to empirically documenting and understanding the contribution middle managers make in the context of corporate entrepreneurship. Thus, it remains unclear which roles these managers play and to what extent they emphasize each of these roles. Despite the paucity of past empirical research in this area, some insights can be gained from reviewing recent writings in the fields of strategic management and international business, both of which have begun to recognize the valuable contributions middle managers can make to the process of strategic change and organizational renewal and to fostering entrepreneurial activities. These two fields also identify key factors that can limit middle managers' contributions and impact.

Bower (1970) was among the very first scholars to draw attention to the importance of middle managers as agents of change in contemporary organizations. However, over the years, little systematic research has been undertaken to define the nature and scope of middle managers' contributions to a company's innovation and entrepreneurship. This situation has changed to some extent as companies sought to revitalize their operations as a means of creating strategic change. Several authors (Drucker, 1985; Kanter, 1983, Peters and Waterman, 1982; Burgelman and Sayles, 1986; Pinchott, 1985) have discussed different aspects of middle managers' contributions to entrepreneurship. Other researchers (e.g., Schuler, 1986; Woolridge and Floyd, 1990) also examined the contributions of middle managers to a company's strategy, a variable that is intimately connected to corporate entrepreneurship (Guth and Ginsberg, 1990; Zahra, 1991).

Quinn (1985) was among the first to recognize the valuable contributions and important roles of middle managers in the innovation process in an established company. Noting senior managers' isolation from actual day-to-day activities, Quinn highlighted the crucial importance of the roles middle managers can play in fostering communication about the company's mission, goals, and priorities. Middle managers interact with diverse employees, which would allow them to use formal and informal approaches to encourage innovation and calculated risk taking. Middle managers also communicate their ideas for innovations to upper management, thereby creating an opportunity where these ideas are evaluated and considered within the context of the firm's overall strategic priorities (Burgelman, 1983a,b).

Other writers (e.g., Peters and Waterman, 1982; Pinchott, 1985) have also observed the important roles middle managers play in informally encouraging employees to innovate and take risks. These middle managers provide political and organizational support for "skunkwork" activities that result in innovative ventures. Kanter (1985, 1988) and Quinn (1985) also note the importance of middle managers in promoting autonomous or informal corporate entrepreneurial activities. Middle managers can do this by providing rewards (mostly intrinsic) that allow employees to experiment with, and explore the feasibility of, innovative ideas. Middle managers can also use different approaches to make the organizational structure less resistant to change thereby allowing corporate entrepreneurial activities to flourish.

As noted earlier, some researchers have sought to examine the roles middle managers play in their company's strategic process. In one such study, Floyd and Woolridge (1992) argue that middle managers frequently play pivotal roles in championing strategic alternatives and making them accessible to senior executives. Middle managers synthesize and integrate information, thereby crystallizing the strategic issues facing the company and setting the stage for strategic change; facilitating adaptability by altering the formal structure; and implementing the formal strategy and providing feedback. This feedback can spur future strategic change and organizational renewal efforts. When Floyd and Woolridge results are connected to the early findings of Burgelman and Sayles (1986), it becomes clearer that middle managers play a key role in shaping their companies' strategic agenda by influencing the types and intensity of corporate entrepreneurial activities.

In their path-breaking analyses of how innovations come about and then create new knowledge that fuels organizational growth, Nonaka and Takeuchi (1995) highlight the central role of middle managers. These researchers suggest that most innovations emanate from the middle of the organization and the promising ones are then sent to upper management for further analysis and evaluation. Those innovations that meet the rigorous standards set by the top management team are then sent back to middle managers who then communicate them to the employees. In this model of innovation, middle managers actively and diligently gather innovation ideas from within and outside the firm. Middle managers work with vendors, observe the market and analyze the competition. As a result, they are well suited to observe areas where innovation and risk taking are needed. Middle managers also become aware of innovation efforts initiated by vendors and competitors. Frequently, middle managers transfer this knowledge to others in their company. Another noteworthy feature of the Nonaka and Takeuchi model is the fact that it recognizes that middle managers frequently work on their ideas, often closely with employees, hoping to refine them and determine their potential. This initial, though informal, testing process can help shape the ideas while creating the administrative structure needed to foster them.

258   J.S. Hornsby et al. / Journal of Business Venturing 17 (2002) 253-273

Building on the work by Nonaka and Takeuchi (1995), Zahra et al. (1999) have also noted the importance of middle managers in facilitating corporate entrepreneurship efforts. Through their effective communication and use of rewards, middle managers create the social capital and trust needed to foster the corporate entrepreneurial process. In a similar fashion, Floyd and Woolridge (1997) observe that this social capital is of great importance because it encourages employees to take risks, without fear for their jobs or reputations.

Scholars from the international business discipline have also discussed and recognized the importance of middle managers in promoting and sustaining innovations. Like other larger corporations, some multinationals develop rigid structures that limit employees' flexibility and willingness to take risks. However, as Bartlett and Ghoshal (1996) observe, middle managers can create an environment in their respective divisions or subsidiaries where innovations and entrepreneurial activities flourish. In turn, this can allow multinationals to capitalize on the unique resources that exist in their different markets and respond to their customers effectively.

Bartlett and Ghoshal (1993) note that the typical multinational has two ongoing but parallel processes. The first centers on integrating the various activities of the firm, aiming to achieve coherence, economies of scope, and economies of scale. The second process is entrepreneurial in nature, centering on creating new businesses and spurring innovation. Bartlett and Ghoshal go on to delineate the different roles of top, middle, and front line managers. In terms of the integration process, middle managers are believed to link different skills, resources, and knowledge in pursuit of those strategic goals defined by senior managers. In terms of the entrepreneurial process, middle managers are viewed as reviewing, developing and supporting initiatives in their units. Recent research by Noble and Birkinshaw (1998) corroborates these assertions. Overall, their research reveals that middle managers influence and shape the types and intensity of various entrepreneurial initiatives of their respective subsidiaries.

The literature also highlights several factors that can limit middle managers' willingness or ability to facilitate corporate entrepreneurship. Some managers have demanding work schedules that leave little time for innovation and experimentation. This is especially true in companies that have initiated restructuring programs (Floyd and Woolridge, 1994). Resources available for innovations are often constrained and middle managers have to work hard to obtain these resources (Pinchott, 1985). Managers also have to work hard to get senior executives' attention to and support of promising innovative ideas. They also have to work through territorial disputes that erupt among different units (groups) in their companies, fearing the consequences of innovation on established lines of communication and access to organizational resources (Kanter, 1988). These are formidable challenges that can stifle middle managers' efforts aimed at encouraging and promoting corporate entrepreneurship.

To summarize, two decades of research in strategic management, international business, and entrepreneurship suggest that middle managers can have pervasive influences on corporate entrepreneurial activities. This influence can, therefore, determine the viability and survival of the various corporate ventures. Yet, it is surprising that little systematic effort has been made to document and understand how middle managers view the various activities they perform in support of different corporate entrepreneurial activities. Given the organiza-

J.S. Hornsby et al. / Journal of Business Venturing 17 (2002) 253–273   259

tional and political barriers that exist in companies, understanding these views can be an important starting point toward appreciating the contribution middle managers make to their companies. One way to capture these views is to consider middle managers' perceptions of the importance they place on the various tasks they perform in support of corporate entrepreneurship. The present study aims to fill this void in the literature.

1.2. Internal factors for corporate entrepreneurship

The impact of corporate entrepreneurial activities on successful company performance has attracted research into the organizational factors that can promote (impede) these activities (Zahra, 1991; Zahra and Covin, 1995). Researchers have sought to identify some of the key variables that can affect a company's pursuit of corporate entrepreneurship, including internal organizational factors such as: the company's incentive and control systems (Sathe, 1985), culture (Kanter, 1985; Hisrich and Peters, 1986; Brazeal, 1993), organizational structure (Covin and Slevin, 1991; Naman and Slevin, 1993), and managerial support (Stevenson and Jarillo, 1990; Kuratko et al., 1993). Individually and in combination, these factors are believed to be important antecedents of corporate entrepreneurship efforts, because they affect the internal environment, which determines interest in and support of entrepreneurial initiatives within an established company. Burgelman's (1983a,b) research clearly shows that internal organizational factors influence the types of corporate entrepreneurship activities a company pursues.

Pearce et al. (1997), Floyd and Woolridge (1990, 1992, 1994), Ginsberg and Hay (1994), among others, recognized the importance of middle managers in enhancing and cultivating such autonomous behavior and thereby fostering corporate entrepreneurship. However, much of this discussion has been general in nature, failing to provide specific guidance on the exact role middle managers can play. While some of these researchers have noted some of the factors that can influence middle managers (Kanter, 1985; Vesper, 1984), there is no universal agreement on which factors matter the most in promoting corporate entrepreneurship efforts. However, recent writings on the topic appear to converge on at least five factors.

The first dimension is the appropriate use of rewards (Scanlan, 1981; Souder,1981; Kanter, 1985; Sathe, 1985; Fry, 1987; Block and Ornati, 1987; Sykes, 1992; Barringer and Milkovich, 1998). Theorists, therefore, stress that an effective reward system that spurs entrepreneurial activity must consider goals, feedback, emphasis on individual responsibility, and results-based incentives. The use of appropriate rewards can also enhance middle managers' willingness to assume the risks associated with entrepreneurial activity.

A second important dimension is management support, which indicates the willingness of managers to facilitate and promote entrepreneurial activity in the firm (Quinn, 1985; Hisrich and Peters, 1986; MacMillian et al., 1986; Sykes and Block, 1989; Sathe, 1989; Stevenson and Jarillo, 1990; Damanpour, 1991; Kuratko et al., 1993; Pearce et al., 1997). This support can take many forms, including championing innovative ideas, providing necessary resources or expertise, or institutionalizing the entrepreneurial activity within the firm's system and processes.

The third dimension is resources (that includes time) and their availability for entrepreneurial activity. Accordingly, employees must perceive the availability of resources for

260 *J.S. Hornsby et al. / Journal of Business Venturing 17 (2002) 253–273*

innovative activities (Von Hippel, 1977; Souder, 1981; Kanter, 1985; Sathe, 1985; Sykes, 1986; Sykes and Block, 1989; Hisrich and Peters, 1986; Katz and Gartner, 1988; Stopford and Baden-Fuller, 1994; Das and Teng, 1997; Slevin and Covin, 1997). The availability of slack resources usually encourages experimentation and risk-taking behaviors (Burgelman and Sayles, 1986).

The fourth dimension is the existence of a supportive organizational structure (Souder, 1981; Sathe, 1985; Hisrich and Peters, 1986; Sykes, 1986; Sykes and Block, 1989; Burgelman and Sayles, 1986; Schuler, 1986; Bird, 1988; Guth and Ginsberg, 1990; Covin and Slevin, 1991; Zahra, 1991, 1993; Brazeal, 1993; Hornsby et al., 1993). The structure also provides the administrative mechanisms by which ideas are evaluated, chosen, and implemented (Burgelman and Sayles, 1986).

The fifth, and final, dimension is risk taking, which indicates the middle managers' willingness to take risks and show a tolerance for failure when it occurs (MacMillian et al., 1986; Sathe, 1985, 1989; Sykes, 1986; Sykes and Block, 1989; Burgelman, 1983a,b, 1984; Quinn, 1985; Kanter, 1985; Ellis and Taylor, 1988; Bird, 1988; Stopford and Baden-Fuller, 1994).

Kuratko et al. (1990) presented an exploratory study that used these five conceptually distinct internal factors that support corporate entrepreneurship (top management support for corporate entrepreneurship, reward and resource availability, organizational structure and boundaries, risk taking, and time availability). However, the empirical analysis conducted by Kuratko et al. reduced these factors were down to three: managerial support, organizational structure, and reward and resource availability. This initial study, while not supporting the hypothesized full five-factor model, established the need for further research on the internal organizational factors that foster entrepreneurship.

The Kuratko et al. (1990) results were reinforced by the findings of a study of 119 Fortune 500 CEO's (Zahra, 1991). This study examined several internal organizational factors as well as the association between corporate entrepreneurship and the financial performance of the firm. Specifically, the study examined internal organizational conditions such as: tangible factors (communication, scanning, integration, differentiation, and control) and intangible factors that refer to dominant organizational values. The results showed both tangible and intangible internal factors influence a company's pursuit of entrepreneurship. Consequently, Zahra (1991) called for additional studies that examine managers' efforts aimed at shaping or creating an organization supportive of corporate entrepreneurship.

Fig. 1 provides a model to illustrate the conceptual idea driving the current study. It suggests that a firm's strategy influences the internal factors that affect corporate entrepreneurship, as argued earlier in past research (Burgelman, 1983a,b). Middle managers' perceptions of these internal factors determine their relative emphasis on the various activities they undertake to encourage or facilitate corporate entrepreneurship (Kuratko et al., 1990, 1993). This model serves to highlight the need to document the extent to which middle managers perceive the various internal factors (discussed earlier) in the context of corporate entrepreneurship. Once we understand these variations and the extent to which these activities are emphasized, the stage is set for examining how these variations translate into differences in corporate entrepreneurship or gains from these activities.

J.S. Hornsby et al. / Journal of Business Venturing 17 (2002) 253–273   261

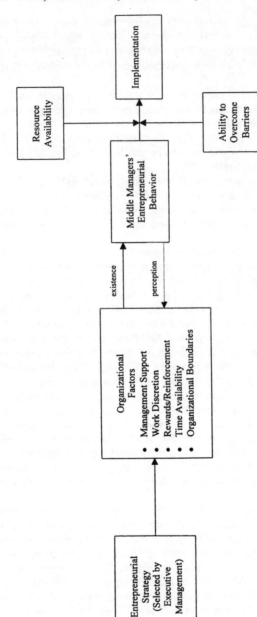

Fig. 1. Middle manager's perception of the internal environment for corporate entrepreneurship.

262   J.S. Hornsby et al. / Journal of Business Venturing 17 (2002) 253–273

With our study's focus in mind, and based on the literature that conceptually identified five critical organizational dimensions, an 84-item CEAI was developed. The objective was to test the existence of these key organizational factors believed to foster a corporate entrepreneurial environment. The psychometric characteristics of the CEAI, including reliability and validity, were then assessed using two samples, as reported in the following section. The following three hypotheses are provided:

Hypothesis 1: The CEAI has a consistent factor structure related to the internal factors identified in the literature.

Hypothesis 2: The resulting factor structure will be duplicated or cross-validated with an independent sample.

Hypothesis 3: The internal consistency reliability of the factors will be high indicating factor stability.

2. Method

In order to investigate the existence of internal organizational factors that encourage corporate entrepreneurship, three analyses were conducted. First, an exploratory factor analysis was conducted to investigate the existence of the factors. Second, using a second sample, a confirmatory factor analysis was conducted to cross-validate the findings of the initial analysis. Third, the internal consistency of each of the resulting factors was determined. This procedure is similar to other recent studies that have endeavored to develop a psychometrically sound entrepreneurial assessment instrument (e.g., Knight, 1997).

2.1. Sample

Data were collected from two separate samples that consisted of 231 and 530 midlevel managers, respectively. For the first sample, managers were recruited from continuing education/training programs for middle managers conducted by a large midwestern university. These respondents held middle management positions in their respective firms. Participation in the study was voluntary, resulting in a response rate of approximately 80%.

For the second sample, participants were recruited from manufacturing, service, and financial organizations throughout the United States and Canada. Potential respondents were randomly selected from trade association membership directories and were asked to participate in the study. These trade associations include the Standard & Poor's Register of Corporations, Directors and Executives, and the Canadian Trade Index of the Canadian Manufacturers Association. A total of 100 were sent and 17 firms agreed to participate (representing a 17% organization participation rate). The participating organizations were asked to identify individuals in middle management positions and give them the survey instrument. Each survey packet included a return envelope to provide confidentiality for respondents. The response rate for managers was approximately 92%.

J.S. Hornsby et al. / Journal of Business Venturing 17 (2002) 253–273   263

As seen in Table 1, the sample demographics for the study's two samples were similar. The only noticeable differences were in average age and organizational tenure. The younger age and shorter tenure of respondents in the first survey may be explained by the fact that they were currently enrolled in middle management training programs. Respondents in the second study, on average, were somewhat more established in their professional careers.

2.2. Data collection procedure

The CEAI was developed to gauge the organizational factors that foster corporate entrepreneurial activity within a company. As noted earlier, even though different labels have been used in the literature to describe the dimensions of corporate entrepreneurship, the most widely acknowledged appear to fall into *five* distinctive areas: management support; organizational structure; risk taking, time availability; and reward and resource availability. These five areas, therefore, constituted the theoretical basis for the 84 items generated for the CEAI. The questionnaire used Likert-type scales with 1 representing *strongly disagree* to 5 representing *strongly agree*. Eleven items were negatively worded to avoid response tendencies by the subjects (Cooper and Emory, 1995) and they were reverse-scored for the analysis. The complete list of items can be found in Table 2.

2.3. Analyses

2.3.1. Factor analysis
Initially an exploratory factor analysis was conducted to uncover key dimensions in the CEAI. Specifically, a principal components factor analysis with varimax rotation was utilized. In interpreting the results, only items with factor loadings of .40 or above were selected for any particular factor. To enhance the interpretation of the factors, items that loaded significantly on more than one factor were dropped.

Next, as stated earlier, the CEAI was administered to a second independent sample. A confirmatory factor analysis was then utilized forcing the factor structure derived in the first factor analysis. Again, only items with an absolute value of .40 factor loading were selected for a given factor, and any item loading significantly on more than one factor was deleted.

Table 1
Sample demographics for experimental samples

Variables	Analysis 1 ($n = 231$)	Analysis 2 ($n = 530$)
Average age (years)	32.54	39.59
Sex		
Males (%)	69	75
Females (%)	31	25
Average organization tenure (years)	6.3	12.2
Average job tenure (years)	3.6	4.5

Table 2
Rotated factor structure for the revised CEAI

	Factor loadings	
Factors	Analysis 1	Analysis 2
Factor 1: Management support for corporate entrepreneurship		
1. My organization is quick to use improved work methods	.65	.51
2. My organization is quick to use improved work methods that are developed by workers.	.66	.56
3. In my organization, developing one's own ideas is encouraged for the improvement of the corporation.	.57	.55
4. Upper management is aware and very receptive to my ideas and suggestions.	.60	.50
5. Promotion usually follows the development of new and innovative ideas.	.53	.42
6. Those employees who come up with innovative ideas on their own often receive management encouragement for their activities.	.63	.23[a]
7. The "doers" are allowed to make decisions on projects without going through elaborate justification and approval procedures.	.55	.51
8. Senior managers encourage innovators to bend rules and rigid procedures in order to keep promising ideas on track.	.49	.56
9. Many top managers have been known for their experience with the innovation process.	.65	.61
10. Money is often available to get new project ideas off the ground.	.56	.61
11. Individuals with successful innovative projects receive additional reward and compensation for their ideas and efforts beyond the standard reward system.	.59	.37[a]
12. There are several options within the organization for individuals to get financial support for their innovative projects and ideas.	.63	.56
13. Individual risk takers are often recognized for their willingness to champion new projects, whether eventually successful or not.	.72	.69
14. People are often encouraged to take calculated risks with new ideas around here.	.68	.67
15. The term "risk taker" is considered a positive attribute for people in my work area.	.65	.61
16. This organization supports many small and experimental projects realizing that some will undoubtedly fail.	.64	.68
17. A worker with a good idea is often given free time to develop that idea.	.60	.54
18. There is considerable desire among people in the organization for generating new ideas without regard to crossing departmental or functional boundaries.	.60	.47
19. People are encouraged to talk to workers in other departments of this organization about ideas for new projects.	.55	.44
Factor 2: Work discretion		
1. I feel that I am my own boss and do not have to double check all of my decisions.	.69	.68
2. Harsh criticism and punishment result from mistakes made on the job.	.45	.43
3. This organization provides the chance to be creative and try my own methods of doing the job.	.55	.61
4. This organization provides freedom to use my own judgment	.66	.68

(continued on next page)

Table 2 (*continued*)

Factors	Factor loadings	
	Analysis 1	Analysis 2
5. This organization provides the chance to do something that makes use of my abilities.	.42	.55
6. I have the freedom to decide what I do on my job.	.69	.77
7. It is basically my own responsibility to decide how my job gets done.	.76	.72
8. I almost always get to decide what I do on my job.	.71	.75
9. I have much autonomy on my job and am left on my own to do my own work.	.69	.74
10. I seldom have to follow the same work methods or steps for doing my major tasks from day to day.	.42	.50
Factor 3: Rewards/reinforcement		
1. My manager helps me get my work done by removing obstacles.	.44	.44
2. The rewards I receive are dependent upon my work on the job.	.45	.56
3. My supervisor will increase my job responsibilities if I am performing well in my job.	.65	.53
4. My supervisor will give me special recognition if my work performance is especially good.	.61	.76
5. My manager would tell his boss if my work was outstanding.	.76	.64
6. There is a lot of challenge in my job.	.49	.27[a]
Factor 4: Time availability		
1. During the past three months, my work load was too heavy to spend time on developing new ideas.	.69	.73
2. I always seem to have plenty of time to get everything done.	.72	.73
3. I have just the right amount of time and work load to do everything well.	.77	.67
4. My job is structured so that I have very little time to think about wider organizational problems.	.48	.57
5. I feel that I am always working with time constraints on my job.	.77	.67
6. My co-workers and I always find time for long-term problem solving.	.48	.54
Factor 5: Organizational boundaries		
1. In the past three months, I have always followed standard operating procedures or practices to do my major tasks.	.49	.55
2. There are many written rules and procedures that exist for doing my major tasks.	.44	.34[a]
3. On my job I have no doubt of what is expected of me.	.57	.60
4. There is little uncertainty in my job.	.57	.53
5. During the past year, my immediate supervisor discussed my work performance with me frequently.	.43	.29[a]
6. My job description clearly specifies the standards of performance on which my job is evaluated.	.49	.51
7. I clearly know what level of work performance is expected from me in terms of amount, quality, and timeliness of output.	.67	.60

[a] Denotes items that did not meet the statistical requirements for inclusion in the CEAI.

2.3.2. Reliability assessment

Internal consistency reliability measures were assessed on the factor structures derived from both analyses reported above, using the Chronbach's procedure available in the SPSSx statistical package.

2.3.3. Managerial level analysis

Respondents were also asked to identify their particular level of middle management. Three categories were provided including lower middle, middle level, and upper middle. In order to asses whether or not middle manager level impacted the perception of the corporate entrepreneurial environment, the resulting factor structure was tested for significant differences across managerial level. A multiple analysis of variance (MANOVA) procedure was utilized to assess differences. Follow-up analysis of variance (ANOVA) for each factor was utilized when a significant MANOVA was found. Also, Scheffe's tests were utilized to determine specific differences for managerial level on each factor. The second sample was selected since it was larger and provided larger sample sizes for each managerial level.

3. Results

3.1. Factor analysis and reliability

3.1.1. Analysis 1

The results of the exploratory factor analysis yielded five significant factors. Each factor was titled based on the items that comprised them. The factors covered were: management support (19 items), work discretion (9 items), rewards/reinforcement (6 items), time availability (6 items), and organizational boundaries (7 items). The five-factor solution accounted for 46% of variance. These results confirm Hypotheses 1 and 2 in that a set of five factors was determined in the exploratory factor analysis and supported in the confirmatory factor analysis.

Next, the items loading on each factor were subjected to an internal consistency reliability analysis. The reliabilities of these factors were then established using Chronbach's α. The resulting reliabilities were .92, .86, .75, .77, and .69 for management support, autonomy, rewards/reinforcement, time, and organizational boundaries, respectively.

3.1.2. Analysis 2

The results of the confirmatory factor analysis also suggested a five-factor solution. The purpose of this analysis was to further confirm that CEAI items fit the pattern predicted by previous theory and research. The resulting factors were: management support (17 items), work discretion (10 items), rewards/reinforcement (5 items), time availability (6 items), and organizational boundaries (5 items). This five-factor solution accounted for 43.3% of variance. However, five items from the original CEAI failed to meet the statistical requirements for inclusion in the second analysis. The results of both

J.S. Hornsby et al. / Journal of Business Venturing 17 (2002) 253–273   267

Table 3
Factor analysis statistics

Factor	Eigenvalue	Percent of variance	Cumulative variance
Analysis 1			
1	11.03	23.0	23.0
2	3.66	7.6	30.6
3	3.24	6.7	37.3
4	2.46	5.1	42.5
5	1.70	3.5	46.0
Analysis 2			
1	10.68	22.2	22.2
2	3.07	6.4	28.6
3	2.90	6.0	34.7
4	2.53	5.3	40.0
5	1.59	3.34	43.3

the exploratory and confirmatory factor analyses are summarized in Tables 2 and 3 and depicted in Fig. 2.

After constructing the relevant corporate entrepreneurship factors, reliability analysis was conducted. The resulting coefficient α's were .89, .87, .75, .77, and .64 for management support, autonomy, rewards/reinforcement, time, and organizational boundaries, respectively. Collectively, the findings from the second sample suggests that the five-factor solution is stable and internally consistent (reliable). These results confirm Hypothesis 3.

Fig. 2. Confirmatory factor analysis results. Percentages in gray overlap areas represent independent variance accounted for in the factor analytic model.

268   *J.S. Hornsby et al. / Journal of Business Venturing 17 (2002) 253–273*

Table 4
ANOVA follow-up results

Dependent variable	Type III sum of squares	df	Mean square	F	Significance
Management support	6.055	2	3.028	8.187	.000
Discretion	8.582	2	4.291	10.905	.000
Rewards/reinforcement	1.233	2	0.617	1.578	.207
Availability	4.478	2	2.239	4.254	.015
Organizational boundaries	4.043	2	2.022	6.885	.001

3.1.3. Analysis 3

The overall MANOVA was significant ($F = 3.486$) indicating a managerial level difference. The follow-up ANOVA for each of the five factors revealed significant differences for four of the five factors (Table 4). The only factor not showing significance was the rewards/reinforcement factor. Scheffe's tests utilized to determine which managerial levels were significantly different on each factor revealed a consistent finding that upper middle management scores on each factor were significantly higher than the other levels (middle and lower middle managers). Table 5 details these findings for each managerial level and each factor.

Table 5
Scheffe's mean comparisons for managerial level analysis

Current job level	Mean	S.D.	n
Management support			
Lower middle management	2.7376	0.5737	181
Middle management	2.8094	0.6021	282
Upper middle management[a]	3.0875	0.7157	67
Discretion			
Lower middle management	3.5333	0.6015	181
Middle management	3.6824	0.6434	282
Upper middle management[a]	3.9478	0.6264	67
Rewards/reinforcement			
Lower middle management	3.4208	0.6029	181
Middle management	3.4655	0.6179	282
Upper middle management[a]	3.5796	0.7097	67
Availability			
Lower middle management	2.3886	0.6867	181
Middle management	2.5267	0.7471	267
Upper middle management[a]	2.6741	0.7348	67
Organizational boundaries			
Lower middle management	2.8904	0.5205	181
Middle management	2.9981	0.5612	282
Upper middle management[a]	3.1733	0.5146	67

[a] Significant difference from other managerial levels.

J.S. Hornsby et al. / Journal of Business Venturing 17 (2002) 253–273   269

4. Discussion

This study contributes to the literature on corporate entrepreneurship by documenting the existence of an underlying set of five stable organizational factors that should be recognized in promoting entrepreneurial activities within an organization. The five factors that were identified (management support, work discretion/autonomy, rewards/reinforcement, time availability, and organizational boundaries) represent a parsimonious description of the internal organizational factors that influence middle managers to foster entrepreneurial activity within established companies. It is important to note that this resulting structure held up on the second confirmatory factor analysis using an entirely separate sample of middle managers.

From a theoretical perspective, the current research provides an important step toward understanding the internal factors that spur middle managers towards corporate entrepreneurship. As previously noted, the literature in this area has been primarily normative in that most researchers have developed conceptual schema that have either never been empirically tested, or are based on limited case study analyses. In contrast, this study presented a two-stage empirical analysis that emphasized the key internal factors that are likely to impact corporate entrepreneurial behavior of middle managers. This focus clearly distinguishes this research from previous studies that tend to be concerned with more generalized assessments of organizations' readiness to initiate corporate entrepreneurship efforts. The results, which help to integrate major writings in this area, can therefore be used to guide further research into corporate entrepreneurship activities. By examining appropriate rewards and incentives, time available for employees to experiment and innovate, and the level of organizational support, researchers will be able to more clearly measure factors that influence middle managers corporate entrepreneurship efforts. Further research efforts into corporate entrepreneurial environments need to give special attention to the five internal factors uncovered in this study.

One of the interesting aspects of this particular study's concentration on middle managers within the domain of corporate entrepreneurship is the difference in perception of the key factors by upper middle managers and middle to lower middle managers. As was demonstrated in the Results section, there were significant differences on all five factors (although the rewards factors demonstrated only slight significance) when comparing between the upper middle level and the middle to lower middle manager level. This emphasizes the importance of future research with the CEAI instrument. Fig. 1 conceptualizes the basis of this research with the existence and perceptions of the organizational factors. It is the perceptual aspect that may become most important for future research, especially if there continues to be significant differences between the levels of management.

The instrument developed in this study also has practical implications for managers. For example, the CEAI can be used as an assessment tool for evaluating corporate training needs in entrepreneurship and innovation. Many companies have initiated such programs in recent years to identify areas needing attention to encourage entrepreneurial and risk-taking activities (Kuratko and Montagno, 1989; McWilliams, 1993). The results of one empirical analysis indicated that a training program designed to enhance corporate entrepreneurship significantly affected perceptions of the environment by managers (Kuratko et al., 1990). Therefore, the instrument developed in this study can be used as a diagnostic tool for determining areas where training may be needed if a company is considering initiating corporate entrepreneurship activities. Determining these training needs can set the stage for improving middle managers' skills and increasing their sensitivity to the challenges of building and supporting a corporate entrepreneurship program.

4.1. Research suggestions

While this study suggests the existence of a stable set of factors necessary for a corporate entrepreneurial environment, additional research addressing the validity of the study's instrument is recommended. First, the instrument needs further empirical work to assess its relationship to such measures as the number of ideas generated in an organization; time spent on entrepreneurial ideas; and employee willingness to break through organizational boundaries. Second, while this study has initiated an important exploration, clarification, and refinement of these factors, it is necessary to further support the relationship between the instrument and measures of individual corporate entrepreneurial activities. For example, researchers may link this instrument's five dimensions to financial measures of organizational performance. While companies initiate corporate entrepreneurship efforts for varying reasons, ultimately, senior management expects corporate entrepreneurship efforts to improve the company's financial position. Consequently, future researchers should investigate the relationship between corporate entrepreneurship dimensions and financial performance measures. One possible methodology is to compare and contrast firms who score high and low on the five factors of the CEAI. Third, would a study involving CEOs result in similar or different corporate entrepreneurship factors? Finally, additional research into whether or not such variables as industry type and culture play a role in the corporate entrepreneurial environment is necessary.

In summary, this study provides empirical evidence regarding the existence of a stable set of five organizational factors believed to enhance corporate entrepreneurship. Grounded in data from two large samples, the current study advances the research on the factors that spur corporate entrepreneurial efforts, and provides researchers with a reliable instrument that examines these factors within an organization. This instrument is used with a sample of middle managers, who are believed to play a key role in determining the success of corporate entrepreneurship. The study's results and proposed instrument offer a foundation for developing a reliable and valid measure of the firm's internal factors for corporate entrepreneurship.

References

Alterowitz, R., 1988. New Corporate Ventures. Wiley, New York.
Baden-Fuller, C., 1995. Strategic innovation, corporate entrepreneurship and matching outside-in to inside-out approaches to strategy research. Br. J. Manage. 6, S3–S16 (special issue).
Barringer, M.S., Milkovich, G.T., 1998. A theoretical exploration of the adoption and design of flexible benefit plans: a case of human resource innovation. Acad. Manage. Rev. 23, 305–324.
Bartlett, C.A., Ghoshal, S., 1993. Beyond the *m*-form: toward a managerial theory of the firm. Strategic Manage. J. 14, 23–45 (special issue).

J.S. Hornsby et al. / Journal of Business Venturing 17 (2002) 253–273   271

Bartlett, C.A., Ghoshal, S., 1996. Release the entrepreneurial hostages from your corporate hierarchy. Strategy Leadership 24 (2), 36–42 (July/August).

Bird, B., 1988. Implementing entrepreneurial ideas: the case for intention. Acad. Manage. Rev. 13, 442–453.

Birkinshaw, J., 1997. Entrepreneurship in multinational corporations: the characteristics of subsidiary initiatives. Strategic Manage. J. 18, 207–229.

Block, Z., Ornati, O.A., 1987. Compensating corporate venture managers. J. Bus. Venturing 2, 41–51.

Bower, J.L., 1970. Managing the Resource Allocation Process. Harvard Business School, Boston, MA.

Brazeal, D.V., 1993. Organizing for internally developed corporate ventures. J. Bus. Venturing 8, 75–90.

Burgelman, R.A., 1983a. A process model of internal corporate venturing in the diversified major firm. Adm. Sci. Q. 28, 223–244.

Burgelman, R.A., 1983b. Corporate entrepreneurship and strategic management: insights from a process study. Manage. Sci. 29, 1349–1363 (December).

Burgelman, R.A., 1984. Designs for corporate entrepreneurship. Calif. Manage. Rev. 26, 154–166.

Burgelman, R.A., Sayles, L.R., 1986. Inside Corporate Innovation: Strategy, Structure, and Managerial Skills. Free Press, New York, NY.

Cooper, D.R., Emory, C.W., 1995. Business Research Methods, fifth ed. Richard D. Irwin, Homewood, IL.

Covin, J.G., Miles, M.P., 1999. Corporate entrepreneurship and the pursuit of competitive advantage. Entrepreneurship Theory Pract. 23 (3), 47–64 (Spring).

Covin, J.G., Slevin, D.P., 1991. A conceptual model of entrepreneurship as firm behavior. Entrepreneurship Theory Pract. 16 (1), 7–25 (Fall).

Damanpour, F., 1991. Organizational innovation: a meta-analysis of effects of determinant and moderators. Acad. Manage. J. 34, 55–390.

Das, T.K., Teng, B.S., 1997. Time and entrepreneurial risk behavior. Entrepreneurship Theory Pract. 22, 69–88.

Dess, G.G., Lumpkin, G.T., McGee, J.E., 1999. Linking corporate entrepreneurship to strategy, structure, and process: suggested research directions. Entrepreneurship Theory Pract. 23 (3), 85–102.

Drucker, P.F., 1985. The discipline of innovation. Harv. Bus. Rev. 63, 67–72 (May/June).

Ellis, R.J., Taylor, N.T., 1988. Success and failure in internal venture strategy: an exploratory study. Frontiers of Entrepreneurship Research 518–533.

Floyd, S.W., Woolridge, B., 1990. The strategy process, middle management involvement, and organizational performance. Strategic Manage. J. 11 (3), 231–242.

Floyd, S.W., Woolridge, B., 1992. Middle management involvement in strategy and its association with strategic type: a research note. Strategic Manage. J. 13, 53–168 (special issue).

Floyd, S.W., Woolridge, B., 1994. Dinosaurs or dynamos? Recognizing middle managements' strategic role. Acad. Manage. Exec. 8 (4), 47–58.

Floyd, S.W., Woolridge, B., 1997. Middle managers strategic influence and organizational performance. J. Manage. Stud. 3 (34), 465–485 (May).

Fry, A., 1987. The Post-It-Note: an entrepreneurial success. SAM Adv. Manage. J. 52, 4–9 (Summer).

Ginsberg, A., Hay, M., 1994. Confronting the challenges of corporate entrepreneurship: guidelines for venture managers. Eur. Manage. J. 12, 82–389.

Guth, W.D., Ginsberg, A., 1990. Corporate entrepreneurship. Strategic Manage. J. 11, 5–15 (special issue).

Hanan, M., 1976. Venturing corporations — think small to stay strong. Harv. Bus. Rev. 54, 139–148.

Hill, R.M., Hlavacek, J.D., 1972. The venture team: a new concept in marketing organizations. J. Mark. 36, 44–50.

Hisrich, R.D., Peters, M.P., 1986. Establishing a new business venture unit within a firm. J. Bus. Venturing 1, 307–322.

Hornsby, J.S., Naffziger, D.W., Kuratko, D.F., Montagno, R.V., 1993. An interactive model of the corporate entrepreneurship process. Entrepreneurship Theory Pract. 17 (2), 29–37 (Spring).

Kanter, R., 1988. When Giants Learn to Dance. Simon & Schuster, New York, NY.

Kanter, R.M., 1983. The Change Masters. Simon & Schuster, New York, NY.

Kanter, R.M., 1985. Supporting innovation and venture development in established companies. J. Bus. Venturing 1, 47–60.

Katz, J., Gartner, W.B., 1988. Properties of emerging organizations. Acad. Manage. Rev. 13, 429–441.

Knight, G.A., 1997. Cross cultural reliability and validity of a scale to measure firm entrepreneurial orientation. J. Bus. Venturing 12 (3), 213–226.

Kuratko, D.F., 1993. Intrapreneurship: developing innovation in the corporation. Adv. Global High Technol. Manage.–High Technol. Venturing 3, 3–14.

Kuratko, D.F., Montagno, R.V., 1989. The intrapreneurial spirit. Train. Dev. J. 43 (10), 83–87 (October).

Kuratko, D.F., Montagno, R.V., Hornsby, J.S., 1990. Developing an intrapreneurial assessment instrument for an effective corporate entrepreneurial environment. Strategic Manage. J. 11, 49–58.

Kuratko, D.F., Hornsby, J.S., Naffziger, D.W., Montagno, R.V., 1993. Implementing entrepreneurial thinking in established organizations. Adv. Manage. J. 58 (1), 28–33 (Winter).

MacMillian, I.C., Block, Z., Narasimha, P.N.S., 1986. Corporate venturing: alternatives, obstacles encountered, and experience effects. J. Bus. Venturing 1, 177–191.

McGrath, R.G., Venkataraman, S., MacMillan, I.C., 1994. The advantage chain: antecedents to rents from internal corporate ventures. J. Bus. Venturing 9, 351–369.

McWilliams, B., 1993. Strengths from within-how today's companies nurture entrepreneurs. Enterprise 6 (4), 43–44 (April).

Merrifield, D.B., 1993. Intrapreneurial corporate renewal. J. Bus. Venturing 8, 383–389.

Miller, D., Friesen, P.H., 1982. Innovation in conservative and entrepreneurial firms: two models of strategic momentum. Strategic Manage. J. 3 (1), 1–25.

Naman, J., Slevin, D., 1993. Entrepreneurship and the concept of fit: a model and empirical tests. Strategic Manage. J. 14, 137–153.

Noble, R., Birkinshaw, J., 1998. Innovation in multinational corporations: control and communication patterns. Strategic Manage. J. 19 (5), 479–496.

Nonaka, I., Takeuchi, H., 1995. The Knowledge Company: How Japanese Companies Create the Dynamics of Innovation. Oxford Univ. Press, New York.

Pearce, J.A., Kramer, T.R., Robbins, D.K., 1997. Effects of managers' entrepreneurial behavior on subordinates. J. Bus. Venturing 12, 147–160.

Peters, T.J., Waterman, R.H., 1982. In Search of Excellence: Lessons from America's Best Run Companies. Harper & Row, New York.

Peterson, R., Berger, D., 1972. Entrepreneurship in organizations. Adm. Sci. Q. 16, 97–106.

Pinchott, G., 1985. Intrapreneurship. Harper & Row, New York.

Quinn, J., 1979. Technological innovation, entrepreneurship, and strategy. Sloan Manage. Rev. 20 (3), 19–30.

Quinn, J.B., 1985. Managing innovation: controlled chaos. Harv. Bus. Rev. 63, 73–84 (May/June).

Sathe, V., 1985. Managing an entrepreneurial dilemma: nurturing entrepreneurship and control in large corporations 636–656. Frontiers of Entrepreneurship Research Babson College, Wesley, Mas.

Sathe, V., 1989. Fostering entrepreneurship in a large diversified firm. Organ. Dyn. 18, 20–32.

Scanlan, B.K., 1981. Creating a climate for achievement. Bus. Horizons 24, 5–9 (March/April).

Schollhammer, H., 1982. Internal corporate entrepreneurship. In: Kent, C., Sexton, D., Vesper, K. (Eds.), Encyclopedia of Entrepreneurship. Prentice-Hall, Englewood Cliffs, NJ, pp. 209–223.

Schuler, R.S., 1986. Fostering and facilitating entrepreneurship in organizations: implications for organization structure and human resource management practices. Hum. Res. Manage. 25, 607–629.

Sharma, P., Chrisman, J.J., 1999. Toward a reconciliation of the definitional issues in the field of corporate entrepreneurship. Entrepreneurship Theory Pract. 23 (3), 11–27.

Slevin, D.P., Covin, J.G., 1997. Time, growth, complexity and transitions: entrepreneurial challenges for the future. Entrepreneurship Theory Pract. 22, 43–68.

Souder, W., 1981. Encouraging entrepreneurship in large corporations. Res. Manage. 24 (3), 18–22 (May).

Stevenson, H.H., Jarillo, J.C., 1990. A paradigm of entrepreneurship: entrepreneurial management. Strategic Manage. J. 11, 17–27 (special issue).

Stopford, J.M., Baden-Fuller, C.W.F., 1994. Creating corporate entrepreneurship. Strategic Manage. J. 15, 521–536.

Sykes, H.B., 1986. The anatomy of a corporate venturing program. J. Bus. Venturing 1, 275–293.

Sykes, H.B., 1992. Incentive compensation for corporate venture personnel. J. Bus. Venturing 7, 253–265.

Sykes, H.B., Block, Z., 1989. Corporate venturing obstacles: sources and solutions. J. Bus. Venturing 4, 159–167.

Vesper, K.H., 1984. Three faces of corporate entrepreneurship: a pilot study. Frontiers of Entrepreneurship Research 294–320.

Von Hippel, E., 1977. Successful and failing internal corporate ventures: an empirical analysis. Ind. Mark. Manage. 6, 163–174.

Woolridge, B., Floyd, S.W., 1990. The strategy process, middle management involvement, and organizational performance. Strategic Manage. J. 11, 231–241.

Zahra, S.A., 1991. Predictors and financial outcomes of corporate entrepreneurship: an exploratory study. J. Bus. Venturing 6, 259–286.

Zahra, S.A., 1993. Environment, corporate entrepreneurship and financial performance: a taxonomic approach. J. Bus. Venturing 8, 319–340.

Zahra, S.A., Covin, J.G., 1995. Contextual influences on the corporate entrepreneurship–performance relationship: a longitudinal analysis. J. Bus. Venturing 10, 43–58.

Zahra, S.A., O'Neil, H.M., 1998. Charting the landscape of global competition: reflections on emerging organizational challenges and their implications for senior executives. Acad. Manage. Exec. 12, 13–21.

Zahra, S.A., Nielsen, A.P., Bogner, W.C., 1999. Corporate entrepreneurship, knowledge, and competence development. Entrepreneurship Theory Pract. 23 (3), 169–190.

[22]

° *Academy of Management Journal*
1996, Vol. 39, No. 6, 1713–1735.

GOVERANCE, OWNERSHIP, AND CORPORATE ENTREPRENEURSHIP: THE MODERATING IMPACT OF INDUSTRY TECHNOLOGICAL OPPORTUNITIES

SHAKER A. ZAHRA
Georgia State University

Corporate entrepreneurship is important for organizational survival, profitability, growth, and renewal. Data from 127 *Fortune* 500 companies show that executive stock ownership and long-term institutional ownership are positively associated with such entrepreneurship. Conversely, short-term institutional ownership is negatively associated with it, as is a high ratio of outside directors on a company's board. Outside directors' stock ownership somewhat mitigates the latter negative association. Outsiders, including stock owners, might lead companies away from internal product development, the traditional route to corporate entrepreneurship. Finally, an industry's technological opportunities moderate the associations observed between corporate governance and ownership variables and corporate entrepreneurship.

This study focuses on entrepreneurial risk taking in the largest U.S. industrial corporations. It examines the association of a company's governance and ownership systems with its level of corporate entrepreneurship, defined here as consisting of innovation aimed at business creation and venturing, and strategic renewal (Zahra & Covin, 1995). The study's argument is that the association of ownership and governance with corporate entrepreneurship is moderated by the level of technological opportunities that exist in the firm's major industry.

Over the past decade there has been a growing awareness that governance and ownership systems can significantly impact corporate entrepreneurship. Porter (1992) called for studies documenting the association of governance and ownership systems with entrepreneurial activity. Researchers have responded to this call by documenting the impact of these systems

---

I acknowledge with much appreciation the many constructive comments of Robert Hoskisson on this article. Jeffrey Covin, Edward Miles, Donald Neubaum, Lynn Shore, Patricia H. Zahra, and this journal's reviewers also provided many useful suggestions. A grant from the College of Business Administration of Georgia State University supported this research. Data collection was supported by the Beebe Institute and Zewerner Chair in Entrepreneurship, both at Georgia State University.

1714   *Academy of Management Journal*   December

on research and development (R&D) spending and outputs (e.g., Baysinger, Kosnik, & Turk, 1991; Daily & Dalton, 1992; Graves, 1988). However, these studies have produced contradictory results. Additional research is, therefore, needed if the association of governance and ownership systems with corporate entrepreneurship is to be better understood. This study was intended to clarify these relationships and to contribute to the literature in three ways.

First, the study emphasizes executives' reports of their companies' corporate entrepreneurship, thereby providing additional insights into the determinants of managerial risk-taking behavior. According to March and Shapira (1987), executives define a risky choice as one that has a possibly poor outcome. Entrepreneurial projects meet this criterion because many of them fail, those that survive may take years to generate a profit (Block & Mac-Millan, 1993), and it is difficult to estimate their results a priori. Hoskisson, Hitt, and Hill also noted that "choices that contain the threat of a very poor outcome are ones that involve a departure from established operating *routines and procedures* . . . [as happens when] a firm tries to adopt an innovation . . . that requires a fundamental change in the way the firm operates" (1991: 298; emphasis in original). Implanting corporate entrepreneurship projects usually requires making fundamental changes in the company's culture, structure, and managerial styles (Zahra, 1991). As these changes create uncertainty, success cannot be achieved without the strong support of senior executives (Zahra & Covin, 1995).

Second, the study examines the association of different groups of institutional investors with corporate entrepreneurship. Rather than treating these owners as a monolithic group, as was done in past research, I recognized that different institutional owners often pursue different goals and, therefore, may view corporate entrepreneurship quite differently. Therefore, I grouped institutional investors in terms of length of investment horizons (Roe, 1994).

Third, the study explores the moderating effect of technological opportunities on the associations of governance and ownership with corporate entrepreneurship. This link is important because there is concern that prevailing governance and ownership systems often harm corporate entrepreneurship, especially in high-technology industries (National Academy of Engineering, 1992) and other industries that have great potential for innovation. These reductions in innovation and other entrepreneurial activities can undermine the global competitive position of U.S. companies (Franko, 1989).

THEORY AND HYPOTHESES

Corporate Entrepreneurship

Corporate entrepreneurship includes radical product innovation, risk taking, and proactiveness (Covin & Slevin, 1991; Miller, 1983). It also includes business venturing and "intrapreneuring" (Kuratko, Montagno, &

Hornsby, 1990) and organizational renewal (Sathe, 1989). A review of the literature by Guth and Ginsberg (1990) concluded that corporate entrepreneurship has two dimensions: innovation aimed at business creation and venturing, and strategic renewal. I adopted this definition in this article because of its conceptual clarity and comprehensiveness.

As a component of corporate entrepreneurship, innovation is a company's commitment to creating and introducing products, production processes, and organizational systems (Covin & Slevin, 1991; Lumpkin & Dess, 1996). Venturing means that the firm will enter new businesses by expanding operations in existing or new markets (Block & MacMillan, 1993). Strategic renewal refers to revitalizing the company's operations by changing the scope of its business, its competitive approach, or both (Stopford & Baden-Fuller, 1994; Zahra, 1993). Strategic renewal also means building or acquiring new capabilities and then creatively leveraging them to add value for shareholders.

Corporate entrepreneurship can enhance shareholders' value by creating a work environment that supports individual and corporate growth, giving employees an opportunity to use their creative skills, quickening a company's response to the market, and creating an organizational culture that fosters cross-functional collaboration. These changes in turn promote entrepreneurial efforts that create new revenue streams (Zahra, 1991).

Despite the potential contributions of entrepreneurial activities to value creation, executives may not support them. Such managerial risk aversion is a widely suspected cause of the perceived decline of the competitiveness of U.S. companies (Franko, 1989; Hoskisson & Hitt, 1994). Careerism and short-term-based reward systems may discourage executives' pursuits of corporate entrepreneurship (Jacobs, 1991). Although investors can usually reduce their risk by holding diversified stock portfolios, executives cannot always diversify their risk, and some entrepreneurial activities have a high probability of failure (Zahra & Covin, 1995), a factor that can depress a company's short-term performance and lower executive compensation. As entrepreneurial failures can also damage executives' reputations and increase their risk of unemployment, they may induce managerial risk aversion. To counter this aversion, shareholders should use boards of directors to monitor executives to ensure a focus on long-term value creation.

Using corporate entrepreneurship as a lens to study managerial risk taking has several advantages. Notably, measuring such activity allows for a more comprehensive variable than the risk-taking proxies commonly used in the literature, such as R&D spending. Multiple manifestations of managerial risk-taking behavior can be examined, and their simultaneous relationships with corporate governance and ownership variables can be documented. Further, corporate entrepreneurship projects usually have longer time horizons than the activities on which the measures used in past research—such as R&D inputs and outputs—are based. R&D–based measures may embody inaccuracies. For instance, high R&D spending may reflect internal inefficiencies, whereby the firm consumes vast resources to generate new prod-

1716   *Academy of Management Journal*   December

ucts or technologies, rather than risk taking. High R&D spending may also reflect high agency costs, with managers attempting to keep funds within a firm rather than distribute them to shareholders. Past researchers also appear to have assumed that high R&D spending means greater product or process innovations, which is questionable (Kochhar & David, 1996). Similarly, the number of a firm's patents does not always indicate the financial viability of those patents.

Corporate entrepreneurship projects often create information asymmetry between inside and outside participants in the corporate governance system. Specifically, because R&D spending figures are among a company's most widely publicized decisions, the financial community is likely to monitor them closely. This factor may limit managers' willingness to significantly reduce these allocations (Laverty, 1993). In contrast, some corporate entrepreneurship initiatives are invisible to external observers, a condition that may encourage managers to forgo investing in them. Some entrepreneurial efforts are like Burgelman's (1983) autonomous strategic behaviors: initiatives that complement a company's formal corporate entrepreneurship activities. Although some entrepreneurial activities may be incomprehensible even to insiders, executives are usually responsible for championing, evaluating, and integrating these projects into a company's formal initiatives. Insiders are, therefore, expected to have more data and more first-hand, tacit knowledge of entrepreneurial initiatives than outsiders. This information asymmetry between insiders and outsiders can affect the criteria used in evaluating corporate entrepreneurship. If financial criteria and controls are used exclusively, such activity may decline (Baysinger & Hoskisson, 1990).[1]

Agency theory suggests that corporate ownership and governance systems can affect managers' willingness to take risks (Jones & Butler, 1992). Ownership determines a company's relationship with shareholders and its investment horizons. When major shareholders exist, they can monitor executives' decisions and ensure attention to corporate entrepreneurship. Also, when investors own stock in a company for a long period, they are in a position to increase executives' interest in corporate entrepreneurship (Jacobs, 1991). The corporate governance system—the mechanisms that regulate the relationship between executives and shareholders—can similarly and profoundly shape managers' commitment to corporate entrepreneurship. Strong, vigilant boards of directors can encourage managers to support and pursue entrepreneurial activities.

---

[1] It should be acknowledged that Baysinger and Hoskisson's propositions on the link of strategic and financial controls with corporate entrepreneurship have not been thoroughly tested, especially in reference to governance issues. However, ownership variables and their associations with different control types have received more empirical attention (e.g., Baysinger et al., 1991).

Governance and Ownership Systems and Corporate Entrepreneurship

According to agency theory (Jacobs, 1991; Zahra & Pearce, 1989), promoting corporate entrepreneurship requires increasing the representation of outside directors on a board, increasing outside directors' ownership interests to give them an incentive to monitor a CEO's commitment to entrepreneurship, increasing the ownership interest of a company's executives to align their goals with those of the shareholders, and ensuring the presence of a major shareholder that monitors the CEO and encourages the pursuit of corporate entrepreneurship. The next section of the article discusses the anticipated associations of these four variables with corporate entrepreneurship.

Insiders and outsiders' board representation. Aligning the interests of managers and shareholders requires active and independent boards, which can be achieved by increasing the representation of outside directors (Daily & Dalton, 1992; Judge & Zeithaml, 1992). A high ratio of outside directors on a board can expand the base of expertise from which a firm's CEO can draw, enhance objectivity in board deliberations, strengthen the system of corporate checks and balances, and increase directors' independence. It can also improve the board's ability to effectively perform its control function and encourage executives to pursue corporate entrepreneurship (Zahra & Pearce, 1989).

With a high ratio of outsiders, a board can tie executive compensation to the pursuit of corporate entrepreneurship and use commitment to it as a criterion in evaluating the CEO's performance. However, research does not universally support the presumed positive association between the ratio of outsiders on a board and corporate entrepreneurship. Indeed, some authors (e.g., Baysinger et al., 1991; Hill & Snell, 1988) have concluded that insiders' dominance on a board is positively associated with R&D spending, an indicator of corporate innovation. This finding is consistent with Porter's statement that "Boards, which have come to be dominated by outside directors with no other links to the company, exert only limited influence on corporate goals . . . . they often lack the time or ability to absorb the vast amounts of information required to understand a company's internal operations. Moreover, most directors have limited stakes in the companies they oversee" (Porter, 1992: 71). These observations also reinforce Kosnik's (1987) statement that "outside directors whose stock ownership in a company is small may have the same tendency to free-ride as small investors" (1987: 136). Lacking an ownership interest, outside directors may have little incentive to monitor a chief executive or promote entrepreneurial activity.

The fact that CEOs play a major role in the selection, remuneration, and retention of outside directors also limits outside directors' power. Currently, 80 percent of the CEOs of large companies also serve as their boards' chairs (Finkelstein & D'Aveni, 1994). Further, because most outside directors are themselves high-ranking officers of other companies, they may grant a CEO great powers (Roe, 1994). Shareholders have filed many suits against direc-

1718   *Academy of Management Journal*   December

tors, but their accountability remains questionable (Jacobs, 1991). Directors have increased their coverage for liability and nearly 85 percent of U.S. public manufacturing companies have amended their bylaws to allow them to indemnify outside directors. These factors can insulate outside directors from the legal consequences of poor decisions.

Baysinger and Hoskisson (1990) observed that inside directors, through their participation in the strategic process, can more reliably assess the merits of corporate entrepreneurship projects. Outsiders, who are not usually as intimately involved in the strategy formulation process as insiders, may rely heavily on financial controls, which may lower corporate entrepreneurship. Inside directors are responsible for creating the administrative structures and the organizational culture necessary for corporate entrepreneurship (Burgelman, 1983; Zahra, 1991) and thus become familiar with these ventures. Insiders are also more capable than outsiders of achieving multifunctional coordination (Hill & Snell, 1988) and of promoting intensive interdepartmental communications.

Promoting corporate entrepreneurship in large organizations also requires changing prevailing corporate cultures and revising existing systems to overcome inertia. These changes frequently create considerable uncertainty, which also favors reliance on inside directors (Hill & Hoskisson, 1987). Also, because of their long-term association with a firm, insiders are usually informed about the sources and implications of this uncertainty. Inside directors are also positioned to observe the individuals and groups responsible for implementing corporate entrepreneurship and, consequently, can identify and address the sources of uncertainty. Further, given that they are typically responsible for monitoring and assessing industry changes (Galbraith, 1973), inside directors usually have access to information about the sources of uncertainty. This is important because entrepreneurial activities are likely to thrive in business environments characterized by dynamism and uncertainty (Zahra, 1991, 1993). Managing the uncertainty associated with or resulting from corporate entrepreneurship is a task best given to qualified inside directors (Baysinger & Hoskisson, 1990). Therefore,

> *Hypothesis 1: A high ratio of outsiders on a company's board of directors is negatively associated with corporate entrepreneurship.*

Involving outside directors through ownership. Outside directors' inability to monitor executives' commitment to corporate entrepreneurship may stem, in part, from a lack of ownership (Porter, 1992). However, outside directors who hold ownership interests will be motivated to monitor a CEO and will thus become more involved with a firm's operations. This involvement can improve outside directors' use of strategic controls (Johnson, Hoskisson, & Hitt, 1993), possibly promoting corporate entrepreneurship: Hoskisson and colleagues (1993) found that when strategic controls were emphasized, managers usually supported risky projects. Given that entrepreneurial ventures can improve a company's performance, they can enhance the value of stock, so stock ownership may therefore further motivate outside directors to promote corporate entrepreneurship (Jacobs, 1991). Thus, stock ownership may weaken the association between the ratio of outside directors and corporate entrepreneurship predicted in Hypothesis 1. Although the effect on entrepreneurship of the interaction of outsiders' representation and their stock ownership should remain negative, the coefficient will be lower than that resulting from a test of Hypothesis 1. Therefore,

> *Hypothesis 2: Stock ownership by outside directors will temper the negative association between the ratio of outside directors on a company's board and corporate entrepreneurship.*

Executive ownership. Executives are sometimes viewed as being more interested in improving a company's short-term performance than in maximizing its long-term value (Jacobs, 1991). Because their compensation is usually based on short-term financial performance, executives may have little incentive to promote internal entrepreneurship, especially when they have low ownership stakes (Malatesta & Walling, 1988). Tying rewards to long-term corporate value can stimulate executives' interest in corporate entrepreneurship (Jones & Butler, 1992). Even though the above discussion suggests a positive association between executives' ownership and corporate entrepreneurship, past research has yielded contradictory results. Some researchers have found a positive but insignificant association between managerial ownership and R&D spending (Hill & Snell, 1988, 1989), and others have reported a positive association between these variables only within particular industries (Hansen & Hill, 1991). These conflicting results highlight a need for additional research on the issue. Still, it is noteworthy that none of the past studies reviewed has found a negative association between executive stock ownership and corporate entrepreneurship. Therefore,

> *Hypothesis 3: Executive stock ownership is positively associated with corporate entrepreneurship.*

Institutional ownership. The presence of a major powerful shareholder encourages a CEO to pursue risky long-term ventures such as corporate entrepreneurship (Jensen & Meckling, 1976). Institutional owners are fast becoming powerful players in the corporate governance system. Yet there is no agreement on the nature of the association between institutional ownership and entrepreneurship. Some authors have suggested that institutional owners will influence corporate entrepreneurship positively because they are better informed than other shareholders about the companies in which they hold stock (Baysinger et al., 1991; Hansen & Hill, 1991) and cannot always dispose of their holdings without a significant loss. Also, the rising activism of some institutional owners, coupled with several regulatory changes that have somewhat eased the requirements for waging proxy contests, have raised hopes that these investors will encourage corporate entrepreneurship. However, other authors have predicted a negative effect

(Graves, 1988), because institutional investors may be driven by short-term, bottom-line considerations.

These conflicting propositions on the association of institutional ownership with entrepreneurship may have arisen from researchers' tendency to view these investors as a monolithic group. This assumption should be empirically tested; different groups of institutional investors may pursue different goals and emphasize different objectives and investment horizons (Kochhar & David, 1996; Roe, 1994). In this study, I grouped institutional investors on the basis of their investment horizons. The first group includes mutual, pension, and retirement funds. Because of the large size and long durations of their investments, managers of such funds may be primarily interested in improving their portfolios' long-term value. Long-term ownership should promote corporate entrepreneurship (Roe, 1994).

The second group is short-term institutional owners, such as investment banks and private funds. These investors have been the subject of much concern in the literature. Because fund managers are evaluated quarterly, they may promote short-term investment horizons (Chaganti & Damanpour, 1991), a condition that might jeopardize corporate entrepreneurship. Further, fund managers usually focus on maximizing their portfolios' annual performance (Jacobs, 1991). If the value of a stock declines, fund managers may discontinue the investment rather than challenge management, a process that can explain frequent stock shuttling by these investors (Porter, 1992). Consequently, these investors are likely to pressure executives to overlook corporate entrepreneurship projects with long payback periods (Graves, 1988; Hill, Hitt, & Hoskisson, 1988). Therefore,

> *Hypothesis 4a: Long-term institutional stock ownership is positively associated with corporate entrepreneurship.*

> *Hypothesis 4b: Short-term institutional stock ownership is negatively associated with corporate entrepreneurship.*

Technological opportunities and the association of governance and ownership with corporate entrepreneurship. To date, researchers have ignored the moderating impact of industry conditions on the associations posited in Hypotheses 1 through 4, a practice that might have contributed to past contradictory findings. As industries vary in governance systems, investment horizons (Jacobs, 1991), and the pursuit of corporate entrepreneurship (Zahra, 1993), there is a need to document the impact of industry variables. The technological opportunities executives believe to exist in an industry can profoundly influence the predicted associations.

Industries vary considerably in their technological opportunities (Geroski, 1990), defined as executive's perceptions of ability to support and generate growth opportunities through product and process innovations. Industries with high levels of perceived technological opportunities are usually characterized by rapid and frequent product and process technology introductions and high levels of R&D spending and patenting. Conversely, industries low in technological opportunities are usually limited in their growth potential and report modest levels of R&D investments.

To succeed in industries with high technological opportunities, executives must quickly process large amounts of information on their competition, market, and customers (Galbraith, 1973). This condition favors having a majority of inside directors on a company's board, as implied in Hypothesis 1. Also, in these industries, a firm must take risks and engage in corporate entrepreneurship, spend heavily on developing products and technologies (Zahra & Covin, 1995), and accept long payback periods for its investments. These factors reinforce the need for highly motivated inside directors and managers who have a vested interest in the company through ownership, as indicated in Hypothesis 3. This ownership stake, which aligns the interests of the managers and shareholders, also bonds the former to the company and ensures steady leadership. Still, if outside directors serve on the board, companies should motivate them through stock ownership, as implied in Hypothesis 2. Finally, in industries with high technological opportunities, companies need long-term institutional owners who provide the patient capital necessary to exploit growth opportunities, as posited in Hypothesis 4a. Short-term institutional owners may pressure executives to forgo long-term investments in high-risk ventures, as implied in Hypothesis 4b. Therefore,

> *Hypothesis 5: Level of perceived technological opportunities will moderate the association between governance and ownership in such a way that the associations posited in Hypotheses 1 through 4 will be stronger in industries with high, rather than low, technological opportunities.*

METHODS

Data

Collection and sample. To test the study's hypotheses, I collected data from secondary sources and through a mail survey that was directed to the CEOs or the highest-ranking executives of the manufacturing companies on the 1988 *Fortune* 500 list. Two mailings, conducted one month apart in 1991, were used to enhance the response rate. A personalized letter accompanied each questionnaire, explaining the study's objective and assuring the executives of the confidentiality of their replies. Responses from 138 firms represented a response rate of 27.6 percent, which was consistent with expectations about this population (Tootelian & Gaedeke, 1987).

To test for absence of response bias, I compared respondents to the first mailing to respondents to the second mailing in terms of company size (assets in millions of dollars), return on sales (ROS), and responses to the survey items. The *t*-tests showed significant differences between the two groups on only two items.[2] Using data from COMPUSTAT, I compared all respondents to nonrespondents on company size measured as both assets in millions and number of full-time employees, ROS, and return on assets (ROA); the *t*-test revealed no significant differences. These results indicated that respondents did not vary significantly from the *Fortune* 500 population. Responding companies averaged 23,093 (s.d. = 15,662) full-time employees and $4,329.2 (s.d. = 2,334.7) million in assets.

The survey targeted the firms' CEOs or most senior executives because of their likely familiarity with company-wide strategic actions, especially corporate entrepreneurship efforts (Miller, 1983; Zahra, 1991). Analysis of the titles of respondents showed that 79 percent were CEOs or presidents, 17 percent were senior vice presidents, and the remaining 4 percent were board secretaries. These figures suggested that the survey data were provided by the firms' senior executives.

Interrater reliability. The questionnaire was also sent to a second randomly selected group of executives in the responding companies (*n* = 138). One mailing yielded 49 completed responses (35.5 percent) that I then matched with replies from the CEOs. The correlation between the two responses was significant (*p* < .001), which indicated strong interrater reliability (Jones, Johnson, Butler, & Main, 1983).

Measures

Ownership and governance. Four variables, averaged over the 1988–90 period, were constructed as follows: *Outsider ratio* was measured by dividing the number of outside directors by the total number of directors on a board. Data were obtained from the 1991 *Corporate* 1000. Following previous research (e.g., Cochran et al., 1985; Gilson, 1990), I considered directors outsiders when they were not former employees (officers) of a firm or its subsidiaries (divisions), did not possess contractual relationships with it, or were not associated with a major supplier to the company. *Outsider equity ownership* was defined as the sum of outsiders' equity divided by a company's common shares. Data came from *Value Line*. *Executive ownership* was measured by the percentage of a company's total stock held by its senior executives, defined as vice presidents and those in higher offices (Chaganti & Damanpour, 1991). Data were obtained from *Standard & Poor's Stock Reports* and were available for only 127 companies. To measure *institutional ownership*, I identified two groups of institutional investors. The first, long-term institutional investors, included mutual, pension, and retirement funds. The second, short-term institutional owners, covered investment bankers and private funds. Both variables were measured as the percentage of a company's stock held by the focal group, calculated by using data from

---

[2] The two items were "This company has reduced its support of new business ventures in markets outside the US," and "This company has encouraged risk taking by managers in its overseas subsidiaries."

Standard and Poor's Stock Reports.

Corporate entrepreneurship. The variable was measured using the survey data. Innovation, venturing, and strategic renewal were addressed in 14 items. Executives rated their firms' actual, rather than preferred, entrepreneurial activities using a five-point scale (1 = strongly disagree, 5 = strongly agree). I then factor-analyzed the items using varimax rotation. As Table 1 shows, three factors with eigenvalues exceeding 1.0 resulted and, combined, explained 57.02 percent of the variance.

The first factor (five items, α = .76) captured a company's commitment to *innovation.* Items covered the creation and introduction of products, emphasis on R&D investments, and commitment to patenting. Items also corresponded to previously used measures of organizational aggressiveness and proactiveness (Lumpkin & Dess, 1996; Miller, 1983), radical product innovation, strong R&D, and patenting (Hitt et al., 1991; Zahra, 1995). The second factor (five items, α = .70) captured a firm's *venturing* activities, such as

TABLE 1
Results of Factor Analysis of the Corporate Entrepreneurship Measures

Items	Factors[a]		
	1	2	3
Over the past three years, this company...			
Has spent heavily (well above your industry average) on research and development (R&D).	**.83**	−.25	.17
Has maintained world-class research and development (R&D) facilities.	**.79**	−.28	.19
Has introduced a large number of new products to the market.	**.71**	.21	−.27
Has acquired significantly more patents than its major competitors.	**.67**	.28	−.21
Has pioneered the development of breakthrough innovations in its industry.	**.53**	−.18	−.16
Has entered many new industries.	.29	**.70**	−.21
Has expanded its international operations significantly.	.25	**.66**	−.13
Has acquired many companies in very different industries.	−.26	**.63**	.17
Has established or sponsored several new ventures.	.23	**.60**	−.14
Has focused on improving the performance of its current business, rather than entering new industries.[b]	.17	**−.53**	.26
Has divested several unprofitable business units.	−.26	−.17	**.69**
Has changed its competitive approach (strategy) for each business units.	.25	.11	**.62**
Has initiated several programs to improve the productivity of business units.	.27	−.19	**−.57**
Has reorganized operations to ensure increased coordination and communication among business units.	.25	−.15	**.54**
Eigenvalve	3.11	2.36	1.88
Percentage of variance explained	24.13	18.31	14.58

[a] Loadings with an absolute value of .50 were considered significant.
[b] Reversed-coded.

entry into new business fields by sponsoring new ventures (Block & Mac-Millan, 1993) and creating new businesses (Zahra, 1991, 1993). The third factor (four items, $\alpha = .73$) covered *strategic renewal* efforts aimed at revitalizing a company's ability to compete (Sathe, 1989; Stopford & Baden-Fuller, 1994) and redefining its business domain by eliminating unprofitable operations while improving internal efficiencies (Hoskisson & Hitt, 1994).

Three steps were used to establish the validity of the corporate entrepreneurship measures. First, I used Miller's (1983) corporate entrepreneurship index ($\alpha = .71$). The items, presented in the Appendix, followed a five-point Likert scale (5 = strongly agree, 1 = strongly disagree). Miller's index was associated ($p < .001$) with innovation ($r = .81$), venturing ($r = .57$), and renewal ($r = .66$). Second, I developed an objective indicator using the three-year averages of a firm's R&D spending as a percentage of sales, the number of products it introduced to the market, and the percentage of its revenue from businesses that did not exist three years earlier. A factor analysis with a varimax rotation produced one significant factor that I labeled "objective CE" (eigenvalue = 1.37). The factor score was then significantly correlated with innovation, venturing, and renewal (all at $p < .001$). Finally, interrater reliability between two executives was significant on the three corporate entrepreneurship measures (all at $p < .001$).

Technological opportunities. To gauge this variable, respondents were asked to focus on their firm's major industry over the three-year period before data collection. Perceptions of this industry usually determine managerial actions (Keats & Hitt, 1988). A four-item index based on the survey was used ($\alpha = .71$); survey items appear in the Appendix.

Control variables. The study also included six control variables that were believed to influence corporate entrepreneurship. The average figure for the 1988–90 period was used for each variable, as follows: *CEO duality* meant that a company's CEO also served as its board's chairperson (Finkelstein & D'Aveni, 1994). Because CEO duality can reduce the ability of outsiders to evaluate corporate entrepreneurship, it was entered as a dummy variable coded 1 if the CEO also served as the chair and 0 otherwise. The *debt-to-common-equity ratio* was also considered because heavily leveraged companies have limited slack resources, which, in turn, reduces corporate entrepreneurship (Hansen & Hill, 1991). Data were collected from COMPUSTAT. *Liquidity* was considered because corporate entrepreneurship requires slack resources. I entered the current ratio, which indicated the availability of these funds, as a control variable and calculated it using data from COMPUSTAT. *Company size* was included in the analysis because I expected a negative association between size and corporate entrepreneurship. It was measured as the logarithm of corporate assets, using data from the *Fortune 500*. *Past performance* was also considered because, when a company performs well, slack resources increase, which encourages entrepreneurial activity. I collected data from *Business Week*, COMPUSTAT, and *Fortune* on ROA, a major indicator of profitability, and calculated a three-year average. Also, because industries varied in their performance, I adjusted past performance data by subtracting a firm's major industry's performance from the firm's rating for the same period. I also controlled for *industry type*. Following Hitt and Ireland (1985), I classified the major industry of a firm (listed in the *Fortune* 500) as consumer nondurable (n = 40), consumer durable (n = 31), producer goods (n = 29), and capital goods (n = 27). Dummy codes were then assigned.

ANALYSIS AND RESULTS

Table 2 presents the means, standard deviations, and correlations among the study's variables. The means for outsider ratio and outsider ownership, executive ownership, total institutional ownership, debt-to-equity ratio, liquidity, and CEO duality are consistent with past research.

Hierarchical regression analysis was used to test the study's hypotheses. I entered the control variables first (step 1), then the independent variables (step 2), then the interaction terms (step 3). One interaction term was the cross product of the ratio of outsiders on a board and outsider stock ownership. The remaining interaction terms were formed using the cross products of technological opportunities and the study's independent variables, as reported in Table 3.

As Hypothesis 1 predicts, the outsider ratio was negatively associated with the three corporate entrepreneurship measures, all at $p < .05$. The results for Hypothesis 2 also showed that although outsider ownership had positive coefficients in the three regression equations, only the beta for venturing was significant ($p < .05$). Also, the coefficients for the interaction of outsider ratio and ownership were negative and insignificant in the three equations. The betas for the interaction terms were smaller than, but not significantly different from, those derived from the outsider ratio only; this finding supported Hypothesis 2.

The data in Table 3 also supported Hypothesis 3, as executive ownership was positively associated with the three corporate entrepreneurship measures (all at $p < .05$). Further, consistent with Hypothesis 4a, long-term institutional investment was positively and significantly associated with innovation ($p < .01$) and venturing ($p < .05$), but not with strategic renewal. Similarly, although short-term institutional investment was negatively associated with innovation ($p < .05$) and venturing ($p < .01$), it was not significantly associated with strategic renewal. These results partially supported Hypothesis 4b.

The results also supported Hypothesis 5. As Table 3 shows, the interaction of technological opportunities with the outsider ratio was significant in the three regression equations ($p < .01$), as was opportunities' interaction with outsider ownership ($p < .05$). The three-way interaction term crossing outsider ratio, outsider ownership, and technological opportunities was negative and insignificant in the three regressions. The interactions of technological opportunities with both executive ownership and long-term institutional ownership were positive and significant in the three equations. The interaction of technological opportunities with short-term institutional own-

TABLE 2
Descriptive Statistics and Correlations[a]

Variables	Mean	s.d.	1	2	3	4	5	6	7	8	9	10	11	12	13
1. Innovation	3.17	1.29													
2. Venturing	2.94	1.47	-.31												
3. Strategic renewal	2.87	1.73	.27	.29											
4. Outsider ratio	0.62	0.25	-.21	-.18	-.20										
5. Outsider ownership	0.03	0.04	.04	.06	.26	.26									
6. Executive ownership	7.13	11.58	.29	.25	.36	-.30	.11								
7. Long-term institutional ownership	15.11	10.89	.27	.22	.05	.31	.14	.16							
8. Short-term institutional ownership	20.83	17.61	-.29	-.33	.09	.21	.09	-.22	.29						
9. Debt-to-equity ratio	0.49	0.46	-.28	.19	-.23	.35	.23	.09	-.09	-.13					
10. Liquidity	2.13	0.66	.18	.19	.21	.03	-.05	.07	.05	.05	.09				
11. CEO duality	0.73	0.29	.11	.09	.14	-.16	.03	.13	-.19	-.21	.06	.09			
12. Perceived technological opportunities	3.01	1.21	.21	-.34	.19	.31	.14	.29	.19	.24	-.13	.13	.06		
13. Company size	6.07	9.14	.10	.15	-.12	.24	.29	-.34	.07	.14	.37	-.20	-.10	-.13	
14. Past ROA	7.91	5.12	.19	.23	.26	.10	.19	.14	.18	.23	-.21	.08	-.03	.29	.26

[a] Correlations greater than or equal to .18 are significant ($p < .05$); $n = 127$.

TABLE 3
Results of Hierarchical Regression Analysis[a]

Step	Variables	Innovation				Venturing				Renewal			
		β	R^2	ΔR^2	F	β	R^2	ΔR^2	F	β	R^2	ΔR^2	F
1	Control												
	Liquidity	.18*				.21*				.23*			
	Debt-to-equity ratio	-.11				-.23*				-.22*			
	CEO duality	.13				.15				.09			
	Company size	.08				.12				.13			
	Past ROA	.23*				.21*				.25*			
	Consumer nondurable	.19*				.10				.21*			
	Consumer durable	.07				.16				.07			
	Capital goods	-.11	.16		4.21**	.13				.15	.15		2.91*
2	Independent												
	Outsider ratio	-.25*				-.19*				-.27*			
	Outsider ownership	.11				.23*				.09			
	Executive ownership	.29*				.20*				.24*			
	Long-term institutional	.31**				.26*				.12			
	Short-term institutional	-.19*	.39	.23	9.53***	-.31*	.38	.17	13.81***	.09	.29	.14	6.01**
3	Interaction terms												
	Outsider ratio × outsider ownership	-.13				-.07				-.03			
	Outsider ratio × perceived technological opportunities	-.39***				-.30**				-.37**			
	Outsider ownership × perceived technological opportunities	.19*				.29*				.19*			
	Outsider ratio × outsider ownership × perceived technological opportunities	-.02				-.03				-.02			
	Executive ownership × perceived technological opportunities	.43***				.31**				.41**			
	Long-term institutional ownership × perceived technological opportunities	.39***				.33**				.21*			
	Short-term institutional ownership × perceived technological opportunities	-.37***	.49	.10	14.37***	-.41**				.29*	.42	.13	10.73***

*p < .05; **p < .01; ***p < .001.

ership had a negative and significant association with both innovation ($p <$ .01) and venturing ($p < .01$); however, its relationship with renewal was positive and significant.

Table 3 shows that of the control variables, liquidity and past ROA had positive and significant associations with corporate entrepreneurship. The debt-to-equity ratio was negatively and significantly associated with venturing and renewal and had a negative but insignificant association with innovation. CEO duality and company size were insignificant in the three regression equations. Finally, only the consumer nondurable group had positive associations with both innovation and renewal.

DISCUSSION

Review of Findings

The results of this study support the importance of corporate governance and ownership variables for explaining commitment to corporate entrepreneurship among the largest U.S. industrial corporations, the *Fortune* 500. Consistent with Hypothesis 1, the results show an inverse but significant association between the proportion of outside directors on a board and corporate entrepreneurship. These results support Baysinger and Hoskisson's (1990) suggestion that inside directors may be better positioned than outsiders to judiciously evaluate entrepreneurial activity. The results also support the conclusions of other researchers (e.g., Baysinger & Butler, 1985; Hill & Snell, 1988; Porter, 1992) who have noted that a high ratio of outsiders on a company's board may have unintended costs, such as low corporate entrepreneurship. One reason is the tendency of some outside directors to engage in free riding and to use financial (not strategic) controls. The results also raise a question about the merits of staffing boards primarily with outside directors, especially in view of the findings relating to Hypothesis 2.

The finding that ownership by outside directors may temper the negative association between outsider's representation and corporate entrepreneurship is consistent with Hypothesis 2. Outside directors' ownership may align their interests with those of other shareholders, encourage monitoring of managerial actions, and increase directors' interest in corporate entrepreneurship. As outside directors' ownership may mitigate the negative association of a high proportion of outsiders with corporate entrepreneurship, companies should consider providing incentives through stock ownership to outside directors. There are upper limits, however, to the potential impact of such stock ownership on the association between outsider representation on a board and corporate entrepreneurship, as evidenced by the negative signs of the interaction term in the three regression equations.

Another concern about outside directors' increased stock ownership is that it promotes control over these directors by a firm's CEO and other senior executives. In fact, following the publication of Cadbury's (1992) report, the United Kingdom prohibited outside directors from holding strong equity positions in their firms. This step was deemed necessary to reduce the prospect of CEOs controlling their boards. This problem is not currently serious in the United States, but if companies increase their use of stock ownership as a means of motivating outside directors, the independence and objectivity of these directors might be compromised.

Besides the declining value as a motivator of incentives through stock ownership, the lack of access to information on corporate entrepreneurship may continue to frustrate even those outside directors who own relatively large blocks of corporate stock. This difficulty may induce some outside directors to encourage managers to pursue a different form of entrepreneurial activity, one that centers on new market entry through venturing rather than on patient new product innovation. Thus, ownership by outsiders may promote acquisition activities rather than internal business and product development, the traditional focus of corporate entrepreneurship activities. Although the extent and implications of such a shift for company performance have not been fully studied, Hoskisson, Johnson, and Moesel (1994) suggested that outside ownership increased debt, which is usually associated with a high number of mergers, acquisitions, and restructurings. Clearly, if long-term pursuit of corporate entrepreneurship is sought, there is a need to reexamine the wisdom of using outside directors and offering them incentives in the form of stock ownership.

Consistent with Hypothesis 3, stock ownership by executives is positively associated with corporate entrepreneurship, which may reflect a closer alignment between the goals of executives and shareholders. Although the results support Jones and Butler's (1992) position, they contradict the insignificant associations between executive ownership and R&D spending Hill and Snell (1988, 1989) found. Perhaps executive ownership is more relevant in the case of corporate entrepreneurship, where managers may have great discretion in the decision-making process. By contrast, R&D allocations are usually monitored by the financial community, which may limit executives' willingness to reduce these investments.

Mixed support emerged for Hypotheses 4a and 4b. Long-term institutional ownership was positively and significantly associated with both innovation and venturing, but the coefficient for strategic renewal was positive and insignificant. Perhaps long-term institutional owners readily appreciate the need to use patient capital to redefine a company's business through innovation and venturing. Concurrently, these investors may view strategic renewal efforts as stopgap measures that do not improve a company's capacity to create long-term value.

A different pattern was observed for short-term institutional ownership, for which strategic renewal had a positive and insignificant beta, while both innovation and venturing had negative and significant betas. These results are consistent with those of Graves (1988), who found a negative association between institutional stock ownership and R&D investments. The present results also support the concerns expressed over the potential impact of short-term institutional investors on innovation and new business creation activities (National Academy of Engineering, 1992). Short-term investors may discourage innovation and venturing because these activities take a long time to pay off.

Combined, the results on Hypotheses 4a and 4b highlight the importance of separating the different types of institutional owners in order to better understand their associations with corporate entrepreneurship. Researchers should further explore the conditions under which investors are willing to exercise their powers and voice their displeasure with managers' inattention to entrepreneurship. By considering the size of institutional holdings, investment time horizons, and disposition to exercise their powers, researchers can identify the conditions under which institutional owners influence corporate entrepreneurship positively and negatively.

A key finding from this study is that perceived technological opportunities may significantly moderate the associations of corporate governance and ownership systems with corporate entrepreneurship. The results support Hypothesis 5 and show that two variables are positively and significantly associated with corporate entrepreneurship in industries with high technological opportunities: high levels of executive ownership and long-term institutional ownership. However, short-term institutional investors and a high proportion outsiders of board have negative and significant associations with entrepreneurial activity. These results indicate that some governance and ownership systems may inhibit corporate entrepreneurship more in industries with high technological opportunities. As predicted by the National Academy of Engineering (1992), transient capital may reduce the innovation and venturing components of corporate entrepreneurship. The same is also true for the increased representation of outside directors on a company's board, even when they have an ownership stake in the company. Finally, the significant, positive coefficient of the three-way interaction of short-term stitutional ownership, technological opportunity, and renewal indicates that short-term institutional investors may be more relevant for strategic renewal in stable environments. Overall, the results for Hypothesis 5 indicate a need to explicitly consider the influence of a firm's competitive setting on the design of its governance system and corporate entrepreneurship.

Managerial and scholarly implications. The results show that executive ownership of a company's stock is positively associated with corporate entrepreneurship. Thus, executives' incentives appear to make a significant difference in creating commitment to entrepreneurial activity. By providing incentives to managers in the form of increased stock ownership, boards can turn managers into owners and increase their support of such activity. To achieve this transformation, a portion of managers' compensation can be given in stock ownership.

Companies also need to reconsider their approach to improving board performance. They need to examine both the composition of a board and the incentives they offer outside directors. Incentives like stock ownership may somewhat mitigate the negative association between a high proportion of outside directors and corporate entrepreneurship. In particular, companies need to explore ways to enhance the motivation of their directors and foster their commitment to such activity. Rather than simply increasing the representation of particular groups of directors on a board, companies should explore other ways to encourage directors' attention to corporate entrepreneurship.

Although the growing power of institutional owners has been a source of concern among executives and public policy makers, the present results offer some hopeful news. Long-term institutional ownership is positively associated with both the innovation and venturing aspects of corporate entrepreneurship. Perhaps executives should work more closely with these investors to explain different initiatives and their potential contributions to value creation. Increased communication with institutional owners might also counter the negative association of short-term institutional investors with corporate entrepreneurship, a major source of concern in industries with high technological opportunities.

Replications with data from companies in other sectors of the U.S. economy are needed to establish the robustness of the present findings. This research would confirm whether governance and ownership systems impede corporate entrepreneurship more in industries with high technological opportunities. Researchers should consider conducting comparative studies of companies in high- and low-technology industries. If the current associations are corroborated, then future efforts directed as reforming corporate boards can be better guided by research findings.

Another area for future research is outside directors' supposed reliance on financial, rather than strategic, controls in evaluating corporate entrepreneurship. This proposition should be verified empirically, using explicit measures of different types of controls. Currently, the bulk of the literature on this issue is speculative and anecdotal.

Researchers should also identify different groups of institutional owners and determine their effect on the different dimensions of corporate entrepreneurship. For example, researchers can classify institutional investors in terms of their long-term staying power, defined as their ability to withstand the pressures resulting from stock market performance (Kochhar & David, 1996) and then examine the commitment of these investor groups to corporate entrepreneurship. Researchers should also distinguish activist from nonactivist institutional investors (Roe, 1994) and document differences between the two regarding corporate entrepreneurship. Understanding the motives and tactics of activist institutional investors should yield a richer appreciation of their effect on entrepreneurial activity. A model that identifies the conditions leading to activism and managerial responses to it would also advance scholarship in this area.

Today, corporate entrepreneurship is essential for ensuring corporate profitability and growth by enhancing a company's innovation, redefining its business concept, and renewing its operations. Nurturing entrepreneurial activities in established companies, however, requires interested management, patient capital, and enlightened investment policies. This study

1732   *Academy of Management Journal*   December

shows that corporate governance and ownership systems can affect corporate entrepreneurship efforts significantly, and this impact varies considerably between industries with low and high technological opportunities.

REFERENCES

Baysinger, B., & Butler, H. 1985. Corporate governance and the board of directors: Performance effects on changes in the board composition. *Journal of Law, Economics, and Organization*, 1: 101–124.

Baysinger, B., & Hoskisson, R. E. 1990. The composition of boards of directors and strategic control: Effects on corporate strategy. *Academy of Management Review*, 15: 72–87.

Baysinger, B. D., Kosnik, R. D., & Turk, T. A. 1991. Effects of board and ownership structure on corporate R&D strategy. *Academy of Management Journal*, 34: 205–214.

Block, Z., & MacMillan, I. 1993. *Corporate venturing*. Cambridge, MA: Harvard Business School Press.

Burgelman, R. 1983. A process model of internal corporate venturing in the diversified major firm. *Administrative Science Quarterly*, 28: 223–244.

Cadbury, A. 1992. *The financial aspects of corporate governance*. London: Committee on the Financial Aspects of Corporate Governance.

Chaganti, R., & Damanpour, F. 1991. Institutional ownership, capital structure, and firm performance. *Strategic Management Journal*, 12: 479–791.

Cochran, P. L., Wood, R. A., & Jones, T. B. 1985. The composition of boards of directors and incidence of golden parachutes. *Academy of Management Journal*, 28: 664–671.

Covin, J. G., & Slevin, D. P. 1991. A conceptual model of entrepreneurship as firm behavior. *Entrepreneurship Theory and Practice*, 16: 7–25.

Daily, C. M., & Dalton, D. R. 1992. The relationship between governance structure and corporate performance in entrepreneurial firms. *Journal of Business Venturing*, 7: 375–386.

Finkelstein, S., & D'Aveni, R. A. 1994. CEO duality as a double-edged sword: How boards of directors balance entrenchment avoidance and unity of command. *Academy of Management Journal*, 37: 1079–1108.

Franko, L. G. 1989. Global corporate competition: Who's winning, who's losing, and the R&D factor as one reason why. *Strategic Management Journal*, 10: 449–474.

Galbraith, J. 1973. *Designing complex organizations*. Reading, MA: Addison-Wesley.

Geroski, P. 1990. Innovation, technological opportunity, and market structure. *Oxford Economic Papers*, 42: 586–602.

Gilson, S. 1990. Bankruptcy, boards, banks, and blockholders. *Journal of Financial Economics*, 26: 355–387.

Graves, S. B. 1988. Institutional ownership and corporate R&D in the computer industry. *Academy of Management Journal*, 31: 417–428.

Guth, W. D., & Ginsberg, A. 1990. Guest editors' introduction: Corporate entrepreneurship. *Strategic Management Journal*, 11: 5–15.

Hansen, G. S., & Hill, C. W. L. 1991. Are institutional investors myopic? A time-series study of four technology-driven industries. *Strategic Management Journal*, 12: 1–16.

Hill, C. W. L., & Hoskisson, R. E. 1987. Strategy and structure in the multiproduct firm. *Academy of Management Review*, 12: 331–341.

Hill, C. W. L., Hitt, M. A., & Hoskisson, R. E. 1988. Declining U.S. competitiveness: Reflections on a crisis. *Academy of Management Executive,* 2: 51–60.

Hill, C. W. L., & Snell, S. A. 1988. External control, corporate strategy, and firm performance in research intensive industries. *Strategic Management Journal,* 9: 577–590.

Hill, C. W., & Snell, S. A. 1989. Effects of ownership structure and control on corporate productivity. *Academy of Management Journal,* 32: 25–46.

Hitt, M. A., & Ireland, R. D. 1985. Corporate distinctive competence, strategy, industry and performance. *Strategic Management Journal,* 6: 273–293.

Hitt, M. A., Hoskisson, R. E., Ireland, R. D., & Harrison, J. 1991. Effects of acquisitions on R&D inputs and outputs. *Academy of Management Journal,* 34: 693–706.

Hoskisson, R. E., & Hitt, M. A. 1994. *Downscoping: How to tame the diversified firm.* New York: Oxford University Press.

Hoskisson, R. E., Hitt, M. A., & Hill, C. W. L. 1991. Managerial risk taking in diversified firms: An evolutionary perspective. *Organization Science,* 2: 296–313.

Hoskisson, R. E., Hitt, M. A., & Hill, C. W. L. 1993. Managerial incentives and investment in R&D in large multiproduct firms. *Organization Science,* 4: 325–341.

Hoskisson, R. E., Johnson, R. A., & Moesel, D. D. 1994. Corporate divestiture intensity in restructuring firms: Effects of governance, strategy, and performance. *Academy of Management Journal,* 37: 1207–1251.

Jacobs, M. T. 1991. *Short-term America: The causes and cures of our business myopia.* Cambridge, MA: Harvard Business School Press.

Jensen, M., & Meckling, W. 1976. Theory of the firm: Managerial behavior, agency cost, and capital structure. *Journal of Financial Economics,* 3: 305–360.

Jones, A., Johnson, L., Butler, M., & Main, D. 1983. Apples and oranges: An empirical comparison of commonly used indices of interrater agreement. *Academy of Management Journal,* 26: 507–519.

Jones, G., & Butler, J. 1992. Managing internal corporate entrepreneurship: An agency theory perspective. *Journal of Management,* 18: 733–749.

Johnson, R., Hoskisson, R., & Hitt, M. 1993. Board of director involvement in restructuring: The effect importance of board versus managerial controls and characteristics. *Strategic Management Journal,* 14(special issue): 33–51.

Judge, W. Q., & Zeithaml, C. P. 1992. Institutional and strategic choice perspectives on board involvement in the strategic decision process. *Academy of Management Journal,* 35: 766–794.

Keats, B., & Hitt, M. 1988. A causal model of linkages among environmental dimensions, macro organizational characteristics, and performance. *Academy of Management Journal,* 31: 570–598.

Kochhar, R., & David, P. 1996. Institutional investors and firm innovation: A test of competing hypotheses. *Strategic Management Journal,* 17: 73–84.

Kosnik, R. D. 1987. Greenmail: A study of board performance in corporate governance. *Administrative Science Quarterly,* 32: 163–183.

Kuratko, D. F., Montagno, R. V., & Hornsby, J. S. 1990. Developing an entrepreneurial assessment instrument for an effective corporate entrepreneurial environment. *Strategic Management Journal,* 11: 49–58.

Laverty, K. J. 1993. How valid are R&D measures in empirical tests of "short-termism"? *Academy of Management Best Papers Proceedings:* 27–31.

1734   *Academy of Management Journal*   December

Lumpkin, G. T., & Dess, G. G. 1996. Clarifying the entrepreneurial orientation construct and linking it to performance. *Academy of Management Review*, 21: 135–172.

Malatesta, P., & Walling, R. 1988. Poison pill securities: Stockholder wealth profitability and ownership structure. *Journal of Financial Economics*, 20: 374–376.

March, J. G., & Shapira, Z. 1987. Managerial perspectives on risk and risk taking. *Management Science*, 33: 1404–1418.

Miller, D. 1983. Entrepreneurship correlates in three types of firms. *Management Science*, 29: 770–791.

National Academy of Engineering. 1992. *Time horizons and technology investments.* Washington, DC: National Academy Press.

Porter, M. E. 1992. Capital disadvantage: America's failing capital investment system. *Harvard Business Review*, 70: 65–82.

Roe, M. J. 1994. *Strong managers, weak owners.* Princeton, NJ: Princeton University Press.

Sathe, V. 1989. Fostering entrepreneurship in the large, diversified firm. *Organizational Dynamics*, 18(1): 20–32.

Stopford, J. M., & Baden-Fuller, C. 1994. Creating corporate entrepreneurship. *Strategic Management Journal*, 15: 521–536.

Tootelian, D. H., & Gaedeke, R. M. 1987. *Fortune* 500 list revisited 12 years later: Still an endangered species for academic research? *Journal of Business Research*, 15: 359–363.

Zahra, S. A. 1991. Predictors and financial outcomes of corporate entrepreneurship: An exploratory study. *Journal of Business Venturing*, 6: 259–285.

Zahra, S. A. 1993. Environment, corporate entrepreneurship and financial performance: A taxonomic approach. *Journal of Business Venturing*, 8: 319–340.

Zahra, S. A. 1995. Corporate entrepreneurship and company performance: The case of management leveraged buyouts. *Journal of Business Venturing*, 10: 225–247.

Zahra, S. A., & Covin, J. 1995. Contextual influences on the corporate entrepreneurship-company performance relationship in established firms: A longitudinal analysis. *Journal of Business Venturing*, 10: 43–58.

Zahra, S. A., & Pearce, J. II 1989. Boards of directors and corporate financial performance: A review and integrative model. *Journal of Management*, 15: 291–344.

APPENDIX

Corporate Entrepreneurship

As reported in the text and in Table 1, 14 items were used to measure corporate entrepreneurship and factor analysis yielded three factors. Three approaches were then used to validate these measures.

1. An overall index was developed by summing scores on these items and then dividing the total by 7 ($\alpha = .71$). This index, developed by Miller (1983), consisted of the following items: "Our company has introduced many new products or services over the past three years," "Our company has made many dramatic changes in the mix of its products and services over the past three years," "Our company has emphasized making major innovations in its products and services over the past three years," "Over the past three years, this company has shown a strong proclivity for high-risk projects (with chances of very high return)," "This company has emphasized taking bold, wide-ranging action in positioning itself and its products (services) over the past three years," "This company has shown a strong commitment to research and development (R&D), technological leadership, and innovation," and "This company has followed strategies that allow it to exploit opportunities in its external environment."

2. An objective corporate entrepreneurship indicator was constructed using the three-year average on three variables, as follows: (a) *R&D spending as a percentage of sales.* Data were collected from the 1988–90 volumes of the *Business Week Corporate R&D Scoreboard.* Because of the uncertain payoff associated with these activities, R&D spending is a widely used measure of corporate innovation and risk taking (Hoskisson et al., 1993). (b) *Number of new products introduced to market.* Like R&D, product innovation involves considerable risks, nearly 80 percent of all new products fail upon market introduction. New products enhance a company's ability to serve current and new customers or penetrate new markets, thus fueling both growth and profitability. New products are a major indicator of corporate entrepreneurship (Zahra, 1993). CEOs were asked to indicate "the total number of new and modified products your company introduced to the market over the past three years." I then collected three years of data for 41 companies (about 30 percent of the sample) from annual reports and trade publications. Survey and archival data were significantly correlated ($r = .72$, $p < .001$). (c) *Percentage of revenues from businesses that did not exist three years earlier.* Executives provided data on the percentage of revenues generated by divisions or strategic business units created within the last three years. This measure captures a firm's involvement in creating new business and venturing activities (Block & MacMillan, 1993; Zahra, 1993). Data were available for 113 companies. To validate the survey measure, I collected data for 37 companies (32.7 percent of the responding companies) from annual reports and COMPUSTAT. The two sources were significantly correlated ($r = .74$, $p < .01$).

3. I also examined the interrater reliability of the three corporate entrepreneurship factors using data from two executives, as reported in the text.

Technological Opportunities

This index consisted of the following items: "Opportunities for product innovation are abundant in our major industry," "Opportunities for technological innovation are abundant in our major industry," "Spending on research and development (R&D) is higher in our major industry than in most industries," and "Opportunities for major technological breakthroughs are abundant in our major industry." The average score on these items was entered into the regression analyses. The items followed a five-point response format (5 = strongly agree, 1 = strongly disagree).

To ensure valid results, I also conducted the analysis using a firm's major industry's past three-year average R&D spending. The results were similar to those found when the survey-based index was used. Hence, only the results from the overall technological opportunities index are reported.

Shaker A. Zahra is a professor of strategic management at the Department of Management, College of Business Administration, Georgia State University. His research centers on corporate governance, corporate innovation and entrepreneurship, and the strategic use of technology.

B
Championing Corporate Entrepreneurship Activities

[23]

It is in the nature of a large organization to oppose upsetting change and innovation, yet change and innovation there must be. The answer to the problem is . . . .

Champions for
Radical New Inventions

By Donald A. Schon

• Why do small companies, large corporations, military laboratory employees, and independent inventors find it so difficult to sell really new inventions to the military services?

• What is the nature of resistance to innovation in military and business organizations?

• What does experience show to be the requirements of successful technical innovation?

• What steps can management take to ensure that the necessary development work will go into promising proposals for radical new products and processes?

The military services hold up to the business community an enormous and only slightly distorted mirror in which patterns surrounding technical innovation stand out clearly. Goaded by the threat of competition and a perceived need for corporate growth, industry seeks new products. In order to "win the arms race" and "meet the Soviet threat," the military seeks new weapons systems. Both depend on technical innovation and lean on technical resources for producing change. Both are caught in the gap between the wish for deliberate and systematic methods of innovation and the uncertainty and risk inherent in this activity. In both, there is a discrepancy between formal organization for innovation and the informal organization and process by which it is sometimes accomplished (though in the military, perhaps because it is a superorganization, the informal routes are more clearly visible).

In this article I shall examine the significance of the resources for invention that are being wasted and the reasons (many of them all too human and understandable) that this waste continues to go on. Then I shall turn to the measures we can take in business and government to cope with the problem. The first and most essential step is recognizing resistance to change and accepting it rather than "driving it underground." There are a series of measures, one of the most important of which has to do with the "product champion" concept, that we can take to promote the development of promising new inventions.

Much of the information and thinking in this discussion is based on a study conducted by Arthur D. Little, Inc., under a contract administered by the National Inventors Council and supported by the military services.

Significant Resource

In the traditional sense, "inventor" means an amateur, untrained, and independent genius of the kind supposedly typified by men like Thomas A. Edison and Samuel F. Morse. Whether or not technical heroes ever did fit this mold, it is clear that they do not fit it now. The growing technical complexity of military and industrial life has made it impossible for individuals to invent effectively without extensive technical experience. Moreover, in our culture today, the official idealization of inventors masks an unofficial contempt. "Inventor" is very nearly a dirty word. With few exceptions, industry and the military alike tend more and more to protect themselves from the apparent dangers of deal-

77

ing with individuals as individuals; and as a result the individuals who might once have called themselves "inventors" are now forming small businesses or filtering into the ranks of large corporations.

For these reasons, "inventors" in the old sense are not the resource we ought to be interested in here. We should be concerned, rather, with innovative, technically trained individuals who have proved their ability to develop new products and processes and who have done so as individuals, without organizational support. We find these people operating as professional independents and in a variety of organizational settings: universities, research institutes, small and large corporations, and the military itself. What is more, our concern should be with radical innovation, such as Robert H. Goddard's early work on rockets and Sir Frank Whittle's work on the jet engine. When it comes to this kind of innovation (which is always easier to identify in retrospect than in advance), a man's residence in an organization does not guarantee him organizational support.

From this point on, when I refer to "inventors" and "inventions," I shall use the terms in the ways just described.

Number of Inventors

How many such men are there; how much have they contributed? This question can be answered only indirectly and by approximation. On the basis of our own estimates and interviews with technical people in military laboratories and large corporations, heads of small businesses, and professional independent inventors themselves, a good guess is that today there are several thousand independent inventors in the United States. To mention some of the pieces of evidence gathered in our study:

• The United States Patent Office was able to give the National Inventors Council a list of 500 inventors who had accumulated many useful patents, working independently. Jacob Schmookler estimates that 40% of the patents currently granted are assigned to such individuals.[1]

• There are about 310,000 small businesses in the United States ("small" by the Small Business Association's standards — less than 500 employees and less than $10,000,000 in annual sales).

• We interviewed 42 small companies which, through technically trained individuals in their employ, had developed an impressive array of new products and processes.

We have no way of estimating the number of independent innovators working without organizational support *in* military laboratories and large corporations.

Value of Contribution

How important a role have such people played in innovation? Evidence for their actual and potential contributions is, as might be expected, elusive. Nevertheless, several different kinds of evidence have been gathered:

❧ Although patents are a doubtful sign of technical innovation, patent studies have been made which are at least indicative. Jacob Schmookler's study covering patents granted during the last decade reveals that a surprisingly high percentage were assigned to individuals working as individuals, rather than to organizations. Indeed, 40% to 60% of the patentees worked outside the organized research teams of industrial laboratories. And John Jewkes, David Sawers, and Richard Stillerman made a study which showed that between 1936 and 1955, in both the United States and Great Britain, the percentage of patents issued to individuals, as opposed to corporations, remained between 40% and 50%.[2]

❧ In a paper presented to the Joint Economic Committee on September 24, 1959, Professor Daniel Hamberg of the University of Maryland stated that 12 of the 18 inventions he had examined resulted from the work of independent individuals and relatively small companies. The authors, in their *The Sources of Invention,* show that 40 of 61 important inventions made since 1900 were the product of independent innovators, working alone, unaffiliated with any industrial laboratory. Another 6 were the product of investigation conducted in small- to medium-size organizations. Their list cuts across technical disciplines and industrial areas, ranging from Bakelite and cellophane to safety razors and ball-point pens.[3]

❧ In the course of our study, we assembled a list of inventions important for military uses, made within roughly the past 50 years. Individuals working without organizational support were either entirely responsible for these inventions or played a major role in their evolution:

> Jet engine — Sir Frank Whittle
> Gyrocompass — H. Anschütz-Kaempfe
> Helicopter — Igor I. Sikorsky
> Rockets — Robert H. Goddard

[1] "Inventors Past and Present," *Review of Economics and Statistics,* August 1957, p. 321.
[2] *The Sources of Invention* (New York, St. Martin's Press, 1959), p. 105.
[3] Ibid., pp. 72, 73.

Many varieties of automatic guns — e.g., the
Lewis gun
Suspension tanks — George Christie
Doron body armor — General Georges F.
Doriot
Noiseless and flashless machine guns —
Stanley Lovell
Cryotron — Dudley Buck
Atomic submarine — Admiral Hyman G.
Rickover
Sidewinder missile — William B. McLean
Project Astron — Nicholas C. Christofilos
Stainless steel — Elwood Haynes
Titanium — W. J. Kroll

Bear in mind that many of these developments,
as well as a number of others which could have
been included, occurred *after* the beginning of the
organized research and development which has
characterized the last 50 years.

It is clear, then, that in recent times individuals working without organizational support
have been responsible for an extraordinarily high
percentage of important, radical commercial developments. In spite of the problems in contributing to the military, they have also been responsible for a number of significant military
changes. Also, these individuals have shown
themselves to be particularly well equipped
to do innovative exploratory work and to do
it quickly in comparison to the research teams
of large corporations. However, as we shall see
presently, much of their potential value to business and the military has been wasted.

What are the reasons for this waste? Let us
begin with a look at the military screening offices, then turn to companies and individuals
who are doing (or might be doing) defense
work. Later we can examine the interesting
parallels with commercial innovation.

Failure to Get Through

Within the military, there is official recognition of the need for technical innovation. Military research and development chiefs and civilian advisers emphasize the need for radically
new developments, for "ideas," and for more exploration. They are apt to express this need in
terms of "meeting the Soviet threat," "winning
the Cold War," "defending the Free World,"
and the like — phrases which play for the military very much the same role that "growth" plays
for the industrial corporation.

The formal channel by which the ideas of

individuals may enter the military is the military screening offices. The major research and
development agencies of each of the three services have such offices, as do major operating
groups like the Army Ordnance Corps and individual military laboratories like the Army Sig-
nal Corps Laboratories. The function of these
agencies is to receive and screen the ideas of
individuals, inside and outside the military, and
to pass on to appropriate technical personnel
those ideas which seem to have most merit.

How much innovation goes through this channel? We interviewed 14 men from 7 screening
offices which receive from 40 to 2,000 ideas a
month. The chief question asked of each man
was whether he could identify an invention
submitted through his office and later used by
the military. *In not one case could he do so.*

For this reason we were led to conclude that
as a means of helping the military to use resources of invention which are not now adequately used, these screening offices are virtually a hindrance. They can be best understood
as a wall, rather than as a screen. They protect
the main body of military R & D from the dis-
turbance of outside inventors and inventions;
they are a device for maintaining good public
relations.

Many of the men we interviewed were perfectly open about this. They had long ago concluded that inventors may as well not submit
inventions to the military services. They pointed to their own problems: cuts in budget, too
few personnel, overlap and repetition of function within and among the services, and difficulties in getting feedback on ideas from the working laboratories. And although these men are
charged officially with a constructive function,
they work under conditions that permit them to
perform only a secondary, defensive one.

In brief, there are significant resources of innovation for which there is expressed need, and
there is a screening organization whose main
function is to serve as a buffer against them.
This is not the simple case of a large organization's discrimination against certain individuals.
The case is much more that of a complicated
social tangle in which people on all sides of the
issue are caught, in spite of their best efforts.

Why Inventors Fail

The problems of contributing to the military
are experienced in different ways by individuals

in varying settings. Let us take a look at four groups — people in the military, large and small business, and independent inventors.

Federal Employees

Individuals in military laboratories, who are inventive and technically competent, have a unique value as a resource. They know what the technical problems are. They have access to prior art in their fields. They are subject to minimum security restrictions. And, unlike individuals in other settings, they are already organized as a resource. It is particularly significant, therefore, that where figures are available, military screening offices report that the rate of rejection of ideas submitted internally through formal channels is as great as the rate of rejection of ideas submitted from the outside.

Some of the reasons for this came out in our interviews with technical personnel in military laboratories. In spite of the fact that many of these people had records of outstanding technical contribution, there was a general sense of discouragement about the possibility of contribution apart from assigned work. The men gave several reasons for this attitude:

(1) In their view self-initiated innovation was not expected of them. And where their function was not limited to testing or administration of contracts, their superiors seemed to fear that self-initiated work would distract them from assigned tasks.

(2) While there was a civilian award program for self-initiated contributions, substantial awards were rarely given. (An exception was the $25,000 award given for the development of the Sidewinder missile at the Navy's China Lake Laboratory.)

(3) Most important of all, discouraging delays were encountered when the men attempted to go through formal channels. This they attributed to a "reverse natural selection" among technical civil service personnel. Relatively low salaries tended to drive many good innovative technical men out of government work, and the dedicated inventors who stayed on had to cope with the remainder — many of whom come into positions of responsibility only through seniority. One laboratory experimented with an "Operation Blue Sky" in order to solicit new technical ideas. But the ideas submitted were reviewed by the same men who were believed to have blocked innovation in the past, and the experiment produced nothing but frustration.

Small Business

In the case of small business, many innovators come from universities and large corporations precisely in order to be freer and more effective in technical innovation. They tend to be men who show unusual enthusiasm for new technical developments and who, by and large, have demonstrated an unusual ability to move quickly from new technical ideas to prototype development. But they do not contribute significantly to the military for these reasons:

(1) Many technically based small companies have not even attempted to gain military R & D contracts. They attribute this to the unprofitability of such contracts, inability to capitalize on later production contracts, the difficulty and cost of selling R & D to the government, and competition with large corporations.

(2) Relatively few small businesss are successful when they attempt to gain technical development contracts with the military, and the successful ones tend to conform to a pattern. Thus —

(a) They gain contracts in a specialized technical area in which one or two of their staff members have considerable technical prestige.

(b) They have a man (or two) in top management experienced in dealing with the military.

(c) They either bid on contracts where the technical requirement is already clearly recognized by the military, or they sponsor their own development work and apply to the military for optimization contracts.

(d) In general, they do not make money on such contracts; they are lucky to break even.

All of this suggests that, in spite of efforts by the military and the Small Business Administration to increase the small business share of R & D contracts, there is still a resource of technically trained innovative individuals in small firms throughout the country whose contributions the military is not getting. This is particularly true of technical needs that the military has not yet clearly recognized and of small companies lacking the qualifications mentioned above.

Big Business

Large corporations are entirely distinct from individuals without organizational support. But the large corporation's advantages in approaching the military — its proven name, its large sales force, its capital, its ability to carry out production contracts — apply only to projects officially sanctioned by top management. Innovative, technically trained individuals within a corporation frequently have technical ideas that never get official sanction. Ideas of this kind may not look to the top management like a source of long-range profit, they may not seem to have commercial application, or they may even lie outside the corporation's pattern of technical growth. And yet they may be of great value to the military. To illustrate:

During World War II, technical staff members of a large corporation proposed water-filled protective capsules for pilots of high-speed aircraft and a new kind of aircraft thermometer. Both ideas were rejected at the time and later produced successfully elsewhere. Most technical directors of large corporations are familiar with similar cases.

Inevitably, corporate managers make some mistakes in judging the value of a proposed development for the corporation, and in many more cases they correctly judge as inappropriate for them a development which might be of great value to the military. The originator of such a development must either sell the idea "uphill" in his own organization; or he must sell it essentially as an individual to the military. The double obstacle is usually insuperable. And, what is more, the technical man usually has no incentive to overcome it. He will have signed away his patent rights, so that he cannot profit from them. He is not eligible for the civilian award program. If his project succeeds, he is likely to gain some status and prestige. But if it fails, he may very well suffer for having wasted time and money.

Independent Operators

Independent inventors constitute a special case in that their problems in relating to large organizations, both in the military and in private business, are classic.

First, there are difficulties inherent in the relation itself. Witness, for instance, the mutually frustrating, but finally successful, efforts of Alexander Zarchin to interest the Israeli government in his salt-water conversion process, and the mutual harassment that characterized the interaction of many inventors in one U.S. industry — an interaction which in the case of at least three major inventors (Rudolph Diesel, Wallace H. Carothers, and William G. Armstrong) ended tragically.

In the case of the U.S. military, this relationship has certain special features. For example, each of the services views itself as being harassed at present by one or two voluble inventors, skillful in appeal to Congressmen, who have made that service their particular target. Unfortunate-

ly for R & D administrators in each of the services, the word "inventor" is apt to conjure up an image of their particular tormentor.

What makes the situation even more delicate is that these men cannot easily be dismissed. There are the stories of Professor Robert H. Goddard who tried in the 1930's, for the most part unsuccessfully, to interest the U.S. military in rocketry; of George Christie, inventor of the suspension system for tanks — rejected by the U.S. Army, later adopted successfully by the Russians; and of Nicholas C. Christofilos, "the crazy Greek" who turned up with Project Astron.

The difficulty with these rare geniuses is that they can be recognized easily only in retrospect, never in prospect. You never know for certain that your present-day tormentor, whom you *think* is a crank, may not turn out to be another Goddard, another Christie, or another Christofilos.

Furthermore, the inventor himself may often show considerable aggressiveness, not to say eccentricity, in his dealings with the military. In many cases, his motives appear to be primarily to show up the professional military man, the professional scientist, or the professional engineer. He may present his invention so aggressively as to suggest that he is aiming not at having it accepted but at being able to complain of its unfair rejection.

At best, the preliminary judgment of new technical developments is precarious, particularly for men who do not have great technical sophistication in the field in question. Often the technical administrator must base his judgments on the soundness of the man at least as much as on the promise of the development itself. And when the man appears in sneakers and an open shirt, when he behaves queerly, or when he refuses (moved by his own perhaps legitimate and perhaps excessive fears about protection of his idea) to reveal the principle of his invention until he has been paid, he makes it extremely difficult for the military decision-maker to act favorably toward him.

While these difficulties are sharpest for the men who call themselves inventors, they extend generally to all kinds of individuals mentioned earlier. For the military, feeling that it has been burned so frequently in its dealings with individual inventors, tends to apply its defensive attitude to *all* "organizationless" individuals. Thus, we are confronted here by a vicious circle of protection and aggression, practiced by both parties.

Need to Resist Change

So far, the complicated social tangle responsible for the record of the military screening offices has been presented mainly from the side of the would-be contributors. But there is another side as well. And here we find striking parallels between military and commercial organizations.

"Normal" Opposition

Individuals approaching the military tend to be inattentive to the military administrator's problems. These problems make it difficult for him to invest in radically new technical developments for which there is no obvious and immediate requirement — especially when these are at the "idea" stage and are to be undertaken by individuals working without organizational support. These problems have to do, in part, with the so-called "weapons systems" approach which characterizes much of the military's technical development work:

"To ensure that no time, money, or effort will be wasted on blind alleys, almost all of the planning is done in terms of the end products that are supposed to emerge from the program — the weapon systems. Before any major project is begun, the planners painstakingly figure out what performance characteristics the weapon system is supposed to have and the technological innovations it will contain. The development program is spelled out stage by stage and then reviewed by numerous agencies within the armed services, by special committees, and by the staff of the Assistant Secretary of Defense for Research and Engineering. After the program is under way, progress is monitored at every step." [4]

Within this sort of approach, certain general technical routes to the goal are chosen. "Technical problems" are problems in implementing these routes. A military technical administrator operating within such a system cannot easily shift his attention to radical technical ideas not obviously related to his requirements, and so he finds it even more difficult to invest in risky individuals who will not be able to carry their innovations into production later on.

There is an even more general sort of resist-

[4] Burton Klein, "A Radical Proposal for R & D," *Fortune*, May 1958, p. 112.

ance to radical technical change. Elting Morison describes it elegantly in his study of the introduction to the Navy of continuous-aim firing (a new combat-tested method, presenting major advantages over old ones, had been rejected by Navy officials until President Theodore Roosevelt intervened):

"The Navy is not only an armed force — it is a society. In the forty years following the Civil War, this society had been forced to accommodate itself to a series of technological changes. . . . These changes wrought extraordinary changes in ship design, and therefore in the concepts of how ships were to be used; that is, in fleet tactics and even in naval strategy. . . . To these numerous innovations, producing as they did a spreading disorder throughout a service with heavy commitments to formal organization, the Navy responded with grudging pain. It is wrong to assume, as civilians frequently do, that this blind reaction to technological change springs exclusively from some causeless Bourbon distemper that invades the military mind. There is a sounder and more attractive base. The opposition, where it occurs, of the soldier and the sailor to such change springs from the normal human instinct to protect oneself and more especially one's way of life. Military organizations are societies built around and upon the prevailing weapon systems. Intuitively and quite correctly the military man feels that a change in weapons portends a change in the arrangements of his society." [5]

What Morison characterizes as the "normal human instinct" to oppose technological change is as true of the military today as it was in Theodore Roosevelt's time.

Justified Ambivalence

We come now to a most important point. Resistance to change is not only normal but in some ways even desirable. An organization totally devoid of resistance to change would fly apart at the seams. It *must* be ambivalent about radical technical innovation. It *must* both seek it out and resist it. Because of commitments to existing technology and to forms of social organization associated with it, management *must* act against the eager acceptance of new technical ideas, even good ones. Otherwise, the technical organization would be perpetually and fruitlessly shifting gears.

This is true in the military and also in almost all walks of private industry. As a matter of

[5] "A Case Study of Innovation," *Engineering and Science*, April 1950.

fact, most corporations are, if anything, *more* intensively defensive than the military. Taking the case of proposals from outside the organization first, only a few companies have maintained a tradition of receptiveness to such ideas. For in addition to sharing with the military reasons like those mentioned, many companies are afraid of being sued. Because some companies have had to pay damages to inventors, most companies have built up elaborate legal defenses. And because some companies have stolen ideas from inventors, many would-be inventors have become gun-shy.

But the most interesting analogies refer to inside, rather than to outside, innovation. Here, too, most large corporations share the military's ambivalence over radical proposals. On the one hand, there is official enthusiasm for growth, expansion, diversification, progressiveness, getting ahead of the competition, and maintaining share of market — all backed up by the axiom that those who do not forge ahead fall behind, as well as by the *Alice in Wonderland* notion that you must run very hard even to stand still.

There is plenty of reality behind this axiom, as witnessed by the fate of many sleepy industries tied to outmoded products and processes. (I seriously wonder, however, if growth is *always* required for corporate health and whether new products are *always* the means to salvation.) The fact stands, nevertheless, that radical product innovation means radical changes in all phases of the business — new technologies, new product techniques, new channels of distribution, and perhaps even a new conception of the market.

Novelty in these areas challenges accepted ways of doing things and long-established skills. It may throw a company, including top management, into areas where it feels inept and uninformed. Also, as in Morison's example of continous-aim firing, changes in technology tend to carry with them major changes in social organization, threatening established hierarchies, undermining the security of positions based on old products.

Moreover, the more radical the product innovation, the higher, in general, the cost of developing it. And this cost curve tends to rise sharply after the preliminary work in which the first models are built and the first market concepts are achieved. In fact, the whole process is marked by increasing risk and takes place in a context where most new product efforts fail. It is not surprising, in view of these tendencies, that a ground swell of covert resistance to change comes into conflict with official enthusiasm for it.

The pernicious part of this problem for both the military and industry is not the resistance to change, but the failure to recognize it. Here again, the rule applies to almost all types of organizations.

In the case of the military, resistance is masked by official assumptions to the effect that the services are wholeheartedly in favor of technical innovation in weapons systems and accept or reject all new ideas objectively, strictly on their merits. These assumptions conflict with reality and mislead potential innovators. For they go hand in hand with other assumptions. It is held, for example, that "civilian resources of invention are ready to be tapped" — that is, solutions to urgent technical problems are there for the taking, in the form of already worked out developments. If this is so, it is only prudent to reject solutions which have not yet been fully developed — and this, of course, includes most ideas submitted to the military.

In short, official assumptions, masking what is often legitimate resistance to change, drive that resistance underground, as in the case of the idea-screening operation itself. Once underground, this resistance to change goes out of control. Thus, the question of its legitimacy never comes up, and potential contributors to the services are bewildered by the discrepancy between words and action.

In industry, too, once resistance to change goes underground, it becomes capable of destroying most product innovation. Underground resistance paves the way for disguised defenses against change. In screening new ideas, many large corporations employ formal committees which are, in effect, buffers against new ideas. Assumptions are found to the effect that new ideas are wholeheartedly desired and are evaluated objectively, strictly on their merits — together with the further assumption that new ideas should be fully developed and ready for plucking. For instance:

In some large companies, the "new idea forms" which must be filled out by innovators require a fullness and precision of detail impossible early in the life of a new product idea. Such screening mechanisms require that each idea be developed before support is given for its development; they have the effect either of discouraging submission of new ideas or of forcing development work underground.

Pattern of Success

Despite the complicated buffers and screens I have described, innovation does take place in government and industry. Radical inventions do find acceptance, and the fact that they do, and the reasons that they do, are tremendously important. Since the military is such a superb case in point, let us take its experience first.

Developments like McLean's Sidewinder missile and Rickover's atomic submarine do not fit the pattern of orderly presentation of promising technical ideas to official judges, favorable objective evaluation, and then orderly marshaling of technical resources for development. These histories look more like crusades or military campaigns, with overtones of fifth-column activity and guerrilla warfare. They present clear illustrations of four major themes.

1. *At the outset, the idea encounters sharp resistance.*

Like Goddard's work on rockets, Whittle's work on the jet engine, and virtually every other significant military technical development, the Sidewinder and the atomic submarine at first were met with indifference and in some cases active resistance from military officials. These innovations appeared to run counter to the most sensible and established technical commitments. They looked expensive and unfeasible.

2. *Next, the idea receives active and vigorous promotion.*

In spite of the myth that valid technical ideas do not need internal sales, it is characteristic of successful technical innovation within the military that the new idea requires and receives active promotion. Often, as in Morison's description of the introduction of continuous-aim firing, there is a division of labor as to invention and promotion. In that instance, the inventor was not equally talented as a promoter, and so a second figure emerged who was able to carry the fight for its introduction and development into the highest Navy circles. In our own time, Admiral Rickover's skill in defending and promoting his ideas is legendary. Techniques for promoting new technical ideas are a matter of serious concern, even at the highest military

levels, as shown by the use for this purpose of outside publication and appeal to Congress.

3. *For the introduction, promotion, and development of these ideas, their proponents make use of the informal, rather than the official, military system.*

In the early stages of development, when the idea was still in its infancy, the Sidewinder was not funded through official contracts from any of the Navy bureaus, but from the small sums detoured from official programs. Only when enough work had been done to show the strength of the idea did it fall into official contract channels. The use of such "bootlegged" research funds is only one example of the use of the informal military network. In many instances ideas now under development or test were submitted originally through personal contracts; in the matter of technical development, particularly across departmental lines, a network of good personal contacts is a cherished resource. The buffering function of the official screening offices virtually forces such a network into existence.

4. *Typically, one man emerges as champion of the idea.*

Many people do know of Goddard, Whittle, Rickover, and McLean. But in the case of less famous developments, for example, the Navy's "Ribbon in the Sky" and the introduction of frangible bullet firing as a training method in World War II, individuals also emerged as champions. There is nothing incidental or exceptional about this happening. Where radical innovation is concerned, the emergence of a champion is required. Given the underground resistance to change described earlier, the new idea either finds a champion *or dies.*

Essentially, the champion must be a man willing to put himself on the line for an idea of doubtful success. He is willing to fail. But he is capable of using any and every means of informal sales and pressure in order to succeed.

No ordinary involvement with a new idea provides the energy required to cope with the indifference and resistance that major technical change provokes. It is characteristic of champions of new developments that they identify with the idea as their own, and with its promotion as a cause, to a degree that goes far beyond the requirements of their job. In fact, many display persistence and courage of heroic quality. For a number of them the price of failure is professional suicide, and a few become martyrs to the championed idea.

All of these requirements apply to commercial organizations as well as to the military. As just one example, Arthur K. Watson has testified to the importance of the third condition at IBM:

"The disk memory unit, the heart of today's random access computer, is not the logical outcome of a decision made by IBM management. It was developed in one of our laboratories as a bootleg project — over the stern warning from management that the project had to be dropped because of budget difficulties. A handful of men ignored the warning. They broke the rules. They risked their jobs to work on a project they believed in." [6]

Product Champions

But perhaps the most challenging part of the pattern described, at least for corporate executives, is the product-champion concept. How can it be made to work (yet not work so well that the organization is in chaos)?

To begin, it is clear that the product champion must have considerable power and prestige in the organization; otherwise he will not have the freedom to play his role. He must know and know how to use the company's informal system of relationships. Also, his interests must cut across the special interests (technology, marketing, production, and finance) which are essential to the product's or the process's development.

But attention to these requirements has a curiously futile ring to it. For one thing, it is extremely difficult *in practice* for top management to admit the need for such a man, since the implication in doing so is that something is wrong with what is euphemistically called the organization's "climate for creativity." Moreover, once the need is admitted, what can be done about it? Is management to bring in individuals whose overt function is to disrupt the company order which has been so carefully built up over the years? And, if it is to do so, what evidence is there that product champions can be selected and fostered?

In fact, there is some evidence that these men can*not* be hired and "developed" the way some others can. In more than one case, com-

panies have brought in men who were specially chosen to initiate radical product change; but since these men were chosen, in part, for their thick-skinned aggressiveness, they succeeded in alienating others on whom they depended, even to the point of ensuring failure. In still other cases, companies brought into this new product role men who were well received within the organization but who lacked the aggressive, risk-taking properties of the product champion, and failed for the opposite reasons.

Nevertheless, there have been instances in which product champions have been successfully introduced from outside, or recognized and supported within, a company. This kind of activity has occurred in at least two different ways:

(1) Management resorts not to sweeping across-the-board change, but to a model for change. It sets up a pilot operation staffed by only a few men but capable of carrying ideas through preliminary development and promoting them vigorously in the informal channels of the organization. This pilot operation can be headed by a man selected because he has the characteristics of the product champion described previously, with the exception of overt aggressiveness, which often is not necessary. The function of the operation is to provide a model of product innovation, small at first, but capable of taking root and spreading.

(2) The company's management makes the decision to adapt to its new technology and to the product champions who accompany that technology, rather than to force innovation into the mold of the established organization. Such a decision crucially affects the company's policy of corporate growth and diversification, since it does not require that new products mesh with existing means of production and distribution. Essentially, it gives support to certain product champions as entrepreneurs, allowing them to push their product through from beginning to end, and establishing a new division for the resulting business (that division need be only loosely related to the existing corporate structure).

More often than not, the champions are drawn from within the organization. They are given freedom to take a technical, production, marketing, and management view of their new product — in effect, to approach its development as though they were setting up a small business with corporate funding and support. They are held responsible for the success of that business, in turn, as though they were an independent corporate entity. The corporation resulting from consistent pursuit of such a policy has the aspect of a loose confedera-

[6] Address to the Eighth International Congress of Accountants, New York City, September 24, 1962.

tion of businesses which may or may not fall into the same product family.

Both of the foregoing patterns share recognition of the need for the product champion, a need created by the organization's own powerful underground resistance to change. The patterns are devices by which top management, shrewdly assessing obstacles to innovation, attempts to manipulate the organization. The success of the manipulation, at least on a temporary basis, is shown by the number of organizations for which one or another of the patterns described has become a standard procedure.

Needless to say, these patterns do not represent the only alternatives. Once the need for the product champion has been recognized, there are many possible social inventions for selecting and supporting him. The important point is that *some* such invention is required.

Conclusion

In perspective, the problem of significant innovation in business and the military raises some basic questions. For instance, it seems fair to ask if the most important aspect for top management is not formal organizational procedures but the social tangle which necessitates bringing the product champion into being in the first place. Why must legitimate resistance to change go underground? Why is it not possible to deal openly in a company with the dangers of innovation, even while proceeding with development work? Why should penalties for failure fall so heavily on one or two men, when the organization as a whole demands innovation?

The product-champion approach grows out of the sharp division between those in top management who dispose and those, lower in the organization, who propose. Product champions would be needed less if the risks of product change were more evenly distributed, that is, if top management were to give up some of its prerogatives to dispose of what others propose. This may be seen as too steep a price to pay for innovation. But a willingness to face the price of innovation is a major part of the problem of technological progress.

[24]

Journal of Management
1995, Vol. 21, No. 5, 931-952

Cultural Differences in
Innovation Championing Strategies

Scott Shane
Georgia Institute of Technology

S. Venkataraman
Rennselear Polytechnic Institute

Ian MacMillan
University of Pennsylvania

This study examines the relationship between national culture and national preferences for innovation championing strategies for a sample of 1228 individuals in 30 countries. The study finds that the more uncertainty avoiding a society is the more people prefer champions to work through organizational norms, rules and procedures to promote innovation. The more power distant a society is the more people prefer champions to focus on gaining the support of those in authority before other actions are taken on an innovation rather than on building a broad base of support among organization members for new ideas. The more collectivist a society is the more people prefer champions to seek cross-functional support for the innovation effort.

Innovation has the capacity to alter the distribution of power, the systems, and the structures of established organizations (Schon, 1973; Shane, Venkataraman and MacMillan, 1994). However, organization members cannot know in advance the direction and magnitude of changes imposed by the innovation process since they cannot foresee the development of technological standards or the products and processes that will gain market acceptance (Venkataraman, MacMillan & McGrath, 1992). The capacity of innovation to impose unforeseen changes on organization member creates resistance to new ideas by many organization members who are uncomfortable with the uncertainty of the innovation process (Van de Ven, 1986).

This resistance creates a need for innovation champions—people who take personal risks to overcome resistance to innovative ideas in established organizations (Schon, 1963; Burgelman, 1983; Van de Ven, 1986; Howell & Higgins, 1991; Frost & Egri, 1991). Recent research on championing has identified the process by which organization members champion new ideas, products and technologies in American organizations.

Direct all correspondence to: Scott Shane, Georgia Institute of Technology, Strategic Management Group, 755 Ferst Drive, Atlanta, GA 30332.

The increasing globalization of innovation efforts by multinational corporations (Ghoshal, 1987) raises the question of whether or not the nature of the championing process identified in research in the United States is the same in other national cultural environments. This issue is of substantive import to managers of multinational corporations. Many organizations create new competitive advantages on the basis of innovations that leverage the internal diversity of the multi-cultural organization. As Ghoshal (1987:431) has argued, internal diversity enhances "the chances that [the firm] will be in possession of the capabilities required to cope with an uncertain future state." The creation of a common approach to innovation and innovation championing reduces this internal diversity. A decentralized approach to innovation in global firms enhances this diversity, but requires senior managers to understand if and how national cultural values influence the championing behavior of their subordinates in different countries around the world.

In this paper, we argue that organizations around the world share features that cause organization members to resist new ideas, thereby requiring a champion to overcome such resistance. However, we argue that it cannot be said with equal confidence that the same championing strategies would be equally effective in all contexts. In fact, the hypothesis that different national cultures induce different norms and behaviors would suggest that preferred championing strategies should vary with national cultural contexts.

We extend and test a theoretical model proposed in Shane et al. (1994) for the relationship between people's preferences for innovation championing strategies and three of Hofstede's (1980) national cultural values: individualism/collectivism, power distance, and uncertainty avoidance/uncertainty acceptance. The basic argument is that national cultural values lead organization members in different countries to prefer different innovation championing strategies.

The paper unfolds along the following lines. In the next section, we present a theoretical argument for why preferences for championing strategies should vary across cultures and offer hypotheses about the effect of individualism, uncertainty avoidance, and power distance on the preferred choice of championing behaviors. Following this, we present the methodology used to test the hypotheses, the data analysis and the results. We close with our conclusions and discussions of the implication of this study for managers.

Theory Development

The objective of this section is to derive a set of hypotheses that link cultural values and preferences for championing strategies. We will begin by explaining why organization members in different countries differ in their cultural values and traits. We will then discuss three dimensions on which culture can vary, following Hofstede (1980). After that, we will identify common organizational obstacles to innovation in large geographically dispersed organizations. Finally, we will show how cultural values systematically influence people's preferences for the behaviors champions employ to promote innovation.

Differences in Cultural Values

Many definitions of culture exist. The definition of culture used in this study is that of Hofstede (1980, p. 25). It is "the collective programming of the mind which distinguishes the members of one human group from another... the interactive aggregate of common characteristics that influence a human group's response to its environment."

People belong to many differe_nt "human groups" at the same time. For example, a person may belong to a nation, a gender, a generation, and an organization all at the same time (Hofstede, 1991). Each of these groups has a culture and each culture influences behavior (Hofstede, 1980, 1991). This paper focuses on only one of these cultures—national culture. National culture is the set of collective beliefs and values that distinguish people of one nationality from those of another (Hofstede, 1991). This paper seeks to examine the effect of national culture on preferences for championing strategies, holding constant the effect of organizational, generational and gender cultures. By controlling for the effect of these other cultures in regression analysis, we can examine the effect of national culture on preferences for championing strategies even though organizational, generational and gender cultures also influence managerial behavior.

To measure national culture, this study examines three of the dimensions of culture identified by Hofstede (1980). These are: uncertainty avoidance, individualism, and power distance. These dimensions are examined here for two reasons. First, these dimensions are pertinent to the issue of innovation. For example, individualism-collectivism has implications for the kind of choices made in the area of rewarding and compensating innovation and innovation participants; uncertainty avoidance has implications for the nature of the innovations pursued—exploratory versus exploitative, high risk versus low risk, radical versus incremental; power distance has implications for the structural choices made for tasks and for governance in carrying out innovations. Second, the validity and reliability of these measures have been shown repeatedly (Hofstede, 1980; Hofstede & Bond, 1984; The Chinese Culture Connection, 1987; Hoppe, 1990).

The three cultural values are defined as follows: "Individualism pertains to societies in which the ties between the individuals are loose: everyone is expected to look after himself or herself and his or her immediate family. Collectivism as its opposite pertains to societies in which people from birth onwards are integrated into strong, cohesive ingroups, which throughout people's lifetime continue to protect them in exchange for unquestioning loyalty (Hofstede, 1991, p. 51)."

"Power distance can be defined as the extent to which the less powerful members of institutions and organizations within a country expect and accept that power is distributed unequally....In the large power distant situation superiors and subordinates consider each other as existentially unequal; the hierarchical system is felt to be based on this existential inequality. Organizations centralize power as much as possible in a few hands. Subordinates are expected to be told what to do (Hofstede, 1991, pp. 28-35)."

'Uncertainty avoidance can ... be defined as the extent to which the members of a culture feel threatened by uncertain or unknown situations (Hofstede, 1991, p. 113)."

These three cultural values influence societal level preferences for championing strategies. We now turn to a description of the domains of championing actions.

Domains of Championing

Organizations resist innovative ideas for reasons ranging from bounded rationality to the allocation of power in organizations and inertia (Shane et al., 1994). To overcome bounded rationality, organizations need to specialize labor (Simon, 1958). This specialization creates resistance to innovation. Specialization focuses the attention of organizational members on their own responsibilities and often leads them to ignore the activities of other organization members. Specialization also limits horizontal information flows to reduce information overload on decision makers. These conditions make people resistant to the cross-functional exchange of information and create a need for champions to bring together organization members with different backgrounds and knowledge for innovation to take place (Shane et al., 1994).

As Venkataraman et al. (1992, p. 502) point out, a second major reason why new ideas may be resisted within organizations is because "of the possibility that the new idea may threaten the existing power and resource distribution within the firm." Innovation causes some organization members to gain influence at the expense of others (Tushman & Romanelli, 1985). This fact was noted by Machiavelli as early as the 1500's. He wrote, "the innovator makes enemies of all those who prospered under the old order, and only lukewarm support from those who would prosper under the new (Cited in Rogers and Shoemaker, 1971, p. 74)." To overcome the resistance introduced by adherence to the power structure, champions provide or acquire the necessary resources and support for the innovation to be developed or implemented.

A third reason why new ideas are resisted in organizations is organizational inertia (Shane et al., 1994). Since innovation often demands many rapid and frequent changes in organizations, flexibility in organizational routines and authority structures is often important to the innovation effort (Quinn, 1985). While flexibility in authority systems is important to innovation, preserving the preexisting system of authority and routines may be essential for the survival of an organization (Nelson & Winter, 1982). Since much investment of resources, time, energy and political capital is expended in building such authority systems, there is pressure not to deviate from the status quo (Cyert & March, 1963; Nelson & Winter, 1982). These systems lead people to believe that there are costs to deviating from prescribed authority systems. As Venkataraman et al., (1992, p. 503) explain, "ideas may also be resisted because they require significant investments in retraining personnel and changing routines and the resource base of the firm. Forces of inertia may make these changes a difficult exercise for managers, hence resisting the idea is easier than implementing it." Thus survival of new ideas and products in the light of these pressures is difficult in ongoing organizations (Schon, 1973; Aldrich & Auster, 1986; Van de Ven, 1986). Hence the prevailing system of authority and routines creates conditions that go against some of the requirements of innovative activity. In order to overcome these obstacles, a champion emerges to do what is necessary to get the job done whether or not these ways are consistent with organizational norms and routines.

In summary, overcoming the obstacles raised by the existence of specialization, systems of authority, and routines requires actions in three different domains in order to move the innovation forward: selection of how to attract organization members to the innovation effort; determination of the locus of support for the innovation; and decisions on the degree of autonomy from organizational norms and routines accorded to innovation participants. We now turn to the task of identifying what specific championing strategies in each of these three domains will be preferred by people in different cultures.

Hypotheses

As was shown in the previous section, one of the forces that overcome organizational resistance to innovation is the champion (Burgelman, 1983). We have argued that the way champions go about overcoming these obstacles will differ across national cultures. This section presents specific hypotheses about the ways in which preferences for championing behaviors are influenced by national culture.

Individualism. As was mentioned above, organizational specialization often creates a need for a champion to bring together people of a diverse background to work together on an innovation. The national cultural value of individualism influences preferences for how champions should create this innovation group. We argue that people in collectivist cultures are more likely than people in individualistic cultures to prefer appeals for cross-functional support for the innovation effort. In collectivist cultures, long tenure in organizations (Dore, 1973), intense employee socialization (Abegglen, 1958), organizational commitment to employees and their welfare (Ouchi, 1980; Dore, 1973) and continual job rotation encourage a degree of loyalty to the organization often higher than that found in individualistic cultures (Shane et al., 1994). These policies create a sense of commitment to the organization that makes people in collectivistic cultures more likely than people in individualistic cultures to prefer a champion who appeals for cross-functional support for the innovation across parts of the organization. This argument leads to the first hypothesis:

> **H1**: *The greater the collectivism of a society, the more people will prefer champions to make cross-functional appeals for support of the innovation effort.*

Power distance. People in high power distant societies tend to adhere more rigidly to organizational hierarchy, to centralize decision making and to disbelieve in participative approaches to management than do people in low power distant societies (Hofstede, 1980; Child & Kieser, 1979; Brossard & Maurice, 1974; Lammers & Hickson, 1979; Wong, 1985; Tayeb, 1988). Therefore, we argue that people in high power distant cultures are more likely than people in low power distant cultures to prefer champions to work closely with those in authority to approve innovative activities before work is conducted on them (Shane et al.,1994). By contrast, in low power distant societies, people prefer champions to adopt participative approaches to management and to create widespread support for an innovation before formal attention by those in authority (Howell & Higgins, 1991). This support enables the participants to convince the decision makers that there is broad-based support in the organization for the innovation. The differences between high and low power distant cultures lead us to the following hypothesis about championing behavior:

> **H2**: *The higher the power distance of a society, the more people in it prefer champions to gather support for the innovation among those in authority before beginning work on an innovation.*

Uncertainty avoidance. People in uncertainty accepting societies are more accepting of new approaches to problem solving (Philips & Wright, 1977; Yates, Zhu, Wang, Shinotsuka & Toda, 1989; Wright, Phillips, Whalley, Choo, Ng, Ian & Wisudha, 1978). They are also more tolerant of non-conformity to social norms (Hofstede, 1980; Milgram, 1961; Mann, 1980). Therefore, we argue that the more uncertainty accepting a society, the more people will prefer a champion to violate organizational rules, norms and procedures to overcome inertia to new ideas. By contrast, in uncertainty avoiding societies, people will prefer champions to adapt the innovation to the norms and rules of the organization or to alter the rules of the organization to accept the innovation (Venkataraman et al., 1992; Shane et al., 1994; Howell & Higgins, 1991). The differences between uncertainty avoiding and uncertainty accepting cultures lead us to the following hypothesis about championing behavior:

> **H3**: *The higher the uncertainty avoidance of a society, the more people in the society prefer to ensure that champions work within the organization's rules and standard operating procedures to develop the innovation.*

Methodology

Sample

The sample consists of 1228 individuals from 30 countries who were members of 4 different organizations: a life and property insurance company, a financial services firm, a petrochemicals firm, and a consumer electronics firm. The selection of the organizations was based on the following rationale. An attempt was made to include organizations from a variety of industries and of a variety of forms. Organizations from different industries were important to ensure that the findings were generalizable beyond the particular industry under investigation.

Administration of the survey occurred during a four month period from December 1991 to March 1992. All the participating organizations had previously agreed to the study and were supportive of it. Participants within each organization were selected randomly. The surveys were administered by mail along with a letter from the first author describing the study and a self-addressed return envelope.

The survey response rate was 42.2 percent. There were no significant differences in response rates across organizations or across nations. Unfortunately, since the organizations were unwilling or unable to provide demographic information on their members, we could not conduct checks for non-response bias. Therefore, there may be differences between respondents and non-respondents. However, we know of no theoretical argument for how differences between respondents and non-respondents could explain the pattern of relationships between cultural values and preferences for championing strategies.

Type of Innovation and Innovation Championing Studied

The innovation literature has shown that the forces explaining the adoption of innovation in established organizations are a-function of the domain of the innovation—technology, products, administration, processes or structure (Aiken, Bacharach & French, 1980; Downs & Mohr, 1976; Damanpour, 1987, 1988, 1991; Evan & Black, 1967; Kimberly & Evanisko, 1981; Knight, 1967; Rowe & Boise, 1974), the radicalness of the innovation (Damanpour, 1987, 1991; Dewar & Dutton, 1986; Ettlie, Bridges & O'Keefe, 1984; Hage, 1980), and the stage of the innovation process (Damanpour, 1991; Marino, 1982; Utterback and Abernathy, 1975; Zaltman, Duncan & Holbek, 1973; Zmud, 1982). Therefore, an understanding of the relationship between cultural values and the championing process which promotes the adoption of innovation must define the stage, domain and radicalness of the innovation studied.

In this study, innovation was defined as any idea that is new to an organization. The study encompasses ideas for administrative, technological, product, process and structural innovations and includes both radical and incremental innovations.

The difficulties of collecting cross-national data led us to use a broad and inclusive definition of innovation that would be salient to as many study participants as was possible. The broadness of this definition may create greater noise in the data than is the case in single nation studies of innovation. However, given the relative lack of cross-cultural work on the topic, we felt that this trade-off was acceptable. Nevertheless, we caution the reader that our study implicitly assumes that the domain and radicalness of innovation do not vary systematically with cultural values when it tests the relationship between cultural values and preferences for championing strategies.

The term innovation champion has been used in many different ways in the innovation management literature (Chakrabarti & Hauschildt, 1989; Frost & Egri, 1991). A number of different championing roles have been identified, including idea champions, product champions, organizational champions, executive champions, and sponsors (Chakrabarti & Hauschildt, 1989; Venkataraman et al., 1992). This study defined the need for championing as occurring when "one member of an organization has a new idea that other members of the organization do not initially support." The champion is defined as the person who "emerges and employs various strategies to get the members of the organization to support the idea." Therefore, we believe that the subjects answering the survey were focusing on a common championing construct. Nevertheless, the reader is cautioned that potential respondent ambiguity about the concept of championing might weaken our results.

Survey Instrument

The parts of the survey used in this study included questions designed to check the country of origin and place of present employment, and to ascertain the age, sex, educational background, and occupational background of the respondents and twenty-four questions about preferences for championing strategies.

In this study we defined the respondent's national culture as that of the country in which the person was born. Comparisons of expatriates and people still living in their country of origin revealed no significant differences in preferences for championing strategies. This suggests that one's culture of origin rather than one's host culture influences championing behavior. In fact, in a review of the international human resource management literature, Schneider (1988) makes the argument that the dominant influence of culture of origin on organizational behavior exists because expatriates stress their culture of origin in reaction to the host culture.

The respondents were primarily managers. However, there were no significant differences between managers and nonmanagers on the championing items. On the cultural values side, Hofstede's (1980) scales were constructed to control for these differences.

The selection of items for the questionnaire was straightforward. The background questions are ones common to most survey questionnaires used by management scholars. The championing questions, which are shown in Appendix 1, come from the received wisdom on innovation championing. They were developed from statements in the literature on innovation championing, primarily the works of Burgelman (1983); Howell and Higgins (1991); Imai, Nonaka & Takeuchi (1985); Kanter (1988); Knight (1987); Pinchot (1987); Schon (1963); Souder (1981); and Van de Ven (1986).

The surveys were distributed in English to individuals residing in the United States, Belgium, Denmark, United Kingdom, South Africa, Ireland, Hong Kong, India, Kenya, The Philippines, Malaysia, Zimbabwe, Turkey, Mauritius, New Zealand and Jamaica. The survey was administered in Spanish to respondents in Spain, Mexico, Chile, Uruguay, and Argentina; in Portuguese to respondents in Portugal and Brazil; in German to respondents in Germany and Switzerland; in French to respondents in France; in Norwegian to respondents in Norway; in Italian to respondents in Italy; in Japanese to respondents in Japan; and in Chinese to respondents in Taiwan.

To minimize translation problems, front and back translation of the survey instrument were used. The large number of countries included in the study also reduced the likelihood of translation bias. In two country studies, translation errors are difficult to rule out since the difference in means between two countries could be as easily explained by a translation error as by hypothesized relationships. However, in a 30 country study that was administered in nine languages, the probability that the support for the hypothesized relationships comes from translation errors is extremely low (Hofstede, Neuijen, Ohayv & Sanders, 1990). This means that we can say with a fair degree of confidence that any relationships that we find between cultural values and preferences for championing strategies are not the result of translation error.

Level of Analysis

This study was designed to examine country-level differences in preferences for championing strategies. The raw data from respondents was transformed into 30 group means for each national unit of the four organizations that existed in the 30 countries. For example, Financial Services Company's (FSC) office in the United Kingdom was one unit, the insurance company's UK office was another, and FSC's office in Switzerland was a third unit. These unit scores represent the unique combination of a particular organization with a given country. If one controls for organizational effects through dummy variables for organization in regression analysis, this approach will show the effect of national culture on preferences for championing strategies net of company effects.

At this point, it may be useful to explain why the analysis was conducted at the group level. First, Hofstede (1980) and Hoppe (1990) demonstrated the ecological fallacy of analyzing these measures at the individual level. Second, research has shown that the group level is the correct one for examining culture (Leung & Bond, 1989; Hofstede et al., 1990). For group level analysis, at least twenty respondents in each group are needed for stable means (Hofstede, 1980; Hoppe, 1990). Therefore, this study includes only the 30 countries from which there were at least 20 respondents per organization. The countries covered and number of respondents per country are shown in Appendix 2.

Cultural Values Measures

The independent variables measuring culture used in this study were Hofstede's (1980) scales for individualism, power distance and uncertainty avoidance. That is, we used the numerical values calculated by Hofstede (1980) as our measure for each of the three national cultural values.

Hofstede's (1980) scores were used as the measure of culture for a number of reasons. First, they have been subject to more checks of internal validity, external validity and reliability than the measures used in any other cross-cultural study (Hambrick & Brandon, 1988; Kogut & Singh, 1988). Second, they were developed in the largest study of cultural values ever undertaken, both in terms of number of countries and number of respondents. Third, the measures have been replicated extensively (Hoppe, 1990). Fourth, by using culture scores from a different study, we can ensure that any relationship between culture and championing that we find is not an artifact of common method bias.

Construction of the Championing Scores

The dependent variables were preferences for championing strategies. These measures were calculated as national unit scores on the championing questions administered to the respondents. Following the logic of Hofstede et al. (1990, p. 298), we argue that to determine the relationship between cultural values and preferences for championing strategies, one can make comparisons at the level of the individual across all units, one can make comparisons at the level of the individual separately for each unit, or one can compare mean scores across units.

Since cultures are attributes of groups not individuals, measures of cultures should be constructed from "mean scores for each of the . . . organizational units, so as to move from the individual level to the social system (Hofstede et al., 1990, p. 297)." This argument means that, in this study, ecological factor analysis is the appropriate methodology for creating the championing scores.

The primary difference between an ecological factor analysis and a traditional factor analysis is that an ecological factor analysis is based on group mean scores rather than on individual scores (Hui & Triandis, 1985). Therefore, to create the championing factors, we calculated mean scores for each championing item across all members of each national offices of each company and then factor analyzed these means.

Researchers have found that in an ecological factor analysis "the stability of the factor structure for ecological matrices does not depend on the number of aggregate cases but on the number of independent individuals who contributed to each case (Hofstede et al., 1990, p. 299)." The ratio in this study is 1228 to 24, a stable ratio.

A factor analysis with orthogonal rotation yielded three robust factors which represent the three dimensions of championing hypothesized earlier in the study. The factors were named: Autonomy from Norms, Cross-Functional Appeal, and Locus of Support. National organizational unit factor scores were computed using the regression method. Table 1 shows the items defining each of the dimensions of championing. Table 2 shows the loadings of the items on the three factors.

We concluded that these factors were robust for the following reasons: First, the factors ranged in eigen values from 6.69 to 2.91, and explained 54.8 percent of the variance in the data. Second, a scree graph confirmed limiting the championing items to three factors. Third, in a test for inter-item reliability, all of the items in each factor had a Cronbach's alpha of greater than 0.70, the recommended threshold (Nunnally, 1978). Fourth, we ensured that the factors were not an artifact of the measures of central tendency used in this

Table 1.   Items Loading 0.50 or Better on the Three Championing Factors

Factor 1: Autonomy

B2   Make it possible for the people working on an innovation to bypass standard operating procedures to develop the innovation (Schon, 1963; Howell & Higgins 1991; Burgelman, 1983).

B3   Be allowed to bypass certain budgetary procedures to get funds for an innovation (Schon 1963; Pinchot, 1987; Burgelman, 1983).

B4   Be allowed to bypass certain personnel procedures to get people committed to an innovation (Howell & Higgins, 1991).

B10   Create support for an innovation among employees before formal approval of the innovation by senior managers (Howell & Higgins, 1991; Burgelman, 1983).

B11   Make it possible for people working on an innovation to make decisions without referring them to higher level officials (Schon, 1963).

B12   Make it possible for people working on an innovation to make decisions outside the traditional hierarchy of the organization (Schon, 1963; Kanter, 1988; Van De Ven, 1986).

B14   Make it possible for the people working on an innovation to avoid having to justify the innovation financially at every stage of the development process (Burgelman, 1984; Souder, 1981).

B16   Make it possible for people working on an innovation to make decisions based on their intuition (Burgelman, 1984).

Factor 2: Cross-Functional Appeal

B8   Test but trust the decisions of people working on an innovation (Kanter, 1988).

B20   Always include the person who developed the idea for an innovation regardless of his or her status in the organization (Knight, 1987).

B21   Convince people in other departments that an innovation deserves their support by showing the benefits of the innovation to them as individuals (Kanter, 1988).

B22   Attempt to get people in other departments to commit their resources to an innovation by showing them the benefit of the innovation to the organization as a whole (Howell & Higgins, 1991).

Factor 3: Locus of Support

B5   Help the people working on an innovation to get a budget to undertake only one stage of the innovation at a time (Imai et al., 1985; Souder, 1981).

B6   Help the people working on an innovation to get authority to undertake only one stage of the innovation at a time (Imai et al., 1985; Souder, 1981).

B7   Not make it possible for people working on an innovation to take initiative on their ideas without getting formal approval for them (Howell & Higgins, 1991; Kanter, 1986).

Items with a negative loading have been reworded to make them conform with factor structure.

study by using alternative measures of central tendency to conduct the factor analysis. These alternative approaches yielded the same factor structures.

Control Variables in the Regression Analyses

Although our central hypothesis is that national cultural differences induce differences in preferences for championing strategies, an observed empirical relationship may also be explained by alternative theoretical viewpoints unless they are controlled for in the empirical analysis. Three dominant theoretical alternatives, each at a different level of analysis, may be identified which could potentially confound our inferences from the results.

Table 2. Factor Structure of the Championing Questions

Question	Autonomy	Cross	Support
Bypass SOPs	.75	-.24	-.05
Bypass Budgets	.65	-.07	-.00
Bypass Personnel	.85	-.10	-.02
Support Among People	.65	.10	.20
Avoid Higher Levels	.54	.05	-.44
Outside Hierarchy	.73	-.06	-.34
Financial Justification	.67	.01	-.34
Use Intuition	.76	-.19	-.16
Test but Trust	-.22	.70	-.13
Idea Generator Included	.07	.61	.29
Individual Benefits	.00	.76	.05
Benefit to all	-.12	.83	.11
Budget by Stage	-.08	.02	.95
Authority by Stage	-.07	.09	.94
Take Initiative	.15	.08	-.56
Bend Rules	.31	.26	-.04
Work with Senior	-.02	.48	-.28
Without Plans	.07	-.20	-.32
All Decide	.16	.07	.13
All Equal	-.38	.34	-.07
Commitment to Firm	-.20	.45	.11
Personal Rewards	.43	-.23	-.01
Financial Updates	-.32	.35	.14
Meet All Members	.14	.29	.01
Eigen Value	6.69	3.55	2.91
Cumulative Percent of Variance	27.9	42.7	54.8
Cronbach's Alpha	0.89	0.77	0.90

The first alternative is a macro-economic one. It may be argued that the prevailing economic conditions in a country may influence workplace behavior and preferences for such behavior, and the construct of national culture may simply be picking up the underlying economic differences between countries rather than any real cultural differences (Hofstede, 1980). In order to control for country-level economic characteristics such as the stage of industrialization, method of capital formation, natural resource endowment and business-government relations that may influence individuals' responses to questions about innovation and championing activities, we included GNP/capita as a proxy for these differences. These figures were taken from the World Bank's *World Development Report*.

The second alternative is at the level of demography. Since the demographic mix of the work force may be different across countries, it can be argued that it is workplace demography, rather than national culture, that induces differences in human behavior or preferences for behavior within organizations (Hofstede, 1980). Unless we control for differences in the demographic mix in the sample of firms studied here, we cannot be sure if the underlying construct of national culture is simply picking up demographic differences. In order to control for demographic differences, we included controls for them.

The demographic differences were measured in the following way: Work experience was measured by the average number of years of work experience of the respondents. Gender was measured by the percentage of female respondents. Championing experience was measured by the percentage of respondents stating that they had championing experience. Education was measured by the average number of years of education of the respondents.

The third alternative explanation is at the level of the organization. Under this argument, organizations differ for reasons that may be independent of national culture. Industry differences or organizational culture differences may induce differences in managerial behavior or preferences for such behaviors. In the absence of a large and representative sample of organizations from each nation, the construct of national culture may simply be picking up differences in organizational cultures, unless organization differences are controlled for. In order to control for company differences, a series of dummy variables of 1 for each company and 0 for all others for three of the four organizations was included in the regression equations.

Results

To test the hypotheses three sets of multiple regressions were run. The demographic, organizational and economic control variables are included in separate regression equations for reasons of sample size. Inclusion of all variables in the same regression equation reduces the number of degrees of freedom to significantly below the accepted norm of thirty.

The first set of regressions sought to control for demographic differences across samples (Model 1, Tables 3-5). These included differences in length of work experience, gender of respondents, their championing experience and their educational level. In these regressions, power distance was significantly related to the preference for seeking support of those in authority before other actions were taken on an innovation ($t=2.10$, $p<.05$). Uncertainty avoidance was significantly related to autonomy from organizational norms and procedures ($t=-3.96$, $p<.001$). Individualism was significantly related appealing for cross-functional support ($t=-1.71$, $p<.10$).

The second set of regressions sought to control for organizational differences through the inclusion of dummy variables for organizational effects (Model 2, Tables 3-5). In these regression analyses two of the three hypotheses remained significant. Power distance was significantly related to the preference for seeking support of those in authority before other actions were taken on an innovation ($t=1.83$, $p<.10$). Uncertainty avoidance was significantly related to autonomy from organizational norms and procedures ($t=-3.23$, $p<.001$). Individualism was signed in the right direction but not significant ($t=-1.49$).

The third set of regressions sought to control for economic differences across countries (Model 3, Tables 3-5). Controlling for differences in per capita

Table 3. Results of the Regression Analyses of Uncertainty Avoidance on Autonomy

Variables	Model 1 N=30 β	Model 1 N=30 t	Model 2 N=30 β	Model 2 N=30 t	Model 3 N=30 β	Model 3 N=30 t
CON	83.01	0.88	126.51	5.08***	85.63	5.96***
UAI	-0.72	-3.96***	-0.58	-3.23***	-0.63	-3.28***
EXP	-2.97	-1.74*	#	#	#	#
CHAMP	-0.31	-0.68	#	#	#	#
GEND	0.65	1.69*	#	#	#	#
EDUC	0.51	0.08	#	#	#	#
FSC	#	#	-38.20	-1.58	#	#
ELE	#	#	-58.75	-2.02**	#	#
INS	#	#	-59.68	-2.18**	#	#
GNP/CAPITA	#	#	#	#	0.00	0.58
R^2	35.5		34.8		25.4	
F	4.19**		4.88**		5.94**	

Notes: * = significant at the $p < .10$ level or better; ** = significant at the $p < .05$ level or better; *** = significant at the $p < .001$ level or better. # = Not included in the regression.

Key:
    CON = Constant
    UAI = Uncertainty Avoidance Index
    EXP = Average Years of Work Experience
    CHAMP = Percentage of Respondents With Championing Experience
    GEND = Percentage of Respondents Who are Female
    EDUC = Average Number of Years of Education
    FSC = Financial Services Company
    ELE = Electronics Company
    INS = Insurance Company
    GNP/CAPITA = Gross National Product Per Capita

income, power distance was significantly related to the preference for seeking support of those in authority before other actions were taken on an innovation ($t=1.70$, $p<.10$). Uncertainty avoidance was significantly related to autonomy from organizational norms and procedures ($t=-3.28$, $p<.001$). Individualism was significantly related to appealing for cross-functional support ($t=-1.81$, $p<.10$). Tables 3 through 5 show these regressions.

    The overall regression equations which include uncertainty avoidance were significant, but the overall regression equations which include power distance and individualism were not. However, this study was not a test of what variables explain championing behavior, but only a test of whether there is a relationship between the culture variable and championing behavior. Therefore, it is only the significance of the culture variable, not the F-value of the overall regression equation that is of interest.

    One alternative hypothesis is that the data are an artifact of the means used to derive the championing dimensions. To rule out this alternative explanation, we used a number of alternative measures to derive the championing dimensions. The data were run using five percent trimmed means in place of the regular mean scores. Five percent trimmed means eliminate the

Table 4. Results of the Regression Analyses of Power Distance on Locus of Support

Variables	Model 1 N=30 β	Model 1 N=30 t	Model 2 N=30 β	Model 2 N=30 t	Model 3 N=30 β	Model 3 N=30 t
CON	-9.57	-0.10	-1.97	-0.08	8.27	0.40
PDI	0.49	2.10**	0.45	1.83*	0.47	1.70*
EXP	-1.26	-0.77	#	#	#	#
CHAMP	-0.06	-0.13	#	#	#	#
GEND	-0.39	-1.04	#	#	#	#
EDUC	3.77	0.58	#	#	#	#
FSC	#	#	11.92	0.47	#	#
ELE	#	#	5.85	0.20	#	#
INS	#	#	8.61	0.30	#	#
GNP/CAPITA	#	#	#	#	-0.00	-0.04
R^2	14.6		1.0		6.6	
F	2.10		1.03		2.02	

Notes: * = significant at the $p < .10$ level or better; ** = significant at the $p < .05$ level or better; *** = significant at the $p < .001$ level or better. # = Not included in the regression.

Key:
CON = Constant
PDI = Power Distance Index
EXP = Average Years of Work Experience
CHAMP = Percentage of Respondents With Championing Experience
GEND = Percentage of Respondents Who are Female
EDUC = Average Number of Years of Education
FSC = Financial Services Company
ELE = Electronics Company
INS = Insurance Company
GNP/CAPITA = Gross National Product Per Capita

distortive effects of extreme outliers (Hildebrand, 1986). The data were analyzed with median values in place of the means to allow for the possibility that the questions are ordinal rather than cardinal scales (Hofstede et al., 1990). In addition, the data were analyzed on three of the four organizations at a time, dropping each of the organizations from the analysis in turn to ensure that the results were not driven by the distributions in a particular organization. None of these alternative approaches produced significantly different results.

Discussion and Conclusions

This study demonstrated support for a relationship between cultural values and preferences for championing strategies. It found that the more collectivist a society is, the more people in it prefer champions to gather support for an innovative idea by making cross-functional appeals for support from organization members. It also found that the more uncertainty accepting a society is, the more people in it prefer champions to overcome organizational inertia to innovation by violating organizational norms, rules and procedures. Finally, it found that the more power distant a society is, the more people in

Table 5. Results of the Regression Analyses of Individualism
on Cross-Functional Appeal

Variables	Model 1 N=30		Model 2 N=30		Model 3 N=30	
	β	t	β	t	β	t
CON	188.11	2.56**	99.46	4.51***	74.63	9.38***
IDV	-0.17	-1.71*	-0.21	-1.49	-0.33	-1.81*
EXP	-1.21	-1.02	#	#	#	#
CHAMP	0.89	2.74**	#	#	#	#
GEND	0.31	1.14	#	#	#	#
EDUC	-10.19	-2.00*	#	#	#	#
FSC	#	#	-22.89	-1.21	#	#
ELE	#	#	-44.81	-2.04**	#	#
INS	#	#	-14.83	-0.68	#	#
GNP/CAPITA	#	#	#	#	-0.00	-1.65*
R^2	24.1		12.8		11.1	
F	2.84		2.07		2.81	

Notes: * = significant at the $p < .10$ level or better; ** = significant at the $p < .05$ level or better; ***
= significant at the $p < .001$ level or better. # = Not included in the regression.

Key: CON = Constant
              IDV = Individualism Index
              EXP = Average Years of Work Experience
          CHAMP = Percentage of Respondents With Championing Experience
           GEND = Percentage of Respondents Who are Female
           EDUC = Average Number of Years of Education
             FSC = Financial Services Company
             ELE = Electronics Company
             INS = Insurance Company
    GNP/CAPITA = Gross National Product Per Capita

it prefer champions to make those in authority the locus of support for efforts
to overcome resistance to innovative ideas.

If we look at the individual variables in regression analyses that controlled
for economic, demographic and company differences, we find that uncertainty
avoidance and power distance are significant throughout. However,
individualism is not significant when we control for the electronics organization.
Therefore, with this sample, we cannot say whether the cultural value of
collectivism is associated with preferences for cross-functional championing
strategies for reasons of national or corporate culture. More systematic data
are required to make this claim.

Limitations of this Study

While this study was the first to provide empirical evidence of a relationship
between cultural values and preferences for championing strategies, it suffered
from a number of limitations imposed by resource constraints. First, only a
few respondents were available for some countries. Second, the controls for
types of organizations and demographic differences across countries were crude.

Third, no controls for stage of the innovation process were included. Fourth, preferences for championing behavior rather than actual championing behavior were measured.

Nevertheless, the results suggest that a relationship exists between national culture and preferences for championing strategies and that future research should further examine this relationship. Given the constraints on conducting large sample cross-cultural survey research in this area, a valued "next step" would be for scholars to undertake in-depth studies of the championing process in two countries for which this study has shown significant differences in approaches to championing. In-depth approaches that included interviews or face-to-face surveys would allow researchers to control for many of the factors influencing championing behavior that could not be controlled in this study. Convergent validity between the findings of such in-depth studies and this large scale survey would provide increased support for the argument that cultural values influence championing practices.

Implications for Managers

Recent research has suggested that multinational corporations have greater opportunities to develop new competitive advantages than do domestic firms because they are present in more environments and these environments create the variation necessary for the development of new competitive advantages (Ghoshal, 1987). Senior managers of these multinational firms need to learn how to harness this diversity. Since the success rate of innovation is enhanced when individuals promoting innovation gain the support of others (Kanter, 1986), learning culturally appropriate innovation championing strategies is important for managers.

Finding appropriate normative recommendations for how to champion innovation in non-American contexts may be difficult for managers, and they are cautioned against generalizing from the American context. The American championing literature is replete with prescriptive recommendations for championing strategy that would be inappropriate in many non-American contexts. For example, many writers have argued against strong financial controls in the innovation process (Quinn, 1979; Burgelman, 1984). Kanter (1988) and Quinn (1985) explain that decisions should be intuitive since innovation moves quickly. Finally, Knight (1987, pp. 289-290) writes, "the more successful firms tend to give the champion a very loose leash. That is tight controls of spending tend to frustrate entrepreneurial personalities." Yet this study found that in uncertainty avoiding societies, organization members prefer innovation champions to stick to budgetary procedures and justify their decisions financially rather than to base decisions on intuition.

Quinn (1979) and Kanter (1988) also advocate locating ventures outside the control of the rest of the organization and exempting them from the organization's formal rules and procedures. Burgelman (1983) cites a McKinsey study which shows that entrepreneurial companies in the United States have strong cultures supporting these strategic approaches. However, in uncertainty avoiding societies, people prefer champions to work through rules, budgets, and standard operating procedures.

Burgelman (1983, p. 238) explains that "organizational championing involved the establishment of contact with top management to keep them informed and enthusiastic about a particular area of development." Knight (1987, p. 295) writes, "the champion should manage the idea all the way to completion. He should not be required to hand it over to a more senior manager." But in less power distant societies, organization members felt that champions should make it possible for people working on an innovation to take initiative on their ideas and to make decisions without having to get the budget or authority for each stage of the innovation at a time.

The contradiction between the normative prescriptions and the results of this study suggests that executives should not export American championing strategies overseas without first evaluating the cultural receptivity to these strategies. Otherwise, inappropriate championing strategies may be employed to the detriment of the innovation effort.

In closing, we argue that as business globalizes, managers must understand that to build new competitive advantages in the global corporation, they need to ensure that the process of innovation championing occurs in culturally appropriate ways in each of their national subsidiaries. Understanding these differences is crucial to the development of new global competitive advantages.

Appendix 1

Championing Questions

A champion is an individual who promotes the development of an innovation within an organization. The need for championing occurs when one member of an organization has a new idea that other members of the organization do not initially support. In response to this need, a champion emerges and employs various strategies to get the members of the organization to support the idea. Listed below are several statements about strategies that champions can use. Using the following scale from 1 (strongly disagree) to 5 (strongly agree), circle the number which indicates the extent to which you agree or disagree with the following statements.

1 = Strongly Disagree   2 = Somewhat Disagree   3 = Neither Agree nor Disagree
4 = Somewhat Agree   5 = Strongly Agree

An innovation champion should...

B1	make it possible for the people working on an innovation to bend the rules of the organization to develop the innovation	1	2	3	4	5
B2	make it possible for the people working on an innovation to bypass standard operating procedures to develop the innovation	1	2	3	4	5
B3	be allowed to bypass certain budgetary procedures to get funds for an innovation	1	2	3	4	5
B4	be allowed to bypass certain personnel procedures to get people committed to an innovation	1	2	3	4	5

(continued)

Appendix 1. (Continued)

1 = Strongly Disagree	2 = Somewhat Disagree	3 = Neither Agree nor Disagree
4 = Somewhat Agree	5 = Strongly Agree	

An innovation champion should...

B5	help the people working on an innovation to get a budget to undertake only one stage of the innovation at a time	1	2	3	4	5
B6	help the people working on an innovation to get authority to undertake only one stage of the innovation at a time	1	2	3	4	5
B7	make it possible for people working on an innovation to take initiative on their ideas without getting formal approval for them	1	2	3	4	5
B8	test but trust the decisions of the people working on an innovation	1	2	3	4	5
B9	work closely with senior management to get their support for an innovation at a very early stage	1	2	3	4	5
B10	create support for an innovation among employees before formal approval of the innovation by senior management	1	2	3	4	5
B11	make it possible for the people working on an innovation to make decisions without referring them to higher level officials	1	2	3	4	5
B12	make it possible for the people working on an innovation to make decisions outside the traditional hierarchy of the organization	1	2	3	4	5
B13	seek the organization's support for an innovation by presenting regular financial updates demonstrating the value of the innovation	1	2	3	4	5
B14	make it possible for the people working on an innovation to avoid having to justify the innovation financially at every stage of the development process	1	2	3	4	5
B15	make it possible for the people working on an innovation to work without being required to write formal plans	1	2	3	4	5
B16	make it possible for the people working on an innovation to make decisions based on their intuition	1	2	3	4	5
B17	meet frequently with all the people working on an innovation rather than just the highest ranking members	1	2	3	4	5
B18	include all the people working on an innovation in its decision making process	1	2	3	4	5
B19	make it possible for all people working on an innovation to participate equally in the planning process regardless of their position in the organization	1	2	3	4	5
B20	always include the person who developed the idea for an innovation regardless of his or her status in the organization	1	2	3	4	5
B21	convince people in other departments that an innovation deserves their support by showing the benefits of the innovation to them as individuals	1	2	3	4	5
B22	attempt to get people in other departments to commit their resources to an innovation by showing them the benefit of the innovation to the organization as a whole	1	2	3	4	5
B23	get people in other departments to contribute manpower to an innovation by appealing to the employees' sense of commitment to the organization	1	2	3	4	5
B24	offer personal rewards to individuals to get them to work on an innovation	1	2	3	4	5

Appendix 2

Number of Respondents per Country

Country	N
United States (USA)	102
United Kingdom (UK)	76
Taiwan (TAI)	76
New Zealand (NZ)	53
India (IND)	52
Mexico (MEX)	49
Mauritius (MAUR)	48
South Africa (SAF)	46
Denmark (DEN)	44
Norway (NOR)	43
Portugal (PORT)	37
Philippines (PHIL)	36
Italy (IT)	35
Chile (CHI)	34
Ireland (IRE)	34
Kenya (KEN)	34
Malaysia (MAL)	33
Argentina (ARG)	32
Jamaica (JAM)	32
Japan (JAP)	31
Germany (GER)	31
Spain (SP)	30
France (FR)	30
Brazil (BRA)	30
Switzerland (SWI)	30
Turkey (TUR)	30
Uruguay (URU)	30
Zimbabwe (ZIM)	30
Hong Kong (HK)	30
Belgium (BEL)	30

References

Abegglen, J. (1958). *The Japanese factory: Aspects of its social organization.* Glencoe, IL: Free Press.

Aiken, M., Bacharach, S. & French, J. (1980). Organizational structure, work process, and proposal making in administrative bureaucracies. *Academy of Management Journal, 23*: 631-652.

Aldrich, H. & Auster, E. (1986). Even dwarfs started small: Liabilities of age and size and their strategic implications. Pp. 165-198 in L.L. Cummings & B.M. Staw (Eds.), *Research in organizational behavior,* Vol. 8. Greenwich, CT: JAI Press.

Brossard, M. & Maurice, M. (1974). Existe-t-il un modele universel des structures d'organisation? *Sociologie du Travail, 4*: 402-426.

Burgelman, R. (1983). A process model of internal corporate venturing in the major diversified firm. *Administrative Science Quarterly, 28*: 223-244.

————. (1984). Managing the internal corporate venturing process. *Sloan Management Review,* (Winter): 33-48.

Chakrabarti, A. & Hauschildt, J. (1989). The division of labor in innovation management. *R&D Management, 19*: 161-171.

Child, J. & Kieser, A. (1979). Organization and managerial roles in British and West German companies: An examination of the culture free thesis. In C. J. Lammers & D. Hickson (Eds.), *Organizations alike and unalike: International and inter-institutional studies in the sociology of organizations.* London: Routledge and Kegan Paul.

Chinese Culture Connection. (1987). Chinese values and the search for culture-free dimensions of culture. *Journal of Cross-Cultural Psychology, 18*(2): 143-164.

Crozier, M. (1964). *The bureaucratic phenomenon.* London: Tavistock.

Cyert, R. & March, J. (1963). *A behavioral theory of the firm.* Englewood Cliffs, NJ: Prentice Hall.

Damanpour, F. (1987). The adoption of technological, administrative , and ancillary innovations: Impact of organizational factors. *Journal of Management, 13*: 675-688.

———. (1988). Innovation type,radicalness, and the adoption process. *Communication Research, 15*: 545-567.

———. (1991). Organizational innovation: A meta-analysis of effects of determinants and moderators. *Academy of Management Journal, 34*(3): 555-590.

Dewar, R. & Dutton, J. (1986). The adoption of radical and incremental innovations: An empirical analysis. *Management Science, 32*: 1422-1433.

Dore, R. (1973). *British factory, Japanese factory: The origins of diversity in industrial relations.* Berkeley: University of California Press.

Downs, G. & Mohr, L. (1976). Conceptual issues in the study of innovation. *Administrative Science Quarterly, 21*: 700-714.

Ettlie, J., Bridges, W. & O'Keefe, R. (1984). Organization strategy and structural differences for radical versus incremental innovation. *Management Science, 30*: 682-695.

Evan, W. & Black, G. (1967). Innovation in business organizations: Some factors associated with success or failure. *Journal of Business, 40*: 519-530.

Frost, P. & Egri, C. (1991). The political process of innovation. Pp. 229-296 in B.M. Staw and L.L. Cummings (Eds.), *Research in organizational behavior,* Vol. 13. Greenwich, CT: JAI Press.

Ghoshal, S. (1987). Global strategy: An organizing framework. *Strategic Management Journal, 8*: 425-440.

Hage, J. (1980). *Theories of organizations.* New York: Wiley.

Hambrick, D. & Brandon, G. (1988). Executive values. In D. Hambrick (Ed.), *The executive effect: Concepts and methods for studying top managers.* Greenwich, CT: JAI Press.

Hildebrand, D. (1986). *Statistical thinking for behavioral scientists.* Boston: Duxbury Press.

Hofstede, G. (1980). *Culture's consequences: International differences in work related values.* Beverly Hills, CA: Sage.

———. (1991). *Cultures and organizations: Software of the mind.* New York: McGraw Hill.

Hofstede, G. & Bond, M. (1984). Hofstede's culture dimensions: An independent validation using Rokeach's value survey. *Journal of Cross-Cultural Psychology, 15*: 417-433.

Hofstede, G., Neuijen, B., Ohayv, D. & Sanders, G. (1990). Measuring organizational cultures: A qualitative and quantitative study across twenty cases. *Administrative Science Quarterly, 35*: 286-316.

Hoppe, M. (1990). *A replication of Hofstede's measures.* Unpublished doctoral dissertation, University of North Carolina, Chapel Hill.

Howell, J. & Higgins, C. (1991). Champions of change: Identifying, understanding, and supporting champions of technological innovations. *Organization Dynamics, 10*(1): 40-55.

Hui, H. & Triandis, H. (1985). Measurement in cross-cultural psychology. *Journal of Cross-Cultural Psychology, 16*: 131-152.

Imai, K., Nonaka, I. & Takeuchi, T. (1985). Managing the new product development process: How Japanese companies learn and unlearn. In K. Clark, R. Hayes & C. Lorenz (Eds.), *The uneasy alliance.* Cambridge: Harvard Business School Press.

Kanter, R. (1986). The new work force meets the changing workplace: Strains, dilemmas, and contradictions in attempts to implement participative and entrepreneurial management. *Human Resource Management, 25*(4): 515-537.

———. (1988). When a thousand flowers bloom: Structural, collective and social conditions for innovation in organization. Pp. 169-211 in B.M. Staw & L.L. Cummings (Eds.), *Research in organizational behavior,* Vol. 10. Greenwich, CT: JAI Press.

Kimberly, J. & Evanisko, M. (1981). Organizational innovation: The influence of individual, organizational, and contextual factors on hospital adoption of technological and administrative innovations. *Academy of Management Journal, 24*: 689-713.

Knight, K. (1967). A descriptive model of the innovation process. *Journal of Business, 40*: 478-496.

Knight, R. (1987). Corporate innovation and entrepreneurship: A Canadian study. *Journal of Product Innovation Management, 4*: 284-297.

Kogut, B. & Singh, H. (1988). The effect of national culture on choice of entry mode. *Journal of International Business Studies, 19*: 411-430.

Lammers, C. & Hickson, D. (1979). *Organizations alike and unalike: International and interinstitutional studies in the sociology of organizations.* London: Routledge and Kegan Paul.

Leung, K. & Bond, M. (1989). On the empirical identification of dimensions for cross-cultural comparisons. *Journal of Cross-Cultural Psychology, 20*(2):133-151.

Mann, L. (1980). Cross-cultural studies of small groups. Pp. 155-209 in H. Triandis and R. Brislin (Eds.), *Handbook of cross cultural psychology*, Vol. 5. Boston: Allyn and Bacon.

Marino, K. (1982). Structural correlations of affirmative action compliance. *Journal of Management, 8*: 75-93.

Milgram, S. (1961). Nationality and conformity. *Scientific American, 205*(6): 45-51.

Nelson, R. & Winter. S. (1982). *An evolutionary theory of economic change*. Cambridge, MA: Belknap.

Nunnally, J. (1978). *Psychometric theory*. New York: McGraw Hill.

Ouchi, W. (1980). Markets, bureaucracies, and clans. *Administrative Science Quarterly, 25*: 129-142.

Phillips, L. & Wright, G. (1977). Cultural differences in viewing uncertainty and assessing probabilities. In H. Jungermann & G. de Zeeuw (Eds.), *Decision making and change in human affairs*. Dordrecht, Holland: Reidel.

Pinchot, G. (1987). Innovation through intrapreneuring. *Research Management*, (March-April): 14-19.

Quinn, J. (1979). Technological innovation, entrepreneurship and strategy. *Sloan Management Review*, (Spring): 19-30.

_____. (1985). Managing innovation: Controlled chaos. *Harvard Business Review, 63*(3): 73-84.

Rogers, E. & Shoemaker, F. (1971). *Communication of innovations*. New York: The Free Press.

Rowe, L. & Boise, W. (1974). Organizational innovation: Current research and evolving concepts. *Public Administration Review, 34*: 284-293.

Schneider, S. (1988). National vs. corporate culture: Implications for human resource management. *Human Resource Management, 27*(2): 231-246.

Schon, D. (1963). Champions for radical new inventions. *Harvard Business Review, 41*: 77-86.

_____. (1973). *Beyond the stable state*. New York: W.W. Norton.

Sekaran, U. (1983). Methodological and theoretical issues and advancements in cross-cultural research. *Journal of International Business Studies, 14*(3): 61-73.

Shane, S., Venkataraman, S. & MacMillan, I. (1994). The effects of cultural differences on new technology championing behavior within firms. *Journal of High Technology Management Research, 5*(2): 163-181.

Simon, H. (1958). *Administrative behavior*. New York: MacMillan.

Souder, W. (1981). Encouraging entrepreneurship in the large corporations. *Research Management*, (May): 18-22.

Tayeb, M. (1988). *Organizations and national culture*. London: Sage.

Tushman, M. & Romanelli, E. (1985). Organizational evolution: A metamorphosis model of convergence and reorientation. Pp. 171-222 in B.M. Staw & L.L. Cummings, (Eds.), *Research in organizational behavior*, Vol. 7. Greenwich, CT: JAI Press.

Utterback, J. & Abernathy, W. (1975). A dynamic model of process and product innovation. *Omega, 3*: 639-656.

Van de Ven, A. (1986). Central problems in the management of innovation. *Management Science, 32*(5): 590-607.

Venkataraman, S, MacMillan, I. & McGrath, R. (1992). Progress in research on corporate venturing. Pp. 487-519 in D. Sexton (Ed.), *State of the art in entrepreneurship*. New York: Kent.

Wong, S. (1985). The Chinese family firm: A model. *British Journal of Sociology, 36*(1): 58-72.

Wright, G., Phillips, L., Whalley, P., Choo, G., Ng, K., Ian, I. & Wisudha, A. (1978). Cultural differences in probabilistic thinking. *Journal of Cross Cultural Psychology, 9*: 285-299.

Yates, J., Zhu, Y., Ronis, D., Wang, D., Shinotsuka, H. & Toda, M. (1989). Probability accuracy: China, Japan, and the United States. *Organizational Behavior and Human Decision Processes, 43*: 145-171.

Zaltman, G., Duncan, R. & Holbek, J. (1973). *Innovation and organizations*. New York: Wiley.

Zmud, R. (1982). Diffusion of modern software practices: Influence of centralization and formalization. *Management Science, 28*: 1421-1431.

Part VI
Effect of External Environment on Corporate Entrepreneurship

[25]

Strategic Management Journal, Vol. 18:9, 677–695 (1997)

ENTREPRENEURIAL STRATEGY MAKING AND FIRM PERFORMANCE: TESTS OF CONTINGENCY AND CONFIGURATIONAL MODELS

GREGORY G. DESS*[1], G. T. LUMPKIN[2], J. G. COVIN[3]

[1]*Carol Martin Gatton College of Business and Economics, University of Kentucky, Lexington, Kentucky, U.S.A.*
[2]*College of Business Administration, University of Illinois at Chicago, Chicago, Illinois, U.S.A.*
[3]*School of Management, Georgia Institute of Technology, Atlanta, Georgia, U.S.A.*

This field study explores the nature of entrepreneurial strategy making (ESM) and its relationship with strategy, environment and performance. In the first phase, we assess the independence of entrepreneurially oriented strategy-making processes through factor analysis. The second phase, using moderated hierarchical regression anlaysis, investigates the relative predictive power of two approaches for exploring the ESM–performance relationship: contingency and configuration. Findings from a sample of 32 firms competing in a wide variety of industries indicate that configurational approaches that align ESM, strategy, and environment have greater predictive power than contingency approaches. However, not all high performing configurations are consistent with normative theory. Thus, alternate theories linking entrepreneurial strategy making to competitive advantage should be developed and tested. © 1997 by John Wiley & Sons, Ltd.

Strat. Mgmt. J. Vol. 18: 677–695, 1997

No of Figures: 0. No of Tables: 5. No of References: 74.

Today's managers, faced with rapidly changing and fast-paced competitive environments, are challenged to manage 'discontinuities created by an interdependent global economy, heightened volatility, hypercompetition, demographic changes, knowledge-based competition, and demassification of some sectors accompanied by enormous growth in others' (Daft and Lewin, 1993: i). Such environmental conditions place intense demands on organizations to actively interpret opportunities and threats when making key strategic decisions. To cope with such chal-

lenges, management theorists have suggested that an entrepreneurial approach to strategy making may be vital for organizational success. An entrepreneurial strategy-making process, referred to as an 'entrepreneurial posture' by Covin and Slevin (1989), and an 'entrepreneurial orientation' by Lumpkin and Dess (1996), is often said to exist in a firm that 'engages in product market innovation, undertakes somewhat risky ventures and is *first* to come up with "proactive" innovations, beating competitors to the punch' (Miller, 1983: 771). This depiction is consistent with the type of organization-wide entrepreneurial strategy-making processes described in previous research. For example, Miller and Friesen (1982) posit that the entrepreneurial firm is the conceptual opposite of the conservative firm which is reluctant to innovate; Mintzberg (1973) argues

Key words: Entrepreneurship; strategy making processes; firm performance
* Correspondence to: Professor Gregory G. Dess, Carol Martin Gatton College of Business and Economics, University of Kentucky, Lexington, KY 40506-0034, U.S.A.

CCC 0143–2095/97/0900677–19 $17.50
© 1997 by John Wiley & Sons, Ltd.

Received 14 July 1995;
Final revision received 10 October 1996

678   *G. G. Dess, G. T. Lumpkin and J. G. Covin*

that firms with an adaptive mode are 'reactive' compared to proactive entrepreneurial firms; and Miles and Snow (1978) suggest that prospector firms are risk takers, unlike defenders that avoid risk in favor of protecting previous gains. For managers confronting challenging and intense competitive environments, therefore, entrepreneurial strategy making (ESM) may represent an important strategy-making process.

What, then, are the performance implications for firms operating in an entrepreneurial strategy-making mode? On the one hand, there often seems to be a strong normative bias toward the inherent value in entrepreneurial behavior and an assumption or explicit depiction of a positive relationship between behavior and desired organizational outcomes such as sales growth and profitability (Covin and Slevin, 1991; Peters and Waterman, 1982; Schollhammer, 1982; Zahra, 1993a). Further, the popular press applauds entrepreneurial behavior and encourages its diffusion throughout the economy (Wallace, 1993). In sharp contrast, however, Hart (1992) suggests that entrepreneurial-type strategy making is more likely to be associated with poor performance. Hart argues that firms with directive, entrepreneurial top managers operating in a command mode and those with autonomous, intrapreneuring organization members operating in a generative mode are likely to be low performers relative to firms using other approaches to strategy making. We suggest that the ESM–performance relationship is an empirical question and agree with Zahra (1993a) who notes that there is 'a paucity of empirical documentation of the effect of entrepreneurship on company financial performance' (1993a: 11). Thus, the purpose of this paper is to explore the ESM construct and its relationship to performance.

The environmental challenges and organizational complexities described above suggest that simple relationships may be inadequate to explain the relationship between entrepreneurial strategy making and performance. Thus, multivariate approaches are needed to explore how the competitive environment and strategies used to compete in a given environment may influence the ESM–performance relationship. As such, both contingency and configurational models are proposed to address the question of performance implications. Given the importance of entrepreneurship as a subject in both the academic

literature and popular press, further understanding the process itself, as well as its relationship to other organizational-level constructs and performance, is an important and timely research objective.

This study consists of two phases. In the first phase, a factor analysis is used to assess the dimensionality of strategy-making processes and the independence of the ESM construct. The second phase explores key relationships between ESM, other organizational-level constructs, and organizational performance for a sample of 32 firms competing in a variety of industries. We compare the predictive power of (1) contingency models which explore how a firm's strategy or competitive environment moderate the relationship between ESM and performance with (2) configuration models which assess the combined effects of ESM, strategy, and environment on performance. Accordingly, the remainder of this paper is divided into four sections. The next section develops hypotheses on the relationships between entrepreneurial strategy-making processes, strategy content, environment, and performance based on previous theory and research. Then, we discuss the research methodology, how the hypotheses will be tested, and how key constructs will be operationalized. Results from testing our hypotheses and a discussion of the study's implications will be addressed in the final two sections.

THEORY DEVELOPMENT AND HYPOTHESES

This paper addresses two related issues: the first issue is an important antecedent to the second issue. First, to avoid premature prescriptions about the nature and effects of entrepreneurial strategy making, it is essential to assess the ESM construct and evaluate its independence with regard to other strategy-making constructs such as rational, adaptive, and participative processes (Hart, 1992; Mintzberg, 1973). The second issue relates to the need to use contingency and configurational approaches when exploring the ESM–performance relationship. Both theory and research suggest that the relationship may be dependent on such factors as a firm's competitive environment, its structure or its strategy. On the one hand, additional insight into the entrepreneurship–performance linkage may be provided by exploring contingent relationships. For example, Covin and Slevin (1988) examined the moderating influence of organization structure on the entrepreneurship-performance relationship and found that an entrepreneurial top management style has a positive effect on organically structured firms. The environment as a contingent variable has also been examined. Small firms in a hostile environment were able to obtain higher financial performance when their strategic posture was entrepreneurial (Covin and Slevin, 1989). Firm performance was also found to be contingent on the strategies and competitive tactics of entrepreneurial firms (Covin, 1991; Covin and Adler, 1989; Zahra, 1986). On the other hand, prior research suggests that configurational approaches may be required to understand complex relationships between organizational or environmental variables and performance (Doty, Glick, and Huber, 1993; Miller, 1988). For example, in one of the few entrepreneurial studies to take a configurational approach to understanding the 'fit' among multiple contingent variables, Naman and Slevin (1993) found that firm performance was positively related to measures of fit among entrepreneurial style, organic structure, and mission strategy. In this study, therefore, the moderating effects of both competitive environments and business-level strategy will be explored, as well as the economic viability of configurations consisting of the multivariate alignment of the two aforementioned constructs with ESM.

The two subsections that follow describe the theory development and hypotheses that relate to the two phases of this research field study.

Phase 1: Defining entrepreneurial strategy making

Strategy making is an organization-level process that encompasses the range of activities firms engage in to formulate and enact their strategic mission and goals. These activities include analysis, planning, decision making, strategic management, and many aspects of the organization's culture, shared value system and corporate vision (Hart, 1992). Some researchers have suggested that there is a finite set of organizational processes from which strategic decisions evolve which take the form of patterns or gestalts that can be characterized and identified across organizations

(e.g., Hart, 1992). In attempting to identify the variables relevant to these gestalts, many researchers have focused on delineating the dimensions of strategy making. Miller and Friesen (1978) identified 11 strategy-making process dimensions including, for example, adaptiveness, analysis, expertise, integration, innovation, and risk taking. In his study of structural influences on decision-making processes, Fredrickson (1986) proposed dimensions such as proactiveness, rationality, comprehensiveness, risk taking, and assertiveness. Lumpkin and Dess (1996) suggested that the dimensions of an entrepreneurial orientation consist of autonomy, innovativeness, risk taking, proactiveness, and competitive aggressiveness.

The concept of strategy making as a gestalt or pattern of dimensions is suggested by the idea of strategy-making modes. Miller (1987) claims the most frequently occurring strategy-making modes are rationality, interaction, and assertiveness. Rationality consists of the systematic, formal planning mode of strategy making, while interaction involves political, bargaining, and consensus-building activities. Assertive strategy making suggests a proactive, risk-seeking orientation. Mintzberg (1973) suggested entrepreneurial, adaptive, and planning modes of strategy making, later adding a bargaining mode (Mintzberg, 1983; Mintzberg, Raisinghani, and Theoret, 1976). Mintzberg's planning mode suggests strategy making via formal analysis, the adaptive mode involves adjusting strategies to meet stakeholder concerns, and the bargaining mode represents a political process among decision-makers with conflicting goals. The entrepreneurial mode refers to opportunity seeking, risk taking and decisive action catalyzed by a strong leader. A similar but more broadly conceived set of strategic types— prospectors, defenders, analyzers, and reactors— was proposed by Miles and Snow (1978).

Hart (1992) proposed an integrative framework of strategy-making processes that includes five 'distinctive modes of strategy making' (1992; 334): command, symbolic, rational, transactive, and generative. Although none of the modes suggested by Hart represent a pure entrepreneurial type, both the command and generative mode include elements of an entrepreneurial orientation. The command mode suggests the kind of opportunity seeking and assertive style suggested by Mintzberg's (1973) interpretation of an entrepreneurial strategy-making mode. The generative mode, where autonomous organization members experiment, take risks, and intrapreneur, is reminiscent of Miller and Friesen's dimensions of innovation and expertise, and Burgelman's (1983) notion of internal venturing via autonomous strategic initiative. Consistent with Hart's (1992) suggestion that his pure types can be combined, we suggest that entrepreneurial strategy making is a distinctive strategy-making mode that combines features of a command mode—bold, directive, opportunity-seeking style—with aspects of the generative mode—risk taking and experimentation. This is consistent with prior theory and research related to entrepreneurial strategy making and reflects the entrepreneurial orientation dimensions identified by Lumpkin and Dess (1996).

The preceding comments notwithstanding, there is still some uncertainty regarding whether entrepreneurial strategy making exists independent of other related organizational phenomena. This uncertainty arises from the fact that entrepreneurial-type behavior in organizations is often empirically examined or theoretically discussed as a contributing element in a larger, coherent organizational gestalt. Mintzberg (1973) describes the entrepreneurial strategy-making mode in terms of a host of theoretically coherent managerial, organizational and enviromental attributes. Similar treatments of entrepreneurial processes in organizations can be found in the writings of, for example, Miller (1988), Zahra (1993b), and Cornwall and Perlman (1990). Collectively, this literature suggests that an entrepreneurial strategy-making process may be subsumed by or parallel to other related processes which are difficult to disentangle in an organizational context. In the interests of resolving this issue, it is hypothesized:

Hypothesis 1: An entrepreneurial strategy-making process in an important strategy-making mode that an organization may exhibit.

Phase 2: Strategy and environment as moderators of the ESM–performance relationship

Drawing on the literature, two variables which would appear to have a strong moderating effect on the ESM–performance relationship are the environment and strategy. The environment poses

an element of uncertainty to organizations (Lawrence and Lorsch, 1967; Duncan, 1972) which has been characterized along a number of dimensions such as unpredictability, dynamism and heterogeneity. Khandwalla (1987), for example, found that firms competing in high-tech or dynamic environments successfully coped with these difficult conditions through risk taking, innovative behavior, and proactive strategies and tactics. Miller and his colleagues have also investigated the relationship between the environment and entrepreneurial activities. Miller, Droge, and Toulouse (1988) found that environmental uncertainty was positively associated with strategic product innovation and Miller and Friesen (1982), in a study of 52 business firms, found that environmental dynamism and heterogeneity were positively associated with a firm's entrepreneurial posture and innovation. Similarly, in Miller's (1983) study, environmental heterogeneity, dynamism, and hostility were significantly and positively related to pioneering, innovation, and risk taking. This relationship was borne out by a variety of firms, including owner-managed firms, firms with high planning orientations, and firms characterized by decentralized, organic structures. Covin and his colleagues had similar findings but also explored performance implications. In these studies (Covin and Slevin, 1989; Zahra and Covin, 1995), firms which competed in hostile environments and adopted an entrepreneurial posture enjoyed superior performance. It can be argued that Zahra and Covin's definition of hostility as 'high levels of competitive intensity, a paucity of readily exploitable market opportunities, tremendous competitive-, market-, and/or product-related uncertainties, and a general vulnerability to influence from forces and elements external to the firm's external environment' (1995: 48) includes elements of uncertainty and heterogeneity.

Developing contingency hypotheses

Taken together, we contend that uncertain and multifaceted environments often necessitate a strong entrepreneurial orientation in strategy making. Such environments characteristically pose numerous strategic challenges for the occupying firms (Miller and Friesen, 1984; Zahra, 1993b). In particular, passive or nonaggressive behaviors in such environments often lead to deteriorating performance because bases for competitive advantage, industry structure, and product performance standards are generally short lived or in a constant state of flux (Karagozoglu and Brown, 1988). Under such challenging circumstances, product–market superiority is typically achieved through competitive aggressiveness which distances the firm from its industry rivals (Covin and Covin, 1990). Therefore, we suggest:

Hypothesis 2: Environmental uncertainty will moderate the relationship between entrepreneurial strategy making and performance: among firms with a strong emphasis on entrepreneurial strategy making, greater environmental uncertainty will be associated with higher performance.

Hypothesis 3: Environmental heterogeneity will moderate the relationship between entrepreneurial strategy making and performance: among firms with a strong emphasis on entrepreneurial strategy making, greater environmental heterogeneity will be associated with higher performance.

Strategy is another important variable that has been found to moderate the ESM–performance relationship (e.g., Covin, 1991; Covin and Adler 1989). Two of the generic strategies identified by Porter (1980) include overall cost leadership and differentiation. The cost leadership strategy is the type pursued by Miles and Snow's (1978) defenders or Hambrick's (1985) 'efficient misers.' A cost leadership strategy suggests an internal orientation whereby a firm concentrates on product efficiencies and cost control in order to be the lowest cost producer relative to competitors. Cost savings are sometimes achieved by tactics such as minimizing expenditures on innovation and advertising and offering no-frills products to customers seeking cost savings rather than brand image. For cost leadership strategies, Porter suggests 'common organizational requirements' such as tight cost controls, structured sets of organizational responsibilities, incentives based on meeting strict quantitive targets, and frequent, detailed control reports (Porter, 1980: 40). Resources expended on activities such as experimentation, risk taking, and environmental scanning and monitoring may be detrimental to effectively implementing a low-cost strategy. Thus, an

entrepreneurial approach to strategy making may work at cross-purposes with a cost leadership strategy, the result being that each negates the potential benefit of the other. Therefore, it is hypothesized:

Hypothesis 4: A cost leadership strategy will moderate the relationship between entrepreneurial strategy making and performance: among firms with a strong emphasis on entrepreneurial strategy making, lower performance will result from greater use of a cost leadership strategy.

Differentiation strategies (Porter, 1980) endeavor to offer customers unique products or services. Differentiators are similar to Miles and Snow's (1978) prospectors and are characterized by risk taking and a proactive external orientation. Miller (1986) identified two distinct types of differentiation: marketing and innovative. Marketing differentiators are characterized by 'salesmanship' and are similar to Miller and Friesen's (1984) mature giants or Kim and Lim's (1988) marketing differentiators. Marketing differentiation is characterized by extensive advertising, image management, and intensive marketing such as offering attractive features, convenience, and service guarantees. Miller (1992) describes innovative differentiators as 'pioneering', similar to adaptive and innovative-type firms found in previous research (Miller and Friesen, 1984). Innovative differentiation is characterized by creativity in product development, original applications of new technologies, up-to-date innovations, and quality design. Overall differentiation strategies appear to fit well in a context of entrepreneurial strategy making given the apparent similarity of purposes and means. Thus, we hypothesize:

Hypothesis 5: A marketing differentiation strategy will moderate the relationship between entrepreneurial strategy making and performance: among firms with a strong emphasis on entrepreneurial strategy making, higher performance will result from greater use of a marketing differentiation strategy.

Hypothesis 6: An innovative differentiation strategy will moderate the relationship between entrepreneurial strategy making and performance: among firms with a strong emphasis on

Strat. Mgmt J.. Vol **18**, 677–695 (1997)

entrepreneurial strategy making, higher performance will result from greater use of an innovative differentiation strategy.

Developing configuration hypotheses

Several theorists researching contingent relationships have argued that multivariate configurations of strategy and environment with organizational processes may offer more useful or complete explanations of complex organizations than those provided by simple bivariate descriptions (Hambrick, 1985; Miller, 1986, 1987; Miller and Mintzberg, 1984). Organizational configurations or gestalts represent an elaboration or extension of contingency approaches into multivariate combinations that express complex interrelations which may have more predictive power than bivariate contingencies (Dess, Newport, and Rasheed, 1993). Miller (1988) investigated configurations by examining multiple interactions among variables and found the highest performance among organizations whose alignment of strategy, environment and structure was consistent with the normative contingency literature. High performance among firms exhibiting simple bivariate relationships was not supported in his study. In Hypotheses 2 and 3 above, the moderating role of environment is hypothesized. Hypotheses 4, 5, and 6 address the moderating role of strategy. However, the configuration perspective would suggest that firms which are configured consistently with normative theory on many constructs would enjoy superior performance to those which are consistent on only two constructs. Therefore, we hypothesize that firms which have both environments and their strategies consistent with the normative guidelines associated with entrepreneurial strategy making will enjoy higher performance. Thus:

Hypothesis 7a: Among firms with a strong emphasis on entrepreneurial strategy making, greater use of a cost leadership strategy in uncertain environments will be associated with lower performance.

Hypothesis 7b: Among firms with a strong emphasis on entrepreneurial strategy making, greater use of a cost leadership strategy in heterogeneous environments will be associated with lower performance.

Hypothesis 8a: Among firms with a strong emphasis on entrepreneurial strategy making, greater use of a marketing differentiation strategy in uncertain environments will be associated with higher performance.

Hypothesis 8b: Among firms with a strong emphasis on entrepreneurial strategy making, greater use of a marketing differentiation strategy in heterogeneous environments will be associated with higher performance.

Hypothesis 9a: Among firms with a strong emphasis on entrepreneurial strategy making, greater use of an innovative differentiation strategy in uncertain environments will be associated with higher performance.

Hypothesis 9b: Among firms with a strong emphasis on entrepreneurial strategy making, greater use of an innovative differentiation strategy in heterogeneous environments will be associated with higher performance.

RESEARCH METHOD

The first phase of the research consists of an exploratory factor analysis to determine the underlying dimensions of organizational strategy making. In the second phase, moderated regression analysis is used to test hypotheses concerning the peformance implications of relationships between generic strategies, environment and the strategy-making process.

Sample

The sample in this research is a judgement sample, a type of purposive sampling used in exploratory research in which the researcher selects a sample to meet specific criteria (Emory and Cooper, 1991; Kerlinger, 1986). The objective was to target a heterogeneous sample of nondiversified firms. Additionally, firms were selected in which a member of its top management team served on the Business Advisory Board of one of the two universities that sponsored the research. Since our research methodology required a high level of involvement, (i.e., onsite interviews with the CEO/President and completion of lengthy questionnaires by multiple members of each participating firm's top management team), this was a practical consideration.

Given the sampling criterion, the sample was heterogeneous regarding factors such as firm size, industry, and ownership. The participating firms included, for example, a small venture capital firm, a privately held engineering firm, a manufacturer of gardening equipment, and a medium-sized food distributor. Variation in the sample has the potential to increase the generalizability of the findings. However, the nonrandom nature of the sample limits the extent to which the findings are applicable to a given firm or industry.

The final sample consisted of firms located in two large metropolitan areas in the southwestern United States. Forty-two of 53 firms initially contacted by mail granted on-site interviews. Responses from 34 firms and 98 executives were included in the data analysis. However, since two of the firms had only single respondents, these two were dropped in order to obtain organization-level measures and help reduce common method variance. The final sample included 96 executives from 32 firms. Participating executives were also interviewed on a variety of issues including decision-making processes, the role of the CEO, and perceptions of industry conditions.

Research instrumentation

Entrepreneurial strategy making was measured using a modification of Hart's (1991) instrument. Hart's instrument was based on two dimensions that are 'central to conceptualizing and understanding strategy-making processes: (1) top management "intentionality," and (2) organizational actor "autonomy"' (1991: 104). He used these dimensions to develop four generic modes of strategy making. The instrument—which related to strategy-making practices and processes, CEO style, and general management orientation—consists of 25 items and associated 5-point Likert scales ranging from 1 'Strongly Disagree' to 5 'Strongly Agree.'

The environment portion of the survey used Miller's (1983) measures of dynamism, unpredictability and heterogeneity. The three dynamism and two unpredictability items used 7-point semantic differential-type scales anchored by descriptive phrases. Since unpredictability and dynamism are considered to be 'the key components of the overarching construct of uncertainty' (Miller, 1988: 291), the dynamism and unpredictability variables were combined into a com-

posite index of environmental uncertainty. The heterogeneity portion consisted of three items (relating to customer buying habits, competition, and technological requirements) and used a 7-point scale. The use of managerial perceptions of environment has been supported by a number of studies based on the relevance of such perceptions to the formulation of strategy (Downey and Slocum, 1975), as well as on their accuracy with respect to objective measures of environmental conditions (Bourgeois, 1985; Dess and Keats, 1987).

The measure of Porter's generic strategies was conducted using a 7-item scale similar to the scale developed by Miller (1988). The scale asks questions regarding the importance of specific competitive tactics and includes two cost leadership items, two innovative differentiation items and three marketing differentiation items. The scale is a 5-point Likert-type scale and responses range from 1 'Not At All Important' to 5 'Extremely Important.'

Performance was measured by obtaining individual responses to three performance indices assessed with a 7-point Liket type scale ranging from 1 'Low Performer' to 7 'High Performer.' The three categories include sales growth, profitability and return on investment, and overall company performance. The questionnaire asked executives to 'assess your organization's performance OVER THE PAST FIVE YEARS relative to your competitors.' Prior research has indicated that subjective measures of performance can be consistent with objective measures, thus enhancing reliability and validity (Dess and Robinson, 1984; Venkatraman and Ramanujam, 1987).

Data analysis

For Phase 1, an exploratory factor analysis using the principal factors method with promax rotation was used to identify underlying dimensions of strategy-making and internal organizational processes. Factor analysis has the ability to produce descriptive summaries of data matrices, which aid in the detection of meaningful patterns among a given set of variables. In Phase 2, a moderated hierarchical regression analysis approach (Cohen and Cohen, 1983) was used. Moderation suggests that the relationship between two variables depends on a third variable. This technique is particularly useful for testing both two-way and

684		*G. G. Dess, G. T. Lumpkin and J. G. Covin*

three-way interactions among the variables of interest.

Control variables

Both organizational size (Blau and Schoenherr, 1971) and industry type (Hitt and Tyler, 1991) may affect the complexity and style of strategy-making processes. In order to investigate potential confounding due to the possible influence of size and industry, these variables were used as controls in the analysis. The log of number of employees was used as a measure of firm size. The sample was also broadly classified into two industry categories: service and manufacturing (dummy coded as 1 and 0).

RESULTS

Phase 1 results

Phase 1 explores whether entrepreneurial strategy making is a distinct strategy-making process. The rotated principal factors solution is shown in Table 1. Using the Kaiser criterion (i.e., eigenvalues >1) seven significant factors emerged from the factor analysis. However, an examination of the slope of a plot of the characteristic roots in a scree test (Cattell, 1965) indicated a significant gap between factors four and five and a flattening trend thereafter. In addition, the four factors that explained the greatest amount of variance suggested a straightforward interpretation which led us to converge on the four-factor solution reported in Table 1.

Overall, 24 of the 25 strategy-making process variables had significant factor loadings (i.e., $\geq \pm 0.40$) on at least one of the four factors. Loadings such as these may be considered consistent with a conservative criterion. Both Hair *et al.* (1979) and Kim and Mueller (1978) consider factor loadings of 0.30 to be significant. An examination of the reference axis matrix provided support for the independence of the factors (Kim and Mueller, 1978), i.e., the degree of correlation among the factors was never larger than 0.31. Kaiser's Measure of Sampling Adequacy (MSA), which measures the extent to which variables are appropriate for factor analysis, was 0.78 overall, indicating a very satisfactory level (0.80 is considered 'meritorious' (Kaiser and Rice, 1974)).

The interpretation and labeling of the underlying dimensions of each factor were straightforward and intuitively appealing. The first factor—'Participative SMP'—includes variables such as 'business planning involves everyone in the organization' (V4) and 'consensus and cooperation across departments and functional areas' (V17 and V24) that are clearly indicative of a participative management style. Two variables with significant negative loadings—'suppression of conflict' (V15) and 'CEO insists on putting mark on everything' (V25)—may be considered the opposite of participation.

The second factor—'Entrepreneurial SMP'—includes variables that suggest strategy making characterized by innovation, experimentation, risk taking, and assertiveness. Variables loading significantly on this factor include 'very dynamic and entrepreneurial' (V14) which suggests an overall entrepreneurial orientation. The variable 'people are encouraged to identify new, innovative approaches or products' (V21) connotes innovativeness, and 'people are willing to take risks' (V12) indicates a risk-taking perspective. Risk taking and proactiveness are also inferred by the 'encouraged to experiment' (V21) variable and by a significant negative loading on the variable 'failure is to be avoided' (V20) which suggests a predisposition to enter markets early and assertively with new products or services. Another variable, 'people are treated the same regardless of rank or status' (V13), may indicate an orientation that encourages autonomy. Thus, we believe our results provide support for the proposition that an entrepreneurial orientation is a salient strategy-making process within organizations.

The third factor—'Adaptive SMP'—suggests an external orientation focused on adapting to customer needs, and responding to cues and feedback from the environment. Among the variables loading significantly on this factor are 'we spend time with customers and key stakeholders, listening to what they say' (V5), 'business and product planning involves customers and suppliers' (V6) and 'continually adapts by making appropriate changes based upon feedback' (V3). The importance of effective adapting is suggested by a concern with 'long-term potential' (V22) and by making decisions 'at the level where the most accurate information is available' (V10).

The fourth factor—'Simplistic SMP'—includes several variables that indicate a well-established

Entrepreneurial Strategy Making and Firm Performance **685**

Table 1. Results of factor analysis of strategy-making process variables

Variable	Factor 1 Participative SMP	Factor 2 Entrepreneurial SMP	Factor 3 Adaptive SMP	Factor 4 Simplistic SMP
1. There is a clear blueprint for this organization's strategy that was set some time ago and has changed very little.	0.11	−0.11	−0.15	0.42[a]
2. Strategy, for this organization, is primarily provided by the president/chief executive and a few of his/her fellow top executives.	−0.42	−0.33	0.31	0.30
3. Our organization continually adapts by making appropriate changes in its strategy based upon feedback from the marketplace.	0.20	0.16	0.41	−0.18
4. Business planning in our organization is ongoing, involving everyone in the process to some degree.	0.81	−0.04	−0.02	−0.06
5. We spend as much time as possible with customers and other key stakeholders, listening to what they have to say about the organization.	0.06	0.02	0.44	0.05
6. Our business and product planning process involves customers, suppliers, and providers of funds.	−0.08	0.07	0.51	−0.16
7. Business and product planning in this organization is largely an internal process, seeking to contain the amount of information leaking to the outside.	−0.23	0.05	−0.04	0.36
8. There is a clear and consistent set of values in this organization that governs the way we do business.	−0.01	0.09	0.09	0.59
9. This organization has a characteristic 'management style' and a common set of management practices.	0.13	−0.24	0.24	0.51
10. Decisions in this organization are usually made at the level where the most accurate information is available.	0.19	0.10	0.44	0.21
11. Most people in this organization have input into the decisions that affect them.	0.50	0.07	0.11	0.04
12. Most people in this organization are willing to take risks.	−0.07	0.61	0.03	0.03
13. Most people in this organization are treated pretty much the same, regardless of rank or status.	−0.04	0.44	−0.22	0.49
14. People in this organization are very dynamic and entrepreneurial.	−0.11	0.70	0.26	−0.02
15. Conflict in this organization is often suppressed rather than dealt with openly.	−0.51	−0.13	−0.11	0.09
16. Specific work roles and expectations are clearly defined in this organization.	0.56	−0.27	0.18	−0.18
17. Cooperation and collaboration across functional roles are actively encouraged.	0.68	−0.03	0.09	0.01
18. People with unpopular views are given a fair hearing in this organization.	0.58	0.01	0.04	0.23
19. Working in this organization is like being part of a team.	0.43	0.27	0.01	0.28
20. Failure is something to be avoided in this organization at all cost.	−0.01	−0.40	0.02	0.02
21. People are encouraged to experiment in this organization so as to identify new, more innovative approaches or products.	0.05	0.43	0.41	−0.08
22. Long-term potential is valued over short-term performance in this organization.	−0.05	−0.04	0.49	0.15
23. The way we do things in this organization is well suited to the business we are in.	0.30	0.12	0.14	0.44
24. Decisions concerning business strategy are made on a consensus basis, involving people from many departments.	0.55	−0.07	−0.25	0.09

686   *G. G. Dess, G. T. Lumpkin and J. G. Covin*

Table 1. Continued

Variable	Factor 1 Participative SMP	Factor 2 Entrepreneurial SMP	Factor 3 Adaptive SMP	Factor 4 Simplistic SMP
25. The chief executive of our organization insists on placing his/her mark on virtually every major initiative.	−0.43	−0.32	0.03	0.07
Eigenvalue	4.74	3.04	2.96	2.98
Percentage of common variance explained	47.0	30.4	29.6	29.8
Percentage of total variance explained	18.8	12.2	11.8	11.9

[a]Factors with loadings ≥±0.40 are underlined.

but limited strategy-making process (Miller, 1993). The idea of a 'characteristic management style and practices' (V9) and 'a blueprint set some time ago that has changed very little' (V1) corresponds to the emphasis on a routine way of conducting business or narrow focus on a dominant element of strategy. Managers using a simplistic approach develop a bias toward a 'one best way' style of doing business suggested by the variable 'clear and consistent set of values that governs' (V8). Another variable, 'the way we do things is well suited to the business we are in' (V23), suggests an entrenched approach to strategy making that focuses on traditional solutions and routines.

It might be noted that these four dimensions of the strategy-making process not only have face validity, but they are also consistent with four of the five key dimensions of top management style identified by Khandwalla (1976/77). Briefly, based on a well-researched review of the management literature, Khandwalla concluded that there are at least five independent dimensions of top management style: risk taking, technocracy, organicity, participation, and coercion. Khandwalla described the risk-taking dimension of top management style as reflecting elements similar to those identified with the 'Entrepreneurial SMP' factor. The technocracy dimension of top management style was described in terms similar to the current 'Simplistic SMP' factor (with a low technocracy emphasis being consistent with a high simplistic SMP score, and vice versa). The 'Adaptive SMP' factor resembles Khandwalla's characterization of the organic dimension of top management style. Finally, the construct of participation is clearly evident in both the current research results and Khandwalla's typology. (The

coercion dimension of top management style has no direct analog in the current research.) Importantly, just as minimal overlap is observed among the four strategy-making process dimensions in the current research, Khandwalla's operationalization of his theoretically derived management style dimensions yielded scales with very low average intercorrelations. This fact corroborates the argument made above that the four empirically derived dimensions observed in the current research are likely to be independent constructs.

To further ensure that these factors represented valid constructs, additional criteria were applied to the statistical analysis. The unit of analysis in this research is the organization. Multiple respondents were used to ensure that responses closely represented organizational viewpoints. Since a construct such as 'SMP' should represent an organizational-level construct, it was decided, *a priori*, that only factors which exhibit a significant F-ratio in a comparison of between-firm vs. within-firm variance should be included in the analysis. Otherwise, it could be argued that the measurement of the SMP construct reflected as much of the 'individual differences' of the participating executives (e.g., experience, functional responsibility, education) as the construct itself. Prior theory and research provide support for the important influence of TMT characteristics on strategy and performance outcomes (Hambrick and Mason, 1984; Murray, 1989).

To test this, the responses of CEOs were compared with those of all other executives using one-way ANOVA. The intent was to determine if there was more agreement among executives within individual firms on the dimensions than that which existed *across* firms. If this were so,

Table 2.   Results of one-way analysis of variance for dimensions of strategy-making processes

Construct	Source	d.f.	SS	MS	F	Prob.
Participative	Between	32	55.3	1.73	3.83	0.000
	Within	63	28.4	0.45		
Entrepreneurial	Between	32	43.4	1.36	2.67	0.000
	Within	63	32.0	0.51		
Adaptive	Between	32	36.0	1.12	1.96	0.011
	Within	63	36.0	0.57		
Simplistic	Between	32	33.8	1.05	1.65	0.046
	Within	63	40.4	0.64		

$N = 96$

it would be reasonable to assume that the measures of SMP were actually representing organizational constructs rather than individual differences. As indicated in Table 2, all four of the dimensions of internal organizational processes exhibit significant F-ratios suggesting that agreement among all other executives as a group was different than argeement among CEOs. The differences, therefore, can be ascribed to their place of work and not to the positions they hold. A similar principle was also used in the analysis of performance conducted in Phase 2: CEO responses were used to represent the entrepreneurial strategy-making variable and the responses of other executives were used for the performance, strategy, and environment measures. This arrangement serves to minimize common method variance.

Phase 2 results

In Phase 2, the moderating influence of strategy and environment on the entrepreneurial strategy making–performance relationship was tested. Factor scores for the ESM factor developed in Phase 1 were used in the regression analysis. Cronbach's alpha for the variables loading ($\geq \pm 0.40$) on the entrepreneurial SMP factor was 0.64. To minimize the potential effects of common method variance, the responses of CEOs were used to represent the entrepreneurial strategy-making variable and responses of other executives (averaged to obtain a firm level score for each firm) were used for strategy, environment, and performance variables. This resulted in a sample size of $N = 32$ for the regression analysis. Table 3 presents the descriptive statistics and Pearson correlations for the variables.

There are several results shown in the correlation matrix that warrant further discussion. First, the low correlations between entrepreneurial strat-

Table 3.   Descriptive statistics and correlations[a]

Variables	Means	S.D.	1	2	3	4	5	6	7	8
1. Entrepreneurial strategy making	0.23	0.58								
2. Uncertainty	3.86	0.63	−0.07							
3. Heterogeneity	3.97	1.21	−0.03	0.18						
4. Cost leadership	3.55	0.86	−0.27	0.16	0.21					
5. Marketing differentiation	3.06	0.45	0.02	0.54	0.17	0.36				
6. Innovative differentiation	2.70	0.69	0.13	−0.01	0.00	−0.17	−0.00			
7. Sales growth	5.52	1.09	0.08	−0.22	−0.04	−0.09	−0.18	0.17		
8. Profitability/ROI	5.08	1.62	0.05	−0.03	0.05	−0.26	−0.07	0.27	0.40	
9. Overall performance	5.50	1.38	0.10	−0.14	0.09	−0.18	0.01	0.38	0.59	0.74

[a]$N = 32$. Correlations greater than 0.36 are significant at $p < 0.05$.

egy making and the three performance variables are consistent with prior research which has shown that, in the short run, the strength of the relationship between entrepreneurial behavior and firm performance tends to be weak (e.g., Covin, Slevin, and Schultz, 1994). While an entrepreneurial strategy-making process is often adopted in pursuit of competitive advantage, it is the fit between this strategic element and its organizational and environmental contexts which appears to promote performance, not the existence of such a process *per se* (Zahra, 1993b; Naman and Slevin, 1993).

Second, the correlation between cost leadership and profitability/ROI is negative, albeit insignificant $(r = -0.26, \ p > 0.05)$. While one might expect that reductions in cost structure would promote short-term profitability, the current cost leadership scale assesses the presence of such a strategy rather than the *change* in a firm's cost structure. If the latter were the case, a positive correlation between this strategy scale and profitability might be expected. However, since the cost leadership scale assesses this strategic attribute rather than the change in this attribute, the negative correlation with profitability is not counterintuitive as it may initially appear.

Finally, Table 3 shows that a cost leadership strategy is positively and modestly correlated with a marketing differentiation strategy $(r = 0.36, \ p < 0.05)$ and negatively but minimally correlated with an innovative differentiation strategy $(r = -0.17, \ p > 0.05)$. What is particularly noteworthy here is the implication that cost leadership is not inherently antithetical to a differentiation strategy. This result is consistent with prior empirical research (e.g., Miller, 1988) and suggests the possibility that similar interaction effects between these strategies and entrepreneurial strategy making could theoretically emerge in the analyses of the current data.

To assess the reliability of the self-reported performance measures, archival data for a 5-year period from a subsample of 10 publicly held firms was analyzed. The correlation between secondary data for sales growth and the self-report sales growth data from our study was 0.754 $(p = 0.01)$. Additionally, the correlations between the self-report measure of profitability/return on investment were significant for secondary data measures of return on sales $(r = 0.576, \ p = 0.08)$ and approached significance for return on total

assets $(r = 0.527, \ p = 0.12)$ for the 5-year period. These results suggest that the self-report measures from the study converged with archival measures of performance.

A moderated hierarchial regression analysis was utilized following the method described by Cohen and Cohen (1983: 320–323). For both the two-way and three-way interactions, size and industry were entered into the regression equation first, then the ESM variable was entered, followed by the specific environment or strategy variable being analyzed. Then, a second regression equation was calculated using the interaction terms and the change in R^2 was evaluated.

The results of the two-way and three-way moderated hierarchial regression analysis are summarized in Tables 4 and 5. Hypotheses 2 and 3 stated that environmental uncertainty and heterogeneity would positively moderate the performance of firms emphasizing entrepreneurial strategy making. Table 4 shows that neither uncertainty nor heterogeneity has a statistically significant moderating effect and, in both cases, the direction of the effect is equivocal (i.e., it varies with the dependent variable being examined). Hypothesis 4 stated that a cost leadership strategy would be negatively related to the performance of entrepreneurial firms. The results indicate that cost leadership and entrepreneurial strategy making interactively impact only the overall company performance variable, but this interaction effect is opposite of the hypothesized direction. Hypotheses 5 and 6 predicted that entrepreneurially oriented firms using either marketing differentiation or innovative differentiation strategies would be positively related to firm performance. Table 4 indicates that the results of the moderated regression analysis are not significant for either type of differentiation strategy. Therefore, none of the hypotheses that predicted significant two-way interactions of strategy or environment with entrepreneurial strategy making was supported.

Table 5 reports results of the three-way interactions of strategy, environment, and entrepreneurial strategy making. Hypothesis 7 stated that peformance would be lower when a firm with an entrepreneurial orientation used a cost leadership strategy in an uncertain or heterogeneous environment. Table 5 indicates that there is a significant three-way interaction between entrepreneurial strategy making, cost leadership, and uncertainty with two of the performance variables, but in the

Table 4. Results of moderated regression analysis: Two-way[a]

Variables	Sales growth		Profitability/ROI		Overall performance	
	b	R^2	b	R^2	b	R^2
Size	-0.17		-0.19		-0.01	
Industry	-0.04		0.39		0.05	
Entrepreneurship	-0.86		3.55		0.03	
Uncertainty	-0.28	0.05	0.13	0.04	-0.26	0.02
Entrepreneurship × Uncertainty	0.26	0.05	-0.94	0.08	0.02	0.02
Size	-0.22		-0.35		-0.15	
Industry	-0.18		0.54		0.13	
Entrepreneurship	-1.05		4.63		2.97	
Heterogeneity	-0.19	0.05	0.06	0.06	0.12	0.02
Entrepreneurship × Heterogeneity	0.27	0.06	-1.01	0.15	-0.60	0.06
Size	-0.25		-0.15		-0.02	
Industry	-0.11		0.50		0.40	
Entrepreneurship	-3.50		-2.69		-8.65	
Cost leadership	-0.42	0.03	-0.64	0.09	-0.95	0.04
Entrepreneurship × Cost leadership	0.99	0.10	0.68	0.11	2.33*	0.20
Size	-0.16		-0.27		-0.12	
Industry	-0.06		0.51		0.16	
Entrepreneurship	-2.27		1.25		-1.60	
Marketing differentiation	-0.57	0.03	0.09	0.06	-0.20	0.02
Entrepreneurship × Marketing differentiation	0.79	0.05	-0.42	0.06	0.58	0.02
Size	-0.08		-0.02		-0.13	
Industry	-0.13		0.66		0.39	
Entrepreneurship	-1.03		-2.18		-2.91	
Innovative differentiation	0.25	0.08	0.60	0.18	1.08	0.21
Entrepreneurship × Innovative differentiation	0.44	0.10	0.74	0.20	1.16	0.27

[a]Regression weights shown are unstandardized coefficients obtained at the final step.
$N = 32$. *$p < 0.05$.

opposite direction from what was hypothesized. The interaction of cost leadership and heterogeneity was positive, but not statistically significant. Therefore Hypothesis 7 is not supported.

Hypothesis 8 predicted that entrepreneurial firms pursuing a marketing differentiation strategy in an uncertain or heterogeneous environment would enjoy higher performance. Table 5 indicates strong support for this contention. The use of a marketing differentiation strategy in a heterogeneous environment is statistically significant and positive for both the profitability/ROI and overall company performance measures. Higher performance is also indicated for marketing differentiation in an uncertain

environment with profitability/ROI as the dependent variable. Hypothesis 9 stated that entrepreneurial firms following an innovative differentiation strategy would also be associated with higher performance. This was supported for firms in an uncertain environment (for sales growth and overall performance), as well as for innovative differentiators in a heterogeneous environment (for overall performance).

The results reported here indicate a general lack of support for the hypotheses that predicted contingent relationships based on two-way interactions. However, configurations of strategy and environment with entrepreneurial strategy

Table 5. Results of moderated regression analysis: Three-way[a,b]

Variables	Sales growth		Profitability/ROI		Overall performance	
	b	R^2	b	R^2	b	R^2
Size	0.25		0.22		0.30	
Industry	0.10		0.49		0.23	
Entrepreneurship	27.76		39.89		21.04	
Cost leadership	−1.67		1.00		−0.99	
Uncertainty	−0.74	0.05	2.76	0.08	0.43	0.05
Entrepreneurship × Cost × Uncertainty	2.33†	0.31	2.67†	0.28	1.85	0.33
Size	−0.07		−0.27		−0.08	
Industry	0.11		0.36		−0.02	
Entrepreneurship	14.69		20.05		21.16	
Cost leadership	1.96		0.99		0.58	
Heterogeneity	2.13	0.05	1.16	0.09	1.02	0.05
Entrepreneurship × Cost × Heterogeneity	1.19	0.24	0.95	0.17	1.76	0.32
Size	−0.19		−0.19		−0.05	
Industry	0.09		0.70		0.34	
Entrepreneurship	41.08		94.95		52.59	
Marketing differentiation	1.31		3.17		0.66	
Uncertainty	0.78	0.05	2.90	0.05	0.76	0.02
Entrepreneurship × Marketing differentiation × Uncertainty	3.46	0.15	7.48*	0.36	4.42	0.18
Size	−0.36		−0.68		−0.49	
Industry	−0.21		−0.02		−0.42	
Entrepreneurship	26.53		70.78		77.74	
Marketing differentiation	0.91		13.57		13.50	
Heterogeneity	0.41	0.05	8.24	0.06	8.38	0.02
Entrepreneurship × Marketing differentiation × Heterogeneity	2.35	0.21	4.74*	0.40	5.69**	0.43
Size	−0.05		−0.01		−0.04	
Industry	0.15		0.55		0.47	
Entrepreneurship	40.61		27.34		43.73	
Innovative differentiation	5.96		6.36		14.64	
Uncertainty	4.36	0.11	5.14	0.13	10.78	0.17
Entrepreneurship × Innovative differentiation × Uncertainty	4.09†	0.30	2.49	0.24	4.20†	0.44
Size	−0.08		−0.19		−0.23	
Industry	0.14		0.62		0.02	
Entrepreneurship	−15.91		17.34		30.21	
Innovative differentiation	0.27		2.54		2.06	
Heterogeneity	−0.15	0.11	1.12	0.18	0.60	0.21
Entrepreneurship × Innovative differentiation × Heterogeneity	−0.86	0.19	0.99	0.36	2.23†	0.40

[a] Two-way interactions included in the regression analysis are not shown here in order to save space.
[b] Regression weights shown are unstandardized coefficients obtained at the final step.
$N = 32$. † $p < 0.10$; * $p < 0.05$; ** $p < 0.01$

making—the three-way interactions—were supported for both marketing and inovative differentiation strategies. There was also statistical significance (two out of six equations) for the three-way interactions associated with cost leadership, but in the direction *opposite* of that hypothesized.

DISCUSSION

This study endeavored to examine the relationship between entrepreneurial strategy making and performance. Some theorists have argued that entrepreneurship will be positively associated with performance (e.g., Covin and Slevin, 1991), while others have claimed that an entrepreneurial approach to strategy making will detract from performance (e.g., Hart, 1992). We suggested that an essential key to understanding the ESM–performance relationship is to analyze the context in which it occurs. In Phase 1, we predicted that ESM would emerge as a salient strategy-making mode that organizations utilize. In Phase 2, we hypothesized that the relationship between ESM and performance is contingent on strategic and environmental factors, and may best be explained by investigating complex configurations.

The present study provides strong support for Phase 1 and somewhat mixed support for Phase 2. In Phase 1, the entrepreneurial strategy-making process which was derived through factor analysis was found to be consistent with the underlying concepts of decision making and behavior that have been frequently suggested in the entrepreneurial process literature (Covin and Slevin, 1991; Lumpkin and Dess, 1996; Miller, 1983; Mintzberg, 1973). Also, the significant one-way F-tests, as earlier stated, provide support for entrepreneurial strategy making as an organization-level construct. The entrepreneurial SMP factor was also independent of the three other SMP factors in the analysis: participativeness, adaptiveness, and simplicity. We believe that this finding has theoretical implications in that it suggests, for example, that an entrepreneurial approach to strategy making may exist independently of the level of participation or degree of adaptiveness that a firm may use in its strategy-making process. Thus, unlike Hart (1992) or Bourgeois and Brodwin (1984), who maintain that entrepreneurial dimensions are subsumed by other strategy-making modes, our findings suggest that entrepreneurial

strategy making represents a distinct strategy-making process characterized by experimentation, innovativeness, risk taking, and proactive assertiveness.

In Phase 2, we found that entrepreneurial strategy making was most strongly associated with performance when it was combined with *both* the appropriate strategy and environmental conditions. This finding is consistent with Miller (1988) and others who suggest a configurational framework—as opposed to a contingency approach—for the purpose of further developing normative and descriptive theory. Lenz (1980), for example, in a study of savings and loan associations concluded that 'neither environment, strategy nor organizational structure is sufficient to explain differences in performance... organizational performance is determined, in part, by the particular coalignment administrators are able to achieve' (1980: 220–221). The findings reported here support the notion that multivariate configurations may be better predictors of firm performance.

Contrary to our hypotheses, however, entrepreneurial strategy making, when matched with high environmental uncertainty as well as a low cost strategy, was also associated with high performance. One might interpret this finding as suggesting that, even when competing on the basis of cost, it may be advisable to proactively monitor the environment, take some risks, and innovate. Perhaps entrepreneurial processes serve as a means of encouraging the use of state-of-the-art process technologies that further lower costs and enhance quality. Such is the nature of several recent practices which have become rather common among many leading-edge organizations. Under names such as 'core process redesign' 'business process improvement,' and 'reengineering' (Hammer and Champy, 1993), such activities can be innovative, proactive, and serve to dramatically enhance a firm's cost position relative to its competitors. Our finding, which suggests that an entrepreneurial strategy-making process is associated with higher performance when accompanied by a cost leadership strategy, is also consistent with Hamel and Prahalad's (1989) observation that successful firms 'build layers of advantage' by combining distinct bases for competitive superiority in their strategic initiatives. A cost leadership strategy and an entrepreneurial strategy-making process are, arguably, dis-

© 1997 by John Wiley & Sons, Ltd.

Strat. Mgmt J., *Vol* 18, 677–695 (1997)

tinct bases on which competitive advantage is sought (albeit at the strategy content vs. the strategy-making process levels). As argued by Miller and Friesen (1984), Covin and Slevin (1989), Lumpkin and Dess (1996), and many others, firms often adopt an entrepreneurial posture in their strategy-making processes as a means to achieve competitive advantage through proactive strategic repositioning and product/market revitalization efforts. A cost leadership strategy is also widely regarded as a potentially effective yet independent (of entrepreneurial posture) means to achieve competitive advantage (Porter, 1980). Importantly, the pursuit of a cost leadership strategy is not inimical to entrepreneurial strategy making. Therefore, companies that exhibit both strategic characteristics are positioned to leverage multiple layers of advantage. This may explain why firms with cost leadership strategies *and* entrepreneurial strategy-making processes excelled in the current sample.

In contrast, it might be argued that differentiation strategies and entrepreneurial strategy-making processes are more congruent strategic constructs. For example, in his study of the competitive strategies of firms with entrepreneurial vs. conservative strategic postures (where strategic posture was operationalized along the same innovation, risk-taking and proactiveness dimensions used in the current study to define an entrepreneurial strategy-making process), Covin (1991) found that differentiation tactics like high price and high product quality were most pronounced among the entrepreneurial firms. This observed congruence between differentiation and entrepreneurial posture suggests that both strategic elements may contribute to a singular basis of competitive advantage. If these two strategic constructs do, in fact, contribute to a singular basis of competitive advantage, superior performance would not be expected to result from the combinations of these factors as multiple bases of advantage will not be realized. In other words, firms with high scores on both factors would not be expected to significantly outperform firms with high scores on one or the other factor. Consistent with this possibility, differentiation strategies and an entrepreneurial strategy-making process did not interact to predict firm performance in the two-way interactions among the sample firms.

It is interesting to speculate about why so many three-way interaction effects were found to

be significant while so many of the two-way effects were not. One obvious rationale is that configurations of attributes—that is, organizational gestalts—are more predictive of firm success because they, by definition, take into account more of the variables that can affect firm success. However, this explanation does not consider the specific variables examined as part of the three-way interaction effects in the current research. Moreover, one might conclude from the preceding explanation that all three-way interactions among variables that are critical contingencies within an organizational system context should, therefore, be more predictive of firm success than any two-way combinations of these same variables. But we know that this will not always be the case.

The presence of so many significant three-way interaction effects among the current study's variables, including similar 'direction' effects for disparate competitive strategy variables, may be at least partially attributable to the fact that high scores on all of the competitive strategy variables (i.e., the differentiation and cost leadership variables) represent, in essence, the presence of a basis for competitive advantage by the firm (Porter, 1980). Such a competitive advantage presence would, arguably, be most beneficial to a firm when (1) the environment is challenging such that a preponderance of the firms operating therein would not necessarily be expected to excel and (2) the firm is inclined to actively exploit this basis of advantage as demonstrated by the existence of an aggressive strategic posture. The first condition would be met among firms high on the environmental uncertainty and heterogeneity scales, and the second condition would be met by firms with entrepreneurial strategy-making processes. In other words, high scores on all three elements of the observed three-way interaction terms can be theoretically defended as the optimal positions to promote firm performance. This is, in fact, what our results show because any positive and significant betas associated with three-way interaction terms imply that high scores across all three contributing variables are positively associated with the dependent (performance) variable in question. The preceding argument may also partially explain why so many of the two-way interaction effects, which do not reflect a competitive strategy element, were not significant.

These findings clearly suggest that to further

understand the relationships between ESM and organizational and environmental factors, future research should investigate the processes by which entrepreneurial behavior enhances a firm's competitive position and performance. Such research may involve, for example, more fine-grained (Harrigan, 1983) methodologies (i.e., intensive field research, case studies) than the present study. Along these lines, Burgelman (1983) explored the implications of formal (induced) and informal (autonomous) entrepreneurial activities. In his study of six internal corporate venturing projects in a large high-tech firm, he found that the 'motor for corporate entrepreneurship resides in the autonomous strategic initiatives of individuals at the operational levels in the organization' (1983: 241). Such fine-grained methodologies could also provide insight into the role of culture and, in the context of the resource-based model of the firm, complex social processes (e.g., Barney, 1992) associated with the elements of an entrepreneurial posture.

Another limitation, as well as another opportunity for future research, relates to our conceptualization of strategy. As suggested earlier, entrepreneurial strategy making is likely to lead to revised or extended concepts of low cost leadership. Entrepreneurially oriented firms may address cost reduction via aggressive technology policy (Zahra and Covin, 1993) or radical innovativeness (Hage, 1980) aimed at reengineering processes and systems to achieve a low-cost advantage. It is well known that such processes can improve differentiation strategies as well in terms of quality and quick response. This serves to further support a growing literature that provides both strong theoretical rationale (Hill, 1988; Jones and Butler, 1988) as well as empirical support (White, 1986; Kim and Lim, 1988) for combining Porter's (1980) generic strategies. Thus, future research could investigate new approaches to configuring sources of competitive advantage.

A limitation of the present research is its cross-sectional design. Future research needs to investigate the organizational and performance implications of entrepreneurial strategy making over time. The present study, of course, implicitly assumes that the culture, processes, and structures associated with an ESM are enduring and stable over time. However, investigating how such behavior evolves over time and its relationship

to environment, strategy, structure, processes, and performance necessitates longitudinal analysis. One of the few studies to have addressed this issue is Zahra and Covin's (1995) research, consisting of three different data bases, which found that the relationship between ESM and performance strengthens over time.

Finally, many would agree that research exploring the relationship between entrepreneurial activities and performance is very timely given the competitive conditions faced by firms of all sizes in today's economy. The present study has used a factor analytic approach to identify the dimensionality and independence of entrepreneurial strategy making and suggests the need for a configurational approach when modeling this construct. Further research is needed to refine measures, explore the underlying processes associated with entrepreneurial behavior—ideally with longitudinal designs—and recognize the multidimensional and configurational nature of entrepreneurial strategy making and its outcomes.

ACKNOWLEDGEMENTS

The authors wish to thank *SMJ*'s reviewers and Richard Priem, Abdul Rasheed and Bruce Walters for their helpful comments on earlier drafts of this manuscript.

REFERENCES

Barney, J. (1992). 'Integrating organizational behavior and strategy formulation research: A resource-base analysis'. In P. Shrivastava, A. Huff, and J. Dutton (eds.), *Advances in Strategic Management*. JAI Press, Greenwich, CT, pp. 39–62.

Blau, P. M. and R. A. Schoenherr (1971). *The Structure of Organizations*. Basic Books, New York.

Bourgeois, L. J. (1985). 'Strategic goals, perceived uncertainty, and economic performance in volatile environments', *Academy of Management Journal*, 28, pp. 548–573.

Bourgeois, L. and D. Brodwin (1984). 'Strategic implementation: Five approaches to an elusive phenomenon', *Strategic Management Journal*, 5(3), pp. 241–264.

Burgelman, R. (1983). 'A process model of internal corporate venturing in the diversified major firm', *Administrative Science Quarterly*, 28, pp. 223–244.

Cattell, R. (1965). 'Factor analysis: An introduction to essentials; (1) the purpose and underlying models, (2) the role of factor analysis in research', *Biometrics*, 21, pp. 190–215.

694   *G. G. Dess, G. T. Lumpkin and J. G. Covin*

Cohen, J. and P. Cohen (1983). *Applied Multiple Regression/Correlation Analysis for the Behavioral Sciences* (2nd ed.). Erlbaum, Hillsdale, NJ.

Cornwall, J. R. and B. Perlman (1990). *Organizational Entrepreneurship.* Irwin, Homewood, IL.

Covin, J. G. (1991) 'Entrepreneurial versus conservative firms: A comparison of strategies and performance', *Journal of Management Studies*, **28**, pp. 439–462.

Covin, J. G. and P. Adler (1989). 'Strategic behavior, strategy patterns, and performance levels of small entrepreneurial and conservative firms', *Southern Management Proceedings*, pp. 250–252.

Covin, J. G. and T. Covin (1990). 'Competitive aggressiveness, environmental context, and small firm performance', *Entrepreneurship: Theory and Practice*, **14**(4), pp. 35–50.

Covin, J. G. and D. Slevin (1988). 'The influence of organization structure on the utility of an entrepreneurial top management style', *Journal of Management Studies*, **25**, pp. 217–234.

Covin, J. G. and D. Slevin (1989). 'Strategic management of small firms in hostile and benign environments', *Strategic Management Journal*, **10**(1), pp. 75–87.

Covin, J. G. and D. Slevin (1991). 'A conceptual model of entrepreneurship as firm behavior', *Entrepreneurship: Theory and Practice*, **16**, pp. 7–24.

Covin, J. G., D. P. Slevin and R. L. Schultz (1994). 'Implementing strategic missions: Effective strategic, structural, and tactical choices', *Journal of Management Studies*, **31**(4), pp. 481–505.

Daft, R. and A. Lewin (1993). 'Where are the theories for the "new" organizational forms? An editorial essay', *Organization Science*, **4**, pp. i–vi.

Dess, G. and B. Keats (1987). 'Environmental assessment and organizational performance: An exploratory field study', *Proceedings of the Academy of Management's annual meeting*, New Orleans, LA, pp. 21–25.

Dess, G., S. Newport and A. Rasheed (1993). 'Configuration research in strategic management: Key issues and suggestions', *Journal of Management*, **19**(4), pp. 775–795.

Dess, G. and R. Robinson (1984). 'Measuring organizational performance in the absence of objective measures: The case of the privately-held firm and conglomerate business unit', *Strategic Management Journal*, **5**(3), pp. 265–273.

Doty, D. H., W. H. Glick and G. P. Huber (1993). 'Fit, equifinality, and organizational effectiveness: A test of two configurational theories', *Academy of Management Journal*, **36**(6), pp. 1196–1250.

Downey, H. and J. Slocum (1975). 'Uncertainty: Measures, research, and sources of variation', *Academy of Management Journal*, **18**, pp. 562–577.

Duncan, R. (1972). 'Characteristics of organizational environments and perceived environmental uncertainty', *Administrative Science Quarterly*, **17**, pp. 313–327.

Emory, C. W. and D. R. Cooper (1991). *Business Research Methods* (4th ed.). Irwin, Homewood IL.

Fredrickson, J. (1986). 'The strategic decision making process and organizational structure', *Academy of Management Review*, **8**, pp. 280–297.

Hage, J. (1980). *Theories of Organization.* Wiley, New York.

Hair, J., R. Anderson, R. Tatham and B. Grablowsky (1979). *Multivariate Data Analysis.* Petroleum Publishing, Tulsa, OK.

Hambrick, D. (1985). 'Strategies for mature industrial product businesses'. In J. H. Grant (ed.), *Strategic Management Frontiers.* JAI Press, Greenwich, CT, pp. 320–356.

Hambrick, D. and P. Mason (1984). 'Upper echelons: The organization as a reflection of its top managers', *Academy of Management Review*, **9**, pp. 193–206.

Hamel, G. and C. K. Prahalad (1989). 'Strategic intent', *Harvard Business Review*, **67**(3), pp. 63–76.

Hammer, M. and J. Champy (1993). *Reengineering the Corporation: A Manifesto for Business Revolution.* Harper Business, New York.

Harrigan, K. R. (1983). 'Research methodologies for contingency approaches to strategy', *Academy of Management Review*, **8**, pp. 398–405.

Hart, S. (1991). 'Intentionality and autonomy in strategy-making process: Modes, archetypes, and firm performance'. In P. Shrivastava, A. Huff and J. Dutton (eds.), *Advances in Strategic Management*, Vol. 7, JAI Press, Greenwich CT, pp. 97–127.

Hart, S. (1992). 'An integrative framework for strategy-making processes', *Academy of Management Review*, **17**, pp. 327–351.

Hill, C. W. L. (1988). 'Differentiation versus low cost or differentiation and low cost: A contingency framework', *Academy of Management Review*, **13**, pp. 401–412.

Hitt, M. and B. Tyler (1991). 'Strategic decision models: Integrating different perspectives', *Strategic Management Journal*, **12**(5), pp. 327–351.

Jones, G. R. and J. E. Butler (1988). 'Costs, revenue, and business-level strategy', *Academy of Management Review*, **13**, pp. 202–213.

Kaiser, H. F. and J. Rice (1974). 'Little Jiffy, Mark IV', *Educational and Psychological Measurement*, **34**, pp. 111–117.

Karagozoglu, N. and W. B. Brown (1988). 'Adaptive responses by conservative and entrepreneurial firms', *Journal of Product Innovation Management*, **5**, pp. 269–281.

Kerlinger, F. N. (1986). *Foundations of Behavioral Research* (3rd ed.). Holt Rinehart and Winston, Fort Worth, TX.

Khandwalla, P. N. (Winter 1976/77). 'Some top management styles, their context and performance', *Organization and Administrative Sciences*, **7**(4), pp. 21–51.

Khandwalla, P. N. (1987). 'Generators of pioneering-innovative management: Some Indian evidence', *Organization Studies*, **8**, pp. 39–59.

Kim, L. and Y. Lim (1988). 'Environment, generic strategies and performance in a rapidly developing country: A taxonomic approach', *Academy of Management Journal*, **31**, pp. 802–827.

Kim, J. and C. Mueller (1978). *Factor Analysis: Sta-*

tistical Methods and Practical Issues. Sage, Beverly Hills, CA.

Lawrence, P. and J. Lorsch (1967). Organization and Environment. Harvard University Press, Cambridge, MA.

Lenz, R. T. (1980). 'Environment, strategy, organizational structure, and performance: Patterns in one industry', Strategic Management Journal, 1(3), pp. 209–226.

Lumpkin, G. T. and G. G. Dess (1996). 'Clarifying the entrepreneurial orientation construct and linking it to performance', Academy of Management Review, 21(1), pp. 135–172.

Miles, R. and C. Snow (1978). Organizational Strategy, Structure, and Process. McGraw-Hill, New York.

Miller, D. (1983). 'The correlates of entrepreneurship in three types of firms', Management Science, 29, pp. 770–791.

Miller, D. (1986). 'Configurations of strategy and structure: Towards a synthesis', Strategic Management Journal, 7(3), pp. 233–249.

Miller, D. (1987). 'Strategy making and structure: Analysis and implications for performance', Academy of Management Journal, 30(1), pp. 7–32.

Miller, D. (1988). 'Relating Porter's business strategies to environment and structure: Analysis and performance implications', Academy of Management Journal, 31, pp. 280–308.

Miller, D. (1992). 'Generic strategies: Classification, combination and context'. In P. Shrivastava, A. Huff and J. Dutton (eds.), Advances in Strategic Management. JAI Press, Greenwich, CT, pp. 391–408.

Miller, D. (1993). 'The architecture of simplicity', Academy of Management Review, 18, pp. 116–138.

Miller, D., C. Droge and J. Toulouse (1988). 'Strategic process and content as mediators between organizational context and structure', Academy of Management Journal, 31, pp. 544–569.

Miller, D. and P. Friesen (1978). 'Archetypes of strategy formulation', Management Science, 24, pp. 921–933.

Miller, D. and P. Friesen (1982). 'Innovation in conservative and entrepreneurial firms: Two models of strategic momentum', Strategic Management Journal, 3(1), pp. 1–25.

Miller, D. and P. Friesen (1984). Organizations: A Quantum View. Prentice-Hall, Englewood Cliffs, NJ.

Miller, D. and H. Mintzberg (1984). 'The case for configuration'. In G. Morgan (ed.), Beyond Method. Sage, Beverly Hills, CA, pp. 57–73.

Mintzberg H. (1973). 'Strategy making in three modes', California Management Review, 16(2), pp. 44–53.

Mintzberg H. (1983). Power in and around organizations. Prentice-Hall, Englewood Cliffs, NJ.

Mintzberg H., D. Raisinghani and A. Theoret (1976). 'The structure of "unstructured" decision processes', Administrative Science Quarterly, 21(2), pp. 246–275.

Murray, A. (1989). 'Top management group heterogeneity and firm performance', Strategic Management Journal, Summer Special Issue, 10, pp. 125–141.

Naman, J. and D. Slevin (1993). 'Entrepreneurship and the concept of fit: A model and empirical test', Strategic Management Journal, 14(2), pp. 137–153.

Peters, T. and R. Waterman (1982). In Search of Excellence. Harper & Row, New York.

Porter, M. (1980). Competitive Strategy. Free Press, New York.

Schollhammer, H. (1982). 'Internal corporate entrepreneurship'. In C. A. Kent, D. L. Sexton and K. H. Vesper (eds.), Encyclopedia of Entrepreneurship. Prentice-Hall, Englewood Cliffs, NJ, pp. 209–223.

Venkatraman, N. and V. Ramanujam (1987). 'Measurement of business economic performance: An examination of method convergence', Journal of Management, 13, pp. 109–122.

Wallace, G. (1993). 'Enterprise', Business Week, Special 1993 Bonus issue.

White, R. E. (1986). 'Generic business strategies, organizational context and performance: An empirical investigation', Strategic Management Journal, 7(3), pp. 217–231.

Zahra, S. (1986). 'A canonical analysis of corporate entrepreneurship antecedents and impact on performance', Proceedings of the Academy of Management's annual meeting, Chicago IL, pp. 71–75.

Zahra, S. (1993a). 'A conceptual model of entrepreneurship as firm behavior: A critique and extension', Entrepreneurship: Theory and Practice, 18, pp. 5–21.

Zahra, S. (1993b). 'Environment, corporate entrepreneurship and financial performance: A taxonomic approach', Journal of Business Venturing, 8, pp. 319–340.

Zahra, S. and J. G. Covin (1993). 'Business strategy, technology policy and firm performance. Strategic Management Journal, 14(6), pp. 451–478.

Zahra, S. and J. G. Covin (1995). 'Contextual influences on the corporate entrepreneurship–performance relationship: A longitudinal analysis', Journal of Business Venturing, 10(1), pp. 43–58.

[26]

CONTEXTUAL INFLUENCES ON THE CORPORATE ENTREPRENEURSHIP– PERFORMANCE RELATIONSHIP: A LONGITUDINAL ANALYSIS

SHAKER A. ZAHRA
Georgia State University

JEFFREY G. COVIN
Georgia Institute of Technology

EXECUTIVE SUMMARY

Over the past several years corporate entrepreneurship has been widely touted by executives and researchers alike as an effective means for revitalizing companies and improving their financial performance. For the most part, the call for greater entrepreneurial behavior on the part of established companies has been accepted on faith as an inherently desirable objective. The implicit logic behind the pervasive belief in the value of corporate entrepreneurship seems to be that risk taking, innovation, and aggressive competitive action—the key elements of entrepreneurial corporations—will help in identifying and pursuing lucrative product/market opportunities and in providing new bases for achieving superior competitive positions.

But what do we really know about the financial consequences of corporate entrepreneurship? Most of the evidence that corporate entrepreneurship "pays off" is anecdotal in nature or based on cross-sectional studies that focus on the short-term implications of entrepreneurial behaviors. As such, in a definitive sense, we know very little about the financial consequences of corporate entrepreneurship.

In an attempt to improve our understanding of this issue, this article describes a study of corporate entrepreneurship and its impact on company financial performance. Data were collected from three different samples over a seven-year period to assess the longitudinal impact of corporate

Address correspondence to Jeffrey G. Covin, School of Management, Georgia Institute of Technology, Atlanta, GA 30332-0520

The authors would like to thank the three anonymous *JBV* reviewers, as well as Donald Neubaum, Mark Simon, Rod Shrader, and Patricia Zahra for their comments on earlier drafts of this article.

0883-9026/95/$9.50
SSDI 0883-9026 (94) 00004-E

entrepreneurship on firm performance. These samples consist of 24 medium-sized manufacturing firms representing 14 industry segments, 39 chemical companies, and 45 Fortune 500 industrial firms representing five industry segments. Data were gathered on each sample using both primary and secondary sources. Regression analysis was then used to analyze the data.

The results suggest that corporate entrepreneurship has a positive impact on financial measures of company performance. This effect on performance, which tends to be modest over the first few years, increases over time, suggesting that corporate entrepreneurship may, indeed, be a generally effective means for improving long-term company financial performance. Moreover, the results indicate that corporate entrepreneurship is a particularly effective practice among companies operating in hostile environments (as opposed to benign environments).

The study has three principal implications for practicing managers. First, the study documents the general financial viability of engaging in corporate entrepreneurship. This is not to suggest that corporate entrepreneurship is a panacea for improving financial performance. However, entrepreneurial behavior, when considered on the whole (i.e., across firms and industries), is associated with superior financial performance. Second, the study suggests a need to use a long-term time horizon in order to adequately judge the financial consequences of corporate entrepreneurship. The use of a shorter evaluation period may not allow sufficient time for entrepreneurial actions to have their full market and corresponding financial impact. Finally, the study identifies the context-specific character of effective entrepreneurial practice. Specifically, corporate entrepreneurship appears to be a particularly effective strategic practice among firms operating in hostile business settings.

INTRODUCTION

Corporate entrepreneurship (CE) provides a potential means for revitalizing established companies. This is accomplished through risk taking, innovation, and proactive competitive behaviors (Guth and Ginsberg 1990). That is, CE is reflected in top management's risk taking with regard to: investment decisions and strategic actions in the face of uncertainty, the extensiveness and frequency of product innovation and the related tendency toward technological leadership, and the pioneering nature of the firm as evident in the propensity to aggressively and proactively compete with industry rivals (Sexton and Bowman-Upton 1991; Zahra 1991).

To date, research has examined the nature of CE (Morris, Davis, and Ewing 1988); its antecedent conditions such as the environment (Covin and Slevin 1991), structure (Burgelman and Sayles 1986; Zajac, Golden, and Shortell 1991), and organizational variables (Miller 1983); and its potential outcomes such as improved company performance (Block and MacMillan 1993; MacMillan and Day 1987). However, despite the fact that CE may take a long time before it significantly impacts company performance (Biggadike 1979; Miller and Camp 1985), little systematic attention has been given to documenting the long-term financial implications of CE activities. This makes it difficult for scholars to develop theories and models that explain the utility of CE. As such, managers have little guidance from the existing literature on the potential time horizon for recouping their investments in CE activities. Information on this investment horizon is important for planning and resource allocation purposes. Moreover, evidence on the pay-off from CE can be useful for managers as they seek senior executives' support in undertaking CE-related activities.

This study contributes to the literature in three specific ways. First, unlike past research, this study focuses on the long-term financial implications of CE. Although some past studies have explored the time horizons over which new ventures typically achieve profitability (Block and MacMillan 1993), they have examined a specific manifestation of CE and its relationship with performance, rather than the CE–performance relationship per se. The present study examines the broader concept of CE and its relationship with company financial performance over time. The operational definition of CE used in the current study is based on Miller's (1983) conceptualization of this construct as a company's commitment to innovation in existing businesses. There are, of course, other ways in which CE can be conceptualized and operationalized. For example, resource allocation patterns intended to revise existing business definitions, competencies, or firm skill bases can be viewed as manifestations of CE (Burgelman 1983), and these activities should be longitudinally examined in future research. Nonetheless, the longitudinal design of the current research is novel among the studies that have adopted Miller's (1983) broadly defined operationalization of CE.

A second contribution of this study is its examination of a key environmental factor that can profoundly influence the level of success associated with the pursuit of CE: environmental hostility. The crucial importance of this variable as a correlate or determinant of strategic behavior has been documented in numerous studies (e.g., Zahra 1993; Miller and Friesen 1984). Dess and Beard (1984) note that hostility's importance stems from the fact that it reflects the extent of environmental support for organizational activities like CE. Hostility may have a particularly strong effect on the success of CE, moderating the relationship between CE and firm financial performance.

A third contribution of this study is its reliance on longitudinal data collected from three diverse samples of companies. The diversity of the samples provides a basis for examining the generalizability of the CE–performance relationship over time. Moreover, one of the samples is composed of firms in a single industry, thus permitting the examination of the longitudinal CE–performance relationship under more controlled environmental conditions. Further, the study has controlled for industry effects on performance, thus removing a factor that could potentially confound the CE–performance relationship.

In short, this study extends our knowledge of the CE–performance relationship by exploring, in several industry settings, the longitudinal impact of CE on company financial performance while simultaneously documenting the effects of a generally recognized contextual influence, hostility, on this relationship.

The following section reviews the literature on the CE–company-performance relationship and concludes by advancing testable hypotheses. The next section outlines the study's data collection approach, measures, and analytical techniques, and this is followed by a presentation of the study's results. The final section outlines the study's limitations and discusses the implications of the findings for managerial action and future research.

THEORY AND HYPOTHESES

The Corporate Entrepreneurship–Performance Relationship

Miller (1983) views CE as encompassing three related components: product innovation, proactiveness, and risk taking. Product innovation refers to the ability of a company to create new products or modify existing ones to meet the demands of current or future markets. Proactiveness refers to a company's capacity to beat competitors in introducing new products, services, or technologies to the market. Finally, CE indicates that a company is willing to engage in business ventures or strategies in which the outcome may be highly uncertain. Together, product innovation, proactiveness, and risk taking capture the essence of CE. This multi-faceted definition builds on Schumpeter's (1934) work and is consistent with recent writings on the topic (Guth and Ginsberg 1990). This definition has also influenced recent research on CE (e.g., Jennings and Seaman 1990; Zahra 1991). Consequently, Miller's definition of CE is adopted in this article.

Current interest in CE arises from its potential usefulness as a means for renewing established organizations and increasing their ability to compete in their chosen markets. Covin and Slevin (1991, p. 19) suggest that "the growing interest in the study of entrepreneurship is a response ... to the belief that such activity can lead to improved performance in established organizations." Schollhammer (1982, p. 210) also suggests that corporate entrepreneurship is "the key element for gaining competitive advantage and consequently greater financial rewards." Similarly, Peters and Waterman (1982) suggest that undertaking CE activities improves a company's financial performance.

Of course, not all CE efforts lead to improved company performance. Citing examples of venturing activities by leading corporations, Fast (1981) argues that CE can be risky and, in fact, detrimental to a firm's short-term financial performance. Moreover, poor organization, lack of strategic focus, and dysfunctional organizational politics often doom corporate entrepreneurial activities (Burgelman and Sayles 1986; Sexton and Bowman-Upton 1991).

Nonetheless, a theoretical link between CE and company financial performance can be readily inferred from the literature. For example, an impressive body of literature suggests that companies which pioneer the creation and introduction of new products or technologies, which would be typical of companies that practice CE, often achieve superior financial performance (e.g., Cheney, Devinney, and Winer 1991; Lengnick-Hall 1992). Pioneers can target premium market segments and charge correspondingly high prices, control access to the market by dominating distribution channels, and establish their products as the industry's standard. These actions help the pioneers to acquire and sustain high market share and achieve profitability. This is not to suggest that pioneering does not have concomitant costs and risks. Pioneers must often invest heavily in developing name recognition, building distribution channels, and safeguarding against imitation by competitors. The returns on these investments can be very disappointing (Rosenbloom and Cusumano 1987; Teece 1986). However, research suggests that under hostile environmental conditions, pioneering will often enable a firm to revise the rules of competition, redefine industry boundaries, and preempt would-be rivals from entering the industry, thereby enhancing the firm's competitive posture (Zahra and Das 1993).

Despite the theoretical link between CE and company financial performance, little empirical research has focused on this relationship to date. Covin and Slevin (1991, p. 19) conclude that "surprisingly little systematic empirical evidence is available to support the belief in a strong positive relationship between entrepreneurial posture and firm performance." Sexton and Bowman-Upton (1991) also note the inconclusiveness of the empirical link between CE and financial performance. Similarly, Zahra (1991) observes that the bulk of the evidence on the CE–financial-performance relationship is anecdotal and testimonial in nature.

Some tentative findings on the CE–performance link have been reported in the literature. For example, Covin and Slevin (1986) reported a simple correlation of $r = .39$ ($p < .001$) between their entrepreneurial posture scale and a multi-item index of firm performance. Zahra (1991) reported a positive association between CE activities and profitability, growth, and risk-related measures of company performance. Moreover, when one- and two-year performance lag effects were considered, Zahra's study revealed that CE continues to be positively associated with company performance over time, and that lagged correlation coefficients may surpass contemporaneous ("concurrent") correlations. Zahra cautioned, however, that a much longer lag time would be needed to adequately document the possible longitudinal effects of CE on company performance.

Consistent with the spirit of the previous findings, past research has indicated that the pay-off of certain CE variables is long-term in nature. Ravenscraft and Scherer (1982) found that a firm's research and development (R&D) spending, a major predictor of innovativeness among established companies, has a positive association with company profitability, lagging four to six years. Franko (1989) also documented the long-term effect of a company's R&D spending on long-term profitability and growth. Because R&D is widely considered to be a major source of new products, technologies, and improved production processes, these results suggest that companies should adopt a long-term perspective in evaluating the potential financial results of CE activities. This same conclusion was drawn in Biggadike's (1979) research on corporate ventures, where it was found that these businesses take, on average, eight years to break even and do not reach their maximum profitability until year 12.

Still, there is much uncertainty regarding the time horizon over which CE activities can reasonably be expected to yield positive returns on investment (Block and MacMillan 1993). Some of this uncertainty stems from inconsistencies in the ways that findings are reported within the literature. For example, in a study of 11 corporate start-ups (which are a form of CE activity), Fast (1981) found that, on average, an 18% ROI was achieved by the third year of operations. Von Hippel (1977), in a study of 18 corporate ventures, reported that 60% became "successful" (defined as having achieved 10% pretax profit) within a three- to five-year period. In a comparative study of corporate venturing practices in U.S. and Japanese companies, Block and Subbanarasimha (1989) reported that the mean time required to break even was 2.7 to 3.0 years, and this held for ventures in both countries. One conclusion of the Block and Subbanarasimha (1989) study was that time-to-profitability cannot be predicted by using any simple formula. Rather, it is affected by a complex set of factors including the structure of the market, the venture's basis for competitive advantage, and the resources applied to the venture.

The preceding arguments suggest that much ambiguity exists regarding the impact of different CE manifestations on company financial performance as well as on the time horizon over which the effects of these manifestations are likely to be felt. Nonetheless, on the whole, the empirical research that has focused on CE, broadly defined, supports the following hypothesis:

H1: *CE is positively associated with a company's financial performance.*

From a theoretical perspective, there are at least two reasons for expecting a positive and increasing relationship between CE activities and subsequent firm performance. First, consistent with arguments made by Miller and Friesen (1984), Pinchot (1985), and others, innovativeness can be a source of competitive advantage for a firm. Innovative companies frequently develop strong, positive market reputations that ensure customer loyalty. They also monitor market changes and respond quickly, thus capitalizing on emerging opportunities. Importantly, sustained innovation can increasingly distance entrepreneurial firms from their industry rivals, thereby resulting in positive and growing returns to the entrepreneurial firm. Second, the fact that firms which pursue CE are proactive by definition often allows them to exploit an additional basis for competitive advantage—that is, quick market response or the availability of a market offer ahead of competitors. Dess and Miller (1993) note that a quick response strategy often results in first-mover advantages (Lieberman and Montgomery 1988) that translate into superior firm performance. These advantages may grow in magnitude as learning and experience curve effects enable entrepreneurial firms to improve their product/market strategies. These arguments support the following hypothesis:

H2: *The strength of the CE–performance relationship will increase over time.*

Contextual Influences on the Corporate Entrepreneurship–Performance Relationship

A growing body of research suggests that contextual influences affect the level of success achieved by firms that practice CE (Dean 1993; Covin and Slevin 1991). These contextual influences can be broadly divided into internal factors (e.g., organizational structure, culture, and systems) and external factors (e.g., industry globalization, product/market life cycle stage, and governmental regulations). The current article focuses on the effects of a significant external factor on the CE–performance relationship. This external factor is environmental hostility.

Research suggests that the CE–performance relationship is contingent upon the nature of the firm's external environment (Zahra 1993; Block and Subbanarashimha 1989), and environmental hostility is a widely recognized dimension of the environment (Keats and Hitt 1988) that has strong theoretical ties to the construct of CE. Hostile environments are characterized by high levels of competitive intensity, a paucity of readily exploitable market opportunities, tremendous competitive-, market-, and/or product-related uncertainties, and a general vulnerability to influence from forces and elements external to the firm's immediate environment (Dess and Beard 1984). They are harsh, overwhelming settings in which survival is often viewed as a major accomplishment (Khandwalla 1977; Miller and Friesen 1984).

Research has shown that CE may be a particularly effective organizational practice among firms operating in hostile environments. For example, in a study of how changing environmental conditions impact entrepreneurial behavior and consequent performance, Miller and Friesen (1983) found that changes in innovative behavior and competitive proactiveness—two of the three dimensions of CE assessed in the current study—were significantly more positively correlated with changes in environmental hostility among a sample of 48 "successful" firms than among a sample of 40 "unsuccessful" firms.

Similar results were reported in Covin and Slevin's (1989) study of 161 manufacturing firms representing 25 industries. They argued that hostile environments afford fewer opportunities for achieving growth and profitability, and that in these settings CE is a logical means for creating and exploiting opportunities that result in competitive superiority. Further, Covin and Slevin suggested that because of the plentiful market opportunities and peaceful coexistence of firms in benign environments, the pursuit of CE in such settings may represent an unnecessary risk. Consistent with their arguments, these authors found that firms exhibiting high levels of CE activity generally performed best in hostile environments, whereas firms exhibiting low levels of CE activity generally performed best in more benign environments.

Finally, in a recent study of 102 manufacturing companies, Zahra (1993) found that environmental hostility is strongly associated with particular manifestations of CE (e.g., product development). His results further suggest that hostility moderates the relationship between several of these individual CE manifestations and company financial performance.

The preceding studies collectively make a strong argument that hostility moderates the CE–performance relationship. One limitation of these studies is their lack of attention to the CE–performance relationship over time. Therefore, whether or not hostility has a consistent, sustained (i.e., longitudinal) impact on the CE–performance relationship is unclear from the current empirical literature. It is plausible, nonetheless, that the effective practice of CE by firms in hostile environments will hasten the decline or demise of weaker firms and, in doing so, create market opportunities which will best be exploited by the stronger firms. Thus, hostility, per se, may amplify the positive impact of CE on firm financial performance over time. It is hypothesized thus:

H3: *The CE–performance relationship is more positive among firms in hostile environments than among firms in benign environments, and this situation holds over time.*

METHODS

Samples

Data collection for this article began in 1983 and ended in 1990. Telephone interviews with company executives were used in conjunction with secondary sources (e.g., companies' publications and annual reports) to make annual updates to the database. The data were collected from three samples that had several qualities in common: (1) they all consisted of domestic (or U.S.-based) manufacturing companies; (2) they all were mature, reflecting the various attributes of mature industries identified by Grant (1991); and (3) they all consisted of established companies, defined as those in existence for at least 10 years. To ensure clarity, the procedures used to collect data from the three samples are described separately below.

Study 1

Data were collected from manufacturing companies in five southeastern states in 1983. A total of 200 companies were contacted by phone or mail and 69 agreed to participate in the study for a response rate of 34.5%. This rate is similar to that reported in field research in this area (Miller and Friesen 1984). Companies that declined the invitation to participate in the study cited lack of time and confidentiality as major reasons for their decision.

T-test comparisons of the respondents and nonrespondents on company age ($t = 1.03$, $p = .41$), number of full-time employees ($t = 1.31$, $p = .23$), value of assets ($t = 1.27$, $p = .26$), and return on assets ($t = 1.02$, $p = .39$) did not reveal significant differences between the two groups. Therefore, it was concluded that responding firms did not differ significantly from the nonrespondents.

Data were collected through interviews with at least two senior executives, thus minimizing potential source bias. The respondents' scores on the study's measures were averaged, and the mean values were used as the company's scores on the individual measures. (The mean inter-rater correlation on the CE measure within this sample was $r = 0.85$, $p < .001$.) The respondents were among the firms' most senior executives, with 40% holding the title of president, 30% were general managers, and the remaining 30% were senior vice presidents. Financial data were collected from company publications and secondary sources. The companies competed in 14 different manufacturing industry sectors.

Study 2

A second database was collected from chemical companies located throughout the U.S. Potential respondents were identified for this study using trade association and government directories. A questionnaire was then mailed to the chief executive officers (CEOs) or highest ranking executives of 125 of the publicly held companies included in the population. Two mailings resulted in 55 completed surveys, but only 50 of these responses were usable, for a response rate of 40%.

To validate responses from the CEOs, a separate mailing was directed to a second senior executive in each of the responding companies. This mailing produced 30 completed responses. T-tests of the two sets of responses (the CEOs and the second respondents) revealed that the two groups differed ($p < .05$) in only 7% of the cases. Moreover, the correlation between the CEO and the second senior respondent on the CE measure for the sample was r = 0.82, *p* < .001. Therefore, it was concluded that responses from the CEOs were representative of the opinions of their top management groups. The CEO responses are used as this study's data.

Responding and nonresponding firms were compared on company age (*t* = 0.96, *p* = .53), number of employees (*t* = 1.41, *p* = .22), value of assets (*t* = 1.09, *p* = .32), and ROA (*t* = 1.16, *p* = .29). The *t*-test comparisons did not reveal any significant differences between the two groups. Thus, it was concluded that the sample did not differ significantly from the nonrespondents.

Study 3

Data were collected from *Fortune 500* industrial corporations. Mailed questionnaires were sent to the CEOs (or presidents) of 199 corporations in five industries. Two mailings resulted in 61 responses, of which 59 were usable, for a response rate of 30%.

As in study 2, a separate mailing was directed to a second senior executive in each of the 59 responding companies. The purpose was to validate the results from the initial survey. The second mailing produced 23 completed responses. *T*-tests of the two sets of responses (CEOs' and second respondents') showed that the two groups differed (*p* < .05) on only 5% of the questionnaire items. As with the prior two samples, there is a high degree of inter-rater reliability among the respondents on the CE measure. Specifically, the average correlation between respondents from the same firm is r = 0.86, *p* < .001. Hence, it was concluded that responses from the CEOs were representative of the opinions of their top management groups. The CEO data were used in the subsequent analyses.

T-tests were used to compare responding and nonresponding firms on company age (*t* = 0.96, *p* = .46), the number of employees (*t* = 1.08, *p* = .31), value of assets (*t* = 1.16, *p* = .25), and ROA (*t* = 0.89, *p* = .62). This comparison did not reveal any significant differences between the two groups. Thus, it was concluded that the sample did not differ from nonresponding firms.

Combined Sample Characteristics

Primary and secondary data were collected on the sampled firms' financial performance and environmental conditions over a six-year period subsequent to initial measurement in 1983. During this time, many of the companies in the initial samples experienced executive turnover that resulted in the loss of contacts in those firms. Mergers, acquisitions, and, in a few instances, bankruptcies also reduced the effective sample size during this period. Finally, incomplete longitudinal data on firm performance or environmental hostility, or incomplete 1983 data on the CE scale, resulted in several firms being dropped from the analysis. Collectively, these selection criteria and sample constraints resulted in a reduction in the overall sample size from 178 to 108. *T*-tests were used to verify that the final sample did not differ (*p* > .05) from the population from which it was drawn on the variables age, number of employees, and value of assets. Included in this final figure of 108 firms are 24 of the 69 medium-sized manufacturing firms, 39 of the 50 chemical companies, and 45 of the 59 *Fortune 500* companies.

This reduction in workable sample size required the collapsing of all three samples into one sample for data analysis purposes. This is clearly a compromise decision. However, the resulting and final sample is conservatively defined in that the same set of firms (with complete data for the same seven-year period) is used in all analyses. Moreover, two analyses were conducted to ascertain the appropriateness of combining all three samples prior to this action. One-way ANOVAs indicated that the three samples exhibit no overall differences (p >.05) in terms of their individual CE, environmental hostility, and financial performance scores. Additionally, Chow tests (Maddala 1977) run on the regression equations derived from the individual samples revealed that the overall structures of the relationships tested in this study do not significantly differ across the three samples. This latter finding is particularly important because it suggests that the same pattern of relationships holds for the two more diverse samples (numbers 1 and 3) as for the sample comprised of firms operating in a single industry (number 2). The 108 firms included in the combined sample have, on average, 6263.4 employees (SD = 2507.1), $1938.4 million in assets (SD = $671.4 million), and are 36.5-years old (SD = 21.9 years).

Measures

The collection and use of retrospective data pose many potential problems for researchers, such as the possibilities of limited recall of the respondents, biased perceptions of past realities, and unfamiliarity with critical issues and events. In order to ensure the existence of valid perceptual data for the current study, the measurement practices proposed by Huber and Power (1985) were followed during data collection. Specifically, in order to ensure that the respondents were familiar with the research issues and could respond accurately, the most senior managers of the sampled firms were targeted for data collection. As noted by Hambrick (1981), CEOs are typically the most knowledgeable persons regarding their companies' strategies and overall business situations. Second, in order to minimize social desirability bias in the measurement of constructs, the respondents were repeatedly reminded that there were no right or wrong answers to the questions being asked of them, and they were guaranteed confidentiality. Third, in order to ensure that the respondents could reasonably be expected to remember the precise and pertinent details necessary for the provision of valid data, the respondents were asked to recall how their companies had behaved over the most recent three-year period, and the study focused on a limited number of issues that fell within the managerial domains of the respondents.

To ensure the comparability of results across the samples, the same measures of CE, environmental hostility, and financial performance were used in the three studies, and the data were collected over the same seven-year time period. The measures are described below.

Corporate Entrepreneurship

Miller and Friesen's (1982) index was used as the primary measure of CE. The scale items are: (1) our company has introduced many new products or services over the past three years. (2) Our company has made many dramatic changes in the mix of its products and services over the past three years. (3) Our company has emphasized making major innovations in its products and services over the past three years. (4) Over the past three years, this company has shown a strong proclivity for high-risk projects (with chances of very high return). (5) This company has emphasized taking bold, wide-ranging actions in positioning itself and its products (services) over the past three years. (6) This company has shown a strong commitment to research and development (R&D), technological leadership, and innovation. (7) This company has followed strategies that allow it to exploit opportunities in its external environment.

This CE measure has been widely used in past research because of its reliability and validity (e.g., Jennings and Lumpkin 1989; Zahra 1991). The measure follows a seven-point scale ranging from 1 = very untrue to 7 = very true. Scores on the items were averaged to produce an overall CE index; a high score on the index shows high involvement in CE activities and vice versa. As mentioned previously, the respondents were asked to provide data on their companies' actual behaviors over the preceding three-year period, were reminded that there are no right or wrong answers, and were promised confidentiality. The index surpassed minimum internal consistency requirements as measured by an alpha coefficient of 0.75. Data for the CE measure were collected in 1983 using both interviews and mail surveys.

Environmental Hostility

Secondary data were used to compute an annual hostility index for each firm's environment over a seven-year period. For each year, three variables were used to construct the hostility index: the inverse of the industry's growth rate, the inverse of the industry's net profit margin, and the number of bankruptcies in an industry divided by the total number of firms in that industry. These variables were examined because they each reflect an environment's diminishing capacity to support business operations. For instance, low industry growth will often discourage innovation and further resource commitments to existing businesses. Declining profit margins can force executives to explore alternative arenas for capital investments, and bankruptcies may reflect an industry's approach to balancing demands and invested resources. When considered in unison, these variables provide an accurate and theoretically defensible operationalization of the environmental hostility construct.

For sampled firms operating in multiple industries, the aforementioned variables were weighted by the firm's share in its top four industries. On an annual basis, these data were factor-analyzed, and the factor loadings were multiplied by the firms' scores on these individual variables. The products were then summed to produce a single environmental hostility index for each firm, where higher scores indicate greater hostility. Importantly, because the hostility index was updated annually, the results reported in this article can be interpreted as having controlled for severe environmental shifts.

Company Financial Performance

Because CE may influence growth and profitability differently, annual secondary data were collected to capture both dimensions of company financial performance. Return on assets (ROA) and return on sales (ROS) were the two profitability measures used in the current research. The ROA and ROS measures were calculated as follows:

ROA = Net Earnings/Total Assets

ROS = Net Earnings/Company Sales Revenues

Growth in revenue (GR) was examined as the company growth measure. The GR measure was constructed on an annual basis as follows:

GR = (Current Year's Revenue – Last Year's Revenue) / (Last Year's Revenue)

Because of high correlations among the financial performance criteria (range of r = 0.48 to r = 0.73), an annual overall performance index was constructed to serve as the dependent variable in the analyses. The ROA, ROS, and GR data were factor-analyzed annually, and the factor loadings were multiplied by the firms' scores on these performance criteria. The products were then summed to produce a single, annual financial performance index for each firm.

ANALYTICAL TECHNIQUES AND RESULTS

Given the cross-sectional nature of the sample, it was decided to control for variations in industry performance prior to testing the hypotheses. This was done following the approach suggested by Sousa de Vasconcellos e Sa and Hambrick (1989). Briefly, the difference between a company's performance score and its industry average was computed, then divided by the industry's average. The outcome of this process was then multiplied by 100. The results showed how much better (or worse) a company performed than its average industry competitor.

After data preparation, the testing of hypotheses 1 and 2 proceeded by first regressing the second year's financial performance index (with the first year's performance subtracted out, as discussed later) with the CE index measured in 1983, then the third year's performance index (again controlling for past performance) was regressed on the 1983 CE index, and so on.

Hypothesis 3 was tested through the use of moderated regression analysis. Specifically, a firm's CE score and the environmental hostility index were entered into a regression equation (that had the financial performance index as the dependent variable). Then a second regression equation was run that included these two independent variables plus their cross-product. This was done every year with annual updates on the financial performance and environmental hostility indexes for each of the seven years of the study. If the inclusion of this cross-product significantly increased the predictive power of the equation, then it could be concluded that CE and environmental hostility interactively influence firm financial performance. Additionally, if the regression coefficient of the cross-product had a positive sign, this would support the relationships indicated in hypothesis 3.

Incorporating time as a variable in the analysis raises the additional concern that serial correlations may exist among the annual performance data, thus making it difficult to determine the true effect that CE has on performance. As such, past performance needed to be controlled in the analysis. Two techniques were used to accomplish this. First, the dependent variable in the yearly regression equations was computed as this year's performance minus last year's performance which, in effect, reduced the impact of momentum in the data. Second, last year's performance was included as an independent variable in the yearly regression equations, and this year's performance was used as the dependent variable in the same equations. Both techniques control for performance trends that may not be attributable to CE. Moreover, similar to results reported by Wiseman and Bromiley (1991), both techniques produced results similar to those obtained when past performance was not controlled. This demonstrated that serial correlations among the annual performance data are not a problem in the current research. Because the second technique for separating out the effect of past performance tends to artificially inflate a regression equation's coefficient of determination, the results presented are based on the first technique, in which the dependent variable in the regression equation is computed as this year's performance minus last year's performance.

Table 1 shows the regression analysis results based on the combined sample of 108 firms. Consistent with hypothesis 1, CE is positively and significantly associated with firm performance over each year of the seven-year period. Consistent with hypothesis 2, the strength of the CE–performance relationship increases over time.

Table 1 also shows the moderated regression analysis results. These results suggest that hostile environments reward CE to a greater extent than do benign environments.

54   S.A. ZAHRA AND J.G. COVIN

TABLE 1   Moderated Regression Analysis Results

Variables in Equation	Cumulative R-squared	Regression Coefficients[a]			F value for Equation
		CE	HOS	CH	
Year 2[b]					
(1) CE, HOS	.08	.18[c]	−.22[c]		3.08[c]
(2) CE, HOS, CH	.10	.20[e]	−.22[c]	2.10[e]	4.73[d]
Year 3					
(1) CE, HOS	.09	.19[c]	−.23[c]		3.14[c]
(2) CE, HOS, CH	.13	.21[c]	−.23[c]	2.14[c]	4.80[d]
Year 4					
(1) CE, HOS	.11	.21[c]	−.22[c]		3.18[c]
(2) CE, HOS, CH	.16	.26[c]	−.22[c]	2.21[c]	4.99[d]
Year 5					
(1) CE, HOS	.12	.26[c]	−.22[c]		3.22[c]
(2) CE, HOS, CH	.21	.32[d]	−.23[c]	2.29[c]	5.78[d]
Year 6					
(1) CE, HOS	.15	.33[d]	−.23[c]	3.36[c]	
(2) CE, HOS, CH	.27	.40[e]	−.23[c]	2.33[d]	7.23[e]
Year 7					
(1) CE, HOS	.18	.35[d]	−.23[c]		3.94[c]
(2) CE, HOS, CH	.29	.46[e]	−.23[c]	2.37[d]	9.31[e]

Abbreviations: CE, corporate entrepreneurship; HOS, environmental hostility; CH, corporate entrepreneurship × environmental hostility.

() Indicates order of entry into regression equations.

[a] The unstandardized regression coefficient is reported for the interaction term. See Southwood (1978) for details.

[b] The analysis begins in year 2 in order to allow for the control of past performance.

[c] $p < .05$.

[d] $p < .01$.

[e] $p < .001$

Specifically, the data indicate that CE and environmental hostility jointly interact to determine firm financial performance, and that this interaction effect, as predicted in hypothesis 3, persists over time. Thus, the results corroborate past research in the area (e.g., Miller and Friesen 1983), yet go beyond this prior research by demonstrating that the moderating effect of environmental hostility on the CE–performance relationship holds over time.

As shown in Table 1, environmental hostility is a significant predictor of financial performance ($p < .05$) over each of the seven years of the study, with standardized regression coefficients ranging from −0.22 to −0.23. Importantly, the predictive power of environmental hostility fluctuates slightly and randomly from year to year, suggesting that it is CE, rather than hostility, which is causing the modest strengthening of the interaction effect over time.

DISCUSSION AND CONCLUSION

The growing scholarly interest in corporate entrepreneurship (CE) has not resulted in commensurate attention to documenting its potential association with company growth and profitability. To date, the empirically based literature has focused primarily on the concurrent relationship between CE and company financial performance, ignoring CE's potential long-term performance implications. The present study has attempted to fill this void in the literature by using a longitudinal design to examine the main effect of CE on company financial performance over time and the long-term moderating effect of environmental hostility on the CE–performance relationship. The current results can be summarized as follows:

First, CE is positively associated with company financial performance, and the strength of this relationship tends to grow over time, even after controlling for past performance. Further, the current results corroborate prior studies that have documented positive concurrent relationships between CE and performance (e.g., Zahra 1991). However, the current research extends prior results by empirically demonstrating that the CE–performance relationship can significantly strengthen (i.e., grow) over time. Importantly, the current results suggest that CE should not be viewed as a short-term "fix," but as a long-term strategy for achieving superior financial performance.

The aforementioned findings have two, clear implications for managerial action. The first is that managers should seriously consider CE activities as means for enhancing company financial performance. Following an era of highly mixed financial results from mergers, acquisitions, and takeovers, it is reassuring that the current results show that CE is generally and positively associated with company performance. Moreover, because of this study's reliance on a single performance index comprising both growth and profitability indicators, the results suggest that CE activities may have a "double pay-off" (MacMillan and Day 1987; Zahra 1993).

A second implication of this study is that managers should adopt a long-term perspective in developing, managing, and evaluating CE. As documented, CE activities may take many years to fully pay off. This fact is particularly significant because such activities are often on the fringes of the formal, traditional concept of the firm (Burgelman and Sayles 1986) and, therefore, vulnerable and in need of considerable support. In order to realize the full benefits of CE, managers must be willing and able to sustain their support for entrepreneurial initiatives over a multi-year period. Without such managerial support, CE activities may be discontinued long before they would reasonably be expected to financially benefit the organization.

Second, the environment in which CE is practiced can have a strong and persistent impact on the effectiveness of an established firm's entrepreneurial behaviors. In the current study, CE was found to be a significantly better predictor of financial performance among firms in hostile environments than among firms in benign environments, and the impact of hostility on the CE–performance relationship grew modestly over time. Clearly, environmental context must be regarded by managers and scholars alike as a variable that may either enhance or stifle the impact of CE on firm performance. Evidence of CE among an industry's leaders would suggest that the industry's markets reward such behavior, and vice versa.

The previous observations should be interpreted with caution for several reasons. First, despite the fact that companies may practice CE over multi-year periods, CE was measured in the current study at a single point in time. The CE measure asked the respondents to indicate their firms' engagement in particular CE-related activities over the most recent three-year period. Nonetheless, it is possible that the length of time over which companies undertake CE (i.e., beyond three years) is a variable that will impact the effectiveness of CE activities. Second, there is a possibility that CE pays off by improving non-financial indicators of company performance (Pinchot 1985). The current data do not capture these improvements or their intervening effects on financial performance. Third, the study's focus on CE and company financial performance may obscure the possibility that both variables are the "outcomes" of other organizational factors (e.g., competitive strategy). Still, because many variables other than CE contribute to a company's performance (Hansen and Wernerfelt 1990), the positive associations between CE and financial performance reported in this article are encouraging. Fourth, although the current research adopted a reliable measure of CE that has been widely used in prior studies, it can be argued that several salient considerations involving CE, such as the locus of CE within an organization, are overlooked by this measure. This raises the possibility that the results reported here may incompletely represent the pay-off from CE, and that different measures may have produced different findings. Finally, there is a possibility that the observed CE–performance relationships may have been affected by industry shifts over the span of this study. Specifically, given the way hostility was measured, improved firm performance could have followed from CE activity but may also have reflected benefits to the surviving companies of bankrupt firms exiting the industry.

The results of this study contribute to a growing body of research that could expand in any number of significant directions. For instance, it may be worthwhile to explore CE-related activities at different levels of the organization. Though the present study has focused only on the corporate level, CE activities may exist at other levels, such at that of the individual, and future research could fruitfully focus on how CE is manifested throughout the organization. Future studies could also measure CE over time in order to explore its dynamic associations with company performance. Another worthwhile extension would be to use market-based measures of performance to gauge an additional potential pay-off from CE that has not been fully captured in this or in other studies. Finally, variables other than environmental hostility will moderate the effectiveness of CE activity; for example, future research could document the moderating effect of organizational culture or business strategy on the CE–performance relationship.

Clearly, research on CE and its implications for company financial performance is fast emerging as an exciting area of scholarly inquiry. It is hoped that this study will encourage additional research to further document the value added from companies' commitments to corporate entrepreneurship.

REFERENCES

Biggadike, R. 1979. The risky business of diversification. *Harvard Business Review* 79(5):103–111.

Block, Z, and MacMillan, I.C. 1993. *Corporate Venturing.* Boston, MA: Harvard Business School Press.

Block, Z., and Subbanarasimha, P.N. 1989. Corporate venturing: practices and performance in the U.S. and Japan. Working paper. New York: Center for Entrepreneurial Studies, Stern School of Business, New York University.

Burgelman, R.A. 1983. Corporate entrepreneurship and strategic management: insights from a process study. *Management Science* 29:1349–1364.

Burgelman, R.A., and Sayles, L.R. 1986. *Inside Corporate Innovation: Strategy, Structure and Managerial Skills.* New York: The Free Press.

Cheney, P.K., Devinney, T., and Winer, R.S. 1991. The impact of new product introductions on the market value of firms. *Journal of Business* 64(4):573–610.

Covin, J.G., and Slevin, D.P. 1986. The development and testing of an organizational-level entrepreneurship scale. In R. Ronstadt, J.A. Hornaday, R. Peterson, and K.H. Vesper, eds., *Frontiers of Entrepreneurship Research—1986.* Wellesley, MA: Babson College, pp. 628–639.

Covin, J.G., and Slevin, D.P. 1989. Strategic management of small firms in hostile and benign environments. *Strategic Management Journal* 10(1):75–87.

Covin, J.G., and Slevin, D.P. 1991. A conceptual model of entrepreneurship as firm behavior. *Entrepreneurship: Theory and Practice* 16:7–24.

Dean, C.C. 1993. Corporate entrepreneurship: strategic and structural correlates and impact on the global presence of United States firms. Unpublished doctoral dissertation, TX: University of North Texas.

Dess, G.G., and Beard, D.W. 1984. Dimensions of organizational task environments. *Administrative Science Quarterly* 29:52–73.

Dess, G.G., and Miller, A. 1993. *Strategic Management.* New York: McGraw-Hill, Inc.

Fast, N. 1981. Pitfalls of corporate venturing. *Research Management* 24(2):21–24.

Franko, L. 1989. Global corporate competition: who's winning, who's losing, and the R&D factor as one reason why. *Strategic Management Journal* 10:449–474.

Grant, R. 1991. *Contemporary Strategy Analysis: Concepts, Techniques, Applications.* New York: Basil Blackwell.

Guth, W., and Ginsberg, A. 1990. Guest editor's introduction: corporate entrepreneurship. *Strategic Management Journal* 11(special issue):5–16.

Hambrick, D.C. 1981. Strategic awareness within top management teams. *Strategic Management Journal* 2:263–279.

Hansen, G., and Wernerfelt, B. 1990. Determinants of firm performance: the relative importance of economic and organizational factors. *Strategic Management Journal* 10:399–411.

Huber, G.P., and Power, D.J. 1985. Retrospective reports of strategic level managers. *Strategic Management Journal* 6:171–180.

Jennings, D.F., and Lumpkin, J.R. 1989. Functionally modeling corporate entrepreneurship: an empirical integrative analysis. *Journal of Management* 15:485–502.

Jennings, D.F., and Seaman, S.L. 1990. Aggressiveness of response to new business opportunities following deregulation: an empirical study of established financial firms. *Journal of Business Venturing* 5:177–189.

Keats, B., and Hitt, M.A. 1988. A causal model of linkages among environmental dimensions, macro organizational characteristics, and performance. *Academy of Management Journal* 31:570–598.

Khandwalla, P.N. 1977. *The Design of Organizations.* New York: Harcourt Brace Jovanovich.

Lengnick-Hall, C.A. 1992. Innovation and competitive advantage: what we know and what we need to learn. *Journal of Management* 18(2):399–429.

Lieberman, M.B., and Montgomery, D.B. 1988. First mover advantages. *Strategic Management Journal* 9:41–58.

MacMillan, I.C., and Day, D.L. 1987. Corporate ventures into industrial markets: dynamics of aggressive entry. *Journal of Business Venturing* 2:29–39.

Maddala, G.S. 1977. *Econometrics.* New York: McGraw-Hill.

Miller, A., and Camp, B. 1985. Exploring determinants of success in corporate ventures. *Journal of Business Venturing* 1(1):87–105.

Miller, D. 1983. The correlates of entrepreneurship in three types of firms. *Management Science* 29:770–791.

Miller, D., and Friesen, P.H. 1984. *Organizations: A Quantum View.* Englewood Cliffs, NJ: Prentice Hall.

Miller, D., and Friesen, P.H. 1983. Strategy-making and environment: the third link. *Strategic Management Journal* 4:221–235.

Miller, D., and Friesen, P.H. 1982. Innovation in conservative and entrepreneurial firms: two models of strategic momentum. *Strategic Management Journal* 3:1–25.

Morris, M., Davis, L., and Ewing, J. 1988. The role of entrepreneurship and marketing in established firms. *Industrial Marketing Management* 17:337–346.

Peters, T.J., and Waterman, R.H., Jr. 1982. *In Search of Excellence.* New York: Harper & Row.

Pinchot, G., III. 1985. *Intrapreneuring.* New York: Harper & Row.

Ravenscraft, D., and Scherer, F.M. 1982. The lag structure of returns to research and development. *Applied Economics* 14:603–620.

Rosenbloom, R.S., and Cusumano, M.A. 1987. Technological pioneering and competitive advantage: the birth of the VCR industry. *California Management Review* 29(4):51–76.

58 S.A. ZAHRA AND J.G. COVIN

Schollhammer, H. 1982. Internal corporate entrepreneurship. In C.A. Kent, D.L. Sexton, and K.H. Vesper, eds., *Encyclopedia of Entrepreneurship*. Englewood Cliffs, NJ: Prentice Hall, pp. 209–223.

Schumpeter, J. 1934. *The Theory of Economic Development.* Cambridge, MA: Harvard University Press.

Sexton, D., and Bowman-Upton, N. 1991. *Entrepreneurship: Creativity and Growth*. New York: Macmillan Publishing Company.

Sousa de Vasconcellos e Sa, J., and Hambrick, D. 1989. Key success factors: test of a general theory in the mature industrial sector. *Strategic Management Journal* 10:367–383.

Southwood, K.E. 1978. Substantive theory and statistical interaction: five models. *American Journal of Sociology* 83:1154–1203.

Teece, D.J. 1986. Profiting from technological innovation: implications for integration, collaboration, licensing and public policy. *Research Policy* 15(6):285–305.

von Hippel, E. 1977. Successful and failing corporate ventures. *Industrial Marketing Management* *6:163–174.*

Wiseman, R.M., and Bromiley, P. 1991. Risk–Return associations: paradox or artifact? An empirically tested explanation. *Strategic Management Journal* 12:231–241.

Zahra, S.A. 1991. Predictors and financial outcomes of corporate entrepreneurship: an exploratory study. *Journal of Business Venturing* 6:258–282.

Zahra, S.A. 1993. Environment, corporate entrepreneurship, and financial performance: a taxonomic approach. *Journal of Business Venturing* 8:319–340.

Zahra, S.A., and Das, S. 1993. Innovation strategy and firm performance in manufacturing companies. *Production and Operations Management*.

Zajac, E., Golden, B., and Shortell, S. 1991. New organizational forms for enhancing innovation: the case of internal corporate joint ventures. *Management Science* 37:170–184.

Part VII
The Dynamic Interplay Between Competitive Strategy and Corporate Entrepreneurship

27

Strategic Management Journal
Strat. Mgmt. J., **20**: 421–444 (1999)

THE RELATIONSHIP BETWEEN CORPORATE ENTREPRENEURSHIP AND STRATEGIC MANAGEMENT

BRUCE R. BARRINGER[1]* AND ALLEN C. BLUEDORN[2]
[1]*College of Business Administration, University of Central Florida, Orlando, Florida, U.S.A.*
[2]*College of Business and Public Administration, University of Missouri—Columbia, Columbia, Missouri, U.S.A.*

This study examines the relationship between corporate entrepreneurship intensity and five specific strategic management practices in a sample of 169 U.S. manufacturing firms. The five strategic management practices include: scanning intensity, planning flexibility, planning horizon, locus of planning, and control attributes. The results of the study indicated a positive relationship between corporate entrepreneurship intensity and scanning intensity, planning flexibility, locus of planning, and strategic controls. The fine-grained nature of these results may be of practical use to firms that are trying to become more entrepreneurial and may help researchers better understand the subtleties of the interface between strategic management and corporate entrepreneurship. Copyright © 1999 John Wiley & Sons, Ltd.

INTRODUCTION

Many authors have singled out corporate entrepreneurship as an organizational process that contributes to firm survival and performance (Covin and Slevin, 1989; Drucker, 1985; Lumpkin and Dess, 1996; Miller, 1983; Zahra, 1993). In short, these authors argue that entrepreneurial attitudes and behaviors are necessary for firms of all sizes to prosper and flourish in competitive environments. As a result of these sentiments, a growing body of literature is evolving to help firms understand the organizational processes that facilitate entrepreneurial behavior (Covin and Slevin, 1991a; Guth and Ginsberg, 1990; Miller, 1983; Sathe, 1988; Zahra, 1991). This stream of research is extremely valuable because a firm's ability to increase its entrepre-

neurial behavior is largely determined by the compatibility of its management practices with its entrepreneurial ambitions (Murray, 1984).

Among the management practices believed to facilitate entrepreneurial behavior are a firm's strategic management practices (e.g., Covin and Slevin, 1991a; Miller, 1983; Murray, 1984; Zahra, 1991). This research is consistent with the general notion that a firm's strategic management practices should be tailored to support its organizational objectives and context (Chakravarthy, 1987; Child, 1972). Unfortunately, no study has focused specifically on the relationship between a firm's strategic management practices and its entrepreneurial intensity. Instead, the studies that have examined the organizational characteristics that facilitate entrepreneurial behavior have looked at a broad array of variables and have not provided extensive insight about the impact of a firm's strategic management practices on its entrepreneurial intensity.

To develop a more comprehensive picture of how a firm's strategic management practices influence its entrepreneurial behavior, we exam-

Key words: corporate entrepreneurship; strategy; planning; scanning; flexibility
* Correspondence to: Prof. B. Barringer, College of Business Administration, University of Central Florida, Orlando, Florida, 32816-1400, USA

CCC 0143–2095/99/050421–24 $17.50
Copyright © 1999 John Wiley & Sons, Ltd.

Received 23 April 1996
Final revision received 27 August 1998

ined the relationship between the strategic management practices and corporate entrepreneurship intensity of a sample of 169 U.S. manufacturing firms. We selected five dimensions of the strategic management process to include in the study, including scanning intensity, planning flexibility, planning horizon, locus of planning, and control attributes. The process of selecting the dimensions of strategic management to include in the study struck a balance between completeness and parsimony. In designing the study, we sought to include enough dimensions of strategic management to reflect the overall essence of the strategic management process while keeping the number of dimensions manageable and theoretically relevant. Accordingly, the dimensions of strategic management were selected through a literature review focused on identifying the areas of strategic management most relevant to the pursuit of corporate entrepreneurship. Thus the approach taken in this study was to examine the relationship between each of the dimensions of strategic management included in the study and a firm's corporate entrepreneurship intensity.

This article proceeds in the following manner. First, we provide a review of the corporate entrepreneurship literature. Second, we examine and discuss the relationship between each of the dimensions of strategic management included in the study and corporate entrepreneurship intensity, and we articulate a research hypothesis to summarize each of the individual discussions. Third, we describe the research design and report the results of the hypothesis tests. Finally, we examine the implications of the results for managers and researchers.

CORPORATE ENTREPRENEURSHIP

Contemporary entrepreneurship research originated in the work of economist Joseph Schumpeter (1883–1950). In his writings, Schumpeter argued that the main agents of economic growth are the entrepreneurs who introduce new products, new methods of production, and other innovations that stimulate economic activity (Schumpeter, 1936, 1950). Schumpeter described entrepreneurship as a process of 'creative destruction,' in which the entrepreneur continually displaces or destroys existing products or methods of pro-

duction with new ones. Schumpeter (1936, 1950) viewed this process favorably, because innovations typically represent an improvement in terms of product or process utility and as a result create greater buyer interest and overall economic activity.

Although Schumpeter's writings focused primarily on the activities of the individual entrepreneur, in many settings entrepreneurship is arguably a firm-level phenomenon (Covin and Slevin, 1991a, 1991b; Miller, 1983; Stevenson and Jarillo, 1990). For example, 3M, one of the world's largest corporations, has a long history of entrepreneurial behavior, transcending the tenures of CEOs and top management teams (Hussey, 1997). Similarly, a recent study of the role of entrepreneurship in reformulating Intel Corporation's corporate strategy suggested that entrepreneurial activities were the outcome of the interaction of individuals and groups at multiple levels within the firm (Burgelman, 1991).

The end result of these and similar observations has been the conceptualization of entrepreneurship as a firm-level phenomenon (e.g., Burgelman, 1983; Covin and Slevin, 1988, 1991a; Miller, 1983; Zahra, 1991, 1993). The main assumption that underlies the notion of corporate entrepreneurship is that it is a behavioral phenomenon and all firms fall along a conceptual continuum that ranges from highly conservative to highly entrepreneurial. Entrepreneurial firms are risk-taking, innovative, and proactive. In contrast, conservative firms are risk-adverse, are less innovative, and adopt a more 'wait and see' posture. The position of a firm on this continuum is referred to as its entrepreneurial intensity.

Against this backdrop, one of the main themes that has emerged in the corporate entrepreneurship literature is that a firm's level of entrepreneurial intensity is influenced by both its external and its internal corporate context (Zahra, 1991). Firms in turbulent vs. stable environments tend to be more innovative, risk-taking, and proactive (Naman and Slevin, 1993). Previous studies have identified attributes of highly entrepreneurial firms that differ from those of firms exhibiting lower levels of entrepreneurial intensity. In the next section of this article, we discuss the relationship between each of the individual dimensions of strategic management included in this study and corporate entrepreneurship intensity.

THE RELATIONSHIP BETWEEN CORPORATE ENTREPRENEURSHIP AND FIVE DIMENSIONS OF STRATEGIC MANAGEMENT

Three variables that underlie a firm's ability to behave in an entrepreneurial manner are consistently mentioned in the literature. These are opportunity recognition (Miller, 1983; Stevenson and Jarrillo-Mossi, 1986; Zahra, 1993), organizational flexibility (Murray, 1984; Naman and Slevin, 1993; Stevenson and Gumpert, 1985), and a firm's ability to measure, encourage, and reward innovative and risk-taking behavior (Sathe, 1988; Zahra, 1993). The strategic management practices included in this study (i.e., scanning intensity, locus of planning, planning flexibility, planning horizon, and control attributes) were selected on the basis of their potential for influencing one or more of these key enablers of firm-level entrepreneurial behavior, and a firm's overall entrepreneurial intensity.

The following is a discussion of each of the strategic management practices included in the study and its effect on firm-level entrepreneurial behavior. A research hypothesis is postulated to summarize each of the discussions. It should be noted that for ease of discussion we refer to the polar ends of the corporate entrepreneurship continuum as 'conservative' (low corporate entrepreneurship intensity) and 'entrepreneurial' (high corporate entrepreneurship intensity).

Scanning intensity

Environmental scanning refers to the managerial activity of learning about events and trends in the organization's environment (Hambrick, 1981). The philosophical roots of the scanning concept date back to the ancient Greeks, who believed that success in combat was dependent upon adequate intelligence for the purpose of making good tactical and strategic decisions (Box, 1991). Today scanning is important to managers for more benign, yet similar reasons. Scanning provides managers with information about events and trends in their relevant environments, which facilitates opportunity recognition (Bluedorn *et al.*, 1994). In addition, scanning is a method of 'uncertainty absorption,' although the uncertainty absorption component of scanning is a two-edged sword. A belief that scanning reduces all uncer-

tainty can produce a false sense of security in managers that makes it easy for them to miss signals coming from the environment. Thus, scanning can help managers cope with uncertainty, but only if they realize that uncertainty can only be reduced, not eliminated. Managers must remain vigilant, regardless of the degree of rigor in their scanning practices.

A high level of environmental scanning is congruent with the entrepreneurial process (Miller, 1983; Stevenson and Jarrillo-Mossi, 1986; Zahra, 1991). Recall that entrepreneurial firms are innovative, risk-taking, and proactive; and a central theme of the innovation literature is that information gathering and analysis is critical to the development and maintenance of successful innovation strategies (Covin, 1991; Kanter, 1988; Zumd, 1983). In addition, industries that pay a premium for innovative behavior require constant monitoring and analysis to remain understood. Examples of environmental settings, called high-velocity environments (Eisenhardt, 1989), that fit this profile include the electronics, computer software, biotechnology, and health care industries (Covin and Slevin, 1991b; Zahra, 1993). These industries are characterized by products and services that have relatively short life cycles. As a result, firms that compete in these industries must adopt short planning horizons and develop scanning mechanisms that focus on detecting shifts in environmental trends that provide opportunities for new products and services.

Scanning also facilitates the risk-taking and proactiveness dimensions of entrepreneurial behavior. As a means of partial uncertainty absorption, scanning may lower the perception of risk associated with a potential entrepreneurial venture, increasing the likelihood that the firm will engage in the venture. Entrepreneurial managers may also realize that scanning is their bridge to remaining competitive. A firm in a turbulent environment must be continually innovative to remain competitive, which requires extensive scanning to recognize and exploit environmental change. As a result, an intensive scanning regime, complemented by a short planning horizon and a flexible planning system, is a practical approach for entrepreneurial firms.

In contrast, scanning is less likely to be a critical strategic management function for conservative firms. Conservative firms are usually

424   *B. R. Barringer and A. C. Bluedorn*

located in industries that compete in stable
environments (Covin, 1991). These environments
generate low levels of uncertainty and, consequently, do not require an extensive search process to remain understood (Covin and Slevin,
1989; Miller and Friesen, 1983). Because product
and service life cycles are longer in stable vs.
turbulent environments, planning horizons can be
longer and scanning activities typically focus on
subtle shifts in environmental trends, quality
improvements, and opportunities to gain market
share. In addition, there is a considerable cost of
environmental scanning in terms of both managerial time and cash outlays (Jennings and Seaman, 1994). Thus an overemphasis on environmental scanning for conservative firms may be
counterproductive. This discussion leads to the
following hypothesis:

*Hypothesis 1: A positive relationship exists
between scanning intensity and corporate
entrepreneurship intensity.*

Planning flexibility

Planning flexibility refers to the capacity of a
firm's strategic plan to change as environmental
opportunities/threats emerge. The notion of planning flexibility was first suggested by Kukalis
(1989) to investigate how environmental and firm
characteristics affect the design of strategic planning systems. Kukalis theorized that firms in
complex environmental settings maximize performance by adopting 'flexible' planning systems.
Flexible planning systems allow firms to adjust
their strategic plans quickly to pursue opportunities and keep up with environmental change
(Stevenson and Jarrillo-Mossi, 1986). Kukalis
theorized that firms in highly complex environments need flexible planning systems because of
the frequency of change in their business environments.

In general, planning flexibility is an organizational design attribute that has not received
much research attention, but scholars have noted
that planning has a natural tendency to engender
inflexibility. Newman (1963: 62) observed that
'The establishment of advanced plans tends to
make administration inflexible; the more detailed
and widespread the plans, the greater the inflexibility.' Both Newman (1951) and Mintzberg
(1994) attribute the inflexibility of planning to

psychological factors. Newman argued that once
an executive prepares a plan there is a tendency
to try to 'make it work' which engenders a
resistance to change as a result of an established
mindset and a fear of loss of face. Similarly,
Mintzberg (1994: 175) argued that 'The more
clearly articulated the strategy, the greater the resistance to change—due to the development of both
psychological and organizational momentum.'

Despite these observations, a number of theorists have argued that the need for flexibility in
all areas of organizational design is increasing
due to the increasingly rapid pace of environmental change (Aaker, 1995; Aaker and Mascarenhas,
1984; Bahrami, 1992; Chakravarthy, 1996).
Applying this notion to strategic management,
Gardner, Rachlin, and Sweeney (1986: 2.22)
observed that 'one of the hallmarks of good
strategies is the willingness of the drafters to
encompass the likelihood of change and consequent uncertainties.' Similarly, Koontz (1958: 55)
wrote, 'effective planning requires that the need
for flexibility be a major consideration in the
selection of plans.'

A concerted effort in the direction of planning
flexibility facilitates a high level of corporate
entrepreneurship intensity for several reasons.
First, a flexible planning system, coupled with
intensive environmental scanning, allows a firm's
strategic plan to remain 'current' and permits a
firm's entrepreneurial initiatives to be planned
rather than to take place in an ad hoc manner
outside the parameters of a strategic plan. This
latter point is important because involvement in
entrepreneurial behavior does not imply an aban-
donment of the rational–deliberate 'scan-
formulate–implement–evaluate' approach to planning. What entrepreneurial behavior does imply
is that the pace of this process must be accelerated and made more flexible because the essence
of entrepreneurship is capitalizing on environmental change (Schumpeter, 1936). Second, although
the entrepreneurial process is intended to keep a
firm in step with environmental change, entrepreneurial firms are not completely free from inertia.
As a result, putting a planning system in place
that is flexible and is by design subject to change
may remove a potential obstacle to change when
it is needed.

In contrast, planning flexibility may undermine
the effectiveness of conservative firms. Because
conservative firms are not innovative, they typi-

cally seek to obtain a competitive advantage through reliability in executing repetitive transactions and routine activities. In this setting, a flexible planning system runs the risk of disrupting rather than facilitating a firm's business activities. There is a danger that plans may change too frequently, more as an artifact of the planning system rather than as a result of competitive necessity (Amburgey, Kelly, and Barnett, 1993). Therefore we propose the following hypothesis:

Hypothesis 2: A positive relationship exists between planning flexibility and corporate entrepreneurship intensity.

Planning horizon

A firm's planning horizon refers to the length of the future time period that decision-makers consider in planning (Das, 1987). For most firms, this period corresponds to the length of time necessary to execute the firm's routine strategies (Camillus, 1982). According to Rhyne (1985), the planning horizon for individual firms can vary from less than one year to more than fifteen years. The rationale for a given planning horizon is that it should be long enough to permit planning for expected changes in strategy and yet be short enough to make reasonably detailed plans available (Das, 1991). Clearly, within this broad framework firms will have a portfolio of planning horizons that are necessitated by the need to manage both short-term and long-term strategies simultaneously (Capon, Farley, and Hulbert, 1987; Judge and Spitzfaden, 1995).

A relatively 'short' average planning horizon (less than 5 years) may be optimal for entrepreneurial firms. These firms typically compete in turbulent environments that are characterized by short product and service life cycles. As a result, the paramount concern of an entrepreneurial firm is product and service innovation, which typically must be accomplished in the short term rather than the long term to maintain a sustainable competitive advantage. A short planning horizon, coupled with intensive environmental scanning and a high degree of organizational and planning flexibility, provides an entrepreneurial firm with the capacity to quickly recognize environmental change and develop appropriate product and service innovations.

The adoption of a relatively long planning horizon is not tenable for entrepreneurial firms. A reliance on a long-term planning horizon may engender a reluctance to deviate from a long-term view of the future despite short-term environmental change, which runs counter to the proactive nature of the entrepreneurial process. In addition, entrepreneurial firms operating in turbulent environments must survive the short term to get to the long term. As a result, a reliance on long-term planning would not be practical.

Conversely, a relatively 'long' planning horizon (more than 5 years) may be optimal for conservative firms. Conservative firms are not predisposed to continually look for opportunities to introduce new products or services as a result of environmental change. As a result, these firms tend to operate in stable, predictable environments (Covin, 1991; Covin and Slevin, 1991a). In these environmental settings, competitive advantage is usually derived from reliability in production and brand awareness rather than speed of new product introduction. Firms achieve reliability of production in part through long-term planning and forecasting, which are compatible with a relatively long-term planning horizon. This discussion leads to the following hypothesis:

Hypothesis 3 A negative relationship exists between planning horizon length (short-term vs. long-term) and corporate entrepreneurship intensity.

Locus of planning

The term locus of planning refers to the depth of employee involvement in a firm's strategic planning activities. Organizations can be characterized as having either a shallow or a deep locus of planning. A deep locus of planning denotes a high level of employee involvement in the planning process, including employees from virtually all hierarchical levels within the firm. Conversely, a shallow locus of planning denotes a fairly exclusive planning process, typically involving only the top managers of a firm. A deep locus of planning is akin to the Japanese style of planning, which is team oriented and places a heavy emphasis on employee participation (Reid, 1989). Although the Japanese style of planning has deep roots in the Japanese culture, it has served as a model for American firms that have tried to make their planning systems more participative.

There are several reasons to believe that a deep locus of planning facilitates a high level of corporate entrepreneurship intensity. First, a high level of employee involvement in planning brings the people 'closest to the customer' into the planning process. This characteristic of employee participation in planning may facilitate opportunity recognition, which is central to the entrepreneurial process (Schumpeter, 1936). Moreover, a deep locus of planning legitimizes the active participation of middle and lower-level managers in the planning process. Doing so avoids the potential of good ideas being overlooked simply because managers at these levels are not involved in the planning process (Burgelman, 1988).

The second reason that a deep locus of planning facilitates the entrepreneurial process is that it maximizes the diversity of viewpoints that a firm considers in formulating its strategic plan. The diversity of viewpoints considered is necessarily limited when planning is restricted to a firm's top managers, not only by the small number of people involved but also by the homogeneous nature of many top management teams (Lant, Milliken, and Batra, 1992). This latter issue can constrain entrepreneurial activity, as evidenced by the results of several studies that have found a negative relationship between top management team homogeneity and an openness to innovation and change (Bantel and Jackson, 1989; Judge and Zeithaml, 1992). In many instances this problem can be overcome by involving a deeper and more diverse mix of employees in the strategic planning process (Dutton and Duncan, 1987).

Conservative firms have less to gain from a high level of employee participation in planning. Although strategic planning may be just as complex in a conservative firm as it is in an entrepreneurial firm, it does not emphasize opportunity recognition and the pursuit of new ideas to the same extent. As a result, deep participation in planning, which is expensive in terms of managerial time and energy, may not be necessary. In addition, there are pitfalls associated with a high degree of employee participation in planning that conservative firms can avoid. For example, a deep locus of planning may necessitate providing a large number of employees with access to proprietary information and other sensitive data. This

access increases the likelihood of a breach of confidentiality, which may damage a firm's competitive stature. This discussion supports the following hypothesis:

Hypothesis 4: A positive relationship exists between a deep locus of planning (i.e., high level of employee involvement) and corporate entrepreneurship intensity.

Control attributes

The purpose of a control system is to make sure that business strategies meet predetermined goals and objectives (Lorange, Morton, and Ghoshal, 1986). In the context of this study, this means that the control systems of entrepreneurial firms must stimulate innovation, proactiveness, and risk-taking. Two forms of control are particularly relevant to a discussion of corporate entrepreneurship. These are strategic controls and financial controls (Hitt, Hoskisson, and Ireland, 1990). In most firms, both forms of control are present (Hoskisson and Hitt, 1988). Financial controls base performance on objective financial criteria such as net income, return on equity, and return on sales (Hitt *et al.*, 1990). In contrast, strategic controls base performance on strategically relevant criteria as opposed to objective financial information (Gupta, 1987; Hoskisson and Hitt, 1988). Examples of strategic control measures include customer satisfaction criteria, new patent registrations, success in meeting target dates for new product or process introductions, and the achievement of quality control standards.

Because strategic controls and financial controls can both be present simultaneously in a firm, they do not represent opposite ends of a conceptual continuum; therefore, we articulate separate hypotheses to summarize our discussion of the relationship between each form of control and corporate entrepreneurship intensity.

Strategic controls

An emphasis on strategic controls is consistent with the entrepreneurial process. Strategic controls are capable of rewarding creativity and the pursuit of opportunity through innovation. These characteristics of strategic controls are important to sustain the innovation process because long time-lags frequently intervene between innovative

Strat. Mgmt. J., **20**: 421–444 (1999)

initiatives and their eventual pay-off (Drucker, 1985; Kanter, 1989). A well-designed strategic control system is capable of rewarding firm employees for incremental but substantive progress on product or process innovations that take a long time to reach market (Goold and Campbell, 1987; Hoskisson, Hitt, and Hill, 1991). Conversely, for conservative firms, strategic controls are less important. Conservative firms do not gain their competitive advantage by pursuing opportunities through innovation. There are costs involved in maintaining strategic controls in terms of managerial time and effort (Goold and Quinn, 1990; Hayes and Abernathy, 1980), which conservative firms can avoid. As a result of this discussion we hypothesize:

Hypothesis 5a: A positive relationship exists between the degree of emphasis on strategic controls and corporate entrepreneurship intensity.

Financial controls

Financial controls are congruent with the distinctive competencies of most conservative firms. Financial controls are clear and unambiguous, which introduces a high degree of discipline into the control process. Financial controls also provide an opportunity for the parties involved to agree on objective performance standards well in advance of any performance evaluation. These factors may be particularly beneficial to conservative firms, which are firms that do not have as salient a need to encourage creativity and innovation as entrepreneurial firms. This discussion leads to the following hypothesis:

Hypothesis 5b: A negative relationship exists between the degree of emphasis on financial controls and corporate entrepreneurship intensity.

RESEARCH DESIGN

Sample and data collection

The sample of firms that participated in the study included 169 manufacturing firms located in the midwestern and southern regions of the United States. We employed two criteria to determine the specific population from which we drew our

sample: (1) to ensure a least a minimal degree of homogeneity among the respondents, we restricted the firms included in the sample to manufacturing firms (SIC codes 2000–4000); and (2) to reduce the confounding effects of diversification, we limited the firms in the sample to those that generate at least 70 percent of their sales from a single industry. The 70 percent figure was based upon Rumelt's (1974) definition of a single or dominant firm.

We collected data from two sources: a self-report mail survey and the Compustat Annual Data Tape. We obtained measures of corporate entrepreneurship, the five dimensions of strategic management included in the study, and two control variables (i.e., environmental turbulence and environmental complexity) from the self-report survey. We collected firm demographic and financial data from the Compustat Annual Data Tape. The administration of the mail survey was preceded by a pilot study, involving the CEOs of 30 midwestern manufacturing firms. The purpose of the pilot study was to assess the face validity and the reliability of the psychometric measures included in the survey. As a result of the feedback obtained, we refined several of the measures and made them more theoretically meaningful.

We administered the self-report survey following a modified Dillman (1978) procedure. Following the completion of the pilot study, we prepared and mailed a revised survey instrument to a member of the top management team in each of 501 midwestern and southern manufacturing firms. Two weeks later we sent a second copy of the survey to the nonrespondents. A total of 169 firms returned usable surveys, resulting in a response rate of 34 percent, which compares favorably to similar studies (e.g., Covin and Slevin, 1988; Naman and Slevin, 1993; Zahra, 1991). The firms that responded to the survey represented a broad cross-section of manufacturing firms, ranging in size from 50 employees to 280,000. The mean number of employees for the responding firms was 4720.

We conducted three tests to check for bias in the self-report survey data, including interrater reliability, common method variance, and nonresponse bias. Bias in self-report data is a threat to validity. First, following the data collection effort described above, we sent an identical copy of the survey to a second top manager in each of the 169 responding firms. A total of 57 firms returned the second survey. We used these data to conduct a check of interrater reliability for the 57 firms that provided two surveys. The results were supportive of good interrater reliability. For each variable except planning horizon, the responses across the matched pair of raters differed by an average of less than 1 scale point on a 7-point Likert scale. For planning horizon, the responses across the matched pair of reviewers differed by an average of 1.44 scale points on a 7-point Likert scale.

We used Harman's one-factor test to check for the presence of common method variance, as suggested by Podsakoff and Organ (1986). To test for this potential threat to validity, we entered the variables in the study into a factor analysis. We then examined the results of the unrotated factor analysis to determine the number of factors that were necessary to account for the variance in the variables. The basic assumption of this procedure is that if a substantial amount of common method variance in the data exists, either a single factor will emerge or one 'general' factor will account for the majority of the covariance among the variables. Harman's one-factor test for common method variance in this study yielded 13 factors with eigenvalues greater than one, and no single factor was dominant. These results suggest that common method variance is not a significant problem in our data.

Finally, to assess the presence of nonresponse bias in our data, we compared the firms that responded to our survey against those that did not on three characteristics: firm sales, number of employees, and 1994 return on assets (ROA). There was no significant difference between responding and nonresponding firms on firm sales and ROA. The respondent firms were larger than the nonrespondents in terms of number of employees (the respondent firms averaged 4720 employees while the nonrespondents averaged 3960, $p < 0.01$). Although this difference is statistically significant, we do not feel it has any practical significance.

Measures

The survey instrument included psychometric scales designed to measure corporate entrepreneurship intensity, the dimensions of strategic management included in the study, and two control variables: environmental complexity and environmental turbulence. Each of the multi-item measures were based on 7-point Likert scales. A copy of these measures, with the exception of the control variables, is included in the Appendix.

Corporate entrepreneurship

We used a nine-item scale to measure a firm's level of corporate entrepreneurship intensity (alpha = 0.87). The scale was developed and validated by Covin and Slevin (1986) based on previous scale development work by Khandwalla (1977) and Miller and Friesen (1982). The scale contains items that measure a firm's tendency toward innovation, risk-taking, and proactiveness, which are the subdimensions of corporate entrepreneurship (Miller, 1983). The mean score, calculated as the average of the nine items, assesses a firm's position on a conservative–entrepreneurial continuum. The higher the score, the more the firm demonstrates an entrepreneurial orientation.

Scanning intensity

We developed a 12-item scale specifically for this study to measure scanning intensity (alpha = 0.83). In this study, we conceptualized scanning as the extent of effort dedicated towards environmental scanning and the comprehensiveness of the environmental scanning process. A separate six-item scale measured each of these subdimensions of scanning. The first set of six items was a modified version of Miller and Friesen's (1982) Effort Dedicated Towards Scanning scale. The second set of six items measured scanning comprehensiveness. These items asked the respondent to assess how thoroughly his or her firm scans elements of the firm's task and societal environments. The mean score, averaged across the 12 items, assesses a firm's degree of scanning intensity.

Planning flexibility

For this study, we developed a nine-item scale to measure planning flexibility (alpha = 0.80). The scale is straightforward and asked the respondents to assess how difficult it is for their firms to change their strategic plans to adjust for each of nine theoretically relevant environmental contingencies. The mean score on the scale, averaged across the nine items, assesses a firm's level of planning flexibility.

Planning horizon

We developed a four-item multipart scale specifically for this study to measure planning horizon (alpha = 0.90). The scale asked the respondent to assess the degree of emphasis his or her firm places on business strategies or firm investments for each of the following predetermined time periods: less than 1 year; 1–3 years; 3–5 years; and more than 5 years. In addition, the respondent was asked to make this assessment for each of the following hierarchical levels in his or her firm: board of directors, top management, middle management, and lower-level management.

Only a portion of the data captured by this scale was actually of interest in this study. We used the other items to sensitize the respondents to the various time horizons that may exist in a firm. We were interested in the amount of emphasis placed on planning horizons of more than 5 years, averaged across the four hierarchical levels. The 5-year plateau is arbitrary but has been used as a heuristic in past management studies as a conceptual dividing line between a 'long' (more than 5 years) and a 'short' (less than 5 years) planning horizon (e.g., Kukalis, 1989; Lindsay and Rue, 1980; Rhyne, 1986).

Locus of planning

We developed specifically for this study a five-item multipart Likert scale to measure locus of planning (alpha = 0.89). The scale measures the extent to which employees from different hierarchical levels in a firm are involved in their firm's strategic planning process. The following hierarchical levels in a firm were included: top management, middle management, lower-level management, and rank-and-file employees. The scale items, including goal formation, environmental scanning, strategy formulation, strategy implementation, and evaluation and control, represent the basic steps in the strategic management process (Schendel and Hofer, 1979). We determined locus of planning by averaging the scores for middle management, lower-level management, and rank-and-file employees across the five steps in the strategic management process.

Control attributes

Control attributes included separate scales for strategic controls and financial controls. We modified a three-item scale used by Johnson, Hoskisson, and Hitt (1993) to measure strategic controls (alpha = 0.64). Similarly, we modified a three-item scale used by Hitt et al. (1996) to measure financial controls (alpha = 0.77). For each scale the mean score, calculated as the average of the three items, assessed a firm's emphasis on the respective type of control.

Control variables

We included five control variables in the data analysis, including two measures of the external environment (turbulence and complexity), two measures of financial stability (debt level and current ratio), and firm size. We used a nine-item scale to measure environmental turbulence (alpha = 0.67). The scale was based on similar turbulence scales used by Naman and Slevin (1993), Miller and Friesen (1982), and Khandwalla (1977). Similarly, we used a five-item, 7-point Likert scale to measure environmental complexity (alpha = 0.73). We developed the environmental complexity scale specifically for this study and it is consistent with Aldrich's (1979) conceptualization of the complexity construct. We obtained archival data pertaining to debt level, current ratio, and firm size from the 1994 Compustat Annual Data Tape.

Data reliability and validity

In evaluating the quality of the psychometric properties of the measures we obtained from the self-report survey, we focused on two properties: reliability and validity.

Reliability

As reported in the previous section, we calculated Cronbach's coefficient alpha to evaluate the reliability of the measures. An alpha level of 0.70 or above is generally considered to be acceptable (Cronbach, 1951). All the measures in the survey exceeded this minimum threshold with the exception of strategic controls (alpha = 0.64) and environmental turbulence (alpha = 0.67). Although the alpha levels for these variables were disappointing, they did not preclude these variables from further analysis. However, they do suggest caution when interpreting results involving these scales.

Validity

Reliability is a form of validity, which we discussed above. Other assessments of validity include theoretical and observational meaningfulness, discriminant validity, and convergent validity (Binning and Barrett, 1989; Venkatraman and Grant, 1986). The following is a discussion of each of these forms of validity as they relate to the variables in our study.

Theoretical and observational meaningfulness. At a basic level, validity is established by developing measures from well-grounded theory. Although entrepreneurship is an old topic, the resurgence of interest in entrepreneurship is a fairly recent phenomenon (Wortman, 1987). Thus, although the corporate entrepreneurship construct measure has good reliability and has performed well in previous studies, it is based on a stream of literature that is still developing. As a result, the theoretical validity of the corporate entrepreneurship construct is still in its formative stage.

In regard to the measures of strategic management included in the study, strong literature bases exist to support the theoretical validity of scanning intensity, control attributes, and planning horizon. Less mature streams of literature support planning flexibility and locus of planning.

Discriminant validity. Discriminant validity shows that a measure is distinct and is empirically different from other measures. We employed exploratory factor analysis to assess the discriminant validity of the variables in this study. Specifically, we conducted a principal components analysis with varimax rotation, constraining the number of factors to seven. The results of this factor analysis are shown in Table 1, and they support the discriminant validity of the measures used in this study.

As shown in Table 1, all the variables in the study loaded cleanly on separate factors. With only three exceptions, the scale items had factors loadings in excess of 0.40, a common threshold for acceptance. We retained these three items

for conceptual reasons. The first two items were Scanning 1a and Scanning 1d, with factor loadings of 0.39 and 0.35 respectively. These items did not load higher on any other factors, and are both part of the Miller and Friesen (1982) Effort Dedicated Towards Scanning scale. The third item that did not reach the 0.40 minimum was Strategic Controls 1c. This item had a factor loading of 0.20 on the strategic controls factor. We retained it to keep the three-item strategic controls scale intact, thereby maintaining consistency with its use in other studies.

For ease of presentation, Table 1 shows only the factor score coefficients greater than or equal to 0.40 and the three additional coefficients retained for conceptual reasons.

Convergent validity. Convergent validity is an assessment of the consistency in measurement across multiple ways of measuring the same variable. The corporate entrepreneurship construct was measured by two different scales in separate portions of the self-report survey. The first scale was the nine-item corporate entrepreneurship scale described earlier. The second scale was a simple one-item, 7-point Likert scale that assessed the respondent's position on the conservative–entrepreneurial continuum. The correlation between these two measures was $r = 0.62$ ($p < 0.0001$), demonstrating good convergent validity across separate measures of this construct.

Overall, the tests reported above, along with the tests designed to check for bias in the self-report survey results, indicate that the measures in this study have good reliability and validity. The most serious area of concern pertains to the planning horizon construct, which may have only moderate validity in this study as evidenced by the relatively low interrater reliability.

Data analysis and hypothesis test results

Data analysis

The respondents ($N = 169$) to the mail survey represented a broad cross-section of the manufacturing sector in the United States. The largest number of respondents ($N = 36$) came from SIC 35, Machinery, Except Electrical. A total of 17 of the 20 SIC codes in the manufacturing sector were represented in the sample, improving the study's generalizability.

Table 1. Results of the principal-components analysis with varimax rotation

Item name	Factor 1 Entrepreneurship	Factor 2 Scanning intensity	Factor 3 Locus of planning	Factor 4 Planning flexibility	Factor 5 Planning horizon	Factor 6 Financial controls	Factor 7 Strategic controls
Entrepreneurship 1a	0.58						
Entrepreneurship 1b	0.73						
Entrepreneurship 1c	0.83						
Entrepreneurship 2a	0.56						
Entrepreneurship 2b	0.66						
Entrepreneurship 3a	0.62						
Entrepreneurship 3b	0.75						
Entrepreneurship 3c	0.61						
Entrepreneurship 4a	0.80						
Scanning 1a		0.39					
Scanning 1b		0.67					
Scanning 1c		0.58					
Scanning 1d		0.35					
Scanning 1e		0.55					
Scanning 1f		0.66					
Scanning 2a		0.41					
Scanning 2b		0.62					
Scanning 2c		0.44					
Scanning 2d		0.65					
Scanning 2e		0.68					
Scanning 2f		0.66					
Planning flexibility 1a				0.63			
Planning flexibility 1b				0.62			
Planning flexibility 1c				0.64			
Planning flexibility 1d				0.50			
Planning flexibility 1e				0.70			
Planning flexibility 1f				0.41			
Planning flexibility 1g				0.51			
Planning flexibility 1h				0.61			
Planning flexibility 1i				0.54			

continued overleaf

Strat. Mgmt. J., **20**: 421–444 (1999)

Table 1. Continued

Item name	Factor 1 Entrepreneurship	Factor 2 Scanning intensity	Factor 3 Locus of planning	Factor 4 Planning flexibility	Factor 5 Planning horizon	Factor 6 Financial controls	Factor 7 Strategic controls
Planning horizon 1a					0.69		
Planning horizon 1b					0.78		
Planning horizon 1c					0.85		
Planning horizon 1d					0.70		
Locus of planning 1a			0.69				
Locus of planning 1b			0.78				
Locus of planning 1c			0.76				
Locus of planning 1d			0.78				
Locus of planning 1e			0.81				
Strategic controls 1a							0.76
Strategic controls 1b							0.77
Strategic controls 1c							0.20
Financial controls 1a						0.69	
Financial controls 1b						0.85	
Financial controls 1c						0.68	
Eigenvalue	8.93	4.77	2.91	2.39	2.18	2.05	1.67

Note: All factor loadings < 0.40 were excluded from the table except the three underlined loadings. The names of the items correspond to the way they are labeled on their measurement scales, as shown in the Appendix.

The means, standard deviations, Pearson product–moment correlations, and coefficient alphas (where applicable) for the variables included in the study are shown in Table 2. The range of responses on all of the variables was broad, avoiding a restriction of range problem in the data. The correlation matrix shows statistically significant correlations in the direction expected between corporate entrepreneurship and four of the six dimensions of strategic management included in the study. Corporate entrepreneurship correlated positively with scanning intensity ($p < 0.05$), planning flexibility ($p < 0.01$), locus of planning ($p < 0.05$), and strategic controls ($p < 0.01$). There was not a significant correlation between corporate entrepreneurship and either planning horizon or financial controls.

As the correlation matrix indicates, the inter-correlations among the dimensions of strategic management included in the study were generally low, thereby minimizing the problem of multi-collinearity. A high level of multicollinearity can result in unstable regression coefficients in linear regression models (Pedhazur, 1982).

Results of the tests of the hypotheses

To test the hypotheses, we used hierarchical regression analysis. For each hypothesis, this approach allowed us to regress corporate entrepreneurship against a set of control variables and then add the respective dimension of strategic management into the equation and test whether the incremental change in R^2 resulting from the addition of the strategic management variable was statistically significant (Pedhazur, 1982). The control variables included environmental turbulence, environmental complexity, firm size, debt level, and current ratio. Previous studies have found that environmental turbulence (Naman and Slevin, 1993) and environmental complexity (Zahra, 1991) are positively related to corporate entrepreneurship. Firm size, debt level (long-term debt divided by firm sales), and the current ratio (current assets divided by current liability) are demographic and financial measures that have been found to influence elements of entrepreneurial behavior (Hitt *et al.*, 1996). We expected negative relationships between corporate entrepreneurship and firm size and debt level; we expected a positive relationship between corporate entrepreneurship and the current ratio.

For each hypothesis we completed a separate hierarchical regression as shown in Table 3. Each hierarchical regression involved two steps. In step one, we regressed corporate entrepreneurship intensity on the control variables. In step two, we regressed corporate entrepreneurship intensity on the control variables and the dimension of strategic management associated with the hypothesis. The F-test that constituted the test of the hypothesis was based on the statistical significance of the change in R^2 between the restricted model (control variables only) and the full model (control variables plus the dimension of strategic management associated with the hypothesis).

Table 3 reports the results of the hypothesis tests. Hypothesis 1 was supported ($p < 0.05$). For the firms in our sample, there is a positive relationship between scanning intensity and corporate entrepreneurship intensity. Hypothesis 2 was also supported ($p < 0.001$), indicating a positive relationship between planning flexibility and corporate entrepreneurship intensity. Hypothesis 3, which postulated a negative relationship between a planning horizon of more than 5 years and corporate entrepreneurship intensity, was not supported. Recall that the planning horizon measure had poor interrater reliability. Thus, the failure of this hypothesis may be due to a bias in the data or a misapplication of the theoretical arguments. Hypothesis 4 was supported, demonstrating a positive relationship between a broad locus of planning and corporate entrepreneurship intensity ($p < 0.01$). Support was also found for Hypothesis 5a, which postulated a positive relationship between an emphasis on strategic controls and corporate entrepreneurship intensity ($p < 0.001$). Hypothesis 5b was not supported. This hypothesis postulated a negative relationship between an emphasis on financial controls and corporate entrepreneurship intensity. Overall, four of the six hypotheses were supported.

DISCUSSION OF THE RESULTS AND CONCLUSION

The results of this study suggest that a firm's entrepreneurial intensity is influenced by the nature of its strategic management practices. This conclusion is not surprising, because a firm's strategic management practices are intended to shape and mold its behavior. For firms that are

Table 2. Pearson product–moment correlation matrix including corporate entrepreneurship, dimensions of strategic management included in the study, and control variables. N ranges from 148 to 167

Variable name	Mean	S.D.	1	2	3	4	5	6	7	8	9	10	11
1. Corporate entrepreneurship	4.48	1.05	(0.87)										
2. Scanning intensity	4.92	0.83	0.16*	(0.83)									
3. Planning flexibility	4.82	0.85	0.34**	0.11	(0.80)								
4. Planning horizon	2.32	1.27	0.13	0.30**	0.25**	(0.90)							
5. Locus of planning	4.11	0.96	0.19*	0.48**	0.25**	0.31**	(0.89)						
6. Strategic controls	5.57	0.92	0.29**	0.33**	0.29**	0.31**	0.33**	(0.64)					
7. Financial controls	5.41	1.04	0.04	0.32**	0.11	0.24**	0.19*	0.33**	(0.77)				
8. Environmental turbulence	3.88	0.80	0.09	0.14+	-0.13	0.12	0.08	-0.11	-0.08	(0.67)			
9. Environmental complexity	3.79	1.12	0.10	0.10	-0.04	0.15+	0.10	-0.05	0.00	0.25**	(0.73)		
10. Firm size	3.67	1.91	-0.21**	0.15*	-0.10	0.22**	-0.02	-0.07	0.28**	0.04	-0.03		
11. Debt level	2.75	2.13	-0.05	-0.11	0.10	-0.10	-0.03	0.04	-0.11	-0.02	-0.09	-0.46**	
12. Current ratio	3.01	3.19	-0.04	-0.06	-0.03	-0.06	-0.01	-0.00	-0.20**	-0.09	-0.00	-0.39**	0.74**

+$p < 0.10$; *$p < 0.05$; **$p < 0.01$

Coefficient alphas are on the diagonal where applicable. Variables 1–9 were measured on 7-point Likert scales (1 low–7 high).

Firm size is the log of the total number of employees. Debt level is long-term debt/firm sales. Current ratio is current assets/current liabilities.

Table 3.   Results of the hypothesis tests using hierarchical regression

	Restricted model Control variables regressed against corporate entrepreneurship	Full models Control variables plus individual dimensions of strategic management regressed against corporate entrepreneurship					
		Hypothesis 1 Scanning intensity	Hypothesis 2 Planning flexibility	Hypothesis 3 Planning horizon	Hypothesis 4 Locus of planning	Hypothesis 5a Strategic controls	Hypothesis 5b Financial controls
Control variables							
Environmental turbulence	0.05	0.01	0.11	0.06	0.00	0.09	0.07
Environmental complexity	0.16+	0.15+	0.12	0.14	0.13	0.15+	0.19*
Firm size	−0.23*	−0.26**	−0.20*	−0.21*	−0.17+	−0.21*	−0.25**
Debt level	−0.02	0.04	−0.09	0.04	0.06	−0.02	0.06
Current ratio	−0.12	−0.16	−0.05	−0.16	−0.16	−0.11	−0.17
Strategic management dimensions							
Environmental scanning		0.21*					
Planning flexibility			0.32***				
Planning horizon				0.15			
Locus of planning					0.26**		
Strategic controls						0.30***	
Financial controls							0.16
F-ratio	2.03+	2.55*	3.98***	1.90+	2.52*	3.98***	2.54*
R^2	0.08	0.12	0.17	0.10	0.12	0.17	0.12
F-ratio testing the Δ in R^2 between the full and partial model		4.95*	12.78***	2.20	5.89*	12.77***	5.00*

+$p < 0.10$; *$p < 0.05$; **$p < 0.01$; ***$p < 0.001$
The *F*-ratio testing the change in R^2 between the full and partial models assesses the significance of each of the dimensions of strategic management beyond the contribution of the control variables.
Regression coefficients shown are standardized coefficients.

attempting to become more entrepreneurial, however, the value-added contribution of this paper lies in providing a sharper picture of exactly how five specific strategic management practices influence a firm's entrepreneurial intensity. This type of fine-grained information is of practical use to managers and helps researchers better understand the subtleties of the strategic management corporate entrepreneurship interface.

This study produced several normative implications. It is clear from the results that scanning intensity is an important correlate of entrepreneurial behavior. This result is consistent with similar findings reported by Miller (1983) and Zahra (1993). What is particularly instructive about this result is that the pursuit of entrepreneurship requires an increase in the intensity of some management practices, such as scanning intensity. Opportunity recognition, which is a precursor to entrepreneurial behavior, is often associated with a flash of genius, but in reality is probably more often than not the end result of a laborious process of environmental scanning and industry awareness. As a result, the fundamental practice of scanning the environment to recognize opportunities and threats should be a principal concern of entrepreneurially minded firms.

The results of the study also depict a strong relationship between planning flexibility and corporate entrepreneurship intensity. Recall that planning flexibility refers to the ease with which a firm can change its strategic plan in response to environmental change. In practice, planning flexibility may be difficult to achieve. Many firms expend enormous effort and cost in developing sophisticated short-term and long-term plans. As a result, in some instances the extent of this effort may actually work against a firm by engendering a hesitancy on the part of managers to deviate from plans for fear that the deviations will be interpreted as flaws in the initial planning process. In addition, as noted by Stevenson and Jarrillo-Mossi (1986: 14), the sentiment that 'good plans do not need to be changed' also hinders the recognition that planning flexibility is necessary. The implication of the results in this area is that entrepreneurially minded firms should work hard to institutionalize flexibility in their planning systems. The manner in which this is accomplished is a potentially fruitful topic for future research.

As reported earlier, we did not find a relationship between the length of a firm's planning horizon and corporate entrepreneurship intensity. The lack of results may be due to the poor reliability of our planning horizon measure. A contributing factor to the poor reliability of the measure may have been the fact that the respondent was asked to assess the planning horizon for four different hierarchical levels in his or her firm, which may have required the respondent to speculate too far beyond his or her personal experience. In addition, dichotomizing a firm's planning horizon as either short (less than 5 years) or long (more than 5 years) may be too simplistic. Capon *et al.* (1987) found that more than 80 percent of the firms in their sample of 258 manufacturers produced plans with more than one planning horizon (typically one short and one long), and some firms produced plans with up to three. The manner in which entrepreneurial firms conceptualize the future and manage their planning horizons is not well understood. An entrepreneurial firm faces the dual challenge of remaining responsive to current environmental trends, which suggests the adoption of a short-term planning horizon, while at the same time remaining visionary, which suggests the adoption of a longer-term perspective. The manner in which entrepreneurial firms resolve this tension represents potentially interesting research.

The positive relationship between locus of planning and corporate entrepreneurship intensity indicates that a high level of employee involvement in planning facilitates firm-level entrepreneurial behavior. This result is supportive of the general notion that employee participation at all levels is an essential key to the entrepreneurial process (e.g., Burgelman, 1984). The result is also consistent with Sathe's (1988) observation that if entrepreneurship is to flourish in an organization, lower-level managers need to be free to identify and pursue promising opportunities. The positive relationship between strategic controls and corporate entrepreneurship intensity is also consistent with the literature (e.g., Sathe, 1988). This result reaffirms the notion that control systems capable of rewarding creativity and the pursuit of opportunity through innovation are an essential part of the entrepreneurial process.

Along with the normative implications discussed above, an important contribution of this study is the development of the psychometric scales used to measure the dimensions of strategic management included in the study. Two of the scales — planning flexibility and locus of planning — are unique to this study and demonstrated good reliability and preliminary evidence of validity. Future researchers may benefit by using these scales in replication studies or to study additional aspects of the interface between strategic management and corporate entrepreneurship.

This study has limitations. We confined our analysis to the study of five specific strategic management practices and corporate entrepreneurship intensity. Obviously, strategic management is a much broader multidimensional construct, and other dimensions of the strategic management process may influence a firm's entrepreneurial behavior. In addition, the study was limited to manufacturing firms. The extent to which the precursors to entrepreneurial behavior differ between manufacturing firms and service firms has not been tested. The strength of our study is that our methodology provided a reasonably fine-grained examination of the influence of each of the strategic management practices included in the study on corporate entrepreneurship intensity.

In conclusion, the compelling theme that emerges from this study is that a firm's strategic management practices influence its entrepreneurial intensity. This study moves the literature forward by examining in a more detailed manner than previously attempted the specific nature of the relationship between five specific strategic management practices and corporate entrepreneurship intensity.

ACKNOWLEDGEMENTS

Support for this research was provided by a Summer Research Fellowship from the College of Business and Public Administration at the University of Missouri — Columbia. The authors would like to thank Richard Johnson, Jeffrey Harrison, and two anonymous reviewers for their helpful comments on earlier versions of this manuscript.

REFERENCES

Aaker, D. A. (1995). *Developing Business Strategies*. Wiley, New York.

Aaker, D. A. and B. Mascarenhas (1984). 'Flexibility: A strategic option', *Journal of Business Strategy*, 15(2), pp. 74–82.

Aldrich, H. E. (1979). *Organizations and Environments*. Prentice-Hall, Englewood Cliffs, NJ.

Amburgey, T. L., D. Kelly and W. P. Barnett (1993). 'Resetting the clock: The dynamics of organizational change and failure', *Administrative Science Quarterly*, 38, pp. 51–73.

Bahrami, H. (1992). 'The emerging flexible organization: Perspectives from Silicon Valley', *California Management Review*, 34(4), pp. 33–52.

Bantel, K. A. and S. E. Jackson (1989). 'Top management and innovations in banking: Does the composition of the top team make a difference?', *Strategic Management Journal*, Summer Special Issue, 10, pp. 107–124.

Binning, J. and G. Barrett (1989). 'Validity of personnel decisions: A conceptual analysis of the inferential and evidential bases', *Journal of Applied Psychology*, 74, pp. 478–494.

Bluedorn, A. C., R. A. Johnson, D. K. Cartwright and B. R. Barringer (1994). 'The interface and convergence of the strategic management and organizational environment domains', *Journal of Management*, 20, pp. 201–262.

Box, T. (1991). 'Performance predictors for entrepreneurial manufacturing', unpublished doctoral dissertation, Oklahoma State University.

Burgelman, R. A. (1983). 'Corporate entrepreneurship and strategic management: Insights from a process study', *Management Science*, 29, pp. 1349–1364.

Burgelman, R. A. (1984). 'Designs for corporate entrepreneurship', *California Management Review*, 26(2), pp. 154–166.

Burgelman, R. A. (1988). 'Strategy making as a social learning process: The case of internal corporate venturing', *Interfaces*, 18, pp. 74–85.

Burgelman, R. A. (1991). 'Intraorganizational ecology of strategy making and organizational adaptation: Theory and field research', *Organization Science*, 2, pp. 239–262.

Camillus, J. (1982). 'Reconciling logical incrementalism and synoptic formalism: An integrated approach to designing strategic planning processes', *Strategic Management Journal*, 3(3), pp. 277–283.

Capon, N., J. Farley and J. Hulbert (1987). *Corporate Strategic Planning*. Columbia University Press, New York.

Chakravarthy, B. S. (1987). 'On tailoring a strategic planning system to its context: Some empirical evidence', *Strategic Management Journal*, 8(6), pp. 517–534.

Chakravarthy, B. S. (1996). 'Flexible commitment: A key to strategic success', *Strategy and Leadership*, 24, pp. 14–20.

Child, J. (1972). 'Organizational structure, environment,

and performance: The role of strategic choice', *Sociology*, **6**, pp. 2–22.

Covin, J. G. (1991). 'Entrepreneurial versus conservative firms: A comparison of strategies and performance', *Journal of Management Studies*, **28**, pp. 439–462.

Covin, J. G. and D. P. Slevin (1986). 'The development and testing of an organizational-level entrepreneurship scale'. In R. Ronstadt, J. A. Hornaday, R. Peterson and K. H. Vesper (eds.), *Frontiers of Entrepreneurship Research*. Babson College, Wellesley, MA, pp. 628–639.

Covin, J. G. and D. P. Slevin (1988). 'The influence of organizational structure on the utility of an entrepreneurial top management style', *Journal of Management Studies*, **25**, pp. 217–234.

Covin, J. G. and D. P. Slevin (1989). 'Strategic management of small firms in hostile and benign environments', *Strategic Management Journal*, **10**(1), pp. 75–87.

Covin, J. G. and D. P. Slevin (1991a). 'A conceptual model of entrepreneurship as firm behavior', *Entrepreneurship Theory and Practice*, **16**, pp. 7–25.

Covin, J. G. and D. P. Slevin (1991b). 'Entrepreneurial versus conservative firms: A comparison of strategies and performance', *Journal of Management Studies*, **28**, pp. 439–462.

Cronbach, L. J. (1951). 'Coefficient alpha and the internal structure of tests', *Psychometrika*, **16**, pp. 297–334.

Das, T. K. (1987). 'Strategic planning and individual temporal orientation', *Strategic Management Journal*, **8**(2), pp. 203–209.

Das, T. K. (1991). 'Time: The hidden dimension in strategic planning', *Long Range Planning*, **24**, pp. 49–57.

Dillman, D. A. (1978). *Mail and Telephone Surveys: The Total Design Method*. Wiley, New York.

Drucker, P. F. (1985). *Innovation and Entrepreneurship*. Harper & Row, New York.

Dutton, J. E. and R. B. Duncan (1987). 'The influence of the strategic planning process on strategic change', *Strategic Management Journal*, **8**(2), pp. 103–116.

Eisenhardt, K. M. (1989). 'Making fast strategic decisions in high-velocity environments', *Academy of Management Journal*, **32**, pp. 543–576.

Gardner, J., R. Rachlin and H. Sweeney (1986). *Handbook of Strategic Planning*. Wiley, New York.

Goold, M. and A. Campbell (1987). *Strategies and Styles*. Blackwell, London.

Goold, M. and J. Quinn (1990). *Strategic Controls*. Addison-Wesley, Reading, MA.

Gupta, A. K. (1987). 'SUB strategies, corporate–SBU relations, and SBU effectiveness in strategy implementation', *Academy of Management Journal*, **30**, pp. 477–500.

Guth, W. and A. Ginsberg (1990). 'Guest editor's introduction: Corporate entrepreneurship', *Strategic Management Journal*, Summer Special Issue, **11**, pp. 5–15.

Hambrick, D. C. (1981). 'Specialization of environmental scanning activities among upper level executives', *Journal of Management Studies*, **18**, pp. 299–320.

Hayes, R. and W. Abernathy (1980). 'Managing our way to economic decline', *Harvard Business Review*, **58**(4), pp. 67–77.

Hitt, M. A., R. E. Hoskisson and R. D. Ireland (1990). 'Mergers and acquisitions and managerial commitment to innovation in M-form firms', *Strategic Management Journal*, Summer Special Issue, **11**, pp. 29–47.

Hitt, M. A., R. E. Hoskisson, R. A. Johnson and D. D. Moesel (1996). 'The market for corporate control and firm innovation', *Academy of Management Journal*, **39**, pp. 1084–1119.

Hoskisson, R. E. and M. A. Hitt (1988). 'Strategic control systems and relative R&D investment in large multiproduct firms', *Strategic Management Journal*, **9**(6), pp. 605–621.

Hoskisson, R. E., M. A. Hitt and C. W. L. Hill (1991). 'Managerial risk taking in diversified firms: An evolutionary perspective', *Organizational Science*, **3**, pp. 296–314.

Hussey, D. (1997). *The Innovative Challenge*. Wiley, New York.

Jennings, D. F. and S. Seaman (1994). 'High and low levels of organizational adaptation: An empirical analysis of strategy, structure, and performance', *Strategic Management Journal*, **15**(6), pp. 459–475.

Johnson, R. A., R. E. Hoskisson and M. A. Hitt (1993). 'Board of director involvement in restructuring: The effects of board versus managerial controls and characteristics', *Strategic Management Journal*, Summer Special Issue, **14**, pp. 33–50.

Judge, W. Q. and M. Spitzfaden (1995). 'The management of strategic time horizons within biotechnology firms: The impact of cognitive complexity on time horizon diversity', *Journal of Management Inquiry*, **4**, pp. 179–196.

Judge, W. Q. and C. P. Zeithaml (1992). 'Institutional and strategic choice perspective on board involvement in the strategic decision process', *Academy of Management Journal*, **35**, pp. 766–794.

Kanter, R. M. (1988). 'When a thousand flowers bloom: Structural, collective and social conditions for innovation in organizations'. In B. M. Staw and L. L. Cummings (eds.), *Research in Organizational Behavior*, Vol. 10. JAI Press, Greenwich, CT, pp. 169–211.

Kanter, R. M. (1989). *When Giants Learn to Dance*. Simon and Schuster, New York.

Khandwalla, P. N. (1977). *The Design of Organizations*. Harcourt Brace Jovanovich, New York.

Koontz, H. (1958). 'A preliminary statement of principles of planning and control', *Academy of Management Journal*, **1**(1), pp. 45–61.

Kukalis, S. (1989). 'The relationship among firm characteristics and design of strategic planning systems in large organizations', *Journal of Management*, **15**, pp. 565–579.

Lant, T., F. Milliken and B. Batra (1992). 'The role of managerial learning and interpretation in strategic persistence and reorientation: An empirical explo-

Strat. Mgmt. J., **20**: 421–444 (1999)

ration', *Strategic Management Journal*, **13**(8), pp. 585–608.

Lindsay, W. M. and L. W. Rue (1980). 'Impact of the organizational environment on the long-range planning process: A contingency view', *Academy of Management Journal*, **23**, pp. 385–404.

Lorange, P., M. Morton and S. Ghoshal (1986). *Strategic Control Systems*. West, St. Paul, MN.

Lumpkin, G. T. and G. G. Dess (1996). 'Clarifying the entrepreneurial orientation construct and linking it to performance', *Academy of Management Review*, **21**, pp. 135–172.

Miller, D. (1983). 'The correlates of entrepreneurship in three types of firms', *Management Science*, **29**, pp. 770–791.

Miller, D. and P. Friesen (1982). 'Innovation in conservative and entrepreneurial firms: Two models of strategic momentum', *Strategic Management Journal*, **3**(1), pp. 1–25.

Miller, D. and P. Friesen (1983). 'Strategic-making and environment: The third link', *Strategic Management Journal*, **4**(3), pp. 221–235.

Mintzberg, H. (1994). *The Rise and Fall of Strategic Planning*. Free Press, New York.

Murray, J. A. (1984). 'A concept of entrepreneurial strategy', *Strategic Management Journal*, **5**(1), pp. 1–13.

Naman, J. and D. Slevin (1993). 'Entrepreneurship and the concept of fit: A model and empirical tests', *Strategic Management Journal*, **14**(2), pp. 137–153.

Newman, W. H. (1951). *Administrative Action: The Techniques of Organization and Management*. Prentice-Hall, Englewood Cliffs, NJ.

Newman, W. H. (1963). *Administrative Action: The Techniques of Organization and Management* (2nd ed.). Prentice-Hall, Englewood Cliffs, NJ.

Pedhazur, E. (1982). *Multiple Regression in Behavioral Research*. Holt, Rinehart & Winston, Fort Worth, TX.

Podsakoff, P. and D. Organ (1986). 'Reports in organizational research: Problems and prospects', *Journal of Management Studies*, **27**, pp. 305–327.

Reid, D. (1989). 'Operationalizing strategic planning', *Strategic Management Journal*, **10**(6), pp. 553–567.

Rhyne, L. C. (1985). 'The relationship of informative usage, characteristics to planning system sophistication: An empirical examination', *Strategic Management Journal*, **6**(4), pp. 319–337.

Rhyne, L. C. (1986). 'The relationship of strategic planning to financial performance', *Strategic Management Journal*, **7**(5), pp. 423–436.

Rumelt, R. P. (1974). *Strategy, Structure, and Economic Performance*. Harvard University Press, Cambridge, MA.

Sathe, V. (1988). 'From surface to deep corporate entrepreneurship', *Human Resource Management*, **27**, pp. 389–411.

Schendel, D. E. and C. Hofer (1979). *Strategic Management: A New Way of Business Policy and Planning*. Little, Brown, Boston, MA.

Schumpeter, J. A. (1936). *The Theory of Economic Development*. Cambridge University Press, Cambridge, U.K.

Schumpeter, J. A. (1950). *Capitalism, Socialism, and Democracy* (3rd edn.). Harper & Row, New York.

Stevenson, H. H. and D. E. Gumpert (1985). 'The heart of entrepreneurship', *Harvard Business Review*, **85**(2), pp. 85–93.

Stevenson, H. H. and J. C. Jarillo (1990). 'A paradigm of entrepreneurship: Entrepreneurship management', *Strategic Management Journal*, Summer Special Issue, **11**, pp. 17–27.

Stevenson, H. H. and J. C. Jarillo-Mossi (1986). 'Preserving entrepreneurship as companies grow', *Journal of Business Strategy*, **7**(1), pp. 10–23.

Venkatraman, N. and J. Grant (1986). 'Construct measurement in strategy research: A critique and proposal', *Academy of Management Review*, **11**, pp. 71–86.

Wortman, M. S. (1987). 'Entrepreneurship: An integrating typology and evaluation of the empirical research in the field', *Journal of Management*, **13**, pp. 259–279.

Zahra, S. A. (1991). 'Predictors and financial outcomes of corporate entrepreneurship', *Journal of Business Venturing*, **6**, pp. 259–285.

Zahra, S. A. (1993). 'Environment, corporate entrepreneurship, and financial performance: A taxonomic approach', *Journal of Business Venturing*, **8**, pp. 319–340.

Zumd, R. (1983). 'The effectiveness of external information channels in facilitating innovation within software development groups', *MIS Quarterly*, **7**, pp. 43–47.

440   *B. R. Barringer and A. C. Bluedorn*

APPENDIX: MEASUREMENT SCALES USED IN THE SELF-REPORT MAIL SURVEY

The Corporate Entrepreneurship Scale (coefficient alpha = 0.87)

The following statements are meant to identify the *collective management style* of your firm's key decision-makers.

Please indicate which response *most closely matches* the management style of your businesses key managers.

1. In general, the top managers of my firm favor ...

a.	A strong emphasis on the marketing of tried and true products and services	1 2 3 4 5 6 7	A strong emphasis on R&D, technological leadership, and innovation
b.	Low-risk projects with normal and certain rates of return	1 2 3 4 5 6 7	High-risk projects with changes of very high returns
c.	A cautious, 'wait and see' posture in order to minimize the probability of making costly decisions when faced with uncertainty	1 2 3 4 5 6 7	A bold, aggressive posture in order to maximize the probability of exploiting potential when faced with uncertainty

2. How many new lines of products or services has your firm marketed in the past 5 years?

a.	No new lines of products or services	1 2 3 4 5 6 7	Many new lines of products or services
b.	Changes in product or service lines have been mostly of a minor nature	1 2 3 4 5 6 7	Changes in product or service lines have usually been quite dramatic

3. In dealing with its competitors, my firm ...

a.	Typically responds to actions which competitors initiate	1 2 3 4 5 6 7	Typically initiates actions to which competitors then respond
b.	Is very seldom the first firm to introduce new products/ services, operating technologies, etc.	1 2 3 4 5 6 7	Is very often the first firm to introduce new products/ services operating technologies, etc.
c.	Typically seeks to avoid competitive clashes, preferring a 'live-and-let-live' posture	1 2 3 4 5 6 7	Typically adopts a very competitive, 'undo-the-competitor' posture

4. In general, the top managers of my firm believe that ...

a.	Owing to the nature of the environment, it is best to	1 2 3 4 5 6 7	Owing to the nature of the environment, bold, wide-

| explore gradually via cautious behavior | ranging acts are necessary to achieve the firm's objectives |

Sources: Items 1a, 2a, and 2b measure innovation; Items 1b, 1c, and 4a measure risk-taking; Items 3a, 3b, and 3c measure proactiveness. Items are based on Khandwalla (1977); Miller and Friesen (1982); Covin and Slevin (1988).

The Scanning Intensity Scale (coefficient alpha = 0.83)

1. Rate the extent to which the following scanning devices are used by your firm to gather information about its business environment.

		Not ever used						Used frequently
a.	Routine gathering of opinions from clients	1	2	3	4	5	6	7
b.	Explicit tracking of the policies and tactics of competitors	1	2	3	4	5	6	7
c.	Forecasting sales, customer preferences, technology, etc.	1	2	3	4	5	6	7
d.	Special marketing research studies	1	2	3	4	5	6	7
e.	Trade magazines, government publications, news media	1	2	3	4	5	6	7
f.	Gathering of information from suppliers and other channel members	1	2	3	4	5	6	7

Sources: The items above measure effort devoted towards scanning. Items 1–4 are from Miller and Friesen (1982). Items 5–6 are original.

2. How often do you collect information to remain abreast of changes in each of the following areas?

		Never						Frequently
a.	Economic trends	1	2	3	4	5	6	7
b.	Technological trends	1	2	3	4	5	6	7
c.	Demographic trends	1	2	3	4	5	6	7
d.	Customer needs and preferences	1	2	3	4	5	6	7
e.	Competitor strategies	1	2	3	4	5	6	7
f.	Supplier strategies	1	2	3	4	5	6	7

Sources: The items above measure scanning comprehensiveness. All items are original.

The Planning Flexibility Scale (coefficient alpha = 0.80)

1. How difficult is it for your firm to change its strategic plan to adjust to each of the following contingencies/possibilities?

		Very difficult						Not at all difficult
a.	The emergence of a new technology	1	2	3	4	5	6	7
b.	Shifts in economic conditions	1	2	3	4	5	6	7
c.	The market entry of new competition	1	2	3	4	5	6	7
d.	Changes in government regulations	1	2	3	4	5	6	7
e.	Shifts in customer needs and preferences	1	2	3	4	5	6	7
f.	Modifications in supplier strategies	1	2	3	4	5	6	7
g.	The emergence of an unexpected opportunity	1	2	3	4	5	6	7

442   *B. R. Barringer and A. C. Bluedorn*

h.   The emergence of an unexpected threat   1 2 3 4 5 6 7
i   Political developments that affect your industry   1 2 3 4 5 6 7

Sources: All items are original.

The Planning Horizon Scale (coefficient alpha = 0.90)

1. Recall that a planning horizon is the length of the future time period that decision-makers consider in planning. At each of the following hierarchical levels in your firm, what degree of emphasis is placed on managing business strategies and firm investments that have the following planning horizons?

                                            Very little emphasis   Considerable emphasis

a.   Board of Directors

      *Length of planning horizon of business strategy
      or firm investment*

      Less than 1 year   1 2 3 4 5 6 7
      1 to 3 years   1 2 3 4 5 6 7
      3 to 5 years   1 2 3 4 5 6 7
      More than 5 years   1 2 3 4 5 6 7

b.   Top management

      Less than 1 year   1 2 3 4 5 6 7
      1 to 3 years   1 2 3 4 5 6 7
      3 to 5 years   1 2 3 4 5 6 7
      More than 5 years   1 2 3 4 5 6 7

c.   Middle management

      Less than 1 year   1 2 3 4 5 6 7
      1 to 3 years   1 2 3 4 5 6 7
      3 to 5 years   1 2 3 4 5 6 7
      More than 5 years   1 2 3 4 5 6 7

d.   Lower-level Management

      Less than 1 year   1 2 3 4 5 6 7
      1 to 3 years   1 2 3 4 5 6 7
      3 to 5 years   1 2 3 4 5 6 7
      More than 5 years   1 2 3 4 5 6 7

Sources: All items are original.

The Locus of Planning Scale (coefficient alpha = 0.89)

1. Strategic management can be broken down into the five phases shown below. To what extent is each of the following categories of employees involved in each of these phases of the strategic management process in your firm?

Corporate Entrepreneurship and Strategic Management 443

	No Involvement						Substantial Involvement

a.   Goal Formation

Top Management	1	2	3	4	5	6	7
Middle Management	1	2	3	4	5	6	7
Lower-level Management	1	2	3	4	5	6	7
Rank-and-file Employees	1	2	3	4	5	6	7

b.   Scanning the Business Environment

Top Management	1	2	3	4	5	6	7
Middle Management	1	2	3	4	5	6	7
Lower-level Management	1	2	3	4	5	6	7
Rank-and-file Employees	1	2	3	4	5	6	7

c.   Strategy Formulation

Top Management	1	2	3	4	5	6	7
Middle Management	1	2	3	4	5	6	7
Lower-level Management	1	2	3	4	5	6	7
Rank-and-file Employees	1	2	3	4	5	6	7

d.   Strategy Implementation

Top Management	1	2	3	4	5	6	7
Middle Management	1	2	3	4	5	6	7
Lower-level Management	1	2	3	4	5	6	7
Rank-and-file Employees	1	2	3	4	5	6	7

e.   Evaluation and control

Top Management	1	2	3	4	5	6	7
Middle Management	1	2	3	4	5	6	7
Lower-level Management	1	2	3	4	5	6	7
Rank-and-file Employees	1	2	3	4	5	6	7

Sources: All items are original.

The Strategic Controls Scale (coefficient alpha = 0.64)

1. How important is each of the following in making sure that your firm's employees and business strategies meet predetermined objectives?

	Unimportant						Important
a. Face-to-face meetings between top managers and business unit or functional area personnel	1	2	3	4	5	6	7
b. Informal face-to-face meetings between top managers and business unit or functional area personnel	1	2	3	4	5	6	7
c. Measuring performance against subjective stra-	1	2	3	4	5	6	7

444   *B. R. Barringer and A. C. Bluedorn*

tegic criteria such as improvements in customer
satisfaction or progress on product innovations

Sources: Items 1–2 are from Johnson *et al.* (1993). Item 3 is original.

The Financial Controls Scale (alpha = 0.77)

1. How important are each of the following factors in evaluating the performance of business
    unit/or functional   area personnel?

		Unimportant						Important
a.	Objective strategic criteria such as return on assets	1	2	3	4	5	6	7
b.	Return on investment	1	2	3	4	5	6	7
c.	Cash-flow	1	2	3	4	5	6	7

Sources: All items are modified from Hitt *et al.* (1996).

28

©Academy of Management Review 1983, Vol. 8, No. 1, 61-70

A Model of the Interaction of Strategic Behavior, Corporate Context, and the Concept of Strategy[1]

ROBERT A. BURGELMAN
Stanford University

Based on a review of previous landmark studies and in the light of findings of recent research on internal corporate venturing, a model of the strategic process in large, complex firms is presented under which the propositions "structure follows strategy" and "strategy follows structure" can both be subsumed. Current corporate strategy induces some strategic behavior but changes in corporate strategy follow other, autonomous, strategic behavior.

The study of the relationships between strategy and structure in large, complex firms remains of central concern to scholars in the fields of strategic management and macro organizational behavior. Previous research has, indeed, produced apparently conflicting propositions regarding the directionality of these relationships. Depending on which body of empirical evidence is used to bolster the argument, "structure follows strategy" and "strategy follows structure" both seem to be valid propositions (Bower & Doz, 1979; Galbraith & Nathanson, 1979; Hall & Saias, 1980). The present paper contributes to the resolution of this apparent contradiction by elucidating further the conditions under which each of these propositions may be valid.

The analysis presented here rests on two critical insights. First, both propositions need to be considered in terms of what they imply about the nature of the strategic *process*. As previous researchers have observed (Bower & Doz, 1979), the strategic process in large, complex firms consists of the strategic activities of managers from different levels in the organization. Second, these strategic activi-

[1] Support for this paper from New York University's Graduate School of Business Administration and from the Strategic Management Program of Stanford University's Graduate School of Business is gratefully acknowledged. Michael L. Tushman (Columbia University), Eric J. Walton (New York University), L. Jay Bourgeois, David B. Jemison, and Steven C. Wheelwright (all of Stanford University) have made helpful comments on earlier drafts of this manuscript.

ties are of two kinds. Most strategic activities are *induced* by the firm's current concept of corporate strategy, but also emerging are some *autonomous* strategic activities, that is, activities that fall outside the scope of the current concept of strategy. The consequences of this distinction for the strategic process have not previously been made the subject of systematic analysis.

Autonomous strategic activities have been documented by the students of unrelated diversification through internal corporate venturing (ICV) (Biggadike, 1979; Burgelman, 1980, Fast, 1979). Fast's study of new venture divisions in large, diversified firms, for instance, has provided incidental evidence of the autonomous nature of the strategic activities involved in new venturing. As a participant in one of the firms in Fast's study observed:

> Top management saw a need for ventures and said, "Go ahead and do it." Nobody really managed or directed it. So the whole company began to get into ventures but there was no clear direction or purpose (1979, p. 76).

Biggadike's (1979) large sample study of new entries at the business level of analysis also suggests the autonomous nature of new venture activities. Even though ICV projects required the commitment of substantial amounts of resources over substantial periods of time and changed the scope of the corporate business portfolio when they were successful, there seemed to come little guidance from the firms' current corporate strategy for these ICV efforts.

Neither Fast nor Biggadike has attempted to conceptualize the corporate strategic process in which new ventures take shape. Yet both researchers have suggested that the research of Bower (1970) and his students could be useful to conceptualize the corporate strategic processes involved in ICV. Independent of these suggestions, Burgelman's (1980) study of ICV project development in the diversified major firm has found that Bower's model is indeed useful but needs to be extended. This study has provided systematic field data from which the category of autonomous strategic behavior has been induced. It also has provided additional insight in the corporate context processes in which ICV project development is embedded (Burgelman, 1982).

These insights concerning the nature of strategic behavior and corporate context processes provide the basis for reanalyzing the landmark studies from which the two apparently contradictory propositions concerning the relationships between strategy and structure have been derived.

Structure Follows Strategy

The proposition that structure follows strategy became firmly established as a result of Chandler's (1962) study of the historical development of major U.S.-based industrial firms in the period 1919-1959. Subsequent empirical research in the multinational context, and in firms situated in other countries of the Western world, generally has corroborated the structure follows strategy proposition (Galbraith & Nathanson, 1979). Relatively little can be learned about the strategic process underlying Chandler's proposition from these large sample, verification-oriented follow-up studies. The original field study, however, can be reexamined to evaluate the extent to which the original theoretical generalizations were grounded.

Strategy Follows Autonomous Strategic Behavior

Chandler's case materials indicate that major structural adjustments followed the experience of severe management problems *after* strategic initiatives had been undertaken in areas unrelated, or only marginally related, to the traditional lines of business of the firm.

The case data also indicate that these strategic initiatives were not the result of an a priori clearly formulated corporate strategy on the part of top management. Rather, the corporate strategy emerged through a somewhat haphazard process. It was the result of final authorizations by top management of strategic projects that had successfully absorbed the firm's excess resources and promised to do so profitably in the future.

Chandler raised the important question: "Why did the new strategy which called for a change in structure, arise in the first place?" (1962, p. 14). He refers to the major changes in the external environment that had created opportunities for the use of existing excess resources of the firm. At the conclusion of the study, Chandler refers to Penrose's (1968) work and suggests that his data supports her theoretical analysis of the growth of the firm.

Penrose's analysis, however, emphasizes the *internal* impulse toward growth. She observes that the recognition of opportunities takes place in the mind of managers and is often independent of changes in the external environment. In fact, Penrose forebodes the concept of the "enacted environment" (Weick, 1979):

> In the last analysis, the "environment" rejects or confirms the soundness of the judgments about it, but the relevant environment is not an objective fact discoverable before the events (Penrose, 1968, p. 41).

Implicit in the affirmation of the relevance of Penrose's analysis seems to be the recognition that corporate development was not really the result of top management taking a fresh look at the environment, then formulating a strategy, and then establishing the appropriate structural arrangements to implement the strategy. In reality, the structural rearrangements reflected efforts to *consolidate* the results of autonomous strategic behavior. The new strategy reflected the recognition of the importance of these strategic actions. In the final analysis, Chandler's study seems to indicate that changes in corporate strategy followed autonomous strategic behavior.

Heroic View of Top Management

Chandler's case data suggest that multiple layers of management were involved in the strategic initiatives that produced the extensive diversification, and in response to which the new strategy and the new structure eventually emerged. The theoretical generalizations, however, collapse this strategic process into a top management activity. Even though the influence of lower levels in the determination of the content of the strategy is recognized, the major emphasis is on the role of top management. Yet, as the du Pont case materials suggest, top management's influence before the reorganization was very limited, with the real influence over strategic behavior situated at the department head level. It was only after H. Fletcher Brown wrote a penetrating analysis of this situation (Chandler, 1962) that the strategic role of the executive committee (representing the whole corporation) became firmly established.

In spite of a preoccupation with the role of top management in the strategic development of the firms studied, Chandler presents data that question the relative importance of this role, ironically even with respect to the decisions to change the structural arrangements:

> At du Pont, General Motors, and Jersey Standard, the initial awareness of the structural inadequacies caused by the new complexity came from executives close to top management, but who were not themselves in a position to make organizational changes. *In all cases, the president gave no encouragement to the proposers of change* (1962, p. 308, emphasis provided).

And after reflecting on the meaning of the data, Chandler puts forward another key question:

> But if the stockholders and the board became captives of the fulltime administrators, were not the professional entrepreneurs themselves captives of their subordinates? Were not the information and alternatives available to the top determined, possibly quite unconsciously, by junior executives down the line? Must not then the enterprise or the organization as a whole be considered responsible for the basic economic decisions? If this is so, then no individual or team of individuals can be identified as the key decision makers in the private sector of the American economy (1962, p. 313).

Chandler concludes that the case data challenge the view that the role of top management was not predominant. This conclusion, however, is based on the observation that the new structure had facilitated top management's role in strategy formulation and entrepreneurship after it had been put in place. The case data relating to the situation before the reorganization do not support the heroic view of the role of top management. Furthermore, the proposition that the new type of structural arrangement would lead to a greater role for top management in the formulation of corporate strategy can be verified in the light of the findings of another major line of research in the field of strategic management.

Strategy Follows Structure

The process oriented line of research in strategic management has taken the concepts of the "decision making" (Cohen, March, & Olsen, 1972; Cyert & March, 1963; March & Simon, 1958) and "institutional" (Selznick, 1957) orientations in organization theory, and the "incrementalist" theory in strategy making (Lindblom, 1959) as its points of departure. These theories allow for a bottom-up conception of strategy formulation in which top management's role is not necessarily critical—one in which the concepts of strategy and structure are not clearly delineated from each other (Bower, 1974), nor are operational decisions delineated from strategic decisions (Ansoff, 1965). Basically, this is Chandler's view upside down. Important empirical research has investigated the usefulness of these theoretical orientations for the understanding of the process whereby key decisions are made in complex organizations. It has extended the theory by clarifying the role of top management in these processes (Aharoni, 1966; Allison, 1971; Carter, 1971).

A landmark study concerning the strategic process is Bower's (1970) carefully designed, longitudinal field study of the management of strategic capital investment projects in the "diversified major" firm. Probably the most complex type of divisionalized firm, the latter encompasses an agglomeration of widely diversified but partially related businesses grouped into major divisions whose general managers report to corporate management.

Strategy Making—A Multilayered Process

Bower's study documents the manner in which the strategic capital investment process in such firms is spread over the management hierarchy. Three major subprocesses could be discerned, each of which, in turn, comprised three major phases related to activities of managers at particular levels in the organization.

At the product/market level in a division, proposals are defined in technical/economic terms. This *definition* process is triggered by a perceived discrepancy between strategic business objectives and existent physical plant capacity available to attain these. Projects survive only if they receive impetus from divisional level management. This _impetus_ process is highly political, because managers at the divisional level are aware that their career prospects depend, to a large extent, on developing a good "batting average" in supporting strategic projects. Thus managers will evaluate proposals in the light of the reward and measurement systems that determine whether it is in their interest to provide impetus for a particular project. At the corporate level, the major contribution is precisely the manipulation of the _structural context_ within which the proposal generation takes shape. Through the manipulation of structural context, top management can influence the type of proposals that will be defined and given impetus.

Whereas definition and impetus are primarily, if not exclusively, bottom-up processes, the design of the structural context is primarily, if again not exclusively, a top-down process. Thus, to the extent that capital investment proposals reflect strategic business planning, it is possible to posit that strategy making is both a bottom-up and top-down multilayered process (Bower, 1974). Because of the effects of structural context on the generation and shaping of strategic projects, it also is possible to posit that strategy follows structure. However, to the extent that the structural context reflects a given concept of corporate strategy, Bower's study actually indicates that corporate strategy induces strategic behavior.

A Less Heroic View of Top Management

Bower's study has provided the basis for further research of the strategic process in various types of organizations and concerning different classes of strategic decisions. These have further elucidated the social and political forces in and around the strategic process (Hofer, 1976).

Recently, Bower and Doz have articulated a major implication of this line of research, which concerns an alternative view of the role of top management in the strategic process:

> Thus, in contrast to strategy formulation as the critical direction-setting general management activity, this new process school of research suggested an alternative, that is, managing the strategic process (1979, p. 158).

Yet, as the authors point out, it is not clear how the management of the corporate phase can be done:

> If structure is to shape strategy, what vision shapes structure and how is that vision to be developed? Who has a say in the process? More research is needed (1979, p. 159).

A Model of the Interaction of Strategic Behavior, Corporate Context, and the Concept of Strategy

Based on the findings of the process study of ICV, and on the insights derived from the preceding review of Chandler's and Bower's studies in the light of these findings, a new model of the strategic process in large, complex firms can be constructed. This new model sheds additional light on the important questions raised by Bower and Doz. It provides a conceptual framework from which the two major, apparently contradictory, propositions in the field of strategic management can be deduced simultaneously. Figure 1 represents this model.

Variation, Enactment, and Strategic Behavior

This model, inductively derived, is isomorphous to the variation-selection-retention model currently emerging as a major conceptual framework for explaining organizational survival, growth, and development (Aldrich, 1979). Its orientation also is in line with current theoretical efforts (White & Hamermesh, 1981) to integrate research done in industrial organization economics, organization theory, and business policy. The model presented here, however, integrates the business and corporate levels of analysis and applies to the class of firms that are large enough and sufficiently resource-rich to be relatively independent of the tight control of external environment selection. Such firms are able to engage in "strategic choice" (Child, 1972) and, as pointed out earlier, their strategic choice process involves substantive inputs from managers from different levels in the organization. Internally generated variation, resulting from the "enactment" (Weick, 1979) of the environment is, at the minimum, a very important source of variation in such firms (Penrose, 1968). Strategic behavior, in the model presented here, refers to such enactments.

The model proposes that two generic categories of strategic behavior can be discerned in such large, complex firms: induced and autonomous. _Induced_ strategic behavior uses the categories provided by the current concepts of strategy to identify oppor-

Figure 1
A Model of the Interaction of Strategic Behavior,
Corporate Context, and the Concept of Strategy

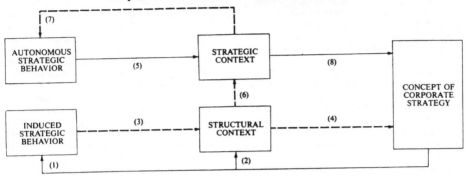

—————— STRONG INFLUENCE
— — — — WEAK INFLUENCE

tunies in the "enactable environment" (Weick, 1979). Being consistent with the existing categories used in the strategic planning system of the firm, such strategic behavior generates little equivocality in the corporate context. Examples of such strategic behavior emerge around, among others, new product development projects for existing businesses, market development projects for existing products, and strategic capital investment projects for existing businesses. Such strategic behavior is shaped by the current structural context. For instance, it can be judged relatively easily in the light of current evaluation and measurement systems. This is the type of strategic behavior documented by Bower (1970). It follows corporate strategy. Hence, the feedback loop (1) in Figure 1 between concept of strategy and induced strategic behavior.

During any given period of time, the bulk of strategic activity in a firm is likely to be of the induced variety. The present model, however, proposes that large, resource-rich firms are likely to possess a reservoir of entrepreneurial potential at operational levels that will express itself in autonomous strategic initiatives. *Autonomous* strategic behavior introduces new categories for the definition of opportunities. Entrepreneurial participants, at the product/market level, conceive new business opportunities, engage in project championing efforts to mobilize corporate resources for these new opportunities, and perform strategic forcing efforts to

create momentum for their further development. Middle level managers attempt to formulate broader strategies for areas of new business activity and try to convince top management to support them. This is the type of strategic behavior encountered in the study of internal corporate venturing (Burgelman, 1980; Roberts, 1980). The strategic initiatives leading up to the corporate managerial problems documented by Chandler (1962) also would seem to fall under this category. Such autonomous strategic initiatives attempt to escape the selective effects of the current structural context, and they make the current concept of corporate strategy problematical. They lead to a redefinition of the corporation's relevant environment and provide the raw material for strategic renewal. They precede changes in corporate strategy.

Corporate Context and Selection

One of the key insights of the study of ICV, reflected in the model presented here, is that the corporate context within which the strategic process takes place encompasses two distinct, selective processes: structural context determination and strategic context determination.

Structural context determination is a broad envelope concept used to denote the various administrative mechanisms that corporate management can manipulate to change the perceived interests of the strategic actors in the organization. In the study of

ICV, it was found to encompass the choices of top management regarding the overall structural configuration, the degree of formalization of positions and relationships, the criteria for project screening, the measures of managerial performance, and the appointment of middle level managers with particular orientations toward entrepreneurial initiative. Bower (1970), of course, had identified earlier the selective nature of this important process.

Structural context determination reflects the efforts of corporate management to fine-tune the selective effects of the administrative arrangements so as to keep (or bring) the strategic proposal generating process in line with the current concept of strategy. This part of the model corresponds to Chandler's proposition that structure follows strategy. Hence, the feedback loop (2) in Figure 1 between concept of strategy and structural context.

Over time, this fine-tuning may make the structural context more elaborate, with more rules applied to the induced strategic behavior. As a result, the range and scope of these strategic behaviors may become narrower while their probability of failure may decrease. One major consequence of the increased selective efficiency of the structural context is that fewer of the selected strategic projects have the potential to force a significant change in the concept of strategy. Standardized, quantitative procedures for project screening, uniform categories of strategic planning unit systems, selection of higher level managers with strong corporate orientation in their decision making, all tend to reduce the variation in the strategic proposals selected by the firm and provide the basis for the proposition that strategy eventually follows structure. Thus, structural context intervenes between induced strategic behavior and the concept of strategy—(3) and (4) in Figure 1. This part of the model corresponds to Bower's findings.

Chandler's proposition focused on the role of top management in bringing structure in line with new strategy. Bower focused on the effects of structure, given strategy. Both studies paid relatively little attention, at least in the conceptualization of the findings, to the role of autonomous strategic behavior in the process through which corporate strategy becomes articulated and changed. The study of ICV has focused on the latter process. This has allowed identification of the process of strategic context determination.

Strategic context determination reflects the efforts of middle level managers to link autonomous strategic behaviors at the product/market level into the corporation's concept of strategy. To do so, the middle level managers must make sense out of these autonomous strategic initiatives and formulate workable, attractive strategies for the corresponding areas of new business development. In addition, they must engage in political activities to convince top management to rationalize, retroactively, these successful initiatives by amending the concept of strategy to accommodate the strategic initiatives. This aspect of the process underlies the proposition that strategy follows autonomous strategic behavior. Thus, strategic context intervenes between autonomous strategic behavior and concept of strategy—(5) and (8) in Figure 1.

The intervening effect of structural context is limited here. In the ICV study, this influence was reflected only in the concerns of the actors to demonstrate large potential size and fast growth rate for the ICV projects. Hence, the dotted arrow (6) from structural context to strategic context in Figure 1.

The degree to which middle management is successful in activating the process of strategic context determination provides guidance for further entrepreneurial initiatives at the operational level. This is represented by the dotted feed-forward loop (7) in Figure 1. It is a feed-forward loop because it guides further strategic initiatives in a particular new area before this area has become incorporated in the concept of strategy of the firm. It is represented as a dotted line because the guidance is relatively tentative and ambiguous.

The Concept of Strategy and Retention

From the perspective of a process study, the concept of strategy of large, complex firms can be viewed as the result of the selective effects of the corporate context on the stream of strategic behaviors at operational levels. The present model proposes that the *concept of corporate strategy* represents the more or less explicit articulation of the firm's theory about its past concrete achievements. This theory defines the identity of the firm at any moment in time. It provides a basis for the maintenance of this identity and for the continuity in strategic activity. It induces further strategic initiative in line with it.

Corporate level managers in large, diversified major firms tend to rise through the ranks, having earned their reputation as head of one or more of the operating divisions. By the time they reach the top management level they have developed a highly reliable frame of reference to evaluate business strategies and resource allocation proposals pertaining to the main lines of business of the corporation. Top managers, basically, are strategies-in-action whose fundamental strategic premises are unlikely to change (Kissinger, 1979). It therefore is not surprising that corporate management focuses on the manipulation of the structural context to keep strategic behavior in line with the current concept of strategy. In the operating system of the firm, this fosters predictability and integration of strategic activity: strategy-making takes on a "planning" mode (Mintzberg, 1973).

To the extent that the current concept of strategy is deeply ingrained in corporate management, its capacity to deal with the substantive issues pertaining to new technological and market developments can be expected to be low. Rather than activating the process of strategic context determination, top management is likely to rely also on the manipulation of the structural context to bring autonomous behavior under control. Ironically, from this analytical perspective, the establishment of a new venture division constitutes a manipulation of the structural context to reduce the variability in the operating divisions rather than the implementation of a strategy of unrelated diversification. Also, from this perspective, Fast's (1979) finding that the position of a new venture division in the corporate context is precarious and Burgelman's (1980) observation of wide oscillations in new venture activity are not surprising. Nor is the finding that the activation of the strategic context requires great conceptual and political skills on the part of middle level managers.

Conclusions and Implications

The widening of the scope of a corporation's business portfolio as a result of successful autonomous strategic activity puts strain on its administrative machinery. Periods of unrelated diversification thus are likely to be followed by periods of consolidation. Chandler's study has documented such cycles during the period 1919-1959, out of which the divisionalized firm emerged as a new generic type. Once the concept of strategy of the firm has been established through top management's ratification of successful autonomous strategic behavior, structures can be designed and refined to select and shape strategic proposals compatible with this concept of strategy. Bower's study has documented the latter processes. Structural design, however, does not work like a well-calibrated sieve. Autonomous strategic activities continue to escape the selective effects of the structural context by mere chance or because alert actors are able to circumvent, or play to their advantage, the selective mechanisms. In any case, the result can be strategic activity falling outside the established strategy. In a more deterministic sense, structure may motivate or impede strategic activity in unanticipated ways (Greiner, 1972; Mintzberg, 1978).

Structure and strategy thus exist in a reciprocal relationship to each other. Depending on which part of the strategic process is observed, both "structure follows strategy" and "strategy follows structure" can be correct propositions.

The present paper has attempted to provide further insight in the strategic process of large, complex firms by focusing on the interaction between the corporate level process of relating structure to strategy, and the process of strategic behavior at the product/market and middle levels in the firm. The model presented here accommodates the conventional, normative proposition that corporate strategy induces strategic behavior. In addition, and perhaps more fundamentally, the model reflects the new proposition that the more dramatic changes in the corporate strategy of large, complex firms are likely to have been preceded by autonomous strategic initiatives at the operational and middle levels of the organization: strategy follows autonomous strategic behavior. The complete list of propositions embedded in the model presented in this paper are summarized in Table 1. It is hoped that these will stimulate further theoretical and empirical research in the field of strategic management.

The present paper focuses the attention of practitioners of strategic management on the dilemmas that result from the opposing tendencies in large, complex firms toward stability and change. Coherence, continuity, and stability in corporate strategy require the institutionalization of strategic behavior through strategic planning systems. Corporate en-

67

Table 1
Propositions Concerning the Interaction of Strategic Behavior, Corporate Context, and the Concept of Strategy

(1) The current concept of strategy induces some but usually not all strategic activity in large, diversified firms. Therefore, at any moment in time, the totality of strategic activity of such firms is usually a mixture of induced and autonomous strategic behavior.

(2) The current concept of strategy leads to the establishment of a structural context aimed at keeping strategic behavior at lower levels in line with the concept of corporate strategy. In this sense, structure follows strategy.

(3) Structural context intervenes in the relationship between induced strategic behavior and concept of strategy. It operates as a selection mechanism on the stream of induced strategic behavior. In this sense, strategy follows structure.

(4) Over time, structural context reduces the variation in induced strategic behavior, and may thereby prevent strategic learning on the part of the firm. This is another aspect of the strategy follows structure proposition.

(5) Strategic context intervenes in the relationship between autonomous strategic behavior and concept of strategy. Through the activation of the process of strategic context determination, autonomous strategic behavior can become integrated in the concept of strategy of the firm.

(6) Structural context intervenes only to a limited extent in the relationship between autonomous strategic behavior and concept of strategy.

(7) The activation of the process of strategic context determination has a weak influence on maintaining the volume of autonomous strategic behavior in the firm.

(8) Over time, changes in the concept of strategy are the result of the retroactive rationalization of autonomous strategic behavior. This, in turn, changes the basis for the further inducement of strategic behavior.

trepreneurship and the resulting strategic renewal of large, complex firms, on the other hand, require the interlocking autonomous strategic initiatives of individuals at operational and middle levels, and an experimentation-and-selection approach at the corporate level. Maintaining a pragmatic balance between these fundamentally different requirements presents a major challenge for top management. This is evident, for instance, in the problems of dealing with performance differences between divisions (Hamermesh, 1977) and in the need to provide strategic guidance for different types of strategic business units (SBUs) in the corporate business portfolio. The present paper suggests that such challenges may be met more readily by recognizing the different requirements of different strategic situations existing simultaneously in the organization.

The distinction between autonomous and induced strategic behavior in the model presented in this paper also provides a theoretical foundation for the deduction of the categories in Miles and Snow's (1978) typology. "Analyzers" are firms high on

both induced and autonomous strategic behavior. They attempt to strike the kind of balance discussed in the previous paragraph. "Prospectors" emphasize autonomous strategic behavior. They, however, face the problem of maintaining coherence and continuity in their corporate strategy. "Defenders" emphasize induced strategic behavior based on a very clear concept of corporate strategy. Such firms face the long run danger of a lack of creativity and renewal in their corporate strategy. Finally, "reactors" have neither a clear corporate strategy to induce strategic behavior nor the entrepreneurial capabilities related to autonomous strategic behavior. They find themselves in a dangerously unstable situation.

The model of the strategic process presented here seems also relevant for the emerging theory of organizational learning. The concept of strategy of a corporation and the corresponding structural arrangements impound the learning of the firm over time. The concept of strategy provides a more or less explicit, and more or less shared, frame of reference or "paradigm" (Duncan & Weiss, 1979; Jelinek, 1979) concerning the bases of the firm's past success. Not unlike the sociological notion of a paradigm (Kuhn, 1970; Masterman, 1970), it provides guidance for further strategic action in line with it. At the same time, it crystallizes the attitudinal and social factors that were selected together with the cognitive, substantive factors underlying the past success. As such, it also is likely to prescribe, often implicitly and tacitly, attitudes and managerial styles and an ideology deemed necessary for the prolongation of the firm's success. Autonomous strategic behavior, identified here as the major source of strategic renewal, thus is likely to encounter nonrational obstacles in its efforts to convince top management that changes in corporate strategy are necessary.

Further research may find it useful to explore these less obvious, potentially entropic (Rifkin, 1980) consequences of a concept of corporate strategy for organizational learning. Such research also could shed more light on the factors—external and/or internal to the firm—that influence the balance between induced and autonomous strategic behavior at any given moment in time, and the evolution of this balance over time. In the same line of thought, further research also could investigate the role of acquisition and divestment as compensatory mechanisms—positive and negative, respectively —for the firm's adaptation efforts through autonomous strategic behavior.

Finally, the present paper illustrates an important characteristic of field research. The conceptual frameworks induced from such research seldom exhaust the full content and meaning of the data. Such research allows progress through an iterative process: new conceptual lenses can be brought to bear on old data to generate new insights. Through this process, the old insights can be refined and/or some of their additional implications revealed.

References

Aharoni, Y. *The foreign investment decision process.* Boston, Mass.: Graduate School of Business Administration, Harvard University, 1966.

Aldrich, H. E. *Organizations and environments.* Englewood Cliffs, N. J.: Prentice Hall, 1979.

Allison, G. T. *Essence of decision.* Boston, Mass.: Little Brown, 1971.

Ansoff, H. T. *Corporate strategy.* New York: McGraw-Hill, 1965.

Biggadike, E. R. *Corporate diversification: Entry, strategy, and performance.* Cambridge, Mass.: Harvard University Press, 1979.

Bower, J. L. *Managing the resource allocation process.* Boston, Mass.: Graduate School of Business Administration, Harvard University, 1970.

Bower, J. L. Planning and Control: Bottom-up or top-down. *Journal of General Management,* 1974, 1, 20-31.

Bower, J. L., & Doz, I. Strategy formulation: A social and political view. In D. E. Schendel & C. W. Hofer (Eds.), *Strategic management.* Boston, Mass.: Little Brown, 1979, 152-166.

Burgelman, R. A. *Managing innovating systems: A study of the process of internal corporate venturing.* Unpublished doctoral dissertation, Columbia University, 1980.

Burgelman, R. A. A process model of internal corporate venturing in the diversified major firm. Research paper #636, Graduate School of Business, Stanford University, 1982.

Carter, E. E. The behavioral theory of the firm and top level corporation decisions. *Administrative Science Quarterly,* 1971, 17, 413-428.

Chandler, A. D. *Strategy and structure.* Cambridge, Mass.: M.I.T. Press, 1962.

Child, J. Organization structure, environment, and performance —The role of strategic choice. *Sociology,* 1972, 6, 1-22.

Cohen, M. D., March, J. G., & Olsen, J. P. A garbage can model of organizational choice. *Administrative Science Quarterly,* 1972, 17, 1-25.

Cyert, R. M., & March, J. G. *A behavioral theory of the firm.* Englewood Cliffs, N. J.: Prentice Hall, 1963.

Duncan, R., & Weiss, A. Organizational learning: Implications for organizational design. In B. Shaw (Ed.), *Research in organizational behavior* (Vol. 1). Greenwich, Conn.: JAI Press, 1979, 75-124.

Fast, N. D. *The rise and fall of corporate new venture divisions.* Ann Arbor, Mich.: U.M.I. Research Press, 1979.

Galbraith, J. R., & Nathanson, D. A. The role of organizational structure and process in strategy implementation. In D. E. Schendel & C. W. Hofer (Eds.), *Strategic management.* Boston, Mass.: Little Brown, 1979, 249-284.

Greiner, L. E. Evolution and revolution as organizations grow. *Harvard Business Review,* 1972, 50 (4), 37-46.

Hall, D. J., & Saias, M. A. Strategy follows structure. *Strategic Management Journal,* 1980, 1, 149-163.

Hamermesh, R. G. Responding to divisional profit crises. *Harvard Business Review,* 1977, 55 (2), 124-130.

Hofer, C. W. Research on strategic planning: A survey of past studies and suggestions for future efforts. *Journal of Business and Economics,* 1976, 28 (3), 261-286.

Jelinek, M. *Institutionalizing innovation.* New York: Praeger, 1979.

Kissinger, H. A. *White house years.* Boston, Mass.: Little Brown, 1979.

Kuhn, T. *The structure of scientific revolutions.* Chicago: Ill.: University of Chicago Press, 1970.

Lindblom, C. E. The science of "muddling through." *Public Administration Review,* 1959, 19, 79-88.

March, J. G., & Simon, H. A. *Organizations.* New York: Wiley, 1958.

Masterman, M. The nature of a paradigm. In I. Lakatos & A. Musgrave (Eds.), *Criticism and the growth of knowledge.* Cambridge University Press, 1970, 59-89.

Miles, R. E., & Snow, C. C. *Organizational strategy, structure, and process.* New York: McGraw-Hill, 1978.

Mintzberg, H. Strategy-making in three modes. *California Management Review,* 1973, 16, 44-53.

Mintzberg, H. Patterns of strategy formation. *Management Science,* 1978, 24, 934-948.

Penrose, E. *The theory of the growth of the firm.* Oxford, England: Blackwell, 1968.

Rifkin, J. *Entropy.* New York: The Viking Press, 1980.

Roberts, E. New ventures for corporate growth. *Harvard Business Review,* 1980, 58 (4), 134-142.

Selznick, P. *Leadership in administration.* New York: Harper & Row, 1957.

Weick, K. *The social psychology of organizing.* Reading, Mass.: Addison-Wesley, 1979.

White, R. E., & Hamermesh, R. G. Toward a model of business unit performance: An integrative approach. *Academy of Management Review,* 1981, 6, 213-223.

Robert A. Burgelman is Assistant Professor of Management in the Graduate School of Business, Stanford University.

Part VIII
National Culture and the Pursuit of Corporate Entrepreneurship

[29]

CORPORATE ENTREPRENEURS AND PRIVATIZED FIRMS IN RUSSIA, UKRAINE, AND BELARUS

IGOR FILATOTCHEV

MIKE WRIGHT

TREVOR BUCK

VLADIMIR ZHUKOV

University of Nottingham Business School

EXECUTIVE SUMMARY

This paper provides a preliminary examination of the development of corporate entrepreneurship in privatized firms in Russia, Belarus, and Ukraine, three countries with a common background as part of the Soviet Union, but with different incentives and constraints on entrepreneurship since the beginning of transition. Using large-scale surveys of newly privatized companies, the paper shows that there are differences in the nature and extent of entrepreneurship in established businesses in the three countries. The paper utilizes representative samples of general directors in 105 privatized Russian enterprises, 100 privatized Ukranian enterprises, and 68 privatized enterprises in Belarus.

Evidence is presented that suggests that Russian privatized firms have lower insider stakes, greater outside ownership, less employee voice, and greater managerial power within the firm than is the case in Belarus and Ukraine. The active monitoring of managers by outsiders may be an important aspect of the transformation of Russian firms to efficient, commercially viable entities. In Ukraine and Belarus a lack of outside involvement in corporate governance may lead to managerial opportunism and low incentives to attract outside strategic investors, including foreign partners. Russia appears to be building a stronger platform for the future development and effectiveness of entrepreneurship than is the case in Ukraine and Belarus. The findings provide evidence of the importance of direct involvement and the

Address correspondence to Igor Filatotchev, University of Nottingham, School of Management and Finance, Nottingham, U.K.; Phone: 44-1159 515 265; Fax: 44-1159 515 252; E-mail: Igor.Filatotchev@Nottingham.ac.uk

The authors wish to thank the Department for International Development for financial support. Comments from the editor and two anonymous reviewers are acknowledged with gratitude.

Journal of Business Venturing **14**, 475–492
0883-9026/99/$–see front matter
PII S0883-9026(98)00028-7

476   I. FILATOTCHEV ET AL.

development of relationships to counteract the shortcomings of the legal infrastructure and financial reporting mechanisms.

In general, the findings of the study for Russia show that in the current hostile and rapidly changing environment, entrepreneurial priorities and actions so far have primarily focused on controlling cash flow, seeking new markets, and redefining businesses through retrenchment and restructuring. Although it is, as yet, too early to examine the longer term effects of the changes in entrepreneurial conditions, the paper presents the first large-scale comparative evidence of the indications of a divergence in entrepreneurial development between the three countries. There was a greater incidence of turnover among the senior management team in Russia. Managers in Ukraine and Belarus had more diverse strategic objectives in contrast to those in Russia where managers have behaved in a more realistic fashion by focusing on retrenchment.

For academics, the study's findings suggest further research is needed to examine the longer term nature and effects of corporate entrepreneurship, compare entrepreneurship in new start-ups in the three countries, and compare with corporate entrepreneurship elsewhere in emerging markets and the barriers to the development of corporate entrepreneurship. For practitioners and policy makers, the study highlights the need to develop and enforce an appropriate regulatory framework which strengthens the rules of the game under which corporate entrepreneurship operates.   © *1999 Elsevier Science Inc.*

INTRODUCTION

The literature on entrepreneurship has traditionally concentrated on new business start-ups, but more recently there has been growing attention to entrepreneurship in established businesses (Cooper and Dunkelberg 1986; Wright et al. 1992; Guth and Ginsberg 1990; Zahra 1995). In this paper we provide the first comparative large-scale analysis of such corporate entrepreneurship in privatized firms in the transition economies of Russia, Ukraine, and Belarus. In general, the findings of the study show that corporate entrepreneurship has primarily focused on controlling cash flow, seeking new markets, and redefining businesses through retrenchment and restructuring.

It is generally agreed that former centrally planned economies (CPEs) involved no significant legal role for individual entrepreneurs, and as a result CPEs ultimately suffered from low customer satisfaction and levels of innovation. Economic reforms were expected to create a solid foundation for the liberation of entrepreneurship. In the former USSR in particular, however, there was a long history of low levels of private business start-ups (Kantorovich 1998). Since 1991 new business start-ups have been mainly restricted to the service sector, such as trade, financial services, and consultancy. The former commanding heights of the former USSR in the manufacturing sector have seen few new private firms (EBRD 1997). Rather, the principal reforms of the manufacturing sector in the former USSR have comprised the gradual withdrawal of the State from enterprise decisions, price liberalization, and a mass privatization program that has generally put the ownership of enterprises into the hands of enterprise incumbents: managers and employees. Control has tended to follow ownership, and privatized manufacturing firms have been described as manager-controlled employee buy-outs (Earle and Estrin 1996).

Former republics of the USSR provide fertile ground for the study of entrepreneurial development under different regimes of economic reform, and in particular different patterns of enterprise ownership and control. To address these issues, this paper presents preliminary evidence from those former republics which were the main industrial regions of the USSR, now independent nations: Russia, Ukraine, and Belarus. From their common starting point as members of the Soviet Union with similar privatization methods in which incumbents obtained significant equity stakes, each country has experienced contrasting constraints on the development of entrepreneurial actions.

The purpose of this paper is to provide an exploratory examination of the nature and extent of corporate entrepreneurship in the former USSR, concentrating on outside influences from owners and lenders on the entrepreneurial decisions of incumbent managers. This analysis abstracts from the degree of product market competition facing firms, but this factor is addressed in the final section. Evidence is provided on the important ownership and control positions held by directors and the generally low involvement of outsiders; these features are particularly marked in Ukraine and Belarus. The paper examines the effects of the ownership changes following privatization on short- and long-term entrepreneurial strategies, but it is too early to examine the longer term effects of the changes in entrepreneurial conditions.

The paper has three parts. First, it outlines the main problems facing entrepreneurship in Russia, Ukraine, and Belarus, and in particular the influences of incentives and constraints on the actions of managers of newly privatized companies. This includes an analysis of the privatization programs in the manufacturing industries of the three countries. Second, the paper goes on to present evidence from a large-scale questionnaire survey of general directors of enterprises in the three countries which involves 105 privatized companies in Russia, 100 in Ukraine, and 68 in Belarus. Third, implications for academics and practitioners are outlined.

CORPORATE ENTREPRENEURSHIP IN THE FORMER SOVIET UNION

Entrepreneurship in the former Soviet Union (USSR) may develop either through the creation of new firms (start-ups, greenfield investment, etc.) or through the entrepreneurial transformation of privatized enterprises, that is, corporate entrepreneurship (Ners 1995). The literature on corporate entrepreneurship within existing corporations recognizes that it has two broad dimensions: innovations aimed at business creation and venturing and innovations concerned with strategic renewal (Block and MacMillan 1993; Guth and Ginsberg 1990; Stopford and Baden-Fuller 1994; Zahra 1993, 1996).

Major surveys by international agencies find that the creation of de novo businesses in the former USSR continues to lag behind the rate of new business creation in other former Communist countries in Central Europe, with the number of officially registered smaller businesses in Russia remaining at only around 1 million in 1997 (EBRD 1997). In contrast, the privatization of State-owned enterprises has been an important tool of economic reform in Russia, though to a much lesser extent in Ukraine and Belarus (Table 1). The form but not the scale of the Russian mass privatization model, involving the distribution of vouchers to citizens and eventual insider control (Boycko et al. 1993), was however, imitated in Belarus and Ukraine (Filatotchev et al. 1996).

A key issue concerns the extent to which managers in the former USSR, whether through starting a business or becoming owners as part of the privatization program, have the characteristics and expertise to engage in entrepreneurial actions. Entrepreneurship has been under-developed in these countries for a considerable period. Hisrich and Grachev (1993) in reviewing the historical development of entrepreneurship in the Russian Empire find that from the 16th to the 19th century, entrepreneurship was generally underdeveloped and entrepreneurs were considered as inferior individuals. During

TABLE 1 Privatization in Russia, Ukraine, and Belarus

	Russia	Ukraine	Belarus
Commencement of privatization program	1992	1994	1993
Coverage of program	All industry*	Selected, listed firms only	Selected, listed firms only
Target number of firms covered	20,000	8,000	8,500
Actual number of firms privatized by 1997	20,000	3,000	212**
Private companies' share of industrial output 1997	89%	40%	12%
Private companies' share of industrial employment 1997	81%	21%	8%

* Excluding certain "strategic" firms in the natural resource and defense-related sectors;
** Plus other so-called "privatized" firms where the State has retained a majority shareholding. Sources: European Bank for Reconstruction and Development, Transition Report 1997, London, EBRD. Belarussky Rinok, March 1997: 7, Minsk.

the period of central planning in the former USSR, most strategic decisions were made at the center with enterprises carrying out routine, planned operations. In effect, entrepreneurship was concentrated in the Ministries which tried to run the country as a single firm (USSR Inc.).

The nature of entrepreneurship, however, reflects the rules of the game (Baumol 1996) and in the former USSR it was often unproductive or even destructive. In practice, many designers and administrators of the plan at all levels diverted economic rents to their own individual benefit (Richman 1965). At the level of the individual enterprise, the actual outcome was described as "reverse entrepreneurship" (Filatotchev et al. 1992) whereby valuable inputs (especially raw materials) were extensively converted into finished goods of low value. Under state control, enterprises operated with soft budget constraints, where state agencies acted as a lender of last resort to enterprises over-demanding resources to reach ratcheted targets set by Ministries. Although under the central planning system there were few rewards for innovation nor penalties for failure, it was nevertheless possible to identify entrepreneurs outside the ministries (Hisrich and Grachev 1993). These individuals either emerged as entrepreneurs through the development of the shadow economy or were employed by factories as 'tolkachi' to identify and obtain scarce material inputs (Filatotchev et al. 1992).

The beginning of economic reforms in the former USSR dramatically changed the conditions in which companies produce and sell their outputs. Managers have to learn to run their companies in a situation where the state is gradually withdrawing from the system of control and funding of enterprises and free-market mechanisms are slowly evolving in all areas of a company's operations. To survive in this rapidly changing environment, there is a need for more entrepreneurial managers (Ernst et al. 1996).

Doubts have been raised about whether the psyche of managers in Russia compared to those in the West predisposes them to act entrepreneurially and make the changes necessary for survival in a market economy (Holt et al. 1994). At the start of the reform process there was a general absence of sufficiently skilled managers in existing businesses trained to compete in a market-based economy (Puffer 1994). Studies of the entrepreneurial characteristics of Russian entrepreneurs who have started a business have found that although they located control internally, they possessed significantly lower internal locus of control scores than entrepreneurs elsewhere (Kaufman et al. 1995) and perceive serious constraints on the starting of a viable business in the manufacturing sector in particular (McCarthy et al. 1993). Within existing enterprises, the so-called Red Directors of the former Soviet system tended to be all-powerful and experienced in dealing with routine functional problems, but were often inflexible regarding the adjustments required in a market economy. Although managers were generally technically excellent or had some relevant training, they were often inexperienced in such functions as marketing, finance, strategic planning, etc. (Linz 1997; Filatotchev et al. 1996b). As managers were chosen by the mainly negative selection of the former regime, they are less likely to display entrepreneurial drive. Moreover, Red Directors may have been so imbued with the modus operandi of the former system that they were unable to effect entrepreneurial actions following privatization (Linz 1996). Krueger (1995), however, argues that the former Red Directors, even the nomenklatura, are more entrepreneurial and have more savvy than is generally believed. Hard budget constraints are a new concept for managers in the former command economies, and time is required to adapt to these changes (Linz and Krueger 1996).

A long-standing importance has been attached to equity ownership as an important aspect of entrepreneurship since ownership rights are crucial to the generation of entrepreneurial profit through the coordination of resources in an uncertain environment (Hawley 1900; Gartner and Shane 1995). The introduction of equity ownership for managers following the privatization of enterprises in the former USSR may thus be expected to provide a stimulus to corporate entrepreneurship. It is expected that managers' acting as corporate entrepreneurs will seek to further concentrate ownership in their hands in all three countries in order to be in a more dominant position to effect longer term restructuring. However, the above problems may affect the willingness or ability of incumbent managers in existing business to undertake entrepreneurial actions, and attention turns to improving their quality using certain mechanisms involving outsiders as shareholders, outside lenders and monitors, and the role of product market competition.

The general reluctance of founders of entrepreneurial businesses to allow influence and involvement by outsiders is well-known (Ang 1991). In established businesses substantial managerial equity stakes may also increase the risk of entrenchment (Morck et al. 1988), with the added problem in the former USSR that managers may be able to prevent sales of their shares to outsiders (Filatotchev et al. 1996). The corollary is that important wealth creation may derive from new entrepreneurial ventures where close relationships are established between entrepreneurs and outside financiers to try and enhance a company's value through counseling and oversight (Bhide 1994). Early evidence suggested that an openness to outside equity finance and the contribution that outsiders can bring to new firms is positively associated with growth (Hutchinson 1975). A more recent literature and debate have developed concerning the financial and monitoring contributions of venture capitalists in entrepreneurial ventures (for example, Wright and Robbie (1998) for a review). This literature has shown that venture capitalists may adopt different approaches to monitoring investees according to circumstances (for example, Sapienza et al. 1996), but there is mixed evidence about investees' views concerning the contribution made by outsiders (Rosenstein et al. 1993). In the context of established businesses, a number of authors have emphasized the need to examine the link between governance and ownership systems and entrepreneurial activity (for example, Bull 1989; Wright et al. 1992; Zahra 1993, 1995, 1996). In particular, Zahra (1995) explicitly examines corporate entrepreneurship activities in management leveraged buy-outs. He points to the importance of the combination of managerial equity

480   I. FILATOTCHEV ET AL.

incentives and governance by outsiders in increasing attention to value-enhancing activities. These activities relate on the one hand to the reduction of opportunism, producing cost reductions, and on the other to an increase in managerial discretion leading to entrepreneurial actions.

There have been similar arguments concerning the potential benefits to be derived from outsiders' involvement in enterprises in the former USSR which would otherwise be dominated by insiders (for example, Frydman et al. 1993). Outside monitoring and control per se may be insufficient to promote entrepreneurial actions (that is, downsizing, modernization of production capacities, re-focusing, etc.) if they are not accompanied by changes in managerial attitudes and skills. A major criticism leveled at large-scale, rapid privatization is that although ownership changed, management largely did not, since the programs themselves were biased towards the acquisition of ownership by incumbents without the need for outside finance (Brada 1996). Outside shareholders may however, be more pre-disposed to achieve such changes by replacing existing inefficient managers with more able and better trained corporate entrepreneurs (Denis et al. 1997). To the extent that managers have greater equity stakes and outsiders have less influence, the degree of replacement of directors is expected to be significantly lower. In the light of Table 1, this suggests that the rate of replacement of managers will be lower in Belarus and Ukraine than it is Russia.

Restricted access to finance may introduce a further constraint on corporate entrepreneurial actions (see Zahra 1996, for a review of the issues). Privatized state-owned firms in the former USSR are likely to have high-investment finance needs and to experience major financial difficulties because of environmental uncertainties, yet at the time of privatization are likely to have access to insignificant amounts of extra capital (Frydman et al. 1993). The underdeveloped financial sector also means that access to equity finance is very limited. Creditors (mainly banks) have an opportunity to impose direct monitoring on managers using a wide variety of channels, such as board representation, performance-related provision of loans, indirect controls, etc. (see, for example, Jensen 1993; Kaplan 1997). However, the existence of under-capitalized banks and a general absence of monitoring skills by bank executives lead to an expectation that such monitoring will be thin.

The nature of corporate entrepreneurship may be influenced by the nature of ownership and control and the nature of the product market environments in which firms are operating (Zahra 1993). Zahra (1996) finds that in large U.S. companies, corporate entrepreneurship is positively associated with long-term institutional share ownership. In contrast, outside investors without this commitment may be associated with reduced corporate entrepreneurship where they use short-term financial rather than longer-term strategic controls. Managers in Russia, Ukraine, and Belarus may be hostile towards outside investors if they are perceived to be only concerned with short-term financial results rather than with longer term entrepreneurial actions involving strategic development and modernization. Earlier survey evidence from Russia suggests that managers of privatized enterprises perceive banks, investment funds, and other financial institutions to be primarily short-term portfolio speculators (Wright et al. 1998). It is, therefore, expected that incumbent managers will be reluctant to cede majority control and significant influence to outsiders.

Zahra (1993) shows that in hostile product market environments involving a reduction in demand and/or increased competition, entrepreneurial decisions by insiders are positively associated with retrenchment and a redefinition of the business through restructuring and a search for innovative ways to manage the hostility. In contrast, incumbent managers are more likely to investigate new business creation in dynamic and growing environments. Managers in the three countries examined here may recognize that products are not competitive on world markets and require considerable investment to achieve such a position. However, the generally hostile market conditions in the three countries lead to an expectation that retrenchment will be an important priority for corporate entrepreneurs. Downsizing and getting rid of less productive divisions and surplus labor may be required to address the problems caused by the high level of 'labor hoarding' which companies have inherited from their central planning past (see for example, Kornai 1980). Sharp falls in demand may also suggest that managers will give priority to seeking new markets.

Impediments to entrepreneurial actions may be exacerbated by the nature of the privatization program. First, the use of voucher privatization techniques enable employees generally to obtain a significant equity stake in privatized enterprises. As such, their already entrenched rights may be strengthened further, with the consequence that even where directors wish to undertake entrepreneurial actions they are frustrated from doing so. Second, differences in the political priority given to privatization programs may also have an impact on corporate entrepreneurship. Although all three countries used mass privatization schemes, privatization programs in Ukraine and Belarus were promoted by their national governments with far less vigor than in Russia. Table 1 shows that the impact of privatization has been greatest in Russia and least in Belarus, with Ukraine in an intermediate position. Indeed in Belarus, the privatization process has been halted since 1996, and in 1997 some privatized firms were re-nationalized as the State reintroduced many of the institutions of central planning. In Ukraine, the government has exhibited an intermediate, stop-start commitment to privatization. Moreover, it seems likely that in Ukraine and Belarus, companies to be privatized were carefully selected by incumbent managers with strong political contacts. Rather than engaging in entrepreneurial actions to improve efficiency, these managers may entrench themselves and resist reform by relying on their contacts in government and a continuing weak market system. This continuation of slack rules of the game (Baumol 1996) may mean that such managers initiate destructive entrepreneurship involving the personal appropriation of the firm's resources (Bim 1996).

DATA

For each of the three countries, a sample of medium- and large-sized industrial firms was sought, covering the main industrial regions, all types of privatized firms and different industrial sectors, concentrating on firms that had been privatized for more than 1 year. In Russia, 105 useable responses were collected, exactly 100 in Ukraine, and 68 in Belarus. Given the importance of synchronicity (Frydman et al. 1997), simultaneous surveys were made in each of the three countries from January to July 1997.

The same questionnaire was applied to each country after being piloted in Moscow and Minsk. The questionnaire design included a combination of two types of questions. The first type related to measurable company characteristics for the 1995–1997 period (employment, market structure, etc.) from companies' unpublished financial reports. The second type related to respondents' perceptions of current entrepreneurial strategies and attitudes with all responses being scaled on a 7-point Likert scale. This approach, and the targeting of General Directors as respondents at the center of strategic developments in their enterprises, was adopted to minimize the problems of respondent recall.

The questions proved to be easily understood by Russian managers, who generally gave full, rational responses. In Belarus and Ukraine, however, managers seemed rather unfamiliar with Western terminology, and it was decided here to invest more resources in the form of face-to-face interviews, using the same questionnaire (adjusted for national currencies, etc.) that was applied through a postal survey in Russia. In each of the three countries, a random 5% of returns were checked by at least two of the authors on a personal visit.

Assessing the representativeness of samples of privatized enterprises in the former USSR is problematical where data relating to the population is often unavailable. However, on the available criteria where it is possible to make comparisons, the samples appear to be reasonably representative. The ownership distribution of the Russian firms in our sample (see below) was compared with those reported in similar surveys of privatized conducted in Russia at approximately the same time (Blasi et al. 1997) and no significant differences were identified. Published statistics of the industry, size, and regional distributions of privatized enterprises in Russia are not available. Comparisons between the Russian sample in this paper and these characteristics of all Russian enterprises (that is, privatized, state-owned, and private) generally show a close match. As regards the distribution of the employment size of Russian firms surveyed there is, not surprisingly, a greater proportion of larger firms in the sample than is the case in the Russian economy as a whole; this is to be expected given the focus here on those enterprises coming within the scope of the main manufacturing enterprise privatization programs as opposed to the tender privatization program, which was mainly aimed at shops and smaller service enterprises, and new start-ups (see Appendix tables). The regional distribution of the sample was generally close to that for Russia as a whole. For Belarus, the representativeness of the sample is indicated by the fact that it comprises 32% of all industrial privatized firms in that country.

RESULTS

The results of these simultaneous surveys are now presented in relation to the different constraints and pressure on incumbent managers in the three countries and their patterns of entrepreneurial responses.

Ownership

The distribution of equity stakes in the three countries is given by Table 2, which also shows the results of tests on the equality of mean ownership distributions across the three countries. These tests indicate the existence of statistically significant differences between the three samples; the Russian sample, as expected, generally being significantly different from the sample for the other two countries. Clearly some market-based ownership restructuring is taking place in a situation where, although managers have significant stockholdings, other employees hold the majority of the equity. Ukraine and Belarus exhibit significantly higher levels of ownership by incumbents than in Russia. Ownership by non-managerial employees in Ukraine and Belarus is also relatively higher (at about 57.7% and 56.9%, respectively, compared with only 38.7% in Russia).

PRIVATIZATION IN RUSSIA, UKRAINE, AND BELARUS **483**

TABLE 2 Distribution of Voting Shares Among Shareholders (percentage of total)

	Russia		Ukraine		Balarus		Anova[i]	
Shareholders	1997	change, 1995–1997	1997	change, 1995–1997	1997	change, 1995–1997	1997	change, 1995–1997
Individual directors in total	15.9%	4.8%	12.2%	0.9%	11.9%	2%	1.2	2.4***
Individual workers in total	387	−5.9	577	−6.2	56.9	2	10.7*	5.7*
Insiders in total	54.6	−1	69.9	−5.3	68.8	4	5.1*	4.2**
Trading partners	4.1	0.5	0.1	0.1	1.1	0.4	3.0***	0.3
Investment funds	3.6	0.8	4.6	1.6	2	1.6	0.6	0.3
Banks	1.7	0.3	0	0	0.6	0.2	2.0	0.2
External private individuals	12.9	1.4	11.7	4.5	10.9	3	0.2	1.8
Holding companies	1.7	0.1	1.4	0	1.5	0	0.03	0.02
Foreign investors	0.6	0.3	1.6	0.5	1.9	1.9	0.9	1.8
Other organizations	15.1	0.4	5.1	1.4	1.7	0.4	7.0*	0.2
Outsiders in total	397	3.8	24.5	8.1	19.7	7.5	9.7*	1.9
The State	5.7	−2.7	5.6	−2.8	11.5	−11.5	1.7	8.8*

Russian sample reduced from 105 to 91 companies as 14 could not distinguish manager and other employee ownership. In Belarus and Ukraine there were 39 and 35 useable responses respectively. Significance Levels: * = p < 0.01; ** = p < 0.05; *** = p < 0.1; [i] Figures are F-ratios. Because of space constraints and for clarity of presentation, significance tests using Pearson chi-squared and Kruskal-Wallis ANOVA across the three countries and pair-wise tests for differences between countries are omitted. Data are available from the authors on request. The Pearson chi-squared and the Kruskal-Wallis tests produced the same significant differences as for the ANOVA. The pair-wise tests involving Russia against Ukraine and Belarus combined constantly show that the Russian mean score for each long run priority variable is significantly different from that for Ukraine/Belarus.

Since 1995 the average equity stake held by management has increased in each of the three countries. but most notably in Russia. In Russia and Ukraine this process of consolidating managerial share ownership has been accompanied by a gradual erosion of employees' stakes. Only in Belarus has employees' share ownership actually increased, by 2% on average. Our survey shows that a substantial proportion of managers in Russia (and less so in Belarus and Ukraine) are trying to promote further changes in the insiders' ownership structure of their companies. In 29.8% of cases, Russian managers have acquired shares from employees compared to 12.2% in Ukraine and 10.4% in Belarus. In almost a third of cases Russian managers have further intentions to purchase shares from employees (36.4% in Ukraine and 31.8% in Belarus).

Russian companies on average display significantly greater involvement by outsiders in their ownership structures than is the case in Ukraine and Belarus. Among outside investors, external private individual holdings account for the highest outside ownership stake in Russia and Ukraine, with the remaining equity being owned by a wide group of interests. In Belarus, the State is the largest outside shareholder. In all three countries, private institutional investors (banks, investment funds, etc.) are still in a minority as shareholders, although there is evidence of a gradual increase in their stakes in 1995–1997.

Outsider Influence on Corporate Entrepreneurship

The potential controlling role of different stakeholders in the decision-making process was identified by looking at the composition of companies' Boards. The survey results suggest a link between insiders' stock and internal voice, although there are striking differences between Russia and the other two countries. Russian managers hold not only significantly more stock on average than their Ukranian and Belarussian counterparts, they also exercise more voice as proxied by Board representation (89 Russian companies reported that managers are represented on the Board in 1997, compared with 59 and 38 in Ukraine and Belarus, respectively) (Table 3). On the other hand, during 1995–1997 there was a slight fall in the number of companies in Russia which had employees sitting on the Board, while in Ukraine and Belarus these numbers increased substantially. Combined with the dynamics of insider ownership patterns this evidence suggests that, as expected, Russian managers are more effectively taking control in the vast majority of companies than their Ukranian and Belarussian counterparts. This may be expected to impact on corporate entrepreneurship.

There are clear signs of the increasing involvement of outside equityholders in companies' Boards, in Russia in particular: 35 companies reported that they have external private individuals represented on the Board in 1997, and 24 companies had other industrial organizations among their Board members (Table 3). Such organizations as banks and investment funds are gradually consolidating their voice in newly privatized companies in Russia and Ukraine and to a much lesser extent in Belarus: 13 Russian companies mentioned investment funds among their Board members (10 cases in Ukraine and only 3 in Belarus), and 6 companies had bank representation (6 in Ukraine and 2 in Belarus). On the other hand, in Belarus, 32 companies had State representatives on the Board at the beginning of 1997, a substantial increase compared to 23 cases in 1995. This indicates that the active role of outsiders in Russia is slowly evolving towards that found in enterprises in the West, while in Belarus in particular, privatization has resulted in the creation of organizations where the State is directly involved in control. This implies again that corporate entrepreneurship should be relatively more active in Russia than in the other two countries.

There is evidence of senior managerial changes in all three countries (Table 4). In the period between 1995 and 1997, the general Director had been replaced in more than a third of cases (a quarter of cases in Ukraine and Belarus). In Russia and Belarus, in almost half of cases other members of the Directorate had been replaced too, with significantly less being replaced in Ukraine (Pearson chi-square = 3.35, p < 0.1). These differential response rates may again reflect relative outsider pressures on boards in the three countries.

However, there is a substantially lower average number of seats held by outside stakeholders on companies' Boards compared to insiders in all three countries, suggesting that their power is currently rather limited. Reflecting the deep mistrust of outsiders noted earlier, there remains a widespread reluctance to cede majority control (Table 5). Only one-third of senior directors in Belarus would agree to give majority control to outside strategic partners, even if they were to provide the capital necessary for restructuring the company, technological expertise and a marketing network. Managers in Russia and Ukraine are somewhat less entrenched than their Belarussian colleagues: almost half of all respondents would agree to swap their controlling stake for strategic investments.

Moreover, there is a direct link between the extent of insider control and managerial hostility to an outside take-over. The majority of directors in the three countries reported that they would seek to prevent an unexpected accumulation of shares especially by outside domestic and foreign investors, with there being no significant difference in this respect between the three countries. Obviously, their strategy is to keep and re-enforce insider voice in the governance mechanism, blocking the acquisition of controlling stakes by outsiders and reducing their ability to intervene.

TABLE 3 Shareholder Board Representation, 1995–1997 (total number of companies reporting a particular shareholder on the board)

Stakeholders	Russia			Ukraine			Belarus		
	1995	1997	change, 1995–1997	1995	1997	change, 1995–1997	1995	1997	change, 1995–1997
Banks	6 (1.2)[1]	6 (1.5)[1]	0 (0.3)	4 (1)[2]	6 (2.2)[2]	2 (1.2)	0 (0)[3]	2 (1.5)[3]	2 (1.5)
Investment funds	10 (1.9)	13 (2.5)	3 (0.6)	5 (2.4)	10 (2.1)	5 (−0.3)	1 (1)	3 (1.3)***	2 (0.3)
External private individuals	24 (1.8)	35 (2)	11 (0.2)	4 (3.2)	10 (1.6)	6 (−1.6)	4 (1.5)	11 (2.5)	7 (1)
Industrial organizations	20 (2.1)	24 (2.3)	4 (2.2)	1 (1)	3 (2)	2 (1)	4 (3)	9 (2.2)	5 (−1.2)
Foreign companies	1 (1.1)	2 (1)	1 (0)	2 (2)	1 (3)	−1 (1)	0 (0)	0 (0)	0 (0)
Managers	84 (3.4)*	89 (3.3)*	5 (−0.1)	40 (5.7)	59 (4.9)	19 (−0.8)	27 (6.1*)	38 (5.3)*	11 (−0.8)
Employees	57 (3.0)	56 (2.7)	−1 (−0.3)	21 (2.9)	32 (2.7)	11 (−0.2)	28 (3.3)	37 (3.0)	9 (−0.3)
The State	27 (1.4)	18 (1.3)	−9 (−0.1)	10 (1.9)	10 (1.8)	0 (−0.1)	23 (1.6)	32 (1.5)	9 (−0.1)

Average number of seats held by each particular shareholder is in brackets. Significance levels: * = $p < 0.01$; ** = $p < 0.05$; *** = $p < 0.1$; [1] Asterisks in columns relate to t-tests on probability of equality in Russian and Ukrainian population means; [2] Asterisks in columns relate to t-tests on probability of equality in Ukrainian and Belarusian population means; [3] Asterisks in columns relate to t-tests on probability of equality in Russian and Belarusian population means.

TABLE 4 Changes to the Directorate Since Privatization (percentage of companies responding 'yes')

	Russia	Ukraine	Belarus	Pearson chi-square
New General Director	35.2[1]	25[2]	27.9[3]	2.66
Replacement of other member of directorate	50***	37.5	47	3.35

Significance level: *** = p < 0.1; [1] Asterisks in columns relate to *t*-tests on probability of equality in Russian and Ukrainian population means; [2] Asterisks in columns relate to *t*-tests on probability of equality in Ukrainian and Belarusian population means; [3] Asterisks in columns relate to *t*-tests on probability of equality in Russian and Belarusian population means.

The survey results support expectations that the usual Western private financial lending channels have been largely inoperative, especially in Belarus: such sources of funding as issue of bonds and equity, selling/leasing of buildings and equipment hardly scored above 3 on average. Credits from domestic banks have been mentioned as the second most important source of funding in Russia and Belarus (average scores 4.5 and 4.3 respectively), and the third in Ukraine (average score 4.9). This may be a sign that privatized companies are gradually shifting to borrowings that are more consistent with market competition in financial provision or soft credits directed by the State.

When asked about banks' involvement, more than 90% of managers in the three countries scored as low influence all bank-related factors suggested in the questionnaire, such as banks appointing Directors, restricting the operational/strategic decisions of managers, and restricting directors remuneration. Among possible channels of banks' influence, only telephone contacts scored significantly on a 7-point scale where 7 = high importance (average score 4.4 in Russia, 4.2 in Belarus, and 3.4 in Ukraine). The second most important channel of control in Russia and Belarus was sending accounts to the bank on a regular basis (average scores 3.6 and 3.7, respectively). Such standard Western channels of bank monitoring and control as representation on a supervisory board (for example, Germany) and monitoring of debt covenants (for example, as in the U.K.) had very minor importance in all three countries. Our survey shows that there is not only a substantial laxity in banks' monitoring and control of industrial companies, but the banks also do not usually impose any serious penalties upon managers failing to meet payments of interest and capital.

Entrepreneurial Strategies

In the light of these influences on the penalties and reward facing corporate entrepreneurs, our survey results provide preliminary evidence on their different responses in privatized enterprises in three countries of the former USSR.

The overwhelming need for entrepreneurial action was revealed by survey questions concerning product quality. There is widespread recognition that products are not competitive on world markets and that considerable investment is required to achieve this position. Fewer than 25% of managers in all three countries consider their main products to be competitive on world markets in terms of price, build quality, design and packaging, and after-sales servicing, with design and after-sales servicing being the worst factors of all. In all three countries, managers' assessments of the most important actions required to achieve world standards were: investment in machinery and equipment (average score above 6 on a 7-point Likert scale where 7 = high importance),

TABLE 5   Managers' Attitudes to a Hostile Take-Over by Other Investors

	Russia	Ukraine	Belarus	Pearson chi-square
Employees	55.8[1]	59.7***[2]	43.9[3]	3.64
Outside domestic investors	68.9	60.9	68.8	1.31
Outside foreign investors	70.6	58.8	70.3	2.73

Percentages of companies answering 'yes' to the question: Will Directors try to prevent an unexpected accumulation of shares by the following investors?

Significance Level: *** = $p < 0.1$; [1] Asterisks in columns relate to t-tests on probability of equality in Russian and Ukrainian population means; [2] Asterisks in columns relate to t-tests on probability of equality in Ukrainian and Belarusian population means; [3] Asterisks in columns relate to t-tests on probability of equality in Russian and Belarusian population means.

followed by investment in marketing (average score above 5), and investment in research and development.

Some important national differences did emerge when enterprise directors were invited to score different entrepreneurial priorities on a 7-point second scale with 7 = 'high priority.' Table 6 shows that directors of privatized companies in all three countries surveyed placed a uniformly high and anticipated emphasis on short-run responses involving cash-flow monitoring and seeking domestic markets for existing products. Besides these ex ante priorities, however, other short-run responses were surveyed relating to the ex post retrenchment of employment levels and productive capacity. According to the surveys, Russian managers on average reduced gross employment levels by 23%, 1995–1997, compared with 19.5% in Ukraine and 14.3% in Belarus. Similarly, actual capacity reductions through the permanent closure of plant and workshops averaged 3.6% of output in Russia over the same period compared with only 2.1% in Belarus and Ukraine. These actual responses may reflect the relatively stronger outside pres-

TABLE 6   Mean Values of Directors' Enterpreneurial Properties (Responses on a 7-point Likert scale where 1 = not important and 7 = very important.[1] Rows ranked in terms of average Russian response)

	Russia (Mean score)	Ukraine (Mean score)	Belarus (Mean score)	ANOVA[2]
Short-term priorities				
Cash flow monitoring	6.1	5.9	5.9	0.6
Seeking new domestic markets, existing products	5.7	6.2	5.3	5.2*
Long-term priorities				
Development of new products for domestic market	5.2	6.0	5.9	4.0*
Seeking new outside investors	4.4	5.6	5.1	6.4*
Marketing and advertising	4.1	5.8	5.5	22.9*
Monitoring firm's return on investment	3.7	5.5	5.4	15.9*
Development of new products for export	3.0	5.6	5.4	32.7*
Seeking new export markets for existing products	2.7	5.6	5.6	52.4*

Significance Levels: * = $p < 0.1$; ** = $p < 0.05$; *** = $p < 0.01$;

[1] Cronbach's alpha for Russia = 0.79, Ukraine = 0.79, and Belarus 0.77; [2] Because of space constraints and for clarity of presentation, significance tests using Pearson chi-squared and Kruskal-Wallis ANOVA across the three countries and pair-wise tests for differences between countries are omitted. Data are available from the authors on request. The Pearson chi-squared and the Kruskal-Wallis tests produced the same significant differences as for the ANOVA. The pair-wise tests involving Russia against Ukraine and Belarus combined consistantly show that the Russian mean score for each long run priority variable is significantly different from that for Ukraine/Belarus.

sures faced by Russian managers. Uniform short-run entrepreneurial priorities should, however, also be interpreted in conjunction with long-run priorities.

Striking national variations were reported in relation to long-run managerial priorities, and this result was consistent with relatively weak corporate governance in Belarus and Ukraine (Table 6). Managers in both Ukraine and Belarus were prepared to disclose high priorities (average 5.6) for increased sales of existing products in export markets, despite the fact that more than 75% of all directors in the three countries had already admitted (see above) that their products in their current forms were uncompetitive on world markets, necessitating infeasibly high levels of investment. These responses suggest that directors in Belarus and Ukraine do not have a structurally focused approach to short-term and long-term stabilization and recovery strategies. This conclusion is reinforced by the comparisons of the long-run priorities listed in Table 6 between Russia and the scores for Belarus and Ukraine. The overall test for equality of mean scores identified significant differences between the three countries, and pair-wise comparisons between Russia and the combined Ukraine and Belarus scores consistently found there to be significant differences in long run priorities.

Russian managers in the middle of a short-run crisis have quite properly focussed on short-run entrepreneurial responses, and in Table 6 report significantly lower current priorities for all long-run factors. It is in this context that the high priorities also reported for short run strategies should be interpreted. Again, these differences in the apparent quality of entrepreneurial responses may be attributable to stronger external constraints on Russian managers. Weaker constraints in Belarus and Ukraine may have contributed to lower executive replacement rates, less retrenchment and a lack of appropriate entrepreneurial priorities compared with Russia.

DISCUSSION AND POLICY IMPLICATIONS

This study has provided preliminary comparative evidence concerning the development of entrepreneurship in privatized enterprises in three republics in the former USSR.

In terms of ownership structure and decision-making mechanisms, our survey evidence across the three countries emphasizes the important potential role of corporate entrepreneurs. However, the evidence indicates that although the three countries started from a common base, their subsequent reforms have not been homogeneous. Russian privatized firms have lower employee stakes, greater outside ownership, and greater managerial power within the firm (vis-a-vis employees) than is the case in Ukraine and Belarus. In Russia, corporate entrepreneurs are, therefore, subject to more outside influence as well as less internal influence from employees. The balance of power within enterprises in Ukraine and Belarus appears to lie very much with inside managers and employees, which may have negative implications for the exercising of corporate entrepreneurship where employees resist managers' attempts at restructuring. In this sense, Russia has arguably built a better platform for the liberation of latent entrepreneurial capacity. Managers of Russian firms are also relatively less hostile to outside investors, but in Belarus the State still represents a significant stakeholder influence. In Russia and Ukraine, firms have been actively using bank loans as a source of funding, but they are still not exposed to any effective scrutiny by the outside providers of finance.

Our preliminary survey results on post-privatization corporate entrepreneurship in the three countries show evidence of strategies aimed at securing enterprise survival in a rapidly changing and hostile market environment. The most obvious changes were in managerial tenure and directors' objectives. Russian enterprises experienced the highest replacement rate of directors, which may be associated with the greater presence of outside shareholders in these companies compared to their counterparts in Ukraine and Belarus. This arrival of new people in companies' decision-making centers may facilitate further long-term corporate entrepreneurship.

Generally, actual and proposed short-run managerial decisions and intended long-run priorities in Russia are consistent with less employee influence and the higher level of involvement of outsiders in Russian privatized firms. Russian managers have properly focussed on short-run priorities in a short-run crisis, while the high priority given to all short and long-run factors in Belarus and Ukraine implies unfocussed and unrealistic entrepreneurial attitudes among managers from these countries. In terms of actual short-run retrenchments, Russian managers have also achieved more.

It must of course be recognized that any improved corporate governance from outside owners and lenders can only be seen as a necessary, and not a sufficient, condition for improved corporate entrepreneurship, in the context of product markets that may not be competitive. Without competitive product markets, greater pressure from capital markets may even induce managerial incumbents to exercise any product market monopoly power they may enjoy, and simply exploit consumers more by raising product prices. To date, no evidence is available on relative product market conditions in the three countries, and important research remains to be done on this key issue.

The findings of the study suggest some implications for policymakers and practitioners. Corporate entrepreneurial behavior appears to be markedly affected by the prevailing conditions in the countries studied here and lower employee (and higher outsider) ownership and control seems to be associated with more realistic managerial decisions and priorities, but these need further support from the market environment.

The legislation essential to the functioning of a market economy, such as company and bankruptcy law, has been successfully enacted in all three countries surveyed (Appendix Tables A1, A2). However, in Russia, Ukraine, and Belarus such laws are often not enforced, and contractual obligations are sometimes ignored with impunity (Black 1996). The legal system in these countries is often replaced by private mechanisms of enforcing agreements and resolving disputes, including organized crime. This lack of law enforcement can mean that corporate entrepreneurial actions may be either destructive or unproductive and dysfunctional managers can remain in post. Hence, there is a need to address continuing shortcomings in the legal and regulatory environment that will strengthen the rules of the game promoting productive entrepreneurship. Western institutions, such as the U.K. Know-How Fund, USAID, KU, etc., could also play a more active role in providing technical assistance and training to emerging corporate entrepreneurs in the former USSR.

Our study also has implications for researchers. First, given the necessarily short period covered by surveys and the exploratory nature of the analysis, there is a need for longitudinal studies in order to compare both the development of corporate entrepreneurial strategies as well as outcomes (that is, performance and life-cycles of enterprises) as well as to consider more fully the different forces at play in each of the three countries examined in this study. Second, there is a need to compare the quality of entrepreneurship in existing firms with entrepreneurship in new ventures in the three countries. Third, there is scope for comparison of corporate entrepreneurship with other countries in Central and Eastern Europe.

Finally, our findings clearly suggest that ownership transformation by itself cannot be relied upon to create extensive long term corporate entrepreneurship and further work remains to be done on the importance of product market competitive conditions and their interplay with corporate governance changes. Privatization is just the beginning of a long-term process. The development of corporate entrepreneurship and the liberation of latent entrepreneurial talents in privatized companies will not happen by itself, over a short period of time. An important role is likely to be played by supportive and robust corporate governance mechanisms combined with the strengthening of the legal framework and the liberalization of capital and product markets.

REFERENCES

Ang, J. 1991. Small business uniqueness and the theory of financial management. *Journal of Small Business Finance* 1(1):1–13.

Baumol, W. 1996. Entrepreneurship: productive, unproductive and destructive. *Journal of Business Venturing* 11(1):3–22.

Bhide, A. 1994. Efficient markets, inefficient governance. *Harvard Business Review* 94(6): 128–139.

Bim, A. 1996. Ownership and control of Russian enterprises and strategies of shareholders. *Communist Economics and Economic Transformation* 8(4):471–500.

Black, B., Kraakman, R., and Hay, J. 1996. Corporate law from scratch: In R. Frydman, C.W. Gray, and A. Rapaczynski, eds., *Corporate Governance in Central Europe and Russia*, vol. 2. Budapest: Central European University Press.

Blasi, J., Kroumova, M., and Kruse, D. 1997. *Kremlin Capitalism. Privatizing the Russian Economy*. Ithaca and London: Cornell University Press.

Block, Z., and MacMillan, I. 1993. *Corporate Venturing*, Boston, MA: Harvard Business School Press.

Boycko, M., Shleifer, A., and Vishny, R. 1993. *Privatizing Russia*. Cambridge, MA: The MIT Press.

Brada, J. 1996. Privatization is transition: or is it? *Journal of Economic Perspectives* 10(2):67–86.

Bull, I. 1989. Financial performance of leveraged buy-outs. *Journal of Business Venturing* 4(4):263–279.

Cooper, A., and Dunkelberg, W. 1986. Entrepreneurship and paths to business ownership. *Strategic Management Journal* 7(1):53–56.

Denis, D., Denis, D. K., and Sarin, A. 1997. Ownership structure and top executive turnover. *Journal of Financial Economics* 45(2):193–221.

Earle, J., and Estrin, S. 1996. Employee ownership in transition. In R. Frydman, C.W. Gray, and A. Rapaczynski, eds., vol. 2, *Corporate Governance in Central Europe and Russia*. Budapest: Central European University Press.

EBRD. 1997. *Transition Report*. London: European Bank for Reconstruction and Development.

Ernst, M., Alexeev, M., and Marer, P. 1996. *Transforming The Core: Restructuring Industrial Enterprises in Russia and Central Europe*. Boulder, CO: Westview Press.

Filatotchev, I., Buck, T., and Wright, M. 1992. Privatization and entrepreneurship in the break-up of the USSR. *World Economy* 15(4):505–524.

Filatotchev, I., Buck, T., Wright, M., and Van Frausum, Y. 1996. Privatization and industrial restructuring in Ukraine. *Communist Economies and Economic Transformation* 8(2):185–203.

Filatotchev, I., Hoskisson, R., Buck, T., and Wright, M. 1996. Corporate restructuring in Russian privatizations: Implications for US investors. *California Management Review* 38(2):87–105.

Frydman, R., Phelps, E., Rapaczyaski, A. and Shleifer, A. 1993. Needed mechanisms of corporate governance and finance in Eastern Europe. *Economics of Transition*; 1(2):171–207.

Frydman, R., Gray, C., Hessel, M., and Rapaczynski, A. 1997. *Private Ownership And Corporate Performance: Some Lessons From Transition Economies*. New York: New York University.

Gartner, W., and Shane, S. 1995. Measuring entrepreneurship over time. *Journal of Business Venturing* 10(4):283–301.

Guth, W., and Ginsberg, A. 1990. Guest editors' introduction: corporate entrepreneurship. *Strategic Management Journal* 11(S):5–15.

Hawley, F. 1900. Enterprise and profit. *Quarterly Journal of Economics* 15(1):75–105.

Hisrich, R., and Grachev, M. 1993. The Russian entrepreneur. *Journal of Business Venturing* 8(6):487–497.

Holt, D., Ralston, D., and Terpstra, R. 1994. Constraints on capitalism in Russia: The managerial psyche, social infrastructure and ideology. *California Management Review* 36(3):124–141.

Hutchinson, P., Piper, J., and Ray, G. 1975. The financing of rapid growth firms up to flotation. *Accounting and Business Research* 5(18):145–151.

Jensen, M. 1993. The modern industrial revolution, exit, and failure of internal control systems. *Journal of Finance* 48(3):831–880.

Kantorovich, V. 1998. New business creation and Russian economic recovery. *Paper presented at the 6th Annual Meeting of the Association for Comparative Economic Studies.* Chicago, Jan. 5th.

Kaplan, S. 1997. Corporate governance and corporate performance: a comparison of Germany, Japan and the US. *Journal of Applied Corporate Finance* 9(4):86–93.

Kaufman, P., Welsh, D., and Bushmarin, N. 1995. Locus of control and entrepreneurship in the Russian Republic. *Entrepreneurship: Theory and Practice* 20(1):43–56.

Kornai, J. 1980. *The Economics of Shortage.* Volumes A and B, Amsterdam: North Holland.

Krueger, G. 1995. Transition strategies of former state-owned enterprises in Russia. *Comparative Economic Studies* 37(4):89–110.

Linz, S. 1996. Red executives in Russia's transition economy. *Post-Soviet Geography and Economics* 37(10):633–651.

Linz, S. 1997. Russian firms in transition: champions, challengers and chaff. *Comparative Economic Studies* 39(2):1–36.

Linz, S., and Krueger, G. 1996. Russia's managers in transition: pilferers or paladins? *Post-Soviet Geography and Economics* 37(7):397–425.

McCarthy, D., Puffer, S., and Shekshnia, S. 1993. The resurgence of an entrepreneurial class in Russia. *Journal of Management Inquiry* 2(2):125–137.

Morck, R., Shleifer, A., and Vishny, R. 1988. Management ownership and market valuation: An empirical analysis. *Journal of Financial Economics* 20(1):293–316.

Ners, K. 1995. Privatization (from above, below or mass privatization) versus generic private enterprise building. *Communist Economies and Economic Transformation* 7(1):105–116.

Puffer, S. 1994. Understanding the bear: A portrait of Russian business leaders. *Academy of Management Executive* 8(1):41–54.

Richman, B. 1965. *Soviet Management,* Englewood Cliffs, NJ: Prentice Hall.

Rosenstein, J., Bruno, A., Bygrave, W., and Taylor, N. 1993. The CEO, venture capitalists, and the board. *Journal of Business Venturing* 8(2):99–113.

Sapienza, H., Manigart, S., and Vermeir, C. 1996. Venture capitalists' governance and value added in four countries. *Journal of Business Venturing* 11(6):439–470.

Stopford, J., and Baden-Fuller, C. 1994. Creating corporate entrepreneurship. *Strategic Management Journal* 15(7):521–536.

World Bank 1996. *Mass Privatization in Ukraine.* State Property Fund of Ukraine, Meeting with World Bank Representatives. Washington, DC.

Wright, M., and Robbie, K. 1998. Venture capital and private equity: a review and synthesis. *Journal of Business Finance and Accounting* 25(5/6):521–570.

Wright, M., Thompson, S., and Robbie, K. 1992. Venture capital and management-led leveraged buyouts: a European perspective. *Journal of Business Venturing* 7(1):47–72.

492   I. FILATOTCHEV ET AL.

Wright, M., Filatotchev, I., and Buck, T. 1996. Entrepreneurship and privatized firms in Russia
    and Ukraine: Evidence on performance. In *Frontiers of Entrepreneurship Research*, Pro-
    ceedings of the 16th Annual Entrepreneurship Conference, Seattle, USA, March 1996.
    Babson College, MA: Center for Entrepreneurial Studies.

Wright, M., Filatotchev, I., Hoskisson, R., and Buck, T. 1998. Revitalizing privatized Russian
    enterprises. *Academy of Management Executive* 12(2):74–85.

Zahra, S. 1993. Environment, corporate entrepreneurship and financial performance: A taxo-
    nomic approach. *Journal of Business Venturing* 8(4):319–340.

Zahra, S. 1995. Corporate entrepreneurship and financial performance: The case of management
    leveraged buy-outs. *Journal of Business Venturing* 10(3):225–248.

Zahra, S. 1996. Governance, ownership and corporate entrepreneurship: the moderating impact
    of industrial technological opportunities. *Academy of Management Journal* 39(6):1713–1735.

APPENDIX: SAMPLE CHARACTERISTICS (RUSSIAN SAMPLE)

TABLE A1   Industrial Structure of Privatized Firms

Industry	Share in Total Non-State Russian Industrial Firms' Employment (%)[1]	Share in the Total Sample in This Survey (%)
Metallurgy	10.95	22.07
Chemical and petrochemical	7.14	2.21
Engineering	41.46	41.23
Timber, forestry, pulp, and paper	10.54	11.94
Building materials	7.44	6.35
Light industries	10.56	10.39
Food	11.92	5.81
Total	100.00	100.00

In 1995; Non-state firms include both privatized and de novo firms where data on the number of privatized firms are
not available. Sources: Goskomstat Russia (1996), Promishlennost Rossii, pp. 30–1, 80–1.

TABLE A2   Employment Distribution

Number of Employees	Share in Total Russian Industrial Output (%)[1]	Share in Total Sample in This Survey's Sales (%)
Less than 200	10.8	4.69
200–499	13.4	10.52
500 or more	75.8	84.79
Total	100.0	100.0

[1] In 1995, excluding Far East. Source: Goskomstat Russia (1996), Promishlennost Rossii, p.18.

[30]

FOSTERING CORPORATE ENTREPRENEURSHIP: CROSS-CULTURAL COMPARISONS OF THE IMPORTANCE OF INDIVIDUALISM VERSUS COLLECTIVISM

Michael H. Morris*
University of the Pacific

Duane L. Davis and Jeffrey W. Allen***
University of Central Florida

Abstract. This study reports on results of a cross-cultural, empirical investigation designed to assess the impact of individualism/ collectivism upon organizational entrepreneurship. The findings indicate individualism/collectivism is an important factor in understanding entrepreneurial behavior in the firm. Implications of these findings are discussed.

INTRODUCTION

While much has been written about the need for established firms to become more entrepreneurial (e.g., Brandt [1986]; Cornwall and Perlman [1990]; MacMillan et al. [1986]; Waterman [1987]), only limited progress has been made in determining exactly how entrepreneurship can be accomplished and sustained in these organizations [Burgelman and Sayles 1986; Jennings and Young 1990; Kanter 1983; Morris and Trotter 1990; Stefflre 1985; Stewart 1989]. Attempts to address this issue appear to emphasize the differences,

*Michael H. Morris holds a Ph.D. in marketing from Virginia Polytechnic Institute and is currently the Fletcher Jones Professor of Entrepreneurship at the University of the Pacific. Dr. Morris has published in numerous journals, is author of several textbooks, and contributes frequently to national and regional conferences. Professor Morris was recently a Fulbright Scholar at the University of Capetown, South Africa.

**Duane L. Davis holds a D.B.A. in marketing from the University of Kentucky and is currently a professor in the Department of Marketing at the University of Central Florida. Dr. Davis is the author of *Business Research for Decision Making*, third edition, and has published extensively in a wide variety of journals. Professor Davis was recently a Fulbright Scholar at the Universidade do Porto and the Universidade do Algarve in Portugal.

***Jeffrey W. Allen holds a D.B.A. in marketing from the University of Kentucky and is currently an assistant professor at the University of Central Florida's Daytona Beach Campus. Dr. Allen has published in a variety of journals and proceedings. Dr. Allen's research interests include social responsibility, distribution management and the development of marketing strategy.

The authors wish to express their appreciation to Professor Carlos Barral and the Instituto Superior De Estudos Empresariais, Universidade do Porto, Porto, Portugal for their assistance and support in this study.

Received: September 1992; Revised: July 1993; Accepted: September 1993.

66   JOURNAL OF INTERNATIONAL BUSINESS STUDIES, FIRST QUARTER 1994

rather than the similarities between independent start-ups and established firms [MacMillan 1983; Miller 1983; Sinetar 1985; Smith and Miner 1983]. The assumption seems to be that entrepreneurship in a corporate setting is a relatively unique phenomenon [Cornwall and Perlman 1990; Pinchot 1985; MacMillan et al. 1986].

This assumption warrants further analysis, as no evidence has been produced to suggest the factors most responsible for successful entrepreneurship are not the same in both settings. Of all the factors effecting entrepreneurial performance, the one receiving the most emphasis in the literature on independent start-ups is the entrepreneur himself or herself (e.g., Brockhaus [1982]; Carland et al. [1984]; Hisrich and Brush [1986]; Homaday and Aboud [1971]; McClelland [1987]; Sexton and Bowman [1986]). Thus, it is argued that without the visionary leadership and persistence demonstrated by this individual, little would be accomplished. Extensive work has been done to identify the characteristics of this individual, and to distinguish him or her from conventional managers, inventors, and society at large [Brandt 1986; Brockhaus 1982; Mancuso 1974; McClelland 1987; Shapero 1982].

At the same time, observers of the corporate environment have argued that the team or group, and not the individual, is essential for accomplishing entrepreneurship [Kanter 1989; Reich 1987; Stewart 1989]. For instance, Reich [1987] has suggested entrepreneurial teams must replace the lone entrepreneurial hero if the United States is to remain globally competitive (see also Stewart [1989]).

The role of individuals versus groups or collectives in facilitating entrepreneurship in organizations may also be culture-bound. Individualism is an intrinsic aspect of American culture, which helps to explain the relatively intensive amount of independent entrepreneurial activity in the U.S. [Birch 1981; Birch and McCracken 1982; Reynolds and Freeman 1987; Peterson 1988]. However, when examining corporate entrepreneurship, the influence of national culture may be moderated by the influence of organizational culture. While organizational culture might be expected to reflect national culture, it may also have its own distinct characteristics [Deal and Kennedy 1982; Frost et al. 1985; Hofstede 1991; Kotter and Heskett 1991].

The purpose of this research is to examine how the relative emphasis on the individual, versus the group or collective, impacts upon organizational entrepreneurship, and to determine if this impact varies across different cultures. It is hypothesized that the relationship between individualism— collectivism is curvilinear, and that progressively higher levels of a group or collective orientation serve to inhibit entrepreneurship. Results are reported of three separate surveys directed at managers within U.S., South African and Portuguese firms. Based on the findings, managerial implications are drawn, and suggestions are made for ongoing research.

INDIVIDUALISM AND COLLECTIVISM DEFINED

Traditionally conceptualized as a continuum, individualism-collectivism has received considerable attention from sociologists and social psychologists [Earley 1989; Hofstede 1980; Hui and Triandis 1986; Triandis et al. 1988; Wagner and Moch 1986]. Individualism refers to a self-orientation, an emphasis on self-sufficiency and control, the pursuit of individual goals that may or may not be consistent with in-group goals, a willingness to confront members of the in-group to which a person belongs, and a culture where people derive pride from their own accomplishments. In an individualistic environment, people are motivated by self-interest and achievement of personal goals. They are hesitant to contribute to collective action unless their own efforts are recognized, preferring instead to benefit from the efforts of others.

Collectivism involves the subordination of personal interests to the goals of the larger work group, an emphasis on sharing, cooperation, and group harmony, a concern with group welfare, and hostility toward out-group members. Collectivists believe that they are an indispensable part of the group, and will readily contribute without concern for advantage being taken of them or for whether others are doing their part. They feel personally responsible for the group product and are oriented towards sharing group rewards.

Individualism-collectivism is a dimension of culture at both the societal and organizational levels, although most of the research has focused on societal or national culture. Thus, Hofstede [1980] has shown that countries such as the United States, Australia, Great Britain, and Canada demonstrate high scores on his individualism-collectivism index, while Venezuela, China, Pakistan, Thailand and Mexico score fairly low.

Although less researched, individualism-collectivism would also appear to be an important dimension of organizational culture. Wagner and Moch [1986] argue that individualism-collectivism is implicit in organizational science, but has received scant attention. Triandis et al. [1988] discuss the need for corporate education programs directed at employees who bring a particular societal orientation, say individualistic, to an organization whose values are more collectivistic.

Individualism and collectivism would seem to have both functional and dysfunctional aspects within an organizational setting. While there is neither universal agreement nor definitive empirical evidence for all these relationships, Table 1 presents some hypothesized pros and cons from the literature (see also Gudykunst, Yoon and Nishida [1987]; Hui and Triandis [1986]; Hsu [1981]; Spence [1985]; Triandis et al. [1988]). For instance, individualistic cultures may foster development of an individual's self-concept and self-confidence. There is also likely to be a greater sense of personal responsibility for performance outcomes, while interpersonal competition may generate a steady stream of ideas for innovative change. However, there is also likely to be an emphasis on personal gain, selfishness, and expediency.

68 JOURNAL OF INTERNATIONAL BUSINESS STUDIES, FIRST QUARTER 1994

TABLE 1
Hypothesized Pros/Cons of Individualism and Collectivism in an Organizational Setting

Individualism	Collectivism
Pros:	**Pros:**
• Employee develops stronger self-concept, more self-confidence	• Greater synergies from combined efforts of people with differing skills
• Consistent with achievement motivation	• Ability to incorporate diverse perspectives and achieve comprehensive view
• Competition among individuals encourages greater numbers of novel concepts and ideas; breakthrough innovations	• Individuals treated as equals
	• Relationships more personalized, synchronized, harmonious, while interpersonal conflicts are discouraged
• Stronger sense of personal responsibility for performance outcomes	• Greater concern for welfare of others, network of social support available
• Linkage between personal effort and rewards creates greater sense of equity	• More consensus regarding direction and priorities
Cons:	• Credit for failures and successes equally shared
• Emphasis on personal gain at expense of others, selfishness, materialism	• Teamwork produces steady, incremental progress on projects
• Individuals have less commitment/ loyalty, are more "up for sale"	
• Differences among individuals are emphasized	**Cons:**
• Interpersonal conflicts are encouraged	• Loss of personal and professional self to group/collective
• Greater levels of personal stress, pressure for individual performance	• Greater emotional dependence of individuals on the group or organization
• Insecurity can result from over-dependence on one's self	• Less personal responsibility for outcomes
• Greater feelings of loneliness, alienation, and anomie	• Individuals "free ride" on efforts of others, rewards not commensurate with effort
• Stronger incentive for unethical behavior, expediency	• Tendency toward "group think"
• Onus of failure falls on the individual	• Outcomes can represent compromises among diverse interests, reflecting need to get along more than need for performance
	• Collectives can take more time to reach consensus, may miss opportunities

Further, high levels of personal stress are a likely by-product of this type of environment, and interpersonal conflict may be encouraged.

Collectivism offers the advantage of more harmonious relationships among individuals. In this type of culture, greater synergies may occur from the combined efforts of people with diverse skills, while individuals may enjoy a network of social support. Alternatively, there is likely to be a loss of one's self to the group or organizational persona, and a greater level of emotional dependence on the organization. Individuals may have a greater tendency to "free ride" on the efforts of others, while outcomes may represent compromises among the differing interests participating in a task.

What remains unclear are the implications of an emphasis on the individual versus the group or collective when attempting to foster entrepreneurial behavior in an organizational setting. Drawing such implications requires that we first expand on the nature of corporate entrepreneurship.

THE ORGANIZATIONAL CONTEXT OF ENTREPRENEURSHIP

Entrepreneurship can be defined as "the process of creating value by bringing together a unique package of resources to exploit an opportunity" [Stevenson et al. 1989]. The process itself consists of the set of activities necessary to identify an opportunity, develop a business concept, assess and acquire the necessary resources, implement the concept, and then manage and harvest the venture. As a process, it has applicability to organizations of all sizes and types.

The entrepreneurship construct has three underlying dimensions: innovativeness, or the development of novel or unique products, services or processes; risk-taking, or a willingness to pursue opportunities having a reasonable chance of costly failure; and proactiveness, or an emphasis on persistence and creativity in overcoming obstacles until the innovative concept is fully implemented [Covin and Slevin 1989; Ginsberg 1985; Jennings and Young 1990; Khandwalla 1977; Miles and Arnold 1991; Miller and Friesen 1983]. Because different levels of innovativeness, risk-taking, and proactiveness are possible in a particular entrepreneurial event, and any number of such events are possible in a given social context, entrepreneurship can be said to occur in varying degrees and amounts [Morris and Lewis 1991; Stevenson and Jarillo 1990; Wortman 1987].

When the social context is an established firm, entrepreneurship takes on unique characteristics, and the process becomes subject to a number of constraints and opportunities not found with most independent start-ups [Brandt 1986; Kao 1989; MacMillan et al. 1986; Pinchot 1985; Zahra 1986]. Corporate entrepreneurship entails a somewhat different role for the entrepreneur. This individual, sometimes referred to as the "intrapreneur" or "champion," is not risking his/her own resources, but those belonging to the company. While personal risk is involved, it is more career-related [Kanter 1983]. Further, this individual does not "own" the entrepreneurial concept, and must be prepared to give credit to others in the organization's hierarchy. In addition, there are real limits on the personal rewards, especially financial, that can be earned by the corporate entrepreneur should the concept be successful.

The established firm offers the entrepreneurial individual an abundance of resources critical for concept development, testing, and implementation. With these resources come a variety of formal policies and procedures, structural constraints, and cultural norms which can hinder innovative efforts [Cornwall and Perlman 1990; Knight 1987; Morris and Trotter 1990; Peters 1988; Souder 1987; Waterman 1987]. The corporate entrepreneur's success in capitalizing on these resources while overcoming such obstacles may require certain political skills, as well as an ability to obtain sponsors, build teams, craft coalitions, and work through others [Jennings and Lumpkin 1989; Kanter 1983; Maidique 1980; Pinchot 1985]. Stated differently, the corporate entrepreneur does not exercise as much personal control over his/her project's destiny as does the independent entrepreneur.

CULTURE AND ENTREPRENEURSHIP

Culture refers to a learned, socially transmitted set of behavioral standards. It is held, expressed, and shared by individuals through their personal values, norms, activities, attitudes, cognitive processes, interpretation of symbols, feelings, ideas, reactions and morals [Douglas and Dubois 1977; Hofstede 1980; Tse et al. 1988]. Culture exists at multiple levels, ranging from broad societal or national cultures to individualized corporate or organizational cultures [Davies and Weiner 1985]. At the broadest level, culture provides a basic framework for social interaction, and represents a cohesive element among the individual members of a society [Douglas and Dubois 1977]. Within an organization, culture serves the same function as personality does to the individual—a hidden yet unifying theme that provides meaning, direction, and mobilization [Kilmann 1989].

The different levels of culture are interrelated with one another. For instance, Moore [1986] indicates a need for the culture of an organization to be in congruence or harmony with at least some dimensions of the broader societal culture in which it is embedded. Beck and Moore [1985] have demonstrated a high degree of congruence between employee perceptions of national character in Canada and their perceptions regarding the culture in branches of large banks (see also Davies and Weiner [1985]).

It appears that entrepreneurship is affected by culture at both the societal and organizational levels. Numerous authors have traced the high levels of entrepreneurship within the United States to such cultural values as freedom, independence, self-sufficiency, individualism, achievement, and materialism (e.g., Gilder [1988]; Peterson [1988]; Spence [1985]; Sundbo [1991]). Similarly, research on corporate entrepreneurship has identified cultural obstacles to successful entrepreneurship, and suggested that entrepreneurship requires a culture built around risk, innovation, emotional commitment, autonomy, and empowerment, among others [Cornwall and Perlman 1990; Peters 1987; Pinchot 1985; Waterman 1987].

INDIVIDUALISM-COLLECTIVISM AND ENTREPRENEURSHIP

Individualism-collectivism would seem to be one of the more salient dimensions of culture insofar as entrepreneurship is concerned. In Hofstede's [1980] global study of national cultures, he demonstrated a relationship between an emphasis on individualism and a country's level of economic development and wealth. Economic development has also been positively linked to levels of entrepreneurship in a society [Birch 1981; Gilder 1988; Schumpeter 1950]. Others have identified relationships between individualism and the willingness of people to violate norms [Verma 1985] as well as their level of achievement motivation [Hofstede 1980; Spence 1985], both of which are commonly associated with entrepreneurship [Brockhaus 1982; Collins and Moore 1964; McClelland 1987].

More fundamentally, perhaps the richest research tradition in the entrepreneurship literature focuses on the psychological traits and sociological characteristics of the individual entrepreneur (e.g., Brockhaus [1982]; Kets de Vries [1977]; Sexton 1980]). Implicit in this research is the assumption that the entrepreneurial process is a highly individualistic pursuit. Moore [1986] and Gartner [1985] have suggested that, of all the elements necessary for successful entrepreneurship, the independent entrepreneur is the most critical.

While individualism may help explain the amount of new business start-up activity in a society, it is less clear how entrepreneurship in existing firms is affected by this dimension of culture. That is, even in highly individualistic societies, established firms are frequently not especially entrepreneurial. This tendency may be due, at least in part, to the intervening impact of corporate culture on entrepreneurship. For example, the corporate culture may be fairly collectivistic, while coexisting in a relatively individualistic society. However, the relationship may be more complicated. For example, the impact of individualism-collectivism on entrepreneurship may differ depending on whether the analysis is performed at the societal or the organizational level.

Wagner and Moch [1986] suggest that overly individualistic corporate cultures may be inappropriate for contemporary organizations in which highly interdependent methods of production, inventory management, and matrix structures are employed. Similar suggestions have been made regarding corporate entrepreneurship [Reich 1987; Stewart 1989; Sundbo 1991]. According to these authors, the individual entrepreneur is overly motivated by self-gain, and can be "bought" by the highest bidder; whereas, the group or collective cannot. Moreover, the corporate setting demands certain political skills and an ability to work with and through others, which may be inconsistent with a strong individualistic orientation. Further, the entrepreneurial process is sufficiently complex and lengthy as to require a well-coordinated group of employees, each having his/her own expertise, to achieve any measure of success. Finally, collectives are viewed as more able to generate a continuous stream of incremental innovations, as opposed to the major breakthroughs that periodically come from individuals.

72   JOURNAL OF INTERNATIONAL BUSINESS STUDIES, FIRST QUARTER 1994

At the same time, others continue to stress the role of the individual in corporate entrepreneurship. Peters [1987] places strong emphasis on the need for organizations to support radical champions within their ranks. Pinchot [1985] argues that achieving innovation in large firms requires that managers find ways to apply the concepts of individual liberty and freedom within the corporate walls. Burgelman and Sayles [1986] claim that individualism does not inherently conflict with big business, and that entrepreneurship depends on new business forms built around the integration of individualism.

RESEARCH HYPOTHESES

For the purposes of further research, a set of hypotheses is presented here regarding the relationship between individualism-collectivism and entrepreneurship, focusing on both variables at the corporate level. The relationship is hypothesized to be curvilinear, reflecting the positive and negative characteristics of individualism-collectivism that were summarized in Table 1.

Beginning with the highly individualistic end of the continuum, it would seem that such cultures will produce strong incentives for entrepreneurial behavior, but will also result in a gamesmanship, zero-sum competition, sequestering of information, and the chaotic pursuit of tangential projects having little strategic fit with the organization's competencies or overall direction [Maidique 1980; Quinn 1985; Reich 1987; Rosenbaum et al. 1980; Steele 1983]. In the absence of any group or team identification, individuals will more likely use organizational resources to satisfy self-interests [Earley 1989; Mitroff 1988; Wagner and Moch 1986]. Further, many tasks will be left incomplete as individuals are unable to obtain cooperation from those having the expertise and resources necessary for implementation of the entrepreneurial concept [Ferguson 1988; Kaplan 1987; Reich 1987; Stewart 1989; Whyte 1956]. The result will be modest levels of entrepreneurship.

At the other extreme, a strongly collectivist environment may actually give rise to an anti-entrepreneurial bias. Group performance and reward systems can encourage "free-rider" or "social loafing" syndromes on the part of specific individuals [Earley 1989; Jones 1984; Albanese and Van Fleet 1985]. Further, tasks become over-segmented, such that individuals lose sight of the larger project and concentrate only on their assigned duties [Peters 1988; Waterman 1987; Whyte 1956]. Compromise is highly valued, as is acceptance of group norms and roles [Earley 1989; Hui 1988; Kilmann 1989]. The result can be mutually acceptable incremental solutions, as opposed to more controversial breakthrough innovations [Gilder 1988; Ferguson 1988; Reich 1987]. In the final analysis, the collective will work to resist significant change, while fostering imitation and adaptation. Tropman and Morningstar [1989, p. 123] explain, "in a firm where unity of interest is the dominant theme, emphasis on the creating of some diversity, heterogeneity, and internal organizational friction are necessary to get the supply of new ideas required for continual achievement."

The highest levels of entrepreneurship will occur when a fairly balanced amount of consideration is given to the needs of the individual and the collective. This quasi-balance would seem consistent with Waterman's [1987] concept of "directed autonomy." Respect for the individual combined with personal incentives (financial and non-financial) are necessary to spur employees to tap their creative potential and develop novel concepts on a continual basis [Balkin and Logan 1988; Maidique 1980; Souder 1987; Tropman and Morningstar 1989]. Moreover, individual autonomy and a sense of ownership of innovation encourage the risk-taking and significant persistence required to implement an entrepreneurial concept [Brandt 1986; Drucker 1985; Jennings and Lumpkin 1989; Maidique 1980; Pinchot 1985; Stevenson and Jarillo 1990]. Rosabeth Kanter, in her book *The Changemasters* [1983], explains (p. 410), "There are times when autonomy and individual responsibility are more important than participation and team responsibility . . . invention and innovation are often not democratic processes." At the same time, the complexity of many new product opportunities, combined with technological constraints, the diversity of markets, governmental restrictions, uncontrollable economic developments, and the need for partnerships with suppliers and distributors suggest a degree of teamwork and well-coordinated task integration are vital for entrepreneurial success [Burgelman and Sayles 1986; Kay 1979; Martin 1984; Reich 1987; Rothwell 1980; Stewart 1989]. Thus the single-minded entrepreneur must be adept at crafting coalitions and building teams who feel a strong sense of joint involvement and contribution [Kanter 1983].

Based on this discussion, the following research hypotheses are proposed:

H1: Extensive emphasis on individualism relative to collectivism will result in low levels of entrepreneurship.

H2: Extensive emphasis on collectivism relative to individualism will result in low levels of entrepreneurship.

H3: A relatively balanced emphasis between individualism and collectivism will result in high levels of entrepreneurship.

RESEARCH DESIGN

These hypotheses were tested with three surveys, one each conducted in the United States, South Africa, and Portugal. While these three countries are all westernized democracies, they differ in significant ways. The U.S. is arguably the most entrepreneurial country in the world, and has one of the highest standards of living. Portugal was a socialized nation until fairly recently, and while its economy is emerging, it is among the poorest nations in the EC. South Africa has an economy consisting of first-, second- and third-world components. It has experienced tremendous turbulence in recent years, due in part to the devastating impact of international trade sanctions, but also related to the dynamic process of internal transformation that continues

74   JOURNAL OF INTERNATIONAL BUSINESS STUDIES, FIRST QUARTER 1994

to unfold. Importantly, these three countries represent the entire range of possible scores on Hofstede's [1980] individualism-collectivism index. On a 100-point scale, with higher scores representing a more individualistic culture, Hofstede reported scores for the U.S., South Africa and Portugal of 91, 64 and 25, respectively.

Instrument Development

In each of the three countries, a research design was employed in which executives from a cross-section of industrial firms participated in a mail survey. A questionnaire was developed consisting of thirty-nine varied response items, twenty-four of which dealt with individualism, fifteen addressing entrepreneurship.

The relative emphasis placed on the individual was measured using three subscales. The first of these was the personal freedom measure developed by Kilmann and Saxton [1983], and labeled IND1. Included here are seven items that have proven effective at measuring culture gaps in personal freedom within a large number of profit and non-profit organizations. These items are a subset of twenty-eight norm pairs that were statistically derived from over four hundred norms identified in studies of a variety of different types of organizations. The items were presented as a series of bipolar paired alternatives.

The second subscale (IND2) was an adaptation of Hofstede's [1980] individualism-collectivism scale, which is based on the earlier work of Breer and Locke [1965]. The original set of twelve items was derived from a number of factor analyses on cross-cultural data. Initially developed for measurement of societal orientations, it was slightly modified to apply in organizations. The resulting nine items were presented as bipolar statements separated by a five-point response scale.

The third subscale (IND3) was developed from Earley's [1989] measures of collectivism and social loafing, and specifically, the subordination of personal for in-group goals. This work builds on the efforts of Triandis et al. [1985] and Wagner and Moch [1986]. The subscale consists of eight items structured as a five-point Likert-type scale (strongly agree-strongly disagree). Earley found these items, when factor analyzed, produced a single factor with loadings from .71 to .87. The reliability (Cronbach's *alpha*) for this composite was .88.

The measurement of entrepreneurship was accomplished using a scale originally developed by Miller and Friesen [1983], and subsequently adapted by Ginsberg [1985], Covin and Slevin [1989], and Morris and Paul [1987]. Twelve items were included which assess the extent to which the respondent's firm is perceived to be innovative, takes calculated risks, and emphasizes a proactive approach to identifying and capitalizing upon opportunities. This scale was labeled ENT. The item response consisted of a five-point (very definitely describes our firm—does not describe our firm at all) scale. Ginsberg reported a reliability (*alpha*) of .75, while Covin and Slevin reported an *alpha* of .87, and Morris and Paul reported a reliability of .78. In addition, self-report measures were included that asked respondents to indicate the number of new products and services to be introduced by their firms during the current calendar year, and the percentage of senior management time devoted to innovation.

It must be noted that other than the Hofstede subscale, the scales were largely constructed and validated using American managers. This limitation is noted in the conclusions of this paper. While this is a limitation of this research, it provides a basis for future cross-cultural scale development. In addition, consistent results in scale performance across the various countries would seem to suggest some level of post-hoc validation.

Questionnaires were administered in English for the U.S. and South African samples, and in Portuguese for that sample. The Portuguese questionnaire was translated, then back-translated by an independent expert in the field to ensure consistency in meaning to the original questionnaire. Both the translator and interpreter agreed the meanings were equivalent for the measurement instrument. Pretests indicated no significant interpretative problems with any of the samples.

Sampling and Data Collection

Similar data collection procedures were employed with the U.S. and South African surveys, with some variations in Portugal. For the U.S. survey, 180 manufacturing companies located within the State of Indiana were randomly selected from the Harris Directory. Senior marketing executives were first contacted by telephone, had the study described to them, and were asked to participate. They were also asked if three surveys could be sent to them, and if they would pass the other two on to the heads of the personnel/human resources and production/operations departments. Once completed, the marketing managers were to collect all three surveys and return them in a stamped, self-addressed envelope that had been provided. Subject companies were guaranteed anonymity, and respondents were offered an executive summary of the results. A total of 252 usable questionnaires were returned from 84 firms, for a 46.6% response rate from the organizations surveyed.

For the South African survey, 300 firms with 100 or more employees were randomly selected from the population of industrial firms registered with the national government. In this case, however, the participating functions were marketing, research and development, and administration. A total of 225 responses were received from 75 firms, for a 25% organization response rate.

In the case of Portugal, severe constraints were placed on the research methodology by local officials. The sample was limited to the random selection of 75 firms from a listing (Dun's Europa) of the 240 largest

76   JOURNAL OF INTERNATIONAL BUSINESS STUDIES, FIRST QUARTER 1994

manufacturing firms (as measured by sales). All firms were Portuguese-held and controlled. In addition, only the senior human resources executive responded for each firm. A total of twenty-five completed surveys were received, for a 33% rate of response for the organizations surveyed.

ANALYSIS AND RESULTS

Analysis of Group Responses

Because of the multiple dependent measures nature of the data, cross-cultural comparisons on responses to each of the entrepreneurship (ENT) and the three individualism-collectivism subscales (IND1, IND2, and IND3) were performed using multivariate analysis of variance (MANOVA). MANOVA does not restrict the number of subjects in subgroups, so that the procedure is appropriate even with the disproportionate numbers of Portuguese to United States and South African managers [Finn and Mattsson 1978]. Significant (p's$\leq$.01) multivariate F-values indicated differences among responses from the three countries on all four of the scales.

Respondents' perceptions of the entrepreneurship and individualism-collectivism dimensions studied are presented in Tables 2 through 5. Each table contains the significance of the univariate F-tests along with group means ($\bar{x}$) and standard deviations (s.d.) for the numbered items in the corresponding scales.

With one exception (i.e., decisions are not compromises) significant ($p<.05$) differences in the items pertaining to the dimensions of entrepreneurship revealed higher importance scores for the South African and Portuguese over the U.S. sample (see Table 2). On average, managers from the U.S. sample tended to rate most items in Table 2 lower than did the others.

As shown in Tables 3 and 4, several differences existed regarding issues of personal freedom, while only one item was significantly different with regard to the individualism-collectivism scale (p's$\leq$.002). Items reported in these tables were measured on bipolar response statements coded from emphasis on the individual (low=1) to emphasis on the collective (high=5). On whether managers should use their own judgement when following rules (item 3), U.S. respondents showed more of a tendency to comply with all rules and regulations. However, the South African managers were more inclined to live for their career or job (6) and to believe in the values of the organization (7). From Table 4, item 3, it can be seen that Portuguese managers perceived slightly more than South Africans that identity should be based with the individual rather than the organization.

A response pattern similar to that in Table 2 emerges from the comparisons on items related to the subordination of personal to in-group goals. The U.S. managers agreed less, and the South African and Portuguese managers more, on the following statements in Table 5: (2) people are encouraged to work independently ($p=.001$), (4) members of work groups are given freedom

TABLE 2
Analysis of Responses to Items in Entrepreneurship Scale (ENT)

| ENT Scale Item | Sample | | | Significance of F | Inc. in Revised Scale |
	(n=252) United States	(n=225) South Africa	(n=25) Portugal		
1. High rate of new product introduction	$\bar{x}$=3.71 s.d.=1.15	3.76 1.12	4.12 1.17	.223	*
2. Continous production improvement	$\bar{x}$=4.39 s.d.=.92	4.20 .87	4.40 .91	.079	*
3. Risk-taking	$\bar{x}$=2.66 s.d.=1.14	2.86 1.06	3.20 1.00	.021	*
4. Do not use "Live and Let Live" philosophy	$\bar{x}$=3.60 s.d.=1.27	3.53 1.12	3.40 .96	.626	
5. Novel solutions by idea men	$\bar{x}$=3.27 s.d.=1.21	3.57 1.12	3.64 1.29	.013	*
6. Spend to develop new products	$\bar{x}$=2.72 s.d.=1.24	2.93 1.09	2.68 .90	.131	*
7. Use a non-cautious approach to decisions	$\bar{x}$=2.71 s.d.=1.16	2.92 1.16	2.48 1.05	.057	*
8. Active opportunity search	$\bar{x}$=3.23 s.d.=1.18	3.61 1.06	3.44 1.19	.001	*
9. Rapid growth is a dominant goal	$\bar{x}$=2.75 s.d.=1.28	3.08 1.14	2.80 .87	.009	*
10. Make bold decisions	$\bar{x}$=2.24 s.d.=1.13	2.67 1.11	2.64 1.15	.000	*
11. Decisions are not compromises	$\bar{x}$=2.92 s.d.=1.09	2.88 1.02	2.36 .81	.039	
12. Decisions not concerned with steady growth	$\bar{x}$=1.75 s.d.=1.10	2.05 .98	2.08 .76	.005	

to pursue their own self-interests even if this sometimes conflicts with the goals of the group (p=.034), and (5) people are more productive when they are alone than when they are part of a group (p=.002). U.S. respondents were more likely to agree that the company is more productive if individual employees put their personal interests above the welfare of the group (p=.000).

Tests of Relationships

Responses to the item sets were next summed to form composite scales; Cronbach *alphas* (α) were calculated across all three samples and item analyses were performed. After deleting three items, a coefficient of .70 resulted for the ENT scale. One item each was deleted from IND1 and IND2 and two items from IND3 producing reliabilities of .59, .70 and .69, in that order (see Tables 2-5 for items in revised scales). Based on the criterion of

78   JOURNAL OF INTERNATIONAL BUSINESS STUDIES, FIRST QUARTER 1994

TABLE 3
Analysis of Responses to Items in Individualism-Collectivism Scale (IND1)—Personal Freedom

IND1 Scale Item	Sample			Significance of F	Inc. in Revised Scale
	(n=252) United States	(n=225) South Africa	(n=25) Portugal		
1. Dress as you like vs. accepted manner	$\bar{x}$=3.76 s.d.=1.12	3.91 1.14	3.46 .72	.098	*
2. Communicate with anyone vs. lines of communication	$\bar{x}$=2.22 s.d.=1.17	2.44 1.18	2.25 1.15	.126	*
3. Use your own judgement vs. comply	$\bar{x}$=3.64 s.d.=1.11	3.18 1.12	2.21 1.02	.000	*
4. Do what pleases you vs. organization	$\bar{x}$=3.84 s.d.=.97	3.81 .90	3.71 .91	.802	*
5. Express personal preferences vs. not	$\bar{x}$=2.46 s.d.=1.09	2.40 1.03	2.63 .88	.569	*
6. Live for yourself vs. job or career	$\bar{x}$=3.02 s.d.=.77	3.46 .88	3.04 .75	.000	
7. Believe in your own values vs. the firm's	$\bar{x}$=3.05 s.d.=1.02	3.37 1.07	3.08 .89	.002	*

.70 [Nunnally 1978], three of the scales, IND2, IND3, and ENT appear to be acceptable. The IND1 subscale was eliminated from further analysis. Separate α's computed for the U.S., South African and Portuguese samples ranging from .65 to .74 for the ENT scale, and .67 to .81, and .63 to .76 for the IND2 and IND3 scales indicate a consistent degree of reliability.

Prior to testing the hypotheses, MANOVAs were performed to determine if differences existed in the perceptions of managers within the U.S. and South African samples regarding the nature of their firms. The Portuguese sample could not be utilized in this analysis because of the limitation of sample size. The U.S. respondents were tested for variation by department type (i.e., marketing, human resources, and production) and organizational size. Size was included because it has been suggested that, as firms become larger, they typically become less entrepreneurial [Cornwall and Perlman 1990; Knight 1987; Zahra 1986]. Based on a median split, managers were divided into groups of organizations with $\leq$\$25 million and >\$25 million in annual sales. Similarly, the sample of South African managers was grouped by department (i.e., marketing, R&D, and administration) and by size. Again, using a median split, managers were divided into organizations with $\leq$200 million and >200 million rand in annual sales (the U.S. dollar was approximately equal to 2.8 South African rand).

For the analyses, two factorial designs were used where group differences were considered as multileveled independent factors and the composite

TABLE 4
Analysis of Responses to Items in Individualism-Collectivism (IND2)—Organizational Orientation

IND2 Scale Item	Sample			Significance of F	Inc. in Revised Scale
	(n=252) United States	(n=225) South Africa	(n=25) Portugal		
1. Take care of him/her self vs. others	$\bar{x}$=3.07 s.d.=1.07	2.96 .99	3.13 .85	.466	*
2. "I" vs. "We" holds sway	$\bar{x}$=3.45 s.d.=.97	3.53 1.04	3.33 1.01	.511	*
3. Individual identity vs. organizational	$\bar{x}$=2.83 s.d.=1.02	3.24 1.12	3.33 1.05	.000	*
4. Emotional independence vs. dependence	$\bar{x}$=3.06 s.d.=1.08	3.14 .86	3.21 .83	.613	*
5. Motivated by self-interests vs. firm's	$\bar{x}$=3.19 s.d.=1.05	3.28 1.03	3.08 1.14	.497	*
6. Emphasis on individual achievements vs. the team's	$\bar{x}$=3.49 s.d.=1.13	3.42 1.09	3.46 .98	.764	*
7. Right to a private life vs. company interference	$\bar{x}$=2.30 s.d.=1.15	2.47 1.14	2.54 .72	.194	
8. Financial security sought from firm vs. provided by firm	$\bar{x}$=3.14 s.d.=1.04	3.16 1.06	3.46 1.06	.351	*
9. Belief in individual decisions vs. group decisions	$\bar{x}$=3.27 s.d.=1.12	3.37 .99	3.04 1.12	.285	*

subscales as related dependent measures. Using the measure of organizational size as a blocking factor and including it as an independent variable in the analyses provides an alternative to analysis of covariance that allows for control over the variables and a more efficient test (see Cox [1957]; Edwards [1987]).

Results of the MANOVAs indicated no significant ($p > .05$) main or interaction effects for any of the variables tested, suggesting that managerial perceptions along the individualism-collectivism and entrepreneurship scales are similar within countries. Because these findings indicate that managers' perceptions are different among the countries, but comparable within each country, the proposed hypotheses were tested for each sample using the individual manager as the unit of analysis. Consequently, three separate trend analyses were performed to illuminate the relationship of entrepreneurship scores along the individualism-collectivism continuum illustrated in Figure 1.

Results of the trend analyses used to test the stated hypotheses are presented by country in Table 6. The three-part table displays the raw *beta* coefficients

80   JOURNAL OF INTERNATIONAL BUSINESS STUDIES, FIRST QUARTER 1994

TABLE 5
Analysis of Responses to Items in Individualism-Collectivism (IND3)—Personal vs. In-Group Goals

IND3 Scale Item	Sample			Significance of F	Inc. in Revised Scale
	(n=252) United States	(n=225) South Africa	(n=25) Portugal		
1. Working alone is better	$\bar{x}$=3.89 s.d.=.87	4.04 .87	3.84 1.07	.140	*
2. Individual work is encouraged	$\bar{x}$=2.85 s.d.=1.00	3.18 1.00	3.28 .94	.001	*
3. Individual responsible for group	$\bar{x}$=2.44 s.d.=1.02	2.54 1.08	2.36 .81	.493	
4. Freedom to pursue self-interest	$\bar{x}$=3.42 s.d.=.98	3.65 .95	3.52 .82	.034	*
5. Individual work is more productive	$\bar{x}$=3.25 s.d.=.97	3.56 .92	3.40 .87	.002	*
6. Group member does what he thinks best	$\bar{x}$=3.41 s.d.=.99	3.25 1.05	3.00 1.12	.073	*
7. Group allows member to pursue interests	$\bar{x}$=3.18 s.d.=1.08	3.12 1.02	2.76 1.05	.169	*
8. Individual needs put above group's	$\bar{x}$=3.85 s.d.=.85	3.52 .93	3.56 1.04	.000	

and associated *p*-values for the curvilinear regressions of ENT onto IND2 and IND3. Significant ($p<.05$) linear and quadratic components with corresponding betas in the predicted direction are indicated only for the IND2 subscale in both the U.S. and South African samples. The predictive contributions (ΔR^2) of IND2^2 over that of IND2 (3.8% and 7.3%, respectively) are significant ($p<.01$). Results support the hypothesis related to IND2 in these two countries. Neither the linear nor quadratic components for IND2 or IND3 achieved significance in the Portuguese sample.

Using the *beta* coefficients from the table, predicted values for ENT are plotted over the relevant ranges of IND2 and IND3 for the U.S. sample and IND2 for the South African sample in Figure 1. The plotted curves in the figure clearly show that in each of these countries, a relatively high emphasis on either individualism or collectivism tends to produce less entrepreneurship than a balanced emphasis.

To assess the overall relationship proposed in Figure 1, a hierarchical modeling technique was applied to test whether the multiple regression of ENT against IND2 and IND3 is curvilinear. To accomplish this, the linear components (IND2 and IND3) were ordered before the linear interaction (IND2×IND3) and quadratic components (IND2^2 and IND3^2) and the increment in variance accounted for (ΔR^2) by the higher order terms was tested

FIGURE 1
Predicted Values for Entrepreneurship Plotted along
the Individualism-Collectivism Continuum

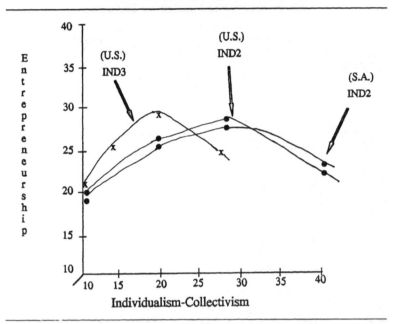

Note: IND2 = Hofstede's societal measure of individualism-collectivism (adapted). Ranges for IND2 were 10-40 for both the U.S. and South African samples. IND3 = Earley's organizational measure of subordination of personal for group interests (adapted). The range for IND3 was 10-28 for the U.S. sample only.

for significance. The proportion of variance explained by the higher order terms was significant for the U.S. sample ($F(3, 246)=4.7433$, $p=.012$) but not for the South African sample, indicating that the regression for the U.S. sample was curvilinear. Both the linear and quadratic terms for IND2 were significant ($p<.05$) in the U.S. model. No significant relationships were found for the Portuguese sample on any of the variables tested.

The two behavioral measures, percentage of time spent on innovation and number of new products/services to be introduced in the next calendar year, were also regressed against the two individualism-collectivism scales for each country. For the U.S. sample, the only significant relationship found was the percent of management time spent on innovation as a function of IND2 ($p<.01$). No significant relationships were found for either IND2 or IND3 as predictors of innovation for the South African or Portuguese samples.

82   JOURNAL OF INTERNATIONAL BUSINESS STUDIES, FIRST QUARTER 1994

TABLE 6
Results of the Curvilinear and Multiple Curvilinear Regressions of Entrepreneurship on Individualism-Collectivism for the U.S., South African and Portuguese Samples

Variables	Tests of Significance			Tests of Fit		
	B	p-value	R^2	ΔR^2	F_Δ	p-value
Part A. U.S. Sample (n=252)						
IND2	1.609	.001	.038	—		
IND2^2	-.029	.003	.073	.035	9.279	.001
Constant	5.619	—				
Multiv. $F(2, 249)$=9.442, p=.002						
IND3	2.340	.019	.005	—		
IND3^2	-.056	.025	.027	.022	5.361	.008
Constant	3.677	—				
Multiv. $F(2, 249)$ = 3.141, p=.045						
IND2	1.343	.016				
IND3	1.752	.087	.038	—		
IND2×IND3	.016	.509				
IND2^2	-.030	.005				
IND3^2	-.054	.035	.092	.056	4.743	.012
Constant	-8.056	—				
Multiv. F (5, 246)=4.639, p=.001						
Part B. South African Sample (n=225)						
IND2	1.305	.018	.004	—		
IND2^2	-.024	.024	.027	.023	5.349	.003
Constant	9.535	—				
Multiv. $F(2, 222)$=3.036, p=.050						
IND3	-.337	.699	.004	—		
IND3^2	.006	.781	.004	.000	.014	.981
Constant	30.969	—				
Multiv. $F(2, 222)$=.466, p=.628						
IND2	1.577	.017				
IND3	-.174	.849	.011	—		
IND2×IND3	-.016	.542				
IND2^2	-.023	.046				
IND3^2	.011	.629	.036	.025	1.527	.279
Constant	8.700	—				
Multiv. $F(5, 219)$=1.640, p=.151						

CONCLUSIONS AND IMPLICATIONS

Based on these results, individualism-collectivism would appear to be a salient dimension of organizational culture across different societies. Evidence was provided of measurable variation in individualism-collectivism within samples of firms from three countries. Both an adapted version of Hofstede's [1980] societal individualism-collectivism scale (IND2) and Earley's [1989]

TABLE 6
(continued)

Part C. Portuguese Sample (*n*=25)

IND2	-2.927	.246	.009	—		
IND2^2	.058	.231	.096	.087	2.214	.142
Constant	64.828	—				

Multiv. $F(2, 22)$=.855, p=.444

IND3^2	-.039	.991	.031	—		
IND3^2	-.006	.949	.031	.000	.010	.987
Constant	32.918	—				

Multiv. $F(2, 22)$=.538, p=.473

IND2	.562	.868				
IND3	-.807	.827	.101	—		
IND2×IND3	-.213	.200				
IND2^2	.077	.218				
IND3^2	.142	.296	.243	.142	1.120	.442
Constant	32.280	—				

Multiv. $F(5, 19)$=.838, p=.546

collectivism and social loafing scale (IND3) produced acceptable reliabilities in all three samples.

Further, unique patterns in individualism-collectivism were observed at the organizational level when compared to Hofstede's [1980] results at the societal level. Hofstede found the U.S. to be the most individualistic society, followed by South Africa and Portugal. However, if the summated scores for individualism-collectivism at the organizational level (IND2) are averaged for each country, U.S. organizations are the most individualistic (with a score of 25.5 on a 40-point scale), but only nominally more so than those in Portugal (26.05) and South Africa (26.1). This finding might suggest a fairly universal tendency for formal organizations to have a collectivizing impact on the attitudes and behaviors of employees.

The results also suggest that individualism-collectivism is a relevant factor for further understanding the entrepreneurial behavior of firms. Using exploratory measures, initial support was provided for a curvilinear relationship between these variables. In both the U.S. and South Africa, it appears that entrepreneurship declines the more collectivism is emphasized. However, it also appears that there may be dysfunctionally high levels of individualism, at least from the standpoint of fostering entrepreneurship. The failure to find the hypothesized relationships within the Portuguese sample may have been due to sample size limitations. However, an alternative explanation might be that Portugal was one of the most collectivist societies in terms of Hofstede's scale, and such a strong societal orientation (at least at the collectivistic end of the continuum) complicates the relationship between organizational culture and entrepreneurship.

84   JOURNAL OF INTERNATIONAL BUSINESS STUDIES, FIRST QUARTER 1994

The major implications of these findings are twofold. First, corporate executives must recognize and proactively manage this dimension of culture. Because of its strategic implications, managers should be aware of the extent to which reward and evaluation systems, administrative policies and procedures, hiring and firing practices, decisionmaking processes, the organization structure, communication systems, and executive behavior reinforce the individual versus the collective. Of course, it must be recognized that this study has not definitely established the direction of causality, because it could be argued that higher levels of entrepreneurship lead to individualism or even that they are both covariates with some independent underlying cause. Yet, much of the extant literature on entrepreneurship stresses the vital and causal role of a dedicated, visionary champion. Further research of a causal nature needs to be undertaken to culturally cross-validate the relevant measurement scales and subsequently specify the exact nature of these relationships.

Second, firms should exercise some caution in completely abandoning the individual and embracing the collective, in spite of conventional wisdom to the contrary. Teams and groups are invaluable in modern organizations, and play a critical role in accomplishing corporate entrepreneurship. However, these findings suggest that individuals matter, and must be given the incentive and autonomy to identify opportunities and champion innovative products and processes.

The key is to balance the need for individual initiative with the spirit of cooperation and group ownership of innovation. This balance occurs over the entrepreneurial process, not all at once, and as micro-level innovation evolves into macro-level organizational change. Individuals are needed to provide the vision, unwavering commitment, and internal salesmanship without which nothing would be accomplished. But as the process unfolds, the entrepreneur requires teams of people with unique skills and resources. These teams may be formal or ad hoc, but their membership is likely to be fluid as people join or depart depending on project requirements. Also, the members of the team do more than provide functional expertise or perform specific tasks. They modify and adapt the innovation as new and unanticipated obstacles arise, all the while being kept on track and spurred on by the individual champion. And, in the final analysis, it is this amorphous group that takes ownership of, and credit for, the end-product.

Whether or not purely team or collective entrepreneurship is possible, as suggested by Reich [1987] and Kanter [1989], remains subject to question. Such a model might apply when the innovation in question involves highly complex, scientific and technological breakthroughs from teams of physicists, chemists, computer engineers, and others.

These findings also serve to provide direction in terms of further research. Additional progress is needed in the area of scale development. Some have proposed that individualism-collectivism may not be merely a continuum, but is multidimensional [Hui and Triandis 1986; Triandis et al. 1988]. The relevant dimensions must be identified, and may be corporate- culture specific. In addition, research efforts should be directed at identifying the organizational policies, procedures, systems, and structural forms that reflect an individualistic versus collectivistic orientation. This also suggests a need for replications of the current study that control for type of industry and organization. Also useful would be research to determine if the appropriateness of a more individualistic or collectivistic orientation is dependent upon the nature and type of innovation sought (e.g., discontinuous versus incremental, new product versus process). Evidence is also needed concerning other causes of entrepreneurial behavior in organizations, including other dimensions of culture, and how these factors interact with the individualism-collectivism construct.

Finally, deeper insights regarding the relationship between individualism-collectivism at the societal and organizational levels are needed. While these results indicate considerably more variability at the societal than the organizational level, the extent to which one is influenced by the other is not apparent. In addition, efforts should be devoted to determining whether individualism-collectivism at the societal level impacts organizational entrepreneurship, and how entrepreneurship is affected when societal and organizational cultures differ significantly from one another. Here, additional research utilizing a larger number of countries would allow one to mask the effects of other external environmental factors such as level of economic development, stability of the economic and political system and other confounding factors.

REFERENCES

Albanese, Robert & David D. Van Fleet. 1985. Rational behavior in groups: The free-riding tendency. *Academy of Management Review*, 10 (April): 244-55.

Balkin, David B. & James W. Logan. 1988. Reward policies that support entrepreneurship. *Compensation and Benefits Review*, 20: 18-25.

Beck, Brenda E. F. & Larry F. Moore. 1985. Linking the host culture to organizational variables. In P. J. Frost et al., *Organizational culture*. Newbury Park, Calif.: Sage Publishers.

Birch, David L. 1981. Who creates jobs? *The Public Interest*, 65: 62-82.

_____ & Stephen McCracken. 1982. *The small business share of job creation: Lessons learned from the use of longitudinal files*. Washington, D.C.: Small Business Administration.

Brandt, Steven. 1986. *Entrepreneuring in established companies*. Homewood, Ill.: Dow Jones-Irwin.

Breer, Paul E. & Edwin A. Locke. 1965. *Task experience as a source of attitudes*. Homewood, Ill.: Dorsey Press.

Brittan, Arthur. 1977. *The privatized world*. London: Routledge & Kegan Paul.

Brockhaus, Robert H. 1982. The psychology of the entrepreneur. In C. Kent, D. Sexton & K. Vesper, editors, *Encyclopedia of entrepreneurship*. Englewood Cliffs, N.J.: Prentice-Hall.

Burgelman, Robert A. & Leonard R. Sayles. 1986. *Inside corporate innovation: Strategy, structure, and managerial skills*. New York: Free Press.

Carland, James W., Frank Hoy, William R. Boulton & Joann A. Carland. 1984. Differentiating entrepreneurs from small business owners: A conceptualization. *Academy of Management Review*, (April): 358.

Collins, Orvis F. & David G. Moore. 1964. *The enterprising man*. East Lansing, Mich.: Board of Trustees of Michigan State University.

Cornwall, Jeffrey R. & Baron Perlman. 1990. *Organizational entrepreneurship*. Homewood, Ill.: Irwin.

Covin, Jeffrey G. & Dennis P. Slevin. 1989. Strategic management of small firms in hostile and benign environments. *Strategic Management Journal*, 10 (January).

Dansereau, Fred. 1989. A multiple level of analysis perspective on the debate about individualism. *American Psychologies*, 44: 959-60.

Davies, Robert J. & Nan Weiner. 1985. A cultural perspective on the study of industrial relations. In P. J. Frost et al., *Organizational culture*. Newbury Park, Calif.: Sage Publishers.

Deal, Terrence E. & Allan A. Kennedy. 1982. *Corporate cultures: The rites and rituals of corporate life*. Reading, Mass.: Addison-Wesley.

Douglas, Susan & Bernard Dubois. 1977. Looking at the cultural environment for international marketing opportunities. *Columbia Journal of World Business*, (Winter): 47-56.

Drucker, Peter. 1985. *Innovation and entrepreneurship: Practice and principles*. New York: Harper & Row.

Earley, P. Christopher. 1989. Social loafing and collectivism: A comparison of the United States and the People's Republic of China. *Administrative Science Quarterly*, 34: 565-81.

Edwards, Allen L. 1987 (fourth edition). *Experimental design in psychological research*. New York: Holt, Rinehart and Winston, Inc.

Ferguson, Charles H. 1988. From the people who brought you voodoo economics. *Harvard Business Review*, 66 (May-June): 55-62.

Finn, Joseph & David Mattsson. 1978. *Multivariate analysis in educational research*. Chicago: National Educational Resources.

Frost, Peter J., Larry F. Moore, Meryl R. Louis, Craig C. Lundberg & Joanne Martin. 1985. *Organizational culture*. London: Sage Publications.

Gartner, William B. 1985. A conceptual framework for describing the phenomenon of new venture creation. *Academy of Management Review*, 10(4): 696-706.

Gilder, George. 1988. The revitalization of everything: The law of the microcosm. *Harvard Business Review*, 66 (March-April): 49-61.

Ginsberg, Allen. 1985. Measuring changes in entrepreneurial orientation following industry deregulation: The development of a diagnostic instrument. In G.B. Roberts, editor, *Proceedings: Discovering entrepreneurship*. Marietta, Ga.: U.S. Affiliate of the International Council for Small Business.

Gudykunst, William, Young-Chul C. Yoon & Tsukasa Nishida. 1987. The influence of individualism-collectivism on perceptions of communication in ingroup and outgroup relationships. *Communication Monographs*, 54: 295-306.

Halpern, Diane F. & Spencer Kagan. 1984. Sex, age, and cultural differences in individualism. *Journal of Genetic Psychology*, 145: 23-35.

Hisrich, Robert D. & Candida G. Brush. 1986. *The women entrepreneurs*. Lexington, Mass.: Lexington Books.

Ho, David Y.F. 1978. The concept of man in Mao Tse-Tung's thought. *Psychiatry*, 41: 391-402.

Hofstede, Geert. 1983. The cultural relativity of organizational practices and theories. *Journal of International Business Studies*, 14(3): 75-89.

_____. 1984. The cultural relativity of the quality of life concept. *Academy of Management Review*, 9(3): 389-98.

_____. 1980. Motivation, leadership, and organization: Do American theories apply abroad? *Organizational Dynamics*, 9(Summer): 42-63.

Hornaday, Jeffrey A. & John Aboud. 1971. Characteristics of successful entrepreneurs. *Personal Psychology*, 24: 141-53.

Hui, C. Harry. 1988. Measurement of individualism-collectivism. *Journal of Research in Personality*, 22: 17-36.

_____ & Harry C. Triandis. 1986. Individualism-collectivism: A study of cross-cultural researchers. *Journal of Cross-Cultural Psychology*, 17: 225-48.

Hui, C. Harry & Marcelo J. Villareal. 1989. Individualism-collectivism and psychological needs, their relationships in two cultures. *Journal of Cross-Cultural Psychology*, 20(3): 310-23.

Jennings, Daniel F. & James R. Lumpkin. 1989. Functionally modeling corporate entrepreneurship: An empirical integrative analysis. *Journal of Management*, 15(3): 485-502.

Jennings, Daniel F. & Dean M. Young. 1990. An empirical comparison between objective and subjective measures of the product innovation domain of corporate entrepreneurship. *Entrepreneurship: Theory and Practice*, 15(1): 53-66.

Jones, Gareth. 1984. Task visibility, free riding, and shirking: Explaining the effect of structure and technology on employee behavior. *Academy of Management Review*, 9(October): 684-95.

Kanter, Rosabeth M. 1983. *The change masters: Innovation and entrepreneurship in the American corporation.* New York: Simon & Schuster.

———. 1989. *When giants learn to dance.* New York: Simon & Schuster.

Kao, John J. 1989. *Entrepreneurship, creativity and organization.* Englewood Cliffs, N.J.: Prentice-Hall.

Kaplan, Roger. 1987. Entrepreneurship reconsidered: The antimanagement bias. *Harvard Business Review*, 65 (May-June): 84-89.

Kay, Neil M. 1979. *The innovating firm.* London: Macmillan.

Kets de Vries, Manfred F.R. 1977. The entrepreneurial personality: A person at the crossroads. *Journal of Management Studies*, 14: 34-57.

Khandwalla, P. N. 1977. *The design of organizations.* New York: Harcourt, Brace & Jovanovich.

Kilmann, Ralph H. 1989. *Managing beyond the quick fix.* San Francisco, Calif.: Jossey-Bass.

——— & M.J. Saxton. 1983. *Kilmann-Saxton culture-gap survey.* Tuxedo, N.Y.: Organizational Design Consultants Inc.

Knight, Russell M. 1987. Corporate innovation and entrepreneurship: A Canadian study. *Journal of Product Innovations Management*, 4(4): 32-41.

Kotter, John P. & James L. Heskett. 1991. *Corporate culture and performance.* New York: Free Press.

Leung, Kwok & Michael H. Bond. 1982. How Chinese and Americans reward task related contributions: A preliminary study. *Psychologia*, 25: 32-39.

MacMillan, Ian C. 1983. The politics of new venture management. *Harvard Business Review*, 61(November-December): 8-12.

———, Zenas Block & Narasimha P.N. Subba. 1986. Corporate venturing: Alternatives, obstacles encountered and experience effects. *Journal of Business Venturing*, 1(2): 121-32.

Maidique, Modesto. 1980. Entrepreneurs, champions, and technological innovation. *Sloan Management Review*, 21(2): 59-76.

Mancuso, Joseph R. 1974. What it takes to be an entrepreneur. *Journal of Small Business Management*, 12(4): 16-22.

Martin, Michael J. 1984. *Managing technological innovation and entrepreneurship.* Reston, Va.: Reston Publishing.

McClelland, David C. 1987. Characteristics of successful entrepreneurs. *Journal of Creative Behavior*, 21: 219-33.

Miles, Morgan P. & Danny R. Arnold. 1991. The relationship between marketing orientation and entrepreneurial orientation. *Entrepreneurship Theory and Practice*, 15(4): 49-65.

Miller, Danny & Peter H. Friesen. 1983. Innovation in conservative and entrepreneurial firms: Two models of strategic momentum. *Strategic Management Journal*, 3: 1-25.

Mitroff, Ian I. 1988. *Business not as usual.* San Francisco, Calif.: Jossey-Bass.

Moore, Carol F. 1986. Understanding entrepreneurial behavior. In J.A. Pearce & R.B. Robinson, editors, *Academy of Management best papers*, Forty-Sixth Annual Meeting, Academy of Management, Chicago.

Morris, Michael H. & Pamela S. Lewis. 1991. Entrepreneurship as a significant factor in social quality of life. *Journal of Business Research*, 23(1): 21-36.

Morris, Michael H. & Gordon W. Paul. 1987. The relationship between entrepreneurship and marketing in established firms. *Journal of Business Venturing*, 2(5): 247-59.

88 JOURNAL OF INTERNATIONAL BUSINESS STUDIES, FIRST QUARTER 1994

Morris, Michael H. & J. Donald Trotter. 1990. Institutionalizing entrepreneurship in a large company: A case study at AT&T. *Industrial Marketing Management*, 19(2): 131-39.

Nunnally, Jum C. 1978. *Psychometric theory*. New York: McGraw-Hill.

Olson, Mancur. 1971. *The logic of collective action*. Cambridge, Mass.: Harvard University Press.

Parsons, Talcott & Edward A. Shils. 1958. *Toward a general theory of action*. Cambridge, Mass.: Harvard Press.

Peters, Thomas. 1987. *Thriving on chaos*. New York: Alfred A. Knopf.

_____ & Robert Waterman. 1982. *In search of excellence*. New York: Harper and Row.

Peterson, Rein. 1988. Understanding and encouraging entrepreneurship internationally. *Journal of Small Business Management*, (April): 1-7.

Pinchot, Gifford, III. 1985. *Intrepreneuring*. New York: Harper and Row.

Quinn, James B. 1985. Managing innovations: Controlled chaos. *Harvard Business Review*, 63(May-June): 73-84.

Reich, Robert B. 1987. Entrepreneurship reconsidered: The team as hero. *Harvard Business Review*. 65(May-June): 77-83.

Reynolds, Paul D. & S. Freeman. 1987. *1986 Pennsylvania new firm study, Vol. two: New firm contributions to Pennsylvania*. Philadelphia, Penn.: University of Pennsylvania, Wharton School.

Rosenbaum, Milton E., Danny L. Moore, John L. Cotton, Michael S. Cook, Rex H. Hieser, M. Niki Shovan & Morris J. Gray. 1980. Group productivity and process: Pure and mixed reward structures and task interdependence. *Journal of Personality and Social Psychology*, 39(4): 626-42.

Rothwell, Robert. 1980. Policies in industry. In D. Pavitt, editor, *Technical innovation and British economic performance*, 300-301. London: Tavistock.

Sampson, Edward. 1988. The debate on individualism: Indigenous psychologies of the individual and their role in personal and societal functioning. *American Psychologist*, 43: 15-22.

Schumpeter, Joseph. 1950. *Capitalism, socialism, and democracy*. New York: Harper and Row.

Schwartz, Shalom H. 1990. Individualism-collectivism: Critique and proposed refinements. *Journal of Cross-Cultural Psychology*, 21(2): 139-57.

Sexton, Donald L. 1980. Characteristics and role demands of successful entrepreneurs. Paper presented to the Academy of Management, Detroit, Michigan.

_____ & Bowman, Nancy B. 1986. Validation of personality index: Comparative psychological characteristics analysis of female entrepreneurs, managers, entrepreneurship students and business students. In Ronstadt et al., editors, *Frontiers of entrepreneurship research*. Wellesley, Mass.: Babson College.

Shapero, Albert. 1982. Inventors and entrepreneurs: Their roles in innovation. WPS 82-35. Columbus, Ohio: Ohio State University, College of Administrative Science.

Sinetar, Marie. 1985. Entrepreneurs, chaos, and creativity—Can creative people really survive large company structure? *Sloan Management Review*, (Winter): 57-62.

Smith, Neil R. & John B. Miner. 1983. Type of entrepreneur, type of firm and managerial motivation: Implications for organizational life cycle theory. *Strategic Management Journal*, 4: 325-40.

Souder, William. 1987. *Managing new product innovations*. Lexington, Mass.: D.C. Heath and Company.

Spence, Janet T. 1985. Achievement American style: The rewards and costs of individualism. *American Psychologist*, 40: 1285-95.

Steele, Lowell. 1983. Managers' misconceptions about technology. *Harvard Business Review*, (November-December): 47-54.

Stefflre, Volney. 1985. Organizational obstacles to innovation: A formulation of the problem. *Journal of Product Innovation Management*, 2: 3-11.

Stevenson, Howard & J. Carlos. 1990. A paradigm of entrepreneurship: Entrepreneurial management. *Strategic Management Journal*, 11: 17-27.

Stevenson, Howard, Michael J. Roberts & Irving Grousbeck. 1989 (third edition). *New business ventures and the entrepreneur*. Homewood, Ill.: Irwin Publishing.

Stewart, Alex. 1989. *Team entrepreneurship*. Newbury Park, Calif.: Sage Publications.

Sundbo, Jon. 1991. Strategic paradigms as a frame of explanation of innovations: A theoretical synthesis. *Entrepreneurship and Regional Development*, 3: 159-73.

Triandis, Harry C., Kwok Leung, Marcelo J. Villareal & Frank Clack. 1985. Allocentric vs. idiocentric tendencies: Convergent and discriminant validation. *Journal of Research in Personality*, 19: 395-415.

Triandis, Harry C., Richard Brislin & C. Harry Hui. 1988. Cross-cultural training across the individualism-collectivism divide. *International Journal of Intercultural Relations*, 12: 269-89.

Tropman, John E. & Gersh Morningstar. 1989. *Entrepreneurial systems for the 1990s*. Westport, Conn.: Quorum Books.

Tse, David K., John K. Wong & Chin Tiong Tan. 1988. Towards some standardized cross-cultural consumption values. *Advances in Consumer Research*, 15: 387-95.

Verma, Jyoti. 1985. The ingroup and its relevance to individual behaviour: A study of collectivism and individualism. *Psychologia*, 28: 173-81.

Wagner, John & Michael K. Moch. 1986. Individualism-collectivism: Concept and measure. *Group & Organization Studies*, 11(3): 280-304.

Waterman, Robert H. 1987. *The renewal factor: How the best get and keep the competitive edge*. New York: Bantam Books.

Wheeler, Ladd, Harry T. Reis & Michael H. Bond. 1989. Collectivism-individualism in everyday social life: The middle kingdom and the melting pot. *Journal of Personality and Social Psychology*, 57: 79-86.

Whyte, William H., Jr. 1956. *The organization man?* New York: Simon & Schuster.

Wortman, Max S. 1987. Entrepreneurship: An integrating typology and evaluation of the empirical research in the field. *Journal of Management*, 13(2): 259-79.

Yatani, Choichiro. 1989. American national character and Japanese management: Individualism and work ethic. *Organization Development Journal*, 12 (Spring): 75-79.

Zahra, Shaker A. 1986. A canonical analysis of corporate entrepreneurship antecedents and impact on performance. In Pearce & Robinson, editors, *Best paper proceedings*, 71-75. 46th Annual Meeting, Academy of Management.

[31]

ELSEVIER

INTERNATIONAL CORPORATE ENTREPRENEURSHIP AND FIRM PERFORMANCE: THE MODERATING EFFECT OF INTERNATIONAL ENVIRONMENTAL HOSTILITY

SHAKER A. ZAHRA
Georgia State University, Atlanta, Georgia

DENNIS M. GARVIS
Washington & Lee University, Lexington, Virginia

EXECUTIVE SUMMARY

Globalization of the world economy has encouraged U.S. companies to leverage their resources and skills by expanding into existing or new foreign markets. U.S. companies have also acquired new capabilities by locating important functional activities overseas, and joining with foreign partners in new markets through alliances and joint ventures. These opportunities, however, are tempered by the constraints imposed by the competitive forces that exist in international environments. Aggressive government intervention, technological changes, and fierce local rivalries all contribute to hostile international environments for U.S. firms' global expansion.

Success in global business operations requires resourcefulness and entrepreneurial risk taking. The

Address correspondence to Dr. S.A. Zahra, Department of Management, J. Mack Robinson College of Business Administration, Georgia State University, Atlanta, GA 30303, (404) 651-2894, E-mail: Szahra @gsu.edu

We acknowledge with gratitude the supportive comments of two anonymous *JBV* reviewers, Brett Matherne and Patricia H. Zahra. An earlier version of this paper appeared in the 1998 *Academy of Management Best Papers' Proceedings*. The financial support of the Beebe Institute to the first author in data collection is also appreciated.

Journal of Business Venturing **15**, 469–492
0883-9026/00/$–see front matter
PII S0883-9026(99)00036-1

activities of U.S. companies in foreign markets, therefore, provide a unique opportunity to examine the effects of international corporate entrepreneurship (ICE) efforts on company performance. ICE is defined as the sum of a company's efforts aimed at innovation, proactiveness, and risk taking. These efforts offer an important means of revitalizing and renewing established companies and improving their performance. Few studies have empirically examined the effects of ICE activities on companies' financial performance.

This study used data from 98 U.S. companies to: (1) determine the impact of ICE efforts on firm performance, and (2) explore the moderating effect that the perceived hostility of the international environment has on the relationship between ICE and company performance. The results showed that ICE was positively associated with a firm's overall profitability and growth as well as its foreign profitability and growth. Those firms that aggressively pursued ICE in international environments with higher levels of hostility had higher return on assets (ROA) but did not achieve significantly higher levels of growth. However, as hostility in the international environment continued to intensify, ROA rose and then fell as companies increased their ICE activities. Thus, there was a point of diminishing returns to a company's aggressive pursuit of ICE under excessive environmental hostility.

The results highlight both the rewards and risks of pursuing ICE. Companies benefit from ICE activities by achieving higher overall performance as well as foreign profits and growth in revenue. However, the aggressive pursuit of ICE does not always guarantee superior performance. Our results show that the payoff from ICE is moderated by executives' perceptions of the hostility of their firm's international business environment. Our findings highlight the importance of ICE for organizational success, both overall and in foreign markets. Yet, the results compellingly suggest that there are upper limits to the potential gains a firm achieves from its aggressive pursuit of ICE when the international environment in which it competes is hostile. © 2000 Elsevier Science Inc.

INTRODUCTION

The globalization of the world economy has created countless opportunities for U.S. companies to grow and achieve profitability. Faced with abundant opportunities, some U.S. companies have sought to creatively leverage their resources and skills in foreign markets. Confronted by strong global rivals, companies have also acquired capabilities from several foreign sources (Leavy 1997). For example, seeking to increase their innovations companies such as Colgate-Palmolive and Intel have built research and development (R&D) activities in multiple centers around the globe (Chiesa 1996). Other companies such as Chrysler, Hewlett-Packard, Mattel, and 3M have built production facilities in several overseas locations to capitalize on local talents (Ferdows 1997) and incorporate this knowledge in new products for customers in foreign markets (Levy and Dunning 1993).

Success in global business operations requires creativity, ingenuity, and calculated risk taking (Bossak and Nagashima 1997), because domestic strengths do not always guarantee success in foreign markets (Hu 1995; Vlasic 1998). Consequently, when expanding internationally, U.S. companies have explored new models of production, management, R&D, human resources, and marketing systems (Bannon 1998; Porter 1990). They have also learned and utilized different skills from those that have been used in their home markets (Smart 1996; Williamson 1997). Developing and exploiting these capabilities requires experimentation and risk taking (McGrath, MacMillan and Venkataraman 1995; Shama 1995). Entrepreneurial activities are, therefore, closely linked to firms' global operations (Dean, Thibodeaux, Beyerlein, Ebrahimi and Molina 1993).

The continuing globalization of business provides an important opportunity to study U.S. companies' entrepreneurial activities in international markets. Even though the motivations for, and effects of, these global activities have been explored from economic and organizational perspectives, rarely have they been viewed through an entrepreneurial lens. This paper fills this gap in the literature by examining U.S. firms' corporate entrepreneurship (CE) activities in international markets. Even though entrepreneurial activities might permeate every aspect of a firm's operations (Pinchot 1985; Zahra 1991), this study focuses on CE undertaken primarily in a company's international operations. We refer to these activities as international corporate entrepreneurship (ICE).

This study views ICE as the sum of a company's innovation, risk taking, and proactiveness (Miller 1983; Covin and Slevin 1989; Zahra 1991). These activities usually seek to increase the firm's innovativeness, adaptation, and agile strategic responses to changes in the external environment. Innovation refers to the firm's ability to create new products and successfully introduce them to the market. It also indicates the company's commitment to process and organizational innovations (Zahra 1993). Proactiveness shows a fie fie fie fie fie fie firm's aggressive pursuit of market opportunities and a strong emphasis on being among the very first to undertake innovations in its industry. Risk taking is defined as the firm's disposition to support innovative projects (e.g., international ventures), even when the payoff from these activities is uncertain. Collectively, these activities can enhance the company's ability to recognize and exploit market opportunities well ahead of its competitors.

Entrepreneurial activities can renew established companies (Kuratko, Montagno and Hornsby 1990; Pinchot 1985; Stopford and Baden-Fuller 1994). Renewal is usually achieved through innovation and venturing activities (Guth and Ginsberg 1990) that give the firm access to different skills, capabilities, and resources (McGrath et al. 1995). Innovation generates new products, processes, and organizational systems that set the company apart from its rivals as it expands its international operations (Hitt, Hoskisson, and Kim 1997). Innovation also revises the firm's knowledge base, allowing it to develop new competitive approaches, which can be exploited in new foreign markets and achieve growth and profitability (Hitt et al. 1997; Hu 1995).

Venturing activities emphasize the creation of new businesses by entering new foreign markets or expanding in existing ones (Bannon 1998; Bossak and Nagashimi 1997; Shama 1995). A firm, therefore, can revise its business base by entering new economic regions or foreign markets, capitalizing on the differences in the resources that may exist in various locations (Porter 1990). International venturing can also enhance a firm's performance by using its existing knowledge and resources in new markets, as happened when many U.S. corporations successfully entered markets in Eastern Europe and the Commonwealth of Independent States (Shama 1995). International venturing can also expand the firm's knowledge base (Schlender 1997), which increases the innovativeness of a firm's products and strategy (Stopford and Baden-Fuller 1994). ICE, through international venturing, can thus renew a company by improving its ability to compete and take risks by redefining its business concept, reorganizing its operations, and introducing system-wide innovations (Miller 1983).

Global business activities clearly offer an attractive setting in which to study entrepreneurship. However, while scholars have recognized the importance of entrepreneurial efforts in foreign markets and have called for research on this issue (e.g., Guth and Ginsberg 1990), only a few empirical studies have specifically examined ICE. One reason for this omission may be researchers' preoccupation with defining the domain of corporate entrepreneurship and establishing its contributions to company performance.

Another reason is the difficulty of obtaining data on ICE. Consequently, little is known today about the effect of ICE on company performance. This study addresses this gap in the literature by exploring the link between ICE and a firm's performance as well as its performance in international operations (hereafter "foreign performance"). Further, given that environmental conditions may vary dramatically between the firm's domestic and foreign markets (Agrawal and Ramaswamy 1992; Miller 1993; Williamson 1997), the study also explores how these differences affect the ICE-performance relationship.

This study extends prior research in two ways. First, it responds to prior studies' call to broaden the research lens beyond domestic CE by examining ICE activities (Guth and Ginsberg 1990). Second, prior research has found significant relationships between the environment, CE, and firm performance (e.g., Covin and Slevin 1989, 1991; Zahra 1993). To date, however, researchers have relied almost exclusively on measures of CE and competitive environments within the firm's domestic operations, failing to include its foreign operations, performance, or external environment. In contrast, this study focuses on the international aspects of CE as well as the firm's environment and explores the moderating effect of the external environment. The results can clarify the effect of ICE on a company's performance under different environmental conditions.

The following section of the paper discusses the theoretical links between ICE and a company's performance, with an emphasis on delineating the domain of ICE. Once this discussion has been completed, attention will focus on the relationships between a firm's ICE and a company's performance. This discussion and related hypotheses will also highlight the moderating role of a firm's international business environment on the ICE-company performance relationship. The next section of the paper will then describe the data and analytical methods used to test the hypotheses. After presenting the results, the paper will discuss the study's key findings and their implications for future research and managerial action.

THEORY AND HYPOTHESES

The relationship between a firm's international activities and company performance has been the subject of much discussion in the literature (Sullivan 1994). Using British (Grant, Jammine, and Thomas 1988), German (Buhner 1987), and U.S. data (Geringer, Beamish, and deCosta 1989; Hennart 1991; Kim and Hwang, and Burgers 1989, 1993), for example, researchers have sought to determine the sources of competitive advantages firms gain from internationalizing their operations. The present study examines entrepreneurial activities that occur in a firm's operations (Dean et al. 1993; Guth and Ginsberg 1990). It suggests that, when undertaken in a firm's international operations, entrepreneurial activities can give a company a competitive advantage in existing or new markets (Miller 1983; Stopford and Baden-Fuller 1994; Zahra and Covin 1995).

Innovation

Entrepreneurial activities influence a company's performance by increasing its commitment to innovation (Miller 1983; Lumpkin and Dess 1996) by offering innovative products or processes. ICE can therefore redefine the way the firm competes or redirecting the scope of its operations towards new segments (Zahra 1991). Established companies such as Chrysler (Vlasic 1998), General Electric (Smart 1996), and Mattel (Bannon 1998) have used this strategy in pursuing global market opportunities. These companies have created innovative products to target new market segments and enter new foreign markets, a process that has renewed their operations and improved their profitability (Baden-Fuller and Stopford 1994). Significant advantages may also be gained from diffusing product and process innovations developed in various national markets throughout a multinational firm's network (Bartlett and Ghoshal 1989).

Currently, the nature of the relationship between international activities and firm performance is far from clear (Dess, Gupta, Hennart and Hill 1995). Prior studies, however, offer some insights into this relationship. For example, Morck and Yeung (1991) found that the interaction of internationalization and a firm's R&D investments are significantly related to company performance, whereas internationalization alone was not. Hitt, Hoskisson, and Ireland (1994) also theorized that expansion into foreign markets results in greater returns from a firm's innovations while reducing the risk of business failure. In essence, internationalization increases a firm's ability to sustain the advantages it gains from innovation before competitors can overcome them. Hitt et al. (1994) also suggested that the presence of product and process innovations in international firms represents an ideal combination of strategic choices that generate optimal financial performance. Several empirical studies have also found that innovation in international operations can enhance a firm's overall performance (e.g., Franko 1989; Kimura 1989).

Innovation can also lead to the development of key capabilities that can improve a firm's performance (Teece, Pisano, and Shuen 1997). The development of these capabilities is intimately linked to the countries in which the firm conducts its operations. Kogut (1991) suggests that competitive capabilities that result in performance differences do not always cross national borders, a factor which explains why firms invest in developing foreign markets as a means of gaining access to sources of innovations (Shan and Hamilton 1991). Florida (1997) also notes that firms increasingly cross international borders to pursue innovation and capitalize on the learning to be gained from local markets. Porter (1990) also argues that multinational firms can draw upon the advantages embedded in foreign countries by diversifying across borders. Access to diverse sources of knowledge can provide firms with significant learning opportunities that intensify product and process innovations. Innovation generates products, goods, processes, services, and systems that can be used to meet customer needs and build a strong international market position (Bannon 1998). Innovation can thus improve the firm's profitability and fuel its growth.

Venturing

ICE may take place also in new foreign markets as the firm utilizes its resources and capabilities in ways that create new revenue streams, as happened when several U.S. companies entered newly opened markets in the former Soviet Bloc (Shama 1995), Middle-Eastern (Dean et al. 1993), and Latin American countries. As these firms gain experience in these markets, they can use their capabilities in building new competitive positions and expand in other foreign markets (McGrath et al. 1995). U.S. companies have gained considerable skills from locating some of their manufacturing operations overseas and then creatively using the knowledge gained from foreign markets to widen their global reach.

A firm may pursue ICE to learn about and enter new foreign markets, and establish gateways for future entry. It can also use its ICE activities proactively to preempt entry by its future rivals, thereby creating a competitive advantage. Porter (1990) suggests that preemptive entry into foreign markets can erect strong mobility barriers that deter or minimize subsequent entry. Mascarenhas (1992a, 1997) concludes that firms that are first entrants have a higher rate of survival in foreign markets. These "first mover" companies can proactively set the rules of competition by setting product and technological standards, investing heavily in establishing and controlling distribution channels, and promoting their products in ways that reduce switching to subsequently entering rival brands. First movers also engage in significant product, process, and organizational innovations that strengthen their market positions and further enhance their profitability (Bannon 1998). For those firms that enter the market later, ICE can also be useful in revising industry boundaries as firms attempt to change the rules of competitive engagement. Late entrants can also use skills and resources that differ significantly from those of the early entrants and then proceed to claim key portions of the market. Some U.S. companies have successfully followed this approach in dethroning prominent multinational corporations in several foreign markets (Dean et al. 1993). These firms have also aggressively targeted new market segments and then shielded them from rivals through product and process innovations (Williamson 1997).

The above-mentioned benefits from venturing into foreign markets are consistent with theories that depict internationalization as a process characterized by various stages of growing commitment (Johanson and Vahlne 1977). The knowledge gained at one stage can profoundly influence a future international expansion, as firms experiment, take risks and learn. International venturing can broaden a firm's knowledge base through learning about new markets, customers, cultures, technologies, and innovation systems, which can enhance a firm's performance. Of course, the benefits from international venturing are not unidirectional. The firm can transfer its best practices from its international operations back to its home market, which further increases the firm's ability to innovate. Companies that are proactive in foreign markets also have available to them a broader base of skills and knowledge which they can exploit in building a distinctive competence (Kogut 1991).

Proactiveness

Some companies undertake ICE to challenge the competition and revise the rules of rivalry in their industries. Proactive ICE indicates a company's determination to pursue promising opportunities, rather than merely responding to competitors' moves (Miller 1983). Morck and Yeung (1991) suggest that the interaction of a firm's proactiveness and internationalization is significantly associated with performance, whereas internationalization alone is not significant.

Proactive ICE, such as pioneering or first entry, can improve company performance. Kimura (1989), for example, has concluded that first entrants enjoyed significant strategic advantages in international markets. Mascarenhas (1992a,b) has also found that oil equipment companies that were first to enter international markets enjoyed important first-mover advantages derived from the barriers erected through technical leadership, resource commitments, and buyer switching costs. First-movers also survived longer in their foreign markets than late entrants. Mascarenhas (1992b) also uncovered a positive relationship between the timing of a firm's market entry and its market share. Pioneering in several foreign markets concurrently, rather than sequentially, was also positively associated with market survival. Consequently, proactiveness in international markets can be conducive to successful firm performance. The above discussion suggests the following hypothesis:

H1: ICE will be positively associated with a firm's financial performance.

Hostility of the International Environment as a Moderator of the ICE-Performance Relationships

Research also suggests that contextual factors can affect the success of the firm's entrepreneurial activities (Covin and Slevin 1991; Zahra 1991). Environmental hostility, in particular, can have a significant moderating influence on the CE-performance relationship (Zahra 1993; Zahra and Covin 1995). This study extends the literature by testing the effects of a firm's international environment on the ICE-company performance relationship. Although the conditions of the home market often influence the firm's success in international operations (Hitt et al. 1994), this study posits that the perceived characteristics of its international environment, especially hostility, will significantly moderate the relationship between ICE and performance.

Environmental hostility indicates unfavorable external forces for a firm's business. Unfavorable environmental conditions result from radical industry changes, intense regulatory burdens placed on the industry, or fierce rivalry among competitors (Werner, Brouthers, and Brouthers 1996). Hostility also results from perceived competitive-, market-, and product-related uncertainties (Dess and Beard 1984). Perceived hostility in the firm's international markets also arises from other sources (Agrawal and Ramaswamy 1992), including changing demand conditions and radical innovations that render the firm's basic technology obsolete. Rivalry, which can cause hostility, reflects the perceived nature of competitive dynamics (Porter 1980), the number of companies competing in an industry, and the intensity of competition in an industry (Grant 1995). Firms, therefore, must devote scarce resources to managing such an unfavorable environment in order to ensure the achievement of their organizational goals (Zahra 1993).

International markets, in general, have been described as hostile (Hitt et al. 1997). One reason is that the external environments firms face in competing internationally are much different in that companies must address diverse and inconsistent laws, national cultures, and industry forces (Rosenzweig and Singh 1991). A firm, therefore, needs to invest heavily in understanding local conditions (Bartlett and Ghoshal 1989; Doz and Prahalad 1987), often for years without any guarantees of success (Vlasic 1998).

Governments' actions and policies in protecting national markets can also increase perceived environmental hostility. U.S. firms venturing into Taiwan, Korea, or Singapore have had to contend with the fact that governments in these countries have used multiple ways to support and protect their country's producers (The Flexible Tiger, *The Economist,* January 3, 1998). Likewise, some European governments have enacted laws that favor their own domestic producers, causing U.S. companies to work harder at finding new sources of competitive advantage (Smart 1996).

This study expects environmental hostility to significantly moderate the ICE-performance relationship. Several factors support this anticipated relationship. Specifically, given the skills and resources necessary to engage in ICE, firms may well be prepared to address problems presented by these environments, as found in some prior research (Miller and Friesen 1984; Covin and Slevin 1989; Zahra 1993; Zahra and Covin 1995). Furthermore, entrepreneurship is a logical means of exploiting business opportunities in hostile environments (Covin and Slevin 1989, 1991). Consequently, as perceived hostility intensifies in a firm's international markets, the payoff from ICE in the form of improved financial performance is expected to increase (Miller 1993).

However, as hostility intensifies, the profits to be gained from ICE might decline because the firm has to work harder at building a strong market position, establishing its brand name recognition, and developing customer loyalty. The firm has to accomplish these goals while addressing a multitude of technological, social, political, and economic uncertainties (Williamson 1997). Under these conditions, the cost of foreign operations can increase, leading to reduced profits, as found in past research using data from U.S. companies' domestic operations (e.g., Zahra 1993).

In an environment characterized by increasing levels of intense hostility, it also becomes more difficult to gain additional market shares. Firms also have to engage in costly innovation and advertising and marketing to protect their market positions (Grant 1995). Growth in these environments is sometimes a zero-sum game insofar as it is achieved primarily by taking market shares away from rivals (Porter 1980). U.S. firms entering South Asian markets, for example, have had to build their positions by battling local and foreign rivals (Williamson 1997), a process that has slowed down their acquisition of market shares. Entry by some U.S. companies into foreign markets has also led local politicians to enact laws and regulations that have made it increasingly difficult to achieve further expansion. Local distributors and other intermediaries were also slow to give U.S. companies access to channels of distribution, further slowing down these companies' expansion plans.

Thus, while environmental hostility may positively influence company performance, the relationship may not be linear. Prior research indicates that excessive entrepreneurship can reduce the firm's profits (Miller and Friesen 1984). As the environment becomes hostile, the payoff from ICE may decline further, as the firm must continually reconfigure its skill and resource bases. Firms that are competing in excessively hostile international environments, therefore, may realize diminishing and negative returns. Given the high costs of this strategy, combined with diminishing returns from additional market shares, increasing ICE efforts might not yield the same profit and growth outcomes achieved under low hostility (i.e., in placid environments). This discussion suggests the study's final two hypotheses:

> *H2:* The relationship between ICE and a company's performance will be moderated by international environmental hostility. Firms that pursue ICE in international environments with higher levels of hostility will have higher profits and higher growth.

> *H3:* The moderator effect of international environmental hostility on the relationship between ICE and company performance is curvilinear. Firms that over-pursue ICE in hostile international environments will generate diminishing profits and lower growth.

METHODS

Sample

To test the hypotheses, data were collected using a mail questionnaire, which was later supplemented and validated with secondary data. Initially, the names of 600 established companies competing in 20 manufacturing industries throughout the U.S were chosen. These industries were chosen because of their global business activities, using the lists developed by Carpano, Chrisman and Roth (1994) and Roth (1992). These researchers recognized that, while these industries were global in their markets and customers, they varied considerably in their international sales, stage of development, intensity of the competition, and profitability. These variations were desirable to provide a reliable test of the hypotheses.

Names and addresses of companies and their senior executives were obtained from multiple sources including *Lexis-Nexis*, most recent corporate annual reports, *Business Week 1000*, and *Fortune 500*. Initially, surveys were mailed to the chief executive officer (CEO) or the highest ranking officer of each firm, who were believed to be the most knowledgeable about their firm's overall and international operations (Carpano et al. 1994; Roth 1992; Roth and O'Donnell 1996). These individuals are informed about their company's ICE efforts (Miller 1983; Werner et al. 1996; Yeoh and Jeong 1995; Zahra 1991). Two mailings were used to ensure a high response rate. Of the 600 surveys, 23 were undeliverable. Completed responses were received from 149 companies, for a response rate of 25.82%, which compared favorably with those achieved in similar studies (e.g., Carpano et al. 1994).

A second copy of the survey questionnaire was also sent to each of the vice presidents for international operations (or equivalent) in the 149 responding companies. Completed responses, which were received from a second group of 73 managers, were significantly correlated with those of the CEOs (or other senior primary respondents) on the study's variables ($p < 0.001$), which supported inter-rater reliability.

To establish the representation of the sample, responding and non-responding companies were compared based on their age, size (full-time employee), and sales volume. T-tests showed that the two groups did not differ significantly in these three variables. The X^2 test also indicated that the association between a firm's primary industry and response to the survey was not significant. Thus, there was no significant association between industry type and participation in the survey. Similarly, when the X^2 test examined the association between company location (by state) and response to the survey, the result was not significant. T-tests also compared the first wave of respondents (those that sent their completed questionnaire in within the first two weeks) and later respondents (those that sent their replies within the third week or later). No differences were found in company age, size (full-time employees), or scores on the study's variables. These results indicated that the sample represented its population.

Measures

Data were collected from multiple sources, as follows:

1. *ICE.* A modified version of Miller's (1983) 7-item measure was used to capture the firm's ICE activities. A 5-point scale (1 = very untrue vs. 5 = very true) was used. Executives were asked to indicate the extent to which each item applied to their international operations (defined as those business activities conducted outside the U.S.) over the preceding 3-year period. Executives were also given the opportunity to indicate "not applicable" when responding to the survey. Miller's measure was used because of its prominence in prior CE studies in domestic business (e.g., Covin and Slevin 1991; Zahra 1991; Zahra and Covin 1995), international operations (e.g., Dean et al. 1993; Knight 1997), and non-U.S. companies' entrepreneurial activities (Werner et al. 1996). Previous researchers also found this measure to be reliable (Covin

and Slevin 1991; Werner et al. 1996; Zahra 1991) and valid (Knight 1997). Responses to the measure's seven items were averaged, and the mean was then used in the analysis. The ICE scale was reliable (α = 0.78).

Items for the ICE scale were: This company shows a great deal of tolerance for high risk projects; this company uses only "tried and true" procedures, systems, and methods (reverse scored); this company challenges, rather than responds to, its major competitors; this company takes bold, wide-ranging strategic actions, rather than minor changes in tactics; this company emphasizes the pursuit of long-term goals and strategies; usually, this company is the first in the industry to introduce new products to the market; and this company rewards taking calculated risks.

Four additional analyses, using data from secondary sources, were performed to validate the ICE measure. Validation data were obtained from *COMPUSTAT, Fortune 500, Global Business 1000, Global Scope,* and *Forbes.* The first analysis examined changes in the firm's diversification over a three-year period, a construct related to corporate venturing (Porter 1987). The ratio of the firm's foreign sales to its total sales was used, as has been done in past research (Buhner 1987; Geringer et al. 1989; Kim et al. 1989, 1993; Ramaswamy, Kroeck, and Renforth 1996; Sambharya 1996; Sullivan 1994; Tallman and Li 1996). The correlation between this ratio and the ICE index was positive and significant (r = 0.59, n = 65, $p < 0.001$).

The second validation analysis followed the literature by constructing an entropy measure of international diversification (Hitt et al. 1997) for a subset of firms. International diversification was a key approach to corporate venturing (Porter 1987). The change score in the entropy measure over a 3-year period was positively and significantly associated with ICE (r = 0.71, n = 53, $p < 0.001$).

The third analysis focused on measures of proactiveness, a key component of ICE (Lumpkin and Dess 1996; Miller 1983). Given that Morck and Yeung (1991) suggest that advertising is an important measure of proactiveness, a company's advertising in foreign markets was positively and significantly correlated with ICE (r = 0.57, n = 0.61, $p < 0.001$), supporting the validity of the ICE measure.

The fourth analysis focused on R&D spending in foreign markets, a measure of innovation (Morck and Yeung 1991). The 3-year average R&D score (for the firm's foreign operations) was positively and significantly correlated with ICE (r = 0.53, n = 58, $p < 0.01$), which supported the validity of the ICE measure.

2. *Hostility.* Although several indicators of perceived hostility have been used in prior research (Dess and Beard 1984), the measures developed and validated by Miller and Friesen (1984) were employed in this study. Other researchers (Covin and Covin 1990; Zahra, 1991, 1993) used variants of this measure.

Executives were asked to evaluate their foreign markets using six items: access to channels of distribution is difficult; access to capital is difficult; access to skilled labor is difficult; bankruptcy among companies in the industry is high; products become obsolete quickly; and demand for industry products is declining. Prior research that concluded that these perceptions shaped CE activities (Zahra and Covin 1995) and international business operations (Miller 1993) supported reliance on managers' perceptions of foreign market conditions. Responses to the six items were averaged, and the mean was used in the analysis. The international business environmental hostility (hereafter "IHOST") scale had a Cronbach α of 0.70.

3. *Company Performance.* The study also used the following indicators of financial performance:

3.1 Overall performance. Companies undertake ICE to improve their overall financial positions (Baden-Fuller and Stopford 1994; Pinchot 1985; Stopford and Baden-Fuller 1994). The following two indicators of overall performance, therefore, were used in this study:

3.1.1 *Return on assets (ROA)* was used because ICE activities require the redeployment of the firm's assets in innovative ways. The use of ROA to gauge the effect of ICE permitted an evaluation of a company's innovative use of its assets in foreign markets. Prior researchers have also used ROA to assess the effect of CE on a company's overall performance (Zahra 1991) and its success in foreign operations (Buhner 1987; Geringer et al. 1989; Grant 1987; Kim et al. 1989; Sambharya 1995, 1996).

ROA data were available from *COMPUSTAT* for a subset of 63 of the 98 responding companies. When the 3-year average ROA for the 63 firms was correlated with the data gathered through the survey, the correlation was positive and significant ($r = 0.84$, $p < 0.001$). This analysis supported the validity of the ROA survey data.

3.1.2 *Sales Growth* was used because ICE involves costly venturing into dynamic and growth markets. Thus, ICE might increase company sales even though profits may lag. The growth measure, therefore, gauged the firm's success in foreign venturing activities. Managers were asked to report "average annual growth (decline) in your company's sales over the past 3 years." To ensure the validity of this measure, two analyses were conducted. The first correlated managers' responses to the above question with their responses to a two-item scale that followed a 5-point response format (5 = top 20% in the industry vs. 1 = lowest 20% in the industry). Items, which covered a 3-year period, were total sales growth and net income growth. The correlation between these two items and the study's growth measured averaged 0.76 ($p < 0.001$). The second analysis used data on sales growth collected from *COMPUSTAT* for 59 of the 98 responding companies, and correlations between the *COMPUSTAT* and survey measure were significant ($r = 0.87$, $p < 0.001$), thus supporting the validity of the survey data.

3.2 Foreign Performance. As noted earlier, companies pursue ICE in foreign markets to achieve profitability (Hitt et al. 1997) and growth (Baden-Fuller and Stopford 1994; Leavy 1997). Obtaining data on foreign performance is difficult, however, because few companies are required to publicly report their international results separate from overall performance. Two measures of foreign performance were used, covering a 3-year period, as follows:

3.2.1 *Foreign Profitability*. Following the literature (Carpano et al. 1994), a firm's profitability in international operations was measured using four items with a 5-point scale. Executives rated their company's foreign operations relative to those of other companies in their industry (1 = lowest 20% in the industry vs. 5 = top 20% in the industry). Items were: return on assets, net profit margins, return on sales, and return on investment. Given that simple correlations among the four items averaged 0.83 ($p < 0.001$), responses were averaged and their mean was used in the analysis.

3.2.2 *Foreign Growth*. Companies pursue ICE to create opportunities for growth (Dean et al. 1993). Growth in international operations was measured by four items with 5-point scales. Executives rated their companies' foreign operations relative to others in their industry (1 = lowest 20% in the industry vs. 5 = top 20% in the industry). Items covered growth in: return on assets, net profit margins, return on sales, and return on investment. Given that simple correlations among these ratings averaged 0.78, the mean response on the four items was used in the analysis.

4. *Control Variables.* The study also controlled for a company's size, age, global business scope, past performance, and industry type, as follows:

4.1 *Company size* was included as a control variable because of the significant association between this variable and corporate innovation and venturing (Zahra 1993), product diversification (Sambharya 1995), and international diversification (Tallman and Li 1996). A positive relationship was expected between company size and ICE because larger firms were expected to possess the slack resources necessary for ICE activities. Size was measured by the *log* of a firm's total number of employees, which ranged from 68 to 14000.

4.2 *Company age* was included in the analysis because it influenced a firm's international operations and entrepreneurial activities (Pinchot 1985; Zahra 1991). The number of years a company has been in operation was used as a control variable.

4.3 *The scope of the firm's international operations* was measured by the number of countries in which a firm sold its products. This variable, therefore, served as a proxy of a firm's global geographic diversity. The greater the global scope of a firm's operations, the greater its opportunities to innovate, take risks, learn new skills, and explore new systems. Successful ICE ventures can also be transferred within a firm's international operations, which can further increase ICE activities (Hitt et al. 1997). International diversification can also generate the capital necessary to support large-scale R&D projects by spreading the risk and providing markets in which the firm can recoup its investments (Kobrin 1991). Finally, global geographic diversity determines the firm's overall performance (Grant 1987; Kim et al. 1989; Tallman and Li 1996). A positive relationship was expected between global scope and ICE.

4.4 *Past company performance* was included as a control variable because it affected the availability of slack resources. When a company performs well, financial slack increases and risk taking rises (Singh 1986). High past firm performance (relative to industry competitors) was expected to be positively associated with ICE. Consequently, the study asked executives to rate their companies' performance on sales growth, return on assets (ROA), and return on investment (ROI) over the preceding three-year period. A 5-point scale was used (5 = top 20% vs. 1 = lowest 20%). Average scores on the three items were used in the analyses.

4.5 *Industry type* was included because of the interindustry differences in entrepreneurial activities, levels and patterns of internationalization (Grant 1995), and opportunities for innovation (Covin and Slevin 1991; Zahra 1993, 1996). For a given industry, therefore, the average for responding firms was subtracted from each firm's score.

ANALYSIS

Table 1 provides the means and standard deviations (S.D.) for the sample. Of the 149 responding firms, 111 reported international business roles. However, missing data on the study's other variables further reduced the number of observations to 98. The 98 companies averaged 23.97 years (SD = 16.35) in age and reported having international operations in 5.21 (SD = 13.37) countries. On average, 29.44% (SD = 24.26) of companies' sales were from foreign markets. The intercorrelation matrix presented in Table 1 showed that multicolinearity was not a problem in the database.

To test the hypotheses, four moderated regression analyses (Cohen and Cohen 1983) were performed. For each of the study's dependent variables, the analysis progressed in four steps. First, to test the effect of ICE on company performance, the dependent variable (Y_{ij}) was regressed on the control variables and ICE. Model 1, therefore, was as follows: Y_{ij} = f (Control variables, ICE). Second, to test the effect of international environmental hostility on performance, Model 2 was developed by adding the measures for IHOST and an interaction term created by multiplying ICE and IHOST. Model 2 was as follows: Y_{ij} = f (Control variables, ICE, IHOST, ICE*IHOST). Third, to test the possible curvilinear relationship between ICE and company performance, Model 3 was Y_{ij} = f (Control variables, ICE, IHOST, ICE^2, $IHOST*ICE^2$). Finally, the moderator effect was analyzed by comparing the R^2s for Models 2 and 3 (Cohen and Cohen 1983). If the partial F-value associated with the change in R^2 was significant, then the moderator effect was significant. The results from these analyses are presented next.

RESULTS

ICE and Company Performance (H1)

Tables 2 and 3 present the regression results for a company's overall and foreign performance. Testing H1 required consideration of the results for Model 1 in both tables.

Table 2, which reports results for overall performance, shows that Model 1 was significant ($p < 00.001$) and explained 13% of variance in ROA. As predicted in H1, ICE was significant and positively related ($p < 0.05$) to ROA. For revenue growth, Model 1 was also significant ($p < 0.05$) and explained 11% of the variance. ICE was also significant and positively related to revenue growth ($p < 0.05$). These results supported H1.

Table 3 reports results for foreign performance. These results indicate support for H1. Model 1 for foreign profits was significant ($p < 0.05$) and explained 11% of the variance. ICE was significant and positive ($p < 0.01$). Model 1 for foreign revenue growth was also significant ($p < 0.05$), explaining 8% of the variance. ICE was also significantly and positively associated with foreign growth ($p < 0.01$). In summary, ICE was a significant and positive explanatory variable in all regression equations examining company performance.

The Moderating Effect of IHOST on the ICE-Company Performance Relationship (H2)

Testing H2 was accomplished by examining Model 2 in Tables 2 and 3. With respect to overall performance reported in Table 2, Model 2 was significant ($p < 0.01$), explaining 19% of the variance in ROA. IHOST was negatively (but not significantly) associated with ROA; this negative sign was consistent with the literature (Dess and Beard 1984; Covin and Slevin 1989). However, as predicted in H2, the interaction term ICE*IHOST was significantly and positively associated with ROA. Following Covin and Slevin (1989), this positive sign indicated that the impact of ICE on ROA was greater under higher levels of environmental hostility.

TABLE 1 Correlations among the Study's Variables (n = 98)

Variables	Ranges	Mean[a]	sd	1	2	3	4	5	6	7	8	9	10
1. ICE	1.2–4.7	2.94	1.51										
2. International E. Hostility [IHOST]	1.1–4.7	2.88	1.01	0.20									
3. Company size	1.83–4.38	2.73	2.61	−0.03	−0.02								
4. Past performance [index]	1.4–4.8	2.79	1.83	0.02	−0.09	0.15							
5. Company age	12–78	23.97	16.35	0.07	0.05	−0.13	0.18						
6. Global scope	1–43	5.17	13.37	0.11	0.16	0.16	0.02	0.11					
7. ROA [overall]	(4.2)–29.7	11.73	14.34	0.23*	−0.02	0.09	0.05	0.28*	0.15				
8. Growth in sales [overall]	(4.7)–51.3	19.88	31.24	0.29*	−0.09	0.17	0.09	0.09	0.25*	0.30*			
9. Foreign profits	(12.1)–58.2	24.43	29.61	0.31*	0.13	0.06	0.14	0.34*	0.13	0.23	0.07		
10. Foreign growth [index]	1.1–4.5	2.39	1.81	0.34*	0.07	0.12	0.14	0.25*	0.31*	0.18	0.34*	0.17	

[a] Means (unadjusted). Correlations were based on figures adjusted for industry; * ( ) indicate a loss or decline; * $p < 0.05$.

TABLE 2   Regression Results for Overall Company Performance

Variable	ROA			Revenue Growth		
Model	#1	#2	#3	#1	#2	#3
Constant	1.09	1.13	0.98	0.67	0.79	0.74
Company size	−0.07	−0.05	−0.07	−0.08	−0.05	−0.01
Company age	0.05	0.02	0.02	0.03	0.01	0.01
Past performance	0.12	0.13	0.13	0.02	0.07	0.05
Global scope	0.09	0.08	0.05	0.08	0.14	0.13
ICE	0.23*	0.29*	0.27*	0.26*	0.33*	0.33**
IHOST		−0.09	−0.04		−0.02	−0.05
ICE *IHOST		0.23*			0.28*	
ICE squared			−0.19*			−0.17*
ICE squared *IHOST			0.15			0.24*
R^2	0.13	0.19	0.21	0.11	0.15	0.18
F value	2.71**	4.05**	4.61**	2.11*	2.31*	3.81**
Change in R^2		0.06	0.02		0.04	0.03
Partial F (Change in R^2)		3.29*	2.22*		2.61*	3.22*

* $p < 0.05$; ** $p < 0.01$; *** $p < 0.001$.

The results for overall revenue growth also supported H2. Model 2 was also significant ($p < 0.05$) and had an R^2 of 15%. IHOST was negatively but insignificantly associated with revenue growth. The interaction term ICE*IHOST, however, was positively and significantly associated with revenue growth ($p < 0.05$). Thus, the positive association between ICE and revenue growth was stronger under higher international environmental hostility.

The data in Table 3 show that Model 2 was significant ($p < 0.05$), explaining 16% of the variance in foreign profitability. The interaction term ICE*IHOST was significantly and positively associated with foreign profitability ($p < 0.01$). The results for foreign revenue growth also supported H2, as Model 2 was significant ($p < 0.05$) and had an R^2 of 15%. The interaction term ICE*IHOST was positively and significantly associated

TABLE 3   Regression Results for Foreign Performance

Variable	Profits			Revenue Growth		
Model	#1	#2	#3	#1	#2	#3
Constant	0.44	0.37	0.38	0.59	0.69	0.41
Company size	0.07	0.05	0.02	0.02	0.03	0.02
Company age	−0.03	−0.01	−0.01	−0.03	−0.02	−0.01
Past performance	−0.07	−0.03	−0.01	−0.03	−0.08	0.04
Global scope	0.13	0.10	0.12	0.19*	0.20*	0.14
ICE	0.37**	0.31**	0.37**	0.34**	0.37**	0.29*
IHOST		−0.03	−0.05		−0.09	−0.04
ICE *IHOST		0.26*			0.25*	
ICE squared			−0.21*			−0.20*
ICE squared *IHOST			0.19*			0.11
R^2	0.11	0.16	0.18	0.08	0.13	0.16
F value	2.69*	2.83*	3.01**	2.19*	2.37*	3.91**
Change in R^2		0.05	0.02		0.06	0.03
Partial F (Change in R^2)		2.65*	2.17*		2.55*	3.14**

* $p < 0.05$; ** $p < 0.01$; *** $p < 0.001$.

with revenue growth ($p < 0.05$). Thus, like the results for overall performance, the positive association between ICE and foreign revenue growth was stronger under higher international environmental hostility.

In all cases, the regression equations including interaction terms used to test H2 explained significantly more variance than the equations without these variables used to test H1. For overall performance, the R^2 for Model 2 (0.19) was significantly higher ($p < 0.05$) than that of Model 1 (0.13) for ROA. For revenue growth, the R^2 for Model 2 (0.15) was significantly higher ($p < 0.05$) than that of Model 1 (0.11). With respect to foreign performance, the R^2 for Model 2 (0.16) was significantly higher ($p < 0.05$) than that of Model 1 (0.11) for foreign profitability. For foreign revenue growth, the R^2 for Model 2 (0.13) was significantly higher ($p < 0.05$) than that of Model 1 (0.08). The ICE*IHOST interaction term was also a significant and positive explanatory variable in all regressions examining performance.

The Curvilinear Relationships between ICE and Performance: The Moderating Role of IHOST (H3)

The results for Model 3, shown in Tables 2 and 3, provide some support for the predicted curvilinear relationship between ICE and performance. With respect to overall performance, Model 3 for ROA was significant ($p < 0.01$) and had an R^2 of 21%. Consistent with H3, Table 2 shows that including ICE^2 and the interaction term ICE^2*IHOST in the regression equation significantly ($p < 0.05$) improves the R^2 above and beyond that found in Model 2 ($R^2 = 0.19$). Also, ICE^2 had a negative and significant coefficient ($p < 0.05$), confirming the predicted non-linear relationship. However, the ICE^2*IHOST interaction term had positive and significant coefficients in the ROA equations, which was contrary to expectations.

Table 2 also shows the regression results for overall revenue growth. Model 3 was significant ($p < 0.01$) with an R^2 of 18%, which was significantly ($p < 0.05$) higher than Model 2 ($R^2 = 0.15$). The ICE^2 coefficient and its interaction with IHOST were positive and significant ($p < 0.05$). These results only partially supported H3 with overall performance.

The data in Table 3 provide support for the predicted curvilinear relationship between ICE and foreign performance. Model 3 for foreign profits was significant ($p < 0.01$), with an R^2 of 18%. The R^2 for Model 3 for foreign profits was significantly ($p < 0.05$) higher than that of Model 2 ($R^2 = 0.16$). The interaction term ICE^2*IHOST was positively and significantly associated with foreign profits ($p < 0.05$), thereby supporting H3. Finally, the results for Model 3 for foreign revenue growth were also significant ($p < 0.01$). Model 3 had an R^2 of 16% which was significantly ($p < 0.01$) higher than the R^2 for Model 2 ($R^2 = 0.13$). Although ICE^2 had a negative and significant coefficient ($p < 0.05$), its interaction with IHOST was positive but insignificant, thus failing to support H3. These results only partially supported H3 with respect to foreign performance.

DISCUSSION

This study examined the association between international corporate entrepreneurship (ICE) and company performance, and explored the moderating effect of hostile international environments on this relationship. Responding to calls for empirical testing of international entrepreneurial activities (Dean et al. 1993; Guth and Ginsberg 1990), the results also clarify the relationships between ICE and company performance (both over-all and foreign), as discussed in the following paragraphs.

ICE and Company Performance

The results support H1, showing a positive relationship between ICE and a company's performance. Findings that ICE is positively related to overall profitability and growth are consistent with prior research examining domestic entrepreneurial activities (e.g., Covin and Slevin 1991; Zahra 1991, 1993). Firms that engage in ICE can realize impor-tant financial benefits from their innovation, risk taking, and new business creation, a finding that supports past results (Baden-Fuller and Stopford 1994).

The results extend the literature by showing that ICE is positively associated with the profitability and growth of foreign operations, which supports past research (Dean et al. 1993). Firms that pursue venturing and innovation in foreign markets can achieve profits and growth, which supports the literature (Bossak and Nagashima 1997). While the variance explained in the regression analyses is modest because many variables in-fluence a company's performance, the results show that ICE can be a source of profit-ability and growth, both overall and foreign.

The results further extend the literature by showing that companies benefit in their profitability and growth when pursuing ICE. This finding supports the anecdotal evi-dence found in the business press (Bannon 1998; Smart 1996). This "double payoff" from entrepreneurial activities also supports some prior research findings (Zahra 1993). Thus, one should not presume *a priori* that tradeoffs exist between foreign growth and profitability as the firm engages in ICE. This potential double payoff from ICE might have been a primary force for the growing internationalization of U.S. companies' oper-ations (Shama 1995; Symonds et al. 1996). These results should be tempered with cau-tion, however, given the study's cross-sectional design. Longitudinal designs would help future researchers to better understand the relationship between ICE and overall per-formance.

The Moderating Impact of IHOST on the ICE-Performance Relationship (H2)

The results also indicate that the association of ICE with performance is contingent on the perceived hostility of a firm's international markets, which supports prior findings from domestic operations (Covin and Slevin 1989, 1991; Zahra and Covin 1995). This finding shows that this moderating effect exists also for the firm's ICE activities, and for the company's overall and foreign performance, measured by both profits and growth. Thus, when hostility is high, ICE can enhance company performance. While some managers' impulse reaction to high international hostility may be to pursue more conservative options, the study highlights the desirability of a more proactive but calcu-lated risk-taking. Managers need to be cautious because excessive pursuit of ICE can be counter-productive when environmental hostility in foreign markets is high.

The Non-Linear Relationships between ICE and Performance: The Moderating Role of IHOST

The results reveal that complex associations exist between ICE and company perfor-mance. As reported earlier, and consistent with H3, firms initially realized profits then experience negative returns from increasing ICE activities. These findings are not surprising, as other studies that have found inverted U-shaped relationships with respect to a firm's innovation (Miller and Friesen 1984) and internationalization activities (Hitt et al. 1997; Tallman and Li 1996). Negative returns may be explained by the difficulties firms may experience in managing their complex foreign operations or from the costliness of coordinating, directing, and managing their venturing and innovation initiatives in multiple foreign markets. The transfer of the best entrepreneurial practices within a company's international network can also be time consuming, costly, and challenging. Although this study did not measure possible causes for these diminishing returns, it shows the risks of excessive pursuit of ICE.

The study also highlights the strong influence of environmental hostility on the relationship between ICE and performance, but in the opposite direction of that hypothesized. In foreign markets where competitive rivalry and hostility were viewed as intense, the performance of those firms engaged in higher levels of ICE was not as adversely influenced as the performance of those firms with low ICE levels. When considered as a predictor, perceived international environmental hostility did not significantly explain differences in a company's financial performance. However, the interaction term ICE^2* IHOST was positively associated with performance, supporting the predicted moderating effect of perceived hostility in international operations. Thus, the negative effects of high ICE levels on firm performance were somewhat reduced in hostile environments.

There are several reasons why firms that aggressively pursue ICE might enjoy higher financial performance than firms that implement fewer ICE programs, even when IHOST is high. One reason is that ICE activities themselves may be the primary source of the hostility experienced in a firm's foreign markets. Innovation or pioneering activities that firms pursue to capture market shares and profits may intensify competitive rivalries in markets that were formerly benign. Firms engaged in higher levels of ICE may be positioned to manage and even profit under high environmental hostility. The resources and skills necessary for successful innovation and venturing can give these firms the ability to take advantage of changing environmental conditions. Entrepreneurial firms are often more flexible in their approach to interacting with their environments, and are quicker than their rivals in seizing strategic initiatives even under challenging environmental conditions. This flexibility can enable the firm to achieve multiple points of distinction across its global operations, which can enhance a company's performance.

Post-Hoc Analyses

To put the above results in perspective, we identified the five companies with the highest ICE scores in placid vs. hostile environments. We conducted an extensive search (using Lexis-Nexis and newspaper data searches) about these companies' ICE activities. Although the small number of observations (n = 10) was too small to confidently generalize findings, there were major differences between the two sets of firms in the objectives, content and effect of their ICE efforts.

Companies in placid environments appeared to explain their high ICE efforts by a desire to: safeguard against strategic surprises, solidify their reputation, exploit their past successes, protect their markets, widen their growth options, and remain strategically focused. In this environment, companies that aggressively pursued ICE believed that their hospitable environment cannot last long, and they wanted to be prepared when change took place in their industries. However, those companies that aggressively pursued ICE in hostile environments appeared to believe in the adage "innovate or die". Therefore, they viewed ICE as a strategic priority, providing a basis for creating new niches and protecting existing markets. ICE served the dual purpose of preempting the competition while maximizing the firms' competitive advantage.

Companies also followed different paths to ICE. In placid environments, the focus was on frequent product upgrades and on being first to do so in the industry. In hostile environments, ICE efforts were more wide ranging, centering on frequent radical innovation, entering new foreign markets, and broadening the firm's scope of global operations and services. Companies espoused an attitude of being on the "frontier" of ongoing global transformation.

Generalizations from a small number of observations about the ICE-company performance link can be hazardous, at best. We caution the readers, therefore, to bear this in mind as they interpret the following observations. In placid environments, the five companies with the highest ICE scores reported higher scores on different measures of performance than other firms in the same environment but with lower ICE scores. Companies with high ICE in placid environments, however, had lower performance than firms with high ICE scores in hostile environments. Companies with low ICE scores in placid and hostile environments reported lower performance levels.

Finally, we were interested in the causes of the curvilinear relationship found between ICE and performance in a hostile environment. One of the five companies we examined provided some important clues. Five years before our study, this company replaced its CEO. The new CEO and top management team made globalization the cornerstone of the company's new competitive strategy. Consequently, the company quickly moved to acquire existing facilities in 11 countries, entered into a series of international strategic alliances, and devoted more resources for R&D both in the U.S. and abroad, generating a dizzying array of new products. The firm also spent heavily on its manufacturing, marketing and distribution, with the goal of achieving a "first-mover" status in several of its markets. Profits continued to rise but, in the past two years, they experienced a drop because of the high costs of global expansion and the unfavorable economic conditions in some of the countries the firm has entered.

Limitations

Having discussed the results, it is important to recognize the study's limitations. The most obvious is the use of survey data in measuring the study's key variables. Despite the fact that secondary data supported the validity of the measures, one cannot totally dismiss source bias. Like other data collection techniques, mail surveys also have limitations that can affect the quality of the findings. Another limitation is the study's short time frame, which does not permit an analysis of causal relationships among the variables. Fortunately, Block and MacMillan (1993) have concluded that the financial payoff from corporate venturing efforts quickly becomes evident. Likewise, the focus on the associations of ICE with firm performance, without exploring the effect of ICE processes, is a third limitation of the study. Detailed analyses such as those conducted by Baden-Fuller and Stopford (1994) would have provided deeper and richer insights into how, when, and why different ICE activities may impact a company's performance. Still, the results have implications for managerial practice and future research on ICE.

Managerial Implications

The findings of this study, in which ICE is positively associated with a company's overall and foreign performance, suggest that firms should consider being actively involved in international entrepreneurial activities, but in moderation. Executives need to encourage and support ICE activities. Though time consuming, politically challenging, and expensive, ICE activities can be financially rewarding by creating opportunities that enhance growth and improve profitability. Nurturing and supporting risky ICE activities, therefore, should remain a top management priority.

It is also clear from the results that the pursuit of ICE can be financially worthwhile, especially when environmental hostility in international markets is perceived as being high. ICE can widen a firm's growth options, enabling it to enter new and profitable business fields (McGrath et al. 1995). ICE activities provide savvy firms with the means to seize advantages created by hostile and uncertain international competitive conditions. Indeed, managers who abandon innovation and risk taking when hostility increases in international markets may place their company's long-term profitability and growth at risk.

Executives need to recognize, however, that there are "upper-limits" to the financial gains from pursuing ICE. Taking calculated risks and promoting innovation can be important for achieving growth and profitability, up to a point where the costs are excessive, managers are over-extended, and firm performance suffers. There are also potential dysfunctional effects for excessive innovation and venturing when the firm's international environment is excessively hostile. Sound judgment and experience can help executives to determine if their firms are approaching the appropriate point of moderation in pursuing ICE.

Finally, managers need to devote the necessary resources to conduct effective competitive analyses and continually scan their international business environment. If perceptions of hostility matter this much in determining ICE and their effects, scanning international markets should be given attention. Scanning enables executives to gather, analyze and interpret the diverse dimensions that can increase or reduce IHOST. Using this information, managers can make effective strategic choices about the appropriate levels of ICE to be pursued.

Implications for Theory and Research

The results reported in this paper indicate a need for studies that empirically explore the link between ICE and a firm's performance. Longitudinal designs, in particular, are necessary to establish the nature and direction of the associations between ICE and company performance. These studies should give more attention to the measurement of ICE and identify its different dimensions and to provide a more complete picture of the benefits companies might gain from undertaking different ICE initiatives. Further, the links between ICE and company performance deserve a closer examination in future study. Given that these links lie predominantly in the learning achieved and the knowledge gained in international markets (McGrath et al. 1995), researchers need to study the impact of ICE or particular international ventures on the firm's ability to generate and use different types of knowledge. This can be done using case studies, mail surveys, archival data or field research. Knowledge is a strategic resource that can spell the difference between success and failure in global markets. Researchers also need to better understand the process by which ICE projects are initiated, managed, and institutionalized. Finally, future researchers need to give more attention to the factors that motivate firms to undertake ICE activities. These motives can explain the types of ICE activities pursued and their effect on a firm's financial and non-financial performance outcomes.

In recent years, U.S. companies have expanded their international business operations (Williamson 1997). Considerable innovation, risk taking and entrepreneurial activities have accompanied this globalization process (Carpano et al. 1994; Tallman and Li 1996). The results show that, even when the environment of foreign markets is considered hostile, international entrepreneurial efforts can enhance the growth and profitability of a firm's performance. These findings should be tempered with caution because there is a risk that the financial payoff from excessive ICE activities in this environment may decline. Executives should not abandon entrepreneurial risk taking in their firms' international business operations; instead, they need to proceed with caution.

REFERENCES

Agrawal, S., and Ramaswamy, N.S. 1992. Choice of foreign market entry mode: Impact of ownership, location and internalization factors. *Journal of International Business Studies* 23(1):1–27.

Baden-Fuller, C., and Stopford, M.J. 1994. *Rejuvenating the mature business*. Boston, MA: Harvard Business School Press.

Bannon, L. 1998. Mattel plans to double sales abroad. *Wall Street Journal* February 11, A3 and A8.

Bartlett, C.A., and Ghoshal, S. 1989. *Managing across borders: The transnational solution*. Boston, MA: Harvard Business School Press.

Block, Z., and MacMillan, I. 1993. *Corporate venturing*. Cambridge, MA: Harvard Business Press.

Bossak, J., and Nagashima, S. 1997. *Corporate strategies for a borderless world: Sharpening your competitive Edge*. Tokyo, Japan: Asian Productivity Organization.

Buhner, R. 1987. Assessing international diversification of West German corporations. *Strategic Management Journal* 8(1):25–37.

Carpano, C., Chrisman, J.J., and Roth, K. 1994. International strategy and environment: An assessment of the performance relationship. *Journal of International Business Studies* 25(3):639–656.

Chiesa, V. 1996. Managing the internationalization of R&D activities. *IEEE Transactions on Engineering Management* 43(1):7–23.

Cohen, J., and Cohen. P. 1983. *Applied multiple regression/correlation analysis for the behavioral sciences*. 2nd ed. Hillsdale, N.J.: L. Erlbaum Associates.

Covin, J.G., and Covin T. 1990. Competitive aggressiveness, environmental context, and small firm performance. *Entrepreneurship: Theory and Practice* 14(4):35–50.

Covin, J.G., and Slevin, D. 1989. Strategic management of small firms in hostile and benign environments. *Strategic Management Journal* 10(1):75–87.

Covin, J.G., and Slevin, D. 1991. A conceptual model of entrepreneurship as firm behavior. *Entrepreneurship: Theory and Practice* 16(1):7–25.

Dean, C.C., Thibodeaux, M.S., Beyerlein, M., Ebrahimi, B., and Molina, D. 1993. Corporate entrepreneurship and competitive aggressiveness: A comparison of U.S. firms operating in eastern Europe and the Commonwealth of Independent States with U.S. firms in other high-risk environments. *Advances in International Comparative Management* 8:31–54.

Dess, G. and Beard, D. 1984. Dimensions of organizational task environments. *Administrative Science Quarterly* 29(1):52–73.

Dess, G., Gupta, A., Hennart, J-F., and Hill, C. 1995. Conducting and integrating strategy research at the international, corporate, and business levels: Issues and directions. *Journal of Management* 21(3):357–393.

Doz, Y., and Prahalad, C.K. 1987. *The multinational mission: Balancing local demands and global vision.* New York, NY: The Free Press.

The Flexible Tiger. 1998. *Economist* 346(8049): January 3, 73.

Florida, R. 1997. The Globalization of R&D: Results of a survey of foreign-affiliated R&D laboratories in the USA. *Research Policy* 26(1):85–103.

Ferdows, K. 1997. Making the most of foreign factories. *Harvard Business Review* 75(2):73–88.

Franko, L.G. 1989. Global corporate competition: Who's winning, who's losing and the R&D factor as one reason Why. *Strategic Management Journal* 10(5):449–474.

Geringer, J.M., Beamish, P.W., and deCosta, R.C. 1989. Diversification strategy and internationalization: Implications for MNE performance. *Strategic Management Journal* 10(2):109–119.

Grant, R.M. 1987. Multinationality and performance among British manufacturing companies. *Journal of International Business Studies* 18(3):79–89.

Grant, R.M. 1995. *Contemporary strategy analysis: Concepts, techniques, applications.* Second Edition, Cambridge, MA: Blackwell Publishers Inc.

Grant, R., Jammine, A., and Thomas, H. 1988. Diversity, diversification, and profitability among British manufacturing companies. *Academy of Management Journal* 31(4):771–801.

Guth, W.D., and Ginsburg, A. 1990. Guest Editors' introduction: Corporate entrepreneurship. *Strategic Management Journal* 11(Summer):5–15.

Hennart, J-F. (1991). The transaction costs theory of joint ventures: An empirical study of Japanese subsidiaries in the United States. *Management Science* 37(4):483–497.

Hitt, M.A., Hoskisson, R.E., and Ireland, R.D. 1994. A mid-range theory of the interactive effects of international and product diversification on innovation and performance. *Journal of Management* 20(2):297–326.

Hitt, M.A., Hoskisson, R.E., and Kim, H. 1997. International diversification: Effects on innovation and firm performance in product-diversified firms. *Academy of Management Journal* 40(4):767–798.

Hu, Y-S. 1995. The international transferability of competitive advantage. *California Management Review* 37(4):73–88.

Johanson, J., and Vahlne, J-E. 1977. The internationalization process of the firm—A model of knowledge development and increasing foreign market commitments. *Journal of International Business Studies* 8(1):23–32.

Kim, W.C., Hwang, P., and Burgers, W.P. 1989. Global diversification strategy and corporate profit performance. *Strategic Management Journal* 10(1):45–57.

Kim, W.C., Hwang, P., and Burgers, W.P. 1993. Multinationals' diversification and the risk-return tradeoff. *Strategic Management Journal* 14(4):275–286.

Kimura, Y. 1989. Firm-specific strategic advantages and FDI behavior of firms: The case of Japanese semiconductor firms. *Journal of International Business Studies* 20(2):296–314.

Knight, G.A. 1997. Cross-cultural reliability and validity of a scale to measure firm entrepreneurial orientation. *Journal of Business Venturing* 12(3):213–225.

Kobrin, S. 1991. An empirical analysis of the determinants of global integration. *Strategic Management Journal* 12(Summer):17–31.

Kogut, B. 1991. Country capabilities and the permeability of borders. *Strategic Management Journal* 12(Summer):33–47.

Kuratko, D., Montagno, R., and Hornsby, J. 1990. Developing an intrapreneurial assessment instrument for effective corporate entrepreneurial environment. *Strategic Management Journal* 11(Summer):49–58.

Leavy, B. 1997. Innovation and the established organization. *Journal of General Management* 22(3):38–52.

Levy, D.L., and Dunning, J.D. 1993. International production and sourcing: trends and issues. *Science Technology and Industry Review* 13(Dec.):13–59.

Lumpkin, G.T., and Dess, G.G. 1996. Clarifying the entrepreneurial orientation construct and linking it to performance. *Academy of Management Review* 21(3):135–172.

Mascarenhas, B. 1992a. First-mover effects in multiple dynamic markets. *Strategic Management Journal* 13(3):237–243.

Mascarenhas, B. 1992b. Order of entry and performance in international markets. *Strategic Management Journal* 13(7):499–510.

Mascarenhas, B. 1997. The order and size of entry into international markets. *Journal of Business Venturing* 12(4):287–299.

McGrath, R.G., MacMillan, I.C., and Venkataraman, S. 1995. Global dimensions of new competencies. *International Entrepreneurship* Birley, S. and MacMillan, I.C. (eds.). New York, NY: Routledge.

Miller, D., and Friesen, P. H. 1984. *Organizations: A quantum view.* New York, NY: Prentice Hall.

Miller, D. 1983. The correlates of entrepreneurship in three types of firms. *Management Science* 29(7):770–791.

Miller, K.D. 1993. Industry and country effects on managers' perceptions of environmental uncertainties. *Journal of International Business Studies* 24(4):693–714.

Morck, R., and Yeung, B. 1991. Why investors value multinationality. *Journal of Business* 64(2):165–187.

Pinchot, III, G. 1985. *Intrapreneuring: Why you don't have to leave the corporation to become entrepreneur.* New York, NY: Harper and Row Publishers.

Porter, M. 1980. *Competitive strategy: Techniques for analyzing industries and competitors.* New York, NY: Free Press.

Porter, M. 1987. From competitive advantage to corporate strategy. *Harvard Business Review* 65(3):43–59.

Porter, M. 1990. *The competitive advantage of nations.* London: Collier-Macmillan.

Ramaswamy, K., Kroeck, G., and Renforth, W. (1996). Measuring the degree of internationalization of a firm: A comment. *Journal of International Business Studies* 27(1):167–178.

Rosenzweig, P., and Singh, J. 1991. Organizational environments and the multinational enterprise. *Academy of Management Review* 16(2):340–361.

Roth, K. 1992. International configuration and coordination archetypes for medium-sized firms in global industries. *Journal of International Business Studies* 23(3):533–549.

Roth, K., and O'Donnell, S. 1996. Foreign subsidiary compensation strategy: An agency theory perspective. *Academy of Management Journal,* 39(3):678–703.

Sambharya, R. 1996. Foreign experience of top management teams and international diversification strategies of U.S. multinational corporations. *Strategic Management Journal* 17(9):739–746.

Sambharya, R. 1995. The combined effect of international diversification and product diversification strategies on the performance of U.S.-based multinational corporations. *Management International Review* 35(3):197–218.

Schendler, B. 1997. Microsoft: First america, now the world. *Fortune* August 18, 214–217.

Shama, A. 1995. Entry strategies of U.S. firms to the former Soviet Bloc and Eastern Europe. *California Management Review* 37(3):90–109.

Shan, W., and Hamilton, W. 1991. Country-specific advantage and international cooperation. *Strategic Management Journal* 12(6):419–432.

Singh, J. 1986. Performance, slack, and risk taking in organizational decision making. *Academy of Management Journal* 29(3):562–585.

Smart, T. 1996. GE's Welch: 'Fighting Like Hell to be No. 1'. *Business Week* July 8, 48.

Stopford, J., and Baden-Fuller, C. 1994. Creating corporate entrepreneurship. *Strategic Management Journal* 15(7):521–536.

Sullivan, D. 1994. Measuring the degree of internationalization of a firm. *Journal of International Business Studies* 25(2):325–342.

Symonds, W.C., Bremner, B., Toy, S., and Miller, K.L. 1996. The Globetrotters take over: Worldwide champions outpace domestic competitors. *Business Week* July 8, 46.

Tallman, S., and Li, J. 1996. Effects of international diversity and product diversity on the performance of multinational firms. *Academy of Management Journal* 39(1):179–196.

Teece, D., Pisano, G., and Shuen, A. 1997. Dynamic capabilities and strategic management. *Strategic Management Journal* 18(7):509–533.

Vlasic, B. 1998. The little car that could carry Chrysler overseas. *Business Week* January 19, 39.

Werner, S., Brouthers, L.E., and Brouthers, K.D. 1996. International risk and perceived environmental uncertainty: The dimensionality and internal consistency of Miller's measure. *Journal of International Business Studies* 27(3):571–587.

Williamson, P.J. 1997. Asia's new competitive game. *Harvard Business Review* 75(5):55–67.

Yeoh, P-L., and Jeong, I. 1995. Contingency relationships between entrepreneurship, export channel structure and environment: A proposed conceptual model of export performance. *European Journal of Marketing* 29(8):95–115.

Zahra, S. 1991. Predictors and financial outcomes of corporate entrepreneurship: An exploratory study. *Journal of Business Venturing* 6(4):259–285.

Zahra, S. 1993. Environment, corporate entrepreneurship and financial performance: A taxonomic approach. *Journal of Business Venturing* 8(4):319–340.

Zahra, S. 1996. Governance, ownership, and corporate entrepreneurship: The moderating impact of industry technological opportunities. *Academy of Management Journal* 39(6):1713–1735.

Zahra, S., and Covin, J.G. 1995. Contextual influences on the corporate entrepreneurship-performance relationship: A longitudinal analysis. *Journal of Business Venturing* 10(1):43–58.

Part IX
Value Creation in Corporate Entrepreneurship

[32]

1042-2587-99-233$1 50
Copyright 1999 by
Baylor University

Corporate Entrepreneurship and the Pursuit of Competitive Advantage

Jeffrey G. Covin
Morgan P. Miles

This paper presents a theoretical exploration of the construct of corporate entrepreneurship. Of the various dimensions of firm-level entrepreneurial orientation identified in the literature, it is argued that innovation, broadly defined, is the single common theme underlying all forms of corporate entrepreneurship. However, the presence of innovation *per se* is insufficient to label a firm entrepreneurial. Rather, it is suggested that this label be reserved for firms that use innovation as a mechanism to redefine or rejuvenate themselves, their positions within markets and industries, or the competitive arenas in which they compete. A typology is presented of the forms in which corporate entrepreneurship is often manifested, and the robustness of this typology is assessed using criteria that have been proposed for evaluating classificational schemata. Theoretical linkages are then drawn demonstrating how each of the generic forms of corporate entrepreneurship may be a path to competitive advantage.

Corporate entrepreneurship has long been recognized as a potentially viable means for promoting and sustaining corporate competitiveness. Schollhammer (1982), Miller (1983), Khandwalla (1987), Guth and Ginsberg (1990), Naman and Slevin (1993), and Lumpkin and Dess (1996), for example, have all noted that corporate entrepreneurship can be used to improve competitive positioning and transform corporations, their markets, and industries as opportunities for value-creating innovation are developed and exploited. However, only in recent years has much empirical evidence been provided which justifies the conventional wisdom that corporate entrepreneurship leads to superior firm performance. Perhaps the best evidence of a strong corporate entrepreneurship-performance relationship is provided in a study by Zahra and Covin (1995). Their study examined the longitudinal impact of corporate entrepreneurship on a financial performance index composed of both growth and profitability indicators. Using data collected from three separate samples and a total of 108 firms, Zahra and Covin (1995) identified a positive and strengthening linkage between corporate entrepreneurial behavior and subsequent financial performance.

Assuming that one accepts as valid the espoused and documented utility of corporate entrepreneurship, the reasons why corporate entrepreneurship "works" still remain something of a mystery. That is, the logic of corporate entrepreneurship has not been adequately explained. Recognized bases for competitive advantage, for example, have not been explicitly and systematically linked to corporate entrepreneurial actions. Moreover, the archetypical forms in which corporate entrepreneurial actions are often manifested have not been consistently or clearly delineated in the literature on this topic. However, until management scholars provide an adequate answer to the question of how corporate entrepreneurship creates competitive advantage, prescriptions for the conduct of corporate entrepreneurship will necessarily remain superficial.

Part of the "problem" in trying to infer from the literature why corporate entrepreneurship works is the fact that while there is general agreement that firms *per se* can be entrepreneurial (e.g., Miles & Arnold, 1991; Morris, Davis & Allen, 1994; Smart & Conant, 1994), there is no consensus on what it means for firms to be entrepreneurial. This situation is exacerbated by the proliferation of labels for entrepreneurial phenomena in organizations. Thus, when management theorists talk about corporate entrepreneurship, they are often talking about different phenomena. And with ambiguity surrounding the nature of the corporate entrepreneurship construct, it is not surprising that a general understanding or theory of why corporate entrepreneurship often creates competitive advantage has failed to emerge.

This paper seeks to contribute to the literature on corporate entrepreneurship in two ways. First, this paper will attempt to clarify what it means for firms to be entrepreneurial. In particular, it will be argued that the proliferation in the literature of diverse and often inconsistent definitions of corporate entrepreneurship has created confusion over the nature of the construct, and that much of the writing on this topic fails to recognize what defines the essence of an entrepreneurial firm-level posture. Second, this paper will propose a typology of the common forms of corporate entrepreneurship. The forms identified here are presented as "pure" types that reflect the generic manifestations of the corporate entrepreneurship phenomenon. The robustness of the typology will be assessed using criteria that have been proposed for evaluating classificational schemata. The reasons why the various forms of corporate entrepreneurship may be paths to competitive advantage will then be discussed.

CLARIFICATION OF THE CORPORATE ENTREPRENEURSHIP CONSTRUCT

The label corporate entrepreneurship has been attached to multiple and sometimes distinct organizational phenomena. Three of the most common phenomena that are often viewed as examples of corporate entrepreneurship include situations where (1) an "established" organization enters a new business; (2) an individual or individuals champion new product ideas within a corporate context; and (3) an "entrepreneurial" philosophy permeates an entire organization's outlook and operations. These phenomena are not inherently alternative (i.e., mutually exclusive) constructs, but may co-exist as separate dimensions of entrepreneurial activity within a single organization.

The first phenomenon, where an "established" organization enters a new business, has typically been referred to as corporate venturing and is well described in the writings of, for example, Block and MacMillan (1993), Burgelman (1983), and Venkatraman, MacMillan, and McGrath (1992). The second phenomenon, where an individual or individuals champion new product ideas within a corporate context, is perhaps best known by the label "intrapreneurship," a term popularized by Pinchot (1985). The process of intrapreneuring is well documented in writings on product and innovation champions (e.g., Shane, 1994; Kanter, 1982; Jelinek & Schoonhoven, 1990). The third phenomenon, where an "entrepreneurial" philosophy permeates an entire organization's outlook and operations, has been discussed using labels such as entrepreneurial management (Stevenson & Jarillo, 1990), entrepreneurial posture (Covin, 1991), entrepreneurial orientation (Ramachandran & Ramnarayan, 1993), firm level entrepreneurship (Morse, 1996), entrepreneurial strategy making (Dess, Lumpkin, & Covin, 1997), and pioneering-innovative management (Khandwalla, 1987). This final phenomenon, whereby firms *per se* act in entrepreneurial manners, is the focus of the current manuscript. That is, the term corporate entrepreneurship is reserved to refer to cases where entire firms, rather than exclusively individuals or other "parts" of firms, act in ways that generally would be described as entrepreneurial.

Nonetheless, ambiguities and inconsistencies persist in how corporate entrepreneurship has been operationalized by those who have adopted a firm-level perspective on the topic. For example, Jennings and Lumpkin (1989) equate firm-level entrepreneurship with product innovation or market development. Specifically, in their study of corporate entrepreneurship within the savings and loan industry, Jennings and Lumpkin (1989) refer to any firm that introduces an above-average number of new products or develops an above-average number of new markets as an entrepreneurial firm. Additional criteria are suggested by other researchers before a firm should be referred to as entrepreneurial. Karagozoglu and Brown (1988), for example, categorized a firm as entrepreneurial only if it engaged in product innovation *and* risk-taking behavior. Morris and Paul (1987), Covin and Slevin (1989, 1990), Miles and Arnold (1991), Dean (1993), and Zahra (1991) have all operationalized corporate entrepreneurship in manners consistent with Miller's (1983) argument that entrepreneurial firm-level behavior implies the existence of (1) product or process innovation, (2) a risk-taking propensity by the firm's key decision makers, *and* (3) evidence of proactiveness with respect to product-market introductions or the early adoption of new administrative techniques or process technologies. (In Miller's earlier research [Miller & Friesen, 1982] this third criterion—proactiveness— was not identified as essential to classifying a firm as entrepreneurial.)

In short, there are significant differences of opinion among corporate entrepreneurship researchers regarding what attributes must be present in order to label a firm entrepreneurial. Fortunately, a recent and excellent paper by Lumpkin and Dess (1996) has gone a long way toward helping to define the dimensions of an "entrepreneurial orientation." In particular, based on a thorough review of the broadly defined corporate entrepreneurship literature, Lumpkin and Dess (1996) identified five dimensions of entrepreneurial orientation—namely, autonomy, innovativeness, risk taking, proactiveness, and competitive aggressiveness. They, nonetheless, conclude that it is unclear whether all five dimensions of entrepreneurial orientation will always be present in entrepreneurial firms, or whether any of these identified dimensions must always be present before the existence of an entrepreneurial orientation should be claimed.

The position taken in this paper is that there *is* a commonality among all firms that could be reasonably described as entrepreneurial. This commonality is the presence of innovation. Consistent with the observations of Burgelman, Kosnik, and van den Pol (1988), innovation, as conceived of here, refers to the introduction of a new product, process, technology, system, technique, resource, or capability to the firm or its markets. As noted by Stevenson and Gumpert (1985), innovation is the "heart of entrepreneurship." Likewise, Stopford and Baden-Fuller (1994, p. 522) observed that "most authors accept that all types of entrepreneurship are based on innovations." Therefore, the label entrepreneurial should not be applied to firms that are not innovative. Innovation is at the center of the nomological network that encompasses the construct of corporate entrepreneurship. Certainly it is easy to envision how the other dimensions of entrepreneurial orientation identified by Lumpkin and Dess (1996) could be antecedents, consequences, or simple correlates of innovation and, thereby, help to define the domain of corporate entrepreneurship. Nonetheless, without innovation there is no corporate entrepreneurship regardless of the presence of these other dimensions.

Still, there appears to be something missing from much of the empirically based as well as purely conceptual literature that purports to focus on corporate entrepreneurship as a firm-level phenomenon. As noted above, corporate entrepreneurship necessarily implies the presence of innovation, but there is more to corporate entrepreneurship than innovation. For example, firms that replace their core production technologies with newer technologies that are disseminating throughout their industries may be engaged in innovations that from an internal, organizational perspective are quite dramatic. However, such innovations will not typically evoke images of corporate entrepreneurship. Integrated U.S. steel manufacturers—like U.S. Steel, Inland, National, LTV, and Bethlehem—are a good case in point. While several of these firms switched during the 1970s and 1980s from open-hearth furnace technology to newer oxygen-based furnace technology, few would identify these as entrepreneurial firms within their industry segments.

Moreover, this additional "missing" element is not simply the presence of autonomy, risk taking, proactiveness, or competitive aggressiveness, although each of these dimensions could easily flourish in entrepreneurial firms. Rather, the element that, we believe, must exist in conjunction with innovation in order to claim an entrepreneurial orientation is the presence of the objective of sustaining high performance or improving competitive standing through actions that radically energize organizations or "shake up" the status quo in their markets or industries. That is, corporate entrepreneurship is engaged in to increase competitiveness through efforts aimed at the rejuvenation, renewal, and redefinition of organizations, their markets, or industries. Corporate entrepreneurship revitalizes, reinvigorates, and reinvents. It is the spark and catalyst that is intended to place firms on the path to competitive superiority or keep them in competitively advantageous positions.

In fairness, the preceding "missing element" of the literature on corporate entrepreneurship—the objective of rejuvenating or purposefully redefining organizations, markets, or industries in order to create or sustain a position of competitive superiority—is evident in some definitions and discussions of this phenomenon. Miller (1983, p. 770), for example, states that corporate entrepreneurship is "the process by which organizations renew themselves and their markets. . . ." Likewise, Zahra (1997) includes a "strategic renewal" element in his empirical operationalization of the construct of corporate entrepreneurship. Nonetheless, one cannot keep from being struck by the fact that this recognition, while having strong face validity and intuitive appeal, is not widely reflected in the corporate entrepreneurship literature.

The importance of recognizing the centrality of this "rejuvenation and redefinition" element to the corporate entrepreneurship construct can hardly be overstated. Corporate entrepreneurship is not just the old wine of organizational innovation in new bottles, as those who are cynical over the constant emergence of new managerial fads might suggest. Rather, corporate entrepreneurship refers to a distinct, multidimensional, and empirically verifiable set of organizational phenomena. Importantly, the complete academic and practitioner legitimacy of corporate entrepreneurship will only be realized when both the innovation and the rejuvenation and redefinition elements are widely recognized as defining the essence of the construct.

THE FORMS OF CORPORATE ENTREPRENEURSHIP

Having defined corporate entrepreneurship as the presence of innovation plus the presence of the objective of rejuvenating or purposefully redefining organizations, markets, or industries in order to create or sustain competitive superiority, it is possible to envision at least four forms of this phenomenon. These forms will be labeled sustained regeneration, organizational rejuvenation, strategic renewal, and domain redefinition. As conceptualized here, these forms relate to the organization's ability to regularly introduce new products or enter new markets, to the organization *per se,* to the organization's strategy for navigating its current environment, and to the organization's creation and exploitation of new product-market arenas, respectively. Significantly, all four corporate entrepreneurship forms are defined by at least one potential basis for competitive advantage, albeit some more clearly than others.

It is important to emphasize that *these forms will often concurrently exist in entrepreneurial organizations.* However, they will be presented separately here in order to clarify what we regard as fundamental to each. It is also acknowledged that, in reality, *organizations typically cannot a-priori determine a particular corporate entrepreneurship outcome.* As noted by Hamel (1997, p. 80), "innovative strategies [like the forms of corporate entrepreneurship presented here] are always, and I mean always, the result of lucky foresight." Thus, the emergence of each of the four forms is not something that is simply a matter of managerial choice. Since the outcomes of entrepreneurial processes are uncertain, a form of corporate entrepreneurship cannot be readily enacted as a deliberate strategy with the expectation that particular outcomes will necessarily be realized. Nonetheless, the four forms of corporate entrepreneurship are presented below to elucidate the characteristics of what would seem to be some of the most common firm-level manifestations of entrepreneurial processes.

Sustained Regeneration

Sustained regeneration is the form of corporate entrepreneurship that is, perhaps, most widely accepted and recognized as evidence of firm-level entrepreneurial activity. In particular, firms that engage in sustained regeneration are those that regularly and continuously introduce new products and services or enter new markets. This ongoing stream of new products and services or new market introductions is intended to capitalize on latent or under-exploited market opportunities using the firm's valued innovation-producing competencies. Firms successful at the sustained regeneration form of corporate entrepreneurship tend to have cultures, structures, and systems supportive of innovation. They also tend to be learning organizations that embrace change and willingly challenge competitors in battles for market share. Moreover, at the same time they are introducing new products and services or entering new markets, these firms will often be culling older products and services from their lines in an effort to improve overall competitiveness through product life cycle management techniques.

Arm & Hammer is a good example of a firm that exhibits both the "new products" and "new markets" variants of sustained regeneration. Although it is a small, narrow-line player within its industry, Arm & Hammer has been able to achieve enviable financial returns through the creative introduction of its core product—baking soda—into new product-market arenas. For example, through the development and introduction of baking soda-based toothpaste and deodorizing products, Arm & Hammer has been able to capitalize on emerging product-market opportunities unseen or underappreciated by competitors in its core industry segment. This strategy is not simply one of product development or related diversification. Rather, the proactive, competence-expanding actions of Arm & Hammer reflect conscious decisions to regularly and strategically expand the business of the company for the purpose of ensuring its long-term competitiveness. This is evidence of sustained regeneration.

Also typical of firms that exhibit evidence of the sustained regeneration form of corporate entrepreneurship are 3M, Motorola, and Mitsubishi. These firms have reputations as innovation machines. Although each is broadly diversified across multiple business segments, they share the common attributes of entrepreneurial cultures, flexible structures, rapid decision making capabilities, and discontent with the status quo. These firms are constantly striving for a broader market presence or greater market share. Significantly, they view their capacities for innovation as essential core competencies that must be protected, nourished, and leveraged through corporate strategies of continual product/service development.

Organizational Rejuvenation

The label organizational rejuvenation is used to refer to the corporate entrepreneurship phenomenon whereby the organization seeks to sustain or improve its competitive standing by altering its internal processes, structures, and/or capabilities. This phenomenon is sometimes referred to as organizational renewal (Hurst, Rush, & White, 1989), corporate renewal (Beer, Eisenstat, & Spector, 1990), or corporate rejuvenation (Stopford & Baden-Fuller, 1990) in the corporate entrepreneurship and competitiveness literatures. However, these latter terms are often used in reference to entrepreneurial phenomena that entail strategy as well as organizational changes. In contrast, the current use of the term organizational rejuvenation is intentionally limited to corporate entrepreneurial phenomena for which the focus and target of innovation is the organization *per se*. This position is adopted because we believe it is important to recognize that firms need not change their strategies in order to be entrepreneurial. Rather, corporate entrepreneurship may involve efforts to sustain or increase competitiveness through the improved execution of particular, pre-existing business strategies. When this is the case, organizational rejuvenation is the label we would attach to the entrepreneurial phenomenon.

Improved strategy execution via organizational rejuvenation frequently entails actions that reconfigure a firm's value chain (Porter, 1980) or otherwise affect the pattern of internal resource allocation. For example, Procter and Gamble has been able to greatly improve its inventory and distribution systems in recent years through the extensive adoption of bar-coding technology. This technology has not only revolutionized the entire outbound logistics function within P&G but has enabled the firm to sustain its position as a leading consumer products company by setting the customer service standard against which competitors are being judged. General Electric has introduced numerous and often radical new administrative techniques, operating policies, and human resource practices over the past fifteen years. Many of these innovations have been aimed at transforming the corporation from a change-resistant firm to a continuous-learning organization. The net effect of these internal changes has been to improve GE's competitiveness across its diversified business portfolio. At Chrysler Corporation, the entire process through which automobiles are designed and produced has been reconfigured in recent years. Using what is referred to as a "platform" team structure, Chrysler brings together managers and employees from across the corporation to achieve strong and effective functional integration. Because of their positive impact on things like product development cycle time and product quality, the process reengineering principles adopted at Chrysler are often credited with enabling the firm to sustain its position as a leader in the global automobile industry.

In each of the above cases the firm in question introduced an innovation or innovations that (1) redefined how some major aspect of its operations was conducted, (2) created value for the firm's customers, and (3) sustained or improved the firm's ability to effectively implement its chosen strategy. Importantly, identifying each of these innovations as an example of corporate entrepreneurship would likely meet with minimal disagreement.

Strategic Renewal

The label strategic renewal is used here to refer to the corporate entrepreneurship phenomenon whereby the organization seeks to redefine its relationship with its markets or industry competitors by fundamentally altering how it competes. Whereas the focal point for organizational rejuvenation is the organization *per se*, the focal point for strategic renewal is the firm within its environmental context and, in particular, the strategy that mediates the organization-environment interface.

It should be acknowledged that there is a risk in adopting the label strategic renewal when referring to this third form of corporate entrepreneurship. Specifically, like the label corporate entrepreneurship, the label strategic renewal has been used in the past to refer to different phenomena. For example, Guth and Ginsberg (1990, p. 5) defined strategic renewal as "the transformation of organizations through renewal of the key ideas on which they are built." In Guth and Ginsberg's (1990) conceptualization of this phenomenon, strategic renewal does not necessarily relate to organizational strategy and could conceivably more closely approximate the aforementioned phenomenon of organizational rejuvenation. In contrast, when Simons (1994) uses the term strategic renewal he is simply referring to the implementation of a "new" business strategy. As conceptualized in the current corporate entrepreneurship typology, the phenomenon of strategic renewal necessarily implies the implementation of a new business strategy. However, the label strategic renewal is intentionally limited to the phenomenon in which new business strategies differ significantly from past practices in ways that better leverage the firm's resources or more fully exploit available product-market opportunities.

Defined in this manner, strategic renewal can be observed in a variety of business scenarios. For example, declining firms facing turnaround situations sometimes embrace new product or process technologies that allow them to redefine how they compete and their industry positions. After years of decline within the motorcycle industry, Harley-Davidson reinvented itself through strategic renewal. In a sharp departure from its not-too-distant past, Harley-Davidson is no longer content to let its reputation as an American company and its production of classically styled motorcycles be its primary bases for competition. Through major investments in product and process R&D and the adoption of what is commonly referred to as a marketing orientation (e.g., Miles & Arnold, 1991; Hills & LaForge, 1992), Harley-Davidson has been able to radically change the bases on which it competes. While still appropriately characterized as pursuing a niche-differentiation strategy, Harley-Davidson is now differentiated on the bases of superior quality, excellent service, and responsiveness to customers' product desires.

The preceding is not meant to imply that only struggling or somehow disadvantaged firms will benefit from strategic renewal. This form of corporate entrepreneurship may also facilitate the maintenance of competitive superiority among industry leaders. In fact, sometimes industry leaders must embrace strategic change to ensure their viability. For example, when IBM introduced the "System 360" line of mainframe computers in the mid-1960s it already held over two-thirds of the mainframe market share. Yet the System 360 line represented not just a new product line for the company but a new strategy for competition in the mainframe computer industry. This new strategy emphasized the technological compatibility (not just performance) of IBM products, an increasingly valued basis for advantage that simply could not be matched by IBM's competitors. According to Maidique and Hayes (1984, p. 21), IBM's System 360 strategy "redefined the rules of competition for decades to come." Still, given the relative reluctance of industry leaders to modify or abandon strategic recipes that produced positive results in the past (see Schwenk & Tang, 1989; Miller, 1990), strategic renewal may not be as pervasive among industry leaders as among those seeking leadership or, at a minimum, improved positions.

The preceding examples are offered as cases where the label strategic renewal applies. These examples are not presented as exhaustive of the specific manifestations of strategic renewal. More important, however, than delineating the various potential manifestations of strategic renewal is communicating the essence of the phenomenon. In every case, it is corporate strategy that is viewed as both the key to energizing the firm and the medium though which long-term competitive advantage is sought. Deliberate and major repositioning actions characterize these strategies of renewal.

Domain Redefinition

Finally, domain redefinition is the label used to refer to the corporate entrepreneurship phenomenon whereby the organization proactively creates a new product-market arena that others have not recognized or actively sought to exploit. By engaging in domain redefinition the firm, in effect, takes the competition to a new arena where its first or early mover status is hoped to create some bases for sustainable competitive advantage. Through domain redefinition firms often seek to imprint the early structure of an industry. Under such a scenario, the entrepreneurial firm may be able to create the industry standard or define the benchmark against which later entrants are judged. Thus, firms that engage in domain redefinition are entrepreneurial by virtue of the fact that they exploit market opportunities in a preemptive fashion, redefining where and how the competitive game is played in the process.

Two specific manifestations of the domain redefinition form of corporate entrepreneurship are bypass strategies and product-market pioneering. Fahey (1989) describes bypass strategies as "attacking by surpassing competitors." This type of business-level strategy is driven by a firm's desire to (1) avoid competitive confrontation in some specific product-market arena or (2) move the competitive battle to a new arena where current or prospective competitors are likely to suffer from later-entrant status. For example, facing stiff and increasing competition in the financial services industry, twenty years ago Merrill Lynch introduced the Cash Management Account, an all-purpose brokerage account. Through this introduction Merrill Lynch succeeded in both decreasing its vulnerability to the hostilities and uncertainties of the financial services industry and in creating a new product-market arena within this industry. It took competitors well over a decade to catch up. Thus, Merrill Lynch effectively bypassed its competition and enhanced its profitability and competency base through redefining its competitive domain.

A similar phenomenon to bypass strategies are product-market pioneering strategies. In fact, these labels can refer to the same phenomenon. However, whereas bypass strategies are strongly motivated by a desire to decrease overall vulnerability to adverse, current competitive conditions, product-market pioneering strategies tend to be more opportunistic in character. That is, they are pursued not so much to avoid the existing but to exploit the potential. In either case, however, the desired effect on the organization is one of increased competitiveness through innovation that positively redefines the firm's product-market domain.

Golder and Tellis (1993, p. 159) define a pioneer as "the first firm to sell in a new product category." The term product category refers to a group of products that consumers view as substitutable for one another yet distinct from those in another product category. Product categories are, in effect, product-market arenas. Established firms that "pioneer" are, by definition, redefining their domains. A good example of this phenomenon is Sony's creation and exploitation of a new product-market arena within the audio portion of the consumer electronics industry. Specifically, over a decade ago Sony introduced the Walkman to a very receptive and enthusiastic public. Numerous competitors have since entered this product-market arena. However, due to Sony's accumulated first-mover advantages (in the areas of, for example, patent protection, channel access, and reputation), these competitors have yet to achieve anything near Sony's level of success.

In each of the preceding cases, the exploration of a new product-market arena helped to energize and reorient the firm. The products introduced were innovative from the perspective of the firm, the industry, and the market. Proactiveness and at least a moderate amount of risk characterized each of these introductions. In short, the dynamics and dimensions of corporate entrepreneurship are clearly manifested in the phenomenon of domain redefinition.

A THEORETICAL EVALUATION OF THE PROPOSED TYPOLOGY

While the proposed typology of corporate entrepreneurship forms may have a certain amount of face validity, it is important to evaluate this typology using criteria suggested for the development of acceptable classificational schemata. Hunt (1983) offers one such set of criteria. According to Hunt (1983, p. 355), for a classification schema to be maximally robust one should be able to answer the majority of the following five questions in the affirmative:

1) Does the schema adequately specify the phenomenon to be classified?
2) Does the schema adequately specify the properties or characteristics that will be doing the classifying?
3) Does the schema have categories that are mutually exclusive?
4) Does the schema have categories that are collectively exhaustive?
5) Is the schema useful?

Regarding the current typology, it is possible to answer the first question in the affirmative because each of the phenomena to be classified—that is, the four forms of corporate entrepreneurship—meets the definitional criteria of corporate entrepreneurship as discussed earlier in this paper. The current typology also fairs well in reference to the second question because the four forms have distinct foci and empirical manifestations that are identified in the descriptions of these forms.

The criterion of mutual exclusivity, as suggested by question three, is not met by the current typology. Mutual exclusivity exists, according to Hunt (1983, p. 359), when no single item will fit into two or more categories. The current typology does not have this characteristic. The strategic renewal form of corporate entrepreneurship is the source of difficulty here. Specifically, any time a firm adopts or begins to strongly exhibit an entrepreneurial behavior pattern that represents a fundamental departure from past strategic behavior for the firm, strategic renewal can be said to exist. The problematic matter here is that this single manifestation or form of corporate entrepreneurship—that is, the newly adopted entrepreneurial behavior pattern—could be categorized as strategic renewal *and* whatever other category of corporate entrepreneurship the entrepreneurial behavior reflects. For example, if a conservative, non-innovative firm were to begin acting entrepreneurially by regularly introducing new products, this single expression of entrepreneurial firm-level behavior—that is, the newly adopted strategy of competing through frequent new product introductions—could be viewed as evidence of both sustained regeneration and strategic renewal. Fortunately, Hunt (1983) notes that the failure of classificational schemata to meet the mutual exclusivity criterion is not a "mortal blow" to a schema, and that many commonly used classifications (such as the distinction between industrial and consumer goods) fall short of this ideal.

Moreover, in defense of the current typology, it might be noted that any of the four forms of corporate entrepreneurship may exist without any of the others existing, and that even an "extreme" manifestation of any of the identified forms of corporate entrepreneurship will not inherently include evidence of any of the other forms. Thus, while sustained regeneration and domain redefinition, for example, may be outcomes of similar entrepreneurial processes, firms that regularly introduce new products or enter new markets (evidence of sustained regeneration) may never have an arena-creating new product-market introduction (evidence of domain redefinition), and firms that achieve the latter may not be frequent new product-market innovators. Similar observations could be made in regard to the other identified forms of corporate entrepreneurship.

The fourth question proposed by Hunt (1983) for assessing the robustness of classificational schemata—Does the schema have categories that are collectively exhaustive?—cannot be definitively answered in the affirmative when applied to the current corporate entrepreneurship typology. This typology contains categories or forms of corporate entrepreneurship that should be widely recognizable to those familiar with firm-level entrepreneurial phenomena. Certainly the typology has content validity. Still, it would be presumptuous to conclude that such phenomena are necessarily limited to those identified in the proposed typology.

The fifth question—Is the schema useful?—can be answered in the affirmative on at least two bases. First, the proposed typology represents a rare attempt to attach some unambiguous definitions to entrepreneurial phenomena for the purpose of facilitating a better understanding of the corporate entrepreneurship construct. Second, the proposed typology can be empirically operationalized for the purpose of theory testing, the results of which may eventually contribute to the effective practice of corporate entrepreneurship.

Overall, it can be concluded that while the proposed four-forms typology is not beyond all criticism, it enjoys many of the properties that make a classification schema theoretically sound and useful. Thus, the current typology represents a reasonable starting point in an attempt to bring some order and concreteness to how the construct of firm-level entrepreneurship might be depicted in theory and observed in practice.

CORPORATE ENTREPRENEURSHIP AND COMPETITIVE ADVANTAGE

Significantly, the seeds of competitive advantage are evident in each of the aforementioned forms of corporate entrepreneurship. There are several fundamental bases for competitive advantage. Porter's writings (1980; 1985) clarified the logic of overall cost leadership and differentiation as bases for competitive advantage. More recently, strategic management scholars have recognized the importance of speed or quick response—that is, having a market offering prior to competitors—as a distinct basis for competitive advantage (e.g., Bhide, 1986, Stalk, 1988). Each of the bases for advantage potentially could be exploited by firms that engage in sustained regeneration, organizational rejuvenation, strategic renewal, or domain redefinition.

However, overall cost leadership may be the basis for competitive advantage one would most typically associate with the organizational rejuvenation form of corporate entrepreneurship. Specifically, it seems plausible that organizational rejuvenation—due to its internal, organizational focus—may most commonly create advantage based on efficiencies achieved through actions that lower an organization's cost structure.

Differentiation-based advantage will likely be common among firms engaged in the sustained regeneration form of corporate entrepreneurship. This expectation follows from at least two rationales. First, a reputational distinction and advantage tends to become associated with the most innovative companies, like Sharp Corp. and Hewlett-Packard. This reputational advantage will often positively differentiate the products of these companies in the minds of prospective consumers. Second, and related to the preceding point, companies that regularly and continuously introduce new products or enter new markets often exploit existing brand names that leverage consumer awareness. Intel Corp., for example, leverages its name recognition in the Pentium line as a basis for competitive differentiation.

Finally, quick response is the basis for competitive advantage one might most commonly associate with the domain redefinition form of corporate entrepreneurship. Domain redefinition implies taking the competitive battle to a new product-market arena. If competitors have yet to enter this arena, then the quick response basis for advantage is necessarily being exploited.

Strategic renewal has the weakest *inherent* link to any of the three bases for competitive advantage. This observation is not meant to suggest that strategic renewal will likely be weakly linked to some basis or bases for competitive advantage. Rather, there is simply not an obvious "most likely" basis for advantage one would associate with the strategic renewal form of corporate entrepreneurship. The particular reasons why strategic renewal could be expected to result in competitive advantage will depend on the specific manifestation or case of strategic renewal in question.

Table 1 summarizes the "focus" of each form of corporate entrepreneurship as well as the "typical basis for competitive advantage" associated with each. This table also summarizes for each form the "typical frequency of new entrepreneurial acts" and the "magnitude of negative impact if new entrepreneurial act is unsuccessful."

A "new entrepreneurial act" is a behavior that reflects the focus of the form of corporate entrepreneurship in question. Thus, as noted in Table 1, a new entrepreneurial act in the context of the sustained regeneration form of corporate entrepreneurship is a new product introduction or the entrance of a new (to the firm) but existing market; for organizational rejuvenation it is a major, internally focused innovation aimed at improv-

Table 1

Some Key Attributes of the Four Forms of Corporate Entrepreneurship

Form of Corporate Entrep.	Focus of Corporate Entrep.	Typical Basis for Competitive Advantage	Typical Frequency of New Entrepreneurial Acts*	Magnitude of Negative Impact if New Entrepreneurial Act is Unsuccessful
Sustained Regeneration	New Products or New Markets	Differentiation	High Frequency	Low
Organizational Rejuvenation	The Organization	Cost Leadership	Moderate Frequency	Low-to-Moderate
Strategic Renewal	Business Strategy	Varies with Specific Form Manifestation	Less Frequent	Moderate-to-High
Domain Redefinition	Creation and Exploitation of Product-Market Arenas	Quick Response	Infrequent	Varies with Specific Form Manifestation and Contextual Considerations

*New Entrepreneurial Acts for

● Sustained Regeneration A new product introduction or the entrance of a new (to the firm) but existing market

● Organizational Rejuvenation A major, internally focused innovation aimed at improving firm functioning or strategy implementation

● Strategic Renewal The pursuit of a new strategic direction

● Domain Redefinition The creation and exploitation of a new, previously unoccupied product/market arena

ing firm functioning or strategy implementation; for strategic renewal it is the pursuit of a new strategic direction; and for domain redefinition it is the act of creating and exploiting a new, previously unoccupied product-market arena.

Table 1 shows that the frequency of new entrepreneurial acts are high, of moderate frequency, less frequent, and infrequent for sustained regeneration, organizational rejuvenation, strategic renewal, and domain redefinition, respectively. The assigned frequency levels are intended to reflect the typical ease with which new entrepreneurial acts are pursued within each form of corporate entrepreneurship. New entrepreneurial acts in the sustained regeneration form are frequent by definition. For most firms, major internal innovations will not be so regularly or easily embraced, so new entrepreneurial acts of organizational rejuvenation are identified as moderate. Changing strategic directions may be even harder for most firms than implementing major internal innovations. Therefore, new entrepreneurial acts of strategic renewal are likely to be even less frequent. Finally, finding ways to bypass competitors or pioneer truly new product-market arenas requires much creativity and marketing savvy, a product like no one else's, and a certain amount of luck. As such, new entrepreneurial acts of domain redefinition may be the most rare.

The information on the "magnitude of negative impact if new entrepreneurial act is unsuccessful" is furnished in Table 1 because of the importance of communicating the potential down-side to corporate entrepreneurship. As with the pursuit of any innovative initiative there will be risk to the organization when pursuing the various forms of corporate entrepreneurship. However, these forms are expected to differ in the extent to which they may jeopardize firm performance or viability.

Specifically, for sustained regeneration, the magnitude of negative impact on firm performance if a new entrepreneurial act fails is rated as low. One bad product or one poor market entry decision will typically not threaten the viability of a highly innovating firm. The risk to firm performance associated with an unsuccessful major, internal innovation could be somewhat greater depending upon the centrality of the innovation to the firm's effective implementation of its business strategy. Considering two of the aforementioned cases, if P&G had failed to successfully and extensively implement bar-coding technology, one portion of its value chain would have been disrupted and the firm may have been rendered temporarily vulnerable to competitor opportunism. Even so, the negative impact on firm performance would likely have been low. However, if Chrysler had failed to implement its "platform" team structure initiative, more negative consequences could have resulted. This is due to the greater relative importance of the operations function—which the platform team structure mainly affects—to the success of Chrysler's business strategy.

A negative impact on firm performance of moderate-to-high magnitude would be expected if new entrepreneurial acts of strategic renewal fail. A failure at strategic renewal implies that a firm has been unable to successfully execute a strategic redirection. Such failures can be costly in both a resource requirement sense and in an opportunity cost sense. The depletion of resources that accompanies failed strategic renewal attempts can easily threaten the viability of a firm. On a similar note, strategies take time to prove themselves, and managers who have committed their firms to new strategies may be unlikely to admit the failure of these new strategies until much time has elapsed and other significant resources have been consumed. At the point of admitting failure, these managers may have sapped so much strength from their businesses that a successful strategic turnaround will be unlikely. Even in the case of a successful firm pursuing a new strategic direction, the prospects of a full recovery from a failed strategic renewal initiative may be slim. For example, if IBM's System 360 strategy had failed, competitors would likely have had an opportunity to gain ground on this industry leader as it struggled to identify yet another new strategy or to reinstitute its past strategy.

Generalizing about the likely impact of failed domain redefinition acts on firm performance is difficult-to-impossible. This is because the percent of total firm resources gambled in individual domain redefinition initiatives will vary greatly according to such things as the size of the firm, the cost to the firm of trying to exploit the new product-market arena, and the firm's confidence in the viability or attractiveness of the new product-market arena. For example, the risk to Sony in trying to create and exploit a product-market arena for its Walkman was quite minimal. Sony was so large, and the resources required so relatively small, that a failure in this new product-market arena would likely have had minimal negative impact on overall firm performance. In stark contrast, many small biotechnology firms, like Biodel, have declared bankruptcy or relinquished involvement in more immediately promising product lines after having squandered significant resources trying to create and exploit potentially lucrative new arenas for genetic engineering products. Accordingly, Table 1 notes that the down-side effect of failed domain redefinition acts on firm performance "varies."

CONCLUSION

This theoretical exploration of the construct of corporate entrepreneurship began with the observation that there is a poor understanding of the reasons why corporate entrepreneurship often produces, or at least is assumed to produce, superior firm performance. Based on the preceding discussions, one response to this uncertainty should be clearer. That is, corporate entrepreneurship has a positive reputation as a generally effective behavioral phenomenon because the organizational actions associated with this phenomenon can often be linked to recognized bases of competitive advantage.

A second reason why corporate entrepreneurship may contribute to firm performance is that at least one of the aforementioned forms of corporate entrepreneurship will represent appropriate, defensible, and value-enhancing behavior in any given firm's specific competitive context. For example, organizational rejuvenation would seem to fit particularly well with dominant or otherwise competitively strong firms since these firms' successful strategies will often not "require" major modification. Rather, an emphasis on organizational rejuvenation may further improve the firms' implementation of a strategy that has already led to high performance. On the other hand, strategic renewal implies some amount of strategic repositioning. Such repositioning may generally be of greater value among weaker or nondominant firms whose current strategies, by definition, have not resulted in strong competitive positions. The attractiveness of domain definition would seem to vary in inverse proportion with the attractiveness of an industry. That is, in industries where the long-term prospects for profitability or growth are uncertain or bleak, domain redefinition may be an especially desirable form of corporate entrepreneurship. Finally, sustained regeneration would seem to be particularly viable among firms operating in the expanding product-market domains of growth industries, or in mature industries where product differentiation and market segmentation efforts are often associated with the leading firms. In short, it might also be claimed that corporate entrepreneurship "works" because there will typically be a form of this phenomenon that is a recognized route to success, taking into account the particulars of any given firm's business strength and industry context.

Yet another reason for corporate entrepreneurship's enviable reputation may relate to how this phenomenon is manifested in organizations. As emphasized above, the forms of corporate entrepreneurship are presented here as distinct manifestations of firm-level entrepreneurship. However, these forms will often concurrently exist in entrepreneurial organizations. AT&T, for example, can be pointed to as a case where both the sustained regeneration and the domain redefinition forms of corporate entrepreneurship are clearly evident—sustained regeneration because of AT&T's steady stream of new product introductions and domain redefinition because of AT&T's arena-defining technological pioneering successes. Since the various forms of corporate entrepreneurship may be associated with different bases on which competitive advantage is being sought, it is plausible that another reason why corporate entrepreneurship works is that entrepreneurial firms will often be leveraging multiple bases for advantage. As observed by Hamel and Prahalad (1989), high performance often results when firms are able to "layer" several bases for competitive advantage. Consistent with this point, recent evidence by Dess et al. (1997) suggests that firms with entrepreneurial postures are likely to benefit from engaging in actions that achieve such layering.

The significance to managers of these observations is potentially great. The linkage between corporate entrepreneurship and firm performance has been empirically documented in methodologically rigorous research. However, it is only after understanding how and why corporate entrepreneurship produces superior firm performance that reservations regarding the possible spuriousness of this relationship can and should be discounted. The insights and arguments presented in this paper suggest that corporate entrepreneurship produces superior firm performance for identifiable, defensible, and strategically valid reasons. Thus, corporate entrepreneurship should be viewed as more than simply one of the more recent panaceas in a long string of managerial quick fixes that have surfaced over the years. The principal challenge to management researchers is to identify the entrepreneurial processes that lead to various forms of corporate entrepreneurship, and then to theoretically predict and empirically verify the forms of this phenomenon that produce the best results for firms in various business and industry contexts. Admittedly, this is a tough challenge. However, the pay-off in terms of improved firm performance should be substantial.

REFERENCES

Beer, M., Eisenstat, R , & Spector, B (1990) *The critical path to corporate renewal.* Boston· Harvard Business School Press.

Bhide, A (1986). Hustle as a strategy *Harvard Business Review, 64*(5), 59-65.

Block, Z., & MacMillan, I C. (1993) *Corporate venturing Creating new businesses within the firm.* Boston. Harvard Business School Press

Burgelman, R. A (1983). A process model of internal corporate venturing in the diversified major firm. *Administrative Science Quarterly, 28*(2), 223-244.

Burgelman, R A , Kosnik, T I. & van den Pol, M. (1988). Toward an innovative capabilities audit framework. In R. A. Burgelman, M A. Maidique, (Eds.), *Strategic management of technology and innovation,* pp 31-44. Homewood, IL: Irwin.

Covin, J. G (1991) Entrepreneurial versus conservative firms. A comparison of strategies and performance. *Journal of Management Studies, 28,* 439-462

Covin, J. G., & Slevin, D. P. (1989). The strategic management of small firms in hostile and benign environments. *Strategic Management Journal, 10*(1), 75-87

Covin, J G , & Slevin, D. P. (1990) New venture strategic posture, structure, and performance· An industry life cycle analysis. *Journal of Business Venturing, 5,* 123-135

Dean, C. C (1993). *Corporate entrepreneurship. Strategic and structural correlates and impact on the global presence of United States firms* Unpublished doctoral dissertation, University of North Texas, Denton, TX

Dess, G. G., Lumpkin, G T , & Covin, J G. (1997) Entrepreneurial strategy making and firm performance: Tests of contingency and configurational models *Strategic Management Journal, 18*(9), 677-695.

Fahey, L. (1989) Bypass strategy. Attacking by surpassing competitors. In L. Fahey, (Ed.), *The strategic planning management reader,* pp. 189-193 Englewood Cliffs, NJ. Prentice Hall

Golder, P N , & Tellis, G. J (1993) Pioneer advantage Marketing logic or marketing legend *Journal of Marketing Research, 30,* 158-170

Guth, W D , & Ginsberg, A (1990) Guest editor's introduction· Corporate entrepreneurship *Strategic Management Journal, 11*(Summer), 5-16.

Hamel, G (1997) Killer strategies that make shareholders rich *Fortune, 135*(12), 70-84

Hamel, G., & Prahalad, C. K (1989). Strategic intent *Harvard Business Review, 67*(3), 63-76

Hills, G E., & LaForge, R W (1992). Marketing and entrepreneurship The state of the art. In D. L. Sexton, & J D Kasarda (Eds), *The state of the art of entrepreneurship,* pp 164-190 Boston· PWS-Kent.

Hunt. S D (1983). *Marketing theory· The philosophy of marketing science* Homewood, IL: Irwin.

Hurst, D K , Rush, J. C , & White, R. E (1989). Top management teams and organizational renewal. *Strategic Management Journal, 10* (Summer), 87-105

Jelinek, M., & Schoonhoven, C B. (1990). *The innovation marathon Lessons from high technology firms* Oxford· Basil Blackwell.

Jennings, D F., & Lumpkin, J. R (1989). Functionally modeling corporate entrepreneurship· An empirical integrative analysis *Journal of Management, 15,* 485-502.

Kanter, R. M. (1982). The middle manager as innovator. *Harvard Business Review, 60*(4), 95-106.

Karagozoglu, N , & Brown, W. B (1988) Adaptive responses by conservative and entrepreneurial firms *Journal of Product Innovation Management, 5,* 269-281.

Khandwalla, P N (1987). Generators of pioneering-innovative management Some Indian evidence. *Organization Studies, 8*(1), 39-59

Lumpkin, G. T , & Dess, G G (1996) Clarifying the entrepreneurial orientation construct and linking it to performance *Academy of Management Review, 21*(1), 135-172.

Maidique, M. A., & Hayes, R. H. (1984) The art of high technology management *Sloan Management Review, 25*(2), 17-31

Miles, M. P., & Arnold, D R (1991) The relationship between marketing orientation and entrepreneurial orientation. *Entrepreneurship Theory & Practice, 15*(4), 49-65

Miller, D. (1983). The correlates of entrepreneurship in three types of firms *Management Science, 29,* 770-791

Miller, D (1990) *The Icarus paradox.* New York HarperCollins

Miller, D . & Friesen, P. H (1982). Innovation in conservative and entrepreneurial firms. Two models of strategic momentum *Strategic Management Journal, 3*(1), 1-26

Morris, M H , Davis, D L , & Allen, J W (1994). Fostering corporate entrepreneurship: Cross-cultural compansons of the importance of individualism versus collectivism. *Journal of International Business Studies, 21,* 65-89.

Morris, M. H., & Paul, G W (1987) The relationship between entrepreneurship and marketing in established firms. *Journal of Business Venturing, 2,* 247-259

Morse, E. A. (1996). Current thought in firm level entrepreneurship. Paper presented at the 1996 Western Academy of Management meeting.

Naman, J. L, & Slevin, D P. (1993). Entrepreneurship and the concept of fit: A model and empirical tests. *Strategic Management Journal, 14,* 137-153.

Pinchot, G. (1985). *Intrapreneuring: Why you don't have to leave the company to become an entrepreneur* New York. Harper & Row.

Porter, M. E. (1980). *Competitive strategy.* New York: Free Press.

Porter, M E. (1985). *Competitive advantage* New York: Free Press.

Ramachandran, K., & Ramnayaran, S. (1993) Entrepreneurial orientation and networking: Some Indian evidence *Journal of Business Venturing, 8*(6), 513-524

Schollhammer, H (1982). Internal corporate entrepreneurship In C. A. Kent, D. L. Sexton, K. H. Vesper, (Eds.), *Encyclopedia of entrepreneurship,* pp. 209-229. Englewood Cliffs, NJ· Prentice Hall.

Schwenk, C. R., & Tang, M. (1989). Economic and psychological explanations for strategic persistence. *Omega, 17,* 559-570.

Shane, S A (1994). Are champions different from non-champions? *Journal of Business Venturing, 9,* 397-421

Simons, R (1994). How new top managers use control systems as levers of strategic renewal *Strategic Management Journal, 15,* 169-189.

Smart, D. T., & Conant, J. S. (1994). Entrepreneurial orientation, distinctive marketing competencies and organizational performance. *Journal of Applied Business Research, 10*(3), 28-38

Stalk, G, Jr. (1988). Time—The next source of competitive advantage *Harvard Business Review, 66*(4), 41-51.

Stevenson, H. H, & Gumpert, D. (1985) The heart of entrepreneurship. *Harvard Business Review, 85*(2), 85-95.

Stevenson, H H., & Jarillo, J. C. (1990) A paradigm of entrepreneurship. Entrepreneurial management *Strategic Management Journal, 11,* Summer, 17-27

Stopford, J. M, & Baden-Fuller, C. W. F. (1990). Corporate rejuvenation. *Journal of Management Studies, 27*(4), 399-415

Stopford, J. M., & Baden-Fuller, C. W F. (1994) Creating corporate entrepreneurship *Strategic Management Journal, 15,* 521-536

Venkatraman, S, MacMillan, I., & McGrath, R. (1992). Progress in research on corporate venturing. In D L. Sexton, & J D Kasarda, (Eds.), *The state of the art of entrepreneurship,* pp. 487-519. Boston: PWS-Kent

Zahra, S A. (1991). Predictors and financial outcomes of corporate entrepreneurship· An exploratory study *Journal of Business Venturing, 6,* 259-285

Zahra, S A. (1993). A conceptual model of entrepreneurship as firm behavior. A critique and extension. *Entrepreneurship Theory & Practice, 17*(4), 5-21

Zahra, S A (1997) Governance, ownership, and corporate entrepreneurship The moderating impact of industry technological opportunities. *Academy of Management Journal, 39*(5), 1713-1735

Zahra, S A , & Covin, J. G. (1995) Contextual influences on the corporate entrepreneurship-performance relationship: A longitudinal analysis. *Journal of Business Venturing, 10*(1), 43-58

Jeffrey G. Covin is Professor of Strategic Management and the Hal and John Smith Chair of Entrepreneurship and Small Business Management at the Georgia Institute of Technology.

Morgan P Miles is Professor of Marketing at Georgia Southern University. He is currently visiting the University of Cambridge as a Senior Research Associate

The authors wish to thank the two anonymous reviewers, Michael Heeley, Patricia McDougall, and Shaker Zahra for their helpful comments on earlier versions of this paper.

[33]

1042-2587-99-233$1 50
Copyright 1999 by
Baylor University

Corporate Entrepreneurship, Knowledge, and Competence Development

Shaker A. Zahra
Anders P. Nielsen
William C. Bogner

The literature highlights the importance of corporate entrepreneurship (CE) for improving a company's market and financial performance. This paper extends the literature by focusing on the knowledge-creation processes within a firm's formal and informal CE activities. This multifaceted knowledge, which encompasses organizational, technical, and social dimensions, is developed by individuals or groups and diffused throughout the organization. Whether radical or incremental, this knowledge can generate new skills, which a company can then use to reconfigure the sources of its competitive advantage. This paper also discusses the role of intrapreneurs and CE champions, particularly in the creation and use of social capital, in the development of dynamic competencies.

The importance of corporate entrepreneurship (CE) for successful organizational performance and renewal has been the subject of interest in the literature over the past three decades. In one of the earliest studies, Peterson and Berger (1971) show that entrepreneurial activities help companies to develop new businesses that create revenue streams. CE activities also enhance a company's success by promoting product and process innovations (Burgelman, 1983a, 1991). Similarly, in one of the most influential studies, Miller (1983) defines CE as embodying risk taking, pro-activeness, and radical product innovations. These CE activities can improve organizational growth and profitability and, depending on the company's competitive environment, their impact may increase over time (e.g., Brazeal, 1993; Kanter, 1985; Zahra, 1991, 1993a, 1993b; Zahra & Covin, 1995). The empirical evidence is compelling that CE improves company performance by increasing the firm's pro-activeness and willingness to take risks, and by pioneering the development of new products, processes, and services (Kuratko, Montagno, & Hornsby, 1990; Lumpkin & Dess, 1996; Zahra, Covin, & Zahra, 1998; Zahra & Pearce, 1994). Given this firmly established base for the effectiveness of CE, we believe that research should now focus on identifying the underlying processes that determine the contributions of CE to a company's performance.

In this paper, we argue that formal and informal CE activities can enrich a company's performance by creating new knowledge that becomes a foundation for building new competencies or revitalizing existing ones. The knowledge-creation process within CE activities and the subsequent strategic use of this knowledge are tightly linked to the firm's learning and unlearning processes (Stopford & Baden-Fuller, 1990; Zahra & Das, 1993b). Executives, intrapreneurs, and CE champions, therefore, need to understand the dynamics of organizational learning, appreciate the nature of the knowledge created by and within CE activities, and use this knowledge to develop new competencies or improve existing ones. Thus, some of the most profound contributions of CE activities may lie in its links with the larger organizational learning processes that increase the company's competencies in assessing its markets or creating and commercializing new knowledge-intensive products, processes, or services (Burgelman, 1983a, 1983b, 1983c; Kanter, 1985; Zahra, 1995). In many areas, CE activities can create new knowledge that can improve the firm's ability to respond to changes in its markets by enhancing the company's competencies and thus determine the results of competitive rivalries among firms. Consequently, understanding the processes associated with a company's knowledge creation and exploitation within CE activities is the subject of this paper.

OBJECTIVES AND CONTRIBUTIONS

Three key concerns in contemporary management research also justify our focus on the development of knowledge within CE activities. The first is the growing recognition of the importance of new knowledge generation in the process of *self-renewal* by established companies (Brown, 1991; Stopford & Baden-Fuller, 1990). This process typically requires the unlearning of old skills while learning new ones. Organizational renewal demands the acquisition and use of new knowledge while shedding old routines, systems, and structures (Zahra, 1993a; Zahra & Garvis, 1999). Yet, both learning and unlearning are time-consuming, complex processes. Cultivating the knowledge created from an organization's learning and unlearning processes is an important managerial challenge, one that requires the resolution of challenging political, financial, organizational, and strategic issues (Brown, 1991; Dougherty & Heller, 1994). Exploiting the knowledge developed in CE activities is important for successful organizational renewal (Stopford & Baden-Fuller, 1990).

Second, new and unique knowledge is important in today's dynamic marketplace (Bettis & Hitt, 1995; Bohn, 1994). Continually generating knowledge is among the major determinants of a firm's ability to develop and sustain core competencies, even when its competitive landscape undergoes radical change (Hamel & Prahalad, 1994, 1996). Knowledge generated in CE activities can shape a company's strategic choices. A well-performing company usually develops an effective competitive strategy that embodies elements of both "stretch and leverage" (Hamel & Prahalad, 1993), and the knowledge produced by CE activities can augment and stretch a company's existing skills and knowledge even in ways unforeseen by senior executives. How firms actually cultivate the knowledge in building new competencies should be understood (Brown, 1991).

Third, the prevailing explanations of organizational evolution depend almost exclusively on the *strategic intent* of some foresighted senior executives and their dedicated investments made in the development of key resources of the organization (Hamel & Prahalad, 1989, 1994; Nelson & Winter, 1982). Strategic intent centers on the pursuit of a challenging competitive goal by using CE activities to overcome resource limitations (Hamel & Prahalad, 1989). The importance of this intent and the necessity of resource dedication have been widely discussed within the strategic choice (Andrews, 1980), the resource (Penrose, 1959; Mahoney & Pandian, 1992), and the evolutionary perspectives of the firm (Nelson & Winter, 1982). Despite this recognition of the importance of strategic intent and organizational vision as contributors to the development and exploitation of organizational competencies, existing theories do not provide a complete explanation of their development (McGrath, MacMillan, & Venkataraman, 1995; Teece, Pisano, & Shuen, 1997). Consequently, we argue that gaining a more complete view of how competencies emerge in established firms starts by examining how these organi-

ENTREPRENEURSHIP THEORY and PRACTICE

zations get the knowledge and insight necessary to identify, target, develop, and dedicate particular resources that build unique competencies.

Presently, many firms in the U.S. and other countries are considering innovative ways to respond to their complex and challenging competitive environments. Companies need to adopt new routines and practices that will allow them to protect any distinctive positions they may possess while simultaneously stretching their competencies to new limits (Zahra & Garvis, 1999). Understanding how the knowledge-creation and exploitation processes operate within CE activities can help mangers to improve the speed and effectiveness of their strategic responses to the challenges of competition (Helfat, 1994). It can also provide insights into the differences between those organizations that appear so capable of remaking and transforming themselves several times (Kanter, 1989), and those that are unable to act even when they possess considerable resources or are provided with some of the most interesting opportunities in their industries. This improved understanding of how the knowledge created from CE activities adds to a firm's reservoir of competencies can also yield deeper insights into the contributions of these activities to organizational value creation. Examining the nature of knowledge creation and utilization can clarify the intangible benefits of CE activities to organizational renewal processes (Zahra, 1993b) and open the "black box" that has hereto pervaded most past research on the relationship between CE and company performance.

Building on the literature (e.g., Bohn, 1994; Dodgson, 1992, 1993), therefore, we suggest a model of CE in which ongoing organizational learning provides a mechanism for creating different types of knowledge and for seeing how a firm's distinctive competence and competitive advantage can be built based on this knowledge. This model also illustrates how knowledge and competencies can be leveraged in creating new work forms, products, and strategies.[1] The various distinctions among different knowledge bases in the model also help to show why certain CE initiatives can immediately improve a firm's performance while others may not directly influence the firm's short-term bottom line. The discussion also draws attention to the importance of all types of knowledge generated within CE activities *and* the necessity of nurturing the managerial processes used in developing, capturing, transferring, and utilizing this knowledge in achieving organizational success.

CE, KNOWLEDGE, AND ORGANIZATIONAL COMPETENCIES: A MODEL

Both the evolutionary (Nelson & Winter, 1982) and the resource perspectives of the firm (Penrose, 1959; Wernerfelt, 1995) posit that the development and deployment of unique resources and idiosyncratic skills are necessary for achieving organizational survival, profitability, and growth. Competencies, which can be viewed as an output of CE activities, represent the skills that add unique value to a firm's products or services. Distinctive new products and processes are natural outputs for those firms that continually develop and improve competencies, the means by which firms can better serve their customers. The development of new competencies can also enlarge a company's strategic options and redefine its competitive arenas, allowing it to pursue new markets or customers where its competence is valued. Sustaining competence requires continuous learning, a factor that underscores the need for effective CE initiatives.

Figure 1 outlines the key processes associated with knowledge creation and exploitation within a firm's CE activities. Grounded in past research (e.g., Covin & Slevin, 1991; Dess, Lumpkin, & Covin, 1997; Lumpkin & Dess, 1996; Zahra, 1991, 1996), the

---

1. In this paper when we use the term "products" we also include services and processes

model recognizes the importance of a firm's external environment (path 1) and internal organizational variables (path 2) for promoting and inducing CE activities. A key feature of the model is its recognition of the potential contributions of formal and informal CE efforts for inducing and improving organizational learning (path 3).

Formal CE activities are developed in pursuit of the firm's established mission and goals (Zahra, 1996). Informal CE activities, however, are initiated by individuals and groups in pursuit of particular areas of interest (Zahra, 1991). Multifaceted learning from formal and informal CE is conducive to replenishing the firm's existing knowledge or creating new knowledge, as depicted in path 4. This knowledge, in turn, becomes a foundation for building or extending organizational competencies.

The model recognizes that gaining an advantage from new knowledge requires the integration of this knowledge with other knowledge that exists within the firm (path 5). The integration of knowledge provides a basis for building or revising the firm's competencies. For analytical convenience, however, the model separates the strategic thrust of competencies (path 6) from their domains (path 7). The *domain* of the competencies refers to the area, arena, or field where an organizational competence can be built, whereas the *thrust* of the competencies refers to whether the knowledge created through CE activities maintains or extends an existing competence or generates a new one. The model also indicates that competence thrust and domain interact to influence the financial (e.g., profitability) and non-financial outcomes of CE activities (path 8). Finally, the model recognizes that the impact of organizational competencies on these outcomes is moderated by the roles managers play in identifying, articulating, transferring, integrating, and exploiting knowledge, and then using it in developing or maintaining important competencies. These activities are referred to as "knowledge deployment" (path 9).

Organizational Learning in CE

Whether formal or informal, CE activities can create significant opportunities for multifaceted organizational learning (Pinchot, 1985), as indicated in path 3 (Figure 1). This learning centers on a firm's external environment, industry, markets, competitors, and internal operations and processes (Zahra, 1991). Learning in CE activities also

Figure 1

Corporate Entrepreneurship (CE), Knowledge, and Organizational Competence Development

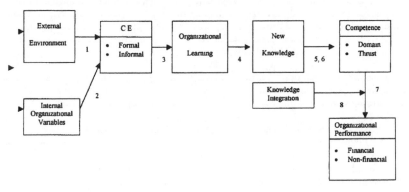

entails the acquisition of new technical, social, and organizational skills (Burgelman, 1983a, 1983b; Stopford & Baden-Fuller, 1990).

The process by which skills are gained through CE activities and used to develop organizational competencies has two distinct but related learning activities (Bogner, Thomas, & McGee, 1998). The first is the development of organizational knowledge through the learning that occurs within the company. This learning and the knowledge it generates can occur within specific technologies (or functions or tasks) *or* by integrating these technologies into an innovative, functioning system (e.g., a new product). The skill of *integrating* this knowledge by making it useful throughout the organization can in itself become a new competence (Hamel & Prahalad, 1994), leading to improved organizational performance (Grant, 1996, 1997) or additional CE activities. This infusion of new ideas can challenge prevailing assumptions and cognitive maps in an organization, revise organizational memory, and extend its existing knowledge bases. This learning can cause a company to reexamine and redefine its mission, competencies, and competitive weapons, which often leads to new knowledge.

A second process, which is akin to Nonaka and Takeuchi's (1995) "conversion" phase, augments a firm's knowledge base by transferring, and later exploiting, new knowledge in the marketplace. This conversion process consists of transferring knowledge from one part of the company to another and then bundling this knowledge into the firm's new product. These observations suggest the following proposition:

P1: Formal and informal CE activities promote organizational learning that leads to the creation of new knowledge.

The competence-based approach to competition places organizational learning at the core of the managerial responsibilities in a company (Prahalad & Hamel, 1990; Pisano, 1996). It suggests that the development and exploitation of idiosyncratic skills and competencies, not just market position in isolation, is the foundation of a sustainable competitive advantage. The role of CE activities in creating this knowledge is well recognized in the literature (Burgelman & Sayles, 1986; Zahra, 1991) because CE activities frequently produce valuable, new, unique, and firm-specific knowledge that can be used to develop new competencies or extend existing ones. This occurs through the process of organizational learning.

Acquisitive vs. Experimental Learning within CE

Broadly speaking, organizational learning can be classified into two types: acquisitive and experimental. Acquisitive learning occurs when a firm acquires and internalizes knowledge that pre-exists externally to its boundaries. Although this knowledge may not provide an immediate distinctive advantage to the firm, its absence can cause sub-par organizational performance. Even though acquisitive learning can improve the organization, it does not always offer a basis for building or extending its competencies. Learning activities identified by Huber (1991) as "vicarious," "grafting," and "search and notice" fall within acquisitive learning.

Experimental learning, however, happens largely internally and generates new knowledge that is distinctive to the organization (Lei, Hitt, & Bettis, 1996). It usually involves individuals (or groups) who have the discretion to experiment *and* a process that translates individual (group) experiences into organizational knowledge. Despite the importance of acquisitive learning it is clearly within experimental learning that CE activities may have the greatest potential to create or reinforce the firm's competitive advantage.

Through experimental learning and the subsequent exploitation of the resulting knowledge, firms can maneuver more efficiently in unstable and turbulent environments

(Grant, 1995) and exponentially expand the range of their possible effective responses to these situations (Nonaka, 1994; Zahra & Garvis, 1999). Experimental learning, therefore, should be among the priorities for any organization attempting to compete in today's dynamic but turbulent markets (Zahra & Garvis, 1999). This learning is also needed for organizational renewal, growth through innovation, and the development of new markets.

However, developing and exploiting unique knowledge through CE activities can be challenging for the firm's top management team. Developing this knowledge frequently requires considering several interrelated and complex strategic, organizational, political, and cultural factors. It also demands the recognition, transfer, integration, and exploitation of multiple learning processes.

The interrelated knowledge-generation and knowledge-exploitation activities that management must address in CE activities are placed, therefore, inside the two ovals labeled "radical" and "incremental" outcomes in Figure 2. These activities can occur within both formal and informal CE activities. Thus, besides the knowledge-generation activities, effective CE activities demand that the knowledge gained from these processes be integrated, transferred, and exploited in developing organizational competencies (Grant, 1996). The transformation of new knowledge into organizational competencies depends on the effective integration of this knowledge.

There are also critical knowledge-flow links between the firm and its markets (Day, 1994). Because executives usually focus on managing the competition in the firm's market, we do not include a double-lined arrow in Figure 2, reserving that indicator only for the internal managerial responsibilities tied directly to knowledge creation in CE activities. Finally, the ovals in Figure 2 in no way represent different organizational units or individuals, just different processes within formal and informal CE activities. Units and individuals in an entrepreneurial organization are dynamic players in the different aspects of these processes. To appreciate the different outcomes of learning within CE activities, we need to consider the outcomes of different types of organizational learning.[2] Knowledge outcomes of CE-based learning are indicated by path 4 in Figure 1.

---

2. A discussion of the cognitive processes involved in learning is beyond this paper. Interested readers should consult Hedlund (1994), Huber (1991), Kim (1997), and Nonaka (1994)

Figure 2

Top Management and CE-Based Knowledge Outcomes

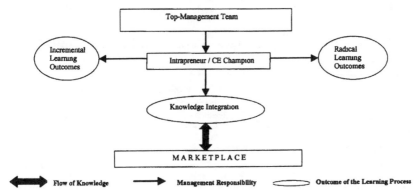

Experimental learning can yield incremental or radical knowledge[3] that can ensure the maintenance of existing competencies *and* the development of new ones, as illustrated in Table 1. Therefore, each cell in Table 1 represents a meaningfully different way in which the outcomes to learning that occur through CE activities can affect a firm's competitive advantage. Although all four activities are at work simultaneously and complement each other, we will address each separately to highlight its distinctive traits.

Knowledge Outcomes of Incremental Learning

As depicted in cell 1, experimental learning within CE can lead to incremental improvements in a firm's operational efficiency and enable a company to maintain and protect its competitiveness in existing operations and markets (Itami, 1987). Incremental improvements in the product components also keep the company's products distinctive, despite rivals' aggressive countermoves, by *extending* a firm's existing competencies (Bogner et al., 1998). Such improvements are critical for sustaining the high returns and positive cash flows that provide funds for future innovation and venturing activities. Further, when improvements in a company's existing competencies lead to a creative new use, they can also produce entirely new streams of revenue. By maintaining and creatively exploiting a firm's existing competencies, intrapreneurs can provide the platform from which this type of CE activity can occur. Frequently, intrapreneurs recognize the existence of under-utilized assets and competencies, which they can creatively utilize in developing new products and processes that give the firm a competitive advantage over time.

A similar incremental learning process can occur in areas where a firm initially does not have a competitive advantage, as depicted in cell 2 (Table 1). Although each individual gain is small, collective improvements can move the firm from a non-distinctive position to one of a competitive advantage through the accumulation of new resources and the development of distinctive skills over time. These progressive improvements may not reveal clear, immediate financial returns. Yet, these activities are often the necessary preliminary steps in organizational stretch processes, which may not have a clear link with current market advantages but are critical to long-term gains. Thus, as

---

3. Later in this paper a third type of experimental learning will be addressed This learning focuses on the transfer and integration of the new knowledge to the firm's ongoing operations and the subsequent commercialization of this new knowledge in the marketplace

Table 1

Links Between Firm Competence and Types of Experimental Learning

	Types of Experimental Learning Outcomes	
Firm Competence	**Incremental**	**Radical**
Existing (leverage)	**Extend** Sustain advantage	**Shift** Leapfrogging
Emerging (stretch)	**Develop** Build Foundation	**Intrapreneurship**

firms use experimental learning to *develop* emerging competencies, the benefit of each gain may be hard to see. Komatsu's decade-long, gap-closing effort relative to Caterpiller illustrates how well this progression can sneak up on and transform the market (Zahra & Das, 1993a, 1993b). As the literature suggests, the measurement of returns, the assignment of cost, and the allocation of rewards are difficult where the progress is incremental and the competence is, at best, probabilistic. Despite these difficulties, the proper management of these incremental gains is critical to successful CE activities and subsequent competence development.

Knowledge Outcomes of Radical Learning

The second type of experimental learning is "radical," which represents the leaps beyond incremental improvements in a company's existing or emerging competencies. As cell 3 of Table 1 indicates, radical learning frequently entails "frame-breaking" changes in the company's competitive and cognitive maps (Huber, 1991) rather than mere extensions of existing frames of reference. Therefore, clear breaks exist between the new offering and what came before. These radical advances in a company's existing products create a major *shift* in the trajectory of its existing product development activities or major advances in an existing trajectory, either of which can significantly change the structure and dynamics of competition (Tushman & Anderson, 1986). Advances within existing competencies also involve learning that focuses on exploiting these competencies in new ways by developing products and serving unmet market needs. These actions usually demand making significant changes in a firm's cognitive maps on how the emerging competence will be exploited (Nonaka, 1994). These shifts in the existing competence, moreover, can generate the sustainable, long-term competitive advantages that yield large returns as the firm's existing competencies are amplified.

The final outcome of experimental learning in cell 4 (Table 1) represents the greatest and the rarest leap in organizational competence. Here, a firm quickly gains an advantage in the market with a major innovation in an area where it had no pre-existing competence. In this case, effective firms are those that have allowed CE activities in cell 2 to take employees wherever their interests and knowledge can take them, even if it is beyond the scope of the current products (Pinchot, 1985). This is true *"intrapreneurship."* Of course, this does not mean that the firm has no prior knowledge in the area; there is usually some relatedness between old and new knowledge bases, but there has also been a major learning jump that opens new markets. Clearly, the learning needed here is quite different from that which happens when firms sustain their existing competencies through incremental improvements. Firms such as Hewlett Packard, Texas Instruments, and 3M have constantly encouraged such intrapreneurship, spinning off successful new products into new business units (Peters & Waterman, 1982; Pinchot, 1985). While it is often impossible to say when a successful CE activity will move from incremental to radical, different managerial challenges emerge as the changes that an organization faces become significant. Therefore, trust, persuasion, and effective use of social capital—key managerial skills to be discussed later—are essential to increase the radical outcomes of CE activities.

Joint Outcomes of Learning Types and Outcomes

The learning processes, the risks, the management challenges, and the outcomes for the organization differ extensively across the four cells of Table 1. Yet, all four are outcomes of effective CE activities that can enrich a firm's knowledge and contribute to the development of its competencies. These activities are also a top managerial responsibility, because each represents knowledge that can lead to a competitive advantage. Even if the firm sells some product components or licenses some of the products resulting from this learning, the revenue it receives for these transactions will still include returns to the knowledge gained through experimental learning.

The above four learning outcomes should not be seen as presenting firms with mutually exclusive options. In an effective CE system, these four learning types interact and mutually reinforce each other. For instance, over time incremental learning can yield important insights that help the firm stretch its resources and competencies in radically new ways. "Skunk-works" (Pinchot, 1985) and "bootlegging" (Peters & Waterman, 1982), or "autonomous" entrepreneurial behaviors (Burgelman, 1983a, 1983b, 1983c), all of which fall within such learning, have promoted the innovation and risk taking that has helped companies to achieve successful performance (Zahra, 1991, 1993a, 1993b). Incremental learning activities have also encouraged companies to pursue radical innovations or enter new domestic and international markets (Zahra, 1997; Zahra & Garvis, 1999).

As noted above, incremental learning can have some unintended consequences. As the insights and experiences gleaned from the incremental learning gained from CE activities are interpreted and comprehended, political pressures to creatively and competitively exploit the insights from within the firm rise, demanding action. Indeed, Burgelman (1983b) suggests that as autonomous CE activities increase, managers frequently have to consider, evaluate, select, and integrate some of these efforts into the firm's established strategy. These actions create a forum where executives become aware of the necessity of strategic change. Autonomous strategic behaviors, consequently, can reflect an emerging pattern of response to changing competitive or market realities. Incremental learning in CE activities, therefore, can accentuate the need for a more radical, strategic reorientation by documenting and highlighting new market realities and showing the viability of emerging competencies. Autonomous CE activities, even those that lead to incremental improvements, can "thaw" organizational inertia that may keep some companies captive of their past choices. As inertial forces slowly thaw, a company's propensity to engage in frame-breaking learning usually intensifies (Zahra & Chaples, 1993) and innovation increases. This discussion leads to the following proposition:

P2: Organizational learning gained through CE can be incremental, radical, or both.

LEARNING AND THE DOMAINS AND THRUSTS OF CE-BASED NEW KNOWLEDGE

The above discussion focused on the four learning outcomes from CE activities. As Figure 1 suggests, organizational learning creates new knowledge that can be used to maintain, extend, or build these competencies. The link between learning and competence lies in the knowledge created in CE activities (path 4 in Figure 1). Executives need to understand what new knowledge can be "about," *and* where new knowledge can have its effect.

THREE TYPES OF CE-BASED NEW KNOWLEDGE

CE activities can lead to three different types of new knowledge. The first type, which is developed with *specific* areas or tasks, provides insights into the nature and properties of particular activities. While this knowledge is key to future product refinements and product line extensions, enhancing fundamental product properties does not always lead to commercially viable new products. Further, although it serves as a foundation for other types of knowledge, this knowledge is seldom sufficient for a company to develop a sustainable competitive advantage. Firms that only emphasize developing and using knowledge in this way rarely see their CE activities yielding significant results in other areas. Companies' increasing ability to copy each others' technologies can also quickly erode the advantages that arise from an incremental change in a single technology (Barney, 1991; Clark & Fujimoto, 1991; D'Aveni, 1994; Zahra & Chaples, 1993; Zahra, Nash, & Bickford, 1995).

A second type of new knowledge is *integrative* in nature. The strategic importance of this knowledge stems from the fact that most products offered by a company are usually embedded in, and integrated with, several (if not hundreds of) knowledge components. Some of the knowledge that may bring these many elements together appear very mundane on the surface, yet collectively they lead to "combinative" knowledge (Kogut & Zander, 1992). This knowledge is further enhanced and expanded by learning. Thus, knowledge creation within CE sometimes centers on the skills of integrating component technologies, a task that demands a thorough understanding of how individual pieces interact and how they can be best integrated (Henderson & Cockburn, 1994). This integrative knowledge is firm-specific and tacit in nature and, therefore, can give the company a competitive advantage (Itami, 1987).

The tacit nature of integrative knowledge, however, often presents a challenge for managers who frequently deal with more concrete and explicit data. The insights needed to integrate component knowledge should be sufficiently articulated so that the new knowledge can be systematically used. Consequently, the integration of knowledge is an important activity separate from, but no less important than, the firm's effort in creating the knowledge, as indicated earlier in Figure 1. In fact, integrating existing areas of knowledge in innovative ways (e.g., new products) actually resembles the conception of entrepreneurship advanced by Schumpeter (1934), who saw the entrepreneur as a re-combinator of resources (including knowledge) for new uses. Though organizationally and politically challenging, the integration of specific knowledge with other resources and skills has the additional benefit of interlinking existing competencies in ways that frustrate rivals' efforts aimed at imitating the firms' products, thus protecting the gains the firm makes from its CE initiatives.

CE activities can also lead to a third type of new knowledge by suggesting or uncovering new ways to *exploit* the technical and integrative organizational knowledge (Huber, 1991). Although some of the knowledge created in CE activities is of crucial importance for a company's success, a firm is not merely a research institute (Brown, 1991). A company, instead, should harvest the fruits of its experimentation and venturing by effectively commercializing its new products, goods, and services (Brown, 1991; Rogers, 1995; Zahra, Nash, & Bickford, 1995). Learning new ways to exploit the firm's resources serves this end. Here, too, we draw on Schumpeter (1934), who viewed entrepreneurship not only as a disposition to take risks, but also as a means of creating rents through calculated risk taking.

Such new market commercializations should not be confined to the unit (or division) where the knowledge is generated. Once again, effective integration is important. New knowledge from any specific area should be transferred and integrated, even if the benefits of this knowledge are not evident *ex ante*. Indeed, while generating an integrated system of knowledge is useful for a company and may give it bragging rights, using this knowledge to create an economic value is equally important (Zahra et al., 1995).

A firm should capitalize on the three types of knowledge mentioned above in pursuit of competitive advantage. The benefits to be gained from exploitative knowledge are often different from those to be obtained from integrative knowledge. Yet, in combination, these benefits can significantly strengthen the firm's market and financial position. This discussion suggests the following proposition:

P3: The knowledge generated from learning in CE activities has technical (specialized), integrative (combinative), and exploitative (use) components.

Domains of organizational competence. Whether incremental or radically new, the knowledge gained from CE activities can determine the potential domain of competencies (path 6 in Figure 1). This domain refers to the area in which a new competence is sought or built; it embodies the firm's cognition, routines and systems, organizational processes, and products. Knowledge gained in CE activities, therefore, can revise the firm's frame of reference, revise its organizational memory, or induce quantum changes (Zahra & Chaples, 1993). This knowledge can also revise the routines, systems, and procedures a firm uses in its operations, thereby setting the stage for assembling different skills and competencies. Changes in these routines, processes, and systems can also alter how a firm views, designs, markets, and packages its products. The knowledge gained in CE activities can also revise and change a firm's internal processes and decision rules—which improves learning and induces knowledge acquisition. In turn, this can determine a firm's view of the market, success factors, competitive dynamics, and area of product differentiation (Baden-Fuller & Stopford, 1994). These observations suggest the following proposition:

P4: Knowledge created by CE activities significantly determines the domains of organizational competencies.

Thrusts of organizational competence. The above discussion shows that CE activities should be woven into every aspect of a firm's organization; each type of knowledge and use described should transcend particular functions, tasks, or departments. When embedded in a firm's organization, CE activities can effectively enhance its technical, organizational, administrative and social competencies. This embeddedness ensures that knowledge is effectively utilized to replenish, upgrade, and protect existing knowledge, or build new knowledge. We refer to this in Figure 1 as the thrust of organizational competencies (path 7).

Rapid technological changes, fierce competition, and radical socioeconomic changes have compelled companies to reconsider where and how to compete (Bogner et al., 1998). The knowledge gained in CE activities and the changes they can cause in the domain of organizational competencies can encourage firms to seek ways that protect their well-established core competencies. Yet, the traditional means of protecting these competencies are fast losing their relevance and currency in today's dynamic industries (Zahra, 1996; Zahra & Bogner, 1998). Given companies' widespread imitation of their rivals' innovations, the best protection of competencies may lie in constant innovation, institutionalizing and embedding these innovations into a firm's culture and structure.

CE activities can also extend a firm's existing competence by promoting the technical, combinative, or exploitative knowledge just discussed (Peters & Waterman, 1982; Pinchot, 1985). Not only do CE activities improve and extend these competencies, but they also frequently enhance the managerial practices associated with using these competencies (Burgelman & Sayles, 1986). The interaction of improved organizational competencies and increased managerial skills in using them can significantly improve organizational performance (Spender & Grant, 1996; Grant, 1997).

Finally, the knowledge gained in CE activities can result in new organizational competencies that revolutionize where and how the firm competes. Corporate venturing, for example, can lead the firm to enter new markets to capitalize on its new knowledge (Zahra, 1993a,b; Zahra & Garvis, 1999). Indeed, in their quest to capitalize on newly acquired technologies and market skills, some U.S. firms have entered new foreign markets where these competencies can be effectively leveraged. Japanese (Kodama, 1995) and Korean (Kim, 1997) companies have done the same thing. International venturing efforts, a key component of CE activities, have been important for acquiring and exploiting new knowledge in creating and sharpening a firm's skills (Zahra, 1997; Zahra & Garvis, 1999). These observations lead to the following proposition:

P5: Knowledge created by CE activities significantly determines the competitive thrusts of organizational competencies.

The three strategic thrusts of organizational competencies just discussed above are interrelated. As the firm attempts to use the knowledge it has gained from CE, it often acquires new insights that extend its competencies. Incremental learning and subsequent accumulation of knowledge also change the way in which the firm assembles and exploits its competencies, leading to major revisions in the firm's competence base (Zahra & Das, 1993a, 1993b). These changes, however, are rarely automatic. Instead, as indicated in Figure 1 (path 9), these changes result from vigilant and effective management. Consequently, the following section examines the managerial roles and skills associated with the effective use of the knowledge generated through CE activities.

KNOWLEDGE INTEGRATION

The creation of new knowledge does not always produce a competence that gives the firm a competitive advantage. New knowledge is often fragmented, vague, and subject to multiple interpretations, and widely dispersed throughout the organization. Yet, establishing a new competence requires the integration of the multiple insights and ideas that developed within the firm's CE formal and informal activities. As indicated in path 5 (Figure 1), managers can overcome some of these problems by integrating new knowledge into the firm's preexisting competencies, laying a foundation for building new competencies (Zahra & Das, 1993b).

Integration is important to understand the nature and amount of knowledge the firm has gained from its CE activities and to explore new competence domains and thrusts that can enrich the firm's performance. Integration also embeds a firm's newly acquired knowledge into its culture, systems, and operations, allowing the firm to develop competencies that can improve organizational competencies and performance. These observations suggest the following proposition:

P6: Knowledge integration determines the domains and thrusts of CE-based organizational competencies.

Successful knowledge integration requires several managerial skills that include: recognition and identification of learning; articulation; focusing and sense making of the new knowledge; and communicating and transferring this knowledge to other parts of the organization. The intraprenur or manager must also rely on his or her social capital to achieve the effective integration of this knowledge.

Recognition and Identification of New Knowledge

Intrapreneurs and managers can determine the fate of emerging learning and knowledge within a firm's CE activities. In particular, their personal insights and experience can affect the knowledge these individuals gain and what they do with it. Opportunity recognition, therefore, is a highly prized quality among intrapreneurs (Pinchot, 1985). This recognition gives meaning to a firm's experiences in formal and informal CE activities, and draws lessons beyond the initial conditions that produced these experiences (Nonaka, 1991, 1994; Nonaka & Takeuchi, 1995). Successful intrapreneurs are "sense makers" who add meaning to the firm's knowledge from formal and informal innovation and venturing activities, and then use the lessons they have learned elsewhere. Without this ability to spot, identify, and interpret emerging knowledge, organizational learning may not materialize within CE activities.

Intrapreneurs, however, do not always recognize the importance of the insights they or members of the CE team have gained. Cognitive biases, limited perspectives, and faulty thinking patterns sometimes limit the intrapreneurs' ability to discern and use new knowledge (Pinchot, 1985). Fortunately, intrapreneurs are not the only "sense-makers" in CE activities. Individuals and groups involved in CE activities often see the potential of emerging knowledge. Other organizational members who are not directly or intimately involved with CE activities can also add richly to these insights. Companies, therefore, need to develop effective organizational processes that enable the intrapreneur to come to grips with the meaning and potential implications of emerging knowledge. For any individual, however, perfection is not expected. By channelling the knowledge flow through the organization, a greater understanding of the nature and effect of this knowledge typically *unfolds* as the ideas are discussed, shared, or used. These observations suggest the following proposition:

P7: Knowledge recognition and identification facilitates the integration of CE-based new knowledge into competence domains and thrusts.

Articulation

Articulation is a managerial skill that focuses on specifying the type and depth of new knowledge that might exist among members of the CE venture. It enhances awareness of the existence of knowledge among the members of the CE team and crystallizes the insights they have gained. Articulation and crystallization make CE team members aware of the knowledge they have gained as well as the significance of this knowledge.

The intrapreneur can play a significant role in articulating the new knowledge gained from formal and informal CE. In particular, the intrapreneur can help to overcome the fragmentation resulting from differences in individual learning processes or functional specialization. Fragmentation of knowledge often results from individuals' lack of self-insight, wherein they do not recognize what they know. Because flashes of creativity are often fleeting and ambiguity surrounds personal insights, alert intrapreneurs are apt to understand that people know more than they actually realize and can help them define what they know. Further, as noted above, specialization usually involves complex routines, which are understood only by insiders (Schein, 1996). An effective intrapreneur therefore can provide a common means of communicating ideas and interpreting events, enabling members of the CE team to interact and communicate effectively.

An intrapreneur also has to overcome the fragmentation of knowledge caused by the ad hoc, autonomous CE efforts. As noted earlier, some of these efforts lack a clear connection to each other or to the firm's formal CE activities (Pinchot, 1985). Integrating autonomous behaviors into shared knowledge requires team work. The complexity associated with the development of knowledge (e.g., the different types of knowledge and the learning process) accentuates this need (McGrath et al., 1995). Intrapreneurs, therefore, can help to resolve conflicts between differing viewpoints (Fiol, 1991, 1994) and develop a shared understanding and interpretation of the information at hand (Weick & Roberts, 1993).

An intrapreneur can also proactively seek to overcome the fragmentation of knowledge within CE by developing a sense of "groupness," defined as the cohesion and smooth functioning of the CE team. Groupness is important for "heedful relating," which exists when the members of a group understand each other, work towards a common goal, and function as one (Weick & Roberts, 1993). To develop this groupness, the intrapreneur has to balance and direct the skills that exist among the CE venture team. These observations suggest the following proposition:

P8: Articulation facilitates the integration of CE-based new knowledge into competence domains and thrusts.

Focusing and Sense Making

Focusing is another important managerial task in the CE-based knowledge integration process. It requires the intrapreneur to make sense of the knowledge the CE team or its members have gained. Consequently, the intrapreneur has to give individual insights meaning by connecting, rearranging, or interpreting them, setting the stage for further learning.

Focusing, as a component of knowledge integration, also requires attention to the social dimension of learning. Data are viewed and interpreted from the prism of organizational objectives, resources, and competencies as well as the political realities that exist within a firm and the diverse agendas that permeate its structure and culture. The particular meaning given to the data also depends on a firm's competitive milieu, and the intrapreneur or CE champion must be adept at recognizing this reality. In turn, an understanding of organizational forces can set the stage for identifying and appreciating the knowledge created in CE activities, which can then determine the potential uses of the data. When the intrapreneur or the CE champion has found organizational meaning for the knowledge created in CE activities, a strong connection to the firm's dominant strategic agenda is established. Linking CE-created knowledge to the firm's competencies, however, requires further investments by the intrapreneur, particularly in sharing and communicating the knowledge created within CE. This discussion suggests the following proposition:

P9: Focusing facilitates the integration of CE-based knowledge into competence domains and thrusts.

Communicating and Transferring Knowledge

Grant (1996, 1997) highlights the role of formal and informal communication and sharing for the effective integration of knowledge. The insights or knowledge gained in CE activities may not have much of an impact on the organization unless they are widely shared with other groups in the firm. Technical discoveries, for example, may not have much effect on the firm's bottom line unless they are shared with, and communicated to, the manufacturing and marketing functions (Zahra & Nielsen, 1998). Here, too, the intrapreneur can play a pivotal role in identifying the key contact persons within the firm and determining the best time and approach to share this information. The intrapreneur can also communicate the information he or she receives from his or her contacts, thus promoting further refinements in the knowledge created through CE activities.

Schein's (1996) discussion of the obstacles to effective organizational learning also reinforces the importance of communication and sharing knowledge. Schein notes that multiple subcultures exist within a firm, with each culture having its dominant values and assumptions. When new ideas, discoveries, or innovations emerge, each subculture is apt to emphasize particular attributes in evaluating the viability of these ideas (innovations). Understanding the key values of these subcultures and recognizing the key power brokers within them can spell the difference in the success or failure of these innovations (Rogers, 1995). The same applies to the knowledge created within CE activities.

Intrapreneurs have to do more than understand organizational subcultures, however. They must work closely with their CE venture group to revise the idea and make it more acceptable to key power brokers and other influential stakeholders in the firm (Pinchot, 1985). These iterative revisions are necessary to realign the CE team's findings to the needs and objectives of the firm. They are an integral part of the knowledge-conversion cycle in the intrapreneurial process because they make the knowledge generated in CE activities politically salient and organizationally relevant (Nonaka & Takeuchi, 1995). This task is accomplished more fully through the effective transfer of knowledge. These observations suggest the following two propositions:

P10: Communication facilitates the integration of new CE-based knowledge into competence domains and thrusts.

P11: Knowledge sharing facilitates the integration of new CE-based knowledge into competence domains and thrusts.

Using Social Knowledge

The preceding section argued that an idea, insight, or discovery should be made accessible to multiple groups and units that may see uses for the new knowledge. The effective transfer of knowledge and its subsequent use in developing or improving competence, however, depends on the intrapreneur's social knowledge. This is defined as the intrapreneur's understanding of the causes and consequences of other organizational members' behaviors and needs, and how to best develop and maintain a sense of groupness.

The intrapreneur's social knowledge can determine the success of knowledge transfer. For instance, this knowledge can help to overcome the fragmentation of knowledge (Kanter, 1985) by inducing sharing, communication, and integration. Some CE ideas (ventures) are more complex than others, and the more complex the idea the greater the need for a systemic or holistic learning that promotes cross-functional integration and collaboration. As integration increases, CE ideas and findings are better understood and their chances of being adopted increase. Collaboration also encourages future learning, as individuals (or groups) with different functional perspectives exchange information and become aware of existing problems and opportunities. Interfunctional learning promotes the development of new competencies (Dodgson, 1992). This suggests the following proposition:

P12: A high degree of social knowledge by the intrapreneur is important for the success of CE activities.

Successful intrapreneurs frequently employ several social skills in creating momentum for transferring and accepting the knowledge created in CE activities. Intrapreneurs persuade, motivate, or coerce to create and later transfer knowledge throughout the organization. Intrapreneurs make use of *social capital* to gain access to resources (Starr & MacMillan, 1990), and overcome weak organizational power bases that sometimes limit their abilities to use the company's formal reward system to provide incentives to followers. Intrapreneurs also use social capital to build support for their projects and gain legitimacy within the organization. This social capital is usually embedded in trust.

Trust is important for embedding the CE team's discoveries into the firm's culture. Some organizational cultures promote sharing and integration of ideas (Nonaka & Takeuchi, 1995). These cultures also encourage autonomous efforts to achieve this integration and support the development of formal organizational systems that capture, integrate, and exploit this knowledge (Hamel & Prahalad, 1994; Szulanski, 1996). Such corporate cultures understand that while autonomous CE activities are inevitable and desirable, organization and communication systems should exist to capture the knowledge that might develop and connect them to other bases of knowledge. These organizational cultures also recognize that new knowledge may contradict the firm's existing definition of competencies, and therefore ways must be found to creatively exploit this tension. The intrapreneur's abilities to link the CE group to the firm's administrative structure and culture ensures that new knowledge is evaluated, interpreted accurately, and creatively exploited. Trust facilitates the effective sharing of information, promotes discussions of its technical, organizational, and political implications, and encourages the firm to connect the knowledge created within its CE activities with other competencies. Thus, when trust prevails, the chances are higher that the CE team and the intrapreneur will receive support from other organizational members in exploiting new knowledge in building competencies. This discussion suggests the following proposition:

P13: A high degree of social knowledge of the intrapreneur is important for the success of CE activities.

KNOWLEDGE DEPLOYMENT

The intrapreneur's success in integrating the knowledge created within the firm's CE activities sets the stage for its effective cultivation in building new competence domains, thrusts, or both (path 8 in Figure 1). We refer to this as knowledge deployment. New or revised competencies can increase a firm's financial and non-financial performance by maximizing its strategic options, reducing its costs, or altering the competitive dynamics of the industry (Burgelman, 1991). These competencies also provide a platform from which the firm can launch new products, develop new systems and processes, or revise the scope of its operations to achieve higher performance. The firm can also use its competencies to achieve flexibility in its operations, improve its responsiveness to its markets, and offer a wider variety of products and services to its customers. Competencies can strengthen a firm's competitive position by linking it to other firms in the same industry or in other industries.

Clearly, the knowledge-conversion cycle envisioned by Nonaka (1991) is incomplete without the deployment of new knowledge. Effective deployment means exploiting the new knowledge created within CE in the firm's operations. It requires the intrapreneur or CE champion to work closely with interested parties in the firm to exploit the new competencies by making use of social capital to explore new strategic directions. CE champions and intrapreneurs can also influence the firm's strategic agenda by demonstrating the strategic benefits of the new knowledge and ways in which it can be effectively harvested. These observations suggest the following, final proposition:

P14: Knowledge deployment moderates the relationship between the domain and thrusts of new competencies and company performance; the relationship between these competencies and performance will be higher when new knowledge is deployed than when it is not.

CONCLUSION

In this paper, we have argued that prior research has overlooked a major contribution of CE activities: improving overall organizational learning and driving the wide range of knowledge creation that becomes the foundation of new organizational competencies. Although some researchers (e.g., Burgelman, 1991; Kanter, 1989; Zahra, 1991) have noted these potential contributions, little systematic attention has been given to showing how effective CE activities induce learning as well as knowledge creation and use, a gap this paper has attempted to overcome.

The paper makes four interrelated points. First, CE efforts are important for successful organizational learning and knowledge creation. Second, creating value from the wide range of new knowledge generated in CE activities requires management of the process of articulating, focusing, sharing, and transferring this knowledge. These processes are essential for the developing and maintaining of competence. The knowledge processes captured by CE activities are multifaceted and complex. Through knowledge articulation and transfer a foundation for building organizational competencies is set. Third, trust is important not only for promoting CE activities, but also for creating and utilizing knowledge resulting from these efforts. Fourth, because learning "is not entirely benign in its consequences" (Levinthal & March, 1993), a firm's culture has a major role in spurring CE efforts, creating knowledge, and making proprietary uses of this knowledge. The organizational culture can profoundly influence the interpretation and subsequent uses of merging knowledge. The intrapreneur has a key role to play in connecting CE activities to the firm's culture and strategic agenda.

Given the important consequences of CE activities for building organizational competence, we believe that the time has come to explicitly consider organizational learning and knowledge creation as outcomes of formal and informal CE activities. If learning and knowledge are important to successful organizational adaptation, then we need also to use these variables as yardsticks in measuring the outcomes of CE activities. Researchers are encouraged to explore the conditions under which formal and informal CE activities encourage learning and promote the development of new knowledge. Knowledge and learning efforts, therefore, can and should be considered key "dependent" variables in future CE research. Linking the learning and knowledge gained through CE activities to organizational performance is also an important future research issue. Studies along these lines can improve our understanding of when and how formal and informal CE activities add value to the firm. We hope this paper will encourage other researchers to explore these issues and deepen our understanding of the role of CE activities in the creation of knowledge and the development of organizational competence.

REFERENCES

Andrews, K R (1980) *The concept of corporate strategy*, second ed Homewood, IL Richard D. Irwin.

Baden-Fuller, C., & Stopford, M. J (1994). *Rejuvenating the mature business*, Boston Harvard Business School Press

Barney, J (1991) Firm resources and sustained competitive advantage. *Journal of Management, 17*, 99-120

Bettis, R A , & Hitt, M A (1995) The new competitive landscape. *Strategic Management Journal, 16* (special issue), 7-19.

Bogner, W. C., Thomas, H., & McGee, J. (1998) *Core competence and competitive advantage. A dynamic, theory-based model* Working Paper, Georgia State University, Atlanta

Bohn, R E. (1994) Measuring and managing technological knowledge *Sloan Management Review, 36*(1), 61-73

Brazeal, D. V. (1993) Organizing for internally developed corporate ventures *Journal of Business Venturing, 8*(1), 75-90

Brown, J S (1991). Research that reinvents the corporation *Harvard Business Review, 69*(1), 102-111

Burgelman, R. A (1983a). A model of the interaction of strategic behavior, corporate context, and the concept of strategy. *Academy of Management Review, 8*(1), 61-70.

Burgelman, R. A (1983b). A process model of internal corporate venturing in the diversified major firm *Administrative Science Quarterly, 28*(2), 223-244

Burgelman, R A. (1983c). Corporate entrepreneurship and strategic management: Insights from a process study *Management Science, 29*(12), 1349-1364.

Burgelman, R. A. (1991) Intraorganizational ecology of strategy-making and organizational adaptation. Theory and field research *Organization Science, 2*, 239-262

Burgelman, R A., & Sayles, L. R. (1986). *Inside corporate innovation strategy, structure and managerial skills* New York: The Free Press.

Clark, K B., & Fujimoto, T. (1991). *Product development performance,* Boston: Harvard Business School Press.

Covin, J. G , & Slevin, D. (1991). A conceptual model of entrepreneurship as firm behavior. *Entrepreneurship Theory and Practice, 16*(1), 7-25.

D'Aveni, R. (1994) *Hypercompetition Managing the dynamics of strategic maneuvering.* New York The Free Press.

Day, G S. (1994). Continuous learning about markets *California Management Review, 36*(4), 9-31

Dess, G. G , Lumpkin, G T., & Covin, J. G. (1997). Entrepreneurial strategy making and firm performance Tests of contingency and configurational models. *Strategic Management Journal, 18*(9), 677-695.

Dodgson, M (1993). Organizational learning: A review of some literatures. *Organization Studies, 14*(3), 375-394.

Dodgson, M. (1992). Technological collaborations: Problems and pitfalls. *Technology Analysis & Strategic Management, 4*(1), 83-88.

Dougherty, D., & Heller, T (1994) The illegitimacy of product innovation in large firms *Organization Science, 5*(2), 200-218.

Fiol, C M (1991). Managing culture as a competitive resource: An identity-based view of sustainable competitive advantage *Journal of Management, 17*, 191-211.

Fiol, C M (1994). Consensus diversity, and learning in organizations. *Organization Science, 5*(3), 403-420.

Grant, R. M. (1995). *Contemporary strategy analysis: Concepts, techniques, applications,* second ed Cambridge, MA: Blackwell Publishers Inc.

Grant, R. M. (1996). Toward a knowledge-based theory of the firm *Strategic Management Journal, 17,* 109-122.

Grant, R. M. (1997). The knowledge-based view of the firm: Implications for management practice. *Long-Range Planning, 30*(3), 450-454

Hamel, G , & Prahalad, C. K. (1989). Strategic intent *Harvard Business Review, 67*(3), 63-76

Hamel, G., & Prahalad, C K (1993) Strategy as stretch and leverage *Harvard Business Review, 71*(2), 75-84.

Hamel, G , & Prahalad, C. K. (1994) *Competing for the future.* Boston: Harvard Business School Press.

Hamel, G , & Prahalad, C. K (1996). Competing in the new economy. Managing out of bounds. *Strategic Management Journal, 17*(3), 237-242.

Hedlund, G. (1994) A model of knowledge management and the N-form corporation. *Strategic Management Journal, 15* (special issue), 73-90

Helfat, C E. (1994) Evolutionary trajectories in petroleum firm R&D. *Management Science, 20*(12), 1720-1747

Henderson, R , & Cockburn, I. (1994). Measuring competence? Exploring firm effects in pharmaceutical research. *Strategic Management Journal, 15* (special issue), 63-84

Huber, G. (1991). Organizational learning. The contributing processes and literatures. *Organization Science, 2*, 88-115.

Itami, H (1987). *Mobilizing invisible assets* Boston Harvard University Press

Kanter, R. (1985) Supporting innovation and venture development in established companies. *Journal of Business Venturing, 1*(1), 47-60.

Kanter, R (1989) *When giants learn to dance.* New York Simon & Schuster

Kim, L (1997) *Imitation to innovation: The dynamics of Korea's technological learning* Boston Harvard Business School Press.

Kodama, F (1995) *Emerging patterns of innovation Sources of Japan's technological edge* Boston Harvard Business School Press

Kogut, B., & Zander, U. (1992). Knowledge of the firm, combinatory capabilities, and the replication of technology *Organization Science, 3*(3), 383-397

Kuratko, D , Montagno, R., & Hornsby, J. (1990). Developing an intrapreneurial assessment instrument for effective corporate entrepreneurial environment *Strategic Management Journal, 11* (Summer), 49-58.

Lei, D., Hitt, M. A , & Bettis, R. (1996) Dynamic core competencies through meta-learning and strategic context. *Journal of Management, 22*(4), 549-569.

Levinthal, D A , & March, J G. (1993) The myopia of learning *Strategic Management Journal, 14* (special issue), 95-112.

Lumpkin, G T , & Dess, G. G (1996) Clarifying the entrepreneurial orientation construct and linking it to performance *Academy of Management Review, 21*(3), 135-172

Mahoney, J. T , & Pandian, J. R (1992) The resource-based view within the conversation of strategic management. *Strategic Management Journal, 13*(5), 363-380.

McGrath, R. G., MacMillan, I. C , & Venkataraman, S (1995). Defining and developing a competence. A strategic process paradigm *Strategic Management Journal, 16*(4), 251-275.

Miller, D (1983). The correlates of entrepreneurship in three types of firms *Management Science, 29*(7), 770-791

Nelson, R , & Winter, S (1982). *An evolutionary theory of economic change.* Cambridge, MA. Harvard University Press

Nonaka, I (1991) The knowledge-creating company *Harvard Business Review, 69*(6), 96-104

Nonaka, I (1994). A dynamic theory of organizational knowledge creation *Organization Science, 5*(1), 14-37.

Nonaka, I., & Takeuchi, H (1995). *The knowledge-creating company. How Japanese companies create the dynamics of innovation* New York Oxford University Press

Penrose, R. (1959) *The theory of the growth of the firm* New York: John Wiley

Peters, T. J., & Waterman, R H., Jr (1982). *In search of excellence.* New York. Harper and Row.

Peterson, R., & Berger, D. (1971). Entrepreneurship in organizations. *Administrative Science Quarterly, 16,* 97-106

Pinchot G, III. (1985) *Intrapreneuring: Why you don't have to leave the corporation to become an entrepreneur* New York: Harper and Row.

Pisano, G P. (1996). Learning-before-doing in the development of new process technology. *Research Policy, 25*(7), 1097-1119.

Prahalad, C. K, & Hamel, G. (1990). The core competence of the corporation. *Harvard Business Review,* May-June, 79-91

Rogers, E. (1995). *Diffusion of innovations,* fourth ed. New York· Free Press.

Schein, E H. (1996). Three cultures of management: The key to organizational learning. *Sloan Management Review, 38*(1), 9-20

Schumpeter, J. (1934). *The theory of economic development* Cambridge, MA· Harvard University Press

Spender, J-C, & Grant, R. M. (1996). Knowledge and the firm: Overview *Strategic Management Journal, 17,* 5-9.

Starr, J. A, & MacMillan, I (1990). Resource cooptation via social contracting· Resource acquisition strategies for new ventures. *Strategic Management Journal, 11,* 79-92.

Stopford, J, & Baden-Fuller, C (1990). Creating corporate entrepreneurship. *Strategic Management Journal, 15*(7), 521-536

Szulanski, G. (1996) Exploring internal stickiness· Impediments to the transfer of best practice within the firm. *Strategic Management Journal, 17* (Winter), 27-43.

Teece, D, Pisano, G., & Shuen, A. (1997). Dynamic capabilities and strategic management *Strategic Management Journal, 18*(7), 509-533.

Tushman, M. L, & Anderson, P. (1986). Technological discontinuities and organizational environments. *Administrative Science Quarterly, 31*(3), 439-465

Weick, K E., & Roberts, K H. (1993). Collective mind in organizations: Heedful interrelating on flight decks. *Administrative Science Quarterly, 38*(3), 357-381.

Wernerfelt, B. (1995) The resource-based view of the firm: Ten years after. *Strategic Management Journal, 16,* 171-174.

Zahra, S. (1991) Predictors and financial outcomes of corporate entrepreneurship: An exploratory study *Journal of Business Venturing, 6*(4), 259-285.

Zahra, S. (1993a). Environment, corporate entrepreneurship and financial performance A taxonomic approach. *Journal of Business Venturing, 8*(4), 319-340

Zahra, S (1993b). A conceptual model of entrepreneurship as firm behavior A critique and extension. *Entrepreneurship Theory and Practice, 14*(4), 5-21

Zahra, S (1995). Corporate entrepreneurship and company performance. The case of management leveraged buyouts *Journal of Business Venturing, 10*(3), 225-247.

Zahra, S. (1996). Governance, ownership and corporate entrepreneurship among the Fortune 500 The moderating impact of industry technological opportunities. *Academy of Management Journal, 39,* 1713-1735.

Zahra, S. (1997) *Research on the international dimensions of corporate entrepreneurship· Opportunities, challenges and rewards* Paper presented at the Academy of Management Meeting (Joint Symposium sponsored by the Entrepreneurship and International Management Divisions), Boston

Zahra, S , & Bogner, W (1998) Technology strategy and software new ventures' performance Exploring the moderating effect of the competitive environment *Journal of Business Venturing*, in press

Zahra, S., & Chaples, S. (1993) Blind spots in competitive analysis *Academy of Management Executive*, 7(2), 7-28

Zahra, S , & Covin, J G. (1995). Contextual influences on the corporate entrepreneurship-performance relationship. A longitudinal analysis. *Journal of Business Venturing*, 10(1), 43-58

Zahra, S , Covin, S., & Zahra, P (1998) Organizational structure and corporate entrepreneurship. Implications for performance. *Journal of Enterprising Culture*, in press

Zahra, S , & Das, S. (1993a). Innovation strategy and financial performance in manufacturing companies An empirical analysis *Production and Operations Management*, 2(1), 15-37.

Zahra, S., & Das, S. (1993b) Building competitive advantage on manufacturing resources. *Long Range Planning*, 26(2), 90-100

Zahra, S , & Garvis, S. (1999) International corporate entrepreneurship and company performance: The moderating effect of international environmental hostility. *Journal of Business Venturing*, in press.

Zahra, S., Nash, S , & Bickford, D. (1995) Transforming technological pioneering into competitive advantage *Academy of Management Executive*, 9(1), 17-31

Zahra, S , & Pearce, J (1994) Corporate entrepreneurship in smaller firms: The role of strategy, environment and organization. *Entrepreneurship, Innovation and Change*, 3(1), 31-44.

Zahra, S , & Nielsen, A. (1998). Integration as a moderator of the relationship between sources manufacturing capabilities and technology commercialization *Academy of Management Best Papers Proceedings*

Shaker A Zahra is Professor of Management at Georgia State University, Atlanta

Anders P Nielsen is at Aslborg University, Denmark

William C. Bogner is at Georgia State University, Atlanta

We acknowledge with appreciation the helpful suggestions of Dennis Garvis, Brett Matherne, and Patricia H Zahra The support of the Beebe Institute at Georgia State University is also gratefully acknowledged.

Address Correspondence to Professor Shaker A. Zahra, Department of Management, College of Business Administration, Georgia State University, Atlanta, GA 30303 [e-mail· szahra @ GSU EDU]

[34]

Pergamon

Journal of Management 2003 29(3) 351–378

JOURNAL OF
MANAGEMENT

Emerging Issues in Corporate Entrepreneurship

Gregory G. Dess*
School of Management, University of Texas at Dallas, Richardson, TX 75083-0688, USA

R. Duane Ireland
Department of Management Systems, Robins School of Business, University of Richmond, Richmond, VA 23173, USA

Shaker A. Zahra
Entrepreneurship Division, Babson College, Babson Park, MA 02157-0310, USA

Steven W. Floyd
School of Business Administration, The University of Connecticut, 368 Fairfield Road, Storrs, CT 06269, USA

Jay J. Janney
Department of Management and Marketing, School of Business Administration, University of Dayton, 300 College Park, Dayton, OH 95469-2271, USA

Peter J. Lane
Department of Management, College of Business, Arizona State University, P.O. Box 874006, Tempe, AZ 85287-4006, USA

Research on corporate entrepreneurship (CE) has grown rapidly over the past decade. In this article, we identify four major issues scholars can pursue to further our understanding about CE. The issues we explore include various forms of CE (e.g., sustained regeneration, domain redefinition) and their implications for organizational learning; the role of leadership and social exchange in the CE process; and, key research opportunities relevant to CE in an international context. To address the latter issue, we propose a typology that separates content from process-related studies and new ventures vs. established companies. We close with a reassessment of the outcomes in CE research, which becomes particularly salient with the increasing importance of social, human, and intellectual capital in creating competitive advantages and wealth in today's knowledge economy. Throughout the article, we use the organizational learning theory as a means of integrating our discussion and highlighting the potential contributions of CE to knowledge creation and effective exploitation.
© 2003 Elsevier Science Inc. All rights reserved.

---

* Corresponding author. Tel.: +1-972-883-2703; fax: +1-972-883-2799.
E-mail addresses: gdess@utdallas.edu (G.G. Dess), direland@richmond.edu (R.D. Ireland), sazahra@hotmail.com (S.A. Zahra), steven@sba.uconn.edu (S.W. Floyd), janney@notes.udayton.edu (J.J. Janney), peter.lane@asu.edu (P.J. Lane).

0149-2063/03/$ – see front matter © 2003 Elsevier Science Inc. All rights reserved.
doi:10.1016/S0149-2063(03)00015-1

352 *G.G. Dess et al. / Journal of Management 2003 29(3) 351–378*

Both scholars and practitioners remain interested in studying and better understanding corporate entrepreneurship (CE) (Ireland, Kuratko & Covin, 2002). CE has been viewed as the driver of new businesses within on-going enterprises as achieved through internal innovation, joint ventures or acquisitions; strategic renewal (Guth & Ginsberg, 1990; Hitt, Nixon, Hoskisson & Kockhar, 1999); product, process, and administrative innovations (Covin & Miles, 1999); diversification (Burgelman, 1991); and processes through which individuals' ideas are transformed into collective actions through the management of uncertainties (Chung & Gibbons, 1997). Sharma and Chrisman define CE as "... the process whereby an individual or a group of individuals, in association with an existing organization, create a new organization, or instigate renewal or innovation within that organization" (1999: 18).

Given its importance to corporate vitality and wealth generation in today's global economy, CE has generated considerable attention in research. This paper identifies emerging issues in CE and suggests research questions for future research. Our analysis highlights the role of CE in inducing and cultivating organizational learning, which is a key source of new knowledge that could be used to develop organizational capabilities. Learning is at the heart of the strategic renewal process that enables the firm to adapt and respond to challenges in their new markets (Zahra, Nielsen & Bogner, 1999). Given the various types of CE (Covin & Miles, 1999), our discussion applies learning theory to show how CE in domestic and international operations creates new knowledge. This discussion also gives attention to the role of leadership in stimulating organizational learning within CE and harvesting new knowledge. Finally, recognizing the vital importance of learning for strategic renewal, we propose that future researchers should incorporate learning among the key outcomes of CE activities.

The organizational learning theory suggests that when companies are exposed to new and diverse stimuli, the stage is set for questioning existing assumptions and beliefs. This process also induces experimentation, which fosters learning by doing. Learning means the acquisition of information and knowledge that is new for a firm. This learning is important for the creation and exploitation of the knowledge necessary for product, process and organizational innovation. Therefore, throughout this article we highlight the importance of CE activities for promoting organizational learning and developing new knowledge that generates advantages.

Our analysis of CE covers four major issues. The first is how knowledge is created through four types of CE—sustained regeneration, organizational rejuvenation, strategic renewal, and domain redefinition. Mediated by two forms of organizational learning, these CE types lead to three forms of new knowledge that are then used differently within the firm.

Next, we identify the critical roles and social exchanges that comprise the CE process. This analysis shows how entrepreneurial roles and information exchanges across multiple levels of management promote the kinds of organizational learning required by the four types of CE. Based on this perspective, we define entrepreneurial leadership as establishing the conditions conducive to role performance and social exchange. These conditions include organization trust, consensus on dominant logic, and appropriate organizational controls.

Third, we address the dynamic interplay between CE and internationalization. We use a typology that separates content from CE process-related studies in new ventures vs. established companies. In addition to reviewing and synthesizing studies conducted in each

G.G. Dess et al. / Journal of Management 2003 29(3) 351–378 353

cell, we highlight major findings from earlier research in each area, identify gaps, and suggest promising avenues for future CE research. The discussion draws attention to knowledge creation and exploitation as important objectives within CE.

Fourth, we address the outcome variables in CE research. We provide examples of how performance indicators must reflect the temporal nature of CE. In addition, we draw on such literatures as knowledge management, options theory, and entrepreneurial failure to discuss how the increasing importance of social, human, and intellectual capital necessitates new conceptualizations of performance. This discussion concludes by highlighting the importance of learning and knowledge creation as dependent variables in future CE research.

CE, Organizational Learning, and Knowledge

Deliberate and intentional in nature, CE is concerned with various forms of newness (e.g., organizational renewal, innovation, and establishing new ventures) and has its consequences for organizational survival, growth, and performance (Kazanjian, Drazin & Glynn, 2001). Increasingly, CE is found to affect firm performance (Zahra & Covin, 1995; Zahra & Nielsen, 2002). From a resource-based perspective, CE is a key means of accumulating, converting, and leveraging resources for competitive purposes (Floyd & Wooldridge, 1999) such as developing and using product, process, and administrative innovations to rejuvenate and redefine the firm and its markets or industries (Covin & Miles, 1999).

An intangible resource vital to 21st century organizations (Hitt & Ireland, 2002; Ireland & Hitt, 1999), *knowledge* can be created through effective CE (Kuratko, Ireland & Hornsby, 2001). In fact, Zahra et al. (1999: 169) argue that, "... formal and informal CE activities can enrich a company's performance by creating new knowledge that becomes a foundation for building new competencies or revitalizing existing ones." Embedded primarily within the firm's human capital (Lepak & Snell, 1999), knowledge is information that is laden with experience, judgment, intuition, and value (Nonaka & Takeuchi, 1995). Both explicit and tacit in nature, knowledge is mutable and can be thought of as true justified belief (von Grogh, Ichijo & Nonaka, 2000).

Given its centrality to forming competitive advantages that often are the path the firm travels to outperform its rivals (Coff, 2002; Grant, 1996), today's firms benefit by facilitating the development and management of knowledge stocks and flows between people and organizational units (Ireland, Hitt, Camp & Sexton, 2001). We argue that through effective CE, firms develop knowledge and use it as a continuous source of innovations to outperform competitors (Kazanjian et al., 2001). In this context, CE is a knowledge enabler as it forms and subsequently uses or applies knowledge (von Grogh et al., 2000)—knowledge that at its best, is valuable, new, unique, and competitively relevant (Zahra et al., 1999).

According to Zahra et al. (1999: 177), "CE activities can lead to three different types of new knowledge." CE's multidimensionality (Covin & Miles, 1999) complicates these relationships. Moreover, we believe that organizational learning mediates the relationships between different CE types and different kinds of knowledge. In turn, the different types of knowledge (i.e., technical, integrative, and exploitative) should be used differently for the organization to gain maximum competitive benefit from them.

354   *G.G. Dess et al. / Journal of Management 2003 29(3) 351–378*

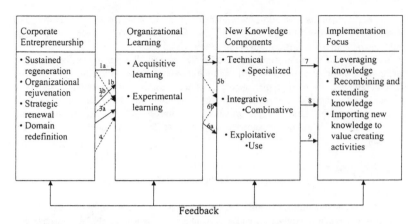

Figure 1. Relationships among CE strategy, organizational learning, knowledge and implementation.

We explore these issues through a series of proposed relationships (see Figure 1) that are drawn primarily from the entrepreneurship and strategic management literatures' theory and empirical results. As stated above, the general expectation of relationships among Figure 1's variables is established (Covin & Miles, 1999; Zahra et al., 1999). However, the relationships we propose between different types of CE and new knowledge, as moderated by two types of organizational learning, have not been specified. As such, the expectations depicted in Figure 1 are untested and represent fertile ground for entrepreneurship and strategic management researchers.

Forms of Corporate Entrepreneurship

Covin and Miles (1999) conceptualize four types of CE, with each one oriented to either rejuvenating or intentionally redefining the organization or establishing innovation. Structurally complex firms such as those engaging in product and/or market diversification may simultaneously use one of more or even all four CE forms in different parts of the company.

Concerned primarily with continuous innovations, *sustained regeneration* is the most frequently recognized CE form. Here, the firm develops cultures, processes, and structures to support and encourage a continuous stream of new product introductions in its current markets as well as entries with existing products into new markets (Covin & Miles, 1999). Firms are aware of product life cycles and often frame product strategies around the competitive expectations associated with them. Commonly viewed as competitors who understand an industry's accepted rules of engagement (Porter, 1980), firms involved with CE commit to the importance of learning and adapting while actively competing against rivals. Demonstrating an ability to introduce new products and enter new markets, Arm and Hammer uses sustained regeneration as it creatively works with baking soda, its core product. According to Covin and Miles (1999: 51): "... through the development and introduction of baking soda-based toothpaste and deodorizing products, Arm and Hammer has been able to capitalize on emerging product-market opportunities unseen or underappreciated by competitors in its core industry segment."

The firm's internal processes, structures, and capabilities are the targets of *oganizational rejuvenation*. Concerned primarily with improving the firm's ability to execute strategies, organizational rejuvenation often entails changes to value chain activities. Demonstrating process and administrative innovations rather than product innovations, organizational rejuvenation shows that firms can become more entrepreneurial through processes and structures as well as by introducing new product and/or entering new markets with existing products. In recent years, GE rejuvenated itself by developing and using what others sometimes viewed as radical administrative routines and operating policies to support them. For the most part, CE efforts oriented to organizational rejuvenation are framed around support activities (e.g., procurement and human resource management) rather than primary (e.g., inbound logistics and operations) activities (Porter, 1980). The most successful organizational rejuvenation efforts renew one or more major aspects of the firm's operations.

Strategic renewal finds the firm seeking to change how it competes. Thus, the nature of rivalry with competitors is altered as the firm concentrates on renewing the strategies it uses to successfully align itself with its external environment. With organizational rejuvenation, the organization itself is the focus of CE efforts. This is in stark contrast to strategic renewal's intention of positively mediating the "organization-environment interface" (Covin & Miles, 1999: 52). At its best, CE as strategic renewal allows the firm to more profitably exploit product-market opportunities. Often, this outcome is achieved when the firm repositions itself in ways that allow simultaneous exploitation of current competitive advantages and exploration for advantages that will lead to future success (Ireland, Hitt & Vaidyanath, 2002). Harley-Davidson's turnaround demonstrates the use of this CE form. Cisco Systems' current attempt to renew itself through internal growth rather than acquisitions highlights this firm's effort to at least partially alter how it competes, given changes in its competitive environment.

Through *domain redefinition*, the firm proactively seeks to create a new product market position that competitors haven't recognized or have underserved (Covin & Miles, 1999). The focus here is exploring for what is possible rather than exploiting what is currently available. The commitment to reenergize the firm by redefining its domain is also intended to establish first mover advantages. As the first firm to sell an offering in a new product category (Golder & Tellis, 1993), the company redefining its domain is proactive and demonstrates a strong entrepreneurial orientation (Lumpkin & Dess, 1996). Sony's introduction of the innovative Walkman illustrates first mover actions that created a new product arena.

Types of Organizational Learning

Organizational learning is a capability allowing firms to create knowledge as the source of improved performance (Hitt & Ireland, 2000). Thus, organizational learning mediates or facilitates the relationships between CE and the development of new types of knowledge.

Organizational learning occurs through several avenues including *action* (called learning by doing) (Lieberman, 1984) and *memory* (the constant repetition of an organization's activities) (Nelson & Winter, 1982). Two major types of learning—acquisitive and experimental—occur as organizations using one or more types of CE learn by doing and through memory, among other avenues (Zahra et al., 1999) (see Figure 1).

356   *G.G. Dess et al. / Journal of Management 2003 29(3) 351–378*

Acquisitive learning takes place when the firm gains access to and subsequently internalizes preexisting knowledge from its external environment. Acquisition knowledge is grounded in public knowledge—that is, knowledge that resides in the public domain (Matusik, 2002). Because of this, acquisitive knowledge is rarely the source of uniqueness firms require to form sustainable competitive advantages (Leonard-Barton, 1995). But, the absence of access to publicly available knowledge and learning places the firm at a competitive disadvantage relative to rivals (Zahra et al., 1999) and reduces its ability to use CE as the path to creating a new organization or to engage in strategic renewal or successful innovation.

Experimental learning occurs inside the firm and generates knowledge that is distinctive to it. Private knowledge, which includes items such as the firm's unique routines, processes, trade secrets, and documentation (Matusik, 2002), is the basis of experimental learning. Because it is the product of firm-specific knowledge that may be valuable, rare, and imperfectly imitable, competitive advantages evolving from experimental learning tend to be more sustainable than are those that are products of acquisitive learning. Thus, acquisitive learning represents a necessary but insufficient condition for competitive success as measured by the firm's ability to develop new knowledge. Moreover, the emphasis on innovation as a source of successful competition in the global economy, in turn, leads to a premium on experimental learning relative to acquisitive learning for firms engaging in CE (Zahra & Garvis, 2000).

As shown in Figure 1, we argue that the different CE types have different relationships with the two types of organizational learning. In turn, three types of new knowledge are products of the interactions among CE forms and the two organizational learning types.

New Knowledge and its Implementation

Traveling through the organization's ability to learn, CE leads to three types of new knowledge. *Technical* knowledge, concerned with insights about the properties of specific activities, is vital to sustained regeneration and results primarily from acquisitive learning. Specialized in nature, technical knowledge helps the firm refine current products and extend product lines, often through process innovations. From an efficiency perspective, technical knowledge is vital to the firm's efforts to create more value by how it completes primary and support activities in its value chain(s). However, this type of knowledge is rarely the foundation for sustainable competitive advantages.

Organizational learning also leads to *integrative* knowledge. Firm-specific and predominately tacit in nature, it is a product of how the firm has learned to creatively and uniquely combine its idiosyncratic resources and capabilities to create value. Grounded in memory, history, and organizational routines, employees creating integrative knowledge do so by recombining and extending the firm's resources and capabilities in manners that demonstrate Schumpeter's (1934) classic conceptualization of an entrepreneur (Zahra et al., 1999). Thus, integrative knowledge results primarily from the combined, relatively indirect effects of acquisitive and experimental learning (Figure 1's dotted lines show the proposed indirect effects).

Exploitative knowledge accumulates as the firm learns how to exploit its resources. Thus, exploitative knowledge expands as the firm learns how to creatively find unique, value-creating ways to exploit its technical and integrative knowledge sets. This learning type is oriented to finding new ways of commercializing the firm's goods or services that evolved from effective applications of its technical and integrative knowledge.

As shown in Figure 1, we believe that a different emphasis is required for the firm to gain maximum benefit from the new knowledge components resulting from its use of CE as mediated by organizational learning. When using technical knowledge, the implementation focus is on leveraging knowledge. In contrast, recombining and extending knowledge is the outcome sought when the firm applies its new integrative knowledge. Lastly, the firm concentrates on importing new technical and integrative knowledge into value-creating primary and support activities when trying to effectively use its new exploitative knowledge.

Research Questions

We believe that relationships shown in Figure 1 should be tested empirically. Testing these relationships would require different specifications among the variables, given the proposed direct and indirect effects.

Our view is that indirect relationships between variables are not as strong as are the direct relationships. For example, sustained regeneration's relationship with acquisitive learning is stronger than is its relationship with experimental learning.

Recall that this type of CE finds the firm trying to learn how to apply its valuable innovation-producing capabilities in ways that will result in new products being introduced into current markets or existing products being introduced into new markets. In both instances, externally-based acquisitive knowledge can be used to help improve the organization as it learns how to continue applying existing advantages in value-creating ways. However, we also argue that sustained regeneration has an indirect relationship with experimental learning in that new products are unlikely to be produced without effort being devoted to developing and then using valuable, idiosyncratic organizational knowledge.

Space limitations preclude discussion of all the relationships are proposed in Figure 1. We encourage scholars to consider the theoretical validity of what we've proposed. If deemed theoretically sound, empirical testing of those relationships could answer interesting research questions as well as contribute to the entrepreneurship and strategic management literatures.

Entrepreneurial Leadership in Corporations: The Roles of Controls, Consensus and Trust

Corporate entrepreneurship often fails because large organizations present hostile environments for creative ideas (Burgelman, 1983a; Sharma & Chrisman, 1999). Innovative proposals are frequently defeated by financial control systems and other formalities that are typical of large bureaucracies (Kanter, 1983). Creating collateral organizations, such as new venture divisions can isolate entrepreneurial processes from the parent organization (Burgelman, 1983b). However, the isolation also makes it less likely that their initiatives will harmonize with the needs of the core business, which, in turn, reduces the likelihood that new ventures receive the support and acceptance, necessary to become commercially

358   *G.G. Dess et al. / Journal of Management 2003 29(3) 351–378*

viable (Sharma, 1999). Even when the CE process is established within the core of a firm, virtually all entrepreneurial initiatives face some degree of survival risk induced either by the structural or strategic context (Burgelman, 1983b). The firm needs to explore how its innovative and competitive capabilities can be redefined, renewed, or replaced while ensuring that the resulting changes in policies, priorities, and procedures will be accepted throughout the organization. Managers' acceptance of the new initiatives is of particular concern because they are the ones responsible for managing the shift from one set of operating routines to another. Indeed, the lack of such acceptance threatens the success of any organizational change effort (Kotter, 1995). Thus, a fundamental challenge in CE is managing the conflict between the new and the old and overcoming the inevitable tensions that such conflict produces for management.

Despite the potential importance of such conflict, prior research on CE leadership has paid little if any attention to the issue. One way to begin to focus on it is to build upon recent work on managers' strategic roles. Floyd and Lane (2000) suggest that strategic change involves a system of social exchanges between managerial roles. These roles form three sub-processes (competence deployment, competence modification, and competence definition). We believe that these processes drive the four types of CE identified above (Covin & Miles, 1999). (See the top rows of Table 1.)

Specifically, in *sustained regeneration* firms seek to create a steady stream of new product introductions and the entry of existing products into new markets. This requires a combination of competence deployment and competence modification. *Organizational rejuvenation* aims at improving the effectiveness of existing strategy by adjusting value chain activities, especially support activities. This requires deploying the firm's existing competence while modifying the organizational processes that enable such deployment. *Strategic renewal* goes beyond adjusting processes to fundamentally rethinking how the firm competes. This is the essence of competence definition. Finally, *domain redefinition* focuses on exploring possible new markets and products to create first-mover advantages. This is the most challenging of Covin and Miles (1999) types, as it typically requires both defining and deploying new competences.

Viewing CE as a system of roles and social exchanges provides a theoretical basis for *connecting* entrepreneurial activity to the organization's on-going agenda. Therefore, it suggests a way to examine how CE leadership may resolve conflicts between old and new priorities. More specifically, this perspective portrays the challenges of CE leadership as managing a social learning process involving roles and relationships among managers at the top, middle and operating levels of the organization. Thus, CE leadership depends not only on the skills and abilities of individuals but also on the quality of interactions within the management hierarchy—in particular, we will argue that it depends on the extent of shared understanding and the level of interpersonal trust in the organization. Researching the contingencies surrounding these attributes requires understanding the nature of the social exchanges in CE, the conflicts that disrupt them, and the resolution mechanisms at a leader's disposal.

CE Leadership as a System of Social Exchanges

The motivation for viewing CE as social exchange is the set of strategic roles shown in Table 1. The literature suggests that these roles are central to both CE and strategic renewal

G.G. Dess et al. / *Journal of Management* 2003 29(3) 351–378

359

Table 1
Social exchanges, managerial roles, and controls in corporate entrepreneurship

	Type of corporate entrepreneurship							
	Sustained regeneration		Organizational rejuvenation		Strategic renewal		Domain redefinition	
Effects on firm's competence	Deploy existing	Modify existing	Deploy existing	Modify existing	Deploy existing	Define new	Define new	Deploy new
Top management roles	Directing	Recognizing	Directing	Recognizing	Directing	Ratifying	Ratifying	Directing
Middle management roles	Implementing	Synthesizing and facilitating	Implementing	Synthesizing and facilitating	Implementing	Championing	Championing	Implementing
Operating management roles	Conforming	Adjusting	Conforming	Adjusting	Conforming	Experimenting	Experimenting	Conforming
Organizational controls needed	A mix of bureaucratic and clan controls	A mix of bureaucratic and clan controls	A mix of bureaucratic and clan controls	A mix of bureaucratic and clan controls	A mix of bureaucratic and market controls	A mix of bureaucratic and market controls	A mix of market and clan controls	A mix of market and clan controls

360   *G.G. Dess et al. / Journal of Management 2003 29(3) 351–378*

(Bartlett & Ghoshal, 1994; Hart, 1992; Nonaka, 1994). Performing in these roles involves processing information and taking action that facilitates organizational change, and it is the need for information to perform in these roles that gives rise to our focus on social exchange as a central feature of CE.

In contrast to bounded rationality or political views, a social exchange perspective of CE (MacNeil, 1974; Rousseau, 1990) highlights its on-going, dynamic quality. Individual actions and decisions are thus seen in a relational context where "no segment of which—past, present, future—can sensibly be viewed independently from other segments" (MacNeil, 1974: 695). As organization members interact and exchange information, roles and role expectations develop which are embedded in relationships specific to the organizational context. These roles enable the organization to engage in many activities including CE.

CE's dependence on relational exchanges among managers has several implications for CE leadership. Leadership should be focused on the social context—both in terms of in-role performance and in architecting broader organizational arrangements. Taking on roles means depending on others to provide information and perform in complementary roles. The role of middle managers as champions, for example, depends on gaining information from experimentation at the operating level and ratification at the top. CE leadership means more than performing in one of the roles, however. It means shaping the internal organizational context in ways that foster effective exchanges between all the roles. This requires articulating a vision, gaining acceptance of the vision within the organization, and creating congruence between the vision and followers' self-interests (Pawar & Eastman, 1997).

Strategic Role Conflict and Exchange Opportunism in CE

Management entails a wide variety of behaviors, including but not limited to the entrepreneurial roles identified in Table 1. This variety of formal and informal behaviors and differences in the expectations of the people with whom a manager interacts—the role senders (Nandram & Klandermans, 1993)—is likely to result in conflicts about which role is appropriate at a given point in time. Adding to the potential for role conflicts are differences in managers' beliefs about the need for organizational change. Differences in managers' belief structures are due to educational background, experience, primary functional area, and position within the corporate hierarchy (Floyd & Lane, 2000; Weick, 1995). The plethora of managerial roles and differing managerial beliefs leads to dissensus over which roles to enact, and as a result, inconsistent role-sending behavior. For example, top management may see a need to fundamentally rethink how the firm competes (the need for strategic renewal) and thus expect operating-level managers to adopt the experimenting role. But if middle managers do not perceive the same need for fundamental change, if they believe, for example, that incremental improvements are of primary importance (the need for sustained regeneration), they will expect operating-level managers to adopt the conforming role. The conflict in the expectations of the two role senders would create tension and uncertainty at the operating level. This tension over which entrepreneurial role a manger should enact is termed *strategic role conflict* (Floyd & Lane, 2000).

Managers caught in role conflict are unlikely to enact entrepreneurial roles successfully, and this will disrupt the information exchanges needed for CE. Managers caught in role

G.G. Dess et al. / Journal of Management 2003 29(3) 351–378 361

conflict may also experience considerable stress that can lead to organizationally dysfunctional coping behaviors such as avoidance, lying, or exit (Grover, 1993; Hirschman, 1970). These coping behaviors deprive the organization of timely access to needed information and therefore have the potential to disrupt CE even further.

Role dissensus also undermines predictability in relational exchanges and weakens interpersonal trust. Lower levels of trust, in turn, increase the risk of opportunism among managers—in the form of dishonesty, infidelity or shirking (Griesenger, 1990). Note that opportunism need not be real to be disruptive. Just the risk of opportunism can be enough to reduce the amount of information shared (Lane, Lyles & Salk, 1998). Well-intended but unexpected behavior may be misinterpreted as opportunistic (Ghoshal & Moran, 1996). When members of a relational exchange system begin to perceive that others are acting opportunistically, trust breaks down even further, and the cycle of misinformation therefore tends to become negatively self-reinforcing.

Differences in strategic role expectations can create uncertainty in all management situations. However, Jones and Butler (1992) suggest that such uncertainty is especially likely in CE. An additional source of uncertainty in CE is that the firm is by definition venturing into new areas for which managers have not yet developed a shared understanding (Weick, 1995). Jones and Butler suggest that this not only creates uncertainty in how opportunities are recognized but also in how the firm should develop structures and transactions to capitalize on them. The differences in managerial perceptions discussed earlier and the uncertainty in CE further elevate the risk of real or perceived managerial opportunism.

Developing CE Consensus and Trust through Organizational Controls

For effective exchanges to occur, an individual must be willing to "buy" what another party wishes to sell. For CE this means that there should be some overlap in managerial beliefs about the substance of strategic priorities and the need for strategic change—what we describe as consensus on the dominant logic. Lacking it, champions are likely to become frustrated by top managers who consistently reject their proposals, for example. Implementers are likely to be confused by directions that are out of sync with their own perceptions of strategy. In addition to the substance of entrepreneurial initiatives, consensus on the dominant logic includes shared understanding on the need for change, i.e., which types of exchanges (regeneration, rejuvenation, renewal, or redefinition) are needed. Lacking this, managers are likely to be working at cross-purposes—operating level managers experimenting when middle managers expect them to conform, for example. In short, consensus on the dominant logic increases the likelihood that managers will share a common set of expectations for role performance and that they will seek and receive the information necessary to perform in role.

A broad consensus on dominant logic also will have indirect benefits. Because consensus reduces uncertainty about expected managerial roles, it reduces both the opportunities for managers to act opportunistically and the chance that well-intended actions will be misconstrued. This sets in another self-reinforcing spiral, an increasingly positive one. The less that members of a relational exchange system perceive that others are acting opportunistically, the more that trust builds up between them, and the less concerned they are about opportunism in the future.

What is needed, therefore, is a mechanism by which leaders can help their organizations develop the consensus and trust needed to support CE. Jones and Butler (1992: 742–746) suggest the problems created by uncertainty in CE can be addressed by providing "an equitable distribution of rewards." However, they caution that effective reward systems may be difficult to develop for CE. They conclude that the ultimate solution may lay in the development of organizational controls that can help address the problems of uncertainty, but provide no insights into what the ideal set of controls might be (1992: 746–747). Floyd and Lane's (2000) prescriptions for minimizing strategic role conflict offer a more detailed answer. They suggest that aligning a firm's organizational controls with the type of environmental change that it faces can minimize strategic role conflict. The alignment creates consistency in behavioral expectations by signaling what cues are important, which behaviors are appropriate and what kind of result is valuable. This, in turn, reduces uncertainty about each role's importance and the kind of information that is valued by the firm.

Approaches to organizational control can be described as a choice between market devices, bureaucratic mechanisms and clan controls (Ouchi, 1980). These controls vary in the types of uncertainty that they can address, but they are not mutually exclusive and can be used in combination to nurture strategic consensus in a variety of contexts (Floyd & Lane, 2000). Market control uses passively observable data to evaluate opportunities and outcomes within the firm (Daft & Weick, 1984). They help address the potential for role conflict in competence definition by clarifying the objective criteria for evaluating new ideas and opportunities. Bureaucratic control entails the use of standardized behavior and performance assessments. Under bureaucracy managers methodically probe to determine how to resolve well-defined problems (Daft & Weick, 1984). These controls are appropriate for competence deployment. Clan control conveys information through traditions and assumes that members' commitment is driven by organizational identification and common culture. Rather than analyzing data or methodically searching for the one right answer, clans reduce uncertainty by creating a communality that reduces opportunism due to similarity of norms, beliefs, and priorities between members. The trust that develops through clan control may be essential if there is uncertainty about whether and how to modify an existing competence, what to keep, what to change, and how.

Combining these insights on organization controls and consensus with the earlier discussion of the relationship between types of CE and change in the firm's competences suggests the alignment of controls and types of CE presented in the bottom rows of Table 1. Here, we propose that by correctly aligning controls with the type of CE, managers can reduce role dissensus and increase dominant logic consensus. If the controls and CE type are misaligned, either the existing strategy will be insufficiently reinforced or needed deviations from the existing strategy will be stifled.

Opportunities for Researching CE Leadership

We offer this model of CE leadership because we believe that it focuses on an important but under researched topic—managing conflicts in the CE process. The social exchange approach we take offers rich opportunities for future research because it acknowledges that managers at multiple levels play a role in CE and because it places interactions between managers at the heart of the CE process. The social exchange perspective also suggests

G.G. Dess et al. / Journal of Management 2003 29(3) 351–378   363

that two new constructs, dominant logic consensus and strategic role conflict, should be examined by future CE leadership studies. Other streams of management research can provide guidance on operationalizing both constructs (see Dess & Priem, 1995; Shenkar & Zeira, 1992). Finally, the model implies that the efficiency of social exchanges may be an indicator of CE leadership effectiveness. This could be operationalized using measures of organizational trust (Rousseau, Sitkin, Burt & Camerer, 1998) or identification-based trust (Lewicki & Bunker, 1995).

While we feel that examining CE leadership though this lens has much promise, it is clearly not the only approach that can be taken to studying this topic. Indeed, our concept of CE leadership resonates with other leadership theories focused on transforming the intraorganizational social context to facilitate change. Pettigrew (1987), for example, describes leadership as a process wherein the leader delegitimates alternative views and seeks to legitimate desired views. Sashkin (1992) describes leadership as a process of instilling new values and organizational culture. Nadler and Tushman (1989) see it as envisioning, energizing, and empowering organizational members. Our view of CE leadership as special context for transformational leadership is perhaps most in line with Kotter's (2001) distinction between managers and leaders. Managers organize people to solve problems. Leaders prepare organizations for change and help them to cope with it.

Corporate Entrepreneurship and Internationalization

A growing body of research seeks to empirically document CE activities as firms internationalize their operations (Zahra & Garvis, 2000). Given that internationalization is a complex, challenging and costly process, the success of CE efforts can significantly influence firm performance. Companies can no longer simply export their domestic business practices to foreign markets and expect to reap the full benefits of internationalization. Success in global markets requires companies to be entrepreneurial in deciding when, how, and where to expand internationally. Internationalization, therefore, provides an important opportunity to study CE activities and their links to performance among new ventures and established companies alike.

As Figure 2 indicates, one way to organize this literature is to separate content from process-related studies in new ventures vs. established companies. Content studies usually focus on the types of strategies and their dimensions that firms use as they internationalize their operations. Process studies examine how a firm's internationalization strategies emerge and change over time. These studies usually assume that the process of internationalization influences a firm's success as well as the types of entrepreneurial activities it pursues. Below, we review key studies that have been conducted to date on each of the four cells in Figure 2.

New Venture Internationalization and Entrepreneurship

Recently, some researchers have begun to examine the different factors that spur successful internationalization by new ventures (i.e., companies eight years or younger). Research indicates that environmental, organizational and strategic factors combine to influence the extent, direction, speed and process of new ventures' internationalization (for a review, see

	New Ventures	Established Companies
Content	Cell 1 Sources: Dana, Entemad & Wright, 1999 Oviatt & McDougall, 1999 Zahra & George, 2002	Cell 3 Sources: Bartlett & Ghoshal, 1988 Zahra & Garvis, 2000 Zahra, Neubaum, & House, 2000
Process	Cell 2 Sources: Schollhammer, 1982	Cell 4 Sources: Birkinshaw, 1997; 1998 D'Cruz, 1986 Ghoshal & Bartlett, 1988; 1989; 1991

Figure 2. A 2 × 2 typology of corporate entrepreneurship research.

Zahra & George, 2002). This research also suggests that new ventures gain access to re-sources and knowledge, especially about technology, by internationalizing their operations (Zahra, Ireland & Hitt, 2000). New ventures also can improve their competitive and finan-cial performance as they enter international markets. The organizational learning theory suggests that new ventures can gain new knowledge from its diverse internationalization efforts. This knowledge, in turn, can promote the development of new organizational skills and capabilities.

Entrepreneurial activities, especially those embodied in CE, pervade new ventures and es-tablished companies alike. Some new ventures are more willing to take risks, introduce more new products, and exhibit greater proactiveness than their rivals. Yet, some researchers tend to equate the creation of a new global business with entrepreneurship. While this practice is consistent with some research (Gartner, 1985), it does not capture those entrepreneurial activities that occur within a new firm after its creation. Thus, this research ignores the variety of post-internationalization entrepreneurial activities and their implications for or-ganizational learning.

Cell 1 (content). This stream of research examines the content of new ventures' in-ternational activities and their potential effect on future performance. Research by Ovi-att and McDougall is most representative of this stream of research (for a review, see Oviatt & McDougall, 1999). These researchers have cataloged the entrepreneurial ac-tivities that managers undertake to develop and grow global start-ups (Dana, Etemad & Wright, 1999) The results of this research have provided a foundation for the proposition that entrepreneurial activities that precede internationalization significantly influence the short-term success of global start-ups. These studies have also examined the survival, growth and profitability of international new ventures, even though these studies remain relatively few in number.

Despite the growing research interest in understanding the factors that influence the success of global start-ups, we could not locate any studies that have examined the en-trepreneurial activities that start-ups undertake once they go international. Differences

G.G. Dess et al. / Journal of Management 2003 29(3) 351–378 365

across different types of global start-ups in their CE activities are also ignored. It is also unclear if such differences, if they exist, vary across the stages of the firm's internationalization process. Thus, these studies have not captured the effect and type of organizational learning (Zahra et al., 1999), as discussed earlier, on future CE activities among global start-ups. Finally, studies that fall within Cell 1 have yet to link post-internationalization entrepreneurial activities to the survival of global start-ups. One probable reason for this gap is that the use of case studies and mail surveys has dominated this body of research, making it difficult to document entrepreneurial activities or learning from these efforts and link them directly to new venture performance.

Cell 2 (process). To date, only a few studies have tracked the evolution of the strategies global start-up firms use or the entrepreneurial activities they undertake over time. Most of these studies have investigated the process by which entrepreneurs assembled resources and put their organizations together in their bid to internationalize their operations. Collectively, these studies highlight the importance of the founder's vision, connections (as commonly manifested by social capital), and access to international networks.

However, researchers have not systematically examined the types of entrepreneurial activities and their intensity as the firm globalizes its operations. Further, the effect of the sequence of a firm's strategic actions to internationalize its operations has not been linked to entrepreneurial activities, learning or financial performance. Changes in the modes of entry and use of coordinative mechanisms to synchronize global strategies have not been connected to the firm's entrepreneurial activities, even though certain modes (e.g., acquisitions) might be conducive to particular CE efforts (Schollhammer, 1982). Thus, it is unclear how entrepreneurial activities influence the evolution, growth, or financial performance of global new ventures. Also, how companies learn and develop new knowledge through internationalization remains unknown. Finally, researchers have not examined how the process of internationalization varies across the four types of CE presented earlier (Covin & Miles, 1999).

Established Companies' Internationalization and Entrepreneurship

More research has been published on the entrepreneurial activities within established global companies than within new ventures. The bulk of this research is descriptive in focus and static in research design, as discussed next.

Cell 3 (content). Content-related studies have explored the types of CE activities in MNCs. Ghoshal and Bartlett (1988) conducted one of the earliest studies, examining the range and content of entrepreneurial activities that occur in MNCs. These researchers proposed that such entrepreneurial activities are crucial for MNCs' successful performance, a factor that has encouraged other researchers to document the conditions under which CE influences company performance. For example, Zahra and Garvis (2000) theorized and empirically found that CE moderates the relationship between a firm's internationalization and its financial performance. Specifically, their findings show that established companies with higher levels of CE were able to achieve higher performance through international expansion than those firms with lower CE scores. The results also indicated that established companies

366   *G.G. Dess et al. / Journal of Management 2003 29(3) 351–378*

that vigorously pursued CE were better positioned to leverage their international venturing activities in ways that improved their financial performance, thereby creating wealth for their owners. Similarly, a recent study found that international venturing by medium-sized US companies was positively related to a company's future performance (Zahra, Neubaum & Huse, 2000).

Despite the insights gained from recent studies examining content-related issues linking CE and internationalization, they remain few in number and limited in focus. These studies also lack clarity as to how firms actually leverage their skills in their international expansion to achieve higher financial performance. These studies have also failed to determine the length and duration of the period where higher CE was conducive to a stronger relationship between a firm's internationalization and its financial performance. Understanding the length of the period where CE improves a firm's financial performance can be useful in guiding strategy-making processes, especially in investing in different CE ventures. Finally, the learning implications of internationalization have not been analyzed in a systematic fashion.

Cell 4 (process). A related body of empirical research has explored the processes associated with CE in MNCs or established companies that are expanding internationally. Three themes dominate this body of research. The first centers on the role managers play in stimulating and fostering CE in the MNC's operations. Ghoshal and Bartlett (1994) aptly described the nature of these roles and the factors that shape their substance and content, proposing that these roles vary by managers' organizational level within the formal structure. While each role can enhance an MNC's overall entrepreneurial activities, serious conflicts might arise as different managers champion and support different initiatives at different levels within the MNC. Therefore, coordination is essential in order to gain the full benefits from these diverse managerial roles. The intuitive appeal of Ghoshal and Bartlett's (1994) conceptual scheme notwithstanding, there exists little empirical validation of their theoretically derived role descriptions and how to ensure effective coordination among these roles within an MNC. The implications of this coordination for CE and subsequent organizational learning are also not well understood in this stream of research.

A second theme in past CE research is how MNCs leverage their international operations in order to build and exploit a set of enduring competitive advantages. Some researchers have examined and evaluated the contributions of MNCs' subsidiaries to the creation and later diffusion of innovations within their parent organizations (Bartlett & Ghoshal, 1989; Birkinshaw, 1999; Birkinshaw & Hood, 1998; D'Cruz, 1986). Findings from this research have improved our understanding of the antecedents and effects of subsidiary entrepreneurship. Less is known, however, about the process by which CE activities actually unfold in subsidiaries or how they are connected later to the MNCs' competitive strategy or formal business definition. This gap in the literature is puzzling especially because early empirical work on CE has focused on these issues (e.g., Burgelman, 1983a, 1983b).

A third theme in prior research has investigated the potential effects of national cultures in shaping CE in established companies. While this research does not examine CE in MNCs *per se*, it has sought to clarify if and how national cultural variables influence CE efforts within established companies. Research by Morris, Davis and Allen (1994) is illustrative of this theme. It shows that certain organizational cultural variables (e.g., individualism) can significantly and positively influence CE in one country but can have the opposite (or

G.G. Dess et al. / Journal of Management 2003 29(3) 351–378 367

no) effect in other countries. The results highlight the contingent nature of the relationship between organizational cultural variables and CE; this relationship depends on national culture. These findings are informative of the vital roles national cultural variables play in influencing CE activities and determining a firm's gains from them. Findings from this research stream can also guide managerial decision-making in different countries, determining the nature, direction, and pace of CE and its implications for entrepreneurial activities.

Despite the important insights gained from process-related research on CE and internationalization (Cell 4), the bulk of this research has been descriptive and lacks a strong theoretical foundation. The dominance of case studies is another source of concern because these analyses that have not yielded original theoretical insights. Finally, reviewing the empirical studies that have been published to date, it is hard to confidently distinguish them from mainstream international business research. Researchers who have pursued this research stream have emphasized the internationalization process rather than entrepreneurial issues.

Synthesis and Future Research Agenda

Clearly, the link between CE and internationalization is an emerging subject of great interest to entrepreneurship, international business, and strategy scholars. Opportunities for productive future research in this young but fast growing area are abundant. For scholars interested in content-related issues (Cells 1 and 3 in Figure 2), an important challenge is to examine and document the types of entrepreneurial activities in established companies, be it MNCs or otherwise. Researchers would benefit also from applying and refining existing classifications or typologies of CE activities (Morris, 1998; Schollhammer, 1982). They would benefit also from examining a firm's entrepreneurial orientation (Lumpkin & Dess, 1996) as well as its actual behavior. Using longitudinal research designs, future researchers can also provide a strong basis to identify different CE activities as they unfold over time. This research can also help fill several gaps in the literature on the effect of national and corporate cultures in promoting different types of CE and how they influence a firm's gains from pursuing different CE activities.

Focusing on process-related issues (Cells 2 and 4), we believe future research can also be informative in showing how firms develop effective structures and systems that spur CE in their international operations. Understanding these structures and systems is essential to tracking the processes by which CE activities come into existence within international operations in new ventures and established companies alike. These systems and structures also influence organizational learning. The various strategies CE champions employ to promote their initiatives within their companies' international operations is another issue worthy of future study. Research is necessary also to document how firms institutionalize their different CE efforts. Toward this end, future researchers need to examine how the processes used to institutionalize CE in a firm's international operations might contribute to organizational learning and acquiring new knowledge. CE institutionalization demands sensitivity to several organizational, political, and strategic issues. It also requires capturing, sharing and integrating the knowledge the firm might have gained in its international CE activities. The process by which the firm captures this knowledge can be useful in crystallizing and integrating the firm's learning. Following the learning theory, knowledge integration ensures

368 *G.G. Dess et al. / Journal of Management 2003 29(3) 351–378*

that internationalization enhances the firm's learning (Zahra et al., 2000) and subsequent financial performance.

Future research should establish whether firms with different CE types (Miles & Snow, 1999) pursue different internationalization strategies that link these differences to organizational performance. Also, researchers should document the effect of CE types on organizational learning as a consequent of internationalization. To do so, researchers need to consider the various types of learning discussed earlier (Zahra et al., 1999), and study the effect of the intensity of CE activities and their types on the content, speed and depth of organizational learning (Zahra, Ireland & Hitt, 2000). Finally, given the potential dynamic interplay between CE and organizational learning, future empirical research should explore the effect of prior learning on changes in CE types and how these changes unfold over time.

Examining the issues above can significantly improve our understanding of potential relationships among CE, internationalization, and performance. In an environment where globalization is the norm, executives and scholars alike can gain rich insights into the dynamic interplay between the internationalization process and CE as a way of creating new competencies that enable firms to enhance firm performance. At the core of this dynamic interplay lies the firm's ability to create and gain new knowledge that can be combined or deployed to renew existing skills while creating and honing new ones (Zahra et al., 1999). The development and acquisition of skills promotes strategic renewal, a process that usually demands creativity. This dynamic renewal process is at the heart of entrepreneurship in both young and established companies.

Conclusion

The dynamic interplay between a firm's CE and internationalization represents an important research opportunity. Managers and researchers should give attention to the firm's entrepreneurial activities that shape these firms' product portfolios and differentiate them from the competition. While we are encouraged by the growing interest in these issues, this review shows that scholarship has not kept up with managerial practice, thereby missing a major opportunity to inform future theory building on the changing foundations of competitive advantages in global markets. The research issues outlined herein offer a roadmap for fruitful inquiry into the potentially rich contributions entrepreneurship can make to a company's successful internationalization and vice versa and the implications of these variables for organizational learning.

Corporate Entrepreneurship and Performance: Reassessing the Dependent Variable

CE in today's global and information economy has important implications for the development of both descriptive and normative theory. As such, the inclusion of outcome constructs and measures that are both reliable and valid is essential for building a coherent body of research that has relevance for both academics and practitioners. Developing normative theory of CE and the development of auxiliary measurement theory cannot be divorced from one another. As noted by Blalock (1982), if a poor fit is observed (in, for

G.G. Dess et al. / Journal of Management 2003 29(3) 351–378 369

example, CE constructs and performance), we are unable to ascertain if the fault lies with the substantive theory, the auxiliary measurement theory, or both. Thus, in addition to the need for reliable and valid measures of CE constructs, the same rigorous criteria must be applied to performance indicators.

In this section, we begin by discussing the need to include multiple measures of the economic and financial outcomes of CE initiatives. Then, we address the value of incorporating a stakeholder perspective, i.e., moving beyond the narrow use of economic and financial indicators. Drawing on Kaplan and Norton's (1992) concept of the "balanced scorecard," we propose that the use of stakeholder analysis need not implicitly involve tradeoffs among the various stakeholders, but rather that symbiotic relationships may exist and that stakeholder groups can be satisfied in an interdependent manner. In the closing section, we focus on the need to emphasize additional forms of capital—human, social, intellectual—in assessing the outcomes of CE endeavors. We posit that concepts such as real options and learning platforms can provide useful insights on the potential benefits of CE initiatives that may not be evident in the short-term. One of the most important consequences of CE is learning that enables the firm to develop new knowledge that renews its skills and capabilities. Consequently, we believe that learning should be considered an outcome of CE.

Economic and Financial Measures

CE research must include multiple measures of economic outcomes such as profitability and sales growth to capture the inherent tradeoffs between efficiency and effectiveness, respectively (Hofer & Schendel, 1978). Furthermore, the desired outcomes of CE initiatives such as investment in R&D, new product development, or re-tooling a production facility with expensive (and risky) new technology may not be realized for several accounting periods. For example, in the biotechnology industry, it can take approximately seven years to go from the initial new drug application to bringing a new product to market—typically at costs in excess of US$ 100 million (Folta, Amburgey & Janney, 1997). Zahra and Covin (1995) and others have argued that the economic benefits of CE efforts may not be readily apparent in the short run, but take several years to come to fruition. In conducting research on the relationship between CE initiatives and performance (especially activities involving the expenditures of significant financial and nonfinancial resources), researchers must make judicial use of lag effects to incorporate the temporal nature of their subject of inquiry.

CE research can also benefit from the inclusion of more sophisticated measures of financial performance. Economic value added (EVA) and market value added (MVA) provide additional insights because they recognize the cost of capital and the inherent riskiness of a firm's operations (Lehn & Makhija, 1996). MVA, for example, provides an indicator of the stock market's estimate of the net present value of a firm's past and future investment projects; it would likely provide a measure of future returns for CE endeavors. Such indicators are not, of course, without controversy. Gary Hamel criticized EVA as a performance indicator because it only measures returns in excess of a firm's cost of capital. Instead, Hamel suggests a measure that he believes better captures the dynamics of corporate performance, i.e., "a company's current share of total market capitalization of its relevant competitive domain with its share a decade ago" (Hamel, 1997: 75). This perspective suggests that

370   *G.G. Dess et al. / Journal of Management 2003 29(3) 351–378*

on-going CE activities aimed at keeping the organization on the cutting edge in terms of proactively seeking new opportunities may make a more lasting contribution to value creation than an occasional attempt to innovate, introduce or adopt entrepreneurial ideas. Clearly, research can benefit from the inclusion of both accounting and market measures of financial performance.

Incorporating Stakeholder Perspectives

Conceptualizing and operationalizing the performance of the "effectiveness" construct is, of course, a highly problematic issue in many research domains. However, it presents particular challenges in the domain of CE. When firms undertake CE initiatives, how can one tell if it augmented (or detracted from) the organization's effectiveness? As Atkinson, Waterhouse and Wells (1997), Freeman and McVea (2001) and others have noted, the modern organization is a complex nexus of contracts, both explicit and implicit, that specifies relationships and involves bargaining among multiple stakeholder groups. Atkinson et al. (1997) identified two groups of stakeholders: *environmental* stakeholders who define the firm's external environment (customers, owners, and the community-at-large) and *process* stakeholders (employees and suppliers) who work "within the environment defined by the external stakeholders to plan, design, implement, and operate the processes that make and deliver the company's products to its customers" (1997: 27). Recognizing the inherent conflicts among an organization's external and internal stakeholders, Hall (1987) has proposed a "contradiction model" of organization effectiveness in which firms face conflicts among multiple and conflicting environmental constraints, multiple and conflicting goals, and multiple and conflicting time frames.

To provide integration of the many diverse issues that firms face in assessing their effectiveness, Kaplan and Norton (1992) have developed the "balanced scorecard" concept. It includes a set of measures that provide managers with a quick but comprehensive view of their business. It complements the financial indicators that reflect the results of actions already taken with indicators of operational measures of customer satisfaction, internal processes, and the organization's innovation and improvement activities. The latter are considered operational measures that can drive future performance.

Such a concept has important implications for assessing the outcomes of CE initiatives. Although CE often revolves around innovation and new venture creation, the balanced scorecard approach provides a reminder that these activities must satisfy several criteria that are weighted differently by different stakeholders.

An underlying tenet of the balanced scorecard approach is the salience of multiple forms of capital to an organization. Clearly, managers should be concerned about enhancing their firm's stock of financial resources. However, in today's knowledge economy, human, social, and customer capital take on an increasing importance. For example, both scholars (e.g., Coff, 1997; Nahapiet & Ghoshal, 1998) as well as writers in the popular press (e.g., Edvinsson & Malone, 1997; Munk, 1998; Stewart, 1997) have argued that human capital is the critical, scarce resource and the key to value creation in the information age. Furthermore, Porter (1985) has articulated the need for organizations to view their firm as part of an expanded value chain consisting of themselves, suppliers, customers, and alliance partners. Such a perspective reinforces the importance of the role of social capital both within

G.G. Dess et al. / Journal of Management 2003 29(3) 351–378 371

organizations as well as between a focal organization and external stakeholders (Dyer & Singh, 1998). A shortcoming of the balanced scorecard is ignoring the learning outcomes of the various CE types, discussed earlier in this paper. This learning requires multiple types of capital, as discussed next.

Recognizing the Increasing Role of Multiple Forms of Capital in Today's Economy

We argue that many of the performance constructs developed in the strategic management literature were originally created within the context of existing firms as well as at a time when physical, financial, and labor resources were a firm's key resources for attaining advantages. And, although many of the measures originally used in the CE literature may remain viable for new ventures, such measures may become less applicable for firms that rely primarily on human, social, and intellectual capital to create advantages. Therefore, future CE researchers should give greater attention to knowledge-based resources and learning outcomes.

Human capital focuses primarily on capabilities, knowledge, skills, and experience, all of which are embodied in and inseparable from the individual. *Intellectual capital* refers "to the knowledge and knowing capabilities of a social collectivity, such as an organization, intellectual community, or professional practice" (Nahapiet & Ghoshal, 1998: 245). *Social capital* is "broadly defined as an asset that inheres in social relations and networks" (Leana & Van Buren, 1998: 538). We believe that as the level of human, social, and intellectual capital inherent in a new venture increases, different perspectives on the outcomes of CE become more important. Such intangible resources or "invisible assets" (Itami & Roehl, 1987) are especially salient in newer firms in emerging industries. Assembling, deploying and leveraging these diverse types of capital create opportunities for knowledge creation and exploitation within CE activities.

In addition to the increasing importance of human, intellectual, and social capital in our discussion of CE, we draw upon the real options literature (Bowman & Hurry, 1993; McDonald & Siegel, 1986; Myers, 1977). A real option is an investment in which the purchaser obtains the right, but not the obligation, to acquire (or divest) an investment at a later date, at contracted terms (McGrath, 1999). The literature suggests that firms can derive an economic value by investing incrementally and delaying a full investment commitment until more information about the decision is known (Dixit & Pindyck, 1994). If the investment decision fares poorly, losses are capped at the amount of the initial investment; at the same time the firm retains the full "upside potential" of the investment decision. This insight encourages firms to place many "small bets" on promising opportunities, pouring funds then into the most promising opportunities. Real options create flexibility for firms; freed from having to extricate themselves from much larger commitments, firms can shift funds from a given opportunity to a more promising one. Using this logic, companies also see far downside risks associated with CE activities. Consequently, they are more willing to experiment, learn and develop new knowledge.

We suggest that real options theory can shed some new light on the outcomes of CE initiatives. For example, as firms make platform investments in order to establish a new technology or early foothold in new markets, they maintain the ability to expand rapidly if conditions warrant. These investments also can enhance the learning consequences of CE.

At the same time, firms embedded in wider networks tend to use the informal relations to facilitate innovation (Starr & MacMillan, 1990), while they enjoy a more accurate assessment of environmental conditions. Therefore, they are able to proactively pursue opportunities more quickly than firms outside of their network. Future CE research should enhance our understanding of how firms employ such intangible forms of capital to create and exploit new opportunities. Additionally, platforms for learning (Grenadier & Weiss, 1997) can moderate the relationship between CE initiatives and company performance. For example, endeavors at innovative product market development—even if unsuccessful at one point in time—may provide substantial economic benefits at a later time if it enables the firm to recombine resources effectively (Kogut & Zander, 1992). Following learning theory, this process can improve learning and knowledge creation within CE activities. Clearly, future CE research could benefit from using longitudinal time lagged variables.

The operationalization of performance constructs in CE research could be revised to recognize the emergence of the importance of intangible assets in the economy. The inclusion of indicators to reflect a new venture's level of intellectual capital should require much more fine-grained measures than those proposed by Edvinsson and Malone (1997) in their path-breaking book, *Intellectual Capital*. Rather than rely on measures such as "new channel development investment," "education unique to noncompany-based employees," and "employee competence and development investment" (1997: 245), we would propose including indicators of "the knowledge and knowing capabilities" (Nahapiet & Ghoshal, 1998) that enable an organization to exploit emerging opportunities. This knowledge should be assessed within a firm's competitive context as a means of providing sustainable competitive advantages, a proposition that is consistent with learning theory. This would require the perspective of both an organization's present product-market-technology and its anticipated endeavors. The question could be posed: How do such intangible resources provide leverage for future entrepreneurial endeavors? The firm's social capital—a viable outcome as well as antecedent to CE endeavors—could be assessed, broadly speaking, by its network of relationships that have the potential for providing it with valuable tangible and intangible resources (Adler & Kwon, 2002).

CE research could build on prior network research that has investigated such substantive issues as alliance networks, executive friendship ties, and corporate director interlocks (e.g., Geletkanycz & Hambrick, 1997; Gulati, 1995; Westphal & Zajac, 1997). Such network ties—both strong and weak—would serve to mitigate the extent of risk taking that is inherent in CE initiatives. For example, firms in deeply embedded networks may better benefit from their strategic initiatives via superior access to financial and knowledge resources. This enables firms to combine resources in a more effective and efficient manner as well as enhance their potential for developing superior learning platforms to exploit future product-market opportunities. Thus, not only would the potential downside or risk taking associated with CE efforts be mitigated, but also the positive economic benefits of proactive and innovative behaviors would be released. Following the learning theory, such outcomes might include rapid, deep and broad learning of new technologies and skills. Such research would benefit from the application of "fine-grained" methodologies (Harrigan, 1983) that would enable one to identify unfolding, emergent processes. This research would help to further improve our understanding of the role of organizational learning as a consequence of the various CE types firms might pursue.

G.G. Dess et al. / Journal of Management 2003 29(3) 351–378 373

Conclusion

In this paper, we have identified four promising research avenues in CE. While other issues are worthy of analysis, we believe the four issues we examined have important implications for organizational learning and the creation of new knowledge. Collectively, these issues help us open the "black box" that pervades the literature on the relationship between CE and performance. These issues also help us to recognize the importance of CE for knowledge creation and exploitation as well as learning. We welcome dialogue, debate, and critique with the goal of enhancing research in an area that holds such promise for rich descriptive and normative theory.

Acknowledgments

The ideas in this paper were initially developed for a panel that was presented at the 2000 Strategic Management Society Meetings in Vancouver, British Columbia, Canada. We thank the reviewers and editors of the *Journal of Management* as well as Tom Lumpkin, Doug Lyon, and Bruce Skaggs for their helpful comments.

References

Adler, P. S., & Kwon, S. W. 2002. Social capital: Prospects for a new concept. *Academy of Management Review*, 27: 17–40.

Atkinson, A. A., Waterhouse, J. J., & Wells, R. B. 1997. A stakeholder approach to strategic performance measurement. *Sloan Management Review*, 38: 25–37.

Bartlett, C. A., & Ghoshal, S. 1989. *Managing across borders: The transnational solution.* Boston, MA: Harvard Business School Press.

Bartlett, C. A., & Ghoshal, S. 1994. Changing the role of top management: Beyond strategy to purpose. *Harvard Business Review*, 72(6): 79–88.

Birkinshaw, J. 1999. The determinants and consequences of subsidiary initiative in multinational corporations. *Entrepreneurship Theory and Practice*, 24(1): 9–36.

Birkinshaw, J., & Hood, N. 1998. Multinational subsidiary evolution: Capability and charter change in foreign-owned subsidiary companies. *Academy of Management Review*, 23: 773–795.

Blalock, H. M. 1982. *Conceptualization and measurement in the social sciences.* Beverly Hills, CA: Sage.

Bowman, E. H., & Hurry, D. 1993. Strategy through the options lens: An integrated view of resource investments and the incremental-choice process. *Academy of Management Review*, 18: 160–782.

Burgelman, R. A. 1983a. A model of the interaction of strategic behavior, corporate context, and the concept of strategy. *Academy of Management Review*, 8: 61–70.

Burgelman, R. A. 1983b. A process model of internal corporate venturing in the diversified major firm. *Administrative Science Quarterly*, 28: 223–244.

Burgelman, R. A. 1991. Intraorganizational ecology of strategy making and organizational adaptation: Theory and field research. *Organizational Science*, 2: 239–262.

Chung, L. H., & Gibbons, P. T. 1997. Corporate entrepreneurship: The roles of ideology and social capital. *Group and Organization Management*, 22: 10–30.

Coff, R. W. 1997. Human assets and management dilemmas: Coping with hazards on the road to resource-based theory. *Academy of Management Review*, 22: 374–402.

Coff, R. W. 2002. Human capital, shared expertise, and the likelihood of impasse in corporate acquisitions. *Journal of Management*, 28: 107–128.

Covin, J. G., & Miles, M. P. 1999. Corporate entrepreneurship and the pursuit of competitive advantage. *Entrepreneurship Theory and Practice*, 23(3): 47–63.

D'Cruz, J. R. 1986. Strategic management of subsidiaries. In H. Etemad & L. S. Dulude (Eds.), *Managing the multinational subsidiary*. London: Croom Helm.

Daft, R. L., & Weick, K. E. 1984. Toward a model of organizational interpretation systems. *Academy of Management Review*, 9: 284–295.

Dana, L.-P., Etemad, H., & Wright, R. 1999. Theoretical foundations of international entrepreneurship. In R. Wright (Ed.), *International entrepreneurship: Globalization of emerging businesses. Research in Global Strategic Management*, 7. Stamford, CT: JAI Press.

Dess, G. G., & Priem, R. L. 1995. Consensus-performance research: Theoretical and empirical extensions. *Journal of Management Studies*, 32: 401–417.

Dixit, A. K., & Pindyck, R. S. 1994. *Investment under uncertainty*. Princeton, NJ: Princeton University Press.

Dyer, J. H., & Singh, H. 1998. The relational view: Cooperative strategy and sources of interorganizational competitive advantage. *Academy of Management Review*, 24: 650–679.

Edvinsson, L., & Malone, M. S. 1997. *Intellectual capital: Realizing your company's true value by finding its hidden brainpower*. New York: Harper Business.

Floyd, S. W., & Lane, P. J. 2000. Strategizing throughout the organization: Managing strategic renewal and strategic role conflict. *Academy of Management Review*, 25: 154–177.

Floyd, S. W., & Wooldridge, B. 1999. Knowledge creation and social networks in corporate entrepreneurship: The renewal of organizational capability. *Entrepreneurship Theory and Practice*, 23(3): 123–143.

Folta, T. B., Amburgey, T. L., & Janney, J. J. 1997. *Private placements and the growth of knowledge of the firm: Quality signals in the biotechnology industry*. Paper presented at the Strategic Management Society Conference, Barcelona, Spain.

Freeman, R. E., & McVea, J. 2001. A stakeholder approach to strategic management. In M. A. Hitt, R. E. Freeman, & J. S. Harrison (Eds.), *Handbook of strategic management*: 189–207. Oxford, UK: Blackwell.

Gartner, W. B. 1985. A conceptual framework for describing the phenomenon of new venture creation. *Academy of Management Review*, 10: 696–706.

Geletkanycz, M. A., & Hambrick, D. C. 1997. The external ties of top executives: Implications for strategic choice and performance. *Administrative Science Quarterly*, 42: 654–681.

Ghoshal, S., & Bartlett, C. 1988. Creation, adoption, and diffusion of innovations by subsidiaries. *Journal of International Business Studies*, 19: 365–388.

Ghoshal, S., & Bartlett, C. A. 1994. Linking organizational context and managerial action: The dimensions of quality of management. *Strategic Management Journal*, 15(Summer Special Issue): 91–112.

Ghoshal, S., & Moran, P. 1996. Bad for practice: A critique of the transaction cost theory. *Academy of Management Review*, 21: 13–47.

Golder, P. N., & Tellis, G. J. 1993. Pioneer advantage: Marketing logic or marketing legend. *Journal of Marketing Research*, 30: 158–170.

Grant, R. M. 1996. Toward a knowledge-based theory of the firm. *Strategic Management Journal*, 17(Special Issue): 109–122.

Grenadier, S. R., & Weiss, A. M. 1997. Investments in technological innovations: An option pricing approach. *Journal of Financial Economics*, 44: 397–416.

Griesenger, D. W. 1990. The human side of economic organization. *Academy of Management Review*, 15: 478–499.

Grover, S. L. 1993. Lying, deceit, and subterfuge: A model of dishonesty in the workplace. *Organization Science*, 4: 478–495.

Gulati, R. 1995. Social structure and alliance formation patterns: A longitudinal analysis. *Administrative Science Quarterly*, 40: 619–652.

Guth, W., & Ginsberg, A. 1990. Guest editor's introduction: Corporate entrepreneurship. *Strategic Management Journal*, 11(Summer Special Issue): 5–15.

Hall, R. H. 1987. *Organizations: Structures, processes, and outcomes* (4th ed.). Englewood Cliffs, NJ: Prentice-Hall.

Hamel, G. 1997, June. Killer strategies. *Fortune*, 23: 70–84.

Harrigan, K. 1983. Research methodologies for contingency approaches to strategy. *Academy of Management Review*, 8: 398–405.

G.G. Dess et al. / Journal of Management 2003 29(3) 351–378 375

Hart, S. 1992. An integrative framework for strategy-making processes. *Academy of Management Review*, 17: 327–351.

Hirschman, A. O. 1970. *Exit, voice, and loyalty*. Cambridge, MA: Harvard University Press.

Hitt, M. A., & Ireland, R. D. 2000. The intersection of entrepreneurship and strategic management research. In D. L. Sexton & H. Landstrom (Eds.), *Handbook of entrepreneurship*: 45–63. Oxford, UK: Blackwell.

Hitt, M. A., & Ireland, R. D. 2002. The essence of strategic leadership: Managing human and social capital. *Journal of Leadership and Organizational Studies*, 9(1): 3–14.

Hitt, M. A., Nixon, R. D., Hoskisson, R. E., & Kochhar, R. 1999. Corporate entrepreneurship and cross-functional fertilization: Activation, process and disintegration of new product design team. *Entrepreneurship Theory and Practice*, 23(3): 145–167.

Hofer, C. W., & Schendel, D. 1978. *Strategy formulation: Analytical concepts*. St. Paul, MN: West Publishing.

Ireland, R. D., & Hitt, M. A. 1999. Achieving and maintaining strategic competitiveness in the 21st century: The role of strategic leadership. *Academy of Management Executive*, 13(1): 43–57.

Ireland, R. D., Hitt, M. A., Camp, S. M., & Sexton, D. L. 2001. Integrating entrepreneurship and strategic management action to create firm wealth. *Academy of Management Executive*, 15(1): 49–63.

Ireland, R. D., Hitt, M. A., & Vaidyanath, D. 2002. Strategic alliances as a pathway to competitive success. *Journal of Management*, 28: 413–446.

Ireland, R. D., Kuratko, D. F., & Covin, J. G. 2002. *Antecedents, elements, and consequences of corporate entrepreneurship strategy*. Working paper, University of Richmond.

Itami, H., & Roehl, T. 1987. *Mobilizing invisible assets*. Cambridge, MA: Harvard University Press.

Jones, G. R., & Butler, J. E. 1992. Managing internal corporate entrepreneurship: An agency theory perspective. *Journal of Management*, 18: 733–749.

Kanter, R. M. 1983. *The change masters*. New York: Simon & Schuster.

Kaplan, R. S., & Norton, D. P. 1992. The balanced scorecard: Measures that drive performance. *Harvard Business Review*, 69(1): 71–79.

Kazanjian, R. K., Drazin, R., & Glynn, M. A. 2001. Implementing strategies for corporate entrepreneurship: A knowledge-based perspective. In M. A. Hitt, R. D. Ireland, S. M. Camp, & D. L. Sexton (Eds.), *Strategic entrepreneurship: Creating a new mindset*: 173–200. Oxford, UK: Blackwell.

Kogut, B., & Zander, V. 1992. Knowledge of the firm, combinative capabilities, and the replication of technology. *Organization Science*, 3: 383–397.

Kotter, J. P. 1995. Leading change: Why transformation efforts fail. *Harvard Business Review*, 73(2): 59–67.

Kotter, J. P. 2001. What leaders really do. *Harvard Business Review*, 71(11): 3–11.

Kuratko, D. F., Ireland, R. D., & Hornsby, J. S. 2001. Improving firm performance through entrepreneurial actions: Acordia's corporate entrepreneurship strategy. *Academy of Management Executive*, 15(4): 60–71.

Lane, P. J., Lyles, M. A., & Salk, J. 1998. Relative absorptive capacity, trust, and interorganizational learning in international joint ventures. In M. A. Hitt, J. E. Ricart, & R. D. Nixon (Eds.), *Managing strategically in an interconnected world*: 374–397. New York: Wiley.

Leana, C. R., & Van Buren, H. J., III. 1998. Organizational social capital and employment practices. *Academy of Management Journal*, 42: 538–555.

Lehn, K., & Makhija, A. K. 1996. EVA & MVA as performance measures and signals for strategic change. *Strategy & Leadership*, May/June: 34–38.

Leonard-Barton, D. F. 1995. *Wellsprings of knowledge: Building and sustaining the source of innovation*. Boston: Harvard Business School Press.

Lepak, D. P., & Snell, S. A. 1999. The human architecture: Toward a theory of human capital allocation and development. *Academy of Management Review*, 24: 31–48.

Lewicki, R. J., & Bunker, B. 1995. Trust in relationships: A model of trust development and decline. In B. Bunker & J. Rubin (Eds.), *Conflict, cooperation and justice*: 133–173. San Francisco: Jossey-Bass.

Lieberman, M. B. 1984. The learning curve and pricing in the chemical processing industries. *RAND Journal of Economics*, 15: 213–228.

Lumpkin, G. T., & Dess, G. G. 1996. Clarifying the entrepreneurial orientation construct and linking it to performance. *Academy of Management Review*, 21: 135–172.

MacNeil, I. R. 1974. The many futures of contract. *Southern California Law Review*, 47: 691–816.

Matusik, S. F. 2002. An empirical investigation of firm public and private knowledge. *Strategic Management Journal*, 23: 457–467.

376   *G.G. Dess et al. / Journal of Management 2003 29(3) 351–378*

McDonald, R., & Siegel, D. R. 1986. The value of waiting to invest. *Quarterly Journal of Economics*, 101: 707–727.

McGrath, R. G. 1999. Falling forward: Real options reasoning and entrepreneurial failure. *Academy of Management Review*, 24: 13–30.

Morris, M. H. 1998. *Entrepreneurial intensity*. Westport, CT: Quorum Books.

Morris, M. H., Davis, D. L., & Allen, J. W. 1994. Fostering corporate entrepreneurship: Cross-cultural comparisons of the importance of individualism versus collectivism. *Journal of International Business Studies*, First Quarter: 65–89.

Munk, N. 1998, March. The new organization man. *Fortune*, 16: 68–72.

Myers, S. C. 1977. Determinants of corporate borrowing. *Journal of Financial Economics*, 5(2): 147–175.

Nadler, D. A., & Tushman, M. L. 1989. Beyond the charismatic leader: Leadership and organizational change. *California Management Review*, 32(2): 77–97.

Nahapiet, J., & Ghoshal, S. 1998. Social capital, intellectual capital, and the organizational advantage. *Academy of Management Review*, 23: 242–266.

Nandram, S. S., & Klandermans, B. 1993. Stress experienced by active members of trade unions. *Journal of Organizational Behavior*, 14(5): 415–431.

Nelson, R. R., & Winter, S. G. 1982. *An evolutionary theory of economic change*. Cambridge, MA: Harvard University Press.

Nonaka, I. 1994. A dynamic theory of organizational knowledge creation. *Organization Science*, 5: 714–737.

Nonaka, I., & Takeuchi, H. 1995. *The knowledge company: How Japanese companies create the dynamics of innovation*. New York: Oxford University Press.

Ouchi, W. G. 1980. Markets, bureaucracies, and clans. *Administrative Science Quarterly*, 25: 120–142.

Oviatt, B., & McDougall, P. 1999. A framework for understanding accelerated international entrepreneurship. In R. Wright (Ed.), *International entrepreneurship: Globalization of emerging businesses. Research in Global Strategic Management*. Stamford, CT: JAI Press.

Pawar, B. S., & Eastman, K. K. 1997. The nature and implications of contextual influences on transformational leadership: A conceptual examination. *Academy of Management Review*, 22: 80–109.

Pettigrew, A. M. 1987. Context and action in the transformation of the firms. *Journal of Management Studies*, 24: 649–670.

Porter, M. E. 1980. *Competitive strategy*. New York: Free Press.

Porter, M. E. 1985. *Competitive advantage*. New York: Free Press.

Rousseau, D. M. 1990. New hire perceptions of their own and their employer's obligations: A study of psychological contracts. *Journal of Organization Behavior*, 11: 389–400.

Rousseau, D., Sitkin, S., Burt, R., & Camerer, C. 1998. Not so different after all: A cross-discipline view of trust. *Academy of Management Review*, 23: 393–412.

Sashkin, M. 1992. Strategic leadership competencies. In R. L. Phillips & J. G. Hunt (Eds.), *Strategic leadership*: 139–160. Westport, CT: Quorum Books.

Schollhammer, H. 1982. Internal corporate entrepreneurship. In C. A. Kent, D. L. Sexton, & K. H. Vesper (Eds.), *Encyclopaedia of entrepreneurship*: 209–229. Englewood Cliffs, NJ: Prentice-Hall.

Schumpeter, J. 1934. *The theory of economic development*. Cambridge, MA: Harvard University Press.

Sharma, A. 1999. Central dilemmas of managing innovation in large firms. *California Management Review*, 41(3): 146–164.

Sharma, P., & Chrisman, J. J. 1999. Toward a reconciliation of the definitional issues in the field of corporate entrepreneurship. *Entrepreneurship Theory and Practice*, 23(3): 11–27.

Shenkar, O., & Zeira, Y. 1992. Role conflict and role ambiguity of chief executive officers in international joint ventures. *Journal of International Business*, 23: 55–75.

Starr, J. A., & MacMillan, I. C. 1990. Resource cooperation and social contracting: Resource acquisition for new ventures. *Strategic Management Journal*, 11: 79–92.

Stewart, T. A. 1997. *Intellectual capital: The new wealth of organizations*. New York: Doubleday/Currency.

von Grogh, G., Ichijo, K., & Nonaka, I. 2000. *Enabling knowledge creation*. New York: Oxford University.

Weick, K. 1995. *Sensemaking in organizations*. Thousand Oaks, CA: Sage.

Westphal, J. D., & Zajac, E. J. 1997. Defections from the inner circle: Social exchange, reciprocity, and the diffusion of board independence in US corporations. *Administrative Science Quarterly*, 42: 161–183.

Zahra, S. A., & Covin, J. G. 1995. Contextual influences on the corporate entrepreneurship–performance relationship: A longitudinal analysis. *Journal of Business Venturing*, 10: 43–58.

Zahra, S. A., & Garvis, D. 2000. International corporate entrepreneurship and company performance: The moderating effect of international environmental hostility. *Journal of Business Venturing*, 15: 469–492.

Zahra, S. A., & George, G. 2002. International entrepreneurship: The current status of the field and future research agenda. In M. A. Hitt, R. D. Ireland, S. M. Camp, & D. L. Sexton (Eds.), *Strategic entrepreneurship: Creating a new mindset*: 255–288. Oxford, UK: Blackwell.

Zahra, S. A., & Nielsen, A. P. 2002. Sources of capabilities, integration and technology commercialization. *Strategic Management Journal*, 23: 377–398.

Zahra, S. A., Ireland, R. D., & Hitt, M. A. 2000. International expansion by new venture firms: International diversity, mode of market entry, technological learning and performance. *Academy of Management Journal*, 43: 925–950.

Zahra, S. A., Neubaum, D. O., & Huse, M. 2000. Entrepreneurship in medium-size companies: Exploring the effects of ownership and governance systems. *Journal of Management*, 26: 947–976.

Zahra, S. A., Nielsen, A. P., & Bogner, W. C. 1999. Corporate entrepreneurship, knowledge, and competence development. *Entrepreneurship Theory and Practice*, 23(3): 169–189.

Gregory G. Dess is the Andrew Cecil Endowed Chair in Management at the University of Texas at Dallas. He has published numerous articles in leading academic and practitioner-oriented journals in strategic management, organization theory, knowledge management, and related topics. He currently serves on the editorial board of *Strategic Management Journal*, *Journal of Business Venturing*, *Journal of Business Research*, and *Organizational Dynamics*. Greg was one of the charter members of the Academy of Management Journals' Hall of Fame and he received his Ph.D. from the University of Washington.

R. Duane Ireland holds the W. David Robbins Chair in Strategic Management in the Robins School of Business, University of Richmond. His research is concerned with strategic alliances, strategic entrepreneurship, and corporate entrepreneurship. In addition to the *Journal of Management*, Duane's articles have appeared in the *Academy of Management Journal*, *Academy of Management Review*, *Academy of Management Executive*, *Strategic Management Journal*, *Administrative Science Quarterly*, *Decision Sciences*, *Human Relations*, *Journal of Management Studies*, and *British Journal of Management*, among others. He has written several textbooks and edited scholarly books. His work has received awards for best papers from the *Academy of Management Journal* (2000) and *Academy of Management Executive* (1999). Duane has received awards for excellence in terms of teaching and service.

Shaker A. Zahra is Paul T. Babson Distinguished Professor in Entrepreneurship in Babson College. His research covers corporate, international, and technological entrepreneurship. Shaker's articles have appeared in the *Academy of Management Journal*, *Academy of Management Review*, *Academy of Management Executive*, *Strategic Management Journal*, *Journal of Management*, *Journal of Business Venturing*, *Journal of Management Studies*, *Entrepreneurship: Theory and Practice*, *Decision Sciences*, *Information Systems Research*, among others. His research has received several awards including best papers in the *Academy of Management Journal*, *Journal of Management*, and *Entrepreneurship: Theory and Practice*. His teaching and service have also received awards of excellence.

Steven W. Floyd is the Cizik Chair in Strategic Management, Technology and Manufacturing, and an Associate Professor in Strategic Management at the School of Business, University of Connecticut. His recent research focuses on the role of social context in the development of strategic initiatives, the contributions of middle-level management to corporate entrepreneurship and strategy-making and the organizational processes associated with strategic renewal. Articles on these and other topics have been published in the *Academy of Management Review*, *Academy of Management Journal*, *Strategic Management Journal*, *Journal of Management*, *Entrepreneurship: Theory and Practice*, and *Journal of Management Studies*.

Jay J. Janney is an Assistant Professor of Management at the University of Dayton. His research interests include the integration of strategic management and entrepreneurship, real options, and the resource-based view of the firm. His work has appeared in *Business Horizons*, *Journal of Business Ethics*, and *Journal of Business Venturing* (in press), among others. Jay earned his Ph.D. from the University of Kentucky, and previously served on the faculty of Purdue University.

Peter J. Lane is an Associate Professor of Management at Arizona State University's College of Business. His research on corporate strategy, strategic processes, and interfirm collaboration has been published in the *Academy of Management Review*, *Academy of Management Executive*, *Strategic Management Journal*, and *Human Relations*. His current research focuses on socio-cognitive influence on strategy innovation both within and across organizations.

[35]

Academy of Management Executive, 2001, Vol. 15, No. 4

Improving firm performance through entrepreneurial actions: Acordia's corporate entrepreneurship strategy

Donald F. Kuratko, R. Duane Ireland, and Jeffrey S. Hornsby

Executive Overview

As the 21st century unfolds, entrepreneurial actions are viewed as critical pathways to competitive advantage and improved performance. One company in the healthcare management field, Acordia, Inc., developed and prospered through its strategic entrepreneurial vision. In the words of Acordia's CEO, Frank C. Witthun: "2000 was another landmark year for Acordia, with important acquisitions, innovative new products, and the foresight of sound, strategic planning fueling our impressive growth. It is our expert vision that has brought us to this point: a vision of what a brokerage firm can and should be in the new millennium, and our expertise in delivering innovative products and services to our clients in a way that not only exceeds their expectations, but fundamentally changes them."

Starting in 1986, entrepreneurial actions were instrumental to how Acordia has conducted business over the last 15 or so years. We use insights from the academic literature and business press as the framework for the story of how one company was able to use entrepreneurial actions as the foundation for its successful corporate entrepreneurship strategy.

Entrepreneurial actions were the medium through which Acordia, Inc., wanted to influence its competitive environment and establish its position, starting in the mid-1980s. Entrepreneurial actions are any newly fashioned behaviors through which companies exploit opportunities others have not noticed or aggressively pursued. Novelty, in terms of new resources, customers, markets, or a new combination of resources, customers, and markets, is the defining characteristic of entrepreneurial actions.[1]

As was the case at Acordia, entrepreneurial actions are the conduit through which entrepreneurship is practiced in organizations.[2] Entrepreneurship includes acts of creation, renewal, or innovation that occur within or outside an organization.[3] When these acts take place in an established firm, particularly a large one, like Acordia, they describe corporate entrepreneurship.[4] Entrepreneurship is especially important for firms facing rapid changes in industry and market structures, cus-

tomers' needs, technology, and societal values.[5] Because Acordia faced all of these conditions as the 1980s were closing, using entrepreneurial actions to form and implement a corporate entrepreneurship strategy was appropriate.

A firm's strategy is the set of commitments and actions taken to develop and exploit a competitive advantage in the marketplace. Because they are the source of how firms create value, being able to develop and exploit one or more competitive advantages is a universal objective of all companies.[6] A competitive advantage "is the result of an enduring value differential between the products or services of one organization and those of its competitors in the minds of customers."[7] Companies able to exploit the competitive advantages they own today, while simultaneously making decisions to shape the advantages they intend to own and use tomorrow, increase the probability of long-term survival, growth, and financial success.[8]

2001 *Kuratko, Ireland, and Hornsby* 61

Acordia wanted to emphasize its current competitive advantages (marketing programs, administrative skills, and computer applications) while using entrepreneurial actions to develop innovation as tomorrow's competitive advantage.

Innovation offers interdependent benefits to firms. First, innovation itself can be an important competitive advantage. Indeed, especially in rapidly changing environments, innovation is a prerequisite to competitive parity as well as being a competitive advantage.[9] In addition, being able to innovatively upgrade current advantages helps the firm derive maximum competitive value from them. An upper-level executive from Enron speaks to this benefit: "Innovation is at the heart of sustaining a company's competitive advantage."[10] As we will see, Acordia's executives were aware of innovation's importance to their firm's current and future performances.

"Innovation is at the heart of sustaining a company's competitive advantage."

Innovations bring something new into being—products, processes for producing an existing product or service, and markets. Sometimes, new markets for the firm's current products are found; in other cases, new products are sold in new markets. Product, process, and market innovations often flow from newly fashioned entrepreneurial actions, through which firms exploit opportunities that others have not noticed or pursued.

The terms we use to frame Acordia's story have an interdependent and sequential relationship. For example, entrepreneurial actions are novel behaviors the firm intends to use to pursue opportunities; entrepreneurship captures the full set of entrepreneurial actions the firm takes to create, renew, or innovate; when practiced in large organizations, entrepreneurial actions are the foundation for corporate entrepreneurship, a specific application of entrepreneurship; and, when entrepreneurial actions are the foundation on which a firm's strategy is built, a corporate entrepreneurship strategy is being implemented. Because novel behaviors (that is, entrepreneurial actions) formed the core of its newly chosen commitments and actions, Acordia clearly chose to implement a corporate entrepreneurship strategy to reverse its fortunes and prepare for a successful future.

The Relationship Between Corporate Entrepreneurship and Firm Performance

The relationship between corporate entrepreneurship and firm performance in large organizations

has been assessed differently across time. During the 1980s, some argued that it was difficult for people to act entrepreneurially in bureaucratic organizational structures.[11] At the same time, others believed that, for companies of any size, entrepreneurial actions were possible, should be encouraged, and could be expected to enhance firm performance.[12]

A virtual revolution about the value of entrepreneurial actions as a contributor to firm performance took place from the late 1980s throughout the 1990s. This was a time during which companies were redefining their businesses, thinking about how to most effectively use human resources, and learning how to compete in the global economy. In short, "Some of the world's best-known companies had to endure painful transformation to become more entrepreneurial. These companies had to endure years of reorganization, downsizing, and restructuring. These changes altered the identity or culture of these firms, infusing a new entrepreneurial spirit throughout their operations... change, innovation, and entrepreneurship became highly regarded words that describe what successful companies must do to survive."[13]

As the 21st century unfolds, entrepreneurial actions continue to be seen as an important path to competitive advantage and improved performance in firms of all types and sizes.[14] Some even believe that the failure to use entrepreneurial actions successfully in the fast-paced and complex global economy is a recipe for failure.[15]

Many factors affect companies' success when using entrepreneurial actions to implement a corporate entrepreneurship strategy.[16] The most important factors concern the firm's ability to establish a vision and for top management to support it,[17] to organize people and tasks in ways that make it possible for entrepreneurial actions to flourish,[18] to have sufficient resources to support entrepreneurial actions,[19] to use rewards and compensation systems that reinforce individuals' and teams' entrepreneurial actions,[20] and to encourage risk taking, as measured by individuals' willingness to accept risks and tolerate failure.[21]

Several topics are explored to tell the story of Acordia, Inc.[22] First, we discuss the entrepreneurial vision, new-venture teams, and compensation that the firm emphasized to design and use its corporate entrepreneurship strategy. A new-venture team is a way of organizing people to promote entrepreneurial actions. Thus the factors Acordia concentrated on parallel three of those that research evidence shows to be critical for successful use of a corporate entrepreneurship strategy.

Figure 1 shows how most of the literature-

FIGURE 1
Entrepreneurial Actions and Implementation of a Corporate Entrepreneurship Strategy

supported factors are involved with designing and implementing a corporate entrepreneurship strategy. The specific manner in which Acordia applied the three factors that it determined were vital to its entrepreneurial efforts is shown in Figure 2. We then discuss the context and details of Acordia's entrepreneurial journey, and discuss its implications for managerial practice.

Entrepreneurial Vision—The Guiding Light

An entrepreneurial vision indicates what a company expects to achieve. Environmental opportunities and the patterns of competition between a firm and its rivals influence this vision.[23] Intended to capitalize on opportunities, an entrepreneurial vision's desired outcomes should be challenging. In a recent annual survey, *Fortune* found that the most admired companies set more challenging goals as compared with those failing to make the list.[24]

The ultimate responsibility for forming a vision rests with top-level executives. An effective entrepreneurial vision allows affected parties to focus on critical tasks as they pursue organizational and personal objectives.[25] A meaningful vision is sensible in employees' eyes, is easily understood, suggests a higher calling,[26] and creates a cultural glue that binds people together in ways that help them share knowledge in competitively relevant ways. Moreover, in the global economy, the most effective vision highlights a firm's commitment to product, process, and market innovations. Talented vision setters know that part of their responsibility is

to coach employees to meet the challenges of organizational life, energize them by their own determination and relentless pursuit of success and opportunity, and facilitate their attempts to achieve more than they thought possible as they strive to help the firm reach its vision.[27]

New-Venture Teams—An Organizational Form for Entrepreneurial Actions

In today's complex business environments, top-level executives don't have access to all of the information needed for their firms to innovate and pursue environmental opportunities. Because information is widely dispersed among employees, teams are formed.[28] Often called new-venture teams, their focus is on collective entrepreneurship rather than solely on the entrepreneurial abilities of a firm's top-level managers.

Collective entrepreneurship results in team-based endeavors in which the whole of the effort exceeds the sum of individuals' contributions.[29] The collective talent of a new-venture team can be particularly effective (as measured by product, process, and market innovations) when its members come from different functions (e.g., marketing, design, and production) and when top-level managers actively support the team's efforts.[30] When forming new-venture teams, firms should draw from their entire talent pool, because the most effective entrepreneurial actions sometimes surface from individuals or teams from whom such output wasn't anticipated.[31] Unexpected, yet valuable, contributions surface because most, if not all, members of an organization have untapped talent and potential.[32]

> *When forming new-venture teams, firms should draw from their entire talent pool, because the most effective entrepreneurial actions sometimes surface from individuals or teams from whom such output wasn't anticipated.*

Several benefits result from productive new-venture teams. First, because effective teams accept responsibility to monitor and control their behavior, managers have more time to engage in entrepreneurial actions, such as those necessary to find new markets. Effective new-venture teams also share their diverse knowledge sets. Integrating knowledge from team members' different functional areas increases the likelihood that the team will develop successful product, process, or market innovations. Research findings, as well as com-

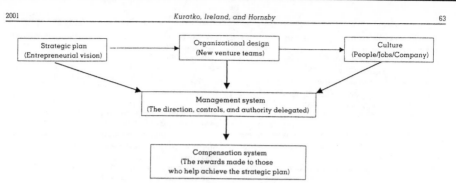

FIGURE 2
Acordia's Corporate Entrepreneurial Actions and Corporate Entrepreneurship Strategy

pany experience, suggest that the most effective new-venture teams have members who feel free to use their knowledge, intelligence, skills, and creativity while working together.[33]

However, new-venture teams sometimes fail to fulfill their promise. Poor intragroup communications, a lack of commitment by all, and ineffective performance incentives are examples of conditions that contribute to failure. An experienced consultant believes that unsuccessful teams are a product of poor planning, preparation, leadership, and assessment.[34] In contrast, high-performance teams are diverse (in terms of members' work background and problem-solving approaches, for example) and characterized by supportive relationships (e.g., communicating with integrity and authenticity[35]).

Compensation—An Important Motivator of Entrepreneurial Actions

Because it is among the most visible indicators of a firm's motivation and reward systems, compensation is a frequent topic of discussion among managers and employees alike. Compensation can have a powerful effect on outcomes resulting from individual and team efforts, and, ultimately, on firm performance.[36]

Broad in scope, compensation can include "more than just money paid in the form of wages, salaries, and bonuses. If the definition is stretched, we could include intrinsic or psychic compensation, such as status, independence, power, and so on."[37] Traditionally, compensation components are grouped into three categories—indirect pay (benefits and services), direct pay (base pay, merit, incentives, and cost-of-living adjustments), and relational forms (recognition, status, security, challenging work, and learning opportunities).[38]

What do we know about compensation's effects on firm performance? A review of the last 10 years or so of research findings suggests several things. First, it seems that the type of compensation system has a greater effect on firm performance than does the amount of compensation. Also, compensation's effect on firm performance is as significant as, if not greater than, the effects of all other human resource activities. And a mixture of variable pay or incentives results in a more significant effect on firm performance than does any single compensation source.[39]

Some top-level managers believe that unique types and combinations of compensation should be used to stimulate entrepreneurial actions and to support implementation of a corporate entrepreneurship strategy. A survey of CEOs in *Fortune* 1000 firms revealed that in over 30 percent of the firms, managers of new ventures are compensated differently from their counterparts in more established organizations. Moreover, more than half of the respondents indicated that venture members' incentives should be based on the venture's ROI, and that incentives should be capped between 50 and 200 percent of an individual's salary. Internal compensation equity, the specification of new-venture goals, and determining how to respond effectively to any shareholder objections about new-venture teams were seen as the major obstacles to using entrepreneurial compensation practices.[40]

Research findings offer additional insights about the relationship among strategies, compensation, and performance.[41] For example, to achieve high performance, companies implementing an innovation strategy (searching continually for new-market opportunities, and developing process, product, and market innovations) should use different compensation policies from firms implementing cost-leadership or differentiation strategies. Compared with cost leaders and differentiators, high-performing innovators assign more importance to the nature of the objectives that influence how new employees are attracted and current ones retained, are more aggressive in their pay level policies, use a wider range of merit raises and extend merit pay to a larger percentage of non-exempt employees, and are more open and participative in administering pay policies. Another significant finding from the study was that inferior firm performance was related to a lack of fit between the pay policy and the strategy being used.[42] Though obvious, the managerial implications of these findings are important for firms seeking to be innovators, as was the case for Acordia, Inc.

> *Another significant finding from the study was that inferior firm performance was related to a lack of fit between the pay policy and the strategy being used.*

Acordia, Inc.—An Entrepreneurial Journey

In the early 1980s, Blue Cross/Blue Shield of Indiana experienced many environmental discontinuities and changes. Studying these conditions, many of which threatened the viability of how the firm had been competing, convinced L. Ben Lytle, the CEO and chairman of the board of directors, that decisive actions were necessary. Believing that the insurance industry's changing competitive environment called for innovation, Lytle was concerned about his firm's innovative ability. In particular, he feared that the company's bureaucratic structure was stifling what were at that time informal attempts by some employees to act entrepreneurially to develop product, process, or market innovations. Lytle's belief is consistent with research evidence suggesting that eliminating organizational structures "that obscure personal responsibility and homogenize individuals' actions"[43] is a prerequisite to successful corporate entrepreneurship. Moreover, Lytle envisioned innovation as the key to exploiting opportunities that were emerging in the external environment. Thus to improve Acordia's current performance and to lay the foundation for future success, Lytle knew that employees had to behave differently, and that incentives were needed to elicit and reinforce those behaviors. He also knew that, in conjunction with the other top-level managers, he had to visibly support emerging entrepreneurial actions if they were to surface across the firm.

Beginning in 1986, Lytle and his company embarked on a multiyear entrepreneurial journey. An entrepreneurial vision, of the firm's becoming the nation's largest supplier of insurance products to mid-market customers, framed this journey. Mid-market customers were defined as cities with populations between 100,000 and 1,000,000, employers with fewer than 5,000 employees and $200,000 annually in property and casualty commissions, and individuals with incomes exceeding $50,000 per year, with a net worth greater than $500,000 but less than $5 million. Selling multiple products to mid-market customers was an opportunity that competitors had not recognized or had chosen not to pursue intensely.

Early in the journey, a corporate-entrepreneurship training program was started to introduce employees to the importance of entrepreneurial actions and to describe what would be done to elicit and support them. Upper-level managers took other early entrepreneurial actions, including changing the firm's name from Blue/Cross Blue Shield of Indiana to The Associated Group, and organizing the new company into operating units. The units were batched by industry, geography, demographics, and products, permitting a focus on mid-market customers' needs. Acordia, Inc., one of the major units created through the reorganization, is the focus of our story. As a subsidiary of The Associated Group, Acordia, Inc., created independent and entrepreneurial companies under its umbrella. Ranging in size from 42 to 200 employees, Acordia's companies (eventually 50 in total) operated independently of each other, with each having profit and loss responsibility. The constant was that each one had to focus on serving mid-market customers' needs. The companies' products included life insurance, property and casualty insurance, insurance brokerage, and health insurance.

Each Acordia company was expected to dominate its current market niche while simultaneously developing new ones it could expect to dominate, typically through innovations. Acordia's corporate entrepreneurship strategy called for identical entrepreneurial processes in all companies, although they differed in terms of products developed and serviced. Thus for each Acordia company, the same routines were used to form a vision, organize new-venture teams, and develop a compensation system that would support and reinforce entrepreneurial actions. Each Acordia company had its own CEO, vice presidents, and board of directors. Those chosen to lead the Acordia companies had experience with innovations, had shown competitive aggressiveness in leading other firms, and had a history of taking appropriate levels of risk when steering firms by relying on entrepreneurial actions.

Acordia's Corporate Entrepreneurship Strategy

The primary objectives of Acordia's corporate entrepreneurship strategy were to use entrepreneurial actions to diversify into other insurance and financial services products with sales patterns that were either noncyclical or counter-cyclical to those of health insurance, expand geographically outside Indiana into growth markets such as the South, West, and Southwest, and strengthen its core healthcare business. Thus Acordia expected its independent companies to use newly fashioned behaviors to exploit opportunities and improve performance as a result.

To stimulate process, product, and market innovations by implementing its corporate entrepreneurship strategy, Acordia executives knew that an entrepreneurial culture was needed in each company. In such a culture, creativity, commitment, dedication, and a desire to innovate are common behavioral norms. To rapidly develop such cultures in the Acordia companies, corporate-entrepreneurship training programs were offered and performance responsibilities were decentralized to each company's CEO. Among several benefits, decentralization facilitated the forming of new-venture teams—teams that were expected to be a primary source of process, product, and market innovations. Including people with different functional backgrounds, teams were organized around discreet customer needs by industry type, geographic area, demographic characteristics, and products.

As previously indicated, Acordia's entrepreneurial vision was to become the nation's largest supplier of insurance products to mid-market clients. The following operational objectives guided the entrepreneurial actions taken to reach the vision.[44]

Creating value

Objective: Demonstrate that value is created for an employer or an individual in selecting an insurance or financial service product, tailoring it to the customer's needs, and servicing the product after the sale.

The continuous restructuring of Acordia to form new companies focusing on distinct customer-segment niches with unique needs was the primary entrepreneurial action taken regarding this objective. Each Acordia company was expected to develop process innovations to reduce its overall cost of distribution and administration. To create more customer value, profitable new products were to be created as well. This expectation resulted in the development of product innovations for segments called "pioneer customers."

Financial performance

Objective: Achieve a level of financial performance for shareholders at least equal to if not superior to the level that could be earned through investment alternatives.

An average of 15-percent annual growth in earnings per share and maintenance of an average annual return on shareholders' equity in the top one-half of comparable companies were the performance metrics used to assess Acordia companies' outcomes. Satisfying these financial criteria was expected to yield the capital required to create new Acordia companies and meet shareholders' expectations.

Market segmentation

Objective: Utilize a market-segmentation strategy designed to continually focus the Acordia companies on efforts to form increasingly specialized market niches.

The purpose of the market-segmentation strategy was to encourage each Acordia company to rely on innovation to identify new segments of existing markets or to locate new customers with specialized needs. Moreover, each company was to perform at a level that resulted in its being ranked no lower than third in the total share of its market. Identifying and then dominating increasingly specialized market niches yielded additional spin-offs from existing Acordia companies. To compensate entrepreneurial team members, stock options were associated with each spin-off.

Entrepreneurial companies

Objective: Maintain and develop small, highly entrepreneurial, expense-sensitive Acordia companies.

Using only two levels of management and preventing any Acordia company from exceeding 200 employees were two important aspects of Acordia's management system that helped reduce each company's operating costs. In addition, flat organizational structures and sophisticated management information systems stimulated the sharing of tacit knowledge[45] among team members as well as between and among the new-venture teams.

Table 1
Acordia's Annual Incentive Plan

Award Calculation Guide
($ expressed per $10,000 of target award)

Financial result (Revenue growth)	Formula award (Cash bonus)	Individual Acordia companies' board of directors' discretion range	Acordia, Inc., parent company discretion range	Total maximum award earned
Threshold = 12%	$6,000	Up to $2,000	Up to $2,000	$10,000
Target = 15%	$8,000	Up to $2,000	Up to $5,000	$15,000
Outstanding = 18%	$10,000	Up to $2,000	Up to $6,000	$18,000
Below threshold	Not eligible for incentive based on formula.			

Increasingly, knowledge is recognized as an important competitive advantage. Of the different types, tacit knowledge, knowledge that can be observed in employees' actions and the outcomes resulting from them, is linked strongly to the development of successful process, product, and market innovations. Because tacit knowledge can't be easily codified, it is difficult for competitors to understand and imitate it. As a result, organizations prefer to rely on tacit knowledge as a primary foundation for their competitive advantages.[46]

Incentive compensation

Objective: Develop a compensation system that continuously elicits, supports, and encourages entrepreneurial actions.

Focused on performance outcomes, the compensation system in the Acordia companies was instrumental to the success of Acordia's corporate entrepreneurship strategy. The compensation system called for cash wages to be consistent with individual market averages for individual positions. Each market average was a combination of base pay plus an annual incentive. The base pay was established at the low end of a market range; the annual incentive, however, was positioned at the range's upper end. This approach allowed high performers to earn more than those working in comparable positions in other organizations.

An individual Acordia company's financial performance, along with an assessment by the company's board of directors and the discretionary input from those managing Acordia, Inc., determined a CEO's annual incentive. A worksheet similar to the one shown in Table 1 was used by each company's board to create clear performance incentives. Incentives were also influenced by customer-satisfaction surveys, the quality of a company's product and geographic diversification, assessed by the board, and surveys of employee satisfaction

with the manager's performance, especially as it related to her or his ability to induce and support entrepreneurial actions. The aggressive incentives were intended to provide significant returns to high performers.

A stock-option plan (see Table 2) was another part of the compensation system. Intended as a long-term incentive and ownership opportunity for all Acordia companies' executives, the plan was framed around the stock of Acordia, Inc. Of course, the value of this stock was influenced by the quality of all Acordia companies' financial performances.

Operationally, the stock-option plan featured a target pool of 1,800 shares of stock annually for each Acordia company. For control and broad-based incentive purposes, an upper limit of 600 shares in any one year for each manager was established. Each company's board followed established guidelines to allocate shares. In total, the relatively rare compensation system facilitated implementation of the corporate entrepreneurship strategy by fostering and supporting an ownership perspective among the companies' executives.

Acordia Corporate Benefits, Inc.: A Product of Entrepreneurial Actions

Acordia Corporate Benefits, Inc., (ABI) was one of the 50 Acordia companies whose development and growth demonstrated Acordia's corporate entrepreneurship strategy.[47]

On December 1, 1990, ABI was incorporated in Indiana as a third-party administrator and insurance agency. Consistent with the entrepreneurial vision of Acordia, Inc., ABI's mission was to develop, market, and administer innovative insurance and insurance-related products to firms with 50 to 1,000 employees. A limited number of manufacturing and service firms were the target market.

ABI started with 97 employees. As with each Acordia company, an immediate interest was to

Table 2
Acordia's Stock-Option Plan

Individual Performance	Operating company growth rate		
	12%	15%	16% & above
Poor	0	0	0
Good	100	150	200
Excellent	200	400	500
Superior	300	500	600

Note: Numbers refer to stock options awarded to each eligible employee.

build an entrepreneurial culture through which ABI could develop process and product innovations and identify new markets with unique needs. ABI's initial organizational structure influenced the company's subsequent culture. Each employee worked for one of four vice presidents, responsible for sales, systems, finance, and underwriting. The vice presidents reported to ABI's CEO. With only two management layers, employee independence and self-control were encouraged and supported.

A new, one-floor facility also proved instrumental to developing an entrepreneurial culture. The building facilitated interactive workflow procedures. Interactions among new-venture team members and among independent teams became grounded in forming and sharing tacit knowledge. Positive feelings surfacing from these interactions and the knowledge they fostered created positive morale in individuals and between employees and their vice president.

A new, one-floor facility also proved instrumental to developing an entrepreneurial culture.

An Employee Advisory Council was created with the primary objective to find ways for ABI to continuously improve its innovation abilities. Elected by peers, council members developed programs (e.g., quarterly all-employee meetings and dress-down day on each payday) that supported ABI's commitment to elicit and support entrepreneurial actions. The council's work was a positive influence on ABI's entrepreneurial culture.

ABI's entrepreneurial actions brought noteworthy results. In its first year, the company earned a pretax return of over 18 percent. Performance results in 1992 were better, with pretax net earnings exceeding 1991's by 22 percent. Moreover, during 1992, ABI earned over 40 percent of its net income from states other than Indiana; non-health insur-

ance businesses accounted for approximately 20 percent of earnings. ABI had become a licensed third-party administrator and life and health insurance agency in over 20 states.

Consistent with the objectives of Acordia's corporate entrepreneurship strategy, ABI continuously evaluated opportunities that might create geographic or product-line diversification. In 1993, Flexible Benefits Administration, a product innovation, was introduced. The product resulted from the sharing of tacit knowledge among team members engaging in entrepreneurial actions. This product innovation generated revenue of over $1 million in its initial year. ABI also acquired a large Indianapolis-based property and casualty insurance agency in 1993.

As we have described, the entrepreneurial actions of ABI's employees contributed to the successful implementation of the corporate entrepreneurship strategy of Acordia, Inc. ABI remained small and tightly focused on unique and specific market niches. Company personnel continued to find new niche markets and serve them with new units such as the Indianapolis-based property and casualty insurance agency. Overall, ABI contributed to the improved performance of Acordia, Inc., through its successful use of entrepreneurial actions.

Corporate Entrepreneurship within Acordia

L. Ben Lytle, CEO of Blue Cross/Blue Shield of Indiana—the predecessor to The Associated Group and to Acordia, Inc., as a part of it—recognized the threats and opportunities the external environment of the 1980s created for his firm. Volatility, unpredictability, and rapid changes had become common in the insurance industry and were altering Blue Cross/Blue Shield of Indiana's familiar and comfortable competitive patterns. Approaching these challenges proactively, Lytle concluded that entrepreneurial actions were the foundation on which the company's future had to be built. As we noted earlier, both corporate experiences and research findings suggest that an entrepreneurial vision, effective new-venture teams, and a compensation system that stimulates and reinforces entrepreneurial actions are linked with a successful corporate entrepreneurship strategy. As we have described, this turned out to be the case for Acordia. The entrepreneurial vision—to become the nation's largest supplier of insurance products to mid-market customers—was bold and energizing. From the outset, it inspired employees and stimulated entrepreneurial cultures in which process, product, and market innovations became desired sources of competitive advantage.

The work of new-venture teams in the Acordia companies was instrumental to their success. Grouping employees by skills required to innovate in ways that could satisfy unique customer needs, rather than organizing people on the basis of their functional expertise (e.g., marketing, production, and finance), facilitated the sharing of tacit knowledge—knowledge that became the foundation of product, process, and administrative innovations. Importantly, too, grouping people by skill type signaled the expectation that employees were to work collaboratively rather than individually. Decentralizing decision-making authority empowered employees to regulate their own behavior and enabled rapid, creative responses to market opportunities as they surfaced.

The Acordia companies' compensation system fostered entrepreneurial actions. An important feature of the system was the decision to use a two-tiered structure. Initially, market rates were used to attract talented people. Importantly, though, significant incentives could be earned when entrepreneurial performance targets were reached or exceeded. Decentralization of decision making to first a company and then to teams within each company made it possible to create incentives that induced superior performances grounded in streams of individual and team entrepreneurial actions.

The Acordia Experience: Implications for Managerial Practice

Acordia's experience with entrepreneurial actions as the foundation of its corporate entrepreneurship strategy offers several insights that inform managerial practice.

Entrepreneurial actions and the corporate entrepreneurship strategy for which they are a foundation result from intentional decisions. Our analysis of the Acordia, Inc., experience suggests that forming an entrepreneurial vision, using new-venture teams, and relying on a compensation system that encourages and supports creative and innovative behaviors are products of careful and deliberate planning.

Upper-level managers must support the importance of entrepreneurial actions, through both words and deeds. Supportive words are one thing. Seeing their leaders behave entrepreneurially creates employee commitment to do the same and has a more significant effect than words. Moreover, watching managers behave entrepreneurially, including actions taken to deal with the consequences of those behaviors, demonstrates that all parties will work together to cope with the disruption to existing work patterns that novel behaviors create.

> **Supportive words are one thing. Seeing their leaders behave entrepreneurially creates employee commitment to do the same and has a more significant effect than words.**

All who will be affected by an entrepreneurial vision should be involved with its development. Visions formed this way take on the characteristics of a commitment, almost an informal contract, between top-level managers and their associates. The commitment to use entrepreneurial actions to improve the firm's performance by reaching the vision sometimes creates bonds that serve the firm well when difficulties are encountered. People and teams bonded tightly through a vision to which they are committed find ways to quickly and effectively resolve issues that have the potential to retard movement toward vision fulfillment.

Effective corporate entrepreneurship strategies consider the value of several types of innovation. Innovative products are important and can create significant value. However, process and market innovations are also valuable outcomes of entrepreneurial actions. Through process innovations, firms discover ways to operate more efficiently. Market innovations contribute to a company's interest in operating more effectively, in that they help the firm identify new market space in which it can compete. Thus the triad of product, process, and market innovations is the most desirable outcome for firms using entrepreneurial actions.

Eliciting entrepreneurial actions is challenging. An obvious indicator of a manager's success is the degree to which employees change their behavior to begin acting entrepreneurially. A second and complementary performance measure is the processes the manager used to elicit those behaviors. For example, did the manager begin to act entrepreneurially? Did he or she involve all relevant parties when forming an entrepreneurial vision, organizing new-venture teams, and developing a compensation system? Particularly in firms unaccustomed to focusing on entrepreneurial actions and innovation, processes are as important as content or outcomes.

Epilogue: Innovation Breeds Success

The corporate entrepreneurship strategy of Acordia, Inc., was a success, with entrepreneurial actions being used throughout the Acordia companies. Innovative processes helped to streamline company operations. The firm became more diversified in its products and markets, in that new products were introduced into multiple markets, while new markets with specific customer needs were regularly identified. The commitment to serve new, highly focused markets led to additional Acordia companies. Using its original competitive advantages, as well as innovation, a new advantage was formed in many of the individual companies. Acordia's entrepreneurial journey proved to be the foundation for The Associated Group's success in the early 1990s.

Impressive financial results were recorded during implementation of the corporate entrepreneurship strategy. At the end of 1991, The Associated Group (TAG), the parent organization for all Acordia companies, was earning more than one-fourth of its $2 billion sales revenue from business lines outside Blue Cross/Blue Shield of Indiana's original core product—health insurance. In early 1992, Acordia, Inc., completed a successful IPO. Subsequently, the firm's stock traded on the NYSE. In June of the same year, *Business Insurance* ranked Acordia, Inc., as the 10th largest insurance broker in the United States and 14th largest in the world.

Not all of Acordia's financial success can be attributed to using entrepreneurial actions within a corporate entrepreneurship strategy. Nonetheless, the corporate entrepreneurship strategy was clearly instrumental in the progress made toward reaching the entrepreneurial vision. A comment from an Acordia company's CEO demonstrates the value of using entrepreneurial actions as the foundation for a corporate entrepreneurship strategy: "We became an employer of empowered employees who look forward to change, new products, and a promising future."

"We became an employer of empowered employees who look forward to change, new products, and a promising future."

The results of a 1995 strategic plan brought change to Acordia and its parent, The Associated Group. As was the case in the early 1980s, a rapidly changing external environment, one that created threats and opportunities, influenced the changes.

Projections resulting from the 1995 analysis of the external environment suggested that the future would find healthcare being delivered, paid for, and administered in substantially different ways. In addition, expectations were that the healthcare industry would consolidate rapidly, resulting in a smaller number of competitors, each of whom would have the size required to develop performance-enhancing economies of scale.

Careful study of these projections and their implications supported TAG's decision that continuing its focus on product and geographic diversification would no longer be effective. TAG executives concluded that refocusing on core healthcare-insurance product lines was best. By concentrating its resources on a narrower product line, the firm felt that it could learn how to meaningfully satisfy customers' anticipated needs.

Actions were taken to refocus TAG so that its financial performance would remain strong. In 1997, Acordia's stock was purchased off the public market. Subsequently, all healthcare insurance businesses were transferred from the Acordia companies to TAG. Without its healthcare businesses, Acordia, Inc., was essentially a property and casualty insurance firm. TAG sold Acordia, Inc., in 1997 to a group of investors and company officers, creating the largest privately held brokerage company in the world as a result.

Contributing to the success Acordia has experienced since becoming a privately held company is its ability to grow by acquiring smaller U.S. brokerage firms. The intent is to identify local firms with outstanding reputations and business philosophies that parallel Acordia's. Each new acquisition benefits from Acordia's large and diverse resource base as it remains focused on providing superior service to its local clients. In 2000, Acordia completed seven major acquisitions of firms located in several states, including Alabama, California, and Minnesota.

Offering global reach with local expertise, Acordia remains committed to developing innovative products and innovative ways of delivering them. In 2000, Acordia debuted eProtector, a package of coverages intended to meet the needs of technology companies by dealing with the risks they face in the digital age. EProtector covers risks that general liability policies have not considered. Strategic partnerships, such as one formed in 2000 with Merck-Medco, have become an innovative means of delivering Acordia products. Merck-Medco is the nation's largest prescription benefits manager. Acordia and this firm pooled their resources to form scriptSMART, a private-label prescription program offered exclusively through Acordia. Offering deep discounts on over-the-counter medicines, vision care, and prescriptions, the program is administered out of Acordia's Cincinnati, OH, office.

With over 3,800 employees committed to providing superior client service, Acordia believes that it is "stretching the definition of what an outstanding brokerage firm should offer its clients."[48] Oriented to continuous product, process, market, and administrative innovations, entrepreneurial actions remain at the core of how Acordia stretches its resources to reach its objectives. Thus the entrepreneurial journey that started by establishing the first Acordia companies continues today as Acordia seeks to provide services that exceed clients' expectations.

Endnotes

[1] Smith, K. G., & Di Gregorio, D. 2002. Bisociation, discovery and the role of entrepreneurial action. In M. A. Hitt, R. D. Ireland, S. M. Camp, & D. L. Sexton, (Eds.), *Strategic entrepreneurship: Creating a new mindset.* New York: Blackwell Publishers, in press.

[2] Ireland, R. D., Hitt, M. A., Camp, S. M., & Sexton, D. L. 2001. Integrating entrepreneurship and strategic management actions to create firm wealth. *The Academy of Management Executive,* 15(1): 49–63.

[3] Sharma, P., & Chrisman, J. J. 1999. Toward a reconciliation of the definitional issues in the field of corporate entrepreneurship. *Entrepreneurship: Theory & Practice,* 23(3): 11–27.

[4] Ibid.

[5] Morris, M. H. 1998. *Entrepreneurial intensity: Sustainable advantages for individuals, organizations, and societies.* Westport, CT: Quorum Books.

[6] Black, J. A., & Boal, K. B. 1994. Strategic resources: Traits, configurations, and paths to sustainable competitive advantage. *Strategic Management Journal,* 15 (Special Issue): 131–148; and Dess, G. G., Lumpkin, G. T., & Covin, J. G. 1997. Entrepreneurial strategy making and firm performances: Tests of contingency and configurational models. *Strategic Management Journal,* 18(9): 677–695.

[7] Duncan, W. J., Ginter, P. M., & Swayne, L. E. 1998. Competitive advantage and internal organizational assessment. *The Academy of Management Executive,* 12(3): 6–16.

[8] Hitt, M. A., Ireland, R. D., & Hoskisson, R. E. 2001. *Strategic management: Competitiveness and globalization,* 4th ed. Cincinnati: South-Western College Publishing.

[9] Hitt, M. A., Nixon, R. D., Hoskisson, R. E., & Kochhar, R. 1999. Corporate entrepreneurship and cross-functional fertilization: Activation, process and disintegration of a new product design team. *Entrepreneurship: Theory & Practice,* 23(3): 145–167.

[10] Stein, N. The world's most admired companies. *Fortune,* 2 October 2000, 182–196.

[11] Morse, C. W. 1986. The delusion of intrapreneurship. *Long Range Planning,* 19(6): 92–95; Duncan, W.J. 1988. Intrapreneuring and the reinvention of the corporation. *Business Horizons,* 31(3): 16–21.

[12] Burgelman, R. A. 1984. Designs for corporate entrepreneurship. *California Management Review,* 26(4): 154–148; Kanter, R. M. 1985. Supporting innovation and venture development in established companies. *Journal of Business Venturing,* 1(1): 47–60; and Kuratko, D. F., & Montagno, R. V. 1989. The intrapreneurial spirit. *Training and Development Journal,* 43(10): 83–87.

[13] Zahra, S. A., Kuratko, D. F., & Jennings, D. F. 1999. Entrepreneurship and the acquisition of dynamic organizational capabilities. *Entrepreneurship: Theory & Practice,* 23(3): 5–10.

[14] Covin, J. G., Slevin, D. P., & Heeley, M. B. 2000. Pioneers and followers: Competitive tactics, environment, and firm growth. *Journal of Business Venturing,* 15(2): 175–210.

[15] Zahra, S. A. 1999. The changing rules of global competitiveness in the 21st century. *The Academy of Management Executive,* 13(1): 36–42.

[16] Brazeal, D. V. 1993. Organizing for internally developed corporate ventures. *Journal of Business Venturing,* 8(1): 75–90;

Covin, J. G., & Slevin, D. P. 1991. A conceptual model of entrepreneurship as firm behavior. *Entrepreneurship: Theory & Practice,* 16(1): 17–25; Hornsby, J. S., Naffziger, D. W., Kuratko, D. F., & Montagno, R. V. 1993. An interactive model of the corporate entrepreneurship process. *Entrepreneurship: Theory & Practice,* 17(2): 29–37; Zahra, S. A. 1991. Predictors and financial outcomes of corporate entrepreneurship: An exploratory study. *Journal of Business Venturing,* 6(4): 259–286.

[17] MacMillan, I. C., Block, Z., & Narasimha, P. N. 1986. Corporate venturing: Alternatives, obstacles encountered, and experienced efforts. *Journal of Business Venturing,* 1(2): 177–191; Quinn, J. B. 1985. Managing innovation: Controlled chaos. *Harvard Business Review,* 63(3): 73–84; Pearce, J. A., Kramer, T. R., & Robbins, D. K. 1997. Effects of managers' entrepreneurial behavior on subordinates. *Journal of Business Venturing,* 12(2): 147–160.

[18] Hisrich, R. D., & Peters, M. P. 1986. Establishing a new business venture unit within a firm. *Journal of Business Venturing,* 1(3): 307–322; Sathe, V. 1989. Encouraging entrepreneurship in large corporations. *Research Management,* 32(3): 18–22; Sathe, V. 1989. Fostering entrepreneurship in large diversified firms. *Organizational Dynamics,* 18(1): 20–32.

[19] Das, T. K., & Bing-Sheng, T. 1997. Time and entrepreneurial risk behavior. *Entrepreneurship: Theory & Practice,* 22(2): 69–88; Guth, W. D., & Ginsberg, A. 1990. Corporate entrepreneurship. *Strategic Management Journal* (Special Issue), 11: 5–15; Kanter, Op. Cit.

[20] Block, Z., & Ornati, O. A. 1987. Compensating corporate venture managers. *Journal of Business Venturing,* 2(1): 41–51; Sykes, H. B. 1992. Incentive compensation for corporate venture personnel. *Journal of Business Venturing,* 7(4): 253–265.

[21] Burgelman, R. A. 1983. Corporate entrepreneurship and strategic management: Insights from a process study. *Management Science,* 29(12): 1349–1363; Stopford, J. M., & Baden-Fuller, C. W. F. 1994. Creating corporate entrepreneurship. *Strategic Management Journal,* 15(7): 521–536; Sykes, H. B., & Block, Z. 1989. Corporate venturing obstacles: Sources and solutions. *Journal of Business Venturing,* 4(3): 159–167.

[22] Barry, D., & Elmes, M. 1997. Strategy retold: Toward a narrative view of strategic discourse. *Academy of Management Review,* 22(2): 429–452; Ireland, R. D., & Hitt, M. A. 1997. Strategy as story: Clarifications and enhancements to Barry and Elmes' arguments. *Academy of Management Review,* 22(4): 844–847.

[23] Tiessen, J. H. 1997. Individualism, collectivism, and entrepreneurship: A framework for international comparative research. *Journal of Business Venturing,* 12(5): 367–384.

[24] Stein, op. cit., 186.

[25] Prokesch, S. E. 1997. Unleashing the power of learning: An interview with John Browne. *Harvard Business Review,* 75(5): 147–168.

[26] Martin, P. Lessons in humility. *Financial Times,* 22 June 1999, 18.

[27] Eggers, J. H. 1999. Developing entrepreneurial growth. *Ivey Business Journal,* 63(4): 76–81.

[28] Edmondson, A. 1999. Psychological safety and learning behavior in work teams. *Administrative Science Quarterly,* 44(2): 350–383; Block, Z., & MacMillan, I. C. 1993. *Corporate venturing.* Boston: Harvard Business School Press.

[29] Reich, R. B. 1987. Entrepreneurship reconsidered: The team as hero. *Harvard Business Review,* 65(3): 77–83.

[30] Hitt, et al., op. cit.

[31] Higdon, Jr., L. I. 2000. Leading innovation. *Executive Excellence,* 17(8): 15–16.

[32] Ireland, R. D. 2001. Unleashing organizational citizens' capabilities: The role of strategic leadership. Working paper, University of Richmond.

[33] Pfeffer, J. 1998. *The human equation: Building profits by putting people first.* Boston: Harvard Business School Press.

[34] Hunt, J. W. The elusive ingredients of team spirit. *Financial Times,* 30 June 1999, 8.

[35] Dess, G. G., & Picken, J. C. 1999. *Beyond productivity: How leading companies achieve superior performance by leveraging their human capital.* AMACOM: New York, 114–117.

[36] Becker, B., & Gerhart, B. 1996. The impact of human resource management in organizational performance: Progress and prospects. *Academy of Management Journal,* 39(4): 779–801; Huselid, M. A. 1995. The impact of human resource management practices on turnover, productivity, and corporate financial performance. *Academy of Management Journal,* 38(3): 635–672; Lepak, D., & Snell, S. 1999. The human resource architecture: Toward a theory of human capital allocation and development. *Academy of Management Review,* 24(1): 31–48; and Roberts, K., Kossek, E., & Ozeki, C. 1998. Managing the global workforce: Challenges and strategies. *The Academy of Management Executive,* 12(4): 93–106.

[37] Baron, J. N., & Kreps, D. M. 1999. *Strategic human resources: Frameworks for general managers.* New York: John Wiley & Sons, 297.

[38] Milkovich, G. T., & Newman, J. M. 1999. *Compensation,* 6th ed. Boston: McGraw-Hill/Irwin.

[39] Barkema, H. G., & Gomez-Mejia, L. R. 1998. Managerial compensation and firm performance: A general research perspective. *Academy of Management Journal,* 41(2): 135–145; Becker, B., & Huselid, M. 1997. High performance work systems and firm performance: A synthesis of research and managerial implications. In G. R. Ferris, (Ed.), *Research in Personnel and Human Resource Management.* Greenwich, CT: JAI Press; Gerhart, B., & Milkovich, G. 1990. Organization differences in managerial compensation and financial performance. *Academy of Management Journal,* 33(4): 663–691; Gomez-Mejia, L. R., & Balkin, D. 1992. *Compensation, organizational strategy, and firm performance.* Cincinnati: South-Western College Publishing; Snell, S. A., & Dean, J. W. 1994. Strategic compensation for integrated manufacturing: The moderating effects of job and organizational inertia. *Academy of Management Journal,* 37(5): 1109–1114; and Stroh, J. B. 1996. Agency theory and variable pay compensation strategies. *Academy of Management Journal,* 39(3): 751–767.

[40] Block, Z., & Ornati, O. 1987. Compensating corporate venture managers. *Journal of Business Venturing,* 2(1): 41–52.

[41] Miles, R. E., & Snow, C. C. 1978. *Organizational strategy, structure, and process.* New York: McGraw-Hill/Irwin.

[42] Montemayor, E. F. 1996. Congruence between pay policy and competitive strategy in high-performing firms. *Journal of Management,* 22(6): 889–908.

[43] Bartlett, C. A., & Ghoshal, S. 1996. Release the entrepreneurial hostages from your corporate hierarchy. *Strategy & Leadership,* July-August: 36–42.

[44] The operational objectives were drawn from Acordia's annual reports for 1992, 1993, and 1994.

[45] Brockmann, E. N., & Anthony, W. P. 1998. The influence of tacit knowledge and collective mind on strategic planning. *Journal of Managerial Issues,* 10(2): 204–222; Miller, C. C., & Ireland, R. D. 2001. Intuition in strategic decision making: Friend or foe in the entrepreneurial millennium? Working paper, Wake Forest University.

[46] Grant, R. M., & Spender, J. -C., (Eds.). 1996. Knowledge and the firm. *Strategic Management Journal,* 17 (Special Issue), December.

[47] The Acordia Corporate Benefits, Inc., story was developed through an on-site interview with Michael D. Houk, the firm's CEO.

[48] About Acordia. September 1, 2001. www.acordia.com.

Donald F. Kuratko is the Stoops Distinguished Professor of Entrepreneurship and founding director of the Entrepreneurship Program, Ball State University. His research interests include corporate entrepreneurship and entrepreneurial strategies. Honored as Ball State University's Outstanding Professor (1996) and Outstanding Researcher (1999), he has authored 18 books. Contact: DKuratko@gw.bsu.edu.

R. Duane Ireland is the W. David Robbins Chair of Business Policy in the E. Claiborne Robins School of Business, University of Richmond. His research interests include the intersection between entrepreneurship and strategic management. His numerous publications include 1999 best paper of the year in *The Academy of Management Executive* and best paper in 2000 in *The Academy of Management Journal.* Contact: direland@richmond.edu.

Jeffrey S. Hornsby is a professor and director of the Human Resource Management Program at Ball State University. His research centers on corporate entrepreneurship, compensation, and human resource management practices. He has coauthored numerous articles appearing in the *Journal of Applied Psychology, Strategic Management Journal, Group and Organizational Management,* and other journals. Contact: JHornsby@gw.bsu.edu.

Name Index